Shakespeare's Comedies

BY COURTESY OF THE NATIONAL PORTRAIT GALLERY, LONDON

EDITORIAL ADVISORY BOARD

Shakespeare's Comedies

Edited by
David Bevington
The University of Chicago

PEARSON
Longman

New York San Francisco Boston
London Toronto Sydney Tokyo Singapore Madrid
Mexico City Munich Paris Cape Town Hong Kong Montreal

Managing Editor: Erika Berg
Development Editor: Michael Greer
Executive Marketing Manager: Ann Stypuloski
Project Coordination and Electronic Page Makeup: Electronic Publishing Services Inc., NYC
Cover Designer/Manager: Wendy Ann Fredericks
Cover Art: Henry Woodward as Petruchio in *The Taming of the Shrew* by Shakespeare 1775 at Drury Lane Theatre, 1756; Gucht, Van Der Benjamin, 1753–94, English; The Art Archive/Garrick Club.
Manufacturing Buyer: Lucy Hebard
Printer and Binder: Hamilton Printing Co.
Cover Printer: Lehigh Press, Inc.

About the cover:
A 1775 portrait by English painter Benjamin Van der Gucht (1753–1794) depicts actor Henry Woodward as Petruchio in *The Taming of the Shrew* in a 1756 production at Drury Lane Theatre in London.

The Library of Congress has cataloged the single volume, hardcover edition as follows:
Shakespeare, William, 1564–1616.
[Works. 2003]
The complete works of Shakespeare / edited by David Bevington.—5th ed.
p. cm.
Includes bibliographical references and index.
ISBN 0-321-09333-X
I. Bevington, David M. II. Title.
PR2754.B4 2003
822.3′3—dc21 2003045975

Please visit us at http://www.ablongman.com

ISBN 0-321-42262-7

2 3 4 5 6 7 8 9 10—HT—09 08 07 06

CONTENTS

PREFACE

I have had the extraordinary privilege of editing and reediting *The Complete Works of Shakespeare* throughout my career as teacher and scholar, beginning in the early 1970s. The work is now in its fifth edition. Each new edition has, I hope, made advances in thoroughness and accuracy. Now seems a good time to publish that edition in four separate volumes. Shakespeare was such a prolific writer that the single-volume edition is heavy and hard to carry around. At the same time, his work can be conveniently and logically divided into four volumes of more or less equal size: the comedies, the English history plays, the tragedies, and the late romances combined with the poems and sonnets. These units can lend themselves well to classroom use or to general reading: sometimes courses in Shakespeare focus during one term on the comedies and histories, and during another on the tragedies and late romances, whereas more general courses in literary study and appreciation may sometimes choose to study the sonnets, or a few particular plays.

My hope is that this four-volume edition, with each volume separately available, can offer to students and general readers an unusually flexible and accessible anthology for study, for pleasure, and for continued reference.

KEY FEATURES OF THE FOUR-VOLUME PORTABLE EDITION

- **Flexible arrangement in volumes of convenient size,** grouped according to genres of comedy, history, tragedy, and romances and poems.
- **Thoroughly revised and updated notes and glosses** provide contemporary readers the support they need to understand Elizabethan language and idioms in accessible and clear modern language, line by line.
- **A richly illustrated general introduction** provides readers with the historical and cultural background required to understand Shakespeare's works in context.
- **Significantly revised introductory essays on each of the plays and poems** offer new insight into major themes, cultural issues, and critical conflicts.
- **Updated appendices** include the most recent information on sources, textual choices, performance history, dating of the works, and bibliographic resources.

From the start of my editing career I have aimed at explaining difficult passages, not just single words, keeping in mind the questions that readers might ask as to possible meanings. In undertaking the latest revision I was astonished to discover how extensively I have wanted to rewrite the commentary notes. The present edition incorporates many such changes. Some notes I had written seemed to me just plain wrong; many others seemed to me in need of greater clarity and accessibility. I have been both abashed to see how much improvement was necessary and grateful to be able to profit from my own experience with these texts in the classroom.

Issues of post-colonialism, gender relations, ethnic conflict, attitudes toward war and politics, ambiguities of language, the canon, dating, multiple authorship, and textual revision have been on the march since the early 1980s especially. These are heady times in which to attempt to practice literary criticism. Introductory essays need to be open to recent as well as more traditional critical approaches; they should open up issues for examination rather than offer pronouncements. I have listened carefully to reviewers who have occasionally found my introductions to earlier editions too confident of my own reading of the plays and poems. I have attempted to make an important correction in this matter, especially by adding some examples of production history and recent criticism that offer radically different readings of the dramatic texts. A teaching text should ask questions and offer the reader alternative possibilities. Discussion of recent film and stage history can enhance our appreciation of the plays in performance while at the same time enriching possibilities of interpretation.

This edition differs from other currently available editions of the *Complete Works* in being presented from the viewpoint of a single editor. That is at once its strength and no doubt its weakness. The viewpoint is, I would venture to say, a moderate and inclusive one, deeply interested in new critical approaches while also attuned to the kinds of responses that Shakespeare has evoked in past generations. I like the fact that this edition began in the Middle West, in Chicago, and that it serves a host of colleges and universities many of which are also in the great heartland of America. This edition attempts to be middle American, intended for a broad spectrum of educational uses and for private enjoyment as well.

I hope that the potential hubris of a single editorship is significantly ameliorated by the way in which this edition, like its predecessors, has made extensive use of editorial consultants. Each consultant was asked to respond to a particular play or work, including the notes and commentary. Many of the responses have been extraordinary and have sharpened issues I could never have addressed sufficiently on my own. The consultants, listed in the front of the book, are experts not only in Shakespeare studies but in the particular work I asked them to consider. I am deeply grateful for their help. Lois Potter, originally asked to serve as a consultant on performance history, presented so many suggestions that Longman and I asked her to write a new essay on the subject.

A BRIEF GUIDE TO THE EDITORIAL PRACTICES AND STYLE USED IN THIS EDITION

The running title at the top of each page of text gives the Through Line Numbers (TLN) of each play based on the *Norton First Folio of Shakespeare*. That facsimile of the original provides line numberings throughout, one number for each line of type. The advantage of this system is that it is universal, applying to all editions whether new or old. Such editions vary in line numbering depending on how the text is divided into scenes and how prose is numbered in columns of varying width. Because the TLN system is truly universal it is often used by textual scholars.

Line numbers in the text indicate that a gloss is to be found at the foot of the column for some word or phrase in the line in question.

Stage directions in square brackets are editorially added. Those without brackets, or in parentheses, are from the original Folio or Quarto text. The same is true of the numberings of acts and scenes.

The notes indicate the place of each scene. These indications should not be read as meaning that the stage needs to "look" like a particular street or house or room. Shakespeare's plays were acted essentially without scenery, as is often the case today. The indications of place are meant solely to give the reader information on the imagined location, as those locations can shift quite rapidly.

When the scansion of verse requires that vowels are to receive a syllable they would not normally receive, the vowel in question is marked with an accent grave. Thus, "lovèd" is to be pronounced in two syllables, "lov-ed." When the word has no such accented vowel it should receive the normal pronunciation. These markings normally correspond with a similar system in the original Folio and Quarto texts, although in those texts "loved" is normally bisyllabic, whereas "lov'd" is monosyllabic.

In the commentary notes, capitalization and end punctuation of each note is determined by how the paraphrase in the note fits into the Shakespearean text it represents. If the phrase being glossed begins a sentence, the note will begin with a capital letter, and correspondingly with end punctuation. The idea here is to make the paraphrase as smoothly compatible with the text as possible.

Any reader interested in further discussion on modernizing of spelling is invited to consult the Preface of the fourth updated edition.

ACKNOWLEDGMENTS

I am grateful to the reviewers who made numerous suggestions for improvements in this new edition. For their detailed and thoughtful suggestions, I would like to thank the following: Nick Barker, Covenant College, Lookout Mountain, Georgia; Celia A. Easton, SUNY Geneseo; Peter Greenfield, University of Puget Sound; Glenn Hopp, Howard Payne University; George Justice, Louisiana State University; Joseph Tate, University of Washington; Ann Tippett, Monroe Community College; Lewis Walker, University of North Carolina, Wilmington; Robert F. Wilson Jr., University of Missouri, Kansas City; and David Wilson-Okamura, East Carolina University.

A number of faculty were generous enough to respond to a survey we conducted to learn more about the undergraduate Shakespeare course market today. Thanks to the following for providing guidance and information: Mark Aune, North Dakota State University; Douglas A. Brooks, Texas A & M University; Robert Cirasa, Kean University; Bill Dynes, University of Indianapolis; Lisa Freinkel, University of Oregon; John Hagge, Iowa State University; Ritchie D. Kendall, University of North Carolina, Chapel Hill; Robert Levine, Boston University; Allen Michie, Iowa State University; Neil Nakadate, Iowa State University; Bonnie Nelson, Kansas State University; Robert O'Brien, California State University, Chico; Arlene Okerlund, San Jose State University; George Rowe, University of Oregon; Lisa S. Starks, University of South Florida; and Nathaniel Wallace, South Carolina State University.

I want to acknowledge a special debt of gratitude to the editorial advisory board members, who provided detailed suggestions on the plays, commentaries, notes, and appendixes. The names of our editorial consultants are listed facing the title page.

Lois Potter of the University of Delaware went far beyond the call of duty by completely rewriting Appendix 3 on Shakespeare in Performance. That her work was done under intense deadline pressure makes the achievement of her wonderful and learned essay all the more impressive.

SUPPLEMENTS

The following supplements are available free when ordered with this text. Please consult your local Longman representative if you would like to set up a value pack.

***Evaluating a Performance,* by Mike Greenwald,** informs students about stage and theatrical performance and helps them to become more critical viewers of dramatic productions (ISBN 0-321-09541-3).

***Screening Shakespeare: Using Film to Understand the Plays,* by Michael Greer,** is a brief, practical guide to select feature films of the most commonly taught plays (ISBN 0-321-19479-9).

***Shakespeare: Script, Stage, Screen,* by David Bevington, Anne Marie Welsh, and Michael L. Greenwald,** is an edition designed for the teaching of Shakespeare plays most usefully studied in these contexts, with extensive discussions and commentary on stage and screen adaptations (ISBN 0-321-19813-1).

I would be most grateful if you would bring to my attention any errors you find. Such errors can be corrected in a subsequent printing. My e-mail address is bevi@uchicago.edu.

David Bevington

GENERAL INTRODUCTION

THE COMEDIES

When Shakespeare's plays were first published in a one-volume complete edition in the so-called First Folio of 1623, seven years after his death, they were grouped by the editors into three categories: comedies, histories, and tragedies. Fourteen of the thirty-six plays in the 1623 edition (which left out *Pericles* entirely, and did not list *Troilus and Cressida* in the contents) were included in the section devoted to comedies. The first play there was *The Tempest,* a very late play (c. 1611) and apparently Shakespeare's swan song or farewell to the theater. It may have been placed first because the editors, John Heminges and Henry Condell, who were Shakespeare's colleagues in the acting company known as the King's Men, regarded *The Tempest* as a shining example of his best work.

The present edition divides the Shakespeare canon into four groupings rather than three. Ever since the late nineteenth century, scholars and readers have seen that Shakespeare's late plays, *Pericles, Cymbeline, The Winter's Tale,* and *The Tempest* (c. 1606–11), are somewhat different in genre from the comedies of his earlier years. The late plays are now generally classified as romances, or tragicomedies, and they are published here under the heading of "Romances."

The differences between the comedies of the earlier era and the late romances should not be overstated. All are comedies in many ways: they generally deal with young people falling in love, and they usually end in marriage. (The important exceptions to this will be discussed shortly.) Even the late *Cymbeline,* which the Folio editors chose to include among the tragedies, ends in reconciliation and marriage. The comedies generally move through the vexing complications of parental opposition or other difficulties toward forgiveness and reunion. Most of Shakespeare's early comedies, through the first half of his career (before 1600), are often described as romantic comedies. The term "romantic" suggests romantic love and sexual attraction, of course, but it also points to "romance" in the sense of adventure, separation, and wandering, leading eventually to a happy coming together at the end. The fact that so many early comedies can be called "romantic comedies" points up the resemblance to the late romances.

The main difference between the romantic comedies and the late romances is only one of degree, and even here one must be careful not to overstate the case. The earlier comedies tend to be funnier and more joyous; they celebrate the joys as well as the perils of young love. The late romances read as though they have been written by a great playwright who, in the interim, has written some of the greatest and most harrowing tragedies in the English language: *Hamlet, Othello, King Lear, Macbeth,* and still others. Have those deeply challenging plays left their mark on the tone and spirit of the late romances? Many readers and theater directors have felt that this is the case: the late romances continually remind us of how fragile human happiness can be, and how close is the approach of death.

The early romantic comedies seem more intent on celebrating the joys of courtship and marriage, and yet even here the threat of disaster and even of death is never very far away. In *The Comedy of Errors,* a framing plot tells of old Egeon, who is told he will be executed at the end of the day unless someone can be found to ransom him. The happy ending saves him from that fate, but only at the last moment. At the very end of *Love's Labor's Lost,* the news of the death of the King of France prompts the Princess and her companion ladies to postpone courtship for at least a year, so that we have no marriages at the end of this otherwise romantic comedy. In *The Two Gentlemen of Verona,* the competition among two young men for the woman they both love nearly leads to mayhem. The same is true in *A Midsummer Night's Dream,* in which Demetrius and Lysander do their best to kill each other until the love juice administered by Puck restores Demetrius to his one-time fondness for Helena. *The Merchant of Venice* is especially harrowing for a so-called romantic comedy: Shylock, a Jewish moneylender, nearly succeeds in cutting out a pound of flesh from his Christian adversary, Antonio. The subplot of *Much Ado About Nothing* is no less distressing: the innocent heroine, Hero, is accused of sexual promiscuity by her intended husband and seems to be doomed to a life of perpetual chastity in a monastery. The sobering realities of usurpation and homicidal sibling rivalry hover over *As You Like It* from first to last. *Twelfth Night* begins with the seeming drowning of Viola's twin brother; it also subjects the steward Malvolio to humiliation for his hypocritical dreams of social advancement that results in his being incarcerated as a madman. Only *The Merry Wives of Windsor,* among this sizable group of plays, is content to avoid the threat of disaster: Falstaff suffers nothing worse than being exposed as a would-be wife-stealer.

Threats of unhappiness in these plays generally serve the purpose of giving the plot a chance to develop through complication toward resolution. Villains such as Don John in *Much Ado* do their insidious work of temptation, but the spirit of comedy is there to rescue the young people and to deepen the happiness of their eventual bliss by showing how preciously it has been achieved. As result, these comedies tend to move toward better self-understanding of the characters and toward a forgiveness of their faults. To learn that one is capable of bitterness and competitive hatred can be a way toward knowing who one is, and these comedies offer forgiveness for such failings. The women in particular learn how to forgive young men for their self-destructive anxieties and their mistrust of women: Claudio in *Much Ado* learns that he has wronged Hero, Proteus in *The Two Gentlemen* must learn to eschew his perfidies and find some way to deserve Julia's steadying faith in him, and so on. Even the women learn about themselves through their own lapses: Helena in *A Midsummer Night's Dream* discovers that she is capable of feeling endlessly persecuted by her friends. Yet women generally become the instructors of the young men in how to think realistically about courtship, and how to regard young women as complex human beings rather than as idealized goddesses placed on a pedestal. Both Rosalind in *As You Like It* and Viola in *Twelfth Night* guide the young men they love toward a mature self-understanding that the young men seem incapable of achieving on their own.

These then are the romantic comedies of this volume, in all their engaging complexity. Toward the end of the present volume, on the other hand, we move into a strange and even scary world of a very different sort of comedy. It is a kind of comedy so fraught with emotional difficulties and spiritual failures that comedy itself becomes threatened and uncertain. Marriages, if achieved at all, are highly problematic. The young women seem less nurturing and more threatening to the young men, even brazen. The fallen nature of humanity bears down so on these plays that they have been categorized, ever since the late nineteenth century, as problem comedies or even (especially in the case of *Troilus and Cressida*) problem plays, dropping the label of "comedy" entirely. Not surprisingly, perhaps, they seem to have been written around the time that Shakespeare was beginning to write major tragedies like *Hamlet* and *Othello,* that is to say, during the years from 1601 to 1604, at a turning point in Shakespeare's career.

All's Well That Ends Well features a heroine, Helena, who dares to pursue a young man who is vastly her social superior and who resists marriage with her in every way he can. She eventually tricks him into accepting her with the device of a substitute bed trick: when he longs to sleep with a young woman he has met, Helena takes that woman's place and then presents her wayward husband with a baby. *Measure for Measure* uses the bed trick again, this time to satisfy Angelo's sexual desire for Isabella (who is on the verge of entering a convent for life) by arranging for the nighttime assignation to be fulfilled by a woman to whom Angelo was previously engaged. This Mariana still loves Angelo, despite his villainous and even murderous intents, and at the end she does claim him in marriage. Whether he is content to be her husband is far from clear, but the marriage at least means that he will not be executed for his crimes. The proposal of marriage by Duke Vincentio to Isabella is no less unexpected and even bizarre, and in modern productions one can never be sure whether she will accept or not. Angelo's fraught soliloquies of self-hatred and of panic at his inability to stop his own lustful desires are as tortured and painful as any of the soliloquies in *Hamlet* or *Othello*.

Troilus and Cressida is the most strange of all to be included in a volume of comedies. The editors of the 1623 Folio must have sensed this, because they inserted it finally between the histories and tragedies, not in the comedy section at all. The play is not named in the table of contents, perhaps suggesting that its inclusion came very late in the printing process; its pagination is also anomalous. If it is a comedy at all, it is what we might call a "black comedy" of satire directed at wars and at lechery in a time of social dissolution. Driven by the grim necessities of the Trojan War, Greek and Trojan fighters alike are embittered, quarrelsome, petty, self-destructive. In such an apocalyptic world, the young lovers of the title, Troilus and Cressida, come together in desire and need for companionship only to be driven apart by military imperatives. The play is like a tragedy in its depiction of the deaths of Hector and Patroclus, among others. It is a history play in its chronicling of the greatest war in classical history—a war that also turns out to be one of the most absurd. Shakespeare's ventures in comedy thus take a new turn around 1600, as he moves toward tragic exploration of the human condition.

LIFE IN SHAKESPEARE'S ENGLAND

England during Shakespeare's lifetime (1564–1616) was a proud nation with a strong sense of national identity, but it was also a small nation by modern standards. Probably not more than five million people lived in the whole of England, considerably fewer than now live in London. England's territories in France were no longer extensive, as they had been during the fourteenth century and earlier; in fact, by the end of Queen Elizabeth's reign (1558–1603), England had virtually retired from the territories she had previously controlled on the Continent, especially in France. Wales was a conquered principality. England's overseas empire in America had scarcely begun, with the Virginia settlement established in the 1580s. Scotland was not yet a part of Great Britain; union with Scotland would not take place until 1707, despite the fact that King James VI of Scotland assumed the English throne in 1603 as James I of England. Ireland, although declared a kingdom under English rule in 1541, was more a source of trouble than of economic strength. The last years of Elizabeth's reign, especially from 1597 to 1601, were plagued by the rebellion of the Irish under Hugh O'Neill, Earl of Tyrone. Thus, England of the sixteenth and early seventeenth centuries was both small and isolated.

The Social and Economic Background

By and large, England was a rural land. Much of the kingdom was still wooded, though timber was being used increasingly in manufacturing and shipbuilding. The area of the Midlands, today heavily industrialized, was at that time still a region of great trees, green fields, and clear streams. England's chief means of livelihood was agriculture. This part of the economy was generally in a bad way, however, and people who lived off the land did not share in the prosperity of many Londoners. A problem throughout the sixteenth century was that of "enclosure": the conversion by rich landowners of croplands into pasturage. Farmers and peasants complained bitterly that they were being dispossessed and starved for the benefit of livestock. Rural uprisings and food riots were common, to the dismay of the authorities. Some Oxfordshire peasants arose in 1596, threatening to massacre the gentry and march on London; other riots had occurred in 1586 and 1591. There were thirteen riots in Kent alone during Elizabeth's reign. Unrest continued into the reign of James I, notably the Midlands' rising of 1607. Although the government did what it could to inhibit enclosure, the economic forces at work were too massive and too inadequately understood to be curbed by governmental fiat. The absence of effective bureaucracies or agencies of coercion compounded the difficulty of governmental control. Pasture used large areas with greater efficiency than crop farming, and required far less labor. The wool produced by the pasturing of sheep was needed in ever increasing amounts for the manufacture of cloth.

The wool industry also experienced occasional economic difficulties, to be sure; overexpansion in the early years of the sixteenth century created a glutted market that collapsed disastrously in 1551, producing widespread unemployment. Despite such fluctuations and reversals, however, the wool industry at least provided handsome profits for some landowners and middlemen. Mining and manufacture in coal, iron, tin, copper, and lead, although insignificant by modern standards, also were expanding at a significant rate. Trading companies exploited the rich new resources of the Americas, as well as of eastern Europe and the Orient. Queen Elizabeth aided economic development by keeping England out of war with her continental enemies as long as possible, despite provocations from those powers and despite the eagerness of some of her advisers to retaliate.

Certainly England's economic condition was better than the economic condition of the rest of the Continent; an Italian called England "the land of comforts." Yet although some prosperity did exist, it was not evenly distributed. Especially during Shakespeare's first years in London, in the late 1580s and the 1590s, the gap between

"Enclosure" was a problem throughout the sixteenth century in England. Crop lands were converted into pasturage. The livelihood of the plowman was threatened by the pasturing of sheep and the growing production of wool.

rich and poor grew more and more extreme. Elizabeth's efforts at peacemaking were no longer able to prevent years of war with the Catholic powers of the Continent. Taxation grew heavier, and inflation proceeded at an unusually rapid rate during this period. A succession of bad harvests compounded the miseries of those who dwelled on the land. When the hostilities on the Continent ceased for a time in about 1597, a wave of returning veterans added to unemployment and crime. The rising prosperity experienced by Shakespeare and other fortunate Londoners was undeniably real, but it was not universal. Nowhere was the contrast between rich and poor more visible than in London.

London

Sixteenth-century London was at once more attractive and less attractive than twenty-first-century London. It was full of trees and gardens; meadows and cultivated lands reached in some places to its very walls. Today we can perhaps imagine the way in which it bordered clear streams and green fields when we approach from a distance some noncommercial provincial city such as Lincoln, York, or Hereford. Partly surrounded by its ancient wall, London was by no means a large metropolis. With 190,000 to 200,000 inhabitants in the city proper and its suburbs, it was nonetheless the largest city of Europe, and its dominance among English cities was even more striking; in 1543–1544, London paid thirty times the subsidy of Norwich, then the second-largest city in the kingdom (15,000 inhabitants). Although London's population had

Sixteenth-century London was a city teeming with activity. Pedestrians were often forced to make way for the livestock being driven through the streets.

expanded into the surrounding area in all directions, the city proper stretched along the north bank of the Thames River from the old Tower of London on the east to St. Paul's Cathedral and the Fleet Ditch on the west—a distance of little more than a mile. Visitors approaching London from the south bank of the Thames (the Bankside) and crossing London Bridge could see virtually all of this exciting city lying before them. London Bridge itself was one of the major attractions of the city, lined with shops and richly decorated on occasion for the triumphal entry of a king or queen.

Yet London had its grim and ugly side as well. On London Bridge could sometimes be seen the heads of executed traitors. The city's houses were generally small and crowded; its streets were often narrow and filthy. In the absence of sewers, open ditches in the streets served to collect and carry off refuse. Frequent epidemics of the bubonic plague were the inevitable result of unsanitary conditions and medical ignorance. Lighting of the streets at night was generally nonexistent, and the constabulary was notoriously unreliable. Shakespeare gives us unforgettable satires of night watchmen and bumbling police officials in *Much Ado About Nothing* (Dogberry and the night watch) and *Measure for Measure* (Constable Elbow). Prostitution thrived in the suburbs, conveniently located, although beyond the reach of the London authorities. Again, we are indebted to Shakespeare for a memorable portrayal in *Measure for Measure* of just such a demimonde (Mistress Overdone the bawd, Pompey her pimp, and various customers). Houses of prostitution were often found in the vicinity of the public theaters, since the theaters also took advantage of suburban locations to escape the stringent regulations imposed by London's Lord Mayor and Council of Aldermen. The famous Globe Theatre, for example, was on the south bank of the Thames, a short distance west of London Bridge. Another theatrical building (called simply "The Theatre"), used earlier by Shakespeare and the Lord Chamberlain's players, was located in Finsbury Fields, a short distance across Moorfields from London's northeast corner. The suburbs also housed various con games and illegal operations,

COURTESY, GUILDHALL LIBRARY, CORPORATION OF LONDON

This detail from a 1572 map of London shows closely packed buildings intersected with throroughfares, with gardens and open spaces on the outskirts.

BY PERMISSION OF THE FOLGER SHAKESPEARE LIBRARY

London Bridge, lined with shops, houses, and severed heads on poles, provided a colorful route for those traveling between the north and south banks of the Thames. A number of Elizabethan theaters, including the Globe, were located on the south bank.

The taverns of Cheapside in London were popular and occasionally rowdy.

some of them brilliantly illustrated (and no doubt exaggerated) in Ben Jonson's *The Alchemist* (1610).

Roughly half of London's total population, perhaps 100,000 people, lived within its walls, and as many more in the suburbs. The royal palace of Whitehall, Westminster Abbey (then known as the Abbey Church of St. Peter), the Parliament House, and Westminster Hall were well outside London, two miles or so to the west on the Thames River. They remain today in the same location, in Westminster, although the metropolis of London has long since surrounded these official buildings.

Travel

Travel was still extremely painful and slow because of the poor condition of the roads. Highway robbers were a constant threat. (The celebrated highway robbery in Shakespeare's *1 Henry IV* takes place at Gads Hill, on the main road between London and Canterbury.) English inns seem to have been good, however, and certainly much better than the inns of the Continent. Travel on horseback was the most common method of transportation, and probably the most comfortable, since coach building was a new and imperfect art. Coaches of state, some of which we see in prints and pictures of the era, were lumbering affairs, no doubt handsome enough in processions, but springless, unwieldly, and hard to pull. Carts and wagons were used for carrying merchandise, but packsaddles were safer and quicker. Under such difficulties, no metropolitan area such as London could possibly have thrived in the interior. London depended for its commercial greatness upon the Thames River and its access to the North Sea.

Commerce

When Elizabeth came to the English throne in 1558, England's chief foreign trade was with Antwerp, Bruges, and other Belgian cities. Antwerp was an especially important market for England's export of wool cloth. This market was seriously threatened, however, since the Low Countries were under the domination of the Catholic King of Spain, Philip II. When Philip undertook to punish his Protestant subjects in the Low Countries for their religious heresy, many of Elizabeth's counselors and subjects urged her to come to the defense of England's Protestant neighbors and trading allies. Elizabeth held back. Philip's armies attacked Antwerp in 1576 and again in 1585, putting an end to the commercial ascendancy of that great northern European metropolis. Perhaps as many as one-third of Antwerp's merchants and artisans settled in London, bringing with them their expert knowledge of commerce and manufacture. The influx of so many skilled workers and merchants into London produced problems of unemployment and overcrowding but contributed nevertheless to London's emergence as a leading port of trade.

English ships assumed a dominant position in Mediterranean trade, formerly carried on mainly by the Venetians. In the Baltic Sea, England competed successfully in trade that had previously been controlled by the Hanseatic League. Bristol thrived on commerce with Ireland and subsequently on trade with the Western Hemisphere. Boston and Hull increased their business with Scandinavian ports. The Russia Company was founded in 1555; the Levant Company became the famous East India Company in 1600; and the Virginia Company opened up trade with the New World in the Western Hemisphere. Fisheries were developed in the North Sea, in the waters north of Ireland, and off the banks of Newfoundland. Elizabeth and her ministers encouraged this commercial expansion.

The Poor Laws and Apprenticeship

Despite the new prosperity experienced by many Elizabethans, especially in London, unemployment remained a serious problem. The suppresssion of the monasteries in 1536–1539, as part of Henry VIII's reformation of the Catholic Church, had dispossessed a large class of persons who were not easily reemployed. Other causes of unemployment, such as the periodic collapse of the wool trade, dispossession of farm workers by enclosure of land, the sudden influx of skilled artisans from Antwerp, and the return of army veterans, have already been mentioned. Elizabethan parliaments attempted to cope with the problem of unemployment but did so in ways that seem unduly harsh today. Several laws were passed between 1531, when the distinction between those poor needing charity and those unwilling to work first became law, and 1597–1598. The harshest of the laws was that of 1547, providing that vagabonds be branded and enslaved for two years; escape was punishable by death or life enslavement. This act was repealed in 1549, but subsequent acts of 1572 and 1576 designated ten classes of vagrants and required municipal authorities to provide work for the healthy unemployed of each town or parish. This localization of responsibility laid the basis for what has been known historically as the "poor rate" (a local tax levied for the support of the poor) and for that sinister institution, the workhouse. The provisions of this act remained in force for centuries. The most comprehensive laws were those of the Parliament of 1597–1598, which repeated many provisions of earlier acts and added harsh, punitive penalties intended to send vagabonds back to the parishes in which they had been born or had last worked. After 1597, no begging was permitted; the poor were supposed to be provided for by the "poor rate" already established.

Regulations for apprentices were no less strict. An act of Parliament of 1563, known as the Statute of Artificers, gave the craft trades of England—still organized as medieval guilds—virtually complete authority over the young persons apprenticed to a trade. The law severely limited access to apprenticeship to sons of families with estates worth at least forty shillings of income. Apprenticeship usually began between the ages of fourteen and seventeen, and lasted for a period of not less than seven years. During this time, the young worker lived with the family of the employer. Without such an extensive apprenticeship, entry into the skilled crafts was virtually impossible. Apprenticeships were not open, however, in all guilds, and the law courts subsequently ruled that apprenticeship rules did not apply to crafts developed after 1563, so that exceptions did exist. All able-bodied workers not bound to crafts were supposed to work in agriculture. Acting companies, such as the company Shakespeare joined, were not technically organized as guilds, though the boys who played women's parts were in some cases at least bound by the terms of apprenticeship; a number of the adult actors belonged to one London guild or another and could use that status to apprentice boys. We do not know whether Shakespeare actually served such an indenture before becoming a full member of his acting company.

Although some Elizabethans rose to great wealth, poverty and unemployment were widespread.

Social Change

The opportunities for rapid economic advance in Elizabethan England, though limited almost entirely to those who were already prosperous, did produce social change and a quality of restlessness in English society. "New men" at court were an increasing phenomenon under the Tudor monarchs, especially Henry VII and Henry VIII, who tended to rely on loyal counselors of humble origin rather than on the once-too-powerful nobility. Cardinal Wolsey, for example, rose from obscurity to become the most mighty subject of Henry VIII's realm, with a newly built residence (Hampton Court) rivaling the splendor of the King's own palaces. He was detested as an upstart by old aristocrats, such as the Duke of Norfolk, and his sudden fall was as spectacular as had been his rise to power. The Earl of Leicester, Queen Elizabeth's first favorite, was a descendant of the Edmund Dudley who had risen from unpretentious beginnings to great eminence under Henry VII, Queen Elizabeth's grandfather. Although Queen Elizabeth did not contribute substantially to the new aristocracy—she created only three peers from 1573 onward—new and influential families were numerous throughout the century. Conversely, the ancient families discovered that they were no longer entrusted with positions of highest authority. To be sure, the aristocracy remained at the apex of England's social structure. New aspirants to power emulated the aristocracy by purchasing land and building splendid residences, rather than defining themselves as a rich new "middle class." Bourgeois status was something the new men put behind them as quickly as they could. Moreover, social mobility could work in both directions: upward and downward. Many men were quickly ruined by the costly and competitive business of seeking favor at the Tudor court. The poor, in a vast majority, enjoyed virtually no rights at all. Nonetheless, the Elizabethan era was one of greater opportunity for rapid social and economic advancement among persons of wealth than England had heretofore known.

Increased economic contacts with the outside world inevitably led to the importation of new styles of living. Such new fashions, together with the rapid changes now possible in social position, produced a reaction of dismay from those who feared the destruction of traditional English values. Attitudes toward Italy veered erratically between condemnation and admiration: on the one hand, Italy was the home of the Catholic Church and originator of many supposedly decadent fashions, whereas, on the other hand, Italy was the cradle of humanism and the country famed for Venice's experiment in republican government. To many conservative Englishmen, the word *Italianate* connoted a whole range of villainous practices, including diabolical methods of torture and revenge: poisoned books of devotion that would kill the unsuspecting victims who kissed them, ingeniously contrived chairs that would close upon the person who sat in them, and the like. The revenge plays of Shakespeare's contemporaries, such as *Antonio's Revenge* by John Marston, *The Revenger's Tragedy* probably by Thomas Middleton, and *The White Devil* by John Webster, offer spectacular caricatures of the so-called Italianate style in murder. The name of Italy was also associated with licentiousness, immorality, and outlandish fashions in clothes. France, too, was accused of encouraging such extravagances in dress as ornamented headdresses, stiffly pleated ruffs, padded doublets, puffed or double sleeves, and richly decorated hose. Rapid changes in fashion added to the costliness of being up to date and thereby increased the outcry against vanity in dress. Fencing, dicing, the use of cosmetics, the smoking of tobacco, the drinking of imported wines, and almost every vice known to humanity were attributed by angry moralists to the corrupting influence from abroad.

Not all Englishmen deplored continental fashion, of course. Persons of advanced taste saw the importation of European styles as a culturally liberating process. Fashion thus became a subject of debate between moral traditionalists and those who welcomed the new styles. The controversy was a bitter one, with religious overtones, in which the reformers' angry accusations became increasingly extreme. This attack on changing fashion was, in fact, an integral part of the Puritan movement. It therefore stressed the sinfulness, not only of extravagance in clothing, but also of the costliness in building great houses and other such worldly pursuits. Those whose sympathies were Puritan became more and more disaffected with the cultural values represented by the court, and thus English society drifted further and further toward irreconcilable conflict.

Shakespeare's personal views on this controversy are hard to determine and do not bear importantly on his achievement as an artist. Generally, however, we can observe that his many references to changes in fashion cater neither to the avant-garde nor to reactionary traditionalists. Shakespeare's audience was, after all, a broadly national one. It included many well-informed Londoners who viewed "Italianate" fashion neither with enthusiasm nor with alarm, but with satiric laughter. Such spectators would certainly have seen the point, for example, in Mercutio's witty diatribe at the expense of the new French style in fencing. The object of his scorn is Tybalt, who, according to Mercutio, "fights as you sing prick song" and fancies himself to be "the very butcher of a silk button." "Is not this a lamentable thing," asks Mercutio rhetorically, "that we should be thus afflicted with these strange flies, these fashionmongers, these pardon-me's, who stand so much on the new form that they cannot sit at ease on the old bench?" (*Romeo and Juliet*,

COURTESY, THE FOLGER SHAKESPEARE LIBRARY

This brothel scene, featuring gambling or dicing, illustrates some of the vices that were attributed to the corrupting influence from abroad.

2.4.20–35). In a similar vein, Shakespeare's audience would have appreciated the joking in *The Merchant of Venice* about England's servile imitation of continental styles in clothes. "What say you, then, to Falconbridge, the young baron of England?" asks Nerissa of her mistress Portia concerning one of Portia's many suitors. Portia replies, "How oddly he is suited! I think he bought his doublet in Italy, his round hose in France, his bonnet in Germany, and his behavior everywhere" (1.2.64–74). Court butterflies in Shakespeare's plays who bow and scrape and fondle their plumed headgear, like Le Beau in *As You Like It* and Osric in *Hamlet*, are the objects of ridicule. Hotspur in *1 Henry IV*, proud northern aristocrat that he is, has nothing but contempt for an effeminate courtier, "perfumèd like a milliner," who has come from King Henry to discuss the question of prisoners (1.3.36). Throughout Shakespeare's plays, the use of cosmetics generally has the negative connotation of artificial beauty used to conceal inward corruption, as in Claudius's reference to "the harlot's cheek, beautied with plast'ring art" (*Hamlet*, 3.1.52). Yet Shakespeare's treatment of newness in fashion is never shrill in tone. Nor does he fail in his dramas to give an honorable place to the ceremonial use of wealth and splendid costuming. His plays thus avoid both extremes in the controversy over changing fashions, though they give plentiful evidence as to the liveliness and currency of the topic.

Shakespeare also reflects a contemporary interest in the problem of usury, especially in *The Merchant of Venice*. Although usury was becoming more and more of a necessity, emotional attitudes toward it changed only slowly. The traditional moral view condemned usury as forbidden by Christian teaching; on the other hand, European governments of the sixteenth century found themselves increasingly obliged to borrow large sums of money. The laws against usury were alternatively relaxed and enforced, according to the economic exigencies of the moment. Shakespeare's plays capture the Elizabethan ambivalence of attitude toward this feared but necessary practice (see Introduction to *The Merchant of Venice*). Similarly, most Englishmen had contradictory attitudes toward what we today would call the law of supply and demand in the marketplace. Conservative moralists complained bitterly when merchants exploited the scarcity of some commodity by forcing up prices; the practice was denounced as excessive profit taking and declared to be sinful, like usury. In economic policy, then, as in matters of changing fashion or increased social mobility, many Englishmen were ambivalent about the perennial conflict between the old order and the new.

Elizabethan Houses

Those fortunate Englishmen who grew wealthy in the reign of Elizabeth took special pleasure in building themselves fine new houses with furnishings to match. Chimneys were increasingly common, so that smoke no longer had to escape through a hole in the roof. Pewter, or even silver dishes, took the place of the wooden spoon and trencher. Beds, and even pillows, became common. Carpets were replacing rushes as covering for the floors; wainscoting, tapestries or hangings, and pictures appeared on the walls; and glass began to be used extensively for windows.

Despite the warnings of those moralists who preached against the vanity of worldly acquisition, domestic comfort made considerable progress in Elizabethan England. Many splendid Tudor mansions stand today, testifying to the important social changes that had taken place between the strife-torn fifteenth century and the era of relative

Tudor mansions were often splendid, with impressive gardens and terraces. Shown here is Little Moreton Hall, in Cheshire, built in 1559.

THE NATIONAL TRUST PHOTOGRAPHIC LIBRARY. PHOTO BY GEOFF MORGAN

peace under Elizabeth. The battlement, the moat, the fortified gate, and the narrow window used for archery or firearms generally disappeared in favor of handsome gardens and terraces. At the lower end of the social scale, the agricultural laborers who constituted the great mass of the English population were generally poor, malnourished, and uneducated, but they seem to have enjoyed greater physical security than did their ancestors in the fifteenth century, and no longer needed to bring their cows, pigs, and poultry into their dwellings at night in order to protect them from thieves. City houses, of which many exist today, were often large and imposing structures, three or four stories in height, and framed usually of strong oak with the walls filled in with brick and plaster. Although the frontage on the streets of London was usually narrow, many houses had trees and handsome gardens at the rear. Of course London also had its plentiful share of tenements for the urban poor.

With the finer houses owned by the fortunate elite came features of privacy that had been virtually unknown to previous generations. Life in the household of a medieval lord had generally focused on the great hall, which could serve variously as the kitchen, dining hall, and sitting room for the entire family and its retainers. The men drank in the hall in the evenings and slept there at night. The new dwellings of prosperous Elizabethans, on the other hand, featured private chambers into which the family and the chief guests could retire.

The Elizabethans built well. Not only do we still admire their houses, but also we can see from their oriel windows and stained glass, their broad staircases, their jewels, and their costumes that they treasured the new beauty of their lives made possible by the culture of the Renaissance. Although the graphic and plastic arts did not thrive in England to the same extent as in Italy, France, and the Low Countries, England made lasting achievements in architecture, as well as in music, drama, and all forms of literature.

The Political and Religious Background

England under the Tudors suffered from almost unceasing religious conflict. The battle over religion affected every aspect of life and none more so than politics. At the very beginning of the Tudor reign, to be sure, England's problem was not religious but dynastic. Henry VII, the first of the Tudor kings, brought an end to the devastating civil wars of the fifteenth century with his overthrow of Richard III at the battle of Bosworth Field in 1485. The civil wars thus ended were the so-called Wars of the Roses, between the Lancastrian House of Henry VI (symbolized by the red rose) and the Yorkist House of Edward IV (symbolized by the white rose). Shakespeare chose these eventful struggles as the subject for his first series of English history plays, from *Henry VI* in three parts to *Richard III*. The House of Lancaster drew its title from John of Gaunt, Duke of Lancaster, father of Henry IV and great-grandfather of Henry VI; the House of York drew its title from Edmund Langley, Duke of York, great-grandfather of Edward IV and Richard III. Because John of Gaunt and Edmund Langley had been brothers, virtually all the noble contestants in this War of the Roses were cousins of one another, caught in a remorseless dynastic struggle for control of the English crown. Many of them lost their lives in the fighting. By 1485, England was exhausted from civil conflict. Although Henry VII's own dynastic claim to the throne was weak, he managed to suppress factional opposition and to give England the respite from war so desperately needed. His son, Henry VIII, inherited a throne in 1509 that was more secure than it had been in nearly a century.

Henry VIII's notorious marital difficulties, however, soon brought an end to dynastic security and civil accord. Moreover, religious conflict within the Catholic Church was growing to the extent that a break with Rome appeared inevitable. Henry's marriage troubles precipitated that momentous event. Because he divorced his first wife, Katharine of Aragon, in 1530 without the consent of Rome, he was excommunicated by the pope. His response in 1534 was to have himself proclaimed "Protector and only Supreme Head of the Church and Clergy of England." This decisive act signaled the

SOCIETY OF ANTIQUARIES OF LONDON

On Sundays crowds gathered to listen to the sermon at St. Paul's Cathedral, the subject of this anonymous painting dated 1616.

The Knights of the Garter belonged to the highest order of knighthood; many were influential courtiers and favorites of Queen Elizabeth. A masterful politician, Elizabeth remained unmarried throughout her life. A marriage would have upset the political balance and would have committed her to one foreign nation or to one constituency at home.

beginning of the Reformation in England, not many years after Martin Luther's momentous break with the papacy in 1517 and the consequent beginning of Lutheran Protestantism on the Continent. In England, Henry's act of defiance split the Church and the nation. Many persons chose Sir Thomas More's path of martyrdom rather than submit to Henry's new title as supreme head of the English church. Henry's later years did witness a period of retrenchment in religion, after the downfall of Thomas Cromwell in 1540, and indeed Henry's break with Rome had had its origin in political and marital strife as well as in matters of dogma and liturgy. Nevertheless, the establishment of an English church was now an accomplished fact. The accession of Henry's ten-year-old son Edward VI in 1547 gave reformers an opportunity to bring about rapid changes in English Protestantism. Archbishop Cranmer's forty-two articles of religion (1551) and his prayer book laid the basis for the Anglican Church of the sixteenth century.

The death of the sickly Edward VI in 1553 brought with it an intense crisis in religious politics and a temporary reversal of England's religious orientation. The Duke of Northumberland, Protector and virtual ruler of England in Edward's last years, attempted to secure a Protestant succession and his own power by marrying his son to Lady Jane Grey, a granddaughter of Henry VII, whom Edward had named heir to the throne, but the proclamation of Lady Jane as Queen ended in failure. She was executed, as were her husband and father-in-law. For five years, England returned to Catholicism under the rule of Edward's elder sister Mary, daughter of the Catholic Queen Katharine of Aragon. The crisis accompanying such changes of government during this midcentury period was greatly exacerbated by the fact that all three of Henry VIII's living children were considered illegitimate by one faction or another of the English people. In Protestant eyes, Mary was the daughter of the divorced Queen Katharine, whose marriage to Henry had never been valid because she had previously been the spouse of Henry VIII's older brother Arthur. This Arthur had died at a young age, in 1502, shortly after his state marriage to the Spanish princess. If, as the Protestants insisted, Arthur had consummated the marriage, then Katharine's subsequent union with her deceased husband's brother was invalid, and Henry was free, instead, to marry Anne Boleyn—the mother-to-be of Elizabeth. In Catholic eyes, however, both Elizabeth and her brother Edward VI (son of Jane Seymour, Henry VIII's third wife) were the bastard issue of Henry's bigamous marriages; Henry's one and only

true marriage in the Catholic faith was that to Katharine of Aragon. Edward and Elizabeth were regarded by many Catholics, at home and abroad, not only as illegitimate children, but also as illegitimate rulers, to be disobeyed and even overthrown by force. Thus, dynastic and marital conflicts became matters of grave political consequence.

Because of these struggles, Elizabeth's accession to the throne in 1558 remained an uncertainty until the last moment. Once she actually became ruler, England returned once more to the Protestant faith. Even then, tact and moderation were required to prevent open religious war. Elizabeth's genius at compromise prompted her to seek a middle position for her church, one that combined an episcopal form of church government (owing no allegiance to the pope) with an essentially traditional form of liturgy and dogma. As much as was practicable, she left matters up to individual conscience; she drew the line, however, where matters of conscience tended to "exceed their bounds and grow to be matter of faction." In practice, this meant that she did not tolerate avowed Catholics on the religious right or Protestant sects who denied the doctrine of the Trinity on the religious left. The foundation for this so-called Elizabethan compromise was the thirty-nine articles, adopted in 1563 and based in many respects upon Cranmer's forty-two articles of 1551. The compromise did not please everyone, of course, but it did achieve a remarkable degree of consensus during Elizabeth's long reign.

Queen Elizabeth and Tudor Absolutism

Elizabeth had to cope with a religiously divided nation and with extremists of both the right and the left who wished her downfall. She was a woman, in an age openly skeptical of women's ability or right to rule. Her success in dealing with such formidable odds was in large measure the result of her personal style as a monarch. Her combination of imperious will and femininity and her brilliant handling of her many contending male admirers have become legendary. She remained unmarried throughout her life, in part, at least, because marriage would have upset the delicate balance she maintained among rival groups, both foreign and domestic. Marriage would have committed her irretrievably to either one foreign nation or to one constituency at home. She chose instead to bestow her favor on certain courtiers, notably Robert Dudley (whom she elevated to be the Earl of Leicester) and, after Leicester's death in 1588, Robert Devereux, second Earl of Essex. Her relationship with these men, despite her partiality to them, was marked by her outbursts of tempestuous jealousy. In addition, she relied on the staid counsel of her hard-working ministers: Lord Burghley, Sir Francis Walsingham, Burghley's son Robert Cecil, and a few others.

In her personal style as monarch, Elizabeth availed herself of the theory of absolute supremacy. Under all the Tudors, England was nominally at least an absolute monarchy in an age when many of England's greatest rivals—France, Spain, the Holy Roman Empire—were also under absolutist rule. "Absolutism" meant that the monarch served for life, could not legally be removed from office, and was normally succeeded by his eldest son—all of this bolstered by claims of divine sanction, though the claims were frequently contested. The rise of absolutism throughout Renaissance Europe was the result of an increase of centralized national power and a corresponding decrease in autonomous baronial influence. Henry VII's strong assertion of his royal authority at the expense of the feudal lords corresponded roughly in time with the ascendancy of Francis I of France (1515) and Charles V of the Holy Roman Empire (1519). Yet England had long enjoyed a tradition of rule by consensus. When Elizabeth came to the throne, England was already in some ways a "limited" monarchy. Parliament, and especially the members of the House of Commons, claimed prerogatives of their own and were steadily gaining in both experience and power. In the mid-1560s, for example, the Commons made repeated attempts to use parliamentary tax-levying authority as a means of obliging Elizabeth to name a Protestant successor to the throne. The attempt, despite its failure to achieve its immediate goal, was significant; the Commons had shown that they were a force to be reckoned with. Even though Elizabeth made skillful rhetorical use of the theory of absolutism, portraying herself as God's appointed deputy on earth, her idea of absolutism should not be confused with despotism. To be sure, Elizabeth learned to avoid parliamentary interference in her affairs whenever possible; there were only thirteen sessions of Parliament in her forty-five years of rule. Still, Parliament claimed the right to establish law and to levy taxes on which the monarchy had to depend. Elizabeth needed all her considerable diplomatic skills in dealing with her parliaments and with the English people, who were self-reliant and proud of their reputation for independence. Elizabeth had more direct authority over her Privy Council, since she could appoint its members herself, yet even here she consulted faithfully with them on virtually everything she did. Nor were her closest advisers reluctant to offer her advice. Many vocal leaders in her government, including Walsingham and Leicester, urged the Queen during the 1570s and 1580s to undertake a more active military role on the Continent against the Catholic powers. So did her later favorite, the Earl of Essex. With remarkable tact, she managed to retain the loyalty of her militant and sometimes exasperated counselors, and yet to keep England out of war with Spain until that country actually launched an invasion attempt in 1588 (the Great Armada).

Catholic Opposition

During her early years, Elizabeth sought through her religious compromise to ease the divisions of her kingdom and attempted to placate her enemies abroad (notably Philip of Spain) rather than involve England in a costly war. For about twelve years, while England's economy gained much-needed strength, this policy of temporizing succeeded. Yet Elizabeth's more extreme Catholic opponents at home and abroad could never be reconciled to the daughter of that Protestant "whore," Anne Boleyn. England's period of relative accommodation came to an end in 1569 and 1570, with Catholic uprisings in the north and with papal excommunication of the English Queen. As a declared heretic, Elizabeth's very life was in danger; her Catholic subjects were encouraged by Rome to disobey her and to seek means for her violent overthrow.

Conspirators did, in fact, make attempts on the Queen's life, notably in the so-called Babington conspiracy of 1586, named for one of the chief participants. This plot, brought to light by Secretary of State Walsingham, sought to place Mary, Queen of Scots on the English throne in Elizabeth's stead. Mary was Elizabeth's kinswoman; Mary's grandmother, sister to Henry VIII, had been married to James IV of Scotland. So long as Elizabeth remained childless, Mary was a prominent heir to the English throne. Catholics pinned their hopes on her succession, by force if necessary; Protestant leaders urged Elizabeth to marry and give birth to a Protestant heir or at least to name a Protestant successor. Mary had abdicated the Scottish throne in 1567 after the sensational murder of her Catholic counselor David Rizzio, the murder of Mary's husband, the Earl of Darnley (in which Mary was widely suspected to have taken part), and her subsequent marriage to Darnley's slayer, the Earl of Bothwell. Taking refuge in England, Mary remained a political prisoner and the inevitable focus of Catholic plotting against Elizabeth for approximately two decades. She, in fact, assented in writing to Babington's plot against Elizabeth. All that long while Elizabeth resisted demands from her Protestant advisers that she execute her kinswoman and thereby end a constant threat to the throne; Elizabeth was reluctant to kill a fellow monarch and agreed fully with Mary's son James that "anointing by God cannot be defiled by man." Nonetheless, Mary's clear involvement in the Babington conspiracy led to the so-called Bond of Association, in which thousands of Englishmen pledged to prevent the succession of any per-

Along with the defeat of the Spanish Armada in 1588, the 1587 beheading of Mary, Queen of Scots, shown holding a crucifix and surrounded by official witnesses in this contemporary illustration, virtually ended any serious Catholic challenge to Elizabeth's throne.

son plotting Elizabeth's death, and then at last to Mary's execution in 1587. By that time, Spain was mounting an invasion against England, the Great Armada of 1588, and Elizabeth's temporizing tactics were no longer feasible. The long years of peace had done their work, however, and England was considerably stronger and more resolute than thirty years before. With Elizabeth's tacit approval, Sir Francis Drake and other naval commanders carried the fighting to Spain's very shore and to her American colonies. The war with Spain continued from 1588 until about 1597.

Elizabeth's great compromise dealt not only with the political dangers of opposition but also with the more central theological issues. England was sorely divided, as was much of Europe, on such matters as whether Christ's body was transubstantially present in the Mass, as Catholic faith maintained; whether good works were efficacious in salvation or whether people could be saved by God's grace alone, as the Reformers insisted; whether a portion of humankind was predeterminately damned, as the Calvinists believed; and the like. During the turbulent years of the Reformation, many people died for their faith. In general, the Elizabethan compromise insisted on allegiance to the English throne, church, and ecclesiastical hierarchy but allowed some latitude in matters of faith. The degree of elaboration in vestments and ritual was also an explosive issue on which the English church attempted to steer a central and pragmatic course, although conflicts inevitably arose within the church itself.

Protestant Opposition

The threat from the Protestant left was no less worrisome than that from the Catholic right. Protestant reformers had experienced their first taste of power at the time of Henry VIII's break with Rome in 1534. Under Thomas Cromwell, Cardinal Wolsey's successor as the King's chief minister, the monasteries were suppressed and William Tyndale's English Bible was authorized. The execution of Cromwell introduced a period of conservative retrenchment, but the accession of Edward VI in 1547 brought reform once more into prominence. Thereafter, Mary's Catholic reign drove most of the reformers into exile on the Continent. When they returned after 1558, many had been made more radical by their continental experience.

To be sure, reform covered a wide spectrum, from moderation to radicalism. Some preferred to work within the existing hierarchical structure of church and state, whereas others were religious separatists. Only the more radical groups, such as the Brownists and Anabaptists, endorsed ideas of equality and communal living. The abusive epithet "Puritan," applied indiscriminately to all reformers, tended to obscure the wide range of difference in the reform movement. The reformers were, to some extent, united by a dislike for formal ritual and ecclesiastical garments, by a preference for a simple and pious manner of living, and by a belief in the literal word of the Bible rather than the traditional teachings of the church fathers. They stressed personal responsibility in religion and were Calvinist in their emphasis on human depravity and the need for grace through election. Yet at first only the more radical were involved in a movement to separate entirely from the established English church.

The radicals on the religious left, even if they represented at first only a minority of the reformers, posed a serious threat to Elizabeth's government. Their program bore an ironic resemblance to that of the Catholic opposition on the religious right. In their theoretical writings, the extreme reformers justified overthrow of what they considered to be tyrannical rule, just as Catholic spokesmen had absolved Elizabeth's subjects of obedience to her on the grounds that she was illegitimate. Both extremes appealed to disobedience in the name of a higher religious law, as enunciated in Romans 13:1–2: "For there is no power but of God." Among the reforming theoreticians was John Ponet, whose *Short Treatise of Politic Power* (1556) argued that a monarch is subject to a social contract and must rule according to laws that are equally subscribed to by Parliament, the clergy, and the people.

The Doctrine of Passive Obedience

Elizabeth's government countered such assaults on its authority, from both the right and the left, with many arguments, of which perhaps the most central was that of passive obedience. This doctrine condemned rebellion under virtually all circumstances. Its basic assumption was that the king or queen is God's appointed deputy on earth. To depose such a monarch must therefore be an act of disobedience against God's will. Since God is all-wise and all-powerful, his placing of an evil ruler in power must proceed from some divine intention, such as the punishment of a wayward people. Rebellion against God's "scourge" merely displays further disobedience to God's will. A people suffering under a tyrant must wait patiently for God to remove the burden, which he will surely do when the proper time arrives.

This doctrine was included in the official book of homilies of the Church of England and was read from the pulpit at regular intervals. The best-known such homily, entitled *Against Disobedience and Willful Rebellion,* had been preceded by such tracts as William Tyndale's *Obedience of a Christian Man* (1528); a book of homilies, published in 1547, including an "Exhortation Concerning Good Order and Obedience"; Thomas Cranmer's *Notes for a Sermon on the Rebellion of 1549;* and Hugh Latimer's *Sermon on the Lord's Prayer* (1552). Shakespeare heard such homilies often, and he expresses their ideas through several of his characters, such as John of Gaunt and the Bishop of Carlisle in *Richard II* (1.2.37–41, 4.1.115–50). This is not to say that he endorses such ideas, for he sets them in dramatic opposition to other and more heterodox concepts. We can say, nevertheless, that Shakespeare's audience would have recognized in Gaunt's speeches a clear expression of a familiar and officially correct position.

The Political Ideas of Machiavelli

The orthodoxies of the Elizabethan establishment were under attack, not only from the Catholic right and the Protestant left, but also from a new and revolutionary point of view that set aside all criteria of religious morality. Tudor defense of order was based, as we have seen, on the assumption that the monarch rules in accord with a divine plan, a higher Law of Nature to which every just ruler is attuned. Political morality must be at one with religious morality. Catholic and Protestant critiques of the Tudor establishment made similar assumptions, even though they appealed to revolution in the name of that religious morality. To Niccolò Machiavelli, on the other hand, politics was a manipulative science best governed by the dictates of social expediency. His philosophy did not, as many accusingly charged, lead necessarily to the cynical promotion of mere self-interest. Nevertheless, he did argue, in his *Discourses* and *The Prince*, that survival and political stability are the first obligations of any ruler. Machiavelli regarded religion as a tool of the enlightened ruler rather than as a morally absolute guide. He extolled in his ideal leader the quality of *virtù*—a mixture of cunning and forcefulness. He saw history as a subject offering practical lessons in the kind of pragmatic statecraft he proposed.

Machiavelli was a hated name in England, and most of his works were never available in an English printed edition during Shakespeare's lifetime. (The *Florentine History* was translated in 1595; *The Prince* was not translated until 1640.) Nevertheless, his writings were available in Italian, French, and Latin editions, and in manuscript English translations. His ideas certainly had a profound impact on the England of the 1590s. Marlowe caricatures the Italian writer in his *The Jew of Malta,* but he clearly was fascinated by what Machiavelli had to say. Shakespeare, too, reveals a complex awareness. However much he may lampoon the Machiavellian type of conscienceless villain in *Richard III,* he shows us more plausible pragmatists in *Richard II* and *1 Henry IV*. Conservative theories of the divine right of kings are set in debate with the more heterodox ambitions of Henry Bolingbroke (who then adopts the most orthodox of political vocabularies once he is king). Bolingbroke is not a very attractive figure, but he does succeed politically where Richard has failed.

Shakespeare thus reveals himself as less a defender of the established order than as a great dramatist able to give sympathetic expression to the aspirations of all sides in a tense political struggle. His history plays have been variously interpreted either as defenses of monarchy or as subtle pleas for rebellion, but the consensus today is that the plays use political conflict as a way of probing the motivations of social behavior. To be sure, the plays do stress the painful consequences of disorder and present, on the whole, an admiring view of monarchy (especially in *Henry V*), despite the manifest limitations of that institution. Certainly, we can sense that Shakespeare's history plays were written for a generation of Englishmen who had experienced political crisis and who could perceive issues of statecraft in Shakespeare's plays that were relevant to England's struggles in the 1580s and the 1590s. The play of *King John,* for example, deals with a king whose uncertain claim to the throne is challenged by France and the papacy in the name of John's nephew, Arthur; Elizabeth faced a similar situation in her dilemma over her kinswoman, Mary, Queen of Scots. Elizabeth also bitterly acknowledged the cogency of a popular analogy comparing her reign with that of King Richard II, and, when Shakespeare's play about Bolingbroke's overthrow of Richard was apparently revived for political purposes shortly before the Earl of Essex's abortive rebellion against Elizabeth in 1601, Shakespeare's acting company had some explaining to do to the authorities (see Introduction to *Richard II*). Nevertheless, Shakespeare's attitudes toward the issues of his own day are ultimately unknowable and unimportant, since his main concern seems to have been with the dramatization of political conflict rather than with the urging of a polemical position.

Shakespeare on Religion

Our impressions of Shakespeare's personal sympathies in religion are similarly obscured by his refusal to use his art for polemical purposes. To be sure, members of his mother's family in Warwickshire seem to have remained loyal to Catholicism, and his father John Shakespeare may conceivably have undergone financial and other difficulties in Stratford for reasons of faith. (See "Shakespeare's Family" below, in the section on Shakespeare's Life and Work.) Certainly Shakespeare himself displays a familiarity with some Catholic practices and theology, as when the Ghost of Hamlet's father speaks of being "Unhousled, disappointed, unaneled" (i.e., not having received last rites) at the time of his murder (*Hamlet,* 1.5.78). Nonetheless, we see in his plays a spectrum of religious attitudes portrayed with an extraordinary range of insight. In matters of doctrine, his characters are at various times acquainted with Catholic theology or with the controversy concerning salvation by faith or good works (see *Measure for Measure,* 1.2.24–5), and yet a consistent polemical bias is absent. Some Catholic prelates are schemers, like Pandulph in *King John*. Ordinarily, however, Shakespeare's satirical digs at ecclesiastical pomposity and hypocrisy have little to do with the Catholic question. Cardinal Beaufort in *1 Henry VI* is a political maneuverer, but so are many of his secular rivals. Cardinal Wolsey in *Henry VIII* is motivated by personal ambition, rather than by any sinister conspiracy of the international church. Many of Shakespeare's nominally Catholic clerics, such as Friar Laurence in *Romeo and Juliet* or Friar Francis in *Much Ado About Nothing,* are gentle and well-intentioned people, even if occasionally bumbling. We can certainly say that Shakespeare consistently avoids the chauvinistic anti-Catholic baiting so often found in the plays of his contemporaries.

The same avoidance of extremes can be seen in his portrayal of Protestant reformers, though the instances in this case are few. Malvolio in *Twelfth Night* is fleetingly compared with a "puritan" (2.3.139–46), although Shakespeare insists that no extensive analogy can be made. Angelo in *Measure for Measure* is sometimes thought to be a critical portrait of the Puritan temperament. Even if this were so, Shakespeare's satire is extremely indirect compared with the lampoons written by his contemporaries Ben Jonson and Thomas Dekker.

Stuart Absolutism

Queen Elizabeth's successor, James I of the Scottish house of Stuarts, reigned from 1603 to 1625. Even more than Elizabeth, he was a strong believer in the divinely appointed authority of kings; whereas she had insisted on divine sanction, James and his successor Charles called it a divine right. Although James succeeded easily to the throne in 1603, since he was Protestant with a legitimate claim of descent from Henry VIII, the English people did not take to this foreigner from the north. James was eccentric in his personal habits, and the English were always inclined to be suspicious of the Scots in any case. As a result, James was less successful in dealing with the heterogeneous and antagonistic forces that Elizabeth had kept in precarious balance. At the Hampton Court Conference of 1604, relations quickly broke down between James and the Puritan wing of the church, so that even its more moderate adherents joined forces with the separatists. James had similar difficulties with an increasingly radical group in the House of Commons. In the widening rift between the absolutists and those who defended the supremacy of Parliament,

James's court moved toward the right. Catholic sympathies at court became common. Civil war was still a long way off and by no means inevitable; the beheading of King Charles I (James's son) would not occur until 1649. Still, throughout James's reign, the estrangement between the right and the left was becoming more and more uncomfortable. The infamous Gunpowder Plot of 1605, in which Guy Fawkes and other Catholic conspirators were accused of having plotted to blow up the houses of Parliament, raised hysteria to a new intensity. Penal laws against papists were harshly enforced. The Parliament of 1614 included in its membership John Pym, Thomas Wentworth, and John Eliot—men who were to become turbulent spokesmen against taxes imposed without parliamentary grant, imprisonment without the stating of specific criminal charges, and other purported abuses of royal power. The polarization of English society naturally affected the London theaters. Popular London audiences (generally sympathetic with religious reform) eventually grew disaffected with the stage, while even the popular acting companies came under the increasing domination of the court. Shakespeare's late plays reflect the increasing influence of a courtly audience.

The Intellectual Background

Renaissance Cosmology

In learning, as in politics and religion, Shakespeare's England was a time of conflict and excitement. Medieval ideas of a hierarchical and ordered creation were under attack but were still widely prevalent, and were used to justify a hierarchical order in society itself. According to the so-called Ptolemaic system of the universe, formulated by Ptolemy of Alexandria in the second century A.D., the earth stood at the center of creation. Around it moved, in nine concentric spheres, the heavenly bodies of the visible universe, in order as follows (from the earth outward): the moon, Mercury, Venus, the sun, Mars, Jupiter, Saturn, the fixed stars on a single plane, and lastly the *primum mobile,* imparting motion to the whole system. (See the accompanying illustration.) Some commentators proposed alternate arrangements or speculated as to the existence of one or two additional spheres, in particular a "crystalline sphere" between the fixed stars and the *primum mobile.* These additional spheres were needed to cope with matters not adequately explained in Ptolemaic astronomy, such as the precession of the equinoxes. More troublesomely, the seemingly erratic retrograde motion of the planets—that is, the refusal of Mars and other planets to move around the earth in steady orbit—called forth increasingly ingenious theories, such as Tycho Brahe's scheme of epicycles. Still, the conservative appeal of the earth-centered cosmos remained very strong. How could one suppose that the earth was not at the center of the universe?

The *primum mobile* was thought to turn the entire universe around the earth once every twenty-four hours. Simultaneously, the individual heavenly bodies moved more slowly around the earth on their individual spheres, constantly changing position with respect to the fixed stars. The moon, being the only heavenly body that seemed subject to change in its monthly waxing and waning, was thought to represent the boundary between the unchanging universe and the incessantly changing world. Beneath the moon, in the "sublunary" sphere, all creation was subject to death as a result of Adam's fall from grace; beyond the moon lay perfection. Hell was imagined to exist deep within the earth, as in Dante's *Inferno,* or else outside the *primum mobile* and far below the created universe in the realm of chaos, as in Milton's *Paradise Lost.*

Heaven or the Empyrean stood, according to most Ptolemaic systems, at the top of the universe. Between heaven and earth dwelled the nine angelic orders, each associated with one of the nine concentric spheres. According to a work attributed to Dionysius the Areopagite, *On the Heavenly Hierarchy* (fifth century A.D.), the nine angelic orders consisted of three hierarchies. Closest to God were the contemplative orders of Seraphim, Cherubim, and Thrones; next, the intermediate orders of Dominions, Powers, and Virtues; and finally the active orders of Principalities, Archangels, and Angels. These last served as God's messengers and intervened from time to time in the affairs of mortals. Ordered life among humans, although manifestly imperfect when compared with the eternal bliss of the angelic orders, still modeled itself on that platonic idea of perfect harmony. Thus the state, the church, and the family all resembled one another because they resembled (however distantly) the kingdom of God. Richard Hooker, in his *Of the Laws of Ecclesiastical Polity* (1594–1597), defends the established Church of England in terms that emanate from a comparable idea of a divine, creative, and ordering law of nature "Whose seat is the bosom of God, whose voice the harmony of the world."

The devils of hell were fallen angels, with Satan as their leader. Such evil spirits might assume any number of shapes, such as demons, goblins, wizards, or witches. Believers in evil spirits generally made no distinction between orthodox Christian explanations of evil and the more primitive folklore of witchcraft. Belief in witchcraft was widespread indeed; King James I took the matter very seriously. So did Reginald Scot's *The Discovery of Witchcraft* (1584), though its author also attempted to confute what he regarded as ignorant superstition and charlatanism. Throughout Shakespeare's lifetime, belief and skepticism about such matters existed side by side.

A similar ambiguity pertained to belief in the Ptolemaic universe itself. All major poets of the Renaissance,

Ptolemy's earth-centered system of the universe (top) was challenged by the sun-centered system of Copernicus (bottom) with the publishing of De revolutionibus orbium coelestium *in 1543. Shakespeare, like other major poets of the English Renaissance, poetically represents the universe in cosmic terms as described by Ptolemy, but also reflects uncertainties generated by the new cosmology.*

including Shakespeare, Spenser, and Milton (who completed *Paradise Lost* after 1660), represented the universe in cosmic terms essentially as described by Ptolemy. Yet Nicolaus Copernicus's revolutionary theory of a sun-centered solar system (*De revolutionibus orbium coelestium*, published on the Continent in 1543) and the discovery of a new star in Cassiopeia in 1572 stimulated much new thought. Galileo Galilei, born in the same year as Shakespeare (1564), published in 1610 the results of his telescopic examinations of the moon, thereby further confirming Copernicus's hypothesis. Although the news of Galileo's astounding discovery came too late to affect any but the latest of Shakespeare's plays, a sense of excitement and dislocation was apparent throughout most of the years of his writing career. Thomas Nashe, in 1595, referred familiarly to Copernicus as the author "who held that the sun remains immobile in the center of the world, and that the earth is moved about the sun" (Nashe, *Works*, ed. R. B. McKerrow, 1904–1910, 3.94). John Donne lamented in 1611–1612 that the "new philosophy" (i.e., the new science) "calls all in doubt." Skeptical uncertainty about the cosmos was on the rise. The poetic affirmations in Renaissance art of traditional ideas of the cosmos can best be understood as a response to uncertainty—a statement of faith in an age of increasing skepticism.

Alchemy and Medicine

In all areas of Renaissance learning, the new and the old science were juxtaposed. Alchemy, for example, made important contributions to learning, despite its superstitious character. Its chief goal was the transformation of base metals into gold, on the assumption that all metals were ranked on a hierarchical scale and could be raised from lower to higher positions on that scale by means of certain alchemical techniques. Other aims of alchemy included the discovery of a universal cure for diseases and of a means for preserving life indefinitely. Such aims encouraged quackery and prompted various exposés, such as Chaucer's "The Canon's Yeoman's Tale" (late fourteenth century) and Jonson's *The Alchemist* (1610). Yet many of the procedures used in alchemy were essentially chemical procedures, and the science of chemistry received a valuable impetus from constant experimentation. Queen Elizabeth was seriously interested in alchemy throughout her life.

In physics, medicine, and psychology, as well, older concepts vied with new. Traditional learning apportioned all physical matter into four elements: earth, air, fire, and water. Each of these was thought to be a different combination of the four "qualities" of the universe: hot, cold, moist, and dry. Earth combined cold and dry; air, hot and moist; fire, hot and dry; and water, cold and moist. Earth and water were the baser or lower elements, confined to the physical world; fire and air were aspiring elements,

Alchemists employed relatively sophisticated equipment in their futile search for the "philosopher's stone," a reputed substance supposed to possess the property of changing other metals into gold and silver.

tending upward. Humans, as a microcosm of the larger universe, contained in themselves the four elements. The individual's temperament, or "humor" or "complexion," depended on which "humor" predominated in that person. The four humors in humans corresponded to the four elements of physical matter. The blood was hot and moist, like air; yellow bile or choler was hot and dry, like fire; phlegm was cold and moist, like water; and black bile was cold and dry, like earth. A predominance of blood in an individual created a sanguine or cheerful temperament (or humor), yellow bile produced a choleric or irascible temperament, phlegm produced a phlegmatic or stolid temperament, and black bile produced a melancholic temperament. Diet could affect the balance among these humors, since an excess of a particular food would stimulate overproduction of one humor. The stomach and the liver, which converted food into humors, were regarded as the seat of human passions. The spleen was thought to be the seat of laughter, sudden impulse, or caprice, and also melancholy. (Hotspur, in *1 Henry IV,* is said to be "governed by a spleen," 5.2.19.) Strong emotional reactions could be explained in terms of the physiology of the humors: in anger, the blood rushed to the head and thereby produced a flush of red color and staring eyes; in fear, the blood migrated to the heart and thus left the face and liver pale, and so on. Sighs supposedly cost the heart a drop of blood, while wine could refortify it (as Falstaff insists in 2 *Henry IV,* 4.3.90–123). The signs of youth were warmth and moisture, as in Desdemona's "hot and moist" hand (*Othello,* 3.4.39); those of age were "a moist eye, a dry hand, a yellow cheek, a white beard, a decreasing leg, an increasing belly" (2 *Henry IV,* 1.2.179–81). A common remedy for illness was to let blood and thereby purge the body of unwanted humors.

The name traditionally associated with such theories was that of Galen, the most celebrated of ancient writers on medicine (c. 130 A.D.). A more revolutionary name was that of Paracelsus, a famous German physician (c. 1493–1541) who attacked the traditional medical learning of his time and urged a more unfettered pragmatic research into pharmacy and medicine. Such experimentalism bore fruit in the anatomical research of Vesalius (1514–1564) and in William Harvey's investigations of the circulation of the blood (c. 1616). Nevertheless, the practice of medicine in Renaissance times remained under the influence of the "humors" theory until quite late, and its ideas are found throughout Shakespeare's writings.

The four humors of black bile, blood, yellow bile or choler, and phlegm, as shown in this illustration from an illuminated manuscript, were believed to govern the human personality by producing a disposition toward melancholic, sanguine, choleric, or phlegmatic temperaments.

Learning

In learning generally, and in theories of education, new ideas conflicted with old. The curriculum of schools and colleges in the Renaissance was inherited largely from the Middle Ages and displayed many traditional characteristics. The curriculum consisted of the seven Liberal Arts: a lower division, called the trivium, comprised of grammar, rhetoric, and logic; and an upper division, called the quadrivium, comprised of arithmetic, geometry, astronomy, and music. In addition, there were the philosophical studies associated chiefly with Aristotle: natural philosophy, ethics, and metaphysics.

Aristotle's name had a towering influence in medieval times and remained important to the Renaissance as well. Even among his Renaissance admirers, however, Aristotle proved more compelling in practical matters than in the abstract scholastic reasoning associated with his name in the Middle Ages. The Italian Aristotelians whose work made its way into England were interested primarily in the science of human behavior. Aristotelian ethics was for them a practical subject, telling people how to live usefully and well and how to govern themselves politically. Rhetoric was the science of persuasion, enabling people to use eloquence for socially useful goals. Poetry was a kind of rhetoric, a language of persuasion which dramatists, too, might use for morally pragmatic ends.

At the same time, new thinkers were daring to attack Aristotle by name as a symbol of traditional medieval thought. The attack was not always fair to Aristotle himself, whose work had been bent to the *a priori* purposes of much medieval scholasticism. Nevertheless, his name had assumed such symbolic importance that he had to be confronted directly. The Huguenot logician Petrus Ramus (1515–1572), defiantly proclaiming that "everything that Aristotle taught is false," argued for rules of logic as derived from observation. He urged, for example, that his students learn about rhetoric from observing in detail Cicero's effect on his listeners, rather than by the rote practice of syllogism. Actually, Ramus's thought was less revolutionary in its concepts of logic than in the tremendous ferment of opinion caused by his iconoclastic teaching.

A basic issue at stake in the anti-Aristotelian movement was that of traditional authority versus independent observation. How do people best acquire true knowledge—through the teachings of their predecessors or through their own discovery? The issue had profound implications for religious truth as well: should individuals heed the collective wisdom of the earthly church or read the Bible with their individual perceptions as their guide? Is "reason" an accretive wisdom handed down by authority or a quality of the individual soul? Obviously, a middle ground exists between the two extremes, and no new thinker of the Renaissance professed to abandon entirely the use of ancient authority. For men like Henricus Agrippa (1486–1535) and Sir Francis Bacon (1561–1626), however, scholastic tradition had exerted its oppressive influence far too long. Authority needed to be examined critically and scientifically. Bacon, in his *The Advancement of Learning* (1605), fought against the blind acceptance of ancient wisdom and argued that "knowledge derived from Aristotle, and exempted from liberty of examination, will not rise again higher than the knowledge of Aristotle." Sir Walter Ralegh and others joined in the excited new search for what human "reason" could discover when set free from scholastic restraint. Such belief in the perfectibility of human reason owed some of its inspiration to Italian Neoplatonic humanists like Giovanni Pico della Mirandola (1463–1494), who, in his *Oration on the Dignity of Man*, celebrated a human race "constrained by no limits" in accordance with the potential of its own free will. The new learning did not seem to trouble these men in their religious faith, although a tension between scientific observation and faith in miracles was to become plentifully evident in the seventeenth century.

The Nature of Humankind

Medieval thought generally assigned to humankind a uniquely superior place in the order of creation on earth. That assumption of superiority rested on biblical and patristic teachings about the hierarchy of creation, in which humanity stood at the apex of physical creation nearest God and the angels. Humankind was thus supreme on earth in the so-called chain of being. Human reason, though subject to error because of sinfulness, enabled humans to aspire toward divinity. Humans were, in the view of medieval philosophers, the great amphibians, as well as the microcosm of the universe, part bestial and part immortal, doomed by Adam's fall to misery and death in this life but promised eternal salvation through Christ's atonement. Right reason, properly employed, could lead to the truths of revealed Christianity and thus give humankind a glimpse of the heavenly perfection one day to be ours. Renaissance Neoplatonism, as expounded, for example, in the writings of Marsilio Ficino, Pico della Mirandola, and Baldassare Castiglione (in *The Courtier*, translated by Sir Thomas Hoby in 1561), offered humanity a vision of a platonic ladder, extending from the perception of physical beauty to contemplation of the platonic idea of beauty and finally to the experiencing of God's transcendent love.

Protestant thought of the Renaissance did not wholly disagree with this formulation, but it did place a major new emphasis on human reprobation. The idea was not new, for Saint Augustine (354–430) had insisted on human depravity and our total dependence on God's inscrutable grace, but, in the years of the Reformation, this theology took on a new urgency. Martin Luther

(1483–1540), by rejecting veneration of the Virgin Mary and the saints, and by taking away the sacraments of confession and penance, by which individual Christians could seek the institutional comforts of the Catholic Church, exposed the individual sinner to agonies of conscience that could result in a sense of alienation and loss. The rewards were great for those who found new faith in God's infinite goodness, but the hazards of predestinate damnation were fearsome to those who were less sure of their spiritual welfare. Luther's God was inscrutable, majestic, and infallible. Luther's God decreed salvation for the elect and damnation for all others, and His will could not be challenged or questioned. The individual was to blame for sin, even though God hardened the hearts of the reprobate. John Calvin (1509–1564) placed even greater stress on predestinate good and evil and insisted that the grace of salvation was founded on God's freely given mercy that humans could not possibly deserve. Salvation was God's to give or withhold as He wished; humans might not repine that in His incomprehensible wisdom God has "barred the door of life to those whom He has given over to damnation." Faced with such a view of human spiritual destiny, the individual Christian's lot was one of potential tragedy. The human soul was a battleground of good and evil.

Michel de Montaigne (1533–1592), Shakespeare's great French contemporary, provided a very different and heterodox way of thinking about human imperfection. In his "Apology for Raymond Sebond" and other of his essays, Montaigne questioned the assumption of humanity's superiority to the animal kingdom, and in doing so gave Shakespeare a fundamentally different way to consider the nature of humankind—a way that reflects itself, for example, in Hamlet's observations on humans as "quintessence of dust." Montaigne stressed humans' arrogance, vanity, and frailty. He was unconvinced of humanity's purported moral superiority to the animals and argued that animals are no less endowed with a soul. Montaigne undermined, in other words, the hierarchy in which the human race was the unquestioned master of the physical world, just as Copernican science overturned the earth-centered cosmos and Machiavelli's political system dismissed as an improbable fiction the divinely constituted hierarchy of the state. Montaigne's very choice of

BY PERMISSION OF THE BRITISH LIBRARY

This guide, graphically setting forth the ideals to which every English gentlewoman and gentleman should aspire, illustrates the Renaissance concept that outward deportment and accomplishments should correctly and invariably mirror a person's inner nature.

the essay as his favorite literary form bespeaks his commitment to attempts and explorations, rather than to definite solutions; etymologically, the very word "essay" signifies an exploration or inquiry. Montaigne was not alone in his skepticism about human nature; his ideas had much in common with Bernardino Telesio's *De Rerum Natura* and with the writings of the Italian Giordano Bruno. Montaigne was followed in the seventeenth century by that overpowering iconoclast, Thomas Hobbes, who extended the concept of mechanical laws governing human society and human psychology. Hobbes postdates Shakespeare, to be sure, but one has only to consider Iago's philosophy of the assertive individual will (in *Othello*) or Edmund's contempt for his father Gloucester's astrological pieties (in *King Lear*) to see the enormous impact on Shakespeare of the new heterodoxies of his age. Shakespeare makes us aware that skeptical thought can be used by dangerous men like Iago, Edmund, and Richard III to promote their own villainies in a world no longer held together by the certitudes of traditional faith, but he also shows us the gullibility of some traditionalists and the abuses of power that can be perpetrated in the name of ancient and divine privilege by a king like Richard II. Above all, Shakespeare delights in the play of mind among competing ideas, inviting us to wonder, for example, if Caliban in *The Tempest* is not invested with natural qualities that Prospero, his Christian colonizer, does not sufficiently understand, and whether some of the other supposedly civilized Europeans who come to Caliban's island do not have a great deal to learn from its uncivilized beauty.

LONDON THEATERS AND DRAMATIC COMPANIES

Throughout Shakespeare's life, the propriety of acting any plays at all was a matter of bitter controversy. Indeed, when one considers the power and earnestness of the opposition, one is surprised that such a wealth of dramatic excellence could come into being and that Shakespeare's plays should reflect so little the anger and hostility generated by this continuing conflict.

Religious and Moral Opposition to the Theater

From the 1570s onward, and even earlier, the city fathers of London revealed an ever-increasing distrust of the public performance of plays. They fretted about the dangers of plague and of riotous assembly. They objected to the fact that apprentices idly wasted their time instead of working in their shops. And always the municipal authorities suspected immorality. Thus, by an order of the Common Council of London, dated December 6, 1574, the players were put under severe restrictions.

The order cites the reasons. The players, it was charged, had been acting in the innyards of the city, which in consequence were haunted by great multitudes of people, especially youths. These gatherings had been the occasions of frays and quarrels, "evil practices of incontinency in great inns"; the players published "uncomely and unshamefast speeches and doings," withdrew the Queen's subjects from divine service on Sundays and holidays, wasted the money of "poor and fond persons," gave opportunity to pick pockets, uttered "busy and seditious matters," and injured and maimed people by the falling of their scaffolds and by weapons and powder used in plays. The order goes on to state the Common Council's fear that if the plays, which had been forbidden on account of the plague, should be resumed, God's wrath would manifest itself by an increase of the infection. Therefore, no innkeeper, tavernkeeper, or other person might cause or suffer to be openly played "any play, interlude, comedy, tragedy, matter, or show" which had not been first licensed by the mayor and the Court of Aldermen.

The mayor and aldermen did not always state their case plainly, because Queen Elizabeth was a patron of the players, and because the players had friends and patrons in the Privy Council and among the nobility; sometimes, however, they did so quite boldly. One sees the case against plays stated syllogistically in the following words of Thomas White, a preacher at Paul's Cross in 1577:

> Look but upon the common plays of London, and see the multitude that flocketh to them and followeth them! Behold the sumptuous theater houses, a continual monument of London prodigality and folly! But I understand they are now forbidden because of the plague. I like the policy well if it hold still, for a disease is but botched and patched up that is not cured in the cause, and the cause of plagues is sin, if you look to it well, and the cause of sin are plays. Therefore the cause of plagues are plays. (From *A Sermon preached at Paul's Cross . . . in the Time of the Plague,* 1578.)

Moved, no doubt, by the prohibition of the Common Council, James Burbage, with a company of actors under the patronage of the Earl of Leicester, leased a site in Shoreditch, a London suburb in Middlesex, beyond the immediate jurisdiction of the official enemies in the Common Council, whose authority extended only to the city limits. By 1576, he had completed the Theatre. Perhaps he called it "the Theatre" because it had no competitor (other than the Red Lion, established in 1567 and used seemingly as a playing place for feasts and festival days in the performance style of Corpus Christi and saints' plays). Burbage erected what may have been England's first permanent commercial theatrical building. In general, the building combined features of the innyard and the animal-baiting house, having a central and probably paved courtyard open to the sky (like an innyard) and

NATIONAL TRUST PHOTOGRAPHIC LIBRARY. PHOTO BY ANDREW SALTER

The George Inn of Southwark, England, London's only surviving galleried inn, was destroyed by fire in 1676 but rebuilt the following year with two galleries instead of the original three. Despite these changes, the George Inn gives us the best picture we have of the kind of space in which traveling companies could mount their plays on bare platform stages.

surrounding galleries on all sides (like an animal-baiting house). Burbage erected a stage at one side of the circular arena and put dressing rooms behind it to form the "tiring house" or backstage area for the actors; the facade of this "tiring house" served as a visible backdrop to the stage itself. Burbage's Theatre became the model for other public playhouses, such as the Curtain, the Swan, and the Globe, which were constructed later.

By building his playhouse in Shoreditch, Burbage gained immunity from the London authorities. The city fathers could not suppress plays or control them with perfect success if they were performed in Middlesex, or in the "liberty" of Blackfriars and similar districts exempted by charters from London's civic authority (see "London's Private Theaters," below), or (in the case of later playhouses) on the Bankside across the Thames in Surrey. In order to get at them in these suburban regions, the city authorities had to petition the Queen's Privy Council to give orders to the magistrates and officers of the law in these counties. The Queen's Privy Council, although always on the most polite terms with the Lord Mayor and his brethren of the city and always open to the argument that the assemblage of crowds caused the spread of the plague, was to a much less degree in sympathy with the moral scruples of the city. Current arguments for the plays, derived from the works of scholars, poets, and playwrights, were numerous and often heard: namely, that classical antiquity gave precedent for dramatic spectacles; that by drawing a true picture of both the bad and the good in life, plays enabled people to choose the good; that people should have wholesome amusement; and that plays provided livelihood for loyal subjects of the Queen.

Of these arguments, to be sure, the Privy Council made little use, resting the case for plays instead on what was, no doubt, an unanswerable argument: that since the players were to appear before Her Majesty, especially during the Christmas/Shrovetide period, the players needed practice in order to prepare themselves to please the royal taste. A good deal of politic fencing ensued, and, so far as orders, complaints, and denunciations were concerned, the reforming opposition had much the better of it. The preachers thundered against plays. Pamphleteers denounced all matters pertaining to the stage: Stephen Gosson in *The School of Abuse, Containing a Pleasant Invective Against Poets, Pipers, Players, Jesters and Suchlike Caterpillars of a Commonwealth* (1579) and other works; Philip Stubbes in *The Anatomy of Abuses* (1583); and finally and most furiously of all, William Prynne in *Histrio-Mastix: The Players' Scourge or Actor's Tragedy* (1633). Gosson spoke of plays as "the inventions of the devil, the offerings of idolatry, the pomp of worldlings, the blossoms of vanity, the root of apostacy, food of iniquity, riot and adultery." "Detest them," he warned. "Players are masters of vice, teachers of wantonness, spurs to impurity, the sons of idleness."

At first, such diatribes represented an extreme reforming opinion obviously not shared by a majority of London viewers. They kept coming to plays, and the flourishing public theaters attracted the talents of the age's leading dramatists. An ominous note of polarization was sounded, however, early in the reign of James I (1603–1625) when the rift between the Puritans and the court broke into open antagonism. After about 1604, when James alienated the Puritans at the Hampton Court Conference, the split between popular audiences and the best drama of the age became increasingly evident. Shakespeare's company, now the King's men, gravitated, whether through choice or necessity, toward the precinct of the court. Although the public theater, with its capacity for large audiences, continued to serve as a lively center of theatrical activity, Puritan opposition to the stage gathered momentum. Many dramatists, in turn, grew more satirical of London customs and more attuned to courtly tastes. Eventually, Puritan hostility to the theater was at least part of the motive behind Parliament's order to close the theaters in 1642.

The Public Theaters

A year or more after Burbage built the Theatre in 1576, the Curtain was put up near it by Philip Henslowe, or possibly by Henry Laneman, or Lanman. About ten years later, Philip Henslowe built the Rose, the first playhouse on the Bankside (the southern bank of the Thames River). In 1599, James Burbage's sons Richard and Cuthbert dismantled the Theatre because of trouble about the lease of the land and rebuilt it as the Globe on the Bankside. This Globe playhouse burned on June 29, 1613, from the discharge of cannon backstage during a performance of *All Is True*, a play thought to be identical with Shakespeare's *Henry VIII*. The Globe was rebuilt, probably in its original polygonal form, that is, essentially round with a large number of sides. In 1600, Henslowe built the Fortune as a theater for the Lord Admiral's men, who were chief rivals to the Lord Chamberlain's men. The companies were differently organized, in that the Lord Chamberlain's men were joint sharers in their own enterprise and owners of their own theatrical building, whereas Henslowe owned the Fortune (and the Rose before it) and served as landlord to the Admiral's men—no doubt profiting handsomely from their activities.

BY PERMISSION OF THE FOLGER SHAKESPEARE LIBRARY

This drawing of an Elizabethan public stage appeared on the title page of the published version of William Alabaster's play Roxana *(1632).*

Various records of these theatrical buildings have survived. One such record is the Fortune contract, preserved at Dulwich College among other invaluable papers of Philip Henslowe, theatrical entrepreneur and father-in-law of the famous Edward Alleyn of the Lord Admiral's men. The contract for building the Fortune was let to the same contractor who had built the new Globe, and, since the specifications required that the Fortune should be like the Globe in all its main features, except that it was to be square instead of polygonal, we may gain from these specifications an idea of the Globe. A second documentary record is a drawing of the Swan, a Bankside theater, accompanying a description of the playhouse by Johannes De Witt, who visited London in 1596. The drawing, which was discovered in the University Library at Utrecht, is the work of one Van Buchell and may be based on drawings by De Witt himself. Besides the Fortune contract and the Swan drawing, we have two or three little pictures of the Elizabethan public stage on the title pages of published plays, the most important being that on the title page of William Alabaster's *Roxana* (1632). Just recently, in 1989, the discovery and excavation of the foundations of the Rose playhouse and partial excavation of the Globe playhouse foundations in Southwark, together with the construction of a modern replica of the Globe playhouse near the site of these two theaters, have added invaluable archeological information about the dimensions of that acting arena.

The London Public Stage

From these documents and pictures and from scattered references to the theaters, as well as from extended studies of stage directions and scenic conditions in plays themselves, we have a fairly clear idea of the public stage in London. Its features are these: a pit about seventy feet in diameter, usually circular and open to the sky; surrounding this, galleries in three tiers, containing the most expensive seats; and a rectangular stage, about forty-three by twenty-seven feet, wider than it was deep, raised about five and one-half feet above the surface of the yard, sometimes built on trestles so that it could be removed if the house was also customarily used for bearbaiting and bullbaiting. The flat, open stage usually contained one trapdoor. Part of the stage was afforded some protection from the weather by a brightly decorated wooden roof supported by posts, constituting the "heavens." Above this roof was a "hut," perhaps containing suspension gear for ascents and descents. (The Rose appears originally to have been generally smaller than what is described here, with a stage that tapered toward the front to a width of only twenty-five feet or so. The building was somewhat expanded in 1592 but was still small compared with other theaters. The original building shows no certain evidence of a roof over the

UNIVERSITEITSBIBLIOTHEEK UTRECHT

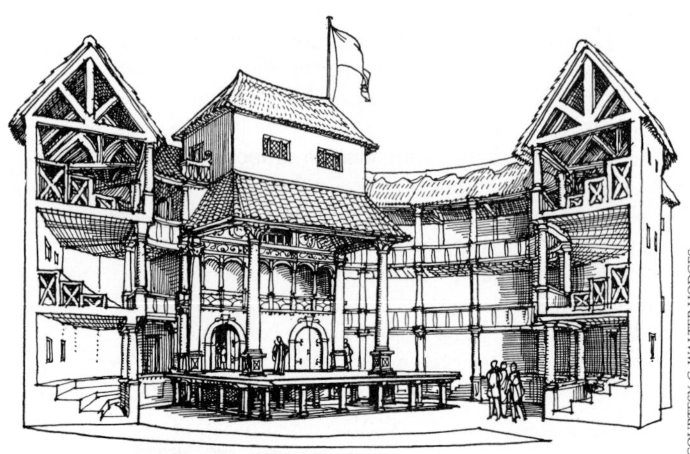

COURTESY, C. WALTER HODGES

This diagram of the Swan Theatre (left) by Van Buchell (c. 1596), based on the observations of Johannes De Witt, shows features of the public playhouse shared by James Burbage's Theatre and the Globe. A modern sketch of the Swan Theatre (right) shows the open, encircling roof and a full view of the tiring house. Like the Globe and other open theaters, the design of the Swan seems to resemble the Elizabethan innyard with an added stage.

stage supported by pillars, but the later building appears to have had roof pillars at the front of the stage.)

At the back of the stage was a partition wall, the "tiring-house facade," with at least two doors in it connecting the stage with the actors' dressing rooms or "tiring house." In the Rose, the tiring-house facade seems to have curved with the polygonal shape of the theater building, but in the DeWitt drawing the Swan facade looks perfectly straight across. Some theaters appear to have had no more than two doors, left and right, as shown in the Swan drawing; other theaters may have had a third door in the center. The arrangement of the Globe playhouse in this important matter cannot be finally determined, although some particular scenes from Shakespeare's plays seem to demand a third door. In any case, the so-called inner stage, long supposed to have stood at the rear of the Elizabeth stage, almost certainly did not exist. A more modest "discovery space" could be provided at one of the curtained doors when needed, as for example in *The Tempest* when Ferdinand and Miranda are suddenly "discovered" at their game of chess by Prospero. Such scenes never called for extensive action within the discovery space, however, and, indeed, the number of such discoveries in Elizabethan plays is very few. Well-to-do spectators who may have been seated in the gallery above the rear of the stage could not see into the discovery space. Accordingly, it was used sparingly and only for brief visual effects. Otherwise, the actors performed virtually all their scenes on the open stage. Sometimes curtains were hung over the tiring-house facade between the doors to facilitate scenes of concealment, as when Polonius and Claudius eavesdrop on Hamlet and Ophelia.

An upper station was sometimes used as an acting space, but not nearly so often as was once supposed. The gallery seats above the stage, sometimes known as the "Lord's room," were normally sold to well-to-do spectators. (We can see such spectators in the Swan drawing and in Alabaster's *Roxana*.) Occasionally, these box seats could be used by the actors, as when Juliet appears at her window (it is never called a balcony). In military sequences, as in the *Henry VI* plays, the tiring-house facade could represent the walls of a besieged city, with the city's defenders appearing "on the walls" (i.e., in the gallery above the stage) in order to parley with the besieging enemy standing below on the main stage. Such scenes were relatively infrequent, however, and usually required only a small number of persons to be aloft. A music room, when needed, could be located in one of the gallery boxes over the stage, but public theaters did not emulate the private stages with music rooms and music between the acts until some time around 1609.

Elizabethan dancers, shown above, perform on a stage below a gallery of musicians. Imported stage designs from Italy made more use of perspective scenery than did the commercial theaters.

The use of scenery was almost wholly unknown on the Elizabethan public stage, although we do find occasional hints of the use of labels to designate a certain door or area as a fixed location (as, perhaps, in *The Comedy of Errors*). For the most part, the scene was unlimited and the concept of space was fluid. No proscenium arch or curtain stood between the actors and the audience, and so the action could not be easily interrupted. Only belatedly did the public companies adopt the private-theater practice of entr'acte music, as we have seen. Most popular Elizabethan plays were written to be performed nonstop. Five-act structure had little currency, especially at first, and the occasional act divisions in the published versions of Shakespeare's plays may be nonauthorial. Acting tempo was brisk. The Prologue of *Romeo and Juliet* speaks of "the two hours' traffic of our stage." Plays were performed in the afternoons and had to be completed by dark in order to allow the audience to return safely to London. During the winter season, playing time was severely restricted. Outbreaks of plague often occasioned the closing of the theaters, especially in warm weather.

A capacity audience for the popular theaters came to about 2,000 to 3,000 persons. (The recently excavated Rose playhouse foundations suggest an audience there of around 2,000.) For the most part, the audience was affluent, consisting chiefly of the gentry and of London's substantial mercantile citizenry who paid two to three pence or more for gallery seats or the "Lord's room," but the ample pit or yard also provided room for small shopkeepers and artisans who stood for a penny. The spectators were lively, demanding, and intelligent. Although Shakespeare does allow Hamlet to refer disparagingly on one occasion to the "groundlings" who "for the most part are capable of nothing but inexplicable dumbshows and noise" (*Hamlet*, 3.2.11–12), Shakespeare appealed to the keenest understanding of his whole audience, thereby achieving a breadth of vision seldom found in continental courtly drama of the same period. The vitality and financial success of the Elizabethan public theater is without parallel in English history. The city of London itself, in 1600 or so, had only about 100,000 inhabitants, yet throughout Shakespeare's career several companies were competing simultaneously for this audience and constantly producing new plays. Most new plays ran for only a few performances, so that the acting companies were always in rehearsal with new shows. The actors needed phenomenal memories and a gift of improvisation as well. Their acting seems to have been of a high caliber, despite the speed with which they worked. Among other things, many of them were expert fencers and singers.

The London public stage inherited many of its practices from native and medieval traditions. The fluid, open stage, with spectators on four sides, recalled the arena staging of many early Corpus Christi cycles, saints' plays, and morality plays. The adult professional companies were, as we have seen, descended from the itinerant troupes that had acted their plays throughout England in guildhalls, private residences, monastic houses and schools, and perhaps occasionally outdoors on booth stages (though the evidence for this last possible venue is scarce). The Elizabethan tiring-house facade and platform stage may have owed much to the kinds of theatrical space that touring actors had known, and perhaps to the arrangement of a booth stage and a trestle platform set up against one wall of an innyard where the guests of the inn could enjoy a performance, along with standing spectators in the yard. When the itinerant actors had set up their plays in noblemen's banqueting halls or at court, at any rate, they encountered another space that had an important influence on their concept of a theater: the Tudor hall. We must next examine the significance of this indoor theatrical setting.

The Tudor Hall

The Tudor banqueting hall played a major part in the staging of much early Tudor drama. Medwall's *Fulgens and Lucrece,* one of the earliest such plays, was written to be performed during the intervals of a state banquet. The patrician guests were seated at tables, while servingmen bustled to and fro or stood crowded together at the doors in the hall "screen." This screen or partition traversed the lower end of the rectangular hall, providing a passageway to the kitchens and to the outside. Its doors—often two, sometimes three—were normally curtained to prevent drafts. This arrangement of the doors bears an interesting resemblance to that of many playhouses in late Elizabethan England, both public and private. Moreover, hall screens and passageways were normally surmounted by a gallery, where musicians could play—an architectural feature markedly resembling the upper galleries of late Elizabethan theaters. Could the Tudor hall screen provide a natural facade for dramatic action? Perhaps it did, although records from Shakespeare's era only rarely document an actual performance in front of the screen, whereas performances were common at the upper end of the hall in front of the dais or in the midst of the hall, where the persons of highest social rank sitting on the dais would have had the best view. The actors of *Fulgens and Lucrece* clearly made use of the doorways in the hall screen, sometimes joking with the servingmen as the actors pushed their way into the hall, but they probably acted in the center, among the spectators' tables. John Heywood's *Play of the Weather* calls for a similar *mise en scène*. Although this ready-made "stage" sufficed for most Tudor plays, the actors sometimes provided additional stage structures; *Weather,* for example, calls for a throne room into which Jupiter can retire without leaving the hall. Similar structures could represent a shop, an orchard, a mountain, or what have you.

Guild and town halls, where players on tour performed before the mayor and council (and sometimes a wider public), provided a similar physical environment except that we cannot be sure that such spaces had galleries in the sixteenth century. Since the gallery is not necessary for many Tudor plays, the players may well have gained experience in halls of this kind that influenced their techniques of staging once they had gravitated to London.

Although both medieval and continental drama offered traditions of multiple staging, in which a series of simultaneously visible and adjacent structures would represent as fixed locations all the playing areas needed for the performance of a play, Tudor indoor staging seems to have made less use of this method than was once supposed. Nor did the various indoor theaters of Tudor England make extensive use of neoclassical staging from Italy, with its street scene in perspective created by means of lath-and-canvas stage "houses." Italian scenery of this sort came into use sooner in the court masque than in regular drama. Nevertheless, we do find in the Tudor indoor theater a neoclassical tendency toward a fixed locale, in preference to the unlimited open stage. *Gammer Gurton's Needle*, for example, acted probably in a university hall, seems to have used one stage structure, or possibly one door, to represent Gammer's house throughout the action, and another to represent Dame Chat's house. Shakespeare may have been influenced by this kind of fixed-locale staging in *The Comedy of Errors*. (Alan Nelson's *Early Cambridge Theaters*, 1994, is an important resource for school staging.)

The Tudor banqueting hall provided a place to "stage" much early Tudor drama. The actors performed on the floor among the tables of the guests. The Middle Temple Hall, shown here, later served as the location for a performance of Shakespeare's Twelfth Night *on February 2, 1602. The Middle Temple is one of the Inns of Court, where young men studied law and occasionally relaxed by staging dramatic entertainments.*

HULTON ARCHIVE PHOTOS/GETTY IMAGES

The Private Stage

Despite such influences on the public stage, the most significant contribution of the Tudor hall and its hall screen was to the so-called private stage of the late Elizabethan period—"private" in the sense of being intended for a more select and courtly audience than that which frequented the "public" theaters. In the 1570s, choir boys began performing professionally to courtly and intellectual audiences in London. The choir boys had long performed plays for the royal and noble households to which they were attached, but in the 1570s they were, in effect, organized into professional acting companies. Sebastian Westcote and the Children of Paul's may have originated this enterprise. Their theater was apparently some indoor hall in the vicinity of St. Paul's in London, outfitted much like the typical domestic Tudor hall to which the boys had grown accustomed. Comparable indoor "private" theaters soon followed at Blackfriars and Whitefriars.

At some point, a low stage was constructed in front of the hall screen, and seats were provided for all the spectators. Many of these seats were in the "pit," or what we would call the "orchestra," facing toward the stage at one end of the rectangular room. Other seats were in galleries along both sides of the room; these were quite elaborate in the so-called Second Blackfriars of 1596 and provided two or three tiers of seats. Elegant box seats stood at either side of the stage itself. The Second Blackfriars had a permanently built tiring house to the rear of the stage, with probably three doors. Above it was a gallery used variously as a lord's room, a music room, and an upper station for occasional acting.

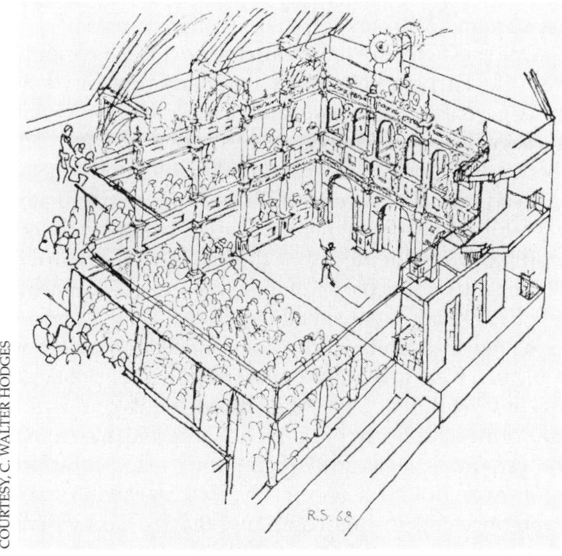

COURTESY, C. WALTER HODGES

A reconstruction of the Second Blackfriars, featuring a rectangular stage, a tiring house with three doors, and a gallery.

The private theater flourished during the 1580s and again after 1598–1599, having been closed down during most of the 1590s because of its satirical activities. Although it was a commercial theater, it was "private" in its clientele, because its high price of admission (sixpence) excluded those who could stand in the yards of the "public" theaters for a penny (roughly the equivalent of an hour's wage for a skilled worker). Plays written for the more select audiences of the "private" theaters tended to be more satirical and oriented to courtly values than those written for the "public" theaters, although the distinction is by no means absolute.

London Private Theaters

The important private theaters of Shakespeare's London were two in the precinct, or "liberty," of Blackfriars, an early one in Whitefriars about which little is known, a later one there, and a theater at Paul's, the exact location and nature of which is not known. In the thirteenth century, the mother house of the Dominican friars, or Blackfriars, was established on the sloping ground between St. Paul's Cathedral and the river. It was a sizable institution, ultimately covering about five acres of ground. It stood on the very border of the city and, after the custom of the time, was made a liberty; that is to say, it had its own local government and was removed from the immediate jurisdiction of the city of London. After the suppression of the friary and the confiscation of its lands, the jealousy existing between the Privy Council, representing the crown, and the mayor and aldermen, representing the city and probably also the rights of property holders, prevented the district of the Blackfriars from losing its political independence of the municipality. It was still a liberty and therefore attractive to players and other persons wishing to avoid the London authorities. At the same time, aristocrats residing in the area required protection, and the crown had certain rights still in its control.

From 1576 to 1584, the Children of the Queen's Chapel, one of the two most important companies of boy actors, had used a hall in the precinct of Blackfriars in which to act their plays. Here were acted at least some of John Lyly's plays. In 1596, James Burbage purchased property in this precinct and seems to have spent a good deal of money in its adaptation for use as an indoor theater (the so-called Second Blackfriars). He probably appreciated its advantages over Cripplegate or the Bankside of greater proximity to London and of protection against the elements, particularly for use in winter. But the aristocratic residents of the Blackfriars by petition to the Privy Council prevented him from making use of his theater. Plays within the city proper had only recently been finally and successfully prohibited, and the petitioners no doubt objected to their intrusion into Blackfriars on the grounds that the plays and their crowds were a nuisance.

Burbage's new indoor theater may have lain idle from the time of its preparation until 1600; but, in any case, in that year it became the scene of many plays. It was let by lease for the use of the Children of the Chapel, who in 1604 became the Children of the Queen's Revels. Their theater managers brought into their service a number of new dramatists—Ben Jonson, John Marston, George Chapman, and later John Webster. The vogue of the plays acted by the Children of the Chapel was so great as to damage the patronage of the established companies and to compel them to go on the road. Out of this rivalry between the children and the adult actors arose that open competition alluded to in *Hamlet* (2.2.328–362) and sometimes referred to today as the "War of the Theaters." The skirmishes were relatively brief, arising in part from a clash of personalities among Jonson, Marston, and Thomas Dekker, but the debate between public and private acting companies was significant as an indication of whether London drama would continue to play to large popular audiences or would increasingly turn to a more courtly clientele. In 1608, the Burbage interests secured the evacuation of the lease, so that the theater in Blackfriars became the winter playhouse of Shakespeare's company from that time forward.

System of Patronage

In 1572, common players of interludes, along with minstrels, bearwards, and fencers, were included within the hard terms of the act for the punishment of vagabonds, provided that such common players were not enrolled as the servants of a baron of the realm or of some honorable person of greater degree. The result was a system of patronage of theatrical companies in Elizabethan and Jacobean times, according to which players became the "servants" of some nobleman or of some member of the royal family.

By the time Shakespeare came to London in the late 1580s, many of these companies were already in existence, some of which long antedated the passage of the act of 1572. Provincial records of the visits of players, to be sure, sometimes failed to distinguish actors from acrobats or other public performers who were similarly organized. Nonetheless, we have evidence that various companies of players performed in London and elsewhere in the late 1580s under the patronage of the Queen, the Earl of Worcester, the Earl of Leicester, the Earl of Oxford, the Earl of Sussex, the Lord Admiral, and Charles, Lord Howard of Effingham. These companies were eventually much reduced in number; usually only three adult companies acted at any given time in London during Shakespeare's prime. In addition, the children's companies, privately controlled, acted intermittently but at times very successfully. The most important of these were the Children of the Chapel and Queen's Revels and the Children of Paul's, but there were also boy players of Windsor, Eton College, the Merchant Taylors, Westminster, and other schools.

Shakespeare and the London Theatrical Companies

We know that by 1592 Shakespeare had arrived in London and had achieved sufficient notice as a young playwright to arouse the resentment of a rival dramatist, Robert Greene. In that year, shortly before he died, Greene—or possibly his editor after Greene's death—lashed out at an "upstart crow, beautified with our feathers," who had had the audacity to fancy himself "the only Shake-scene in a country" (*Groats-worth of Wit*). This petulant outburst was plainly directed at Shakespeare, since Greene included in his remarks a parody of some lines from *3 Henry VI*. As a university man and an established dramatist, Greene seems to have resented the intrusion into his profession of a mere player who was not university trained. This "upstart crow" was achieving a very real success on the London stage. Shakespeare had probably already written *The Comedy of Errors*, *Love's Labor's Lost*, *The Two Gentlemen of Verona*, the *Henry VI* plays, and *Titus Andronicus*, and perhaps also *Richard III* and *The Taming of the Shrew*.

For which acting company or companies had he written these plays, however? By 1594, we know that Shakespeare was an established member of the Lord Chamberlain's company, important enough, in fact, to have been named, along with Will Kempe and Richard Burbage, as payee for court performances on December 26 and 28 of 1594. But when had he joined the Chamberlain's men, and for whom had he written and acted previously? These are the problems of the so-called dark years, during which Shakespeare came to London (perhaps around 1587) and got started on his career.

One prestigious acting company he could have joined was the Earl of Leicester's company, led by James Burbage, father of Shakespeare's later colleague, Richard Burbage. Leicester was a favorite minister of Queen Elizabeth until his death in 1588, and his company of actors received from the Queen in 1574 an extraordinary patent to perform plays anywhere in England, despite all local prohibitions, provided that the plays were approved beforehand by the master of the Queen's Revels. Since an act of 1572 had outlawed all unlicensed troupes, Leicester's men and similar companies attached to important noblemen were given a virtual monopoly over public acting. In 1576, Burbage built the Theatre for his company in the northeast suburbs of London. This group also toured the provinces: Leicester's company visited Stratford-upon-Avon in 1587. Conceivably, Shakespeare served an apprenticeship in this company, though no evidence exists to prove a connection. Leicester's company had lost some of its prominence in 1583, when several of its best men joined the newly formed Queen's men, with Richard

Tarlton as its most famous actor. The remaining members of Leicester's company disbanded in 1588 upon the death of the Earl, and many of its principal actors ultimately became part of Lord Strange's company. These probably included George Bryan, Will Kempe, and Thomas Pope, all of whom subsequently went on to become Lord Chamberlain's men.

Lord Strange's (The Earl of Derby's) Men

The Queen's men gained an extraordinary prominence in the 1580s, as Scott McMillin and Sally-Beth MacLean have shown in the *Queen's Men and Their Plays* (1998). This acting group was assembled under royal sponsorship as an instrument of furthering the Protestant Reformation through its performances of plays, and did so with notable success, although it then declined rapidly in the early 1590s chiefly because as a touring company it was unprepared to compete with the new companies that learned how to succeed in the metropolis by staging a wide variety of plays in a fixed London theater. Prominent among the acting companies to which Shakespeare could have belonged when he came to London, probably in the late 1580s, were Lord Strange's men, the Lord Admiral's men, the Earl of Pembroke's men, and the Earl of Sussex's men. Scholars have long speculated that Shakespeare may have joined the company of Ferdinando Stanley, Lord Strange (who in 1593 became the Earl of Derby). The names of George Bryan, Will Kempe, and Thomas Pope appear on a roster of Strange's company in 1593, along with those of John Heminges and Augustine Phillips. All of these men later became part of the Lord Chamberlain's company, most of them when it was first formed in 1594. Shakespeare's name does not appear on the 1593 Lord Strange's list (which was a license for touring in the provinces), but he may possibly have stayed in London to attend to his writing while the company toured. Certainly, an important number of his later associates belonged to this group.

During the years from 1590 to 1594, some of Lord Strange's men appear to have joined forces on occasion with Edward Alleyn and others of the Admiral's men. This impressive combination of talents enjoyed a successful season in 1591–1592, with six performances at court. Alleyn's father-in-law, Philip Henslowe, recorded in his *Diary* the performances of the combined players in early 1592, probably at the Rose Theatre. Their repertory included a *Harey the vj* and a *Titus & Vespacia*. The latter play is, however, no longer thought to have any connection with Shakespeare's *Titus Andronicus;* and the *Harey the vj* may or may not have been Shakespeare's, since *3 Henry VI* was (according to its 1595 title page) acted by Pembroke's men, rather than Lord Strange's men. If Shakespeare was a member of the Strange-Admiral's combination in 1591–1592, we are at a loss to explain why Henslowe's 1592 list records so many performances of

Clowns were enormously popular on the Elizabethan stage. Of the many Elizabethan clowns whose names are known to us, Richard Tarlton is one of the most famous. (Will Kempe, in Shakespeare's company, the Lord Chamberlain's men, is another; see pp. lxviii-lxix.) Tarlton is shown here inside an elaborate letter T, dancing a jig with his pipe and tabor. Such jigs were often used at the conclusion of a play.

plays by Marlowe, Greene, Kyd, and others, but none that are certainly by Shakespeare. On the other hand, the *Harey the vj* may be his, and the title page of the 1594 Quarto of *Titus Andronicus* does list the Earl of Derby's men as performers of the play, in addition to the Earl of Pembroke's and the Earl of Sussex's men. (Lord Strange's men became officially known as the Earl of Derby's men when Lord Strange was made an earl in September 1593.) At any rate, the company disbanded when the Earl died in April 1594, leaving them without a patron. The connection with the Admiral's men was discontinued, with Alleyn returning to the Admiral's men and the rest of the group forming a new company under the patronage of Henry Carey, first Lord Hunsdon, the Lord Chamberlain.

The Earl of Pembroke's Men

The other company to which Shakespeare is most likely to have belonged prior to 1594 is the Earl of Pembroke's company. This group came to grief in 1593–1594, evidently as a result of virulent outbursts of the plague, which had kept the theaters closed during most of 1592 and 1593. Pembroke's men were forced to tour the provinces and then to sell a number of their best plays to the booksellers. Henslowe wrote to Alleyn in September

1593 of the extreme financial plight of Pembroke's company: "As for my lord of Pembroke's [men], which you desire to know where they be, they are all at home and has been this five or six weeks, for they cannot save their charges [expenses] with travel, as I hear, and were fain to pawn their parell [apparel] for their charge." Soon thereafter this company disbanded.

Pembroke's men were associated with a significant number of Shakespeare's early plays. Among the playbooks they evidently sold in 1593–1594 were *The Taming of a Shrew* and *The True Tragedy of Richard Duke of York*. The first of these was published in 1594 with the assertion that it had been "sundry times acted by the Right Honorable the Earle of Pembroke his Servants." Although the text of this quarto is not Shakespeare's play as we know it but, instead, an anonymous version, most scholars now feel certain that it was an imitation of Shakespeare's play and that the work performed by Pembroke's men was, in fact, Shakespeare's. The same conclusion pertains to a performance in 1594 of "*the Tamynge of a Shrowe*" at Newington Butts, a playhouse south of London Bridge. Henslowe's *Diary* informs us that the actors on this occasion were either the Lord Chamberlain's or the Lord Admiral's men. The probability, then, is that Shakespeare's *The Taming of the Shrew* passed from Pembroke's men to the Chamberlain's men when Pembroke's company collapsed in 1593–1594.

The True Tragedy of Richard Duke of York, published in 1595, was a seemingly unauthorized quarto of Shakespeare's *3 Henry VI*. Its title page declared that it had been "sundry times acted by the Right Honorable the Earl of Pembroke his Servants." Probably they acted *2 Henry VI* as well, to which part three was a sequel. In addition, the 1594 Quarto of *Titus Andronicus* mentions on its title page the Earl of Pembroke's servants, although the Earl of Derby's and the Earl of Sussex's men are named there as well. Thus, Pembroke's men performed as many as four of Shakespeare's early plays—more than we can assign to any other known company. Nevertheless, their claim to Shakespeare remains uncertain. We simply do not know who acted several of Shakespeare's earliest plays, such as *The Comedy of Errors*, *Love's Labor's Lost*, and *The Two Gentlemen of Verona*. Lord Strange's (Derby's) men, as we have seen, did act something called *Harey the vj* and are named on the 1594 title page of *Titus Andronicus*. Sussex's men may conceivably have owned for a time some early Shakespearean plays that later went to the Lord Chamberlain's men, such as *Titus Andronicus*. The Queen's men, although associated with no known Shakespeare play, other than the old *King Lear* (acted jointly with Sussex's men in 1593), were a leading company during the years in question. All we can say for sure is that the difficulties of 1592–1593 with the plague and the death of the Earl of Derby in 1594 led to a major reshuffling of the London acting companies. From this reshuffling emerged in 1594 the Lord Chamberlain's company, with Shakespeare and Richard Burbage (whose earlier history is also difficult to trace) as two of its earliest and most prominent members.

SHAKESPEARE'S LIFE AND WORK

The Early Years, 1564–c. 1594

Stratford-upon-Avon

About Shakespeare's place of birth, Stratford-upon-Avon, there is no doubt. He spent his childhood there and returned periodically throughout his life. During most or all of his long professional career in London, his wife and children lived in Stratford. He acquired property and took some interest in local affairs. He retired to Stratford and chose to be buried there. Its Warwickshire surroundings lived in his poetic imagination.

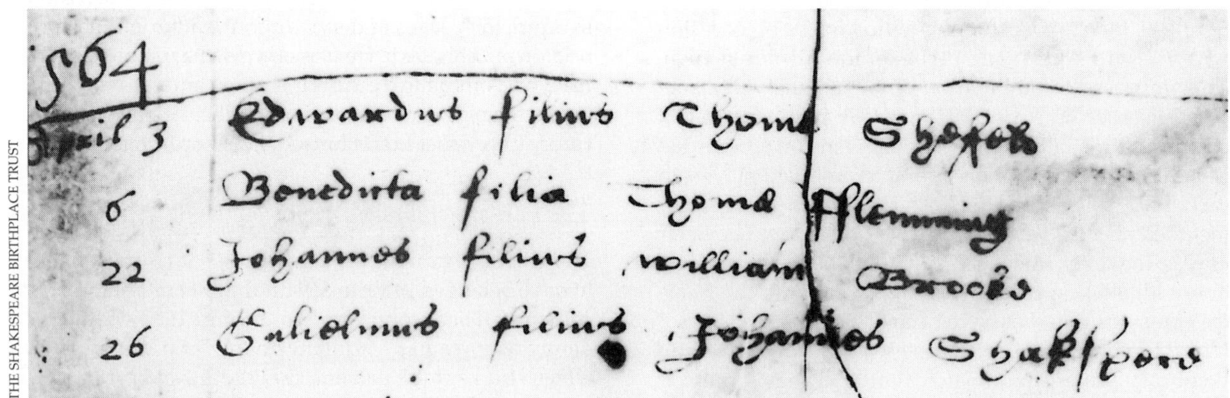
1564
April 3 Edwardus filius Thome Shefe
6 Bonedicta filia Thome Flemming
22 Johannes filius William Brookes
26 Gulielmus filius Johannes Shakspere

THE SHAKESPEARE BIRTHPLACE TRUST

The earliest written reference to William Shakespeare is this record of his christening in the register of Holy Trinity Church at Stratford, April 26, 1564. The entry reads, "Gulielmus filius Johannes Shakspere."

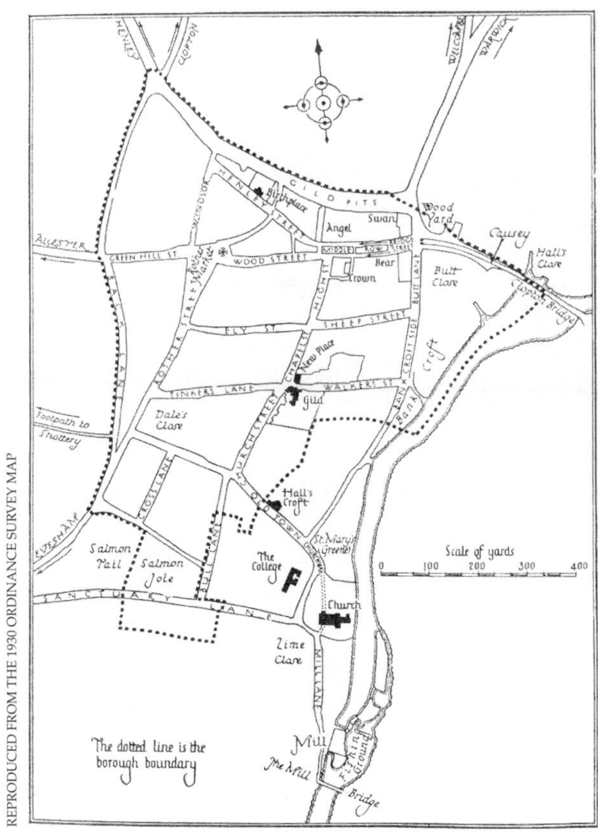

The town of Stratford-upon-Avon as Shakespeare knew it. The house in which he is considered to have been born is on Henley Street; the larger house he purchased in 1597, New Place, is on Chapel Street.

The Stratford of Shakespeare's day was a "handsome small market town" (as described by William Camden) of perhaps 1,500 inhabitants, with fairly broad streets and half-timbered houses roofed with thatch. It could boast of a long history and an attractive setting on the river Avon. A bridge of fourteen arches, built in 1496 by Sir Hugh Clopton, Lord Mayor of London, spanned the river. Beside the Avon stood Trinity Church, built on the site of a Saxon monastery. The chapel of the Guild of the Holy Trinity, dating from the thirteenth century, and an old King Edward VI grammar school were buildings of note. Stratford had maintained a grammar school at least since 1424 and probably long before that. It was a town without the domination of clergy, aristocracy, or great wealth. It lay in a rich agricultural region, in the county of Warwickshire. To the north of Stratford lay the Forest of Arden.

Shakespeare's Family

The family that bore the name of Shakespeare was well distributed throughout England, but was especially numerous in Warwickshire. A name "Saquespee," in various spellings, is found in Normandy at an early date. It means, according to J. Q. Adams, "to draw out the sword quickly." That name, in the form "Sakspee," with many variants, is found in England; also the name "Saksper," varying gradually to the form "Shakespeare." It may have been wrought into that form by the obvious military meaning of "one who shakes the spear."

Our first substantial records of the family begin with Richard Shakespeare, who was, in all probability, Shakespeare's grandfather, a farmer living in the village of Snitterfield four miles from Stratford. He was a tenant on the property of Robert Arden of Wilmcote, a wealthy man with the social status of gentleman. Richard Shakespeare died about 1561, possessed of an estate valued at the very respectable sum of thirty-eight pounds and seventeen shillings.

His son John made a great step forward in the world by his marriage with Mary Arden, daughter of his father's landlord. John Shakespeare had some property of his own and through his wife acquired a good deal more. He moved from Snitterfield to Stratford at some date before 1552. He rose to great local importance in Stratford and bought several houses, among which was the one on Henley Street traditionally identified as Shakespeare's birthplace. William Shakespeare was born in 1564 and was baptized on April 26. The exact date of his birth is not known, but traditionally we celebrate it on April 23, the feast day of St. George, England's patron saint. (The date is at least plausible in view of the practice of baptizing infants shortly after birth.) The house in which Shakespeare was probably born, though almost entirely rebuilt and changed in various and unknown ways during the years that have intervened since Shakespeare's birth, still stands. It is of considerable size, having four rooms on the ground floor, and must, therefore, have been an important business house in the Stratford of those days. John Shakespeare's occupation seems to have been that of a tanner and glover; that is, he cured skins, made gloves and some other leather goods, and sold them in his shop. He was also a dealer in wool, grain, malt, and other farm produce.

The long story, beginning in 1552, of John Shakespeare's success and misfortunes in Stratford is attested to by many borough records. He held various city offices. He was ale taster (inspector of bread and malt), burgess (petty constable), affeeror (assessor of fines), city chamberlain (treasurer), alderman, and high bailiff of the town—the highest municipal office in Stratford. At some time around 1576, he applied to the Herald's office for the right to bear arms and style himself a gentleman. This petition was later to be renewed and successfully carried through to completion by his famous son. In 1577 or 1578, however, when William was as yet only thirteen or fourteen years old, John Shakespeare's fortunes began a sudden and

THE SHAKESPEARE BIRTHPLACE TRUST

This house on Henley Street in Stratford is considered to have been the birthplace of Shakespeare. Its considerable size shows what must have been an important house of business. Shakespeare's father dealt chiefly in leather goods, though he also traded in wool, grain, and other farm produce.

mysterious decline. He absented himself from council meetings. He had to mortgage his wife's property and showed other signs of being in financial difficulty. He became involved in serious litigation and was assessed heavy fines. Although he kept his position on the corporation council until 1586 or 1587, he was finally replaced as alderman because of his failure to attend. Conceivably, John Shakespeare's sudden difficulties were the result of persecution for his Catholic faith, since John's wife's family had remained loyal to Catholicism, and the old faith was being attacked with new vigor in the Warwickshire region in 1577 and afterwards. This hypothesis is unsubstantial, however, especially in view of the fact that some Catholics and Puritans seemed to have held posts of trust and to have remained prosperous in Stratford during this period. In the last analysis, we have little evidence as to John Shakespeare's religious faith or as to the reasons for his sudden reversal of fortune.

The family of Shakespeare's mother could trace its ancestry back to the time of William the Conqueror, and Shakespeare's father, in spite of his troubles, was a citizen of importance. John Shakespeare made his mark, instead of writing his name, but so did other men of the time who we know could read and write. His offices, particularly that of chamberlain, and the various public functions he discharged indicate that he must have had some education.

Shakespeare in School

Nicholas Rowe, who published in 1709 the first extensive biographical account of Shakespeare, reports the tradition that Shakespeare studied "for some time at a Free-School." Although the list of students who actually attended the King's New School at Stratford-upon-Avon in the late sixteenth century has not survived, we cannot doubt that Rowe is reporting accurately. Shakespeare's father, as a leading citizen of Stratford, would scarcely have spurned the benefits of one of Stratford's most prized institutions. The town had had a free school since the thirteenth century, at first under the auspices of the Church. During the reign of King Edward VI (1547–1553), the Church lands were expropriated by the crown and the town of Stratford was granted a corporate charter. At this time, the school was reorganized as the King's New School, named in honor of the reigning monarch. It prospered. Its teachers, or "masters," regularly held degrees from Oxford during Shakespeare's childhood and received salaries that were superior to those of most comparable schools.

Much has been learned about the curriculum of such a school. A child would first learn the rudiments of reading and writing English by spending two or three years in a "petty" or elementary school. The child learned to

THE SHAKESPEARE BIRTHPLACE TRUST

The interior of the Stratford grammar school: a late and not very reliable tradition claims that Shakespeare's desk was third from the front on the left-hand side.

read from a "hornbook," a single sheet of paper mounted on a board and protected by a thin transparent layer of horn, on which was usually printed the alphabet in small and capital letters and the Lord's Prayer. The child would also practice an ABC book with catechism. When the child had demonstrated the ability to read satisfactorily, the child was admitted, at about the age of seven, to the grammar school proper. Here the day was a rigorous one, usually extending from 6 A.M. in the summer or 7 A.M. in the winter until 5 P.M. Intervals for food or brief recreation came at midmorning, noon, and midafternoon. Holidays occurred at Christmas, Easter, and Whitsuntide (usually late May and June), comprising perhaps forty days in all through the year. Discipline was strict, and physical punishment was common.

Latin formed the basis of the grammar school curriculum. The scholars studied grammar, read ancient writers, recited, and learned to write in Latin. A standard text was the *Grammatica Latina* by William Lilly or Lyly, grandfather of the later Elizabethan dramatist John Lyly. The scholars also became familiar with the *Disticha de Moribus* (moral proverbs) attributed to Cato, *Aesop's Fables,* the *Eclogues* of Baptista Spagnuoli Mantuanus or Mantuan (alluded to in *Love's Labor's Lost*), the *Eclogues* and *Aeneid* of Virgil, the comedies of Plautus or Terence (sometimes performed in Latin by the children), Ovid's *Metamorphoses* and other of his works, and possibly some Horace and Seneca.

Shakespeare plentifully reveals in his dramatic writings an awareness of many of these authors, especially Plautus (in *The Comedy of Errors*), Ovid (in *A Midsummer Night's Dream* and elsewhere), and Seneca (in *Titus Andronicus*). Although he often consulted translations of these authors, he seems to have known the originals as well. He had, in Ben Jonson's learned estimation, "small Latin and less Greek"; the tone is condescending, but the statement does concede that Shakespeare had some of both. He would have acquired some Greek in the last years of his grammar schooling. By twentieth-century standards, Shakespeare had a fairly comprehensive

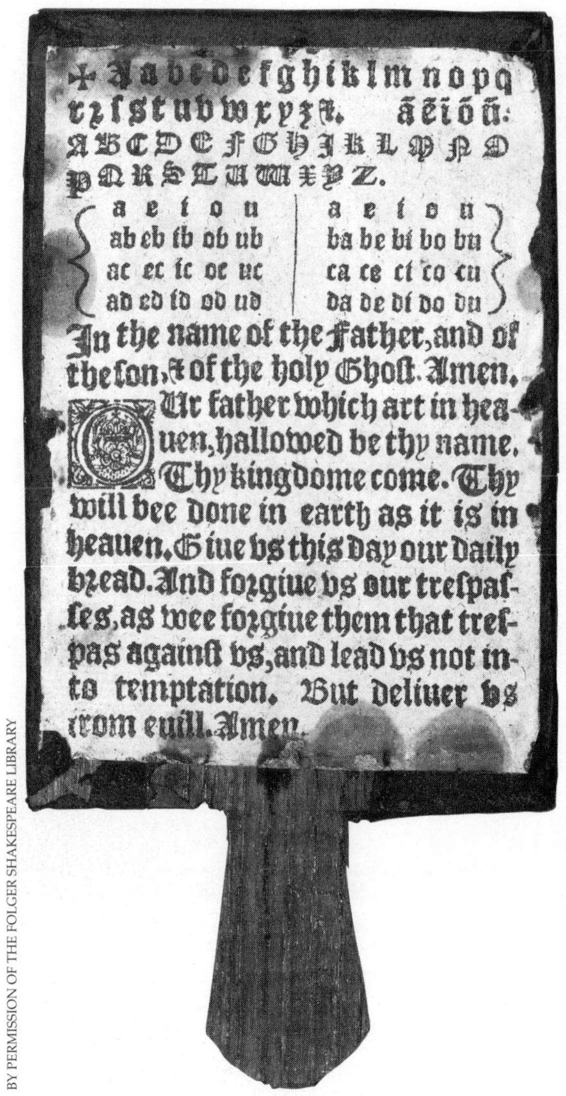

The hornbook pictured here—showing the alphabet and the Lord's Prayer—was part of a child's education in Shakespeare's time.

amount of training in the ancient classics, certainly enough to account for the general, if unscholarly, references we find in the plays.

Shakespeare's Marriage

When Shakespeare was eighteen years old, he married Anne Hathaway, a woman eight years his senior. (The inscription on her grave states that she was sixty-seven when she died in August 1623.) The bishop's register of Worcester, the central city of the diocese, shows for November 27, 1582, the issue of a bishop's license for the marriage of William Shakespeare and Anne "Whately"; the bond of sureties issued next day refers to her as "Hathaway." She has been identified with all reasonable probability as Agnes (or Anne) Hathaway, daughter of the then recently deceased Richard Hathaway of the hamlet of Shottery, a short distance from Stratford.

The obtaining of a license was not normally required for a marriage. William Shakespeare and Anne Hathaway seem to have applied for a license on this occasion because they wished to be married after only one reading of the banns rather than the usual three. (The reading of the banns, or announcement in church of a forthcoming marriage, usually on three successive Sundays, enabled any party to object to the marriage if he or she knew of any legal impediment.) Since the reading of all banns was suspended for long periods during Advent (before Christmas) and Lent (before Easter), a couple intending to marry shortly before Christmas might have had to wait until April before the banns could be read thrice. Accordingly, the bishop not uncommonly granted a license permitting couples to marry during the winter season with only one reading of the banns. To obtain such a license, two friends of the bride's family had to sign a bond obligating themselves to pay the bishop up to forty pounds, should any impediment to the marriage result in a legal action against the bishop for having issued the license.

The actual record of the marriage in a parish register has not survived, but presumably the couple were married shortly after obtaining the license. They may have been married in Temple Grafton, where Anne had relatives. The couple took up residence in Stratford. Anne was already pregnant at the time of the marriage, for she gave birth to a daughter, Susanna, on May 26, 1583. The birth of a child six months after the wedding may explain the need for haste the previous November. These circumstances, and Anne's considerable seniority in age to William, have given rise to much speculation about matters that can never be satisfactorily resolved. We do know that a formal betrothal in the presence of witnesses could legally validate a binding relationship, enabling a couple to consummate their love without social stigma. We know also that Shakespeare dramatized the issue of premarital contract and pregnancy in *Measure for Measure*. Whether Shakespeare entered into such a formal relationship with Anne is, however, undiscoverable.

On February 2, 1585, Shakespeare's only other children, the twins Hamnet and Judith, were baptized in Stratford Church. The twins seem to have been named after Shakespeare's friends and neighbors, Hamnet Sadler, a baker, and his wife, Judith.

The Seven "Dark" Years

From 1585, the year in which his twins were baptized, until 1592, when he was first referred to as an actor and dramatist of growing importance in London, Shakespeare's activities are wholly unknown. Presumably, at

J. KOMENSKY, "ORBIS SENSUALUM PICTUS," 1659

A schoolroom in Tudor England.

some time during this period he made his way to London and entered its theatrical world, but otherwise we can only record traditions and guesses as to what he did between the ages of 21 and 28.

One of the oldest and most intriguing suggestions comes from John Aubrey, who, in collecting information in the late seventeenth century about actors and dramatists for his "Minutes of Lives," sought the help of one

THE SHAKESPEARE BIRTHPLACE TRUST

The substantial farmhouse owned by the Hathaways of Shottery, originally known as "Hewland" but now almost universally famous as Anne Hathaway's Cottage.

William Beeston. John Dryden believed Beeston to be "the chronicle of the stage," and Aubrey seems also to have had a high opinion of Beeston's theatrical knowledge. In his manuscript, Aubrey made a note to himself: "W. Shakespeare—quaere [i.e., inquire of] Mr. Beeston, who knows most of him." Aubrey then cites Beeston as his authority for this tradition about Shakespeare:

> Though, as Ben Jonson says of him, that he had but little Latin and less Greek, he understood Latin pretty well, for he had been in his younger years a schoolmaster in the country.

Beeston had been a theatrical manager all his life. He was the son of the actor Christopher Beeston, who had been a member of Shakespeare's company, probably from 1596 until 1602, and who therefore had occasion to know Shakespeare well.

Shakespeare's own grammar school education would not have qualified him to be the master of a school, but he could have served as "usher" or assistant to the master. The idea that Shakespeare may have taught in this way is not unattractive. Although, as we have seen, he had some acquaintance with Plautus, Ovid, and other classical writers through his own grammar school reading, a stint as schoolmaster would have made these authors more familiar and readily accessible to him when he began writing his plays and nondramatic poems. His earliest works—*The Comedy of Errors, Love's Labor's Lost, Titus Andronicus, Venus and Adonis, The Rape of Lucrece*—show most steadily and directly the effect of his classical reading. Schoolteaching experience might have encouraged his ambitions to be a writer, like Marlowe or Greene, who went to London not to be actors but to try their hands at poetry and playwriting. All in all, however, it seems more probable that Shakespeare became a young actor rather than a schoolteacher.

Another tradition about the years from 1585 to 1592 asserts that Shakespeare served part of an apprenticeship in Stratford. This suggestion comes to us from one John Dowdall, who, traveling through Warwickshire in 1693, heard the story from an old parish clerk who was showing him around the town of Stratford. According to this parish clerk, Shakespeare had been bound as apprentice to a butcher but ran away from his master to London where he was received into a playhouse as "servitor." John Aubrey records a similar tradition: "When he [Shakespeare] was a boy he exercised his father's trade." Aubrey believed this trade to have been that of a butcher. Moreover, says Aubrey, "When he killed a calf, he would do it in a high style, and make a speech." No other evidence confirms, however, that Shakespeare was a runaway apprentice. The allusion to "killing a calf" may, instead, refer to an ancient rural amusement in which the slaughter of a calf was staged behind a curtain for the entertainment of visitors at county fairs. Conceivably, Shakespeare's participation in such a game during his youth may have given rise to the tradition that he had been a butcher's apprentice.

Another legend, that of Shakespeare's deer stealing, has enjoyed wide currency. We are indebted for this story to the Reverend Richard Davies, who, some time between 1688 and 1709, jotted down some gossipy interpolations in the manuscripts of the Reverend William Fulman. (Fulman himself was an antiquarian who had collected a number of notes about Shakespeare and Stratford.) According to Davies, Shakespeare was "much given to all unluckiness in stealing venison and rabbits, particularly from Sir —— Lucy, who had him oft whipped and sometimes imprisoned and at last made him fly his native country, to his great advancement." This tradition has led to speculation by Nicholas Rowe that Justice Shallow of *2 Henry IV* and *The Merry Wives of Windsor* is a satirical portrait of Sir Thomas Lucy of Charlecote Hall and that Shakespeare even composed an irreverent ballad about Lucy that added to the urgency of Shakespeare's departure for London. In fact, however, there is no compelling reason to believe that Shallow is based on Lucy, on Justice William Gardiner of Surrey (as Leslie Hotson insists), or on any live Elizabethan. We don't know that Shakespeare ever drew contemporary portraits in his plays, as is sometimes alleged; is Polonius in *Hamlet* Lord Burghley, for example, or is he Shakespeare's original portrait of a minister of state who is also a busybody? Nor do we know if the deer-slaying incident took place at all. It makes interesting fiction but unreliable biography.

Shakespeare's Arrival in London

Because of the total absence of reliable information concerning the seven years from 1585 to 1592, we do not know how Shakespeare got his start in the theatrical world. He may have joined one of the touring companies that came to Stratford and then accompanied the players to London. Edmund Malone offered the unsupported statement (in 1780) that Shakespeare's "first office in the theater was that of prompter's attendant." Presumably, a young man from the country would have had to begin at the bottom. Shakespeare's later work certainly reveals an intimate and practical acquaintance with technical matters of stagecraft. In any case, his rise to eminence as an actor and a writer seems to have been rapid. He was fortunate also in having at least one prosperous acquaintance in London, Richard Field, formerly of Stratford and the son of an associate of Shakespeare's father. Field was a printer, and in 1593 and 1594 he published two handsome editions of Shakespeare's first serious poems, *Venus and Adonis* and *The Rape of Lucrece.*

"The Only Shake-scene in a Country"

The first allusion to Shakespeare after his Stratford days is a vitriolic attack on him. It occurs in *Greene's Groatsworth of Wit Bought with a Million of Repentance,* written by Robert Greene during the last months of his wretched existence (he died in poverty in September 1592). A famous passage in this work lashes out at the actors of the public theaters for having deserted Greene and for bestowing their favor instead on a certain upstart dramatist. The passage warns three fellow dramatists and University Wits, Christopher Marlowe, Thomas Nashe, and George Peele, to abandon the writing of plays before they fall prey to a similar ingratitude. The diatribe runs as follows:

> . . . Base minded men all three of you, if by my misery you be not warned. For unto none of you (like me) sought those burs to cleave—those puppets, I mean, that spake from our mouths, those antics garnished in our colors. Is it not strange that I, to whom they all have been beholding, is it not like that you, to whom they all have been beholding, shall (were ye in that case as I am now) be both at once of them forsaken? Yes, trust them not. For there is an upstart crow, beautified with our feathers, that with his "Tiger's heart wrapped in a player's hide" supposes he is as well able to bombast out a blank verse as the best of you, and, being an absolute *Johannes Factotum,* is in his own conceit the only Shake-scene in a country.

The "burs" here referred to are the actors who have forsaken Greene in his poverty for the rival playwright "Shake-scene"—an obvious hit at Shakespeare. The sneer at a *"Johannes Factotum"* suggests another dig at Shakespeare for being a jack-of-all-trades—actor, playwright, poet, and theatrical handyman in the directing and producing of plays. The most unmistakable reference to Shakespeare, however, is to be found in the burlesque line, "Tiger's heart wrapped in a player's hide," modeled after "Oh, tiger's heart wrapped in a woman's hide!" from *3 Henry VI* (1.4.137). Shakespeare's success as a dramatist had led to an envious outburst from an older, disappointed rival. (Did Shakespeare possibly have this attack in mind some years later when he has Polonius object, in *Hamlet,* 2.2.111–12, "'beautified' is a vile phrase"?)

Soon after Greene's death, Henry Chettle, who had seen the manuscript through the press (and who today some believe to have written the attack himself), issued an apology in his *Kind-Heart's Dream* that may refer to Shakespeare. The apology begins with a disclaimer of all personal responsibility for the incident and with Chettle's insistence that he has neither known nor wishes to know Marlowe (whom Greene's pamphlet had accused of atheism). Toward another unidentified playwright, on the other hand, Chettle expresses genuine concern and regret that Chettle had not done more to soften the acerbity of Greene's vitriol:

> The other, whom at that time I did not so much spare as since I wish I had, for that, as I have moderated the heat of living writers and might have used my own discretion (especially in such a case, the author being dead), that I did not I am as sorry as if the original fault had been my fault; because myself have seen his demeanor no less civil than he excellent in the quality he professes. Besides, divers of worship have reported his uprightness of dealing, which argues his honesty and his facetious grace in writing that approves his art.

If the unnamed person here is to be understood as Shakespeare, it represents him in a most attractive light. Chettle freely admits to having been impressed by this person's civility. He praises the dramatist as "excellent in the quality he professes," that is, excellent as an actor. Chettle notes with approval that the man he is describing enjoys the favor of certain persons of importance, some of whom have borne witness to his uprightness in dealing. *Greene's Groatsworth of Wit,* then, with its rancorous attack on Shakespeare, has paradoxically led to the plausible inference (though not certain in its identification) that in 1592 Shakespeare was regarded as a man of pleasant demeanor, honest reputation, and acknowledged skill as an actor and writer.

Dramatic Apprenticeship

By the end of the year 1594, when after the long plague the theatrical companies were again permitted to act before London audiences, we find Shakespeare as a member of the Lord Chamberlain's company. Probably he had already written *The Comedy of Errors, Love's Labor's Lost, The Two Gentlemen of Verona, the Henry VI* plays, and *Titus Andronicus.* (*A Love's Labor's Won,* mentioned by Francis Meres in 1598, is possibly either a lost play or an alternate title for one of the extant comedies.) He may also have completed *The Taming of the Shrew, A Midsummer Night's Dream, Richard III, King John,* and *Romeo and Juliet.* Although some scholars still question his authorship in part or all of *Titus* and the *Henry VI* plays, no one questions that they are from the period around 1590.

Shakespeare's early development is hard to follow because of difficulties in exact dating of the early plays and because some of the texts (such as *Love's Labor's Lost*) may have been later revised. As a learner making rapid progress in the skill of his art, Shakespeare was also subjected to outside influences that can only partly be determined. Among these influences, we may be sure, were the plays of his contemporary dramatists. If we could define these influences and form an idea of the kinds of plays acceptable on the stage during Shakespeare's early period, we could better understand the milieu in which he began his work.

Fortunately, we know a fair amount concerning the dramatic repertory in London during Shakespeare's early years. Henslowe's *Diary,* for example, records the daily performances of plays by the Lord Strange's men, in conjunction with the Admiral's men, from February 19, 1592 to June 22, 1592. Many of their plays unfortunately are lost, but enough of them are preserved to indicate the sorts of drama then in vogue. The Strange-Admiral's repertory included Christopher Marlowe's *The Jew of Malta,* Robert Greene's *Orlando Furioso* and *Friar Bacon and Friar Bungay,* Robert Greene and Thomas Lodge's *A Looking Glass for London and England,* Thomas Kyd's *The Spanish Tragedy,* the anonymous *A Knack to Know a Knave,* and possibly George Peele's *The Battle of Alcazar,* and Shakespeare's *1 Henry VI.* We find, in other words, a tragedy with a villain as hero, a romantic comedy masquerading as a heroic play, a love comedy featuring a lot of magic, a biblical moral, England's first great revenge tragedy, a popular satiric comedy aimed at dissolute courtiers and usurers, a history play about Portugal's African empire, and an English history play. The titles of other works now lost suggest a similar amalgam of widely differing genres.

Comparatively few plays may have been written during the period when plays were forbidden because of the long plague of 1592–1594. When the Lord Chamberlain's men and the Lord Admiral's men acted under Henslowe's management at the suburban theater of Newington Butts from June 3–13, 1594, their repertories seem to have consisted largely of old plays. In this brief period, they are thought to have acted *Titus Andronicus, Hamlet* (the pre-Shakespearean version), *The Taming of a Shrew* (quite possibly Shakespeare's version), *The Jew of Malta,* a lost play called *Hester and Ahasuerus,* and others.

The Lord Admiral's men probably moved soon afterwards in 1594 to the Rose on the Bankside, across the river Thames from the city of London, where they continued to play under Henslowe's management until 1603. During the years 1594–1597, Henslowe kept in his *Diary* a careful record of their plays and of the sums of money taken in. This circumstance enables us to know a great deal more about the repertory of Shakespeare's rival company than we can ever know about his own. When the Lord Admiral's men began again in 1594, they had five of Marlowe's plays. They seem also to have had Peele's *Edward I,* Kyd's *The Spanish Tragedy,* and a Henry V play. They may also have had plays by both Greene and Peele (Henslowe's chaotic spelling makes it hard to determine), although some of the principal dramas of these two authors had probably ceased to be acted.

We do not know as much about the repertory of the Lord Chamberlain's company as we do about that of the Lord Admiral's men. We know enough, however, to be sure that in 1594 both companies were acting the same sorts of plays that had been on the boards in 1592. We have, therefore, grounds for assuming that, in spite of the loss of many plays (some of which may have been important), the chief contemporary influences upon Shakespeare during his early period were those of Marlowe, Greene, Peele, and Kyd. As an actor possibly in Lord Strange's company or the Earl of Pembroke's company, he would have been familiar with their plays.

Shakespeare learned also from Lyly, though perhaps more from reading Lyly's plays than from actually seeing or performing in them. The boy actors for whom Lyly wrote were forced by the authorities to suspend acting in about 1591 because of their tendency toward controversial satire, and a number of Lyly's plays were printed at that time. As a theatrical figure, therefore, Lyly belonged really to the previous decade.

The Early Plays

Although Shakespeare's genius manifests itself in his early work, his indebtedness to contemporary dramatists and to classical writers is also more plainly evident than in his later writings. His first tragedy, *Titus Andronicus* (c. 1589–1592), is more laden with quotations and classical references than any other tragedy he wrote. Its genre owes much to the revenge play that had been made so popular by Thomas Kyd. Like Kyd, Shakespeare turns to Seneca but also reveals on stage a considerable amount of sensational violence in a manner that is distinctly not classical. For his first villain, Aaron the Moor, Shakespeare borrows some motifs from the morality play and its gleefully sinister tempter, the Vice. Shakespeare may also have had in mind the boastful antics of Marlowe's Vicelike Barabas, in *The Jew of Malta.* Certainly, Shakespeare reveals an extensive debt in his early works to Ovid and to the vogue of Ovidian narrative poetry in the early 1590s, as, for example, in his repeated allusions to the story of Philomela and Tereus (in *Titus Andronicus*) and in his Ovidian poems, *Venus and Adonis* and *The Rape of Lucrece* (1593, 1594).

Shakespeare was still questing for a suitable mode in tragedy and was discovering that the English drama of the 1590s offered no single, clear model. His only other early tragedy, *Romeo and Juliet* (c. 1594–1596), proved to be as different a tragedy from *Titus Andronicus* as could be imagined. Revenge is still prominent in *Romeo and Juliet* but is ultimately far less compelling a theme than the brevity of love and the sacrifice the lovers make of themselves to one another. Shakespeare's source is not the revenge drama of Seneca or Kyd, but a romantic love narrative derived from the fiction of Renaissance Italy. Elements of comedy so predominate in the play's first half that one senses a closer affinity to *A Midsummer Night's Dream* than to *The Spanish Tragedy.*

Shakespeare discovered his true bent more quickly in comedy than in tragedy. Again, however, he experimented with a wide range of models and genres. *The Comedy of Errors* (c. 1589–1594) brings together elements of two plots from the Latin drama of Plautus. The character types and situations are partly derivative, but Shakespeare still reveals an impressive skill in plot construction. *Love's Labor's Lost* (c. 1588–1597) is Shakespeare's most Lylyan early comedy, with its witty debates and its amicable, if brittle, war between the sexes. The play also features an

A contemporary illustration of Titus Andronicus, *the earliest of Shakespeare's tragedies. Shakespeare's early plays demonstrated that he was more than a slavish imitator of predecessors such as Kyd and Marlowe.*

THE GREAT POND AT ELVETHAM
arranged for the Second Day's Entertainment.
A. Her Majestie's presence seate and traine. B. Nereus and his followers. C. The pinnace of Neæra and her musicke. D. The Ship-ile. E. A boate with musicke, attending on the pinnace of Neæra. F. The Fort-mount. G. The Snaile-mount. H. The Roome of Estate. I Her Majestie's Court. K. Her Majestie's Wardrop. L. The place whence Silvanus and his companie issued.

An entertainment presented by the Earl of Hertford to Queen Elizabeth during her visit to Elvetham in 1591 is seemingly referred to by Shakespeare in A Midsummer Night's Dream, *2.1.157–64. The scene shows an elaborate water pageant in honor of the Queen, who appears enthroned at the left of the picture.*

array of humorous characters, including a clownish bumpkin, a country slut, a fantastic courtier, a pedant, a country curate, and the like, whose mannerisms and wordplay add to the rich feast of language in a play that centers its attention on proper and improper styles. *The Two Gentlemen of Verona* (c. 1590–1594) and *The Taming of the Shrew* (c. 1590–1593) are derived from Italianate romantic fiction and comedy. In both, Shakespeare skillfully combines simultaneous plots that offer contrasting views on love and friendship. (*The Taming of the Shrew* makes effective use of a "frame" plot involving a group of characters who serve as audience for the rest of the play.) *A Midsummer Night's Dream* (c. 1595), with its four brilliantly interwoven actions involving court figures, lovers, fairies, and Athenian tradesmen, shows us Shakespeare already at the height of his powers in play construction, even though the comic emphasis on love's irrationality in this play is still in keeping with Shakespeare's early style. The early comedies do not ignore conflict and danger, as we see in the threatened execution of Egeon in *The Comedy of Errors* and the failure of courtships in *Love's Labor's Lost*, but these plays do not as yet fully explore the social dilemmas of *The Merchant of Venice*, the narrowly averted catastrophe of *Much Ado About Nothing*, or the melancholy vein of *As You Like It* and *Twelfth Night*. On stage, early comedies such as *The Comedy of Errors* and *The Taming of the Shrew* are as hilariously funny as anything Shakespeare ever wrote.

Shakespeare's early history plays show a marked affinity with those of Marlowe, Peele, and Greene. Yet today Shakespeare is given more credit for pioneering in the genre of the English history play than he once was. If all the *Henry VI* plays (c. 1589–1592) are basically his, as scholars now often allow, he had more imitators in this genre than predecessors. He scored a huge early success with the heroic character of Lord Talbot in *1 Henry VI*, and by the time Richard Duke of Gloucester had emerged from the *Henry VI* plays to become King Richard III, Shakespeare's fame as a dramatist was assured. He had, of course, learned much from Marlowe's "mighty line" in *Tamburlaine* (1587–1588) and perhaps from Peele's *The Battle of Alcazar* (1588–1589). The anonymous *Famous Victories of Henry V* (1583–1588) must have preceded and influenced his work. Even so, Shakespeare had done much more than simply "beautify" himself with the "feathers" of earlier dramatists, as Greene (or Chettle) enviously charged. Even in his earliest work, Shakespeare already displayed an extraordinary ability to transcend the models from which he learned.

Shakespeare in the Theater, c. 1594–1601

By the year 1594, Shakespeare had already achieved a considerable reputation as a poet and dramatist. We should not be surprised that many of his contemporaries thought of his nondramatic writing as his most significant literary achievement. Throughout his lifetime, in fact, his contemporary fame rested, to a remarkable degree, on his nondramatic poems, *Venus and Adonis, The Rape of Lucrece,* and the *Sonnets* (which were circulated in manuscript prior to their unauthorized publication in 1609). One of the earliest tributes suggesting the importance of the poems is found in an anonymous commendatory verse prefixed to Henry Willobie's *Willobie His Avisa* (1594). It summarizes the plot and theme of *The Rape of Lucrece*:

> Though *Collatine* have dearly bought,
> To high renown, a lasting life,
> And found—that most in vain have sought—
> To have a fair and constant wife,
> Yet Tarquin plucked his glittering grape,
> And Shakespeare paints poor Lucrece' rape.

Richard Barnfield, in his *Poems in Divers Humors* (1598), praised the "honey-flowing vein" of Shakespeare's *Venus and Adonis* and *The Rape of Lucrece*.

Yet Shakespeare's plays were also highly regarded by his contemporaries, even if those plays were accorded a literary status below that given to the narrative and lyrical poems. Francis Meres insisted, in 1598, that Shakespeare deserved to be compared not only with Ovid for his verse but also with Plautus and Seneca for his comedies and tragedies:

> As the soul of Euphorbus was thought to live in Pythagoras, so the sweet, witty soul of Ovid lives in mellifluous and honey-tongued Shakespeare: witness his *Venus and Adonis,* his *Lucrece,* his sugared sonnets among his private friends, etc.
>
> As Plautus and Seneca are accounted the best for comedy and tragedy among the Latins, so Shakespeare among the English is the most excellent in both kinds for the stage: for comedy, witness his *Gentlemen of Verona,* his *Errors,* his *Love's Labor's Lost,* his *Love's Labor's Won,* his *Midsummer Night's Dream,* and his *Merchant of Venice;* for tragedy, his *Richard the II, Richard the III, Henry the IV, King John, Titus Andronicus,* and his *Romeo and Juliet.*

Comedy and tragedy were, after all, literary forms sanctioned by classical precept. By calling some of Shakespeare's English history plays "tragedies," Meres endowed them with the respectability of an ancient literary tradition, recognizing, too, that many of Shakespeare's historical plays culminate in the death of an English king.

John Weever, too, in his epigram *Ad Gulielmum Shakespeare* in *Epigrams in the Oldest Cut and Newest Fashion* (1599), mentioned not only the ever-popular narrative poems but also *Romeo and Juliet* and a history play about one of the Richards:

> Honey-tongued Shakespeare! When I saw thine issue,
> I swore Apollo got them and none other:
> Their rosy-tainted features clothed in tissue,
> Some heaven-born goddess said to be their mother;
> Rose-cheeked Adonis, with his amber tresses,
> Fair fire-hot Venus, charming him to love her;
> Chaste Lucretia virgin-like her dresses,
> Proud lust-stung Tarquin seeking still to prove her;
> *Romeo, Richard*—more whose names I know not.
> Their sugared tongues and power-attractive beauty
> Say they are saints, although that saints they show not,
> For thousands vows to them subjective duty;
> They burn in love thy children. Shakespeare het them.
> Go, woo thy muse more nymphish brood beget them.

Even Gabriel Harvey, an esteemed classical scholar and friend of Edmund Spenser, considered Shakespeare's play *Hamlet* to be worthy of no less praise than the best of the Ovidian poems. Harvey's comments are to be found in a marginal note to a copy of Speght's *Chaucer,* written down some time between 1598 and 1601:

> The younger sort takes much delight in Shakespeare's *Venus and Adonis,* but his *Lucrece* and his tragedy of *Hamlet, Prince of Denmark* have it in them to please the wiser sort.

Shakespeare's growing fame was even such that his dramatic characters began to enter into the intellectual life of the time. The name of Falstaff became a byword almost as soon as he made his appearance on the stage. The references were not always friendly. A play written to be performed by the rival Admiral's company in answer to *1 Henry IV*, called *Sir John Oldcastle* (1599), took Falstaff to task for being a "pampered glutton" and an "aged counsellor to youthful sin." Evidently, the authors of this attack were offended by the fact that Falstaff had been named "Oldcastle" in an early version of *1 Henry IV,* thereby dishonoring the name of one whom many Puritans regarded as a martyr to their cause (see the Introduction to

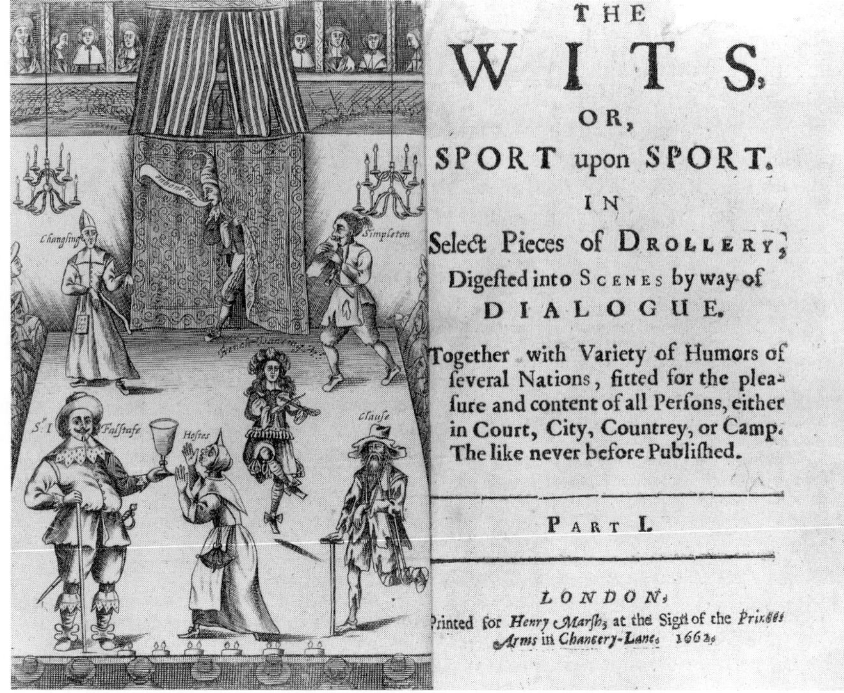

THE

WITS,

OR,

SPORT upon SPORT.

IN

Select Pieces of DROLLERY,

Digeſted into SCENES by way of

DIALOGUE.

Together with Variety of Humors of ſeveral Nations, fitted for the pleaſure and content of all Perſons, either in Court, City, Countrey, or Camp. The like never before Publiſhed.

PART I.

LONDON,

Printed for *Henry Marſh*, at the Sign of the *Princes Arms* in *Chancery-Lane*, 1662.

Falstaff and Mistress Quickly are shown here in a composite theatrical illustration of about 1662. The engraving, used as the frontispiece to Francis Kirkman's The Wits, or Sport upon Sport, *also shows other theatrical types. Visible are candelabras and footlights for stage lighting and a curtained area used perhaps for "discoveries." Spectators are visible in the gallery above, as they are also in the De Witt drawing of the Swan Theatre on p. xlvi and in Alabaster's* Roxana *on p. xlv.*

1 Henry IV). Generally, however, the references during this period to Falstaff and his cronies were fond. In a letter to a friend in London, for example, Sir Charles Percy fretted jocosely that his prolonged stay in the country among his rustic neighbors might cause him to "be taken for Justice Silence or Justice Shallow" (1600). In another letter, from the Countess of Southampton to her husband (written seemingly in 1599), Falstaff's name had become so familiar that it was used apparently as a privately understood substitute for the name of some real person in an item of court gossip:

> All the news I can send you, that I think will make you merry, is that I read in a letter from London that Sir John Falstaff is by his Mistress Dame Pintpot made father of a godly miller's thumb, a boy that's all head and very little body; but this is a secret.

Shakespeare's immense popularity as a dramatist was bound to invite some resentment. One irreverent reaction is found in the so-called *Parnassus* trilogy (1598–1603). The three plays in this series consist of *The Pilgrimage to Parnassus* and *The Return from Parnassus,* in two parts, all of which were acted by the students of St. John's College, Cambridge.

These *Parnassus* plays take a mordantly satirical view of English life around 1600, from the point of view of university graduates attempting to find gainful employment. The graduates discover, to their vocal dismay, that they must seek the patronage of fashion-mongering courtiers, complacent justices of the peace, professional acting companies who offer them pitifully small wages, and the like. One especially foolish patron, to whom the witty Ingenioso applies for a position, is a poetaster named Gullio. This courtly fop aspires to be a fashionable poet himself, and agrees to hire Ingenioso if the latter will help him with his verse writing. In fact, however, as Ingenioso scornfully observes in a series of asides, Gullio's verses are "nothing but pure Shakespeare and shreds of poetry that he hath gathered at the theaters." Most of all, Gullio loves to plagiarize from *Venus and Adonis* and *Romeo and Juliet*. With unparalleled presumption, he actually requests Ingenioso to compose poems "in two or three divers veins, in Chaucer's, Gower's and Spenser's and Mr. Shakespeare's," which Gullio will then pass off as his own inspiration. When Ingenioso does so extempore, producing, among other things, a fine parody of *Venus and Adonis*, Gullio is as delighted as a child. Although he admires Spenser, Chaucer, and Gower, Gullio confesses that Shakespeare is his favorite; he longs to hang Shakespeare's portrait "in my study at the court" and vows he will sleep with *Venus and Adonis* under his pillow (*The Return from Parnassus*, Part I, 1009–1217). Later on (lines 1875–1880), some university graduates trying out as actors in Shakespeare's company are requested to recite a few famous lines from the beginning of *Richard III*—lines that, in the satirical context of this play, sound both stereotyped and bombastic. Shakespeare's fame made him an easy target for university "wits" who regarded the theater of London as lowbrow. Still, the portrait throughout is more satirical

Henry Fuseli's nineteenth-century interpretation of Falstaff shows him in the tavern in Eastcheap with Doll Tearsheet on his lap while Prince Hal and Poins, disguised as tapsters, enter from behind. Falstaff is perhaps saying, "Peace, good Doll, do not speak like a death's-head" (2 Henry IV, *2.4.232–3).*

of those who plagiarize and idolize Shakespeare than of the dramatist's own work. In their backhanded tribute, the *Parnassus* authors make plain that Shakespeare was a household name even at the universities.

Shakespeare's Career and Private Life

During the years from 1594 to 1601, Shakespeare seems to have prospered as an actor and writer for the Lord Chamberlain's men. Whether he had previously belonged to Lord Strange's company or to the Earl of Pembroke's company, or possibly to some other group, is uncertain, but we know that he took part in 1594 in the general reorganization of the companies, out of which emerged the Lord Chamberlain's company. In 1595, his name appeared, for the first time, in the accounts of the Treasurer of the Royal Chamber as a member of the Chamberlain's company of players, which had presented two comedies before Queen Elizabeth at Greenwich in the Christmas season of 1594. This company usually performed at the Theatre, northeast of London, from 1594 until 1599, when they moved to the Globe playhouse south of the Thames. They seem to have been the victors in the intense economic rivalry between themselves and the Lord Admiral's company at the Rose playhouse under Philip Henslowe's management. Fortunately for all the adult companies, the boys' private theatrical companies were shut down during most of the 1590s. Shakespeare's company enjoyed a phenomenal success, and in short time it became the most successful theatrical organization in England.

The nucleus of the Chamberlain's company in 1594 was the family of Burbage. James Burbage, the father, was owner of the Theatre, Cuthbert Burbage was a manager, and Richard Burbage became the principal actor of the troupe. Together the Burbages owned five "shares" in the company, entitling them to half the profits. Shakespeare and four other principal actors—John Heminges, Thomas Pope, Augustine Phillips, and Will Kempe—owned one share each. Not only was Shakespeare a full sharing actor, but also he was the principal playwright of the company. He was named as a chief actor in the 1616 edition of Ben Jonson's *Every Man in His Humor,* performed by the Chamberlain's company in 1598. Later tradition reports, with questionable reliability, that Shakespeare specialized in "kingly parts" or in the roles of older men, such as Adam in *As You Like It* and the Ghost in *Hamlet*. Shakespeare was more celebrated as a playwright than as an actor, and his acting responsibilities may well have diminished as his writing reputation grew. The last occasion on which he is known to have acted was in Jonson's *Sejanus* in 1603.

His prosperity appears in the first record of his residence in London. The tax returns, or Subsidy Rolls, of a parliamentary subsidy granted to Queen Elizabeth for the year 1596 show that Shakespeare was a resident in the parish of St. Helen's, Bishopsgate, near the Theatre, and was assessed at the respectable sum of five pounds. By the next year, Shakespeare had evidently moved to Southwark, near the Bear Garden, for the returns from

First among the actors in Shakespeare's company was Richard Burbage (1567–1619). He played Hamlet, Othello, King Lear, and presumably other major roles including Macbeth, Antony, Coriolanus, and Prospero.

Bishopsgate show his taxes delinquent. He was later located and the taxes paid.

In 1596, Shakespeare suffered a serious personal loss: the death of his only son Hamnet, at the age of eleven. Hamnet was buried at Stratford in August.

Shakespeare acquired property in Stratford during these years, as well as in London. In 1597 he purchased New Place, a house of importance and one of the two largest in the town. Shakespeare's family entered the house as residents shortly after the purchase and continued to live there until long after Shakespeare's death. The last of his family, his granddaughter, Lady Bernard, died in 1670, and New Place was sold.

Shakespeare was also interested in the purchase of land at Shottery in 1598. He was listed among the chief holders of corn and malt in Stratford that same year and sold a load of stone to the Stratford corporation in 1599.

No less suggestive of Shakespeare's rapid rise in the world is his acquisition of the right to bear arms, or, in other words, his establishment in the rank and title of gentleman. The Herald's College in London preserves two drafts of a grant of arms to Shakespeare's father, devised by one William Dethick and dated October 20, 1596. Although we may certainly believe that the application was put forward by William Shakespeare, John Shakespeare was still living, and the grant was drawn up in the father's name. The device for Shakespeare's coat of arms makes a somewhat easy use of the meaning of his name:

> Gold on a bend sables, a spear of the first steeled argent. And for his crest of cognizance a falcon, his wings displayed argent, standing on a wreath of his colors, supporting a spear, gold steeled as aforesaid, set upon a helmet with mantles and tassels, as hath been accustomed and doth more plainly appear depicted on this margent.

According to one of the documents in the grant, John Shakespeare, at the height of his prosperity as a Stratford burgher, had applied twenty years before to the Herald's College for authority to bear arms. The family may not have been able to meet the expense of seeing the application through, however, until William Shakespeare had made his fortune. The grant of heraldic honors to John Shakespeare was confirmed in 1599.

A lawsuit during this period gives us a rather baffling glimpse into Shakespeare's life in the theater. From a writ discovered by Leslie Hotson (*Shakespeare Versus Shallow,* 1931) in the records of the Court of the Queen's Bench, Michaelmas term 1596, we learn that a person named William Wayte sought "for fear of death" to have William Shakespeare, Francis Langley, and two unknown women bound over to keep the peace. Earlier in the same term, moreover, Francis Langley had sworn out a similar writ against this same William Wayte and his stepfather William Gardiner, a justice of the peace in Surrey. Langley was owner of the Swan playhouse on the bankside, near the later-built Globe. His quarrel with Gardiner and Wayte appears to have jeopardized all the acting companies that performed plays south of the Thames, for William Gardiner's jurisdiction included the Bankside theater district. Gardiner and Wayte vengefully tried to drive the theaters out of the area. Possibly Shakespeare's company acted occasionally at the Swan in 1596. Hotson speculates that Shakespeare retaliated by immortalizing

This recreation of what New Place purportedly looked like during Shakespeare's ownership suggests that it must have indeed been an imposing structure. It was warmed by ten fireplaces and had surrounding grounds that included two gardens and two barns.

Gardiner and Wayte as Shallow and Slender in *The Merry Wives of Windsor*. The date of 1596 is too early for that play, and we do not know that Shakespeare drew contemporary portraits in his drama, but we can wonder if lawsuits of this sort gave him no very high opinion of the law's delay and the insolence of office.

During this period Shakespeare's plays began to appear occasionally in print. His name was becoming such a drawing card that it appeared on the title pages of the Second and Third Quartos of *Richard II* (1598), the Second Quarto of *Richard III* (1598), *Love's Labor's Lost* (1598), and the Second Quarto of *1 Henry IV* (1599).

In 1599, the printer William Jaggard sought to capitalize unscrupulously on Shakespeare's growing reputation by bringing out a slender volume of twenty or twenty-one poems called *The Passionate Pilgrim,* attributed to Shakespeare. In fact, only five of the poems were assuredly his, and none of them was newly composed for the occasion. Three came from *Love's Labor's Lost* (published in 1598) and two from Shakespeare's as yet unpublished sonnet sequence.

Contemporary Drama

Shakespeare was without doubt the leading dramatist of the period from 1594 to 1601, not only in our view, but also in that of his contemporaries. The earlier group of dramatists from whom he had learned so much—Lyly, Greene, Marlowe, Peele, Kyd, Nashe—were either dead or no longer writing plays. The group of dramatists who were to rival him in the 1600s and eventually surpass him in contemporary popularity had not yet become well known.

Ben Jonson's early career is obscure. He may have written an early version of his *A Tale of a Tub* in 1596 and *The Case Is Altered* in 1597, though both were later revised. Unquestionably, his first major play was *Every Man in His Humor* (1598), in which Shakespeare acted. This comedy did much to establish the new vogue of comedy of humors, a realistic and satirical kind of drama featuring "humors" characters whose personalities are dominated by some exaggerated trait. We are invited to laugh at the country simpleton, the jealous husband, the overly careful father, the cowardly braggart soldier, the poetaster, and the like. Shakespeare responded to the vogue of humors comedy in his *Henry IV* plays and *The Merry Wives*. Jonson followed his great success with *Every Man Out of His Humor* (1599), an even more biting vision of human folly. George Chapman also deserves important credit for the establishment of humors comedy, with his *The Blind Beggar of Alexandria* (1596) and *An Humorous Day's Mirth* (1597).

Despite the emergence of humors comedy, however, with its important anticipations of Jacobean and even Restoration comedy of manners, the prevailing comedy to be seen on the London stage between 1595 and 1601 was romantic comedy. William Haughton wrote *Englishmen for My Money* in 1598. Thomas Dekker's *Old Fortunatus,* the dramatization of a German folktale, appeared in 1599. Dekker's *The Shoemaker's Holiday* (1599), despite its seemingly realistic touches of life among the apprentices of London, is a thoroughly romanticized saga of rags to riches. A young aristocrat disguises himself as a shoemaker to woo a mayor's daughter; love conquers social rank, and the King himself sentimentally blesses the union. Thomas Heywood wrote heroical romances and comedies, perhaps including *Godfrey of Boulogne* (1594), although most of his early works have disappeared. The boys' private theaters were closed during most of the 1590s, until 1598–1599, and thus the child actors could not perform the satirical comedies at which they were so adept.

Patriotic history drama also continued to flourish on the public stage during those years when Shakespeare wrote his best history plays. Heywood wrote the two parts of *Edward IV* between 1592 and 1599. The anonymous *Edward III* appeared in 1595 or earlier, enough in the vein of Shakespeare's histories that it is sometimes attributed (albeit on uncertain and impressionistic grounds) to him. *Sir Thomas More,* by Munday, Dekker, Chettle, and perhaps Heywood, was written sometime in the later 1590s and very probably revised by Shakespeare himself. Chettle and Munday wrote a trilogy of plays about *Robert, Earl of Huntingdon,* or Robin Hood (1598–1599), on themes that remind us of Shakespeare's *As You Like It*. These plays were performed by the Admiral's men, who also produced the two parts of *Sir John Oldcastle* (1599–1600) by Drayton, Hathway, Munday, and others, in rivalry with Shakespeare's *Henry IV* plays.

Shakespeare's Work

Shakespeare thus wrote his greatest history plays for an audience that knew the genre well. The history play had first become popular just at the start of Shakespeare's career, during the patriotic aftermath of the defeat of the Spanish Armada (1588). Shakespeare himself did much to establish the genre. He wrote first his four-play series dealing with the Lancastrian wars of the fifteenth century, and then went backwards in historical time to King John's reign and to the famous reigns of Henry IV and Henry V.

His romantic comedies were also written for audiences that knew what to expect from the genre. From the comedies of Greene, Peele, Munday, and the rest, as well as Shakespeare himself, Elizabethan audiences were thoroughly familiar with such conventions as fairy charms, improbable adventures in forests, heroines disguised as young men, shipwrecks, love overcoming differences in social rank, and the like. Yet the conventions also demanded more than mere horseplay or foolish antics. Plays of this sort customarily affirmed "wholesome" moral values and appealed to generosity and decency. They were written, like the history plays, for a socially diversified, though generally intelligent and well-to-do, audience.

Several critical terms have been used to suggest the special quality of Shakespeare's comedies during this period of the later 1590s. "Romantic comedy" implies first of all a story in which the main action is about love, but it can also imply elements of the improbable and the miraculous. (The difference between the "romantic comedies" of the later 1590s and the "romances" of Shakespeare's last years, 1606–1613, is that, in part at least, romantic comedy seeks to "make wonder familiar," whereas the romances seek to make the familiar wonderful.) "Philosophical comedy" emphasizes the moral and sometimes Christian idealism underlying many of these comedies of the 1590s: the quest for deep and honest understanding between men and women in *Much Ado About Nothing,* the awareness of an eternal and spiritual dimension to love in *The Merchant of Venice,* and the theme of love as a mysterious force able to regenerate a corrupted social world from which it has been banished in *As You Like It*. "Love-game comedy" pays particular attention to the witty battle of the sexes that we find in several of these plays. "Festive comedy" urges the celebratory nature of comedy, especially in *Twelfth Night* and the *Henry IV* plays, in which Saturnalian revelry must contend against grim and disapproving forces of sobriety. "Comedy of forgiveness," although applicable to only a limited number of plays of this period (especially *Much Ado*), stresses the unexpected second chance that the world of comedy extends to even the most undeserving of heroes; Claudio is forgiven his ill treatment of Hero, although the play's villain, Don John, is not.

Shakespeare in the Theater, c.1601–1608

When the Globe, the most famous of the London public playhouses, was built in 1599, one-half interest in the property was assigned to the Burbage family, especially to the brothers Cuthbert and Richard Burbage. The other half was divided among five actor-sharers: Shakespeare, Will Kempe, Thomas Pope, Augustine Phillips, and John Heminges. Kempe left the company, however, in 1599 and subsequently became a member of the Earl of Worcester's men. His place as leading comic actor was taken by Robert Armin, an experienced man of the theater and occasional author, whose comic specialty was the role of the wise fool. We can observe in Shakespeare's plays the effects of Kempe's departure and of Armin's arrival. Kempe had apparently specialized in clownish and rustic parts, such as those of Dogberry in *Much Ado,* Lancelot Gobbo in *The Merchant of Venice,* and Bottom in *A Midsummer Night's Dream.* (We know that he played Dogberry because his name appears in the early Quarto, derived from the play manuscript; similar evidence links his name to the role of Peter in *Romeo and Juliet.*) For Armin, on the other hand, Shakespeare evidently created such roles as Touchstone in *As You Like It,* Feste in *Twelfth Night,* Lavatch in *All's Well That Ends Well,* and the Fool in *King Lear*.

Other shifts in personnel can sometimes be traced in Shakespeare's plays, especially changes in the number and ability of the boy actors (whose voices would suddenly start to crack at puberty). Shakespeare makes an amusing point about the relative size of two boy actors, for example, in *A Midsummer Night's Dream* and in *As You Like It*; this option may have been available to him only at certain times. On the other hand, not all changes in the company roster can be related meaningfully to Shake-

Among the members of Shakespeare's acting company were John Lowin, William Sly, and Nathaniel Field.

BY PERMISSION OF THE FOLGER SHAKESPEARE LIBRARY

BY PERMISSION OF THE HUNTINGTON LIBRARY, SAN MARINO, CALIFORNIA

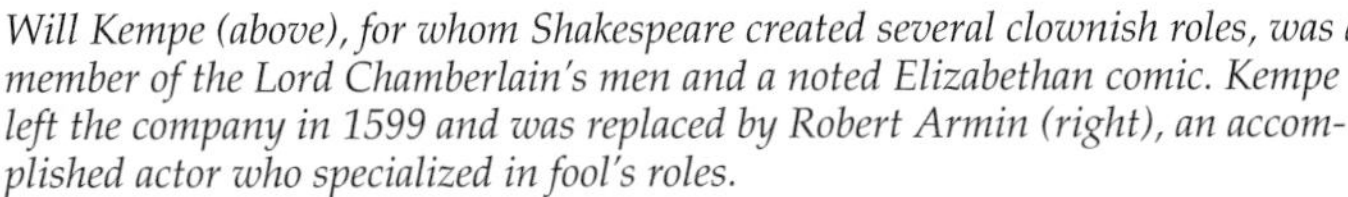

Will Kempe (above), for whom Shakespeare created several clownish roles, was a member of the Lord Chamberlain's men and a noted Elizabethan comic. Kempe left the company in 1599 and was replaced by Robert Armin (right), an accomplished actor who specialized in fool's roles.

speare's dramatic development. Augustine Phillips, who died in 1605, was a full actor-sharer of long standing in the company, but his "type" of role was probably not sharply differentiated from that of several of his associates. Shakespeare's plays, after all, involve many important supporting roles, and versatility in the undertaking of such parts must have been more common than specialization. (Phillips is remembered also for his last will and testament: he left a bequest of "a thirty shillings piece in gold" to "my fellow, William Shakespeare," and similar bequests to other members of the troupe.)

With the reopening of the boys' acting companies in 1598–1599, a serious economic rivalry sprang up between them and the adult companies. The Children of the Chapel Royal occupied the theater in Blackfriars, and the Children of Paul's probably acted in their own singing school in St. Paul's churchyard. Their plays exploited a new vogue for satire. The satiric laughter was often directed at the city of London and its bourgeois inhabitants: socially ambitious tradesmen's wives, Puritan zealots, and the like. Other favorite targets included parvenu knights at court, would-be poets, and hysterical governmental officials. The price of admission at the private theaters was considerably higher than at the Globe or Rose, so the clientele tended to be more fashionable. Sophisticated authors like Ben Jonson, George Chapman, and John Marston tended to find writing for the boy actors more rewarding literarily than writing for the adult players.

One manifestation of the rivalry between public and private theaters was the so-called War of the Theaters, or Poetomachia. In part, this was a personal quarrel between Jonson on one side and Marston and Thomas Dekker on the other. Underlying this quarrel, however, was a serious hostility between a public theater and one that catered more to the elite. Dekker, with Marston's encouragement, attacked Jonson as a literary dictator and snob—one who subverted public decency. Jonson replied with a fervent defense of the artist's right to criticize everything that the artist sees wrong. The major plays in the exchange (1600–1601) were Jonson's *Cynthia's Revels,* Dekker and Marston's *Satiromastix*, and Jonson's *The Poetaster*.

Shakespeare allows Hamlet to comment on the theatrical rivalry (2.2.330–62), with seeming regret for the fact that the boys have been overly successful and that many adult troupes have been obliged to tour the provinces. Most of all, though, Hamlet's remarks deplore the needless bitterness on both sides. The tone of kindly remonstrance makes it seem unlikely that Shakespeare took an active part in the fracas. To be sure, in the Cambridge play *2 Return from Parnassus* (1601–1603), the character called Will Kempe does assert that his fellow actor, Shakespeare, had put down the famous Ben Jonson:

> Why, here's our fellow Shakespeare puts them all down, ay, and Ben Jonson, too. O, that Ben Jonson is a pestilent fellow! And he brought up Horace giving the poets a pill, but our fellow Shakespeare hath given him a purge that made him bewray his credit (lines 1809–1813).

Nevertheless, no play exists in which Shakespeare did put down Jonson, and the reference may be instead to *Satiromastix,* which was performed by Shakespeare's company. Or perhaps "put down" means simply "surpassed." In fact, Shakespeare and Jonson remained on cordial terms, despite their differences in artistic outlook.

Upon the death of Queen Elizabeth in 1603 and the accession to the throne of King James I, Shakespeare's company added an important new success to their already great prosperity. According to a document of instruction from King James to his Keeper of the Privy Seal, dated May 19, 1603, and endorsed as "The Players' Privilege," the acting company that had formerly been the Lord Chamberlain's men now became the King's company. The document names Shakespeare, Richard Burbage, Augustine Phillips, John Heminges, Henry Condell, Will Sly, Robert Armin, Richard Cowley, and Lawrence Fletcher—the last, an actor who had played before the King and the Scottish court in 1599 and 1601. These players are accorded the usual privileges of exercising their art anywhere within the kingdom and are henceforth to be known as the King's company. The principal members of the troupe also were appointed to the honorary rank of Grooms of the Royal Chamber. We therefore find them duly recorded in the Accounts of the Master of the Wardrobe on March 15, 1604, as recipients of the customary grants of red cloth, so that they, dressed in the royal livery, might take part in the approaching coronation procession of King James. The same men are mentioned in these grants as in the Players' Privilege. Shakespeare's name stands second in the former document and first in the latter. In a somewhat similar manner, the King's players, as Grooms of the Royal Chamber, were called in attendance on the Spanish ambassador at Somerset House in August 1604.

The Revels Accounts of performances at court during the winter season of 1604–1605 contain an unusually full entry, listing several of Shakespeare's plays. The list includes *Othello, The Merry Wives of Windsor, Measure for Measure, "The play of Errors," Love's Labor's Lost, Henry V,* and *The Merchant of Venice.* The last play was "again commanded by the King's majesty," and so was performed a second time. This list also sporadically notes the names of "the poets which made the plays," ascribing three of these works to "Shaxberd." (Probably the final *d* is an error for *e*, since the two characters are easily confused in Elizabethan handwriting; the word represents "Shaxbere" or "Shaxpere.") The entire entry was once called into question as a possible forgery but is now generally regarded as authentic.

A number of records during this period show us glimpses of Shakespeare as a man of property. On May 1, 1602, John and William Combe conveyed to Shakespeare one hundred and seven acres of arable land, plus twenty acres of pasture in the parish of Old Stratford, for the sizable payment of three hundred and twenty pounds. The deed was delivered to Shakespeare's brother Gilbert and not to the poet, who was probably at that time occupied in London. On September 28 of the same year, Shakespeare acquired the title to "one cottage and one garden by estimation a quarter of an acre," located opposite his home (New Place) in Stratford.

Shakespeare made still other real-estate investments in his home town. In 1605 he purchased an interest in the tithes of Stratford and adjacent villages from one Ralph Hubaud for the considerable sum of four hundred and forty pounds. The purchasing of tithes was a common financial transaction in Shakespeare's time, though unknown today. Tithes were originally intended for the support of the Church but had, in many cases, become privately owned and hence negotiable. The owners of tithes paid a fixed rental sum for the right to collect as many of these taxes as they could, up to the total amount due under the law. Shakespeare seems, on this occasion in 1605, to have bought from Ralph Hubaud a one-half interest, or "moiety," in certain tithes of Stratford and vicinity. Later, probably in 1609, Shakespeare was one of those who brought a bill of complaint before the Lord Chancellor, requesting that certain other titheholders be required to come into the High Court of Chancery and make answer to the complaints alleged, namely, that they had not paid their proportional part of an annual rental of twenty-seven pounds, thirteen shillings, and four pence on the whole property in the tithes to one Henry Barker. This Barker had the theoretical right to foreclose on the entire property if any one of the forty-two titheholders failed to contribute his share of the annual fee. The suit was, in effect, a friendly one, designed to ensure that all those who were supposed to contribute did so on an equitable and businesslike basis.

We learn from the Stratford Registers of baptism, marriage, and burial of the changes in Shakespeare's family during this period. His father died in 1601, his brother Edmund in 1607, and his mother in 1608. On June 5, 1607, his daughter Susanna was married to Dr. John Hall in Holy Trinity Church, Stratford. Their first child, and Shakespeare's first grandchild, Elizabeth, was christened in the same church on February 21, 1608.

Shakespeare's Reputation, 1601–1608

Allusions to Shakespeare are frequent during this period of his life. One amusing reference is not literary but professes to tell about Shakespeare's prowess as a lover and rival of his good friend and theatrical colleague, Richard Burbage. Perhaps the joke was just a good bawdy story and should not be taken too seriously, but it is nonetheless one of the few anecdotes that date from Shakespeare's lifetime. Our informant is John Manningham, a young law student, who notes in his commonplace book in 1602 the following:

13 March 1601 [1602] . . . Upon a time, when Burbage played Richard III there was a citizen grew so far in liking with him

that, before she went to the play, she appointed him to come that night unto her by the name of Richard the Third. Shakespeare, overhearing their conclusion, went before, and was entertained and at his game ere Burbage came. Then message being brought that Richard the Third was at the door, Shakespeare caused return to be made that William the Conqueror was before Richard the Third. Shakespeare's name William.

Other allusions of the time are more literary. Shakespeare's greatness is, by this time, taken for granted. Anthony Scoloker, for example, in his epistle prefatory to *Diaphantus, or the Passions of Love* (1604), attempts to describe an excellent literary work in this way:

It should be like the never-too-well read Arcadia . . . or to come home to the vulgar's element, like friendly Shakespeare's tragedies, where the comedian rides, when the tragedian stands on tip-toe. Faith, it should please all, like Prince Hamlet.

The antiquarian William Camden includes Shakespeare's name among his list of England's greatest writers in his *Remains of a Greater Work Concerning Britain* (1605):

These may suffice for some poetical descriptions of our ancient poets. If I would come to our time, what a world could I present to you out of Sir Philip Sidney, Edmund Spenser, Samuel Daniel, Hugh Holland, Ben Jonson, Thomas Campion, Michael Drayton, George Chapman, John Marston, William Shakespeare, and other most pregnant wits of these our times, whom succeeding ages may justly admire.

An attempt to use one of Shakespeare's plays for political purposes had some potentially serious repercussions. Two days before the abortive rebellion of the Earl of Essex on February 7, 1601, Shakespeare's company was commissioned to perform a well-known play in its repertory about King Richard II. This play must almost surely have been Shakespeare's. Evidently, the purpose of this extraordinary performance was to awaken public sympathy for Essex by suggesting that Queen Elizabeth was another Richard II, surrounded by corrupt favorites and deaf to the pleas of her subjects. Essex's avowed intention was to remove from positions of influence those men whom he considered his political enemies. Fortunately, Shakespeare's company was later exonerated of any blame in the affair (see the Introduction to *Richard II*).

Perhaps no other allusion to Shakespeare during this period can suggest so well as the following quotation the extent to which Shakespeare's plays had become familiar to English citizens everywhere. The quotation is taken from the notes of a certain Captain Keeling, commander of the East India Company's ship *Dragon*, off Sierra Leone, in the years 1607 and 1608:

1607, Sept. 5. I sent the interpreter, according to his desire, aboard the *Hector*, where he broke fast, and after came aboard me, where we gave the tragedy of *Hamlet*.

30. Captain Hawkins dined with me, where my companions acted *King Richard the Second*.

[March 31.] I invited Captain Hawkins to a fish dinner and had *Hamlet* acted aboard me, which I permit to keep my people from idleness and unlawful games or sleep.

Other Drama of the Period

Even without Shakespeare, the early Jacobean drama in England would rank as one of the most creative periods in the history of all theater. (The word *Jacobean* is derived from *Jacobus,* the Latin form of the name of King James I.) Shakespeare's earlier contemporaries—Lyly, Greene, Marlowe, Peele, Kyd—were dead or silent, but another generation of playwrights was at hand. George Chapman, John Marston, and Ben Jonson all began writing plays shortly before 1600. So did Thomas Dekker and Thomas Heywood, whose dramatic output, often in collaboration, would prove to be considerable. Francis Beaumont, John Fletcher, Cyril Tourneur, and Thomas Middleton emerged into prominence in about 1606 or 1607. John Webster collaborated with Dekker and others in such plays as *Westward Ho* and *Sir Thomas Wyatt* around 1604, although he did not write his great tragedies until 1609–1614. Lesser talents, such as Henry Chettle, Anthony Munday, Henry Porter, John Day, and William Haughton, continued to pour forth an abundant supply of workmanlike plays. As Shakespeare's career developed, therefore, he enjoyed the fellowship and, no doubt, the rivalry of a remarkably gifted and diverse group of practicing dramatists.

Early Jacobean drama is, on the whole, characteristically different from the late Elizabethan drama that had preceded it. Other dramatists besides Shakespeare mirror his shift of focus from romantic comedies and patriotic histories to "problem" plays and tragedies. The boys' companies, reopening in 1598–1599 after virtually a decade of silence, did much to set the new tone. They avoided almost entirely the English history play, with its muscularly heroic style, so unsuited for the acting capabilities of boys. Besides, sophisticated audiences were sated with jingoistic fare, and even in the public theaters the genre had pretty well run its course. The fashion of the moment turned instead to revenge tragedy and satiric comedy.

The Jacobean revenge play owed much of its original inspiration to Thomas Kyd's *The Spanish Tragedy* (c. 1587), with its influential conventions: the intervention of supernatural forces, the feigned madness of the avenger, his difficulty in ascertaining the true facts of the murder, his morbid awareness of the conflict between human injustice and divine justice, his devising of a play within the play, and his invention of ingenious methods of slaughter in the play's gory ending. Kyd may also have written an early version of *Hamlet* featuring similar motifs. Shakespeare confronted cosmic issues of justice and human depravity in his revenge tragedy, *Hamlet* (c. 1599–1601), as indeed Kyd had done, but most followers of Kyd preferred to revel in the sensationalism of the genre. Some private-theater dramatists, such as Marston, subjected the conventions of the genre to caricature. Marston's revenge plays, written chiefly for Paul's boys and (after 1604) for the Children of the Queen's Revels, include *Antonio's Revenge* (1599–1601) and *The Malcontent* (1600–1604). These dramas are marked by flamboyantly overstated cynicism and are, in many ways, as close to satire as they are to tragedy. Marston had, in fact, made his first reputation as a nondramatic satirist, with *The Metamorphosis of Pygmalion's Image* and *The Scourge of Villainy* in 1598. His plays represent a continuation in dramatic form of the techniques of the Roman satirist. The typical Marstonian avenger, such as Malevole in *The Malcontent,* is an exaggeratedly unattractive authorial spokesman, pouring forth venomous hatred upon the loathsome and degenerate court in which he finds himself.

Similar in their exaggerated pursuit of the grotesque and the morbid are Cyril Tourneur's *The Atheist's Tragedy* (1607–1611) and a play formerly attributed to Tourneur but probably by Thomas Middleton, *The Revenger's Tragedy* (1606–1607). These plays are brilliant in the plotting of impossible situations and in the invention of cunning Italianate forms of torture and murder. Any sympathetic identification with the characters of these plays is sacrificed in the interests of technical virtuosity. As a result, the plays are more ironic than cathartic in their effect; we are overwhelmed by life's dark absurdities rather than ennobled by a vision of humanity's tragic grandeur. *The Tragedy of Hoffman, or A Revenge for a Father* by Henry Chettle (Admiral's men, 1602) is similarly grotesque and lacking in sympathy for its revenger hero. To be sure, George Chapman's *Bussy D'Ambois* (1600–1604) and its sequel, *The Revenge of Bussy D'Ambois* (1607–1612), are thoughtful plays about human aspiration, in the vein of Marlowe's *Tamburlaine,* but even these plays employ a good deal of Senecan bloody melodrama.

The revenge play enjoyed a great popularity on the public stage and (in a caricatured form) on the private stage. The public theater did, however, cater also to its Puritan-leaning audiences with more pious and moral tragedy. *Arden of Feversham* (c. 1591) is a good early example of what has come to be called domestic or homiletic tragedy. In the studiously plain style of a broadside ballad, it sets forth the facts of an actual murder that had occurred in 1551 and had been reported in Holinshed's *Chronicles.* The play interprets those events earnestly and providentially. The most famous play in the genre of domestic tragedy is Thomas Heywood's *A Woman Killed with Kindness* (1603). It tells, not of a murder, but of an adultery, for which the goodhearted but offending wife must be perpetually banished by her grieving husband. The play succeeds in elevating the private sorrows of its ordinary characters to tragic stature. The moral stances appear to be unambiguous: adultery is a heinous offense but can be transcended by Christian forgiveness; dueling is evil. Still, a mix of sympathies is perhaps reflective of shifting public attitudes toward the role of women in marriage. Other plays in the vein of domestic tragedy include *A Yorkshire Tragedy* (1605–1608), *The Miseries of Enforced Marriage* (1605–1606), and *Two Lamentable Tragedies* (c. 1594–1598).

In comedy, the greatest writer of the period besides Shakespeare was Ben Jonson. His predilection was toward the private theater, though he continued to write occasionally for the public stage as well. To an ever-increasing extent, he fixed his satirical gaze on those values and institutions which Thomas Heywood cherished: the city of London, its bourgeois citizens, its traditional approach to morality, and its religious zeal. *Every Man Out of His Humor* (1599), written for the Chamberlain's men, features a foolish uxorious citizen, his socially aspiring wife, and her fashionmongering lover—humors types that were to appear again and again in the genre of satirical comedy known as "city comedy." (See Brian Gibbons, *Jacobean City Comedy,* 1968.) *Volpone* (1605–1606), though technically not a London city comedy, since it purportedly takes place in Venice, castigates greed among lawyers, businessmen, and other professional types. *The Alchemist* (1610) ridicules the affectations of petty shopkeepers, lawyers' clerks, Puritan divines, and others. *Bartholomew Fair* (1614) and *The Alchemist* give us Jonson's most memorable indictment of the Puritans.

Numerous other writers contributed to humors comedy and city comedy. George Chapman probably deserves more credit than he usually receives for having helped determine the shape of humors comedy in his *The Blind Beggar of Alexandria* (1596), *An Humorous Day's Mirth* (1597), *All Fools* (1599–1604), *May-Day* (1601–1609), *The Gentleman Usher* (1602–1604), and others. Francis Beaumont, assisted perhaps by John Fletcher, ridicules London grocers and apprentices for their naive tastes in romantic chivalry in *The Knight of the Burning Pestle* (1607–1610). Some satire in this vein, to be sure, is reasonably good-humored. *Eastward Ho* (1605), by Chapman, Jonson, and Marston, is genially sympathetic toward the lifestyle of the small shopkeeper, even though the play contains a good deal of satire directed at social climbing and sharp business practices. Thomas Dekker's collaboration with Thomas Middleton on *The Honest Whore* (Part I, 1604) gives us an amused and yet warm portrayal of a linen draper who succeeds in business by insisting that the customer is always right. Dekker often shows a wry but generous appreciation of bourgeois ethics, as in *The Shoemaker's Holiday* (1599). Yet even he turns against the Puritans in *If This Be Not a Good Play, the Devil Is in It* (1611–1612).

Marston shows his talent for city comedy in *The Dutch Courtesan* (1603–1605). Perhaps the most ingratiating and truly funny of the writers of city comedy, however, is Middleton. His *A Trick to Catch the Old One* (1604–1607) illustrates the tendency of Jacobean comedy to move away both from Shakespeare's romantic vein and Jonson's morally satirical vein toward a more lighthearted comedy of manners, anticipating the style of Restoration comedy. One of Middleton's most hilarious and philosophically unpretentious plays, though plotted with great ingenuity of situation, is *A Mad World, My Masters* (1604–1607). *Michaelmas Term,* written about the same time, exposes the sharp practices of usurers and lawyers. All these Middleton plays were written for Paul's boys.

Romantic comedy, though overshadowed by humors and city comedy during the 1600s, still held forth at the public theaters. A leading exponent was Thomas Heywood, in such plays as *The Fair Maid of the West,* or *A Girl Worth Gold* (1597–1610). Heywood also wrote English history plays designed to prove the sturdiness and historical importance of the London citizenry he so loved, as in *Edward IV* (1597–1599), *The Four Prentices of London* (c. 1600), and *If You Know Not Me You Know Nobody* (1605). Classical tragedy also continued to be written, despite the vogue of revenge tragedy. Ben Jonson rather dogmatically illustrated his classical theories of tragedy in *Sejanus* (1603) and *Catiline* (1611). Samuel Daniel wrote *Philotas* in 1604 and a revision of his *Cleopatra* in 1607. Heywood's *The Rape of Lucrece* appeared in 1606–1608. These are not, however, the immortal tragedies for which the Jacobean period is remembered.

Shakespeare's Work, 1601–1608

Shakespeare's plays of this period are characteristically Jacobean in their fascination with the dark complexities of sexual jealousy, betrayal, revenge, and social conflict. The comedies are few in number and lack the joyous affirmation we associate with *Twelfth Night* and earlier plays. *Measure for Measure,* for example, is not about young men and women happily in love, but about premarital sex and the insoluble problems that arise when vice-prone men attempt to legislate morality for their fellow mortals. Angelo, self-hating and out of emotional control, is a tragic hero providentially rescued from his own worst self. The Duke and Isabella must use ethically dubious means—the bed trick—to effect their virtuous aims. Comedy in the play deals darkly in terms of prostitution, slander, and police inefficiency.

All's Well That Ends Well, though less grim than *Measure for Measure* in its confrontation of human degeneracy, does apply a similar bed trick as its central plot device. Just as important, the obstacles to love are internal and psychological, rather than external; that is, the happy union of Bertram and Helena is delayed, not by parental objections or by accident (as in *Romeo and Juliet* and *A Midsummer Night's Dream*), but by Bertram's unreadiness for the demands of a mature marital relationship. *Troilus and Cressida* is a play in which love is paralyzed by a combination of external and internal forces. Troilus must hand Cressida over to the Greeks because his code of honor bids him put his country's cause before his own, and yet that code of "honor" is based on Paris's rape of Helen. Cressida simply gives herself up to Diomedes, knowing she is not strong enough to stand alone in a moral wilderness. The combatants in the greatest war in all history turn out to be petty bickerers who play nasty games on one another and sulk when their reputations are impugned. The cause for which both sides fight is squalid and senseless.

Raphael Holinshed's Chronicles of England, Scotland, and Ireland, *which was published (1577, 2nd edition in 1587) before Shakespeare's career began, served as principal historic source for many plays, including* Macbeth, King Lear, *and* Cymbeline, *as well as the history plays. Here, in a woodcut from the* Chronicles, *Macbeth and Banquo are shown encountering the three weird sisters.*

In *Hamlet,* Shakespeare explores similar dilemmas posed by human carnality. Women, in Hamlet's misogynistic angst, are too often frail; men are too often importunate and brutal. How is a thoughtful person to justify his or her own existence? Should one struggle actively against injustice and personal wrong? How can one know what is really true or foresee the complex results of action? How, in *Othello,* can the protagonist resist temptation and inner weakness, prompting him to destroy the very thing on which his happiness depends? Is Macbeth tempted to sin by the weird sisters and his wife, or is the choice to murder Duncan ultimately his? To what extent is humanity responsible for its tragic fate? Most of all, in *King Lear,* are the heavens themselves indifferent to human bestiality? Must Cordelia die? Yet, despite these overwhelmingly pessimistic questions, and the tragic consequences they imply for all human life, Shakespeare's "great" tragedies affirm at least the nobility of humanity's striving to know itself, and the redeeming fact that human goodness does exist (in Desdemona, Duncan, Cordelia), even if those who practice goodness are often slaughtered.

The Roman or classical tragedies are something apart from the "great" tragedies. They are more ironic in tone, more dispiriting, though they, too, affirm an essential nobility in humanity. Brutus misguidedly leads a revolution against Caesar but dies loyal to his great principles. Timon of Athens proves the appalling ingratitude of his fellow creature and resolutely cuts himself off from all human contact. Coriolanus proclaims himself an enemy of the Roman people and seeks to destroy them for their ingratitude, though he is compromised and destroyed at last by his promptings of human feeling. Antony, too, is pulled apart by an irreconcilable conflict. Yet, in this play at least, Shakespeare achieves, partly through the greatness of Cleopatra, a triumph over defeat that seems to offer a new resolution of humanity's tragic dilemma.

The Late Years: 1608–1616

In the summer of 1608, Shakespeare's acting company signed a twenty-one-year lease for the use of the Blackfriars playhouse, an indoor and rather intimate, artificially lighted theater inside the city of London, close to the site of St. Paul's cathedral. A private theater had existed on this spot since 1576, when the Children of the Chapel and then Paul's boys began acting their courtly plays for paying spectators in a building that had once belonged to the Dominicans, or Black Friars. James Burbage had begun construction in 1596 of the so-called Second Blackfriars theater in the same building. Although James encountered opposition from the residents of the area and died before he could complete the work, James's son Richard did succeed in opening the new theater in 1600. At first, he leased it (for twenty-one years) to a children's company, but when that company was suppressed in 1608 for offending the French ambassador in a play by George Chapman, Burbage seized the opportunity to take back the unexpired lease and to set up Blackfriars as the winter playhouse for his adult company, the King's men. By this time, the adult troupes could plainly see that they needed to cater more directly to courtly audiences than they once had done. Their popular audiences were becoming increasingly disenchanted with the drama. Puritan fulminations against the stage gained in effect, especially when many playwrights refused to disguise their satirical hostility toward Puritans and the London bourgeoisie.

Several of Shakespeare's late plays may have been acted both at the Globe and at Blackfriars. The plays he wrote after 1608–1609—*Cymbeline, The Winter's Tale,* and *The Tempest*—all show the distinct influence of the dramaturgy of the private theaters. Also, we know that an increasing number of Shakespeare's plays were acted at the court of King James. *Othello, King Lear,* and *The Tempest* are named in court revels accounts, and *Macbeth* dramatizes Scottish history with a seemingly explicit reference to King James as the descendant of Banquo who bears the "twofold balls and treble scepters" (4.1.121); James had received a double coronation as King of England and Scotland, and took seriously his assumed title as King of Great Britain, France, and Ireland. On the other hand, Shakespeare's plays certainly continued to be acted at the Globe to the very end of his career. The 1609 Quarto of *Pericles* advertises that it was acted "by his Majesty's Servants, at the Globe on the Bankside." The 1608 Quarto of *King Lear* mentions a performance at court and assigns the play to "his Majesty's servants playing usually at the Globe on the Bankside." Simon Forman saw *Macbeth, Cymbeline,* and *The Winter's Tale* at the Globe. Finally, a performance of *Henry VIII* on June 29, 1613, resulted in the burning of the Globe to the ground, though afterwards it soon was rebuilt.

Shakespeare's last plays, written with a view to Blackfriars and the court, as well as to the Globe, are now usually called "romances" or "tragicomedies," or sometimes both. Although they were not known by these terms in Shakespeare's day—they were grouped with the comedies in the First Folio of 1623, except for *Cymbeline,* which was placed among the tragedies—the very ambiguity about the genre in this arrangement is suggestive of an uncertainty as to whether they were seen as predominantly comic or tragic. The term "romance" suggests a return to the kind of story Robert Greene had derived from Greek romance: tales of adventure, long separation, and tearful reunion, involving shipwreck, capture by pirates, riddling prophecies, children set adrift in boats or abandoned on foreign shores, the illusion of death and subsequent restoration to life, the revelation of the identity of long-lost children by birthmarks, and the like. The term "tragicomedy" suggests

COURTESY, GUILDHALL LIBRARY, CORPORATION OF LONDON

This section of Wenceslaus Hollar's "Long View" of London dates from 1647, some years after Shakespeare's death, but gives nonetheless a fine view of two theater buildings on the south bank of the Thames River, across from the city. The two labels of "The Globe" and "Beere bayting" should in fact be reversed; the Globe (rebuilt in 1613) appears to the left and below the bearbaiting arena.

a play in which the protagonist commits a seemingly fatal error or crime, or (as in *Pericles*) suffers an extraordinarily adverse fortune to test his patience; in either event, he must experience agonies of contrition and bereavement until he is providentially delivered from his tribulations. The tone is deeply melancholic and resigned, although suffused also with a sense of gratitude for the harmonies that are mysteriously restored.

The appropriateness of such plays to the elegant atmosphere of Blackfriars and the court is subtle but real. Although one might suppose at first that old-fashioned naiveté would seem out of place in a sophisticated milieu, the naiveté is only superficial. Tragicomedy and pastoral romance were, in the period from 1606 to 1610, beginning to enjoy a fashionable courtly revival. The leading practitioners of the new genre were Beaumont and Fletcher, though Shakespeare made a highly significant contribution. Perhaps sophisticated audiences responded to pastoral and romantic drama as the nostalgic evocation of an idealized past, a chivalric "golden world" fleetingly recovered through an artistic journey back to naiveté and innocence. The evocation of such a world demands the kind of studied but informal artifice we find in many tragicomic plays of the period: the elaborate masques and allegorical shows, the descents of enthroned gods from the heavens (as in *Cymbeline*), the use of quaint Chorus figures like Old Gower or Time (in *Pericles* and *The Winter's Tale*), and the quasi-operatic blend of music and spectacle. At their best, such plays powerfully compel belief in the artistic world thus artificially created. The very improbability of the story becomes, paradoxically, part of the means by which an audience must "awake its faith" in a mysterious truth.

Shakespeare did not merely ape the new fashion in tragicomedy and romance. In fact, he may have done much to establish it. His *Pericles,* written seemingly in about 1606–1608 for the public stage before Shakespeare's company acquired Blackfriars, anticipated many important features, not only of Shakespeare's own later romances, but also of Beaumont and Fletcher's *The Maid's Tragedy* and *Philaster* (c. 1608–1611). Still, Shakespeare was on the verge of retirement, and the future belonged to Beaumont and Fletcher. Gradually, Shakespeare disengaged himself, spending more and more time in Stratford. His last-known stint as an actor was in Jonson's *Sejanus* in 1603. Some time in 1611 or 1612, he probably gave up his lodgings in London, though he still may have returned for such occasions as the opening performance of *Henry VIII* in 1613. He continued to be one of the proprietors of the newly rebuilt Globe, but his involvement in its day-to-day operations dwindled.

Shakespeare's Reputation, 1608–1616

Shakespeare's reputation among his contemporaries was undiminished in his late years, even though Beaumont and Fletcher were the new rage at the Globe and Blackfriars. Among those who apostrophized Shakespeare was John Davies of Hereford in *The Scourge of Folly* (entered in the Stationers' Register in 1610):

> To our English Terence, Mr. Will Shakespeare.
>
> Some say, good Will, which I, in sport, do sing:
> Hadst thou not played some kingly parts in sport,
> Thou hadst been a companion for a king,
> And been a king among the meaner sort.
> Some others rail. But, rail as they think fit,
> Thou hast no railing, but a reigning, wit.
> And honesty thou sow'st, which they do reap,
> So to increase their stock which they do keep.

The following sonnet is from *Run and a Great Cast* (1614) by Thomas Freeman:

> To Master W. Shakespeare.
>
> Shakespeare, that nimble Mercury thy brain

Lulls many hundred Argus-eyes asleep,
So fit, for all thou fashionest thy vein,
At th' horse-foot fountain thou hast drunk full deep.
Virtue's or vice's theme to thee all one is.
Who loves chaste life, there's *Lucrece* for a teacher;
Who list read lust, there's *Venus and Adonis,*
True model of a most lascivious lecher.
Besides, in plays thy wit winds like Meander,
Whence needy new composers borrow more
Than Terence doth from Plautus or Menander.
But to praise thee aright, I want thy store.
Then let thine own works thine own worth upraise,
And help t' adorn thee with deservèd bays.

Ben Jonson took a more critical view, though he also admired Shakespeare greatly. In the Induction to his *Bartholomew Fair* (1631 edition), Jonson compared the imaginary world he presented in his play with the more improbable fantasies of romantic drama:

If there be never a servant-monster i' the fair, who can help it? He [the author, Jonson] says; nor a nest of antics? He is loath to make Nature afraid in his plays, like those that beget tales, Tempests, and suchlike drolleries to mix his head with other men's heels.

From this, one judges that Jonson had in mind not only *The Tempest* but also Shakespeare's other late romances. He similarly protested in the Prologue to his 1616 edition of *Every Man in His Humor* that his own playwriting was free of the usual romantic claptrap:

Where neither Chrous wafts you o'er the seas,
Nor creaking throne comes down the boys to please,
Nor nimble squib is seen to make afeard
The gentlewomen, nor rolled bullet heard
To say it thunders, nor tempestuous drum
Rumbles to tell you when the storm doth come.

Still, Shakespeare's reputation was assured. John Webster paid due homage, in his note To the Reader accompanying *The White Devil* (1612), to "the right happy and copious industry of M. *Shakespeare,* M. *Dekker,* & M. *Heywood,*" along with Chapman, Jonson, Beaumont, and Fletcher.

Records of the Late Years

Shakespeare's last recorded investment in real estate was the purchase of a house in Blackfriars, London, in 1613. There is no indication he lived there, for he had retired to Stratford. He did not pay the full purchase price of one hundred and forty pounds, and the mortgage deed executed for the unpaid balance furnishes one of the six unquestioned examples of his signature.

John Combe, a wealthy bachelor of Stratford and Shakespeare's friend, left him a legacy of five pounds in his will at the time of Combe's death in 1613. At about the same time, John's kinsman William Combe began a controversial attempt to enclose Welcombe Common, that is, to convert narrow strips of arable land to pasture. Presumably, Combe was interested in a more efficient means of using the land. Enclosure was, however, an explosive issue, since many people feared they would lose the right to farm the land and would be evicted to make room for cattle and sheep. Combe attempted to guarantee Shakespeare and other titheholders that they would lose no money. He offered similar assurances to the Stratford Council, but the townspeople were adamantly opposed. Shakespeare was consulted by letter as a leading titheholder. The letter is lost, but, presumably, it set forth the Council's reasons for objecting to enclosure. Shakespeare's views on the controversy remain unknown. Eventually, the case went to the Privy Council, where Combe was ordered to restore the land to its original use.

One of the most interesting documents from these years consists of the records of a lawsuit entered into in 1612 by Stephen Belott against his father-in-law, Christopher Mountjoy, a Huguenot maker of women's ornamental headdresses who resided on Silver Street, St. Olave's parish, London. Belott sought to secure the payment of a dower promised him at the time of his marriage to Mountjoy's daughter. In this suit, Shakespeare was summoned as a witness and made deposition on five interrogatories. From this document we learn that Shakespeare was a lodger in Mountjoy's house at the time of the marriage in 1604 and probably for some time before that, since he states in his testimony that he had known Mountjoy for more than ten years. Shakespeare admitted that, at the solicitation of Mountjoy's wife, he had acted as an intermediary in the arrangement of the marriage between Belott and Mountjoy's daughter. Shakespeare declared himself unable, however, to recall the exact amount of the portion or the date on which it was to have been paid. Shakespeare's signature to his deposition is authentic and one of the best samples of his handwriting that we have.

In January of 1615 or 1616, Shakespeare drew up his last will and testament with the assistance of his lawyer Francis Collins, who had aided him earlier in some of his transactions in real estate. On March 25, 1616, Shakespeare revised his will in order to provide for the marriage of his daughter Judith and Thomas Quiney in that same year. Shakespeare's three quavering signatures, one on each page of this document, suggest that he was in failing health. The cause of his death on April 23 is not known. An intriguing bit of Stratford gossip is reported by John Ward, vicar of Holy Trinity in Stratford from 1662 to 1689, in his diary: "Shakespeare, Drayton, and Ben Jonson had a merry meeting, and it seems drank too hard, for Shakespeare died of a fever there contracted." The report comes fifty years after Shakespeare's death, however, and is hardly an expert medical opinion.

The will disposes of all the property of which Shakespeare is known to have died possessing, the greater share of it going to his daughter Susanna. His recently married daughter Judith received a dowry, a provision for any children that might be born of her marriage, and other gifts. Ten pounds went to the poor of Stratford; Shakespeare's sword went to Mr. Thomas Combe; twenty-six shillings and eight pence apiece went to Shakespeare's fellow actors Heminges, Burbage, and Condell to buy them mourning rings; and other small bequests went to various other friends and relatives.

An interlineation contains the bequest of Shakespeare's "second best bed with the furniture," that is, the hangings, to his wife. Anne's name appears nowhere else in the will. Some scholars, beginning with Edmund Malone, have taken this reference as proof of an unhappy marriage, confirming earlier indications, such as the hasty wedding to a woman who was William's senior by eight years and his prolonged residence in London for twenty years or more seemingly without his family. The evidence is inconclusive, however. Shakespeare certainly supported his family handsomely, acquired much property in Stratford, and retired there when he might have remained still in London. Although he showed no great solicitude for Anne's well-being in the will, her rights were protected by law; a third of her husband's estate went to her without having to be mentioned in the will. New Place was to be the home of Shakespeare's favorite daughter Susanna, wife of the distinguished Dr. John Hall. Anne Shakespeare would make her home with her daughter and, with her dower rights secured by law, would be quite as wealthy as she would need to be.

The date of Shakespeare's death (April 23, 1616) and his age (his fifty-third year) are inscribed on his monument. This elaborate structure, still standing in the chancel of Trinity Church, Stratford, was erected some time before 1623 by the London stonecutting firm of Gheerart Janssen and his sons. Janssen's shop was in Southwark, near the Globe, and may have been familiar to the actors. The bust of Shakespeare is a conventional sort of statuary for its time. Still, it is one of the only two contemporary likenesses we have. The other is the Droeshout engraving of Shakespeare in the Folio of 1623.

The epitaph on the monument reads as follows:

Iudicio Phylium, genio Socratem, arte Maronem;
Terra tegit, populus maeret, Olympus habet.
Stay passenger. Why goest thou by so fast?

THE NATIONAL ARCHIVES, LONDON PROB 1/4 F3

As with so many other things in his life, the curious terms of Shakespeare's will have led to endless and provocative conjecture.

MR. WILLIAM
SHAKESPEARES
COMEDIES,
HISTORIES, &
TRAGEDIES.
Publifhed according to the True Originall Copies.

LONDON
Printed by Isaac Iaggard, and Ed. Blount. 1623.

BY PERMISSION OF THE FOLGER SHAKESPEARE LIBRARY

Martin Droeshout's engraving on the title page of the First Folio is one of only two authentic likenesses of Shakespeare in existence.

Read, if thou canst, whom envious Death hath placed
Within this monument: Shakespeare, with whom
Quick Nature died, whose name doth deck this tomb
Far more than cost, sith all that he hath writ
Leaves living art but page to serve his wit.

Obiit anno domini 1616,
Aetatis 53, die 23 April.

These lines, of which the beginning Latin couplet compares Shakespeare with Nestor (King of Pylos) for wise judgment, Socrates for genius, and Virgil (Maro) for poetic art, and avers that the earth covers him, people grieve for him, and Mount Olympus (that is, heaven) has him, indicate the high reputation he enjoyed at the time of his death. More widely known, perhaps, are the four lines inscribed over Shakespeare's grave near the north wall of the chancel. A local tradition assigns them to Shakespeare himself and implies that he wrote them "to suit the capacity of clerks and sextons," whom he wished apparently to frighten out of the idea of opening the grave to make room for a new occupant:

Good friend, for Jesus' sake forbear
To dig the dust enclosèd here.
Blest be the man that spares these stones,
And curst be he that moves my bones.

Whether Shakespeare actually wrote these lines cannot, however, be determined.

Other Dramatists

The most significant new development in the drama of the period from about 1608 to 1616, apart from Shakespeare's new interest in romance and tragicomedy, was the emergence of the famous literary partners Francis Beaumont and John Fletcher. Beaumont, the son of a distinguished lawyer, studied for a while at Oxford and then at the Inner Temple before drifting into a literary career. In 1613, he married an heiress and retired almost completely from the theater. John Fletcher was the son of Richard Fletcher, Queen Elizabeth's chaplain and later Bishop of London. The young man probably studied at Cambridge. The father died in 1596 heavily in debt, leaving the young Fletcher to support a family of eight children. Fletcher became a professional writer, earning his living as chief dramatist for the King's men. He was Shakespeare's successor. Fletcher's cousins, Giles and Phineas Fletcher, gained some reputation as poets. Beaumont and Fletcher, who were close friends, regarded themselves also as poets and as members of the "tribe of Ben"—the disciples of the great Ben Jonson who often gathered together at the Mermaid Tavern for an evening of witty literary conversation.

What things have we seen
Done at the Mermaid! heard words that have been
So nimble, and so full of subtle flame,
As if that every one from whence they came
Had meant to put his whole wit in a jest,
And had resolved to live a fool the rest
Of his dull life!

(Master Francis Beaumont's Letter to Ben Jonson)

Beaumont and Fletcher actually collaborated on only about seven plays: *The Woman Hater,* a comedy (1606); *The Maid's Tragedy*, a tragedy (1608–1611); *Philaster,* a tragicomedy (1608–1610); *Cupid's Revenge,* a tragedy (c. 1607–1612); *The Coxcomb,* a comedy (1608–1610); *A King and No King,* a tragicomedy (1611); *The Scornful Lady,* a tragicomedy (1613–1616); and perhaps one or two others. They may have collaborated on *The Knight of the Burning Pestle* (c. 1607–1610), though it was chiefly Beaumont's. Beaumont also wrote *Mask of the Inner Temple and Gray's Inn* (1613). Fletcher unassisted wrote *The Faithful Shepherdess* (1608–1609), *The Night Walker* (c. 1611), *Bonduca* (1611–1614), *Valentinian* (1610–1614), and others. He also collaborated with several other writers, including Massinger, Middleton, Field, and Rowley. Importantly, he seems to have collaborated with Shakespeare on *The Two Noble Kinsmen* (1613–1616) and, probably, on *Henry VIII.* Eventually, most of these various dramatic enterprises were gathered together in 1647 as the works of Beaumont and Fletcher. They have remained known as such ever since, partly because the original collaboration of these two men did so much to set a new style in coterie drama.

The plays they wrote together, such as *The Maid's Tragedy* and *Philaster,* offer an interesting comparison with Shakespeare's contemporary writing in a similar genre. Beaumont and Fletcher often employ exotic settings, like Rhodes or Sicily. In such an environment, refined aristocratic characters are caught in dynastic struggles or in a rarified conflict between love and honor. They must cope with stereotyped villains, such as tyrants or shamelessly lustful courtiers. The sentiments are lofty, the rhetoric is mannered; elaborately contrived situations are offered with no pretense of verisimilitude. The characters live according to lofty chivalric codes and despise ill breeding above all else. In the plotting of the tragicomic reversal, the audience is sometimes deliberately deceived into believing something that is not true, so that the sudden happy outcome arrives as a theatrically contrived surprise. Disguising and masking are common motifs. The audience is deliberately made aware throughout of the play's theatrical artifice, statuesque scene building, and titillating sensationalism.

Although Shakespeare wrote no tragedies after *Coriolanus,* great tragedy did continue to appear on the Jacobean stage. John Webster wrote his two most splendid plays, *The White Devil* and *The Duchess of Malfi,* between 1609 and 1614. Both contain elements of the still-popular revenge tradition. They also manage to achieve a vision of triumphant human dignity in defeat that merits comparison with Shakespeare's greatest tragic achievement. Still to come were *The Changeling* (1622) by Thomas Middleton and William Rowley, *Women Beware Women* (c. 1620–1627) by Middleton, *'Tis Pity She's a Whore* (1629?–1633) by John Ford, and others. Although these tragedies are more concerned with the grotesque than are Shakespeare's great tragedies, and more obsessed with abnormal human psychology (incest, werewolfism, and the like), they are nonetheless sublime achievements in art. The genius of the age for tragedy did not die with Shakespeare. During Shakespeare's last years, George Chapman was also writing his best tragedies, including *Charles Duke of Byron* in 1608, *The Revenge of Bussy D'Ambois* in about 1610, and *Chabot, Admiral of France* between 1611 and 1622. Ben Jonson's *Catiline His Conspiracy,* a classical tragedy, appeared in 1611; Marston's *The Insatiate Countess*, in about 1610.

The Anti-Stratfordian Movement

What we know of Shakespeare's life is really quite considerable. The information we have is just the kind one would expect. It hangs together and refers to one man and one career. Though lacking in the personal details we should like to have, it is both adequate and plausible. Yet the past hundred years or so have seen the growth of a tendency to doubt Shakespeare's authorship of the plays and poems ascribed to him. The phenomenon is sometimes called the "anti-Stratfordian" movement, since its attack is leveled at the literary credentials of the man who was born in Stratford and later became an actor in London. Although based on no reliable evidence, the movement has persisted long enough to become a kind of myth. It also has the appeal of a mystery thriller: who really wrote Shakespeare's plays? A brief account must be made here of the origins of the anti-Stratfordian movement.

Beginning in the late eighteenth century, and especially in the mid nineteenth century, a few admirers of Shakespeare began to be troubled by the scantiness of information about England's greatest author. As we have already seen, good reasons exist for the scarcity: the great London fire of 1666 that destroyed many records, the relatively low social esteem accorded to popular dramatists during the Elizabethan period, and the like. Also, we do actually know more about Shakespeare than about most of his contemporaries in the theater, despite the difficulties imposed by the passage of time. Still, some nineteenth-century readers saw only that they knew far less about Shakespeare than about many authors of more recent date.

Moreover, the impressions of the man did not seem to square with his unparalleled literary greatness. William Shakespeare had been brought up in a small country town; were his parents cultured folk or even literate? No record of his schooling has been preserved; was Shakespeare himself able to read and write, much less write immortal plays and poems? The anti-Stratfordians did not deny the existence of a man called Shakespeare from Stratford-upon-Avon, but they found it incredible that such a person should be connected with the works ascribed to him. Mark Twain, himself an anti-Stratfordian, was fond of joking that the plays were not by Shakespeare but by another person of the same name. Beneath the humor in this remark lies a deep-seated mistrust: how could a country boy have written so knowledgeably and eloquently about the lives of kings and queens? Where could such a person have learned so much about the law, about medicine, about the art of war, about heraldry? The puzzle seemed a genuine one, even though no one until the late eighteenth century had thought to question Shakespeare's authorship of the plays—least of all his colleagues and friends, such as Ben Jonson, who admitted that Shakespeare's classical learning was "small" but insisted that Shakespeare was an incomparable genius.

The first candidate put forward in the anti-Stratfordian cause as the "real" author of the plays was Sir Francis Bacon, a reputable Elizabethan writer with connections at court and considerable cultural attainments. Yet the ascription of the plays to Bacon was based on no documentary evidence. It relied, instead, on the essentially snobbish argument that Bacon was better born and purportedly better educated than Shakespeare—an argument that appealed strongly to the nineteenth century in which a university education was becoming more and more a distinctive mark of the cultivated person. The assertion of Bacon's authorship was also based on a conspiratorial theory of history; that is, its believers had to assume the existence of a mammoth conspiracy in Elizabethan times in which Shakespeare would allow his name to be used by Bacon as a *nom de plume* and in which Shakespeare's friends, such as Ben Jonson, would take part. (Jonson knew Shakespeare too well, after all, to have been duped for a period of almost twenty years.) The motive for such an arrangement, presumably, was that Bacon did not deign to lend his dignified name to the writing of popular plays (since they were considered subliterary) and so chose a common actor named Shakespeare to serve as his alter ego. This theory of an elaborate hoax involving England's greatest literary giant has proved powerfully attractive to modern writers like Mark Twain who have sometimes referred to themselves as rebels against the cultural "Establishment" of their own times.

The claim that Bacon wrote Shakespeare's works was soon challenged in the name of other prominent Elizabethans: the Earl of Oxford, the Earl of Southampton, Anthony Bacon, the Earl of Rutland, the Earl of Devonshire, Christopher Marlowe, and others. Since documentary claims as to Bacon's authorship of the Shakespearen canon were nonexistent, other Elizabethans could be proposed to fill his role just as satisfactorily as Bacon himself. The anti-Stratfordian movement gained momentum and came to include several prominent persons, including Delia Bacon and Sigmund Freud, as well as Mark Twain. One of the appeals of the anti-Stratfordian movement in recent years has proved to be a kind of amateur sleuthing or scholarship, carried on by professional lawyers, doctors, and the like, who have explored Shakespeare's interest in law and medicine as a hobby and have convinced themselves that Shakespeare's wisdom in these subjects entitles him to claim a better birth than that of a glover's son from Stratford. Ingenious efforts at "deciphering" hidden meanings in the works have been adduced to prove one authorship claim or another. The academic "Establishments" of modern universities have been accused of perpetuating Shakespeare's name out of mere vested self-interest: Shakespeare scholarship is an industry, and its busy workers need to preserve their source of income.

We must ask in all seriousness, however, whether such assertions are not offering answers to nonexistent questions. Responsible scholarship has admirably dispelled the seeming mystery of Shakespeare's humble beginnings. T. W. Baldwin, for example, in *William Shakespeare's Petty School* (1943) and *William Shakspere's Small Latine and Lesse Greeke* (1944), has shown just what sort of classical training Shakespeare almost surely received in the free grammar school of Stratford. It is precisely the sort of training that would have enabled him to use classical authors as he does, with the familiarity of one who likes to read. His Latin and Greek were passable but not strong; he often consulted modern translations, as well as classical originals. Just as importantly, Shakespeare's social background was, in fact, typical of many of the greatest writers of the English Renaissance. He earned his living by his writing, and thus had one of the strongest of motives for success. So did his contemporaries Marlowe (who came from a shoemaker's family) and Jonson (whose stepfather was a brickmason). Greene, Peele, Nashe, and many others sold plays and other writings for a livelihood. Although a few wellborn persons, such as Bacon and Sir Philip Sidney, also made exceptional contributions to literature, and although a number of courtiers emulated Henry VIII and Elizabeth as gifted amateurs in the arts, the court was not the direct or major source of England's literary greatness. Most courtiers were not, like Shakespeare, professional writers. A man like Bacon lacked Shakespeare's connection with a commercial acting company. Surely the theater was a more relevant "university" for Shakespeare than Oxford or Cambridge, where most of his studies would have been in ancient languages and in divinity.

SHAKESPEARE'S LANGUAGE: HIS DEVELOPMENT AS POET AND DRAMATIST

Language and Artistic Development

One indication of Shakespeare's greatness is his extraordinary development. As he worked through his writing career of more than twenty years, he constantly explored new themes, perfected genres and moved on to new ones, and saw ever more deeply into the human condition. Many of the works that have made him immortal were not written until he was nearly forty years old or more. The study of his development is, in itself, an interesting and complex subject. It is one that requires an accurate dating of his plays and poems.

The First Folio, published in 1623 as the first "complete edition" of Shakespeare's plays in the large and handsome folio format for which the printed sheet was folded only once, gives no help in determining the order of composition of Shakespeare's plays. They are arranged in three groups—comedies, histories, and tragedies—without regard for dates of composition. The first comedy in the Folio is *The Tempest*, known to be one of Shakespeare's latest plays; the second is *The Two Gentlemen of Verona*, one of the earliest. The histories are arranged in order of the English kings whose reigns they treat, although Shakespeare clearly did not write them in that order. The tragedies show no discernible arrangement by date. Information about dating can partially be recovered from the fact that eighteen of the thirty-six plays in the First Folio had previously been published in single quarto volumes at various times, with dates on their title pages. *Pericles*, which was not included in the First Folio, appeared in quarto format in 1609. (The quarto format required that the printed sheet be folded twice, resulting in a smaller page than that of a folio volume.) All the quarto editions, except *Romeo and Juliet* and *Love's Labor's Lost*, were entered in the Register of the Stationers' Company of London; two other plays, *As You Like It* (entered in the Stationers' Register in 1600) and *Antony and Cleopatra* (S.R. 1608), although not printed in quarto, were entered in the Stationers' Register possibly in order to forestall publication by printers who had no right to them. The date of entry of a play in the register indicates that, at least by that time, the play was in existence. The quarto editions also have certain information on their title pages regarding date, author, and publisher, and sometimes tell what theatrical company acted the play. Other kinds of external evidence of date include references to Shakespeare's plays in diaries, journals, or accounts of the period, and quotations from his plays in the literary works of Elizabethan and Jacobean writers. Allusions in Shakespeare's plays themselves to contemporary events, although difficult to prove beyond dispute, can sometimes be helpful. See Appendix 1, at the end of this volume, for a detailed discussion on "Canon, Dates, and Early Texts" of each of Shakespeare's plays.

Once Shakespeare's plays have been arranged in approximate chronological order on the basis of the kinds of external evidence already described, we can perceive that his style underwent a continuous development from his earliest work to the end of his career as a dramatist. Matters of style are not easy to talk about precisely, and

A CATALOGVE

of the ſeuerall Comedies, Hiſtories, and Tragedies contained in this Volume.

COMEDIES.

The Tempeſt.	*Folio* 1.
The two Gentlemen of Verona.	20
The Merry Wiues of Windſor.	38
Meaſure for Meaſure.	61
The Comedy of Errours.	85
Much adoo about Nothing.	101
Loues Labour loſt.	122
Midſommer Nights Dreame.	145
The Merchant of Venice.	163
As you Like it.	185
The Taming of the Shrew.	208
All is well, that Ends well.	230
Twelfe-Night, or what you will.	255
The Winters Tale.	304

HISTORIES.

The Life and Death of King John.	*Fol.* 1.
The Life & death of Richard the ſecond.	23
The Firſt part of King Henry the fourth.	46
The Second part of K. Henry the fourth.	74
The Life of King Henry the Fift.	69
The Firſt part of King Henry the Sixt.	96
The Second part of King Hen. the Sixt.	120
The Third part of King Henry the Sixt.	147
The Life & Death of Richard the Third.	173
The Life of King Henry the Eight.	205

TRAGEDIES.

The Tragedy of Coriolanus.	*Fol.* 1.
Titus Andronicus.	31
Romeo and Juliet.	53
Timon of Athens.	80
The Life and death of Julius Cæſar.	109
The Tragedy of Macbeth.	131
The Tragedy of Hamlet.	152
King Lear.	283
Othello, the Moore of Venice.	310
Anthony and Cleopater.	346
Cymbeline King of Britaine.	369

John Heminges and Henry Condell, Shakespeare's fellow actors, gathered contents for the First Folio, published in 1623. They collected thirty-six plays in the volume, omitting Pericles *and* The Two Noble Kinsmen. Troilus and Cressida *is included in most copies of the First Folio but is not listed here in the contents.*

we can hardly expect to be able to date a particular passage as having been written in 1604, say, as distinguished from 1602. Overall, on the other hand, the early and late Shakespeare are strikingly distinguishable. Take, for example, the following two passages. One is from the Duke of Clarence's description of his dream in *Richard III* (1.4.21–33), written in about 1591–1594, near the start of Shakespeare's career:

> Oh, Lord, methought what pain it was to drown!
> What dreadful noise of waters in my ears!
> What sights of ugly death within my eyes!
> Methoughts I saw a thousand fearful wracks;
> Ten thousand men that fishes gnawed upon;
> Wedges of gold, great anchors, heaps of pearl,
> Inestimable stones, unvalued jewels,
> All scattered in the bottom of the sea.
> Some lay in dead men's skulls, and in the holes
> Where eyes did once inhabit there were crept,
> As 'twere in scorn of eyes, reflecting gems,
> That wooed the slimy bottom of the deep
> And mocked the dead bones that lay scattered by.

The second is Prospero's description of his magic in *The Tempest* (5.1.33–50), from about 1610–1611 when Shakespeare was on the verge of retirement:

> Ye elves of hills, brooks, standing lakes, and groves,
> And ye that on the sands with printless foot
> Do chase the ebbing Neptune, and do fly him
> When he comes back; you demi-puppets that
> By moonshine do the green sour ringlets make,
> Whereof the ewe not bites; and you whose pastime
> Is to make midnight mushrooms, that rejoice
> To hear the solemn curfew; by whose aid,
> Weak masters though ye be, I have bedimmed
> The noontide sun, called forth the mutinous winds,
> And twixt the green sea and the azured vault
> Set roaring war; to the dread rattling thunder
> Have I given fire, and rifted Jove's stout oak
> With his own bolt; the strong-based promontory
> Have I made shake, and by the spurs plucked up
> The pine and cedar; graves at my command
> Have waked their sleepers, oped, and let 'em forth
> By my so potent art.

These two passages have been chosen for comparison, in part because they are both set speeches in blank verse, rich in formal characteristics. Put side by side, they reveal a stylistic shift that we can observe in other less formal poetry and even in prose. The shift is away from rhetorical balance toward a freedom from verse restraint, a deliberate syncopation of blank verse rhythms, and a complication of syntax.

Completely regular blank verse, invariably consisting of ten syllables to each unrhymed line, with an accent falling on every other syllable, soon becomes monotonous. The iambic pattern can, however, be varied by a number of subtle changes. Extra syllables, accented and unaccented, can be added to the line, or a line may occasionally be short by one or more syllables. The regular alternation of accented and unaccented syllables, producing the effect of five iambic "feet" in each line (each foot consisting of an accented and an unaccented syllable), can be interrupted by the occasional inversion of a foot. Pauses, or caesuras, may occur at several points in the line. Most importantly, the line can be "end-stopped"—with a strong pause at the end of the line—or "run on" without interruption into the next line. Variations of this sort can transform blank verse from a formal and rhetorical vehicle into one that is highly conversational and supple.

Shakespeare increasingly abandons formal end-stopped verse for a fluid and more conversational style. In the preceding two passages, the first introdues a grammatical stop at the end of every line, except the ninth, whereas the second passage tends to run on past the end of the line; it does so in all but the fifth and tenth lines. Similarly, the passage from *The Tempest* is more apt to introduce a grammatical pause in the middle of a verse line, whereas the passage from *Richard III* stops between clauses in midline only in line 9. Shakespeare's later style is freer in its use of so-called feminine ends at the ends of lines, that is, endings with an unstressed syllable added on to the final stress of the iambic pattern; "fly him," "pastime," and "thunder" are good examples of this. A corollary of Shakespeare's increased use of feminine line endings and nonstopped blank verse is that the lines of his later verse are more apt to end in conjunctions, prepositions, auxiliary verbs, possessive pronouns, and other lightly stressed words. The *Richard III* passage generally ends in strong verbs and nouns, such as "drown," "ears," "eyes," and so on, whereas the *Tempest* passage makes use of "that," "up," and "forth."

Stylistic traits such as these can be quantified to demonstrate a fairly steady course of progression from the early to later plays. Early plays have low percentages of run-on lines in relation to the total number of lines: *1 Henry VI* has 10.4 percent, *2 Henry VI* 11.4 percent, *3 Henry VI* 9.5 percent, *The Comedy of Errors* 12.9 percent, and *The Two Gentlement of Verona* 12.4 percent, whereas *Cymbeline* has 46.0 percent, *The Winter's Tale* 37.5 percent, *The Tempest* 41.5 percent, and *Henry VIII* 46.3 percent. Feminine or "double" endings run from a total of 9 in *Love's Labor's Lost* and 29 in *A Midsummer Night's Dream* to 708 in *Coriolanus*, 726 in *Cymbeline*, and 1,195 in *Henry VIII*. The actual number of light or weak endings increases from none in *The Comedy of Errors* and *The Two Gentlemen of Verona* to 104 in *Coriolanus*, 130 in *Cymbeline*, and 100 in *The Tempest*.

Other stylistic characteristics, though not discernible in the two examples from *Richard III* and *The Tempest*, spell out a similar development toward flexibility. For example, Shakespeare increasingly divides a verse line between two or more speakers. *The Comedy of Errors* and *1 Henry VI* do so hardly at all, whereas in *Cymbeline* the figures rise to a remarkable 85 percent of all instances in which one speaker stops speaking and another begins; *The Winter's Tale* does so in 87.6 percent of such instances, and *The Tempest*, in 84.5 percent.

Shakespeare's use of prose in his plays depends, to a significant extent, on genre, especially in his early work. At the start of his career, Shakespeare seldom uses prose, except in the speeches of clowns, servants, and rustics, whereas blank verse is his common vehicle of expression in speeches of heightened oratory or dramatic seriousness. *1 Henry VI* and *3 Henry VI*, *King John*, and *Richard II* are essentially written throughout in verse—usually blank verse. Prose is more common in the early comedies because of the presence of the Dromios, Christopher Sly, and Bottom the Weaver, but the love scenes are generally in verse. Poetry is important to the lyric plays of the mid-1590s, such as *The Merchant of Venice*, *A Midsummer Night's Dream*, and *Romeo and Juliet*. Prose assumes a major function, on the other hand, in plays of comic wit in the later 1590s, including *1 Henry IV* (45 percent), *2 Henry IV* (54 percent), *Much Ado About Nothing* (74 percent), and *The Merry Wives of Windsor* (81 percent), and here we see that comedy is used not for wisecracking servants so much as for Falstaff, Beatrice, and Benedick. Thereafter, prose is essential to Shakespeare's comic world. It also takes on a major function in *Hamlet* (31 percent), as, for instance, when Hamlet converses with his onetime friends Rosencrantz and Guildenstern, when he plagues Polonius with his satirical wit, or when he philosophizes with Horatio, though verse is, of course, appropriate for the soliloquies and the moments of confrontation with Claudius. In the other great tragedies as well, prose has become for Shakespeare an instrument of limitless flexibility. Although the mixture of prose and blank verse is thus hard to quantify in any steady progression of percentages, the pattern of increased versatility is undeniable. Many of the late plays make less use of prose because of their choice of subject, but all excel in prose comic scenes for Autolycus, Caliban, and many others.

In his use of rhyme, as well, Shakespeare's practice changes from the early to late plays. Early plays and those of the lyric period, such as *A Midsummer Night's Dream* and *Romeo and Juliet*, use a great deal of rhyme, whereas late plays, such as *The Tempest*, use practically none. The commonest form of rhyme is the iambic pentameter measure rhymed in couplet, as when Phoebe, quoting Marlowe's *Hero and Leander*, says in *As You Like It* (3.5.81–2):

> Dead shepherd, now I find thy saw of might,
> "Who ever loved that loved not at first sight?"

Shakespeare does not limit his use of rhyme to the couplet, however. *Romeo and Juliet* and *Love's Labor's Lost* each contains a number of complete sonnets, as well as rhymed sequences made up of a quatrain followed by a couplet, and a good deal of alternate rhyme. Doggerel lines of verse appear in some of the early plays.

One quite formal use of the rhymed couplet does not conform to the statistical pattern that we observe generally in the use of rhyme. Because the Elizabethan theater lacked a front curtain to mark a pause between scenes in a play, Elizabethan dramatists often gave emphasis to a scene ending by means of a rhymed couplet. Possibly the device served also as a cue to those actors backstage who were waiting to begin the next scene. At any rate, the use of scene-ending couplets is common in some plays that otherwise make little use of rhyme. For example, Act 1, scene 5 of *Hamlet* virtually ends with the following concluding statement by the protagonist:

> The time is out of joint. O cursèd spite,
> That ever I was born to set it right!

Apart from this convention, however, use of rhyme in Shakespeare is normally indicative of early style. His lovers in the early plays often speak in rhyme; later, they tend to use prose.

Impossible to quantify, but no less significant in any study of the evolution of Shakespeare's art, is his use of imagery. Images are key to his poetic imagination, and, in part, they can be appreciated out of chronological context, because Shakespeare's mind dwells incessantly on certain image clusters: the family as a metaphor for the state, the garden as an image of social order and disorder, images of medicine and healing applied to the ills of the individual and the commonwealth, images of sexual desire and activity, images of hunting and of other sports, biblical images (Eden, Cain and Abel, Christ's ministry, his Passion, the Last Judgment, etc.), mythological allusions (Danae, Actaeon, Phaethon, Noah, Niobe), and many others. Patterns of imagery have been well studied by Caroline Spurgeon in her *Shakespeare's Imagery and What It Tells Us* (1935), Maurice Charney in *The Function of Imagery in the Drama* (1961), and others. In addition, we can see throughout Shakespeare's career the evolution of an imagistic style, as convincingly demonstrated by Wolfgang Clemen in *The Development of Shakespeare's Imagery* (1951). The early Shakespeare uses figures of speech for decoration and amplification, and learns only gradually to integrate these figures into a presentation of theme, subject, and individual character. In Shakespeare's later work, simile is often transformed into metaphor and assumes an organic function in relation to the entire play. By the end of his career, virtually every aspect of his style has been transformed from one of formal and rhetorical regularity to one of vast flexibility and range.

Shakespeare's English

Pronunciation

How would Shakespeare's plays have sounded to our ears? The distance between Shakespearean and modern English is clearly not as great as in the case of Chaucer, and yet significant differences remain. Spoken English, especially in the pronunciation of vowel sounds, has undergone many striking changes since the early seventeenth century. We can assume that however much Shakespeare's own speech may have been colored by his Warwickshire boyhood, his acting company as a whole was most heavily influenced by London dialect. This form of English had become notably more dominant than in Chaucer's day, though it also included an admixture of northern, eastern, and southern forms because of the cosmopolitan character of the city. Shakespeare often pokes fun at regional dialects in his plays, especially at Welsh, Scottish, and Irish, and at the accents of Frenchmen or other foreigners attempting to speak English (see, for example, *Henry V* and *The Merry Wives of Windsor*).

Reconstructing how early modern English would have sounded is, to be sure, not always easy, since dialect did vary substantially from region to region, and since the ascertaining of pronunciations is often based on rhymes when we cannot be sure how either word in a rhyming pair was pronounced and cannot safely assume that rhymes were exact. Nevertheless, here, in summary form, are some approximate suggestions for pronouncing words in Shakespeare that are not similarly pronounced today. These examples can be applied to similar words: for example, *way* and *say* have the same vowel sound as *day; night,* the same vowel sound as *wide.*

folk (sound the *l*)
gnaw (sound the *g*)
knife (sound the *k; i* as in *wide,* below)
brush (rhymes with *push; r* somewhat trilled)
dull (rhymes with *pull*)
seam (pronounced *same,* with open *a*)
old (pronounced *auld*)
now (pronounced *noo*)
house (pronounced *hoos*)
soul (pronounced *saul*)
know (pronounced *knaw,* with sounded *k*)
own (pronounced *awn*)
tune (pronounced *tiwn*)
rule (pronounced *riwl; r* somewhat trilled)
day (pronounced *die*)
time (pronounced *toime*)
wide (pronounced *woide*)
join (rhymes with *line*)
creeping (pronounced *craypin,* with open *a*)
dissention (in four syllables, without *sh* sound)
persuasion (in four syllables, without *zh* sound)

A matter of more practical importance than phonetic changes is that of differences in Shakespeare's English and ours in the accentuation of syllables. Many cases of variable stress can be found in which he seems to have been at liberty to accent the word in two different ways; in other cases, words were customarily accented on a different syllable from that in current speech. For example, the following accentuations are either usual or frequent: *aspect´, charac´ter, com´mendable, com´plete, con´cealed, con´fessor, consort´* (as a noun), *contract´* (noun), *de´testable, dis´tinct, envy´, for´lorn, hu´mane, instinct´, ob´scure, persev´er, pi´oner, ple´beians, portents´, pur´sue, record´* (noun), *reven´ue, se´cure, sinis´ter, welcome´.*

Not only are *-tion* and *-sion* regularly pronounced as two syllables, but the same situation causes other words in which *e* or *i* stand before vowels to be uttered in Shakespeare's language with one more syllable than in ours; for example, *oce-an, courti-er, marri-age.* We may even have *cre-ature, tre-asure,* and *venge-ance.* Nasals and liquids are frequently pronounced as if an extra vowel were introduced between them and a preceding letter. Accordingly, we have *wrest(e)ler, Eng(e)land, assemb(e)ly,* and *ent(e)rance,* as well as *de-ar, you(e)r,* and *mo-re.* Final *-er* often has a greater syllabic importance than it has in later poetry. Final *-(e)s* in the genitive singular and the plural of nouns not ending in an *-s* sound may constitute a separate syllable; for example, "To show his teeth as white as whale's bone" (*Love's Labor's Lost,* 5.2.333).

The study of metrics is fraught with peril. Knowledge of syllabification can often be circular in that it has to assume a kind of metrical regularity in the line of a verse. Even so, in scanning of Shakespeare's verse it helps to ascertain as accurately as we can how many syllables he intended a given word to have. As compared to modern-day English, a Shakespearean word may have (1) an additional syllable, or (2) one fewer syllables, or (3) two adjoining syllables in adjoining words that coalesce or elide. Spelling may not always indicate these differences to a modern reader.

1. The following lines give us extra-syllable words in *moon's, juggler, entrance,* and *complexion*:

> I do wander everywhere,
> Swifter than the moon's sphere.
> (*A Midsummer Night's Dream,* 2.1.6–7)

> O me! You juggler! You cankerblossom!
> (*A Midsummer Night's Dream,* 3.2.282)

> After the prompter, for our entrance.
> (*Romeo and Juliet,* 1.4.8)

> Mislike me not for my complexion.
> (*The Merchant of Venice,* 2.1.1)

Similarly, the words *captain, monstrous, esperance, this* (*this is*), *George* (*Richard III*, 5.5.9), *valiant, villain,* and *jealous* sometimes have extra syllables in pronunciation.

2. In the following line, *marry* is elided into one syllable:

> Good mother, do not *marry* me to yond fool.
> (*The Merry Wives of Windsor,* 3.4.83)

Similarly, the words *lineal, journeying, carrion, celestial, herald, royal, malice, absolute, perjury, madame, needle, taken, heaven, spirit, devil, gentleman, unpeople, forward, gather, innocent, violet, Africa, eagle, listen,* and *venomous* have usually one fewer syllables than in current English.

3. The following examples are of elision between the syllables of adjoining words:

> Why should I joy in *an abortive* birth?
> (*Love's Labor's Lost,* 1.1.104)

> The *lover, all* as frantic,
> (*A Midsummer Night's Dream,* 5.1.10)

> Romans, *do me* right.
> (*Titus Andronicus,* 1.1.204)

Differences in accentuation and lengthening or shortening of words thus have great importance in the reading and scanning of Shakespeare's verse. Shortening of words by elision or by slurring is common in Shakespeare, but at least in this matter modern practice forms a good guide. Syllables ending in vowels are not infrequently elided before words beginning with a vowel, as in "How cáme / *we a*shóre" (*The Tempest*, 1.2.159) and "too hárd / a knót / for mé / *t' un*tie" (*Twelfth Night,* 2.2.41). Syncopation, or the omission of a syllable, often occurs in words with *r,* as in "I wár-*rant* / it wíll" (*Hamlet,* 1.2.248); and in final *-er, -el,* and *-le,* as in "Tráv*el* you / farre ón" (*The Taming of the Shrew,* 4.2.74). The following words and other similar ones may be treated as monosyllabic in Shakespeare's verse: *whether, ever, hither, other, father, evil, having.* Almost any unaccented syllable of a polysyllabic word (especially if it contains an *i*) may be softened and ignored. This syncopation is frequent in polysyllabic words and proper names: "Thoughts spéc*u* / latíve" (*Macbeth,* 5.4.19) and "Did sláy / this Fór*tinbras;* / who by / a seáled / compáct" (*Hamlet,* 1.1.90). Other occasions for slurring, as listed by Abbott in his *Shakespearian Grammar,* are light vowels preceded by heavy vowels, as in *power, dying,* and so on; plurals and possessives of nouns ending in an *s* sound, as in *empress'* and *Mars';* final *-ed* following *d* or *t,* as in "you háve / exceéd*ed* / all prómise" (*As You Like It,* 1.2.234); and the *-est* of superlatives (pronounced *-st*) after dentals and liquids, as "the stérn'st / good-níght" (*Macbeth,* 2.2.4) and "thy éldest / son's són" (*King John,* 2.1.177).

Grammar and Rhetoric

Shakespeare's grammar presents but few differences in forms from the grammar of current modern English. The *-eth* ending in the third person singular of the present tense, indicative mood, was very commonly used, especially in serious prose. Shakespeare frequently uses this older form, especially *hath, doth,* and *saith,* but seems to prefer the form in *-s* or *-es.* In a few cases, he also seems to use the old northern plural in *-s* or *-es* in the third person of the present indicative, as " . . . at those springs, / On chaliced flowers that *lies*" (*Cymbeline,* 2.3.22–3). He does not always agree with modern usage in the forms of the past tenses and the perfect participles of the verbs that he employs. He retains some lost forms of the strong verbs, sometimes ignores distinctions we make between the past tense and the perfect participle, and treats some verbs as weak (or regular) which are now strong (or irregular). For example, he uses *arose* for *arisen, swam* for *swum, foughten* for *fought, gave* for *given, took* for *taken, sprung* for *sprang, writ* for *wrote, blowed* for *blew, weaved* for *wove,* and *shaked* for *shaken.* Forms like *degenerate* for *degenerated* and *exhaust* for *exhausted* are especially common. A few instances are to be found of the archaic *y-* with the past participle, as in *yclad.* For the possessive case of the neuter personal pronoun *it,* Shakespeare normally uses the regular form at that time, *his;* but he also uses the possessive form *it,* and in his plays first published in the First Folio in 1623 we find several occurrences of the new form *its.* Shakespeare uses the old form *moe,* as well as *more,* and *enow* as the plural of *enough,* though these forms have been modernized in this edition because they are used so inconsistently. He uses *near* and *next* along with *nearer* and *nearest,* as the comparative and superlative of *nigh.* These are the most obvious of the formal differences between Shakespeare's grammar and our own.

The functional differences are more considerable. Elizabethan language exercised an extraordinary freedom, even for English, in the use of one part of speech for another. Shakespeare uses verbs, adjectives, adverbs, and pronouns as nouns. He makes verbs out of nouns and adjectives and, of course, uses nouns as adjectives, for this is a distinguishing characteristic of English speech, but he also uses adverbs, verbs, and prepositional phrases as adjectives, as in "Looks he as freshly as he did . . . ?" (*As You Like It,* 3.2.227). Almost any adjective may be freely used as an adverb, as in "And in my house you shall be friendly lodged" (*The Taming of the

Shrew, 4.2.109). He makes active words—both adjectives and verbs—discharge a passive function, as in "the sightless [invisible] couriers of the air" (*Macbeth*, 1.7.23) and "this aspect of mine / Hath feared the valiant," that is, caused the valiant to be afraid (*The Merchant of Venice*, 2.1.8–9). He makes wider use of the infinitive as a verbal noun or as a gerundive participle than do we: "This to be true / I do engage my life" (*As You Like It*, 5.4.164–5), "My operant powers their functions leave to do" (*Hamlet*, 3.2.172), "Nor do I now make moan to be abridged" (*The Merchant of Venice*, 1.1.126), and "You might have saved me my pains, to have taken [by having taken] it away yourself" (*Twelfth Night*, 2.2.5–7). The functions of prepositions in Elizabethan English were so various that one can only refer the student to the notes to the text or to a dictionary.

In certain other features, however, as, for example, in the use of modal auxiliaries, Shakespeare's language is as restricted and conventional as ours is at formal levels, or even more so. *Shall* is regularly used in Shakespeare to express something inevitable in future time and is, therefore, the usual future tense for all persons. *Will*, which originally expressed intention, determination, or willingness, was, to be sure, beginning to encroach on *shall* for the expression of futurity in the second and third persons, but its use usually still retains in Shakespeare a consciousness of its original meaning. *Should* and *would* had their original senses of obligation and volition, respectively, and had other peculiarities, then as now, of considerable difficulty. The subjunctive mood was vital to Shakespeare as a means of expressing condition, doubt, concession, command, wish, or desire, and, in dependent clauses, indefinitiveness, purpose, or sometimes simple futurity. Note the following examples:

> But if my father *had* not scanted me . . .
> Yourself, renownèd prince, then *stood* as fair.
> (*The Merchant of Venice*, 2.1.17, 20)

> *Live* a thousand years,
> I *shall* not find myself so apt to die.
> (*Julius Caesar*, 3.1.161–2)

> Lest your retirement do *amaze* your friends.
> (*1 Henry IV*, 5.4.6)

> *'Twere* best he speak no harm of Brutus here.
> (*Julius Caesar*, 3.2.70)

> *Melt* Egypt into Nile, and kindly creatures
> *Turn* all to serpents!
> (*Antony and Cleopatra*, 2.5.79–80)

> Yet were it true
> To say this boy *were* like me.
> (*The Winter's Tale*, 1.2.134–5)

> And may direct his course as *please* himself.
> (*Richard III*, 2.2.129)

Some other features of Shakespeare's grammar are as follows: he often omits the relative pronoun; he often uses the nominative case of the pronoun for the accusative case, and vice versa; he uses *him, her, me,* and *them* as true reflexives to mean *himself, herself, myself,* and *themselves;* he employs double negatives and double comparatives and superlatives; he shows a consciousness in the use of *thee* and *thou* of their application to intimates and inferiors and of their insulting quality when addressed to strangers (e.g., "If thou 'thou'-est him some thrice, it shall not be amiss," *Twelfth Night*, 3.2.43–4); he employs *which* to refer to both persons and things; and he does not discriminate closely between *ye*, nominative, and *you*, objective. He makes frequent use of the dative constructions, that is, the objective forms of the pronouns, *me, thee, you, him, her,* and so on, without prepositions where the meaning is "by me," "for me," "with me," "to me," "of me," and the like. For example:

> I am appointed *him* [by him] to murder you.
> (*The Winter's Tale*, 1.2.411)

> She looks *us* [to us] like
> A thing made more of malice than of duty.
> (*Cymbeline*, 3.5.32–3)

One prominent feature of Shakespeare's grammar is his use of the ethical dative, a construction in which the pronoun is generally used to indicate the person interested in the statement. In *King John* (3.4.146), the phrase "John lays you plots," means something like "John lays plots which you may profit by." In the following, *me* means "to my detriment" or "to my disadvantage":

> See how this river comes *me* cranking in
> And cuts *me* from the best of all my land
> A huge half-moon.
> (*1 Henry IV*, 3.1.95–7)

"Whip *me* such honest knaves" (*Othello*, 1.1.51) means "In my judgment such knaves should be whipped." In Quickly's description of Mistress Page, the dative *you* is equivalent to "mark you," "take notice":

> . . . a civil modest wife, and one, I tell you, that will not miss *you* morning nor evening prayer, as any is in Windsor.
> (*The Merry Wives of Windsor*, 2.2.92–4)

At times, however, the ethical dative is idiomatic and virtually without equivalent meaning in modern English; the sense of the passage is best obtained by omitting the pronoun.

Shakespeare, like other Renaissance poets, makes extensive use of the forms and figures of rhetoric. He is fond, for example, of using the abstract for the concrete, as in the words addressed by Surrey to Cardinal Wolsey: "Thou scarlet sin" (*Henry VIII*, 3.2.255). Transpositions are numerous, as are inversions, ellipses, and broken or confused constructions, as in the following examples:

> That thing you speak of,
> I took it for a man. (*Absolute construction.*)
> (*King Lear*, 4.6.77–8)

> Souls and bodies hath he divorced three. (*Transposition of adjective.*)
> (*Twelfth Night*, 3.4.238–9)

> A happy gentleman in blood and lineaments. (*Transposition of adjectival phrase.*)
> (*Richard II*, 3.1.9)

> Your state of fortune and your due of birth. (*Transposition of pronoun.*)
> (*Richard III*, 3.7.120)

> She calls me proud, and [says] that she could not love me. (*Ellipsis.*)
> (*As You Like It*, 4.3.17)

> Returning were as tedious as [to] go o'er. (*Ellipsis.*)
> (*Macbeth*, 3.4.139)

> They call him Doricles, and boasts himself
> To have a worthy feeding. (*Ellipsis of nominative.*)
> (*The Winter's Tale*, 4.4.168–9)

> Of all men else I have avoided thee. (*Confusion of two constructions.*)
> (*Macbeth*, 5.8.4)

> The venom of such looks, we fairly hope,
> Have lost their quality. (*Confusion of number arising from proximity.*)
> (*Henry V*, 5.2.18–19)

> Rather proclaim it, Westmorland, through my host
> That he which hath no stomach to this fight,
> Let him depart. (*Construction changed by change of thought.*)
> (*Henry V*, 4.3.34–6)

> For always I am Caesar. (*Inversion of adverb.*)
> (*Julius Caesar*, 1.2.212)

Shakespeare often uses rhetorical figures for symmetrical effects, especially in the early, ornamental style of *Richard III* and the nondramatic poems. Following are definitions of some of the most popular figures he uses, with illustrations from *Venus and Adonis:*

1. *Parison.* The symmetrical repetition of words in grammatically parallel phrases: "How love makes young men thrall, and old men dote" (line 837).
2. *Isocolon.* The symmetrical repetition of sounds and words in phrases of equal length, as in the previous example, and in this: "Or as the wolf doth grin before he barketh, /Or as the berry breaks before it staineth" (lines 459–60). Parison and isocolon are frequently combined.
3. *Anaphora.* The symmetrical repetition of a word at the beginning of a sequence of clauses or sentences, often at the beginning of lines. Anaphora is frequently combined with parison and isocolon, as in the second example already given, and in this: " 'Give me my hand,' saith he. 'Why dost thou feel it?' / 'Give me my heart,' saith she, 'and thou shalt have it' " (lines 373–4).
4. *Antimetabole.* The symmetrical repetition of words in inverted order: "She clepes him king of graves and grave for kings" (line 995).
5. *Anadiplosis.* The beginning of a phrase with the final words of the previous phrase: "O, thou didst kill me; kill me once again!" (line 499).
6. *Epanalepsis.* The symmetrical repetition of a word or words at the beginning and ending of a line: "He sees his love, and nothing else he sees" (line 287).
7. *Ploce.* The insistent repetition of a word within the same line or phrase: "Then why not lips on lips, since eyes in eyes?" (line 120).
8. *Epizeuxis.* An intensified form of ploce, repeating the word without another intervening word: " 'Ay me!' she cries, and twenty times, 'Woe, woe!' / And twenty echoes twenty times cry so" (lines 833–4).
9. *Antanaclasis.* The shifting of a repeated word from one meaning to another: "My love to love is love but to disgrace it," or " 'Where did I leave?' 'No matter where,' quoth he, / 'Leave me' " (lines 412, 715–6).

For other figures and illustrations, see Sister Miriam Joseph, *Shakespeare's Use of the Arts of Language* (1947) and Brian Vickers, "Shakespeare's Use of Rhetoric," in *A New Companion to Shakespeare Studies,* edited by Kenneth Muir and S. Schoenbaum (1971).

Vocabulary

Renaissance English was hospitable to foreign importation. Many words taken directly from Latin became a permanent part of the language, serving to enrich its power to express thought and its rhythmical capabilities; others were ultimately discarded. The principal borrowings were in the realm of learning and culture. Such words usually retained a vital sense of their original Latin meaning. Sometimes such words have not replaced native words of the same meaning, so that we have such pairs of synonyms as *acknowledge* and *confess,* just as Shakespeare had *wonder* and *admiration.* Because of this

Latin heritage, even a slight knowledge of Latin is a great advantage in the correct understanding of Elizabethan writers, since many Latin borrowings have taken on since the sixteenth century a different shade of meaning from that in which they were borrowed. The Latin sense of *aggravate* ("to add weight to") still struggles for recognition; but *apparent* no longer means primarily "visible to sight," and *intention* does not convey the idea of "intentness." The *Oxford English Dictionary* (*OED*) provides a wealth of information about derivations and changes in meaning.

Latin words were often taken over in their Latin forms, as *objectum* and *subjectum, statua* and *aristocratia,* and later were made to conform to English spelling and stress, though a few, such as *decorum,* still have a Latin form. French continued to be drawn upon and sometimes caused a new Latin borrowing to be adopted in a French form, just as, on the other hand, such words as *adventure* were supplied with a *d* to make them conform to Latin spelling. This principle is illustrated in the pedantry of Holofernes when he objects (*Love's Labor's Lost,* 5.1.20) to "det" as the pronunciation of "debt." Spanish, Italian, and Dutch also supplied many terms. Spanish gave words having to do with commerce, religion, and the New World, such as *mosquito, alligator, ambuscado,* and *grandee.* From Italian came terms of art, learning, and dueling: *bandetto, portico, canto, stoccato*. The Dutch contributed many nautical and oriental words.

These foreign borrowings were a part of what might be called the linguistic ambition of the age, a desire for forcible expression. Language was in a plastic state, so that it had an unparalleled freedom in both vocabulary and form. With this freedom, to be sure, came some confusion, since the Elizabethan era saw few efforts at grammatical precision. Such efforts were later to be made by the age of Dryden and the Royal Society, and by learned men ever since, prompted by an awareness that English was too vague and irregular for use as a means of scientific expression. Still, we readily perceive that English profited from its Renaissance expansion and its subsequent absorption with Shakespeare and the English Bible. It gained, for example, an increased facility in making compounds. Shakespeare, with his *cloud-capped towers* and his *home-keeping wits,* was a genius at this. Also from Shakespeare's time came the English adaptability in the use of prefixes, such as *dis-, re-,* and *en-*, and of suffixes, such as *-ful, -less, -ness,* and *-hood.*

SHAKESPEARE CRITICISM

In his own time, Shakespeare achieved a reputation for immortal greatness that is astonishing when we consider the low regard in which playwrights were then generally held. Francis Meres compared him to Ovid, Plautus, and Seneca, and proclaimed Shakespeare to be England's most excellent writer in both comedy and tragedy. John Weever spoke of "honey-tongued Shakespeare." The number of such praising allusions is high. Even Ben Jonson, a learned writer strongly influenced by the classical tradition, lauded Shakespeare as "a monument without a tomb," England's best poet, exceeding Chaucer, Spenser, Beaumont, Kyd, and Marlowe. In tragedy, Jonson compared Shakespeare with Aeschylus, Euripides, and Sophocles; in comedy, he insisted Shakespeare had no rival even in "insolent Greece or haughty Rome." This tribute appeared in Jonson's commendatory poem written for the Shakespeare First Folio of 1623.

To be sure, Jonson had more critical things to say about Shakespeare. Even in the Folio commendatory poem, Jonson could not resist a dig at Shakespeare's "small Latin, and less Greek." To William Drummond of Hawthornden, he objected that Shakespeare "wanted art" because in a play (*The Winter's Tale*) he "brought in a number of men saying they had suffered shipwreck in Bohemia, where there is no sea near by some hundred miles." In *Timber,* or *Discoveries*, Jonson chided Shakespeare for his unrestrained facility in writing. "The players have often mentioned it as an honor to Shakespeare, that in his writing, whatsoever he penned he never blotted out [a] line. My answer hath been, would he had blotted a thousand." In a preface to his own play, *Every Man in His Humor* (1616 edition), Jonson satirized English history plays (such as Shakespeare's) that "with three rusty swords, / And help of some few foot-and-half-foot words, / Fight over York and Lancaster's long jars, / And in the tiring-house bring wounds to scars." He also jeered at plays lacking unity of time in which children grow to the age of sixty or older and at nonsensical romantic plays featuring fireworks, thunder, and a chorus that "wafts you o'er the seas."

These criticisms are all of a piece. As a classicist himself, Jonson held in high regard the classical unities. He deplored much English popular drama, including some of Shakespeare's plays, for their undisciplined mixture of comedy and tragedy. Measured against his cherished ideals of classical decorum and refinement of language, Shakespeare's histories and the late romances—*Pericles, Cymbeline, The Winter's Tale,* and *The Tempest*—seemed irritatingly naive and loose-jointed. Yet Jonson knew that Shakespeare had an incomparable genius, superior even to his own. Jonson's affection and respect for Shakespeare seem to have been quite unforced. In the midst of his critical remarks in *Timber,* he freely conceded that "I loved the man, and do honor his memory (on this side idolatry) as much as any. He was indeed honest, and of an open and free nature, had an excellent fantasy, brave notions, and gentle expressions."

The Age of Dryden and Pope

Jonson's attitude toward Shakespeare lived on into the Restoration period of the late seventeenth century. A commonplace of that age held it proper to "admire" Ben Jonson but to "love" Shakespeare. Jonson was the more correct poet, the better model for imitation. Shakespeare often had to be rewritten according to the sophisticated tastes of the Restoration (see Appendix 3 for an account of Restoration stage adaptations of Shakespeare), but he was also regarded as a natural genius. Dryden reflected this view in his *Essay of Dramatic Poesy* (1668) and his *Essay on the Dramatic Poetry of the Last Age* (1672). Dryden condemned *The Winter's Tale, Pericles,* and several other late romances for "the lameness of their plots" and for their "ridiculous incoherent story" which is usually "grounded on impossibilities." Not only Shakespeare, he charged, but several of his contemporaries "neither understood correct plotting nor that which they call *the decorum of the stage.*" Had Shakespeare lived in the Restoration, Dryden believed, he would doubtless have written "more correctly" under the influence of a language that had become more "courtly" and a wit that had grown more "refined." Shakespeare, he thought, had limitless "fancy" but sometimes lacked "judgment." Dryden regretted that Shakespeare had been forced to write in "ignorant" times and for audiences who "knew no better." Like Jonson, nevertheless, Dryden had the magnanimity to perceive that Shakespeare transcended his limitations. Shakespeare, said Dryden, was "the man who of all modern and perhaps ancient poets had the largest and most comprehensive soul." From a classical writer, this was high praise indeed.

Alexander Pope's edition of Shakespeare (1725) was based upon a similar estimate of Shakespeare as an untutored genius. Pope freely "improved" Shakespeare's language, rewriting lines and excising those parts he considered vulgar, in order to rescue Shakespeare from the barbaric circumstances of his Elizabethan milieu. Other critics of the Restoration and early eighteenth century who stressed Shakespeare's "natural" genius and imaginative powers were John Dennis, Joseph Addison, and the editors Nicholas Rowe and Lewis Theobald.

The Age of Johnson

Shakespeare was not without his detractors during the late seventeenth and early eighteenth centuries; after all, classical criticism tended to distrust imagination and fancy. Notable among the harsher critics of the Restoration period was Thomas Rymer, whose *Short View of Tragedy* (1692) included a famous attack on *Othello* for making too much out of Desdemona's handkerchief. In the eighteenth century, Voltaire spoke out sharply against Shakespeare's violation of the classical unities, though Voltaire also had some admiring things to say.

The most considered answer to such criticism in the later eighteenth century was that of Dr. Samuel Johnson, in his edition of Shakespeare's plays and its great preface (1765). Shakespeare, said Johnson, is the poet of nature who "holds up to his readers a faithful mirror of manners and of life. His characters are not modified by the customs of particular places, unpracticed by the rest of the world. . . . In the writings of other poets a character is too often an individual; in those of Shakespeare it is commonly a species." Johnson's attitudes were essentially classical in that he praised Shakespeare for being universal, for having provided a "just representation of general nature," and for having stood the test of time. Yet Johnson also magnanimously praised Shakespeare for having transcended the classical rules. Johnson triumphantly vindicated the mixture of comedy and tragedy in Shakespeare's plays and the supposed indecorum of his characters.

Of course, Johnson did not praise everything he saw. He objected to Shakespeare's loose construction of plot, careless huddling together of the ends of his plays, licentious humor, and, above all, the punning wordplay. He deplored Shakespeare's failure to satisfy the demands of poetic justice, especially in *King Lear,* and he regretted that Shakespeare seemed more anxious to please than to instruct. Still, Johnson did much to free Shakespeare from the constraint of an overly restrictive classical approach to criticism.

The Age of Coleridge

With the beginning of the Romantic period, in England and on the Continent, Shakespeare criticism increasingly turned away from classical precept in favor of a more spontaneous and enthusiastic approach to Shakespeare's creative genius. The new Shakespeare became indeed a rallying cry for those who now deplored such "regular" dramatic poets as Racine and Corneille. Shakespeare became a seer, a bard with mystic powers of insight into the human condition. Goethe, in *Wilhelm Meister* (1796), conceived of Hamlet as the archetypal "Romantic" poet: melancholic, delicate, and unable to act.

Critical trends in England moved toward similar conclusions. Maurice Morgann, in his *Essay on the Dramatic Character of Sir John Falstaff* (1777), glorified Falstaff into a rare individual of courage, dignity, and—yes—honor. To do so, Morgann had to suppress much evidence as to Falstaff's overall function in the *Henry IV* plays. Dramatic structure, in fact, did not interest him; his passion was "character," and his study of Falstaff reflected a new Romantic preoccupation with character analysis. Like other character critics who followed him, Morgann tended to move away from the play itself and into a world where the dramatic personage being considered might lead an independent existence. What would it have been like to know Falstaff as a real person? How would he have behaved on occasions other than those reported by Shakespeare? Such questions fascinated Morgann and others because they led into grand speculations about human psychology and philosophy. Shakespeare's incomparably penetrating insights into character prompted further investigations of the human psyche.

Other late eighteenth-century works devoted to the study of character included Lord Kames's *Elements of Criticism* (1762), Thomas Whately's *Remarks on Some of the Characters of Shakespeare* (1785), William Richardson's *Philosophical Analysis and Illustration of Some of Shakespeare's Remarkable Characters* (1774), and William Jackson's *Thirty Letters on Various Subjects* (1782). Morgann spoke for this school of critics when he insisted, "It may be fit to consider them [Shakespeare's characters] rather as historic than dramatic beings; and, when occasion requires, to account for their conduct from the whole of character, from general principles, from latent motives, and from policies not avowed."

Samuel Taylor Coleridge, the greatest of the English Romantic critics, was profoundly influenced by character criticism, both English and continental. He himself made important contributions to the study of character. His conception of Hamlet, derived in part from Goethe and Hegel, as one who "vacillates from sensibility, and procrastinates from thought, and loses the power of action in the energy of resolve," was to dominate nineteenth-century interpretations of Hamlet. His insight into Iago's evil nature—"the motive-hunting of a motiveless malignity"— was also influential.

Nevertheless, Coleridge did not succumb to the temptation, as did so many character critics, of ignoring the unity of an entire play. Quite to the contrary, he affirmed in Shakespeare an "organic form" or "innate" sense of shape, developed from within, that gave new meaning to Shakespeare's fusion of comedy and tragedy, his seeming anachronisms, his improbable fictions, and his supposedly rambling plots. Coleridge heaped scorn on the eighteenth-century idea of Shakespeare as a "natural" but untaught genius. He praised Shakespeare not for having mirrored life, as Dr. Johnson had said, but for having created an imaginative world attuned to its own internal harmonies. He saw Shakespeare as an inspired but deliberate artist who fitted together the parts of his imaginative world with consummate skill. "The judgment of Shakespeare is commensurate with his genius."

In all this, Coleridge was remarkably close to his German contemporary and rival, August Wilhelm Schlegel, who insisted that Shakespeare was "a profound artist, and not a blind and wildly luxuriant genius." In Shakespeare's plays, said Schlegel, "The fancy lays claim to be considered as an independent mental power governed according to its own laws." Between them, Coleridge and Schlegel utterly inverted the critical values of the previous age, substituting "sublimity" and "imagination" for universality and trueness to nature.

Other Romantic critics included William Hazlitt (*Characters of Shakespear's Plays*, 1817), Charles Lamb (*On the Tragedies of Shakespeare*, 1811), and Thomas De Quincey (*On the Knocking at the Gate in Macbeth*, 1823). Hazlitt reveals a political liberalism characteristic of a number of Romantic writers in his skeptical view of Henry V's absolutism and his imperialist war against the French. John Keats has some penetrating things to say in his letters about Shakespeare's "negative capability," or his ability to see into characters' lives with an extraordinary self-effacing sympathy. As a whole, the Romantics were enthusiasts of Shakespeare, and sometimes even idolaters. Yet they consistently refused to recognize him as a man of the theater. Lamb wrote, "It may seem a paradox, but I cannot help being of opinion that the plays of Shakespeare are less calculated for performance on a stage than those of almost any other dramatist whatever." Hazlitt similarly observed: "We do not like to see our author's plays acted, and least of all, *Hamlet*. There is no play that suffers so much in being transferred to the stage." These hostile attitudes toward the theater reflected, in part, the condition of the stage in nineteenth-century England. In part, however, these attitudes were the inevitable result of character criticism, or what Lamb called the desire "to know the internal workings and movements of a great mind, of an Othello or a Hamlet for instance, the *when* and the *why* and the *how far* they should be moved." This fascination with character swept everything before it during the Romantic period.

A. C. Bradley and the Turn of the Century

The tendency of nineteenth-century criticism, then, was to exalt Shakespeare as a poet and a philosopher rather than as a playwright, and as a creator of immortal characters whose "lives" might be studied as though existing independent of a dramatic text. Not infrequently, this critical approach led to a biographical interpretation of Shakespeare through his plays, on the assumption that what he wrote was his own spiritual autobiography and a key to his own fascinating character. Perhaps the most famous critical study in this line was Edward Dowden's *Shakspere: A Critical Study of His Mind and Art* (1875), in which he traced a progression from Shakespeare's early exuberance and passionate involvement through brooding pessimism to a final philosophical calm.

At the same time, the nineteenth century also saw the rise of a more factual and methodological scholarship, especially in the German universities. Dowden, in fact, reflected this trend as well, for one of the achievements of philological study was to establish with some accuracy the dating of Shakespeare's plays and thus make possible an analysis of his artistic development. Hermann Ulrici's *Über Shakespeares dramatische Kunst* (1839) and Gottfried Gervinus's edition of 1849 were among the earliest studies to interest themselves in Shakespeare's chronological development.

The critic who best summed up the achievement of nineteenth-century Shakespeare criticism was A. C. Bradley, in his *Shakespearean Tragedy* (1904) and other studies. *Shakespearean Tragedy* dealt with the four "great" tragedies: *Hamlet, Othello, King Lear,* and *Macbeth*. Bradley revealed his Romantic tendencies in his focus on psychological analysis of character, but he also brought to his work a scholarly awareness of the text that had been missing in some earlier character critics. His work continues to have considerable influence today, despite modern tendencies to rebel against nineteenth-century idealism. To Bradley, Shakespeare's tragic world was ultimately explicable and profoundly moral. Despite the overwhelming impression of tragic waste in *King Lear*, he argued, we as audience experience a sense of compensation and completion that implies an ultimate pattern in human life. "Good, in the widest sense, seems thus to be the principle of life and health in the world; evil, at least in these worst forms, to be a poison. The world reacts against it violently, and, in the struggle to expel it, is driven to devastate itself." Humanity must suffer because of its fatal tendency to pursue some extreme passion, but humanity learns through suffering about itself and the nature of its world. We as audience are reconciled to our existence through purgative release; we smile through our tears. Cordelia is wantonly destroyed, but the fact of her transcendent goodness is eternal. Although in one sense she fails, said Bradley, she is "in another sense superior to the world in which [she] appears; is, in some way which we do not seek to define, untouched by the doom that overtakes [her]; and is rather set free from life than deprived of it."

Historical Criticism

The first major twentieth-century reaction against character criticism was that of the so-called historical critics. (On the later critical movement known as the New Historicism, see below, following "Jan Kott and the Theater of the Absurd.") These critics insisted on a more hardheaded and skeptical appraisal of Shakespeare through better understanding of his historical milieu: his theater, his audience, and his political and social environment. In good part, this movement was the result of a new professionalism of Shakespearean studies in the twentieth century. Whereas earlier critics—Dryden, Pope, Johnson, and Coleridge—had generally been literary amateurs in the best sense, early twentieth-century criticism became increasingly the province of those who taught in universities. Historical research became a professional activity. Bradley himself was Professor of English Literature at Liverpool and Oxford, and did much to legitimize the incorporation of Shakespeare into the humanities curriculum. German scholarship produced the first regular periodical devoted to Shakespeare studies, *Shakespeare-Jahrbuch,* to be followed in due course in England and America by *Shakespeare Survey* (beginning in 1948), *Shakespeare Quarterly* (1950), and *Shakespeare Studies* (1965).

From the start, historical criticism took a new look at Shakespeare as a man of the theater. Sir Walter Raleigh (Professor of English Literature at Oxford, not to be confused with his Elizabethan namesake) rejected the Romantic absorption in psychology and turned his attention instead to the artistic methods by which plays affect theater-going spectators. The poet Robert Bridges insisted that Shakespeare had often sacrificed consistency and logic for primitive theatrical effects designed to please his vulgar audience. Bridges's objections were often based on serious lack of information about Shakespeare's stage, but they had a healthy iconoclastic effect nonetheless on the scholarship of his time. In Germany, Levin Schücking pursued a similar line of reasoning in his *Character Problems in Shakespeare's Plays* (1917, translated into English in 1922). Schücking argued that Shakespeare had disregarded coherent structure and had striven instead for vivid dramatic effect ("episodic intensification") in his particular scenes. Schücking's *The Meaning of Hamlet* (1937) explained the strange contradictions of that play as resulting from primitive and brutal Germanic source materials which Shakespeare had not fully assimilated.

A keynote for historical critics of the early twentieth century was the concept of artifice or convention in the construction of a play. Perhaps the leading spokesman for this approach was E. E. Stoll, a student of G. L. Kittredge of Harvard University, himself a leading force in historical scholarship in America. Stoll vigorously insisted, in such works as *Othello: An Historical and Comparative Study* (1915), *Hamlet: An Historical and Comparative Study* (1919), and *Art and Artifice in Shakespeare* (1933), that a critic must never be sidetracked by moral, psychological, or biographical interpretations. A play, he argued, is an artifice arising out of its historical milieu. Its conventions are implicit agreements between playwright and spectator. They alter with time, and a modern reader who is ignorant of Elizabethan conventions is all too apt to be misled by his own post-Romantic preconceptions. For example, a calumniator like Iago in *Othello* is conventionally supposed to be believed by the other characters on stage. We do not need to speculate about the "realities" of Othello's being duped, and, in fact, we are likely to be led astray by such Romantic speculations. Stoll went so far as to affirm, in fact, that Shakespearean drama intentionally distorts reality through its theatrical conventions in order to fulfill its own existence as artifice. *Hamlet* is not a play about delay but a revenge story of a certain length, containing many conventional revenge motifs, such as the ghost and the "mousetrap" scheme used to test the villain, and deriving many of its circumstances from Shakespeare's sources; delay is a conventional device needed to continue the story to its conclusion.

Stoll's zeal led to excessive claims for historical criticism, as one might expect in the early years of a pioneering movement. At its extreme, historical criticism came close to implying that Shakespeare was a mere product of his environment. Indeed, the movement owed many of its evolutionist assumptions to the supposedly scientific "social Darwinism" of Thomas Huxley and other late nineteenth-century social philosophers. In more recent years, however, the crusading spirit has given way to a more moderate historical criticism that continues to be an important part of Shakespearean scholarship.

Alfred Harbage, for example, in *As They Liked It* (1947) and *Shakespeare and the Rival Traditions* (1952), has analyzed the audience for which Shakespeare wrote and the rivalry between popular and elite theaters in the London of his day. Harbage sees Shakespeare as a popular dramatist writing for a highly intelligent, enthusiastic, and socially diversified audience. More recently, in *The Privileged Playgoers of Shakespeare's London, 1576–1642* (1981), Ann Jennalie Cook has qualified Harbage's view, arguing that Shakespeare's audience was, for the most part, affluent and well connected. G. E. Bentley has amassed an invaluable storehouse of information about *The Jacobean and Caroline Stage* (1941–1968), just as E. K. Chambers earlier had collected documents and data on *The Elizabethan Stage* (1923). Other studies by these historical scholars include Chambers's *William Shakespeare: A Study of Facts and Problems* (1930), and Bentley's *Shakespeare and His Theatre* (1964) and *The Profession of Dramatist in Shakespeare's Time* (1971). T. W. Baldwin exemplifies the historical scholar who, like Stoll, claims too much for the method; nevertheless, much information on Shakespeare's schooling, reading, and professional theatrical life is available in such works as *William Shakspere's Small Latine and Lesse Greeke* (1944) and *The Organization and Personnel of the Shakespearean Company* (1927). Hardin Craig uses historical method in *An Interpretation of Shakespeare* (1948).

Historical criticism has contributed greatly to our knowledge of the staging of Shakespeare's plays. George Pierce Baker, in *The Development of Shakespeare as a Dramatist* (1907), continued the line of investigation begun by Walter Raleigh. Harley Granville-Barker brought to his *Prefaces to Shakespeare* (1930, 1946) a wealth of professional theatrical experience of his own. Ever since his time, the new theatrical method of interpreting Shakespeare has been based to an ever increasing extent on a genuine revival of interest in Shakespearean production. John Dover Wilson shows an awareness of the stage in *What Happens in Hamlet* (1935) and *The Fortunes of Falstaff* (1943). At its best, as in John Russell Brown's *Shakespeare's Plays in Performance* (1966), in John Styan's *Shakespeare's Stagecraft* (1967), in Michael Goldman's *Shakespeare and the Energies of Drama* (1972), and in Alan Dessen's *Elizabethan Drama and the Viewer's Eye* (1977) and his *Recovering Shakespeare's Theatrical Vocabulary* (1995), this critical method reveals many insights into the text that are hard to obtain without an awareness of theatrical technique.

Supporting this theatrical criticism, historical research has learned a great deal about the physical nature of Shakespeare's stage. J. C. Adams's well-known model of the Globe Playhouse, as presented in Irwin Smith's *Shakespeare's Globe Playhouse: A Modern Reconstruction* (1956), is now generally discredited in favor of a simpler building, as reconstructed by C. Walter Hodges (*The Globe Restored,* 1953, 2nd edition, 1968), Bernard Beckerman (*Shakespeare at the Globe,* 1962, 2nd edition, 1967), Richard Hosley ("The Playhouses and the Stage" in *A New Companion to Shakespeare Studies,* edited by K. Muir and S. Schoenbaum, 1971, and several other good essays), T. J. King (*Shakespearean Staging,* 1599–1642, 1971), and others. Information on the private theaters, such as the Blackfriars, where Shakespeare's plays were also performed, appears in William Armstrong, *The Elizabethan Private Theatres* (1958); Richard Hosley, "A Reconstruction of the Second Blackfriars" (*The Elizabethan Theatre,* 1969); Glynne Wickham, *Early English Stages* (1959–1972); and others. For further information on innyard theaters and on courtly or private theaters, see the contributions of Herbert Berry, D. F. Rowan, W. Reavley Gair, and others cited in the bibliography at the end of this volume.

A related pursuit of historical criticism has been the better understanding of Shakespeare through his dramatic predecessors and contemporaries. Willard Farnham, in *The Medieval Heritage of Elizabethan Tragedy* (1936), traces the evolution of native English tragedy through the morality plays of the early Tudor period. J. M. R. Margeson's *The Origins of English Tragedy* (1967) broadens the pattern to include still other sources for Elizabethan ideas on dramatic tragedy. Bernard Spivack, in *Shakespeare and the Allegory of Evil* (1958), sees Iago, Edmund, Richard III, and other boasting villains in Shakespeare as descendants of the morality Vice. In *Shakespeare and the Idea of the Play* (1962), Anne Righter (Barton) traces the device of the play-within-the-play and the metaphor of the world as a stage back to medieval and classical ideas of dramatic illusion. Irving Ribner's *The English History Play in the Age of Shakespeare* (1959, revised 1965) examines Shakespeare's plays on English history in the context of the popular Elizabethan genre to which they belonged. Robert Weimann's *Shakespeare and the Popular Tradition in the Theatre* (translated from the German in 1978) is a Marxist study in the social dimension of dramatic form and function. Many other studies of this sort could be cited, including Glynne Wickham's *Shakespeare's Dramatic Heritage* (1969), Oscar J. Campbell's *Shakespeare's Satire* (1943), M. C. Bradbrook's *Themes and Conventions of Elizabethan Tragedy* (1935), and S. L. Bethell's *Shakespeare and the Popular Dramatic Tradition* (1944).

Another important concern of historical criticism has been the relationship between Shakespeare and the ideas of his age—cosmological, philosophical, and political. Among the first scholars to study Elizabethan cosmology were Hardin Craig in *The Enchanted Glass* (1936) and A. O. Lovejoy in *The Great Chain of Being* (1936). As their successor, E. M. W. Tillyard provided in *The Elizabethan World Picture* (1943) a definitive view of the conservative and hierarchical values that Elizabethans were supposed to have espoused. In *Shakespeare's History Plays* (1944), Tillyard extended his essentially conservative view of Shakespeare's philosophical outlook to the histories, arguing that they embody a "Tudor myth" and thereby lend support to the Tudor state. Increasingly, however, critics have disputed the extent to which Shakespeare in fact endorsed the "establishment" values of the Elizabethan world picture. Theodore Spencer, in *Shakespeare and the Nature of Man* (1942), discusses the impact on Shakespeare of radical new thinkers like Machiavelli, Montaigne, and Copernicus. In political matters, Henry A. Kelly's *Divine Providence in the England of Shakespeare's Histories* (1970) has challenged the existence of a single "Tudor myth" and has argued that Shakespeare's history plays reflect contrasting political philosophies set dramatically in conflict with one another. M. M. Reese's *The Cease of Majesty* (1961) also offers a graceful corrective to Tillyard's lucid but occasionally one-sided interpretations. Revisions in this direction continue in the work of the so-called new historicists and cultural materialists, to be discussed below.

Historical criticism has also yielded many profitable specialized studies, in which Shakespeare is illuminated by a better understanding of various sciences of his day. Lily Bess Campbell approaches Shakespearean tragedy through Renaissance psychology in *Shakespeare's Tragic Heroes: Slaves of Passion* (1930). Paul Jorgensen uses Elizabethan documents on the arts of war and generalship in his study *Shakespeare's Military World* (1956). Many similar studies examine Shakespeare in relation to law, medicine, and other professions.

"New" Criticism

As we have seen, historical criticism is still an important part of Shakespeare criticism; for better or worse, it is the stuff of some research-oriented universities and their Ph.D. programs. Since its beginning, however, historical criticism has had to face a critical reaction, generated, in part, by its own utilitarian and fact-gathering tendencies. The suggestions urged by Stoll and others that Shakespeare was the product of his cultural and theatrical environment tended to obscure his achievement as a poet. Amassing of information about Shakespeare's reading or his theatrical company often seemed to inhibit the scholar from responding to the power of words and images.

Such at any rate was the rallying cry of the *Scrutiny* group in England, centered on F. R. Leavis, L. C. Knights, and Derek Traversi, and the "new" critics in America, such as Cleanth Brooks. The new critics demanded close attention to the poetry without the encumbrance of historical research. Especially at first, the new critics were openly hostile to any criticism distracting readers from the text. The satirical force of the movement can perhaps best be savored in L. C. Knights's "How Many Children Had Lady Macbeth?" (1933), prompted by the learned appendices in Bradley's *Shakespearean Tragedy*: "When was the murder of Duncan first plotted? Did Lady Macbeth really faint? Duration of the action in *Macbeth.* Macbeth's age. 'He has no children.'"

In part, the new critical movement was (and still is) a pedagogical movement, a protest against the potential dryness of historical footnoting and an insistence that classroom study of Shakespeare ought to focus on a response to his language. Cleanth Brooks's "The Naked Babe and the Cloak of Manliness" (in *The Well Wrought Urn,* 1947) offers to the teacher a model of close reading that focuses on imagery and yet attempts to see a whole vision of the play through its language. G. Wilson Knight concentrates on imagery and verbal texture, sometimes to the exclusion of the play as a whole, in his *The Wheel of Fire* (1930), *The Imperial Theme* (1931), *The Shakespearian Tempest* (1932), *The Crown of Life* (1947), and others. William Empson is best known for his *Seven Types of Ambiguity* (1930) and *Some Versions of Pastoral* (1935). Derek Traversi's works include *An Approach to Shakespeare* (1938), *Shakespeare: The Last Phase* (1954), *Shakespeare: From Richard II to Henry V* (1957), and *Shakespeare: The Roman Plays* (1963). Perhaps the greatest critic of this school has been L. C. Knights, whose books include *Explorations* (1946), *Some Shakespearean Themes* (1959), *An Approach to Hamlet* (1960), and *Further Explorations* (1965). T. S. Eliot's perceptive and controversial observations have also had an important influence on critics of this school. Other studies making good use of the new critical method include Robert Heilman's *This Great Stage* (1948) and *Magic in the Web* (1956). Many of these critics are concerned not only with language but also with the larger moral and structural implications of Shakespeare's plays as discovered through a sensitive reading of the text.

More specialized studies of Shakespearean imagery and language include Caroline Spurgeon's *Shakespeare's Imagery and What It Tells Us* (1935). Its classifications are now recognized to be overly statistical and restricted in definition, but the work has nonetheless prompted valuable further study. Among later works are Sister Miriam Joseph's *Shakespeare's Use of the Arts of Language* (1947, partly reprinted in *Rhetoric in Shakespeare's Time,* 1962), Wolfgang Clemen's *The Development of Shakespeare's Imagery* (1951), and M. M. Mahood's *Shakespeare's Wordplay* (1957). The study of prose has not received as much attention as that of poetry, although Brian Vickers's *The Artistry of Shakespeare's Prose* (1968) and Milton Crane's *Shakespeare's Prose* (1951) make significant contributions. See also Edward Armstrong's *Shakespeare's Imagination* (1963) and Kirby Farrell's *Shakespeare's Creation: The Language of Magic and Play* (1975).

A more recent development in studies of Shakespeare's imagery has led to the examination of visual images in the theater as part of Shakespeare's art. Reginald Foakes ("Suggestions for a New Approach to Shakespeare's Imagery," *Shakespeare Survey,* 5, 1952, 81–92) and Maurice Charney (*Shakespeare's Roman Plays: The Function of Imagery in the Drama,* 1961) were among the first to notice that Caroline Spurgeon and other "new" critics usually excluded stage picture in their focus on verbal image patterns. Yet Shakespeare's extensive involvement with the practicalities of theatrical production might well lead one to suspect that he arranges his stage with care and that the plays are full of hints as to how he communicates through visual means. Costume, properties, the theater building, the blocking of actors in visual patterns onstage, expression, movement—all of these contribute to the play's artistic whole. Francis Fergusson analyzes the way in which the Elizabethan theatrical building provides *Hamlet* with an eloquently expressive idea of order and hierarchy, against which are ironically juxtaposed Claudius's acts of killing a king and marrying his widow (*The Idea of a Theater,* 1949). Other studies of stage imagery include Ann Pasternak Slater's *Shakespeare the Director* (1982) and David Bevington's *Action Is Eloquence: Shakespeare's Language of Gesture* (1984).

Another call for expansion of the occasionally narrow limits of "new" criticism comes from the so-called Chicago school of criticism, centered on R. S. Crane, Richard McKeon, Elder Olson, Bernard Weinberg, and others, who, in the 1950s and 1960s, espoused a formal or structural approach to criticism, using Aristotle as its point of departure. Crane was reacting to the new critics who, in his view, restricted the kinds of answers they could obtain by limiting themselves to one methodology. Critics hostile to the Chicago school have responded, to be sure, that Crane's own approach tends to produce its own dogmatism. Formalist analyses of Shakespeare plays are to be found, for example, in the work of W. R. Keast, Wayne Booth, and Norman Maclean; see *Critics and Criticism,* edited by R. S. Crane (1952) and the bibliography at the back of this book.

Psychological Criticism

In a sense, Freudian and other psychological criticism continues the "character" criticism of the nineteenth century. Freudian critics sometimes follow a character into a world outside the text, analyzing Hamlet (for instance) as though he were a real person whose childhood traumas can be inferred from the symptoms he displays. The most famous work in this vein is *Hamlet and Oedipus* (1910, revised 1949), by Freud's disciple, Ernest Jones. According to Jones, Hamlet's delay is caused by an oedipal trauma. Hamlet's uncle, Claudius, has done exactly what Hamlet himself incestuously and subconsciously wished to do: kill his father and marry his mother. Because he cannot articulate these forbidden impulses to himself, Hamlet is paralyzed into inactivity. Jones's critical analysis thus assumes, as did such Romantic critics as Coleridge, that the central problem of *Hamlet* is one of character and motivation: why does Hamlet delay? (Many modern critics would deny that this is a problem or would insist, at least, that by setting such a problem, Jones has limited the number of possible answers. Avi Erlich proposes an entirely different psychological reading of the play in *Hamlet's Absent Father,* 1972.) Psychological criticism sometimes also reveals its affinities with nineteenth-century character criticism in its attempt to analyze Shakespeare's personality through his plays, as though the works constituted a spiritual autobiography. The terminology of psychological criticism is suspect to some readers because it is at least superficially anachronistic when dealing with a Renaissance writer. The terminology is also sometimes overburdened with technical jargon.

Nonetheless, psychological criticism has afforded many insights into Shakespeare not readily available through other modes of perception. Jones's book makes clear the intensity of Hamlet's revulsion toward women as a result of his mother's inconstancy. At a mythic level, Hamlet's story certainly resembles that of Oedipus, and Freudian criticism is often at its best when it shows us this universal aspect of the human psyche. Freudian terminology need not be anachronistic when it deals with timeless truths. Psychological criticism can reveal to us Shakespeare's preoccupation with certain types of women in his plays, such as the domineering and threatening masculine type (Joan of Arc, Margaret of Anjou) or, conversely, the long-suffering and patient heroine (Helena in *All's Well,* Hermione in *The Winter's Tale*). Psychological criticism is perhaps most useful in studying family relationships in Shakespeare. It also has much to say about the psychic or sexual connotations of symbols. Influential books include Norman O. Brown's *Life Against Death: The Psychoanalytical Meaning of History* (1959) and Norman Holland's *Psychoanalysis and Shakespeare* (1966) and *The Shakespearean Imagination* (1964).

Richard Wheeler's *Turn and Counter-Turn: Shakespeare's Development and the Problem Comedies* (1981) applies psychoanalytic method to a study of Shakespeare's development, in which, as Wheeler sees it, the sonnets and the problem plays are pivotal as Shakespeare turns from the safely contained worlds of romantic comedy (with non-threatening heroines) and the English history play (in which women are generally denied anything more than a marginal role in state affairs) to the tragedies, in which sexual conflict is shown in all its potentially terrifying destructiveness. Wheeler's completion of C. L. Barber's *The Whole Journey: Shakespeare's Power of Development* (1986) continues the study of Shakespeare's development in the late plays. The dichotomies of gender and genre urged in these studies and continued by Linda Bamber (*Comic Women, Tragic Men: A Study of Gender and Genre in Shakespeare*, 1982), among others, have been challenged by Jonathan Goldberg in his essay, "Shakespearean Inscriptions: The Voicing of Power," in *Shakespeare and the Question of Theory* (edited by Patricia Parker and Geoffrey Hartman, 1985). A collection of essays under the editorship of Murray Schwartz and Coppélia Kahn, *Representing Shakespeare* (1980), affords a sample of work by Janet Adelman, David Willbern, Meredith Skura, David Sundelson, Madelon Gohlke Sprengnether, Joel Fineman, and others.

Much psychoanalytic criticism of the 1980s has sought to displace Freud's emphasis upon the relation of son and father in the oedipal triangle in favor of attention to the mother and child preoedipal relation; a model here is the work of Karen Horney (e.g., *Neurosis and Human Growth: The Struggle Toward Self-Realization*, 1950). Jacques Lacan (*Écrits*, translated by Alan Sheridan, 1977) and Erik Erikson (*Childhood and Selfhood*, 1978) are also prominent theorists in the post-Freudian era. Despite such changes, the psychoanalytic critic still attempts to discover in the language of the play the means by which he or she can reconstruct an early stage in the development of one or more of the dramatic characters.

Mythological Criticism

Related to psychological criticism is the search for archetypal myth in literature, as an expression of the "collective unconscious" of the human race. Behind such an approach lie the anthropological and psychological assumptions of Jung and his followers. One of the earliest studies of this sort was Gilbert Murray's *Hamlet and Orestes* (1914), analyzing the archetype of revenge for a murdered father. Clearly this custom goes far back into tribal prehistory and emerges in varying but interrelated forms in many different societies. This anthropological universality enables us to look at Hamlet as the heightened manifestation of an incredibly basic story. *Hamlet* gives shape to urgings that are a part of our innermost social being. The struggle between the civilized and the primitive goes on in us as in the play *Hamlet*.

The vast interdisciplinary character of mythological criticism leaves it vulnerable to charges of speculativeness and glib theorizing. At its best, however, mythological criticism can illuminate the nature of our responses as audience to a work of art. Northrop Frye argues, in *A Natural Perspective* (1965), that we respond to mythic patterns by imagining ourselves participating in them communally. The Greek drama emerged, after all, from Dionysiac ritual. All drama celebrates in one form or another the primal myths of vegetation, from the death of the year to the renewal or resurrection of life. In his most influential book, *Anatomy of Criticism* (1957), Frye argues that mythic criticism presents a universal scheme for the investigation of all literature, or all art, since art is itself the ordering of our most primal stirrings. Frye sees in drama (as in other literature) a fourfold correspondence to the cyclical pattern of the year: comedy is associated with spring, romance with summer, tragedy with autumn, and satire with winter. Historically, civilization moves through a recurrent cycle from newness to decadence and decay; this cycle expresses itself culturally in a progression from epic and romance to tragedy, to social realism, and, finally, to irony and satire before the cycle renews itself. Thus, according to Frye, the genres of dramatic literature (and of other literary forms as well) have an absolute and timeless relationship to myth and cultural history. That is why we as audience respond so deeply to form and meaning as contained in genre. C. L. Barber, in *Shakespeare's Festive Comedy* (1959), makes a similar argument: our enjoyment of comedy arises from our intuitive appreciation of such "primitive" social customs as Saturnalian revels, May games, and fertility rites. John Holloway offers an anthropological study of Shakespeare's tragedies in *The Story of the Night* (1961).

Frye's critical system has not been without its detractors. For example, Frederick Crews (*Psychoanalysis and Literary Process*, 1970) argues that Frye's system is too self-contained in its ivory tower and too much an abstract artifact of the critical mind to be "relevant" to the social purposes of art. Nevertheless, Frye continues to be one of the most influential critics of the late twentieth century.

Typological Criticism

Another controversy of the later twentieth century has to do with the Christian interpretation of Shakespeare. Do the images and allusions of Shakespeare's plays show him to be deeply immersed in a Christian culture inherited from the Middle Ages? Does he reveal a typological cast of mind, so common in medieval literature, whereby a story can suggest through analogy a universal religious archetype? For example, does the mysterious Duke in *Measure for Measure* suggest to us a God figure, hovering unseen throughout the play to test human will and then to present humanity with an omniscient but merciful judgment? Is the wanton slaughter of the good Cordelia in *King Lear* reminiscent of the Passion of Christ? Can Portia in *The Merchant of Venice* be seen as an angelic figure descending from Belmont into the fallen human world of Venice? Often the operative question we must ask is: "How far should such analogy be pursued?" Richard II unquestionably likens himself to Christ betrayed by the disciples, and at times the play evokes images of Adam banished from Paradise, but do these allusions coalesce into a sustained analogy?

Among the most enthusiastic searchers after Christian meaning are J. A. Bryant, in *Hippolyta's View* (1961); Roy Battenhouse, in *Shakespearean Tragedy: Its Art and Christian Premises* (1969); and R. Chris Hassel, in *Renaissance Drama and the English Church* (1979) and *Faith and Folly in Shakespeare: Romantic Comedies* (1980). Their efforts have encountered stern opposition, however. One notable dissenter is Roland M. Frye, whose *Shakespeare and Christian Doctrine* (1963) argues that Shakespeare cannot be shown to have known much Renaissance theology and that, in any case, his plays are concerned with human drama rather than with otherworldly questions of damnation or salvation. Frye's argument stresses the incompatibility of Christianity and tragedy, as do also D. G. James's *The Dream of Learning* (1951) and Clifford Leech's *Shakespeare's Tragedies and Other Studies in Seventeenth-Century Drama* (1950). Virgil Whitaker's *The Mirror Up to Nature* (1965) sees religion as an essential element in Shakespeare's plays but argues that Shakespeare uses the religious knowledge of his audience as a shortcut to characterization and meaning, rather than as an ideological weapon. The controversy will doubtless long continue, even though the typological critics have had to assume a defensive posture.

Jan Kott and the Theater of the Absurd

At an opposite extreme from the Christian idealism of most typological critics is the iconoclasm of those who have been disillusioned by recent events in history. One who brilliantly epitomizes political disillusionment in the aftermath of World War II, especially in Eastern Europe, is Jan Kott. The evocative debunking of romantic idealism set forth in his *Shakespeare Our Contemporary* (1964, translated from the Polish) has enjoyed enormous influence since the 1960s, especially in the theater. Kott sees Shakespeare as a dramatist of the absurd and the grotesque. In this view, Shakespearean plays are often close to "black" comedy or comedy of the absurd, as defined by Antonin Artaud (*The Theatre and Its Double,* 1958) and Jerzy Grotowski (*Towards a Poor Theatre,* 1968). Indeed, Kott has inspired productions that expose traditional values to skepticism and ridicule. Portia and Bassanio in *The Merchant of Venice* become scheming adventurers; Henry V becomes a priggish warmonger. History is for Kott a nightmare associated with his country's experience in World War II, and Shakespeare's modernity can be seen in his sardonic portrayal of political opportunism and violence. Even *A Midsummer Night's Dream* is a play of disturbingly erotic brutality, Kott argues. Here is an interpretation of Shakespeare that was bound to have an enormous appeal in a world confronted by the assassinations of the Kennedys and Martin Luther King, Jr.; by incessant war in the Middle East, Southeast Asia, and much of the third world; by the threat of nuclear annihilation and ecological disaster; and by political leadership generally perceived as interested only in the public-relations techniques of self-preservation. An essentially ironic view of politics and, more broadly, of human nature has informed a good deal of criticism since Kott's day and has led to the dethronement of E. M. W. Tillyard and his essentially positive view of English patriotism and heroism in the history plays.

New Historicism and Cultural Materialism

A more recent way of investigating Shakespeare through the demystifying perspective of modern experience—the so-called new historicism— has focused on the themes of political self-fashioning and role playing in terms of power and subversion. This critical school has paid close attention to historians and cultural anthropologists like Lawrence Stone (*The Crisis of the Aristocracy,* 1558–1641, 1965) and Clifford Geertz (*Negara: The Theatre State in Nineteenth-Century Bali,* 1980), who explore new ways of looking at the relationship between historical change and the myths generated to bring it about or to retain power. Geertz analyzes the way in which the ceremonies and myths of political rule can, in effect, become a self-fulfilling reality; kings and other leaders, acting out their roles in ceremonials designed to encapsulate the myth of their greatness and divine origin, essentially become what they have created in their impersonations of power. Such a view of political authority is an inherently skeptical one, seeing government as a process of manipulating illusions. When Shakespeare's English history plays—or indeed any plays dealing with conflicts of authority—are analyzed in these terms, subversion and containment become important issues. Do the plays of Shakespeare and other Renaissance dramatists celebrate the power of the Tudor monarchs, or do they question and undermine assumptions of hierarchy? Did Elizabethan drama serve to increase skepticism and pressure for change, or was it, conversely, a way of easing that pressure so that the power structure could remain in force?

The "new historicism" is a name applied to a kind of literary criticism practiced in America, prominently by Stephen Greenblatt. Especially influential have been his *Renaissance Self-Fashioning* (1980), *Shakespearean Negotiations* (1988), and his editing of the journal *Representations.* Those who pursue similar concerns, including Louis Montrose, Stephen Orgel, Richard Helgerson, Don E. Wayne, Frank Whigham, Richard Strier, Jonathan Goldberg, David Scott Kastan, and Steven Mullaney, share Greenblatt's goals to a greater or lesser extent and think of themselves only with important reservations as "new historicists"; the term is misleadingly categorical, and Greenblatt, among others, is eager to enlarge the parameters of the method rather than to allow it to harden into an orthodoxy. (Greenblatt, in fact, prefers the term "poetics of culture" to "new historicism," even though the latter phrase remains better known.) Still, these critics do generally share a number of common concerns. Among the ways in which new historicists seek to separate themselves from earlier historical critics is by denying that the work of art is a unified and self-contained product of an independent creator in masterful control of the meaning of the work. Instead, the new historicists represent the work as shot through with the multiple and contradictory discourses of its time. New historicists also deny the notion that art merely "reflects" its historical milieu; instead, they argue that art is caught up in, and contributes to, the social practices of its time. Although the boundary between new and old historical criticism is often hard to draw, in general the new historicists are apt to be skeptical of the accepted canon of literary texts and are drawn to a markedly politicized reading of Renaissance plays. One finds everywhere in the new historicism a deep ambivalence toward political authority.

Mikhail Bakhtin's provocative ideas on carnival (*L'Oeuvre de François Rabelais et la Culture Populaire du Moyen Age,* 1970) have had an important influence in new historical circles, as reflected, for example, in the work of Michael Bristol (*Carnival and Theatre: Plebeian Culture and the Structure of Authority in Renaissance England,* 1985), Peter Stallybrass, Gail Paster, and others. Like new historicism, this critical approach looks at so-called high cultural entertainment, including Shakespeare, in relation to the practices of popular culture, thereby breaking down the distinction between "high" and "popular." Literary and nonliterary texts are subjected to the same kind of serious scrutiny. Popular origins of the theater receive new attention, as in Robert Weimann's *Shakespeare and the Popular Tradition in the Theater: Studies in the Social Dimension of Dramatic Form and Function* (published in German in 1967 and in English translation in 1978).

Cultural materialism, in Britain, takes an analogous approach to the dethroning of canonical texts and the emphasis on art as deeply implicated in the social practices of its time but differs from American new historicism on the issue of change. New historicism is sometimes criticized for its lack of a model for change and for its reluctant belief, instead (in Greenblatt's formulation especially), that all attempts at subversion through art are destined to be contained by power structures in society; art permits the expression of heterodox points of view, but only as a way of letting off steam, as it were, and thereby easing the pressures for actual radical change. British cultural materialism, in contrast, is more avowedly committed not only to radical political interpretation but also to rapid political change, partly in response to what are perceived to be more deeply rooted class differences than are found in America. Jonathan Dollimore's *Radical Tragedy* (1984) and *Political Shakespeare* (1985), edited by Dollimore and Alan Sinfield, enlist the dramatist on the side of class struggle. So do *Alternative Shakespeares,* edited by John Drakakis (1985), and Terry Eagleton's *Shakespeare and Society* (1967) and *William Shakespeare* (1986). Raymond Williams, not himself a Shakespearean critic, is an acknowledged godfather of the movement.

Feminist Criticism

Feminist criticism is such an important and diverse field that it has necessarily and productively reached into a number of related disciplines, such as cultural anthropology and its wealth of information about family structures. In his *The Elementary Structures of Kinship* (1949, translated 1969) and other books, Claude Lévi-Strauss analyzes the way in which men, as fathers and as husbands, control the transfer of women from one family to another in an "exogamous" marital system designed to strengthen commercial and other ties among men. Recent feminist criticism has had a lot to say about patriarchal structures in the plays and poems of Shakespeare, some of it building upon Lévi-Strauss's analysis of patriarchy; see, for example, Karen Newman, "Portia's Ring: Unruly Women and Structures of Exchange in *The Merchant of Venice,*" *Shakespeare Quarterly,* 38 (1987), 10–33, and Lynda Boose, "The Father and the Bride in Shakespeare," *PMLA,* 97 (1982), 325–47. Coppélia Kahn has examined the ideology of rape in *The Rape of Lucrece,* showing how the raped woman is devalued by the shame that attaches to her husband, even though she is innocent (*Shakespeare Studies,* 9, 1976, 45–72).

Another important source of insight for feminist criticism is the anthropological work on rites of passage by Arnold Van Gennep (*The Rites of Passage,* translated by M. B. Vizedom and G. L. Caffee, 1960) and Victor Turner (*The Ritual Process,* 1969), among others. The focus here is on the dangers of transition at times of birth, puberty, marriage, death, and other turning points of human life. Feminist criticism, in dealing with such crises of transition, concerns itself not only with women's roles but also, more broadly, with gender relations, with family structures, and with the problems that males encounter in their quest for mature sexual identity. Coppélia Kahn's *Man's Estate; Masculine Identity in Shakespeare* (1981) looks particularly at the difficulty of the male in confronting the hazards of maturity. Robert Watson's *Shakespeare and the Hazards of Ambition* (1984) also looks at the male in the political context of career and self-fashioning. Marjorie Garber's *Coming of Age in Shakespeare* (1981) takes a broad look at maturation.

As these titles suggest, the models are often psychological, as well as anthropological. One focus of feminist criticism is the role of women in love and marriage. Feminist critics disagree among themselves as to whether the portrait painted by Shakespeare and other Elizabethan dramatists is a hopeful one, as argued, for example, by Juliet Dusinberre in *Shakespeare and the Nature of Women* (1975, 1996), or repressive, as argued by Lisa Jardine in *Still Harping on Daughters: Women and Drama in the Age of Shakespeare* (1983). Recent historians add an important perspective, especially Lawrence Stone in his *The Family, Sex, and Marriage in England, 1500–1800* (1977). Did the Protestant emphasis on marriage as a morally elevated and reciprocal relationship have the paradoxical effect of arousing in men an increased hostility and wariness toward women and a resulting increase in repression and violence? Or, as David Underdown suggests, should we look to economic explanations of hostility and wariness toward women in the Renaissance? His studies indicate that repression of women is greatest in regions of the country where their place in the economy offers the possibility of their having some control over family finances. (See *Revel, Riot, and Rebellion: Popular Culture in England,* 1603–1660, 1985, pp. 73–105, especially p. 99.)

Certainly, recent criticism has paid a lot of attention to male anxieties about women in Shakespeare's plays, as various male protagonists resolve to teach women a lesson (*The Taming of the Shrew*), succumb to dark fantasies of female unfaithfulness (*Much Ado About Nothing, Othello*), or are overwhelmed by misogynistic revulsion (*Hamlet, King Lear*). It is as though Shakespeare, in his plays and poems, works through the problems that men experience throughout their lives in their relationships with women, from the insecurities of courtship to the desire for possession and control in marriage, and from jealous fears of betrayal to the longing for escape into middle-age sexual adventure (as in *Antony and Cleopatra*). The late plays show us the preoccupation of the aging male with the marriages of his daughters (another form of betrayal) and with the approach of death.

Recently, feminist criticism has begun to increase its historical consciousness. Critics such as Gail Paster, Jean Howard, Phyllis Rackin, Dympna Callaghan, Lorraine Helms, Jyotsna Singh, Alison Findlay, Lisa Jardine, and Karen Newman focus on the construction of gender in early modern England in terms of social and material conditions, abandoning the nonhistorical psychological model of earlier feminist criticism. See the bibliography at the end of this book for feminist studies by these and other feminist critics, including Catherine Belsey, Carol Neely, Peter Erickson, Meredith Skura, Marianne Novy, Margo Hendricks, Kim Hall, Philippa Berry, Frances Dolan, Mary Beth Rose, Valerie Traub, Susan Zimmerman, Lynda Boose, and Ania Loomba. Gender studies concerned with issues of same-sex relationships have made important contributions in recent years, in the work of Bruce Smith, Laurie Shannon, Jonathan Goldberg, Stephen Orgel, Leonard Barkan, Mario DiGangi, and others.

Poststructuralism and Deconstruction

A major influence today in Shakespeare criticism, as in virtually all literary criticism of recent date, is the school of analysis known as poststructuralism or deconstruction; the terms, though not identical, significantly overlap. This school derives its inspiration originally from the work of certain French philosophers and critics, chief among whom are Ferdinand de Saussure, a specialist in linguistics, Michel Foucault, a historian of systems of discourse, and Jacques Derrida, perhaps the most highly visible exponent and practitioner of deconstruction. The ideas of these men were first introduced into American literary criticism by scholars at Yale such as Geoffrey Hartman, J. Hillis Miller, and Paul de Man. The ideas are controversial and difficult.

Poststructuralism and deconstruction begin with an insistence that language is a system of difference—one in which the signifiers (such as words and gestures) are essentially arbitrary to the extent that "meaning" and "authorial intention" are virtually impossible to fix precisely; that is, language enjoys a potentially infinite subjectivity. To an extent, this approach to the subjectivity of meaning in a work of art resembles "new" criticism in its mistrust of "message" in literature, but the new method goes further. It resists all attempts at paraphrase, for example, insisting that the words of a text cannot be translated into other words without altering something vital; indeed, there is no way of knowing if an author's words will strike any two readers or listeners in the same way. The very concept of an author has been challenged by Michel Foucault ("What Is an Author?" in *Language, Counter-Memory, Practice,* edited by Donald F. Bouchard, 1977). Deconstruction proclaims that there is no single identifiable author in the traditional sense; instead of a single text, we have a potentially infinite number of texts.

Both the theory and practice of deconstruction remain highly controversial. Although poststructuralism and deconstruction owe a debt to the general philosophical theory of signs and symbols known as semiotics, in which the function of linguistic signs is perceived to be artificially constructed, the new method also calls into question the very distinctions on which the discipline of semiotics is based. Derrida builds upon the work of Saussure and yet goes well beyond him in an insistence that words (signifiers) be left in play rather than attached to their alleged meaning (signifieds). Frank Lentricchia (*After the New Criticism,* 1980) takes the Yale school critics to task for interpreting Derrida in too formalist and apolitical a sense. Despite disagreements among theorists, nevertheless, the approach has deeply influenced Shakespeare criticism as a whole by urging critics to consider the suppleness with which signifiers (words) in the Shakespearean text are converted by listeners and readers into some approximation of meaning.

The ramifications of poststructuralism and deconstruction are increasingly felt in other forms of criticism, even those at least nominally at odds with poststructuralist assumptions. Some radical textual critics, for example, are fascinated by the unsettling prospects of the deconstructed text. What does one edit and how does one go about editing when words are to be left in play, to the infinite regress of meaning? The problems are acutely examined in a collection of essays called *The Division of the Kingdom,* edited by Gary Taylor and Michael Warren, on the two early and divergent texts of *King Lear* (1983). The method of linguistic analysis known as "speech-act theory," developed by the philosopher J. L. Austin as a way of exploring how we perform certain linguistic acts when we swear oaths or make asseverations and the like, is sharply at variance with deconstruction in its premises about a correlation between speech and intended meaning, and yet it, too, can help us understand the instability of spoken or written language in Shakespeare. Joseph Porter's *The Drama of Speech Acts* (1979), for example, looks at ways in which Shakespeare's characters in the plays about Henry IV and Henry V reveal, through their language of oath making and oath breaking, asseveration, and the like, their linguistic adaptability or lack of adaptability to historical change. Richard II resists historical change in the very way he speaks; Prince Hal embraces it. A third related field of analysis that is interested in the instability of meaning in Shakespeare's texts is metadramatic criticism, where the focus is on ways in which dramatic texts essentially talk about the drama itself, about artistic expression, and about the artist's quest for immortality in art. James Calderwood's *Shakespearean Metadrama* (1971) is an influential example.

At its extreme, then, deconstructive criticism comes close to undermining all kinds of "meaningfulness" in artistic utterance and to being thus at war with other methods of interpretation. Still, deconstruction continues to remain influential, because it also usefully challenges complacent formulations of meaning and because it promotes such a subtle view of linguistic complexity.

At its best, late twentieth-century criticism transcends the splintering effect of a heterogeneous critical tradition to achieve a synthesis that is at once unified and multiform in its vision. The pluralistic approach aims at overall balance and a reinforcement of one critical approach through the methodology of another. Many of the works already cited in this introduction refuse to be constricted by methodological boundaries. The best historical criticism makes use of close explication of the text where appropriate; image patterns can certainly reinforce mythological patterns; typological interpretation, when sensibly applied, serves the cause of image study. Some fine books are so eclectic in their method that one hesitates to apply the label of any one critical school. Among such works are Maynard Mack's *King Lear in Our Time* (1965), David Young's *Something of Great Constancy: The Art of A Midsummer Night's Dream* (1966), R. G. Hunter's *Shakespeare and the Comedy of Forgiveness* (1965), Janet Adelman's *The Common Liar: An Essay on "Antony and Cleopatra"* (1973), Stanley Cavell's "The Avoidance of Love: A Reading of King Lear," in *Must We Mean What We Say?* (1969, reprinted in *Disowning Knowledge in Six Plays of Shakespeare,* 1987), and Paul Jorgensen's *Our Naked Frailties: Sensational Art and Meaning in Macbeth* (1971).

Into the Twenty-First Century

The sense of where we are in the twenty-first century in Shakespeare criticism reflects the uncertainties and guardedly hopeful expectations of the academic profession as a whole. The period of the 1970s and 1980s, described previously, was one of extraordinary ferment, brought on by a host of developments: the Vietnam War and its aftermath, the assassinations of the Kennedys and Martin Luther King, the impact of French linguistic and philosophical thought on American intellectual writing, the frustrations of many academics with Reaganomics and their consequent fascination with British Marxism, emerging demands on behalf of minorities and women, a revolution in social and sexual mores accompanied by a backlash in the name of "family values," conflict over American foreign policy in the Middle East (Israel, Iraq), and much more. The result was what must be regarded as a genuine revolution in methods of critical analysis and reading. The literary text became multivalent, ambiguous, deconstructed, dethroned as a unique artifact, and was seen, instead, as a product of and contributing to its social and intellectual environment. The author became a construction of criticism and of a new kind of literary history.

Shakespeare studies have taken a lead in all of this new exploration. Although one of the postmodern demands has been for a recanonizing of literature in favor of newer literature, works by women and minorities, and works from countries other than Britain and the United States instead of the traditional canon of dead white European males, Shakespeare not only has survived this recanonization but also has become more prominent than ever. Other Renaissance writers such as

Ben Jonson, John Webster, Thomas Dekker, Thomas Nashe, John Lyly, Edmund Spenser, and even Christopher Marlowe, John Milton, and John Donne have been the victims of declining enrollments in classes generally, but Shakespeare triumphs. Why?

One compelling answer is that Shakespeare is simply indispensable to postmodern critical inquiry. His texts are so extraordinarily responsive that new questions put to them—about the changing role of women, about cynicism in the political process, about the protean near-indeterminacy of meaning in language—evoke insights that are hard to duplicate in other literary texts. Shakespeare does not seem out of date. The very impulse of so much recent criticism to claim Shakespeare as "our contemporary," attuned to our own skepticisms and disillusionment and even despair (as in the writings of Jan Kott, for example), attests to his unparalleled engagement with the issues about which we care so deeply. Even those who argue that Shakespeare exhibits the male hang-ups of a patriarchal society and that he is a social snob who glorifies aristocracy and warfare do not see Shakespeare as a writer who is out of touch with the values of our contemporary society but, rather, as one who gives eloquent testimonial to structures that were alive in our cultural past and with which we sense a continuum today even if outward circumstances have changed. The best scholarship does not condemn Shakespeare for believing in kingship or for sometimes showing men as victorious in the battle of the sexes; instead, that criticism is interested in the whole process of the literary text's participation in the creation of culture. Even when recent scholarship is concerned with examining class and gender issues to clarify some of the systematic oppressiveness of early modern culture, it does so generally in an attempt to negotiate the relationship of the present to the past, rather than assuming a superiority in our modern world's approaches to issues of class, gender, and ethnicity.

To be sure, a number of Shakespeare's plays are in trouble today because they make us uncomfortable about these issues. *The Merchant of Venice* is, in the eyes of many, almost unproduceable, because the anti-Semitic emotions it explores are so distasteful. It is less often assigned now in classrooms than it once was, even though, when it is taught or produced onstage, it can lead to extraordinarily searching discussions of painful but real issues. The same is true of *The Taming of the Shrew,* which is being taken from the shelves of more than a few libraries because of its apparent flaunting of sexist behavior toward women. *Othello* offends some readers and viewers because of its racist language and, in the view of some, racial stereotypes. Yet, the power of Shakespeare's language continues to exert its spell despite, and in part because of, these troubling conflicts over the role of dramatic art in modern society.

The world of Shakespeare criticism today, after two decades or so of revolution, is seemingly one of consolidation. At a March 1995 meeting of the Shakespeare Association of America in Chicago, many conferees wondered: Where is the profession going? What are the hot new issues? Who are the new critics that no one wants to miss? And, in fact, there seemed to be little dramatic excitement of this sort, little agreement as to any discernible new trend. To some, this is frustrating. Where does one turn for real creativity after a thoroughgoing revolution such as we have experienced?

To others, a time of stocktaking is potentially healthy. There seems to be relatively little interest in turning the clock back; postmodernism and indeterminacy have changed the critical landscape for better and for worse. Now that this new landscape begins to seem familiar, however, new members of the profession seem less anxious to resolve their own identity crises in terms of affiliating with some critical school or other. The critical challenges are there, not so stridently new as they were ten years ago, and adaptable to various uses.

The result is increasing variety in the kinds of critical work being done. Some of it is recognizably traditional, dealing with stage history and conditions of performance during Shakespeare's lifetime, as, for example, in T. J. King, *Casting Shakespeare's Plays: London Actors and Their Roles* (1992); William Ingram, *The Business of Playing: The Beginnings of the Adult Professional Theater in Elizabethan London* (1992); David Bradley, *From Text to Performance in the Elizabethan Theatre: Preparing the Play for the Stage* (1992); David Mann, *The Elizabethan Player: Contemporary Stage Representation* (1991); John H. Astington, ed., *The Development of Shakespeare's Theater* (1992); Andrew Gurr, *Playgoing in Shakespeare's London* (1987, 2nd edition, 1996) and *The Shakespearian Playing Companies* (1996); and Roslyn Lander Knutson, *The Repertory of Shakespeare's Company, 1594–1613* (1991). Background and historical studies of the conditions that helped produce Shakespeare's theater can sometimes be informatively revisionist in the sense of toppling cherished older notions without at the same time being postmodern in approach. Examples here might include Richard Dutton, *Mastering the Revels: The Regulation and Censorship of English Renaissance Drama* (1991); Scott McMillin and Sally-Beth MacLean, *The Queen's Men and Their Plays* (1998); and Leeds Barroll, *Politics, Plague, and Shakespeare's Theater: The Stuart Years* (1991).

Other studies are more openly revisionist in a postmodern vein, sometimes in dealing with hypotheses about bibliography and textual studies, as in Margreta de Grazia, *Shakespeare Verbatim: The Reproduction of*

Authenticity and the 1790 Apparatus (1991) and Grace Ioppolo, *Revising Shakespeare* (1991). The New Folger Library Shakespeare, edited by Barbara Mowat and Paul Werstine (1992—), gives a more measured approach. The Arden Shakespeare is currently bringing out new critical editions of all the plays in individual volumes (Arden 3), as are the New Cambridge Shakespeare and the Oxford Shakespeare. Occasionally a conservative counterblast is heard, as in Brian Vickers's entertaining, learned, and feisty polemic, *Appropriating Shakespeare: Contemporary Critical Quarrels* (1993). A forum of essays edited by Ivo Kamps, called *Shakespeare Left and Right*, gives us a chance to weigh arguments from various sides.

What the contemporary critical scene does best is to free critics to be who they are and to write without paying dues to any particular affiliation. The results are refreshingly diverse. Among the books that show this spread of critical approaches are Karen Newman, *Fashioning Femininity and the English Renaissance Drama* (1991); Bruce R. Smith, *Homosexual Desire in Shakespeare's England* (1991); Janet Adelman, *Suffocating Mothers: Fantasies of Maternal Origin in Shakespeare's Plays, "Hamlet" to "The Tempest"* (1992); Alan Sinfield, *Faultlines: Cultural Materialism and the Politics of Dissident Reading* (1992); Valerie Traub, *Desire and Anxiety: Circulations of Sexuality in Shakespearean Drama* (1992); Richard Burt, *Licensed by Authority: Ben Jonson and the Discourses of Censorship* (1993); Linda Charnes, *Notorious Identity: Materializing the Subject in Shakespeare* (1993); Lars Engle, *Shakespearean Pragmatism: Market of His Time* (1993); Gail Kern Paster, *The Body Embarrassed: Drama and the Disciplines of Shame in Early Modern England* (1993); Meredith Anne Skura, *Shakespeare the Actor and the Purposes of Playing* (1993); Frances E. Dolan, *Dangerous Familiars: Representations of Domestic Crime in England, 1550–1700* (1994); Kim F. Hall, *Things of Darkness: Economies of Race and Gender in Early Modern England* (1994); Jean Howard, *The Stage and Social Struggle in Early Modern England* (1994); Robert Watson, *The Rest Is Silence: Death as Annihilation in the English Renaissance* (1994); Katharine Eisaman Maus, *Inwardness and Theatre in the English Renaissance Drama* (1995); Louis Montrose, *The Purpose of Playing: Shakespeare and the Cultural Politics of the Elizabethan Theatre* (1996); Patricia Parker, *Shakespeare from the Margins: Language, Culture, Context* (1996); Jean E. Howard and Phyllis Rackin, *Engendering a Nation: A Feminist Account of Shakespeare's English Histories* (1997); Anthony B. Dawson and Paul Yachnin, *The Culture of Playgoing in Shakespeare's England* (2001); David Scott Kastan, *Shakespeare and the Book* (2001); Mary Beth Rose, *Gender and Heroism in Early Modern English Literature* (2002); and Stephen Orgel, *The Authentic Shakespeare* (2002). For other suggestions, see recent entries in the bibliography at the back of this volume.

The Comedies

The Comedy of Errors

Love's Labor's Lost

The Two Gentlemen of Verona

The Taming of the Shrew

A Midsummer Night's Dream

The Merchant of Venice

The Merry Wives of Windsor

As You Like It

Twelfth Night; or, What You Will

All's Well That Ends Well

Measure for Measure

Troilus and Cressida

Much Ado About Nothing

The Comedy of Errors

The Comedy of Errors is a superb illustration of Shakespeare's "apprenticeship" in comedy. It is more imitative of classical comedy, especially of Plautus, than is Shakespeare's mature work. Its verbal humor, including the scatological jokes about breaking wind, the bawdy jests about cuckold's horns, and the overly ingenious banter (as in 2.2), is at times adolescent. The play abounds in the farcical humor of physical abuse, so endearing to children of all ages. It is perhaps the most uncomplicatedly funny of all Shakespeare's plays. Yet the softening touches of Shakespeare's maturity are unmistakably present as well. Shakespeare frames his farce of mistaken identity with old Egeon's tragicomic story of separation, threatened death, and eventual reunion. He adds characters to his chief sources, Plautus's *Menaechmi* and *Amphitruo* (see Appendix 2), in order to enhance the love interest and to reconcile Plautus with English moral conventions. He touches upon themes of illusion, madness, and revelry that are to figure prominently in *A Midsummer Night's Dream* and in *Twelfth Night*, a later comedy of mistaken identity. In these respects, *The Comedy of Errors* is both a fascinating prelude to Shakespeare's later development and a rich achievement in its own right. On stage, it has not attracted the greatest Shakespearean actors, since it offers no complex or dominating roles, but it has seldom failed to delight audiences.

We cannot be sure precisely how early the play was written. A performance took place on December 28, 1594, at Gray's Inn, one of the Inns of Court, before an unruly assembly of lawyers, law students, and their guests. This was probably not the first performance, however. Topical allusions offer hints of an earlier date. When Dromio of Syracuse speaks of France as "armed and reverted, making war against her heir" (3.2.123–4), he clearly is referring to the Catholic League's opposition to Henry of Navarre, who was the heir apparent to the French throne until 1593, when he became king. Another allusion, to Spain's sending "whole armadas of carracks" (lines 135–6), would possibly have lost its comic point soon after the Invincible Armada of 1588. The play's style, characterization, and imitative construction are all consistent with a date between 1589 and 1593.

Whatever the exact date, Shakespeare's youthful fascination with Plautus is manifest. Shakespeare's command of Latin, though sneered at by Ben Jonson, was undoubtedly good enough to have let him read Plautus with pleasure. He must have been drilled in Latin for years as a student in the town of Stratford-upon-Avon. Indeed, the influence of not only Plautus but also Ovid and Seneca (together with touches of Horace, Catullus, etc.) is a prominent feature of Shakespeare's early work, dramatic and nondramatic. Shakespeare may have consulted Plautus both in the original and in a contemporary translation, as was frequently his custom with non-English sources. From Renaissance Latin editions of Plautus, he apparently took the odd designation "Antipholis Sereptus" (i.e., "surreptus," snatched away), which appears in the Folio text in a stage direction at 2.1.0 to indicate the twin who was separated from his father. On the other hand, a translation of the *Menaechmi* by "W. W." (? William Warner), published in 1595, was registered in 1594 and might have been available earlier to Shakespeare in manuscript.

Plautus had much to offer Shakespeare and his fellow dramatists, especially in the way of tightly organized and complex plot construction. Native English drama of the sixteenth century tended to be episodic and panoramic in its design. Shakespeare's apprenticeship in neoclassical form can be seen in his precise observation of the unities of time and place—those unities which he openly disregarded in most of his later plays. At the play's beginning, Egeon is informed that he has until sundown to raise his ransom money, and the play then moves toward that point in time with periodic observations that it is now noon, now two o'clock, and so on. (At one point, time even seems to go backwards, but that is part of the illusion of madness.) The action is restricted to the city of Ephesus; events that have happened elsewhere, at an earlier time (such as the separation of the Antipholus family), are told to us by persons in the play, such as old Egeon. Although Shakespeare's company did not employ the sort of painted scenery drawn in perspective used by continental neoclassicists, with fixed locations for houses facing on a street, the original production of this play may nonetheless have used one stage "house" or door to represent the dwelling of Antipholus of Ephesus (the Phoenix) throughout the drama. The entire play can be staged as if all the action occurs in the vicinity of this single "house," with the Courtesan's establishment and abbey near at hand. Never again does Shakespeare utilize such a neoclassical stage.

These unities of time and place are mechanical matters, but they do also harmonize with a more essential unity of action. The story moves, as though in perfect accord with neoclassical five-act theory, from exposition and complication to climax, anagnoresis (discovery), and peripeteia (reversal of fortune). The brilliance of the plotting is decidedly Plautine. Shakespeare pushes to its limit the interweaving of comic misunderstandings only to unravel all these seemingly tightly woven knots with ease. Yet the imitation of Plautus, even in matters of construction, is by no means slavish, for Shakespeare borrows both from Plautus' farce on the mistaken identity of twins (*Menaechmi*) and from Plautus's best-known comedy (*Amphitruo*), in which a husband and his servant are excluded from their own house while a disguised visitor usurps the master's role within. Such ingenious adaptations and rearrangements were common among neoclassical dramatists like Ludovico Ariosto, and, although Shakespeare seems not to have used any of the sixteenth-century analogues to this play, he does reveal an acquaintance with neoclassical comedy and an ability to compete with the best that Europe had to offer in this vein. Such versatility is noteworthy in a young dramatist who was to reveal himself in time as far less of a neoclassicist than a native English writer. Moreover, even if his self-imposed neoclassical training was only an apprenticeship, it was to prove invaluable to Shakespeare. Despite his later tendency toward "romantic" plotting—toward the depiction of multiple actions extending over widely separated spaces and extended periods of time—Shakespeare's greatest comedies continue to point toward the same gratifying resolution of dramatic conflict in a single and well-structured denouement.

For all its Plautine skill of design, *The Comedy of Errors* is quite far removed from *The Menaechmi* in tone and spirit. Gone are the cynicism, the satirical hardness, and the amoral tone of the Roman original. The characters, though still recognizable as types, are humanized. The familiar Plautine parasite is excluded entirely. The usual clever servant happily becomes the Dromio twins. Plautus's quack Doctor, Medicus, is hilariously transmuted into Dr. Pinch, a pedantic schoolmaster. The Courtesan's role is no longer prominent. Instead, Shakespeare creates Luciana, the virtuous sister of Adriana, who pleads the cause of forbearance in marriage and who eventually becomes the bride of Antipholus of Syracuse. *The Comedy of Errors* does not end, as do most of Shakespeare's later comedies, with a parade of couples to the altar, but the marriage of Antipholus and Luciana is at least one important step in that direction. Besides, we are told of yet another marriage still to come—that of Dromio of Ephesus to Luce, the kitchen wench. This belowstairs parody of wedded affection is thoroughly English in character and recalls a similar mirroring of courtship among the comic servants of Henry Medwall's *Fulgens and Lucrece* (c. 1497). The motif is not sufficiently stressed to threaten the unity of the main plot, but the potentiality for double plotting is unmistakable.

An even more significant contrast to Plautine farce is to be found in the romantic saga of old Egeon and his long-lost wife, the Abbess. Their story is one not of mistaken identity (though that contributes to the denouement) but of painful separation, wandering, and reunion. Indeed, the note struck at the beginning of the play might seem tragic were we not already attuned to the conventional romantic expectation that separated members of a family are likely to be restored to one another again. Egeon, threatened with immediate execution, unfolds to us a narrative of wedded bliss interrupted by the malignancy of Fortune. In contrast to the tightly controlled unity of time of the farcical action, the romantic narrative extends (by recollection) over many years of error and suffering. Egeon's tragicomic story of testing and of patient endurance is very much like that of *Apollonius of Tyre*, a popular tale used by Shakespeare in his late romance *Pericles* (c. 1606–1608). The conventions of this sort of romance, ultimately Greek in origin, stress improbability: identical twins who can be told apart only by birthmarks, a storm at sea splitting a vessel in half and neatly dividing a family, and so on. The sea is emblematic of unpredictable Fortune, taking away with one hand and restoring with the other. The wife who is lost at sea, like her counterpart in *Apollonius* or *Pericles*, takes to a life of cloistered devotion, suggesting a pattern of symbolic death, healing, and ultimate rebirth. The ending of *The Comedy of Errors* has just a hint of death restored mysteriously to life: "After so long grief, such nativity!" (5.1.407).

Egeon's story of endurance counterpoints the farce in yet another way. His arraignment before the Duke of Ephesus introduces into the play a "tragic" world of law, punishment, and death. Egeon's date with the executioner is not illusory. His predicament is the result of the bitter "mortal and intestine jars" (1.1.11) between two cities caught in a frenzy of economic reprisals. The law cannot be merciful, even though the unfairness of Egeon's plight is manifest to everyone, including the Duke. These potentially tragic factors must not be overstressed, for the first scene is brief and we are reassured by the play's hilarious tone (and by our surmising that Egeon is father of the Antipholus twins) that all will be well. Still, Shakespeare's addition of this romance plot suggests his restlessness with pure farce. As in his later comedies, which are virtually all threatened by catastrophes, the denouement of *The Comedy of Errors* is deepened into something approaching miraculous recovery. Moreover, the backdrop of a near-tragic world of genuine suffering heightens our appreciation of comic unreality in the self-contained world of Plautine farce and stresses the illusory nature of the dilemmas arising out of purely mistaken identity. Such delusions are all the more comic because they are the delusions that supposedly sane people suffer: contentiousness and jealousy in marriage, concern for respectable appearances among one's neighbors, and the suspicion that one is always being cheated in money matters. These are the chimeras that, by being made to look so plausible and yet so patently insane, are farcically exploited in Shakespeare's comic device: the inversion of madness and sanity, dreaming and waking, illusion and reality.

What happens when the behavior of one twin is mistaken for that of the other? The situation is, of course, amusing in itself, but it also serves as a test of the other characters, to discover what mad hypotheses they will construct. Adriana, faced with her husband's seeming refusal to come home to dinner, launches into a jealous tirade against husbands who neglect their wives for courtesans. The illusory situation, in other words, brings out her latent fears. We understand better now why she acts shrewishly: she fears rejection and the fading of her beauty, and she imagines that her fading beauty may be the cause of her husband's neglect. Actually, even as she speaks, her husband is busy making arrangements about a chain he means to give Adriana; but, when subsequently he is locked out of his own house and jumps to the conclusion that Adriana is being faithless, he resolves in his fury to bestow the chain on a courtesan in order to "spite my wife." He would actually do so were he not saved from this destructively revengeful impulse by the beneficently comic action of the farcical plot: through mistaken identity, the chain is delivered into the hands of his twin. Once again, illusion has prompted a character to assume the worst, to reveal his suspicions of a plot against him. And so it goes when Antipholus of Ephesus is arrested for nonpayment of the chain (he assumes that all merchants are thieves) or is denied his bail money by the servant he thinks he sent to fetch it (he assumes that all servants are thieves). We laugh at the endless capacity of the human mind for distortions of this self-punishing sort.

The metaphor used most often to convey this sense of bewilderment, even a confusion about one's own identity, is that of metamorphosis. All have drunk of Circe's cup (5.1.271) and have been transformed into animals—most of them into asses. All have hearkened to the mermaid's song and are enchanted. Ephesus, they conclude, must be haunted by sorcerers, witches, goblins, and spirits (4.3.11 ff.). Ephesus is, in fact, associated in the Bible with exorcism (Acts 19:13 ff.), and "Circe" suggests that Antipholus of Syracuse is a becalmed Odysseus. In such a mad world, the characters assume a license to embark on Saturnalian holiday. The experience of transformation thus leads to various forms of "release" from ordinary social behavior, but the experience is also disturbing and continually reminds the characters of exorcism, hell, and devils. The threat of incest hovers over the comic business of two brothers sharing a wife, and indeed there is a dark subtext to the twinning that is unavoidably present throughout the play: the twinned cities of Ephesus and Syracuse, the twinned brothers, the twinned servants, all of whom are trying to discover their identities amid the paradoxes of singleness and doubleness. The play's farcical action is never far from violence. Witches and fat kitchen wenches suggest a fascination with unruly women. The characters can explain their inverted world only by assuming that all men are lunatic, all honest women whores, and all true men thieves. "Do you know me, sir? . . . Am I myself?" "Am I in earth, in heaven, or in hell?/Sleeping or waking, mad or well advised?" (3.2.73–4, 2.2.211–12). Perhaps, as Barbara Freeman suggests, the whole play can be looked at as Egeon's dream. It is both reassuring and hilariously anticlimactic that these questionings can finally be dispelled by the most mundane of explanations: there are two Antipholuses and two Dromios.

Contained within this framework of madness and waking is a playful yet serious examination of the dynamics of courtship and marriage. The two most important women in the play are meaningfully paired and contrasted. Adriana, the shrewish wife, frets at social custom that allows her husband Antipholus to roam abroad while she is domestically confined. Her unmarried sister Luciana endorses the traditional view that husbands enjoy a precedence found everywhere in nature: males "are masters to their females, and their lords" (2.1.24). What Luciana calls obedience (line 29) her married sister calls "servitude" (line 26). Who is right? The debate, left unresolved, nonetheless raises skeptical questions about marital hierarchies. The plot also probes and tests through fantasies of inversion. A wife, believing herself rejected for having aged in her wifely obedience, locks her husband out of the house and dines with a stranger. Luciana meantime finds herself courted by what appears to be her own brother-in-law and thus must face a conflict between desire and loyalty to her sister. Of course, Adriana does not know that she is inverting authority by excluding her husband from his own hearth, but the plot of mistaken identities does allow her to act out her self-assertiveness without being, in fact, guilty of disloyalty. Her husband's role is to play the wandering male and to be eventually forgiven by his wife; presumably his exposure in Act 5 will make him a more tolerant husband, like Count Almaviva in Mozart's *The Marriage of Figaro*. The discovery of identities in Act 5 allows Luciana to marry the man she has learned to love, but without the guilt of her fantasy experience. Patriarchal values are restored by the play's conclusion, yet the partners in love and marriage have been, to some extent, liberated by their role playing in a plot of metamorphosis. These issues of domestic relations will be further explored in *The Taming of the Shrew, Othello,* and other plays.

The playfulness about illusion should not be overemphasized, for the play expends most of its energies in farce. The Dromios, with their incessant drubbings, are often the center of interest in performance, and rightly so. Shakespeare employs no behind-the-scenes manipulator of illusion, such as Puck in *A Midsummer Night's Dream* or the Duke in *Measure for Measure*. His interest in the metaphor of the world as a stage is discernible only as the foreshadowing of greatness to come. Nevertheless, Shakespeare's alterations of Plautus amply reveal the philosophic and idealistic direction that his subsequent comedy is to take.

The Comedy of Errors

[*Dramatis Personae*

SOLINUS, *Duke of Ephesus*
EGEON, *a merchant of Syracuse*
EMILIA, *Lady Abbess at Ephesus, and Egeon's wife*

ANTIPHOLUS OF EPHESUS, ANTIPHOLUS OF SYRACUSE, } *twin brothers, sons of Egeon and Emilia*

DROMIO OF EPHESUS, DROMIO OF SYRACUSE, } *twin brothers, bondsmen to the two Antipholuses*

ADRIANA, *wife of Antipholus of Ephesus*
LUCIANA, *her sister*
LUCE, *Adriana's kitchen maid (also known as* NELL*)*

BALTHASAR, *a merchant*
ANGELO, *a goldsmith*
FIRST MERCHANT, *friend to Antipholus of Syracuse*
SECOND MERCHANT, *to whom Angelo is a debtor*
DOCTOR PINCH, *a conjuring schoolmaster*
A COURTESAN
AN OFFICER
A MESSENGER

Jailer, Headsman, Officers, and other Attendants

SCENE: *Ephesus*]

1.1

Enter the Duke of Ephesus, with [*Egeon*] *the merchant of Syracuse, Jailer, and other attendants.*

1.1. Location: Some editors argue that the play was staged according to classical practice with three visible doors backstage representing three "houses"—that of Antipholus of Ephesus (in the center), that of the Courtesan, and that of the Priory—with the stage itself representing a marketplace or open area. More probably, the stage may have been open and unlocalized. The present scene may be at the Duke's court.

EGEON
Proceed, Solinus, to procure my fall,
And by the doom of death end woes and all.
DUKE
Merchant of Syracusa, plead no more.
I am not partial to infringe our laws.
The enmity and discord which of late
Sprung from the rancorous outrage of your Duke

2 doom judgment **3 Syracusa** Syracuse, in Sicily **4 partial** predisposed, biased **6 outrage** violence

To merchants, our well-dealing countrymen,
Who, wanting guilders to redeem their lives,
Have sealed his rigorous statutes with their bloods,
Excludes all pity from our threat'ning looks.
For since the mortal and intestine jars
Twixt thy seditious countrymen and us,
It hath in solemn synods been decreed,
Both by the Syracusians and ourselves,
To admit no traffic to our adverse towns.
Nay, more, if any born at Ephesus
Be seen at any Syracusian marts and fairs;
Again, if any Syracusian born
Come to the bay of Ephesus, he dies,
His goods confiscate to the Duke's dispose,
Unless a thousand marks be leviѐd
To quit the penalty and to ransom him.
Thy substance, valued at the highest rate,
Cannot amount unto a hundred marks;
Therefore by law thou art condemned to die.

EGEON
Yet this my comfort: when your words are done,
My woes end likewise with the evening sun.

DUKE
Well, Syracusian, say in brief the cause
Why thou departed'st from thy native home
And for what cause thou cam'st to Ephesus.

EGEON
A heavier task could not have been imposed
Than I to speak my griefs unspeakable.
Yet, that the world may witness that my end
Was wrought by nature, not by vile offense,
I'll utter what my sorrow gives me leave.
In Syracusa was I born, and wed
Unto a woman, happy but for me,
And by me, had not our hap been bad.
With her I lived in joy; our wealth increased
By prosperous voyages I often made
To Epidamnum, till my factor's death
And the great care of goods at random left
Drew me from kind embracements of my spouse;
From whom my absence was not six months old
Before herself, almost at fainting under
The pleasing punishment that women bear,
Had made provision for her following me,
And soon and safe arrivѐd where I was.
There had she not been long but she became
A joyful mother of two goodly sons,
And, which was strange, the one so like the other
As could not be distinguished but by names.
That very hour and in the selfsame inn
A mean woman was deliverѐd
Of such a burden male, twins both alike.
Those, for their parents were exceeding poor,
I bought and brought up to attend my sons.
My wife, not meanly proud of two such boys,
Made daily motions for our home return;
Unwilling I agreed. Alas, too soon
We came aboard.
A league from Epidamnum had we sailed
Before the always-wind-obeying deep
Gave any tragic instance of our harm.
But longer did we not retain much hope;
For what obscurѐd light the heavens did grant
Did but convey unto our fearful minds
A doubtful warrant of immediate death,
Which, though myself would gladly have embraced,
Yet the incessant weepings of my wife—
Weeping before for what she saw must come—
And piteous plainings of the pretty babes,
That mourned for fashion, ignorant what to fear,
Forced me to seek delays for them and me.
And this it was, for other means was none:
The sailors sought for safety by our boat
And left the ship, then sinking-ripe, to us.
My wife, more careful for the latter-born,
Had fastened him unto a small spare mast
Such as seafaring men provide for storms;
To him one of the other twins was bound,
Whilst I had been like heedful of the other.
The children thus disposed, my wife and I,
Fixing our eyes on whom our care was fixed,
Fastened ourselves at either end the mast,
And, floating straight, obedient to the stream,
Was carried towards Corinth, as we thought.
At length the sun, gazing upon the earth,
Dispersed those vapors that offended us,
And by the benefit of his wishѐd light
The seas waxed calm, and we discoverѐd
Two ships from far, making amain to us,
Of Corinth that, of Epidaurus this.
But ere they came—Oh, let me say no more!
Gather the sequel by that went before.

DUKE
Nay, forward, old man. Do not break off so,
For we may pity, though not pardon thee.

8 wanting guilders lacking money; the guilder was a Dutch coin worth about one shilling eight pence. **redeem** ransom **9 sealed** ratified. **bloods** i.e., lives. (The grim analogy is to red sealing wax.) **11 mortal . . . jars** deadly civil quarrels **13 synods** assemblies **15 To . . . towns** to allow no trade between our hostile towns. **16 Ephesus** a port on the Aegean coast of modern Turkey **17 marts** markets **20 confiscate** confiscated. **dispose** disposal **21 marks** money worth thirteen shillings four pence **22 quit** pay **23 Thy substance** The sum total of your wealth **32 unspeakable** indescribable. (But with a punning oxymoron on the literal sense: Egeon will speak that which cannot be spoken.) **34 by nature** i.e., by natural affection; here, a father's love **35 gives me leave** allows me. **37–8 happy . . . bad** happy except for my misfortune, and happy indeed through me if we had not suffered misfortune. **41 Epidamnum** (So spelled in Plautus's *The Menaechmi*); Epidamnus, a port on the coast of modern Albania. **factor's** agent's **42 care of** anxiety about

52 As that they **54 mean** of low birth **58 not meanly** to no small degree **59 motions** proposals, entreaties **62 league** a measure of distance, about three miles **64 instance** proof, sign **68 doubtful** dreadful **72 plainings** wailings **73 for fashion** in imitation **74 delays** i.e., delays from death **77 sinking-ripe** ready to sink **78 careful** anxious. **latter-born** (Compare line 124, however, from which we learn that the younger or "latter-born" was saved with the father.) **84 whom** those on whom, or, him on whom **86 straight** at once **89 vapors** clouds **92 making amain** proceeding at full speed **93 Epidaurus** a Greek town southwest of Athens and Corinth; or possibly Dubrovnik, on the Adriatic coast **95 that** that which

EGEON

Oh, had the gods done so, I had not now
Worthily termed them merciless to us!
For, ere the ships could meet by twice five leagues,
We were encountered by a mighty rock,
Which being violently borne upon,
Our helpful ship was splitted in the midst,
So that in this unjust divorce of us
Fortune had left to both of us alike
What to delight in, what to sorrow for.
Her part, poor soul, seeming as burdenèd
With lesser weight, but not with lesser woe,
Was carried with more speed before the wind,
And in our sight they three were taken up
By fishermen of Corinth, as we thought.
At length, another ship had seized on us,
And, knowing whom it was their hap to save,
Gave healthful welcome to their shipwrecked guests,
And would have reft the fishers of their prey
Had not their bark been very slow of sail;
And therefore homeward did they bend their course.
Thus have you heard me severed from my bliss,
That by misfortunes was my life prolonged,
To tell sad stories of my own mishaps.

DUKE

And, for the sake of them thou sorrowest for,
Do me the favor to dilate at full
What have befall'n of them and thee till now.

EGEON

My youngest boy, and yet my eldest care,
At eighteen years became inquisitive
After his brother, and importuned me
That his attendant—so his case was like,
Reft of his brother, but retained his name—
Might bear him company in the quest of him,
Whom whilst I labored of a love to see,
I hazarded the loss of whom I loved.
Five summers have I spent in farthest Greece,
Roaming clean through the bounds of Asia,
And, coasting homeward, came to Ephesus—
Hopeless to find, yet loath to leave unsought
Or that or any place that harbors men.
But here must end the story of my life,
And happy were I in my timely death
Could all my travels warrant me they live.

DUKE

Hapless Egeon, whom the fates have marked
To bear the extremity of dire mishap!

98 had . . . so i.e., had the gods shown pity **99 Worthily** justly **103 helpful ship** i.e., the mast **106 What** something **107 as** as if **114 healthful** saving **115 reft** bereft **116 bark** sailing vessel **122 dilate at full** relate at length **127 so . . . like** in a similar situation **128 Reft . . . name** (Evidently Egeon, presuming that the lost son and servant are dead, has given their names to the surviving twin brothers.) **130–1 Whom . . . loved** i.e., while I labored lovingly to find the lost twin, I ran the risk of losing my younger son, whom I loved no less. **133 clean** entirely. **bounds** boundaries, territories **134 coasting** traveling along the coast **135 Hopeless** despairing **136 Or** either **138 timely** speedy, opportune **139 travels** "travails," or hardships, as well as travels. **warrant** assure **141 mishap** (Punning on *Hapless* in line 140.)

Now, trust me, were it not against our laws,
Against my crown, my oath, my dignity,
Which princes, would they, may not disannul,
My soul should sue as advocate for thee.
But though thou art adjudgèd to the death,
And passèd sentence may not be recalled
But to our honor's great disparagement,
Yet will I favor thee in what I can.
Therefore, merchant, I'll limit thee this day
To seek thy health by beneficial help.
Try all the friends thou hast in Ephesus;
Beg thou, or borrow, to make up the sum,
And live; if no, then thou art doomed to die.—
Jailer, take him to thy custody.

JAILER

I will, my lord.

EGEON

Hopeless and helpless doth Egeon wend,
But to procrastinate his lifeless end. *Exeunt.*

✣

[1.2]

Enter Antipholus [*of Syracuse*], [*First*] *Merchant, and Dromio* [*of Syracuse*].

FIRST MERCHANT

Therefore give out you are of Epidamnum,
Lest that your goods too soon be confiscate.
This very day a Syracusian merchant
Is apprehended for arrival here
And, not being able to buy out his life,
According to the statute of the town
Dies ere the weary sun set in the west.
There is your money that I had to keep.
[*He gives money.*]

S. ANTIPHOLUS [*giving the money to S. Dromio*]

Go bear it to the Centaur, where we host,
And stay there, Dromio, till I come to thee.
Within this hour it will be dinnertime.
Till that, I'll view the manners of the town,
Peruse the traders, gaze upon the buildings,
And then return and sleep within mine inn,
For with long travel I am stiff and weary.
Get thee away.

S. DROMIO

Many a man would take you at your word
And go indeed, having so good a mean.
Exit Dromio [*of Syracuse*].

S. ANTIPHOLUS

A trusty villain, sir, that very oft,
When I am dull with care and melancholy,

143 dignity high office **144 would they** even if they wished. **disannul** annul, cancel **146 the death** i.e., death by judicial sentence **147 recalled** revoked **148 But** except **150 limit** allow, appoint **158 procrastinate** postpone
1.2. Location: The street.
1 give out say **8 keep** safeguard. **9 Centaur** the name of an inn, identified by its sign over the door. In mythology, a centaur is half horse, half man. **host** lodge **11 dinnertime** i.e., noon. **18 mean** (1) opportunity (2) money. **19 villain** servant. (Said good-humoredly.)

Lightens my humor with his merry jests. 21
What, will you walk with me about the town
And then go to my inn and dine with me?

FIRST MERCHANT
I am invited, sir, to certain merchants,
Of whom I hope to make much benefit;
I crave your pardon. Soon at five o'clock, 26
Please you, I'll meet with you upon the mart
And afterward consort you till bedtime. 28
My present business calls me from you now.

S. ANTIPHOLUS
Farewell till then. I will go lose myself 30
And wander up and down to view the city.

FIRST MERCHANT
Sir, I commend you to your own content. *Exit.*

S. ANTIPHOLUS
He that commends me to mine own content
Commends me to the thing I cannot get.
I to the world am like a drop of water 35
That in the ocean seeks another drop,
Who, falling there to find his fellow forth, 37
Unseen, inquisitive, confounds himself. 38
So I, to find a mother and a brother,
In quest of them, unhappy, lose myself.

Enter Dromio of Ephesus.

Here comes the almanac of my true date.— 41
What now? How chance thou art returned so soon? 42

E. DROMIO
Returned so soon? Rather approached too late:
The capon burns, the pig falls from the spit,
The clock hath strucken twelve upon the bell;
My mistress made it one upon my cheek. 46
She is so hot because the meat is cold; 47
The meat is cold because you come not home;
You come not home because you have no stomach; 49
You have no stomach, having broke your fast.
But we that know what 'tis to fast and pray
Are penitent for your default today. 52

S. ANTIPHOLUS
Stop in your wind, sir. Tell me this, I pray: 53
Where have you left the money that I gave you?

E. DROMIO
Oh—sixpence that I had o'Wednesday last
To pay the saddler for my mistress' crupper? 56
The saddler had it, sir; I kept it not.

S. ANTIPHOLUS
I am not in a sportive humor now.
Tell me, and dally not: where is the money?
We being strangers here, how dar'st thou trust
So great a charge from thine own custody? 61

E. DROMIO
I pray you, jest, sir, as you sit at dinner.
I from my mistress come to you in post; 63
If I return, I shall be post indeed, 64
For she will scour your fault upon my pate. 65
Methinks your maw, like mine, should be your clock 66
And strike you home without a messenger.

S. ANTIPHOLUS
Come, Dromio, come, these jests are out of season;
Reserve them till a merrier hour than this.
Where is the gold I gave in charge to thee?

E. DROMIO
To me, sir? Why, you gave no gold to me.

S. ANTIPHOLUS
Come on, sir knave, have done your foolishness,
And tell me how thou hast disposed thy charge. 73

E. DROMIO
My charge was but to fetch you from the mart
Home to your house, the Phoenix, sir, to dinner; 75
My mistress and her sister stays for you.

S. ANTIPHOLUS
Now, as I am a Christian, answer me
In what safe place you have bestowed my money,
Or I shall break that merry sconce of yours 79
That stands on tricks when I am undisposed. 80
Where is the thousand marks thou hadst of me?

E. DROMIO
I have some marks of yours upon my pate,
Some of my mistress' marks upon my shoulders,
But not a thousand marks between you both.
If I should pay Your Worship those again,
Perchance you will not bear them patiently.

S. ANTIPHOLUS
Thy mistress' marks? What mistress, slave, hast thou?

E. DROMIO
Your Worship's wife, my mistress at the Phoenix,
She that doth fast till you come home to dinner
And prays that you will hie you home to dinner. 90

S. ANTIPHOLUS
What, wilt thou flout me thus unto my face,
Being forbid? There, take you that, sir knave.
[*He beats Dromio of Ephesus.*]

E. DROMIO
What mean you, sir? For God sake, hold your hands!
Nay, an you will not, sir, I'll take my heels. 94
Exit Dromio of Ephesus.

S. ANTIPHOLUS
Upon my life, by some device or other
The villain is o'erraught of all my money. 96
They say this town is full of cozenage, 97
As nimble jugglers that deceive the eye,

21 humor mood, disposition **26 Soon at** About **28 consort** accompany **30 lose myself** roam freely **35 to** in relation to **37 to . . . forth** to find his companion **38 confounds himself** mingles indistinguishably. **41 the almanac . . . date** (Being born in the same hour, Dromio serves as an almanac by which Antipholus can see his age.) **42 How chance** How comes it **46 My . . . cheek** i.e., your wife slapped my cheek. (Dromio puns on the idea of the clock *striking* the hour.) **47 hot** angry **49 stomach** appetite **52 penitent** doing penance (i.e., suffering hunger). **default** fault **53 wind** i.e., words **56 crupper** leather strap on a saddle that is passed under the horse's tail in order to keep the saddle from riding forward. **61 charge** responsibility

63 post haste **64 post** door-post of a tavern used for keeping reckonings **65 scour** beat. (With a pun on the idea of keeping score.) **66 maw** stomach. (Applied usually to animals.) **73 disposed** disposed of **75 the Phoenix** the sign of Antipholus of Ephesus's shop. (He lives and carries on his business in the same dwelling.) In mythology, a phoenix is a fabulous bird that periodically is regenerated from its own ashes. **79 sconce** head **80 stands on** insists on, engages in **90 hie** hasten **94 an** if. **take my heels** take to my heels. **96 The . . . money** the rascal has cheated me out of all my money. **97 cozenage** cheating

Dark-working sorcerers that change the mind,
Soul-killing witches that deform the body,
Disguisèd cheaters, prating mountebanks,
And many suchlike liberties of sin.
If it prove so, I will be gone the sooner.
I'll to the Centaur to go seek this slave.
I greatly fear my money is not safe. *Exit.*

✤

2.1

Enter Adriana, wife to Antipholus [*of Ephesus*], *with Luciana, her sister.*

ADRIANA
Neither my husband nor the slave returned
That in such haste I sent to seek his master?
Sure, Luciana, it is two o'clock.

LUCIANA
Perhaps some merchant hath invited him,
And from the mart he's somewhere gone to dinner.
Good sister, let us dine, and never fret.
A man is master of his liberty;
Time is their master, and when they see time
They'll go or come. If so, be patient, sister.

ADRIANA
Why should their liberty than ours be more?

LUCIANA
Because their business still lies out o'door.

ADRIANA
Look when I serve him so, he takes it ill.

LUCIANA
Oh, know he is the bridle of your will.

ADRIANA
There's none but asses will be bridled so.

LUCIANA
Why, headstrong liberty is lashed with woe.
There's nothing situate under heaven's eye
But hath his bound, in earth, in sea, in sky.
The beasts, the fishes, and the wingèd fowls
Are their males' subjects and at their controls.
Man, more divine, the master of all these,
Lord of the wide world and wild wat'ry seas,
Endued with intellectual sense and souls,
Of more preeminence than fish and fowls,
Are masters to their females, and their lords.
Then let your will attend on their accords.

ADRIANA
This servitude makes you to keep unwed.

LUCIANA
Not this, but troubles of the marriage bed.

ADRIANA
But, were you wedded, you would bear some sway.

LUCIANA
Ere I learn love, I'll practice to obey.

ADRIANA
How if your husband start some other where?

LUCIANA
Till he come home again, I would forbear.

ADRIANA
Patience unmoved! No marvel though she pause;
They can be meek that have no other cause.
A wretched soul, bruised with adversity,
We bid be quiet when we hear it cry;
But were we burdened with like weight of pain,
As much or more we should ourselves complain.
So thou, that hast no unkind mate to grieve thee,
With urging helpless patience would relieve me;
But if thou live to see like right bereft,
This fool-begged patience in thee will be left.

LUCIANA
Well, I will marry one day, but to try.
Here comes your man; now is your husband nigh.

Enter Dromio of Ephesus.

ADRIANA
Say, is your tardy master now at hand?

E. DROMIO Nay, he's at two hands with me, and that my two ears can witness.

ADRIANA
Say, didst thou speak with him? Know'st thou his
mind?

E. DROMIO
I? Ay, he told his mind upon mine ear.
Beshrew his hand, I scarce could understand it.

LUCIANA
Spake he so doubtfully thou couldst not feel his
meaning?

E. DROMIO Nay, he struck so plainly I could too well feel his blows, and withal so doubtfully that I could scarce understand them.

ADRIANA
But say, I prithee, is he coming home?
It seems he hath great care to please his wife.

E. DROMIO
Why, mistress, sure my master is horn-mad.

ADRIANA
Horn-mad, thou villain?

E. DROMIO I mean not cuckold-mad,
But sure he is stark mad.
When I desired him to come home to dinner,

101 mountebanks charlatans **102 liberties of sin** persons allowed improper freedom to sin. (With a suggestion of certain districts, as in the London area, that were exempt from civic jurisdiction and were, in a punning sense, places of "license.")
2.1 Location: The house of Antipholus of Ephesus.
8 Time Time alone. **see time** see fit **11 still** constantly **12 Look when** Whenever **15 Why . . . woe** Headstrong liberty (in a wife) is whipped and punished with unhappiness. (Luciana argues that a wife is better off obeying her husband.) **17 his** its **22 intellectual sense** reason **25 accords** consent.

30 start . . . where i.e., goes off elsewhere, after other women. **33 other cause** cause to be otherwise. **34 A wretched soul** i.e., A fussy, crying baby **39 helpless** passive **40–1 But . . . left** i.e., but if you live to see your rights similarly taken away, you will abandon this foolishly urged patience. **42 but to try** i.e., just to put it to the test. **43 man** servant **45 at two hands** (Alluding to the beating he received at 1.2.92.) **48 told** (Punning on "tolled.") **49 Beshrew** Bad luck to. **understand** (With pun on "stand up under"; also in line 53.) **50 doubtfully** ambiguously **52 doubtfully** dreadfully **56 horn-mad** mad as a horned beast. (With a quibble on the sense of rage at being made a cuckold.)

He asked me for a thousand marks in gold.
" 'Tis dinnertime," quoth I. "My gold!" quoth he.
"Your meat doth burn," quoth I. "My gold!" quoth he.
"Will you come home?" quoth I. "My gold!" quoth he.
"Where is the thousand marks I gave thee, villain?"
"The pig," quoth I, "is burned." "My gold!" quoth he.
"My mistress, sir—" quoth I. "Hang up thy mistress!
I know not thy mistress. Out on thy mistress!"

LUCIANA Quoth who?

E. DROMIO Quoth my master.
"I know," quoth he, "no house, no wife, no mistress."
So that my errand, due unto my tongue,
I thank him, I bare home upon my shoulders;
For, in conclusion, he did beat me there.

ADRIANA
Go back again, thou slave, and fetch him home.

E. DROMIO
Go back again and be new beaten home?
For God's sake, send some other messenger.

ADRIANA
Back, slave, or I will break thy pate across.

E. DROMIO
And he will bless that cross with other beating.
Between you I shall have a holy head.

ADRIANA
Hence, prating peasant! Fetch thy master home.
[*She beats Dromio.*]

E. DROMIO
Am I so round with you as you with me,
That like a football you do spurn me thus?
You spurn me hence, and he will spurn me hither.
If I last in this service, you must case me in leather.
[*Exit.*]

LUCIANA
Fie, how impatience loureth in your face!

ADRIANA
His company must do his minions grace,
Whilst I at home starve for a merry look.
Hath homely age th'alluring beauty took
From my poor cheek? Then he hath wasted it.
Are my discourses dull? Barren my wit?
If voluble and sharp discourse be marred,
Unkindness blunts it more than marble hard.
Do their gay vestments his affections bait?
That's not my fault; he's master of my state.
What ruins are in me that can be found
By him not ruined? Then is he the ground
Of my defeatures. My decayèd fair
A sunny look of his would soon repair.
But, too unruly deer, he breaks the pale
And feeds from home. Poor I am but his stale.

LUCIANA
Self-harming jealousy! Fie, beat it hence!

ADRIANA
Unfeeling fools can with such wrongs dispense.
I know his eye doth homage otherwhere,
Or else what lets it but he would be here?
Sister, you know he promised me a chain.
Would that alone o' love he would detain,
So he would keep fair quarter with his bed!
I see the jewel best enamelèd
Will lose his beauty; yet the gold bides still
That others touch, and often touching will
Wear gold; and no man that hath a name
By falsehood and corruption doth it shame.
Since that my beauty cannot please his eye,
I'll weep what's left away, and weeping die.

LUCIANA
How many fond fools serve mad jealousy!
Exeunt.

✤

[2.2]

Enter Antipholus of Syracuse.

S. ANTIPHOLUS
The gold I gave to Dromio is laid up
Safe at the Centaur, and the heedful slave
Is wandered forth in care to seek me out
By computation and mine host's report.
I could not speak with Dromio since at first
I sent him from the mart. See, here he comes.

Enter Dromio of Syracuse.

How now, sir, is your merry humor altered?
As you love strokes, so jest with me again.
You know no Centaur? You received no gold?
Your mistress sent to have me home to dinner?
My house was at the Phoenix? Wast thou mad,
That thus so madly thou didst answer me?

S. DROMIO
What answer, sir? When spake I such a word?

66 Hang up i.e., To hell with **71 due . . . tongue** which I should have delivered by my tongue **72 I bare . . . shoulders** I took in the form of a beating **78 he . . . cross** i.e., he will add further devotion in the form of a beating. (There is a pun on "to bless," to wound, from the French *blesser*. *Cross* is a quibble on *across* in the previous line.) **79 holy** (Punning on the sense "full of holes.") **81 round** plainspoken. (With pun on the sense of "spherical.") **85 loureth** frowns, scowls **86 His . . . grace** He bestows favors on his darling paramours **88 took** taken **89 wasted** (1) squandered (2) laid waste to, ruined **90 discourses** conversations **91–2 If . . . hard** i.e., If my fluent and sometimes too shrewish discourse seems peevish to my husband, unkindness on his part simply blunts it even more than when a sharp instrument is struck against hard marble. **93 his affections bait** entice his passions. **94 state** outward estate, condition, i.e., clothes. **96 ground** cause

97 defeatures disfigurements. **decayèd fair** impaired or perished beauty **99 pale** enclosure **100 from** away from. **stale** rejected lover who has become a laughingstock. (With a pun on *stale*, tiresomely lacking in freshness; she is stale to him, he dear [*deer*] to her.) **102 Unfeeling . . . dispense** Only an insensitive fool would condone such wrongs. **104 lets** hinders **106 Would . . . detain** Would that he would withhold only that token of his affection **107 So . . . bed!** provided he would remain faithful to his marriage bed! **108–12 I see . . . shame** (A difficult passage. Adriana comments that a showy jewel, like a gaudily dressed woman [as in line 93], will lose its beauty in time, whereas a true wife is like gold, which, if properly handled, remains unsullied; no husband of good reputation should be ashamed of virtuous use like this in his wife.) **109 his** its **115 fond** doting
2.2 Location: The street before Antipholus of Ephesus' house.
4 computation estimation, reckoning **8 strokes** blows

S. ANTIPHOLUS
Even now, even here, not half an hour since.

S. DROMIO
I did not see you since you sent me hence
Home to the Centaur with the gold you gave me.

S. ANTIPHOLUS
Villain, thou didst deny the gold's receipt
And told'st me of a mistress and a dinner,
For which I hope thou felt'st I was displeased.

S. DROMIO
I am glad to see you in this merry vein.
What means this jest? I pray you, master, tell me.

S. ANTIPHOLUS
Yea, dost thou jeer and flout me in the teeth?
Think'st thou I jest? Hold, take thou that, and that.
Beats Dromio.

S. DROMIO
Hold, sir, for God's sake! Now your jest is earnest.
Upon what bargain do you give it me?

S. ANTIPHOLUS
Because that I familiarly sometimes
Do use you for my fool and chat with you,
Your sauciness will jest upon my love
And make a common of my serious hours.
When the sun shines let foolish gnats make sport,
But creep in crannies when he hides his beams.
If you will jest with me, know my aspect
And fashion your demeanor to my looks,
Or I will beat this method in your sconce.

S. DROMIO "Sconce" call you it? So you would leave battering, I had rather have it a head. An you use these blows long, I must get a sconce for my head and insconce it too, or else I shall seek my wit in my shoulders. But I pray, sir, why am I beaten?

S. ANTIPHOLUS Dost thou not know?

S. DROMIO Nothing, sir, but that I am beaten.

S. ANTIPHOLUS Shall I tell you why?

S. DROMIO Ay, sir, and wherefore; for they say every why hath a wherefore.

S. ANTIPHOLUS "Why," first—for flouting me; and then, "wherefore"—for urging it the second time to me.

S. DROMIO
Was there ever any man thus beaten out of season,
When in the why and the wherefore is neither rhyme
nor reason?
Well, sir, I thank you.

S. ANTIPHOLUS Thank me, sir, for what?

S. DROMIO Marry, sir, for this something that you gave me for nothing.

S. ANTIPHOLUS I'll make you amends next, to give you nothing for something. But say, sir, is it dinnertime?

S. DROMIO No, sir, I think the meat wants that I have.

S. ANTIPHOLUS In good time, sir, what's that?

S. DROMIO Basting.

S. ANTIPHOLUS Well, sir, then 'twill be dry.

S. DROMIO If it be, sir, I pray you, eat none of it.

S. ANTIPHOLUS Your reason?

S. DROMIO Lest it make you choleric and purchase me another dry basting.

S. ANTIPHOLUS Well, sir, learn to jest in good time. There's a time for all things.

S. DROMIO I durst have denied that before you were so choleric.

S. ANTIPHOLUS By what rule, sir?

S. DROMIO Marry, sir, by a rule as plain as the plain bald pate of Father Time himself.

S. ANTIPHOLUS Let's hear it.

S. DROMIO There's no time for a man to recover his hair that grows bald by nature.

S. ANTIPHOLUS May he not do it by fine and recovery?

S. DROMIO Yes, to pay a fine for a periwig and recover the lost hair of another man.

S. ANTIPHOLUS Why is Time such a niggard of hair, being, as it is, so plentiful an excrement?

S. DROMIO Because it is a blessing that he bestows on beasts, and what he hath scanted men in hair he hath given them in wit.

S. ANTIPHOLUS Why, but there's many a man hath more hair than wit.

S. DROMIO Not a man of those but he hath the wit to lose his hair.

S. ANTIPHOLUS Why, thou didst conclude hairy men plain dealers without wit.

S. DROMIO The plainer dealer, the sooner lost. Yet he loseth it in a kind of jollity.

S. ANTIPHOLUS For what reason?

S. DROMIO For two, and sound ones too.

S. ANTIPHOLUS Nay, not sound, I pray you.

S. DROMIO Sure ones, then.

S. ANTIPHOLUS Nay, not sure, in a thing falsing.

S. DROMIO Certain ones, then.

S. ANTIPHOLUS Name them.

S. DROMIO The one, to save the money that he spends in tiring; the other, that at dinner they should not drop in his porridge.

S. ANTIPHOLUS You would all this time have proved there is no time for all things.

22 in the teeth to my face. **24 earnest** serious. (With a pun on the financial sense: money paid as an installment to secure a bargain.) **28 jest upon** trifle with **29 common** public playground **32 aspect** look, expression; also, astrological favor or disfavor of a planet **34 sconce** head. (With pun on the meaning "fort" in line 35 and "helmet" or "protective covering" in line 37; the *battering*, lines 35–6, is both a beating and assault by a battering ram.) **36 An** If **37–8 insconce** shelter within a sconce or fortification **38–9 I shall . . . shoulders** i.e., my head will be beaten into my shoulders. **47 out of season** inappropriately **51 Marry** i.e., Truly. (A shortened form of the oath "by the Virgin Mary.")

55 wants that lacks that which **56 In good time** Indeed **57 Basting** (1) Moistening with butter or drippings during cooking (2) Beating. **61 choleric** (Hot or dry food was thought to produce or aggravate the choleric or irascible humor.) **62 dry basting** hard beating. **73 fine and recovery** a legal procedure for converting an entailed estate, one in which the property is limited to specified heirs, into a fee simple, one in which the owner has unqualified ownership. **77 excrement** outgrowth (of hair). **83–4 he . . . hair** (A reference to the venereal diseases in which loss of hair was a symptom.) **87 dealer** i.e., dealer with women **88 a kind of jollity** i.e., sexual pleasure. **91 not sound** invalid. (With a pun on "venereally diseased.") **93 falsing** deceptive. (Continuing the joke on venereal disease.) **97 tiring** dressing the hair

S. DROMIO Marry, and did, sir; namely, e'en no time to recover hair lost by nature.

S. ANTIPHOLUS But your reason was not substantial why there is no time to recover.

S. DROMIO Thus I mend it: Time himself is bald and therefore to the world's end will have bald followers.

S. ANTIPHOLUS I knew 'twould be a bald conclusion.
But soft, who wafts us yonder?

Enter Adriana [*beckoning*], *and Luciana.*

ADRIANA
Ay, ay, Antipholus, look strange and frown.
Some other mistress hath thy sweet aspects;
I am not Adriana, nor thy wife.
The time was once when thou unurged wouldst vow
That never words were music to thine ear,
That never object pleasing in thine eye,
That never touch well welcome to thy hand,
That never meat sweet-savored in thy taste,
Unless I spake, or looked, or touched, or carved to thee.
How comes it now, my husband, oh, how comes it,
That thou art then estrangèd from thyself?
Thyself I call it, being strange to me
That, undividable, incorporate,
Am better than thy dear self's better part.
Ah, do not tear away thyself from me!
For know, my love, as easy mayst thou fall
A drop of water in the breaking gulf,
And take unmingled thence that drop again
Without addition or diminishing,
As take from me thyself and not me too.
How dearly would it touch thee to the quick,
Shouldst thou but hear I were licentious
And that this body, consecrate to thee,
By ruffian lust should be contaminate!
Wouldst thou not spit at me, and spurn at me,
And hurl the name of husband in my face,
And tear the stained skin off my harlot brow,
And from my false hand cut the wedding ring,
And break it with a deep-divorcing vow?
I know thou canst, and therefore see thou do it.
I am possessed with an adulterate blot;
My blood is mingled with the crime of lust.
For if we two be one, and thou play false,
I do digest the poison of thy flesh,
Being strumpeted by thy contagion.
Keep then fair league and truce with thy true bed,
I live distained, thou undishonorèd.

S. ANTIPHOLUS
Plead you to me, fair dame? I know you not.
In Ephesus I am but two hours old,
As strange unto your town as to your talk,
Who, every word by all my wit being scanned,
Wants wit in all one word to understand.

LUCIANA
Fie, brother, how the world is changed with you!
When were you wont to use my sister thus?
She sent for you by Dromio home to dinner.

S. ANTIPHOLUS By Dromio?

S. DROMIO By me?

ADRIANA
By thee; and this thou didst return from him:
That he did buffet thee and in his blows
Denied my house for his, me for his wife.

S. ANTIPHOLUS
Did you converse, sir, with this gentlewoman?
What is the course and drift of your compact?

S. DROMIO
I, sir? I never saw her till this time.

S. ANTIPHOLUS
Villain, thou liest, for even her very words
Didst thou deliver to me on the mart.

S. DROMIO
I never spake with her in all my life.

S. ANTIPHOLUS
How can she thus then call us by our names,
Unless it be by inspiration?

ADRIANA
How ill agrees it with your gravity
To counterfeit thus grossly with your slave,
Abetting him to thwart me in my mood!
Be it my wrong you are from me exempt,
But wrong not that wrong with a more contempt.
Come, I will fasten on this sleeve of thine.
[*She clings to him.*]
Thou art an elm, my husband, I a vine,
Whose weakness, married to thy stronger state,
Makes me with thy strength to communicate.
If aught possess thee from me, it is dross,
Usurping ivy, brier, or idle moss,
Who, all for want of pruning, with intrusion
Infect thy sap and live on thy confusion.

S. ANTIPHOLUS [*aside*]
To me she speaks; she moves me for her theme.

105 Time . . . bald (Time is conventionally personified as an old bald man, with only a forelock of hair; one must seize opportunity by the forelock, i.e., quickly, or the occasion will be lost.) **107 bald** i.e., senseless, stupid. (Continuing the joke about baldness.) **108 soft** gently, wait a minute. **wafts** beckons **109 strange** estranged, distant **110 aspects** glances **119 then** therefore. **estrangèd from thyself** (1) behaving unlike yourself (2) estranged from me, your other half. **124 fall** let fall **125 breaking gulf** surf-crested sea **128 and. . . too** without taking me from myself (since we are inseparable and indivisible). **129 the quick** the most sensitive or vulnerable part **131 consecrate** consecrated **132 contaminate** contaminated. **133 spurn** kick **138–43 I know . . . contagion** i.e., Go ahead and divorce me, since you have the right to do it; because we are one flesh as husband and wife, when you commit adultery it taints me also with the guilt of having been a strumpet. (Said with bitter irony.)

144 Keep . . . bed If you remain faithful to your marriage vows **145 distained** unstained (by contagion) **149–50 Who . . . understand** i.e., and I, though listening intently to every word, cannot understand one word of what you've said. **152 use** treat **160 compact** plot. **167 gravity** social dignity **168 grossly** obviously **169 Abetting** helping. **mood** anger. **170–1 Be . . . contempt** i.e., It's bad enough that I have to endure your seeing other women; don't make it worse with your contempt. **175 with . . . communicate** share in your strength. **176 If . . . dross** If anything usurps my possession of you, it is an impure substance **177 idle** unprofitable **178 Who** which. **want** lack. **intrusion** forced entry **179 confusion** ruin. **180 moves . . . theme** appeals to me as her subject of discourse.

What, was I married to her in my dream?
Or sleep I now and think I hear all this?
What error drives our eyes and ears amiss?
Until I know this sure uncertainty, 184
I'll entertain the offered fallacy. 185

LUCIANA
Dromio, go bid the servants spread for dinner. 186

S. DROMIO
Oh, for my beads! I cross me for a sinner. 187
[*He crosses himself.*]
This is the fairy land. Oh, spite of spites,
We talk with goblins, elves, and sprites! 189
If we obey them not, this will ensue:
They'll suck our breath or pinch us black and blue. 191

LUCIANA
Why prat'st thou to thyself and answer'st not? 192
Dromio, thou drone, thou snail, thou slug, thou sot! 193

S. DROMIO
I am transformèd, master, am not I?

S. ANTIPHOLUS
I think thou art in mind, and so am I.

S. DROMIO
Nay, master, both in mind and in my shape.

S. ANTIPHOLUS
Thou hast thine own form.

S. DROMIO No, I am an ape. 197

LUCIANA
If thou art changed to aught, 'tis to an ass.

S. DROMIO
'Tis true; she rides me and I long for grass. 199
'Tis so, I am an ass; else it could never be
But I should know her as well as she knows me.

ADRIANA
Come, come, no longer will I be a fool,
To put the finger in the eye and weep
Whilst man and master laughs my woes to scorn.
Come, sir, to dinner.—Dromio, keep the gate.—
Husband, I'll dine above with you today 206
And shrive you of a thousand idle pranks.— 207
Sirrah, if any ask you for your master, 208
Say he dines forth, and let no creature enter.— 209
Come, sister.—Dromio, play the porter well.

S. ANTIPHOLUS [*aside*]
Am I in earth, in heaven, or in hell?
Sleeping or waking, mad or well-advised? 212
Known unto these, and to myself disguised?
I'll say as they say, and persever so,
And in this mist at all adventures go. 215

S. DROMIO
Master, shall I be porter at the gate?

ADRIANA
Ay, and let none enter, lest I break your pate.

LUCIANA
Come, come, Antipholus, we dine too late.
[*Exeunt. Dromio of Syracuse remains as porter, visible to the audience but not to those approaching the door.*]

3.1

Enter Antipholus of Ephesus, his man Dromio, Angelo the goldsmith, and Balthasar the merchant.

E. ANTIPHOLUS
Good Signor Angelo, you must excuse us all;
My wife is shrewish when I keep not hours. 2
Say that I lingered with you at your shop
To see the making of her carcanet 4
And that tomorrow you will bring it home.—
But here's a villain that would face me down 6
He met me on the mart, and that I beat him
And charged him with a thousand marks in gold, 8
And that I did deny my wife and house.— 9
Thou drunkard, thou, what didst thou mean by this?

E. DROMIO
Say what you will, sir, but I know what I know.
That you beat me at the mart, I have your hand to show. 12
If the skin were parchment and the blows you gave were ink,
Your own handwriting would tell you what I think.

E. ANTIPHOLUS
I think thou art an ass.

E. DROMIO Marry, so it doth appear
By the wrongs I suffer and the blows I bear.
I should kick, being kicked, and, being at that pass, 17
You would keep from my heels and beware of an ass.

E. ANTIPHOLUS
You're sad, Signor Balthasar. Pray God our cheer 19
May answer my good will and your good welcome here. 20

BALTHASAR
I hold your dainties cheap, sir, and your welcome dear. 21

E. ANTIPHOLUS
Oh, Signor Balthasar, either at flesh or fish,
A table full of welcome makes scarce one dainty dish. 23

184 Until . . . uncertainty Until I can fathom the meaning of what is certainly a mystery. (Stated as an oxymoron.) **185 entertain** accept. **fallacy** delusive notion, error. **186 spread** set the table **187 beads** rosary beads. **189 sprites** spirits. **191 suck our breath** (This piece of folklore was perhaps connected with the old idea that the breath of a person was that person's soul. Fairies were famous for sucking and pinching.) **192 prat'st thou** do you chatter **193 sot** fool. **197 ape** i.e., counterfeit. **199 for grass** for freedom (as a horse put out to pasture). **206 above** i.e., on the second floor, above Antipholus's shop **207 shrive** hear confession and give absolution **208 Sirrah** (Customary form of address to servants.) **209 forth** away from home **212 well-advised** in my right mind. **215 at all adventures** whatever may happen

3.1 Location: Before the house of Antipholus of Ephesus. The scene is continuous with the previous one.
2 keep not hours am not punctual. **4 carcanet** necklace (the *chain* of 2.1.105 and line 115 below) **6 face me down** maintain to my face that **8 charged him with** entrusted him with possession of **9 deny** disown **12 hand** i.e., handiwork on my body. (With a pun on "handwriting.") **17 at that pass** in that situation **19 sad** serious. **cheer** entertainment **20 answer** agree with, match **21 dainties** delicacies. **cheap** of minor importance. **dear** of primary importance. **23 makes scarce** scarcely equals

BALTHASAR
Good meat, sir, is common; that every churl affords.

E. ANTIPHOLUS
And welcome more common, for that's nothing
but words.

BALTHASAR
Small cheer and great welcome makes a merry feast.

E. ANTIPHOLUS
Ay, to a niggardly host and more sparing guest.
But though my cates be mean, take them in good
part;
Better cheer may you have, but not with better heart.
[*They approach the door of Antipholus of Ephesus's house.*]
But soft! My door is locked. [*To Dromio*] Go bid them
let us in.

E. DROMIO [*calling*]
Maud, Bridget, Marian, Cicely, Gillian, Ginn!

S. DROMIO [*speaking from the other side of the door*]
Mome, malt-horse, capon, coxcomb, idiot, patch!
Either get thee from the door or sit down at the
hatch.
Dost thou conjure for wenches, that thou call'st for
such store
When one is one too many? Go, get thee from the
door.

E. DROMIO
What patch is made our porter? My master stays in
the street.

S. DROMIO
Let him walk from whence he came, lest he catch cold
on 's feet.

E. ANTIPHOLUS
Who talks within there? Ho, open the door!

S. DROMIO
Right, sir, I'll tell you when, an you'll tell me
wherefore.

E. ANTIPHOLUS
Wherefore? For my dinner. I have not dined today.

S. DROMIO
Nor today here you must not. Come again when
you may.

E. ANTIPHOLUS
What art thou that keep'st me out from the house I
owe?

S. DROMIO
The porter for this time, sir, and my name is Dromio.

E. DROMIO
O villain! Thou hast stol'n both mine office and my
name.
The one ne'er got me credit, the other mickle blame.
If thou hadst been Dromio today in my place,
Thou wouldst have changed thy face for a name or
thy name for an ass.

Enter Luce [*above, concealed from Antipholus of Ephesus and his companions*].

LUCE
What a coil is there, Dromio? Who are those at the
gate?

E. DROMIO
Let my master in, Luce.

LUCE
Faith, no, he comes too late,
And so tell your master.

E. DROMIO
Oh, Lord, I must laugh!
Have at you with a proverb: Shall I set in my staff?

LUCE
Have at you with another: that's—When, can you
tell?

S. DROMIO
If thy name be called Luce, Luce, thou hast answered
him well.

E. ANTIPHOLUS [*to Luce*]
Do you hear, you minion? You'll let us in, I hope?

LUCE
I thought to have asked you.

S. DROMIO
And you said no.

E. DROMIO
So, come help. [*They beat the door.*] Well struck!
There was blow for blow.

E. ANTIPHOLUS [*to Luce*]
Thou baggage, let me in.

LUCE
Can you tell for whose sake?

E. DROMIO
Master, knock the door hard.

LUCE
Let him knock till it ache.

E. ANTIPHOLUS
You'll cry for this, minion, if I beat the door down.
[*He knocks.*]

LUCE
What needs all that, and a pair of stocks in the town?

Enter Adriana [*above, concealed, like Luce and Dromio of Syracuse, from those at the door*].

24 every churl i.e., everyone **27 sparing** self-denying **28 cates** provisions, dainties. **mean** plain, simple **32 s.d.** ***speaking . . . door*** (Dromio of Syracuse has remained onstage since the end of the previous scene, visible to the audience but not to those at the door. Alternatively, he could exit at the end of 2.2 and speak now *within*, or enter at this point, but neither solution seems satisfactory. Compare the entrances of Luce and Adriana at lines 47 and 60.) **32 Mome** Dolt, blockhead. **malt-horse** brewer's horse; stupid person. **patch** fool, clown. **33 hatch** half-door that can be kept closed while the upper half is opened. **34 conjure for** summon as if by magic. **store** quantity **36 What . . . porter?** i.e., What clown is this who is acting as gatekeeper? **stays** waits **37 on 's** in his **39 an** if. **wherefore** why. **42 owe** own.

45 The one . . . blame i.e., My name has never benefited me, my office of servant has got me much blame. **47 Thou . . . ass** i.e., you would have been glad to change places with someone else (since I was beaten like a beast of burden). **47.1** ***Enter Luce*** [***above***] (Luce here and then Adriana at line 70 may enter above in such a way that the audience understands them not to be visible to those who are calling at the door.) **48 coil** noise, disturbance **51 Have . . . staff** Let me come at you with a proverb: Shall I take up my abode here? (With a phallic joke.) **52 When . . . tell?** i.e., Never. (Another proverbial expression, used derisively to turn aside a question.) **54 minion** hussy. **hope** (A line following with an answering rhyme may be missing; perhaps it would have cleared up the present obscurity of lines 55 and 56.) **57 baggage** good-for-nothing **60 What . . . town?** i.e., Why do we need to put up with this disturbance, when the town provides stocks for punishment?

ADRIANA
Who is that at the door that keeps all this noise?

S. DROMIO
By my troth, your town is troubled with unruly boys.

E. ANTIPHOLUS
Are you there, wife? You might have come before.

ADRIANA
Your wife, sir knave? Go get you from the door.
[*Exit with Luce.*]

E. DROMIO
If you went in pain, master, this "knave" would go sore.

ANGELO
Here is neither cheer, sir, nor welcome. We would fain have either.

BALTHASAR
In debating which was best, we shall part with neither.

E. DROMIO
They stand at the door, master. Bid them welcome hither.

E. ANTIPHOLUS
There is something in the wind, that we cannot get in.

E. DROMIO
You would say so, master, if your garments were thin.
Your cake is warm within; you stand here in the cold.
It would make a man mad as a buck to be so bought and sold.

E. ANTIPHOLUS
Go fetch me something. I'll break ope the gate.

S. DROMIO
Break any breaking here, and I'll break your knave's pate.

E. DROMIO
A man may break a word with you, sir, and words are but wind,
Ay, and break it in your face, so he break it not behind.

S. DROMIO
It seems thou want'st breaking. Out upon thee, hind!

E. DROMIO
Here's too much "Out upon thee!" I pray thee, let me in.

S. DROMIO
Ay, when fowls have no feathers and fish have no fin.
[*Exit.*]

E. ANTIPHOLUS
Well, I'll break in. Go borrow me a crow.

E. DROMIO
A crow without feather? Master, mean you so?
For a fish without a fin, there's a fowl without a feather.—
If a crow help us in, sirrah, we'll pluck a crow together.

E. ANTIPHOLUS
Go, get thee gone. Fetch me an iron crow.

BALTHASAR
Have patience, sir. Oh, let it not be so!
Herein you war against your reputation
And draw within the compass of suspect
Th'unviolated honor of your wife.
Once this: your long experience of her wisdom,
Her sober virtue, years, and modesty,
Plead on her part some cause to you unknown;
And doubt not, sir, but she will well excuse
Why at this time the doors are made against you.
Be ruled by me. Depart in patience,
And let us to the Tiger all to dinner,
And about evening come yourself alone
To know the reason of this strange restraint.
If by strong hand you offer to break in
Now in the stirring passage of the day,
A vulgar comment will be made of it,
And that supposèd by the common rout
Against your yet ungallèd estimation,
That may with foul intrusion enter in
And dwell upon your grave when you are dead;
For slander lives upon succession,
Forever housèd where it gets possession.

E. ANTIPHOLUS
You have prevailed. I will depart in quiet,
And, in despite of mirth, mean to be merry.
I know a wench of excellent discourse,
Pretty and witty, wild and yet, too, gentle.
There will we dine. This woman that I mean,
My wife—but, I protest, without desert—
Hath oftentimes upbraided me withal.
To her will we to dinner. [*To Angelo*] Get you home
And fetch the chain; by this I know 'tis made.
Bring it, I pray you, to the Porcupine,
For there's the house. That chain will I bestow—
Be it for nothing but to spite my wife—
Upon mine hostess there. Good sir, make haste.
Since mine own doors refuse to entertain me,
I'll knock elsewhere, to see if they'll disdain me.

61 keeps keeps up **65 If . . . sore** i.e., Yourself and this "knave" she mentions are the same person. **went** i.e., were **66 fain** gladly **67 part** depart **68 They . . . hither** i.e., Both cheer and welcome have been barred at the door, master. Invite them in. (Said ironically, as an impossibility.) **69 something . . . wind** something strange going on **70 You . . . thin** i.e., If you were more thinly dressed (like me), master, you'd say it's a cold wind indeed that shuts you out this way. (Dromio takes the proverbial wind of line 69 in a literal sense.) **72 as a buck** i.e., as a male deer in rutting season. (Compare *horn-mad,* 2.1.57.) **bought and sold** i.e., betrayed, ill-treated. **75 break a word** exchange words. (Punning on *break* in the previous lines.) **76 behind** i.e., in farting. **77 thou . . . breaking** you need to be broken in by a beating. **hind** boor, menial. **79 s.d. *Exit*** (If Dromio of Syracuse has been visible to the audience, he probably leaves at this point.)

80 crow crowbar. (Introducing a quibble by Dromio of Ephesus.) **83 pluck . . . together** pick a bone together, settle accounts. **87 draw . . . suspect** bring under suspicion **89 Once this** To be brief, in short **90 virtue** merit, general excellence **92 excuse** justify **93 made** fastened **95 the Tiger** (Presumably an inn.) **98 offer** attempt **99 stirring passage** bustle **100 vulgar** public **101 And . . . rout** and it will be presumed true by everyone **102 yet . . . estimation** still unsullied reputation **105 lives upon succession** passes from generation to generation **108 in . . . mirth** despite my not feeling mirthful, or, in spite of the mockery **112 desert** my deserving it **115 this** this time **116 Porcupine** (The name of the Courtesan's house.)

ANGELO
I'll meet you at that place some hour hence.
E. ANTIPHOLUS
Do so. This jest shall cost me some expense. *Exeunt.*

[3.2]

Enter Luciana with Antipholus of Syracuse.

LUCIANA
And may it be that you have quite forgot 1
A husband's office? Shall, Antipholus, 2
Even in the spring of love, thy love springs rot? 3
Shall love, in building, grow so ruinous?
If you did wed my sister for her wealth,
Then for her wealth's sake use her with more kindness;
Or if you like elsewhere, do it by stealth:
Muffle your false love with some show of blindness. 8
Let not my sister read it in your eye;
Be not thy tongue thy own shame's orator;
Look sweet, speak fair, become disloyalty; 11
Apparel vice like virtue's harbinger. 12
Bear a fair presence, though your heart be tainted;
Teach sin the carriage of a holy saint; 14
Be secret-false. What need she be acquainted?
What simple thief brags of his own attaint? 16
'Tis double wrong to truant with your bed 17
And let her read it in thy looks at board. 18
Shame hath a bastard fame, well managèd; 19
Ill deeds is doubled with an evil word. 20
Alas, poor women! Make us but believe,
Being compact of credit, that you love us. 22
Though others have the arm, show us the sleeve;
We in your motion turn and you may move us. 24
Then, gentle brother, get you in again.
Comfort my sister, cheer her, call her wife.
'Tis holy sport to be a little vain 27
When the sweet breath of flattery conquers strife.
S. ANTIPHOLUS
Sweet mistress—what your name is else, I know not, 29
Nor by what wonder you do hit of mine— 30
Less in your knowledge and your grace you show not 31
Than our earth's wonder, more than earth divine. 32
Teach me, dear creature, how to think and speak;
Lay open to my earthy-gross conceit, 34
Smothered in errors, feeble, shallow, weak,
The folded meaning of your words' deceit. 36
Against my soul's pure truth why labor you 37
To make it wander in an unknown field? 38
Are you a god? Would you create me new?
Transform me then, and to your power I'll yield.
But if that I am I, then well I know
Your weeping sister is no wife of mine,
Nor to her bed no homage do I owe.
Far more, far more to you do I decline. 44
Oh, train me not; sweet mermaid, with thy note, 45
To drown me in thy sister's flood of tears!
Sing, siren, for thyself, and I will dote.
Spread o'er the silver waves thy golden hairs,
And as a bed I'll take them and there lie, 49
And in that glorious supposition think
He gains by death that hath such means to die. 51
Let Love, being light, be drownèd if she sink! 52
LUCIANA
What, are you mad, that you do reason so? 53
S. ANTIPHOLUS
Not mad, but mated—how, I do not know. 54
LUCIANA
It is a fault that springeth from your eye.
S. ANTIPHOLUS
For gazing on your beams, fair sun, being by. 56
LUCIANA
Gaze where you should, and that will clear your sight.
S. ANTIPHOLUS
As good to wink, sweet love, as look on night. 58
LUCIANA
Why call you me "love"? Call my sister so.
S. ANTIPHOLUS
Thy sister's sister.
LUCIANA That's my sister.
S. ANTIPHOLUS No,
It is thyself, mine own self's better part,
Mine eye's clear eye, my dear heart's dearer heart,
My food, my fortune, and my sweet hope's aim,
My sole earth's heaven, and my heaven's claim. 64
LUCIANA
All this my sister is, or else should be.
S. ANTIPHOLUS
Call thyself sister, sweet, for I am thee. 66

3.2 Location: Antipholus of Ephesus's house or in front of it, certainly so by line 163.
1 may can **2 office** duty. **3 love springs** tender shoots of love **8 Muffle** hide. **show of blindness** deceptive appearance. **11 fair** courteously. **become disloyalty** carry off your infidelity gracefully **12 harbinger** messenger, forerunner. **14 carriage** demeanor **16 simple** simple-minded. **attaint** stain, dishonor. **17 truant with** be faithless to **18 board** table. **19–20 Shame . . . word** i.e., Shameful behavior, if cleverly managed, can assume a false reputation for humble conduct, whereas sin is made twice as heinous by callous boasting of it. **22 Being . . . credit** i.e., we who are wholly inclined to believe you **24 We . . . turn** we in your orbit are governed by your motion (referring to the motion of the heavenly spheres) **27 holy sport** virtuous jesting. (An oxymoron.) **vain** false **29 else** otherwise **30 wonder** miracle. **hit of** hit upon, guess **31–2 Less . . . divine** i.e., you seem no less wise and graceful than our divine queen, wonder of the earth. (Seemingly a flattering reference to Queen Elizabeth.)

34 Lay . . . conceit explain to my dull understanding **36 folded** concealed **37–8 Against . . . field?** Why do you strive against the pure yearning of my soul, as if desiring it to seek elsewhere? **44 decline** incline. **45 train** entice. **mermaid** siren. (In classical myth, one of a group of nymphs who lured sailors to destruction with their sweet singing.) **note** song **49 take** use **51 die** cease to live. (With a pun on "achieve sexual climax.") **52 Let . . . sink!** i.e., Love is supposed to be light and frivolous, but this experience of mine would be like drowning in love, dying thus happily. **53 reason** talk, argue **54 mated** amazed, confounded. (With quibble on the sense of "matched with a wife.") **56 by** near. **58 As . . . night** i.e., If I were to close my eyes or avert my gaze from you, I might as well be in darkness, unable to see at all. **64 My sole . . . claim** my sole heaven on earth and my claim on heaven hereafter. **66 Call . . . thee** i.e., You and I are indivisible, as it were, through the bond of spiritual love, and therefore the sister I love is yourself.

Thee will I love and with thee lead my life;
Thou hast no husband yet, nor I no wife.
Give me thy hand.

LUCIANA Oh, soft, sir! Hold you still.
I'll fetch my sister, to get her good will. *Exit.*

Enter Dromio [*of*] *Syracuse,* [*running*].

S. ANTIPHOLUS Why, how now, Dromio, where runn'st thou so fast?

S. DROMIO Do you know me, sir? Am I Dromio? Am I your man? Am I myself?

S. ANTIPHOLUS Thou art Dromio, thou art my man, thou art thyself.

S. DROMIO I am an ass, I am a woman's man, and besides myself.

S. ANTIPHOLUS What woman's man? And how besides thyself?

S. DROMIO Marry, sir, besides myself I am due to a woman: one that claims me, one that haunts me, one that will have me.

S. ANTIPHOLUS What claim lays she to thee?

S. DROMIO Marry, sir, such claim as you would lay to your horse; and she would have me as a beast—not that, I being a beast, she would have me, but that she being a very beastly creature, lays claim to me.

S. ANTIPHOLUS What is she?

S. DROMIO A very reverend body; ay, such a one as a man may not speak of without he say "sir-reverence." I have but lean luck in the match, and yet is she a wondrous fat marriage.

S. ANTIPHOLUS How dost thou mean, a fat marriage?

S. DROMIO Marry, sir, she's the kitchen wench, and all grease, and I know not what use to put her to but to make a lamp of her and run from her by her own light. I warrant her rags and the tallow in them will burn a Poland winter. If she lives till doomsday, she'll burn a week longer than the whole world.

S. ANTIPHOLUS What complexion is she of?

S. DROMIO Swart like my shoe, but her face nothing like so clean kept. For why? She sweats a man may go over shoes in the grime of it.

S. ANTIPHOLUS That's a fault that water will mend.

S. DROMIO No, sir, 'tis in grain. Noah's flood could not do it.

S. ANTIPHOLUS What's her name?

S. DROMIO Nell, sir; but her name and three quarters—that's an ell and three quarters—will not measure her from hip to hip.

S. ANTIPHOLUS Then she bears some breadth?

S. DROMIO No longer from head to foot than from hip to hip. She is spherical, like a globe. I could find out countries in her.

S. ANTIPHOLUS In what part of her body stands Ireland?

S. DROMIO Marry, sir, in her buttocks. I found it out by the bogs.

S. ANTIPHOLUS Where Scotland?

S. DROMIO I found it by the barrenness, hard in the palm of the hand.

S. ANTIPHOLUS Where France?

S. DROMIO In her forehead, armed and reverted, making war against her heir.

S. ANTIPHOLUS Where England?

S. DROMIO I looked for the chalky cliffs, but I could find no whiteness in them. But I guess it stood in her chin, by the salt rheum that ran between France and it.

S. ANTIPHOLUS Where Spain?

S. DROMIO Faith, I saw it not, but I felt it hot in her breath.

S. ANTIPHOLUS Where America, the Indies?

S. DROMIO Oh, sir, upon her nose, all o'er embellished with rubies, carbuncles, sapphires, declining their rich aspect to the hot breath of Spain, who sent whole armadas of carracks to be ballast at her nose.

S. ANTIPHOLUS Where stood Belgia, the Netherlands?

S. DROMIO Oh, sir, I did not look so low. To conclude, this drudge or diviner laid claim to me, called me Dromio, swore I was assured to her, told me what privy marks I had about me—as the mark of my shoulder, the mole in my neck, the great wart on my left arm, that I amazed ran from her as a witch.
And, I think, if my breast had not been made of
faith and my heart of steel,
She had transformed me to a curtal dog and made
me turn i'the wheel.

S. ANTIPHOLUS
Go, hie thee presently; post to the road.

70 good will approval. (This is perhaps a mere excuse, but it may be a sign she is attracted.) **77–8 besides myself** also myself. (With a pun on the sense of "out of my mind.") **79 besides** (A further quibble: "in addition to.") **86 a beast** (With a pun on "abased," reflecting Elizabethan pronunciation of beast as "baste.") **91 without** unless. **"sir-reverence"** i.e.; save your reverence, an expression used in apology for the remark that follows it. **92 lean** poor, meager **96 grease** (With a pun on "grace," reflecting Elizabethan pronunciation.) **98–9 a Poland winter** i.e., a long, cold winter. **102 Swart** Swarthy, dark **103 She sweats a man** She sweats so much that a man **103–4 over shoes** ankle-deep. (Her sweat makes mud of her face's grime, so deep that a man would be ankle deep in it.) **106 in grain** indelible, fast dyed. **109 Nell** (The maidservant appearing in 3.1 is named Luce; usually the two are assumed to be one person.)

110 an ell forty-five inches. (With a pun on "a Nell.") **120 barrenness** callused hardness and dryness. (Perhaps with a pun on "barren ness," a barren promontory.) **123 reverted** in rebellion. (See the Introduction for an explanation of the reference to the French war.) **124 heir** (With a pun on "hair" and a joke about syphilis as causing baldness.) **126 chalky cliffs** i.e., her teeth. (In his geographic metaphor, Dromio of Syracuse identifies white teeth with the cliffs of Dover.) **127 them** i.e., her teeth. **128 salt rheum** nasal discharge. (Here Dromio jokingly makes a comparison to the English Channel.) **133–6 Oh . . . nose** (Dromio imagines whole fleets of Spanish galleons taking on ballast at this woman's nose, embellished as it is with pimples and boils that resemble the treasures pillaged by the Spanish in the Americas. A *carbuncle* is both a precious jewel and a pimple. The eruptions on her nose pay homage (*declining their rich aspect*) to the hot breath of Spain, suggesting both her foul breath and the hot importunity of the Spanish.) **138 so low** (A joke about the female genitalia. The Netherlands were known as the Low Countries.) **139 diviner** sorceress **140 assured** affianced **141 privy** secret, personal **145 curtal dog** dog with a docked tail. (And hence not used in hunting.) **turn i'the wheel** run in a wheel to turn the spit. **146 hie thee presently** hasten at once. **post** hasten. **road** harbor, roadstead.

An if the wind blow any way from shore, 147
I will not harbor in this town tonight.
If any bark put forth, come to the mart, 149
Where I will walk till thou return to me.
If everyone knows us and we know none,
'Tis time, I think, to trudge, pack, and be gone. 152

S. DROMIO
As from a bear a man would run for life,
So fly I from her that would be my wife. *Exit.*

S. ANTIPHOLUS
There's none but witches do inhabit here,
And therefore 'tis high time that I were hence.
She that doth call me husband, even my soul
Doth for a wife abhor. But her fair sister,
Possessed with such a gentle sovereign grace, 159
Of such enchanting presence and discourse,
Hath almost made me traitor to myself.
But, lest myself be guilty to self-wrong, 162
I'll stop mine ears against the mermaid's song.

Enter Angelo with the chain.

ANGELO
Master Antipholus—

S. ANTIPHOLUS
Ay, that's my name.

ANGELO
I know it well, sir. Lo, here's the chain.
I thought to have ta'en you at the Porcupine; 166
The chain unfinished made me stay thus long.
[*He presents the chain.*]

S. ANTIPHOLUS
What is your will that I shall do with this?

ANGELO
What please yourself, sir. I have made it for you. 169

S. ANTIPHOLUS
Made it for me, sir? I bespoke it not. 170

ANGELO
Not once, nor twice, but twenty times you have.
Go home with it and please your wife withal,
And soon at suppertime I'll visit you
And then receive my money for the chain.

S. ANTIPHOLUS
I pray you, sir, receive the money now,
For fear you ne'er see chain nor money more.

ANGELO
You are a merry man, sir. Fare you well. *Exit.*

S. ANTIPHOLUS
What I should think of this, I cannot tell.
But this I think: there's no man is so vain 179
That would refuse so fair an offered chain.
I see a man here needs not live by shifts, 181
When in the streets he meets such golden gifts.
I'll to the mart and there for Dromio stay;
If any ship put out, then straight away. *Exit.* 184

✤

147 An if If **149 bark** ship **152 pack** depart **159 Possessed with** having possession of **162 to** of **166 ta'en** overtaken, met up with **169 What please yourself** Whatever you please **170 bespoke** requested **179 vain** foolish **181 shifts** stratagems, tricks **184 straight** at once

4.1

Enter a [*Second*] *Merchant,* [*Angelo the*] *goldsmith, and an Officer.*

SECOND MERCHANT [*to Angelo*]
You know since Pentecost the sum is due, 1
And since I have not much importuned you, 2
Nor now I had not, but that I am bound
To Persia and want guilders for my voyage. 4
Therefore make present satisfaction, 5
Or I'll attach you by this officer. 6

ANGELO
Even just the sum that I do owe to you 7
Is growing to me by Antipholus, 8
And in the instant that I met with you
He had of me a chain. At five o'clock
I shall receive the money for the same.
Pleaseth you walk with me down to his house, 12
I will discharge my bond and thank you too.

Enter Antipholus [*and*] *Dromio of Ephesus from the Courtesan's.*

OFFICER
That labor may you save. See where he comes.

E. ANTIPHOLUS [*to Dromio of Ephesus*]
While I go to the goldsmith's house, go thou
And buy a rope's end; that will I bestow 16
Among my wife and her confederates
For locking me out of my doors by day.
But soft! I see the goldsmith. Get thee gone. 19
Buy thou a rope and bring it home to me.

E. DROMIO
I buy a thousand pound a year! I buy a rope! 21
Exit Dromio.

E. ANTIPHOLUS [*to Angelo*]
A man is well holp up that trusts to you! 22
I promisèd your presence and the chain, 23
But neither chain nor goldsmith came to me.
Belike you thought our love would last too long 25
If it were chained together, and therefore came not.

ANGELO [*showing a paper*]
Saving your merry humor, here's the note 27
How much your chain weighs to the utmost carat,
The fineness of the gold and chargeful fashion, 29
Which doth amount to three odd ducats more 30
Than I stand debted to this gentleman.

4.1. Location: The street.
1 Pentecost the commemoration of the descent of the Holy Ghost upon the Apostles, celebrated on the seventh Sunday after Easter **2 since** since then. **importuned** harassed with demands, bothered **4 want guilders** lack money **5 present satisfaction** immediate payment **6 attach** arrest, seize **7 Even just** Precisely **8 growing** due, accruing **12 Pleaseth** May it please **16 a rope's end** a fragment of rope (to be used as a whip). **bestow** employ **19 soft** i.e., wait a minute. **21 I . . . rope!** (An obscure line. Dromio may mean that in buying a rope as he is bidden, he is purchasing for himself a thousand poundings or beatings a year.) **22 holp up** helped **23 promisèd** was promised **25 Belike** Perhaps **27 Saving** With respect for **29 chargeful fashion** expensive workmanship **30 ducats** gold coins (of several European countries)

I pray you, see him presently discharged,
For he is bound to sea and stays but for it.

E. ANTIPHOLUS
I am not furnished with the present money;
Besides, I have some business in the town.
Good signor, take the stranger to my house,
And with you take the chain, and bid my wife
Disburse the sum on the receipt thereof.
Perchance I will be there as soon as you.

ANGELO
Then you will bring the chain to her yourself?

E. ANTIPHOLUS
No, bear it with you, lest I come not time enough.

ANGELO
Well, sir, I will. Have you the chain about you?

E. ANTIPHOLUS
An if I have not, sir, I hope you have,
Or else you may return without your money.

ANGELO
Nay, come, I pray you, sir, give me the chain.
Both wind and tide stays for this gentleman,
And I, too blame, have held him here too long.

E. ANTIPHOLUS
Good Lord! You use this dalliance to excuse
Your breach of promise to the Porcupine.
I should have chid you for not bringing it,
But, like a shrew, you first begin to brawl.

SECOND MERCHANT [*to Angelo*]
The hour steals on. I pray you, sir, dispatch.

ANGELO
You hear how he importunes me. The chain!

E. ANTIPHOLUS
Why, give it to my wife and fetch your money.

ANGELO
Come, come, you know I gave it you even now.
Either send the chain or send me by some token.

E. ANTIPHOLUS
Fie, now you run this humor out of breath.
Come, where's the chain? I pray you, let me see it.

SECOND MERCHANT
My business cannot brook this dalliance.
Good sir, say whe'er you'll answer me or no.
If not, I'll leave him to the officer.

E. ANTIPHOLUS
I answer you? What should I answer you?

ANGELO
The money that you owe me for the chain.

E. ANTIPHOLUS
I owe you none till I receive the chain.

ANGELO
You know I gave it you half an hour since.

E. ANTIPHOLUS
You gave me none. You wrong me much to say so.

ANGELO
You wrong me more, sir, in denying it.
Consider how it stands upon my credit.

SECOND MERCHANT
Well, officer, arrest him at my suit.

OFFICER [*to Angelo*]
I do, and charge you in the Duke's name to obey me.

ANGELO [*to Antipholus of Ephesus*]
This touches me in reputation.
Either consent to pay this sum for me,
Or I attach you by this officer.

E. ANTIPHOLUS
Consent to pay thee that I never had?
Arrest me, foolish fellow, if thou dar'st.

ANGELO
Here is thy fee. Arrest him, officer. [*He gives money.*]
I would not spare my brother in this case
If he should scorn me so apparently.

OFFICER [*to Antipholus of Ephesus*]
I do arrest you, sir. You hear the suit.

E. ANTIPHOLUS
I do obey thee till I give thee bail.—
But, sirrah, you shall buy this sport as dear
As all the metal in your shop will answer.

ANGELO
Sir, sir, I shall have law in Ephesus,
To your notorious shame, I doubt it not.

Enter Dromio [*of*] *Syracuse, from the bay.*

S. DROMIO
Master, there's a bark of Epidamnum
That stays but till her owner comes aboard,
And then she bears away. Our freightage, sir,
I have conveyed aboard, and I have bought
The oil, the balsamum, and aqua vitae.
The ship is in her trim; the merry wind
Blows fair from land; they stay for naught at all
But for their owner, master, and yourself.

E. ANTIPHOLUS
How now? A madman? Why, thou peevish sheep,
What ship of Epidamnum stays for me?

S. DROMIO
A ship you sent me to, to hire waftage.

E. ANTIPHOLUS
Thou drunken slave, I sent thee for a rope
And told thee to what purpose and what end.

S. DROMIO
You sent me for a rope's end as soon.
You sent me to the bay, sir, for a bark.

E. ANTIPHOLUS
I will debate this matter at more leisure
And teach your ears to list me with more heed.

32 discharged paid **34 present** available **41 time enough** in time. **47 too blame** too blameworthy **48 dalliance** idle delay **50 chid** chided **53 importunes** solicits urgently **56 send me . . . token** send me with some object of yours authorizing me to receive payment. **57 run . . . breath** i.e., carry the joke too far. **59 brook** endure **60 whe'er** whether. **answer me** pay, give me satisfaction

68 how . . . credit how it affects my reputation for honesty. **69 at my suit** on my petition. **71 touches** injures, affects **78 apparently** openly. **84.1** ***from the bay*** i.e., presumably from a side entry which we understand to represent the direction of the bay. **89 balsamum** balm, a fragrant and healing resin. **aqua vitae** strong liquor. **90 in her trim** rigged and ready to sail **93 peevish** silly. **sheep** (With play on *ship* in next line.) **95 waftage** passage. **98 a rope's end** i.e., a whipping, or perhaps a hangman's noose; see line 16 and note **101 list** listen to

To Adriana, villain, hie thee straight. [*He gives a key.*]
Give her this key, and tell her, in the desk
That's covered o'er with Turkish tapestry
There is a purse of ducats; let her send it.
Tell her I am arrested in the street,
And that shall bail me. Hie thee, slave, begone!
On, officer, to prison till it come.
Exeunt [*all but Dromio of Syracuse*].

S. DROMIO
To Adriana! That is where we dined,
Where Dowsabel did claim me for her husband.
She is too big, I hope, for me to compass.
Thither I must, although against my will,
For servants must their masters' minds fulfill. *Exit.*

✤

[4.2]

Enter Adriana and Luciana.

ADRIANA
Ah, Luciana, did he tempt thee so?
Mightst thou perceive austerely in his eye
That he did plead in earnest, yea or no?
Looked he or red or pale, or sad or merrily?
What observation mad'st thou in this case
Of his heart's meteors tilting in his face?

LUCIANA
First he denied you had in him no right.

ADRIANA
He meant he did me none; the more my spite.

LUCIANA
Then swore he that he was a stranger here.

ADRIANA
And true he swore, though yet forsworn he were.

LUCIANA
Then pleaded I for you.

ADRIANA And what said he?

LUCIANA
That love I begged for you he begged of me.

ADRIANA
With what persuasion did he tempt thy love?

LUCIANA
With words that in an honest suit might move.
First he did praise my beauty, then my speech.

ADRIANA
Didst speak him fair?

LUCIANA Have patience, I beseech.

ADRIANA
I cannot, nor I will not, hold me still.
My tongue, though not my heart, shall have his will.
He is deformèd, crooked, old, and sere,
Ill faced, worse bodied, shapeless everywhere;
Vicious, ungentle, foolish, blunt, unkind,
Stigmatical in making, worse in mind.

LUCIANA
Who would be jealous then of such a one?
No evil lost is wailed when it is gone.

ADRIANA
Ah, but I think him better than I say,
And yet would herein others' eyes were worse.
Far from her nest the lapwing cries away;
My heart prays for him, though my tongue do curse.

Enter Dromio of Syracuse, [*running, with the key*].

S. DROMIO
Here, go—the desk, the purse! Sweet, now, make
haste.

LUCIANA
How hast thou lost thy breath?

S. DROMIO By running fast.

ADRIANA
Where is thy master, Dromio? Is he well?

S. DROMIO
No, he's in Tartar limbo, worse than hell.
A devil in an everlasting garment hath him,
One whose hard heart is buttoned up with steel;
A fiend, a fairy, pitiless and rough;
A wolf, nay, worse, a fellow all in buff;
A back friend, a shoulder clapper, one that
countermands
The passages of alleys, creeks, and narrow lands;
A hound that runs counter and yet draws dryfoot
well;
One that before the judgment carries poor souls to
hell.

ADRIANA Why, man, what is the matter?

S. DROMIO
I do not know the matter. He is 'rested on the case.

ADRIANA
What, is he arrested? Tell me at whose suit.

S. DROMIO
I know not at whose suit he is arrested well;

110 Dowsabel (Used ironically for Nell or Luce; derived from the French *douce et belle*, "gentle and beautiful.") **111 compass** achieve. (With added meaning of "put my arms around.")
4.2. Location: The house of Antipholus of Ephesus.
2 austerely objectively, strictly **4 or red** either red-faced. **or sad** either sad **6 meteors tilting** i.e., passions warring. (The next line begins a passage of stichomythia, dialogue in which each speech consists of a single line, much used in classical drama.) **7 no** i.e., any **8 spite** vexation, grief. **10 true . . . were** i.e., though no foreigner, he spoke true in the sense that he is a stranger to my heart and thus false to his vows. **14 honest** honorable **16 Didst . . . fair?** Did you encourage him?

18 his its **19 sere** withered **20 shapeless** misshapen **22 Stigmatical in making** deformed in appearance **26 And . . . worse** i.e., and yet I wish that others would look disapprovingly at his behavior, or would find him less attractive. **27 Far . . . away** i.e., I am like the lapwing (a bird that flies away from its nest to divert the attention of intruders from its young) in that what I say is very different from what I feel **29 Sweet** (An inoffensive term of endearment. Some editors emend it to *Sweat.*) **32 Tartar limbo** Tartarus or pagan hell, worse than Christian hell **33 everlasting garment** i.e., buff leather attire of the police officer; everlasting both because of its durability and because of the joke about perpetual durance in limbo or jail. (*Everlasting* is itself the name of a coarse woolen fabric sometimes used for the uniforms of petty officers of justice.) **35 fairy** i.e., malevolent spirit **37–9 one . . . well** i.e., one who prohibits the movement of people in alleys and narrow passages; a hound that follows a trail in the direction opposite to that which the game has taken (with a quibble on *counter*, a prison) and skillfully tracks game by the mere scent of the footprint **40 judgment** legal decision. (With a pun on "Judgment Day," continuing the joke about jail as Tartar limbo.) **42 'rested on the case** arrested in a lawsuit.

But is in a suit of buff which 'rested him, that can I tell.
Will you send him, mistress, redemption, the money in his desk?

ADRIANA
Go fetch it, sister. *Exit Luciana.*
This I wonder at,
That he, unknown to me, should be in debt.
Tell me, was he arrested on a band?

S. DROMIO
Not on a band, but on a stronger thing:
A chain, a chain! Do you not hear it ring?

ADRIANA What, the chain?

S. DROMIO
No, no, the bell. 'Tis time that I were gone.
It was two ere I left him, and now the clock strikes one.

ADRIANA
The hours come back! That did I never hear.

S. DROMIO
Oh, yes, if any hour meet a sergeant, 'a turns back for very fear.

ADRIANA
As if Time were in debt. How fondly dost thou reason!

S. DROMIO
Time is a very bankrupt and owes more than he's worth to season.
Nay, he's a thief too. Have you not heard men say
That Time comes stealing on by night and day?
If 'a be in debt and theft, and a sergeant in the way,
Hath he not reason to turn back an hour in a day?

Enter Luciana [with the purse].

ADRIANA
Go, Dromio, there's the money. Bear it straight,
And bring thy master home immediately.
[Exit Dromio, with the purse.]
Come, sister. I am pressed down with conceit—
Conceit, my comfort and my injury. *Exeunt.*

✤

[4.3]

Enter Antipholus of Syracuse, [wearing the chain].

S. ANTIPHOLUS
There's not a man I meet but doth salute me
As if I were their well-acquainted friend,
And everyone doth call me by my name.
Some tender money to me; some invite me;
Some other give me thanks for kindnesses;
Some offer me commodities to buy.
Even now a tailor called me in his shop
And showed me silks that he had bought for me
And therewithal took measure of my body.
Sure, these are but imaginary wiles,
And Lapland sorcerers inhabit here.

Enter Dromio of Syracuse, [with the purse].

S. DROMIO Master, here's the gold you sent me for. What, have you got the picture of old Adam new-appareled?

S. ANTIPHOLUS What gold is this? What Adam dost thou mean?

S. DROMIO Not that Adam that kept the Paradise, but that Adam that keeps the prison; he that goes in the calf's skin that was killed for the Prodigal; he that came behind you, sir, like an evil angel, and bid you forsake your liberty.

S. ANTIPHOLUS I understand thee not.

S. DROMIO No? Why, 'tis a plain case: he that went, like a bass viol, in a case of leather, the man, sir, that, when gentlemen are tired, gives them a sob and 'rests them; he, sir, that takes pity on decayed men and gives them suits of durance; he that sets up his rest to do more exploits with his mace than a morris-pike.

S. ANTIPHOLUS What, thou mean'st an officer?

S. DROMIO Ay, sir, the sergeant of the band; he that brings any man to answer it that breaks his band; one that thinks a man always going to bed, and says, "God give you good rest!"

S. ANTIPHOLUS Well, sir, there rest in your foolery. Is there any ships puts forth tonight? May we be gone?

S. DROMIO Why, sir, I brought you word an hour since that the bark *Expedition* put forth tonight, and then were you hindered by the sergeant to tarry for the hoy *Delay.* Here are the angels that you sent for to deliver you. *[He gives the purse.]*

45 suit (1) suit of clothes (2) lawsuit **49 band** bond. (But Dromio puns on the sense "neckband" in the next line.) **54 one** (*One* and *on* were pronounced very much alike; the word here rhymes with *gone.*) **56 if . . . fear** Time appears to go backwards, like a person in debt (an "over,"punning on *hour*), or a whore (pronounced like *hour*) running away from an arresting officer. **'a** it, she, he **57 fondly** foolishly **58 Time . . . season** i.e., Having overspent itself, Time is so much in debt that it is of little worth when it comes to fruition. (With a probable pun on *season* and *seisin*, legal possession.) **to season** to bring to fruition, make acceptable. **61 theft** i.e., a thief. **in the way** lying in wait to arrest **63 straight** straightaway, immediately **65 conceit** imaginings **66 Conceit . . . injury** (Adriana is filled with imaginings, both of the wrongs she has suffered and the comfort she can provide her wayward husband.)
4.3. Location: The street.

4 tender offer **5 other** others **10 imaginary wiles** tricks of the imagination **11 Lapland sorcerers** (Lapland was said to surpass all nations in the practice of witchcraft and sorcery.) **13–14 What . . . new-appareled?** (Dromio wonders how his master has managed to evade the arresting officer who apprehended Antipholus (of Ephesus, not Syracuse) in 4.1. *New-appareled* plays on [1] a new suit of clothes [2] a new lawsuit. Adam, *new-appareled* in beasts' skins after the fall of man [Genesis 3:21], reminds Dromio of the correcting officer in his buff leather jerkin or jacket.) **16 kept the Paradise** (This sounds like an allusion to an inn of which the innkeeper was named Adam.) **18 calf's . . . Prodigal** (An allusion to the fatted calf killed for the Prodigal Son's return; see Luke 15:23.) **23 case** (With a pun on *plain case*, line 22.) **24 a sob** (1) a sob of pity; see next line (2) a breathing-space given to a horse to allow it to recover from its exertions **24–5 'rests them** (1) arrests them (2) gives them respite **25 decayed** financially ruined. (With a pun on the usual sense.) **26 durance** a kind of long-wearing cloth like buff. (With a pun on "imprisonment.") **sets . . . rest** stakes his all. (With a continuing pun on *'rest*; the metaphor of staking all one's venture is from the game of primero.) **27 mace** staff of office carried by a constable. **morris-pike** a weapon, supposedly of Moorish origin **29 band** troop **30 band** bond **32 rest** (Continuing the wordplay on *arrest.*) **37 hoy** a small coastal vessel **38 angels** gold coins worth about ten shillings

S. ANTIPHOLUS
The fellow is distract, and so am I,
And here we wander in illusions.
Some blessèd power deliver us from hence!

Enter a Courtesan.

COURTESAN
Well met, well met, Master Antipholus.
I see, sir, you have found the goldsmith now.
Is that the chain you promised me today?

S. ANTIPHOLUS
Satan, avoid! I charge thee, tempt me not.

S. DROMIO Master, is this Mistress Satan?

S. ANTIPHOLUS It is the devil.

S. DROMIO Nay, she is worse, she is the devil's dam, and here she comes in the habit of a light wench; and thereof comes that the wenches say, "God damn me," that's as much to say, "God make me a light wench." It is written they appear to men like angels of light; light is an effect of fire, and fire will burn; ergo, light wenches will burn. Come not near her.

COURTESAN
Your man and you are marvelous merry, sir.
Will you go with me? We'll mend our dinner here.

S. DROMIO Master, if you do, expect spoon meat, or bespeak a long spoon.

S. ANTIPHOLUS Why, Dromio?

S. DROMIO Marry, he must have a long spoon that must eat with the devil.

S. ANTIPHOLUS [*to the Courtesan*]
Avoid then, fiend! What tell'st thou me of supping?
Thou art, as you are all, a sorceress.
I conjure thee to leave me and be gone.

COURTESAN
Give me the ring of mine you had at dinner
Or, for my diamond, the chain you promised,
And I'll be gone, sir, and not trouble you.

S. DROMIO
Some devils ask but the parings of one's nail,
A rush, a hair, a drop of blood, a pin,
A nut, a cherrystone;
But she, more covetous, would have a chain.
Master, be wise. An if you give it her,
The devil will shake her chain and fright us with it.

COURTESAN
I pray you, sir, my ring, or else the chain!
I hope you do not mean to cheat me so?

S. ANTIPHOLUS
Avaunt, thou witch!—Come, Dromio, let us go.

S. DROMIO
"Fly pride," says the peacock. Mistress, that you
know. *Exeunt* [*Antipholus and Dromio of Syracuse*].

COURTESAN
Now, out of doubt Antipholus is mad,
Else would he never so demean himself.
A ring he hath of mine worth forty ducats,
And for the same he promised me a chain;
Both one and other he denies me now.
The reason that I gather he is mad,
Besides this present instance of his rage,
Is a mad tale he told today at dinner
Of his own doors being shut against his entrance.
Belike his wife, acquainted with his fits,
On purpose shut the doors against his way.
My way is now to hie home to his house
And tell his wife that, being lunatic,
He rushed into my house and took perforce
My ring away. This course I fittest choose,
For forty ducats is too much to lose. [*Exit.*]

✤

[4.4]

Enter Antipholus of Ephesus with a Jailer [*or Officer*].

E. ANTIPHOLUS
Fear me not, man, I will not break away.
I'll give thee ere I leave thee so much money
To warrant thee as I am 'rested for.
My wife is in a wayward mood today
And will not lightly trust the messenger.
That I should be attached in Ephesus,
I tell you, 'twill sound harshly in her ears.

Enter Dromio of Ephesus with a rope's end.

Here comes my man. I think he brings the money.—
How now, sir? Have you that I sent you for?

E. DROMIO [*giving the rope*]
Here's that, I warrant you, will pay them all.

E. ANTIPHOLUS But where's the money?

E. DROMIO
Why, sir, I gave the money for the rope.

E. ANTIPHOLUS
Five hundred ducats, villain, for a rope?

E. DROMIO
I'll serve you, sir, five hundred at the rate.

40 distract deranged, distracted **46 avoid!** begone! (See Matthew 4:10.) **49 dam** mother **50 habit** demeanor, manner; also, dress. **light** wanton **51 damn me** i.e., dam me, make me a mother. **53 angels of light** (See 2 Corinthians 11:14, where Satan is referred to as transformed into an angel of light.) **54 ergo** therefore **55 will burn** i.e., will transmit venereal disease. **57 mend** supplement, complete **58 spoon meat** food for infants, hence delicacies **59 bespeak** order **61–2 he . . . devil** (A proverbial idea.) **63 What** Why **73 An If** If **77 Avaunt** Begone

78 "Fly . . . peacock (The peacock, symbol of vanity, warns hypocritically against pride; similarly, in Dromio's view, this cheating courtesan accuses Antipholus of cheating her. *Pride* can also mean "sexual desire.") **80 demean** conduct **85 rage** madness **88 Belike** Presumably **90 My way** My best course **92 perforce** forcibly **93 fittest** as most appropriate

4.4 Location: The street.

3 warrant thee guarantee your security **4 wayward** perverse, ill tempered **5 lightly trust** easily believe **6 attached** arrested **14 I'll . . . rate** I'll supply you with five hundred ropes, sir, for that amount.

E. ANTIPHOLUS
To what end did I bid thee hie thee home?

E. DROMIO To a rope's end, sir; and to that end am I returned.

E. ANTIPHOLUS
And to that end, sir, I will welcome you.
[*He starts to beat Dromio of Ephesus.*]

OFFICER Good sir, be patient.

E. DROMIO Nay, 'tis for me to be patient. I am in adversity.

OFFICER Good now, hold thy tongue.

E. DROMIO Nay, rather persuade him to hold his hands.

E. ANTIPHOLUS Thou whoreson, senseless villain!

E. DROMIO I would I were senseless, sir, that I might not feel your blows.

E. ANTIPHOLUS Thou art sensible in nothing but blows, and so is an ass.

E. DROMIO I am an ass, indeed; you may prove it by my long ears. I have served him from the hour of my nativity to this instant and have nothing at his hands for my service but blows. When I am cold, he heats me with beating; when I am warm, he cools me with beating. I am waked with it when I sleep, raised with it when I sit, driven out of doors with it when I go from home, welcomed home with it when I return. Nay, I bear it on my shoulders, as a beggar wont her brat, and I think when he hath lamed me I shall beg with it from door to door.

Enter Adriana, Luciana, Courtesan, and a schoolmaster called Pinch.

E. ANTIPHOLUS
Come, go along. My wife is coming yonder.

E. DROMIO [*to Adriana*] Mistress, *respice finem*, respect your end; or rather, to prophesy like the parrot, "Beware the rope's end."

E. ANTIPHOLUS Wilt thou still talk? *Beats Dromio.*

COURTESAN [*to Adriana*]
How say you now? Is not your husband mad?

ADRIANA
His incivility confirms no less.—
Good Doctor Pinch, you are a conjurer;
Establish him in his true sense again,
And I will please you what you will demand.

LUCIANA
Alas, how fiery and how sharp he looks!

COURTESAN
Mark how he trembles in his ecstasy!

PINCH [*to Antipholus*]
Give me your hand, and let me feel your pulse.

E. ANTIPHOLUS [*striking him*]
There is my hand, and let it feel your ear.

PINCH
I charge thee, Satan, housed within this man,
To yield possession to my holy prayers
And to thy state of darkness hie thee straight!
I conjure thee by all the saints in heaven!

E. ANTIPHOLUS
Peace, doting wizard, peace! I am not mad.

ADRIANA
Oh, that thou wert not, poor distressèd soul!

E. ANTIPHOLUS
You minion, you, are these your customers?
Did this companion with the saffron face
Revel and feast it at my house today,
Whilst upon me the guilty doors were shut
And I denied to enter in my house?

ADRIANA
Oh, husband, God doth know you dined at home,
Where would you had remained until this time,
Free from these slanders and this open shame!

E. ANTIPHOLUS
Dined at home? [*To E. Dromio*] Thou villain, what
sayest thou?

E. DROMIO
Sir, sooth to say, you did not dine at home.

E. ANTIPHOLUS
Were not my doors locked up and I shut out?

E. DROMIO
Pardie, your doors were locked and you shut out.

E. ANTIPHOLUS
And did not she herself revile me there?

E. DROMIO
Sans fable, she herself reviled you there.

E. ANTIPHOLUS
Did not her kitchen maid rail, taunt, and scorn me?

E. DROMIO
Certes, she did. The kitchen vestal scorned you.

E. ANTIPHOLUS
And did not I in rage depart from thence?

E. DROMIO
In verity you did. My bones bears witness,
That since have felt the vigor of his rage.

ADRIANA
Is't good to soothe him in these contraries?

PINCH
It is no shame. The fellow finds his vein,
And yielding to him humors well his frenzy.

22 Good now Pray you **27 sensible in** sensitive to; also, made sensible by **30 ears** (With a pun on "years"; Dromio says he is an ass for having served his master so long.) **37 wont** is accustomed to (bear) **41 *respice finem*** consider your end. (A pious sentiment on the brevity of life and the approach of death; with a play on *respice funem*, "consider the hangman's rope." A parrot might be taught to say *respice finem*, or perhaps "rope.") **47 Doctor** (An honorific term for any learned person. Pinch is not a medical doctor.) **conjurer** (Being able to speak Latin, Pinch could conjure spirits.) **48 true sense** right mind **49 please** pay **50 sharp** angry **51 ecstasy** fit, frenzy.

60 minion hussy, i.e., Adriana **61 companion** fellow, i.e., Pinch. **saffron** yellow **66 would** I wish **71 Pardie** (An oath, from the French *pardieu*, "by God.") **73 Sans** Without **75 Certes** Certainly. **kitchen vestal** (Ironically, her task was like that of the vestal virgins of ancient Rome, to keep the fire burning.) **79 soothe** encourage, humor. **contraries** denials, lies. **80–1 It . . . frenzy** i.e., Such a humoring of Antipholus is not reprehensible. Dromio grasps the nature of his master's madness, and giving in this way can soothe the patient's frenzy.

E. ANTIPHOLUS [*to Adriana*]
Thou hast suborned the goldsmith to arrest me. 82

ADRIANA
Alas, I sent you money to redeem you
By Dromio here, who came in haste for it.

E. DROMIO
Money by me? Heart and good will you might, 85
But surely, master, not a rag of money. 86

E. ANTIPHOLUS
Went'st not thou to her for a purse of ducats?

ADRIANA
He came to me, and I delivered it.

LUCIANA
And I am witness with her that she did.

E. DROMIO
God and the rope maker bear me witness
That I was sent for nothing but a rope!

PINCH [*to Adriana*]
Mistress, both man and master is possessed;
I know it by their pale and deadly looks. 93
They must be bound and laid in some dark room. 94

E. ANTIPHOLUS [*to Adriana*]
Say wherefore didst thou lock me forth today? 95
[*To E. Dromio*] And why dost thou deny the bag of gold?

ADRIANA
I did not, gentle husband, lock thee forth.

E. DROMIO
And, gentle master, I received no gold.
But I confess, sir, that we were locked out.

ADRIANA
Dissembling villain, thou speak'st false in both.

E. ANTIPHOLUS
Dissembling harlot, thou art false in all
And art confederate with a damnèd pack 102
To make a loathsome abject scorn of me! 103
But with these nails I'll pluck out those false eyes
That would behold in me this shameful sport.
[*He threatens Adriana.*]

ADRIANA
Oh, bind him, bind him! Let him not come near me. 106

Enter three or four, and offer to bind him. He strives.

PINCH
More company! The fiend is strong within him.

LUCIANA
Ay me, poor man, how pale and wan he looks!

E. ANTIPHOLUS
What, will you murder me?—Thou jailer, thou,
I am thy prisoner. Wilt thou suffer them
To make a rescue?

OFFICER Masters, let him go. 111
He is my prisoner, and you shall not have him.

PINCH
Go bind his man, for he is frantic too.
[*They bind Dromio of Ephesus.*]

ADRIANA
What wilt thou do, thou peevish officer? 114
Hast thou delight to see a wretched man
Do outrage and displeasure to himself? 116

OFFICER
He is my prisoner. If I let him go,
The debt he owes will be required of me.

ADRIANA
I will discharge thee ere I go from thee. 119
Bear me forthwith unto his creditor,
And, knowing how the debt grows, I will pay it. 121
Good Master Doctor, see him safe conveyed
Home to my house. Oh, most unhappy day! 123

E. ANTIPHOLUS Oh, most unhappy strumpet!

E. DROMIO
Master, I am here entered in bond for you. 125

E. ANTIPHOLUS
Out on thee, villain! Wherefore dost thou mad me? 126

E. DROMIO Will you be bound for nothing? Be mad, good master; cry, "The devil!"

LUCIANA
God help, poor souls, how idly do they talk! 129

ADRIANA
Go bear him hence. Sister, go you with me. 130
Exeunt [*Pinch and his assistants, carrying off Antipholus and Dromio of Ephesus*]. *Manent Officer, Adriana, Luciana, Courtesan.*
Say now, whose suit is he arrested at?

OFFICER
One Angelo, a goldsmith. Do you know him?

ADRIANA
I know the man. What is the sum he owes?

OFFICER
Two hundred ducats.

ADRIANA Say, how grows it due?

OFFICER
Due for a chain your husband had of him.

ADRIANA
He did bespeak a chain for me, but had it not. 136

COURTESAN
Whenas your husband all in rage today 137
Came to my house and took away my ring—
The ring I saw upon his finger now—
Straight after did I meet him with a chain.

ADRIANA
It may be so, but I did never see it.—
Come, jailer, bring me where the goldsmith is.
I long to know the truth hereof at large. 143

Enter Antipholus and Dromio [*of*] *Syracuse with their rapiers drawn.*

82 suborned induced **85 Heart . . . might** You might have sent love and good wishes by me **86 rag** scrap **93 deadly** deathlike
94 bound . . . room (The regular treatment for lunacy in Shakespeare's day.) **95 forth** out. (Also in line 97.) **102 pack** i.e., of conspirators
103 abject scorn despicable object of contempt **106.1** ***offer*** attempt
111 make a rescue take a prisoner by force from legal custody.
Masters Good sirs

114 peevish silly, senseless **116 displeasure** injury, wrong **119 discharge** pay, clear the debt for **121 knowing . . . grows** when I know how the debt accrued **123 unhappy** fatal, miserable **125 entered in bond** (1) bound up, tied (2) pledged **126 mad** exasperate **129 idly** senselessly **130.2** ***Manent*** They remain onstage **136 bespeak** order
137 Whenas When **143 at large** in full, in detail.

LUCIANA
God, for thy mercy! They are loose again.

ADRIANA
And come with naked swords. Let's call more help
To have them bound again.

OFFICER
Away! They'll kill us.

Run all out. Exeunt omnes, as fast as may be, frighted. [*Antipholus and Dromio of Syracuse remain.*]

S. ANTIPHOLUS
I see these witches are afraid of swords.

S. DROMIO
She that would be your wife now ran from you.

S. ANTIPHOLUS
Come to the Centaur. Fetch our stuff from thence.
I long that we were safe and sound aboard.

S. DROMIO Faith, stay here this night. They will surely do us no harm. You saw they speak us fair, give us gold. Methinks they are such a gentle nation that, but for the mountain of mad flesh that claims marriage of me, I could find in my heart to stay here still and turn witch.

S. ANTIPHOLUS
I will not stay tonight for all the town.
Therefore, away, to get our stuff aboard. *Exeunt.*

✤

5.1

Enter the [*Second*] *Merchant and* [*Angelo*] *the goldsmith.*

ANGELO
I am sorry, sir, that I have hindered you;
But I protest he had the chain of me,
Though most dishonestly he doth deny it.

SECOND MERCHANT
How is the man esteemed here in the city?

ANGELO
Of very reverend reputation, sir,
Of credit infinite, highly beloved,
Second to none that lives here in the city.
His word might bear my wealth at any time.

SECOND MERCHANT
Speak softly. Yonder, as I think, he walks.

Enter Antipholus and Dromio [*of Syracuse*] *again,* [*Antipholus wearing the chain*].

ANGELO
'Tis so, and that self chain about his neck
Which he forswore most monstrously to have.
Good sir, draw near to me. I'll speak to him.—
Signor Antipholus, I wonder much
That you would put me to this shame and trouble
And, not without some scandal to yourself,
With circumstance and oaths so to deny
This chain which now you wear so openly.
Beside the charge, the shame, imprisonment,
You have done wrong to this my honest friend,
Who, but for staying on our controversy,
Had hoisted sail and put to sea today.
This chain you had of me. Can you deny it?

S. ANTIPHOLUS
I think I had. I never did deny it.

SECOND MERCHANT
Yes, that you did, sir, and forswore it too.

S. ANTIPHOLUS
Who heard me to deny it or forswear it?

SECOND MERCHANT
These ears of mine, thou know'st, did hear thee.
Fie on thee, wretch! 'Tis pity that thou liv'st
To walk where any honest men resort.

S. ANTIPHOLUS
Thou art a villain to impeach me thus.
I'll prove mine honor and mine honesty
Against thee presently, if thou dar'st stand.

SECOND MERCHANT
I dare, and do defy thee for a villain. *They draw.*

Enter Adriana, Luciana, [*the*] *Courtesan, and others.*

ADRIANA
Hold, hurt him not, for God sake! He is mad.
Some get within him; take his sword away.
Bind Dromio too, and bear them to my house.

S. DROMIO
Run, master, run; for God sake, take a house!
This is some priory. In, or we are spoiled!

Exeunt [*Antipholus and Dromio of Syracuse*] *to the priory.*

Enter [*Emilia, the*] *Lady Abbess.*

ABBESS
Be quiet, people. Wherefore throng you hither?

ADRIANA
To fetch my poor distracted husband hence.
Let us come in, that we may bind him fast
And bear him home for his recovery.

ANGELO
I knew he was not in his perfect wits.

SECOND MERCHANT
I am sorry now that I did draw on him.

ABBESS
How long hath this possession held the man?

ADRIANA
This week he hath been heavy, sour, sad,
And much different from the man he was;
But till this afternoon his passion

145 naked drawn **146.1** ***omnes*** all **149 stuff** goods, baggage **152 speak us fair** speak courteously to us **155 still** always
5.1. Location: Before the priory and Antipholus of Ephesus's house.
1 hindered you delayed your journey **8 might bear** is worth **10 self** same **11 forswore** denied under oath

16 circumstance details, particulars **18 charge** cost **19 honest** honorable **20 on** as a result of **29 impeach** accuse **31 presently** at once. **stand** take a fighting stance, put yourself to the test. **32 defy** challenge. **villain** base person. **34 within him** under his guard **36 take** take refuge in **37 spoiled** ruined, done for. **45 This week** All this week. **sad** melancholy

Ne'er brake into extremity of rage.

ABBESS
Hath he not lost much wealth by wreck of sea?
Buried some dear friend? Hath not else his eye
Strayed his affection in unlawful love—
A sin prevailing much in youthful men,
Who give their eyes the liberty of gazing?
Which of these sorrows is he subject to?

ADRIANA
To none of these, except it be the last,
Namely, some love that drew him oft from home.

ABBESS
You should for that have reprehended him.

ADRIANA
Why, so I did.

ABBESS Ay, but not rough enough.

ADRIANA
As roughly as my modesty would let me.

ABBESS
Haply in private.

ADRIANA And in assemblies too.

ABBESS Ay, but not enough.

ADRIANA
It was the copy of our conference.
In bed he slept not for my urging it;
At board he fed not for my urging it;
Alone, it was the subject of my theme;
In company I often glancèd it;
Still did I tell him it was vile and bad.

ABBESS
And thereof came it that the man was mad.
The venom clamors of a jealous woman
Poisons more deadly than a mad dog's tooth.
It seems his sleeps were hindered by thy railing,
And thereof comes it that his head is light.
Thou say'st his meat was sauced with thy upbraidings.
Unquiet meals make ill digestions;
Thereof the raging fire of fever bred,
And what's a fever but a fit of madness?
Thou sayest his sports were hindered by thy brawls.
Sweet recreation barred, what doth ensue
But moody and dull melancholy,
Kinsman to grim and comfortless despair,
And at her heels a huge infectious troop
Of pale distemperatures and foes to life?
In food, in sport, and life-preserving rest
To be disturbed would mad or man or beast.
The consequence is, then, thy jealous fits
Hath scared thy husband from the use of wits.

LUCIANA
She never reprehended him but mildly,
When he demeaned himself rough, rude, and wildly.
[*To Adriana*] Why bear you these rebukes and
answer not?

ADRIANA
She did betray me to my own reproof.—
Good people, enter and lay hold on him.

ABBESS
No, not a creature enters in my house.

ADRIANA
Then let your servants bring my husband forth.

ABBESS
Neither. He took this place for sanctuary,
And it shall privilege him from your hands
Till I have brought him to his wits again
Or lose my labor in assaying it.

ADRIANA
I will attend my husband, be his nurse,
Diet his sickness, for it is my office,
And will have no attorney but myself;
And therefore let me have him home with me.

ABBESS
Be patient, for I will not let him stir
Till I have used the approvèd means I have,
With wholesome syrups, drugs, and holy prayers,
To make of him a formal man again.
It is a branch and parcel of mine oath,
A charitable duty of my order.
Therefore depart and leave him here with me.

ADRIANA
I will not hence and leave my husband here;
And ill it doth beseem your holiness
To separate the husband and the wife.

ABBESS
Be quiet and depart. Thou shalt not have him. [*Exit.*]

LUCIANA [*to Adriana*]
Complain unto the Duke of this indignity.

ADRIANA
Come, go. I will fall prostrate at his feet
And never rise until my tears and prayers
Have won His Grace to come in person hither
And take perforce my husband from the Abbess.

SECOND MERCHANT
By this, I think, the dial points at five.
Anon, I'm sure, the Duke himself in person
Comes this way to the melancholy vale,
The place of death and sorry execution
Behind the ditches of the abbey here.

ANGELO Upon what cause?

SECOND MERCHANT
To see a reverend Syracusian merchant,
Who put unluckily into this bay
Against the laws and statutes of this town,
Beheaded publicly for his offense.

ANGELO
See where they come. We will behold his death.

LUCIANA
Kneel to the Duke before he pass the abbey.

48 brake broke. **rage** madness. **49 wreck of** shipwreck at **51 Strayed** led astray **57 reprehended** rebuked **60 Haply** Perhaps **62 copy** topic, theme. **conference** conversation. **63 for** because of **66 glancèd** alluded to **67 Still** continually **69 venom** venomous **82 distemperatures** physical disorder, illness **84 mad or** madden either **88 demeaned** behaved, conducted

90 She . . . reproof i.e., She led me to see my own faults. **97 assaying** attempting **99 office** duty **100 attorney** agent, deputy **103 approvèd** proved, tested **105 formal** normal, made in proper form **106 parcel** integral part **118 By this** By this time. **dial** sun-dial or watch dial **121 sorry** sad

Enter the Duke of Ephesus and [*Egeon*] *the merchant of Syracuse, barehead* [*and bound*], *with the Headsman and other officers.*

DUKE
Yet once again proclaim it publicly,
If any friend will pay the sum for him,
He shall not die; so much we tender him. 132

ADRIANA [*kneeling*]
Justice, most sacred Duke, against the Abbess!

DUKE
She is a virtuous and a reverend lady.
It cannot be that she hath done thee wrong.

ADRIANA
May it please Your Grace, Antipholus my husband,
Who I made lord of me and all I had,
At your important letters, this ill day 138
A most outrageous fit of madness took him,
That desperately he hurried through the street— 140
With him his bondman, all as mad as he— 141
Doing displeasure to the citizens 142
By rushing in their houses, bearing thence
Rings, jewels, anything his rage did like. 144
Once did I get him bound and sent him home,
Whilst to take order for the wrongs I went 146
That here and there his fury had committed.
Anon, I wot not by what strong escape, 148
He broke from those that had the guard of him,
And with his mad attendant and himself,
Each one with ireful passion, with drawn swords,
Met us again and, madly bent on us, 152
Chased us away, till raising of more aid
We came again to bind them. Then they fled
Into this abbey, whither we pursued them;
And here the Abbess shuts the gates on us
And will not suffer us to fetch him out,
Nor send him forth that we may bear him hence.
Therefore, most gracious Duke, with thy command
Let him be brought forth and borne hence for help. 160

DUKE [*raising Adriana*]
Long since, thy husband served me in my wars,
And I to thee engaged a prince's word, 162
When thou didst make him master of thy bed,
To do him all the grace and good I could.—
Go, some of you, knock at the abbey gate
And bid the Lady Abbess come to me.
I will determine this before I stir. 167

Enter a [*Servant as*] *messenger.*

SERVANT
Oh, mistress, mistress, shift and save yourself! 168
My master and his man are both broke loose,
Beaten the maids a-row, and bound the doctor, 170
Whose beard they have singed off with brands of fire,
And ever as it blazed they threw on him
Great pails of puddled mire to quench the hair. 173
My master preaches patience to him, and the while
His man with scissors nicks him like a fool; 175
And sure, unless you send some present help,
Between them they will kill the conjurer.

ADRIANA
Peace, fool! Thy master and his man are here,
And that is false thou dost report to us.

SERVANT
Mistress, upon my life, I tell you true.
I have not breathed almost since I did see it.
He cries for you, and vows, if he can take you,
To scorch your face and to disfigure you. 183
Cry within.
Hark, hark! I hear him, mistress. Fly, begone!

DUKE
Come, stand by me. Fear nothing.—Guard with
halberds! 185

ADRIANA
Ay me, it is my husband! Witness you
That he is borne about invisible.
Even now we housed him in the abbey here, 188
And now he's there, past thought of human reason.

Enter Antipholus and Dromio of Ephesus.

E. ANTIPHOLUS
Justice, most gracious Duke, oh, grant me justice!
Even for the service that long since I did thee,
When I bestrid thee in the wars and took 192
Deep scars to save thy life; even for the blood
That then I lost for thee, now grant me justice.

EGEON
Unless the fear of death doth make me dote,
I see my son Antipholus and Dromio.

E. ANTIPHOLUS
Justice, sweet prince, against that woman there!
She whom thou gav'st to me to be my wife,
That hath abusèd and dishonored me 199
Even in the strength and height of injury!
Beyond imagination is the wrong
That she this day hath shameless thrown on me.

DUKE
Discover how, and thou shalt find me just. 203

E. ANTIPHOLUS
This day, great Duke, she shut the doors upon me
While she with harlots feasted in my house. 205

DUKE
A grievous fault. Say, woman, didst thou so?

132 so . . . him so much consideration we grant him. (With suggestion also of "value" and "have pity on.") **138 important** importunate, pressing. **letters** (Adriana would seem to have been ward to the Duke and married at his importunate urging.) **140 That desperately** so that recklessly **141 all** totally **142 displeasure** wrong, injury **144 rage** madness, insanity **146 take order** settle, make reparation **148 wot** know. **strong** violent **152 bent** turned **160 help** cure. **162 engaged** pledged **167 determine** settle **168 shift** escape, depart

170 a-row one after another **173 puddled** from filthy puddles **175 nicks . . . fool** gives him a fantastic haircut in the short fashion of the court fool **183 scorch** (Compare the singeing of Pinch's beard at line 171; also, score, slash.) **185 halberds** long-handled spears with blades. **188 housed him in** i.e., drove him into **192 bestrid** stood over (to defend when fallen in battle) **199 abusèd** maltreated **203 Discover** Reveal **205 harlots** rascals, vile companions

ADRIANA
No, my good lord. Myself, he, and my sister
Today did dine together. So befall my soul 208
As this is false he burdens me withal. 209

LUCIANA
Ne'er may I look on day nor sleep on night 210
But she tells to Your Highness simple truth.

ANGELO
Oh, perjured woman!—They are both forsworn.
In this the madman justly chargeth them.

E. ANTIPHOLUS
My liege, I am advisèd what I say, 214
Neither disturbèd with the effect of wine
Nor heady-rash provoked with raging ire,
Albeit my wrongs might make one wiser mad.
This woman locked me out this day from dinner.
That goldsmith there, were he not packed with her, 219
Could witness it, for he was with me then;
Who parted with me to go fetch a chain, 221
Promising to bring it to the Porcupine,
Where Balthasar and I did dine together.
Our dinner done, and he not coming thither,
I went to seek him. In the street I met him,
And in his company that gentleman.
[*Indicating the Second Merchant.*]
There did this perjured goldsmith swear me down 227
That I this day of him received the chain,
Which, God he knows, I saw not; for the which
He did arrest me with an officer.
I did obey, and sent my peasant home
For certain ducats. He with none returned.
Then fairly I bespoke the officer 233
To go in person with me to my house.
By th' way we met
My wife, her sister, and a rabble more
Of vile confederates. Along with them
They brought one Pinch, a hungry, lean-faced villain,
A mere anatomy, a mountebank, 239
A threadbare juggler and a fortune-teller, 240
A needy, hollow-eyed, sharp-looking wretch,
A living dead man. This pernicious slave,
Forsooth, took on him as a conjurer 243
And, gazing in mine eyes, feeling my pulse,
And with no face, as 'twere, outfacing me, 245
Cries out I was possessed. Then all together 246
They fell upon me, bound me, bore me thence,
And in a dark and dankish vault at home
There left me and my man, both bound together,
Till, gnawing with my teeth my bonds in sunder,
I gained my freedom and immediately
Ran hither to Your Grace, whom I beseech
To give me ample satisfaction
For these deep shames and great indignities.

ANGELO
My lord, in truth, thus far I witness with him,
That he dined not at home but was locked out.

DUKE
But had he such a chain of thee, or no?

ANGELO
He had, my lord, and when he ran in here
These people saw the chain about his neck.

SECOND MERCHANT [*to E. Antipholus*]
Besides, I will be sworn these ears of mine
Heard you confess you had the chain of him
After you first forswore it on the mart,
And thereupon I drew my sword on you;
And then you fled into this abbey here,
From whence, I think, you are come by miracle.

E. ANTIPHOLUS
I never came within these abbey walls,
Nor ever didst thou draw thy sword on me.
I never saw the chain, so help me heaven!
And this is false you burden me withal.

DUKE
Why, what an intricate impeach is this! 270
I think you all have drunk of Circe's cup. 271
If here you housed him, here he would have been.
If he were mad, he would not plead so coldly. 273
[*To Adriana*] You say he dined at home; the goldsmith here
Denies that saying. [*To E. Dromio*] Sirrah, what say you?

E. DROMIO
Sir, he dined with her there, at the Porcupine.

COURTESAN
He did, and from my finger snatched that ring.

E. ANTIPHOLUS
'Tis true, my liege. This ring I had of her.

DUKE [*to the Courtesan*]
Saw'st thou him enter at the abbey here?

COURTESAN
As sure, my liege, as I do see Your Grace.

DUKE
Why, this is strange. Go call the Abbess hither.
I think you are all mated or stark mad. 282
Exit one to the Abbess.

EGEON
Most mighty Duke, vouchsafe me speak a word.
Haply I see a friend will save my life
And pay the sum that may deliver me.

DUKE
Speak freely, Syracusian, what thou wilt.

EGEON [*to E. Antipholus*]
Is not your name, sir, called Antipholus?
And is not that your bondman, Dromio?

E. DROMIO
Within this hour I was his bondman, sir,
But he, I thank him, gnawed in two my cords.
Now am I Dromio and his man, unbound.

208 So . . . soul i.e., As I hope to be saved **209 he . . . withal** he charges me with. **210 on** at **214 am advisèd** know very well **219 packed** in conspiracy **221 parted with** departed from **227 swear me down** swear in the face of my denials **233 fairly** civilly. **bespoke** requested **239 mere anatomy** absolute skeleton. **mountebank** quack, charlatan **240 juggler** sorcerer **243 took . . . as** pretended to be **245 And . . . me** i.e., and blandly staring me down. (With wordplay on "face" and "outfacing.") **246 possessed** mad.

270 intricate impeach involved accusation **271 Circe's cup** the charmed cup, a draft of which turned men into beasts (as told in Homer's *Odyssey*). **273 coldly** calmly, rationally. **282 mated** stupefied

EGEON
I am sure you both of you remember me.

E. DROMIO
Ourselves we do remember, sir, by you;
For lately we were bound, as you are now.
You are not Pinch's patient, are you, sir?

EGEON
Why look you strange on me? You know me well.

E. ANTIPHOLUS
I never saw you in my life till now.

EGEON
Oh, grief hath changed me since you saw me last,
And careful hours with Time's deformèd hand 299
Have written strange defeatures in my face. 300
But tell me yet, dost thou not know my voice?

E. ANTIPHOLUS Neither.

EGEON Dromio, nor thou?

E. DROMIO No, trust me, sir, nor I.

EGEON I am sure thou dost.

E. DROMIO Ay, sir, but I am sure I do not; and whatsoever a man denies, you are now bound to believe him.

EGEON
Not know my voice! O time's extremity,
Hast thou so cracked and splitted my poor tongue
In seven short years, that here my only son
Knows not my feeble key of untuned cares? 311
Though now this grainèd face of mine be hid 312
In sap-consuming winter's drizzled snow 313
And all the conduits of my blood froze up,
Yet hath my night of life some memory,
My wasting lamps some fading glimmer left, 316
My dull deaf ears a little use to hear.
All these old witnesses—I cannot err—
Tell me thou art my son Antipholus.

E. ANTIPHOLUS
I never saw my father in my life.

EGEON
But seven years since, in Syracusa, boy, 321
Thou know'st we parted. But perhaps, my son,
Thou sham'st to acknowledge me in misery.

E. ANTIPHOLUS
The Duke and all that know me in the city
Can witness with me that it is not so.
I ne'er saw Syracusa in my life.

DUKE
I tell thee, Syracusian, twenty years
Have I been patron to Antipholus,
During which time he ne'er saw Syracusa.
I see thy age and dangers make thee dote.

Enter the Abbess, with Antipholus and Dromio of Syracuse.

ABBESS
Most mighty Duke, behold a man much wronged.
All gather to see them.

ADRIANA
I see two husbands, or mine eyes deceive me.

DUKE
One of these men is genius to the other; 333
And so of these, which is the natural man,
And which the spirit? Who deciphers them? 335

S. DROMIO
I, sir, am Dromio. Command him away.

E. DROMIO
I, sir, am Dromio. Pray, let me stay.

S. ANTIPHOLUS
Egeon art thou not? Or else his ghost?

S. DROMIO
Oh, my old master! Who hath bound him here?

ABBESS
Whoever bound him, I will loose his bonds
And gain a husband by his liberty.
Speak, old Egeon, if thou be'st the man
That hadst a wife once called Emilia
That bore thee at a burden two fair sons. 344
Oh, if thou be'st the same Egeon, speak,
And speak unto the same Emilia!

EGEON
If I dream not, thou art Emilia.
If thou art she, tell me where is that son
That floated with thee on the fatal raft?

ABBESS
By men of Epidamnum he and I
And the twin Dromio all were taken up;
But by and by rude fishermen of Corinth 352
By force took Dromio and my son from them,
And me they left with those of Epidamnum.
What then became of them I cannot tell;
I to this fortune that you see me in.

DUKE
Why, here begins his morning story right: 357
These two Antipholus', these two so like,
And these two Dromios, one in semblance— 359
Besides her urging of her wreck at sea— 360
These are the parents to these children,
Which accidentally are met together.
Antipholus, thou cam'st from Corinth first?

S. ANTIPHOLUS
No, sir, not I. I came from Syracuse.

DUKE
Stay, stand apart. I know not which is which.

E. ANTIPHOLUS
I came from Corinth, my most gracious lord—

E. DROMIO And I with him.

E. ANTIPHOLUS
Brought to this town by that most famous warrior,
Duke Menaphon, your most renownèd uncle.

ADRIANA
Which of you two did dine with me today?

299 careful care-filled **300 defeatures** disfigurements, blemishes **311 my . . . cares** my voice enfeebled by discordant cares. **312 grainèd** lined, furrowed **313 In . . . snow** i.e., by my white hairs, that have dried up the sap of my youth **316 wasting lamps** i.e., dimming eyes **321 But** Only

333 genius attendant spirit **335 deciphers** distinguishes **344 burden** birth **352 rude** rough, simple **357 his morning story** i.e., the history Egeon related this morning **359 semblance** appearance **360 urging** urgent account

S. ANTIPHOLUS
I, gentle mistress.
ADRIANA And are not you my husband?
E. ANTIPHOLUS No, I say nay to that.
S. ANTIPHOLUS
And so do I. Yet did she call me so,
And this fair gentlewoman, her sister here,
Did call me brother. [*To Luciana*] What I told you then
I hope I shall have leisure to make good, 376
If this be not a dream I see and hear.
ANGELO [*pointing to the chain Antipholus of Syracuse wears*]
That is the chain, sir, which you had of me.
S. ANTIPHOLUS
I think it be, sir. I deny it not.
E. ANTIPHOLUS [*to Angelo*]
And you, sir, for this chain arrested me.
ANGELO
I think I did, sir. I deny it not.
ADRIANA [*to Antipholus of Ephesus*]
I sent you money, sir, to be your bail,
By Dromio, but I think he brought it not.
E. DROMIO No, none by me.
S. ANTIPHOLUS [*showing his purse to Adriana*]
This purse of ducats I received from you,
And Dromio my man did bring them me.
I see we still did meet each other's man, 387
And I was ta'en for him, and he for me,
And thereupon these errors are arose.
E. ANTIPHOLUS [*offering money*]
These ducats pawn I for my father here.
DUKE
It shall not need. Thy father hath his life. 391
COURTESAN [*to E. Antipholus*]
Sir, I must have that diamond from you.
E. ANTIPHOLUS [*giving the ring*]
There, take it, and much thanks for my good cheer.
ABBESS
Renownèd Duke, vouchsafe to take the pains 394
To go with us into the abbey here
And hear at large discoursèd all our fortunes, 396
And all that are assembled in this place,
That by this sympathizèd one day's error 398
Have suffered wrong. Go, keep us company,
And we shall make full satisfaction.
Thirty-three years have I but gone in travail
Of you, my sons, and till this present hour
My heavy burden ne'er deliverèd.
The Duke, my husband, and my children both,
And you the calendars of their nativity, 405
Go to a gossips' feast, and joy with me; 406
After so long grief, such nativity!
DUKE
With all my heart I'll gossip at this feast. 408
Exeunt omnes. Manent the two Dromios and two brothers [*Antipholus*].
S. DROMIO [*to Antipholus of Ephesus*]
Master, shall I fetch your stuff from shipboard?
E. ANTIPHOLUS
Dromio, what stuff of mine hast thou embarked?
S. DROMIO
Your goods that lay at host, sir, in the Centaur. 411
S. ANTIPHOLUS
He speaks to me.—I am your master, Dromio.
Come, go with us. We'll look to that anon.
Embrace thy brother there; rejoice with him.
Exeunt [*the two brothers Antipholus*].
S. DROMIO
There is a fat friend at your master's house
That kitchened me for you today at dinner. 416
She now shall be my sister, not my wife. 417
E. DROMIO
Methinks you are my glass and not my brother. 418
I see by you I am a sweet-faced youth.
Will you walk in to see their gossiping? 420
S. DROMIO Not I, sir, you are my elder.
E. DROMIO That's a question. How shall we try it?
S. DROMIO We'll draw cuts for the senior. Till then, lead thou first. 423
E. DROMIO Nay, then, thus:
We came into the world like brother and brother,
And now let's go hand in hand, not one before another. *Exeunt.*

376 leisure opportunity **387 still** continually **391 life** pardon. **394 vouchsafe** deign, agree **396 at large** at length **398 sympathizèd** shared in by all equally

405 calendars . . . nativity i.e., the Dromios, since the servants were born at the same time as their masters **406 a gossips' feast** a christening feast, here to celebrate, belatedly, the start of life for the two sets of twins, who were not truly born till now; also, a feast of companionship **408 gossip** i.e., be a hearty companion, take part **411 lay at host** were put up at the inn **416 kitchened** entertained in the kitchen **417 sister** sister-in-law **418 glass** mirror **420 gossiping** merrymaking. **423 cuts** lots

Love's Labor's Lost

In much the same way that *The Comedy of Errors* is Shakespeare's apprenticeship to Plautus and neoclassical comedy, *Love's Labor's Lost* is his apprenticeship to John Lyly's courtly drama of the 1580s, to the court masque, and to conventions of Petrarchan lyric poetry. The play is word conscious and stylistically mannered to an extent that is unusual even for the pun-loving Shakespeare. The humor abounds in the pert repartee for which juvenile actors were especially fitted, and an extraordinarily high percentage of roles are assigned to boys: four women and a diminutive page (Mote) among seventeen named roles. The social setting is patrician and the entertainments aristocratic. In some ways, little seems to happen in *Love's Labor's Lost*. Fast-moving plot is replaced by a structure that includes a series of debates on courtly topics reminiscent of John Lyly: love versus honor, the flesh versus the spirit, pleasure versus instruction, art versus nature. The songs and sonnets composed by the courtiers for the ladies (4.3.23–116) gracefully caricature the excesses of the Petrarchan love convention (named for the influential Italian sonneteer, Francesco Petrarch): the lovers are "sick to death" with unrequited passion, they catalogue the charms of their proud mistresses, they express their exquisitely tortured emotions through elaborate poetical metaphors, and so on. Stage movements are often masquelike; characters group themselves and then pair off two by two, as in a formal dance. Actual masques and pageants, presented by the courtiers or devised for their amusement, are essential ingredients of the spectacle.

Yet beneath the brightly polished surfaces of this sophisticated comedy, we often catch glimpses of a candor and a simplicity that offset the tinsel and glitter. The wits ultimately disclaim (with some qualification) their wittiness, and the ladies confess they have tried too zealously to put down the men; both sides disavow the extreme postures they have striven so hard to maintain. The clowns, though deflated by mocking laughter for their naiveté and pomposity, deflate the courtiers, in turn, for lack of compassion. From this interplay among various forms of courtly wit, Petrarchism, pedantry, and rustic speech emerges a recommended style that is witty but not irresponsibly so, courtly yet sincere, polished and yet free of affectation or empty verbal ornament. This new harmony is aptly expressed by Berowne and Rosaline, whose witty quest for self-understanding in love foreshadows that of Benedick and Beatrice in *Much Ado About Nothing*. The perfect expression of the true style is found in the song at the end of the play; taking the form of a medieval literary debate between Spring and Winter, it beautifully fuses the natural and the artificial into a concordant vision transcending the mundane.

Like *The Comedy of Errors*, *Love's Labor's Lost* is an early comedy that is hard to date with precision. It was published in quarto in 1598 "as it was presented before Her Highness this last Christmas" (1597). The text also purports to be "newly corrected and augmented," though we know of no earlier published version. Perhaps a play that was already several years old may have seemed in need of stylistic revision. Act 4 does, in fact, contain two long duplicatory passages, suggesting that a certain amount of rewriting did take place. The revisions alter the meaning only slightly, however, and give little support to the widely held notion that Shakespeare must have reworked the ending of his play. The unresolved ending, in which no marriages take place and in which the Princess's territorial claims to Aquitaine are left unsettled, should be regarded not as unfinished but as highly imaginative and indeed indispensable. The title, after all, assures us that "love's labors" will be lost, and the Princess affirms the principle of "form confounded."

Some stylistic tests suggest a date between 1592 and 1595, although these characteristics might point to an early play that had been "new corrected and augmented." Topical hypotheses arise from the quest for Shakespeare's sources. Since the plot of *Love's Labor's Lost* is derived from no known literary source, may it have been drawn instead from the Elizabethan contemporary scene, poking fun at the pretentiousness of literary figures and intellectuals, such as John Florio, Thomas Nashe, Gabriel Harvey, Sir Walter Ralegh, and George Chapman? Or should we seek topical meaning in the undoubted currency of such names as Navarre (Henry of Navarre, King Henry IV of France), Berowne (Biron, Henry IV's general), Dumaine (De Mayenne, brother of the Catholic Guise), and others? From the point of view of dating the play, however, such names would have been distastefully controversial in a courtly comedy after 1589. That date saw the beginning in France of a bitter civil conflict between the Catholic Guise and Protestant Navarre, continuing until Henry abjured Protestantism in 1593 and assumed the French throne. In the late 1580s, on the other hand, the tiny kingdom of Navarre would have seemed charmingly appropriate as a setting for Shakespeare's play. Such an early date, although by no means certain, would also help explain the Lylyan tone of the comedy and its early techniques of versification: the high percentage of rhymed lines in couplets and quatrains, the end-stopped blank verse, the use of various sonnet forms and of seven-stress (septenary) couplets, and the like.

The world of *Love's Labor's Lost* seems uneventful at first and remarkably unthreatened by danger or evil; only hintingly do reminders of mortality intrude upon the never-never-land of Navarre. There are, to be sure, occasional references to the Princess's "bedrid" father, to the plague, and to a "death's head," but the courtiers and we as audience are little prepared for the sudden appearance of Marcade in 5.2 and his announcement that the Princess's royal father is dead and that all lighthearted entertainments must now give way to mourning. Prior to this belated moment of reversal, the male characters are menaced by nothing worse than loss of dignity through breaking of their oaths. And although oath breaking was a matter of great seriousness to Elizabethan gentlemen, their doing so here is partly excused by the constancy of their devotion once they have fallen in love. In such an artificial world, the preservation of one's self-esteem assumes undue importance. Using the criteria of wit and self-awareness, Mote and Boyet, as manipulators and controllers of point of view, show us how to laugh at folly in love and pomposity in language. They present to us variations on a theme of courtly behavior, creating, in effect, a scale of manners ranging from the most aristocratic (the King and the Princess, Berowne and Rosaline) to the most absurdly pretentious (Armado, Holofernes, Nathaniel, and Dull). Nearly all the characters are mocked, but those at the lower end of the scale are especially vulnerable because they are grossly un-self-aware and hence unteachable.

The King and his companions deserve to be mocked because of their transparent lack of self-knowledge, their affectation, and the futility of their vows against love. As Berowne concedes from the start, such defiance of love is at odds with a fundamental natural rhythm that ultimately cannot be thwarted—a rhythm that provides a counterpoint and corrective to the frequently artificial rhythms of courtly life. This natural rhythm asserts itself throughout the play until it becomes starkly insistent in the death of the Princess's royal father and in the resulting twelve-month delay of all marriages.

Hypocritical defiance of love is doomed to comic failure and satirical punishment. The basic devices used to expose this hypocrisy are misdirected love letters and overheard speech, both devices of unmasking. Appropriately, the young ladies administer their most amusing comeuppance to the men by seeing through their Muscovite masks. The code governing this merry conflict is one of "mock for mock" and "sport by sport o'erthrown" (5.2.140, 153). In a prevailing legal metaphor, the young men are guilty of forswearing their written oaths, and must be punished for their perjury. Love is metaphorically a war, a siege, a battle of the sexes in which the women come off virtually unscathed. The language of love is that of parry and thrust (with occasional bawdy overtones). The men naturally are chagrined to be put down by the ladies but are on their way to a cure: they learn to laugh at their own pretentiousness and, even if hyperbolically, vow to cast aside all "affectation" and "maggot ostentation" in favor of "russet yeas and honest kersey noes" (lines 403–16). At the same time, Berowne's renunciation of artful language is cast in the form of a perfect fourteen-line sonnet; Shakespeare is having it both ways.

The clownish types are generally more victimized by their affectations. The fantastical Don Armado, as lover of Jaquenetta the country wench, apes the courtly conventions of the aristocrats to whose company he aspires. Enervated by base passion, penning wretched love letters, and worshiping a dairymaid as though she were an unapproachable goddess, he is a caricature of the Petrarchan lover. Generally, however, the affectations of the comic characters have to do with language rather than love. Armado himself is known as a phrasemaker, "a plume of feathers," a "weathercock": "Did you ever hear better?" (4.1.94–5). His letter to Jaquenetta, read aloud for the Princess's amusement, is an exquisite spoof of John Lyly's exaggeratedly mannered style, called Euphuism: "Shall I command thy love? I may. Shall I enforce thy love? I could. Shall I entreat thy love? I will. What shalt thou exchange for rags? Robes. For tittles? Titles. For thyself? Me" (lines 80–3). Here we see the repeated antitheses, the balanced structure (reflected also in the structure of the play), and the alliterative effects that so intoxicated literary sophisticates of the 1580s. In a similar spirit, other comic types are distinguished by their verbal habits: Constable Dull by his malapropisms (anticipating Dogberry and Elbow); Holofernes by his Latinisms, philological definitions, and varied epithets; Nathaniel by his deference to Holofernes as a fellow bookman; and Costard by his amiable but unlettered confusion over such grandiose terms as "remuneration" and "guerdon" (3.1.167–71). The word-conscious humor of the play gives us parodies of excruciatingly bad verse (as in Holofernes's "extemporal epitaph on the death of the deer," 4.2.49–61), teeth-grating puns (enfranchise, one Frances, 3.1.118–19), and the longest Latin word in existence (*honorificabilitudinitatibus*, 5.1.41).

A little of this sort of thing goes a long way, and occasional scenes of verbal sparring are overdone. Shakespeare tries to have it both ways, reveling in linguistic self-consciousness while laughing at its excesses. Yet the self-possessed characters do at least come to a realization that verbal overkill, like Petrarchan posturing, must be cast aside in favor of decorum and frankness in speech. There will always be "style," but it must be an appropriate style. The comic characters at their best help emphasize this same point. Costard especially is blessed with a pragmatic folk wisdom and simplicity that enable him to stand up unflinchingly to the ladies and gentlemen. He does not hesitate to tell the Princess that she is the "thickest and the tallest" of the ladies, for "truth is truth" (4.1.48). His forbearing description of Nathaniel as "a little o'erparted" (5.2.580–1) in the role of Alexander serves as a gentle rebuke to the wits, whose caustic observations on "The Nine Worthies" have gotten out of hand. Even Holofernes justly chides, before retiring in confusion as Judas Maccabaeus, that "This is not generous, not gentle, not humble" (line 626).

Even if the stylistic self-consciousness makes for labored reading at times, the play can be wonderfully funny in the theater. It provides numerous opportunities for sight gags, and it revels in comic character types who are funny even when their jokes are feeble. For all his indebtedness to Lyly's courtly drama in this play, Shakespeare has shaped it to the demands of a popular audience. Perhaps the greatest source of amusement is in Shakespeare's depiction of the war of the sexes. Nowhere else does he give us male characters who are so consistently baffled and tormented by women. The young women know from the start who they are and what men they are attracted to; we never see the women fall in love, for they have evidently made up their minds already. The men, conversely, flounder about absurdly from one inelegant posture to another, from futile asceticism to curiosity, infatuation, betrayal of their oaths, attempts to conceal their lovesickness from one another, and collapse of all pretenses when they are caught out. They have yet to come to terms with their own inner feelings and must be taught—and tortured—by the self-possessed young ladies. The men are at their most absurd when, having confessed to falling in love, they now rival one another in boasting of their respective mistresses and in striving to see who will succeed first. It never crosses their minds that they might be rejected now that they have deigned to come forward as suitors.

The masquing in Act 5 is thus a device by which the women can test and even humiliate the young men to show them how flighty and uncontrolled are their unfamiliar new emotions. The uncompleted ending of the play expresses an unfinished process: the young men must still apprentice themselves to mature self-reflection before they can be deemed worthy as husbands. Ironically, the young women consign the men to the very sort of celibate exercise in self-understanding that the men thought they were committing themselves to at the play's start. In these terms, too, we can see that some of the play's subplot characters are variations on a theme of male folly in love: Costard is the self-assured peasant, while Armado is the self-abnegating aristocrat. Armado exaggerates everything foolish that the aristocratic men have undergone and in Act 5 is fittingly the center of an absurd pageant, through which he becomes the comic scapegoat. Watching his performance in the pageant of "The Nine Worthies," the young aristocrats can laugh at the absurdities of male posturing and self-abasement that they are now slowly learning to control in themselves.

Above all, then, it is the play's unexpected ending that introduces an invaluable new insight on the courtiers' brittle war of wits. The death of the Princess's father brings everyone back to reality, to sober responsibility, to an awareness that marriage requires thoughtful decision. Devouring Time has entered the never-never-land of Navarre's park. The song at the end, appropriately cast in the form of a dialogue or debate, gives us the two voices of Spring and Winter, love and death, carnival and Lent, to remind us that human happiness and self-understanding are complex and perishable. And the song reminds us as well, in its "living art," of that subtle power of the imagination, which transforms time, love, and death into artistic creation.

Love's Labor's Lost

[*Dramatis Personae*

FERDINAND, *King of Navarre*
BEROWNE, LONGAVILLE, DUMAINE, } *lords attending the King*

THE PRINCESS OF FRANCE
ROSALINE, MARIA, KATHARINE, } *ladies attending the Princess*
BOYET, *a French lord attending the Princess*
MARCADE, *a French gentleman acting as messenger*
Two French LORDS

DON ADRIANO DE ARMADO, *a Spanish braggart*
MOTE, *his page*
NATHANIEL, *a curate*
HOLOFERNES, *a schoolmaster, called a pedant*
DULL, *a constable*
COSTARD, *a rustic, also referred to as a clown*
JAQUENETTA, *a dairymaid*
A FORESTER

Lords and Attendants; Attendants disguised as blackamoors

SCENE: *Navarre*]

[1.1]

Enter Ferdinand, King of Navarre, Berowne, Longaville, and Dumaine.

KING
Let fame, that all hunt after in their lives,
Live registered upon our brazen tombs, 2
And then grace us in the disgrace of death, 3
When, spite of cormorant devouring Time, 4
Th'endeavor of this present breath may buy 5
That honor which shall bate his scythe's keen edge 6
And make us heirs of all eternity.
Therefore, brave conquerors—for so you are,
That war against your own affections 9
And the huge army of the world's desires—
Our late edict shall strongly stand in force. 11
Navarre shall be the wonder of the world;
Our court shall be a little academe, 13
Still and contemplative in living art. 14
You three, Berowne, Dumaine, and Longaville,
Have sworn for three years' term to live with me
My fellow scholars and to keep those statutes
That are recorded in this schedule here. 18
[*He shows a document.*]
Your oaths are passed; and now subscribe your names, 19
That his own hand may strike his honor down 20
That violates the smallest branch herein. 21
If you are armed to do as sworn to do, 22
Subscribe to your deep oaths, and keep it, too.

LONGAVILLE [*signing*]
I am resolved. 'Tis but a three years' fast.
The mind shall banquet, though the body pine. 25
Fat paunches have lean pates, and dainty bits 26
Make rich the ribs but bankrupt quite the wits.

1.1 Location: The King of Navarre's park. (The locale remains the same throughout the play, sometimes immediately outside the gates of Navarre's court.)
2 registered recorded. **brazen** brass **3 grace** honor. **the disgrace of death** (1) the taking away of the grace of life by death (2) the overthrowing of death by proper fame **4 spite of** despite. **cormorant** ravenous, rapacious. (The cormorant is a large, voracious seabird.) **5 breath** breathing time, i.e., life itself; also, speech **6 bate** abate, blunt **9 affections** emotions, passions **11 late** recent

13 academe academy. (From the name of the grove near Athens where Plato and his followers gathered.) **14 Still** constant, calm. **living art** (1) the art of living (an idea probably derived from the *ars vivendi* of the Roman Stoics) (2) infusing learning (*art*) with vitality. **18 schedule** document **19 passed** pledged **20 hand** (1) armed hand of a warrior (2) handwriting **21 branch** i.e., clause **22 armed** i.e., prepared. (With a play on the military sense, as in *hand*, line 20.) **25 pine** languish, waste away. **26 pates** heads. **dainty bits** delicate morsels

DUMAINE [*signing*]
My loving lord, Dumaine is mortified.
The grosser manner of these world's delights
He throws upon the gross world's baser slaves.
To love, to wealth, to pomp I pine and die,
With all these living in philosophy.

BEROWNE
I can but say their protestation over.
So much, dear liege, I have already sworn,
That is, to live and study here three years.
But there are other strict observances:
As, not to see a woman in that term,
Which I hope well is not enrollèd there;
And one day in a week to touch no food,
And but one meal on every day beside,
The which I hope is not enrollèd there;
And then to sleep but three hours in the night,
And not be seen to wink of all the day—
When I was wont to think no harm all night,
And make a dark night too of half the day—
Which I hope well is not enrollèd there.
Oh, these are barren tasks, too hard to keep:
Not to see ladies, study, fast, not sleep!

KING
Your oath is passed to pass away from these.

BEROWNE
Let me say no, my liege, an if you please.
I only swore to study with Your Grace
And stay here in your court for three years' space.

LONGAVILLE
You swore to that, Berowne, and to the rest.

BEROWNE
By yea and nay, sir, then I swore in jest.
What is the end of study, let me know?

KING
Why, that to know which else we should not know.

BEROWNE
Things hid and barred, you mean, from common
sense?

KING
Ay, that is study's godlike recompense.

BEROWNE
Come on, then, I will swear to study so
To know the thing I am forbid to know,
As thus: to study where I well may dine,
When I to feast expressly am forbid;
Or study where to meet some mistress fine,
When mistresses from common sense are hid;
Or, having sworn too-hard-a-keeping oath,
Study to break it and not break my troth.
If study's gain be thus, and this be so,
Study knows that which yet it doth not know.
Swear me to this, and I will ne'er say no.

KING
These be the stops that hinder study quite,
And train our intellects to vain delight.

BEROWNE
Why, all delights are vain, but that most vain
Which, with pain purchased, doth inherit pain:
As, painfully to pore upon a book
To seek the light of truth, while truth the while
Doth falsely blind the eyesight of his look.
Light seeking light doth light of light beguile;
So, ere you find where light in darkness lies,
Your light grows dark by losing of your eyes.
Study me how to please the eye indeed
By fixing it upon a fairer eye,
Who dazzling so, that eye shall be his heed
And give him light that it was blinded by.
Study is like the heaven's glorious sun,
That will not be deep searched with saucy looks.
Small have continual plodders ever won
Save base authority from others' books.
These earthly godfathers of heaven's lights,
That give a name to every fixèd star,
Have no more profit of their shining nights
Than those that walk and wot not what they are.
Too much to know is to know naught but fame;
And every godfather can give a name.

KING
How well he's read, to reason against reading!

DUMAINE
Proceeded well, to stop all good proceeding.

LONGAVILLE
He weeds the corn and still lets grow the weeding.

28 mortified i.e., dead to worldly desire. **30 throws upon** leaves to. **baser slaves** i.e., slaves to passion and pleasure. **32 With . . . philosophy** i.e., thereby choosing instead the philosophical life. (*These* may mean "these acts of renunciation.") **33 say . . . over** repeat their vows. **34 liege** lord **43 wink of all** close the eyes at any time during **44 wont** accustomed. **think no harm** i.e., think it no harm to sleep soundly **50 an if** if **52 space** time. **54 By . . . nay** (A pious equivocation found in Matthew 5:33–7, frequently invoked by those not having a proper answer.) **55 end** goal **57 common sense** ordinary observation or intelligence. **58 recompense** compensation, payment. **59 Come on** (With a quibble on *common*, line 57.)

65 too . . . oath an oath too hard to keep **66 troth** faith. **67–8 If . . . know** If the true purpose of study should be as I've defined it—and indeed it is—then study offers unexpected rewards. **70 stops** obstacles **71 train** lure, entice. **vain** (1) foolish (2) overly proud **73 Which . . . pain** which, acquired by dint of effort and suffering, gains nothing but more pain **74 painfully** laboriously. **upon** over **75–6 while truth . . . look** i.e., while truth meantime eludes the reader's gaze. (Too much study, poorly directed, is counterproductive.) **77–9 Light . . . eyes** i.e., Searching for truth by excessive study paradoxically blinds the reader; and so, before you can bring illumination out of darkness, you lose your ability to see at all. **80 Study me** Let me study **81 fairer** i.e., of a fair lady **82–3 Who dazzling . . . by** i.e., which dazzling eye will occupy all the man's attention and bestow upon him the very light that first blinded him. **85 That . . . looks** i.e., that refuses to be searched or analyzed (literally, penetrated as in "searching" a wound) with insolent gazes. **86 Small** Little **87 Save** except. **base** commonplace, lower **88–9 These . . . star** i.e., Those complacent astronomers who have the audacity to name the stars, as if the astronomers were the stars' godfathers **90 their** i.e., the stars' **91 wot** know **92–3 Too . . . name** i.e., The acquiring of superfluous knowledge leads only to an empty reputation, since anyone who acts as godparent can do what the astronomers do (that is, give a name to something or someone). **95 Proceeded** Advanced. (In the academic sense of taking a degree.) **96 He . . . weeding** He pulls out the wheat and allows the weeds to grow.

BEROWNE
The spring is near when green geese are a-breeding. 97
DUMAINE
How follows that?
BEROWNE Fit in his place and time. 98
DUMAINE
In reason nothing.
BEROWNE Something then in rhyme. 99
KING
Berowne is like an envious sneaping frost 100
That bites the firstborn infants of the spring. 101
BEROWNE
Well, say I am. Why should proud summer boast 102
Before the birds have any cause to sing?
Why should I joy in an abortive birth? 104
At Christmas I no more desire a rose
Than wish a snow in May's newfangled shows, 106
But like of each thing that in season grows. 107
So you to study, now it is too late, 108
Climb o'er the house to unlock the little gate. 109
KING
Well, sit you out. Go home, Berowne. Adieu. 110
BEROWNE
No, my good lord, I have sworn to stay with you.
And though I have for barbarism spoke more 112
Than for that angel knowledge you can say,
Yet, confident, I'll keep what I have sworn
And bide the penance of each three years' day. 115
Give me the paper. Let me read the same,
And to the strictest decrees I'll write my name.
[*He takes the paper.*]
KING
How well this yielding rescues thee from shame!
BEROWNE [*reads*] "Item, That no woman shall come within a mile of my court—" Hath this been proclaimed?
LONGAVILLE Four days ago.
BEROWNE Let's see the penalty—"on pain of losing her tongue." Who devised this penalty?
LONGAVILLE
Marry, that did I.
BEROWNE Sweet lord, and why? 125
LONGAVILLE
To fright them hence with that dread penalty.
BEROWNE
A dangerous law against gentility! 127
[*He reads.*] "Item, If any man be seen to talk with a woman within the term of three years, he shall endure such public shame as the rest of the court can possibly devise."
This article, my liege, yourself must break,
For well you know here comes in embassy 133
The French King's daughter with yourself to speak—
A maid of grace and complete majesty— 135
About surrender up of Aquitaine
To her decrepit, sick, and bed-rid father. 137
Therefore this article is made in vain,
Or vainly comes th'admirèd Princess hither.
KING
What say you, lords? Why, this was quite forgot.
BEROWNE
So study evermore is overshot. 141
While it doth study to have what it would, 142
It doth forget to do the thing it should,
And when it hath the thing it hunteth most, 144
'Tis won as towns with fire—so won, so lost. 145
KING
We must of force dispense with this decree. 146
She must lie here, on mere necessity. 147
BEROWNE
Necessity will make us all forsworn 148
Three thousand times within this three years' space;
For every man with his affects is born, 150
Not by might mastered, but by special grace. 151
If I break faith, this word shall speak for me: 152
I am forsworn on "mere necessity."
So to the laws at large I write my name. [*He signs.*] 154
And he that breaks them in the least degree
Stands in attainder of eternal shame. 156
Suggestions are to other as to me; 157
But I believe, although I seem so loath, 158
I am the last that will last keep his oath. 159
But is there no quick recreation granted? 160
KING
Ay, that there is. Our court, you know, is haunted 161
With a refinèd traveler of Spain, 162
A man in all the world's new fashion planted, 163
That hath a mint of phrases in his brain; 164
One who the music of his own vain tongue 165
Doth ravish like enchanting harmony;
A man of compliments, whom right and wrong 167

97 The . . . a-breeding (Berowne may be hinting that his fellows are all foolish, but Dumaine, in lines 98–9, misses the point; to him, Berowne's quip does not seem to follow logically from what preceded.) **98 Fit in his** Appropriate to its **99 In reason nothing** i.e., It doesn't follow at all logically. **rhyme** (Berowne, answering Dumaine, plays upon the proverbial phrase "neither rhyme nor reason": if what I said doesn't seem to follow logically, at least it rhymes.) **100 envious** malignant. **sneaping** biting, nipping **101 infants** buds **102 proud** glorious **104 abortive** monstrous, unnatural **106 May's . . . shows** i.e., the display of spring flowers **107 like of** approve of. **in season** i.e., in its proper season **108 too late** i.e., too late in our lives to be students **109 Climb . . . gate** i.e., you begin at the wrong end. **110 sit you out** don't take part. **112 for barbarism** on the side of ignorance **115 bide** endure. **each . . . day** every day of the three years. **125 Marry** (A mild oath, derived from "by the Virgin Mary.") **127 gentility** civilized custom.

133 in embassy as an ambassador **135 complete** perfect **137 bed-rid** bedridden **141 overshot** wide of the mark by shooting over the target, mistaken. **142 would** desires **144–5 And . . . lost** i.e., and when study achieves its desire, it does so by consuming what it sought, much as towns are conquered by being burned to the ground or destroyed by artillery. **146 of force** necessarily **147 lie** lodge. **on mere** out of absolute **148 forsworn** guilty of breaking an oath, perjured **150 affects** natural passions **151 might** i.e., his own strength. **special grace** divine intervention. **152 word** motto **154 at large** as a whole, in general **156 in attainder** under penalty **157 Suggestions . . . me** i.e., Temptations affect others as much as they do me. **158 loath** reluctant (to sign) **159 I . . . oath** I that speak last will be the last to break my oath. (But with an equivocal meaning also of being the last person to keep his oath to the last.) **160 quick** lively **161–2 haunted With** frequented by **163 planted** rooted **164 a mint** i.e., a vast sum. (Literally, a place where money is coined.) **165 who** whom **167 compliments** gentlemanly mannerisms

Have chose as umpire of their mutiny.
This child of fancy, that Armado hight,
For interim to our studies shall relate
In high-borne words the worth of many a knight
From tawny Spain, lost in the world's debate.
How you delight, my lords, I know not, I,
But I protest I love to hear him lie,
And I will use him for my minstrelsy.

BEROWNE
Armado is a most illustrious wight,
A man of fire-new words, fashion's own knight.

LONGAVILLE
Costard the swain and he shall be our sport;
And so to study three years is but short.

Enter [Dull,] a constable, with Costard, with a letter.

DULL Which is the Duke's own person?

BEROWNE This, fellow. What wouldst?

DULL I myself reprehend his own person, for I am His Grace's farborough. But I would see his own person in flesh and blood.

BEROWNE This is he.

DULL Señor Arm–Arm–commends you. There's villainy abroad. This letter will tell you more.
[*He gives the letter to the King.*]

COSTARD Sir, the contempts thereof are as touching me.

KING A letter from the magnificent Armado.

BEROWNE How low soever the matter, I hope in God for high words.

LONGAVILLE A high hope for a low heaven. God grant us patience!

BEROWNE To hear, or forbear hearing?

LONGAVILLE To hear meekly, sir, and to laugh moderately, or to forbear both.

BEROWNE Well, sir, be it as the style shall give us cause to climb in the merriness.

COSTARD The matter is to me, sir, as concerning Jaquenetta. The manner of it is, I was taken with the manner.

BEROWNE In what manner?

COSTARD In manner and form following, sir—all those three. I was seen with her in the manor house, sitting with her upon the form, and taken following her into the park; which, put together, is "in manner and form following." Now, sir, for the manner—it is the manner of a man to speak to a woman. For the form—in some form.

BEROWNE For the "following," sir?

COSTARD As it shall follow in my correction; and God defend the right!

KING Will you hear this letter with attention?

BEROWNE As we would hear an oracle.

COSTARD Such is the sinplicity of man to hearken after the flesh.

KING [*reads*] "Great deputy, the welkin's vicegerent, and sole dominator of Navarre, my soul's earth's god, and body's fostering patron—"

COSTARD Not a word of Costard yet.

KING [*reads*] "So it is—"

COSTARD It may be so, but if he say it is so, he is, in telling true, but so.

KING Peace!

COSTARD Be to me and every man that dares not fight.

KING No words!

COSTARD Of other men's secrets, I beseech you.

KING [*reads*] "So it is, besieged with sable-colored melancholy, I did commend the black oppressing humor to the most wholesome physic of thy health-giving air, and, as I am a gentleman, betook myself to walk. The time when? About the sixth hour, when beasts most graze, birds best peck, and men sit down to that nourishment which is called supper. So much for the time when. Now for the ground which—which, I mean, I walked upon. It is yclept thy park. Then for the place where—where, I mean, I did encounter that obscene and most preposterous event that draweth from my snow-white pen the ebon-colored ink which here thou viewest, beholdest, surveyest, or see'st. But to the place where. It standeth north-northeast and by east from the west corner of thy curious-knotted

168 mutiny discord. (This man of judgment and discretion is able to sort out right from wrong.) **169 child of fancy** fantastic or grotesque creature. **hight** is called. (An archaic, affected term.) **170–2 For . . . debate** i.e., For an interlude in our studies, Armado will tell, in lofty and patrician terms, sagas of many an adventurous knight from sunburned Spain that might otherwise be lost to debate. **173 How you delight** What delights you **175 minstrelsy** i.e., entertainment. **176 wight** person **177 fire-new** newly coined **178 Costard** (The name means a large apple; the term is frequently applied humorously or derisively to the head.) **swain** rustic young fellow **180 Duke's** i.e., King's **181 fellow** (Customary form of address to a servant.) **182 reprehend** (Malapropism for "represent.") **183 farborough** (Malapropism for "tharborough" or "third borough," a petty constable.) **186 commends you** sends you his greetings **188 contempts** (Malapropism for "contents.") **189 magnificent Armado** boastful or grandiose Armado. (With an allusion to the great Armada of Spain.) **190 How low soever** However debased **191 high** lofty, exalted **192 low heaven** i.e., small blessing. **197 be it** so be it. **style** (With a pun on "stile," giving point to *climb* in the next line.) **199 is to** applies to **200 with the manner** with the stolen goods. (An Anglo-French law term *mainoure*, from *manoeuvre*.)

202 In manner and form (A familiar legal formula of the time.) **202–3 those three** i.e., manner and form following. (Costard proceeds to illustrate each term as it applies to his case.) **203 manor** (Playing upon "manner.") **204 form** bench. (Playing upon *form* in line 202, as also with *following*.) **210 correction** punishment **210–11 God defend the right**! (Prayer before mortal combat.) **214 sinplicity** (This Quarto reading may be a malapropism and has an ironic fitness, although it could also be a simple misprint or variant spelling for "simplicity." Whether the joke is audible in the theater is hard to say.) **216 welkin's vicegerent** heaven's deputy. (A pompous phrase, as most in the letter are.) **217 dominator** ruler **218 fostering** nurturing **222 but so** i.e., not saying much. **224 Be to me** (Costard punningly changes the King's "Peace"—i.e., "Be silent!"—to suit his own purposes; *Peace be to me* means "may I go undisturbed with the law's blessing.") **226 Of . . . secrets** (As in line 224, Costard changes the King's meaning with witty wordplay: "Let's have no talk of other men's secrets, which can get a person into trouble.") **227 sable-colored** i.e., black **228–9 black oppressing humor** black bile or melancholy, oppressing with its black essence **229 physic** medicine **235 yclept** called. (Archaic usage.) **237 obscene** disgusting **238 snow-white pen** i.e., white goose quill. **ebon-colored** i.e., black. (Like ebony.) **241 curious-knotted** delicately or intricately designed

garden. There did I see that low-spirited swain, that base minnow of thy mirth—"

COSTARD Me?

KING [*reads*] "that unlettered, small-knowing soul—"

COSTARD Me?

KING [*reads*] "that shallow vassal—"

COSTARD Still me?

KING [*reads*] "which, as I remember, hight Costard—"

COSTARD Oh! Me.

KING [*reads*] "sorted and consorted, contrary to thy established proclaimed edict and continent canon, with, with—oh, with—but with this I passion to say wherewith—"

COSTARD With a wench.

KING [*reads*] "with a child of our grandmother Eve, a female; or, for thy more sweet understanding, a woman. Him I, as my ever-esteemed duty pricks me on, have sent to thee, to receive the meed of punishment, by Thy sweet Grace's officer, Anthony Dull, a man of good repute, carriage, bearing, and estimation."

DULL Me, an't shall please you. I am Anthony Dull.

KING [*reads*] "For Jaquenetta—so is the weaker vessel called which I apprehended with the aforesaid swain—I keep her as a vessel of thy law's fury, and shall at the least of thy sweet notice bring her to trial. Thine, in all compliments of devoted and heart-burning heat of duty, Don Adriano de Armado."

BEROWNE This is not so well as I looked for, but the best that ever I heard.

KING Ay, the best for the worst.—But, sirrah, what say you to this?

COSTARD Sir, I confess the wench.

KING Did you hear the proclamation?

COSTARD I do confess much of the hearing it, but little of the marking of it.

KING It was proclaimed a year's imprisonment to be taken with a wench.

COSTARD I was taken with none, sir. I was taken with a damsel.

KING Well, it was proclaimed "damsel."

COSTARD This was no damsel neither, sir. She was a virgin.

BEROWNE It is so varied too, for it was proclaimed "virgin."

COSTARD If it were, I deny her virginity. I was taken with a maid.

KING This "maid" will not serve your turn, sir.

COSTARD This maid will serve my turn, sir.

KING Sir, I will pronounce your sentence: you shall fast a week with bran and water.

COSTARD I had rather pray a month with mutton and porridge.

KING
And Don Armado shall be your keeper.
My Lord Berowne, see him delivered o'er.
And go we, lords, to put in practice that
Which each to other hath so strongly sworn.
[*Exeunt the King, Longaville, and Dumaine.*]

BEROWNE
I'll lay my head to any goodman's hat,
These oaths and laws will prove an idle scorn.
Sirrah, come on.

COSTARD I suffer for the truth, sir; for true it is, I was taken with Jaquenetta, and Jaquenetta is a true girl; and therefore, welcome the sour cup of prosperity! Affliction may one day smile again, and till then, sit thee down, sorrow! *Exeunt.*

✤

[1.2]

Enter Armado and Mote, his page.

ARMADO Boy, what sign is it when a man of great spirit grows melancholy?

MOTE A great sign, sir, that he will look sad.

ARMADO Why, sadness is one and the selfsame thing, dear imp.

MOTE No, no, oh, Lord, sir, no.

ARMADO How canst thou part sadness and melancholy, my tender juvenal?

MOTE By a familiar demonstration of the working, my tough señor.

ARMADO Why "tough señor"? Why "tough señor"?

MOTE Why "tender juvenal"? Why "tender juvenal"?

ARMADO I spoke it, tender juvenal, as a congruent epitheton appertaining to thy young days, which we may nominate "tender."

MOTE And I, tough señor, as an appertinent title to your old time, which we may name "tough."

ARMADO Pretty and apt.

MOTE How mean you, sir? I pretty and my saying apt? Or I apt and my saying pretty?

242 low-spirited ignoble **243 minnow** contemptible little creature **245 unlettered** illiterate **247 vassal** slavish fellow **249 hight** is called. (Archaic usage.) **252 sorted and consorted** associated **253 continent canon** law-enforcing restraint **254 passion** grieve **259 pricks** spurs **260 meed** reward **263 estimation** reputation. **264 an't . . . you** if you please. **265 For** As for. **weaker vessel** i.e., woman. (See 1 Peter 3:7.) **268 at . . . notice** i.e., at your first hint **268–9 bring her to trial** (With perhaps a bawdy double meaning of testing her mettle as a woman.) **273 best . . . worst** i.e., best example of the worst. **sirrah** (Ordinary form of address to inferiors.) **278 the marking of it** paying attention to it. **286 so varied** alternatively phrased (in typical legal jargon) **289 serve your turn** i.e., get you out of your difficulty. (But Costard, in the next line, interprets the phrase in a ribald sense.)

293–4 mutton and porridge mutton broth. (With a pun on "mutton," whore.) **296 delivered o'er** handed over. **299 lay** wager. **goodman's** i.e., yeoman's **300 idle scorn** worthless object of mockery. **303 true** honest **304 prosperity** (Malapropism for "adversity"?) **305 Affliction** (Costard mixes this up with "prosperity.") **305–6 sit thee down** i.e., stay, settle down with me
1.2. Location: The same. Navarre's park.
0.1 *Mote* (The word in the First Quarto is *Moth*, pronounced identically with *mote* and meaning "dust speck." The sense of "moth" or tiny winged creature may also be present. There may possibly be a play also on *mot*, French for "word.") **1 sign is it** is it a sign of **5 imp** young shoot, child. **7 part** distinguish between **8 juvenal** youth; satirist (after Juvenal, the Roman satirist). **9 familiar** plain, easily understood. **working** operation (of these emotions) **10 señor** sir. (With pun on "senior.") **13–14 congruent epitheton** appropriate epithet **14 appertaining** belonging, suiting **15 nominate** call **16 appertinent** appropriate

ARMADO Thou pretty, because little.

MOTE Little pretty, because little. Wherefore apt?

ARMADO And therefore apt, because quick.

MOTE Speak you this in my praise, master?

ARMADO In thy condign praise.

MOTE I will praise an eel with the same praise.

ARMADO What, that an eel is ingenious?

MOTE That an eel is quick.

ARMADO I do say thou art quick in answers. Thou heat'st my blood.

MOTE I am answered, sir.

ARMADO I love not to be crossed.

MOTE [*aside*] He speaks the mere contrary; crosses love not him.

ARMADO I have promised to study three years with the Duke.

MOTE You may do it in an hour, sir.

ARMADO Impossible.

MOTE How many is one thrice told?

ARMADO I am ill at reckoning; it fitteth the spirit of a tapster.

MOTE You are a gentleman and a gamester, sir.

ARMADO I confess both. They are both the varnish of a complete man.

MOTE Then I am sure you know how much the gross sum of deuce-ace amounts to.

ARMADO It doth amount to one more than two.

MOTE Which the base vulgar do call three.

ARMADO True.

MOTE Why, sir, is this such a piece of study? Now here is three studied ere ye'll thrice wink; and how easy it is to put "years" to the word "three" and study three years in two words, the dancing horse will tell you.

ARMADO A most fine figure!

MOTE [*aside*] To prove you a cipher.

ARMADO I will hereupon confess I am in love; and as it is base for a soldier to love, so am I in love with a base wench. If drawing my sword against the humor of affection would deliver me from the reprobate thought of it, I would take Desire prisoner and ransom him to any French courtier for a new-devised curtsy. I think scorn to sigh; methinks I should outswear Cupid. Comfort me, boy. What great men have been in love?

MOTE Hercules, master.

ARMADO Most sweet Hercules! More authority, dear boy, name more; and, sweet my child, let them be men of good repute and carriage.

MOTE Samson, master; he was a man of good carriage, great carriage, for he carried the town gates on his back like a porter; and he was in love.

ARMADO O well-knit Samson! Strong-jointed Samson! I do excel thee in my rapier as much as thou didst me in carrying gates. I am in love too. Who was Samson's love, my dear Mote?

MOTE A woman, master.

ARMADO Of what complexion?

MOTE Of all the four, or the three, or the two, or one of the four.

ARMADO Tell me precisely of what complexion.

MOTE Of the sea-water green, sir.

ARMADO Is that one of the four complexions?

MOTE As I have read, sir; and the best of them, too.

ARMADO Green indeed is the color of lovers; but to have a love of that color, methinks Samson had small reason for it. He surely affected her for her wit.

MOTE It was so, sir, for she had a green wit.

ARMADO My love is most immaculate white and red.

MOTE Most maculate thoughts, master, are masked under such colors.

ARMADO Define, define, well-educated infant.

MOTE My father's wit and my mother's tongue, assist me!

ARMADO Sweet invocation of a child, most pretty and pathetical!

MOTE

If she be made of white and red,
 Her faults will ne'er be known,
For blushing cheeks by faults are bred,
 And fears by pale white shown.
Then if she fear, or be to blame,
 By this you shall not know,
For still her cheeks possess the same
 Which native she doth owe.

21 Thou . . . little. (Armado refers to the commonplace "little things are pretty.") **23 quick** quick-witted. **25 condign** worthily deserved **28 quick** quick at maneuvering. **29–30 Thou . . . blood.** You make me angry. **32 crossed** thwarted, opposed. **33 mere** absolute. **crosses** coins. (So called because many of them were impressed with crosses.) **36 Duke** i.e., King **39 told** counted. **40 ill at reckoning** no good at arithmetic **41 tapster** bartender. **42 gamester** gambler **43 varnish** finish, ornament **44 complete** accomplished **46 deuce-ace** are a throw of two and one in dice **48 vulgar** common people **50 piece** masterpiece **53 dancing horse** (Probably a reference to a famous trained horse brought to London in 1591, named Morocco, that could count by tapping with its hoof.) **54 figure** figure of speech. **55 cipher** zero. (Mote takes Armado's *figure* in line 54 to mean "numeral.") **58–9 humor of affection** inclination to passion **59 deliver me** save me. **reprobate** depraved, degrading **61 new-devised curtsy** newfangled manner of bowing; any new fashion. **61–2 think scorn** disdain **62 outswear** overcome by swearing or, swear to do without

67 carriage bearing. (With pun on "ability to carry" in the following speech; see Judges 16:3 for the account of Samson's deed.) **71 well-knit** well-proportioned **72 in my rapier** in my swordsmanship. (The rapier replaced the old-fashioned long sword in the 1590s.) **76 complexion** skin color; also temperament. (The four complexions were sanguine, choleric, phlegmatic, and melancholic, and were supposedly determined by the relative proportions of the four humors.) **83 Green** (A reference to lovers' "greensickness," an anemic condition of puberty.) **85 affected** loved. **wit** intelligence. **86 green** immature. (With a punning reference perhaps to the seven green withes with which Samson was bound, Judges 16:7–9.) **88 maculate** stained, polluted **89 colors** (With a pun on "pretexts.") **90 Define** Explain **94 pathetical** moving. **95 be made of** i.e., has a complexion that is. (With a play on "maid." Mote also hints that the red and white are cosmetic.) **96 Her . . . known** i.e., she will never be betrayed by blushes or pallor, since the red and white (perhaps cosmetic) will mask those effects **97 by faults are bred** are caused by an awareness of being at fault **98 fears** i.e., fears of detection **100 this** i.e., her complexion or coloring (which is perhaps produced by cosmetics) **101–2 For . . . owe** i.e., for her cheeks are always (and therefore suspiciously) colored with the red and white of her supposedly natural coloration.

A dangerous rhyme, master, against the reason of white and red.

ARMADO Is there not a ballad, boy, of the King and the Beggar?

MOTE The world was very guilty of such a ballad some three ages since, but I think now 'tis not to be found; or, if it were, it would neither serve for the writing nor the tune.

ARMADO I will have that subject newly writ o'er, that I may example my digression by some mighty precedent. Boy, I do love that country girl that I took in the park with the rational hind Costard. She deserves well.

MOTE [*aside*] To be whipped; and yet a better love than my master.

ARMADO Sing, boy. My spirit grows heavy in love.

MOTE [*aside*] And that's great marvel, loving a light wench.

ARMADO I say, sing.

MOTE Forbear till this company be past.

Enter [*Costard the*] *clown,* [*Dull the*] *constable, and* [*Jaquenetta, a*] *wench.*

DULL Sir, the Duke's pleasure is that you keep Costard safe, and you must suffer him to take no delight nor no penance, but 'a must fast three days a week. For this damsel, I must keep her at the park. She is allowed for the deywoman. Fare you well.

ARMADO [*aside*] I do betray myself with blushing.—Maid!

JAQUENETTA Man?

ARMADO I will visit thee at the lodge.

JAQUENETTA That's hereby.

ARMADO I know where it is situate.

JAQUENETTA Lord, how wise you are!

ARMADO I will tell thee wonders.

JAQUENETTA With that face?

ARMADO I love thee.

JAQUENETTA So I heard you say.

ARMADO And so, farewell.

JAQUENETTA Fair weather after you!

DULL Come, Jaquenetta, away!

Exeunt [*Dull and Jaquenetta*].

ARMADO Villain, thou shalt fast for thy offenses ere thou be pardoned.

COSTARD Well, sir, I hope when I do it I shall do it on a full stomach.

ARMADO Thou shalt be heavily punished.

COSTARD I am more bound to you than your fellows, for they are but lightly rewarded.

ARMADO [*to Mote*] Take away this villain. Shut him up.

MOTE Come, you transgressing slave, away!

COSTARD Let me not be pent up, sir. I will fast, being loose.

MOTE No, sir, that were fast and loose. Thou shalt to prison.

COSTARD Well, if ever I do see the merry days of desolation that I have seen, some shall see.

MOTE What shall some see?

COSTARD Nay, nothing, Master Mote, but what they look upon. It is not for prisoners to be too silent in their words, and therefore I will say nothing. I thank God I have as little patience as another man, and therefore I can be quiet. *Exit* [*with Mote*].

ARMADO I do affect the very ground, which is base, where her shoe, which is baser, guided by her foot, which is basest, doth tread. I shall be forsworn, which is a great argument of falsehood, if I love. And how can that be true love which is falsely attempted? Love is a familiar; Love is a devil. There is no evil angel but Love. Yet was Samson so tempted, and he had an excellent strength; yet was Solomon so seduced, and he had a very good wit. Cupid's butt shaft is too hard for Hercules' club, and therefore too much odds for a Spaniard's rapier. The first and second cause will not serve my turn; the passado he respects not, the duello he regards not. His disgrace is to be called boy, but his glory is to subdue men. Adieu, valor! Rust, rapier! Be still, drum! For your manager is in love; yea, he loveth. Assist me, some extemporal god of rhyme, for I am sure I shall turn sonnet. Devise, wit; write, pen; for I am for whole volumes in folio. *Exit.*

103–4 A dangerous . . . red i.e., A warning in rhyme against trusting in white and red complexions. (The sentence plays on the contrast of *rhyme* and *reason*.) **105–6 ballad . . . Beggar** ballad of King Cophetua and the beggar maid. (Compare 4.1.66–7.) **108 since** ago **109–10 it would . . . tune** i.e., both the lyrics and the tune would seem out of date. **serve** suffice **111 writ o'er** written up **112 example . . . by** justify my own waywardness by **114 rational** capable of reason. (Said patronizingly.) **hind** rustic or clown **116–17 To be . . . master** i.e., She deserves to be whipped, as prostitutes are whipped, and yet even at that she deserves a better lover than Armado. **119 light** wanton. (With a play on the opposite of *heavy*, line 118.) **121 Forbear** Hold off **123 suffer** allow **124 penance** (Malapropism for "pleasance," i.e., joy.) **'a** he. **For** As for **125–6 allowed . . . deywoman** approved or assigned to serve as dairymaid. **130 hereby** close by. **131 situate** located. **134 With that face?** (A colloquial sarcasm, like "You don't mean it?") **140 Villain** (1) Servant (2) Rascal

142–3 on a full stomach (1) when I've had plenty to eat (2) with manly courage. **145 bound** (1) obliged (2) tied. **fellows** servants **146 but lightly** only slightly. (Playing on *heavily*, line 144.) **149–50 I will . . . loose** I promise to fast if you give me my liberty. **151 fast and loose** a cheating trick. **Thou shalt** You will go **153–4 desolation** (Malapropism for "consolation"?) **154 some shall see** (Costard seems to imply that some who have wronged him will see how he can revenge, although he refuses to say so when Mote queries his meaning.) **157–8 It is . . . words** (Costard means to say that prisoners should be careful what they utter.) **159 patience** (Costard means the opposite of what he says.) **161 affect** love **163 be forsworn** break my oath **164 argument** proof **166 familiar** attendant evil spirit **169 butt shaft** unbarbed arrow, used in archery practice **170 too much odds** at too great an advantage **171 first . . . cause** (An allusion to certain situations that necessitated a duel according to the code of honor. Armado complains that Cupid will not follow this code of honor.) **172 passado** forward thrust with the sword, one foot being advanced at the same time. **duello** established code of duelists **175 manager** skilled practitioner **176 extemporal . . . rhyme** god of impromptu poetry **177 sonnet** i.e., sonneteer **178 am for** am destined to produce. **folio** large format.

[2.1]

Enter the Princess of France, with three attending Ladies [*Rosaline, Maria, and Katharine*] *and three Lords* [*one being Boyet*].

BOYET

Now, madam, summon up your dearest spirits.
Consider who the King your father sends,
To whom he sends, and what's his embassy:
Yourself, held precious in the world's esteem,
To parley with the sole inheritor
Of all perfections that a man may owe,
Matchless Navarre; the plea of no less weight
Than Aquitaine, a dowry for a queen.
Be now as prodigal of all dear grace
As Nature was in making graces dear
When she did starve the general world beside
And prodigally gave them all to you.

PRINCESS

Good Lord Boyet, my beauty, though but mean,
Needs not the painted flourish of your praise.
Beauty is bought by judgment of the eye,
Not uttered by base sale of chapmen's tongues.
I am less proud to hear you tell my worth
Than you much willing to be counted wise
In spending your wit in the praise of mine.
But now to task the tasker. Good Boyet,
You are not ignorant all-telling fame
Doth noise abroad Navarre hath made a vow:
Till painful study shall outwear three years,
No woman may approach his silent court.
Therefore to 's seemeth it a needful course,
Before we enter his forbidden gates,
To know his pleasure; and in that behalf,
Bold of your worthiness, we single you
As our best-moving fair solicitor.
Tell him the daughter of the King of France,
On serious business craving quick dispatch,
Importunes personal conference with His Grace.
Haste, signify so much, while we attend,
Like humble-visaged suitors, his high will.

BOYET

Proud of employment, willingly I go.

PRINCESS

All pride is willing pride, and yours is so.
Exit Boyet.
Who are the votaries, my loving lords,
That are vow-fellows with this virtuous duke?

A LORD

Lord Longaville is one.

PRINCESS Know you the man?

MARIA

I know him, madam. At a marriage feast,
Between Lord Perigord and the beauteous heir
Of Jaques Falconbridge, solemnizèd
In Normandy, saw I this Longaville.
A man of sovereign parts he is esteemed,
Well fitted in arts, glorious in arms.
Nothing becomes him ill that he would well.
The only soil of his fair virtue's gloss—
If virtue's gloss will stain with any soil—
Is a sharp wit matched with too blunt a will,
Whose edge hath power to cut, whose will still wills
It should none spare that come within his power.

PRINCESS

Some merry mocking lord, belike. Is't so?

MARIA

They say so most that most his humors know.

PRINCESS

Such short-lived wits do wither as they grow.
Who are the rest?

KATHARINE

The young Dumaine, a well-accomplished youth,
Of all that virtue love for virtue loved;
Most power to do most harm, least knowing ill,
For he hath wit to make an ill shape good
And shape to win grace though he had no wit.
I saw him at the Duke Alençon's once,
And much too little of that good I saw
Is my report to his great worthiness.

ROSALINE

Another of these students at that time
Was there with him, if I have heard a truth.
Berowne they call him; but a merrier man,
Within the limit of becoming mirth,
I never spent an hour's talk withal.
His eye begets occasion for his wit,

2.1. Location: The same. Outside the gates of Navarre's court.
1 dearest spirits best thoughts and courage. **5 parley** negotiate **6 owe** own **7 the plea . . . weight** the point at issue being of no less consequence **9 Be . . . grace** Be now as lavish of your divine gracefulness **10 dear** scarce, costly **11 When . . . beside** when she deprived everyone else of her graces **12 prodigally** extravagantly, too generously **13 mean** average, moderate **14 flourish** adornment **16 uttered** (1) spoken (2) offered for sale. **chapmen's** merchants' **17 tell** (1) speak of (2) reckon **20 task** (1) chastise (2) lay a task upon **21 ignorant** unaware that. **fame** rumor **22 noise** spread the news **25 to 's** to us. (The royal "we.") **needful** necessary **27 in that behalf** for that purpose **28 Bold of** confident of. **single** choose **29 best-moving** most eloquent **32 Importunes** requests **33 Haste . . . much** Quickly deliver this message to him

36 All . . . so (The Princess reminds Boyet that pride is self-glorifying and thus sinful, however much he may have meant that he was honored to be asked to serve.) **37 votaries** those who have taken vows **38 vow-fellows** individuals bound by the same vow **41 beauteous** beautiful **44 sovereign parts** excellent qualities **45 fitted in arts** furnished with learning **46 Nothing . . . well** Nothing is unbecoming in him that he undertakes to do well. **47–9 The only . . . will** i.e., The only blot on the appearance of his general excellence, if virtue's fair appearance can sustain any blemish, is a sharp wit matched with too much bluntness **50 Whose** i.e., the wit's. **still** continually **51 his** its **52 belike** most likely. **57–60 Of . . . wit** i.e., esteemed for his virtue by those who love virtue; one whose graces give him the power to do much harm, even though he has no such intent, for he has intelligence enough to put a good appearance on things that are not good and an appearance so attractive that he would win favor even if he lacked intelligence. **62 little** short, inadequate **63 to** compared with **67 becoming** suitable **68 withal** with. **69 begets occasion** creates opportunities

For every object that the one doth catch
The other turns to a mirth-moving jest,
Which his fair tongue, conceit's expositor,
Delivers in such apt and gracious words
That agèd ears play truant at his tales,
And younger hearings are quite ravishèd,
So sweet and voluble is his discourse.

PRINCESS
God bless my ladies! Are they all in love,
That every one her own hath garnishèd
With such bedecking ornaments of praise?

A LORD
Here comes Boyet.

Enter Boyet.

PRINCESS Now, what admittance, lord?

BOYET
Navarre had notice of your fair approach,
And he and his competitors in oath
Were all addressed to meet you, gentle lady,
Before I came. Marry, thus much I have learned:
He rather means to lodge you in the field,
Like one that comes here to besiege his court,
Than seek a dispensation for his oath
To let you enter his unpeopled house.

Enter [the King of] Navarre, Longaville, Dumaine, and Berowne.

Here comes Navarre.

KING Fair Princess, welcome to the court of Navarre.

PRINCESS "Fair" I give you back again, and "welcome" I have not yet. The roof of this court is too high to be yours, and welcome to the wide fields too base to be mine.

KING
You shall be welcome, madam, to my court.

PRINCESS
I will be welcome, then. Conduct me thither.

KING
Hear me, dear lady: I have sworn an oath.

PRINCESS
Our Lady help my lord! He'll be forsworn.

KING
Not for the world, fair madam, by my will.

PRINCESS
Why, will shall break it—will and nothing else.

KING
Your Ladyship is ignorant what it is.

PRINCESS
Were my lord so, his ignorance were wise,
Where now his knowledge must prove ignorance.
I hear Your Grace hath sworn out housekeeping.
'Tis deadly sin to keep that oath, my lord,
And sin to break it.
But pardon me, I am too sudden-bold;
To teach a teacher ill beseemeth me.
Vouchsafe to read the purpose of my coming,
And suddenly resolve me in my suit.
[*The King is handed a paper.*]

KING
Madam, I will, if suddenly I may.

PRINCESS
You will the sooner that I were away,
For you'll prove perjured if you make me stay.
[*The King reads silently.*]

BEROWNE [*to Rosaline*]
Did not I dance with you in Brabant once?

ROSALINE
Did not I dance with you in Brabant once?

BEROWNE
I know you did.

ROSALINE How needless was it then
To ask the question!

BEROWNE You must not be so quick.

ROSALINE
'Tis long of you, that spur me with such questions.

BEROWNE
Your wit's too hot. It speeds too fast; 'twill tire.

ROSALINE
Not till it leave the rider in the mire.

BEROWNE
What time o'day?

ROSALINE
The hour that fools should ask.

BEROWNE
Now fair befall your mask!

ROSALINE
Fair fall the face it covers!

BEROWNE
And send you many lovers!

ROSALINE
Amen, so you be none.

BEROWNE
Nay, then will I be gone. [*He stands aside.*]

KING [*to the Princess*]
Madam, your father here doth intimate
The payment of a hundred thousand crowns,
Being but the one half of an entire sum
Disbursèd by my father in his wars.
But say that he or we—as neither have—
Received that sum, yet there remains unpaid
A hundred thousand more, in surety of the which

72 conceit's expositor the part of him that gives expression to his clever ideas **74 play truant** i.e., neglect important business **76 voluble** fluent **80 admittance** reception **82 competitors** associates **83 addressed** prepared **88 unpeopled** inadequately staffed with servants **92 The roof of this court** i.e., The sky **99 by my will** willingly. (A common mild oath.) **100 will** intent **101 what it is** what it is that we have sworn. **102–3 Were . . . ignorance** i.e., A better self-knowledge on your part would teach you the wisdom of knowing your own ignorance and thus might save you from the consequences of that imperfect knowledge.

104 sworn out housekeeping renounced hospitality. **108 ill beseemeth me** suits me badly. **109 Vouchsafe** Deign, agree **110 suddenly resolve** quickly answer **112 that . . . away** to procure my departure **114 Brabant** a province in central Belgium **117 quick** sharp. **118 long of** on account of. **spur** goad **119 hot** ardent, eager. **121 What . . . day?** What time of day is it? **123 fair befall** good luck to **124 Fair fall** Good luck to **128 intimate** refer to, discuss, imply **129 The payment** i.e., that he has already paid **131 his** i.e., the king of France's **132 he** i.e., my father **134 in surety** as a guarantee

One part of Aquitaine is bound to us,
Although not valued to the money's worth.
If then the King your father will restore
But that one half which is unsatisfied,
We will give up our right in Aquitaine
And hold fair friendship with His Majesty.
But that, it seems, he little purposeth,
For here he doth demand to have repaid
A hundred thousand crowns, and not demands,
On payment of a hundred thousand crowns,
To have his title live in Aquitaine—
Which we much rather had depart withal,
And have the money by our father lent,
Than Aquitaine, so gelded as it is.
Dear Princess, were not his requests so far
From reason's yielding, your fair self should make
A yielding 'gainst some reason in my breast
And go well satisfied to France again.

PRINCESS
You do the King my father too much wrong,
And wrong the reputation of your name,
In so unseeming to confess receipt
Of that which hath so faithfully been paid.

KING
I do protest I never heard of it;
And, if you prove it, I'll repay it back
Or yield up Aquitaine.

PRINCESS We arrest your word.
Boyet, you can produce acquittances
For such a sum from special officers
Of Charles, his father.

KING Satisfy me so.

BOYET
So please Your Grace, the packet is not come
Where that and other specialties are bound.
Tomorrow you shall have a sight of them.

KING
It shall suffice me, at which interview
All liberal reason I will yield unto.
Meantime, receive such welcome at my hand
As honor, without breach of honor, may
Make tender of to thy true worthiness.
You may not come, fair Princess, within my gates,
But here without you shall be so received
As you shall deem yourself lodged in my heart,
Though so denied fair harbor in my house.
Your own good thoughts excuse me, and farewell.
Tomorrow shall we visit you again.

PRINCESS
Sweet health and fair desires consort Your Grace!

KING
Thy own wish wish I thee in every place.
Exit [with Longaville and Dumaine].

BEROWNE [*to Rosaline*] Lady, I will commend you to mine own heart.

ROSALINE Pray you, do my commendations. I would be glad to see it.

BEROWNE I would you heard it groan.

ROSALINE Is the fool sick?

BEROWNE Sick at the heart.

ROSALINE
Alack, let it blood.

BEROWNE
Would that do it good?

ROSALINE
My physic says "ay."

BEROWNE
Will you prick't with your eye?

ROSALINE
Non point, with my knife.

BEROWNE
Now, God save thy life!

ROSALINE
And yours from long living!

BEROWNE
I cannot stay thanksgiving. *Exit.*

Enter Dumaine.

DUMAINE [*to Boyet*]
Sir, I pray you, a word. What lady is that same?

BOYET
The heir of Alençon, Katharine her name.

DUMAINE
A gallant lady. Monsieur, fare you well. *Exit.*

[*Enter Longaville.*]

LONGAVILLE [*to Boyet*]
I beseech you a word. What is she in the white?

BOYET
A woman sometimes, an you saw her in the light.

LONGAVILLE
Perchance light in the light. I desire her name.

BOYET
She hath but one for herself; to desire that were a shame.

136 valued equal in value **141 little purposeth** scarcely intends **142 demand . . . repaid** insists he has already repaid **143 and not demands** i.e., instead of proposing or stipulating **145 To have . . . Aquitaine** i.e., to regain his title to Aquitaine by paying the 100,000 crowns that are owed to Navarre **146 depart withal** part with **148 gelded** emasculated, weakened in value (with one part cut away) **151 A yielding . . . breast** i.e., a willingness on my part to compromise, despite the fact that right is on my side **155 unseeming** being apparently unwilling **159 arrest** take as security **160 acquittances** receipts for payment of a debt **162 his father** i.e., the King of Navarre's father (referred to in lines 131 and 147). **Satisfy me so** Prove to me that this is true. **164 specialties** warrants, special documents **167 All . . . unto** I will freely yield to all reasonable terms. **170 Make tender of** offer **172 without** outside **173 As** that

177 consort attend **178 Thy . . . place** I return your good wishes wherever you may be. **184 the fool** (A term of endearment or gentle raillery.) **186 let it blood** bleed it. (A reference to the medical practice of drawing blood.) **188 physic** medical knowledge **189 Will . . . eye?** i.e., Will you stab me through the heart with your glance, smiting me as with Cupid's arrow? (With wordplay on *eye* and *ay* in line 188.) **190 *Non* . . . knife** (By playfully proposing to stab Berowne's heart with a knife point, rather than a mere glance of her "killing" eye, Rosaline deflates his flowery metaphors with a dose of reality.) **193 I . . . thanksgiving** I can't stay to thank you for that. (Rosaline has just put Berowne down by saying, in effect, "May you not live long!") **197 What** Who **198 an** if **199 light in the light** wanton when her conduct is known or brought to light. **200 She . . . shame** (Boyet wittily replies as though Longaville, in desiring her name, had asked to take Maria's name away from her.)

LONGAVILLE
Pray you, sir, whose daughter?
BOYET
Her mother's, I have heard.
LONGAVILLE
God's blessing on your beard! 203
BOYET
Good sir, be not offended.
She is an heir of Falconbridge.
LONGAVILLE
Nay, my choler is ended. 206
She is a most sweet lady.
BOYET
Not unlike, sir. That may be. *Exit Longaville.* 208

Enter Berowne.

BEROWNE
What's her name in the cap?
BOYET
Rosaline, by good hap. 210
BEROWNE
Is she wedded or no?
BOYET
To her will, sir, or so. 212
BEROWNE
Oh, you are welcome, sir. Adieu.
BOYET
Farewell to me, sir, and welcome to you. 214
Exit Berowne.
MARIA
That last is Berowne, the merry madcap lord.
Not a word with him but a jest.
BOYET And every jest but a word. 216
PRINCESS
It was well done of you to take him at his word. 217
BOYET
I was as willing to grapple as he was to board. 218
KATHARINE
Two hot sheeps, marry.
BOYET And wherefore not ships? 219
No sheep, sweet lamb, unless we feed on your lips.
KATHARINE
You sheep, and I pasture. Shall that finish the jest? 221
BOYET
So you grant pasture for me. [*Offering to kiss her.*]
KATHARINE Not so, gentle beast. 222
My lips are no common, though several they be. 223
BOYET
Belonging to whom?
KATHARINE To my fortunes and me.
PRINCESS
Good wits will be jangling; but, gentles, agree. 225
This civil war of wits were much better used
On Navarre and his bookmen, for here 'tis abused. 227
BOYET
If my observation, which very seldom lies,
By the heart's still rhetoric disclosèd with eyes, 229
Deceive me not now, Navarre is infected.
PRINCESS With what?
BOYET
With that which we lovers entitle "affected." 232
PRINCESS Your reason?
BOYET
Why, all his behaviors did make their retire 234
To the court of his eye, peeping thorough desire. 235
His heart, like an agate, with your print impressed, 236
Proud with his form, in his eye pride expressed. 237
His tongue, all impatient to speak and not see, 238
Did stumble with haste in his eyesight to be; 239
All senses to that sense did make their repair, 240
To feel only looking on fairest of fair. 241
Methought all his senses were locked in his eye,
As jewels in crystal for some prince to buy, 243
Who, tend'ring their own worth from where they
were glassed, 244
Did point you to buy them, along as you passed. 245
His face's own margent did quote such amazes 246
That all eyes saw his eyes enchanted with gazes.
I'll give you Aquitaine and all that is his, 248
An you give him for my sake but one loving kiss. 249
PRINCESS
Come to our pavilion. Boyet is disposed. 250
BOYET
But to speak that in words which his eye hath
disclosed. 251
I only have made a mouth of his eye,
By adding a tongue which I know will not lie.
ROSALINE
Thou art an old lovemonger and speakest skillfully.
MARIA
He is Cupid's grandfather, and learns news of him.

203 God's . . . beard! (To insult or pluck a man's beard was a standard Elizabethan way to challenge someone to a duel.) **206 choler** anger **208 unlike** unlikely **210 hap** fortune. **212 or so** or something of that kind. **214 Farewell . . . you** You bid me "farewell" and I will say "you're welcome to go." **216 Not . . . jest** Everything he says is a joke. **217 take . . . word** (1) vie with him in wordplay (2) take him literally. **218 grapple, board** (Tactics of sea warfare, here applied to the badinage, with bawdy overtones.) **219 sheeps, ships** (Pronounced nearly alike by Elizabethans.) **221 pasture** (With a play on "pastor," shepherd.) **222 So** Provided **223 common** common land for pasturing. (With a bawdy suggestion of "available to all men.") **223 several** (1) private enclosed land (2) more than one (3) parted

225 jangling quarreling. **gentles** gentlefolk **227 bookmen** scholars. **abused** misapplied. **229 By . . . eyes** seen with the eyes and thus interpreted by the heart's silent rhetoric **232 affected** being in love. **234 behaviors** actions. **make their retire** withdraw, retire. (Navarre was dumbstruck, unable to do anything except gaze at the Princess.) **235 thorough** through **236 agate** (An allusion to small figures cut in agate stones.) **print impressed** image engraved **237 Proud . . . expressed** proud of the form (of the Princess) imprinted on it, expressed that pride through the look in his eye. **238 to speak . . . see** at being able to speak only and not to see **239 in his . . . be** to take part in his seeing **240 that sense** i.e., the eyesight. **make their repair** go **241 To . . . fair** to express themselves solely through looking upon the most beautiful of women. **243 in crystal** enclosed within crystal glass **244 Who . . . glassed** which, proclaiming their worth from the crystal glass of the eyes in which they lay encased **245 point** appoint, direct, invite **246 His . . . amazes** i.e., His expression of amazement offered such a visible commentary on what his eyes saw. (*Margents* or margins of books often bore commentary on the text proper.) **248 I'll give you** i.e., I warrant you can have **249 An** if **250 disposed** inclined (to be merry). **251 But** Merely. **his** i.e., the King's

KATHARINE
Then was Venus like her mother, for her father is
but grim.

BOYET
Do you hear, my mad wenches?

MARIA No.

BOYET What then, do you see?

KATHARINE
Ay, our way to be gone.

BOYET You are too hard for me.

Exeunt omnes.

✤

[3.1]

Enter [*Armado the*] *braggart and* [*Mote,*] *his boy.*

ARMADO Warble, child. Make passionate my sense of hearing.

MOTE [*singing*] Concolinel.

ARMADO Sweet air! Go, tenderness of years. [*He gives a key.*] Take this key, give enlargement to the swain, bring him festinately hither. I must employ him in a letter to my love.

MOTE Master, will you win your love with a French brawl?

ARMADO How meanest thou? Brawling in French?

MOTE No, my complete master, but to jig off a tune at the tongue's end, canary to it with your feet, humor it with turning up your eyelids, sigh a note and sing a note, sometime through the throat as if you swallowed love with singing love, sometime through the nose as if you snuffed up love by smelling love, with your hat penthouse-like o'er the shop of your eyes, with your arms crossed on your thin-belly doublet like a rabbit on a spit, or your hands in your pocket like a man after the old painting, and keep not too long in one tune, but a snip and away. These are compliments, these are humors; these betray nice wenches that would be betrayed without these, and make them men of note—do you note?—men that most are affected to these.

ARMADO How hast thou purchased this experience?

MOTE By my penny of observation.

ARMADO But oh, but oh—

MOTE "The hobbyhorse is forgot."

ARMADO Call'st thou my love "hobbyhorse"?

MOTE No, master; the hobbyhorse is but a colt, and your love perhaps a hackney. But have you forgot your love?

ARMADO Almost I had.

MOTE Negligent student, learn her by heart.

ARMADO By heart and in heart, boy.

MOTE And out of heart, master. All those three I will prove.

ARMADO What wilt thou prove?

MOTE A man, if I live; and this, "by," "in," and "without," upon the instant: "by" heart you love her because your heart cannot come by her; "in" heart you love her because your heart is in love with her; and "out" of heart you love her, being out of heart that you cannot enjoy her.

ARMADO I am all these three.

MOTE And three times as much more—[*aside*] and yet nothing at all.

ARMADO Fetch hither the swain. He must carry me a letter.

MOTE [*aside*] A message well sympathized—a horse to be ambassador for an ass.

ARMADO Ha, ha! What sayest thou?

MOTE Marry, sir, you must send the ass upon the horse, for he is very slow-gaited. But I go.

ARMADO The way is but short. Away!

MOTE As swift as lead, sir.

ARMADO The meaning, pretty ingenious?
Is not lead a metal heavy, dull, and slow?

MOTE
Minime, honest master; or rather, master, no.

ARMADO
I say lead is slow.

MOTE You are too swift, sir, to say so.
Is that lead slow which is fired from a gun?

ARMADO Sweet smoke of rhetoric!
He reputes me a cannon, and the bullet, that's he.
I shoot thee at the swain.

MOTE Thump, then, and I flee.

[*Exit.*]

ARMADO
A most acute juvenal, voluble and free of grace!
By thy favor, sweet welkin, I must sigh in thy face.

256 Then . . . grim i.e., Boyet isn't nearly handsome enough to have given Venus her beauty. **257 Do you hear** i.e., Won't you listen to me. (But the ladies parry Boyet's *hear* and *see* to their own witty purposes.) **mad** high-spirited **258 our . . . gone** the way out of here. **hard** sharp, difficult to outwit **258.1** ***omnes*** all.

3.1. Location: Navarre's park.

1 passionate impassioned, responsive **3 Concolinel** (Unidentified; perhaps the name or refrain of a song.) **4 air** song **5 enlargement** release from confinement **6 festinately** quickly **9 brawl** a French dance figure. **10 Brawling** Quarreling **11 complete** accomplished. **jig . . . tune** sing a jiglike tune **12 canary** dance. (From the name of a lively dance; compare *jig*.) **17 penthouse-like** like the projecting second story of a house built out to shelter the shop on the ground floor **18 arms crossed** (Betokening melancholy; compare 4.3.131.) **thin-belly doublet** (1) man's jacket over his thin belly, thin because of lovesickness (2) a jacket thinly padded in the waist **19 after** in the style of **20 old painting** (If Mote refers here to a specific painting, it remains unidentified, but he may merely mean "some old painting.") **21 a snip and away** a snippet or scrap of one song and then on to another. **compliments** gentlemanly accomplishments. (Or perhaps *complements*, those things that complete or make perfect.) **22 humors** moods. **nice** coy

23 note (1) distinction (2) musical notation **24 affected** inclined, drawn **27–8 But oh . . . forgot.** (Probably the refrain of a popular song; it turns up again in *Hamlet*, 3.2.133. The hobbyhorse was the figure of a horse made of light material and fastened over the torso and head of a morris dancer.) **30–1 hobbyhorse, colt, hackney** (Slang terms for prostitutes or wanton persons.) **37 prove** demonstrate. (But Mote then uses the word in line 39 also to mean "turn out to be.") **41 come by** possess **43 out of heart** discouraged, depressed **48 me** for me **50 sympathized** matched **59** ***Minime*** Not at all **64 Thump** (Representing the sound of cannon.) **65 voluble** quick-witted **66 favor** good will, permission. **welkin** sky

Most rude melancholy, valor gives thee place.
My herald is returned.

Enter [*Mote the*] *page and* [*Costard the*] *clown.*

MOTE
A wonder, master! Here's a costard broken in a shin.

ARMADO
Some enigma, some riddle. Come, thy *l'envoi*; begin.

COSTARD No egma, no riddle, no *l'envoi*, no salve in the mail, sir. Oh, sir, plantain, a plain plantain. No *l'envoi*, no *l'envoi*, no salve, sir, but a plantain.

ARMADO By virtue, thou enforcest laughter; thy silly thought, my spleen; the heaving of my lungs provokes me to ridiculous smiling. Oh, pardon me, my stars! Doth the inconsiderate take "salve" for *l'envoi*, and the word *l'envoi* for a salve?

MOTE
Do the wise think them other? Is not *l'envoi* a salve?

ARMADO
No, page, it is an epilogue or discourse to make plain
Some obscure precedence that hath tofore been sain.
I will example it:
The fox, the ape, and the humble-bee
Were still at odds, being but three.
There's the moral. Now the *l'envoi.*

MOTE
I will add the *l'envoi*. Say the moral again.

ARMADO
The fox, the ape, and the humble-bee
Were still at odds, being but three.

MOTE
Until the goose came out of door,
And stayed the odds by adding four.
Now will I begin your moral, and do you follow with my *l'envoi*.
The fox, the ape, and the humble-bee
Were still at odds, being but three.

ARMADO
Until the goose came out of door,
Staying the odds by adding four.

MOTE A good *l'envoi*, ending in the goose. Would you desire more?

COSTARD
The boy hath sold him a bargain—a goose, that's flat.
Sir, your pennyworth is good, an your goose be fat.
To sell a bargain well is as cunning as fast and loose.
Let me see: a fat *l'envoi*—ay, that's a fat goose.

ARMADO
Come hither, come hither. How did this argument begin?

MOTE
By saying that a costard was broken in a shin.
Then called you for the *l'envoi.*

COSTARD True, and I for a plantain. Thus came your argument in; then the boy's fat *l'envoi*, the goose that you bought; and he ended the market.

ARMADO But tell me, how was there a costard broken in a shin?

MOTE I will tell you sensibly.

COSTARD Thou hast no feeling of it, Mote. I will speak that *l'envoi*:
I Costard, running out, that was safely within,
Fell over the threshold and broke my shin.

ARMADO We will talk no more of this matter.

COSTARD Till there be more matter in the shin.

ARMADO Sirrah Costard, I will enfranchise thee.

COSTARD Oh, marry me to one Frances! I smell some *l'envoi*, some goose, in this.

ARMADO By my sweet soul, I mean setting thee at liberty, enfreedoming thy person. Thou wert immured, restrained, captivated, bound.

COSTARD True, true, and now you will be my purgation and let me loose.

ARMADO I give thee thy liberty, set thee from durance, and in lieu thereof impose on thee nothing but this: Bear this significant [*giving a letter*] to the country maid Jaquenetta. There is remuneration. [*He gives money.*] For the best ward of mine honor is rewarding my dependents. —Mote, follow. [*Exit.*]

MOTE
Like the sequel, I. Seigneur Costard, adieu. [*Exit.*]

67 gives thee place gives way to you. **69 Here's . . . shin** Here's an apple or a head with a bruised shin. (An *enigma*, as Armado points out, since apples and heads don't have shins, though Mote means simply that Costard is limping.) **70 *l'envoi*** i.e., postscript or commendatory statement to the reader attached to a composition; here, an explanation **71 egma** (Costard's attempt at *enigma*; he evidently mistakes this strange name, along with *riddle* and *l'envoi*, as a kind of salve for his hurt shin.) **salve** (With a play seemingly on *salve*, meaning "hail!" Armado points out in his next speech that Costard has mistaken *salve*, a salutation, for *l'envoi*, a farewell.) **72 mail** pouch, bag. (Suggesting the bag of a mountebank or seller of cures.) **plantain** an old-fashioned herbal remedy (which Costard prefers to the strange-sounding *egma*, etc.) **74 By virtue** (A colorful oath.) **75 spleen** i.e., laughter. (The *spleen*, supposedly the seat of emotions and passions, was held to be the organ that controlled excessive mirth or anger.) **76 ridiculous** scornful. (But with unintended meaning of "absurd.") **my stars** the stars that govern my destiny. **77 inconsiderate** mindless fellow. **salve** (Here it is used in the Latin sense of "hail.") **81 precedence** preceding discourse. **tofore** previously. **sain** said. **82 example** give an example of **83 humble-bee** bumblebee **84 still** continually. **at odds** (1) at enmity (2) an odd number, i.e., three **85 moral** riddle or allegory. **90 stayed the odds** (1) stopped the enmity (2) changed odd to even. **four** a fourth.

97 *l'envoi*...goose (Mote's joke is based on the fact that *l'envoi* ends with the same sound as the French word for goose, *oie*. Armado has made himself the goose by playing Mote's game.) **99 sold . . . bargain** i.e., outwitted him. **flat** certain. **100 your . . . good** i.e., you got your money's worth. **an** if **101 fast and loose** a cheating trick. (See 1.2.151.) **104 broken in a shin** with a cut or bruised shin. **108 and . . . market** (Costard refers to the proverbial expression "Three women and a goose make a market.") **109 how** in what sense **111 sensibly** feelingly. (But Costard protests that Mote cannot personally know what it *feels* like.) **117 matter** pus. (Playing on *matter*, business, in line 116.) **118 enfranchise** release from confinement. (Costard hears this as *en-Frances*, "provide with a Frances.") **120 goose** (Slang for "prostitute.") **122 immured** imprisoned **124–5 be my purgation** purge me of guilt. (With pun on the sense of giving a purgative so that Costard's bowels will be *let loose*.) **126 set** release. **durance** imprisonment. **128 significant** sign, token **129 remuneration** payment. **130 ward** guard **132 the sequel** that which follows; *l'envoi*

COSTARD
My sweet ounce of man's flesh, my incony Jew! Now will I look to his remuneration. [*He looks at his money.*] Remuneration! Oh, that's the Latin word for three farthings. Three farthings—remuneration. "What's the price of this inkle?"—"One penny."—"No, I'll give you a remuneration." Why, it carries it. Remuneration! Why, it is a fairer name than French crown. I will never buy and sell out of this word.

Enter Berowne.

BEROWNE My good knave Costard, exceedingly well met.

COSTARD Pray you, sir, how much carnation ribbon may a man buy for a remuneration?

BEROWNE What is a remuneration?

COSTARD Marry, sir, halfpenny farthing.

BEROWNE Why, then, three farthing worth of silk.

COSTARD I thank Your Worship. God be wi' you!
[*He starts to leave.*]

BEROWNE Stay, slave, I must employ thee.
As thou wilt win my favor, good my knave,
Do one thing for me that I shall entreat.

COSTARD When would you have it done, sir?

BEROWNE This afternoon.

COSTARD Well, I will do it, sir. Fare you well.

BEROWNE Thou knowest not what it is.

COSTARD I shall know, sir, when I have done it.

BEROWNE Why, villain, thou must know first.

COSTARD I will come to Your Worship tomorrow morning.

BEROWNE It must be done this afternoon. Hark, slave, it is but this:
The Princess comes to hunt here in the park,
And in her train there is a gentle lady;
When tongues speak sweetly, then they name her name,
And Rosaline they call her. Ask for her,
And to her white hand see thou do commend
This sealed-up counsel. There's thy guerdon; go.
[*Giving him a letter and a shilling.*]

COSTARD Gardon, O sweet gardon! Better than remuneration, a 'levenpence farthing better. Most sweet gardon! I will do it, sir, in print. Gardon! Remuneration! *Exit.*

BEROWNE
And I, forsooth, in love! I that have been Love's whip,
A very beadle to a humorous sigh,
A critic, nay, a night-watch constable,
A domineering pedant o'er the boy,
Than whom no mortal so magnificent!
This wimpled, whining, purblind, wayward boy,
This Senior Junior, giant dwarf, Dan Cupid,
Regent of love rhymes, lord of folded arms,
Th'anointed sovereign of sighs and groans,
Liege of all loiterers and malcontents,
Dread prince of plackets, king of codpieces,
Sole imperator and great general
Of trotting paritors—Oh, my little heart!
And I to be a corporal of his field
And wear his colors like a tumbler's hoop!
What? I love, I sue, I seek a wife?
A woman, that is like a German clock,
Still a-repairing, ever out of frame,
And never going aright, being a watch,
But being watched that it may still go right?
Nay, to be perjured, which is worst of all;
And, among three, to love the worst of all—
A whitely wanton with a velvet brow,
With two pitch-balls stuck in her face for eyes;
Ay, and, by heaven, one that will do the deed
Though Argus were her eunuch and her guard.
And I to sigh for her, to watch for her,
To pray for her! Go to, it is a plague
That Cupid will impose for my neglect
Of his almighty dreadful little might.
Well, I will love, write, sigh, pray, sue, groan.
Some men must love milady, and some Joan. [*Exit.*]

133 incony fine, rare, delicate. **Jew** (Here it is a term of playful insult, possibly suggested by *juvenile*.) **136 farthings** coins worth a quarter of a penny. **137 inkle** a kind of linen tape. **138 carries it** wins the day. **139–40 French crown** (1) a coin (2) a bald head, the result of syphilis or "the French disease." **140 out of** i.e., without using **141–2 exceedingly well met** i.e., how fortunate to see you just now. **143 carnation** flesh-colored **146 halfpenny farthing** i.e., three farthings (a *halfpenny*, worth two farthings, plus one farthing). **149 slave** i.e., fellow, rascal **150 good my knave** my good fellow **166 commend** entrust **167 counsel** private or secret communication. **guerdon** reward. **167.1 *shilling*** a silver coin worth twelve pence **168 Gardon** (Costard anglicizes the French *guerdon*.) **168–9 Better . . . better** (Costard delights that the shilling he has been given is worth eleven pence and a farthing more than the three farthings he had.) **170 in print** i.e., most exactly.

173 beadle parish officer responsible for whipping minor offenders. **humorous** moody **175 pedant** schoolmaster **177 wimpled** blindfolded. **purblind** quite blind **178 Dan** Don, Sir. (From the Latin *dominus*.) **179 Regent** ruler. **folded arms** (Betokening melancholy; see 3.1.18.) **182 plackets** slits in petticoats. (Referring bawdily to women.) **codpieces** flaps or pouches concealing the opening in the front of men's breeches. (Referring bawdily to men.) **183 imperator** absolute ruler **184 paritors** apparitors, summoners of ecclesiastical courts (who could make a profit by spying out sexual offenders) **185 a corporal . . . field** Cupid's field officer. **186 tumbler's hoop** (Such hoops were usually brightly decorated with silks and ribbons.) **189 Still a-repairing** Always in need of repair. **frame** order **191 But being watched** unless it is watched carefully (like a wandering wife) **194 whitely** pale of complexion. (Considered beautiful; but compare 4.3.250–73, where the lords joke about the darkness of Rosaline's features.) **velvet** i.e., soft-skinned **195 pitch-balls** balls made of pitch, a viscous black substance created by distilling tar **196 do the deed** engage in sex **197 Argus** a fabulous monster with a hundred eyes, some of which were always awake. (Juno gave Argus custody over Io, of whom Jove was enamored.) **eunuch** i.e., guard in a seraglio **198 watch** lose sleep, stay awake **199 Go to** (An expression of impatience.) **202 sue** plead **203 milady, Joan** (Opposite types on the social scale—one a lady or quality and one a peasant woman.)

[4.1]

Enter the Princess, a Forester, her Ladies, and her Lords [*Boyet and others*].

PRINCESS
Was that the King that spurred his horse so hard
Against the steep uprising of the hill?

BOYET
I know not, but I think it was not he.

PRINCESS
Whoe'er 'a was, 'a showed a mounting mind.
Well, lords, today we shall have our dispatch;
On Saturday we will return to France.
Then, Forester, my friend, where is the bush
That we must stand and play the murderer in?

FORESTER
Hereby, upon the edge of yonder coppice,
A stand where you may make the fairest shoot.

PRINCESS
I thank my beauty, I am fair that shoot,
And thereupon thou speak'st "the fairest shoot."

FORESTER
Pardon me, madam, for I meant not so.

PRINCESS
What, what? First praise me and again say no?
Oh short-lived pride! Not fair? Alack, for woe!

FORESTER
Yes, madam, fair.

PRINCESS Nay, never paint me now.
Where fair is not, praise cannot mend the brow.
Here, good my glass, take this for telling true.
[*She gives him money.*]
Fair payment for foul words is more than due.

FORESTER
Nothing but fair is that which you inherit.

PRINCESS
See, see, my beauty will be saved by merit!
Oh, heresy in fair, fit for these days!
A giving hand, though foul, shall have fair praise.
But come, the bow. [*She takes the bow.*] Now mercy goes to kill,
and shooting well is then accounted ill.
Thus will I save my credit in the shoot:
Not wounding, pity would not let me do't;
If wounding, then it was to show my skill,
That more for praise than purpose meant to kill.
And, out of question, so it is sometimes,
Glory grows guilty of detested crimes,
When for fame's sake, for praise, an outward part,
We bend to that the working of the heart,
As I for praise alone now seek to spill
The poor deer's blood that my heart means no ill.

BOYET
Do not curst wives hold that self-sovereignty
Only for praise' sake when they strive to be
Lords o'er their lords?

PRINCESS
Only for praise, and praise we may afford
To any lady that subdues a lord.

Enter [*Costard the*] *clown* [*with a letter*].

BOYET
Here comes a member of the commonwealth.

COSTARD God-i-good-e'en all! Pray you, which is the head lady?

PRINCESS Thou shalt know her, fellow, by the rest that have no heads.

COSTARD Which is the greatest lady, the highest?

PRINCESS The thickest and the tallest.

COSTARD
The thickest and the tallest! It is so; truth is truth
An your waist, mistress, were as slender as my wit,
One o' these maids' girdles for your waist should be fit.
Are not you the chief woman? You are the thickest here.

PRINCESS What's your will, sir? What's your will?

COSTARD I have a letter from Monsieur Berowne to one Lady Rosaline.

PRINCESS [*to Rosaline*]
Oh, thy letter, thy letter! He's a good friend of mine.
Stand aside, good bearer. Boyet, you can carve;
Break up this capon. [*The letter is given to Boyet.*]

BOYET I am bound to serve.
This letter is mistook; it importeth none here.
It is writ to Jaquenetta.

4.1. Location: Navarre's park. A hunter's station at the edge of a coppice.
4 'a he. **mounting** (1) rising (2) aspiring **5 dispatch** settlement and dismissal **9 coppice** grove of trees **10 stand** hunter's station, toward which the game is driven. **fairest** most favorable. (The Princess chooses to play on the word in a compliment to herself.) **14 again** i.e., then **16 paint** flatter **17 fair** beauty. **brow** forehead, i.e., face. **18 good my glass** my true mirror. (I.e., a counselor who will not flatter. The Princess amuses herself with Renaissance commonplaces about the value of honest counselors to a true prince, much to the discomfort of the Forester.) **20 inherit** possess. **21 my . . . merit** i.e., my beauty is complimented again in return for my giving a gratuity. (To be *saved by merit* was, however, a heresy according to orthodox Anglican doctrine, which taught salvation by faith rather than by merit or good works.) **22 in fair** regarding beauty. **these days** i.e., these times of religious controversy. **24 mercy** i.e., the Princess, who as a royal woman is an emblem of mercy **25 then** i.e., when a merciful person like the Princess goes hunting **26 credit** reputation **27 Not . . . do't** i.e., I can claim, if I miss, that pity restrained me **29 That . . . kill** i.e., I shot to earn praise for my skill rather than for the sake of killing. **30–1 And . . . crimes** And undoubtedly it is occasionally true that an excessive desire for glory prompts us to commit detestable crimes **32 an outward part** a superficial thing **33 We . . . heart** we deflect the promptings of our heart into an excessive desire for fame **34 As** just as **35 The poor . . . ill** the blood of the poor deer that means me no harm. **36–8 Do . . . lord?** Don't shrewish wives show pride when they claim sole sovereignty in marriage? (But the Princess, in her reply in lines 39–40, defends and honors such assertive wives.) **41 commonwealth** ordinary citizenry. **42 God-i-good-e'en** God give you good afternoon **47 The thickest . . . tallest** (The Princess quips that *greatest* could be defined this way. Costard, in his reply, lines 48–51, undiplomatically observes that the terms could indeed be applied to her.) **49 An** if **55 He's . . . mine** (Perhaps the Princess says this to explain her excitement over the letter. *He's* seems to refer to Berowne.) **56 carve** (1) cut up, i.e., open (2) make courtly gestures. **57 Break up** cut up (a technical term in carving), i.e., open. **capon** (Like the French *poulet, capon* designates figuratively a love letter.) **bound** obliged **58 mistook** mis-taken, misdirected. **importeth** concerns

PRINCESS We will read it, I swear.
Break the neck of the wax, and everyone give ear.

BOYET (*reads*) "By heaven, that thou art fair is most infallible; true that thou art beauteous; truth itself that thou art lovely. More fairer than fair, beautiful than beauteous, truer than truth itself, have commiseration on thy heroical vassal! The magnanimous and most illustrate King Cophetua set eye upon the pernicious and indubitate beggar Zenelophon; and he it was that might rightly say, '*Veni, vidi, vici*'; which to annothanize in the vulgar—Oh, base and obscure vulgar!—videlicet, 'He came, saw, and overcame.' He came, one; saw, two; overcame, three. Who came? The King. Why did he come? To see. Why did he see? To overcome. To whom came he? To the beggar. What saw he? The beggar. Who overcame he? The beggar. The conclusion is victory. On whose side? The King's. The captive is enriched. On whose side? The beggar's. The catastrophe is a nuptial. On whose side? The King's—no, on both in one, or one in both. I am the King, for so stands the comparison; thou the beggar, for so witnesseth thy lowliness. Shall I command thy love? I may. Shall I enforce thy love? I could. Shall I entreat thy love? I will. What shalt thou exchange for rags? Robes. For tittles? Titles. For thyself? Me. Thus, expecting thy reply, I profane my lips on thy foot, my eyes on thy picture, and my heart on thy every part.

Thine, in the dearest design of industry,
Don Adriano de Armado.

Thus dost thou hear the Nemean lion roar
'Gainst thee, thou lamb, that standest as his prey.
Submissive fall his princely feet before,
And he from forage will incline to play.
But if thou strive, poor soul, what art thou then?
Food for his rage, repasture for his den."

PRINCESS
What plume of feathers is he that indited this letter?
What vane? What weathercock? Did you ever hear better?

BOYET
I am much deceived but I remember the style.

PRINCESS
Else your memory is bad, going o'er it erewhile.

BOYET
This Armado is a Spaniard that keeps here in court,
A phantasime, a Monarcho, and one that makes sport
To the Prince and his bookmates.

PRINCESS [*to Costard*] Thou fellow, a word.
Who gave thee this letter?

COSTARD I told you—my lord.

PRINCESS
To whom shouldst thou give it?

COSTARD From my lord to my lady.

PRINCESS
From which lord to which lady?

COSTARD
From my lord Berowne, a good master of mine,
To a lady of France that he called Rosaline.

PRINCESS
Thou hast mistaken his letter. Come, lords, away.
[*To Rosaline*] Here, sweet, put up this; 'twill be thine another day. [*Exeunt Princess and attendants.*]

BOYET
Who is the shooter? Who is the shooter?

ROSALINE Shall I teach you to know?

BOYET
Ay, my continent of beauty.

ROSALINE Why, she that bears the bow.
Finely put off!

BOYET
My lady goes to kill horns, but if thou marry,
Hang me by the neck if horns that year miscarry.
Finely put on!

ROSALINE
Well, then, I am the shooter.

BOYET And who is your deer?

ROSALINE
If we choose by the horns, yourself come not near.
Finely put on, indeed!

MARIA
You still wrangle with her, Boyet, and she strikes at the brow.

60 wax seal **62 infallible** certain, incontrovertible **64 commiseration** pity **65 vassal** humble servant. **66 illustrate** illustrious. **King Cophetua.** (See 1.2.105–6 and note.) **pernicious** (Armado may mean "penurious," or the text may be in error.) **67 indubitate** undoubted. **Zenelophon** Penelophon, the beggar maid in the ballad about King Cophetua **68 *Veni, vidi, vici*** I came, I saw, I overcame. (The words are Julius Caesar's terse account of his victory over King Pharnaces.) **68–9 annothanize** annotate (pseudo-Latin), or, anatomize, explain, interpret **69 vulgar** vernacular **70 videlicet** namely **77 catastrophe** conclusion **78–9 for . . . comparison** according to this analogy **80 lowliness** low social standing. **83 tittles** insignificant specks or dots. **84 profane** desecrate **86 dearest . . . industry** most excellent pattern of zealous gallantry **88 Nemean lion** lion slain by Hercules in the first of his twelve labors **90 Submissive fall** If you fall submissively **91 forage** raging, ravening. **incline** turn, shift **92 strive** resist **93 repasture** food **94 What . . . feathers** What kind of bird, dandy. **indited** wrote **95 vane . . . weathercock** weathervane (because showy and constantly shifting) **96 I . . . but I** i.e., unless my memory fails me, I

97 Else Otherwise. **going o'er it** (1) reading it over (2) climbing over a *stile*, playing on "style." **erewhile** just now. **98 keeps** lives, dwells **99 phantasime** one who entertains fantastic notions. **Monarcho** (The nickname of an eccentric Italian at the Elizabethan court who fancied himself the emperor of the world; hence, anyone who displays absurd pretensions.) **100 To** for. **bookmates** fellow scholars. **106 mistaken** incorrectly delivered **107 up** away. **'twill be thine** i.e., it will be your turn. **s.d. *attendants*** (Perhaps the Forester exits here.) **108 shooter** archer. (With a pun on "suitor." Boyet may be asking who is to shoot, now that the Princess has left. Perhaps Rosaline has been given the bow.) **109 continent of** container of all **110 put off** answered evasively. **111 horns** i.e., deer **112 horns** i.e., cuckolds' horns. (Boyet saucily suggests that, if Rosaline marries, cuckolds' horns will not be in short supply.) **miscarry** do not appear. **113 put on** urged, applied. **114 deer** (With pun on "dear"; Rosaline is the natural target of all this double entendre about the huntress who is hunting for a husband, since Berowne is known to have written her a love letter.) **115 If . . . near** (Rosaline retorts to Boyet acerbically by intimating that he couldn't possibly be her choice.) **117 she . . . brow** i.e., she takes good aim at you. (With pun on the idea that she has also put Boyet down with a joke about cuckoldry.)

BOYET
But she herself is hit lower. Have I hit her now?

ROSALINE Shall I come upon thee with an old saying that was a man when King Pépin of France was a little boy, as touching the hit it?

BOYET So I may answer thee with one as old, that was a woman when Queen Guinevere of Britain was a little wench, as touching the hit it.

ROSALINE
"Thou canst not hit it, hit it, hit it,
Thou canst not hit it, my good man."

BOYET
"An I cannot, cannot, cannot,
An I cannot, another can." *Exit* [*Rosaline*].

COSTARD
By my troth, most pleasant. How both did fit it!

MARIA
A mark marvelous well shot, for they both did hit it.

BOYET
A mark! Oh, mark but that mark! "A mark," says my lady!
Let the mark have a prick in't to mete at, if it may be.

MARIA
Wide o'the bow hand! I' faith, your hand is out.

COSTARD
Indeed, 'a must shoot nearer, or he'll ne'er hit the clout.

BOYET [*to Maria*]
An if my hand be out, then belike your hand is in.

COSTARD
Then will she get the upshoot by cleaving the pin.

MARIA
Come, come, you talk greasily; your lips grow foul.

COSTARD
She's too hard for you at pricks, sir. Challenge her to bowl.

BOYET
I fear too much rubbing. Good night, my good owl.
[*Exeunt Boyet, Maria, and Katharine.*]

COSTARD
By my soul, a swain, a most simple clown!
Lord, Lord, how the ladies and I have put him down!
O' my troth, most sweet jests, most incony vulgar wit!
When it comes so smoothly off, so obscenely, as it were, so fit.
Armado o'th'one side—oh, a most dainty man!
To see him walk before a lady and to bear her fan!
To see him kiss his hand, and how most sweetly 'a will swear!
And his page o't'other side, that handful of wit!
Ah, heavens, it is a most pathetical nit! *Shout within.*
Sola, sola! *Exit* [*Costard, running*].

✤

[4.2]

Enter Dull, Holofernes the pedant, and Nathaniel.

NATHANIEL Very reverend sport, truly, and done in the testimony of a good conscience.

HOLOFERNES The deer was, as you know, *sanguis*, in blood, ripe as the pomewater, who now hangeth like a jewel in the ear of *caelo*, the sky, the welkin, the heaven, and anon falleth like a crab on the face of *terra*, the soil, the land, the earth.

NATHANIEL Truly, Master Holofernes, the epithets are sweetly varied, like a scholar at the least. But, sir, I assure ye, it was a buck of the first head.

HOLOFERNES Sir Nathaniel, *haud credo.*

DULL 'Twas not a *haud credo*, 'twas a pricket.

HOLOFERNES Most barbarous intimation! Yet a kind of insinuation, as it were, *in via*, in way, of explication; *facere*, as it were, replication, or rather, *ostentare*, to show, as it were, his inclination, after his undressed, unpolished, uneducated, unpruned, untrained, or rather, unlettered, or, ratherest, unconfirmed fashion, to insert again my *haud credo* for a deer.

DULL I said the deer was not a *haud credo*, 'twas a pricket.

HOLOFERNES Twice-sod simplicity, *bis coctus!*
O thou monster Ignorance, how deformed dost thou look!

118 hit lower i.e., in the heart, or, more bawdily, in the genital region. **hit her** scored on her in this game of wit, described her situation aright **119 come upon thee** answer or hit back. (Continuing the metaphor of hunting and marksmanship.) **120 was a man** i.e., was already old. **King Pépin** Carolingian king (died 768) **121 as . . . hit it** concerning a catch or round, to be sung dancing. (The song itself is obviously bawdy.) **122 So** As long as, or similarly **123 Guinevere** King Arthur's unfaithful queen **129 fit it** fit the lyrics to the tune. (*Fit it* often has a bawdy meaning as well.) **130 mark** target **132 prick** spot in the center of the target, the bull's-eye. (With sexual double meaning, as throughout this passage. *Mark* here suggests "pudendum.") **mete at** measure with the eye, aim at **133 Wide . . . hand** Wide of the mark on the left side, too far to the left. **out** inaccurate, out of practice. **134 clout** mark at the center of the target. (Continuing the bawdry.) **135 An if . . . is in** i.e., If I'm out of practice (sexually as well as at shooting), no doubt you're in practice. **belike** most likely **136 upshoot** leading or best shot. **cleaving the pin** splitting exactly the small nail holding the clout in place. (With sexual suggestion, as Maria observes in the next line.) **137 greasily** indecently. (Referring to sexual double entendre in *cleaving, hit it, prick, your hand is in*, etc.) **138 pricks** archery. (With sexual pun.) **139 rubbing** grazing or striking together of the bowling balls. (With sexual pun.) **owl** (Maria is so addressed because the owl is a bird of night and because to "take owl" is to take offense; also with a bawdy hint at "hole," rhyming with *bowl*.)

140 swain peasant **142 incony** fine, rare **143 obscenely** (Perhaps a malapropism for "seemly," with unintended appropriateness to the preceding passage.) **fit** suitable. **144 dainty** refined, elegant **148 it** he. **pathetical nit** i.e., touching little fellow. (A *nit* is the egg of a small insect.) **149 Sola** (A hunting cry.)
4.2. Location: Navarre's park.
1 reverend worthy of respect **1–2 in the testimony** with the warrant **3–4 in blood** in prime condition **4 pomewater** a kind of apple. **who now** which at one moment **5 welkin** sky **6 anon** at the next moment. **crab** crab apple **9 at the least** to say the least. **10 of . . . head** in its fifth year, hence with newly full antlers. **11 Sir** (Term of address for ordinary clergymen.) ***haud credo*** I cannot believe it. **12 *haud credo*** (Dull mistakes the Latin for something like "old gray doe.") **pricket** buck in its second year **13 intimation** intrusion. **14 insinuation** hint, suggestion, beginning **15 *facere*** to make. **replication** explanation **18 unconfirmed** inexperienced **19 insert again** substitute, interpret **22 Twice-sod** Twice sodden or cooked, boiled. ***bis coctus.*** twice cooked. (Holofernes is incensed at Dull's twice insisting on his error.)

NATHANIEL
Sir, he hath never fed of the dainties that are bred
in a book. 24
He hath not eat paper, as it were; he hath not drunk 25
ink. His intellect is not replenished. He is only an ani-
mal, only sensible in the duller parts; 27
And such barren plants are set before us that we
thankful should be—
Which we of taste and feeling are—for those parts
that do fructify in us more than he. 29
For as it would ill become me to be vain, indiscreet,
or a fool,
So were there a patch set on learning to see him
in a school. 31
But *omne bene*, say I, being of an old Father's mind: 32
"Many can brook the weather that love not the wind." 33

DULL
You two are bookmen. Can you tell me by your wit
What was a month old at Cain's birth that's not
five weeks old as yet?

HOLOFERNES
Dictynna, goodman Dull, Dictynna, goodman Dull. 36

DULL What is Dictima?

NATHANIEL A title to Phoebe, to Luna, to the moon. 38

HOLOFERNES
The moon was a month old when Adam was no
more, 39
And raught not to five weeks when he came to
fivescore. 40
Th'allusion holds in the exchange. 41

DULL 'Tis true indeed. The collusion holds in the ex- 42
change.

HOLOFERNES God comfort thy capacity! I say, th'allu- 44
sion holds in the exchange.

DULL And I say the pollution holds in the exchange, for 46
the moon is never but a month old; and I say beside
that 'twas a pricket that the Princess killed.

HOLOFERNES Sir Nathaniel, will you hear an extemporal 49
epitaph on the death of the deer? And, to humor the
ignorant, call I the deer the Princess killed a pricket.

NATHANIEL *Perge*, good Master Holofernes, *perge*, so it 52
shall please you to abrogate scurrility. 53

HOLOFERNES I will something affect the letter, for it ar- 54
gues facility. 55
The preyful Princess pierced and pricked a pretty
pleasing pricket; 56
Some say a sore, but not a sore till now made sore
with shooting. 57
The dogs did yell. Put "l" to "sore," then sorel jumps
from thicket, 58
Or pricket sore, or else sorel. The people fall a-hooting. 59
If sore be sore, then "l" to "sore" makes fifty sores
o' sorel. 60
Of one sore I an hundred make by adding but one
more "l."

NATHANIEL A rare talent!

DULL [*aside*] If a talent be a claw, look how he claws 63
him with a talent.

HOLOFERNES This is a gift that I have, simple, simple—
a foolish extravagant spirit, full of forms, figures,
shapes, objects, ideas, apprehensions, motions, revo- 67
lutions. These are begot in the ventricle of memory, 68
nourished in the womb of *pia mater*, and delivered 69
upon the mellowing of occasion. But the gift is good 70
in those in whom it is acute, and I am thankful for it.

NATHANIEL Sir, I praise the Lord for you, and so may
my parishioners, for their sons are well tutored by
you, and their daughters profit very greatly under you. 74
You are a good member of the commonwealth.

HOLOFERNES *Mehercle*, if their sons be ingenious, they 76
shall want no instruction; if their daughters be capa- 77
ble, I will put it to them. But *vir sapit qui pauca loquitur*. 78
A soul feminine saluteth us.

Enter Jaquenetta and [*Costard*] *the clown.*

JAQUENETTA God give you good morrow, Master Person. 80

HOLOFERNES Master Person, *quasi* pierce-one. And if 81
one should be pierced, which is the one? 82

24 of on. **dainties** delicacies **25 eat** eaten. (Pronounced "et.") **27 sensible** capable of perception **29 fructify** grow fruitful. **he** in him. **31 were . . . learning** (1) it would be setting a fool or dolt to learn (2) it would be a disgrace to learning itself **32 *omne bene*** all is well. **being . . . mind** agreeing as I do with one of the Fathers of the early Christian Church **33 Many . . . wind** i.e., One must endure what one cannot change. (A proverb, and hardly the wisdom of the Church Fathers.) **brook** put up with **36, 38 Dictynna, Phoebe, Luna** (Classical names for the moon. The first is uncommon and is appropriate to the pedant. It occurs in Golding's translation of Ovid, a book that Shakespeare knew.) **39 no more** no older **40 raught** reached, attained **41 Th'allusion . . . exchange** i.e., The riddle is still valid even if Cain's name (see line 35) is substituted for Adam's. **42 collusion** conspiracy. (Dull's error for "allusion.") **44 comfort** have pity on **46 pollution** (Another error for "allusion," with perhaps unintended relevance to the linguistic *pollution* of Holofernes' Latin.) **49 extemporal** impromptu **52 Perge** Proceed **52–3 so . . . scurrility** if you will be so good as to refrain from bawdry.

54 something . . . letter somewhat make use of alliteration **54–5 argues** demonstrates **56 preyful** intent upon prey **57 sore** buck in its fourth year. **made sore** wounded **58 Put "l" to "sore"** (The "l" is like a yelling noise that alarms the buck.) **sorel** buck in its third year **59 Or** Either **60 If sore be sore** If it's a sore buck that is wounded. **"l"** ("L" is Roman numeral fifty.) **63 talent** i.e., talon. **claws** (1) scratches (2) flatters **67 motions** impulses **67–8 revolutions** turns of thought. **68 ventricle of memory** one of the three sections of the brain, believed to contain the memory **69 *pia mater*** the membrane surrounding the brain; the brain itself **69–70 delivered . . . occasion** born when the moment is propitious. **74 under you** under your instruction. (With unintended sexual double meaning.) **76 *Mehercle*** By Hercules. **ingenious** clever **77 want** lack **77–8 capable** (1) apt as pupils (2) able to bear children (an unconscious sexual pun that goes back to *under you* in line 74) **78 put it to them** (With unintended sexual meaning.) **78 *vir . . . loquitur*** he is a wise man who says little. **80 Person** (Normally pronounced "parson" in Elizabethan English, but here pronounced "person," in rustic speech, thereby eliciting a pedantic witticism from Holofernes.) **81 *quasi*** that is, as if **82 pierced** (Pronounced "persed"; playing on *pers-one*, "pierce one." This is sometimes taken as an allusion to Nashe's *Pierce Penniless, His Supplication to the Devil*, a fantastic satire in which the author, in the character of Pierce, comments on the vices of the times; also to Harvey's answer, *Pierce's Supererogation*, in which Pierce is referred to as "the hogshead of wit"; compare line 85.)

COSTARD Marry, Master Schoolmaster, he that is likeliest to a hogshead.

HOLOFERNES Of piercing a hogshead! A good luster of conceit in a turf of earth; fire enough for a flint, pearl enough for a swine. 'Tis pretty, it is well.

JAQUENETTA Good Master Person, be so good as read me this letter. It was given me by Costard and sent me from Don Armado. I beseech you, read it.

[*She hands the letter to Nathaniel.*]

HOLOFERNES *"Fauste, precor gelida quando pecus omne sub umbra ruminat,"* and so forth. Ah, good old Mantuan! I may speak of thee as the traveler doth of Venice:

Venezia, Venezia,
Chi non ti vede, chi non ti prezia.

Old Mantuan, old Mantuan! Who understandeth thee not, loves thee not. [*He sings.*] Ut, re, sol, la, mi, fa. [*To Nathaniel, who is examining the letter.*] Under pardon, sir, what are the contents? Or rather, as Horace says in his—What, my soul, verses?

NATHANIEL Ay, sir, and very learned.

HOLOFERNES Let me hear a staff, a stanza, a verse. *Lege, domine.*

NATHANIEL [*reads*]

"If love make me forsworn, how shall I swear to love?
Ah, never faith could hold, if not to beauty vowed!
Though to myself forsworn, to thee I'll faithful prove;
Those thoughts to me were oaks, to thee like osiers bowed.
Study his bias leaves and makes his book thine eyes,
Where all those pleasures live that art would comprehend.
If knowledge be the mark, to know thee shall suffice;
Well learnd is that tongue that well can thee commend,
All ignorant that soul that sees thee without wonder;
Which is to me some praise that I thy parts admire.
Thy eye Jove's lightning bears, thy voice his dreadful thunder,
Which, not to anger bent, is music and sweet fire.
Celestial as thou art, oh, pardon love this wrong,
That sings heaven's praise with such an earthly tongue."

HOLOFERNES You find not the apostrophus, and so miss the accent. Let me supervise the canzonet. [*He takes the letter.*] Here are only numbers ratified, but, for the elegancy, facility, and golden cadence of poesy—*caret*. Ovidius Naso was the man. And why indeed "Naso" but for smelling out the odoriferous flowers of fancy, the jerks of invention? *Imitari* is nothing. So doth the hound his master, the ape his keeper, the tired horse his rider. But, damosella virgin, was this directed to you?

JAQUENETTA Ay, sir, from one Monsieur Berowne, one of the strange queen's lords.

HOLOFERNES I will overglance the superscript: "To the snow-white hand of the most beauteous Lady Rosaline. "I will look again on the intellect of the letter for the nomination of the party writing to the person written unto: "Your Ladyship's in all desired employment, Berowne." Sir Nathaniel, this Berowne is one of the votaries with the King, and here he hath framed a letter to a sequent of the stranger queen's, which accidentally, or by the way of progression, hath miscarried.—Trip and go, my sweet; deliver this paper into the royal hand of the King. It may concern much. [*He gives her the letter.*] Stay not thy compliment. I forgive thy duty. Adieu.

JAQUENETTA Good Costard, go with me.—Sir, God save your life!

COSTARD Have with thee, my girl.

Exit [*with Jaquenetta*].

NATHANIEL Sir, you have done this in the fear of God, very religiously; and, as a certain Father saith—

HOLOFERNES Sir, tell not me of the Father, I do fear colorable colors. But to return to the verses: did they please you, Sir Nathaniel?

NATHANIEL Marvelous well for the pen.

HOLOFERNES I do dine today at the father's of a certain pupil of mine, where, if before repast it shall please you to gratify the table with a grace, I will, on my privilege I have with the parents of the foresaid child or pupil,

84 likeliest most like. **hogshead** barrel. (With a suggestion also of "fathead.") **85 piercing a hogshead** broaching a barrel, i.e., getting drunk. **85–6 A good . . . earth** A good spark of fancy in one who is close to the soil **91–2 *Fauste . . . ruminat*** (The first line of the first eclogue of the Italian Renaissance poet Mantuan. It was a well-known text in the schools. The passage means "Faustus, I beg, while all the cattle chew their cud in the cool shade.") **94–5 *Venezia . . . prezia*** Venice, Venice, only he who sees you not loves you not. **97 Ut** (Equivalent to the modern *do*. If Holofernes intends to sing the scale, *do, re, mi, fa, sol, la*, he displays his ignorance, but he may be singing a fragment of a melody.) **98 Under pardon** i.e., Excuse me **102 staff** stanza **102–3 *Lege, domine*** Read, master. **104–17 If . . . tongue** (These lines were printed with minor changes in *The Passionate Pilgrim*, 1599, a collection of poems by various authors but attributed to Shakespeare. Two others of the volume are also from this play—that read by Longaville, 4.3.56–69, and that by Dumaine, 4.3.97–116.) **107 osiers** willows **108 Study . . . leaves** i.e., The student leaves his studious inclination **110 mark** target, goal **113 Which . . . admire** which reflects well on me in that I sing your praises. **115 bent** turned, directed **116 pardon . . . wrong** excuse this failure in my loving. (Or else, "Oh, pardon, love, this wrong.")

118 find heed. **apostrophus** apostrophes, marks of elision used to indicate omitted vowels and shortened pronunciation of a word **119 supervise the canzonet** peruse the poem. **120 only numbers ratified** i.e., merely language made metrical **122 *caret*** it is lacking. **Ovidius Naso** The Roman poet Ovid, born in 43 B.C. (*Naso*, his surname, is derived from *nasus*, nose.) **124 fancy** imagination. **jerks of invention** strokes of imagination. ***Imitari*** To imitate **129 strange** foreign. (Either Jaquenetta believes mistakenly that Berowne is attached to the Princess's retinue, or she means that the Princess and her ladies regard the young aristocratic men as their "lords," their beaux.) **130 superscript** address **132 intellect** meaning, import, contents **133 nomination** name **134–5 all desired employment** any service you require of me **136 votaries** those who have taken a vow **137 sequent** follower, attendant **138 by . . . progression** in process of delivery **139 Trip and go** Move nimbly and swiftly. (A phrase from a popular song.) **140–1 concern much** be of importance. **141–2 Stay . . . compliment** i.e., Don't stand on ceremony. **142 I forgive thy duty** I set aside the requirement of a curtsy. **145 Have with thee** I'll go with you **147 Father** Church Father **149 colorable colors** i.e., specious authorities. **151 pen** penmanship, or style. **153 repast** the meal **154 gratify** (1) delight (2) grace. **the table** i.e., those at the table

undertake your *ben venuto*; where I will prove those verses to be very unlearned, neither savoring of poetry, wit, nor invention. I beseech your society.

NATHANIEL And thank you too; for society, saith the text, is the happiness of life.

HOLOFERNES And certes the text most infallibly concludes it. [*To Dull*] Sir, I do invite you too. You shall not say me nay. *Pauca verba*. Away! The gentles are at their game, and we will to our recreation. *Exeunt.*

✣

[4.3]

Enter Berowne, with a paper in his hand, alone.

BEROWNE The King, he is hunting the deer; I am coursing myself. They have pitched a toil; I am toiling in a pitch—pitch that defiles. Defile! A foul word. Well, set thee down, sorrow! For so they say the fool said, and so say I—and I the fool. Well proved, wit! By the Lord, this love is as mad as Ajax. It kills sheep; it kills me, I a sheep. Well proved again o' my side! I will not love; if I do, hang me. I' faith, I will not. Oh, but her eye! By this light, but for her eye I would not love her. Yes, for her two eyes. Well, I do nothing in the world but lie, and lie in my throat. By heaven, I do love, and it hath taught me to rhyme and to be melancholy; and here is part of my rhyme, and here my melancholy. Well, she hath one o' my sonnets already. The clown bore it, the fool sent it, and the lady hath it—sweet clown, sweeter fool, sweetest lady! By the world, I would not care a pin, if the other three were in. Here comes one with a paper. God give him grace to groan! *He stands aside.*

The King entereth [*with a paper*].

KING Ay me!

BEROWNE [*aside*] Shot, by heaven! Proceed, sweet Cupid. Thou hast thumped him with thy bird-bolt under the left pap. In faith, secrets!

KING [*reads*]
"So sweet a kiss the golden sun gives not
To those fresh morning drops upon the rose
As thy eyebeams, when their fresh rays have smote
The night of dew that on my cheeks down flows.
Nor shines the silver moon one-half so bright
Through the transparent bosom of the deep
As doth thy face, through tears of mine, give light;
Thou shin'st in every tear that I do weep.
No drop but as a coach doth carry thee;
So ridest thou triumphing in my woe.
Do but behold the tears that swell in me,
And they thy glory through my grief will show.
But do not love thyself; then thou wilt keep
My tears for glasses, and still make me weep.
O queen of queens! How far dost thou excel,
No thought can think nor tongue of mortal tell."
How shall she know my griefs? I'll drop the paper.
Sweet leaves, shade folly. Who is he comes here?

Enter Longaville [*with papers*]. *The King steps aside.*

What, Longaville, and reading! Listen, ear.

BEROWNE [*aside*]
Now, in thy likeness, one more fool appear!

LONGAVILLE Ay me, I am forsworn!

BEROWNE [*aside*]
Why, he comes in like a perjure, wearing papers.

KING [*aside*]
In love, I hope. Sweet fellowship in shame!

BEROWNE [*aside*]
One drunkard loves another of the name.

LONGAVILLE
Am I the first that have been perjured so?

BEROWNE [*aside*]
I could put thee in comfort: not by two that I know.
Thou makest the triumviry, the corner-cap of society,
The shape of Love's Tyburn, that hangs up simplicity.

LONGAVILLE
I fear these stubborn lines lack power to move.
[*Reading*] "O sweet Maria, empress of my love!"—
These numbers will I tear, and write in prose.
[*He tears the paper.*]

BEROWNE [*aside*]
Oh, rhymes are guards on wanton Cupid's hose;

156 undertake your *ben venuto* ensure your welcome **158 society** company. **161–2 certes . . . concludes it** certainly the biblical text you allude to (perhaps Ecclesiastes 4:8–12) infallibly demonstrates the point. **163 *Pauca verba*** Few words. **gentles** gentlefolk **164 game** i.e., hunting

4.3 Location: Navarre's park.

2 coursing pursuing. **pitched a toil** set a snare **2–3 toiling . . . pitch** i.e., struggling in the toils of love. (*Pitch* means both "sticky tar" and "a fixed opinion," with a quibbling reference to Rosaline's eyes, which he has earlier, in 3.1.195, called *two pitch-balls.*) **3 defiles** corrupts. (See Ecclesiasticus 13:1: "Whoso toucheth pitch shall be defiled withal.")
4 set thee down i.e., stay, settle down with me. (See 1.1.305–6.) **4 they . . . said** people attribute that saying to a fool **5 and I the fool** and the fool turns out to be myself. **6 mad as Ajax** (An allusion to the story of Ajax, who, maddened by his failure in a contest for Achilles's armor, attacked a flock of sheep, supposing them to be those who had denied him the prize.) **11 in my throat** i.e., utterly. **17 in** involved (i.e., in love).
18 God . . . groan! i.e., May God grant that he be moved to groan for love!
18.1 *He stands aside* (Possibly Berowne hides in some elevated place understood to be a tree; see 4.3.75, 161.) **21 bird-bolt** blunt arrow for shooting birds **22 left pap** left breast . (Where the heart is located.)
In faith, secrets! i.e., In truth, we will now hear a confession of love!

25 smote struck **26 night of dew** i.e., tears that flow nightly
28 the deep a body of water reflecting the moonlight **36 glasses** mirrors. **still** continually **40 shade** conceal **42 thy** i.e., the King's
44 perjure perjurer. **wearing papers** (An allusion to the custom of attaching to a convicted perjurer's breast the papers involved in and setting forth his offense—in this case, the poem, which is an open indication of Longaville's having forsworn his vow to eschew love.)
46 One . . . name A drunkard finds comfort in the drunkenness of another; misery loves company. **49 Thou . . . society** You make up the triumvirate, the three-cornered cap of our fellowship **50 Tyburn** (A place of public execution in London; with reference here to the triangular structure of the gallows.) **51 stubborn** rough, harsh
53 numbers verses **54 guards** trim, decorative embroideries.
hose breeches

Disfigure not his shop.

LONGAVILLE [*taking another paper*] This same shall go.

(*He reads the sonnet.*)

"Did not the heavenly rhetoric of thine eye,
'Gainst whom the world cannot hold argument,
Persuade my heart to this false perjury?
Vows for thee broke deserve not punishment.
A woman I forswore, but I will prove,
Thou being a goddess, I forswore not thee.
My vow was earthly, thou a heavenly love.
Thy grace being gained cures all disgrace in me.
Vows are but breath, and breath a vapor is.
Then thou, fair sun, which on my earth dost shine,
Exhal'st this vapor vow; in thee it is.
If broken, then, it is no fault of mine.
If by me broke, what fool is not so wise
To lose an oath to win a paradise?"

BEROWNE [*aside*]
This is the liver vein, which makes flesh a deity,
A green goose a goddess. Pure, pure idolatry.
God amend us, God amend! We are much out
o'the way.

Enter Dumaine [*with a paper*].

LONGAVILLE
By whom shall I send this?—Company! Stay.
[*He steps aside.*]

BEROWNE [*aside*]
All hid, all hid—an old infant play.
Like a demigod here sit I in the sky,
And wretched fools' secrets heedfully o'ereye.
More sacks to the mill! Oh, heavens, I have my wish!
Dumaine transformed! Four woodcocks in a dish!

DUMAINE O most divine Kate!

BEROWNE [*aside*] O most profane coxcomb!

DUMAINE
By heaven, the wonder in a mortal eye!

BEROWNE [*aside*]
By earth, she is not, Corporal. There you lie.

DUMAINE
Her amber hairs for foul hath amber quoted.

BEROWNE [*aside*]
An amber-colored raven was well noted.

DUMAINE
As upright as the cedar.

BEROWNE [aside] Stoop, I say!
Her shoulder is with child.

DUMAINE As fair as day.

BEROWNE [*aside*]
Ay, as some days; but then no sun must shine.

DUMAINE
Oh, that I had my wish!

LONGAVILLE [aside] And I had mine!

KING [*aside*]
And I mine too, good Lord!

BEROWNE [*aside*]
Amen, so I had mine. Is not that a good word?

DUMAINE
I would forget her, but a fever she
Reigns in my blood and will remembered be.

BEROWNE [*aside*]
A fever in your blood! Why, then incision
Would let her out in saucers. Sweet misprision!

DUMAINE
Once more I'll read the ode that I have writ.

BEROWNE [*aside*]
Once more I'll mark how love can vary wit.

DUMAINE (*reads his sonnet*)
"On a day—alack the day!—
Love, whose month is ever May,
Spied a blossom passing fair
Playing in the wanton air.
Through the velvet leaves the wind,
All unseen, can passage find,
That the lover, sick to death,
Wished himself the heaven's breath.
'Air,' quoth he, 'thy cheeks may blow;
Air, would I might triumph so!
But, alack, my hand is sworn
Ne'er to pluck thee from thy thorn—
Vow, alack, for youth unmeet,
Youth so apt to pluck a sweet!
Do not call it sin in me
That I am forsworn for thee,
Thou for whom Jove would swear
Juno but an Ethiop were,
And deny himself for Jove,
Turning mortal for thy love.' "
This will I send, and something else more plain,

55 Disfigure . . . shop Don't deface Cupid's place of workmanship (where love's embroideries are fashioned). **56–69 Did . . . paradise?** (See the note on 4.2.104–17.) **57 whom** i.e., which **63 Thy . . . me** i.e., The fact that you are a goddess exculpates me, since I vowed only to forswear the company of women, not goddesses. **66 Exhal'st** draws up. (It was thought that the sun drew up vapors from the earth, thereby producing meteors, will-o'-the-wisps, etc.) **68 If** Even if **69 To** As to **70 the liver vein** i.e., the vein or style of a lover. (Since the liver was assumed to be the seat of the passions.) **71 green goose** gosling, i.e., a young girl, a strumpet **72 much...way** far gone. **74 infant play** child's game of hide and seek. (But with a suggestion also of a medieval religious play, in which God appears above.) **75 in the sky** (Berowne speaks as though he were looking down on the others from some elevated position, possibly the gallery above the stage; see also 4.3.161.) **76 heedfully o'ereye** attentively observe. **77 More . . . mill** (A proverbial expression, here suggesting that more food for laughter appears to be on its way.) **78 woodcocks** (Birds noted for their stupidity.) **81 mortal** human **82 Corporal** i.e., field officer for Cupid (see 3.1.185). With a play on "corporeal," fleshly.) **83 quoted** designated. (Dumaine hyperbolically insists that her amber hair makes real amber seem foul, ugly, by comparison.)

84 An . . . noted i.e. (ironically), Dumaine has aptly described a black fowl (with pun on "foul") as amber-colored. **85 Stoop** (1) Stooped, Stunted (2) Dumaine should avoid such lofty comparisons **86 is with child** i.e., is swollen, unshapely. **90 Is . . . word?** (1) Isn't that kind of me? (2) Isn't *amen* known to be a good word? **91 a fever** as a fever **92 and . . . be** and cannot be ignored. **93 incision** letting blood **94 in saucers** (1) by the bowlful (2) into bowls to catch the blood. **misprision** (1) mistake (2) being released from confinement (of the veins). **96 can vary wit** can inspire variety of expression. **97–116 On . . . love** (See the note on 4.2.104–17.) **99 passing** surpassingly **100 wanton** frolicsome **102 can** began to **103 That** so that **109 unmeet** inappropriate **114 Ethiop** Ethiopian, black African. (Used here as an example of ugliness.) **115 for Jove** to be Jove

That shall express my true love's fasting pain.
Oh, would the King, Berowne, and Longaville
Were lovers too! Ill, to example ill,
Would from my forehead wipe a perjured note,
For none offend where all alike do dote.

LONGAVILLE [*advancing*]
Dumaine, thy love is far from charity,
That in love's grief desir'st society.
You may look pale, but I should blush, I know,
To be o'erheard and taken napping so.

KING [*advancing*]
Come, sir, you blush! As his, your case is such;
You chide at him, offending twice as much.
You do not love Maria? Longaville
Did never sonnet for her sake compile,
Nor never lay his wreathèd arms athwart
His loving bosom to keep down his heart?
I have been closely shrouded in this bush
And marked you both, and for you both did blush.
I heard your guilty rhymes, observed your fashion,
Saw sighs reek from you, noted well your passion.
"Ay me!" says one. "O Jove!" the other cries;
One, her hairs were gold, crystal the other's eyes.
[*To Longaville*] You would for paradise break faith and troth;
[*To Dumaine*] And Jove, for your love, would infringe an oath.
What will Berowne say when that he shall hear
Faith infringèd, which such zeal did swear?
How will he scorn! How will he spend his wit!
How will he triumph, leap, and laugh at it!
For all the wealth that ever I did see
I would not have him know so much by me.

BEROWNE [*advancing*]
Now step I forth to whip hypocrisy.
Ah, good my liege, I pray thee, pardon me.
Good heart, what grace hast thou, thus to reprove
These worms for loving, that art most in love?
Your eyes do make no coaches; in your tears
There is no certain princess that appears;
You'll not be perjured, 'tis a hateful thing—
Tush, none but minstrels like of sonneting!
But are you not ashamed? Nay, are you not,
All three of you, to be thus much o'ershot?
[*To Longaville*] You found his mote; the King your mote did see;
But I a beam do find in each of three.
Oh, what a scene of foolery have I seen,
Of sighs, of groans, of sorrow, and of teen!
Oh, me, with what strict patience have I sat,
To see a king transformèd to a gnat!
To see great Hercules whipping a gig,
And profound Solomon to tune a jig,
And Nestor play at pushpin with the boys,
And critic Timon laugh at idle toys!
Where lies thy grief, oh, tell me, good Dumaine?
And, gentle Longaville, where lies thy pain?
And where my liege's? All about the breast.—
A caudle, ho!

KING Too bitter is thy jest.
Are we betrayed thus to thy overview?

BEROWNE
Not you to me, but I betrayed by you.
I, that am honest, I, that hold it sin
To break the vow I am engagèd in,
I am betrayed by keeping company
With men like you, men of inconstancy.
When shall you see me write a thing in rhyme?
Or groan for Joan? Or spend a minute's time
In pruning me? When shall you hear that I
Will praise a hand, a foot, a face, an eye,
A gait, a state, a brow, a breast, a waist,
A leg, a limb— [*He starts to leave.*]

KING Soft! Whither away so fast?
A true man or a thief, that gallops so?

BEROWNE
I post from love. Good lover, let me go.

Enter Jaquenetta [*with a letter*], *and* [*Costard the*] *clown.*

JAQUENETTA
God bless the King!

KING What present hast thou there?

COSTARD
Some certain treason.

KING What makes treason here?

COSTARD
Nay, it makes nothing, sir.

KING If it mar nothing neither,
The treason and you go in peace away together.

JAQUENETTA
I beseech Your Grace, let this letter be read.
Our parson misdoubts it; 'twas treason, he said.
[*She gives the letter.*]

KING Berowne, read it over.
He [*Berowne*] *reads the letter* [*silently*].
[*To Jaquenetta*] Where hadst thou it?

118 fasting hungering **120 Ill . . . ill** i.e., Then perjury, by serving as an example and precedent of sin **121 note** mark, document. (See 4.3.44.) **122 dote** love dotingly. **123 charity** Christian love **124 That . . . society** you who, in your suffering from love, uncharitably desire others to suffer also. (Proverbial: "Misery loves company.") **131 lay . . . athwart** i.e., fold his arms in the conventional sign of melancholy; compare 3.1.18 **139 troth** loyalty **140 infringe** break **141 when that** when **146 by** about **149 grace** graciousness; privilege. **reprove** rebuke, condemn **151 Your . . . coaches** (Alluding to the King's sonnet, 4.3.31–2.) **152 certain** particular **154 like** approve **156 o'ershot** wide of the mark, shooting beyond it; i.e., in error. **157, 158 mote, beam** i.e., small speck, large defect. (See Matthew 7:3–5, Luke 6:41–2.) **160 teen** affliction, grief.

162 a gnat i.e., a tiny creature. (With a play perhaps on *mote*.) **163 whipping a gig** spinning a top **164 tune** play or sing **165 Nestor** wise old Greek chieftain in the Trojan War. **pushpin** a child's game **166 critic** critical, censorious. **Timon** a fifth-century Athenian notorious for his misanthropy. **laugh . . . toys** take delight in mindless entertainments. **170 caudle** warm drink given to sick people **179 pruning me** preening, i.e., trimming, dressing up myself. **181 state** attitude, bearing **183 true** honest **184 post** hasten **186 What makes treason** What is treason doing **187–8 If . . . together** (The King acerbically suggests that all will be well if Costard and Jaquenetta just leave. With a play on the common saying, "to make or to mar.") **190 misdoubts** suspects

JAQUENETTA Of Costard.
KING [*to Costard*] Where hadst thou it?
COSTARD Of Dun Adramadio, Dun Adramadio.
[*Berowne tears the letter.*]

KING
How now, what is in you? Why dost thou tear it?

BEROWNE
A toy, my liege, a toy. Your Grace needs not fear it.

LONGAVILLE
It did move him to passion, and therefore let's hear it.

DUMAINE [*gathering up the pieces*]
It is Berowne's writing, and here is his name.

BEROWNE [*to Costard*]
Ah, you whoreson loggerhead! You were born to do
me shame.—
Guilty, my lord, guilty! I confess, I confess.

KING What?

BEROWNE
That you three fools lacked me fool to make up the
mess.
He, he, and you—and you, my liege!—and I,
Are pickpurses in love, and we deserve to die.
Oh, dismiss this audience, and I shall tell you more.

DUMAINE
Now the number is even.

BEROWNE True, true, we are four.
Will these turtles be gone?

KING [*to Costard and Jaquenetta*] Hence, sirs. Away!

COSTARD
Walk aside the true folk, and let the traitors stay.
[*Exeunt Costard and Jaquenetta.*]

BEROWNE
Sweet lords, sweet lovers, oh, let us embrace!
As true we are as flesh and blood can be.
The sea will ebb and flow, heaven show his face;
Young blood doth not obey an old decree.
We cannot cross the cause why we were born;
Therefore of all hands must we be forsworn.

KING
What, did these rent lines show some love of thine?

BEROWNE
Did they, quoth you? Who sees the heavenly Rosaline,
That, like a rude and savage man of Ind
At the first opening of the gorgeous east,
Bows not his vassal head and, strucken blind,
Kisses the base ground with obedient breast?
What peremptory eagle-sighted eye
Dares look upon the heaven of her brow
That is not blinded by her majesty?

KING
What zeal, what fury hath inspired thee now?
My love, her mistress, is a gracious moon,
She an attending star, scarce seen a light.

BEROWNE
My eyes are then no eyes, nor I Berowne.
Oh, but for my love, day would turn to night!
Of all complexions the culled sovereignty
Do meet as at a fair in her fair cheek,
Where several worthies make one dignity,
Where nothing wants that want itself doth seek.
Lend me the flourish of all gentle tongues—
Fie, painted rhetoric! Oh, she needs it not.
To things of sale a seller's praise belongs;
She passes praise, then praise too short doth blot.
A withered hermit, fivescore winters worn,
Might shake off fifty, looking in her eye.
Beauty doth varnish age, as if newborn,
And gives the crutch the cradle's infancy.
Oh, 'tis the sun that maketh all things shine!

KING
By heaven, thy love is black as ebony.

BEROWNE
Is ebony like her? Oh, word divine!
A wife of such wood were felicity.
Oh, who can give an oath? Where is a book,
That I may swear Beauty doth beauty lack
If that she learn not of her eye to look?
No face is fair that is not full so black.

KING
Oh, paradox! Black is the badge of hell,
The hue of dungeons and the school of night;
And beauty's crest becomes the heavens well.

BEROWNE
Devils soonest tempt, resembling spirits of light.
Oh, if in black my lady's brows be decked,
It mourns that painting and usurping hair
Should ravish doters with a false aspect;
And therefore is she born to make black fair.
Her favor turns the fashion of the days,

197 toy trifle **200 whoreson loggerhead** i.e., infernal blockhead **203 mess** group of four at table. **205 pickpurses** pickpockets (i.e., cheaters) **208 turtles** turtledoves, lovers. **sirs** (An acceptable form of address for both women and men.) **209 Walk . . . folk** i.e., Those who tell the truth are sent away for their efforts. (Costard's wry comment need not be offered as an aside.) **214 We . . . born** We cannot continue to defy natural instinct (i.e., to love) **215 of all hands** inevitably, in every way, on every side **216 rent lines** torn verses **217 quoth you** forsooth. **218 rude** ignorant. **Ind** India **219 opening** i.e., dawning **222 peremptory** bold. **eagle-sighted** (The eagle was believed to be the only bird able to look directly at the sun.)

227 She i.e., Rosaline. **scarce . . . light** a light scarcely visible. **229 my love** the woman I love **230 the culled sovereignty** those chosen as supreme **232 worthies** excellences. **dignity** i.e., supreme example of beauty **233 wants** is lacking. **want** desire **234 flourish** adornment, eloquence. **gentle** noble **235 painted** artificial **236 of sale** for sale **237 She . . . blot** she surpasses all praise, and thus any praise of her falls short and stains her name. **238 fivescore . . . worn** a hundred years old **240 Beauty . . . newborn** Beauty is able to transform old age, giving it a new lease on life **245 were** would be **246 book** i.e., Bible **248 If . . . look?** unless Beauty herself learns from Rosaline's eyes how beauty should truly appear? **249 full** fully **251 the school of night** The King regards a dark beauty as a contradiction in terms, like a school (either Holofernes's kind of school for youngsters or the "academy" to which the gentlemen earlier professed allegiance) devoted to studying dark things. **252 And . . . well** whereas true beauty in all its glory is the adornment of the heavens. **253 spirits of light** angels. (This warning against false appearances is extended in Berowne's following diatribe against cosmetics. Rosaline's dark beauty need not be covered up in this way.) **254 decked** adorned **255–6 It . . . aspect** she is in black as though in mourning for the sad fact that cosmetics and wigs are so often used to seduce doting males with deceptive appearances **258 Her favor turns** Her beauty inverts

For native blood is counted painting now;
And therefore red, that would avoid dispraise,
Paints itself black to imitate her brow.

DUMAINE
To look like her are chimney sweepers black.

LONGAVILLE
And since her time are colliers counted bright.

KING
And Ethiops of their sweet complexion crack.

DUMAINE
Dark needs no candles now, for dark is light.

BEROWNE
Your mistresses dare never come in rain,
For fear their colors should be washed away.

KING
'Twere good yours did; for, sir, to tell you plain,
I'll find a fairer face not washed today.

BEROWNE
I'll prove her fair, or talk till doomsday here.

KING
No devil will fright thee then so much as she.

DUMAINE
I never knew man hold vile stuff so dear.

LONGAVILLE [*showing his shoe*]
Look, here's thy love; my foot and her face see.

BEROWNE
Oh, if the streets were pavèd with thine eyes,
Her feet were much too dainty for such tread!

DUMAINE
Oh, vile! Then, as she goes, what upward lies
The street should see as she walked overhead.

KING
But what of this? Are we not all in love?

BEROWNE
Nothing so sure, and thereby all forsworn.

KING
Then leave this chat, and, good Berowne, now prove
Our loving lawful and our faith not torn.

DUMAINE
Ay, marry, there, some flattery for this evil.

LONGAVILLE
Oh, some authority how to proceed,
Some tricks, some quillets, how to cheat the devil.

DUMAINE
Some salve for perjury.

BEROWNE Oh, 'tis more than need.
Have at you, then, Affection's men-at-arms!
Consider what you first did swear unto:
To fast, to study, and to see no woman—
Flat treason 'gainst the kingly state of youth.
Say, can you fast? Your stomachs are too young,
And abstinence engenders maladies.
Oh, we have made a vow to study, lords,
And in that vow we have forsworn our books.
For when would you, my liege, or you, or you,
In leaden contemplation have found out
Such fiery numbers as the prompting eyes
Of beauty's tutors have enriched you with?
Other slow arts entirely keep the brain,
And therefore, finding barren practicers,
Scarce show a harvest of their heavy toil;
But love, first learnèd in a lady's eyes,
Lives not alone immurèd in the brain,
But with the motion of all elements
Courses as swift as thought in every power,
And gives to every power a double power
Above their functions and their offices.
It adds a precious seeing to the eye;
A lover's eyes will gaze an eagle blind.
A lover's ear will hear the lowest sound,
When the suspicious head of theft is stopped.
Love's feeling is more soft and sensible
Than are the tender horns of cockled snails.
Love's tongue proves dainty Bacchus gross in taste.
For valor, is not Love a Hercules,
Still climbing trees in the Hesperides?
Subtle as Sphinx, as sweet and musical
As bright Apollo's lute strung with his hair.
And when Love speaks, the voice of all the gods
Make heaven drowsy with the harmony.
Never durst poet touch a pen to write
Until his ink were tempered with Love's sighs.
Oh, then his lines would ravish savage ears
And plant in tyrants mild humility.
From women's eyes this doctrine I derive:
They sparkle still the right Promethean fire;
They are the books, the arts, the academes
That show, contain, and nourish all the world;

259 For . . . now for nowadays a natural, ruddy complexion is suspected of being cosmetically put on **260 dispraise** disparagement, censure **263 colliers** coal miners **264 of . . . crack** boast to have attractive complexions. **266 come in** walk in, be exposed to **267 colors** makeup **269 I'll . . . today** i.e., many unwashed faces are cleaner and fairer than hers. **271 then** i.e., on doomsday **272 hold . . . dear** value worthless things so highly. **274–5 Oh, . . . tread!** Oh, even if the street were paved with your soft and delicate eyeballs, her feet would be too dainty to walk on such a surface! **276 what upward lies** (Dumaine bawdily suggests that a street paved with his eyes would be able to look up constantly under her dress.) **281 torn** broken. **282 some . . . evil** i.e., give us some plausible way to put a good face on this difficulty. **284 quillets** verbal niceties, subtle distinctions **285 'tis . . . need** such a comfort is very needful. **286 Have at you** I come at you, i.e., here it is. **Affection's** Love's

289 state (1) condition (2) majesty **291 maladies** (The Quarto here supplies twenty-two lines that appear to be a first start for lines 292–339; seemingly they were meant to be canceled. See Textual Notes.) **295–7 In . . . with?** have found in the dull study of books the inspiration to write passionate verses in the way that the prompting eyes of beauty have tutored you to do? **298 arts** branches of knowledge. **keep** dwell within **302 immurèd** walled up, imprisoned **303 elements** i.e., earth, air, fire, and water **304 Courses** runs. **power** faculty, natural capacity **306 Above . . . offices** above and beyond their ordinary functions. **308 gaze** stare **310 When . . . stopped** even when the most sensitive alertness to the danger of being robbed hears nothing. **311 sensible** sensitive **312 cockled** having a shell **313 Bacchus** god of wine and revelry **314 For** as for **315 Hesperides** where the golden apples grew (the gaining of which was the eleventh of Hercules's twelve labors) **316 Sphinx** mythological creature of ancient Thebes who destroyed all passersby who could not solve her riddle. **317 Apollo's lute** (Apollo was the Greek god of music, poetry, and prophecy.) **320 durst** dares **321 tempered** blended, softened **325 They . . . fire** they continually emit the true heavenly fire. (From the legend that Prometheus stole fire from heaven and gave it to humankind.)

Else none at all in aught proves excellent.
Then fools you were these women to forswear,
Or, keeping what is sworn, you will prove fools.
For wisdom's sake, a word that all men love,
Or for love's sake, a word that loves all men,
Or for men's sake, the authors of these women,
Or women's sake, by whom we men are men,
Let us once lose our oaths to find ourselves,
Or else we lose ourselves to keep our oaths.
It is religion to be thus forsworn,
For charity itself fulfills the law,
And who can sever love from charity?

KING
Saint Cupid, then! And, soldiers, to the field!

BEROWNE
Advance your standards, and upon them, lords;
Pell-mell, down with them! But be first advised
In conflict that you get the sun of them.

LONGAVILLE
Now to plain dealing. Lay these glozes by.
Shall we resolve to woo these girls of France?

KING
And win them, too. Therefore let us devise
Some entertainment for them in their tents.

BEROWNE
First, from the park let us conduct them thither;
Then homeward every man attach the hand
Of his fair mistress. In the afternoon
We will with some strange pastime solace them,
Such as the shortness of the time can shape;
For revels, dances, masques, and merry hours
Forerun fair Love, strewing her way with flowers.

KING
Away, away! No time shall be omitted
That will betime and may by us be fitted.

BEROWNE
Allons! Allons! Sowed cockle reaped no corn,
And justice always whirls in equal measure.
Light wenches may prove plagues to men forsworn;
If so, our copper buys no better treasure. [*Exeunt.*]

✤

[5.1]

Enter [Holofernes] the pedant, [Nathaniel] the curate, and Dull [the constable].

HOLOFERNES *Satis quod sufficit.*

NATHANIEL I praise God for you, sir. Your reasons at dinner have been sharp and sententious, pleasant without scurrility, witty without affection, audacious without impudency, learned without opinion, and strange without heresy. I did converse this quondam day with a companion of the King's who is intituled, nominated, or called Don Adriano de Armado.

HOLOFERNES *Novi hominem tanquam te.* His humor is lofty, his discourse peremptory, his tongue filed, his eye ambitious, his gait majestical, and his general behavior vain, ridiculous, and thrasonical. He is too picked, too spruce, too affected, too odd, as it were, too peregrinate, as I may call it.

NATHANIEL A most singular and choice epithet.
[*He*] *draw*[*s*] *out his table book.*

HOLOFERNES He draweth out the thread of his verbosity finer than the staple of his argument. I abhor such fanatical phantasimes, such insociable and point-devise companions, such rackers of orthography, as to speak "dout," fine, when he should say "doubt"; "det"when he should pronounce "debt"—d, e, b, t, not d, e, t. He clepeth a calf "cauf," half "hauf"; neighbor *vocatur* "nebor"; neigh abbreviated "ne." This is abhominable—which he would call "abbominable." It insinuateth me of insanie. *Ne intelligis, domine?* To make frantic, lunatic.

NATHANIEL *Laus Deo, bone intelligo.*

HOLOFERNES *"Bone?" "Bone"* for *"bene?"* Priscian a little scratched; 'twill serve.

328 Else otherwise. **aught** anything **332 loves** is lovable to, inspires with love **333–4 Or . . . men** (Conventionally, men are the active principle in the creation of human life, while women are the vessels in which all infants are nurtured.) **335 once** for once, one time. **lose** break **338 For . . . law** (From Romans 13:8: "for he that loveth another hath fulfilled the law.") **341 Advance . . . lords** Advance your standards, raise high your banners. (The military metaphor is not only amorous but bawdy.) **342 Pell-mell** without keeping ranks, in hand-to-hand combat. **be first advised** take care first of all **343 get . . . them** i.e., take field position so that the sun is in their eyes. (With a play on the idea of "begetting a son.") **344 glozes** sophistries **349 attach** seize **351 strange** novel, fresh. **solace** entertain **354 Forerun** come before, prepare the way for **356 betime** happen. **fitted** used. (The King resolves to take advantage of every minute.) **357** *Allons!* Come on, let's go! **cockle** a weed. **corn** wheat. (Berowne says that without well-planned efforts there will be no results.) **358 measure** proportion. (Again suggesting that reward comes only from effort.) **359 Light** Giddy, teasing **360 copper** coin of little value. (Berowne's point is that, as beggars and forswearers, the men cannot afford to be choosers.)

5.1. Location: Navarre's park.
1 ***Satis quod sufficit*** Enough is as good as a feast. **2 reasons** discussions, discourses **4 affection** affectation **5 opinion** arrogance, dogmatism **6 strange** novel, new. **this quondam** the other **7 intituled** entitled, named **9** ***Novi . . . te*** I know the man as well as I know you. **10 peremptory** positive, overbearing. **filed** polished **12 thrasonical** boastful. (From Thraso, a braggart soldier in Terence's play *Eunuchus*.) **13 picked** fastidious. **spruce** dapper **14 peregrinate** touristy **15.1** ***table book*** notebook. **17 staple** fiber, thread. **argument** subject matter **18 phantasimes** persons who entertain fantastic notions. **insociable** unsociable, unpleasant **18–19 such . . . companions** such unsociable and pedantically precise fellows **19 rackers of orthography** torturers of spelling. (Holofernes's tirade reflects a conscious attempt of some Renaissance educators to bring the English spelling and pronunciation of certain borrowed words more nearly to their Latin originals.) **20 fine** mincingly, too thinly. (Or perhaps an error for "*sine* b," "without b.") **22 clepeth** calls **23** ***vocatur*** is called **24 abhominable . . . abominable** (This is pedantic to the point of being simply wrong, since the supposed derivation of *abhominable* from *abhomine*, away from mankind, inhuman, is a false one, but it is a derivation that Shakespeare seems elsewhere to have accepted.) **24–5 It . . . insanie** (1) To me it savors of insanity (2) It drives me mad. **25** ***Ne intelligis, domine?*** Do you understand me, sir? **27** ***Laus . . . intelligo*** Praise God, I understand well. **28** ***"Bone"*** **for** ***"bene"*** i.e., The Latin should be *bene*, "well." **28–9 Priscian . . . scratched** i.e., Your Latin is a little faulty. (Priscian was a grammarian of the fifth or sixth century whose textbooks were considered standard.)

Enter [Armado the] braggart, [Mote, his] boy, [and Costard].

NATHANIEL *Videsne quis venit?*

HOLOFERNES *Video, et gaudeo.*

ARMADO *[to Mote]* Chirrah!

HOLOFERNES *Quare* "chirrah," not "sirrah"?

ARMADO Men of peace, well encountered.

HOLOFERNES Most military sir, salutation.

MOTE *[aside to Costard]* They have been at a great feast of languages and stolen the scraps.

COSTARD *[to Mote]* Oh, they have lived long on the alms basket of words. I marvel thy master hath not eaten thee for a word, for thou art not so long by the head as *honorificabilitudinitatibus*. Thou art easier swallowed than a flapdragon.

MOTE *[to Costard]* Peace! The peal begins.

ARMADO *[to Holofernes]* Monsieur, are you not lettered?

MOTE Yes, yes, he teaches boys the hornbook. What is "a, b" spelled backward, with the horn on his head?

HOLOFERNES Ba, *pueritia*, with a horn added.

MOTE Ba, most silly sheep with a horn! You hear his learning.

HOLOFERNES *Quis, quis*, thou consonant?

MOTE The last of the five vowels, if you repeat them; or the fifth, if I.

HOLOFERNES I will repeat them: a, e, i—

MOTE The sheep. The other two concludes it—o, u.

ARMADO Now, by the salt wave of the *Mediterraneum*, a sweet touch, a quick venue of wit! Snip, snap, quick and home. It rejoiceth my intellect. True wit!

MOTE Offered by a child to an old man—which is wit-old.

HOLOFERNES What is the figure? What is the figure?

MOTE Horns.

HOLOFERNES Thou disputes like an infant. Go whip thy gig.

MOTE Lend me your horn to make one, and I will whip about your infamy *manu cita*—a gig of a cuckold's horn.

COSTARD An I had but one penny in the world, thou shouldst have it to buy gingerbread. Hold, there is the very remuneration I had of thy master, thou halfpenny purse of wit, thou pigeon egg of discretion. *[He gives money.]* Oh, an the heavens were so pleased that thou wert but my bastard, what a joyful father wouldst thou make me! Go to, thou hast it *ad dunghill*, at the fingers' ends, as they say.

HOLOFERNES Oh, I smell false Latin! "Dunghill" for "*unguem*."

ARMADO Arts-man, *preambulate*. We will be singuled from the barbarous. Do you not educate youth at the charge-house on the top of the mountain?

HOLOFERNES Or *mons*, the hill.

ARMADO At your sweet pleasure, for the mountain.

HOLOFERNES I do, sans question.

ARMADO Sir, it is the King's most sweet pleasure and affection to congratulate the Princess at her pavilion in the posteriors of this day, which the rude multitude call the afternoon.

HOLOFERNES The posterior of the day, most generous sir, is liable, congruent, and measurable for the afternoon. The word is well culled, choice, sweet, and apt, I do assure you, sir, I do assure.

ARMADO Sir, the King is a noble gentleman, and my familiar, I do assure ye, very good friend. For what is inward between us, let it pass. I do beseech thee, remember thy courtesy. I beseech thee, apparel thy head. And, among other importunate and most serious designs, and of great import indeed, too—but let that pass; for I must tell thee it will please His Grace, by the world, sometime to lean upon my poor shoulder and with his royal finger thus dally with my excrement, with my mustachio; but, sweetheart, let that pass. By the world, I recount no fable! Some certain special honors it pleaseth his greatness to impart to Armado, a soldier, a man of travel, that hath seen the world, but let that pass. The very all of all is—but, sweetheart, I do implore secrecy—that the King would have me present the Princess, sweet chuck, with some delightful ostentation, or show, or pageant, or antic, or firework. Now, understanding that the curate and your sweet self are good at such eruptions and sudden

30 *Videsne quis venit*? Do you see who comes? **31 *Video, et gaudeo*** I see and I rejoice. (This trivial Latin dialogue is after the manner of schoolboys' exercises.) **32 Chirrah!** (A dialectal corruption of the Greek *chaere*, "hail," or merely a dialectal pronunciation of *sirrah*, a term of address to a social inferior.) **33 *Quare*** Why **39 alms basket** a basket used to gather scraps for the poor **40 for a word** (Mote's name puns on the French *mot*, "word.") **40–1 so long . . . head** i.e., as tall **41 *honorificabilitudinitatibus*** (Once considered the longest word in existence. It is the dative or ablative plural of a Latin word meaning something like "honorableness.") **42 flapdragon** the raisin or plum in burning brandy to be snapped with the mouth in the game of snapdragon. **43 peal** i.e., clatter of tongues, like a peal of bells **44–5 lettered** i.e., educated. (Mote replies as though *lettered* meant "able to teach boys their letters.") **46 hornbook** printed sheets of paper, covered by a protective thin layer of horn; used for teaching children their alphabet. (The *horn* sets up a joke on the sheep's or cuckold's horn.) **48 *pueritia*** child **51 *Quis* . . . consonant?** i.e., Who, who, you nonentity? (A consonant cannot be sounded without also sounding the vowels.) **52 last** (An error for *third*?) **55 The sheep** i.e., Holofernes, by saying "i," that is, "I," has labeled himself the sheep. **concludes it** (1) completes the list of the five vowels (2) proves my point. **o, u** i.e., oh, you. **57 venue** sally, thrust. (A fencing term, continued in *quick and home*, to the quick.) **wit** intellect **60 wit-old** mentally feeble. (With a pun on "wittol," a contented cuckold.) **61 figure** metaphor, figure of speech. **63 Thou disputes** You reason **63–4 whip thy gig** spin your spinning-top (as a child might do).

66 *manu cita* with a ready hand **68 An** If **70–1 halfpenny purse** a tiny purse **71 pigeon egg** i.e., tiny object **77 *unguem*** i.e., *ad unguem*, "to the fingernail," perfectly **78 Arts-man . . . singuled** Scholar, walk with me. We will set ourselves apart **80 charge-house** some kind of school **83 sans** without **85 affection to congratulate** desire to greet **86 in the posteriors** at the end. **rude** ignorant **88 generous** cultivated, wellborn **89 liable** apt. **measurable** fitted **90 culled** selected **93 familiar** intimate acquaintance **94 inward** private. **let it pass** never mind about that **95 remember thy courtesy** i.e., remember to use your hat courteously. **99 by the world** (A mild oath.) **101 excrement** outgrowth (of hair). **sweetheart** (A term of endearment, here spoken in friendship.) **102 I . . . fable!** I'm telling the truth! **105 very all of all** sum of everything **107 chuck** chick. (A term of endearment.) **108 ostentation** display. **antic** a pageant or entertainment using fantastic costumes **109 firework** pyrotechnic display.

breaking out of mirth, as it were, I have acquainted
you withal, to the end to crave your assistance. 112

HOLOFERNES Sir, you shall present before her the Nine 114
Worthies.—Sir Nathaniel, as concerning some enter- 115
tainment of time, some show in the posterior of this
day, to be rendered by our assistance, the King's command, and this most gallant, illustrate, and learned
gentleman, before the Princess—I say none so fit as to 119
present the Nine Worthies.

NATHANIEL Where will you find men worthy enough to present them?

HOLOFERNES Joshua, yourself; myself; and this gallant 123
gentleman, Judas Maccabaeus; this swain, because of 124
his great limb or joint, shall pass Pompey the Great; 125
the page, Hercules— 126

ARMADO Pardon, sir, error. He is not quantity enough for that Worthy's thumb. He is not so big as the end of his club.

HOLOFERNES Shall I have audience? He shall present 130
Hercules in minority. His enter and exit shall be stran- 131
gling a snake; and I will have an apology for that 132
purpose.

MOTE An excellent device! So, if any of the audience 134
hiss, you may cry, "Well done, Hercules! Now thou 135
crushest the snake!" That is the way to make an 136
offense gracious, though few have the grace to do it.

ARMADO For the rest of the Worthies?

HOLOFERNES I will play three myself.

MOTE Thrice-worthy gentleman!

ARMADO Shall I tell you a thing?

HOLOFERNES We attend. 142

ARMADO We will have, if this fadge not, an antic. I be- 143
seech you, follow.

HOLOFERNES *Via*, goodman Dull! Thou hast spoken no 145
word all this while.

DULL Nor understood none neither, sir.

HOLOFERNES *Allons!* We will employ thee. 148

DULL
I'll make one in a dance or so, or I will play 149
On the tabor to the Worthies, and let them dance
the hay. 150

HOLOFERNES
Most dull, honest Dull! To our sport, away!
Exeunt.

[5.2]

Enter the ladies [the Princes, Katharine, Rosaline, and Maria].

PRINCESS
Sweethearts, we shall be rich ere we depart,
If fairings come thus plentifully in. 2
A lady walled about with diamonds! 3
Look you what I have from the loving King.
[*She shows a jewel.*]

ROSALINE
Madam, came nothing else along with that?

PRINCESS
Nothing but this? Yes, as much love in rhyme
As would be crammed up in a sheet of paper,
Writ o'both sides the leaf, margent and all, 8
That he was fain to seal on Cupid's name. 9

ROSALINE
That was the way to make his godhead wax, 10
For he hath been five thousand year a boy. 11

KATHARINE
Ay, and a shrewd unhappy gallows, too. 12

ROSALINE
You'll ne'er be friends with him. 'A killed your sister. 13

KATHARINE
He made her melancholy, sad, and heavy, 14
And so she died. Had she been light, like you, 15
Of such a merry, nimble, stirring spirit,
She might ha' been a grandam ere she died. 17
And so may you, for a light heart lives long.

ROSALINE
What's your dark meaning, mouse, of this light word? 19

KATHARINE
A light condition in a beauty dark. 20

ROSALINE
We need more light to find your meaning out.

KATHARINE
You'll mar the light by taking it in snuff; 22
Therefore I'll darkly end the argument. 23

112 withal with this **114–15 Nine Worthies** (A conventional subject familiar to Shakespeare's audience in poems, pageants, and tapestries. The nine were three pagans, Hector of Troy, Alexander the Great, and Julius Caesar; three Jews, Joshua, David, and Judas Maccabaeus; and three Christians, Arthur, Charlemagne, and Godfrey of Boulogne. The list varied, but Shakespeare makes an unusual departure when he introduces Pompey and Hercules.) **119 gentleman** i.e., Armado **123–6 Joshua . . . Hercules** (The assignment of parts here and in line 139 does not correspond with the actual casting of parts in 5.3.543 ff. Presumably, changes occur in rehearsal.) **130 have audience** be heard. **131 in minority** as a child. **enter** entrance **131–2 strangling a snake** (According to legend, Hercules as an infant displayed his great strength by strangling two serpents sent by the envious Juno to destroy him in his cradle.) **132 apology** explanatory prologue **134–6 if . . . snake** (Any hissing by the audience can thus be explained away as the hissing of the snake.) **142 attend** listen. **143 if this fadge not** i.e., even if this fails. **an antic** i.e., a show of some sort, perhaps of "The Owl and the Cuckoo." **145 *Via*** Onward! (A cry of encouragement to troops.) **148 *Allons*!** Let's go! **149 make one** take part **150 tabor** small drum. **the hay** a country dance

5.2. Location: Navarre's park. Near the ladies' tents.
2 fairings gifts such as might be bought at a fair **3 A lady . . . diamonds** (The Princess has evidently received a brooch with a diamond-studded frame enclosing a portrait of a lady.) **8 margent** margin **9 That . . . name** i.e., that there was no room for the wax seal other than on top of Cupid's name. **10 to make . . . wax** to make Cupid increase in years. (With pun on the wax of the seal.) **11 he hath . . . boy** i.e., Cupid has remained young ever since the world began. **12 shrewd unhappy gallows** wicked, mischievous knave, deserving to be hanged **13 'A killed your sister** (A mocking hint of a story, not developed here, of a young woman who died for love.) **'A** He **14 heavy** depressed **15 light** (1) merry (2) unchaste **17 grandam** grandmother **19 dark** hidden. **mouse** (A term of endearment.) **light word** frivolous speech. **20 light condition** wanton temperament **22 taking . . . snuff** (1) trimming the burning candlewick (2) taking offense **23 darkly** obscurely, mysteriously

ROSALINE
Look what you do, you do it still i'the dark.
KATHARINE
So do not you, for you are a light wench.
ROSALINE
Indeed I weigh not you, and therefore light.
KATHARINE
You weigh me not? Oh, that's you care not for me.
ROSALINE
Great reason, for past cure is still past care.
PRINCESS
Well bandied both! A set of wit well played.
But, Rosaline, you have a favor too.
Who sent it? And what is it?
ROSALINE I would you knew.
An if my face were but as fair as yours,
My favor were as great. Be witness this.
[*She shows a love token.*]
Nay, I have verses too, I thank Berowne;
The numbers true, and, were the numbering, too,
I were the fairest goddess on the ground.
I am compared to twenty thousand fairs.
Oh, he hath drawn my picture in his letter!
PRINCESS Anything like?
ROSALINE
Much in the letters, nothing in the praise.
PRINCESS
Beauteous as ink—a good conclusion.
KATHARINE
Fair as a text B in a copybook.
ROSALINE
Ware pencils, ho! Let me not die your debtor,
My red dominical, my golden letter.
Oh, that your face were not so full of O's!
PRINCESS
A pox of that jest! And I beshrew all shrows.
But, Katharine, what was sent to you from fair
Dumaine?
KATHARINE
Madam, this glove. [*She shows a glove.*]
PRINCESS Did he not send you twain?
KATHARINE
Yes; madam, and moreover
Some thousand verses of a faithful lover,
A huge translation of hypocrisy,
Vilely compiled, profound simplicity.
MARIA [*showing a letter and a pearl necklace*]
This, and these pearls, to me sent Longaville.
The letter is too long by half a mile.
PRINCESS
I think no less. Dost thou not wish in heart
The chain were longer and the letter short?
MARIA
Ay, or I would these hands might never part.
PRINCESS
We are wise girls to mock our lovers so.
ROSALINE
They are worse fools to purchase mocking so.
That same Berowne I'll torture ere I go.
Oh, that I knew he were but in by th' week!
How I would make him fawn, and beg, and seek,
And wait the season, and observe the times,
And spend his prodigal wits in bootless rhymes,
And shape his service wholly to my hests,
And make him proud to make me proud that jests!
So pair-taunt-like would I o'ersway his state
That he should be my fool and I his fate.
PRINCESS
None are so surely caught when they are catched
As wit turned fool. Folly in wisdom hatched
Hath wisdom's warrant and the help of school
And wit's own grace to grace a learnèd fool.
ROSALINE
The blood of youth burns not with such excess
As gravity's revolt to wantonness.
MARIA
Folly in fools bears not so strong a note
As fool'ry in the wise when wit doth dote,
Since all the power thereof it doth apply
To prove, by wit, worth in simplicity.

Enter Boyet.

PRINCESS
Here comes Boyet, and mirth is in his face.

24 look what Whatever. **do it . . . i'the dark** (With obvious sexual meaning.) **26 weigh not you** don't weigh as much as you **27 weigh** regard seriously. **that's** that means **28 Great reason** With good reason. **past cure . . . care** what can't be helped shouldn't be worried about. (Proverbial.) Rosaline implies that Katharine is incurable, and puns on *care*, "have fondness," in line 27. **29 Well bandied both!** i.e., Both of you have wittily traded insults. (A tennis term, continued in *set*.) **30 favor** love token **31 would** wish **32–3 An . . . this** If only my face were as attractive as yours, I might have received as great a gift as love token. Here's the evidence. (*Favor* here also plays on the meaning "personal appearance.") **35 numbers** meter. **numbering** reckoning **36 were** would be **37 fairs** beautiful women **40 Much . . . praise** The lettering (i.e., handwriting) is recognizable, but the praise is unrecognizable (i.e., execessive). **41 ink** (Referring to Rosaline's dark complexion.) **42 a text B** (Perhaps a heavily ornamented capital B, for Berowne, boldly dark like Rosaline's complexion.) **43 Ware pencils** i.e., Be wary of such drawings or paintings. (*Pencils* here are fine-tipped brushes.) **43–5 Let . . . O's!** (Said to Katharine): I'll get even with you, my fine red-cheeked beauty. Oh, if only your face weren't full of smallpox scars! (*Red dominical* is red lettering used in calendars to mark Sundays and holy days; from *Dies dominica*, "the Lord's day." *Golden* suggests both fair hair and the reddish color of gold.) **46 A pox of** i.e., A curse on. (Playing also on the *O's* or smallpox in Katharine's face.) **beshrew all shrows** I wish a plague on all shrews or scolds. (The Quarto/Folio spelling of "beshrow all Shrowes" makes plain the rhyme with *O's*.)

48 twain two. **51 translation** expression **52 simplicity** silliness. **57 would** wish. (Perhaps Maria makes an imploring gesture with her joined hands.) **59 purchase** earn, invite **61 in . . . week** i.e., caught, trapped permanently. **63 And wait . . . times** i.e., and wait until it suits me, follow my schedule **64 bootless** fruitless **65 hests** behests **66 And . . . jests** and make him take satisfaction in glorifying me, the one who mocks him. **67 pair-taunt-like** like one holding a winning hand (pair-taunt) in the card game of "post-and-pair." (With a pun on *taunt*.) **68 his fate** the controller of his destiny. **69 surely** securely **70–1 Folly . . . fool** Folly in a seemingly wise person can have the appearance of wisdom, learning, and graceful wit, all serving to grace one who is only a learned fool. **74 As gravity's revolt** as when a wise man turns **75–8 Folly . . . simplicity** Folly in a genuine fool is not so remarkable as foolishness in doting wise persons, since in the latter case wit uses all its ingenuity.

BOYET
Oh, I am stabbed with laughter! Where's Her Grace?

PRINCESS
Thy news, Boyet?

BOYET
Prepare, madam, prepare!
Arm, wenches, arm! Encounters mounted are
Against your peace. Love doth approach disguised,
Armèd in arguments. You'll be surprised.
Muster your wits, stand in your own defense,
Or hide your heads like cowards and fly hence.

PRINCESS
Saint Denis to Saint Cupid! What are they
That charge their breath against us? Say, scout, say.

BOYET
Under the cool shade of a sycamore
I thought to close mine eyes some half an hour,
When, lo, to interrupt my purposed rest,
Toward that shade I might behold addressed
The King and his companions. Warily
I stole into a neighbor thicket by
And overheard what you shall overhear—
That, by and by, disguised they will be here.
Their herald is a pretty knavish page
That well by heart hath conned his embassage.
Action and accent did they teach him there:
"Thus must thou speak," and "thus thy body bear."
And ever and anon they made a doubt
Presence majestical would put him out;
"For," quoth the King, "an angel shalt thou see;
Yet fear not thou, but speak audaciously."
The boy replied, "An angel is not evil;
I should have feared her had she been a devil."
With that, all laughed and clapped him on the shoulder,
Making the bold wag by their praises bolder.
One rubbed his elbow thus, and fleered, and swore
A better speech was never spoke before.
Another, with his finger and his thumb,
Cried, "*Via*! We will do't, come what will come."
The third he capered and cried, "All goes well!"
The fourth turned on the toe, and down he fell.
With that, they all did tumble on the ground
With such a zealous laughter, so profound,
That in this spleen ridiculous appears,
To check their folly, passion's solemn tears.

PRINCESS
But what, but what? Come they to visit us?

BOYET
They do, they do, and are appareled thus,
Like Muscovites or Russians, as I guess.
Their purpose is to parle, to court, and dance;
And everyone his love suit will advance
Unto his several mistress, which they'll know
By favors several which they did bestow.

PRINCESS
And will they so? The gallants shall be tasked;
For, ladies, we will every one be masked,
And not a man of them shall have the grace,
Despite of suit, to see a lady's face.
Hold, Rosaline, this favor thou shalt wear,
And then the King will court thee for his dear.
Hold, take thou this, my sweet, and give me thine.
So shall Berowne take me for Rosaline.
[*The Princess and Rosaline exchange favors.*]
And change you favors too. So shall your loves
Woo contrary, deceived by these removes.
[*Katharine and Maria exchange favors.*]

ROSALINE
Come on, then, wear the favors most in sight.

KATHARINE
But in this changing what is your intent?

PRINCESS
The effect of my intent is to cross theirs.
They do it but in mockery merriment,
And mock for mock is only my intent.
Their several counsels they unbosom shall
To loves mistook, and so be mocked withal
Upon the next occasion that we meet,
With visages displayed, to talk and greet.

ROSALINE
But shall we dance, if they desire us to't?

PRINCESS
No, to the death we will not move a foot,
Nor to their penned speech render we no grace,
But while 'tis spoke each turn away her face.

BOYET
Why, that contempt will kill the speaker's heart
And quite divorce his memory from his part.

PRINCESS
Therefore I do it; and I make no doubt
The rest will ne'er come in, if he be out.
There's no such sport as sport by sport o'erthrown,
To make theirs ours and ours none but our own.

82 Encounters mounted are Skirmishes or assailants are readied, set in position **84 surprised** assaulted in a surprise attack. **87 Saint Denis** patron saint of France. **to** against **88 charge their breath** aim their words. (To *charge* is to attack at full gallop or to level, as in aiming a weapon.) **92 I . . . addressed** I could see approaching **95 overhear** hear over again **98 conned his embassage** memorized his message. **99 Action** Gesture **101 ever and anon** every now and then. **made a doubt** expressed a fear (that) **102 put him out** leave him confused and tongue-tied **104 audaciously** boldly. **108 wag** young man **109 rubbed his elbow** (in a gesture of satisfaction, like rubbing the hands). **fleered** grinned **111 with . . . thumb** i.e., snapping his fingers **112 *Via*!** Onward! **113 capered** skipped, danced **114 turned on the toe** pirouetted **117 spleen ridiculous** ludicrous fit of laughter

121 Muscovites or Russians (Costumes not uncommon in court masquerades.) **guess** (The unrhymed word suggests a missing line.) **122 parle** parley **124 several** respective, particular. **which** whom **126 tasked** tried, tested **129 suit** petition, entreaty. (With a play on "suit of clothes.") **132–3 Hold . . . Rosaline** (Possibly Shakespeare intended this couplet to replace lines 130–1.) **134 change** exchange **135 removes** exchanges. **136 most in sight** conspicuously. **138 cross** thwart **139 mockery** mocking **141–2 Their . . . mistook** They will disclose their various private intentions to the wrong ladies **144 With visages displayed** we with our masks removed, showing our faces **146 to the death** (as in "fight to the death") **147 penned speech** speech composed and written out with care. **grace** favor **152 The rest . . . out** The others will give up if the first speaker forgets his lines. **154 To . . . own** to make their intended sport into one that is ours and ours alone.

So shall we stay, mocking intended game,
And they, well mocked, depart away with shame.
Sound trumpet [*within*].

BOYET
The trumpet sounds. Be masked; the maskers come.
[*The ladies mask.*]

Enter blackamoors with music; [*Mote,*] *the boy, with a speech, and* [*the King, Berowne, and*] *the rest of the lords disguised* [*as Russians, and visored*].

MOTE
All hail, the richest beauties on the earth!

BEROWNE [*aside*]
Beauties no richer than rich taffeta.

MOTE
A holy parcel of the fairest dames
The ladies turn their backs to him
That ever turned their—backs—to mortal views!

BEROWNE [*prompting Mote*] "Their eyes," villain,
"their eyes."

MOTE
That ever turned their eyes to mortal views!
Out—

BOYET True; out indeed.

MOTE
Out of your favors, heavenly spirits, vouchsafe
Not to behold—

BEROWNE [*to Mote*] "Once to behold," rogue.

MOTE
Once to behold with your sun-beamèd eyes—
With your sun-beamèd eyes—

BOYET
They will not answer to that epithet.
You were best call it "daughter-beamèd eyes."

MOTE
They do not mark me, and that brings me out.

BEROWNE
Is this your perfectness? Begone, you rogue!
[*Exit Mote.*]

ROSALINE [*speaking as the Princess*]
What would these strangers? Know their minds,
Boyet.
If they do speak our language, 'tis our will
That some plain man recount their purposes.
Know what they would.

BOYET What would you with the Princess?

BEROWNE
Nothing but peace and gentle visitation.

ROSALINE What would they, say they?

BOYET
Nothing but peace and gentle visitation.

ROSALINE
Why, that they have, and bid them so be gone.

BOYET
She says you have it, and you may be gone.

KING
Say to her we have measured many miles
To tread a measure with her on this grass.

BOYET
They say that they have measured many a mile
To tread a measure with you on this grass.

ROSALINE
It is not so. Ask them how many inches
Is in one mile. If they have measured many,
The measure then of one is eas'ly told.

BOYET
If to come hither you have measured miles,
And many miles, the Princess bids you tell
How many inches doth fill up one mile.

BEROWNE
Tell her we measure them by weary steps.

BOYET
She hears herself.

ROSALINE How many weary steps,
Of many weary miles you have o'ergone,
Are numbered in the travel of one mile?

BEROWNE
We number nothing that we spend for you.
Our duty is so rich, so infinite,
That we may do it still without account.
Vouchsafe to show the sunshine of your face,
That we, like savages, may worship it.

ROSALINE
My face is but a moon, and clouded too.

KING
Blessed are clouds, to do as such clouds do!
Vouchsafe, bright moon, and these thy stars, to shine,
Those clouds removed, upon our watery eyne.

ROSALINE
Oh, vain petitioner! Beg a greater matter;
Thou now requests but moonshine in the water.

KING
Then in our measure do but vouchsafe one change.
Thou bid'st me beg; this begging is not strange.

ROSALINE
Play, music, then! Nay, you must do it soon.
[*Music plays.*]
Not yet? No dance! Thus change I like the moon.

157.2 *blackamoors* i.e., attendants in blackface **159 Beauties . . . taffeta** Handsome women no richer in beauty than their masks or rich taffeta cloth. (Some editors assign the speech to Boyet.) **160 parcel** company **166 out** i.e., having forgotten his lines **167 Out . . . vouchsafe** Have the goodness, heavenly spirits, to deign **173 daughter-beamèd** (Substituting *daughter* for *sun*, i.e., son.) **174 mark** pay attention to **175 Is . . . perfectness?** Is this your idea of a perfectly memorized speech? **176 What . . . minds** What do these strangers want? Learn their intentions. (Rosaline, masquerading as the Princess, presides.) **178 plain** plainspoken **180 visitation** visit.

185 measured traversed **186 tread a measure** perform a dance **190 measured** (1) traversed (2) taken the measurement of **201 account** reckoning. **204 a moon . . . too** i.e., changeable and soon clouded over with a frown. **205 to do . . . do** i.e., to be close to such heavenly beauty (as the masks are close to the ladies' faces). **206 stars** i.e., ladies **207 clouds** i.e., the masks. **eyne** eyes. **209 moonshine . . . water** i.e., nothing at all, mere foolishness. (Proverbial.) **210 Then . . . change** Then deign to dance one dance with us. (With a play on the idea of the moon's changing.)

KING
Will you not dance? How come you thus estranged? 214

ROSALINE
You took the moon at full, but now she's changed.

KING
Yet still she is the moon, and I the man. 216
The music plays; vouchsafe some motion to it. 217

ROSALINE
Our ears vouchsafe it.

KING But your legs should do it. 218

ROSALINE
Since you are strangers and come here by chance, 219
We'll not be nice. Take hands. We will not dance. 220
[*She offers her hand.*]

KING
Why take we hands, then?

ROSALINE Only to part friends.
Curtsy, sweethearts, and so the measure ends.

KING
More measure of this measure! Be not nice. 223

ROSALINE
We can afford no more at such a price.

KING
Price you yourselves. What buys your company? 225

ROSALINE
Your absence only.

KING That can never be.

ROSALINE
Then cannot we be bought. And so, adieu—
Twice to your visor, and half once to you. 228

KING
If you deny to dance, let's hold more chat. 229

ROSALINE
In private, then.

KING I am best pleased with that.
[*They converse apart.*]

BEROWNE [*to the Princess*]
Whitehanded mistress, one sweet word with thee.

PRINCESS [*speaking as Rosaline*]
Honey, and milk, and sugar—there is three. 232

BEROWNE
Nay, then, two treys, an if you grow so nice— 233
Metheglin, wort, and malmsey. Well run, dice! 234
There's half a dozen sweets.

PRINCESS Seventh sweet, adieu.
Since you can cog, I'll play no more with you. 236

BEROWNE
One word in secret.

PRINCESS Let it not be sweet.

BEROWNE
Thou grievest my gall.

PRINCESS Gall! Bitter.

BEROWNE Therefore meet. 238
[*They converse apart.*]

DUMAINE [*to Maria*]
Will you vouchsafe with me to change a word? 239

MARIA [*speaking as Katharine*]
Name it.

DUMAINE Fair lady—

MARIA Say you so? Fair lord! 240
Take that for your "fair lady."

DUMAINE Please it you,
As much in private, and I'll bid adieu.
[*They converse apart.*]

KATHARINE [*speaking as Maria*]
What, was your vizard made without a tongue? 243

LONGAVILLE
I know the reason, lady, why you ask.

KATHARINE
Oh, for your reason! Quickly, sir, I long.

LONGAVILLE
You have a double tongue within your mask 246
And would afford my speechless vizard half. 247

KATHARINE
"Veal," quoth the Dutchman. Is not "veal" a calf? 248

LONGAVILLE
A calf, fair lady!

KATHARINE No, a fair lord calf.

LONGAVILLE
Let's part the word.

KATHARINE No, I'll not be your half. 250
Take all and wean it; it may prove an ox. 251

LONGAVILLE
Look how you butt yourself in these sharp mocks! 252
Will you give horns, chaste lady? Do not so.

KATHARINE
Then die a calf, before your horns do grow.

LONGAVILLE
One word in private with you, ere I die.

214 How . . . estranged? Why are you disaffected? **216 man** i.e., man in the moon. (This unrhymed word suggests a missing line.) **217 vouchsafe some motion** deign to dance **218 Our . . . it** i.e., I deign to hear your *motion* or proposal. (Rosaline pretends not to understand an invitation to dance.) **219 strangers** foreigners **220 nice** coy. **223 More . . . nice** i.e., We wish more quantity of dancing. Don't be coy. **225 Price you yourselves** Set your own price on yourselves. **228 Twice . . . you** (Rosaline, posing as the Princess, saucily offers more curtsies to the King's visor than to the person behind the mask.) **229 deny** refuse **232 Honey . . . sugar** (These are words of sweetness, appropriate to women.) **233–4 Nay . . . dice!** i.e., Let me counter with three words of my own—words for a spiced drink made from herbs and honey, a sweet unfermented beer, and a strong sweet wine (words that are characteristically masculine). Such is my gambit, my throw of the dice. **236 cog** deceive

238 Thou . . . gall i.e., You distress me. (*Gall* is bile, a bitter secretion of the liver.) **Therefore meet** i.e., Then let us converse. **239 vouchsafe . . . word** deign to speak with me. (*Change* means "exchange.") **240 Say . . . lord** (Maria mischievously takes Dumaine's request for a *word* literally and so cuts off his reply at "Fair lady.") **243 What . . . tongue?** i.e., Cat got your tongue? **246–7 You . . . half** i.e., You speak with a duplicitous tongue and thus can talk enough for the two of us. (The speech may refer also to a leather "tongue" inside some masks, held in the mouth to keep the mask in place.) **248 Veal** i.e., as a Dutchman would pronounce "well." (With a possible pun on *veil*, mask, as well as *veal*, calf; also, in lines 245 and 248, Katharine punningly pronounces Longaville's name—*long veal*—and implies that he is a calf or dunce.) **250 Let's part the word** i.e., Let's reach a compromise. (But Katharine wittily insists on the literal meaning; he must take all the word *calf* to himself.) **your half** (1) sharer with you of two halves (2) your partner in marriage. **251 wean** i.e., raise. **ox** (A type of stupidity.) **252 butt** injure. (With play on *give horns* in the next line, meaning both to butt with horns and to make a cuckold.)

KATHARINE
Bleat softly then. The butcher hears you cry.
[*They converse apart.*]

BOYET
The tongues of mocking wenches are as keen
As is the razor's edge invisible;
Cutting a smaller hair than may be seen;
Above the sense of sense, so sensible 260
Seemeth their conference. Their conceits have wings 261
Fleeter than arrows, bullets, wind, thought, swifter things.

ROSALINE
Not one word more, my maids. Break off, break off!
[*The ladies break away from the gentlemen.*]

BEROWNE
By heaven, all dry-beaten with pure scoff! 264

KING
Farewell, mad wenches. You have simple wits.
Exeunt [*King, lords, and blackamoors. The ladies unmask.*]

PRINCESS
Twenty adieus, my frozen Muscovits.
Are these the breed of wits so wondered at?

BOYET
Tapers they are, with your sweet breaths puffed out. 268

ROSALINE
Well-liking wits they have; gross, gross; fat, fat. 269

PRINCESS
Oh, poverty in wit, kingly-poor flout! 270
Will they not, think you, hang themselves tonight?
Or ever but in vizards show their faces?
This pert Berowne was out of count'nance quite. 273

ROSALINE
They were all in lamentable cases! 274
The King was weeping-ripe for a good word. 275

PRINCESS
Berowne did swear himself out of all suit. 276

MARIA
Dumaine was at my service, and his sword.
"*Non point,*" quoth I. My servant straight was mute. 278

KATHARINE
Lord Longaville said I came o'er his heart;
And trow you what he called me?

PRINCESS
Qualm, perhaps. 280

KATHARINE
Yes, in good faith.

PRINCESS
Go, sickness as thou art!

ROSALINE
Well, better wits have worn plain statute-caps. 282
But will you hear? The King is my love sworn.

PRINCESS
And quick Berowne hath plighted faith to me. 284

KATHARINE
And Longaville was for my service born.

MARIA
Dumaine is mine, as sure as bark on tree. 286

BOYET
Madam, and pretty mistresses, give ear: 287
Immediately they will again be here
In their own shapes, for it can never be 289
They will digest this harsh indignity. 290

PRINCESS
Will they return?

BOYET
They will, they will, God knows,
And leap for joy, though they are lame with blows.
Therefore change favors, and when they repair, 293
Blow like sweet roses in this summer air. 294

PRINCESS
How "blow"? How "blow"? Speak to be understood.

BOYET
Fair ladies masked are roses in their bud;
Dismasked, their damask sweet commixture shown, 297
Are angels vailing clouds, or roses blown. 298

PRINCESS
Avaunt, perplexity!—What shall we do 299
If they return in their own shapes to woo?

ROSALINE
Good madam, if by me you'll be advised,
Let's mock them still, as well known as disguised. 302
Let us complain to them what fools were here,
Disguised like Muscovites in shapeless gear, 304
And wonder what they were, and to what end
Their shallow shows and prologue vilely penned
And their rough carriage so ridiculous 307
Should be presented at our tent to us.

BOYET
Ladies, withdraw. The gallants are at hand.

PRINCESS
Whip to our tents, as roes run o'er land. 310
Exeunt [*Princess, Rosaline, Katharine, and Maria*].

260–1 Above . . . conference The pert talk of women seems so quick-witted as to be beyond the reach of normal sense. **261 conceits** fancies **264 dry-beaten** beaten soundly without blood drawn
268 Tapers . . . out They are like candles puffed out with your sweet breaths. **269 Well-liking . . . fat** Their wits are amiable but gross. **270 Oh . . . flout** i.e., Their wits and floutings are paradoxically both kinglike and poor. **273 out of count'nance** flustered, embarrassed. (With a play on the literal meaning, "without a face," i.e., masked.) **274 cases** (1) situations (2) masks. **275 weeping-ripe** ready to weep. **good** kind **276 out of all suit** excessively and to no avail. (With a play on the idea of "costume.") **278 *Non point*** Not at all. (Quibbling also on the *point* of his sword. See the note on 2.1.190.) **servant** servant in love, admirer. **straight** immediately **280 trow you** would you believe. **Qualm** i.e., Heartburn. (With a play perhaps on *came*, line 279, as suggested by Elizabethan pronunciation.)

282 better . . . statute-caps i.e., one could find better wits even among London apprentices (who were required by statute to wear identifiable caps). **284 plighted faith** pledged his love **286 sure** firmly united **287 give ear** listen **289 In their own shapes** i.e., having put off their disguises **290 digest** stomach, put up with **293 change favors** i.e., return the love tokens to their original owners. **repair** return **294 Blow** bloom. (But the Princess wonders if *blow* might mean to give *blows*, as in line 292.) **297–8 Dismasked . . . blown** unmasked, with their sweet mingling of red and white complexion shown to view, they are angels trailing clouds (of glory) or fully blooming roses. **299 Avaunt, perplexity!** i.e., Away, you tease! **302 as . . . disguised.** in their familiar appearances just as previously in their disguises. **304 shapeless gear** unshapely apparel **307 rough carriage** awkward bearing **310 Whip** Move quickly. **roes** female or roe deer. (With a pun on a *rose* sending out runners.)

Enter the King and the rest [Berowne, Longaville, and Dumaine, in their proper dress].

KING
Fair sir, God save you! Where's the Princess?

BOYET
Gone to her tent. Please it Your Majesty
Command me any service to her thither? 313

KING
That she vouchsafe me audience for one word.

BOYET
I will, and so will she, I know, my lord. *Exit.*

BEROWNE
This fellow pecks up wit as pigeons pease,
And utters it again when God doth please. 317
He is wit's peddler, and retails his wares
At wakes and wassails, meetings, markets, fairs; 319
And we that sell by gross, the Lord doth know, 320
Have not the grace to grace it with such show. 321
This gallant pins the wenches on his sleeve. 322
Had he been Adam, he had tempted Eve. 323
'A can carve too, and lisp. Why, this is he 324
That kissed his hand away in courtesy. 325
This is the ape of form, Monsieur the Nice, 326
That, when he plays at tables, chides the dice 327
In honorable terms. Nay, he can sing 328
A mean most meanly; and in ushering 329
Mend him who can. The ladies call him sweet. 330
The stairs, as he treads on them, kiss his feet.
This is the flower that smiles on everyone,
To show his teeth as white as whale's bone;
And consciences that will not die in debt
Pay him the due of "honey-tongued Boyet."

KING
A blister on his sweet tongue, with my heart,
That put Armado's page out of his part! 337

Enter the ladies [wearing their original favors, with Boyet].

BEROWNE
See where it comes! Behavior, what wert thou 338
Till this madman showed thee? And what art thou
now? 339

KING
All hail, sweet madam, and fair time of day!

PRINCESS
"Fair" in "all hail" is foul, as I conceive. 341

KING
Construe my speeches better, if you may. 342

PRINCESS
Then wish me better. I will give you leave. 343

KING
We came to visit you, and purpose now 344
To lead you to our court. Vouchsafe it, then. 345

PRINCESS
This field shall hold me, and so hold your vow. 346
Nor God nor I delights in perjured men. 347

KING
Rebuke me not for that which you provoke. 348
The virtue of your eye must break my oath. 349

PRINCESS
You nickname virtue. "Vice," you should have
spoke, 350
For virtue's office never breaks men's troth. 351
Now by my maiden honor, yet as pure 352
As the unsullied lily, I protest,
A world of torments though I should endure,
I would not yield to be your house's guest,
So much I hate a breaking cause to be 356
Of heavenly oaths, vowed with integrity.

KING
Oh, you have lived in desolation here,
Unseen, unvisited, much to our shame.

PRINCESS
Not so, my lord. It is not so, I swear.
We have had pastimes here and pleasant game:
A mess of Russians left us but of late. 362

KING
How, madam? Russians?

PRINCESS
Ay, in truth, my lord.
Trim gallants, full of courtship and of state. 364

ROSALINE
Madam, speak true.—It is not so, my lord.
My lady, to the manner of the days, 366
In courtesy gives undeserving praise.
We four indeed confronted were with four
In Russian habit. Here they stayed an hour
And talked apace; and in that hour, my lord, 370
They did not bless us with one happy word. 371
I dare not call them fools; but this I think,

313 Command . . . thither? Do you wish me to take any message to her there? **317 utters** (1) speaks (2) peddles. **when . . . please** i.e., on any occasion. **319 wakes and wassails** festivals and revels **320–1 And . . . show** i.e., and even we who deal wholesale in wit are unable to deliver it with such gracefulness as he. **322 This . . . sleeve** i.e., This dashing fellow is quite a ladies' man, wearing their favors on his garments. **323 had** would have **324–5 'A . . . courtesy** i.e., He can woo courteously, too, and speak with courtly affectation. He kisses his hand so often he might wear it away. **326 ape of form** imitator of courtly manners. **Nice** Fastidious **327 tables** backgammon **328–30 Nay . . . who can** He can sing the tenor part well enough, and, as for fulfilling the role of gentleman-usher, let anyone who would like to do better just try. **337 That . . . part** that caused Mote to forget his lines. **338 it** i.e., Boyet. **Behavior** i.e., Elegant manners **339 Till . . . now?** i.e., till this madcap (Boyet) showed just how elegant manners can be? And see to what a state of art courtly manners have arrived!

341 all hail (The Princess deliberately misconstrues the King to have referred to a hailstorm, foul weather.) **conceive** understand the matter. **342 Construe** Interpret **343 Then . . . leave** i.e., In that case you must greet me better. I will give you permission to try again. **344 purpose** intend **345 Vouchsafe it** Consent to it **346 This . . . vow** i.e., I will stay right here; that way you can still hold true on your vow (not to admit women). **347 Nor** Neither **348 Rebuke . . . provoke** Don't blame me for something which you started (by your enchanting eye). **349 virtue** power. (But the Princess, in the next line, insists on interpreting the word as "moral goodness," the opposite of "vice.") **350 nickname** misname, mention in error **351 office** action. **troth** faith. **352 yet** still **356 a breaking . . . to be** to be the cause of your breaking **362 mess** foursome **364 Trim** Spruce, neatly got up. **courtship** courtliness **366 to . . . days** in the fashion of the time **370 talked apace** spoke rapidly, i.e., chattered **371 happy** felicitous

When they are thirsty, fools would fain have drink.

BEROWNE
This jest is dry to me. Gentle sweet,
Your wits makes wise things foolish. When we greet,
With eyes' best seeing, heaven's fiery eye,
By light we lose light. Your capacity
Is of that nature that to your huge store
Wise things seem foolish and rich things but poor.

ROSALINE
This proves you wise and rich, for in my eye—

BEROWNE
I am a fool, and full of poverty.

ROSALINE
But that you take what doth to you belong,
It were a fault to snatch words from my tongue.

BEROWNE
Oh, I am yours, and all that I possess!

ROSALINE
All the fool mine?

BEROWNE I cannot give you less.

ROSALINE
Which of the vizards was it that you wore?

BEROWNE
Where? When? What vizard? Why demand you this?

ROSALINE
There, then, that vizard, that superfluous case
That hid the worse and showed the better face.

KING [*aside to his lords*]
We were descried. They'll mock us now downright.

DUMAINE [*aside to the lords*]
Let us confess and turn it to a jest.

PRINCESS
Amazed, my lord? Why looks Your Highness sad?

ROSALINE
Help, hold his brows! He'll swoon! Why look you pale?
Seasick, I think, coming from Muscovy.

BEROWNE
Thus pour the stars down plagues for perjury.
Can any face of brass hold longer out?
Here stand I, lady. Dart thy skill at me.
Bruise me with scorn, confound me with a flout,
Thrust thy sharp wit quite through my ignorance,
Cut me to pieces with thy keen conceit,
And I will wish thee nevermore to dance,
Nor nevermore in Russian habit wait.
Oh, never will I trust to speeches penned,
Nor to the motion of a schoolboy's tongue,
Nor never come in vizard to my friend,
Nor woo in rhyme, like a blind harper's song!
Taffeta phrases, silken terms precise,
Three-piled hyperboles, spruce affectation,
Figures pedantical—these summer flies
Have blown me full of maggot ostentation.
I do forswear them, and I here protest,
By this white glove—how white the hand, God knows!—
Henceforth my wooing mind shall be expressed
In russet yeas and honest kersey noes.
And to begin, wench—so God help me, law!—
My love to thee is sound, sans crack or flaw.

ROSALINE
Sans "sans," I pray you.

BEROWNE Yet I have a trick
Of the old rage. Bear with me, I am sick;
I'll leave it by degrees. Soft, let us see:
Write "Lord have mercy on us" on those three.
They are infected; in their hearts it lies;
They have the plague, and caught it of your eyes.
These lords are visited; you are not free,
For the Lord's tokens on you do I see.

PRINCESS
No, they are free that gave these tokens to us.

BEROWNE
Our states are forfeit. Seek not to undo us.

ROSALINE
It is not so, for how can this be true,
That you stand forfeit, being those that sue?

BEROWNE
Peace! For I will not have to do with you.

ROSALINE
Nor shall not, if I do as I intend.

BEROWNE [*to the other lords*]
Speak for yourselves. My wit is at an end.

KING
Teach us, sweet madam, for our rude transgression
Some fair excuse.

PRINCESS The fairest is confession.
Were not you here but even now disguised?

373 When . . . drink i.e., the gentlemen are indistinguishable from fools. **374 dry** stupid, dull. (Playing on *thirsty* in line 373.) **375–9 Your . . . poor** You wittily invert wisdom into folly. When we human beings look directly at the sun, we blind ourselves by too much light. You, like the sun, are of such godlike capacity that, in comparison to your huge store of wisdom, ordinary sagacity seems foolish and normal supplies of intelligence seem inadequate. **380–1 This . . . poverty** (Paradoxically, the beginning of true wisdom is to know that one is an unknowing fool.) **382–3 But . . . tongue** If you weren't so right to acknowledge folly in yourself, it would be impolite of you to anticipate what I was about to say. **386 vizards** masks **387 demand** ask **388 case** covering, mask. **390 descried** discovered. **392 Amazed** Bewildered **393 brows** forehead. **396 face of brass** brazen manner **397 Dart thy skill** Shoot your verbal dexterity **398 confound** overthrow. **flout** jeer, insult **401 wish** entreat **402 habit** dress. **wait** be in attendance

405 friend sweetheart **406 harper's** minstrel's **407 precise** fastidious **408 Three-piled** deep-piled, as in costly velvet. **spruce** fashionable **409 Figures** figures of speech **410 blown me** filled me with maggot eggs, made me foul. **ostentation** pretension, vanity. **414 russet** simple homespun, russet brown in color. **kersey** plain woolen cloth **415 law** lo, indeed **416 sans** without. (But, as Rosaline points out in the next line, he is still using French expressions.) **417 Yet** Still. **trick** trace **418 rage** fever. **420 Lord . . . us** (Sign posted on houses containing the infectious plague within.) **those three** i.e., his companions. **422 of** from **423 visited** infested by the plague. **free** free of infection. (But the Princess also quibbles on the meaning "generous with gifts.") **424 the Lord's tokens** (1) plague sores as visible signs of infection (2) the love tokens given by the lords, *the lords' tokens* **425 free** i.e., generous, openhanded. (Playing on *free*, plague-free, in line 423.) **426 Our . . . us** i.e., We are at your mercy. Do not ruin us. (Berowne introduces a legal metaphor that Rosaline pursues in lines 427–8.) **427–8 It . . . sue?** How can you be legally in danger of forfeiture, being the plaintiffs who bring suit? (With a pun on *sue*, woo.) **429 have** have anything **434 but even now** a short while ago

KING
Madam, I was.
PRINCESS And were you well advised?
KING
I was, fair madam.
PRINCESS When you then were here,
What did you whisper in your lady's ear?
KING
That more than all the world I did respect her.
PRINCESS
When she shall challenge this, you will reject her.
KING
Upon mine honor, no.
PRINCESS Peace, peace! Forbear.
Your oath once broke, you force not to forswear.
KING
Despise me when I break this oath of mine.
PRINCESS
I will, and therefore keep it.—Rosaline,
What did the Russian whisper in your ear?
ROSALINE
Madam, he swore that he did hold me dear
As precious eyesight, and did value me
Above this world, adding thereto moreover
That he would wed me or else die my lover.
PRINCESS
God give thee joy of him! The noble lord
Most honorably doth uphold his word.
KING
What mean you, madam? By my life, my troth,
I never swore this lady such an oath.
ROSALINE
By heaven, you did. And to confirm it plain,
You gave me this. But take it, sir, again.
[*She offers him the Princess's favor.*]
KING
My faith and this the Princess I did give.
I knew her by this jewel on her sleeve.
PRINCESS
Pardon me, sir, this jewel did she wear,
And Lord Berowne, I thank him, is my dear.
[*To Berowne*] What, will you have me, or your pearl
again? [*She offers Rosaline's favor.*]
BEROWNE
Neither of either. I remit both twain.
I see the trick on't: here was a consent,
Knowing aforehand of our merriment,
To dash it like a Christmas comedy.
Some carry-tale, some please-man, some slight zany,
Some mumble-news, some trencher-knight, some
Dick,
That smiles his cheek in years and knows the trick
To make my lady laugh when she's disposed,
Told our intents before; which once disclosed,
The ladies did change favors, and then we,
Following the signs, wooed but the sign of she.
Now, to our perjury to add more terror,
We are again forsworn, in will and error.
Much upon this 'tis. [*To Boyet*] And might not you
Forestall our sport, to make us thus untrue?
Do not you know my lady's foot by th' squier,
And laugh upon the apple of her eye?
And stand between her back, sir, and the fire,
Holding a trencher, jesting merrily?
You put our page out. Go, you are allowed;
Die when you will, a smock shall be your shroud.
You leer upon me, do you? There's an eye
Wounds like a leaden sword.
BOYET Full merrily
Hath this brave manage, this career, been run.
BEROWNE
Lo, he is tilting straight! Peace, I have done.

Enter [*Costard the*] *clown.*

Welcome, pure wit! Thou part'st a fair fray.
COSTARD
Oh, Lord, sir, they would know
Whether the three Worthies shall come in or no.
BEROWNE
What, are there but three?
COSTARD No, sir, but it is vara fine,
For every one pursents three.
BEROWNE And three times thrice is nine.
COSTARD
Not so, sir, under correction, sir, I hope it is not so.
You cannot beg us, sir, I can assure you, sir; we
know what we know.
I hope, sir, three times thrice, sir—
BEROWNE Is not nine?
COSTARD Under correction, sir, we know whereuntil it
doth amount.
BEROWNE By Jove, I always took three threes for nine.
COSTARD Oh, Lord, sir, it were pity you should get your
living by reckoning, sir.

435 And . . . advised? And did you know what you were doing? **438 respect** value, regard **441 force not** have no hesitation **460 either** the two. **remit both twain** give up both of them. **461 on't** of it. **consent** agreement, plot **463 dash** shatter **464–5 Some . . . Dick** Some gossipmonger, some flatterer, some pitiable clown, some prattler, some huge feeder, some very ordinary person (as in "Tom, Dick, and Harry." A *trencher* is a wooden dish.) **466 That . . . years** i.e., who smiles ingratiatingly so hard that he puts wrinkles of seeming age into his face

467 disposed i.e., disposed to be merry(?) **469 change** exchange **470 wooed . . . she** wooed the mere outward appearance of what we took to be our own sweethearts. **473 Much . . . 'tis** i.e., It must have happened much this way. **475–6 Do not . . . eye?** i.e., Don't you know how to suit Rosaline's fancy, and know how to keep her amused by wittily catching her eye? (*Squier*, rhyming with *fire* in line 477, means "square," carpenter's rule; Boyet should know the length of her foot. *Apple* means "pupil of the eye.") **477–8 And . . . merrily?** And stand near her at the fire, at her back, ready to offer her refreshment (in a *trencher,* or wooden dish) and to amuse her? **479 you are allowed** i.e., you are an allowed fool, free to make jests **480 Die . . . shroud** i.e., You are such a ladies' man, so obsequious in attending on them, that you'll be buried with a petticoat as your shroud. **481–2 There's . . . sword** i.e., Your disapproving glance is about as threatening to me as a sword of lead. **482–3 Full . . . run** i.e., What a fine horseback maneuver and gallop you just executed with your wit! (Said sardonically.) **484 Lo . . . straight!** i.e., There he goes, tilting at me again with a quip! **485 Thou . . . fray** You interrupt a fine battle. **488 vara** very **490 under** subject to **491 beg us** i.e., take us for fools, take us for granted **493 whereuntil** to what **496–7 it . . . reckoning** it would be a shame if you had to earn your living by doing sums

BEROWNE How much is it?

COSTARD Oh, Lord, sir, the parties themselves, the actors, sir, will show whereuntil it doth amount. For mine own part, I am, as they say, but to parfect one man in one poor man—Pompion the Great, sir.

BEROWNE Art thou one of the Worthies?

COSTARD It pleased them to think me worthy of Pompey the Great. For mine own part, I know not the degree of the Worthy, but I am to stand for him.

BEROWNE Go bid them prepare.

COSTARD
We will turn it finely off, sir. We will take some care.
Exit.

KING
Berowne, they will shame us. Let them not approach.

BEROWNE
We are shame-proof, my lord; and 'tis some policy
To have one show worse than the King's and his company.

KING I say they shall not come.

PRINCESS
Nay, my good lord, let me o'errule you now.
That sport best pleases that doth least know how,
Where zeal strives to content, and the contents
Dies in the zeal of that which it presents.
Their form confounded makes most form in mirth,
When great things laboring perish in their birth.

BEROWNE [*to the King*]
A right description of our sport, my lord.

Enter [Armado the] braggart.

ARMADO [*to the King*] Anointed, I implore so much expense of thy royal sweet breath as will utter a brace of words. [*He delivers the king a paper.*]

PRINCESS [to *Berowne*] Doth this man serve God?

BEROWNE Why ask you?

PRINCESS 'A speaks not like a man of God his making.

ARMADO That is all one, my fair, sweet, honey monarch, for, I protest, the schoolmaster is exceeding fantastical, too, too vain, too, too vain; but we will put it, as they say, to *fortuna de la guerra.* I wish you the peace of mind, most royal couplement! *Exit.*

KING [*consulting the paper*] Here is like to be a good presence of Worthies. He presents Hector of Troy, the swain Pompey the Great, the parish curate Alexander, Armado's page Hercules, the pedant Judas Maccabaeus;
And if these four Worthies in their first show thrive,
These four will change habits and present the other five.

BEROWNE
There is five in the first show.

KING
You are deceived. 'Tis not so.

BEROWNE
The pedant, the braggart, the hedge-priest, the fool, and the boy.
Abate throw at novum, and the whole world again
Cannot pick out five such, take each one in his vein.

KING
The ship is under sail, and here she comes amain.

Enter [Costard, as] Pompey.

COSTARD
"I Pompey am—"

BEROWNE You lie; you are not he.

COSTARD
"I Pompey am—"

BOYET With leopard's head on knee.

BEROWNE
Well said, old mocker. I must needs be friends with thee.

COSTARD
"I Pompey am, Pompey surnamed the Big—"

DUMAINE "The Great."

COSTARD
It is "Great," sir.—"Pompey surnamed the Great,
That oft in field, with targe and shield, did make my foe to sweat.
And traveling along this coast, I here am come by chance,
And lay my arms before the legs of this sweet lass of France." [*He lays down his weapons.*]
If Your Ladyship would say "Thanks, Pompey," I had done.

PRINCESS Great thanks, great Pompey.

COSTARD 'Tis not so much worth; but I hope I was perfect. I made a little fault in "Great."

BEROWNE My hat to a halfpenny Pompey proves the best Worthy. [*Costard stands aside.*]

Enter [Nathaniel the] curate, for Alexander.

NATHANIEL
"When in the world I lived, I was the world's commander;
By east, west, north, and south, I spread my conquering might.
My scutcheon plain declares that I am Alisander—"

501 parfect (He means "perform," "present.") **502 Pompion** Pumpkin. (Malapropism for *Pompey*.) **506 degree** rank. **stand for** represent, play **508 turn . . . off** perform it well **510 some policy** a shrewd stratagem **515–16 and the . . . presents** and the (feeble) substance of what they perform is obscured by the zeal of the presentation. **517 Their . . . mirth** i.e., Their confusion as performers will provide mirth for us **518 laboring** striving to be born **519 right** apt. **our sport** i.e., our appearance as Muscovites **520 Anointed** i.e., King **522 brace** pair **525 God his** God's **529 *fortuna . . . guerra*** the fortune of war. **530 couplement** couple. **531 like** likely. **presence** assembly **534 pedant** schoolmaster **536 habits** costumes

537 five (Berowne corrects "These four" in lines 536–7 to five, since Armado's paper has named five.) **538 You . . . so** (The King's point is that only four will have to change costumes.) **539 hedge-priest** illiterate, rural priest **540 Abate . . . novum** Set aside a lucky throw of the dice in the game of *novum* or nines—a game that has five and nine as its principal throws. (With a joke on the business of offering nine characters with just five actors.) **541 take . . . vein** character by character. **542 amain** with full force. **544 leopard's head** (A part of Pompey's ridiculous coat of arms or costume.) **545 I . . . thee** Let's be friends. (Berowne is prepared to forget his quarrel with Boyet; they join forces, now mocking the pageant.) **549 targe** shield **555–6 I . . . perfect** I hope I recited correctly. **557 My hat to** I'll wager my hat against **558.1 *for*** as. (Also at 583.2.) **561 scutcheon** coat of arms

BOYET
Your nose says, no, you are not; for it stands too right.
BEROWNE [*to Boyet*]
Your nose smells "no" in this, most tender-smelling knight.
PRINCESS
The conqueror is dismayed. Proceed, good Alexander.
NATHANIEL
"When in the world I lived, I was the world's commander—"
BOYET
Most true; 'tis right. You were so, Alisander.
BEROWNE [*to Costard*] Pompey the Great—
COSTARD Your servant, and Costard.
BEROWNE Take away the conqueror. Take away Alisander.
COSTARD [*to Nathaniel*] Oh, sir, you have overthrown Alisander the conqueror! You will be scraped out of the painted cloth for this. Your lion, that holds his poleax sitting on a closestool, will be given to Ajax; he will be the ninth Worthy. A conqueror, and afeard to speak? Run away for shame, Alisander.

[*Exit Nathaniel.*]

There, an't shall please you, a foolish mild man, an honest man, look you, and soon dashed. He is a marvelous good neighbor, faith, and a very good bowler. But, for Alisander—alas, you see how 'tis—a, little o'erparted. But there are Worthies a-coming will speak their mind in some other sort.
PRINCESS Stand aside, good Pompey.

[*Costard stands aside.*]

Enter [*Holofernes the*] *pedant, for Judas, and* [*Mote*] *the boy, for Hercules.*

HOLOFERNES [*as presenter*]
"Great Hercules is presented by this imp,
Whose club killed Cerberus, that three-headed *canus;*
And when he was a babe, a child, a shrimp,
Thus did he strangle serpents in his *manus.*
Quoniam he seemeth in minority,
Ergo I come with this apology."
[*To Mote*] Keep some state in thy exit, and vanish.

Exit Boy.

[*As Judas*] "Judas I am—"
DUMAINE A Judas!
HOLOFERNES Not Iscariot, sir.
"Judas I am, yclept Maccabaeus."
DUMAINE Judas Maccabaeus clipped is plain Judas.
BEROWNE A kissing traitor. How art thou proved Judas?
HOLOFERNES "Judas I am—"
DUMAINE The more shame for you, Judas.
HOLOFERNES What mean you, sir?
BOYET To make Judas hang himself.
HOLOFERNES Begin, sir. You are my elder.
BEROWNE Well followed. Judas was hanged on an elder.
HOLOFERNES I will not be put out of countenance.
BEROWNE Because thou hast no face.
HOLOFERNES [*pointing to his own face*] What is this?
BOYET A citternhead.
DUMAINE The head of a bodkin.
BEROWNE A death's face in a ring.
LONGAVILLE The face of an old Roman coin, scarce seen.
BOYET The pommel of Caesar's falchion.
DUMAINE The carved-bone face on a flask.
BEROWNE Saint George's half-cheek in a brooch.
DUMAINE Ay, and in a brooch of lead.
BEROWNE Ay, and worn in the cap of a tooth drawer. And now forward, for we have put thee in countenance.
HOLOFERNES You have put me out of countenance.
BEROWNE False. We have given thee faces.
HOLOFERNES But you have outfaced them all.
BEROWNE
An thou wert a lion, we would do so.

562 right straight. (Alexander was supposed to have had a wry neck that twisted his head to one side.) **563 Your . . . this** (Alexander was reputed to have a body odor of "marvelous good savor," according to Plutarch, as translated by Thomas North.) **tender-smelling** sensitive to smells **568 Your . . . Costard** Costard, at your service. **572–3 You will . . . for this** (The Nine Worthies were frequently depicted in tapestry.) **573–4 Your lion . . . closestool** (A Renaissance memorial emblem of Alexander described a lion sitting on a throne, holding a battle-ax. Costard here substitutes a *closestool,* or privy, for the throne.) **574 Ajax** legendary Greek chieftain at the Trojan War who coveted the slain Achilles's armor. (With a pun on *jakes,* privy.) **577 an't . . . you** if you please **578 dashed** rattled, daunted. **581 o'erparted** having a part too difficult. **582 sort** manner. **584 presented** played, represented. **imp** child **585 Cerberus** three-headed dog at the entrance to Hades, the capturing of which was one of Hercules's twelve labors. ***canus*** i.e., *canis,* "dog" in Latin. (*Canus* is needed for the rhyme.) **587 *manus*** hands. **588 *Quoniam* . . . minority** Since he is a child **589 *Ergo*** therefore

590 state dignity **592 A Judas** i.e., A traitor. (The lords deliberately confuse the military hero Judas Maccabaeus with Judas Iscariot, who betrayed Christ.) **594 yclept** called **595 clipped** shortened. (With a play on *yclept* in line 594.) **596 A kissing traitor** i.e., a reference to Judas's embrace and kiss of Jesus by which he betrayed his master. (Playing on *clipped* in line 595, in the sense of "embraced" or "kissed.") **601 You . . . elder** i.e., You are my senior and so should take precedence. **602 Well . . . elder** (Berowne answers Holofernes with a pun on *elder,* "elder tree," traditionally the tree on which Judas hanged himself.) **603 put out of countenance** disconcerted. **604 Because . . . face** (Berowne counters by taking Holofernes's *countenance* in its literal sense, "face.") **606 citternhead** head of a cithern or guitar (often grotesquely carved). **607 bodkin** a long, jeweled pin for a lady's hair, or a small dagger (similarly carved). **608 A death's . . . ring** i.e., A death's-head ring worn as a *memento mori.* **609–10 scarce seen** i.e., worn almost smooth. **611 falchion** curved sword. (The *pommel* or rounded knob on the hilt would be carved.) **612 flask** i.e., horn powder flask. **613 half-cheek** profile **614 of lead** i.e., of inferior quality. **615 tooth drawer** (Tooth extractors were not highly regarded; a brooch worn by such people in the cap might be of an inferior sort.) **616–17 we . . . countenance** i.e., (1) we've reversed our putting you *out of countenance,* line 603 (2) we've drawn your portrait. **618 You . . . countenance** (Holofernes protests: "You've made me forget my lines.") **620 outfaced them** i.e., mocked them, put them down. (Playing on *faces* in line 619.) **621 An** If. **lion** (One of Aesop's fables tells of an ass that wears a lion's skin until he is betrayed by his bray.)

BOYET
Therefore, as he is an ass, let him go.
And so adieu, sweet Jude! Nay, why dost thou stay?

DUMAINE For the latter end of his name.

BEROWNE
For the ass to the Jude? Give it him. Jud-as, away!

HOLOFERNES
This is not generous, not gentle, not humble.

BOYET
A light for Monsieur Judas! It grows dark; he may
stumble. [*Exit Holofernes.*]

PRINCESS
Alas, poor Maccabaeus, how hath he been baited!

Enter [*Armado the*] *braggart* [*as Hector*].

BEROWNE Hide thy head, Achilles! Here comes Hector in arms.

DUMAINE Though my mocks come home by me, I will now be merry.

KING Hector was but a Trojan in respect of this.

BOYET But is this Hector?

KING I think Hector was not so clean-timbered.

LONGAVILLE His leg is too big for Hector's.

DUMAINE More calf, certain.

BOYET No, he is best endued in the small.

BEROWNE This cannot be Hector.

DUMAINE He's a god or a painter, for he makes faces.

ARMADO
"The armipotent Mars, of lances the almighty,
Gave Hector a gift—"

DUMAINE A gilt nutmeg.

BEROWNE A lemon.

LONGAVILLE Stuck with cloves.

DUMAINE No, cloven.

ARMADO Peace!—
"The armipotent Mars, of lances the almighty,
Gave Hector a gift, the heir of Ilion;
A man so breathed that certain he would fight, yea
From morn till night, out of his pavilion.
I am that flower—"

DUMAINE That mint.

LONGAVILLE That columbine.

ARMADO Sweet Lord Longaville, rein thy tongue.

LONGAVILLE I must rather give it the rein, for it runs against Hector.

DUMAINE Ay, and Hector's a greyhound.

ARMADO The sweet warman is dead and rotten. Sweet chucks, beat not the bones of the buried. When he breathed, he was a man. But I will forward with my device. [*To the Princess*] Sweet royalty, bestow on me the sense of hearing.

Berowne steps forth [*to whisper to Costard, and then resumes his place*].

PRINCESS
Speak, brave Hector. We are much delighted.

ARMADO I do adore thy sweet Grace's slipper.

BOYET Loves her by the foot.

DUMAINE He may not by the yard.

ARMADO
"This Hector far surmounted Hannibal—"

COSTARD The party is gone. Fellow Hector, she is gone! She is two months on her way.

ARMADO What meanest thou?

COSTARD Faith, unless you play the honest Trojan, the poor wench is cast away. She's quick; the child brags in her belly already. 'Tis yours.

ARMADO Dost thou infamonize me among potentates? Thou shalt die.

COSTARD Then shall Hector be whipped for Jaquenetta that is quick by him and hanged for Pompey that is dead by him.

DUMAINE Most rare Pompey!

BOYET Renowned Pompey!

BEROWNE Greater than "Great"! Great, great, great Pompey! Pompey the Huge!

DUMAINE Hector trembles.

BEROWNE Pompey is moved. More Ates, more Ates! Stir them on, stir them on!

DUMAINE Hector will challenge him.

BEROWNE Ay, if 'a have no more man's blood in his belly than will sup a flea.

ARMADO By the North Pole, I do challenge thee.

COSTARD I will not fight with a pole, like a northern man. I'll slash; I'll do it by the sword. I bepray you, let me borrow my arms again.

DUMAINE Room for the incensed Worthies!

COSTARD I'll do it in my shirt. [*He takes off his doublet.*]

DUMAINE Most resolute Pompey!

625 Jud-as (Jude's *latter end* turns out to be his ass.) **626 gentle** courteous **628 baited** set upon, attacked. **629 Achilles . . . Hector** (These two were great antagonists in the Trojan War.) **631 by me** to mock me **633 a Trojan . . . this** i.e., (1) a resident of Troy (2) a jolly companion, a roisterer in comparison with Armado. **635 clean-timbered** well built. **637 calf** (1) lower part of leg (2) dolt **638 best . . . small** well endowed in the part of the leg below the calf. **640 makes faces** (1) creates images as a god or a painter might do (2) grimaces (being a bad actor). **641 armipotent** powerful in arms **643 gilt** glazed with egg yolk, saffron, etc. **646 No, cloven** i.e., No, "cloven" is more appropriate to a *leman* or lover (varied from *lemon* in line 644) who is *cloven* in the act of love. **649 Ilion** Troy **650 so breathed** in such fit condition **651 pavilion** tent or camp to which the combatant retired when not engaged in fight **652 flower** (Armado is trying to say "flower of chivalry.") **655 rein** restrain, control **656 give it the rein** allow it to run freely

658 a greyhound i.e., famed for his speed as a runner. **659 warman** warrior **661 forward** go forward, continue **662 device** i.e., speech. **667 yard** (Dumaine puns on the slang sense, "penis.") **669 The party is gone** i.e., Jaquenetta has disappeared. (Costard may have received this news from Berowne when Berowne whispered to him.) **670 on her way** i.e., pregnant. **672 play . . . Trojan** i.e., do the honest thing by her **673 quick** pregnant **675 infamonize** slander **678–9 and hanged . . . him** (Costard seems to mean that Armado will have to kill him, the actor of Pompey, if he does not do right by Jaquenetta; Costard will challenge Armado to a duel.) **680 rare** excellent **685 Ates** i.e., incitements to mischief. (Ate was the goddess of discord.) **688 if 'a** even if he **689 sup** feed **691–2 a northern man** a boorish ruffian from the north (for whom the stave or *pole* was a traditional weapon). **692–3 let . . . again** (Costard asks if he can borrow the weapons he lay down before the Princess in line 551.) **694 Room . . . Worthies!** Make room for the incensed Worthies to fight!

MOTE [*to Armado*] Master, let me take you a buttonhole lower. Do you not see Pompey is uncasing for the combat? What mean you? You will lose your reputation.

ARMADO Gentlemen and soldiers, pardon me. I will not combat in my shirt.

DUMAINE You may not deny it. Pompey hath made the challenge.

ARMADO Sweet bloods, I both may and will.

BEROWNE What reason have you for't?

ARMADO The naked truth of it is, I have no shirt. I go woolward for penance.

BOYET True, and it was enjoined him in Rome for want of linen; since when, I'll be sworn, he wore none but a dishclout of Jaquenetta's, and that 'a wears next his heart for a favor.

Enter a messenger, Monsieur Marcade.

MARCADE God save you, madam!

PRINCESS Welcome, Marcade,
But that thou interruptest our merriment.

MARCADE
I am sorry, madam, for the news I bring
Is heavy in my tongue. The King your father—

PRINCESS
Dead, for my life!

MARCADE Even so. My tale is told.

BEROWNE
Worthies, away! The scene begins to cloud.

ARMADO For mine own part, I breathe free breath. I have seen the day of wrong through the little hole of discretion, and I will right myself like a soldier.

Exeunt [the] Worthies.

KING How fares Your Majesty?

PRINCESS
Boyet, prepare. I will away tonight.

KING
Madam, not so. I do beseech you, stay.

PRINCESS
Prepare, I say. I thank you, gracious lords,
For all your fair endeavors, and entreat,
Out of a new-sad soul, that you vouchsafe
In your rich wisdom to excuse or hide
The liberal opposition of our spirits,
If overboldly we have borne ourselves
In the converse of breath; your gentleness
Was guilty of it. Farewell, worthy lord!
A heavy heart bears not a humble tongue.
Excuse me so, coming too short of thanks
For my great suit so easily obtained.

KING
The extreme parts of time extremely forms
All causes to the purpose of his speed,
And often at his very loose decides
That which long process could not arbitrate.
And though the mourning brow of progeny
Forbid the smiling courtesy of love
The holy suit which fain it would convince,
Yet since love's argument was first on foot,
Let not the cloud of sorrow jostle it
From what it purposed, since to wail friends lost
Is not by much so wholesome-profitable
As to rejoice at friends but newly found.

PRINCESS
I understand you not. My griefs are double.

BEROWNE
Honest plain words best pierce the ear of grief,
And by these badges understand the King.
For your fair sakes have we neglected time,
Played foul play with our oaths. Your beauty, ladies,
Hath much deformed us, fashioning our humors
Even to the opposèd end of our intents,
And what in us hath seemed ridiculous—
As love is full of unbefitting strains,
All wanton as a child, skipping and vain,
Formed by the eye and therefore, like the eye,
Full of strange shapes, of habits, and of forms,
Varying in subjects as the eye doth roll
To every varied object in his glance;
Which parti-coated presence of loose love
Put on by us, if in your heavenly eyes
Have misbecomed our oaths and gravities,
Those heavenly eyes that look into these faults
Suggested us to make. Therefore, ladies,
Our love being yours, the error that love makes
Is likewise yours. We to ourselves prove false
By being once false forever to be true
To those that make us both—fair ladies, you.
And even that falsehood, in itself a sin,
Thus purifies itself and turns to grace.

697 take . . . lower (1) help remove your doublet (2) "take you down a peg," humiliate you. **698 uncasing** undressing **699 You . . . reputation** (A gentleman would lose status fighting with a country bumpkin like Costard.) **701 combat** duel, fight **704 bloods** men of mettle and rank **706–7 go woolward for penance** i.e., with woolen clothing next to the skin and no linen underwear. (Armado's lame excuse is that he does so to punish the flesh.) **708 enjoined** required of **708–9 want of linen** lack of a clean shirt, etc. (Boyet sees through the excuse.) **710 dishclout** dishcloth **711 favor** love token. **719–21 For . . . discretion** i.e., For my part, I have things under control. I now perceive how wrongly I have behaved **721 right myself** i.e., make honorable amends, do the right thing **728 hide** overlook **729 liberal opposition** too-free antagonism **731 in . . . breath** in conversation. **gentleness** courtesy **731–2 your . . . of it** i.e., your courteous forbearance encouraged us to tease you so.

733 A heavy . . . tongue My sad heart prevents me from speaking with a proper humility. **734 so** therefore **735 suit** i.e., the mission on which the came (which the King evidently has granted) **736–7 The . . . speed** i.e., A few last moments demand quick decisions **737, 738 his** i.e., time's **738 loose** release, discharge. (An archery term.) **740 the mourning brow of progeny** i.e., mourning worn by the Princess to honor her dead father **741 Forbid** deny to us **742 The . . . convince** the virtuous love suit it wishes to pursue **745 to wail . . . lost** to lament for the dead **746 by much** nearly **748 double** i.e., because of my father's death, and because I don't understand you. **750 badges** signs, i.e., my honest, plain words **754 opposèd** opposite **756 strains** impulses **757 wanton** frivolous. **vain** foolish **761 his** its **762 Which . . . love** which jesting appearance of unrestrained love **764 misbecomed** been unbecoming to **766 Suggested us to make** tempted us to commit all these follies of love. **767 Our love being yours** i.e., since our love for you is really your fault **768–70 We . . . you** i.e., We have been false to our vows this once, abandoning the studies we vowed to pursue in order to be true forever to you, fair ladies, who make us both false and true: false to our former vow but true to you.

PRINCESS
We have received your letters full of love,
Your favors, the ambassadors of love,
And in our maiden council rated them
At courtship, pleasant jest, and courtesy,
As bombast and as lining to the time.
But more devout than this in our respects
Have we not been, and therefore met your loves
In their own fashion, like a merriment.

DUMAINE
Our letters, madam, showed much more than jest.

LONGAVILLE
So did our looks.

ROSALINE We did not quote them so.

KING
Now, at the latest minute of the hour,
Grant us your loves.

PRINCESS A time, methinks, too short
To make a world-without-end bargain in.
No, no, my lord, Your Grace is perjured much,
Full of dear guiltiness, and therefore this:
If for my love—as there is no such cause—
You will do aught, this shall you do for me:
Your oath I will not trust, but go with speed
To some forlorn and naked hermitage,
Remote from all the pleasures of the world;
There stay until the twelve celestial signs
Have brought about the annual reckoning.
If this austere insociable life
Change not your offer made in heat of blood;
If frosts and fasts, hard lodging, and thin weeds
Nip not the gaudy blossoms of your love,
But that it bear this trial, and last love;
Then, at the expiration of the year,
Come challenge me, challenge me by these deserts,
And, by this virgin palm now kissing thine,
[*giving him her hand*]
I will be thine; and till that instance shut
My woeful self up in a mourning house,
Raining the tears of lamentation
For the remembrance of my father's death.
If this thou do deny, let our hands part,
Neither entitled in the other's heart.

KING
If this, or more than this, I would deny,
To flatter up these powers of mine with rest,
The sudden hand of death close up mine eye!
Hence, hermit, then. My heart is in thy breast.
[*They converse apart.*]

DUMAINE [*to Katharine*]
But what to me, my love? But what to me?
A wife?

KATHARINE A beard, fair health, and honesty.
With threefold love I wish you all these three.

DUMAINE
Oh, shall I say, "I thank you, gentle wife"?

KATHARINE
Not so, my lord. A twelvemonth and a day
I'll mark no words that smooth-faced wooers say.
Come when the King doth to my lady come;
Then, if I have much love, I'll give you some.

DUMAINE
I'll serve thee true and faithfully till then.

KATHARINE
Yet swear not, lest ye be forsworn again.
[*They converse apart.*]

LONGAVILLE
What says Maria?

MARIA At the twelvemonth's end
I'll change my black gown for a faithful friend.

LONGAVILLE
I'll stay with patience, but the time is long.

MARIA
The liker you. Few taller are so young.
[*They converse apart.*]

BEROWNE [*to Rosaline*]
Studies my lady? Mistress, look on me.
Behold the window of my heart, mine eye,
What humble suit attends thy answer there.
Impose some service on me for thy love.

ROSALINE
Oft have I heard of you, my Lord Berowne,
Before I saw you; and the world's large tongue
Proclaims you for a man replete with mocks,
Full of comparisons and wounding flouts,
Which you on all estates will execute
That lie within the mercy of your wit.
To weed this wormwood from your fruitful brain,
And therewithal to win me, if you please,
Without the which I am not to be won,
You shall this twelvemonth term from day to day
Visit the speechless sick and still converse
With groaning wretches, and your task shall be
With all the fierce endeavor of your wit
To enforce the painèd impotent to smile.

BEROWNE
To move wild laughter in the throat of death?
It cannot be. It is impossible.
Mirth cannot move a soul in agony.

774 favors love tokens **775–6 rated them At** evaluated them as **777 bombast** (1) a loosely made fabric used for padding or stuffing garments, for *lining* (2) puffed-up rhetoric, fit only to fill up the time **778–9 But . . . been** i.e., For our part, we have not taken the matter any more seriously than we judged you to have done **782 quote** interpret **787 dear** grievous and precious **788 as . . . cause** i.e., though I can't see why it should inspire you in that way **789 aught** anything **791 naked** austere, isolated **793 twelve celestial signs** signs of the zodiac (encompassing one year) **797 hard lodging** uncomfortable accommodations. **weeds** garments **799 last** remain, continue as **801 challenge** claim. **deserts** meritorious actions **803 instance** instant **808 entitled in** having a claim to **810 To . . . rest** to pamper my five senses with sensual ease **811 The sudden** may the sudden

812 Hence, hermit then i.e., Then off I go to be a hermit. **814 A beard** i.e., May you grow up to be a man **818 smooth-faced** (1) beardless (2) smooth-talking **824 friend** sweetheart. **825 stay** wait **826 The . . . young** i.e., That's just like you. Few tall young men are so callow and impatient. **827 Studies my lady?** i.e., Are you in a brown study? **829 attends** awaits **832 the world's large tongue** i.e., universal report **834 comparisons** sardonic similes. **flouts** jeers, insults **835 all estates** all classes of people **837 weed** i.e., remove. **wormwood** (A bitter-tasting herb, hence, "bitterness.") **841 still converse** constantly associate **844 the painèd impotent** helpless sufferers

ROSALINE
Why, that's the way to choke a gibing spirit, 848
Whose influence is begot of that loose grace 849
Which shallow laughing hearers give to fools.
A jest's prosperity lies in the ear
Of him that hears it, never in the tongue
Of him that makes it. Then if sickly ears,
Deafed with the clamors of their own dear groans, 854
Will hear your idle scorns, continue then,
And I will have you and that fault withal; 856
But if they will not, throw away that spirit,
And I shall find you empty of that fault,
Right joyful of your reformation.

BEROWNE
A twelvemonth? Well, befall what will befall,
I'll jest a twelvemonth in an hospital.

PRINCESS [*to the King*]
Ay, sweet my lord, and so I take my leave.

KING
No, madam, we will bring you on your way. 863

BEROWNE
Our wooing doth not end like an old play;
Jack hath not Jill. These ladies' courtesy
Might well have made our sport a comedy.

KING
Come, sir, it wants a twelvemonth and a day, 867
And then 'twill end.

BEROWNE That's too long for a play.

Enter [*Armado the*] *braggart.*

ARMADO [*to the King*] Sweet Majesty, vouchsafe me—
PRINCESS Was not that Hector?
DUMAINE The worthy knight of Troy.
ARMADO I will kiss thy royal finger, and take leave. I am
a votary; I have vowed to Jaquenetta to hold the plow 873
for her sweet love three year. But, most esteemed
greatness, will you hear the dialogue that the two 875
learned men have compiled in praise of the owl 876
and the cuckoo? It should have followed in the end of
our show.
KING Call them forth quickly. We will do so.
ARMADO [*calling*] Holla! Approach.

Enter all [*Holofernes, Nathaniel, Mote, Costard, Jaquenetta, and others. They stand in two groups.*]

This side is Hiems, Winter, this Ver, the Spring; the
one maintained by the owl, th'other by the cuckoo. 882
Ver, begin.

The Song

SPRING [*sings*]
When daisies pied and violets blue, 884
And lady-smocks all silver-white, 885
And cuckoo-buds of yellow hue 886
Do paint the meadows with delight,
The cuckoo then on every tree
Mocks married men, for thus sings he:
Cuckoo!
Cuckoo, cuckoo! Oh, word of fear,
Unpleasing to a married ear! 892

When shepherds pipe on oaten straws,
And merry larks are plowmen's clocks, 894
When turtles tread, and rooks and daws, 895
And maidens bleach their summer smocks,
The cuckoo then on every tree
Mocks married men, for thus sings he:
Cuckoo!
Cuckoo, cuckoo! Oh, word of fear,
Unpleasing to a married ear!

WINTER [*sings*]
When icicles hang by the wall,
And Dick the shepherd blows his nail, 903
And Tom bears logs into the hall,
And milk comes frozen home in pail,
When blood is nipped, and ways be foul, 906
Then nightly sings the staring owl:
Tu-whit, tu-whoo! A merry note,
While greasy Joan doth keel the pot. 909

When all aloud the wind doth blow,
And coughing drowns the parson's saw, 911
And birds sit brooding in the snow,
And Marian's nose looks red and raw,
When roasted crabs hiss in the bowl, 914
Then nightly sings the staring owl:
Tu-whit, tu-whoo! A merry note,
While greasy Joan doth keel the pot.

ARMADO The words of Mercury are harsh after the 918
songs of Apollo. You that way; we this way. 919
Exeunt, [*separately*].

848 gibing mocking, scornful **849 loose grace** carelessly given approval. (Rosaline is saying that Berowne's mocking manner has been nurtured by the fact that others have laughed shallowly and too easily at his foolish raillery.) **854 dear** heartfelt **856 withal** in addition **863 bring** accompany **867 wants** lacks **873 hold the plow** i.e., labor at farming **875 dialogue** debate **875–6 the two learned men** i.e., Holofernes and Nathaniel **882 maintained** defended, championed

884 pied parti-colored **885 lady-smocks** cuckooflowers **886 cuckoo-buds of yellow** buttercups (?) **892 Unpleasing** i.e., because the cuckoo suggests cuckoldry **894 clocks** i.e., because plowmen "rise with the lark" **895 turtles tread** turtledoves mate. **rooks and daws** black birds related to the crow **903 blows his nail** blows on his fingernails (i.e., to keep warm, and waiting patiently with nothing to do) **906 nipped** chilled. **ways** pathways **909 keel** skim and stir; cool to prevent boiling **911 saw** maxim, moral observation **914 crabs** crab apples **918 Mercury** messenger of the gods and associated with eloquence or sophistry, in antithesis to Apollo, the god of music **919 You . . . this way** (Armado may be directing those who have presented Winter to exit in one direction and those who have presented Spring, in another; he may also be referring to the audience.)

The Two Gentlemen of Verona

If by "romantic comedy" we mean a love story in which the lovers overcome parental obstacles, jealousies, separations, and dangers to be united at last in married bliss, then *The Two Gentlemen of Verona* is perhaps Shakespeare's first. Although *The Comedy of Errors* may be an earlier play, it is a farce of mistaken identity, with only a secondary interest in marriage, whereas *Love's Labor's Lost* is a courtly confection ending in the postponement of all marriages. No mention of *The Two Gentlemen of Verona* occurs until it is mentioned in Francis Meres's *Palladis Tamia: Wit's Treasury* of 1598, but the play is often dated around 1590–1594 on the basis of style: rhymed couplets, end-stopped verse, passages of excessive wit combat, and the like. *The Taming of the Shrew* (c. 1592–1594) is often dated a little later than *The Two Gentlemen of Verona*, if only because its double plotting is more complex and its exploration of the perils and rewards of courtships more challenging. In any event, *The Two Gentlemen of Verona* helps define, at an early stage, the genre of Shakespeare's best-known "festive" comedies, from *A Midsummer Night's Dream* to *Twelfth Night*.

The Two Gentlemen of Verona is also Shakespeare's apprenticeship to the romantic fiction of Italy and other southern European countries, whence he later derived so many plots of threatened love. He locates his story in Italy and gives some of his characters Italian names. He uses the conventional plot devices of romantic fiction: inconstancy in love and in friendship, the disguise of the heroine as a page, the overhearing of false vows, banishment, elopement, capture by outlaws, and so on. Virtually all the characters have a recognizable ancestry, not only in continental fiction but in neoclassical drama as well: Lucetta is the conventional female companion of the heroine, Thurio is the rich but unwelcome rival wooer (the pantaloon), Antonio and the Duke are typically strong-willed fathers opposing the romantic marriages of their children, Speed and Lance are at least supposed to be the clever servants who deliver messages and arrange rendezvous, and the four young lovers are the romantic protagonists.

Even in this early apprenticeship, to be sure, Shakespeare departs from the neoclassical norm of his continental sources. The setting remains nominally Italian, but the tone is often heartily English, and Shakespeare's attitude toward his romantic models borders occasionally on the irreverent. Lucetta is a true friend of Julia and a virtuous counselor in love; the jest about her being a "broker" or a go-between (1.2.41) reminds us how unlike a bawdy duenna of neoclassical comedy she really is. Thurio, Antonio, and the Duke are all portrayed with such amiable forbearance that they often seem inadequately motivated as the opponents of romantic happiness. Most of all, Speed and Lance have departed from their traditional roles as comic manipulators to become vaudeville jokesters.

Moreover, the very conventions of love and friendship are presented in such a way as to cast those conventions in an improbable light. What are we to make of the inconstant Proteus, who rejects his faithful Julia the moment he is away from her, tries instead to win the lady-fair of his dearest friend Valentine, informs the Duke of Valentine's plan to elope with Silvia, and then attempts a violent assault on Silvia's chastity? What sort of romantic hero is this, and why should he be rewarded by being forgiven and restored to his Julia? Most puzzling of all, is it credible that Valentine should respond to all this perfidy by offering to relinquish Silvia to Proteus? By the same token, isn't it absurd that the outlaws in the forest near Mantua should turn out to be gentlemen in exile and that they should offer command of their group to Valentine, whom they have just captured? Isn't the Duke's forgiveness of his eloped daughter Silvia rather sudden and unconvincing? These problems, which have troubled many readers of the play (though they generally seem less formidable to spectators of an actual production), can perhaps best be analyzed in two ways: as a result of Shakespeare's having combined two sources with conflicting conventions, thereby subjecting those conventions to a playfully ironic perspective, and as a result of Shakespeare's conscious interest in the theme of unexpected forgiveness for his erring protagonist.

Using a device of plotting that was to become customary in his romantic comedies, Shakespeare combines two fictional sources and thereby sets up a dramatic tension between the two. His chief source appears to have been *Diana*, a popular pastoral romance in Spanish by the Portuguese Jorge de Montemayor (1520–1561). Its heroine, Felismena (corresponding to Julia), is wooed by Don Felix (Proteus), whose father (Antonio) disapproves of the match and sends Don Felix away to court. Felismena, following after him disguised as a page, stops at an inn and is invited by the Host to listen to some music, whereupon she overhears Don Felix protesting his love to a new lady, Celia (Silvia). At this point, the resemblance between *Diana* and Shakespeare's play breaks off. Even thus far, despite several striking resemblances, the story provides no counterpart for Valentine, Proteus's best friend and the faithful lover of Silvia. Montemayor's romance is primarily concerned with inconstancy in love.

For the motif of true friendship, Shakespeare may have turned to the story of Titus and Gisippus, as told by Sir Thomas Elyot in *The Governor* (1531). Here Gisippus, upon learning that his dear friend Titus has fallen in love with Gisippus's ladylove, not only relinquishes the lady to Titus but also actually smuggles him into bed with her, all unbeknownst to the lady. The point of this story, as of other well-known treatises on friendship, such as John Lyly's *Euphues* (1578) and *Endymion* (1588) or Richard Edwards's *Damon and Pythias* (1565), is that friendship is a higher form of human affection than erotic love, since it is disinterested, platonically pure, and capable of teaching selflessness to others. Such a tale of perfect friendship provides, however, no counterpart for Julia, the lady abandoned by Proteus. Shakespeare has neatly dovetailed the two stories, making a quartet of lovers out of two triangular situations. The false lover of the first story becomes also the false friend of the second—only to be overwhelmed at the end by the generosity of his true friend.

The dramatic problem created by combining these two stories is that they arouse different expectations. The one is dedicated to the virtue of constancy in love; the other, to friendship. Valentine's ultimate function is to demonstrate the triumph of selfless friendship over love, and yet his function in the plot of love rivalry is to demonstrate true loyalty to his Silvia. His relinquishing of her to Proteus seems inconsistent with his vows as a lover. Conversely, Proteus's double perfidy, toward his lover Julia and his friend Valentine, seems to render him unworthy of the generous action Valentine bestows on him. Proteus's very name is synonymous with inconstancy; his namesake in the *Odyssey* was infamous for his ability to change shapes at will. (Valentine's name, on the other hand, betokens constancy in love.) The coupling of the two plots simultaneously intensifies Proteus's guilt and Valentine's magnanimity.

Yet Shakespeare makes a virtue out of the seeming lack of credibility. First, the very implausibility of Valentine's selflessness in love and of Proteus's sudden conversion to virtue allows Shakespeare to mock gently the literary commonplaces of his sources. At the same time, Shakespeare finds serious value in his conventional topics of love and friendship, through the device of paradox. The more unlikely Valentine's actions seem, the more transcendent and wondrous they are bound to appear. Shakespeare prepares for his climactic scene of forgiveness in several ways. First, he presents Proteus as an essentially noble person who has fallen through a single fault. Proteus is wellborn, accomplished, and handsome. The worthy Julia loves him for his good qualities, and he responds with sincerity and passion. He is equally ardent as a friend to Valentine. Only when he sees Silvia does Proteus become helpless, "dazzlèd" (2.4.207). He cannot completely be blamed for being overwhelmed by passion, for the other lovers are no less obedient to love's command. According to the code of love that infuses this play, love cannot choose its object. Proteus's unhappy fate is to love Silvia. Yet he must also be held responsible for his actions and, indeed, blames himself for the desertion that he has consciously committed. His self-hatred increases as he turns flatterer, liar, betrayer, and finally would-be rapist. Like Angelo in *Measure for Measure*, Proteus is compulsively driven to abhorrent sin, but the choice is ultimately his. The psychological insight of that later dark comedy is lacking—the soliloquies do not create the suffocating atmosphere of a nightmare—but the pattern of a guilty fall is still manifest.

We are probably on the wrong track if we attempt to psychoanalyze Valentine too closely; the choice he must sort out between love and friendship is more a conventional debate on a favorite Renaissance theme than a realistic portrayal of a man caught between conflicting ideals. Shakespeare makes no attempt to conceal what is absurd about Valentine's sudden renunciation of the woman who has been unswervingly loyal to him and who has no wish to be traded from one lover to another as though she were the object of some kind of moralistic barter. Nonetheless, the very implausibility of Valentine's offer to relinquish Silvia accentuates the noble intent behind the gesture. We are surprised, even comically surprised, because we don't expect such selflessness in human nature; but, if friendship is to be seen as a supreme achievement of the human spirit, it must transcend humanity's all-too-common penchant for rivalry and ingratitude. Valentine's generosity is not achieved without inner struggle. In the climactic scene of attempted rape, his first natural reaction is angry denunciation. What changes his mind is the depth and earnestness of Proteus's confession and desire for forgiveness: "If hearty sorrow / Be a sufficient ransom for offense, / I tender't here" (5.4.74–6). Valentine responds in the name of mercy and at the prompting of divine example: "By penitence th'Eternal's wrath's appeased" (line 81). The more undeserved the pardon, the more selfless the act of him who pardons. Only by conquering his desire for Silvia can Valentine teach his friend selflessness and thus reunite all four lovers in perfect joy. *The Two Gentlemen of Verona* is thus in part a comedy of forgiveness, anticipating later plays in which the romantic protagonist is equally culpable and yet equally forgiven: *Much Ado About Nothing, Measure for Measure, All's Well That Ends Well, Cymbeline*, and others (see R. G. Hunter's *Shakespeare and the Comedy of Forgiveness*, 1965.) *The Two Noble Kinsmen*, written very late (c. 1613) in collaboration with John Fletcher, is a sophisticated return to issues of friendship and sexual rivalry that are so prominent in *The Two Gentlemen of Verona*.

Forgiveness of Proteus must proceed no less from Julia than from Valentine. She, too, has much to pardon; as Proteus contritely observes, "O heaven! Were man / But constant, he were perfect" (5.4.110–11). Julia initiates a line of Shakespearean heroines, including Hero, Isabella, Helena, and Imogen in the plays already named, who must similarly cure inconstancy by their constancy. Like many Shakespearean heroines, Julia is plucky, resourceful, modest but witty, patiently obedient in love and yet coyly flirtatious, a true friend, and long-suffering. Disguised as a page, she overhears her lover's infidelity and yet never loses her faith in him. She patiently delivers Proteus' messages to her rival (like Viola in *Twelfth Night*) and gently acts as conscience to her erring master.

Julia's use of male disguise anticipates more complex analyses, in later comedies, of the ambivalent and partly illusory nature of the differences between male and female. When Julia determines to don a male disguise in order to follow Proteus to Milan, she and Lucetta laugh at the necessity of Julia's tying up her hair and dressing herself in breeches festooned with a codpiece (2.7.39–61). Since a boy actor is playing a young woman in disguise as a young male, the theatrical playfulness and artifice positively invite us to see gender as something largely defined by role-playing and social expectations. The scene is an amused reflection on the different ways in which young men and women present themselves to the world.

The repeated device of overhearing, as in later comedies, provides a test for the protagonists' intentions. Thinking themselves unobserved, they reveal their true natures for better or for worse. In the ingeniously devised if improbable climactic scene (5.4), Proteus as would-be ravisher is overheard by both his rejected mistress and his betrayed friend. Conversely, Silvia proves loyal and chaste whenever she is silently observed by Julia (disguised as Sebastian) or by Valentine in the forest scenes. These overhearings suggest not only that humanity's good and evil deeds are witnessed but also that a beneficent providence will protect the virtuous. Valentine's unseen presence assures that Silvia will be saved from rape and that Proteus will be prevented from committing an actual crime of violence. As in later comedies of this sort, forgiveness is possible because the guilt remains one of intent only.

These slightly absurd but happy resolutions of conflict take place in a forest near Mantua, the first of what Northrop Frye calls Shakespeare's "green worlds" (*English Institute Essays 1948*, pp. 58–73). Although sketchily presented, this forest does anticipate the Forest of Arden and other sylvan restorative landscapes. Its inhabitants are banished men protesting the injustice of society at court or fugitives from unkind love. Valentine learns to prefer "unfrequented woods" to "flourishing peopled towns." His "wild faction" of outlaws desist from attacking "silly women or poor passengers" and appropriately swear "By the bare scalp of Robin Hood's fat friar" (5.4.2–3; 4.1.36–7). The outlaws are charmingly suited to their role of threatening and then reuniting the lovers, providentially capturing Silvia just as she is on her way to find Valentine. Their actions are highly improbable and poke fun at the very conventions they illustrate, but then the same can be said of Valentine's forgiveness of Proteus and the Duke's sudden reconciliation with his prospective son-in-law, Valentine. Like Arden, this forest is a strange place in which such changes of heart are expected to occur. The aura of improbability may also partly explain the play's carelessness about social distinctions and the realities of geography: the Duke is sometimes called the Emperor, and at one point Valentine sets sail from Verona to Milan (both located inland).

The buffoonish comedy of Lance and Speed performs a function similar to that of romantic improbability by undercutting the artifice and melodrama of the love story. How can we worry long over Valentine's banishment when Lance bursts out, "Sir, there is a proclamation that you are vanished" (3.1.217)? Or how can we fret about Proteus' courtship of Silvia when the love token he sends her is transformed into Lance's odoriferous dog? This sort of absurd anticlimax occurs at every turn. Lance's first soliloquy, about the dog's refusal to mourn their departure from Verona (2.3), is a brilliant example of what we would call vaudeville or stand-up comic joking, but it also comments on the immediately preceding scene of Proteus' tearful farewell to Julia. Lance's friendship for Speed, and especially his friendship for the dog, delightfully blaspheme the play's serious interest in true friendship. In one of Lance's funniest scenes (4.4.1–38), he describes how he has selflessly taken on himself the punishment meted out to the dog for urinating on Silvia's hooped petticoat. Similarly, the spectacle of Lance in love, cataloguing his mistress's virtues and vices, insures us against too deep an involvement in the hazards of Cupid. The play continually reminds us of the folly of love without denying its exquisite joys or its highest potential for selflessness.

The Two Gentlemen of Verona

The Names of All the Actors

DUKE [OF MILAN], *father to Silvia*
VALENTINE, } *the two gentlemen*
PROTEUS, }
ANTONIO, *father to Proteus*
THURIO, *a foolish rival to Valentine*
EGLAMOUR, *agent for Silvia in her escape*
HOST [*of the inn*] *where Julia lodges*
OUTLAWS *with Valentine*

SPEED, *a clownish servant to Valentine*
LANCE, *the like to Proteus*
PANTHINO, *servant to Antonio*

JULIA, *beloved of Proteus*
SILVIA, *beloved of Valentine*
LUCETTA, *waiting-woman to Julia*

[*Servants, Musicians*

SCENE: *Verona; Milan; the frontiers of Mantua*]

1.1

[*Enter*] *Valentine* [*and*] *Proteus.*

VALENTINE
Cease to persuade, my loving Proteus;
Home-keeping youth have ever homely wits. 2
Were't not affection chains thy tender days 3
To the sweet glances of thy honored love,
I rather would entreat thy company
To see the wonders of the world abroad
Than, living dully sluggardized at home,
Wear out thy youth with shapeless idleness. 8
But since thou lov'st, love still, and thrive therein,
Even as I would when I to love begin.

PROTEUS
Wilt thou be gone? Sweet Valentine, adieu!
Think on thy Proteus when thou haply see'st 12
Some rare noteworthy object in thy travel.
Wish me partaker in thy happiness
When thou dost meet good hap; and in thy danger, 15
If ever danger do environ thee,
Commend thy grievance to my holy prayers, 17
For I will be thy beadsman, Valentine. 18

VALENTINE
And on a love book pray for my success? 19

PROTEUS
Upon some book I love I'll pray for thee.

VALENTINE
That's on some shallow story of deep love, 21
How young Leander crossed the Hellespont. 22

PROTEUS
That's a deep story of a deeper love,
For he was more than over shoes in love.

VALENTINE
'Tis true; for you are over boots in love,
And yet you never swam the Hellespont.

PROTEUS
Over the boots? Nay, give me not the boots. 27

VALENTINE
No, I will not, for it boots thee not. 28

PROTEUS What?

VALENTINE
To be in love, where scorn is bought with groans,
Coy looks with heartsore sighs, one fading moment's mirth
With twenty watchful, weary, tedious nights. 32
If haply won, perhaps a hapless gain; 33
If lost, why then a grievous labor won;
However, but a folly bought with wit, 35
Or else a wit by folly vanquishèd.

PROTEUS
So by your circumstance you call me fool. 37

1.1. Location: Verona. A street.
2 homely dull, simple **3 affection** passion, love. **tender** youthful **8 shapeless** aimless **12 haply** by chance **15 hap** fortune **17 Commend thy grievance** commit your distress **18 beadsman** one engaged to pray for others, using the beads of the rosary **19 love book** manual of courtship or a love story (rather than a prayer book)

21 shallow . . . deep (Playing on the oppositions of shallow and deep water, superficial and heartfelt love.) **22 Leander** famous lover of Greek legend who drowned as he swam the Hellespont to see his love Hero **27 give . . . boots** i.e., don't make fun of me. **28 boots** profits, avails. (With play on *boots* in line 27. This passage is full of punning, on *shallow* and *deep, over shoes, over boots*, etc.) **32 watchful** wakeful **33 hapless** unlucky **35 However . . . wit** in either case, being in love is nothing but foolishness acquired through much ingenuity **37 circumstance** account

VALENTINE
So by your circumstance I fear you'll prove.

PROTEUS
'Tis love you cavil at. I am not Love.

VALENTINE
Love is your master, for he masters you;
And he that is so yokèd by a fool
Methinks should not be chronicled for wise.

PROTEUS
Yet writers say, as in the sweetest bud
The eating canker dwells, so eating love
Inhabits in the finest wits of all.

VALENTINE
And writers say, as the most forward bud
Is eaten by the canker ere it blow,
Even so by love the young and tender wit
Is turned to folly, blasting in the bud,
Losing his verdure even in the prime,
And all the fair effects of future hopes.
But wherefore waste I time to counsel thee
That art a votary to fond desire?
Once more adieu! My father at the road
Expects my coming, there to see me shipped.

PROTEUS
And thither will I bring thee, Valentine.

VALENTINE
Sweet Proteus, no. Now let us take our leave.
To Milan let me hear from thee by letters
Of thy success in love, and what news else
Betideth here in absence of thy friend;
And I likewise will visit thee with mine.

PROTEUS
All happiness bechance to thee in Milan!

VALENTINE
As much to you at home! And so, farewell. *Exit.*

PROTEUS
He after honor hunts, I after love.
He leaves his friends to dignify them more;
I leave myself, my friends, and all, for love.
Thou, Julia, thou hast metamorphized me,
Made me neglect my studies, lose my time,
War with good counsel, set the world at naught;
Made wit with musing weak, heart sick with thought.

[Enter] Speed.

SPEED
Sir Proteus, save you! Saw you my master?

PROTEUS
But now he parted hence to embark for Milan.

SPEED
Twenty to one, then, he is shipped already,
And I have played the sheep in losing him.

PROTEUS
Indeed, a sheep doth very often stray,
An if the shepherd be awhile away.

SPEED You conclude that my master is a shepherd, then, and I a sheep?

PROTEUS I do.

SPEED Why then, my horns are his horns, whether I wake or sleep.

PROTEUS A silly answer, and fitting well a sheep.

SPEED This proves me still a sheep.

PROTEUS True; and thy master a shepherd.

SPEED Nay, that I can deny by a circumstance.

PROTEUS It shall go hard but I'll prove it by another.

SPEED The shepherd seeks the sheep, and not the sheep the shepherd; but I seek my master, and my master seeks not me. Therefore I am no sheep.

PROTEUS The sheep for fodder follow the shepherd; the shepherd for food follows not the sheep. Thou for wages followest thy master; thy master for wages follows not thee. Therefore thou art a sheep.

SPEED Such another proof will make me cry "Baa."

PROTEUS But dost thou hear? Gav'st thou my letter to Julia?

SPEED Ay, sir. I, a lost mutton, gave your letter to her, a laced mutton, and she, a laced mutton, gave me, a lost mutton, nothing for my labor.

PROTEUS Here's too small a pasture for such store of muttons.

SPEED If the ground be overcharged, you were best stick her.

PROTEUS Nay, in that you are astray. 'Twere best pound you.

SPEED Nay, sir, less than a pound shall serve me for carrying your letter.

PROTEUS You mistake. I mean the pound—a pinfold.

SPEED
From a pound to a pin? Fold it over and over,

38 circumstance situation, condition **39 cavil at** carp at, find fault with. **Love** i.e., Cupid. **42 chronicled for wise** set down as being wise. **44 canker** cankerworm **45 Inhabits** dwells **46 forward** early **47 blow** bloom **49 blasting** withering **50 his verdure** its flourishing vigor. **prime** spring **51 fair . . . hopes** bright fulfillment of future happiness. **52 wherefore** why **53 votary** worshiper. **fond** foolish **54 road** roadstead, harbor **55 shipped** aboard. (Shakespeare evidently assumes that Verona and Milan are connected by water; Proteus also travels by ship, though Julia later makes the journey by land.) **56 bring** accompany **58 To Milan** By letters sent to Milan **60 Betideth** occurs **61 visit** enrich with a similar benefit **65 friends** (including family). **dignify** i.e., honor (by increasing his own fame) **66 leave** neglect **68 lose** waste **69 War . . . counsel** reject good advice **70 Made . . . thought** You have caused me to weaken my intellect by fanciful imaginings and to make sick my heart through melancholy.

71 save you God save you. **72 But now** Just now. **parted** departed **74 played the sheep** behaved sheepishly. (With a pun on *sheep* and *ship;* the words were pronounced similarly.) **76 An if** if **80 Why . . . his horns** i.e., Then you hint that I and my master are alike in that we are both horned. (Traditionally, husbands whose wives deceived them were supposed to grow cuckolds' horns.) **85 circumstance** process of reasoning. **86 It . . . I'll** I'll be doing pretty badly if I cannot **94 Baa** (With a pun on *bah,* as in "bah, humbug.") **95 dost thou hear** i.e., listen here. **97 to her** (At 1.2.39–40 we learn that Speed gave the letter to Lucetta.) **97–8 a lost mutton . . . a laced mutton** a lost sheep . . . a whore with tightly laced bodice or laced slashing in her dress. (With a pun on *lost/laced*, similarly pronounced.)
102 overcharged overcrowded **103 stick** (1) stab—with a bawdy suggestion of penetration (2) shut up in a pen **104 astray** (1) wandering like a lost sheep (2) going too far, missing the point.
105 pound (1) impound, shut up in an animal pen (2) beat
106 pound (1) twenty shillings (2) a beating **108 pinfold** pen for stray animals. **109 a pin** i.e., an object worth very little. **Fold** (1) as in folding a letter (2) multiply. (*Pin? Fold* plays on *pinfold* in line 108).

'Tis threefold too little for carrying a letter to your lover.
PROTEUS But what said she?
SPEED [*first nodding*] Ay.
PROTEUS Nod—ay—why, that's "noddy." 113
SPEED You mistook, sir. I say she did nod, and you ask me if she did nod, and I say, "Ay."
PROTEUS And that set together is "noddy."
SPEED Now you have taken the pains to set it together, take it for your pains. 118
PROTEUS No, no, you shall have it for bearing the letter.
SPEED Well, I perceive I must be fain to bear with you. 120
PROTEUS Why, sir, how do you bear with me?
SPEED Marry, sir, the letter, very orderly, having noth- 122
ing but the word "noddy" for my pains.
PROTEUS Beshrew me, but you have a quick wit. 124
SPEED And yet it cannot overtake your slow purse.
PROTEUS Come, come, open the matter in brief. What 126
said she?
SPEED Open your purse, that the money and the matter may be both at once delivered. 129
PROTEUS [*giving him money*] Well, sir, here is for your pains. What said she?
SPEED Truly, sir, I think you'll hardly win her.
PROTEUS Why? Couldst thou perceive so much from her?
SPEED Sir, I could perceive nothing at all from her, no, 134
not so much as a ducat for delivering your letter. And 135
being so hard to me that brought your mind, I fear 136
she'll prove as hard to you in telling your mind. Give 137
her no token but stones, for she's as hard as steel. 138
PROTEUS What said she? Nothing?
SPEED No, not so much as "Take this for thy pains." To
testify your bounty, I thank you, you have testerned 141
me; in requital whereof, henceforth carry your letters 142
yourself. And so, sir, I'll commend you to my master. 143
PROTEUS
Go, go, begone, to save your ship from wreck,
Which cannot perish having thee aboard, 145
Being destined to a drier death on shore. 146
[*Exit Speed.*]
I must go send some better messenger.
I fear my Julia would not deign my lines, 148
Receiving them from such a worthless post. *Exit.* 149

✤

113 noddy a simpleton. **118 take . . . pains** take it as your reward. (With wordplay in *taken the pain / take it for your pains.*) **120 fain** content. **bear with** (1) put up with (2) carry for. (Speed sees he is to get no tip.) **122 Marry** i.e., Indeed. (Originally an oath, "by the Virgin Mary.") **124 Beshrew me** (A mild oath.) **126 open** disclose. (Anticipating a pun in line 128 on *opening* a purse.) **129 delivered** (1) handed over (said of the *money*) (2) reported (said of the *matter* or business being discussed). **134 perceive** receive. (Punning on *perceive,* "understand," in the previous line.) **135 a ducat** a silver or gold coin **136 mind** desires, intentions **137 in telling** for telling **138 stones** (1) jewels such as diamonds, harder than steel and well suited to hard-hearted ladies (2) testicles **141–2 testerned me** given me a testern, sixpence (a small tip) **143 commend you** deliver your greetings **145–6 Which . . . shore** (An allusion to the proverb "He that is born to be hanged shall never be drowned.") **148 deign** deign to accept **149 post** (1) messenger (2) blockhead.

1.2

Enter Julia and Lucetta.

JULIA
But say, Lucetta, now we are alone,
Wouldst thou then counsel me to fall in love?
LUCETTA
Ay, madam, so you stumble not unheedfully. 3
JULIA
Of all the fair resort of gentlemen 4
That every day with parle encounter me, 5
In thy opinion which is worthiest love? 6
LUCETTA
Please you repeat their names, I'll show my mind 7
According to my shallow simple skill.
JULIA
What think'st thou of the fair Sir Eglamour? 9
LUCETTA
As of a knight well-spoken, neat, and fine;
But, were I you, he never should be mine.
JULIA
What think'st thou of the rich Mercatio?
LUCETTA
Well of his wealth, but of himself, so-so.
JULIA
What think'st thou of the gentle Proteus?
LUCETTA
Lord, Lord, to see what folly reigns in us!
JULIA
How now? What means this passion at his name? 16
LUCETTA
Pardon, dear madam, 'tis a passing shame 17
That I, unworthy body as I am,
Should censure thus on lovely gentlemen. 19
JULIA
Why not on Proteus, as of all the rest?
LUCETTA
Then thus: of many good I think him best.
JULIA Your reason?
LUCETTA
I have no other but a woman's reason:
I think him so because I think him so.
JULIA
And wouldst thou have me cast my love on him?
LUCETTA
Ay, if you thought your love not cast away.
JULIA
Why, he of all the rest hath never moved me. 27
LUCETTA
Yet he of all the rest I think best loves ye.
JULIA
His little speaking shows his love but small.
LUCETTA
Fire that's closest kept burns most of all.

1.2. Location: Verona. Julia's house.
3 so provided that **4 resort** company, assemblage **5 parle** talk **6 worthiest love** most worthy of love. **7 Please** If it please **9 Eglamour** (Not to be identified with Silvia's friend of the same name.) **16 passion** passionate outburst **17 passing** surpassing **19 censure** pass judgment **27 moved** urged (with a suit of love)

JULIA
They do not love that do not show their love.
LUCETTA
Oh, they love least that let men know their love.
JULIA I would I knew his mind.
LUCETTA [*giving a letter*] Peruse this paper, madam.
JULIA "To Julia." Say, from whom?
LUCETTA That the contents will show.
JULIA Say, say, who gave it thee?
LUCETTA
Sir Valentine's page; and sent, I think, from Proteus.
He would have given it you, but I, being in the way,
Did in your name receive it. Pardon the fault, I pray.
JULIA
Now, by my modesty, a goodly broker!
Dare you presume to harbor wanton lines?
To whisper, and conspire against my youth?
Now, trust me, 'tis an office of great worth,
And you an officer fit for the place.
There, take the paper. See it be returned,
Or else return no more into my sight.
[*She gives the letter back.*]
LUCETTA
To plead for love deserves more fee than hate.
JULIA
Will ye be gone?
LUCETTA That you may ruminate. *Exit.*
JULIA
And yet I would I had o'erlooked the letter.
It were a shame to call her back again
And pray her to a fault for which I chid her.
What 'fool is she, that knows I am a maid
And would not force the letter to my view!
Since maids, in modesty, say no to that
Which they would have the profferer construe ay.
Fie, fie, how wayward is this foolish love
That, like a testy babe, will scratch the nurse
And presently, all humbled, kiss the rod!
How churlishly I chid Lucetta hence,
When willingly I would have had her here!
How angerly I taught my brow to frown,
When inward joy enforced my heart to smile!
My penance is to call Lucetta back
And ask remission for my folly past.
What ho! Lucetta!

[*Enter Lucetta.*]

LUCETTA What would Your Ladyship?
JULIA
Is't near dinnertime?
LUCETTA I would it were,
That you might kill your stomach on your meat
And not upon your maid.
[*She drops the letter and stoops to pick it up.*]
JULIA
What is't that you took up so gingerly?
LUCETTA Nothing.
JULIA Why didst thou stoop, then?
LUCETTA
To take a paper up that I let fall.
JULIA And is that paper nothing?
LUCETTA Nothing concerning me.
JULIA
Then let it lie for those that it concerns.
LUCETTA
Madam, it will not lie where it concerns,
Unless it have a false interpreter.
JULIA
Some love of yours hath writ to you in rhyme.
LUCETTA
That I might sing it, madam, to a tune,
Give me a note. Your ladyship can set.
JULIA
As little by such toys as may be possible.
Best sing it to the tune of "Light o' Love."
LUCETTA
It is too heavy for so light a tune.
JULIA
Heavy! Belike it hath some burden then?
LUCETTA
Ay, and melodious were it, would you sing it.
JULIA
And why not you?
LUCETTA I cannot reach so high.
JULIA
Let's see your song. How now, minion?
[*She takes the letter.*]
LUCETTA
Keep tune there still; so you will sing it out.
And yet methinks I do not like this tune.
JULIA You do not?
LUCETTA No, madam, 'tis too sharp.
JULIA You, minion, are too saucy.
LUCETTA Nay, now you are too flat,
And mar the concord with too harsh a descant.

39 being . . . way i.e., happening to encounter him **41 broker** intermediary. **42–3 Dare . . . youth?** (Said ironically.) **48 more fee** better recompense **49 That . . . ruminate.** (I'm leaving) so that you can think carefully about this. **50 o'erlooked** read **52 to a fault** to commit a fault **53 'fool** a fool **58 testy** fretful **59 presently** immediately afterward. **rod** spanking rod. **62 angerly** angrily **68 kill your stomach** (1) satisfy your appetite (2) appease your anger. **meat** (Pronounced "mate," with wordplay on *maid* in the next line.)

77 lie where it concerns tell falsehoods in matters of importance. (Punning on the meaning "be left for those whose business it is" in the preceding line.) **80 That** In order that **81 note** (With a punning reference to Proteus's letter.) **set** (1) set to music (2) write a letter. (But Julia takes the word in the sense of setting store by something, regarding it of value.) **82 toys** trifles **83 "Light o' Love"** (A familiar tune of the time.) **84 heavy** serious **85 Belike** Perhaps. **burden** (1) bass accompaniment to a melody (2) heavy load (with an added sexual suggestion of the burden women must bear) **86 melodious . . . it** it would be melodious if you would sing it. **87 reach so high** (1) sing so high (2) aspire to a person of Proteus's rank. **88 minion** hussy. (With a pun on *minim*, half-note.) **89 tune** (1) pitch (2) temper, mood. **so . . . out** (1) if you do so, you'll be able to sing the song completely (2) that way you'll get over your bad mood. **92 sharp** (1) high in pitch (2) saucy, bitter. (Perhaps Julia pinches or slaps Lucetta here and at line 94, or perhaps Lucetta is referring to her mistress' tone of voice.) **94 flat** (1) low in pitch (2) blunt **95 descant** (1) soprano counterpoint sung above the melody (2) carping criticism.

There wanteth but a mean to fill your song.

JULIA
The mean is drowned with your unruly bass.

LUCETTA
Indeed, I bid the base for Proteus.

JULIA
This babble shall not henceforth trouble me.
Here is a coil with protestation!
[*She tears the letter and drops the pieces.*]
Go, get you gone, and let the papers lie.
You would be fing'ring them to anger me.

LUCETTA
She makes it strange, but she would be best pleased
To be so angered with another letter. [*Exit.*]

JULIA
Nay, would I were so angered with the same!
[*She picks up some fragments.*]
O hateful hands, to tear such loving words!
Injurious wasps, to feed on such sweet honey
And kill the bees that yield it with your stings!
I'll kiss each several paper for amends.
Look, here is writ "kind Julia." Unkind Julia!
As in revenge of thy ingratitude,
I throw thy name against the bruising stones,
Trampling contemptuously on thy disdain.
[*She throws down a fragment.*]
And here is writ "love-wounded Proteus."
Poor wounded name! My bosom as a bed
Shall lodge thee till thy wound be throughly healed;
And thus I search it with a sovereign kiss.
But twice or thrice was "Proteus" written down.
Be calm, good wind, blow not a word away
Till I have found each letter in the letter,
Except mine own name; that some whirlwind bear
Unto a ragged, fearful, hanging rock
And throw it thence into the raging sea!
Lo, here in one line is his name twice writ,
"Poor forlorn Proteus, passionate Proteus,
To the sweet Julia." That I'll tear away;
And yet I will not, sith so prettily
He couples it to his complaining names.
Thus will I fold them, one upon another.
Now kiss, embrace, contend, do what you will.
[*She puts some folded papers in her bosom.*]

[*Enter Lucetta.*]

LUCETTA Madam,
Dinner is ready, and your father stays.

JULIA Well, let us go.

LUCETTA
What, shall these papers lie like telltales here?

JULIA
If you respect them, best to take them up.

LUCETTA
Nay, I was taken up for laying them down;
Yet here they shall not lie, for catching cold.
[*She gathers up the remaining fragments.*]

JULIA
I see you have a month's mind to them.

LUCETTA
Ay, madam, you may say what sights you see;
I see things too, although you judge I wink.

JULIA Come, come, will 't please you go? *Exeunt.*

✣

1.3

Enter Antonio and Panthino.

ANTONIO
Tell me, Panthino, what sad talk was that
Wherewith my brother held you in the cloister?

PANTHINO
'Twas of his nephew Proteus, your son.

ANTONIO
Why, what of him?

PANTHINO He wondered that Your Lordship
Would suffer him to spend his youth at home,
While other men, of slender reputation,
Put forth their sons to seek preferment out:
Some to the wars, to try their fortune there,
Some to discover islands far away,
Some to the studious universities.
For any or for all these exercises
He said that Proteus your son was meet,
And did request me to importune you
To let him spend his time no more at home,
Which would be great impeachment to his age
In having known no travel in his youth.

ANTONIO
Nor need'st thou much importune me to that
Whereon this month I have been hammering.
I have considered well his loss of time,
And how he cannot be a perfect man,
Not being tried and tutored in the world.
Experience is by industry achieved

96 wanteth but is lacking only. **mean** (1) middle or tenor voice between the *descant* and the *bass,* i.e., Proteus (2) opportunity **97 unruly bass** (With pun on "base behavior.") **98 bid the base for** i.e., act in behalf of, intercede for. (Referring to the game of "prisoner's base,"and with a pun on *base,* "bass, low.") **99 babble** i.e., idle chatter; or else *bauble,* foolish trifle—the letter **100 coil with protestation** commotion or fuss about protestations of love (i.e., about Proteus's letter). **103 makes it strange** pretends indifference. (Lucetta says this speech for the audience's benefit, but it is a catty third-person reference to Julia rather than an aside, and Julia makes it clear in line 105 that she has heard it.) **105 Nay . . . same!** i.e., Indeed, I wish I had this same letter intact to pretend to be angry about! **107 wasps** i.e., fingers **109 several paper** separate scraps of paper **110 Unkind** Unnatural, cruel **111 As** As if, or, Thus **116 throughly** thoroughly **117 search** probe, cleanse (as one would a wound). **sovereign** healing **121 that . . . bear** may some whirlwind bear *that,* my name **127 sith** since

132 stays waits. **135 respect** prize, esteem. **best to take** it were best you take **136 taken up** scolded. (With a play on *take them up* in the preceding line.) **137 for** for fear of **138 month's mind** inclination, liking **140 wink** close the eyes.

1.3. Location: Verona. Antonio's house.

1 sad serious **2 the cloister** any covered arcade attached to a building. **5 suffer** allow **6 of slender reputation** i.e., of lower station than yourself **7 Put . . . out** send their sons away from home to seek advancement **12 meet** fitted **13 importune** urge **15 impeachment to his age** detriment or cause for reproach to him in his mature years **18 hammering** beating (an idea) into shape. **20 perfect** i.e., educated, mature **21 tried** tested

And perfected by the swift course of time.
Then tell me, whither were I best to send him?

PANTHINO
I think Your Lordship is not ignorant
How his companion, youthful Valentine,
Attends the Emperor in his royal court.

ANTONIO I know it well.

PANTHINO
'Twere good, I think, Your Lordship sent him thither.
There shall he practice tilts and tournaments,
Hear sweet discourse, converse with noblemen,
And be in eye of every exercise
Worthy his youth and nobleness of birth.

ANTONIO
I like thy counsel. Well hast thou advised,
And, that thou mayst perceive how well I like it,
The execution of it shall make known.
Even with the speediest expedition
I will dispatch him to the Emperor's court.

PANTHINO
Tomorrow, may it please you, Don Alphonso,
With other gentlemen of good esteem,
Are journeying to salute the Emperor
And to commend their service to his will.

ANTONIO
Good company. With them shall Proteus go—

[Enter] *Proteus,* *[reading a letter].*

And in good time! Now will we break with him.

PROTEUS *[to himself]*
Sweet love, sweet lines, sweet life!
Here is her hand, the agent of her heart;
Here is her oath for love, her honor's pawn.
Oh, that our fathers would applaud our loves
To seal our happiness with their consents!
Oh, heavenly Julia!

ANTONIO
How now? What letter are you reading there?

PROTEUS
May't please Your Lordship, 'tis a word or two
Of commendations sent from Valentine,
Delivered by a friend that came from him.

ANTONIO
Lend me the letter. Let me see what news.

PROTEUS
There is no news, my lord, but that he writes
How happily he lives, how well beloved
And daily gracèd by the Emperor,
Wishing me with him, partner of his fortune.

ANTONIO
And how stand you affected to his wish?

PROTEUS
As one relying on Your Lordship's will,
And not depending on his friendly wish.

ANTONIO
My will is something sorted with his wish.
Muse not that I thus suddenly proceed,
For what I will, I will, and there an end.
I am resolved that thou shalt spend some time
With Valentinus in the Emperor's court.
What maintenance he from his friends receives,
Like exhibition thou shalt have from me.
Tomorrow be in readiness to go.
Excuse it not, for I am peremptory.

PROTEUS
My lord, I cannot be so soon provided.
Please you, deliberate a day or two.

ANTONIO
Look what thou want'st shall be sent after thee.
No more of stay. Tomorrow thou must go.—
Come on, Panthino. You shall be employed
To hasten on his expedition.
[Exeunt Antonio and Panthino.]

PROTEUS
Thus have I shunned the fire for fear of burning
And drenched me in the sea, where I am drowned.
I feared to show my father Julia's letter
Lest he should take exceptions to my love,
And with the vantage of mine own excuse
Hath he excepted most against my love.
Oh, how this spring of love resembleth
The uncertain glory of an April day,
Which now shows all the beauty of the sun,
And by and by a cloud takes all away!

[Enter Panthino.]

PANTHINO
Sir Proteus, your father calls for you.
He is in haste; therefore, I pray you, go.

PROTEUS
Why, this it is: my heart accords thereto,
And yet a thousand times it answers no. *Exeunt.*

✣

2.1

Enter Valentine [and] Speed.

SPEED
Sir, your glove. *[Offering a glove.]*

VALENTINE Not mine. My gloves are on.

SPEED Why, then, this may be yours, for this is but one.

VALENTINE
Ha! Let me see. Ay, give it me, it's mine.

24 were I best would it be best for me **27 the Emperor** i.e., the Duke of Milan. (An apparent inconsistency.) **30 practice** perform, take part in **32 in eye of** in a position to see **33 Worthy** worthy of **37 expedition** swiftness **42 commend** commit, dedicate **44 in good time** i.e., just at the right time (here he comes). **break with** reveal, disclose the plan to **47 pawn** pledge. **49 seal** ratify **53 commendations** greetings **58 gracèd** favored **60 stand you affected** are you disposed, inclined

63 something sorted rather in accordance **64 Muse** Wonder **68 maintenance** allowance. **friends** i.e., relatives **69 exhibition** allowance of money **71 Excuse it not** Offer no excuses. **peremptory** resolved. **72 provided** equipped. **74 Look what** Whatever **75 No more of stay** No more talk of delay. **83 excepted most against** most effectively hindered

2.1. Location: Milan. Perhaps at the Duke's palace, or in some unspecified location.

2 one (Pronounced like "on," thus providing a pun on the previous line.)

Sweet ornament that decks a thing divine!
Ah, Silvia, Silvia!

SPEED [*calling*] Madam Silvia! Madam Silvia!

VALENTINE How now, sirrah?

SPEED She is not within hearing, sir.

VALENTINE Why, sir, who bade you call her?

SPEED Your Worship, sir, or else I mistook.

VALENTINE Well, you'll still be too forward.

SPEED And yet I was last chidden for being too slow.

VALENTINE Go to, sir. Tell me, do you know Madam Silvia?

SPEED She that Your Worship loves?

VALENTINE Why, how know you that I am in love?

SPEED Marry, by these special marks: first, you have learned, like Sir Proteus, to wreathe your arms, like a malcontent; to relish a love song, like a robin redbreast; to walk alone, like one that had the pestilence; to sigh, like a schoolboy that had lost his A B C; to weep, like a young wench that had buried her grandam; to fast, like one that takes diet; to watch, like one that fears robbing; to speak puling, like a beggar at Hallowmas. You were wont, when you laughed, to crow like a cock; when you walked, to walk like one of the lions. When you fasted, it was presently after dinner; when you looked sadly, it was for want of money. And now you are metamorphized with a mistress, that when I look on you I can hardly think you my master.

VALENTINE Are all these things perceived in me?

SPEED They are all perceived without ye.

VALENTINE Without me? They cannot.

SPEED Without you? Nay, that's certain, for, without you were so simple, none else would. But you are so without these follies that these follies are within you, and shine through you like the water in an urinal, that not an eye that sees you but is a physician to comment on your malady.

VALENTINE But tell me, dost thou know my lady Silvia?

SPEED She that you gaze on so as she sits at supper?

VALENTINE Hast thou observed that? Even she I mean.

SPEED Why, sir, I know her not.

VALENTINE Dost thou know her by my gazing on her, and yet know'st her not?

SPEED Is she not hard-favored, sir?

VALENTINE Not so fair, boy, as well-favored.

SPEED Sir, I know that well enough.

VALENTINE What dost thou know?

SPEED That she is not so fair as, of you, well-favored.

VALENTINE I mean that her beauty is exquisite but her favor infinite.

SPEED That's because the one is painted and the other out of all count.

VALENTINE How painted? And how out of count?

SPEED Marry, sir, so painted to make her fair that no man counts of her beauty.

VALENTINE How esteem'st thou me? I account of her beauty.

SPEED You never saw her since she was deformed.

VALENTINE How long hath she been deformed?

SPEED Ever since you loved her.

VALENTINE I have loved her ever since I saw her, and still I see her beautiful.

SPEED If you love her, you cannot see her.

VALENTINE Why?

SPEED Because Love is blind. Oh, that you had mine eyes, or your own eyes had the lights they were wont to have when you chid at Sir Proteus for going ungartered!

VALENTINE What should I see then?

SPEED Your own present folly and her passing deformity; for he, being in love, could not see to garter his hose, and you, being in love, cannot see to put on your hose.

VALENTINE Belike, boy, then you are in love, for last morning you could not see to wipe my shoes.

SPEED True, sir. I was in love with my bed. I thank you, you swinged me for my love, which makes me the bolder to chide you for yours.

VALENTINE In conclusion, I stand affected to her.

SPEED I would you were set; so your affection would cease.

VALENTINE Last night she enjoined me to write some lines to one she loves.

SPEED And have you?

VALENTINE I have.

SPEED Are they not lamely writ?

VALENTINE No, boy, but as well as I can do them. Peace, here she comes.

[*Enter*] *Silvia.*

SPEED [*aside*] Oh, excellent motion! Oh, exceeding puppet! Now will he interpret to her.

7 sirrah fellow. (Form of address to inferiors.) **11 still** always **13 Go to** (An expression of remonstrance.) **18 wreathe** fold. (Folded arms were a conventional gesture of melancholy, such as love melancholy.) **19 relish** sing, warble **21 A B C** primer **22 grandam** grandmother **23 takes diet** diets for reasons of health. **watch** lie awake, sit up at night **24 puling** whiningly. **Hallowmas** All Saints' Day, November 1 (a day when beggars asked special alms). **26 like . . . lions** i.e., proudly, manfully. **28 want** lack **29 with** by. **that** so that **32 without ye** from your outside appearance. **33 Without me?** In my absence? **34 without** unless **35 would** i.e., would perceive them. **35–6 you are . . . follies** i.e., you so surround and encompass these follies **37 urinal** glass container for medical examination of urine **46 hard-favored** ugly **47 fair** beautiful, blond-haired. **well-favored** gracious, charming; also, good-looking. (But Speed takes the word in the sense of "looked upon with approval.")

50 of by. **well-favored** approved of. **52 favor** grace, charm **53 painted** achieved by cosmetics **54 out of all count** incalculable. **57 counts of** esteems **58 How . . . me?** i.e., Are you impugning my judgment? **account of** esteem **60 deformed** i.e., transformed by the distorting perspective of Valentine's love for her. **67 Love** i.e., Cupid, traditionally represented as blind **68 lights** sight **69–70 going ungartered** i.e., neglecting appearance in dress, a traditional sign of love melancholy. **72 passing** surpassing, very great **74–5 cannot . . . hose** i.e., you are in even worse shape than Proteus, and he was perfectly helpless. **76 Belike** Probably **79 you . . . love** you thrashed me for being too fond of lying abed **81 I stand affected to** I am in love with **82 set** (1) settled, finished (2) seated, as contrasted with *stand* in line 81 (3) no longer in a condition of *standing*, being erect (giving a bawdy sense to Valentine's innocent use of *stand*) **90 Peace** Be quiet **91 motion** puppet show. **puppet** i.e., Silvia. **92 interpret** i.e., supply dialogue or commentary, as for a puppet show

VALENTINE Madam and mistress, a thousand good-morrows.

SPEED [*aside*] Oh, give ye good even! Here's a million of manners.

SILVIA Sir Valentine and servant, to you two thousand.

SPEED [*aside*] He should give her interest, and she gives it him.

VALENTINE
As you enjoined me, I have writ your letter
Unto the secret, nameless friend of yours,
Which I was much unwilling to proceed in
But for my duty to Your Ladyship. [*Giving a letter.*]

SILVIA
I thank you, gentle servant. 'Tis very clerkly done.

VALENTINE
Now trust me, madam, it came hardly off,
For, being ignorant to whom it goes,
I writ at random, very doubtfully.

SILVIA
Perchance you think too much of so much pains?

VALENTINE
No, madam. So it stead you, I will write—
Please you command—a thousand times as much.
And yet—

SILVIA
A pretty period! Well, I guess the sequel.
And yet I will not name it. And yet I care not.
And yet take this again. And yet I thank you,
Meaning henceforth to trouble you no more.
[*She offers him the letter.*]

SPEED [*aside*]
And yet you will, and yet another "yet."

VALENTINE
What means Your Ladyship? Do you not like it?

SILVIA Yes, yes. The lines are very quaintly writ,
But since unwillingly, take them again.
Nay, take them. [*She gives back the letter.*]

VALENTINE Madam, they are for you.

SILVIA
Ay, ay. You writ them, sir, at my request,
But I will none of them. They are for you.
I would have had them writ more movingly.

VALENTINE
Please you, I'll write Your Ladyship another.

SILVIA
And when it's writ, for my sake read it over.
And if it please you, so; if not, why, so.

VALENTINE
If it please me, madam? What then?

SILVIA
Why, if it please you, take it for your labor.
And so good morrow, servant. *Exit Silvia.*

SPEED [*aside*]
Oh, jest unseen, inscrutable, invisible
As a nose on a man's face, or a weathercock on a steeple!
My master sues to her, and she hath taught her suitor,
He being her pupil, to become her tutor.
Oh, excellent device! Was there ever heard a better,
That my master, being scribe, to himself should write the letter?

VALENTINE How now, sir? What, are you reasoning with yourself?

SPEED Nay, I was rhyming. 'Tis you that have the reason.

VALENTINE To do what?

SPEED To be a spokesman from Madam Silvia.

VALENTINE To whom?

SPEED To yourself. Why, she woos you by a figure.

VALENTINE What figure?

SPEED By a letter, I should say.

VALENTINE Why, she hath not writ to me.

SPEED What need she, when she hath made you write to yourself? Why, do you not perceive the jest?

VALENTINE No, believe me.

SPEED No believing you, indeed, sir. But did you perceive her earnest?

VALENTINE She gave me none, except an angry word.

SPEED Why, she hath given you a letter.

VALENTINE That's the letter I writ to her friend.

SPEED And that letter hath she delivered, and there an end.

VALENTINE I would it were no worse.

SPEED I'll warrant you, 'tis as well.
For often have you writ to her, and she, in modesty,
Or else for want of idle time, could not again reply;
Or fearing else some messenger that might her mind discover,
Herself hath taught her love himself to write unto her lover.
All this I speak in print, for in print I found it. Why muse you, sir? 'Tis dinnertime.

VALENTINE I have dined.

SPEED Ay, but hearken, sir: though the chameleon Love can feed on the air, I am one that am nourished by my

95 give i.e., God give. **a million** i.e., an excessive amount **97 servant** male admirer devoted to serving a lady in love **98–9 He . . . him** i.e., He is the one who should be showing *interest* in her, as her *servant,* and yet she gives him *interest* by doubling what he has given her. (Playing on the financial meaning of *interest.*) **103 duty** obedience, submission **104 clerkly** in a scholarly manner. (And perhaps with good penmanship.) **105 Now . . . off** Believe me, madam, it was done with difficulty **107 doubtfully** uncertainly. **108 Perchance . . . pains?** Perhaps you think I have given you too much trouble? **109 So** So long as. **stead** benefit **112 A pretty period!** A fine conclusion! i.e., To finish your eloquent protestation of devoted service with "And yet" is to spoil all that came before it. **114 again** back. **118 quaintly** ingeniously **126 so** well and good

132 sues to wooes, pleads with **136, 138 reasoning . . . rhyming** (Playing on the antithesis of *rhyme* and *reason.*) **143 figure** device. **150 No believing you** There's no believing anything you say. (Playing on *No, believe me* in the previous line.) **151 earnest** to be serious. (But Valentine, in line 152, takes the word as a noun meaning "money paid as an installment to secure a bargain.") **155–6 there an end** (1) there's no more to be said (2) that's where the matter should end, with the letter delivered to you as the intended recipient. **163 All . . . found it** I say all this with assurance, having seen it in writing. **165 dined** i.e., feasted on the sight of Silvia. **166 chameleon Love** (The chameleon was popularly thought to be able to live on air. Love is also a chameleon because it is so changeable.)

victuals, and would fain have meat. Oh, be not like your mistress; be moved, be moved! *Exeunt.*

2.2

Enter Proteus [*and*] *Julia.*

PROTEUS Have patience, gentle Julia.

JULIA I must, where is no remedy.

PROTEUS
When possibly I can, I will return.

JULIA
If you turn not, you will return the sooner.
Keep this remembrance for thy Julia's sake.
[*She gives him a ring.*]

PROTEUS
Why, then, we'll make exchange. Here, take you this.
[*He gives her a ring.*]

JULIA
And seal the bargain with a holy kiss. [*They kiss.*]

PROTEUS
Here is my hand for my true constancy;
And when that hour o'erslips me in the day
Wherein I sigh not, Julia, for thy sake,
The next ensuing hour some foul mischance
Torment me for my love's forgetfulness!
My father stays my coming. Answer not.
The tide is now—nay, not thy tide of tears;
That tide will stay me longer than I should.
Julia, farewell! [*Exit Julia.*]
What, gone without a word?
Ay, so true love should do; it cannot speak,
For truth hath better deeds than words to grace it.

[*Enter*] *Panthino.*

PANTHINO
Sir Proteus, you are stayed for.

PROTEUS Go. I come, I come.
Alas! This parting strikes poor lovers dumb. *Exeunt.*

2.3

Enter Lance [*with his dog, Crab*].

LANCE Nay, 'twill be this hour ere I have done weeping. All the kind of the Lances have this very fault. I have received my proportion, like the prodigious son, and am going with Sir Proteus to the Imperial's court. I think Crab, my dog, be the sourest-natured dog that lives. My mother weeping, my father wailing, my sister crying, our maid howling, our cat wringing her hands, and all our house in a great perplexity, yet did not this cruel-hearted cur shed one tear. He is a stone, a very pebblestone, and has no more pity in him than a dog. A Jew would have wept to have seen our parting. Why, my grandam, having no eyes, look you, wept herself blind at my parting. Nay, I'll show you the manner of it. This shoe is my father. No, this left shoe is my father. No, no, this left shoe is my mother. Nay, that cannot be so neither. Yes, it is so, it is so—it hath the worser sole. This shoe with the hole in it is my mother, and this my father. A vengeance on't! There 'tis. Now, sir, this staff is my sister, for, look you, she is as white as a lily and as small as a wand. This hat is Nan, our maid. I am the dog. No, the dog is himself, and I am the dog—Oh, the dog is me, and I am myself. Ay, so, so. Now come I to my father: "Father, your blessing." Now should not the shoe speak a word for weeping. Now should I kiss my father. Well, he weeps on. Now come I to my mother. Oh, that she could speak now like a wood woman! Well, I kiss her. Why, there 'tis. Here's my mother's breath up and down. Now come I to my sister; mark the moan she makes. Now the dog all this while sheds not a tear nor speaks a word; but see how I lay the dust with my tears.

[*Enter*] *Panthino.*

PANTHINO Lance, away, away, aboard! Thy master is shipped, and thou art to post after with oars. What's the matter? Why weep'st thou, man? Away, ass! You'll lose the tide if you tarry any longer.

LANCE It is no matter if the tied were lost, for it is the unkindest tied that ever any man tied.

PANTHINO What's the unkindest tide?

LANCE Why, he that's tied here, Crab, my dog.

PANTHINO Tut, man, I mean thou'lt lose the flood, and in losing the flood, lose thy voyage, and in losing thy voyage, lose thy master, and in losing thy master, lose thy service, and in losing thy service—[*Lance puts his hand over Panthino's mouth.*] Why dost thou stop my mouth?

LANCE For fear thou shouldst lose thy tongue.

PANTHINO Where should I lose my tongue?

LANCE In thy tale.

PANTHINO In thy tail!

LANCE Lose the tide, and the voyage, and the master, and the service, and the tied? Why, man, if the river were dry, I am able to fill it with my tears; if the wind were down, I could drive the boat with my sighs.

PANTHINO Come, come away, man. I was sent to call thee.

168 fain gladly **169 be moved** (1) be not hard-hearted (2) be persuaded to go to dinner
2.2. Location: Verona. Julia's house.
2 where is where there is **4 turn not** do not prove to be unfaithful **9 o'erslips me** slips by me unnoticed **13 stays** awaits **14 The tide** The high tide for departure by ship **18 grace** adorn
2.3. Location: Verona. A street.
2 kind kindred, race **3 proportion** (A malapropism for "portion, allotment.") **prodigious** (A malapropism for "prodigal.") **4 Imperial's** i.e., Emperor's

14 This shoe . . . father (Lance demonstrates.) **17 sole** (With a pun on "soul." Lance refers to a common debate as to whether a woman's soul is inferior to a man's.) **the hole in it** (Suggesting a bawdy joke about the feminine sexual anatomy.) **18 A vengeance on't** (A mild curse, probably occasioned by the difficulty Lance has in pulling his shoe off. *There 'tis* in lines 18–19 signals his success in doing so.) **20 small** slim **27 wood** mad, distraught. (With punning allusion to a wooden shoe.) **28 up and down** i.e., exactly. **33 post** hasten. **with oars** i.e., in a rowboat, in order to reach the sailing vessel at anchor. **36 the tied** i.e., the dog that is tied. (With a pun on *tide.*) **40 lose the flood** miss the tide **46 lose** (1) lose (2) loose **54 call** summon

LANCE Sir, call me what thou dar'st.
PANTHINO Wilt thou go?
LANCE Well, I will go. *Exeunt.*

✣

2.4

Enter Valentine, Silvia, Thurio, [*and*] *Speed.*

SILVIA Servant!
VALENTINE Mistress?
SPEED [*aside to Valentine*] Master, Sir Thurio frowns on you.
VALENTINE Ay, boy, it's for love.
SPEED Not of you.
VALENTINE Of my mistress, then.
SPEED 'Twere good you knocked him. [*Exit.*]
SILVIA [*to Valentine*] Servant, you are sad.
VALENTINE Indeed, madam, I seem so.
THURIO Seem you that you are not?
VALENTINE Haply I do.
THURIO So do counterfeits.
VALENTINE So do you.
THURIO What seem I that I am not?
VALENTINE Wise.
THURIO What instance of the contrary?
VALENTINE Your folly.
THURIO And how quote you my folly?
VALENTINE I quote it in your jerkin.
THURIO My "jerkin" is a doublet.
VALENTINE Well, then, I'll double your folly.
THURIO How?
SILVIA What, angry, Sir Thurio? Do you change color?
VALENTINE Give him leave, madam; he is a kind of chameleon.
THURIO That hath more mind to feed on your blood than live in your air.
VALENTINE You have said, sir.
THURIO Ay, sir, and done too, for this time.
VALENTINE I know it well, sir; you always end ere you begin.
SILVIA A fine volley of words, gentlemen, and quickly shot off.
VALENTINE 'Tis indeed, madam, we thank the giver.
SILVIA Who is that, servant?
VALENTINE Yourself, sweet lady, for you gave the fire. Sir Thurio borrows his wit from Your Ladyship's looks, and spends what he borrows kindly in your company.
THURIO Sir, if you spend word for word with me, I shall make your wit bankrupt.
VALENTINE I know it well, sir; you have an exchequer of words, and, I think, no other treasure to give your followers, for it appears, by their bare liveries, that they live by your bare words.
SILVIA No more, gentlemen, no more. Here comes my father.

[*Enter the*] *Duke.*

DUKE
Now, daughter Silvia, you are hard beset.—
Sir Valentine, your father is in good health.
What say you to a letter from your friends
Of much good news?
VALENTINE My lord, I will be thankful
To any happy messenger from thence.
DUKE
Know ye Don Antonio, your countryman?
VALENTINE
Ay, my good lord, I know the gentleman
To be of worth and worthy estimation,
And not without desert so well reputed.
DUKE Hath he not a son?
VALENTINE
Ay, my good lord, a son that well deserves
The honor and regard of such a father.
DUKE You know him well?
VALENTINE
I know him as myself, for from our infancy
We have conversed and spent our hours together.
And though myself have been an idle truant,
Omitting the sweet benefit of time
To clothe mine age with angel-like perfection,
Yet hath Sir Proteus—for that's his name—
Made use and fair advantage of his days;
His years but young, but his experience old;
His head unmellowed, but his judgment ripe.
And in a word—for far behind his worth
Comes all the praises that I now bestow—
He is complete in feature and in mind
With all good grace to grace a gentleman.
DUKE
Beshrew me, sir, but if he make this good,
He is as worthy for an empress' love
As meet to be an emperor's counselor.
Well, sir, this gentleman is come to me
With commendation from great potentates,
And here he means to spend his time awhile.
I think 'tis no unwelcome news to you.

56 call me what call me whatever names
2.4. Location: Milan. The Duke's palace.
7 'Twere . . . him You'd better hit him. **10 that** what **11 Haply** Perhaps **16 instance** proof **18 quote** notice, observe. (Pronounced like *coat,* enabling Valentine to pun on that idea.) **19 jerkin** close-fitting jacket worn over, or in place of, the doublet **20 My . . . doublet** What you ignorantly call my "jerkin" is in fact a doublet, i.e., another kind of men's jacket. (With a play on *double* in the next line.) **22 How?** (An expression of annoyance or incredulity.) **26 That** i.e., One who **27 in your air** (1) in the air you breathe, i.e., near you (2) listening to your talk. (Chameleons were supposed to be able to live on air alone.)
28 You have said i.e., That's a lot of fine talk **29 done** (1) acted, in contrast to *said* (2) finished. (Thurio hints here that he's prepared to duel with Valentine at some future date.) **30–1 end . . . begin** i.e., stop before you come to actual blows. **36 fire** i.e., spark to set off the volley.

38 kindly fittingly, naturally, affectionately **41 exchequer** treasury **43 bare liveries** threadbare uniforms **44 bare** mere **47 hard beset** strongly besieged (with two wooers at once). **51 happy messenger** bringer of good tidings **55 without desert** undeservedly **63 Omitting** neglecting **68 unmellowed** i.e., unmixed with gray hair **71 complete in feature** perfect in shape of body and personal appearance **73 Beshrew me** (A mild oath.) **make this good** i.e., match your description **75 meet** suited

VALENTINE
Should I have wished a thing, it had been he.

DUKE
Welcome him then according to his worth.
Silvia, I speak to you, and you, Sir Thurio;
For Valentine, I need not cite him to it. 83
I will send him hither to you presently. [*Exit.*]

VALENTINE
This is the gentleman I told Your Ladyship
Had come along with me, but that his mistress 86
Did hold his eyes locked in her crystal looks.

SILVIA
Belike that now she hath enfranchised them 88
Upon some other pawn for fealty. 89

VALENTINE
Nay, sure, I think she holds them prisoners still.

SILVIA
Nay, then he should be blind, and being blind
How could he see his way to seek out you?

VALENTINE
Why, lady, Love hath twenty pair of eyes.

THURIO
They say that Love hath not an eye at all.

VALENTINE
To see such lovers, Thurio, as yourself.
Upon a homely object Love can wink. 96

SILVIA
Have done, have done. Here comes the gentleman. 97

[*Enter*] *Proteus.*

VALENTINE
Welcome, dear Proteus!—Mistress, I beseech you,
Confirm his welcome with some special favor.

SILVIA
His worth is warrant for his welcome hither,
If this be he you oft have wished to hear from.

VALENTINE
Mistress, it is. Sweet lady, entertain him 102
To be my fellow servant to Your Ladyship.

SILVIA
Too low a mistress for so high a servant.

PROTEUS
Not so, sweet lady, but too mean a servant 105
To have a look of such a worthy mistress. 106

VALENTINE
Leave off discourse of disability. 107
Sweet lady, entertain him for your servant.

PROTEUS
My duty will I boast of, nothing else. 109

SILVIA
And duty never yet did want his meed. 110
Servant, you are welcome to a worthless mistress.

PROTEUS
I'll die on him that says so but yourself. 112

SILVIA
That you are welcome?

PROTEUS
That you are worthless.

[*Enter a Servant.*]

SERVANT
Madam, my lord your father would speak with you.

SILVIA
I wait upon his pleasure. [*Exit Servant.*]
Come, Sir Thurio,
Go with me.—Once more, new servant, welcome.
I'll leave you to confer of home affairs.
When you have done, we look to hear from you.

PROTEUS
We'll both attend upon Your Ladyship.
[*Exeunt Sylvia and Thurio.*]

VALENTINE
Now tell me, how do all from whence you came?

PROTEUS
Your friends are well and have them much
commended. 121

VALENTINE
And how do yours?

PROTEUS
I left them all in health.

VALENTINE
How does your lady, and how thrives your love?

PROTEUS
My tales of love were wont to weary you.
I know you joy not in a love discourse.

VALENTINE
Ay, Proteus, but that life is altered now.
I have done penance for contemning Love, 127
Whose high imperious thoughts have punished me
With bitter fasts, with penitential groans,
With nightly tears, and daily heartsore sighs;
For in revenge of my contempt of love
Love hath chased sleep from my enthrallèd eyes
And made them watchers of mine own heart's sorrow. 133
O gentle Proteus, Love's a mighty lord,
And hath so humbled me as I confess 135
There is no woe to his correction, 136
Nor to his service no such joy on earth. 137
Now, no discourse except it be of love.
Now can I break my fast, dine, sup, and sleep
Upon the very naked name of love. 140

PROTEUS
Enough. I read your fortune in your eye.
Was this the idol that you worship so?

VALENTINE
Even she. And is she not a heavenly saint?

PROTEUS
No, but she is an earthly paragon.

83 cite urge **86 Had** would have **88 Belike that** Perhaps **88–9 enfranchised . . . fealty** set free his eyes in return for some other pledge of fidelity, or, to pledge his fidelity somewhere else, or, now that some other lover has pledged his service to her. **96 homely** plain. **wink** close the eyes. **97 Have done** Cease this bickering **102 entertain** take into service **105 mean** lowly, unworthy **106 of** from **107 Leave . . . disability** Stop talking about your unworthiness. **109 duty** i.e., to Silvia **110 want his meed** lack its reward.

112 die on die fighting with **121 have . . . commended** have sent warm greetings. **127 contemning** scorning **133 watchers** wakeful beholders **135 as** that **136 to his correction** compared to the woe of his punishment **137 to his service** i.e., compared to serving Love **140 very naked** mere

VALENTINE
Call her divine.
PROTEUS I will not flatter her.
VALENTINE
Oh, flatter me, for love delights in praises.
PROTEUS
When I was sick, you gave me bitter pills,
And I must minister the like to you.
VALENTINE
Then speak the truth by her: if not divine,
Yet let her be a principality,
Sovereign to all the creatures on the earth.
PROTEUS
Except my mistress.
VALENTINE Sweet, except not any,
Except thou wilt except against my love.
PROTEUS
Have I not reason to prefer mine own?
VALENTINE
And I will help thee to prefer her, too.
She shall be dignified with this high honor:
To bear my lady's train, lest the base earth
Should from her vesture chance to steal a kiss
And, of so great a favor growing proud,
Disdain to root the summer-swelling flower,
And make rough winter everlastingly.
PROTEUS
Why, Valentine, what braggartism is this?
VALENTINE
Pardon me, Proteus, all I can is nothing
To her whose worth makes other worthies nothing.
She is alone.
PROTEUS Then let her alone.
VALENTINE
Not for the world. Why, man, she is mine own,
And I as rich in having such a jewel
As twenty seas, if all their sand were pearl,
The water nectar, and the rocks pure gold.
Forgive me that I do not dream on thee,
Because thou see'st me dote upon my love.
My foolish rival, that her father likes
Only for his possessions are so huge,
Is gone with her along, and I must after;
For love, thou know'st, is full of jealousy.
PROTEUS But she loves you?
VALENTINE
Ay, and we are betrothed. Nay, more, our marriage hour,
With all the cunning manner of our flight,
Determined of—how I must climb her window,
The ladder made of cords, and all the means
Plotted and 'greed on for my happiness.
Good Proteus, go with me to my chamber,
In these affairs to aid me with thy counsel.
PROTEUS
Go on before. I shall inquire you forth.
I must unto the road, to disembark
Some necessaries that I needs must use,
And then I'll presently attend you.
VALENTINE Will you make haste?
PROTEUS I will. *Exit [Valentine].*
Even as one heat another heat expels,
Or as one nail by strength drives out another,
So the remembrance of my former love
Is by a newer object quite forgotten.
Is it mine eye, or Valentine's praise,
Her true perfection, or my false transgression
That makes me, reasonless, to reason thus?
She is fair; and so is Julia that I love—
That I did love, for now my love is thawed,
Which like a waxen image 'gainst a fire
Bears no impression of the thing it was.
Methinks my zeal to Valentine is cold,
And that I love him not as I was wont.
Oh, but I love his lady too, too much,
And that's the reason I love him so little.
How shall I dote on her with more advice,
That thus without advice begin to love her?
'Tis but her picture I have yet beheld,
And that hath dazzlèd my reason's light;
But when I look on her perfections,
There is no reason but I shall be blind.
If I can check my erring love, I will;
If not, to compass her I'll use my skill. *Exit.*

✤

2.5

Enter, [meeting,] Speed and Lance [with his dog, Crab].

SPEED Lance, by mine honesty, welcome to Milan!

LANCE Forswear not thyself, sweet youth, for I am not welcome. I reckon this always, that a man is never undone till he be hanged, nor never welcome to a place till some certain shot be paid and the hostess say, "Welcome!"

SPEED Come on, you madcap, I'll to the alehouse with you presently, where, for one shot of five pence, thou shalt have five thousand welcomes. But sirrah, how did thy master part with Madam Julia?

148 by about **149 a principality** a member of one of the nine orders of angels **151 Sweet** (A term of affection used with both men and women.) **152 Except . . . except** unless you want to cast aspersions **154 prefer** advance. (With wordplay on *prefer*, like better, in line 153.) **159 root** provide rooting for **162 can** i.e., can say of her **163 To her** compared to her **164 is alone** is peerless. (But Proteus plays on the sense of "let her be.") **169 that . . . thee** i.e., that I seem neglectful of you **172 for** because **178 Determined of** is decided, arranged

183 I . . . forth I will ask after your whereabouts and find you. **184 road** roadstead, harbor **189 Even . . . expels** (The application of heat was thought to relieve the pain of a burn.) **195 reasonless** without justification, wrongly **201 wont** accustomed. **204–5 How . . . her?** How will I adore her on further consideration, I who have fallen in love with her so suddenly and rashly? (With wordplay on *advice.*) **206 picture** i.e., outer appearance **208 perfections** true qualities, not immediately apparent to view **209 no reason but** no doubt but that **210 check** restrain **211 compass** obtain

2.5. Location: Milan. A street.

1 by mine honesty upon my word **3–4 undone** ruined **5 shot** tavern reckoning **8 one . . . pence** a fivepenny drink

LANCE Marry, after they closed in earnest they parted 11
very fairly in jest. 12
SPEED But shall she marry him?
LANCE No.
SPEED How then? Shall he marry her?
LANCE No, neither.
SPEED What, are they broken? 17
LANCE No, they are both as whole as a fish. 18
SPEED Why, then, how stands the matter with them?
LANCE Marry, thus: when it stands well with him, it 20
stands well with her.
SPEED What an ass art thou! I understand thee not.
LANCE What a block art thou, that thou canst not! My 23
staff understands me.
SPEED What thou say'st?
LANCE Ay, and what I do too. Look thee, I'll but lean,
and my staff under-stands me.
SPEED It stands under thee, indeed.
LANCE Why, stand-under and under-stand is all one.
SPEED But tell me true, will't be a match?
LANCE Ask my dog. If he say ay, it will; if he say no, it
will; if he shake his tail and say nothing, it will.
SPEED The conclusion is then that it will.
LANCE Thou shalt never get such a secret from me but
by a parable. 35
SPEED 'Tis well that I get it so. But Lance, how say'st 36
thou, that my master is become a notable lover? 37
LANCE I never knew him otherwise.
SPEED Than how?
LANCE A notable lubber, as thou reportest him to be. 40
SPEED Why, thou whoreson ass, thou mistak'st me. 41
LANCE Why, fool, I meant not thee. I meant thy
master.
SPEED I tell thee my master is become a hot lover.
LANCE Why, I tell thee I care not, though he burn 45
himself in love. If thou wilt, go with me to the 46
alehouse; if not, thou art an Hebrew, a Jew, and not
worth the name of a Christian.
SPEED Why?
LANCE Because thou hast not so much charity in thee as
to go to the ale with a Christian. Wilt thou go? 51
SPEED At thy service. *Exeunt.*

11 **closed** (1) embraced (2) came to terms **12 fairly** kindly, gently. **jest** (Playing on the antithesis of *earnest* and *jest.*) **17 broken** no longer engaged. (But Lance plays on the word in the sense of "smashed to pieces.") **18 whole as a fish** (A proverbial comparison.) **20 stands well** (With a bawdy pun about erection.) **23 block** blockhead **35 a parable** enigmatic talk. **36–7 how say'st thou** what do you say to this **40 lubber** big, clumsy fellow. (With obvious pun on "lover.") **41 whoreson** (A friendly term of abuse.) **thou mistak'st me** you mistake my meaning. (But Lance replies to the sense of "you mistake me [Speed] for Valentine.") **45–6 burn himself in love** (With a punning sense of "acquire venereal disease.) **51 go . . . Christian** i.e., go to a church-ale, a village festival used to raise money for the church

2.6

Enter Proteus solus.

PROTEUS
To leave my Julia shall I be forsworn;
To love fair Silvia shall I be forsworn;
To wrong my friend I shall be much forsworn.
And ev'n that power which gave me first my oath 4
Provokes me to this threefold perjury.
Love bade me swear, and Love bids me forswear.
O sweet-suggesting Love, if thou hast sinned, 7
Teach me, thy tempted subject, to excuse it! 8
At first I did adore a twinkling star,
But now I worship a celestial sun.
Unheedful vows may heedfully be broken, 11
And he wants wit that wants resolvèd will 12
To learn his wit t'exchange the bad for better. 13
Fie, fie, unreverent tongue, to call her bad
Whose sovereignty so oft thou hast preferred 15
With twenty thousand soul-confirming oaths! 16
I cannot leave to love, and yet I do; 17
But there I leave to love where I should love.
Julia I lose, and Valentine I lose.
If I keep them, I needs must lose myself.
If I lose them, thus find I by their loss
For Valentine, myself; for Julia, Silvia.
I to myself am dearer than a friend,
For love is still most precious in itself, 24
And Silvia—witness heaven, that made her fair!—
Shows Julia but a swarthy Ethiop. 26
I will forget that Julia is alive,
Rememb'ring that my love to her is dead;
And Valentine I'll hold an enemy,
Aiming at Silvia as a sweeter friend.
I cannot now prove constant to myself
Without some treachery used to Valentine.
This night he meaneth with a corded ladder
To climb celestial Silvia's chamber window,
Myself in counsel, his competitor. 35
Now presently I'll give her father notice
Of their disguising and pretended flight, 37
Who, all enraged, will banish Valentine;
For Thurio, he intends, shall wed his daughter.
But Valentine being gone, I'll quickly cross 40
By some sly trick blunt Thurio's dull proceeding. 41
Love, lend me wings to make my purpose swift,
As thou hast lent me wit to plot this drift! *Exit.* 43

2.6. Location: Milan. The Duke's palace.
0.1 *solus* alone **4 that power** i.e., Love **7 sweet-suggesting** sweetly seductive **7–8 if thou . . . it** i.e., if even you, Love, have committed falsehoods or follies in love, teach frail me how to excuse myself by your example. **11 Unheedful** Ill-considered. **heedfully** after careful consideration **12 wants wit** lacks sense **13 learn** teach **15 preferred** recommended, urged **16 soul-confirming** sworn on the soul **17 leave** cease **24 love . . . itself** i.e., charity begins at home **26 Shows Julia but** reveals Julia to be by comparison no more than. **Ethiop** i.e., dark-skinned, the antithesis of beauty to Elizabethans. **35 in counsel** taken into confidence. **competitor** associate, partner **37 pretended** intended **40 cross** thwart **41 blunt** stupid **43 drift** scheme.

2.7

Enter Julia and Lucetta.

JULIA
Counsel, Lucetta. Gentle girl, assist me;
And ev'n in kind love I do conjure thee,
Who art the table wherein all my thoughts
Are visibly charactered and engraved,
To lesson me and tell me some good mean
How, with my honor, I may undertake
A journey to my loving Proteus.

LUCETTA
Alas, the way is wearisome and long!

JULIA
A true-devoted pilgrim is not weary
To measure kingdoms with his feeble steps;
Much less shall she that hath Love's wings to fly,
And when the flight is made to one so dear,
Of such divine perfection, as Sir Proteus.

LUCETTA
Better forbear till Proteus make return.

JULIA
Oh, know'st thou not his looks are my soul's food?
Pity the dearth that I have pinèd in
By longing for that food so long a time.
Didst thou but know the inly touch of love,
Thou wouldst as soon go kindle fire with snow
As seek to quench the fire of love with words.

LUCETTA
I do not seek to quench your love's hot fire,
But qualify the fire's extreme rage,
Lest it should burn above the bounds of reason.

JULIA
The more thou dam'st it up, the more it burns.
The current that with gentle murmur glides,
Thou know'st, being stopped, impatiently doth rage;
But when his fair course is not hinderèd,
He makes sweet music with th'enameled stones,
Giving a gentle kiss to every sedge
He overtaketh in his pilgrimage,
And so by many winding nooks he strays
With willing sport to the wild ocean.
Then let me go, and hinder not my course.
I'll be as patient as a gentle stream
And make a pastime of each weary step,
Till the last step have brought me to my love,
And there I'll rest, as after much turmoil
A blessèd soul doth in Elysium.

LUCETTA
But in what habit will you go along?

JULIA
Not like a woman, for I would prevent
The loose encounters of lascivious men.
Gentle Lucetta, fit me with such weeds
As may beseem some well-reputed page.

LUCETTA
Why, then, Your Ladyship must cut your hair.

JULIA
No, girl, I'll knit it up in silken strings
With twenty odd-conceited true-love knots.
To be fantastic may become a youth
Of greater time than I shall show to be.

LUCETTA
What fashion, madam, shall I make your breeches?

JULIA
That fits as well as "Tell me, good my lord,
What compass will you wear your farthingale?"
Why, ev'n what fashion thou best likes, Lucetta.

LUCETTA
You must needs have them with a codpiece, madam.

JULIA
Out, out, Lucetta! That will be ill-favored.

LUCETTA
A round hose, madam, now's not worth a pin,
Unless you have a codpiece to stick pins on.

JULIA
Lucetta, as thou lov'st me, let me have
What thou think'st meet and is most mannerly.
But tell me, wench, how will the world repute me
For undertaking so unstaid a journey?
I fear me it will make me scandalized.

LUCETTA
If you think so, then stay at home and go not.

JULIA Nay, that I will not.

LUCETTA
Then never dream on infamy, but go.
If Proteus like your journey when you come,
No matter who's displeased when you are gone.
I fear me he will scarce be pleased withal.

JULIA
That is the least, Lucetta, of my fear.
A thousand oaths, an ocean of his tears,
And instances of infinite of love
Warrant me welcome to my Proteus.

LUCETTA
All these are servants to deceitful men.

JULIA
Base men, that use them to so base effect!
But truer stars did govern Proteus' birth;
His words are bonds, his oaths are oracles,
His love sincere, his thoughts immaculate,
His tears pure messengers sent from his heart,

2.7. Location: Verona. Julia's house.
3 table tablet **4 charactered** inscribed **5 lesson** teach **10 measure** traverse **16 dearth** famine **18 inly** inward **22 qualify** control, moderate **28 enameled** having shiny, polished surfaces; variegated **29 sedge** grassy, rushlike plant **39 habit** apparel **40 prevent** forestall

42 weeds garments **43 beseem** suit **46 odd-conceited** strangely devised **47 fantastic** flamboyantly dressed **48 Of greater time** of more years **51 compass** fullness. **farthingale** hooped petticoat. **53 must needs** will have to. **codpiece** bagged appendage to the front of close-fitting hose or breeches, often conspicuous and ornamented **54 Out** (An expression of reproach or indignation.) **ill-favored** unsightly. **55 round hose** padded breeches **56 stick pins on** (One method used to decorate the codpiece.) **58 meet** suitable **60 unstaid** immodest, unconventional **67 withal** with it. **70 infinite** infinity **75 oracles** infallible indicators

His heart as far from fraud as heaven from earth.

LUCETTA

Pray heav'n he prove so when you come to him!

JULIA

Now, as thou lov'st me, do him not that wrong
To bear a hard opinion of his truth. 81
Only deserve my love by loving him,
And presently go with me to my chamber
To take a note of what I stand in need of
To furnish me upon my longing journey. 85
All that is mine I leave at thy dispose, 86
My goods, my lands, my reputation;
Only, in lieu thereof, dispatch me hence.
Come, answer not, but to it presently.
I am impatient of my tarriance. *Exeunt.* 90

3.1

Enter [*the*] *Duke, Thurio,* [*and*] *Proteus.*

DUKE

Sir Thurio, give us leave, I pray, awhile. 1
We have some secrets to confer about. [*Exit Thurio.*]
Now, tell me, Proteus, what's your will with me?

PROTEUS

My gracious lord, that which I would discover 4
The law of friendship bids me to conceal;
But when I call to mind your gracious favors
Done to me, undeserving as I am,
My duty pricks me on to utter that 8
Which else no worldly good should draw from me.
Know, worthy prince, Sir Valentine, my friend,
This night intends to steal away your daughter.
Myself am one made privy to the plot. 12
I know you have determined to bestow her
On Thurio, whom your gentle daughter hates;
And should she thus be stol'n away from you,
It would be much vexation to your age.
Thus, for my duty's sake, I rather chose
To cross my friend in his intended drift 18
Than, by concealing it, heap on your head
A pack of sorrows which would press you down,
Being unprevented, to your timeless grave. 21

DUKE

Proteus, I thank thee for thine honest care,
Which to requite, command me while I live. 23
This love of theirs myself have often seen,
Haply when they have judged me fast asleep,
And oftentimes have purposed to forbid
Sir Valentine her company and my court.
But, fearing lest my jealous aim might err, 28
And so unworthily disgrace the man—
A rashness that I ever yet have shunned—
I gave him gentle looks, thereby to find
That which thyself hast now disclosed to me.
And, that thou mayst perceive my fear of this,
Knowing that tender youth is soon suggested, 34
I nightly lodge her in an upper tower,
The key whereof myself have ever kept;
And thence she cannot be conveyed away.

PROTEUS

Know, noble lord, they have devised a means
How he her chamber window will ascend
And with a corded ladder fetch her down;
For which the youthful lover now is gone,
And this way comes he with it presently, 42
Where, if it please you, you may intercept him.
But, good my lord, do it so cunningly
That my discovery be not aimèd at; 45
For, love of you, not hate unto my friend,
Hath made me publisher of this pretense. 47

DUKE

Upon mine honor, he shall never know
That I had any light from thee of this.

PROTEUS

Adieu, my lord. Sir Valentine is coming. [*Exit.*]

[*Enter*] *Valentine,* [*hurrying elsewhere, concealing a rope ladder beneath his cloak*].

DUKE

Sir Valentine, whither away so fast?

VALENTINE

Please it Your Grace, there is a messenger
That stays to bear my letters to my friends,
And I am going to deliver them.

DUKE Be they of much import?

VALENTINE

The tenor of them doth but signify
My health and happy being at your court.

DUKE

Nay then, no matter. Stay with me awhile.
I am to break with thee of some affairs 59
That touch me near, wherein thou must be secret. 60
'Tis not unknown to thee that I have sought
To match my friend Sir Thurio to my daughter.

VALENTINE

I know it well, my lord, and sure the match
Were rich and honorable. Besides, the gentleman 64
Is full of virtue, bounty, worth, and qualities
Beseeming such a wife as your fair daughter. 66
Cannot Your Grace win her to fancy him?

DUKE

No, trust me. She is peevish, sullen, froward, 68
Proud, disobedient, stubborn, lacking duty,
Neither regarding that she is my child
Nor fearing me as if I were her father.

81 truth faithfulness. **85 my longing journey** the journey I long to make. **86 at thy dispose** in thy charge **90 tarriance** delaying.
3.1. Location: Milan. The Duke's palace.
1 give us leave (A polite form of dismissal.) **4 discover** reveal
8 pricks spurs **12 Myself . . . plot** I am one who has been given private knowledge of the plot. **18 cross** thwart. **drift** scheme
21 timeless untimely **23 command me** ask any favor of me
28 jealous aim suspicious conjecture

34 suggested tempted **42 presently** now **45 discovery** disclosure. **aimèd at** guessed **47 publisher** discloser. **pretense** intention.
59 I am . . . thee of I wish to disclose to you **60 touch me near** are of vital concern to me **64 Were** would be **66 Beseeming** befitting
68 trust believe. **peevish** willful. **froward** perverse

And, may I say to thee, this pride of hers,
Upon advice, hath drawn my love from her;
And, where I thought the remnant of mine age
Should have been cherished by her childlike duty,
I now am full resolved to take a wife,
And turn her out to who will take her in.
Then let her beauty be her wedding dower,
For me and my possessions she esteems not.

VALENTINE
What would Your Grace have me to do in this?

DUKE
There is a lady in Verona here
Whom I affect, but she is nice and coy
And naught esteems my agèd eloquence.
Now therefore would I have thee to my tutor—
For long agone I have forgot to court;
Besides, the fashion of the time is changed—
How and which way I may bestow myself
To be regarded in her sun-bright eye.

VALENTINE
Win her with gifts if she respect not words.
Dumb jewels often in their silent kind
More than quick words do move a woman's mind.

DUKE
But she did scorn a present that I sent her.

VALENTINE
A woman sometimes scorns what best contents her.
Send her another. Never give her o'er,
For scorn at first makes after-love the more.
If she do frown, 'tis not in hate of you,
But rather to beget more love in you.
If she do chide, 'tis not to have you gone,
Forwhy the fools are mad if left alone.
Take no repulse, whatever she doth say;
For "Get you gone," she doth not mean "Away!"
Flatter and praise, commend, extol their graces;
Though ne'er so black, say they have angels' faces.
That man that hath a tongue, I say, is no man
If with his tongue he cannot win a woman.

DUKE
But she I mean is promised by her friends
Unto a youthful gentleman of worth,
And kept severely from resort of men,
That no man hath access by day to her.

VALENTINE
Why then I would resort to her by night.

DUKE
Ay, but the doors be locked and keys kept safe,
That no man hath recourse to her by night.

VALENTINE
What lets but one may enter at her window?

DUKE
Her chamber is aloft, far from the ground,
And built so shelving that one cannot climb it
Without apparent hazard of his life.

VALENTINE
Why then, a ladder quaintly made of cords
To cast up, with a pair of anchoring hooks,
Would serve to scale another Hero's tower,
So bold Leander would adventure it.

DUKE
Now, as thou art a gentleman of blood,
Advise me where I may have such a ladder.

VALENTINE
When would you use it? Pray, sir, tell me that.

DUKE
This very night; for Love is like a child
That longs for everything that he can come by.

VALENTINE
By seven o'clock I'll get you such a ladder.

DUKE
But hark thee, I will go to her alone.
How shall I best convey the ladder thither?

VALENTINE
It will be light, my lord, that you may bear it
Under a cloak that is of any length.

DUKE
A cloak as long as thine will serve the turn?

VALENTINE
Ay, my good lord.

DUKE
Then let me see thy cloak.
I'll get me one of such another length.

VALENTINE
Why, any cloak will serve the turn, my lord.

DUKE
How shall I fashion me to wear a cloak?
I pray thee, let me feel thy cloak upon me.
[*He pulls open Valentine's cloak.*]
What letter is this same? What's here? "To Silvia"?
And here an engine fit for my proceeding.
I'll be so bold to break the seal for once. [*He reads.*]
"My thoughts do harbor with my Silvia nightly,
And slaves they are to me, that send them flying.
Oh, could their master come and go as lightly,
Himself would lodge where, senseless, they are lying!
My herald thoughts in thy pure bosom rest them,
While I, their king, that thither them importune,
Do curse the grace that with such grace hath blessed them,
Because myself do want my servants' fortune.

73 Upon advice after some careful consideration **74 where** whereas **77 who** whoever **81 Verona** (An error for Milan, seemingly, but *Verona* fits the line metrically. Some editors emend "in Verona" to "of Verona.") **82 affect** am fond of. **nice** difficult to please **83 naught** not at all **84 to** as, for **85 agone** ago. **forgot** forgotten how **87 bestow** behave, conduct **89 respect** heed **90 kind** nature **91 quick** lively (as contrasted with *Dumb,* silent) **99 Forwhy the fools** because women **101 For** by **103 black** dark of complexion **106 friends** i.e., relatives **109 That** so that. (Also in line 112.) **113 lets** hinders

115 shelving projecting, overhanging **116 apparent** plain, evident **117 quaintly** skillfully **119–20 Hero's . . . Leander** (See the note to 1.1.22.) **120 So** provided **121 blood** good family **130 of any length** tolerably long. **131 turn** purpose. **133 such another** the same **138 engine** contrivance, i.e., the rope ladder **140 harbor** reside **141 that . . . flying** I who send those thoughts as messages. **142 lightly** easily, quickly **143 senseless** insensible. **lying** dwelling. **144 them** themselves **145 importune** command **146–7 Do . . . fortune** do curse the happiness that is bestowed so gracefully on them, because I lack the good fortune enjoyed by my servants, i.e., my thoughts. (They are able to be with you, while I am not.)

I curse myself for they are sent by me, 148
That they should harbor where their lord should be."
What's here?
"Silvia, this night I will enfranchise thee."
'Tis so; and here's the ladder for the purpose.
Why, Phaëthon, for thou art Merops' son, 153
Wilt thou aspire to guide the heavenly car,
And with thy daring folly burn the world?
Wilt thou reach stars because they shine on thee? 156
Go, base intruder, overweening slave! 157
Bestow thy fawning smiles on equal mates, 158
And think my patience, more than thy desert,
Is privilege for thy departure hence. 160
Thank me for this more than for all the favors
Which, all too much, I have bestowed on thee.
But if thou linger in my territories
Longer than swiftest expedition 164
Will give thee time to leave our royal court,
By heaven, my wrath shall far exceed the love
I ever bore my daughter or thyself.
Begone! I will not hear thy vain excuse,
But, as thou lov'st thy life, make speed from hence.
[*Exit.*]

VALENTINE
And why not death rather than living torment?
To die is to be banished from myself,
And Silvia is myself. Banished from her
Is self from self—a deadly banishment!
What light is light, if Silvia be not seen?
What joy is joy, if Silvia be not by?
Unless it be to think that she is by
And feed upon the shadow of perfection. 177
Except I be by Silvia in the night, 178
There is no music in the nightingale;
Unless I look on Silvia in the day,
There is no day for me to look upon.
She is my essence, and I leave to be 182
If I be not by her fair influence 183
Fostered, illumined, cherished, kept alive.
I fly not death, to fly his deadly doom; 185
Tarry I here, I but attend on death, 186
But, fly I hence, I fly away from life.

[*Enter Proteus and*] *Lance.*

PROTEUS Run, boy, run, run, and seek him out.
LANCE So-ho, so-ho! 189
PROTEUS What see'st thou?
LANCE Him we go to find. There's not a hair on 's head 191
but 'tis a Valentine. 192
PROTEUS Valentine?
VALENTINE No.
PROTEUS Who then? His spirit?
VALENTINE Neither.
PROTEUS What then?
VALENTINE Nothing.
LANCE Can nothing speak? Master, shall I strike? 199
PROTEUS Who wouldst thou strike?
LANCE Nothing.
PROTEUS Villain, forbear.
LANCE Why, sir, I'll strike nothing. I pray you—
PROTEUS Sirrah, I say, forbear.—Friend Valentine, a word.

VALENTINE
My ears are stopped and cannot hear good news,
So much of bad already hath possessed them.

PROTEUS
Then in dumb silence will I bury mine, 208
For they are harsh, untunable, and bad. 209

VALENTINE Is Silvia dead?
PROTEUS No, Valentine.

VALENTINE
No Valentine, indeed, for sacred Silvia. 212
Hath she forsworn me?

PROTEUS No, Valentine.

VALENTINE
No Valentine, if Silvia have forsworn me.
What is your news?

LANCE Sir, there is a proclamation that you are vanished.

PROTEUS
That thou art banished—Oh, that's the news!—
From hence, from Silvia, and from me thy friend.

VALENTINE
Oh, I have fed upon this woe already,
And now excess of it will make me surfeit.
Doth Silvia know that I am banished?

PROTEUS
Ay, ay; and she hath offered to the doom— 223
Which, unreversed, stands in effectual force— 224
A sea of melting pearl, which some call tears.
Those at her father's churlish feet she tendered;
With them, upon her knees, her humble self,
Wringing her hands, whose whiteness so became them
As if but now they waxèd pale for woe.
But neither bended knees, pure hands held up,
Sad sighs, deep groans, nor silver-shedding tears
Could penetrate her uncompassionate sire,
But Valentine, if he be ta'en, must die. 233

148 for since, in that **153 Phaëthon, Merops** (Phaëthon was the son of Helios, the sun god, and of Clymene, lawful wife of Merops. Phaëthon aspired to guide the sun god's *car* [line 154] or chariot and was slain by Zeus for his presumption after he had scorched a large portion of the earth.) **for** just because **156 reach** reach for **157 overweening** presumptuous **158 equal mates** i.e., women of your own social status **160 Is privilege for** authorizes **164 expedition** speed **177 shadow** image **178 Except** Unless **182 leave** cease **183 influence** (An astrological term for the emanations supposed to flow from the stars and to have power over the destinies of men.) **185 I . . . doom** I shall not escape death by flying from the Duke's sentence of death, or, from death's deadly sentence **186 Tarry I** if I tarry. **attend on** wait for **189 So-ho** (Hunting cry used when the game is sighted.)

191 hair (With pun on "hare.") **192 Valentine** (His name means "token of true love.") **199 shall I strike** (Lance wonders if he should strike at a *spirit,* line 195, to ward off evil effects, as in *Hamlet,* 1.1.144.) **208 mine** i.e., my news **209 they** i.e., the news **212 No Valentine** (Valentine jests bitterly on the inappropriateness of his name and on the loss of his very identity, playing on *No, Valentine* in the previous line.) **223 to the doom** to this news of the sentence **224 Which . . . force** which, if not reversed, must certainly take effect **233 But** but that

Besides, her intercession chafed him so,
When she for thy repeal was suppliant,
That to close prison he commanded her,
With many bitter threats of biding there.

VALENTINE
No more, unless the next word that thou speak'st
Have some malignant power upon my life;
If so, I pray thee, breathe it in mine ear,
As ending anthem of my endless dolor.

PROTEUS
Cease to lament for that thou canst not help,
And study help for that which thou lament'st.
Time is the nurse and breeder of all good.
Here if thou stay thou canst not see thy love;
Besides, thy staying will abridge thy life.
Hope is a lover's staff; walk hence with that
And manage it against despairing thoughts.
Thy letters may be here, though thou art hence,
Which, being writ to me, shall be delivered
Even in the milk-white bosom of thy love.
The time now serves not to expostulate.
Come, I'll convey thee through the city gate,
And ere I part with thee confer at large
Of all that may concern thy love affairs.
As thou lov'st Silvia, though not for thyself,
Regard thy danger, and along with me!

VALENTINE
I pray thee, Lance, an if thou see'st my boy,
Bid him make haste and meet me at the north gate.

PROTEUS [*to Lance*]
Go, sirrah, find him out.—Come, Valentine.

VALENTINE
O my dear Silvia! Hapless Valentine!

[*Exeunt Valentine and Proteus.*]

LANCE I am but a fool, look you, and yet I have the wit to think my master is a kind of a knave. But that's all one, if he be but one knave. He lives not now that knows me to be in love, yet I am in love. But a team of horse shall not pluck that from me, nor who 'tis I love. And yet 'tis a woman, but what woman, I will not tell myself. And yet 'tis a milkmaid. Yet 'tis not a maid, for she hath had gossips. Yet 'tis a maid, for she is her master's maid, and serves for wages. She hath more qualities than a water spaniel, which is much in a bare Christian. [*Pulling out a paper*] Here is the catalog of her condition. "Imprimis: She can fetch and carry." Why, a horse can do no more. Nay, a horse cannot fetch, but only carry; therefore is she better than a jade. "Item: She can milk." Look you, a sweet virtue in a maid with clean hands.

[*Enter*] *Speed.*

SPEED How now, Signor Lance, what news with Your Mastership?

LANCE With my master's ship? Why, it is at sea.

SPEED Well, your old vice still: mistake the word. What news, then, in your paper?

LANCE The black'st news that ever thou heard'st.

SPEED Why, man, how "black"?

LANCE Why, as black as ink.

SPEED Let me read them.

LANCE Fie on thee, jolt-head! Thou canst not read.

SPEED Thou liest. I can.

LANCE I will try thee. Tell me this: who begot thee?

SPEED Marry, the son of my grandfather.

LANCE Oh, illiterate loiterer! It was the son of thy grandmother. This proves that thou canst not read.

SPEED Come, fool, come. Try me in thy paper.

LANCE There. [*Giving him the paper*] And Saint Nicholas be thy speed!

SPEED [*reads*] "Imprimis: She can milk."

LANCE Ay, that she can.

SPEED "Item: She brews good ale."

LANCE And thereof comes the proverb: "Blessing of your heart, you brew good ale."

SPEED "Item: She can sew."

LANCE That's as much as to say, "Can she so?"

SPEED "Item: She can knit."

LANCE What need a man care for a stock with a wench, when she can knit him a stock?

SPEED "Item: She can wash and scour."

LANCE A special virtue, for then she need not be washed and scoured.

SPEED "Item: She can spin."

LANCE Then may I set the world on wheels, when she can spin for her living.

SPEED "Item: She hath many nameless virtues."

LANCE That's as much as to say bastard virtues, that indeed know not their fathers and therefore have no names.

SPEED Here follow her vices.

LANCE Close at the heels of her virtues.

SPEED "Item: She is not to be kissed fasting, in respect of her breath."

LANCE Well, that fault may be mended with a breakfast. Read on.

235 repeal recall from exile **236 close** tightly enclosed **237 biding** permanently remaining **241 ending anthem** requiem **242 that** what **243 study** devise **248 manage** wield **252 expostulate** discuss at length. **254 confer at large** discuss at length **256 though not for thyself** even though not for your own sake **263–4 that's . . . knave** i.e., it's all right so long as he's knavish in one thing only (that is, in love). **264 He lives not now** There is no one alive **266 horse** horses **269 gossips** i.e., godparents to a child of hers. **maid** (Lance quibbles on [1] maidservant [2] virgin. She is the first, even if no longer the second.) **271 water spaniel** (A fawning, subservient kind of dog.) **bare** (1) mere (2) naked, hairless **273 condition** qualities. **Imprimis** In the first place (to be followed, in a list, with each particular marked *Item*) **274–5 cannot fetch** cannot be ordered to go and fetch something

276 jade (1) ill-conditioned horse (2) hussy. **280 at sea** (1) on the high seas (2) adrift, at loose ends. **281 vice** (With added meaning of *Vice,* comic character in morality plays who speaks with double meaning.) **286 them** the news. **287 jolt-head** blockhead. **291 loiterer** idle person, lazy student. **294 Saint Nicholas** patron saint of scholars **295 speed** protection. (With a play on Speed's name.) **304 stock** dowry **305 stock** stocking. **308 scoured** (1) scrubbed (2) beaten, drubbed. (*Washed* probably has a similar double meaning.) **310 set . . . wheels** i.e., take life easy **311 spin for her living** (Probably with a sexual double meaning, as in *Twelfth Night,* 1.3.100–2: "I hope to see a huswife take thee between her legs and spin it off.") **312 nameless** inexpressible **318–9 in respect of** on account of

SPEED "Item: She hath a sweet mouth."

LANCE That makes amends for her sour breath.

SPEED "Item: She doth talk in her sleep."

LANCE It's no matter for that, so she sleep not in her talk.

SPEED "Item: She is slow in words."

LANCE Oh, villain, that set this down among her vices! To be slow in words is a woman's only virtue. I pray thee, out with't, and place it for her chief virtue.

SPEED "Item: She is proud."

LANCE Out with that too. It was Eve's legacy, and cannot be ta'en from her.

SPEED "Item: She hath no teeth."

LANCE I care not for that neither, because I love crusts.

SPEED "Item: She is curst."

LANCE Well, the best is, she hath no teeth to bite.

SPEED "Item: She will often praise her liquor."

LANCE If her liquor be good, she shall. If she will not, I will, for good things should be praised.

SPEED "Item: She is too liberal."

LANCE Of her tongue she cannot, for that's writ down she is slow of; of her purse she shall not, for that I'll keep shut. Now, of another thing she may, and that cannot I help. Well, proceed.

SPEED "Item: She hath more hair than wit, and more faults than hairs, and more wealth than faults."

LANCE Stop there; I'll have her. She was mine and not mine twice or thrice in that last article. Rehearse that once more.

SPEED "Item: She hath more hair than wit—"

LANCE More hair than wit? It may be: I'll prove it. The cover of the salt hides the salt, and therefore it is more than the salt; the hair that covers the wit is more than the wit, for the greater hides the less. What's next?

SPEED "And more faults than hairs—"

LANCE That's monstrous. Oh, that that were out!

SPEED "And more wealth than faults."

LANCE Why, that word makes the faults gracious. Well, I'll have her; and if it be a match, as nothing is impossible—

SPEED What then?

LANCE Why, then will I tell thee—that thy master stays for thee at the north gate.

SPEED For me?

LANCE For thee? Ay, who art thou? He hath stayed for a better man than thee.

SPEED And must I go to him?

LANCE Thou must run to him, for thou hast stayed so long that going will scarce serve the turn.

SPEED Why didst not tell me sooner? Pox of your love letters! *[Exit.]*

LANCE Now will he be swinged for reading my letter—an unmannerly slave, that will thrust himself into secrets! I'll after, to rejoice in the boy's correction. *Exit.*

✤

322 sweet mouth sweet tooth. (With a wanton sense.) **325 sleep** (With a pun on "slip"; pronunciation was similar.) **331 proud** (With additional meaning of "lascivious.") **336 curst** shrewish. **341 liberal** free. **344 another thing** (With bawdy suggestion, playing on the idea of *her purse*, which her husband is to *keep shut* to strangers.) **349 Rehearse** Repeat **353 cover of the salt** lid of the salt cellar **364 stays** waits **370 going** walking **371 Pox** i.e., A plague on **373 swinged** thrashed **375 correction** punishment.

3.2

Enter [the] Duke [and] Thurio.

DUKE
Sir Thurio, fear not but that she will love you,
Now Valentine is banished from her sight.

THURIO
Since his exile she hath despised me most,
Forsworn my company, and railed at me,
That I am desperate of obtaining her.

DUKE
This weak impress of love is as a figure
Trenchèd in ice, which with an hour's heat
Dissolves to water and doth lose his form.
A little time will melt her frozen thoughts,
And worthless Valentine shall be forgot.

[Enter] Proteus.

How now, Sir Proteus? Is your countryman,
According to our proclamation, gone?

PROTEUS Gone, my good lord.

DUKE
My daughter takes his going grievously.

PROTEUS
A little time, my lord, will kill that grief.

DUKE
So I believe, but Thurio thinks not so.
Proteus, the good conceit I hold of thee—
For thou hast shown some sign of good desert—
Makes me the better to confer with thee.

PROTEUS
Longer than I prove loyal to Your Grace
Let me not live to look upon Your Grace.

DUKE
Thou know'st how willingly I would effect
The match between Sir Thurio and my daughter.

PROTEUS I do, my lord.

DUKE
And also, I think, thou art not ignorant
How she opposes her against my will.

PROTEUS
She did, my lord, when Valentine was here.

DUKE
Ay, and perversely she persevers so.
What might we do to make the girl forget
The love of Valentine, and love Sir Thurio?

PROTEUS
The best way is to slander Valentine
With falsehood, cowardice, and poor descent,
Three things that women highly hold in hate.

DUKE
Ay, but she'll think that it is spoke in hate.

PROTEUS
Ay, if his enemy deliver it;
Therefore it must with circumstance be spoken
By one whom she esteemeth as his friend.

3.2. Location: Milan. The Duke's palace.
5 That so that **6 impress** impression **7 Trenchèd** cut **8 his** its **17 conceit** opinion **19 the better** the rather, more willingly **26 her** herself **35 deliver** speak **36 circumstance** confirming detail

DUKE
Then you must undertake to slander him.
PROTEUS
And that, my lord, I shall be loath to do.
'Tis an ill office for a gentleman,
Especially against his very friend.
DUKE
Where your good word cannot advantage him
Your slander never can endamage him.
Therefore the office is indifferent,
Being entreated to it by your friend.
PROTEUS
You have prevailed, my lord. If I can do it
By aught that I can speak in his dispraise,
She shall not long continue love to him.
But say this weed her love from Valentine,
It follows not that she will love Sir Thurio.
THURIO
Therefore, as you unwind her love from him,
Lest it should ravel and be good to none
You must provide to bottom it on me;
Which must be done by praising me as much
As you in worth dispraise Sir Valentine.
DUKE
And, Proteus, we dare trust you in this kind
Because we know, on Valentine's report,
You are already Love's firm votary
And cannot soon revolt and change your mind.
Upon this warrant shall you have access
Where you with Silvia may confer at large;
For she is lumpish, heavy, melancholy,
And, for your friend's sake, will be glad of you,
Where you may temper her by your persuasion
To hate young Valentine and love my friend.
PROTEUS
As much as I can do, I will effect.
But you, Sir Thurio, are not sharp enough.
You must lay lime to tangle her desires
By wailful sonnets, whose composèd rhymes
Should be full-fraught with serviceable vows.
DUKE
Ay, much is the force of heaven-bred poesy.
PROTEUS
Say that upon the altar of her beauty
You sacrifice your tears, your sighs, your heart.
Write till your ink be dry, and with your tears
Moist it again, and frame some feeling line
That may discover such integrity.
For Orpheus' lute was strung with poets' sinews,
Whose golden touch could soften steel and stones,
Make tigers tame, and huge leviathans
Forsake unsounded deeps to dance on sands.
After your dire-lamenting elegies,
Visit by night your lady's chamber window
With some sweet consort. To their instruments
Tune a deploring dump. The night's dead silence
Will well become such sweet-complaining grievance.
This, or else nothing, will inherit her.
DUKE
This discipline shows thou hast been in love.
THURIO
And thy advice this night I'll put in practice.
Therefore, sweet Proteus, my direction-giver,
Let us into the city presently
To sort some gentlemen well skilled in music.
I have a sonnet that will serve the turn
To give the onset to thy good advice.
DUKE About it, gentlemen!
PROTEUS
We'll wait upon Your Grace till after supper,
And afterward determine our proceedings.
DUKE
Even now about it. I will pardon you. *Exeunt.*

✣

4.1

Enter certain Outlaws.

FIRST OUTLAW
Fellows, stand fast. I see a passenger.
SECOND OUTLAW
If there be ten, shrink not, but down with 'em.

[*Enter*] *Valentine* [*and*] *Speed.*

THIRD OUTLAW
Stand, sir! And throw us that you have about ye.
If not, we'll make you sit, and rifle you.
SPEED [*to Valentine*]
Sir, we are undone. These are the villains
That all the travelers do fear so much.
VALENTINE My friends—
FIRST OUTLAW
That's not so, sir. We are your enemies.
SECOND OUTLAW Peace! We'll hear him.
THIRD OUTLAW
Ay, by my beard will we, for he is a proper man.
VALENTINE
Then know that I have little wealth to lose.
A man I am, crossed with adversity;
My riches are these poor habiliments,
Of which if you should here disfurnish me
You take the sum and substance that I have.
SECOND OUTLAW Whither travel you?

41 very true **42 advantage** profit **44 indifferent** neither good nor bad **45 your friend** i.e., the Duke. **49 say . . . Valentine** even supposing this should root out the love she feels for Valentine **53 bottom** wind, as a skein of thread **62 lumpish** dull, spiritless **64 temper** mold **68 lime** birdlime, a sticky substance smeared on twigs to ensnare small birds **70 Should . . . vows** should be fully laden with vows of service. **75 frame** compose **76 discover** reveal. **integrity** true devotion. **77 Orpheus** legendary musician whose music had the power to move inanimate objects as well as animals. **sinews** nerves **79 leviathans** whales

83 consort company of musicians. **84 deploring dump** doleful, sad melody. **85 grievance** grief. **86 inherit** put you in possession of **87 discipline** teaching **91 sort** choose **93 To . . . to** to set in motion **97 pardon you** i.e., excuse you your *waiting upon* or attending upon me.
4.1. Location: The frontiers of Mantua. A forest.
1 passenger traveler. **2 If** Even if **3 Stand** Halt. (But the Third Outlaw puns on *sit,* line 4, as the opposite of "stand up.") **4 rifle** plunder **10 proper** good-looking **12 crossed with** thwarted by **14 disfurnish** deprive

VALENTINE To Verona.
FIRST OUTLAW Whence came you?
VALENTINE From Milan.
THIRD OUTLAW Have you long sojourned there?
VALENTINE
Some sixteen months, and longer might have stayed
If crooked fortune had not thwarted me.
FIRST OUTLAW What, were you banished thence?
VALENTINE I was.
SECOND OUTLAW For what offense?
VALENTINE
For that which now torments me to rehearse:
I killed a man, whose death I much repent,
But yet I slew him manfully in fight
Without false vantage or base treachery.
FIRST OUTLAW
Why, ne'er repent it, if it were done so.
But were you banished for so small a fault?
VALENTINE
I was, and held me glad of such a doom.
SECOND OUTLAW Have you the tongues?
VALENTINE
My youthful travel therein made me happy,
Or else I had been often miserable.
THIRD OUTLAW
By the bare scalp of Robin Hood's fat friar,
This fellow were a king for our wild faction!
FIRST OUTLAW We'll have him. Sirs, a word.
[*The Outlaws confer in whispers.*]
SPEED Master, be one of them;
It's an honorable kind of thievery.
VALENTINE Peace, villain!
SECOND OUTLAW [*returning to Valentine*]
Tell us this: have you anything to take to?
VALENTINE Nothing but my fortune.
THIRD OUTLAW
Know, then, that some of us are gentlemen,
Such as the fury of ungoverned youth
Thrust from the company of awful men.
Myself was from Verona banishèd
For practicing to steal away a lady,
An heir, and near allied unto the Duke.
SECOND OUTLAW
And I from Mantua, for a gentleman
Who, in my mood, I stabbed unto the heart.
FIRST OUTLAW
And I for suchlike petty crimes as these.
But to the purpose—for we cite our faults
That they may hold excused our lawless lives;
And partly, seeing you are beautified
With goodly shape, and by your own report
A linguist, and a man of such perfection
As we do in our quality much want—
SECOND OUTLAW
Indeed, because you are a banished man,
Therefore, above the rest, we parley to you.
Are you content to be our general?
To make a virtue of necessity
And live, as we do, in this wilderness?
THIRD OUTLAW
What say'st thou? Wilt thou be of our consort?
Say ay, and be the captain of us all.
We'll do thee homage and be ruled by thee,
Love thee as our commander and our king.
FIRST OUTLAW
But if thou scorn our courtesy, thou diest.
SECOND OUTLAW
Thou shalt not live to brag what we have offered.
VALENTINE
I take your offer and will live with you,
Provided that you do no outrages
On silly women or poor passengers.
THIRD OUTLAW
No, we detest such vile, base practices.
Come, go with us. We'll bring thee to our crews
And show thee all the treasure we have got,
Which, with ourselves, all rest at thy dispose. *Exeunt.*

✤

4.2

Enter Proteus.

PROTEUS
Already have I been false to Valentine,
And now I must be as unjust to Thurio.
Under the color of commending him
I have access my own love to prefer.
But Silvia is too fair, too true, too holy
To be corrupted with my worthless gifts.
When I protest true loyalty to her,
She twits me with my falsehood to my friend.
When to her beauty I commend my vows,
She bids me think how I have been forsworn
In breaking faith with Julia, whom I loved.
And notwithstanding all her sudden quips,
The least whereof would quell a lover's hope,
Yet, spaniel-like, the more she spurns my love,
The more it grows and fawneth on her still.
But here comes Thurio. Now must we to her window
And give some evening music to her ear.

[*Enter*] *Thurio* [*and*] *musicians.*

22 crooked perverse, malignant **26 rehearse** repeat **27 I killed a man** (A lie, presumably intended to impress the outlaws.) **32 held . . . doom** was pleased with such a light sentence. **33 the tongues** ability in foreign languages. **34 travel** (The Folio spelling, "trauaile," may also suggest "laborious study.") **happy** proficient **36 friar** i.e., Friar Tuck **37 were** would be suitable as. **faction** band, set of persons. **41 villain** i.e., you rogue. **42 anything to take to** any prospect of a position or occupation. **46 awful** law-abiding **48 practicing** plotting **51 mood** anger, displeasure **54 hold excused** justify

58 quality profession. **want** lack **60 above the rest** for this reason chiefly. **parley to** confer with, negotiate with **64 consort** company **72 silly** defenseless. **passengers** travelers. **74 crews** bands **76 dispose** disposal.
4.2. Location: Milan. Outside the Duke's palace, under Silvia's window.
3 color pretext **4 prefer** urge. **9 commend** offer, direct **12 quips** sharp, sarcastic remarks

THURIO
How now, Sir Proteus, are you crept before us?

PROTEUS
Ay, gentle Thurio, for you know that love
Will creep in service where it cannot go.

THURIO
Ay, but I hope, sir, that you love not here.

PROTEUS
Sir, but I do, or else I would be hence.

THURIO
Who? Silvia?

PROTEUS Ay, Silvia—for your sake.

THURIO
I thank you for your own.—Now, gentlemen,
Let's tune, and to it lustily awhile.

[Enter, at a distance, the] Host *[of the inn, and]* Julia *[disguised as a page. They talk apart.]*

HOST Now, my young guest, methinks you're allycholly. I pray you, why is it?

JULIA Marry, mine host, because I cannot be merry.

HOST Come, we'll have you merry. I'll bring you where you shall hear music and see the gentleman that you asked for.

JULIA But shall I hear him speak?

HOST Ay, that you shall.

JULIA That will be music. *[Music plays.]*

HOST Hark, hark!

JULIA Is he among these?

HOST Ay, but peace! Let's hear 'em.

Song

MUSICIAN

Who is Silvia? What is she,
That all our swains commend her?
Holy, fair, and wise is she;
The heaven such grace did lend her,
That she might admirèd be.

Is she kind as she is fair?
For beauty lives with kindness.
Love doth to her eyes repair
To help him of his blindness,
And, being helped, inhabits there.

Then to Silvia let us sing,
That Silvia is excelling.
She excels each mortal thing
Upon the dull earth dwelling.
To her let us garlands bring.

HOST How now? Are you sadder than you were before?
How do you, man? The music likes you not.

JULIA You mistake. The musician likes me not.

HOST Why, my pretty youth?

JULIA He plays false, father.

HOST How? Out of tune on the strings?

JULIA Not so, but yet so false that he grieves my very heartstrings.

HOST You have a quick ear.

JULIA Ay, I would I were deaf. It makes me have a slow heart.

HOST I perceive you delight not in music.

JULIA Not a whit, when it jars so.

HOST Hark, what fine change is in the music!

JULIA Ay, that change is the spite.

HOST You would have them always play but one thing?

JULIA I would always have one play but one thing. But Host, doth this Sir Proteus that we talk on often resort unto this gentlewoman?

HOST I tell you what Lance, his man, told me: he loved her out of all nick.

JULIA Where is Lance?

HOST Gone to seek his dog, which tomorrow, by his master's command, he must carry for a present to his lady.

JULIA
Peace! Stand aside. The company parts.
[Julia and the Host stand aside.]

PROTEUS
Sir Thurio, fear not you. I will so plead
That you shall say my cunning drift excels.

THURIO
Where meet we?

PROTEUS At Saint Gregory's well.

THURIO Farewell.
[Exeunt Thurio and the musicians.]

[Enter] Silvia *[above, at her window].*

PROTEUS
Madam, good even to Your Ladyship.

SILVIA
I thank you for your music, gentlemen.
Who is that that spake?

PROTEUS
One, lady, if you knew his pure heart's truth,
You would quickly learn to know him by his voice.

SILVIA Sir Proteus, as I take it.

PROTEUS
Sir Proteus, gentle lady, and your servant.

SILVIA
What's your will?

PROTEUS That I may compass yours.

SILVIA
You have your wish. My will is even this:
That presently you hie you home to bed.

20 go walk at an ordinary pace. **24 I thank . . . own** i.e., It's just as well, for your own safety, that you added that disclaimer. **25 lustily** heartily, with a will **26–7 allycholly** (A colloquial form of *melancholy.*) **31 asked for** inquired about. **39 swains** youths, wooers **42 admirèd** wondered at **45 repair** hasten, visit **54 likes** pleases **55 likes me not** (1) displeases me with his music (2) does not love me. (The first meaning is intended for the Host; the second is hidden except from the audience.)

57 plays false (1) plays out of tune (2) is unfaithful. **father** (A form of address to an older man.) **62 slow** heavy. (Playing also on *slow* as the opposite of *quick* in line 61.) **65 jars** is discordant **66 change** modulation. (But Julia plays on the sense of "fickleness.") **67 spite** injury, annoyance. **68 play but one thing** play only one musical piece. (But Julia plays on the sense of "play only one role as lover.") **70 talk on** talk of **73 out of all nick** i.e., beyond all reckoning. **80 drift** scheme **89 compass yours** (1) obtain your good will (2) perform your every wish. **91 presently** immediately. **hie** hasten

Thou subtle, perjured, false, disloyal man!
Think'st thou I am so shallow, so conceitless,
To be seducèd by thy flattery,
That hast deceived so many with thy vows?
Return, return, and make thy love amends.
For me, by this pale queen of night I swear,
I am so far from granting thy request
That I despise thee for thy wrongful suit,
And by and by intend to chide myself
Even for this time I spend in talking to thee.

PROTEUS
I grant, sweet love, that I did love a lady,
But she is dead.

JULIA [*aside*] 'Twere false, if I should speak it,
For I am sure she is not burièd.

SILVIA
Say that she be, yet Valentine, thy friend,
Survives, to whom—thyself art witness—
I am betrothed. And art thou not ashamed
To wrong him with thy importunacy?

PROTEUS
I likewise hear that Valentine is dead.

SILVIA
And so suppose am I, for in his grave,
Assure thyself, my love is burièd.

PROTEUS
Sweet lady, let me rake it from the earth.

SILVIA
Go to thy lady's grave and call hers thence.
Or, at the least, in hers sepulchre thine.

JULIA [*aside*] He heard not that.

PROTEUS
Madam, if your heart be so obdurate,
Vouchsafe me yet your picture for my love,
The picture that is hanging in your chamber.
To that I'll speak, to that I'll sigh and weep;
For since the substance of your perfect self
Is else devoted, I am but a shadow,
And to your shadow will I make true love.

JULIA [*aside*]
If 'twere a substance, you would, sure, deceive it
And make it but a shadow, as I am.

SILVIA
I am very loath to be your idol, sir.
But since your falsehood shall become you well
To worship shadows and adore false shapes,
Send to me in the morning, and I'll send it.
And so, good rest.

PROTEUS As wretches have o'ernight
That wait for execution in the morn.
[*Exeunt Proteus and Silvia separately.*]

JULIA Host, will you go?

HOST By my halidom, I was fast asleep.

JULIA Pray you, where lies Sir Proteus?

HOST Marry, at my house. Trust me, I think 'tis almost day.

JULIA
Not so; but it hath been the longest night
That e'er I watched, and the most heaviest. [*Exeunt.*]

✤

4.3

Enter [*Sir*] *Eglamour.*

EGLAMOUR
This is the hour that Madam Silvia
Entreated me to call and know her mind.
There's some great matter she'd employ me in.—
Madam, madam!

[*Enter*] *Silvia* [*above, at her window*].

SILVIA Who calls?

EGLAMOUR Your servant and your friend;
One that attends Your Ladyship's command.

SILVIA
Sir Eglamour, a thousand times good morrow.

EGLAMOUR
As many, worthy lady, to yourself.
According to Your Ladyship's impose,
I am thus early come to know what service
It is your pleasure to command me in.

SILVIA
O Eglamour, thou art a gentleman—
Think not I flatter, for I swear I do not—
Valiant, wise, remorseful, well accomplished.
Thou art not ignorant what dear good will
I bear unto the banished Valentine,
Nor how my father would enforce me marry
Vain Thurio, whom my very soul abhors.
Thyself hast loved, and I have heard thee say
No grief did ever come so near thy heart
As when thy lady and thy true love died,
Upon whose grave thou vowed'st pure chastity.
Sir Eglamour, I would to Valentine,
To Mantua, where I hear he makes abode;
And, for the ways are dangerous to pass,
I do desire thy worthy company,
Upon whose faith and honor I repose.
Urge not my father's anger, Eglamour,

92 subtle crafty **93 conceitless** witless **94 To be** as to be **97 this pale . . . night** i.e., the moon, Diana, goddess of chastity **103 if . . . it** i.e., even if I should say such a thing in the sense that I am slain in my heart by Proteus's faithlessness and thus transformed into "Sebastian" **108 importunacy** importunity. **114 sepulchre** bury **115 He heard not that** i.e., He will turn a deaf ear to such unwelcome talk. **121 else** elsewhere **121–2 I am . . . love** (Proteus plays on two meanings of *shadow*: I am reduced to being nothing, but I will at least worship your picture.) **123–4 If . . . I am** (Julia's rueful aside plays on the antithesis of *substance and shadow:* she fears that Proteus's idea of love is as insubstantial as a mere picture or shadow, and that his love for Silvia is no more realistic or capable of fidelity than his love for Julia has proved to be.) **126 since . . . well** i.e., since it befits your false nature **128 Send** i.e., send a messenger

129 As wretches i.e., I will enjoy just about as much rest as poor convicts **132 halidom** (Originally, a holy relic; here, a mild oath.) **133 lies** lodges **134 Marry** Indeed. (Originally, an oath, "by the Virgin Mary.") **house** inn. **Trust me** i.e., On my honor **136 watched** stayed awake through

4.3. Location: The same, early in the morning (and perhaps only a short time after 4.2, which ends as it is "almost day," line 134).
10 impose command **15 remorseful** compassionate **16 dear** affectionate **24 would** wish to go **26 for** because

But think upon my grief, a lady's grief,
And on the justice of my flying hence
To keep me from a most unholy match,
Which heaven and fortune still rewards with plagues. 33
I do desire thee, even from a heart
As full of sorrows as the sea of sands,
To bear me company and go with me;
If not, to hide what I have said to thee,
That I may venture to depart alone.

EGLAMOUR
Madam, I pity much your grievances,
Which, since I know they virtuously are placed,
I give consent to go along with you,
Recking as little what betideth me 42
As much I wish all good befortune you. 43
When will you go?

SILVIA This evening coming.

EGLAMOUR
Where shall I meet you?

SILVIA At Friar Patrick's cell,
Where I intend holy confession.

EGLAMOUR
I will not fail Your Ladyship.
Good morrow, gentle lady.

SILVIA
Good morrow, kind Sir Eglamour.
Exeunt [*separately*].

✤

4.4

Enter Lance [*with his dog, Crab*].

LANCE When a man's servant shall play the cur with
him, look you, it goes hard—one that I brought up of 2
a puppy, one that I saved from drowning when three
or four of his blind brothers and sisters went to it. I 4
have taught him, even as one would say precisely,
"Thus I would teach a dog." I was sent to deliver him
as a present to Mistress Silvia from my master, and I
came no sooner into the dining chamber but he steps
me to her trencher and steals her capon's leg. Oh, 'tis 9
a foul thing when a cur cannot keep himself in all 10
companies! I would have, as one should say, one that 11
takes upon him to be a dog indeed, to be, as it were, a 12
dog at all things. If I had not had more wit than he, to 13
take a fault upon me that he did, I think verily he had 14
been hanged for't; sure as I live, he had suffered for't.
You shall judge. He thrusts me himself into the company of three or four gentlemanlike dogs, under the
Duke's table. He had not been there—bless the 18
mark!—a pissing while but all the chamber smelt him. 19
"Out with the dog!" says one. "What cur is that?" says
another. "Whip him out," says the third. "Hang him
up," says the Duke. I, having been acquainted with the
smell before, knew it was Crab, and goes me to the 23
fellow that whips the dogs. "Friend," quoth I, "you
mean to whip the dog?" "Ay, marry do I," quoth he.
"You do him the more wrong," quoth I. " 'Twas I did
the thing you wot of." He makes me no more ado, but 27
whips me out of the chamber. How many masters
would do this for his servant? Nay, I'll be sworn I have
sat in the stocks for puddings he hath stolen, otherwise 30
he had been executed. I have stood on the pillory for
geese he hath killed, otherwise he had suffered for't.—
Thou think'st not of this now. Nay, I remember the
trick you served me when I took my leave of Madam
Silvia. Did not I bid thee still mark me and do as I do?
When didst thou see me heave up my leg and make
water against a gentlewoman's farthingale? Didst 37
thou ever see me do such a trick?

[*Enter*] *Proteus* [*and*] *Julia* [*disguised*].

PROTEUS [*to Julia*]
Sebastian is thy name? I like thee well,
And will employ thee in some service presently.

JULIA
In what you please. I'll do what I can.

PROTEUS
I hope thou wilt. [*To Lance*] How now, you whoreson
peasant, 42
Where have you been these two days loitering?

LANCE Marry, sir, I carried Mistress Silvia the dog you
bade me.

PROTEUS And what says she to my little jewel? 46

LANCE Marry, she says your dog was a cur, and tells
you currish thanks is good enough for such a present. 48

PROTEUS But she received my dog?

LANCE No, indeed, did she not. Here have I brought
him back again. [*He points to his dog.*]

PROTEUS What, didst thou offer her this from me?

LANCE Ay, sir, the other squirrel was stolen from me by 53
the hangman boys in the marketplace, and then I 54
offered her mine own, who is a dog as big as ten of
yours, and therefore the gift the greater.

PROTEUS
Go, get thee hence, and find my dog again,
Or ne'er return again into my sight.
Away, I say! Stayest thou to vex me here?
[*Exit Lance with Crab.*]
A slave, that still an end turns me to shame!— 60

33 still rewards always reward **42 Recking** heeding, caring
43 befortune befall

4.4. Location: The same, some hours later.
2 of from **4 blind** i.e., with eyes not yet opened. **to it** i.e., to drowning. **9 me** i.e., to my injury, to my detriment. (Compare lines 16, 23, and 27.) **trencher** wooden dish or plate. **capon's leg** leg of a rooster, castrated to make the flesh succulent. **10 keep** restrain **11–12 one that . . . him** such a dog as undertakes **12–13 a dog at** adept at. (But with literal meaning as well.) **13–14 to take . . . did** to take the blame upon myself for the fault he did

18–19 bless the mark (A phrase used to apologize for indecorous language.) **19 a pissing while** a short while. (But with literal meaning as well.) **23 goes me** i.e., I went **27 wot of** know about. **makes me** makes **30 puddings** sausages made by stuffing animal entrails with spicy minced meat, etc. **37 farthingale** hooped petticoat. **42 whoreson peasant** (A term of jocular familiarity.) **46 jewel** (Proteus is thinking of the small, elegant dog he intended as a present to Silvia.) **48 currish** i.e., mean-spirited. (With a play on *cur*.) **53 squirrel** i.e., little dog **54 hangman** i.e., fit for the hangman, rascally **60 A slave . . . shame** A wretch that continually brings shame upon me.

Sebastian, I have entertainèd thee, 61
Partly that I have need of such a youth
That can with some discretion do my business—
For 'tis no trusting to yond foolish lout—
But chiefly for thy face and thy behavior,
Which, if my augury deceive me not,
Witness good bringing up, fortune, and truth. 67
Therefore know thou, for this I entertain thee.
Go presently and take this ring with thee.
[*He gives a ring.*]
Deliver it to Madam Silvia.
She loved me well delivered it to me. 71

JULIA
It seems you loved not her, to leave her token. 72
She is dead, belike?

PROTEUS Not so. I think she lives. 73

JULIA Alas!

PROTEUS Why dost thou cry "Alas"?

JULIA I cannot choose but pity her.

PROTEUS Wherefore shouldst thou pity her?

JULIA
Because methinks that she loved you as well
As you do love your lady Silvia.
She dreams on him that has forgot her love; 80
You dote on her that cares not for your love. 81
'Tis pity love should be so contrary;
And thinking on it makes me cry "Alas!"

PROTEUS [*giving a letter*]
Well, give her that ring and therewithal 84
This letter. That's her chamber. Tell my lady
I claim the promise for her heavenly picture.
Your message done, hie home unto my chamber,
Where thou shalt find me sad and solitary. [*Exit.*]

JULIA
How many women would do such a message?
Alas, poor Proteus! Thou hast entertained
A fox to be the shepherd of thy lambs.
Alas, poor fool, why do I pity him 92
That with his very heart despiseth me?
Because he loves her, he despiseth me;
Because I love him, I must pity him.
This ring I gave him when he parted from me,
To bind him to remember my good will;
And now am I, unhappy messenger,
To plead for that which I would not obtain,
To carry that which I would have refused,
To praise his faith which I would have dispraised. 101
I am my master's true-confirmèd love,
But cannot be true servant to my master
Unless I prove false traitor to myself.
Yet will I woo for him, but yet so coldly
As, heaven it knows, I would not have him speed. 106

[*Enter*] *Silvia* [*attended*].

Gentlewoman, good day! I pray you, be my mean
To bring me where to speak with Madam Silvia. 108

SILVIA
What would you with her, if that I be she?

JULIA
If you be she, I do entreat your patience
To hear me speak the message I am sent on.

SILVIA From whom?

JULIA From my master, Sir Proteus, madam.

SILVIA Oh, he sends you for a picture?

JULIA Ay, madam.

SILVIA Ursula, bring my picture there.
[*A servant, Ursula, brings a picture.*]
Go, give your master this. Tell him from me,
One Julia, that his changing thoughts forget,
Would better fit his chamber than this shadow.

JULIA
Madam, please you peruse this letter.—
[*She offers a letter but then withdraws it.*]
Pardon me, madam, I have unadvised 121
Delivered you a paper that I should not.
[*She gives another letter.*]
This is the letter to Your Ladyship.

SILVIA
I pray thee, let me look on that again. 124

JULIA
It may not be. Good madam, pardon me.

SILVIA There, hold!
I will not look upon your master's lines.
I know they are stuffed with protestations
And full of newfound oaths, which he will break 129
As easily as I do tear his paper. [*She tears the letter.*]

JULIA [*offering the ring*]
Madam, he sends Your Ladyship this ring.

SILVIA
The more shame for him that he sends it me,
For I have heard him say a thousand times
His Julia gave it him at his departure.
Though his false finger have profaned the ring,
Mine shall not do his Julia so much wrong.

JULIA She thanks you.

SILVIA What say'st thou?

JULIA
I thank you, madam, that you tender her. 139
Poor gentlewoman! My master wrongs her much.

SILVIA Dost thou know her?

61 entertainèd taken into service **67 Witness** bear witness to **71 delivered** who gave **72 leave** part with **73 belike** perhaps. **80 She . . . that** i.e., Julia dreams on Proteus, who **81 her** i.e., Silvia **84 therewithal** with it **92 poor fool** i.e., Julia herself **101 would have** desire to have

106 speed succeed. **106.1** ***Enter Silvia*** This entrance is presumably onto the main stage, still imagined as below Silvia's window in her father's palace, where the scene has been located since the beginning of 4.2. Proteus gestures towards her window in line 85 above when he says, "That's her chamber." Silvia is perhaps on her way to confession at Friar Patrick's cell (4.3.45–6) as part of her plan of escape to Mantua with Eglamour's assistance (4.3.24–7). **108 where to** where I may **121 unadvised** inadvertently **124 that** i.e., the first letter **129 newfound** recently devised **139 tender** feel sympathetically toward

JULIA
Almost as well as I do know myself.
To think upon her woes I do protest
That I have wept a hundred several times.

SILVIA
Belike she thinks that Proteus hath forsook her?

JULIA
I think she doth, and that's her cause of sorrow.

SILVIA Is she not passing fair?

JULIA
She hath been fairer, madam, than she is.
When she did think my master loved her well,
She, in my judgment, was as fair as you;
But since she did neglect her looking glass
And threw her sun-expelling mask away,
The air hath starved the roses in her cheeks
And pinched the lily tincture of her face,
That now she is become as black as I.

SILVIA How tall was she?

JULIA
About my stature; for at Pentecost,
When all our pageants of delight were played,
Our youth got me to play the woman's part,
And I was trimmed in Madam Julia's gown,
Which servèd me as fit, by all men's judgments,
As if the garment had been made for me.
Therefore I know she is about my height.
And at that time I made her weep agood,
For I did play a lamentable part:
Madam, 'twas Ariadne, passioning
For Theseus' perjury and unjust flight;
Which I so lively acted with my tears
That my poor mistress, movèd therewithal,
Wept bitterly; and would I might be dead
If I in thought felt not her very sorrow!

SILVIA
She is beholding to thee, gentle youth.
Alas, poor lady, desolate and left!
I weep myself to think upon thy words.
Here, youth, there is my purse. [*She gives money.*] I give
thee this
For thy sweet mistress' sake, because thou lov'st her.
Farewell. [*Exit Silvia, with attendants.*]

JULIA
And she shall thank you for't, if e'er you know her—
A virtuous gentlewoman, mild and beautiful!
I hope my master's suit will be but cold,
Since she respects my mistress' love so much.
Alas, how love can trifle with itself!
Here is her picture. [*She looks at the picture.*] Let me
see, I think
If I had such a tire, this face of mine
Were full as lovely as is this of hers;
And yet the painter flattered her a little,
Unless I flatter with myself too much.
Her hair is auburn, mine is perfect yellow;
If that be all the difference in his love,
I'll get me such a colored periwig.
Her eyes are gray as glass, and so are mine.
Ay, but her forehead's low, and mine's as high.
What should it be that he respects in her
But I can make respective in myself,
If this fond Love were not a blinded god?
Come, shadow, come, and take this shadow up,
For 'tis thy rival. [*She picks up the picture.*] O thou
senseless form,
Thou shalt be worshiped, kissed, loved, and adored!
And, were there sense in his idolatry,
My substance should be statue in thy stead.
I'll use thee kindly for thy mistress' sake,
That used me so; or else, by Jove I vow,
I should have scratched out your unseeing eyes,
To make my master out of love with thee! *Exit.*

✣

5.1

Enter [*Sir*] *Eglamour.*

EGLAMOUR
The sun begins to gild the western sky,
And now it is about the very hour
That Silvia at Friar Patrick's cell should meet me.
She will not fail, for lovers break not hours
Unless it be to come before their time,
So much they spur their expedition.

[*Enter*] *Silvia.*

See where she comes.—Lady, a happy evening!

SILVIA
Amen, amen! Go on, good Eglamour,
Out at the postern by the abbey wall.
I fear I am attended by some spies.

EGLAMOUR
Fear not. The forest is not three leagues off.
If we recover that, we are sure enough. *Exeunt.*

✣

144 several different **147 passing** surpassingly **152 sun-expelling mask** mask to keep the complexion fair. (Considered more beautiful than a tan.) **155 black** of a dark complexion, tanned **157 Pentecost** Whitsuntide (seven weeks after Easter) **158 pageants of delight** delightful entertainments **159 Our youth** the youth of our village **160 trimmed** dressed up **164 agood** in earnest **166 Ariadne** daughter of Minos, King of Crete. (Ariadne, having fallen in love with one of her father's captives, Theseus, gave him a clew of thread by which he was able to find his way out of the labyrinth. He fled with her but abandoned her on the island of Naxos.) **passioning** sorrowing **172 beholding** indebted, beholden **180 cold** vain **181 my mistress'** (Julia ironically refers thus to herself, as formerly beloved by her master, Proteus.)

184 tire headdress **187 flatter with myself** (1) praise myself with flattery (2) flatter myself with deceiving hopes **192 mine's as high** i.e., my forehead's no lower than hers. (High foreheads were much admired, as was yellow hair.) **194 But . . . myself** that I cannot make worthy of regard in myself. (With wordplay on *respects / respective* in lines 193–4.) **195 fond** foolish **196 shadow . . . shadow** i.e., the mere shadow of myself . . . the picture of Silvia. (See also 4.2.120–4.) **take . . . up** (1) pick up this picture (2) oppose, accept a challenge. **197 senseless** insensible **199 sense** reason **200 My . . . stead** i.e., my real person would be the object of his veneration, his idol, instead of Silvia's mere picture.
5.1. Location: Milan. An abbey.
6 expedition haste. **9 postern** small back or side door **10 attended** followed (for hostile purposes) **12 recover** reach. **sure** safe

5.2

Enter Thurio, Proteus, [*and*] *Julia* [*disguised in page's attire*].

THURIO
Sir Proteus, what says Silvia to my suit?
PROTEUS
Oh, sir, I find her milder than she was,
And yet she takes exceptions at your person.
THURIO What, that my leg is too long?
PROTEUS No, that it is too little.
THURIO
I'll wear a boot, to make it somewhat rounder.
JULIA [*aside*]
But love will not be spurred to what it loathes.
THURIO What says she to my face?
PROTEUS She says it is a fair one.
THURIO
Nay then, the wanton lies. My face is black.
PROTEUS
But pearls are fair, and the old saying is,
Black men are pearls in beauteous ladies' eyes.
JULIA [*aside*]
'Tis true, such pearls as put out ladies' eyes,
For I had rather wink than look on them.
THURIO How likes she my discourse?
PROTEUS Ill, when you talk of war.
THURIO
But well, when I discourse of love and peace.
JULIA [*aside*]
But better, indeed, when you hold your peace.
THURIO What says she to my valor?
PROTEUS Oh, sir, she makes no doubt of that.
JULIA [*aside*]
She needs not, when she knows it cowardice.
THURIO What says she to my birth?
PROTEUS That you are well derived.
JULIA [*aside*] True; from a gentleman to a fool.
THURIO Considers she my possessions?
PROTEUS Oh, ay, and pities them.
THURIO Wherefore?
JULIA [*aside*] That such an ass should owe them.
PROTEUS That they are out by lease.

[*Enter the*] *Duke.*

JULIA Here comes the Duke.
DUKE
How now, Sir Proteus? How now, Thurio?
Which of you saw Eglamour of late?
THURIO Not I.
PROTEUS Nor I.
DUKE Saw you my daughter?
PROTEUS Neither.
DUKE Why then,
She's fled unto that peasant Valentine,
And Eglamour is in her company.
'Tis true, for Friar Laurence met them both
As he in penance wandered through the forest.
Him he knew well, and guessed that it was she,
But, being masked, he was not sure of it.
Besides, she did intend confession
At Patrick's cell this even, and there she was not.
These likelihoods confirm her flight from hence.
Therefore, I pray you, stand not to discourse,
But mount you presently and meet with me
Upon the rising of the mountain foot
That leads toward Mantua, whither they are fled.
Dispatch, sweet gentlemen, and follow me. [*Exit.*]
THURIO
Why, this it is to be a peevish girl,
That flies her fortune when it follows her.
I'll after, more to be revenged on Eglamour
Than for the love of reckless Silvia. [*Exit.*]
PROTEUS
And I will follow, more for Silvia's love
Than hate of Eglamour that goes with her. [*Exit.*]
JULIA
And I will follow, more to cross that love
Than hate for Silvia, that is gone for love. *Exit.*

✤

5.3

[*Enter*] *Silvia,* [*led by*] *Outlaws.*

FIRST OUTLAW Come, come,
Be patient. We must bring you to our captain.
SILVIA
A thousand more mischances than this one
Have learned me how to brook this patiently.
SECOND OUTLAW Come, bring her away.
FIRST OUTLAW
Where is the gentleman that was with her?
THIRD OUTLAW
Being nimble-footed, he hath outrun us,
But Moses and Valerius follow him.
Go thou with her to the west end of the wood;
There is our captain. We'll follow him that's fled.
The thicket is beset; he cannot scape.
[*Exeunt all but the First Outlaw and Silvia.*]

5.2. Location: Milan. The Duke's palace.
3 takes exceptions at finds fault with **7 spurred** incited. (With a quibble on *boot*, i.e., "riding boot," in the preceding line.) **9 fair** i.e., pale. (Beneath the seeming compliment is a suggestion of effeminacy or fair-faced deception.) **10 black** dark, tanned (as contrasted with *fair*, "light-skinned"). **12 pearls** i.e., rare and beautiful objects **13 pearls** i.e., cataracts **14 wink** close the eyes **16 Ill . . . war** i.e., (1) You upset her with frightening talk of war (2) Your absurd talk of war shows how ill-suited you are for manly pursuits. **18 hold your peace** are silent. (With quibble on *peace* in previous line.) **20 makes . . . of** has no uncertainty about. (Another deliberately ambiguous reply.) **23 derived** descended. **24 from . . . fool** (Julia plays on *derived* in another sense—"fallen away from, lowered"—than in line 23.) **26 pities** (1) shows concern for (2) despises **28 owe** own **29 out by lease** (1) rented out (2) beyond Thurio's control.

38 peasant i.e., base scoundrel **43 being masked** i.e., since Silvia was masked—perhaps with a *sun-expelling mask* (4.4.152) rather than a disguise **45 even** evening **48 presently** immediately **51 Dispatch** Make haste **52 peevish** perverse **53 flies her fortune** flees from her good fortune **55 reckless** uncaring
5.3. Location: The frontiers of Mantua. The forest.
4 learned taught. **brook** endure **6 gentleman** i.e., Sir Eglamour **11 beset** surrounded

FIRST OUTLAW
Come, I must bring you to our captain's cave.
Fear not. He bears an honorable mind
And will not use a woman lawlessly.

SILVIA
O Valentine, this I endure for thee! *Exeunt.*

5.4

Enter Valentine.

VALENTINE
How use doth breed a habit in a man!
This shadowy desert, unfrequented woods
I better brook than flourishing peopled towns.
Here can I sit alone, unseen of any,
And to the nightingale's complaining notes
Tune my distresses and record my woes.
O thou that dost inhabit in my breast,
Leave not the mansion so long tenantless,
Lest, growing ruinous, the building fall
And leave no memory of what it was!
Repair me with thy presence, Silvia;
Thou gentle nymph, cherish thy forlorn swain!
[*Shouting is heard within.*]
What halloing and what stir is this today?
These are my mates, that make their wills their law,
Have some unhappy passenger in chase.
They love me well, yet I have much to do
To keep them from uncivil outrages.
Withdraw thee, Valentine. Who's this comes here?
[*He stands aside.*]

[*Enter*] *Proteus, Silvia,* [*and*] *Julia* [*disguised as Sebastian*].

PROTEUS
Madam, this service I have done for you—
Though you respect not aught your servant doth—
To hazard life and rescue you from him
That would have forced your honor and your love:
Vouchsafe me for my meed but one fair look;
A smaller boon than this I cannot beg,
And less than this, I am sure, you cannot give.

VALENTINE [*aside*]
How like a dream is this I see and hear!
Love, lend me patience to forbear awhile.

SILVIA
Oh, miserable, unhappy that I am!

PROTEUS
Unhappy were you, madam, ere I came;
But by my coming I have made you happy.

SILVIA
By thy approach thou mak'st me most unhappy.

JULIA [*aside*]
And me, when he approacheth to your presence.

SILVIA
Had I been seizèd by a hungry lion,
I would have been a breakfast to the beast
Rather than have false Proteus rescue me.
Oh, heaven be judge how I love Valentine,
Whose life's as tender to me as my soul!
And full as much—for more there cannot be—
I do detest false, perjured Proteus.
Therefore begone. Solicit me no more.

PROTEUS
What dangerous action, stood it next to death,
Would I not undergo for one calm look?
Oh, 'tis the curse in love, and still approved,
When women cannot love where they're beloved!

SILVIA
When Proteus cannot love where he's beloved.
Read over Julia's heart, thy first, best love,
For whose dear sake thou didst then rend thy faith
Into a thousand oaths, and all those oaths
Descended into perjury, to love me.
Thou hast no faith left now, unless thou'dst two,
And that's far worse than none. Better have none
Than plural faith, which is too much by one.
Thou counterfeit to thy true friend!

PROTEUS
In love
Who respects friend?

SILVIA
All men but Proteus.

PROTEUS
Nay, if the gentle spirit of moving words
Can no way change you to a milder form,
I'll woo you like a soldier, at arms' end,
And love you 'gainst the nature of love—force ye.

SILVIA
O heaven!

PROTEUS [*assailing her*] I'll force thee yield to my desire.

VALENTINE [*coming forward*]
Ruffian, let go that rude, uncivil touch,
Thou friend of an ill fashion!

PROTEUS
Valentine!

VALENTINE
Thou common friend, that's without faith or love!
For such is a friend now. Treacherous man,
Thou hast beguiled my hopes. Naught but mine eye
Could have persuaded me. Now I dare not say
I have one friend alive; thou wouldst disprove me.
Who should be trusted, when one's right hand
Is perjured to the bosom? Proteus,
I am sorry I must never trust thee more,
But count the world a stranger for thy sake.
The private wound is deepest. Oh, time most accurst,
'Mongst all foes that a friend should be the worst!

PROTEUS
My shame and guilt confounds me.
Forgive me, Valentine. If hearty sorrow
Be a sufficient ransom for offense,

5.4. Location: The forest.
1 use custom **2 desert** deserted region **6 record** sing **15 Have** Who have. **unhappy passenger** unlucky traveler **20 respect** heed **23 meed** reward. **fair** kind **31 approach** amorous advances

37 tender dear **42 undergo** undertake. **calm** gentle, kind **43 still approved** continually reaffirmed by experience **47 rend** tear **50 thou'dst** thou hast **54 respects** takes into consideration **57 arms' end** sword's point. (With bawdy suggestion.) **61 fashion** kind, sort. **62 common** vulgar, superficial

I tender't here. I do as truly suffer
As e'er I did commit.

VALENTINE Then I am paid,
And once again I do receive thee honest.
Who by repentance is not satisfied
Is nor of heaven nor earth. For these are pleased;
By penitence th'Eternal's wrath's appeased.
And, that my love may appear plain and free,
All that was mine in Silvia I give thee.

JULIA Oh, me unhappy! *[She swoons.]*

PROTEUS Look to the boy.

VALENTINE Why, boy! Why, wag! How now? What's the matter? Look up. Speak.

JULIA *[recovering]* Oh, good sir, my master charged me to deliver a ring to Madam Silvia, which, out of my neglect, was never done.

PROTEUS
Where is that ring, boy?

JULIA *[giving her own ring]* Here 'tis. This is it.

PROTEUS How? Let me see.
Why, this is the ring I gave to Julia.

JULIA
Oh, cry you mercy, sir, I have mistook.
This is the ring you sent to Silvia.
[She offers another ring.]

PROTEUS
But how cam'st thou by this ring? At my depart
I gave this unto Julia.

JULIA
And Julia herself did give it me;
And Julia herself hath brought it hither.
[She reveals her identity.]

PROTEUS How? Julia?

JULIA
Behold her that gave aim to all thy oaths
And entertained 'em deeply in her heart.
How oft hast thou with perjury cleft the root!
Oh, Proteus, let this habit make thee blush!
Be thou ashamed that I have took upon me
Such an immodest raiment, if shame live
In a disguise of love.
It is the lesser blot, modesty finds,
Women to change their shapes than men their minds.

PROTEUS
Than men their minds? 'Tis true. Oh, heaven! Were man
But constant, he were perfect. That one error
Fills him with faults, makes him run through all th'sins;
Inconstancy falls off ere it begins.
What is in Silvia's face but I may spy
More fresh in Julia's, with a constant eye?

VALENTINE
Come, come, a hand from either.
Let me be blest to make this happy close;
'Twere pity two such friends should be long foes.
[Proteus and Julia join hands.]

PROTEUS
Bear witness, heaven, I have my wish forever.

JULIA And I mine.

[Enter the] Duke *[and]* Thurio, *[led by]* Outlaws.

OUTLAWS A prize, a prize, a prize!

VALENTINE
Forbear, forbear, I say! It is my lord the Duke.
[The Duke and Thurio are released.]
Your Grace is welcome to a man disgraced,
Banishèd Valentine.

DUKE Sir Valentine!

THURIO *[advancing]*
Yonder is Silvia, and Silvia's mine.

VALENTINE *[drawing his sword]*
Thurio, give back, or else embrace thy death.
Come not within the measure of my wrath.
Do not name Silvia thine; if once again,
Verona shall not hold thee. Here she stands.
Take but possession of her with a touch;
I dare thee but to breathe upon my love.

THURIO
Sir Valentine, I care not for her, I.
I hold him but a fool that will endanger
His body for a girl that loves him not.
I claim her not, and therefore she is thine.

DUKE
The more degenerate and base art thou,
To make such means for her as thou hast done
And leave her on such slight conditions.—
Now, by the honor of my ancestry,
I do applaud thy spirit, Valentine,
And think thee worthy of an empress' love.
Know then I here forget all former griefs,
Cancel all grudge, repeal thee home again,
Plead a new state in thy unrivaled merit,
To which I thus subscribe: Sir Valentine,
Thou art a gentleman and well derived.
Take thou thy Silvia, for thou hast deserved her.

VALENTINE
I thank Your Grace. The gift hath made me happy.
I now beseech you, for your daughter's sake,
To grant one boon that I shall ask of you.

DUKE
I grant it, for thine own, whate'er it be.

76 tender't offer it **77 commit** sin. **78 receive** believe, acknowledge **80 nor of** neither of. **these** i.e., heaven and earth **82 love** friendship **86 wag** (A term of endearment for a youth.) **94 cry you mercy** I beg your pardon. **100 gave aim to** was the object of **103 habit** i.e., page's costume **105–6 if shame . . . love** if a disguise undertaken for love can be thought shameful; or, if one who feigns love (such as Proteus) can feel shame.

112 Inconstancy . . . begins i.e., inconstant love falls away from loving almost before it has even begun. **114 constant** steady, loyal **116 close** union, conclusion **125 give back** stand back **126 measure** reach **128 Verona** (Again, probably an error for *Milan;* see 3.1.81.) **hold thee** keep you safe. **136 means** exertions **137 on . . . conditions** for such a paltry reason. **141 griefs** grievances **142 repeal** recall **143 Plead . . . state** argue or maintain a new state of affairs

VALENTINE

These banished men, that I have kept withal,
Are men endued with worthy qualities.
Forgive them what they have committed here,
And let them be recalled from their exile.
They are reformèd, civil, full of good,
And fit for great employment, worthy lord.

DUKE

Thou hast prevailed. I pardon them and thee.
Dispose of them as thou know'st their deserts.
Come, let us go. We will include all jars
With triumphs, mirth, and rare solemnity.

VALENTINE

And, as we walk along, I dare be bold
With our discourse to make Your Grace to smile.
What think you of this page, my lord?

DUKE

I think the boy hath grace in him. He blushes.

VALENTINE

I warrant you, my lord, more grace than boy.

DUKE What mean you by that saying?

VALENTINE

Please you, I'll tell you as we pass along,
That you will wonder what hath fortunèd.
Come, Proteus, 'tis your penance but to hear
The story of your loves discoverèd.
That done, our day of marriage shall be yours;
One feast, one house, one mutual happiness.

Exeunt.

151 kept withal lived with **159 include all jars** conclude all discords **160 triumphs** festive celebrations. **rare solemnity** marvelous festivity.

168 That . . . fortunèd in such a way that you will marvel at what has happened. **170 discoverèd** declared, disclosed.

The Taming of the Shrew

The Taming of the Shrew (c. 1592–1594) shows Shakespeare's comic genius at its best. At the same time, it shares with his other early plays an anticipation of the directions that his genius is to take in *Much Ado about Nothing* and other comedies of the later 1590s. By skillfully juxtaposing two plots and an induction, or framing plot, it offers contrasting views on the battle of the sexes. This debate on the nature of the love relationship will continue through many later comedies. The play also adroitly manipulates the device of mistaken identity, as in *The Comedy of Errors,* inverting appearance and reality, dreaming and waking, and the master-servant relationship in order to create a transformed Saturnalian world anticipating that of *A Midsummer Night's Dream* and *Twelfth Night*.

The induction sets up the theme of illusion, using an old motif known as "The Sleeper Awakened" (as found, for example, in *The Arabian Nights*). This device frames the main action of the play, giving to it an added perspective. *The Taming of the Shrew* purports, in fact, to be a play within a play, an entertainment devised by a witty nobleman as a practical joke on a drunken tinker, Christopher Sly. The jest is to convince Sly that he is not Sly at all, but an aristocrat suffering delusions. Outlandishly dressed in new finery, Sly is invited to witness a play from the gallery over the stage. In a rendition called *The Taming of a Shrew* (printed in 1594 and now generally thought to be taken from an earlier version of Shakespeare's play, employing a good deal of conscious originality along with some literary borrowing and even plagiarism), the framing plot concludes by actually putting Sly back out on the street in front of the alehouse where he was found. He awakes, recalls the play as a dream, and proposes to put the vision to good use by taming his own wife. Whether this ending reflects an epilogue now lost from the text of Shakespeare's play cannot be said, but it does reinforce the idea of the play as Sly's fantasy. Like Puck at the end of *A Midsummer Night's Dream,* urging us to dismiss what we have seen as the product of our own slumbering, Sly continually reminds us that the play is only an illusion or shadow.

With repeated daring, Shakespeare calls attention to the contrived nature of his artifact, the play. When, for example, Sly is finally convinced that he is, in fact, a noble lord recovering from madness and lustily proposes to hasten off to bed with his long-neglected wife, we are comically aware that the "wife" is an impostor, a young page in disguise. Yet this counterfeiting of roles is no more unreal than the employment of Elizabethan boy-actors for the parts of Katharina and Bianca in the "real" play. As we watch Sly watching a play, levels of meaning intersect in this evocative fashion. Again, the paintings offered to Sly by his new attendants call attention to art's ability to confound illusion and reality. In one painting, Cytherea is hidden by reeds "Which seem to move and wanton with her breath, / Even as the waving sedges play wi'th'wind," and, in another painting, Io appears "As lively painted as the deed was done" (Induction, 2.50–6). Sly's function, then, is that of the naive observer who inverts illusion and reality in his mind, concluding that his whole previous life of tinkers and alehouses and Cicely Hackets has been unreal. As his attendants explain to him, "These fifteen years you have been in a dream, / Or when you waked, so waked as if you slept." We as audience laugh at Sly's naiveté, and yet we, too, are moved and even transformed by an artistic vision that we know to be illusory.

Like Sly, many characters in the main action of the play are persuaded, or contrive, to be what they are not. Lucentio and Tranio exchange roles of master and servant. Bianca's supposed tutors are, in fact, her wooers, using their lessons to disguise messages of love. Katharina is prevailed upon by her husband, Petruchio, to declare that the sun is the moon and that an old gentleman (Vincentio) is a fair young maiden. Vincentio is publicly informed that he is an impostor and that the "real" Vincentio (the Pedant) is at that very moment looking at him out of the window of his son Lucentio's house. This last ruse does not fool the real Vincentio, but it nearly succeeds in fooling everyone else. Baptista Minola is about to commit Vincentio to jail for the infamous slander of asserting that the supposed Lucentio is only a servant in disguise. Vincentio, as the newly arrived stranger, is able to see matters as they really are, but the dwellers of Padua have grown so accustomed to the mad and improbable fictions of their life that they are not easily awakened to reality.

Such illusions have the effect of challenging the norms of social order. If a servant can playact at being the master so successfully that no one can tell the difference, are we to understand that social distinctions are mere arbitrary constructions? If Sly can become a lord by wearing the right clothes and speaking blank verse (as in the Induction, 2.68 and following), might audience members similarly raise their status? The theater promotes such skeptical questions, since it is in the business of dressing actors up as persons of whatever rank the playwright chooses. Surely one of the pleasures of theatrical performance for Elizabethan audiences was that of dreaming of social advancement or social control. At the same time, this theater treats such a liberating experience as holiday or farcical nightmare, and as Saturnalian escape; we realize as audience that we will return to the norms of our daily lives after having visited an imagined space where anything is possible.

Shakespeare multiplies his devices of illusion by combining two entirely distinct plots, each concerned, at least in part, with the comic inversion of appearance and reality: the shrew-taming plot involving Petruchio and Kate, and the more conventional romantic plot involving Lucentio and Bianca. The latter plot is derived from the *Supposes* of George Gascoigne, a play first presented at Gray's Inn (one of the Inns of Court) in 1566, as translated from Ariosto's neoclassical comedy, *I Suppositi,* 1509. (Ariosto's work, in turn, was based upon Terence's *Eunuchus* and Plautus's *Captivi.*) The "Supposes" are mistaken identities or misunderstandings, the kind of hilarious farcical mix-ups with which Shakespeare had already experimented in *The Comedy of Errors.* Shakespeare has, as usual, both romanticized his source and moralized it in a characteristically English way. The heroine, who in the Roman comedy of Plautus and Terence would have been a courtesan, and who in *Supposes* is made pregnant by her clandestine lover, remains thoroughly chaste in Shakespeare's comedy. Consequently, she has no need for a pander, or go-between, such as the bawdy Duenna or Nurse of *Supposes.* The satire directed at the heroine's unwelcome old wooer Gremio is far less savage than in *Supposes,* where the "pantaloon," Dr. Cleander, is a villainously corrupt lawyer epitomizing the depravity of "respectable" society. Despite Shakespeare's modifications, however, the basic plot remains an effort to foil parental authority. The young lovers, choosing each other for romantic reasons, must fend off the materialistic calculations of their parents.

In a stock situation of this sort, the character types are also conventional. Gremio, the aged wealthy wooer, is actually labeled a "pantaloon" in the text (3.1.36–7) to stress his neoclassical ancestry. (Lean and foolish old wooers of this sort were customarily dressed in pantaloons, slippers, and spectacles on the Italian stage.) Gremio is typically "the graybeard," and Baptista Minola is "the narrow-prying father" (3.2.145–6). Even though Shakespeare renders these characters far less unattractive than in *Supposes,* their worldly behavior still invites reprisal from the young. Since Baptista Minola insists on selling his daughter Bianca to the highest bidder, it is fitting that her wealthiest suitor (the supposed Lucentio) should turn out in the end to be a penniless servant (Tranio) disguised as a man of affluence and position. In his traditional role as the clever servant of neoclassical comedy, Tranio skillfully apes the mannerisms of respectable society. He can deal in the mere surfaces—clothes or reputation—out of which a man's social importance is created, and can even furnish himself with a rich father. Gremio and Baptista deserve to be foiled, because they accept the illusion of respectability as real.

Even the romantic lovers of this borrowed plot are largely conventional. To be sure, Shakespeare emphasizes their virtuous qualities and their sincerity. He adds Hortensio (not in *Supposes*) to provide Lucentio with a genuine, if foolish, rival and Bianca with two wooers closer to her age than old Gremio. Lucentio and Bianca deserve their romantic triumph; they are self-possessed, witty, and steadfast to each other. Yet we know very little about them, nor have they seen deeply into each other. Lucentio's love talk is laden with conventional images in praise of Bianca's dark eyes and scarlet lips. At the play's end, he discovers, to his surprise, that she can be willful, even disobedient. Has her appearance of virtue concealed something from him and from us? Because the relationship between these lovers is superficial, they are appropriately destined to a superficial marriage as well. The passive Bianca becomes the proud and defiant wife.

By contrast, Petruchio and Kate are the more interesting lovers, whose courtship involves mutual self-discovery. Admittedly, we must not overstate the case. Especially at first, these lovers are also stock types: the shrew tamer and his proverbially shrewish wife. (The word *shrew,* originally signifying a wicked or malignant man, often applied to the devil or to a malignant planet, had come to mean a scolding or turbulent wife.) Although Shakespeare seems not to have used any single source for this plot, he was well acquainted with crude, misogynistic stories demonstrating the need for putting women in their place. In a ballad called *A Merry Jest of a Shrewd and Curst Wife, Lapped in Morel's Skin* (printed c. 1550), for example, the husband tames his shrewish wife by flaying her bloody with birch rods and then wrapping her in the freshly salted skin of a plow horse named Morel. (This shrewish wife, like Kate, has an obedient and gentle younger sister who is their father's favorite.) Other features of Shakespeare's plot can be found in similar tales: the tailor scolded for devising a gown of outlandish fashion (Gerard Legh's *Accidence of Armory,* 1562), the wife obliged to agree with her husband's assertion of some patent falsehood (Don Juan Manuel's *El Conde Lucanor,* c. 1335), and the three husbands' wager on their wives' obedience (*The Book of the Knight of La Tour-Landry,* printed 1484). In the raw spirit of this sexist tradition, so unlike the refined Italianate sentiment of his other plot, Shakespeare introduces Petruchio as a man of reckless bravado who is ready to marry the ugliest or sharpest-tongued woman alive so long as she is rich. However much he may be later attracted by Kate's fiery spirit, his first attraction to her is crassly financial. Kate is, moreover, a troublesomely defiant young woman at first, described by the men who know her as "intolerable curst / And shrewd and froward," and aggressive in her bullying of Bianca. She and Petruchio meet as grotesque comic counterparts.

At the play's end, the traditional pattern of male dominance and female acquiescence is still prominent. Kate is allowed food, sleep, and sex only when she yields to a socially ordained patriarchal framework in which a husband is the princely ruler of his wife. Kate is not like the young heroines of many other Shakespearean comedies (Portia in *The Merchant of Venice* and Rosalind in *As You Like It,* for example) who wittily guide their immature and overly romantic young men toward a pragmatic view of love and marriage; in this play, Kate is the one who must be mastered by the self-assured male. Her shrewishness is an open threat to male control in the marital bond, and, accordingly, the play's comic finale celebrates containment of this threat in her, along with a sharp reminder of the resistance to be endured by other husbands who have failed to tame their shrews.

Within this male-oriented frame of reference, however, Petruchio and Kate are surprisingly like Benedick and Beatrice of *Much Ado about Nothing*. Petruchio, for all his rant, is increasingly drawn to Kate by her spirit. As wit-combatants, they are worthy of one another's enmity—or love. No one else in the play is a fit match for either of them. Kate, too, is attracted to Petruchio, despite her war of words. Her anger is part defensive protection, part testing of his sincerity. If she is contemptuous of the wooers she has seen till now, she has good reason to be. We share her condescension toward the aged Gremio or the laughably inept Hortensio. She rightly fears that her father wishes to dispose of her so that he may auction off Bianca to the wealthiest competitor. Kate's jaded view of such marriage brokering is entirely defensible. Not surprisingly, she first views Petruchio, whose professed intentions are far from reassuring, as another mere adventurer in love. She is impressed by his "line" in wooing her but needs to test his constancy and sincerity. Marriage for her would be a serious step, since social convention allows a dominant role for the husband; can she hope that she and Petruchio will arrive at some sort of understanding in which her role as wife and partner will be an honorable one? She puts down most men with a shrewish manner that challenges their very masculinity; Petruchio is the first man to counter her wit and energy with his own. Can she learn to live with this man?

Kate's rejection of men has not left her very happy, however genuine her disdain is for most of those who have come to woo. Petruchio's "schooling" can be seen as addressing that unhappiness, even if his purpose is unremittingly masculine in its assumption that a rebellious wife has to be "tamed" as one would tame a hawk. Having wooed and partly won her, Petruchio tests her with his late arrival at the marriage, his unconventional dress, and his crossing all her desires. Like the hawk-tamer, Petruchio uses harsh physical means, including deprivation of food and drink. He treats Kate as his chattle, and never wavers in his certainty that he is right to do so. Other males applaud his success and wish only to follow his example. The resolution is in these terms manifestly more sexist than in *Much Ado About Nothing*; it is as though Shakespeare works his way through the problems of sexual conflict from this early, very masculine play to a more complex and mutual accommodation in his later comedies.

At the same time, it is possible to see *The Taming of the Shrew* as a play in which a genuine accommodation is reached, even if it is on the man's terms with the woman being given no choice. The play may encourage the view that Petruchio's treatment of Kate, no matter how temporarily harsh, is ultimately benign in its intent. Petruchio, by his outlandish behavior of overturning tables and scolding servants, shows Kate an ugly picture of what her refractoriness is like. He succeeds by insisting on what, arguably, she may desire too: a well- defined relationship tempered by mutual respect and love. In this interpretation, Kate may gain something by the play's end. Her closing speech, with its fine blend of irony and self-conscious hyperbole, together with its seriousness of concern, can be read as expressing the way in which her independence of spirit and her newfound acceptance of a domestic rule are successfully fused, enabling her to gain widespread applause instead of opprobrium.

This is by no means the only way of reading the final scene, as modern productions often make clear: Kate emerges in various stage productions as more or less contented, or as simply resigned, or as cruelly brainwashed, or as only playing the role of obedient wife to get what she wants. The uncertainty of interpretation is one of the great pleasures and challenges today, in a world for which ideas about marriage have manifestly shifted since Shakespeare wrote. Even so, the play offers common ground in its appreciation for the seriousness of the issue and in its wonderful transparency as a text that offers itself up for rival interpretations.

The Taming of the Shrew

[*Dramatis Personae*

CHRISTOPHER SLY, *a tinker and beggar,* HOSTESS *of an alehouse,* A LORD, A PAGE, SERVANTS, HUNTSMEN, PLAYERS,	*Persons in the Induction*

BAPTISTA, *a rich gentleman of Padua*
KATHARINA, *the shrew, also called Katharine and Kate, Baptista's elder daughter*
BIANCA, *Baptista's younger daughter*

PETRUCHIO, *a gentleman of Verona, suitor to Katharina*
GRUMIO, *Petruchio's servant*
CURTIS, NATHANIEL, PHILIP, JOSEPH, NICHOLAS, PETER, *and other servants of Petruchio*

GREMIO, *elderly suitor to Bianca*
HORTENSIO, *suitor to Bianca*
LUCENTIO, *son of Vincentio, in love with Bianca*
TRANIO, *Lucentio's servant*
BIONDELLO, *Lucentio's servant*
VINCENTIO, *a gentleman of Pisa*
A PEDANT *(or Merchant) of Mantua*
A WIDOW, *courted by Hortensio*

A TAILOR
A HABERDASHER
AN OFFICER
Other Servants of Baptista and Lucentio

SCENE: *Padua, and Petruchio's country house in Italy; the Induction is located in the countryside and at a Lord's house in England*]

[Induction.1]

Enter Beggar (Christopher Sly) and Hostess.

SLY I'll feeze you, in faith.

HOSTESS A pair of stocks, you rogue!

SLY You're a baggage. The Slys are no rogues. Look in the chronicles; we came in with Richard Conqueror. Therefore *paucas pallabris,* let the world slide. Sessa!

HOSTESS You will not pay for the glasses you have burst?

SLY No, not a denier. Go by, Saint Jeronimy, go to thy cold bed and warm thee.

HOSTESS I know my remedy; I must go fetch the thirdborough. [*Exit.*]

SLY Third, or fourth, or fifth borough, I'll answer him by law. I'll not budge an inch, boy. Let him come, and kindly. *Falls asleep.*

Wind horns [*within*]. *Enter a Lord from hunting, with his train.*

LORD
Huntsman, I charge thee, tender well my hounds.
Breathe Merriman—the poor cur is embossed—
And couple Clowder with the deep-mouthed brach.
Saw'st thou not, boy, how Silver made it good
At the hedge corner, in the coldest fault?

Induction.1. Location: Before an alehouse and, subsequently, before the Lord's house nearby. (See lines 75, 135.)
1 feeze you i.e., fix you, get even with you **2 A . . . stocks** i.e., I'll have you put in the stocks **3 baggage** contemptible woman or prostitute. **4 Richard** (Sly's mistake for "William.") **5 *paucas pallabris*** i.e., *pocas palabras,* "few words." (Spanish.) **Sessa** (Of doubtful meaning; perhaps "be quiet," "cease," or "let it go.") **8 denier** French copper coin of little value. **Go . . . Jeronimy** (Sly's variation of an often quoted line from Kyd's *The Spanish Tragedy,* urging caution.) **8–9 go . . . thee** (Perhaps a proverb; see *King Lear,* 3.4.46–7.)

10–11 thirdborough constable. **12 Third** (Sly shows his ignorance; the *third* in "thirdborough" derives from the Old English word *frith,* "peace.") **13 by law** in the law courts. **14 kindly** welcome. (Said ironically.) **14.1 *Wind*** Blow **14.2 *train*** retinue. **15 tender** care for **16 Breathe Merriman** Give the dog Merriman time to recover its breath. **embossed** foaming at the mouth from exhaustion **17 couple** leash together. **deep-mouthed brach** bitch hound with the deep baying voice. **18 made it good** i.e., picked up the lost scent **19 in the coldest fault** when the scent was lost by a *fault* or break in the scent.

I would not lose the dog for twenty pound.

FIRST HUNTSMAN
Why, Bellman is as good as he, my lord.
He cried upon it at the merest loss,
And twice today picked out the dullest scent.
Trust me, I take him for the better dog.

LORD
Thou art a fool. If Echo were as fleet,
I would esteem him worth a dozen such.
But sup them well and look unto them all.
Tomorrow I intend to hunt again.

FIRST HUNTSMAN I will, my lord.

LORD [*seeing Sly*]
What's here? One dead, or drunk? See, doth he
breathe?

SECOND HUNTSMAN [*examining Sly*]
He breathes, my lord. Were he not warmed with ale,
This were a bed but cold to sleep so soundly.

LORD
Oh, monstrous beast, how like a swine he lies!
Grim death, how foul and loathsome is thine image!
Sirs, I will practice on this drunken man.
What think you, if he were conveyed to bed,
Wrapped in sweet clothes, rings put upon his fingers,
A most delicious banquet by his bed,
And brave attendants near him when he wakes,
Would not the beggar then forget himself?

FIRST HUNTSMAN
Believe me, lord, I think he cannot choose.

SECOND HUNTSMAN
It would seem strange unto him when he waked.

LORD
Even as a flatt'ring dream or worthless fancy.
Then take him up, and manage well the jest.
Carry him gently to my fairest chamber,
And hang it round with all my wanton pictures.
Balm his foul head in warm distillèd waters,
And burn sweet wood to make the lodging sweet.
Procure me music ready when he wakes,
To make a dulcet and a heavenly sound.
And if he chance to speak, be ready straight,
And with a low submissive reverence
Say, "What is it Your Honor will command?"
Let one attend him with a silver basin
Full of rosewater and bestrewed with flowers;
Another bear the ewer, the third a diaper,
And say, "Will 't please Your Lordship cool your
hands?"
Someone be ready with a costly suit,
And ask him what apparel he will wear;
Another tell him of his hounds and horse,
And that his lady mourns at his disease.
Persuade him that he hath been lunatic,
And when he says he is, say that he dreams,
For he is nothing but a mighty lord.
This do, and do it kindly, gentle sirs.
It will be pastime passing excellent,
If it be husbanded with modesty.

FIRST HUNTSMAN
My lord, I warrant you we will play our part
As he shall think by our true diligence
He is no less than what we say he is.

LORD
Take him up gently, and to bed with him,
And each one to his office when he wakes.
[*Some bear out Sly.*] *Sound trumpets* [*within*].
Sirrah, go see what trumpet 'tis that sounds.
[*Exit a Servingman.*]
Belike some noble gentleman that means,
Traveling some journey, to repose him here.

Enter [*a*] *Servingman.*

How now? Who is it?

SERVINGMAN An't please Your Honor, players
That offer service to Your Lordship.

Enter Players.

LORD
Bid them come near.—Now, fellows, you are welcome.

PLAYERS We thank Your Honor.

LORD
Do you intend to stay with me tonight?

FIRST PLAYER
So please Your Lordship to accept our duty.

LORD
With all my heart. This fellow I remember
Since once he played a farmer's eldest son.—
'Twas where you wooed the gentlewoman so well.
I have forgot your name, but sure that part
Was aptly fitted and naturally performed.

SECOND PLAYER
I think 'twas Soto that Your Honor means.

LORD
'Tis very true. Thou didst it excellent.
Well, you are come to me in happy time,
The rather for I have some sport in hand
Wherein your cunning can assist me much.
There is a lord will hear you play tonight.
But I am doubtful of your modesties,
Lest, overeyeing of his odd behavior—
For yet His Honor never heard a play—
You break into some merry passion

22 cried . . . loss bayed to signal his recovery of the scent after it had been completely lost **27 sup them well** feed them a good supper **34 image** likeness (since sleep was regarded as a likeness of death). **35 practice on** play a joke on **37 sweet** perfumed **38 banquet** light repast **39 brave** finely arrayed **41 cannot choose** is bound to. **43 fancy** flight of imagination. **47 Balm** Bathe, anoint **50 dulcet** melodious **51 straight** at once **52 reverence** bow **56 ewer** jug, pitcher. **diaper** towel **60 horse** horses **61 disease** i.e., mental derangement.

63 when . . . is i.e., when he says he must be mad indeed. (The *is* is stressed.) **65 kindly** naturally (and thus persuasively). **gentle** kind **66 passing** surpassingly **67 husbanded with modesty** managed with decorum. **69 As** so that. **by** as a result of **72 office** duty **73 Sirrah** (Usual form of address to inferiors.) **74 Belike** Perhaps **76 An't** If it **81 So please** If it please. **duty** expression of respect and dutiful service. **89 happy** opportune **90 The rather for** the more so since **91 cunning** professional skill **93 doubtful** apprehensive. **modesties** discretion, self-control **94 overeyeing of** witnessing **96 merry passion** outburst of laughter

And so offend him; for I tell you, sirs,
If you should smile, he grows impatient.

FIRST PLAYER
Fear not, my lord, we can contain ourselves,
Were he the veriest antic in the world.

LORD [*to a Servingman*]
Go, sirrah, take them to the buttery,
And give them friendly welcome every one.
Let them want nothing that my house affords.
Exit one with the Players.
Sirrah, go you to Barthol'mew my page,
And see him dressed in all suits like a lady.
That done, conduct him to the drunkard's chamber,
And call him "madam," do him obeisance.
Tell him from me, as he will win my love,
He bear himself with honorable action
Such as he hath observed in noble ladies
Unto their lords by them accomplishèd.
Such duty to the drunkard let him do
With soft low tongue and lowly courtesy,
And say, "What is't Your Honor will command,
Wherein your lady and your humble wife
May show her duty and make known her love?"
And then with kind embracements, tempting kisses,
And with declining head into his bosom,
Bid him shed tears, as being overjoyed
To see her noble lord restored to health,
Who for this seven years hath esteemèd him
No better than a poor and loathsome beggar.
And if the boy have not a woman's gift
To rain a shower of commanded tears,
An onion will do well for such a shift,
Which in a napkin being close conveyed
Shall in despite enforce a watery eye.
See this dispatched with all the haste thou canst.
Anon I'll give thee more instructions.
Exit a Servingman.
I know the boy will well usurp the grace,
Voice, gait, and action of a gentlewoman.
I long to hear him call the drunkard husband,
And how my men will stay themselves from laughter
When they do homage to this simple peasant.
I'll in to counsel them. Haply my presence
May well abate the overmerry spleen
Which otherwise would grow into extremes.
[*Exeunt.*]

✤

100 veriest antic oddest buffoon or eccentric **101 buttery** pantry, or a room for storing liquor (in butts) and other provisions **103 want** lack **105 in all suits** in every detail. (With a pun on *suits* of clothes.) **107 do him obeisance** show him dutiful respect. **108 him** i.e., the page Bartholomew. **as he will** if he wishes to **111 by them accomplishèd** performed by the ladies. **121 him** himself **125 shift** purpose **126 napkin** handkerchief. **close** secretly **127 in despite** i.e., notwithstanding a natural inclination to laugh rather than cry **129 Anon** Soon **130 usurp** assume **133 And how** i.e., and to see how **135 I'll in** I'll go in **136 spleen** mood. (The spleen was the supposed seat of laughter and anger.)

[Induction.2]

Enter aloft the drunkard [*Sly*], *with attendants; some with apparel, basin, and ewer and other appurtenances; and Lord.*

SLY For God's sake, a pot of small ale.

FIRST SERVINGMAN
Will't please Your Lordship drink a cup of sack?

SECOND SERVINGMAN
Will't please Your Honor taste of these conserves?

THIRD SERVINGMAN
What raiment will Your Honor wear today?

SLY I am Christophero Sly. Call not me "Honor" nor "Lordship." I ne'er drank sack in my life; and if you give me any conserves, give me conserves of beef. Ne'er ask me what raiment I'll wear, for I have no more doublets than backs, no more stockings than legs, nor no more shoes than feet—nay, sometimes more feet than shoes, or such shoes as my toes look through the overleather.

LORD
Heaven cease this idle humor in Your Honor!
Oh, that a mighty man of such descent,
Of such possessions and so high esteem,
Should be infusèd with so foul a spirit!

SLY What, would you make me mad? Am not I Christopher Sly, old Sly's son of Burton-heath, by birth a peddler, by education a cardmaker, by transmutation a bearherd, and now by present profession a tinker? Ask Marian Hacket, the fat alewife of Wincot, if she know me not. If she say I am not fourteen pence on the score for sheer ale, score me up for the lyingest knave in Christendom. What, I am not bestraught: here's—

THIRD SERVINGMAN
Oh, this it is that makes your lady mourn!

SECOND SERVINGMAN
Oh, this is it that makes your servants droop!

LORD
Hence comes it that your kindred shuns your house,
As beaten hence by your strange lunacy.
Oh, noble lord, bethink thee of thy birth.
Call home thy ancient thoughts from banishment,
And banish hence these abject lowly dreams.
Look how thy servants do attend on thee,
Each in his office ready at thy beck.

Induction.2. Location: A bedchamber in the Lord's house.
0.1 *aloft* i.e., in the gallery over the rear facade of the stage **1 small** weak (and therefore cheap) **2 sack** sweet Spanish wine (suited for a gentleman to drink). **3 conserves** candied fruit. **7 conserves of beef** preserved (salted) beef. **9 doublets** men's jackets **11 as** that **12 overleather** upper leather of the shoe. **13 idle humor** foolish whim **18 Burton-heath** (Perhaps Barton on the Heath, about sixteen miles from Stratford, the home of Shakespeare's aunt.) **19 cardmaker** maker of cards or combs used to prepare wool for spinning **20 bearherd** keeper of a performing bear. **tinker** pot mender. **21 alewife** woman who keeps an alehouse. **Wincot** small village about four miles from Stratford. (The parish register shows that there were Hackets living there in 1591.) **22–3 on the score** in debt (since such reckonings were originally notched or scored on a stick) **23 sheer** nothing but. **score me up for** reckon me to be **24 bestraught** distracted **29 As** as if **31 ancient** former **34 beck** nod.

Wilt thou have music? Hark, Apollo plays, *Music.*
And twenty cagèd nightingales do sing.
Or wilt thou sleep? We'll have thee to a couch,
Softer and sweeter than the lustful bed
On purpose trimmed up for Semiramis.
Say thou wilt walk; we will bestrew the ground.
Or wilt thou ride? Thy horses shall be trapped,
Their harness studded all with gold and pearl.
Dost thou love hawking? Thou hast hawks will soar
Above the morning lark. Or wilt thou hunt?
Thy hounds shall make the welkin answer them
And fetch shrill echoes from the hollow earth.

FIRST SERVINGMAN
Say thou wilt course, thy greyhounds are as swift
As breathèd stags, ay, fleeter than the roe.

SECOND SERVINGMAN
Dost thou love pictures? We will fetch thee straight
Adonis painted by a running brook,
And Cytherea all in sedges hid,
Which seem to move and wanton with her breath,
Even as the waving sedges play wi'th'wind.

LORD
We'll show thee Io as she was a maid,
And how she was beguilèd and surprised,
As lively painted as the deed was done.

THIRD SERVINGMAN
Or Daphne roaming through a thorny wood,
Scratching her legs that one shall swear she bleeds,
And at that sight shall sad Apollo weep,
So workmanly the blood and tears are drawn.

LORD
Thou art a lord, and nothing but a lord.
Thou hast a lady far more beautiful
Than any woman in this waning age.

FIRST SERVINGMAN
And till the tears that she hath shed for thee
Like envious floods o'errun her lovely face,
She was the fairest creature in the world;
And yet she is inferior to none.

SLY
Am I a lord? And have I such a lady?
Or do I dream? Or have I dreamed till now?
I do not sleep: I see, I hear, I speak,
I smell sweet savors, and I feel soft things.
Upon my life, I am a lord indeed,
And not a tinker nor Christopher Sly.
Well, bring our lady hither to our sight,
And once again a pot o'th' smallest ale.

SECOND SERVINGMAN
Will 't please Your Mightiness to wash your hands?
Oh, how we joy to see your wit restored!
Oh, that once more you knew but what you are!
These fifteen years you have been in a dream,
Or when you waked, so waked as if you slept.

SLY
These fifteen years! By my fay, a goodly nap.
But did I never speak of all that time?

FIRST SERVINGMAN
Oh, yes, my lord, but very idle words;
For though you lay here in this goodly chamber,
Yet would you say ye were beaten out of door,
And rail upon the hostess of the house,
And say you would present her at the leet
Because she brought stone jugs and no sealed quarts.
Sometimes you would call out for Cicely Hacket.

SLY
Ay, the woman's maid of the house.

THIRD SERVINGMAN
Why, sir, you know no house, nor no such maid,
Nor no such men as you have reckoned up,
As Stephen Sly, and old John Naps of Greet,
And Peter Turf, and Henry Pimpernel,
And twenty more such names and men as these,
Which never were, nor no man ever saw.

SLY
Now Lord be thankèd for my good amends!

ALL
Amen.

Enter [the Page as a] lady, with Attendants.

SLY I thank thee. Thou shalt not lose by it.

PAGE
How fares my noble lord?

SLY Marry, I fare well,
For here is cheer enough. Where is my wife?

PAGE
Here, noble lord. What is thy will with her?

SLY
Are you my wife, and will not call me husband?
My men should call me "lord"; I am your goodman.

PAGE
My husband and my lord, my lord and husband;
I am your wife in all obedience.

SLY
I know it well.—What must I call her?

LORD Madam.

35 Apollo i.e., as god of music **39 Semiramis** legendary queen of Assyria, famous for her voluptuousness. **40 bestrew** i.e., scatter rushes on **41 trapped** adorned **45 welkin** sky, heavens **47 course** hunt the hare **48 breathèd** in good physical condition, with good wind. **roe** small, swift deer. **50 Adonis** a young huntsman with whom Venus is vainly in love. (See Ovid's *Metamorphoses,* Book 10, and Shakespeare's poem, *Venus and Adonis.*) **51 Cytherea** one of the names for Venus (because of her association with the island of Cythera). **sedges** grassy marsh plants **52 wanton** play seductively **54 Io** a woman who, according to Ovid, was seduced by Jove concealed in a mist and afterwards transformed into a heifer **56 as** as if **57 Daphne** a wood nymph beloved by Apollo, changed by Diana into a laurel tree to preserve her from Apollo's assault (*Metamorphoses,* Book 1) **60 workmanly** skillfully **63 waning** degenerate **65 envious** spiteful **67 yet** even today

77 wit mental faculties **78 knew but** only knew **81 fay** faith **82 of** during **86 house** tavern **87 present** bring accusation against. **leet** manorial court **88 sealed quarts** quart containers officially stamped as a guarantee of that capacity. (The irregular stoneware quarts might be used to cheat customers.) **93 Stephen . . . Greet** (A Stephen Sly lived in Stratford during Shakespeare's day. *Greet* is a Gloucestershire hamlet not far from Stratford. The Folio reading, "Greece," is an easy misreading if Shakespeare wrote "Greete.") **97 amends** recovery. **98 Thou . . . it** i.e., I will reward your solicitude toward me. **99 Marry** (A mild oath, derived from "by Mary.") **fare well** (1) am fine (2) have plenty of good *cheer* (line 100), refreshment **103 goodman** (A homely term for "husband.")

SLY Al'ce madam, or Joan madam?

LORD
Madam, and nothing else. So lords call ladies.

SLY
Madam wife, they say that I have dreamed
And slept above some fifteen year or more.

PAGE
Ay, and the time seems thirty unto me,
Being all this time abandoned from your bed.

SLY 112
'Tis much.—Servants, leave me and her alone.—
Madam, undress you and come now to bed.

PAGE
Thrice-noble lord, let me entreat of you
To pardon me yet for a night or two,
Or, if not so, until the sun be set.
For your physicians have expressly charged,
In peril to incur your former malady,
That I should yet absent me from your bed.
I hope this reason stands for my excuse.

SLY Ay, it stands so that I may hardly tarry so long. But
I would be loath to fall into my dreams again. I will 122
therefore tarry in despite of the flesh and the blood.

Enter a [*Servingman as*] *messenger.*

SERVINGMAN
Your Honor's players, hearing your amendment,
Are come to play a pleasant comedy,
For so your doctors hold it very meet,
Seeing too much sadness hath congealed your blood, 127
And melancholy is the nurse of frenzy.
Therefore they thought it good you hear a play
And frame your mind to mirth and merriment,
Which bars a thousand harms and lengthens life.

SLY Marry, I will let them play it. Is not a comonty a
Christmas gambold or a tumbling-trick? 133

PAGE 134
No, my good lord, it is more pleasing stuff.

SLY What, household stuff?

PAGE It is a kind of history. 136

SLY Well, we'll see 't. Come, madam wife, sit by my side 137
and let the world slip; we shall ne'er be younger.
[*They sit over the stage.*] *Flourish.* 139

112 abandoned banished **122 stands** (1) is the case (2) punningly, "is giving me an erection." The joke picks up on *stands*, meaning "serves," in line 121. **127 meet** suitable **133 Marry . . . play it** (Perhaps the Folio punctuation should be emended to "Marry, I will. Let them play it.") **comonty** (Sly's approximation of "comedy.") **134 gambold** (Sly's version of "gambol," frolicsome merry-making and leaping about.) **136 household stuff** i.e., domestic doings. **137 history** story. **139.1 *They sit over the stage*** (Possibly the Lord and some servingmen exeunt here or at line 113. At 1.1.249 ff., a servingman, the Page, and Sly speak, while the Lord is no longer heard from.)

1.1

Enter Lucentio and his man, Tranio.

LUCENTIO
Tranio, since for the great desire I had
To see fair Padua, nursery of arts, 2
I am arrived fore fruitful Lombardy, 3
The pleasant garden of great Italy,
And by my father's love and leave am armed
With his good will and thy good company,
My trusty servant, well approved in all, 7
Here let us breathe and haply institute 8
A course of learning and ingenious studies. 9
Pisa, renownèd for grave citizens,
Gave me my being, and my father first— 11
A merchant of great traffic through the world, 12
Vincentio, come of the Bentivolii. 13
Vincentio's son, brought up in Florence, 14
It shall become to serve all hopes conceived 15
To deck his fortune with his virtuous deeds. 16
And therefore, Tranio, for the time I study, 17
Virtue and that part of philosophy
Will I apply that treats of happiness 19
By virtue specially to be achieved.
Tell me thy mind, for I have Pisa left
And am to Padua come as he that leaves
A shallow plash to plunge him in the deep, 23
And with satiety seeks to quench his thirst.

TRANIO
Mi perdonate, gentle master mine. 25
I am in all affected as yourself, 26
Glad that you thus continue your resolve
To suck the sweets of sweet philosophy.
Only, good master, while we do admire
This virtue and this moral discipline,
Let's be no stoics nor no stocks, I pray, 31
Or so devote to Aristotle's checks 32
As Ovid be an outcast quite abjured. 33
Balk logic with acquaintance that you have, 34
And practice rhetoric in your common talk. 35
Music and poesy use to quicken you; 36

1.1 Location: Padua. A street before Baptista's house.
2 Padua . . . arts (Padua's was one of the most renowned of universities during Shakespeare's time.) **3 am arrived fore** have arrived at, or at the gates of, before. (Padua is not in Lombardy, but imprecise maps may have allowed Shakespeare to think of Lombardy as comprising all of northern Italy.) **7 approved** tested and proved trustworthy **8 breathe** pause, settle down. **haply institute** begin, as circumstances permit **9 ingenious** i.e., "ingenuous," liberal, befitting a wellborn person **11 first** i.e., before me **12 of great traffic** involved in extensive trade **13 come of** descended from
14–16 Vincentio's . . . deeds It will befit Vincentio's son, brought up in Florence, to fulfill all the hopes of his family by adding virtuous deeds to what fortune has bestowed on him. **17 for . . . study** for my term of study **19 apply** study. **treats of** discusses, concerns
23 plash pool **25 *Mi perdonate*** Pardon me **26 affected** disposed
31 stocks persons devoid of feeling, like wooden posts. (With a play on *stoics*.) **32 devote** devoted. **checks** restraints **33 As** so that. **Ovid** Latin love poet. (Used here to typify amorous light entertainment, as contrasted with the constraining philosophic study of Aristotle.) **34 Balk logic** Argue, bandy words. **acquaintance** acquaintances **35 common talk** ordinary conversation.
36 Music . . . you Use music and poetry to refresh yourself

The mathematics and the metaphysics,
Fall to them as you find your stomach serves you.
No profit grows where is no pleasure ta'en.
In brief, sir, study what you most affect.

LUCENTIO
Gramercies, Tranio, well dost thou advise.
If, Biondello, thou wert come ashore,
We could at once put us in readiness
And take a lodging fit to entertain
Such friends as time in Padua shall beget.
But stay awhile, what company is this?

TRANIO
Master, some show to welcome us to town.

Enter Baptista with his two daughters, Katharina and Bianca; Gremio, a pantaloon; [*and*] *Hortensio, suitor to Bianca. Lucentio* [*and*] *Tranio stand by.*

BAPTISTA
Gentlemen, importune me no farther,
For how I firmly am resolved you know:
That is, not to bestow my youngest daughter
Before I have a husband for the elder.
If either of you both love Katharina,
Because I know you well and love you well,
Leave shall you have to court her at your pleasure.

GREMIO
To cart her rather. She's too rough for me.
There, there, Hortensio, will you any wife?

KATHARINA [*to Baptista*]
I pray you, sir, is it your will
To make a stale of me amongst these mates?

HORTENSIO
"Mates," maid? How mean you that? No mates for you,
Unless you were of gentler, milder mold.

KATHARINA
I'faith, sir, you shall never need to fear;
Iwis it is not halfway to her heart.
But if it were, doubt not her care should be
To comb your noddle with a three-legged stool,
And paint your face, and use you like a fool.

HORTENSIO
From all such devils, good Lord deliver us!

GREMIO And me too, good Lord!

TRANIO [*aside to Lucentio*]
Husht, master, here's some good pastime toward.
That wench is stark mad or wonderful froward.

LUCENTIO [*aside to Tranio*]
But in the other's silence do I see
Maid's mild behavior and sobriety.
Peace, Tranio!

TRANIO [*aside to Lucentio*]
Well said, master. Mum, and gaze your fill.

BAPTISTA
Gentlemen, that I may soon make good
What I have said—Bianca, get you in.
And let it not displease thee, good Bianca,
For I will love thee ne'er the less, my girl.

KATHARINA A pretty peat! It is best
Put finger in the eye, an she knew why.

BIANCA
Sister, content you in my discontent.—
Sir, to your pleasure humbly I subscribe.
My books and instruments shall be my company,
On them to look and practice by myself.

LUCENTIO [*aside to Tranio*]
Hark, Tranio, thou mayst hear Minerva speak.

HORTENSIO
Signor Baptista, will you be so strange?
Sorry am I that our good will effects
Bianca's grief.

GREMIO Why will you mew her up,
Signor Baptista, for this fiend of hell,
And make her bear the penance of her tongue?

BAPTISTA
Gentlemen, content ye. I am resolved.
Go in, Bianca. [*Exit Bianca.*]
And for I know she taketh most delight
In music, instruments, and poetry,
Schoolmasters will I keep within my house
Fit to instruct her youth. If you, Hortensio,
Or, Signor Gremio, you know any such,
Prefer them hither; for to cunning men
I will be very kind, and liberal
To mine own children in good bringing up.
And so farewell.—Katharina, you may stay,
For I have more to commune with Bianca. *Exit.*

KATHARINA
Why, and I trust I may go too, may I not?
What, shall I be appointed hours,
As though, belike, I knew not what to take,
And what to leave? Ha! *Exit.*

GREMIO You may go to the devil's dam. Your gifts are so good, here's none will hold you.—Their love is not

38 stomach inclination, appetite **40 affect** find pleasant. **41 Gramercies** Many thanks **42 Biondello** (Lucentio apostrophizes his absent servant.) **come ashore** (Padua, though inland, is given a harbor by Shakespeare, unless he is thinking of the canals that crossed northern Italy in the sixteenth century.) **47.2 *pantaloon*** foolish old man, a stock character in Italian comedy **55 cart** carry in a cart through the streets by way of punishment or public exposure. (With a play on *court*.) **58 stale** laughingstock. (With a play on the meaning "harlot," since a harlot might well be carted.) **mates** rude fellows. (But Hortensio takes the word in the sense of "husband.") **62 Iwis . . . heart** indeed, marriage is not even halfway suited to my inclination. (Katharina speaks of herself in the third person here and in line 63.) **64 comb your noddle** rake your head **65 paint** i.e., make red with scratches **68 toward** in prospect.

69 wonderful froward incredibly perverse. **78–9 A . . . why** i.e., A fine spoiled darling she is! She does well to put on a show of weeping, knowing what's good for her. (Said sardonically.) **81 pleasure** will. **subscribe** submit. **84 Minerva** goddess of wisdom **85 strange** distant, unfeeling. **86 effects** causes **87 mew** coop (as one would a falcon) **89 her . . . her** i.e., Bianca . . . Katharina's **92 for** because **97 Prefer** recommend. **cunning** skillful, learned **101 commune** discuss **103 appointed hours** given a timetable **104–5 As . . . leave?** as though, forsooth, I didn't know how to choose for myself? **106 dam** mother. **gifts** endowments. (Said ironically.) **107 hold** detain. **Their love** i.e., The love of women

so great, Hortensio, but we may blow our nails to- 108
gether and fast it fairly out. Our cake's dough on both 109
sides. Farewell. Yet, for the love I bear my sweet 110
Bianca, if I can by any means light on a fit man to teach
her that wherein she delights, I will wish him to 112
her father.

HORTENSIO So will I, Signor Gremio. But a word, I pray.
Though the nature of our quarrel yet never brooked 115
parle, know now, upon advice, it toucheth us both, 116
that we may yet again have access to our fair mistress
and be happy rivals in Bianca's love, to labor and effect
one thing specially.

GREMIO What's that, I pray?

HORTENSIO Marry, sir, to get a husband for her sister.

GREMIO A husband? A devil.

HORTENSIO I say a husband.

GREMIO I say a devil. Think'st thou, Hortensio, though
her father be very rich, any man is so very a fool to be 125
married to hell?

HORTENSIO Tush, Gremio, though it pass your patience 127
and mine to endure her loud alarums, why, man, there 128
be good fellows in the world, an a man could light on 129
them, would take her with all faults, and money 130
enough.

GREMIO I cannot tell. But I had as lief take her dowry 132
with this condition: to be whipped at the high cross 133
every morning.

HORTENSIO Faith, as you say, there's small choice in
rotten apples. But come, since this bar in law makes us 136
friends, it shall be so far forth friendly maintained till
by helping Baptista's eldest daughter to a husband we
set his youngest free for a husband, and then have to't 139
afresh. Sweet Bianca! Happy man be his dole! He that 140
runs fastest gets the ring. How say you, Signor 141
Gremio?

GREMIO I am agreed, and would I had given him the
best horse in Padua to begin his wooing that would
thor-oughly woo her, wed her, and bed her and rid the
house of her! Come on. *Exeunt ambo. Manent* 146
Tranio and Lucentio.

TRANIO
I pray, sir, tell me, is it possible
That love should of a sudden take such hold?

LUCENTIO
Oh, Tranio, till I found it to be true,
I never thought it possible or likely.
But see, while idly I stood looking on,
I found the effect of love in idleness, 152
And now in plainness do confess to thee,
That art to me as secret and as dear 154
As Anna to the Queen of Carthage was, 155
Tranio, I burn, I pine, I perish, Tranio,
If I achieve not this young modest girl.
Counsel me, Tranio, for I know thou canst;
Assist me, Tranio, for I know thou wilt.

TRANIO
Master, it is no time to chide you now.
Affection is not rated from the heart. 161
If love have touched you, naught remains but so,
"Redime te captum quam queas minimo." 163

LUCENTIO
Gramercies, lad. Go forward. This contents; 164
The rest will comfort, for thy counsel's sound. 165

TRANIO
Master, you looked so longly on the maid, 166
Perhaps you marked not what's the pith of all. 167

LUCENTIO
Oh, yes, I saw sweet beauty in her face,
Such as the daughter of Agenor had, 169
That made great Jove to humble him to her hand, 170
When with his knees he kissed the Cretan strand. 171

TRANIO
Saw you no more? Marked you not how her sister
Began to scold and raise up such a storm
That mortal ears might hardly endure the din?

LUCENTIO
Tranio, I saw her coral lips to move,
And with her breath she did perfume the air.
Sacred and sweet was all I saw in her.

TRANIO [*aside*]
Nay, then, 'tis time to stir him from his trance.—
I pray, awake, sir. If you love the maid,
Bend thoughts and wits to achieve her. Thus it stands:
Her elder sister is so curst and shrewd 181
That till the father rid his hands of her,
Master, your love must live a maid at home, 183
And therefore has he closely mewed her up,
Because she will not be annoyed with suitors. 185

LUCENTIO
Ah, Tranio, what a cruel father's he!
But art thou not advised he took some care 187
To get her cunning schoolmasters to instruct her? 188

TRANIO
Ay, marry, am I, sir; and now 'tis plotted.

108–9 blow . . . together i.e., twiddle our thumbs, wait patiently **109 fast . . . out** abstain as best we can. **109–10 Our cake's . . . sides** i.e., We're both out of luck, getting nowhere. **112 wish** commend **115-16 brooked parle** tolerated conference **116 advice** reflection. **toucheth** concerns **125 very a** utterly a **127 pass** exceed **128 alarums** i.e., loud, startling noises. (In military terms, a call to arms.) **129 an** if **130 would** who would **132 I cannot tell** i.e., I don't know about that, don't know what to say. **had as lief** would as willingly **133 high cross** cross set on a pedestal in a marketplace or center of a town **136 bar in law** legal impediment, i.e., Baptista's refusal to receive suitors for Bianca **139 have to't** renew combat **140 Happy . . . dole**! i.e., May happiness be the reward of him who wins! (Proverbial.) **141 the ring** (An allusion to the sport of riding at the ring, with quibble on "wedding ring" and also sexual sense, "vulvar ring.") **146 s.d. *ambo*** both. ***Manent*** They remain onstage

152 love in idleness i.e., (1) desire bred by idleness (2) a popular name for the pansy, thought to induce love **154 secret** trusted, intimate **155 Anna** confidante of her sister Dido, Queen of Carthage, beloved of Aeneas **161 rated** driven away by chiding **163 *Redime . . . minimo*** Buy yourself out of bondage for as little as you can. (From Terence's *Eunuchus* as quoted in William Lilly's *Latin Grammar*.) **164 Gramercies** Thanks **165 The rest** the rest of what you have to say **166 so longly** (1) for such a long time (2) so longingly **167 marked** noted. **pith** core, essence **169 daughter of Agenor** Europa, beloved of Jove; Jove took the form of a bull in order to abduct her **170 him** himself **171 kissed** i.e., knelt on **181 curst and shrewd** shrewish and ill-natured **183 must . . . home** must remain unattached, unmated **185 Because** so that **187 advised** aware (that) **188 cunning** expert

LUCENTIO
I have it, Tranio.
TRANIO Master, for my hand, 190
Both our inventions meet and jump in one. 191
LUCENTIO
Tell me thine first.
TRANIO You will be schoolmaster
And undertake the teaching of the maid:
That's your device.
LUCENTIO It is. May it be done?
TRANIO
Not possible; for who shall bear your part
And be in Padua here Vincentio's son,
Keep house and ply his book, welcome his friends, 197
Visit his countrymen, and banquet them?
LUCENTIO
Basta, content thee, for I have it full. 199
We have not yet been seen in any house,
Nor can we be distinguished by our faces
For man or master. Then it follows thus:
Thou shalt be master, Tranio, in my stead,
Keep house, and port, and servants, as I should. 204
I will some other be, some Florentine,
Some Neapolitan, or meaner man of Pisa. 206
'Tis hatched and shall be so. Tranio, at once
Uncase thee. Take my colored hat and cloak. 208
When Biondello comes, he waits on thee,
But I will charm him first to keep his tongue. 210
TRANIO So had you need.
In brief, sir, sith it your pleasure is, 212
And I am tied to be obedient—
For so your father charged me at our parting,
"Be serviceable to my son," quoth he,
Although I think 'twas in another sense—
I am content to be Lucentio,
Because so well I love Lucentio.
[*They exchange clothes.*]
LUCENTIO
Tranio, be so, because Lucentio loves.
And let me be a slave t'achieve that maid
Whose sudden sight hath thralled my wounded eye. 221

Enter Biondello.

Here comes the rogue.—Sirrah, where have you been?
BIONDELLO
Where have I been? Nay, how now, where are you?
Master, has my fellow Tranio stol'n your clothes?
Or you stol'n his? Or both? Pray, what's the news?
LUCENTIO
Sirrah, come hither. 'Tis no time to jest,
And therefore frame your manners to the time. 227
Your fellow Tranio here, to save my life,
Puts my apparel and my countenance on, 229
And I for my escape have put on his;
For in a quarrel since I came ashore,
I killed a man, and fear I was descried. 232
Wait you on him, I charge you, as becomes, 233
While I make way from hence to save my life.
You understand me?
BIONDELLO I, sir?—Ne'er a whit. 235
LUCENTIO
And not a jot of Tranio in your mouth.
Tranio is changed into Lucentio.
BIONDELLO
The better for him. Would I were so, too!
TRANIO
So could I, faith, boy, to have the next wish after,
That Lucentio indeed had Baptista's youngest daughter.
But, sirrah, not for my sake, but your master's, I advise
You use your manners discreetly in all kind of companies.
When I am alone, why, then I am Tranio,
But in all places else your master Lucentio.
LUCENTIO Tranio, let's go.
One thing more rests, that thyself execute: 246
To make one among these wooers. If thou ask me why,
Sufficeth my reasons are both good and weighty. 248
Exeunt.

The presenters above speak.

FIRST SERVINGMAN
My lord, you nod. You do not mind the play. 249
SLY Yes, by Saint Anne, do I. A good matter, surely.
Comes there any more of it?
PAGE [*as lady*] My lord, 'tis but begun.
SLY 'Tis a very excellent piece of work, madam lady.
Would 'twere done! *They sit and mark.* 254

✤

[1.2]

Enter Petruchio and his man, Grumio.

PETRUCHIO
Verona, for a while I take my leave
To see my friends in Padua, but of all 2
My best belovèd and approvèd friend,
Hortensio; and I trow this is his house. 4
Here, sirrah Grumio, knock, I say.
GRUMIO Knock, sir? Whom should I knock? Is there any
man has rebused Your Worship? 7
PETRUCHIO Villain, I say, knock me here soundly. 8

190 for my hand (A mild oath.) **191 inventions** plans. **jump** tally, agree **197 Keep . . . book** entertain guests and pursue his studies **199 *Basta*** Enough. **full** i.e., fully thought out. **204 port** state, style of living **206 meaner** of a lower social class **208 Uncase thee** remove your outer garments. **210 charm** i.e., command, persuade **212 sith** since **221 Whose . . . thralled** the sudden sight of whom has captured **227 frame** adapt, suit **229 countenance** bearing, manner

232 descried observed. **233 as becomes** as is suitable **235 I, sir** (Lucentio may hear this as "Ay, sir.") **Ne'er a whit** Not in the least. **246 rests** remains to be done **248 Sufficeth** it suffices that **248.2 *presenters*** characters of the Induction, whose role it is to "present" the play proper **249 mind** attend to **254 s.d. *mark*** observe.
1.2. Location: Padua. Before Hortensio's house.
2 of all above all **4 trow** believe **7 rebused** (A blunder for "abused.") **8 Villain** i.e., Wretch. (A term of abuse.) **me** i.e., for me. (But Grumio, perhaps intentionally, misunderstands.)

GRUMIO Knock you here, sir? Why, sir, what am I, sir, that I should knock you here, sir?

PETRUCHIO
Villain, I say, knock me at this gate,
And rap me well, or I'll knock your knave's pate.

GRUMIO
My master is grown quarrelsome. I should knock
you first,
And then I know after who comes by the worst.

PETRUCHIO Will it not be?
Faith, sirrah, an you'll not knock, I'll ring it.
I'll try how you can *sol fa* and sing it.
He wrings him by the ears.

GRUMIO
Help, masters, help! My master is mad.

PETRUCHIO
Now knock when I bid you, sirrah villain.

Enter Hortensio.

HORTENSIO How now, what's the matter? My old friend Grumio and my good friend Petruchio? How do you all at Verona?

PETRUCHIO
Signor Hortensio, come you to part the fray?
Con tutto il cuore ben trovato, may I say.

HORTENSIO
Alla nostra casa ben venuto,
Molto onorato signor mio Petruchio.—
Rise, Grumio, rise. We will compound this quarrel.

GRUMIO Nay, 'tis no matter, sir, what he 'leges in Latin. If this be not a lawful cause for me to leave his service! Look you, sir: he bid me knock him and rap him soundly, sir. Well, was it fit for a servant to use his master so, being perhaps, for aught I see, two-and-thirty, a pip out?
Whom would to God I had well knocked at first!
Then had not Grumio come by the worst.

PETRUCHIO
A senseless villain! Good Hortensio,
I bade the rascal knock upon your gate,
And could not get him for my heart to do it.

GRUMIO Knock at the gate? Oh, heavens! Spake you not these words plain, "Sirrah, knock me here, rap me here, knock me well, and knock me soundly"? And come you now with "knocking at the gate"?

PETRUCHIO
Sirrah, begone, or talk not, I advise you.

HORTENSIO
Petruchio, patience. I am Grumio's pledge.
Why, this's a heavy chance twixt him and you,
Your ancient, trusty, pleasant servant Grumio.
And tell me now, sweet friend, what happy gale
Blows you to Padua here from old Verona?

PETRUCHIO
Such wind as scatters young men through the world
To seek their fortunes farther than at home,
Where small experience grows. But in a few,
Signor Hortensio, thus it stands with me:
Antonio, my father, is deceased,
And I have thrust myself into this maze,
Happily to wive and thrive as best I may.
Crowns in my purse I have, and goods at home,
And so am come abroad to see the world.

HORTENSIO
Petruchio, shall I then come roundly to thee
And wish thee to a shrewd, ill-favored wife?
Thou'dst thank me but a little for my counsel.
And yet I'll promise thee she shall be rich,
And very rich. But thou'rt too much my friend,
And I'll not wish thee to her.

PETRUCHIO
Signor Hortensio, twixt such friends as we
Few words suffice. And therefore, if thou know
One rich enough to be Petruchio's wife—
As wealth is burden of my wooing dance—
Be she as foul as was Florentius' love,
As old as Sibyl, and as curst and shrewd
As Socrates' Xanthippe, or a worse,
She moves me not, or not removes, at least,
Affection's edge in me, were she as rough
As are the swelling Adriatic seas.
I come to wive it wealthily in Padua;
If wealthily, then happily in Padua.

GRUMIO Nay, look you, sir, he tells you flatly what his mind is. Why, give him gold enough and marry him to a puppet or an aglet-baby, or an old trot with ne'er a tooth in her head, though she have as many diseases as two-and-fifty horses. Why, nothing comes amiss, so money comes withal.

11 gate door **13–14 I should . . . worst** i.e., You're asking me to hit you—and I know who then will get the worst of it. **15 Will it not be?** i.e., Aren't you going to do what I said? **16 an** if. **ring it** sound loudly, using a circular knocker or a bell. (With a pun on *wring*.) **17 I'll . . . sing it** i.e., I'll make you cry out. (To *sol fa* is to sing a scale.) **18 masters** i.e., sirs. (Addressed to the audience.) **24 *Con . . . trovato*** With all my heart, well met **25–6 *Alla . . . Petruchio*** Welcome to our house, my much-honored Signor Petruchio. (Italian.) **27 compound** settle **28 'leges** alleges **32–3 two . . . out** i.e., drunk, or not quite right in the head. (Derived from the card game called *one-and-thirty*.)

33 a pip a spot on a playing card. (Hence, *a pip out* means "off by one," or "one in excess of thirty one.") **38 for my heart** i.e., for my life **42 come you now with** do you now change your tune to

44 pledge surety. **45 this's . . . chance** this is a sad occurrence **46 ancient** long-standing. **pleasant** merry **51 in a few** in short **55 Happily** with good luck. (*Happily* and *haply* were not always distinguished.) **56 Crowns** Gold coins **58 come roundly** speak plainly **59 shrewd** shrewish. **ill-favored** ill-natured (? Kate is not "ugly," the usual meaning of this term; see line 85.) **67 burden** undersong, i.e., basis **68 foul** ugly. **Florentius' love** (An allusion to John Gower's version in *Confessio Amantis* of the fairy tale of the knight who promises to marry an ugly old woman if she solves the riddle he must answer. After the fulfillment of all promises, she becomes young and beautiful. Another version of this story is Chaucer's "Tale of the Wife of Bath," from *The Canterbury Tales*.) **69 Sibyl** prophetess of Cumae, to whom Apollo gave as many years of life as she held grains of sand in her hand **70 Xanthippe** the philosopher's notoriously shrewish wife **71 moves** affects, disturbs. (Setting up wordplay on *removes*.) **72 Affection's edge** the keen edge of desire **78 aglet-baby** small figure carved on the metal tip of a lace, i.e., a tiny baby. **trot** hag **80 so** provided **81 withal** with it.

HORTENSIO
Petruchio, since we are stepped thus far in,
I will continue that I broached in jest.
I can, Petruchio, help thee to a wife
With wealth enough, and young and beauteous,
Brought up as best becomes a gentlewoman.
Her only fault, and that is faults enough,
Is that she is intolerable curst
And shrewd, and froward, so beyond all measure
That, were my state far worser than it is,
I would not wed her for a mine of gold.

PETRUCHIO
Hortensio, peace! Thou know'st not gold's effect.
Tell me her father's name and 'tis enough;
For I will board her, though she chide as loud
As thunder when the clouds in autumn crack.

HORTENSIO
Her father is Baptista Minola,
An affable and courteous gentleman.
Her name is Katharina Minola,
Renowned in Padua for her scolding tongue.

PETRUCHIO
I know her father, though I know not her,
And he knew my deceasèd father well.
I will not sleep, Hortensio, till I see her;
And therefore let me be thus bold with you
To give you over at this first encounter,
Unless you will accompany me thither.

GRUMIO [*to Hortensio*] I pray you, sir, let him go while the humor lasts. O' my word, an she knew him as well as I do, she would think scolding would do little good upon him. She may perhaps call him half a score knaves or so. Why, that's nothing; an he begin once, he'll rail in his rope tricks. I'll tell you what, sir: an she stand him but a little, he will throw a figure in her face and so disfigure her with it that she shall have no more eyes to see withal than a cat. You know him not, sir.

HORTENSIO
Tarry, Petruchio, I must go with thee,
For in Baptista's keep my treasure is.
He hath the jewel of my life in hold,
His youngest daughter, beautiful Bianca,
And her withholds from me and other more,
Suitors to her and rivals in my love,
Supposing it a thing impossible,
For those defects I have before rehearsed,
That ever Katharina will be wooed.
Therefore this order hath Baptista ta'en,
That none shall have access unto Bianca
Till Katharine the curst have got a husband.

GRUMIO Katharine the curst!
A title for a maid of all titles the worst.

HORTENSIO
Now shall my friend Petruchio do me grace,
And offer me disguised in sober robes
To old Baptista as a schoolmaster
Well seen in music, to instruct Bianca,
That so I may by this device at least
Have leave and leisure to make love to her,
And unsuspected court her by herself.

Enter Gremio [with a paper], and Lucentio disguised [as a schoolmaster].

GRUMIO Here's no knavery! See, to beguile the old folks, how the young folks lay their heads together! Master, master, look about you. Who goes there, ha?

HORTENSIO
Peace, Grumio, it is the rival of my love.
Petruchio, stand by awhile. [*They stand aside.*]

GRUMIO [*aside*]
A proper stripling and an amorous!

GREMIO [*to Lucentio*]
Oh, very well, I have perused the note.
Hark you, sir, I'll have them very fairly bound—
All books of love, see that at any hand—
And see you read no other lectures to her.
You understand me. Over and beside
Signor Baptista's liberality,
I'll mend it with a largess. Take your paper too,
[*giving Lucentio the note*]
And let me have them very well perfumed,
For she is sweeter than perfume itself
To whom they go to. What will you read to her?

LUCENTIO
Whate'er I read to her, I'll plead for you
As for my patron, stand you so assured,
As firmly as yourself were still in place—
Yea, and perhaps with more successful words
Than you, unless you were a scholar, sir.

GREMIO
Oh, this learning, what a thing it is!

GRUMIO [*aside*]
Oh, this woodcock, what an ass it is!

PETRUCHIO Peace, sirrah!

HORTENSIO [*coming forward*]
Grumio, mum!—God save you, Signor Gremio.

GREMIO
And you are well met, Signor Hortensio.
Trow you whither I am going? To Baptista Minola.

83 that I broached what I began **88–9 intolerable . . . froward** intolerably ill-natured and willful **90 state** estate **94 board** woo aggressively, accost, have intercourse with, rape **95 crack** make an explosive noise. **104 give you over** leave you **107 humor** whim. **O' my word, an** On my word, if **111 he'll . . . tricks** i.e., he has tricks up his sleeve to answer her scolding. **112–14 he will . . . cat** i.e., he will utterly dazzle and disable her with his rhetorical tricks. (A *figure* is a figure of speech.) **116 keep** (1) place to store treasure (2) keeping **117 in hold** (1) in his custody (2) in his stronghold **119 And . . . more** and witholds her from me and others besides **122 rehearsed** related, described **124 this order** these measures

129 grace a favor **132 seen** skilled **134 make love to** woo **136 Here's no knavery!** (Said sarcastically.) **141 proper stripling** handsome young fellow. (Said ironically, in reference to Gremio.) **142 note** (Evidently, a list of books for Bianca's tutoring.) **144 see** see to. **at any hand** in any case **145 read . . . lectures** teach no other lessons **148 mend** improve, increase. **largess** gift of money. **149 them** i.e., the books **154 as** as if. **still in place** present all the time **158 woodcock** (A bird easily caught; proverbially stupid.) **161 you are well met** i.e., how opportune to meet you just now **162 Trow** Know

I promised to inquire carefully
About a schoolmaster for the fair Bianca,
And by good fortune I have lighted well
On this young man, for learning and behavior
Fit for her turn, well read in poetry
And other books—good ones, I warrant ye.

HORTENSIO
'Tis well. And I have met a gentleman
Hath promised me to help me to another,
A fine musician to instruct our mistress.
So shall I no whit be behind in duty
To fair Bianca, so beloved of me.

GREMIO
Beloved of me, and that my deeds shall prove.

GRUMIO [*aside*] And that his bags shall prove.

HORTENSIO
Gremio, 'tis now no time to vent our love.
Listen to me, and if you speak me fair,
I'll tell you news indifferent good for either.
Here is a gentleman whom by chance I met,
Upon agreement from us to his liking,
Will undertake to woo curst Katharine,
Yea, and to marry her, if her dowry please.

GREMIO So said, so done, is well.
Hortensio, have you told him all her faults?

PETRUCHIO
I know she is an irksome brawling scold.
If that be all, masters, I hear no harm.

GREMIO
No? Say'st me so, friend? What countryman?

PETRUCHIO
Born in Verona, old Antonio's son.
My father dead, his fortune lives for me,
And I do hope good days and long to see.

GREMIO
Oh, sir, such a life with such a wife were strange.
But if you have a stomach, to't, i' God's name.
You shall have me assisting you in all.
But will you woo this wildcat?

PETRUCHIO Will I live?

GRUMIO
Will he woo her? Ay, or I'll hang her.

PETRUCHIO
Why came I hither but to that intent?
Think you a little din can daunt mine ears?
Have I not in my time heard lions roar?
Have I not heard the sea, puffed up with winds,
Rage like an angry boar chafèd with sweat?
Have I not heard great ordnance in the field,
And heaven's artillery thunder in the skies?
Have I not in a pitchèd battle heard
Loud 'larums, neighing steeds, and trumpets' clang?
And do you tell me of a woman's tongue,
That gives not half so great a blow to hear
As will a chestnut in a farmer's fire?
Tush, tush! Fear boys with bugs.

GRUMIO For he fears none.

GREMIO Hortensio, hark.
This gentleman is happily arrived,
My mind presumes, for his own good and ours.

HORTENSIO
I promised we would be contributors
And bear his charge of wooing, whatsoe'er.

GREMIO
And so we will, provided that he win her.

GRUMIO
I would I were as sure of a good dinner.

Enter Tranio, brave [*as Lucentio*], *and Biondello.*

TRANIO
Gentlemen, God save you. If I may be bold,
Tell me, I beseech you, which is the readiest way
To the house of Signor Baptista Minola?

BIONDELLO He that has the two fair daughters, is't he you mean?

TRANIO Even he, Biondello.

GREMIO
Hark you, sir, you mean not her to—

TRANIO
Perhaps him and her, sir. What have you to do?

PETRUCHIO
Not her that chides, sir, at any hand, I pray.

TRANIO
I love no chiders, sir.—Biondello, let's away.

LUCENTIO [*aside*]
Well begun, Tranio.

HORTENSIO Sir, a word ere you go.
Are you a suitor to the maid you talk of, yea or no?

TRANIO
An if I be, sir, is it any offense?

GREMIO
No, if without more words you will get you hence.

TRANIO
Why, sir, I pray, are not the streets as free
For me as for you?

GREMIO But so is not she.

TRANIO
For what reason, I beseech you?

GREMIO For this reason, if you'll know,
That she's the choice love of Signor Gremio.

165 lighted alighted **167 Fit for her turn** suited to her needs. (Something that is true in more ways than Gremio realizes.) **170 Hath . . . another** who has promised to help me to obtain another **175 bags** moneybags **176 vent** express **177 speak me fair** deal with me courteously **178 indifferent** equally **180 Upon . . . liking** who, if we agree to terms satisfactory to him **183 So . . . is well** i.e., That's all very well, when his deeds match his words (which may not be soon). **186 masters** good sirs **190 And . . . see** and I hope to see many happy days. **191 were** would be **192 a stomach** an appetite, inclination **201 ordnance** artillery. **field** battlefield

203 a pitchèd battle a planned battle set in orderly array (unlike a skirmish) **204 'larums** calls to arms **207 chestnut** (Chestnuts roasted will pop open or explode with a loud report.) **208 Fear . . . bugs** Frighten children with bugbears, bogeymen. **210 happily** fortunately, just when needed **213 charge** expense **215.1** ***brave*** elegantly dressed **221 Even he** Yes, precisely, he **223 Perhaps . . . do?** i.e., Perhaps I mean to woo both Baptista Minola and Katharina, sir. What's that to you? **224 at any hand** on any account

HORTENSIO
That she's the chosen of Signor Hortensio.
TRANIO
Softly, my masters! If you be gentlemen,
Do me this right: hear me with patience.
Baptista is a noble gentleman,
To whom my father is not all unknown;
And were his daughter fairer than she is,
She may more suitors have, and me for one.
Fair Leda's daughter had a thousand wooers;
Then well one more may fair Bianca have,
And so she shall. Lucentio shall make one,
Though Paris came in hope to speed alone.
GREMIO
What, this gentleman will out-talk us all!
LUCENTIO
Sir, give him head. I know he'll prove a jade.
PETRUCHIO
Hortensio, to what end are all these words?
HORTENSIO [*to Tranio*]
Sir, let me be so bold as ask you,
Did you yet ever see Baptista's daughter?
TRANIO
No, sir, but hear I do that he hath two,
The one as famous for a scolding tongue
As is the other for beauteous modesty.
PETRUCHIO
Sir, sir, the first's for me. Let her go by.
GREMIO
Yea, leave that labor to great Hercules,
And let it be more than Alcides' twelve.
PETRUCHIO
Sir, understand you this of me, in sooth:
The youngest daughter, whom you hearken for,
Her father keeps from all access of suitors,
And will not promise her to any man
Until the elder sister first be wed.
The younger then is free, and not before.
TRANIO
If it be so, sir, that you are the man
Must stead us all, and me amongst the rest;
And if you break the ice and do this feat,
Achieve the elder, set the younger free
For our access, whose hap shall be to have her
Will not so graceless be to be ingrate.
HORTENSIO
Sir, you say well, and well you do conceive.
And since you do profess to be a suitor,
You must, as we do, gratify this gentleman,
To whom we all rest generally beholding.
TRANIO
Sir, I shall not be slack. In sign whereof,
Please ye we may contrive this afternoon,
And quaff carouses to our mistress' health,
And do as adversaries do in law—
Strive mightily, but eat and drink as friends.
GRUMIO, BIONDELLO
Oh, excellent motion! Fellows, let's be gone.
HORTENSIO
The motion's good indeed, and be it so.
Petruchio, I shall be your *ben venuto.* *Exeunt.*

✣

[2.1]

Enter Katharina and Bianca [*with her hands tied*].

BIANCA
Good sister, wrong me not, nor wrong yourself,
To make a bondmaid and a slave of me.
That I disdain. But for these other goods,
Unbind my hands, I'll pull them off myself,
Yea, all my raiment, to my petticoat,
Or what you will command me will I do,
So well I know my duty to my elders.
KATHARINA
Of all thy suitors here I charge thee tell
Whom thou lov'st best. See thou dissemble not.
BIANCA
Believe me, sister, of all the men alive
I never yet beheld that special face
Which I could fancy more than any other.
KATHARINA
Minion, thou liest. Is't not Hortensio?
BIANCA
If you affect him, sister, here I swear
I'll plead for you myself but you shall have him.
KATHARINA
Oh, then belike you fancy riches more.
You will have Gremio to keep you fair.
BIANCA
Is it for him you do envy me so?
Nay, then, you jest, and now I well perceive
You have but jested with me all this while.
I prithee, sister Kate, untie my hands.
KATHARINA (*strikes her*)
If that be jest, then all the rest was so.

Enter Baptista.

238 all entirely **241 Leda's daughter** Helen of Troy **244 Though . . . alone** even if Paris (who abducted Helen from her husband, Menelaus) were to come in hopes of succeeding above all others. **246 Sir . . . jade** Sir, give him a loose bridle; i.e., let him talk freely. I know he'll prove to be a worthless horse, soon tired. **248 as ask** as to ask **253 Let her go by** Pass over her. **255 And . . . twelve** (Hercules, called *Alcides* because he was the reputed grandson of Alcaeus, had to perform twelve huge labors.) **256 of me** from me. **sooth** truth **257 hearken for** seek to win **263 Must stead** who must help **266 whose hap** he whose good fortune **267 to be ingrate** as to be ungrateful. **268 conceive** understand. **270 gratify this gentleman** reward Petruchio

271 beholding beholden, indebted. **273 contrive** manage our affairs, pass the time **274 quaff carouses** drink toasts **275 adversaries** opposing lawyers **277 motion** suggestion. **279 *ben venuto*** welcome, i.e., host.

2.1. Location: Padua. Baptista's house.

3 for as for. **goods** i.e., clothes, jewels, love tokens **4 Unbind** if you will unbind **13 Minion** Hussy **14 affect** love **15 but . . . him** if necessary for you to win him. **16 belike** perhaps **17 fair** resplendent with finery.

BAPTISTA
Why, how now, dame, whence grows this insolence?—
Bianca, stand aside. Poor girl, she weeps.
Go ply thy needle, meddle not with her.—
For shame, thou hilding of a devilish spirit,
Why dost thou wrong her that did ne'er wrong thee?
When did she cross thee with a bitter word?

KATHARINA
Her silence flouts me, and I'll be revenged.
[She] flies after Bianca.

BAPTISTA
What, in my sight? Bianca, get thee in. *Exit [Bianca].*

KATHARINA
What, will you not suffer me? Nay, now I see
She is your treasure, she must have a husband;
I must dance barefoot on her wedding day,
And for your love to her lead apes in hell.
Talk not to me. I will go sit and weep
Till I can find occasion of revenge. *[Exit.]*

BAPTISTA
Was ever gentleman thus grieved as I?
But who comes here?

Enter Gremio, Lucentio [as a schoolmaster] in the habit of a mean man, Petruchio, with [Hortensio as a musician, and] Tranio [as Lucentio] with his boy [Biondello] bearing a lute and books.

GREMIO Good morrow, neighbor Baptista.

BAPTISTA Good morrow, neighbor Gremio. God save you, gentlemen.

PETRUCHIO
And you, good sir. Pray, have you not a daughter
Called Katharina, fair and virtuous?

BAPTISTA
I have a daughter, sir, called Katharina.

GREMIO
You are too blunt. Go to it orderly.

PETRUCHIO
You wrong me, Signor Gremio; give me leave.—
I am a gentleman of Verona, sir,
That, hearing of her beauty and her wit,
Her affability and bashful modesty,
Her wondrous qualities and mild behavior,
Am bold to show myself a forward guest
Within your house, to make mine eye the witness
Of that report which I so oft have heard.
And, for an entrance to my entertainment,
I do present you with a man of mine,
[presenting Hortensio]
Cunning in music and the mathematics,
To instruct her fully in those sciences,
Whereof I know she is not ignorant.
Accept of him, or else you do me wrong.
His name is Litio, born in Mantua.

BAPTISTA
You're welcome, sir, and he, for your good sake.
But for my daughter Katharine, this I know,
She is not for your turn, the more my grief.

PETRUCHIO
I see you do not mean to part with her,
Or else you like not of my company.

BAPTISTA
Mistake me not, I speak but as I find.
Whence are you, sir? What may I call your name?

PETRUCHIO
Petruchio is my name, Antonio's son,
A man well known throughout all Italy.

BAPTISTA
I know him well. You are welcome for his sake.

GREMIO
Saving your tale, Petruchio, I pray,
Let us that are poor petitioners speak too.
Bacare! You are marvelous forward.

PETRUCHIO
Oh, pardon me, Signor Gremio, I would fain be doing.

GREMIO
I doubt it not, sir, but you will curse your wooing.—
Neighbors, this is a gift very grateful, I am sure of it. *[To Baptista]* To express the like kindness, myself, that have been more kindly beholding to you than any, freely give unto you this young scholar *[presenting Lucentio]*, that hath been long studying at Rheims, as cunning in Greek, Latin, and other languages as the other in music and mathematics. His name is Cambio. Pray, accept his service.

BAPTISTA A thousand thanks, Signor Gremio.—Welcome, good Cambio. *[To Tranio]* But, gentle sir, methinks you walk like a stranger. May I be so bold to know the cause of your coming?

TRANIO
Pardon me, sir, the boldness is mine own,
That, being a stranger in this city here,
Do make myself a suitor to your daughter,
Unto Bianca, fair and virtuous.
Nor is your firm resolve unknown to me
In the preferment of the eldest sister.
This liberty is all that I request,
That, upon knowledge of my parentage,
I may have welcome 'mongst the rest that woo,
And free access and favor as the rest.

25 meddle not with have nothing to do with **26 hilding** vicious (hence worthless) beast **28 cross** contradict, thwart **29 flouts** mocks, insults **31 suffer me** let me have my own way. **33, 34 dance . . . day, lead . . . hell** (Popularly supposed to be the fate of old maids.) **38.2** ***habit*** dress. ***mean*** of low social station. (Said here of a schoolmaster.) **45 orderly** in a properly orderly manner. **46 give me leave** excuse me, let me do this my way. **54 entrance** entrance fee. **entertainment** reception **56 Cunning** skillful **57 sciences** subjects, branches of knowledge **59 Accept of** Accept **62 for** as for **65 like not of** do not like **70 know** know of. (See also lines 104–5.) **71 Saving** With all due respect for **73** ***Bacare***! Stand back! **74 fain** gladly. **doing** getting on with the business. (With sexual suggestion.) **76 grateful** pleasing **82 the other** i.e., Hortensio **83 Cambio** (In Italian, appropriately, the word means "change" or "exchange.") **93 In the preferment of** in the precedence you give to **95 upon knowledge of** when you know about **97 favor** leave, permission

And toward the education of your daughters
I here bestow a simple instrument,
And this small packet of Greek and Latin books.
If you accept them, then their worth is great.
[*Biondello brings forward the lute and books.*]

BAPTISTA
Lucentio is your name? Of whence, I pray? 102

TRANIO
Of Pisa, sir, son to Vincentio.

BAPTISTA
A mighty man of Pisa. By report
I know him well. You are very welcome, sir.
[*To Hortensio*] Take you the lute, [*to Lucentio*] and
you the set of books;
You shall go see your pupils presently.—
Holla, within!

Enter a Servant.

Sirrah, lead these gentlemen
To my daughters, and tell them both
These are their tutors. Bid them use them well.
[*Exit Servant, with Lucentio and Hortensio.*]
We will go walk a little in the orchard,
And then to dinner. You are passing welcome, 112
And so I pray you all to think yourselves.

PETRUCHIO
Signor Baptista, my business asketh haste,
And every day I cannot come to woo.
You knew my father well, and in him me,
Left solely heir to all his lands and goods,
Which I have bettered rather than decreased.
Then tell me, if I get your daughter's love,
What dowry shall I have with her to wife?

BAPTISTA
After my death the one half of my lands,
And in possession twenty thousand crowns. 122

PETRUCHIO
And for that dowry I'll assure her of 123
Her widowhood, be it that she survive me, 124
In all my lands and leases whatsoever.
Let specialties be therefore drawn between us, 126
That covenants may be kept on either hand.

BAPTISTA
Ay, when the special thing is well obtained,
That is, her love; for that is all in all.

PETRUCHIO
Why, that is nothing, for I tell you, father, 130
I am as peremptory as she proud-minded;
And where two raging fires meet together,
They do consume the thing that feeds their fury.
Though little fire grows great with little wind,
Yet extreme gusts will blow out fire and all.
So I to her, and so she yields to me, 136
For I am rough and woo not like a babe.

BAPTISTA
Well mayst thou woo, and happy be thy speed! 138
But be thou armed for some unhappy words.

PETRUCHIO
Ay, to the proof, as mountains are for winds, 140
That shakes not, though they blow perpetually. 141

Enter Hortensio [*as Litio*], *with his head broke.*

BAPTISTA
How now, my friend, why dost thou look so pale?

HORTENSIO
For fear, I promise you, if I look pale. 143

BAPTISTA
What, will my daughter prove a good musician?

HORTENSIO
I think she'll sooner prove a soldier. 145
Iron may hold with her, but never lutes. 146

BAPTISTA
Why then, thou canst not break her to the lute? 147

HORTENSIO
Why, no, for she hath broke the lute to me.
I did but tell her she mistook her frets, 149
And bowed her hand to teach her fingering,
When, with a most impatient devilish spirit,
"Frets, call you these?" quoth she, "I'll fume with
them."
And with that word she struck me on the head,
And through the instrument my pate made way;
And there I stood amazèd for a while, 155
As on a pillory, looking through the lute, 156
While she did call me rascal fiddler
And twangling Jack, with twenty such vile terms, 158
As had she studied to misuse me so. 159

PETRUCHIO
Now, by the world, it is a lusty wench! 160
I love her ten times more than e'er I did.
Oh, how I long to have some chat with her!

BAPTISTA [*to Hortensio*]
Well, go with me, and be not so discomfited.
Proceed in practice with my younger daughter; 164
She's apt to learn and thankful for good turns.—
Signor Petruchio, will you go with us,
Or shall I send my daughter Kate to you?

PETRUCHIO
I pray you, do. *Exeunt. Manet Petruchio.*
I'll attend her here, 168
And woo her with some spirit when she comes.

102 Lucentio . . . name? (Baptista may have learned this information from a note accompanying the books and lute.) **112 passing** exceedingly **122 in possession** in immediate possession **123 for** in exchange for **124 widowhood** i.e., widow's share of the estate. **be it that she** if she should **126 specialties** terms of contract **130 father** father-in-law **136 So I** i.e., So I behave, like an extreme gust of wind

138 happy . . . speed! may fortune give you success! **140 to the proof** i.e., in armor, proof against her shrewishness **141 shakes** shake **141.1 *broke*** with a bleeding cut. (Hortensio usually appears on stage with his head emerging through a broken lute.) **143 promise** assure **145 I think . . . soldier** i.e., She's better suited for the manly career of soldiering. **146 hold with** hold out against **147 break** train. (With pun in the next line.) **149 frets** ridges or bars on the fingerboard of the lute. (But Kate puns on the sense of "fume," "be indignant.") **155 amazèd** bewildered **156 As on a pillory** as if with my head in a wooden collar used as punishment **158 Jack** knave **159 As . . . so** as if she had planned how to abuse me so. **160 lusty** lively **164 practice** instruction **168 s.d. *Manet*** He remains onstage

Say that she rail, why then I'll tell her plain
She sings as sweetly as a nightingale.
Say that she frown, I'll say she looks as clear 172
As morning roses newly washed with dew.
Say she be mute and will not speak a word,
Then I'll commend her volubility
And say she uttereth piercing eloquence. 176
If she do bid me pack, I'll give her thanks, 177
As though she bid me stay by her a week.
If she deny to wed, I'll crave the day 179
When I shall ask the banns and when be married. 180
But here she comes; and now, Petruchio, speak.

Enter Katharina.

Good morrow, Kate, for that's your name, I hear.

KATHARINA
Well have you heard, but something hard of hearing. 183
They call me Katharine that do talk of me.

PETRUCHIO
You lie, in faith, for you are called plain Kate,
And bonny Kate, and sometimes Kate the curst;
But Kate, the prettiest Kate in Christendom,
Kate of Kate Hall, my superdainty Kate,
For dainties are all Kates, and therefore, Kate, 189
Take this of me, Kate of my consolation: 190
Hearing thy mildness praised in every town,
Thy virtues spoke of, and thy beauty sounded, 192
Yet not so deeply as to thee belongs,
Myself am moved to woo thee for my wife. 194

KATHARINA
Moved? In good time! Let him that moved you hither 195
Remove you hence. I knew you at the first
You were a movable.

PETRUCHIO Why, what's a movable? 197

KATHARINA
A joint stool.

PETRUCHIO Thou hast hit it. Come, sit on me. 198

KATHARINA
Asses are made to bear, and so are you. 199

PETRUCHIO
Women are made to bear, and so are you.

KATHARINA
No such jade as you, if me you mean. 201

PETRUCHIO
Alas, good Kate, I will not burden thee, 202
For knowing thee to be but young and light. 203

KATHARINA
Too light for such a swain as you to catch, 204
And yet as heavy as my weight should be.

PETRUCHIO
Should be? Should—buzz!

KATHARINA Well ta'en, and like a buzzard. 206

PETRUCHIO
Oh, slow-winged turtle, shall a buzzard take thee?

KATHARINA
Ay, for a turtle, as he takes a buzzard.

PETRUCHIO
Come, come, you wasp, i'faith you are too angry. 209

KATHARINA
If I be waspish, best beware my sting.

PETRUCHIO
My remedy is then to pluck it out.

KATHARINA
Ay, if the fool could find it where it lies.

PETRUCHIO
Who knows not where a wasp does wear his sting?
In his tail.

KATHARINA In his tongue.

PETRUCHIO Whose tongue?

KATHARINA
Yours, if you talk of tales, and so farewell. 217

PETRUCHIO
What, with my tongue in your tail? Nay, come again.
Good Kate, I am a gentleman—

KATHARINA That I'll try.

She strikes him.

PETRUCHIO
I swear I'll cuff you if you strike again.

KATHARINA So may you lose your arms.
If you strike me, you are no gentleman,
And if no gentleman, why then no arms. 223

PETRUCHIO
A herald, Kate? Oh, put me in thy books! 224

KATHARINA What is your crest, a coxcomb? 225

PETRUCHIO
A combless cock, so Kate will be my hen. 226

KATHARINA
No cock of mine. You crow too like a craven. 227

172 clear serene **176 piercing** moving **177 pack** begone **179 deny** refuse. **crave the day** ask her to name the day **180 ask the banns** have a reading of the required announcement in church of a forthcoming marriage **183 heard, hard** (Pronounced nearly alike.) **189 all Kates** (With a quibble on "cates," confections, delicacies.) **190 of me** from me. **consolation** comfort **192 sounded** proclaimed. (With a quibble on "plumbed," as indicated by *deeply* in the next line.) **194 moved** impelled. (Followed by wordplay on the more literal meaning of *move* and *remove*.) **195 In good time!** Forsooth! Indeed! **197 movable** (1) one easily changed or dissuaded (2) an article of furniture. **198 A joint stool** a well-fitted stool made by an expert craftsman. **199 bear** carry. (With puns in the following lines suggesting "bear children" and "support a man during sexual intercourse.") **201 jade** an ill-conditioned horse **202 burden** (1) oppress with a heavy load—a term appropriate to *asses* and *bear* in line 199, since asses are beasts of *burden* (2) lie on during sexual intercourse, impregnate. (See notes on lines 199 and 203.)

203 For knowing because I know. **light** (1) of delicate stature (2) lascivious (3) lacking a *burden* (see previous line) in the musical sense of lacking a bass undersong or accompaniment (4) elusive (in the following line). **204 swain** young rustic in love **206 Should . . . buzz!** (Petruchio puns on *be* and "bee," and uses *buzz* in perhaps three senses: [1] an interjection of impatience or contempt [2] a bee's sound [3] a rumor being buzzed about, to which, he implies, Kate had better listen.) **buzzard** (1) figuratively, a fool (2) in the next line, an inferior kind of hawk, fit only to overtake a slow-winged *turtle* or turtledove, as Petruchio might overtake Kate (3) a buzzing insect, caught by a turtledove. **209 wasp** i.e., waspish, scolding woman. (But suggested by *buzzard,* buzzing insect.) **217 talk of tales** i.e., idly tell stories. (With pun on "tail.") **223 no arms** no coat of arms. (With pun on *arms* as limbs of the body.) **224 books** (1) books of heraldry, heraldic registers (2) grace, favor. **225 crest** (1) armorial device (2) a rooster's comb, setting up the joke on *coxcomb,* the cap of the court fool **226 A combless cock** i.e., A gentle rooster. (With suggestion of the male sexual organ.) **so** provided that **227 a craven** a cock that is not "game" or willing to fight.

PETRUCHIO
Nay, come, Kate, come. You must not look so sour.
KATHARINA
It is my fashion when I see a crab.
PETRUCHIO
Why, here's no crab, and therefore look not sour.
KATHARINA There is, there is.
PETRUCHIO
Then show it me.
KATHARINA Had I a glass, I would.
PETRUCHIO What, you mean my face?
KATHARINA Well aimed of such a young one.
PETRUCHIO
Now, by Saint George, I am too young for you.
KATHARINA
Yet you are withered.
PETRUCHIO 'Tis with cares.
KATHARINA I care not.
PETRUCHIO
Nay, hear you, Kate. In sooth, you scape not so.
KATHARINA
I chafe you if I tarry. Let me go.
PETRUCHIO
No, not a whit. I find you passing gentle.
'Twas told me you were rough, and coy, and sullen,
And now I find report a very liar,
For thou art pleasant, gamesome, passing courteous,
But slow in speech, yet sweet as springtime flowers.
Thou canst not frown, thou canst not look askance,
Nor bite the lip, as angry wenches will,
Nor hast thou pleasure to be cross in talk;
But thou with mildness entertain'st thy wooers,
With gentle conference, soft and affable.
Why does the world report that Kate doth limp?
Oh, sland'rous world! Kate like the hazel twig
Is straight and slender, and as brown in hue
As hazelnuts, and sweeter than the kernels.
Oh, let me see thee walk. Thou dost not halt.
KATHARINA
Go, fool, and whom thou keep'st command.
PETRUCHIO
Did ever Dian so become a grove
As Kate this chamber with her princely gait?
Oh, be thou Dian, and let her be Kate,
And then let Kate be chaste and Dian sportful!
KATHARINA
Where did you study all this goodly speech?
PETRUCHIO
It is extempore, from my mother wit.
KATHARINA
A witty mother! Witless else her son.
PETRUCHIO Am I not wise?
KATHARINA Yes, keep you warm.
PETRUCHIO
Marry, so I mean, sweet Katharine, in thy bed.
And therefore, setting all this chat aside,
Thus in plain terms: your father hath consented
That you shall be my wife; your dowry 'greed on;
And will you, nill you, I will marry you.
Now, Kate, I am a husband for your turn,
For by this light, whereby I see thy beauty—
Thy beauty that doth make me like thee well—
Thou must be married to no man but me.

Enter Baptista, Gremio, [and] Tranio [as Lucentio].

For I am he am born to tame you, Kate,
And bring you from a wild Kate to a Kate
Conformable as other household Kates.
Here comes your father. Never make denial;
I must and will have Katharine to my wife.
BAPTISTA
Now, Signor Petruchio, how speed you with my
daughter?
PETRUCHIO
How but well, sir, how but well?
It were impossible I should speed amiss.
BAPTISTA
Why, how now, daughter Katharine, in your dumps?
KATHARINA
Call you me daughter? Now, I promise you,
You have showed a tender fatherly regard,
To wish me wed to one half-lunatic,
A madcap ruffian and a swearing Jack,
That thinks with oaths to face the matter out.
PETRUCHIO
Father, 'tis thus: yourself and all the world
That talked of her have talked amiss of her.
If she be curst, it is for policy,
For she's not froward, but modest as the dove.
She is not hot, but temperate as the morn.
For patience she will prove a second Grissel,
And Roman Lucrece for her chastity.
And to conclude, we have 'greed so well together
That upon Sunday is the wedding day.

229 crab crab apple. **234 aimed of** guessed for. **young** i.e., inexperienced. (But Petruchio picks up the word in the sense of "strong," "virile.") **237 scape** escape **238 chafe** irritate, arouse **239 passing** very. (Also in line 242.) **240 coy** disdainful **241 a very** an utter **242 pleasant, gamesome** merry, spirited **243 But slow** never anything but slow **244 askance** scornfully **246 cross in talk** always contradicting **247 entertain'st** receive **248 conference** conversation **253 halt** limp. **254 whom thou keep'st command** i.e., order about those whom you employ, your servants, not me. **255 Dian** Diana, goddess of the hunt and of chastity. **become** adorn **258 sportful** amorous. **259 study** memorize **260 mother wit** native intelligence.

261 Witless . . . son i.e., Without the intelligence inherited from her, he would have none at all. **262–3 wise . . . warm** (An allusion to the proverbial phrase "enough wit to keep oneself warm.") **268 will you, nill you** whether you're willing or not **269 for your turn** to suit you **274 wild Kate** (With a quibble on "wildcat.") **275 Conformable** compliant **278 speed** fare, get on **281 in your dumps** in low spirits. **282 promise** assure **285 Jack** ill-mannered fellow **286 face** brazen **289 policy** cunning, ulterior motive **290 froward** willful, perverse **292 Grissel** patient Griselda, the epitome of wifely patience and devotion (whose story was told by Chaucer in "The Clerk's Tale" of *The Canterbury Tales* and earlier by Boccaccio and Petrarch) **293 Roman Lucrece** Lucretia, a Roman lady who took her own life after her chastity had been violated by the Tarquin prince, Sextus. (Shakespeare tells the story in *The Rape of Lucrece*.)

KATHARINA
I'll see thee hanged on Sunday first.

GREMIO Hark, Petruchio, she says she'll see thee hanged first.

TRANIO
Is this your speeding? Nay then, good night our part!

PETRUCHIO
Be patient, gentlemen. I choose her for myself.
If she and I be pleased, what's that to you?
'Tis bargained twixt us twain, being alone,
That she shall still be curst in company.
I tell you, 'tis incredible to believe
How much she loves me. Oh, the kindest Kate!
She hung about my neck, and kiss on kiss
She vied so fast, protesting oath on oath,
That in a twink she won me to her love.
Oh, you are novices! 'Tis a world to see
How tame, when men and women are alone,
A meacock wretch can make the curstest shrew.—
Give me thy hand, Kate. I will unto Venice
To buy apparel gainst the wedding day.—
Provide the feast, father, and bid the guests.
I will be sure my Katharine shall be fine.

BAPTISTA
I know not what to say. But give me your hands.
God send you joy, Petruchio! 'Tis a match.

GREMIO, TRANIO
Amen, say we. We will be witnesses.

PETRUCHIO
Father, and wife, and gentlemen, adieu.
I will to Venice. Sunday comes apace.
We will have rings, and things, and fine array;
And kiss me, Kate. We will be married o'Sunday.

Exeunt Petruchio and Katharine [*separately*].

GREMIO
Was ever match clapped up so suddenly?

BAPTISTA
Faith, gentlemen, now I play a merchant's part,
And venture madly on a desperate mart.

TRANIO
'Twas a commodity lay fretting by you;
'Twill bring you gain, or perish on the seas.

BAPTISTA
The gain I seek is quiet in the match.

GREMIO
No doubt but he hath got a quiet catch.
But now, Baptista, to your younger daughter.
Now is the day we long have lookèd for.
I am your neighbor, and was suitor first.

TRANIO
And I am one that love Bianca more
Than words can witness, or your thoughts can guess.

GREMIO
Youngling, thou canst not love so dear as I.

TRANIO
Graybeard, thy love doth freeze.

GREMIO But thine doth fry.
Skipper, stand back. 'Tis age that nourisheth.

TRANIO
But youth in ladies' eyes that flourisheth.

BAPTISTA
Content you, gentlemen, I will compound this strife.
'Tis deeds must win the prize, and he of both
That can assure my daughter greatest dower
Shall have my Bianca's love.
Say, Signor Gremio, what can you assure her?

GREMIO
First, as you know, my house within the city
Is richly furnishèd with plate and gold,
Basins and ewers to lave her dainty hands;
My hangings all of Tyrian tapestry;
In ivory coffers I have stuffed my crowns;
In cypress chests my arras counterpoints,
Costly apparel, tents, and canopies,
Fine linen, Turkey cushions bossed with pearl,
Valance of Venice gold in needlework,
Pewter and brass, and all things that belongs
To house or housekeeping. Then at my farm
I have a hundred milch kine to the pail,
Sixscore fat oxen standing in my stalls,
And all things answerable to this portion.
Myself am struck in years, I must confess,
And if I die tomorrow, this is hers,
If whilst I live she will be only mine.

TRANIO
That "only" came well in.—Sir, list to me:
I am my father's heir and only son.
If I may have your daughter to my wife,
I'll leave her houses three or four as good,
Within rich Pisa walls, as any one
Old Signor Gremio has in Padua,
Besides two thousand ducats by the year
Of fruitful land, all which shall be her jointure.—
What, have I pinched you, Signor Gremio?

GREMIO
Two thousand ducats by the year of land!
[*Aside*] My land amounts not to so much in all.—
That she shall have, besides an argosy

299 speeding success. **good night our part** good-bye to what we hoped to get. **307 vied** went me one better, kiss for kiss **309 a world** worth a whole world **311 meacock** cowardly **313 gainst** in anticipation of **315 fine** elegantly dressed. **322 kiss me** (Petruchio probably kisses her.) **323 clapped up** settled (by a shaking of hands) **324 Faith** In faith **325 desperate mart** risky venture. **326 lay fretting** i.e., which lay in storage being destroyed by moths, weevils, or spoilage. (With a pun on "chafing.") **329 quiet catch** (Said ironically; Gremio is sure that Kate will be anything but quiet.)

337 Skipper Flighty fellow **339 compound** settle **340 deeds** (1) actions (2) legal deeds. **he of both** the one of you two **341 dower** portion of a husband's estate settled on his wife in his will. (Also at line 387 and 4.4.45.) **345 plate** silver utensils **346 ewers to lave** pitchers to wash **347 hangings** draperies hung on beds and walls. **Tyrian** dark red or purple **348 crowns** five-shilling coins **349 arras counterpoints** counterpanes of tapestry **350 tents** bed curtains **351 Turkey** Turkish. **bossed** embossed **352 Valance** fringes of drapery around the canopy or bed frame **355 milch kine to the pail** dairy cattle **357 answerable to** on the same scale as **358 struck** advanced **367 ducats** gold coins **368 Of** from. **jointure** marriage settlement. **372 argosy** merchant vessel of the largest size

That now is lying in Marseilles road.
[*To Tranio*] What, have I choked you with an argosy?

TRANIO
Gremio, 'tis known my father hath no less
Than three great argosies, besides two galliases
And twelve tight galleys. These I will assure her,
And twice as much, whate'er thou off'rest next.

GREMIO
Nay, I have offered all. I have no more,
And she can have no more than all I have.
[*To Baptista*] If you like me, she shall have me and
mine.

TRANIO
Why then, the maid is mine from all the world,
By your firm promise. Gremio is outvied.

BAPTISTA
I must confess your offer is the best;
And, let your father make her the assurance,
She is your own; else, you must pardon me.
If you should die before him, where's her dower?

TRANIO
That's but a cavil. He is old, I young.

GREMIO
And may not young men die, as well as old?

BAPTISTA
Well, gentlemen, I am thus resolved:
On Sunday next, you know
My daughter Katharine is to be married.
Now, on the Sunday following shall Bianca
Be bride [*to Tranio*] to you, if you make this assurance;
If not, to Signor Gremio.
And so I take my leave, and thank you both. *Exit.*

GREMIO
Adieu, good neighbor.—Now I fear thee not.
Sirrah, young gamester, your father were a fool
To give thee all, and in his waning age
Set foot under thy table. Tut, a toy!
An old Italian fox is not so kind, my boy. *Exit.*

TRANIO
A vengeance on your crafty withered hide!
Yet I have faced it with a card of ten.
'Tis in my head to do my master good.
I see no reason but supposed Lucentio
Must get a father, called supposed Vincentio—
And that's a wonder. Fathers commonly
Do get their children; but in this case of wooing,
A child shall get a sire, if I fail not of my cunning.
Exit.

✤

373 road roadstead, harbor. **376 galliases** heavy, low-built vessels **377 tight** watertight **383 outvied** outbidden. **385 let** provided **388 but a cavil** merely a frivolous objection. **400 Set . . . toy!** i.e., become a dependent in your household. Tut, nonsense! **403 faced . . . ten** brazened it out with only a ten-spot of cards. **408 get** beget. (With a play on *get,* "obtain," in line 406.)

3.1

Enter Lucentio [as Cambio], Hortensio [as Litio], and Bianca.

LUCENTIO
Fiddler, forbear. You grow too forward, sir.
Have you so soon forgot the entertainment
Her sister Katharine welcomed you withal?

HORTENSIO
But, wrangling pedant, this is
The patroness of heavenly harmony.
Then give me leave to have prerogative,
And when in music we have spent an hour,
Your lecture shall have leisure for as much.

LUCENTIO
Preposterous ass, that never read so far
To know the cause why music was ordained!
Was it not to refresh the mind of man
After his studies or his usual pain?
Then give me leave to read philosophy,
And, while I pause, serve in your harmony.

HORTENSIO
Sirrah, I will not bear these braves of thine.

BIANCA
Why, gentlemen, you do me double wrong
To strive for that which resteth in my choice.
I am no breeching scholar in the schools;
I'll not be tied to hours nor 'pointed times,
But learn my lessons as I please myself.
And, to cut off all strife, here sit we down.
[*To Hortensio*] Take you your instrument, play you the
whiles;
His lecture will be done ere you have tuned.

HORTENSIO
You'll leave his lecture when I am in tune?

LUCENTIO
That will be never. Tune your instrument.
[*Hortensio moves aside and tunes.*]

BIANCA Where left we last?

LUCENTIO Here, madam. [*He reads.*]
"Hic ibat Simois; hic est Sigeia tellus;
Hic steterat Priami regia celsa senis."

BIANCA Conster them.

LUCENTIO *"Hic ibat,"* as I told you before, *"Simois,"* I am Lucentio, *"hic est,"* son unto Vincentio of Pisa, *"Sigeia tellus,"* disguised thus to get your love; *"Hic steterat,"* and that Lucentio that comes a-wooing, *"Priami,"* is my man Tranio, *"regia,"* bearing my port, *"celsa senis,"* that we might beguile the old pantaloon.

3.1. Location: The same.
4 this i.e., Bianca **6 prerogative** precedence **8 lecture** lesson **10 To know** as to know **12 usual pain** regular labors. **13 read** teach **14 serve in** present, serve up **15 braves** insults **18 breeching scholar** i.e., schoolboy liable to be whipped **22 the whiles** meantime **28–9** ***Hic . . . senis*** Here flowed the river Simois; here is the Sigeian land; here stood the lofty palace of old Priam. (Ovid, *Heroides,* 1.33–4.) **30 Conster** Construe **35 bearing my port** i.e., pretending to be me **36–7 pantaloon** foolish old man, i.e., Gremio.

HORTENSIO Madam, my instrument's in tune.
BIANCA Let's hear. [*He plays.*] Oh, fie! The treble jars.
LUCENTIO Spit in the hole, man, and tune again.
[*Hortensio moves aside.*]

BIANCA Now let me see if I can conster it: *"Hic ibat Simois,"* I know you not, *"hic est Sigeia tellus,"* I trust you not; *"Hic steterat Priami,"* take heed he hear us not, *"regia,"* presume not, *"celsa senis,"* despair not.

HORTENSIO
Madam, 'tis now in tune. [*He plays again.*]
LUCENTIO All but the bass.
HORTENSIO
The bass is right, 'tis the base knave that jars.
[*Aside*] How fiery and forward our pedant is!
Now, for my life, the knave doth court my love.
Pedascule, I'll watch you better yet.
BIANCA [*to Lucentio*]
In time I may believe, yet I mistrust.
LUCENTIO
Mistrust it not, for, sure, Aeacides
Was Ajax, called so from his grandfather.
BIANCA
I must believe my master; else, I promise you,
I should be arguing still upon that doubt.
But let it rest.—Now, Litio, to you:
Good master, take it not unkindly, pray,
That I have been thus pleasant with you both.
HORTENSIO [*to Lucentio*]
You may go walk, and give me leave awhile.
My lessons make no music in three parts.
LUCENTIO
Are you so formal, sir? Well, I must wait.
[*Aside*] And watch withal; for, but I be deceived,
Our fine musician groweth amorous.
[*He moves aside.*]
HORTENSIO
Madam, before you touch the instrument,
To learn the order of my fingering,
I must begin with rudiments of art,
To teach you gamut in a briefer sort,
More pleasant, pithy, and effectual
Than hath been taught by any of my trade.
And there it is in writing, fairly drawn.
[*He gives her a paper.*]
BIANCA
Why, I am past my gamut long ago.
HORTENSIO
Yet read the gamut of Hortensio.
BIANCA [*reads*]
"Gamut I am, the ground of all accord,
A re, to plead Hortensio's passion;
B mi, Bianca, take him for thy lord,
C fa ut, that loves with all affection.
D sol re, one clef, two notes have I;
E la mi, show pity, or I die."
Call you this gamut? Tut, I like it not.
Old fashions please me best; I am not so nice
To change true rules for odd inventions.

Enter a [*Servant as*] *messenger.*

SERVANT
Mistress, your father prays you leave your books
And help to dress your sister's chamber up.
You know tomorrow is the wedding day.
BIANCA
Farewell, sweet masters both. I must be gone.
LUCENTIO
Faith, mistress, then I have no cause to stay.
[*Exeunt Bianca, Servant, and Lucentio.*]
HORTENSIO
But I have cause to pry into this pedant.
Methinks he looks as though he were in love.
Yet if thy thoughts, Bianca, be so humble
To cast thy wandering eyes on every stale,
Seize thee that list. If once I find thee ranging,
Hortensio will be quit with thee by changing. *Exit.*

✤

[3.2]

Enter Baptista, Gremio, Tranio [*as Lucentio*], *Katharine, Bianca,* [*Lucentio as Cambio*], *and others, attendants.*

BAPTISTA [*to Tranio*]
Signor Lucentio, this is the 'pointed day
That Katharine and Petruchio should be married,
And yet we hear not of our son-in-law.
What will be said? What mockery will it be,
To want the bridegroom when the priest attends
To speak the ceremonial rites of marriage?
What says Lucentio to this shame of ours?

40 Spit in the hole i.e., to make the peg stick **49 *Pedascule*** (A word contemptuously coined by Hortensio, presumably the vocative of an invented Latinism, *pedasculus,* "little pedant.") **51 Mistrust** (Lucentio plays upon Bianca's *mistrust* in line 50, in which she expresses skepticism about his secret wooing; his answer seeks to reassure her, while at the same time in "Litio's" hearing he seems to emphasize the truth of his instruction as he goes on with his lesson from the *Heroides*. Her reply is ambiguous in the same way.) **Aeacides** descendant of Aeacus, King of Aegina, father of Telamon and grandfather of Ajax **57 pleasant** merry **60 formal** precise **61 but** unless **64 order** method **66 gamut** the scale, from the alphabet name (*gamma*) of the first note plus *ut*, its syllable name, now commonly called *do*. (The *gamut* of Hortensio begins on G instead of on C.) **69 drawn** set out, copied.

72 ground bass note, foundation. **accord** harmony **74 *B mi*** (With a suggestion of "be my.") **75 *fa ut*** (The note C is the fourth note, or *fa*, of a scale based on G but is the first note, *ut*, or *do*, of the more universal major scale based on C. Similarly, D is the fifth note, or *sol*, in the G scale but is the second, or *re*, in the C scale; similarly, with E as sixth and third.) **76 two notes** (Hinting at Hortensio's disguise.) **77 *E la mi*** (Suggesting "Ill am I.") **79 nice** capricious **89 stale** ridiculous rival **90 Seize . . . list** let him who wants you have you. **ranging** inconstant. (The metaphor is that of a straying hawk.) **91 be quit** get even. **changing** loving another.
3.2. Location: Padua. Before Baptista's house.
4 What . . . said? What will people say? **5 want** lack

KATHARINA
No shame but mine. I must, forsooth, be forced
To give my hand opposed against my heart
Unto a mad-brain rudesby full of spleen,
Who wooed in haste and means to wed at leisure.
I told you, I, he was a frantic fool,
Hiding his bitter jests in blunt behavior.
And, to be noted for a merry man,
He'll woo a thousand, 'point the day of marriage,
Make friends, invite, and proclaim the banns,
Yet never means to wed where he hath wooed.
Now must the world point at poor Katharine
And say, "Lo, there is mad Petruchio's wife,
If it would please him come and marry her!"

TRANIO
Patience, good Katharine, and Baptista, too.
Upon my life, Petruchio means but well,
Whatever fortune stays him from his word.
Though he be blunt, I know him passing wise;
Though he be merry, yet withal he's honest.

KATHARINA
Would Katharine had never seen him, though!
Exit weeping.

BAPTISTA
Go, girl, I cannot blame thee now to weep,
For such an injury would vex a very saint,
Much more a shrew of thy impatient humor.

Enter Biondello.

BIONDELLO Master, master! News, and such old news as you never heard of!

BAPTISTA Is it new and old too? How may that be?

BIONDELLO Why, is it not news to hear of Petruchio's coming?

BAPTISTA Is he come?

BIONDELLO Why, no, sir.

BAPTISTA What, then?

BIONDELLO He is coming.

BAPTISTA When will he be here?

BIONDELLO When he stands where I am and sees you there.

TRANIO But say, what to thine old news?

BIONDELLO Why, Petruchio is coming in a new hat and an old jerkin; a pair of old breeches thrice turned; a pair of boots that have been candle-cases, one buckled, another laced; an old rusty sword ta'en out of the town armory, with a broken hilt, and chapeless; with two broken points; his horse hipped, with an old mothy saddle and stirrups of no kindred; besides, possessed with the glanders and like to mose in the chine, troubled with the lampass, infected with the fashions, full of windgalls, sped with spavins, rayed with the yellows, past cure of the fives, stark spoiled with the staggers, begnawn with the bots, swayed in the back and shoulder-shotten; near-legged before, and with a half-cheeked bit and a headstall of sheep's leather which, being restrained to keep him from stumbling, hath been often burst and now repaired with knots; one girth six times pieced, and a woman's crupper of velour, which hath two letters for her name fairly set down in studs, and here and there pieced with packthread.

BAPTISTA Who comes with him?

BIONDELLO Oh, sir, his lackey, for all the world caparisoned like the horse; with a linen stock on one leg and a kersey boot-hose on the other, gartered with a red and blue list; an old hat, and the humor of forty fancies pricked in 't for a feather—a monster, a very monster in apparel, and not like a Christian footboy or a gentleman's lackey.

TRANIO
'Tis some odd humor pricks him to this fashion;
Yet oftentimes he goes but mean-appareled.

BAPTISTA I am glad he's come, howsoe'er he comes.

BIONDELLO Why, sir, he comes not.

BAPTISTA Didst thou not say he comes?

BIONDELLO Who? That Petruchio came?

BAPTISTA Ay, that Petruchio came.

BIONDELLO No, sir, I say his horse comes, with him on his back.

BAPTISTA Why, that's all one.

BIONDELLO
Nay, by Saint Jamy,

10 rudesby unmannerly fellow. **spleen** i.e., changeable temper **14 to be noted for** in order to get a reputation as **16 banns** wedding announcement **23 Whatever . . . word** whatever accident keeps him from fulfilling his promise. **24 passing** exceedingly **25 merry** given to joking **30 old** rare; and referring to Petruchio's old clothes **42 to** about **44 jerkin** man's jacket. **turned** i.e., with the material reversed to get more wear **45 candle-cases** i.e., discarded boots, used only as a receptacle for candle ends **47 chapeless** without the chape, the metal plate or mounting of a scabbard, especially that which covers the point **48 points** tagged laces for attaching hose to doublet. **hipped** lamed in the hip. (Almost all the diseases here named are described in Gervase Markham's *How to Choose, Ride, Train, and Diet both Hunting Horses and Running Horses . . . Also a Discourse of Horsemanship*, probably first published in 1593.)

49 of no kindred that don't match **50 glanders** contagious disease in horses causing swelling beneath the jaw and mucous discharge from the nostrils. **mose in the chine** suffer from glanders **51 lampass** a thick, spongy flesh growing over a horse's upper teeth and hindering his eating. **fashions** i.e., farcins, or farcy, a disease like glanders **52 windgalls** soft tumors or swellings generally found on the fetlock joint, so called from having been supposed to contain air. **sped** far gone. **spavins** a disease of the hock, marked by a small bony enlargement inside the leg. **rayed** bespattered, defiled **52–3 yellows** jaundice **53 fives** avives, a glandular disease causing swelling behind the ear **53–4 stark . . . staggers** completely destroyed by a disease causing palsylike staggering **54 bots** parasitic worms **55 shoulder-shotten** with sprained or dislocated shoulder. **near-legged before** with knock-kneed forelegs **55–6 half-cheeked bit** one to which the bridle is attached halfway up the cheek or sidepiece and thus not giving sufficient control over the horse **56 headstall** part of the bridle over the head. **sheep's leather** (i.e., of inferior quality; pigskin was used for strongest harness) **57 restrained** drawn back **59 girth** saddle-strap passing under the horse's belly. **pieced** mended. **crupper** leather loop passing under the horse's tail and fastened to the saddle **60 velour** velvet. **two . . . name** her initials **62 packthread** twine for securing parcels. **64–5 for . . . caparisoned** in all respects outfitted **65 stock** stocking **66 kersey boot-hose** overstocking of coarse material for wearing under boots **67 list** strip of cloth **67–8 the humor . . . feather** a trite motto incised in it instead of a feather **68 pricked** pinned. **for** in place of **71 humor pricks** whim that spurs **72 mean-appareled** poorly dressed. **80 all one** the same thing.

I hold you a penny,
A horse and a man
Is more than one,
And yet not many.

Enter Petruchio and Grumio.

PETRUCHIO
Come, where be these gallants? Who's at home?
BAPTISTA You are welcome, sir.
PETRUCHIO And yet I come not well.
BAPTISTA And yet you halt not.
TRANIO
Not so well appareled as I wish you were.
PETRUCHIO
Were it better, I should rush in thus.
But where is Kate? Where is my lovely bride?
How does my father? Gentles, methinks you frown.
And wherefore gaze this goodly company,
As if they saw some wondrous monument,
Some comet, or unusual prodigy?
BAPTISTA
Why, sir, you know this is your wedding day.
First were we sad, fearing you would not come,
Now sadder that you come so unprovided.
Fie, doff this habit, shame to your estate,
An eyesore to our solemn festival!
TRANIO
And tell us, what occasion of import
Hath all so long detained you from your wife
And sent you hither so unlike yourself?
PETRUCHIO
Tedious it were to tell, and harsh to hear.
Sufficeth I am come to keep my word,
Though in some part enforcèd to digress,
Which at more leisure I will so excuse
As you shall well be satisfied withal.
But where is Kate? I stay too long from her.
The morning wears; 'tis time we were at church.
TRANIO
See not your bride in these unreverent robes.
Go to my chamber. Put on clothes of mine.
PETRUCHIO
Not I, believe me. Thus I'll visit her.
BAPTISTA
But thus, I trust, you will not marry her.
PETRUCHIO
Good sooth, even thus. Therefore ha' done with words.
To me she's married, not unto my clothes.
Could I repair what she will wear in me
As I can change these poor accoutrements,
'Twere well for Kate and better for myself.
But what a fool am I to chat with you,
When I should bid good morrow to my bride
And seal the title with a lovely kiss! *Exit.*
TRANIO
He hath some meaning in his mad attire.
We will persuade him, be it possible,
To put on better ere he go to church.
BAPTISTA
I'll after him, and see the event of this.
Exit [with all but Tranio and Lucentio].
TRANIO
But, sir, to love concerneth us to add
Her father's liking, which to bring to pass,
As I before imparted to Your Worship,
I am to get a man—whate'er he be
It skills not much, we'll fit him to our turn—
And he shall be Vincentio of Pisa
And make assurance here in Padua
Of greater sums than I have promisèd.
So shall you quietly enjoy your hope
And marry sweet Bianca with consent.
LUCENTIO
Were it not that my fellow schoolmaster
Doth watch Bianca's steps so narrowly,
'Twere good, methinks, to steal our marriage,
Which once performed, let all the world say no,
I'll keep mine own, despite of all the world.
TRANIO
That by degrees we mean to look into,
And watch our vantage in this business.
We'll overreach the graybeard, Gremio,
The narrow-prying father, Minola,
The quaint musician, amorous Litio,
All for my master's sake, Lucentio.

Enter Gremio.

Signor Gremio, came you from the church?
GREMIO
As willingly as e'er I came from school.
TRANIO
And is the bride and bridegroom coming home?
GREMIO
A bridegroom, say you? 'Tis a groom indeed,
A grumbling groom, and that the girl shall find.
TRANIO
Curster than she? Why, 'tis impossible.
GREMIO
Why, he 's a devil, a devil, a very fiend.
TRANIO
Why, she's a devil, a devil, the devil's dam.

82 hold wager **88 I come not well** i.e., I am not made to feel welcome; or, I come admittedly not well appareled. **89 halt** limp, move slowly **91 Were it** Even if it (my apparel) were. **rush** come quickly. (Referring to *halt not* in line 89.) **95 monument** portent **96 prodigy** omen. **99 unprovided** ill equipped. **100 habit** outfit. **estate** position, station **106 Sufficeth** It is enough that **107 digress** i.e., deviate **116 Good sooth** i.e., Yes, indeed **118 Could . . . me** If I could amend in my character what she'll have to put up with

123 lovely loving **127 event** outcome **128 to love . . . add** besides obtaining the love of the lady, it behooves us to add **130 to Your Worship** (Tranio privately drops the fiction that he is Lucentio's master.) **132 skills** matters **140 steal our marriage** elope **144 watch our vantage** look out for our best opportunity, advantage **146 narrow-prying** suspicious, watchful **147 quaint** skillful **152 'Tis a groom indeed** A fine bridegroom he is. (Said ironically, with pun on the sense of "servant," "rough fellow.") **156 dam** mother.

GREMIO
Tut, she's a lamb, a dove, a fool to him. 157
I'll tell you, Sir Lucentio. When the priest
Should ask if Katharine should be his wife, 159
"Ay, by Gog's wouns," quoth he, and swore so loud 160
That all amazed the priest let fall the book,
And as he stooped again to take it up,
This mad-brained bridegroom took him such a cuff 163
That down fell priest and book, and book and priest.
"Now take them up," quoth he, "if any list." 165

TRANIO
What said the wench when he rose again?

GREMIO
Trembled and shook, forwhy he stamped and swore 167
As if the vicar meant to cozen him. 168
But after many ceremonies done
He calls for wine. "A health!" quoth he, as if
He had been aboard, carousing to his mates 171
After a storm; quaffed off the muscatel
And threw the sops all in the sexton's face, 173
Having no other reason
But that his beard grew thin and hungerly 175
And seemed to ask him sops as he was drinking. 176
This done, he took the bride about the neck
And kissed her lips with such a clamorous smack
That at the parting all the church did echo.
And I seeing this came thence for very shame,
And after me, I know, the rout is coming. 181
Such a mad marriage never was before. *Music plays.*
Hark, hark! I hear the minstrels play.

Enter Petruchio, Kate, Bianca, Hortensio [*as Litio*], *Baptista,* [*with Grumio, and train*].

PETRUCHIO
Gentlemen and friends, I thank you for your pains.
I know you think to dine with me today,
And have prepared great store of wedding cheer;
But so it is my haste doth call me hence,
And therefore here I mean to take my leave.

BAPTISTA
Is't possible you will away tonight?

PETRUCHIO
I must away today, before night come.
Make it no wonder. If you knew my business, 191
You would entreat me rather go than stay.
And, honest company, I thank you all 193
That have beheld me give away myself
To this most patient, sweet, and virtuous wife.
Dine with my father, drink a health to me,
For I must hence; and farewell to you all.

TRANIO
Let us entreat you stay till after dinner.

PETRUCHIO
It may not be.

GREMIO Let me entreat you.

PETRUCHIO
It cannot be.

KATHARINA Let me entreat you.

PETRUCHIO
I am content.

KATHARINA Are you content to stay?

PETRUCHIO
I am content you shall entreat me stay;
But yet not stay, entreat me how you can.

KATHARINA
Now, if you love me, stay.

PETRUCHIO Grumio, my horse. 204

GRUMIO Ay, sir, they be ready. The oats have eaten the 205
horses. 206

KATHARINA Nay, then,
Do what thou canst, I will not go today,
No, nor tomorrow—not till I please myself.
The door is open, sir; there lies your way.
You may be jogging whiles your boots are green. 211
For me, I'll not be gone till I please myself. 212
'Tis like you'll prove a jolly, surly groom, 213
That take it on you at the first so roundly. 214

PETRUCHIO
Oh, Kate, content thee. Prithee, be not angry.

KATHARINA
I will be angry. What hast thou to do?— 216
Father, be quiet. He shall stay my leisure. 217

GREMIO
Ay, marry, sir, now it begins to work. 218

KATHARINA
Gentlemen, forward to the bridal dinner.
I see a woman may be made a fool
If she had not a spirit to resist.

PETRUCHIO
They shall go forward, Kate, at thy command.—
Obey the bride, you that attend on her.
Go to the feast, revel and domineer, 224
Carouse full measure to her maidenhead, 225
Be mad and merry, or go hang yourselves.
But for my bonny Kate, she must with me. 227
Nay, look not big, nor stamp, nor stare, nor fret; 228
I will be master of what is mine own.
She is my goods, my chattels; she is my house,
My household stuff, my field, my barn,
My horse, my ox, my ass, my anything; 232
And here she stands, touch her whoever dare.

157 a fool to i.e., a pitiable weak creature compared with
159 Should ask came to the point (in the service) where he is directed to ask **160 Gog's wouns** God's (Christ's) wounds **163 took** gave, struck **165 list** choose. **167 forwhy** for **168 cozen** cheat
171 aboard aboard ship **173 sops** cakes or bread soaked in the wine
175 hungerly hungry looking, having a starved or famished look
176 And . . . drinking and seemed to invite the throwing in his face of what Petruchio was drinking. **181 rout** crowd, wedding party
191 Make it no wonder Don't be surprised. **193 honest** worthy, kind

204 horse horses. **205–6 oats . . . horses** (A comic inversion.)
211 be . . . green (Proverbial for "getting an early start," with a sarcastic allusion to his unseemly attire.) **green** fresh, new. **212 For** As for **213 like** likely. **jolly** (Said sarcastically.) **214 take it on you** i.e., throw your weight around. **roundly** unceremoniously.
216 What . . . do? What business is it of yours? **217 stay my leisure** wait until I am ready. **218 now . . . work** now it starts. **224 domineer** feast riotously **225 to her maidenhead** to her loss of virginity
227 for as for **228 big** threatening **232 ox . . . anything** (This catalogue of a man's possessions is from the Tenth Commandment.)

I'll bring mine action on the proudest he
That stops my way in Padua.—Grumio,
Draw forth thy weapon. We are beset with thieves.
Rescue thy mistress, if thou be a man.—
Fear not, sweet wench, they shall not touch thee, Kate!
I'll buckler thee against a million.

Exeunt Petruchio, Katharina, [*and Grumio*].

BAPTISTA
Nay, let them go—a couple of quiet ones!

GREMIO
Went they not quickly, I should die with laughing.

TRANIO
Of all mad matches never was the like.

LUCENTIO
Mistress, what's your opinion of your sister?

BIANCA
That, being mad herself, she's madly mated.

GREMIO
I warrant him, Petruchio is Kated.

BAPTISTA
Neighbors and friends, though bride and bridegroom wants
For to supply the places at the table,
You know there wants no junkets at the feast.
Lucentio, you shall supply the bridegroom's place,
And let Bianca take her sister's room.

TRANIO
Shall sweet Bianca practice how to bride it?

BAPTISTA
She shall, Lucentio.—Come, gentlemen, let's go.

Exeunt.

✤

[4.1]

Enter Grumio.

GRUMIO Fie, fie on all tired jades, on all mad masters, and all foul ways! Was ever man so beaten? Was ever man so rayed? Was ever man so weary? I am sent before to make a fire, and they are coming after to warm them. Now, were not I a little pot and soon hot, my very lips might freeze to my teeth, my tongue to the roof of my mouth, my heart in my belly, ere I should come by a fire to thaw me. But I with blowing the fire shall warm myself; for, considering the weather, a taller man than I will take cold.—Holla, ho! Curtis!

Enter Curtis.

CURTIS Who is that calls so coldly?

GRUMIO A piece of ice. If thou doubt it, thou mayst slide from my shoulder to my heel with no greater a run but my head and my neck. A fire, good Curtis!

CURTIS Is my master and his wife coming, Grumio?

GRUMIO Oh, ay, Curtis, ay, and therefore fire, fire! Cast on no water.

CURTIS Is she so hot a shrew as she's reported?

GRUMIO She was, good Curtis, before this frost. But, thou know'st, winter tames man, woman, and beast; for it hath tamed my old master and my new mistress and myself, fellow Curtis.

CURTIS Away, you three-inch fool! I am no beast.

GRUMIO Am I but three inches? Why, thy horn is a foot, and so long am I, at the least. But wilt thou make a fire, or shall I complain on thee to our mistress, whose hand—she being now at hand—thou shalt soon feel, to thy cold comfort, for being slow in thy hot office?

CURTIS I prithee, good Grumio, tell me, how goes the world?

GRUMIO A cold world, Curtis, in every office but thine, and therefore fire. Do thy duty, and have thy duty, for my master and mistress are almost frozen to death.

CURTIS There's fire ready, and therefore, good Grumio, the news.

GRUMIO Why, "Jack boy, ho, boy!" and as much news as wilt thou.

CURTIS Come, you are so full of coney-catching.

GRUMIO Why, therefore fire, for I have caught extreme cold. Where's the cook? Is supper ready, the house trimmed, rushes strewed, cobwebs swept, the servingmen in their new fustian, the white stockings, and every officer his wedding garment on? Be the Jacks fair within, the Jills fair without, the carpets laid, and everything in order?

CURTIS All ready; and therefore, I pray thee, news.

GRUMIO First, know my horse is tired, my master and mistress fallen out.

CURTIS How?

GRUMIO Out of their saddles into the dirt—and thereby hangs a tale.

234 action (1) lawsuit (2) attack **236 Draw** (Perhaps Petruchio and Grumio actually draw their swords.) **239 buckler** shield, defend **245 Kated** (Gremio's invention for "mated and matched with Kate.") **246–7 wants For to supply** are not present to fill **248 there wants no junkets** there is no lack of sweetmeats **251 bride it** play the bride.

4.1. Location: Petruchio's country house. A table is set out, with seats.

1 jades ill-conditioned horses **2 ways** roads. **3 rayed** bespattered. **5 a little . . . hot** (Proverbial expression for a person of small stature soon angered.) **8 come by** find **10 taller** (With play on the meaning "better," "finer.")

14 run running start **16–17 Cast . . . water** (Alludes to the round "Scotland's burning," in which the phrase "Fire, fire!" is followed by "Pour on water, pour on water.") **23 three-inch fool** (Another reference to Grumio's size.) **I am no beast** (Curtis protests being called *fellow* by Grumio, since Grumio in line 20 has paralleled himself with *beast.*) **24–5 Why . . . least** (Grumio hints that Curtis is a beast with a prominent *horn,* and hence a cuckold; suggesting too that Grumio's *horn,* i.e., *penis,* is as long as Curtis's or longer.) **28 hot office** i.e., duty of providing a fire. **32 have thy duty** have what's coming to you, your due **36 Jack . . . boy** (The first line of another round or catch.) **38 coney-catching** cheating, trickery. (With wordplay on *catch,* or round, like "Jack boy, ho, boy" in line 36.)

41 rushes (Used to cover the floor.) **42 fustian** coarse cloth of cotton and flax **43 officer** household servant. **Jacks** (1) servingmen (2) drinking vessels, usually of leather and hence needing to be clean *within* **44 Jills** (1) maidservants (2) "gills," drinking vessels holding a quarter pint, often of metal and hence in need of polishing *without.* (Grumio may joke that the maidservants cannot be expected to be clean *within.*) **48 fallen out** quarreling. (But with a pun on the literal sense in line 50.) **50–1 thereby hangs a tale** there's quite a story to tell about that. (But with a risible suggestion of hanging by one's tail.)

CURTIS Let's ha 't, good Grumio.

GRUMIO Lend thine ear.

CURTIS Here.

GRUMIO There. *[He cuffs Curtis.]*

CURTIS This 'tis to feel a tale, not to hear a tale.

GRUMIO And therefore 'tis called a sensible tale, and this cuff was but to knock at your ear and beseech listening. Now I begin: Imprimis, we came down a foul hill, my master riding behind my mistress—

CURTIS Both of one horse?

GRUMIO What's that to thee?

CURTIS Why, a horse.

GRUMIO Tell thou the tale. But hadst thou not crossed me, thou shouldst have heard how her horse fell and she under her horse; thou shouldst have heard in how miry a place, how she was bemoiled, how he left her with the horse upon her, how he beat me because her horse stumbled, how she waded through the dirt to pluck him off me, how he swore, how she prayed that never prayed before, how I cried, how the horses ran away, how her bridle was burst, how I lost my crupper, with many things of worthy memory, which now shall die in oblivion and thou return unexperienced to thy grave.

CURTIS By this reckoning he is more shrew than she.

GRUMIO Ay, and that thou and the proudest of you all shall find when he comes home. But what talk I of this? Call forth Nathaniel, Joseph, Nicholas, Philip, Walter, Sugarsop, and the rest. Let their heads be sleekly combed, their blue coats brushed, and their garters of an indifferent knit; let them curtsy with their left legs, and not presume to touch a hair of my master's horsetail till they kiss their hands. Are they all ready?

CURTIS They are.

GRUMIO Call them forth.

CURTIS *[calling]* Do you hear, ho? You must meet my master to countenance my mistress.

GRUMIO Why, she hath a face of her own.

CURTIS Who knows not that?

GRUMIO Thou, it seems, that calls for company to countenance her.

CURTIS I call them forth to credit her.

Enter four or five Servingmen.

GRUMIO Why, she comes to borrow nothing of them.

NATHANIEL Welcome home, Grumio!

PHILIP How now, Grumio?

JOSEPH What, Grumio!

NICHOLAS Fellow Grumio!

NATHANIEL How now, old lad?

GRUMIO Welcome, you; how now, you; what, you; fellow, you—and thus much for greeting. Now, my spruce companions, is all ready, and all things neat?

NATHANIEL All things is ready. How near is our master?

GRUMIO E'en at hand, alighted by this; and therefore be not—Cock's passion, silence! I hear my master.

Enter Petruchio and Kate.

PETRUCHIO
Where be these knaves? What, no man at door
To hold my stirrup nor to take my horse?
Where is Nathaniel, Gregory, Philip?

ALL SERVANTS Here, here, sir, here, sir.

PETRUCHIO
Here, sir! Here, sir! Here, sir! Here, sir!
You loggerheaded and unpolished grooms!
What, no attendance? No regard? No duty?
Where is the foolish knave I sent before?

GRUMIO
Here, sir, as foolish as I was before.

PETRUCHIO
You peasant swain, you whoreson, malt-horse drudge!
Did I not bid thee meet me in the park
And bring along these rascal knaves with thee?

GRUMIO
Nathaniel's coat, sir, was not fully made,
And Gabriel's pumps were all unpinked i'the heel.
There was no link to color Peter's hat,
And Walter's dagger was not come from sheathing.
There were none fine but Adam, Ralph, and Gregory;
The rest were ragged, old, and beggarly.
Yet, as they are, here are they come to meet you.

PETRUCHIO
Go, rascals, go and fetch my supper in.
Exeunt Servants.
[He sings.] "Where is the life that late I led?
Where are those—" Sit down, Kate, and welcome.—
[They sit at table.]
Soud, soud, soud, soud!

Enter Servants with supper.

Why, when, I say?—Nay, good sweet Kate, be merry.—
Off with my boots, you rogues! You villains, when?
[A Servant takes off Petruchio's boots.]
[He sings.] "It was the friar of orders gray,
As he forth walkèd on his way—"

52 ha 't have it **57 sensible** (1) capable of being felt (2) showing good sense **59 Imprimis** In the first place **60 foul** muddy **61 of** on **64 crossed** thwarted, interrupted **67 bemoiled** befouled with mire **73 crupper** (See 3.2.59.) **of worthy** worthy of **78 what** why **81 blue coats** (Usual dress for servingmen.) **82 indifferent** well-matched, identical **89 countenance** pay respects to. (With a following pun on the meaning "face.") **94 credit** pay respects to. (With another pun following, on "extend financial credit.")

103 spruce lively, trim in appearance **107 Cock's passion** By God's (Christ's) suffering **109 hold my stirrup** i.e., help me dismount **115 before** ahead. (With pun in next line on "previously.") **117 swain** rustic. **whoreson . . . drudge** worthless plodding work animal, such as would be used on a treadmill to grind malt. **121 pumps** low-cut shoes. **unpinked** lacking in eyelets or in ornamental tracing in the leather **122 link** blacking made from burnt "links" or torches **123 sheathing** being fitted with a sheath. **124 fine** well clothed **128–9 Where . . . those** (A fragment of a lost ballad, probably lamenting the man's loss of freedom in marriage.) **130 Soud** (A nonsense song, or expression of impatience, or perhaps "food!") **131 when** (An exclamation of impatience.) **133–4 "It . . . way"** (A fragment of a lost ballad, probably bawdy.)

Out, you rogue! You pluck my foot awry.
[He kicks the Servant.]
Take that, and mend the plucking of the other.—
Be merry, Kate.—Some water, here. What, ho!

Enter one with water.

Where's my spaniel Troilus? Sirrah, get you hence,
And bid my cousin Ferdinand come hither—
[Exit Servant.]
One, Kate, that you must kiss and be acquainted with.
Where are my slippers? Shall I have some water?
Come, Kate, and wash, and welcome heartily.
[A Servant offers water, but spills some.]
You whoreson villain, will you let it fall?
[He strikes the Servant.]

KATHARINA
Patience, I pray you, 'twas a fault unwilling.

PETRUCHIO
A whoreson, beetleheaded, flap-eared knave!—
Come, Kate, sit down. I know you have a stomach.
Will you give thanks, sweet Kate, or else shall I?—
What's this? Mutton?

FIRST SERVANT Ay.

PETRUCHIO Who brought it?

PETER I.

PETRUCHIO
'Tis burnt, and so is all the meat.
What dogs are these? Where is the rascal cook?
How durst you, villains, bring it from the dresser
And serve it thus to me that love it not?
There, take it to you, trenchers, cups, and all.
[He throws the meat, etc., at them.]
You heedless jolt-heads and unmannered slaves!
What, do you grumble? I'll be with you straight.
[They run out.]

KATHARINA
I pray you, husband, be not so disquiet.
The meat was well, if you were so contented.

PETRUCHIO
I tell thee, Kate, 'twas burnt and dried away,
And I expressly am forbid to touch it;
For it engenders choler, planteth anger,
And better 'twere that both of us did fast,
Since, of ourselves, ourselves are choleric,
Than feed it with such overroasted flesh.
Be patient. Tomorrow 't shall be mended,
And for this night we'll fast for company.
Come, I will bring thee to thy bridal chamber.
Exeunt.

Enter Servants severally.

NATHANIEL Peter, didst ever see the like?

PETER He kills her in her own humor.

Enter Curtis.

GRUMIO Where is he?

CURTIS In her chamber,
Making a sermon of continency to her,
And rails, and swears, and rates, that she, poor soul,
Knows not which way to stand, to look, to speak,
And sits as one new risen from a dream.
Away, away! For he is coming hither. *[Exeunt.]*

Enter Petruchio.

PETRUCHIO
Thus have I politicly begun my reign,
And 'tis my hope to end successfully.
My falcon now is sharp and passing empty,
And till she stoop she must not be full-gorged,
For then she never looks upon her lure.
Another way I have to man my haggard,
To make her come and know her keeper's call:
That is, to watch her, as we watch these kites
That bate and beat and will not be obedient.
She ate no meat today, nor none shall eat.
Last night she slept not, nor tonight she shall not.
As with the meat, some undeservèd fault
I'll find about the making of the bed,
And here I'll fling the pillow, there the bolster,
This way the coverlet, another way the sheets.
Ay, and amid this hurly I intend
That all is done in reverent care of her.
And in conclusion she shall watch all night,
And if she chance to nod I'll rail and brawl,
And with the clamor keep her still awake.
This is a way to kill a wife with kindness;
And thus I'll curb her mad and headstrong humor.
He that knows better how to tame a shrew,
Now let him speak. 'Tis charity to show. *Exit.*

✤

[4.2]

Enter Tranio [as Lucentio] and Hortensio [as Litio].

TRANIO
Is't possible, friend Litio, that Mistress Bianca
Doth fancy any other but Lucentio?
I tell you, sir, she bears me fair in hand.

135 Out (Exclamation of anger or reproach.) **136 mend the plucking of** do a better job of pulling off **144 unwilling** not intentional. **145 beetleheaded** i.e., blockheaded (since a *beetle* is a pounding tool) **146 stomach** appetite. (With a suggestion also of "temper.") **147 give thanks** say grace **151 dresser** one who "dresses" or prepares the food; or, sideboard **153 trenchers** wooden dishes or plates **154 jolt-heads** blockheads **155 with you straight** after you at once (to get even for this). **157 if . . . contented** if you had chosen to be pleased with it. **160 choler** the humor or bodily fluid, hot and dry in character, that supposedly produced ill temper and was thought to be aggravated by the eating of roast meat **162 of ourselves** by our natures **165 for company** together. **166.2 *severally*** separately.

168 He . . . humor He subdues her shrewishness with his own greater shrewishness. **171 sermon of continency** lecture on self-restraint **172 rates** scolds. **that** so that **176 politicly** with skillful calculation **178 sharp** hungry. **passing** very **179 stoop** fly down to the lure **181 man** tame, assert masculine authority over. **haggard** wild female hawk; hence, an intractable woman **183 watch her** keep her watching, i.e., awake. **kites** a kind of hawk. (With a pun on *Kate*.) **184 bate and beat** beat the wings impatiently and flutter away from the hand or perch **191 hurly** commotion. **intend** pretend **193 watch** stay awake **197 humor** disposition. **199 'Tis charity to show** This is to perform an act of Christian benevolence. (On the rhyme with *shrew*, see also the play's final lines.)
4.2. Location: Padua. Before Baptista's house.
3 bears . . . hand gives me encouragement, leads me on.

HORTENSIO
Sir, to satisfy you in what I have said,
Stand by and mark the manner of his teaching.
[*They stand aside.*]

Enter Bianca [*and Lucentio as Cambio*].

LUCENTIO
Now, mistress, profit you in what you read?
BIANCA
What, master, read you? First resolve me that.
LUCENTIO
I read that I profess, *The Art to Love*.
BIANCA
And may you prove, sir, master of your art!
LUCENTIO
While you, sweet dear, prove mistress of my heart!
[*They move aside and court each other.*]
HORTENSIO [*to Tranio, coming forward*]
Quick proceeders, marry! Now, tell me, I pray,
You that durst swear that your mistress Bianca
Loved none in the world so well as Lucentio.
TRANIO
Oh, despiteful love! Unconstant womankind!
I tell thee, Litio, this is wonderful.
HORTENSIO
Mistake no more. I am not Litio,
Nor a musician, as I seem to be,
But one that scorn to live in this disguise
For such a one as leaves a gentleman
And makes a god of such a cullion.
Know, sir, that I am called Hortensio.
TRANIO
Signor Hortensio, I have often heard
Of your entire affection to Bianca;
And since mine eyes are witness of her lightness,
I will with you, if you be so contented,
Forswear Bianca and her love forever.
HORTENSIO
See how they kiss and court! Signor Lucentio,
Here is my hand, and here I firmly vow
[*giving his hand*]
Never to woo her more, but do forswear her,
As one unworthy all the former favors
That I have fondly flattered her withal.
TRANIO
And here I take the like unfeignèd oath,
Never to marry with her though she would entreat.
Fie on her, see how beastly she doth court him!
HORTENSIO
Would all the world but he had quite forsworn!
For me, that I may surely keep mine oath,
I will be married to a wealthy widow,
Ere three days pass, which hath as long loved me
As I have loved this proud disdainful haggard.
And so farewell, Signor Lucentio.
Kindness in women, not their beauteous looks,
Shall win my love. And so I take my leave,
In resolution as I swore before. [*Exit.*]
TRANIO [*as Lucentio and Bianca come forward again*]
Mistress Bianca, bless you with such grace
As 'longeth to a lover's blessèd case!
Nay, I have ta'en you napping, gentle love,
And have forsworn you with Hortensio.
BIANCA
Tranio, you jest. But have you both forsworn me?
TRANIO
Mistress, we have.
LUCENTIO Then we are rid of Litio.
TRANIO
I' faith, he'll have a lusty widow now,
That shall be wooed and wedded in a day.
BIANCA God give him joy!
TRANIO Ay, and he'll tame her.
BIANCA He says so, Tranio?
TRANIO
Faith, he is gone unto the taming-school.
BIANCA
The taming-school! What, is there such a place?
TRANIO
Ay, mistress, and Petruchio is the master,
That teacheth tricks eleven-and-twenty long
To tame a shrew and charm her chattering tongue.

Enter Biondello.

BIONDELLO
Oh, master, master, I have watched so long
That I am dog-weary, but at last I spied
An ancient angel coming down the hill
Will serve the turn.
TRANIO What is he, Biondello?
BIONDELLO
Master, a marcantant, or a pedant,
I know not what, but formal in apparel,
In gait and countenance surely like a father.
LUCENTIO And what of him, Tranio?
TRANIO
If he be credulous and trust my tale,
I'll make him glad to seem Vincentio,
And give assurance to Baptista Minola

4 satisfy convince **6 read** (Evidently, both Bianca and "Cambio" carry books.) **7 resolve** answer **8 I read . . . *Love*** I read what I practice, Ovid's *Ars Amatoria*. **11 proceeders** (1) workers, doers (2) candidates for academic degrees (as suggested by the phrase *master of your art* in line 9) **14 despiteful** cruel **15 wonderful** cause for wonder. **18 scorn** scorns **19 such a one** i.e., Bianca **20 cullion** base fellow. (Referring to "Cambio"; literally, *cullion* means "testicle.") **23 entire** sincere **24 lightness** wantonness **31 fondly** foolishly **35 Would . . . forsworn!** i.e., May everyone in the world forsake her except the penniless "Cambio," and may she thus get what she deserves!

36 For As for **39 haggard** wild hawk. **43 In resolution** determined **45 'longeth** belongs **46 ta'en you napping** taken you by surprise **50 lusty** merry, lively **58 eleven . . . long** i.e., right on the money. (Alluding to the card game called "one-and-thirty" referred to at 1.2.32–3.) **62 ancient angel** i.e., fellow of the good old stamp. (Literally, an "angel" or gold coin bearing the stamp of the archangel Michael and thus distinguishable from more recent debased coinage.) **63 Will . . . turn** who will serve our purposes. **64 marcantant** merchant. **pedant** schoolmaster. (Though at lines 90–1 he speaks more like a merchant.)

As if he were the right Vincentio.
Take in your love, and then let me alone.
[*Exeunt Lucentio and Bianca.*]

Enter a Pedant.

PEDANT
God save you, sir!

TRANIO
And you sir! You are welcome.
Travel you farre on, or are you at the farthest?

PEDANT
Sir, at the farthest for a week or two,
But then up farther, and as far as Rome,
And so to Tripoli, if God lend me life.

TRANIO
What countryman, I pray?

PEDANT
Of Mantua.

TRANIO
Of Mantua, sir? Marry, God forbid!
And come to Padua, careless of your life?

PEDANT
My life, sir? How, I pray? For that goes hard.

TRANIO
'Tis death for anyone in Mantua
To come to Padua. Know you not the cause?
Your ships are stayed at Venice, and the Duke,
For private quarrel twixt your Duke and him,
Hath published and proclaimed it openly.
'Tis marvel, but that you are but newly come,
You might have heard it else proclaimed about.

PEDANT
Alas, sir, it is worse for me than so,
For I have bills for money by exchange
From Florence, and must here deliver them.

TRANIO
Well, sir, to do you courtesy,
This will I do, and this I will advise you—
First, tell me, have you ever been at Pisa?

PEDANT
Ay, sir, in Pisa have I often been,
Pisa renownèd for grave citizens.

TRANIO
Among them know you one Vincentio?

PEDANT
I know him not, but I have heard of him;
A merchant of incomparable wealth.

TRANIO
He is my father, sir, and, sooth to say,
In count'nance somewhat doth resemble you.

BIONDELLO [*aside*] As much as an apple doth an oyster, and all one.

TRANIO
To save your life in this extremity,
This favor will I do you for his sake;
And think it not the worst of all your fortunes
That you are like to Sir Vincentio.
His name and credit shall you undertake,
And in my house you shall be friendly lodged.
Look that you take upon you as you should.
You understand me, sir. So shall you stay
Till you have done your business in the city.
If this be courtesy, sir, accept of it.

PEDANT
Oh, sir, I do, and will repute you ever
The patron of my life and liberty.

TRANIO
Then go with me to make the matter good.
This, by the way, I let you understand:
My father is here looked for every day
To pass assurance of a dower in marriage
Twixt me and one Baptista's daughter here.
In all these circumstances I'll instruct you.
Go with me to clothe you as becomes you.
Exeunt.

4.[3]

Enter Katharina and Grumio.

GRUMIO
No, no, forsooth, I dare not for my life.

KATHARINA
The more my wrong, the more his spite appears.
What, did he marry me to famish me?
Beggars that come unto my father's door
Upon entreaty have a present alms;
If not, elsewhere they meet with charity.
But I, who never knew how to entreat,
Nor never needed that I should entreat,
Am starved for meat, giddy for lack of sleep,
With oaths kept waking, and with brawling fed.
And that which spites me more than all these wants,
He does it under name of perfect love,
As who should say, if I should sleep or eat
'Twere deadly sickness or else present death.
I prithee, go and get me some repast,
I care not what, so it be wholesome food.

GRUMIO What say you to a neat's foot?

KATHARINA
'Tis passing good. I prithee, let me have it.

GRUMIO
I fear it is too choleric a meat.
How say you to a fat tripe finely broiled?

KATHARINA
I like it well. Good Grumio, fetch it me.

GRUMIO
I cannot tell. I fear 'tis choleric.
What say you to a piece of beef and mustard?

72 let me alone leave things to me. **74 farre** farther **81 goes hard** is serious indeed. **84 stayed** detained **89 than so** than that **90 bills . . . exchange** promissory notes **103 all one** no matter.

108 credit reputation **110 take upon you** play your part **114 repute you** regard you as **116 make . . . good** carry out the plan. **119 pass assurance** convey a legal guarantee
4.3. Location: Petruchio's house. A table is set out, with seats.
2 my wrong the wrong done to me **5 present** immediate. (As in line 14.) **13 As who** as if one **16 so** so long as **17 neat's** ox's **18 passing** extremely **22 I cannot tell** I don't know what to say.

KATHARINA
A dish that I do love to feed upon.
GRUMIO
Ay, but the mustard is too hot a little.
KATHARINA
Why then, the beef, and let the mustard rest.
GRUMIO
Nay then, I will not. You shall have the mustard,
Or else you get no beef of Grumio.
KATHARINA
Then both, or one, or anything thou wilt.
GRUMIO
Why then, the mustard without the beef.
KATHARINA
Go, get thee gone, thou false, deluding slave,
[She] beats him.
That feed'st me with the very name of meat!
Sorrow on thee and all the pack of you,
That triumph thus upon my misery!
Go, get thee gone, I say.

Enter Petruchio and Hortensio with meat.

PETRUCHIO
How fares my Kate? What, sweeting, all amort?
HORTENSIO
Mistress, what cheer?
KATHARINA Faith, as cold as can be.
PETRUCHIO
Pluck up thy spirits; look cheerfully upon me.
Here, love, thou see'st how diligent I am
To dress thy meat myself and bring it thee.
I am sure, sweet Kate, this kindness merits thanks.
What, not a word? Nay, then thou lov'st it not,
And all my pains is sorted to no proof.—
Here, take away this dish.
KATHARINA I pray you, let it stand.
PETRUCHIO
The poorest service is repaid with thanks,
And so shall mine before you touch the meat.
KATHARINA I thank you, sir.
HORTENSIO
Signor Petruchio, fie, you are to blame.
Come, Mistress Kate, I'll bear you company.
PETRUCHIO *[aside to Hortensio]*
Eat it up all, Hortensio, if thou lovest me.—
Much good do it unto thy gentle heart!
Kate, eat apace. And now, my honey love,
Will we return unto thy father's house
And revel it as bravely as the best,
With silken coats and caps and golden rings,
With ruffs, and cuffs, and farthingales, and things,
With scarves, and fans, and double change of brav'ry,
With amber bracelets, beads, and all this knav'ry.
What, hast thou dined? The tailor stays thy leisure,
To deck thy body with his ruffling treasure.

Enter Tailor [with a gown].

Come, tailor, let us see these ornaments.
Lay forth the gown.

Enter Haberdasher [with a cap].

What news with you, sir?
HABERDASHER
Here is the cap Your Worship did bespeak.
PETRUCHIO
Why, this was molded on a porringer—
A velvet dish. Fie, fie, 'tis lewd and filthy.
Why, 'tis a cockle or a walnut shell,
A knack, a toy, a trick, a baby's cap.
Away with it! Come, let me have a bigger.
KATHARINA
I'll have no bigger. This doth fit the time,
And gentlewomen wear such caps as these.
PETRUCHIO
When you are gentle, you shall have one too,
And not till then.
HORTENSIO *[aside]* That will not be in haste.
KATHARINA
Why, sir, I trust I may have leave to speak,
And speak I will. I am no child, no babe.
Your betters have endured me say my mind,
And if you cannot, best you stop your ears.
My tongue will tell the anger of my heart,
Or else my heart, concealing it, will break.
And rather than it shall, I will be free
Even to the uttermost, as I please, in words.
PETRUCHIO
Why, thou say'st true. It is a paltry cap,
A custard-coffin, a bauble, a silken pie.
I love thee well in that thou lik'st it not.
KATHARINA
Love me or love me not, I like the cap,
And it I will have, or I will have none.
[Exit Haberdasher.]
PETRUCHIO
Thy gown? Why, ay. Come, tailor, let us see't.
Oh, mercy, God, what masquing stuff is here?
What's this, a sleeve? 'Tis like a demicannon.
What, up and down carved like an apple tart?
Here's snip, and nip, and cut, and slish and slash,
Like to a censer in a barber's shop.
Why, what i' devil's name, tailor, call'st thou this?

26 let . . . rest i.e., forget about the mustard. **32 very** mere **36 all amort** dejected, dispirited. **40 dress** prepare **43 is . . . proof** have proved to be to no purpose. **54 bravely** splendidly **56 farthingales** hooped petticoats **57 brav'ry** finery

59 stays awaits **60 ruffling treasure** finery trimmed with ruffles. **63 bespeak** order. **64 porringer** porridge bowl **65 lewd** vile **66 cockle** cockleshell **67 trick** trifle **69 fit the time** suit the current fashion **71 gentle** mild. (Petruchio plays on Kate's *gentlewomen*, line 70, i.e., women of high social station.) **75 endured me say** suffered me to say **82 custard-coffin** pastry crust for a custard **87 masquing** i.e., suited only for a masque **88 demicannon** large cannon. **89 What . . . tart?** What, carved from one end to the other with slits like those in the crust of an apple tart? (Such slits in gowns were designed to reveal the fabric underneath.) **91 censer** perfuming pan having an ornamental lid

HORTENSIO [*aside*]
I see she's like to have neither cap nor gown.

TAILOR
You bid me make it orderly and well,
According to the fashion and the time.

PETRUCHIO
Marry, and did. But if you be remembered,
I did not bid you mar it to the time.
Go hop me over every kennel home,
For you shall hop without my custom, sir.
I'll none of it. Hence, make your best of it.

KATHARINA
I never saw a better fashioned gown,
More quaint, more pleasing, nor more
commendable.
Belike you mean to make a puppet of me.

PETRUCHIO
Why, true, he means to make a puppet of thee.

TAILOR
She says Your Worship means to make a puppet of her.

PETRUCHIO
Oh, monstrous arrogance! Thou liest, thou thread,
thou thimble,
Thou yard, three-quarters, half-yard, quarter, nail!
Thou flea, thou nit, thou winter cricket, thou!
Braved in mine own house with a skein of thread?
Away, thou rag, thou quantity, thou remnant,
Or I shall so be-mete thee with thy yard
As thou shalt think on prating whilst thou liv'st!
I tell thee, I, that thou hast marred her gown.

TAILOR
Your Worship is deceived. The gown is made
Just as my master had direction.
Grumio gave order how it should be done.

GRUMIO I gave him no order. I gave him the stuff.

TAILOR
But how did you desire it should be made?

GRUMIO Marry, sir, with needle and thread.

TAILOR
But did you not request to have it cut?

GRUMIO Thou hast faced many things.

TAILOR I have.

GRUMIO Face not me. Thou hast braved many men; brave not me. I will neither be faced nor braved. I say unto thee, I bid thy master cut out the gown, but I did not bid him cut it to pieces. Ergo, thou liest.

TAILOR Why, here is the note of the fashion to testify.
[*He displays his bill.*]

PETRUCHIO Read it.

GRUMIO The note lies in 's throat if he say I said so.

TAILOR [*reads*] "Imprimis, a loose-bodied gown—"

GRUMIO Master, if ever I said loose-bodied gown, sew me in the skirts of it and beat me to death with a bottom of brown thread. I said a gown.

PETRUCHIO Proceed.

TAILOR [*reads*] "With a small compassed cape—"

GRUMIO I confess the cape.

TAILOR [*reads*] "With a trunk sleeve—"

GRUMIO I confess two sleeves.

TAILOR [*reads*] "The sleeves curiously cut."

PETRUCHIO Ay, there's the villainy.

GRUMIO Error i'the bill, sir, error i'the bill. I commanded the sleeves should be cut out and sewed up again, and that I'll prove upon thee, though thy little finger be armed in a thimble.

TAILOR This is true that I say. An I had thee in place where, thou shouldst know it.

GRUMIO I am for thee straight. Take thou the bill, give me thy mete-yard, and spare not me.

HORTENSIO God-a-mercy, Grumio, then he shall have no odds.

PETRUCHIO Well, sir, in brief, the gown is not for me.

GRUMIO You are i'the right, sir, 'tis for my mistress.

PETRUCHIO Go, take it up unto thy master's use.

GRUMIO [*to the Tailor*] Villain, not for thy life! Take up my mistress' gown for thy master's use!

PETRUCHIO Why sir, what's your conceit in that?

GRUMIO
Oh, sir, the conceit is deeper than you think for:
Take up my mistress' gown to his master's use!
Oh, fie, fie, fie!

PETRUCHIO [*aside to Hortensio*]
Hortensio, say thou wilt see the tailor paid.
[*To Tailor*] Go, take it hence. Begone, and say no more.

HORTENSIO [*aside to the Tailor*]
Tailor, I'll pay thee for thy gown tomorrow.
Take no unkindness of his hasty words.
Away, I say. Commend me to thy master.
Exit Tailor.

PETRUCHIO
Well, come, my Kate. We will unto your father's
Even in these honest, mean habiliments.
Our purses shall be proud, our garments poor,
For 'tis the mind that makes the body rich;
And as the sun breaks through the darkest clouds,

93 like likely **96 Marry . . remembered** I did indeed. But if you recollect **98 hop . . . home** hop on home over every street gutter **102 quaint** elegant **103 Belike** Perhaps **106–10 thou thread . . . remnant** Petruchio attacks the tailor's proverbial thinness and effeminacy using metaphors from tailoring. **107 nail** a measure of length for cloth: 2 ¼ inches. **108 nit** louse egg **109 Braved** Defied. **with** by **110 quantity** fragment **111 be-mete** measure, i.e., thrash. **yard** yardstick **112 think on prating** i.e., remember this thrashing and think twice before talking so again **117 stuff** material.
121 faced trimmed, decked **123 Face** Bully. **braved** dressed finely
124 brave defy **126 Ergo** Therefore

129 lies in 's throat i.e., lies utterly **130 Imprimis** First **131 loose-bodied gown** (Grumio plays on *loose,* "wanton"; a gown fit for a prostitute.) **133 bottom** i.e., ball or skein. (A weaver's term for the bobbin.) **135 compassed** flared, cut on the bias so as to fall in a circle **137 trunk** full, wide **139 curiously** elaborately **143 prove upon thee** prove by fighting you **145–6 in place where** in a suitable place **147 bill** (1) the note ordering the gown (2) a weapon, a halberd **148 mete-yard** measuring stick **149 God-a-mercy** Thanks **150 no odds** no advantage. (The contest between Grumio and the Tailor will be evenly matched.) **153 take it up** take it away. **use** i.e., whatever use he can make of it. (But Grumio deliberately misinterprets both expressions in a bawdy sense.) **156 conceit** idea **157 deeper** more serious. (But continuing the sexual idea of lifting up the dress and entering for sexual "use," as in lines 155 and 158.) **166 honest, mean habiliments** respectable, plain clothes.

So honor peereth in the meanest habit.
What, is the jay more precious than the lark
Because his feathers are more beautiful?
Or is the adder better than the eel
Because his painted skin contents the eye?
Oh, no, good Kate; neither art thou the worse
For this poor furniture and mean array.
If thou account'st it shame, lay it on me.
And therefore frolic; we will hence forthwith,
To feast and sport us at thy father's house.
[*To Grumio*] Go call my men, and let us straight to him;
And bring our horses unto Long Lane end.
There will we mount, and thither walk on foot.
Let's see, I think 'tis now some seven o'clock,
And well we may come there by dinnertime.

KATHARINA
I dare assure you, sir, 'tis almost two,
And 'twill be suppertime ere you come there.

PETRUCHIO
It shall be seven ere I go to horse.
Look what I speak, or do, or think to do,
You are still crossing it.—Sirs, let 't alone.
I will not go today, and ere I do,
It shall be what o'clock I say it is.

HORTENSIO [*aside*]
Why, so this gallant will command the sun.

[*Exeunt.*]

✤

[4.4]

Enter Tranio [*as Lucentio*], *and the Pedant dressed like Vincentio* [*booted*].

TRANIO
Sir, this is the house. Please it you that I call?

PEDANT
Ay, what else? And but I be deceived,
Signor Baptista may remember me,
Near twenty years ago, in Genoa—

TRANIO
Where we were lodgers at the Pegasus.—
'Tis well; and hold your own in any case
With such austerity as 'longeth to a father.

Enter Biondello.

PEDANT
I warrant you. But, sir, here comes your boy.
'Twere good he were schooled.

TRANIO
Fear you not him.—Sirrah Biondello,
Now do your duty throughly, I advise you.
Imagine 'twere the right Vincentio.

BIONDELLO Tut, fear not me.

TRANIO
But hast thou done thy errand to Baptista?

BIONDELLO
I told him that your father was at Venice
And that you looked for him this day in Padua.

TRANIO [*giving money*]
Thou'rt a tall fellow. Hold thee that to drink.
Here comes Baptista. Set your countenance, sir.

Enter Baptista, and Lucentio [*as Cambio*]. [*The*] *Pedant* [*stands*] *bareheaded.*

Signor Baptista, you are happily met.
[*To the Pedant*] Sir, this is the gentleman I told you of.
I pray you, stand good father to me now;
Give me Bianca for my patrimony.

PEDANT Soft, son!—
Sir, by your leave, having come to Padua
To gather in some debts, my son Lucentio
Made me acquainted with a weighty cause
Of love between your daughter and himself;
And, for the good report I hear of you
And for the love he beareth to your daughter
And she to him, to stay him not too long,
I am content, in a good father's care,
To have him matched. And if you please to like
No worse than I, upon some agreement
Me shall you find ready and willing
With one consent to have her so bestowed;
For curious I cannot be with you,
Signor Baptista, of whom I hear so well.

BAPTISTA
Sir, pardon me in what I have to say.
Your plainness and your shortness please me well.
Right true it is your son Lucentio here
Doth love my daughter, and she loveth him,
Or both dissemble deeply their affections.
And therefore, if you say no more than this,
That like a father you will deal with him
And pass my daughter a sufficient dower,
The match is made, and all is done.
Your son shall have my daughter with consent.

TRANIO
I thank you, sir. Where then do you know best
We be affied and such assurance ta'en
As shall with either part's agreement stand?

170 peereth . . . habit peeps through the humblest attire. **174 painted** colorfully patterned **176 furniture** furnishings of attire **184 dinnertime** i.e., about noon. **188 Look what** Whatever **189 still crossing** always contradicting or defying **192 so** at this rate
4.4. Location: Padua. Before Baptista's house.
0.2 *booted* (signifying travel) **2 but** unless **3–4 Signor . . . Genoa** (The Pedant rehearses what he is to say.) **5 Where . . . Pegasus** (Tranio is coaching the Pedant in further details of his story.) **the Pegasus** i.e., an inn, so named after the famous winged horse of classical myth. **6 hold your own** play your part **9 schooled** i.e., rehearsed in his part.

11 throughly thoroughly **12 right** real **13 fear not me** don't worry about my doing my part. **17 tall** fine. **Hold . . . drink** Take that and buy a drink. **18 Set your countenance** i.e., Put on the expression of an austere father (line 7). **19 happily** fortunately **23 Soft** i.e., Steady, take it easy **28 for** because of **30 to stay him not** not to keep him waiting **32 like** i.e., approve of the match **35 one** i.e., firm **36 curious** overly particular **45 pass** settle on, give
48–50 Where . . . stand? Where in your view is the best place for us to be betrothed and for legal assurances to be made that will confirm an agreement satisfactory to both parties?

BAPTISTA
Not in my house, Lucentio, for you know
Pitchers have ears, and I have many servants.
Besides, old Gremio is heark'ning still,
And happily we might be interrupted.

TRANIO
Then at my lodging, an it like you.
There doth my father lie, and there this night
We'll pass the business privately and well.
Send for your daughter by your servant here.
[He indicates Lucentio, and winks at him.]
My boy shall fetch the scrivener presently.
The worst is this, that at so slender warning
You are like to have a thin and slender pittance.

BAPTISTA
It likes me well. Cambio, hie you home,
And bid Bianca make her ready straight.
And if you will, tell what hath happened:
Lucentio's father is arrived in Padua,
And how she's like to be Lucentio's wife.
[Exit Lucentio.]

BIONDELLO
I pray the gods she may with all my heart!

TRANIO
Dally not with the gods, but get thee gone.
Exit [Biondello].
Signor Baptista, shall I lead the way?
Welcome! One mess is like to be your cheer.
Come, sir, we will better it in Pisa.

BAPTISTA I follow you.
Exeunt [Tranio, Pedant, and Baptista].

Enter Lucentio [as Cambio] and Biondello.

BIONDELLO Cambio!

LUCENTIO What say'st thou, Biondello?

BIONDELLO You saw my master wink and laugh upon you?

LUCENTIO Biondello, what of that?

BIONDELLO Faith, nothing; but he's left me here behind to expound the meaning or moral of his signs and tokens.

LUCENTIO I pray thee, moralize them.

BIONDELLO Then thus. Baptista is safe, talking with the deceiving father of a deceitful son.

LUCENTIO And what of him?

BIONDELLO His daughter is to be brought by you to the supper.

LUCENTIO And then?

BIONDELLO The old priest at Saint Luke's church is at your command at all hours.

LUCENTIO And what of all this?

BIONDELLO I cannot tell, except they are busied about a counterfeit assurance. Take you assurance of her *cum privilegio ad imprimendum solum.* To th' church take the priest, clerk, and some sufficient honest witnesses.
If this be not that you look for, I have no more to say,
But bid Bianca farewell forever and a day.
[Biondello starts to leave.]

LUCENTIO Hear'st thou, Biondello?

BIONDELLO I cannot tarry. I knew a wench married in an afternoon as she went to the garden for parsley to stuff a rabbit, and so may you, sir. And so, adieu, sir. My master hath appointed me to go to Saint Luke's, to bid the priest be ready to come against you come with your appendix. *Exit.*

LUCENTIO
I may, and will, if she be so contented.
She will be pleased; then wherefore should I doubt?
Hap what hap may, I'll roundly go about her.
It shall go hard if Cambio go without her. *Exit.*

[4.5]

Enter Petruchio, Kate, [and] Hortensio.

PETRUCHIO
Come on, i'God's name, once more toward our father's.
Good Lord, how bright and goodly shines the moon!

KATHARINA
The moon? The sun. It is not moonlight now.

PETRUCHIO
I say it is the moon that shines so bright.

KATHARINA
I know it is the sun that shines so bright.

PETRUCHIO
Now, by my mother's son, and that's myself,
It shall be moon, or star, or what I list
Or ere I journey to your father's house.—
Go on, and fetch our horses back again—
Evermore crossed and crossed, nothing but crossed!

HORTENSIO *[to Katharina]*
Say as he says, or we shall never go.

KATHARINA
Forward, I pray, since we have come so far,
And be it moon, or sun, or what you please;
An if you please to call it a rush candle,

53 heark'ning still continually listening **54 happily** haply **55 an it like** if it please **56 lie** lodge **57 pass** transact **59 scrivener** notary, one to draw up contracts. **presently** at once. **61 like** likely. **slender pittance** i.e., scanty banquet. **70 mess** dish. **cheer** entertainment. **72.1** ***Exeunt*** (Technically, the cleared stage may mark a new scene, but the conversation of Lucentio and Biondello suggests that they come creeping back on stage as the others leave rather than doing the errands Baptista and Tranio bid them.) **79 moral** hidden meaning **81 moralize** elucidate **82 safe** i.e., safely out of the way

91 except unless **92 counterfeit assurance** pretended betrothal agreement. **Take . . . of her** Legalize your claim to her (by marriage) **93** ***cum . . . solum*** with exclusive printing rights. (A copyright formula often appearing on the title pages of books, here jokingly applied to the marriage and to procreation as an act of imprinting.) **94 sufficient** meeting the legal requirement in number and social standing **96 that you look for** what you are looking for **103 against you come** in anticipation of your arrival **104 appendix** something appended, i.e., the bride. (Continuing the metaphor of printing.) **107 roundly . . . her** set about marrying her in no uncertain terms. **108 It . . . her** i.e., I'm determined to have her. (With pun about erection.)
4.5. Location: A road on the way to Padua.
1 our father's our father's house. **7 list** please **8 Or ere** before
14 a rush candle a rush dipped into tallow; hence a very feeble light

Henceforth I vow it shall be so for me.
PETRUCHIO
I say it is the moon.
KATHARINA I know it is the moon.
PETRUCHIO
Nay, then you lie. It is the blessèd sun.
KATHARINA
Then, God be blessed, it is the blessèd sun.
But sun it is not, when you say it is not,
And the moon changes even as your mind.
What you will have it named, even that it is,
And so it shall be so for Katharine.
HORTENSIO
Petruchio, go thy ways. The field is won.
PETRUCHIO
Well, forward, forward. Thus the bowl should run,
And not unluckily against the bias.
But soft! Company is coming here.

Enter Vincentio.

[*To Vincentio*] Good morrow, gentle mistress. Where away?—
Tell me, sweet Kate, and tell me truly too,
Hast thou beheld a fresher gentlewoman?
Such war of white and red within her cheeks!
What stars do spangle heaven with such beauty
As those two eyes become that heavenly face?—
Fair lovely maid, once more good day to thee.—
Sweet Kate, embrace her for her beauty's sake.
HORTENSIO [*aside*]
'A will make the man mad, to make a woman of him.
KATHARINA [*embracing Vincentio*]
Young budding virgin, fair, and fresh, and sweet,
Whither away, or where is thy abode?
Happy the parents of so fair a child!
Happier the man whom favorable stars
Allots thee for his lovely bedfellow!
PETRUCHIO
Why, how now, Kate? I hope thou art not mad.
This is a man, old, wrinkled, faded, withered,
And not a maiden, as thou say'st he is.
KATHARINA
Pardon, old father, my mistaking eyes,
That have been so bedazzled with the sun
That everything I look on seemeth green.
Now I perceive thou art a reverend father.
Pardon, I pray thee, for my mad mistaking.
PETRUCHIO
Do, good old grandsire, and withal make known
Which way thou travelest—if along with us,
We shall be joyful of thy company.
VINCENTIO
Fair sir, and you, my merry mistress,
That with your strange encounter much amazed me,
My name is called Vincentio, my dwelling Pisa,
And bound I am to Padua, there to visit
A son of mine, which long I have not seen.
PETRUCHIO
What is his name?
VINCENTIO Lucentio, gentle sir.
PETRUCHIO
Happily met, the happier for thy son.
And now by law as well as reverend age
I may entitle thee my loving father.
The sister to my wife, this gentlewoman,
Thy son by this hath married. Wonder not,
Nor be not grieved. She is of good esteem,
Her dowry wealthy, and of worthy birth;
Besides, so qualified as may beseem
The spouse of any noble gentleman.
Let me embrace with old Vincentio,
And wander we to see thy honest son,
Who will of thy arrival be full joyous.
[*He embraces Vincentio.*]
VINCENTIO
But is this true? Or is it else your pleasure,
Like pleasant travelers, to break a jest
Upon the company you overtake?
HORTENSIO
I do assure thee, father, so it is.
PETRUCHIO
Come, go along, and see the truth hereof,
For our first merriment hath made thee jealous.
Exeunt [*all but Hortensio*].
HORTENSIO
Well, Petruchio, this has put me in heart.
Have to my widow! And if she be froward,
Then hast thou taught Hortensio to be untoward.
Exit.

✤

[5.1]

Enter Biondello, Lucentio [*no longer disguised*], *and Bianca. Gremio is out before* [*and stands aside*].

BIONDELLO Softly and swiftly, sir, for the priest is ready.
LUCENTIO I fly, Biondello. But they may chance to need thee at home; therefore leave us.
BIONDELLO Nay, faith, I'll see the church a' your back, and then come back to my master's as soon as I can.
[*Exeunt Lucentio, Bianca, and Biondello.*]

23 go thy ways i.e., well done, carry on. **25 against the bias** off its proper course. (The *bias* is an off-center weight in a bowling ball enabling the bowler to roll the ball in an oblique or curving path.) **27 Where away?** Where are you going? **35 'A** He **40 Allots** allot **46 green** young and fresh.

62 by this by this time **63 esteem** reputation **65 so qualified** having such qualities. **beseem** befit **68 wander** go (having changed plans) **71 pleasant** humorous, jocular. **break a jest** play a practical joke **75 jealous** suspicious. **76 put me in heart** encouraged me. **77 Have to** i.e., Now for. **froward** perverse **78 untoward** unmannerly.
5.1. Location: Padua. Before Lucentio's house.
0.2 *out before* i.e., onstage first. (Gremio does not see Biondello, Lucentio, and Bianca as they steal to church, or else he does not recognize Lucentio in his own person.) **5 a' your back** at your back, behind you. (Biondello first wants to see them in church and safely married.)

GREMIO
I marvel Cambio comes not all this while.

Enter Petruchio, Kate, Vincentio, Grumio, with attendants.

PETRUCHIO
Sir, here's the door. This is Lucentio's house.
My father's bears more toward the marketplace;
Thither must I, and here I leave you, sir.

VINCENTIO
You shall not choose but drink before you go.
I think I shall command your welcome here,
And by all likelihood some cheer is toward. *Knock.*

GREMIO [*advancing*] They're busy within. You were best knock louder.

Pedant looks out of the window.

PEDANT What's he that knocks as he would beat down the gate?

VINCENTIO Is Signor Lucentio within, sir?

PEDANT He's within, sir, but not to be spoken withal.

VINCENTIO What if a man bring him a hundred pound or two to make merry withal?

PEDANT Keep your hundred pounds to yourself. He shall need none, so long as I live.

PETRUCHIO [*to Vincentio*] Nay, I told you your son was well beloved in Padua.—Do you hear, sir? To leave frivolous circumstances, I pray you, tell Signor Lucentio that his father is come from Pisa and is here at the door to speak with him.

PEDANT Thou liest. His father is come from Padua and here looking out at the window.

VINCENTIO Art thou his father?

PEDANT Ay, sir, so his mother says, if I may believe her.

PETRUCHIO [*to Vincentio*] Why, how now, gentleman! Why, this is flat knavery, to take upon you another man's name.

PEDANT Lay hands on the villain. I believe 'a means to cozen somebody in this city under my countenance.

Enter Biondello.

BIONDELLO [*aside*] I have seen them in the church together, God send 'em good shipping! But who is here? Mine old master Vincentio! Now we are undone and brought to nothing.

VINCENTIO [*seeing Biondello*] Come hither, crackhemp.

BIONDELLO I hope I may choose, sir.

VINCENTIO Come hither, you rogue. What, have you forgot me?

BIONDELLO Forgot you? No, sir. I could not forget you, for I never saw you before in all my life.

VINCENTIO What, you notorious villain, didst thou never see thy master's father, Vincentio?

BIONDELLO What, my old worshipful old master? Yes, marry, sir, see where he looks out of the window.

VINCENTIO Is't so, indeed? *He beats Biondello.*

BIONDELLO Help, help, help! Here's a madman will murder me. [*Exit.*]

PEDANT Help, son! Help, Signor Baptista! [*Exit from the window.*]

PETRUCHIO Prithee, Kate, let's stand aside and see the end of this controversy. [*They stand aside.*]

Enter [*below*] *Pedant with servants, Baptista,* [*and*] *Tranio* [*as Lucentio*].

TRANIO Sir, what are you that offer to beat my servant?

VINCENTIO What am I, sir? Nay, what are you, sir? O immortal gods! Oh, fine villain! A silken doublet, a velvet hose, a scarlet cloak, and a copintank hat! Oh, I am undone, I am undone! While I play the good husband at home, my son and my servant spend all at the university.

TRANIO How now, what's the matter?

BAPTISTA What, is the man lunatic?

TRANIO Sir, you seem a sober ancient gentleman by your habit, but your words show you a madman. Why, sir, what 'cerns it you if I wear pearl and gold? I thank my good father, I am able to maintain it.

VINCENTIO Thy father! Oh, villain, he is a sailmaker in Bergamo.

BAPTISTA You mistake, sir, you mistake, sir. Pray, what do you think is his name?

VINCENTIO His name! As if I knew not his name! I have brought him up ever since he was three years old, and his name is Tranio.

PEDANT Away, away, mad ass! His name is Lucentio, and he is mine only son, and heir to the lands of me, Signor Vincentio.

VINCENTIO Lucentio! Oh, he hath murdered his master! Lay hold on him, I charge you, in the Duke's name. Oh, my son, my son! Tell me, thou villain, where is my son Lucentio?

TRANIO Call forth an officer.

[*Enter an Officer.*]

Carry this mad knave to the jail. Father Baptista, I charge you see that he be forthcoming.

VINCENTIO Carry me to the jail?

GREMIO Stay, officer, he shall not go to prison.

BAPTISTA Talk not, Signor Gremio. I say he shall go to prison.

9 father's i.e., father-in-law's, Baptista's. **bears** lies. (A nautical term.) **11 You . . . but** i.e., I insist that **13 cheer is toward** entertainment is in prospect. **15.1** ***window*** i.e., probably the gallery to the rear, over the stage. **19 withal** with. **26 circumstances** matters **29 from Padua** i.e., from Padua, where we are right now. (Often emended to "from Mantua," "from Pisa," "to Padua," etc.) **35 flat** downright **38 cozen** cheat. **under my countenance** by pretending to be me. **40 good shipping** bon voyage, good fortune. **43 crackhemp** i.e., rogue likely to end up being hanged. **44 choose** do as I choose

59 offer dare, presume **62 copintank** high-crowned, sugar-loaf shape **63 good husband** careful provider, manager **69 habit** clothing **70 'cerns** concerns **71 maintain** afford **88 forthcoming** ready to stand trial when required.

GREMIO Take heed, Signor Baptista, lest you be coney- 93
catched in this business. I dare swear this is the right 94
Vincentio.

PEDANT Swear, if thou dar'st.

GREMIO Nay, I dare not swear it.

TRANIO Then thou wert best say that I am not Lucentio. 98

GREMIO Yes, I know thee to be Signor Lucentio.

BAPTISTA Away with the dotard! To the jail with him!

Enter Biondello, Lucentio, and Bianca.

VINCENTIO Thus strangers may be haled and abused. 101
—Oh, monstrous villain!

BIONDELLO Oh! We are spoiled and—yonder he is. 103
Deny him, forswear him, or else we are all undone.

Exeunt Biondello, Tranio, and Pedant as fast as may be. [*Lucentio and Bianca*] *kneel.*

LUCENTIO
Pardon, sweet father.

VINCENTIO Lives my sweet son?

BIANCA
Pardon, dear father.

BAPTISTA How hast thou offended?
Where is Lucentio?

LUCENTIO Here's Lucentio,
Right son to the right Vincentio,
That have by marriage made thy daughter mine,
While counterfeit supposes bleared thine eyne. 110

GREMIO
Here's packing, with a witness, to deceive us all! 111

VINCENTIO
Where is that damnèd villain Tranio,
That faced and braved me in this matter so? 113

BAPTISTA
Why, tell me, is not this my Cambio?

BIANCA
Cambio is changed into Lucentio. 115

LUCENTIO
Love wrought these miracles. Bianca's love
Made me exchange my state with Tranio, 117
While he did bear my countenance in the town, 118
And happily I have arrivèd at the last
Unto the wishèd haven of my bliss.
What Tranio did, myself enforced him to;
Then pardon him, sweet father, for my sake.

VINCENTIO I'll slit the villain's nose, that would have sent me to the jail.

BAPTISTA [*to Lucentio*] But do you hear, sir? Have you married my daughter without asking my good will?

VINCENTIO Fear not, Baptista, we will content you. Go 127
to. But I will in, to be revenged for this villainy. 128
Exit.

BAPTISTA And I, to sound the depth of this knavery.
Exit.

LUCENTIO Look not pale, Bianca. Thy father will not frown. *Exeunt* [*Lucentio and Bianca*].

GREMIO
My cake is dough, but I'll in among the rest, 132
Out of hope of all but my share of the feast. [*Exit.*] 133

KATHARINA Husband, let's follow, to see the end of this ado.

PETRUCHIO First kiss me, Kate, and we will.

KATHARINA What, in the midst of the street?

PETRUCHIO What, art thou ashamed of me?

KATHARINA No, sir, God forbid, but ashamed to kiss.

PETRUCHIO
Why, then let's home again. [*To Grumio*] Come, sirrah, let's away.

KATHARINA
Nay, I will give thee a kiss. [*She kisses him.*] Now pray thee, love, stay.

PETRUCHIO
Is not this well? Come, my sweet Kate.
Better once than never, for never too late. *Exeunt.* 143

5.[2]

Enter Baptista, Vincentio, Gremio, the Pedant, Lucentio, and Bianca; [*Petruchio, Kate, Hortensio,*] *Tranio, Biondello, Grumio, and* [*the*] *Widow; the servingmen with Tranio bringing in a banquet.*

LUCENTIO
At last, though long, our jarring notes agree, 1
And time it is, when raging war is done,
To smile at scapes and perils overblown. 3
My fair Bianca, bid my father welcome,
While I with selfsame kindness welcome thine.
Brother Petruchio, sister Katharina,
And thou, Hortensio, with thy loving widow,
Feast with the best, and welcome to my house.
My banquet is to close our stomachs up 9
After our great good cheer. Pray you, sit down, 10
For now we sit to chat as well as eat. [*They sit.*]

PETRUCHIO
Nothing but sit and sit, and eat and eat!

BAPTISTA
Padua affords this kindness, son Petruchio.

PETRUCHIO
Padua affords nothing but what is kind.

93–4 coney-catched tricked **98 wert best** might as well
101 haled hauled about, maltreated **103 spoiled** ruined **110 supposes** suppositions, false appearances. (With an allusion to Gascoigne's *Supposes,* an adaptation of *I Suppositi* by Ariosto, from which Shakespeare took the Lucentio-Bianca plot of intrigue.)
eyne eyes. **111 Here's . . . all!** Here's evidence of a conspiracy, no mistake about it! **113 faced and braved** stood up to and defied
115 Cambio is changed (A pun. *Cambio* in Italian means "change" or "exchange.") **117 state** social station **118 countenance** appearance, identity

127–8 Go to i.e., Don't worry. (An expression of impatience or annoyance.) **132 My . . . dough** i.e., I'm out of luck, I failed
133 Out . . . but having hope for nothing other than **143 once** at some time. (Compare with "better late than never.")
5.2. Location: Padua. Lucentio's house.
1 long after long time **3 scapes** close calls **9 stomachs** (1) appetites (2) quarrels **10 cheer** i.e., wedding feast.

HORTENSIO
For both our sakes, I would that word were true.

PETRUCHIO
Now, for my life, Hortensio fears his widow. 16

WIDOW
Then never trust me if I be afeard. 17

PETRUCHIO
You are very sensible, and yet you miss my sense:
I mean Hortensio is afeard of you.

WIDOW
He that is giddy thinks the world turns round.

PETRUCHIO
Roundly replied.

KATHARINA Mistress, how mean you that? 21

WIDOW Thus I conceive by him. 22

PETRUCHIO
Conceives by me! How likes Hortensio that?

HORTENSIO
My widow says, thus she conceives her tale. 24

PETRUCHIO
Very well mended. Kiss him for that, good widow.

KATHARINA
"He that is giddy thinks the world turns round":
I pray you, tell me what you meant by that.

WIDOW
Your husband, being troubled with a shrew,
Measures my husband's sorrow by his woe. 29
And now you know my meaning.

KATHARINA
A very mean meaning.

WIDOW Right, I mean you. 31

KATHARINA
And I am mean indeed, respecting you. 32

PETRUCHIO To her, Kate! 33

HORTENSIO To her, widow!

PETRUCHIO
A hundred marks, my Kate does put her down. 35

HORTENSIO That's my office.

PETRUCHIO
Spoke like an officer. Ha' to thee, lad! 37
[*He*] *drinks to Hortensio.*

BAPTISTA
How likes Gremio these quick-witted folks?

GREMIO
Believe me, sir, they butt together well. 39

BIANCA
Head, and butt! An hasty-witted body 40
Would say your head and butt were head and horn. 41

VINCENTIO
Ay, mistress bride, hath that awakened you?

BIANCA
Ay, but not frighted me. Therefore I'll sleep again.

PETRUCHIO
Nay, that you shall not. Since you have begun,
Have at you for a bitter jest or two! 45

BIANCA
Am I your bird? I mean to shift my bush; 46
And then pursue me as you draw your bow.
You are welcome all.
Exit Bianca [*with Katharina and the Widow*].

PETRUCHIO
She hath prevented me. Here, Signor Tranio, 49
This bird you aimed at, though you hit her not. 50
Therefore a health to all that shot and missed. 51
[*He offers a toast.*]

TRANIO
Oh, sir, Lucentio slipped me like his greyhound, 52
Which runs himself and catches for his master.

PETRUCHIO
A good swift simile, but something currish. 54

TRANIO
'Tis well, sir, that you hunted for yourself.
'Tis thought your deer does hold you at a bay. 56

BAPTISTA
Oho, Petruchio! Tranio hits you now.

LUCENTIO
I thank thee for that gird, good Tranio. 58

HORTENSIO
Confess, confess, hath he not hit you here?

PETRUCHIO
'A has a little galled me, I confess; 60
And as the jest did glance away from me,
'Tis ten to one it maimed you two outright.

BAPTISTA
Now, in good sadness, son Petruchio, 63
I think thou hast the veriest shrew of all.

PETRUCHIO
Well, I say no. And therefore for assurance 65
Let's each one send unto his wife;
And he whose wife is most obedient
To come at first when he doth send for her
Shall win the wager which we will propose.

HORTENSIO
Content. What's the wager?

LUCENTIO Twenty crowns.

PETRUCHIO Twenty crowns!
I'll venture so much of my hawk or hound, 72
But twenty times so much upon my wife.

16 for my life upon my life. **fears** is afraid of **17 afeard** frightened (by Hortensio). **21 Roundly** Boldly, bluntly **22 Thus . . . him** i.e., That's what I think of him, Petruchio. (But Petruchio takes up *conceives* in the sense of "is made pregnant.") **24 conceives** intends, interprets. (With a possible pun on *tale* and "tail.") **29 his** his own **31 very mean** contemptible. (But the Widow takes up *mean* in the sense of "have in mind," and Kate replies in the sense of "moderate in shrewishness.") **32 respecting** compared to **33 To her** (A cry used to egg on fighting roosters.) **35 marks** coins worth thirteen shillings four pence. **put her down** overcome her. (But Hortensio takes up the phrase in a bawdy sense.) **37 officer** (playing on Hortensio's speaking of his *office* or function). **Ha'** Have, i.e., Here's **39 butt** butt heads **40 An hasty-witted body** A quick-witted person **41 head and horn** (Alluding to the familiar joke about cuckolds' horns.)

45 Have at you for Here comes **46 Am . . . bush** i.e., If you mean to shoot your barbs at me, I intend to move out of the way, as a bird would fly to another bush. (With a possible bawdy double meaning; *bush* can suggest pubic hair.) **49 prevented** forestalled **50 This bird** i.e., Bianca, whom Tranio courted (*aimed at*) in his disguise as Lucentio **51 a health** a toast **52 slipped** unleashed **54 swift** (1) quick-witted (2) concerning swiftness. **currish** (1) ignoble (2) concerning dogs. **56 deer** (Punning on "dear.") **does . . . bay** turns on you like a cornered animal and holds you at a distance. **58 gird** sharp, biting jest **60 galled** scratched, chafed **63 sadness** seriousness **65 assurance** proof **72 of** on

LUCENTIO A hundred then.
HORTENSIO Content.
PETRUCHIO A match. 'Tis done.
HORTENSIO Who shall begin?
LUCENTIO That will I.
Go, Biondello, bid your mistress come to me.
BIONDELLO I go. *Exit.*
BAPTISTA
Son, I'll be your half Bianca comes.
LUCENTIO
I'll have no halves; I'll bear it all myself.

Enter Biondello.

How now, what news?
BIONDELLO
Sir, my mistress sends you word
That she is busy and she cannot come.
PETRUCHIO
How? She's busy and she cannot come?
Is that an answer?
GREMIO Ay, and a kind one too.
Pray God, sir, your wife send you not a worse.
PETRUCHIO I hope better.
HORTENSIO
Sirrah Biondello, go and entreat my wife
To come to me forthwith. *Exit Biondello.*
PETRUCHIO Oho, entreat her!
Nay, then she must needs come.
HORTENSIO I am afraid, sir,
Do what you can, yours will not be entreated.

Enter Biondello.

Now, where's my wife?
BIONDELLO
She says you have some goodly jest in hand.
She will not come. She bids you come to her.
PETRUCHIO
Worse and worse. She will not come!
Oh, vile, intolerable, not to be endured!—
Sirrah Grumio, go to your mistress.
Say I command her come to me. *Exit* [*Grumio*].
HORTENSIO
I know her answer.
PETRUCHIO What?
HORTENSIO She will not.
PETRUCHIO
The fouler fortune mine, and there an end.

Enter Katharina.

BAPTISTA
Now, by my halidom, here comes Katharina!
KATHARINA
What is your will, sir, that you send for me?
PETRUCHIO
Where is your sister, and Hortensio's wife?
KATHARINA
They sit conferring by the parlor fire.
PETRUCHIO
Go fetch them hither. If they deny to come,
Swinge me them soundly forth unto their husbands.
Away, I say, and bring them hither straight.
[*Exit Katharina.*]
LUCENTIO
Here is a wonder, if you talk of a wonder.
HORTENSIO
And so it is. I wonder what it bodes.
PETRUCHIO
Marry, peace it bodes, and love, and quiet life,
An aweful rule, and right supremacy,
And, to be short, what not that's sweet and happy.
BAPTISTA
Now, fair befall thee, good Petruchio!
The wager thou hast won, and I will add
Unto their losses twenty thousand crowns,
Another dowry to another daughter,
For she is changed, as she had never been.
PETRUCHIO
Nay, I will win my wager better yet,
And show more sign of her obedience,
Her new-built virtue and obedience.

Enter Kate, Bianca, and [*the*] *Widow.*

See where she comes and brings your froward wives
As prisoners to her womanly persuasion.—
Katharine, that cap of yours becomes you not.
Off with that bauble. Throw it underfoot.
[*She obeys.*]
WIDOW
Lord, let me never have a cause to sigh
Till I be brought to such a silly pass!
BIANCA
Fie, what a foolish duty call you this?
LUCENTIO
I would your duty were as foolish, too.
The wisdom of your duty, fair Bianca,
Hath cost me a hundred crowns since suppertime.
BIANCA
The more fool you, for laying on my duty.
PETRUCHIO
Katharine, I charge thee tell these headstrong women
What duty they do owe their lords and husbands.
WIDOW
Come, come, you're mocking. We will have no telling.
PETRUCHIO
Come on, I say, and first begin with her.
WIDOW She shall not.
PETRUCHIO
I say she shall—and first begin with her.

81 be your half take half your bet **102 there an end** that's that. **103 by my halidom** (Originally an oath by the holy relics, but confused with an oath to the Virgin Mary.)

108 Swinge thrash. **me** i.e., at my behest. (*Me* is used colloquially.) **113 aweful rule** authority commanding awe or respect **115 fair befall thee** good luck to you, and congratulations **119 as . . . been** as if she had never existed, i.e., she is totally changed. **128 pass** state of affairs. **133 laying** wagering

KATHARINA
Fie, fie! Unknit that threatening, unkind brow,
And dart not scornful glances from those eyes
To wound thy lord, thy king, thy governor.
It blots thy beauty as frosts do bite the meads, 143
Confounds thy fame as whirlwinds shake fair buds, 144
And in no sense is meet or amiable.
A woman moved is like a fountain troubled, 146
Muddy, ill-seeming, thick, bereft of beauty;
And while it is so, none so dry or thirsty 148
Will deign to sip or touch one drop of it.
Thy husband is thy lord, thy life, thy keeper,
Thy head, thy sovereign; one that cares for thee,
And for thy maintenance commits his body
To painful labor both by sea and land, 153
To watch the night in storms, the day in cold, 154
Whilst thou liest warm at home, secure and safe;
And craves no other tribute at thy hands
But love, fair looks, and true obedience—
Too little payment for so great a debt.
Such duty as the subject owes the prince,
Even such a woman oweth to her husband;
And when she is froward, peevish, sullen, sour, 161
And not obedient to his honest will, 162
What is she but a foul contending rebel
And graceless traitor to her loving lord?
I am ashamed that women are so simple 165
To offer war where they should kneel for peace,
Or seek for rule, supremacy, and sway,
When they are bound to serve, love, and obey.
Why are our bodies soft, and weak, and smooth,
Unapt to toil and trouble in the world, 170
But that our soft conditions and our hearts 171
Should well agree with our external parts?
Come, come, you froward and unable worms! 173
My mind hath been as big as one of yours, 174
My heart as great, my reason haply more,
To bandy word for word and frown for frown;
But now I see our lances are but straws,
Our strength as weak, our weakness past compare, 178
That seeming to be most which we indeed least are. 179
Then vail your stomachs, for it is no boot, 180
And place your hands below your husband's foot,
In token of which duty, if he please,
My hand is ready; may it do him ease. 183

PETRUCHIO
Why, there's a wench! Come on, and kiss me, Kate.
[*They kiss.*]

LUCENTIO
Well, go thy ways, old lad, for thou shalt ha 't. 185

VINCENTIO
'Tis a good hearing when children are toward. 186

LUCENTIO
But a harsh hearing when women are froward.

PETRUCHIO Come, Kate, we'll to bed.
We three are married, but you two are sped. 189
[*To Lucentio*] 'Twas I won the wager, though you hit
the white, 190
And, being a winner, God give you good night! 191
Exit Petruchio [*with Katharina*].

HORTENSIO
Now go thy ways. Thou hast tamed a curst shrew. 192

LUCENTIO
'Tis a wonder, by your leave, she will be tamed so.
[*Exeunt.*]

143 meads meadows **144 Confounds thy fame** ruins your reputation **146 moved** angry **148 none . . . thirsty** there is no one so thirsty that he **153 painful** onerous **154 watch** stay awake throughout **161 peevish** obstinate **162 to his honest will** (Kate may suggest that she will be obedient when his will is decent and virtuous, not that his will is always so.) **165 simple** foolish **170 Unapt to** unfit for **171 conditions** qualities

173 unable worms i.e., poor feeble creatures. **174 big** haughty **178 as weak** i.e., as weak as straws **179 That seeming to be** seeming to be that **180 Then . . . boot** Then lower your pride, for it is no use striving **183 do him ease** give him pleasure. **185 go thy ways** well done. **ha 't** have it, the prize. **186 'Tis . . . toward** i.e., One likes to hear when children are obedient. **189 We . . . sped** i.e., All we three men have taken wives, but you two are done for (*sped*) through disobedient wives. **190 the white** the center of the target. (With quibble on the name of Bianca, which in Italian means "white.") **191 being** since I am **192 shrew** pronounced "shrow" (and thus spelled in the Folio). See also 4.1.198 and 5.2.28.

A Midsummer Night's Dream

One of the many astonishing achievements in *A Midsummer Night's Dream* (c. 1594–1595) is its development of the motif of love as an imaginative journey from a world of social conflict into a fantasy world created by the artist, ending in a return to a reality that has itself been partly transformed by the experience of the journey. As the lovers in this play flee from the Athenian law to lose themselves in the forest, they reveal and discover in themselves the simultaneously hilarious and horrifying effects of sexual desire. Moreover, their journey suggests the extent to which love or desire is itself an act of imagination, not unlike the imagination that underlies the creation of art. The fifth act especially invites us to see theatrical experience as like a dream, at times nightmarish but at its best an emancipating foray into an imagined space wholly beyond the realm of ordinary human happenings. Shakespeare gives us an earlier hint of an imaginary sylvan landscape in *The Two Gentlemen of Verona*, but not until *A Midsummer Night's Dream* is the idea fully realized. The motif of contrasting worlds, one of social convention and the other of visionary fantasy, will remain an enduring preoccupation of Shakespeare to the very last. This visionary world haunts the imagination with some of the most poetic passages of the entire Shakespeare canon, from Titania's evocation of her bond of affection with her votaress "in the spicèd Indian air by night" (2.1.123–37) to Oberon's memory of a mermaid singing on a dolphin's back (2.1.150–4). Containing the highest percentage of rhymed verse in all of Shakespeare's plays, *A Midsummer Night's Dream* calls attention to the seemingly magical capacity of words to weave spells not only on the characters but on the audience as well.

In construction, *A Midsummer Night's Dream* is a skillful interweaving of four plots involving four groups of characters: the court party of Theseus, the four young lovers, the fairies, and the "rude mechanicals" or would-be actors. Felix Mendelssohn's incidental music for the play evokes the contrasting textures of the various groups: Theseus's hunting horns and ceremonial wedding marches, the lovers' soaring and throbbing melodies, the fairies' pianissimo staccato, the tradesmen's clownish bassoon. Moreover, each plot is derived from its own set of source materials. The action involving Theseus and Hippolyta, for example, owes several details to Thomas North's translation (1579) of Plutarch's *Lives of the Noble Grecians and Romans*, to Chaucer's *Knight's Tale* and perhaps to his *Legend of Good Women*, and to Ovid's *Metamorphoses* (in the Latin text or in Arthur Golding's popular Elizabethan translation). The lovers' story, meanwhile, is Italianate and Ovidian in tone and also, in the broadest sense, follows the conventions of plot in Plautus's and Terence's Roman comedies, although no particular source is known. Shakespeare's rich fairy lore, by contrast, is part folk tradition and part learned. For some of his material he seems to have turned to written sources, such as the French romance *Huon of Bordeaux* (translated into English by 1540), Robert Greene's play *James IV* (c. 1591), and Edmund Spenser's *The Faerie Queene*, II.i.8 (1590). Similarly, he may have taken Titania's name from the *Metamorphoses*, where it is used as an epithet for both Diana and Circe. At the same time, in his creation of Mustardseed, Cobweb, Mote, and Peaseblossom, Shakespeare also pays homage to a rich body of unwritten sources that are, for the most part, no longer accessible. Changeling children, mortals kidnapped by fairy queens, men transformed to beasts by evil spells: these were the stuff of oral tales circulated by firesides on winter nights. Finally, for Bottom the weaver and company, Shakespeare's primary inspiration was doubtless his own theatrical experience, although even here he is indebted to Ovid for the story of Pyramus and Thisbe, and probably to Apuleius's *Golden Ass* (translated by William Adlington, 1566) for Bottom's transformation.

Each of the four main plots in *A Midsummer Night's Dream* contains one or more pairs of lovers whose happiness has been frustrated by misunderstanding or parental opposition. Theseus and Hippolyta, once enemies in battle, become husband and wife; their court marriage, constituting the overplot of the play, provides a framework for other dramatic actions that similarly oscillate between conflict and harmony. In fact, Theseus's actions are instrumental in setting in motion and finally resolving the tribulations of the other characters. In the beginning of the play, for example, the lovers flee from Theseus's Athenian law; at the end, they are awakened by him from their dream. As the king and queen of fairies come to Athens to celebrate Theseus's wedding, they exchange jealous accusations: Oberon accuses his queen of being overly partial to Theseus, while she is critical of Oberon's attentions to Hippolyta. These plots of the Athenian and the fairy monarchs are drawn even more closely together by the common practice in today's theater of doubling the parts of Theseus and Oberon, Hippolyta and Titania (also, frequently, Philostrate and Puck). The broadly comic action of Bottom the Weaver and his companions is drawn into the overall design by means of their deciding to use the forest of Athens as the place where they will rehearse their performance of "Pyramus and Thisbe" in anticipation of the wedding festivities.

The tragic love story of Pyramus and Thisbe, although it seems absurdly ill suited to a wedding, reminds us of the discord and potentially fatal misunderstandings that threaten even the best of relationships between men and women. For all his graceful bearing and princely authority, Theseus is a conquering male who freely admits that he has won the love of Hippolyta with his sword, doing her "injuries" (1.1.17). He never questions that the accord between them should now be stated in terms of male ascendancy over the female. The Amazonian Hippolyta may accept with good grace the marriage she previously resisted with all her might, like Kate in *The Taming of the Shrew*, and yet, in many recent stage productions, the actress playing Hippolyta has found it easy to cast doubt on the presumed tranquility of this forthcoming marriage by a display of feminist impatience at Theseus's urbanely patriarchal ways. The reconciliation of Oberon and Titania, meanwhile, reinforces the hierarchy of male over female in no uncertain terms. Having taught Titania a lesson for trying to keep a changeling boy from him, Oberon relents and eventually frees Titania from her debasing enchantment. She does not reproach him with so much as a word when she is awakened from her "vision." Even so, the very existence of the abundantly female space of Titania's bower where, surrounded by her attendants, she has acted out desires that she thought were her own, poses an alternative to patriarchy. The four young lovers end up happily paired, but only after they have experienced rejection, rivalry, hatred, and the desire to kill; the final resolution of this plot would not be possible if Demetrius were not left under the spell of the fairy love-juice. Thus, Theseus's wedding provides a ceremonial occasion of harmony and reconciliation but in such a way as to highlight the difficulties that have beset the drama's various couples.

Despite Theseus's cheerful preoccupation with marriage, his court embodies at first a stern attitude toward young love. As administrator of the law, Theseus must accede to the remorseless demands of Hermia's father, Egeus. The inflexible Athenian law sides with parentage, age, male dominance, wealth, and position against youth and romantic choice in love. The penalties are harsh: death or perpetual virginity—and virginity is presented in this comedy (despite the nobly chaste examples of Christ, St. Paul, and Queen Elizabeth) as a fate worse than death. Egeus is a familiar type, the interfering parent found in the Roman comedy of Plautus and Terence (and in Shakespeare's *Romeo and Juliet*). Indeed, the lovers' story is distantly derived from Roman comedy, which conventionally celebrated the triumph of young love over the machinations of age and wealth. Lysander reminds us that "the course of true love never did run smooth," and he sees its enemies as being chiefly external: the conflicting interests of parents or friends; mismating with respect to years and blood, war, death, or sickness (1.1.134–42). This description clearly applies to "Pyramus and Thisbe," and it is tested by the action of *A Midsummer Night's Dream* as a whole (as well as by other early Shakespearean plays, such as *Romeo and Juliet*). The archetypal story, whether ending happily or sadly, is an evocation of love's difficulties in the face of social hostility and indifference.

While Shakespeare uses several elements of Roman comedy in setting up the basic conflicts of his drama, he also introduces important modifications from the beginning. For example, he discards one conventional confrontation of classical and neoclassical comedy, in which the heroine must choose between an old, wealthy suitor supported by her family and the young but impecunious darling of her heart. Lysander is equal to his rival in social position, income, and attractiveness. Egeus's demand, therefore—that Hermia marry Demetrius rather than Lysander—seems simply arbitrary and unjust. Shakespeare emphasizes in this way the irrationality of Egeus's harsh insistence on being obeyed and of Theseus's rather complacent acceptance of the law's inequity. Spurned by an unfeeling social order, Lysander and Hermia are compelled to elope. To be sure, in the end Egeus proves to be no formidable threat; even he must admit the logic of permitting the lovers to couple as they ultimately desire. Thus, the obstacles to love are seen from the start as fundamentally superficial and indeed almost whimsical. Egeus is as heavy a villain as we are likely to find in this *jeu d'esprit*. Moreover, the very irrationality of his position prepares the way for an ultimate resolution of the conflict. Nevertheless, by the end of the first act, the supposedly rational world of conformity and duty, by its customary insensitivity to youthful happiness, has set in motion a temporary escape to a fantasy world where the law cannot reach.

In the forest, all the lovers—including Titania and Bottom—undergo a transforming experience engineered by the mischievous Puck. This experience demonstrates the universal power of love, which can overcome the queen of fairies as readily as the lowliest of humans. It also suggests the irrational nature of love and its affinity to enchantment, witchcraft, and even madness. Love is seen as an affliction taken in through the frail senses, particularly the eyes. When it strikes, the victim cannot choose but to embrace the object of his or her infatuation. By his amusing miscalculations, Puck shuffles the four lovers through various permutations with mathematical predictability. First, two gentlemen compete for one lady, leaving the second lady sadly unrequited in love; then everything is at cross-purposes, with each gentleman pursuing the lady who is in love with the other man; then the two gentlemen compete for the lady they both previously ignored. Finally, of course, Jack shall have his Jill—whom else should he have? The couples are properly united, as they evidently were at some time prior to the commencement of the play, when Demetrius had been romantically attached to Helena and Lysander to Hermia.

Their experience in the forest is an unsettling one for the four young lovers. Although some of them seek out the forest as a refuge from the Athenian law, the place rapidly takes on the darker aspect of a nightmare. Hermia awakens from sleep to find Lysander gone and soon discovers that her dream of a serpent eating her heart away while Lysander watches smiling (2.2.155–6) is all too prophetically true. The forest is a place of testing of the lovers, and the test appears at first to show how they are all their own worst enemies. Helena, having been rejected by Demetrius, can only suppose that she is being mocked, with Lysander and Demetrius both paying court to her. Next, it occurs to her that Hermia must be part of their conspiracy, too. Even though Hermia and Helena recall to each other the selfless devotion they have known as young friends, they become hated rivals in their present mood of self-pity and injured self-regard. The threshold of sexual awakening, it would seem, confronts them with a hazardous rite of passage—one that is especially threatening to the nonsexual friendship of their adolescent years. The two young men respond to similar conflicts by turning on one another in characteristically aggressive male ways. Puck allows them to playact their intended mayhem in a way that cannot harm them and then brings all four lovers together where they can awaken from their nightmare of imagined persecution. How much do they remember? Have they been changed by their journey in the forest? The lovers convey a sense of confusion, of an unreconciled dissonance of perspective in which "everything seems double" (4.1.189). As the lovers return to the daylight world of Athens and the court, their experiences assume the unreality of a remembered dream, like "far-off mountains turnèd into clouds" (4.1.187). When they thus awaken and return to the daylight world of Athens and the court, their renewed love and friendship are presumably deepened by their perception of how narrowly they have escaped from their own self-destructive imaginings. Their new happiness, they see, is better than they have deserved.

We sense that Puck is by no means unhappy about his knavish errors and manipulations: "Lord, what fools these mortals be!" Along with the other fairies in this play, Puck takes his being and his complex motivation from many denizens of the invisible world. As the agent of all-powerful love, Puck compares himself to Cupid. The love juice he administers comes from Cupid's flower, "love-in-idleness." Like Cupid, Puck acts at the behest of the gods, and yet he wields a power that the chiefest of the gods themselves cannot resist. Essentially, however, Puck is less a classical love deity than a prankish folk spirit, such as we find in every folklore: gremlin, leprechaun, hobgoblin, and the like. Titania's fairies recognize Puck as the folk figure Robin Goodfellow, able to deprive a beer barrel of its yeast so that it spoils rather than ferments. Puck characterizes himself as a practical joker, pulling stools out from under old ladies.

Folk wisdom imagines the inexplicable and unaccountable events in life to be caused by invisible spirits who laugh at mortals' discomfiture and mock them for mere sport. Puck is related to these mysterious spirits dwelling in nature, who must be placated with gifts and ceremonies. Although Shakespeare restricts Puck to a benign sportive role in dealing with the lovers or with Titania, the actual folk legends about Puck mentioned in this play are frequently disquieting. Puck is known to "mislead night wanderers, laughing at their harm"; indeed, he demonstrates as much with Demetrius and Lysander, leading them on through the forest to the point of exhaustion, even though we perceive the sportful intent. At the play's end, Puck links himself and his fellows with the ghoulish apparitions of death and night: wolves howling at the moon, screech owls, shrouds, gaping graves. Associations of this sort go beyond mere sportiveness to the witchcraft and demonology involving spirits rising from the dead. Even Oberon's assurance that the fairies will bless all the marriages of this play, shielding their progeny against mole, harelip, or other birth defects, carries the implication that such misfortunes can be caused by offended spirits. The magic of this play is thus explicitly related to deep irrational powers and forces capable of doing great harm, although, to be sure, the spirit of comedy keeps such veiled threats safely at a distance in *A Midsummer Night's Dream*.

Oberon and Titania, in their view of the relationship between gods and humans, reflect yet another aspect of the fairies' spiritual ancestry. The king and queen of fairies assert that, because they are immortal, their regal quarrels in love must inevitably have dire consequences on earth, either in the love relationship of Theseus and Hippolyta or in the management of the weather. Floods, storms, diseases, and sterility abound, "And this same progeny of evils comes / From our debate, from our dissension. / We are their parents and original" (2.1.115–17). This motif of the gods' quarreling over human affairs reminds us of Homer and Virgil. At the same time, in this lighthearted play the motif is more nearly mock-epic than truly epic. The consequences of the gods' anger are simply mirth-provoking, most of all in Titania's love affair with Bottom the weaver.

The story of Bottom and Titania is simultaneously classical and folk in nature. In a playfully classical mode, this love affair between a god and an earthy creature underscores humanity's double nature. Bottom himself becomes half man and half beast, even if he is more ludicrously comic than the centaurs, satyrs, griffins, sphinxes, and other amphibious beings of classical mythology. Some ballads of the early modern period tell of humans transformed into beasts, or of mortals kidnapped by a fairy queen; see, for example, "Tam Lin" and "Thomas Rhymer." Bottom is an especially comic example of metamorphosis because he reverses the usual pattern of a human head and an animal body: instead, his head is animal, his body human. His very name suggests the solid nature of his fleshly being (*bottom* is appropriately also a weaving term). He and Titania represent the opposites of flesh and spirit, miraculously yoked for a time in a twofold vision of humankind's absurd and ethereal nature.

A play bringing together fairies and mortals inevitably raises questions of illusion and reality. These questions reach their greatest intensity in the presentation of "Pyramus and Thisbe." This play within a play focuses our attention on the familiarly Shakespearean metaphor of art as illusion and of the world itself as a stage on which men and women are merely players. As Theseus observes, apologizing for the ineptness of the tradesmen's performance, "the best in this kind are but shadows" (5.1.210); that is, Shakespeare's own play is of the same order of reality as Bottom's play. Puck too, in his epilogue, invites any spectator offended by Shakespeare's play to dismiss it as a mere dream—as, indeed, the play's very title suggests. Theseus goes even further, linking dream to the essence of imaginative art, although he does so in a clearly critical and rather patronizing way. The artist, he says, is like the maniac or the lover in his or her frenzy of inspiration, giving "to airy nothing / A local habitation and a name" (5.1.16–17). Artistic achievements are too unsubstantial for Theseus; from his point of view they are the products of mere fantasy and irrationality, mere myths or fairy stories or old wives' tales. Behind this critical persona defending the "real" world of his court, however, we can hear Shakespeare's characteristically self-effacing defense of "dreaming."

"Pyramus and Thisbe," like the larger play surrounding it, attempts to body forth "the forms of things unknown." The play within the play gives us personified moonshine, a speaking wall, and an apologetic lion. Of course, it is an absurdly bad play, full of lame epithets, bombastic alliteration, and bathos. In part, Shakespeare here is satirizing the abuses of a theater he had helped reform. The players' chosen method of portraying imaginative matters is ridiculous and calls forth deliciously wry comments from the courtly spectators on stage: "Would you desire lime and hair to speak better?" (5.1.164–5). At the same time, those spectators on stage are actors in our play. Their sarcasms render them less sympathetic in our eyes; we see that their kind of sophistication is as restrictive as it is illuminating. Bottom and his friends have conceived moonshine and lion as they did because these simple men are so responsive to the terrifying power of art. A lion might frighten the ladies and get the men hanged. Theirs is a primitive faith, naive but strong, and in this sense it contrasts favorably with the jaded rationality of the court party. Theseus's valuable reminder that all art is only "illusion" is thus juxtaposed with Bottom's insistence that imaginative art has a reality of its own.

Theseus above all embodies the sophistication of the court in his description of art as a frenzy of seething brains. Ironically, Theseus's genial scoffing at "These antique fables" and "these fairy toys" (5.1.3) would seem to efface his own identity as the figure of legend. Limited by his own skepticism, Theseus seems to have forgotten his own forest wanderings, led by Titania through the "glimmering night" (2.1.77). Bottom, contrastingly, has experienced "a most rare vision," such a dream as is "past the wit of man to say what dream it was" (4.1.203–5). He alone can claim to have been the lover of the queen of fairies; and, although his language cannot adequately describe the experience, Bottom will see it made into a ballad called "Bottom's Dream." Shakespeare leaves the status of his fantasy world deliberately complex; Theseus's lofty denial of dreaming is too abrupt. Even if the Athenian forest world can be made only momentarily substantial in the artifact of Shakespeare's play, we as audience respond to its tantalizing vision. We emerge back into our lives wondering if the fairies were "real"; that is, we are puzzled by the relationship of these artistic symbols to the tangible concreteness of our daily existence. Unless our perceptions have been thus enlarged by sharing in the author's dream, we have not surrendered to the imaginative experience.

Recent performances of this enduringly popular play suggest how open it is to varying interpretation and especially to postmodern views of love and politics as thoroughly unsettling in their irrationality. Nineteenth-century staging generally preferred to see the play as a gossamer delight of diminutive gilded-winged fairies and prankish hobgoblins, all underscored by the romantic strains of Mendelssohn's incidental music. More recently, and especially after World War II, theater and film versions have responded to a darker view. Inspired by Jan Kott's *Shakespeare Our Contemporary* (1964), a book written from the perspective of Soviet-dominated eastern Europe of the Cold War, Peter Brook's brilliantly revisionary stage version for the Royal Shakespeare Theater in 1970 set the play in a brightly lit white box peopled with jugglers and athletic trapeze artists who tumbled and dashed about after one another with abandon. Bottom the Weaver, sporting the button nose of a circus clown, rode atop the shoulders of a fellow worker who thrust his clenched fist between Bottom's legs in a gesture of phallic aggression.

Brook's avowed aim of freeing the play from what he saw as an oppressive tradition has proved to be immensely influential. Ever since, the young lovers have learned to express their sexual energies through vigorous pursuit and physical contact. Feminist insights have enriched the role of Queen Hippolyta: formerly a captive queen resigned to her marriage to Theseus, she has become in many productions a champion of Hermia's right to resist her father's patriarchal insistence on his will. Puck, in many a recent production, is the denizen of a drug culture, with the love potion as the weed he gleefully distributes. The experience of the forest becomes a drug-induced "high," for audiences as for the actors. The fairies, sometimes played by adult and hairy males, can exhibit a steak of cruelty. The doubling of some central roles, notably Theseus/Oberon, Hippolyta/Titania, and Philostrate/Puck, has given ironic emphasis to parallels between human society and fairyland. Throughout, modern productions have tended to exploit disenchantment with traditional social structures and the surging energy of sexual self-discovery. These modern interpretations are arguably neither more nor less "true" to Shakespeare's text than earlier or more "traditional" versions. What they do demonstrate is the play's remarkable permeability and openness to differing views.

A Midsummer Night's Dream

[*Dramatis Personae*

THESEUS, *Duke of Athens*

HIPPOLYTA, *Queen of the Amazons, betrothed to Theseus*
PHILOSTRATE, *Master of the Revels*
EGEUS, *father of Hermia*

HERMIA, *daughter of Egeus, in love with Lysander*
LYSANDER, *in love with Hermia*
DEMETRIUS, *in love with Hermia and favored by Egeus*
HELENA, *in love with Demetrius*

OBERON, *King of the Fairies*
TITANIA, *Queen of the Fairies*
PUCK, *or* ROBIN GOODFELLOW

PEASEBLOSSOM, COBWEB, MOTE, MUSTARDSEED, } *fairies attending Titania*
Other FAIRIES *attending*

PETER QUINCE, *a carpenter,*	*representing*	PROLOGUE
NICK BOTTOM, *a weaver,*		PYRAMUS
FRANCIS FLUTE, *a bellows mender,*		THISBE
TOM SNOUT, *a tinker,*		WALL
SNUG, *a joiner,*		LION
ROBIN STARVELING, *a tailor,*		MOONSHINE

Lords and Attendants on Theseus and Hippolyta

SCENE: *Athens, and a wood near it*]

[1.1]

Enter Theseus, Hippolyta, [and Philostrate,] with others.

THESEUS
Now, fair Hippolyta, our nuptial hour
Draws on apace. Four happy days bring in
Another moon; but, oh, methinks, how slow
This old moon wanes! She lingers my desires,
Like to a stepdame or a dowager
Long withering out a young man's revenue.

HIPPOLYTA
Four days will quickly steep themselves in night;
Four nights will quickly dream away the time;
And then the moon, like to a silver bow
New bent in heaven, shall behold the night
Of our solemnities.

THESEUS Go, Philostrate,
Stir up the Athenian youth to merriments.
Awake the pert and nimble spirit of mirth.
Turn melancholy forth to funerals;
The pale companion is not for our pomp.
[*Exit Philostrate.*]
Hippolyta, I wooed thee with my sword
And won thy love doing thee injuries;
But I will wed thee in another key,
With pomp, with triumph, and with reveling.

Enter Egeus and his daughter Hermia, and Lysander, and Demetrius.

EGEUS
Happy be Theseus, our renownèd duke!

THESEUS
Thanks, good Egeus. What's the news with thee?

EGEUS
Full of vexation come I, with complaint
Against my child, my daughter Hermia.—
Stand forth, Demetrius.—My noble lord,
This man hath my consent to marry her.—
Stand forth, Lysander.—And, my gracious Duke,
This man hath bewitched the bosom of my child.—
Thou, thou Lysander, thou hast given her rhymes
And interchanged love tokens with my child.
Thou hast by moonlight at her window sung
With feigning voice verses of feigning love,
And stol'n the impression of her fantasy
With bracelets of thy hair, rings, gauds, conceits,
Knacks, trifles, nosegays, sweetmeats—messengers
Of strong prevailment in unhardened youth.
With cunning hast thou filched my daughter's heart,
Turned her obedience, which is due to me,
To stubborn harshness. And, my gracious Duke,
Be it so she will not here before Your Grace
Consent to marry with Demetrius,
I beg the ancient privilege of Athens:
As she is mine, I may dispose of her,
Which shall be either to this gentleman
Or to her death, according to our law
Immediately provided in that case.

THESEUS
What say you, Hermia? Be advised, fair maid.
To you your father should be as a god—
One that composed your beauties, yea, and one
To whom you are but as a form in wax
By him imprinted, and within his power
To leave the figure or disfigure it.
Demetrius is a worthy gentleman.

HERMIA
So is Lysander.

THESEUS In himself he is;
But in this kind, wanting your father's voice,
The other must be held the worthier.

HERMIA
I would my father looked but with my eyes.

THESEUS
Rather your eyes must with his judgment look.

HERMIA
I do entreat Your Grace to pardon me.
I know not by what power I am made bold,
Nor how it may concern my modesty
In such a presence here to plead my thoughts;
But I beseech Your Grace that I may know
The worst that may befall me in this case
If I refuse to wed Demetrius.

THESEUS
Either to die the death or to abjure
Forever the society of men.
Therefore, fair Hermia, question your desires,
Know of your youth, examine well your blood,
Whether, if you yield not to your father's choice,
You can endure the livery of a nun,
For aye to be in shady cloister mewed,
To live a barren sister all your life,
Chanting faint hymns to the cold fruitless moon.
Thrice blessèd they that master so their blood
To undergo such maiden pilgrimage;
But earthlier happy is the rose distilled
Than that which, withering on the virgin thorn,
Grows, lives, and dies in single blessedness.

1.1. Location: Athens. Theseus's court.
4 lingers frustrates **5 stepdame** stepmother. **a dowager** i.e., a widow (whose right of inheritance from her dead husband is eating into her son's estate) **6 withering out** causing to dwindle
7 Four . . . night (The image is of the day sinking into the ocean as night comes on.) **11 solemnities** festive ceremonies of marriage.
15 companion fellow. (A pale complexion is linked to melancholy.) **pomp** ceremonial magnificence. **16 with my sword** i.e., in a military engagement against the Amazons, when Hippolyta was taken captive **19 triumph** public festivity **31 feigning** (1) counterfeiting (2) faining, desirous **32 And . . . fantasy** and made her fall in love with you (imprinting your image on her imagination) by stealthy and dishonest means **33 gauds, conceits** playthings, fanciful trifles

34 Knacks . . . sweetmeats knicknacks, trinkets, bouquets, candies
35 prevailment in influence on **39 Be it so** if **45 Immediately** directly, with nothing intervening **51 leave** i.e., leave unaltered
54 kind respect. **wanting** lacking. **voice** approval **65 die the death** be executed by legal process **68 blood** passions **70 livery** habit, costume **71 aye** ever. **mewed** shut in. (Said of a hawk, poultry, etc.) **76 earthlier happy** happier as respects this world.
distilled i.e., to make perfume

HERMIA

So will I grow, so live, so die, my lord,
Ere I will yield my virgin patent up 80
Unto His Lordship, whose unwishèd yoke
My soul consents not to give sovereignty.

THESEUS

Take time to pause, and by the next new moon—
The sealing day betwixt my love and me
For everlasting bond of fellowship—
Upon that day either prepare to die
For disobedience to your father's will,
Or else to wed Demetrius, as he would,
Or on Diana's altar to protest 89
For aye austerity and single life.

DEMETRIUS

Relent, sweet Hermia, and, Lysander, yield
Thy crazèd title to my certain right. 92

LYSANDER

You have her father's love, Demetrius;
Let me have Hermia's. Do you marry him.

EGEUS

Scornful Lysander! True, he hath my love,
And what is mine my love shall render him.
And she is mine, and all my right of her
I do estate unto Demetrius. 98

LYSANDER

I am, my lord, as well derived as he, 99
As well possessed; my love is more than his; 100
My fortunes every way as fairly ranked, 101
If not with vantage, as Demetrius'; 102
And, which is more than all these boasts can be,
I am beloved of beauteous Hermia.
Why should not I then prosecute my right?
Demetrius, I'll avouch it to his head, 106
Made love to Nedar's daughter, Helena,
And won her soul; and she, sweet lady, dotes,
Devoutly dotes, dotes in idolatry
Upon this spotted and inconstant man. 110

THESEUS

I must confess that I have heard so much,
And with Demetrius thought to have spoke thereof;
But, being overfull of self-affairs, 113
My mind did lose it. But, Demetrius, come,
And come, Egeus, you shall go with me;
I have some private schooling for you both. 116
For you, fair Hermia, look you arm yourself 117
To fit your fancies to your father's will, 118
Or else the law of Athens yields you up—
Which by no means we may extenuate— 120
To death or to a vow of single life.
Come, my Hippolyta. What cheer, my love?
Demetrius and Egeus, go along. 123

80 patent privilege **89 protest** vow **92 crazèd** cracked, unsound **98 estate unto** settle or bestow upon **99 as well derived** as well born and descended **100 possessed** endowed with wealth **101 fairly** handsomely **102 vantage** superiority **106 head** i.e., face **110 spotted** i.e., morally stained **113 self-affairs** my own concerns **116 schooling** admonition **117 look you arm** take care you prepare **118 fancies** likings, thoughts of love **120 extenuate** mitigate, relax **123 go** i.e., come

I must employ you in some business
Against our nuptial, and confer with you 125
Of something nearly that concerns yourselves. 126

EGEUS

With duty and desire we follow you.
Exeunt [all but Lysander and Hermia].

LYSANDER

How now, my love, why is your cheek so pale?
How chance the roses there do fade so fast?

HERMIA

Belike for want of rain, which I could well 130
Beteem them from the tempest of my eyes. 131

LYSANDER

Ay me! For aught that I could ever read,
Could ever hear by tale or history,
The course of true love never did run smooth;
But either it was different in blood— 135

HERMIA

Oh, cross! Too high to be enthralled to low. 136

LYSANDER

Or else misgrafted in respect of years— 137

HERMIA

Oh, spite! Too old to be engaged to young.

LYSANDER

Or else it stood upon the choice of friends— 139

HERMIA

Oh, hell, to choose love by another's eyes!

LYSANDER

Or if there were a sympathy in choice, 141
War, death, or sickness did lay siege to it,
Making it momentany as a sound, 143
Swift as a shadow, short as any dream,
Brief as the lightning in the collied night 145
That in a spleen unfolds both heaven and earth, 146
And ere a man hath power to say "Behold!"
The jaws of darkness do devour it up.
So quick bright things come to confusion. 149

HERMIA

If then true lovers have been ever crossed, 150
It stands as an edict in destiny.
Then let us teach our trial patience, 152
Because it is a customary cross,
As due to love as thoughts, and dreams, and sighs,
Wishes, and tears, poor fancy's followers. 155

LYSANDER

A good persuasion. Therefore, hear me, Hermia: 156
I have a widow aunt, a dowager
Of great revenue, and she hath no child.
From Athens is her house remote seven leagues; 159
And she respects me as her only son. 160

125 Against in preparation for **126 nearly that** that closely **130 Belike** Very likely **131 Beteem** grant, afford **135 blood** hereditary rank **136 cross** vexation. **137 misgrafted** ill grafted, badly matched **139 friends** relatives **141 sympathy** agreement **143 momentany** lasting but a moment **145 collied** blackened (as with coal dust), darkened **146 in a spleen** in a swift impulse, in a violent flash. **unfolds** reveals **149 confusion** ruin. **150 ever crossed** always thwarted **152 teach . . . patience** i.e., teach ourselves patience in this trial **155 fancy's** amorous passion's **156 persuasion** doctrine. **159 seven leagues** about 21 miles **160 respects** regards

There, gentle Hermia, may I marry thee,
And to that place the sharp Athenian law
Cannot pursue us. If thou lovest me, then,
Steal forth thy father's house tomorrow night;
And in the wood, a league without the town,
Where I did meet thee once with Helena
To do observance to a morn of May,
There will I stay for thee.

HERMIA
My good Lysander!
I swear to thee, by Cupid's strongest bow,
By his best arrow with the golden head,
By the simplicity of Venus' doves,
By that which knitteth souls and prospers loves,
And by that fire which burned the Carthage queen
When the false Trojan under sail was seen,
By all the vows that ever men have broke,
In number more than ever women spoke,
In that same place thou hast appointed me
Tomorrow truly will I meet with thee.

LYSANDER
Keep promise, love. Look, here comes Helena.

Enter Helena.

HERMIA
God speed, fair Helena! Whither away?

HELENA
Call you me fair? That "fair" again unsay.
Demetrius loves your fair. Oh, happy fair!
Your eyes are lodestars, and your tongue's sweet air
More tunable than lark to shepherd's ear
When wheat is green, when hawthorn buds appear.
Sickness is catching. Oh, were favor so,
Yours would I catch, fair Hermia, ere I go;
My ear should catch your voice, my eye your eye,
My tongue should catch your tongue's sweet melody.
Were the world mine, Demetrius being bated,
The rest I'd give to be to you translated.
Oh, teach me how you look and with what art
You sway the motion of Demetrius' heart.

HERMIA
I frown upon him, yet he loves me still.

HELENA
Oh, that your frowns would teach my smiles such skill!

HERMIA
I give him curses, yet he gives me love.

HELENA
Oh, that my prayers could such affection move!

HERMIA
The more I hate, the more he follows me.

HELENA
The more I love, the more he hateth me.

HERMIA
His folly, Helena, is no fault of mine.

HELENA
None, but your beauty. Would that fault were mine!

HERMIA
Take comfort. He no more shall see my face.
Lysander and myself will fly this place.
Before the time I did Lysander see
Seemed Athens as a paradise to me.
Oh, then, what graces in my love do dwell,
That he hath turned a heaven unto a hell?

LYSANDER
Helen, to you our minds we will unfold.
Tomorrow night, when Phoebe doth behold
Her silver visage in the watery glass,
Decking with liquid pearl the bladed grass,
A time that lovers' flights doth still conceal,
Through Athens' gates have we devised to steal.

HERMIA
And in the wood, where often you and I
Upon faint primrose beds were wont to lie,
Emptying our bosoms of their counsel sweet,
There my Lysander and myself shall meet,
And thence from Athens turn away our eyes
To seek new friends and stranger companies.
Farewell, sweet playfellow. Pray thou for us,
And good luck grant thee thy Demetrius!
Keep word, Lysander. We must starve our sight
From lovers' food till morrow deep midnight.

LYSANDER
I will, my Hermia. *Exit Hermia.*
Helena, adieu!
As you on him, Demetrius dote on you!
Exit Lysander.

HELENA
How happy some o'er other some can be!
Through Athens I am thought as fair as she.
But what of that? Demetrius thinks not so;
He will not know what all but he do know.
And as he errs, doting on Hermia's eyes,
So I, admiring of his qualities.
Things base and vile, holding no quantity,
Love can transpose to form and dignity.
Love looks not with the eyes, but with the mind,
And therefore is winged Cupid painted blind.

165 without outside **167 To do . . . May** to perform the ceremonies of May Day **170 best arrow** (Cupid's best gold-pointed arrows were supposed to induce love; his blunt leaden arrows, aversion.) **171 simplicity** innocence. **doves** i.e., those that drew Venus's chariot **173, 174 Carthage queen, false Trojan** (Dido, Queen of Carthage, immolated herself on a funeral pyre after having been deserted by the Trojan hero Aeneas.) **180 fair** fair-complexioned. (Generally regarded by the Elizabethans as more beautiful than a dark complexion.) **182 your fair** your beauty (even though Hermia is dark complexioned). **happy fair** lucky fair one. **183 lodestars** guiding stars. **air** music **184 tunable** tuneful, melodious **186 favor** appearance, looks **190 bated** excepted **191 translated** transformed. **193 sway the motion** control the impulses

197 Oh, that . . . move! Would that my prayers could arouse such desire! **204–5 Before . . . to me** (Love has led to complications and jealousies, making Athens hell for Hermia.) **209 Phoebe** Diana, the moon **210 glass** reflecting surface (of a lake, etc.) **211 liquid pearl** i.e., dew **212 still** always **215 faint** pale **216 counsel** secret thought **219 stranger companies** the company of strangers. **226 o'er . . . can be** can be in comparison to some others. **232 holding no quantity** i.e., unsubstantial, unshapely

Nor hath Love's mind of any judgment taste;
Wings and no eyes figure unheedy haste.
And therefore is Love said to be a child,
Because in choice he is so oft beguiled.
As waggish boys in game themselves forswear,
So the boy Love is perjured everywhere.
For ere Demetrius looked on Hermia's eyne,
He hailed down oaths that he was only mine;
And when this hail some heat from Hermia felt,
So he dissolved, and showers of oaths did melt.
I will go tell him of fair Hermia's flight.
Then to the wood will he tomorrow night
Pursue her; and for this intelligence
If I have thanks, it is a dear expense.
But herein mean I to enrich my pain,
To have his sight thither and back again. *Exit.*

✤

[1.2]

Enter Quince the carpenter, and Snug the joiner, and Bottom the weaver, and Flute the bellows mender, and Snout the tinker, and Starveling the tailor.

QUINCE Is all our company here?

BOTTOM You were best to call them generally, man by man, according to the scrip.

QUINCE Here is the scroll of every man's name which is thought fit, through all Athens, to play in our interlude before the Duke and the Duchess on his wedding day at night.

BOTTOM First, good Peter Quince, say what the play treats on, then read the names of the actors, and so grow to a point.

QUINCE Marry, our play is "The most lamentable comedy and most cruel death of Pyramus and Thisbe."

BOTTOM A very good piece of work, I assure you, and a merry. Now, good Peter Quince, call forth your actors by the scroll. Masters, spread yourselves.

QUINCE Answer as I call you. Nick Bottom, the weaver.

BOTTOM Ready. Name what part I am for, and proceed.

QUINCE You, Nick Bottom, are set down for Pyramus.

BOTTOM What is Pyramus? A lover or a tyrant?

QUINCE A lover, that kills himself most gallant for love.

BOTTOM That will ask some tears in the true performing of it. If I do it, let the audience look to their eyes. I will move storms; I will condole in some measure. To the rest—yet my chief humor is for a tyrant. I could play Ercles rarely, or a part to tear a cat in, to make all split.

"The raging rocks
And shivering shocks
Shall break the locks
Of prison gates;
And Phibbus' car
Shall shine from far
And make and mar
The foolish Fates."

This was lofty! Now name the rest of the players. This is Ercles' vein, a tyrant's vein. A lover is more condoling.

QUINCE Francis Flute, the bellows mender.

FLUTE Here, Peter Quince.

QUINCE Flute, you must take Thisbe on you.

FLUTE What is Thisbe? A wandering knight?

QUINCE It is the lady that Pyramus must love.

FLUTE Nay, faith, let not me play a woman. I have a beard coming.

QUINCE That's all one. You shall play it in a mask, and you may speak as small as you will.

BOTTOM An I may hide my face, let me play Thisbe too. I'll speak in a monstrous little voice: "Thisne, Thisne!" "Ah, Pyramus, my lover dear! Thy Thisbe dear, and lady dear!"

QUINCE No, no, you must play Pyramus, and Flute, you Thisbe.

BOTTOM Well, proceed.

QUINCE Robin Starveling, the tailor.

STARVELING Here, Peter Quince.

QUINCE Robin Starveling, you must play Thisbe's mother. Tom Snout, the tinker.

SNOUT Here, Peter Quince.

QUINCE You, Pyramus' father; myself, Thisbe's father; Snug, the joiner, you, the lion's part; and I hope here is a play fitted.

SNUG Have you the lion's part written? Pray you, if it be, give it me, for I am slow of study.

QUINCE You may do it extempore, for it is nothing but roaring.

BOTTOM Let me play the lion too. I will roar that I will do any man's heart good to hear me. I will roar that I will make the Duke say, "Let him roar again, let him roar again."

QUINCE An you should do it too terribly, you would fright the Duchess and the ladies, that they would shriek; and that were enough to hang us all.

ALL That would hang us, every mother's son.

BOTTOM I grant you, friends, if you should fright the ladies out of their wits, they would have no more discretion but to hang us; but I will aggravate my voice so that I will roar you as gently as any sucking dove; I will roar you an 'twere any nightingale.

236 Nor . . . taste i.e., Nor has Love, which dwells in the fancy or imagination, any least bit of judgment or reason **237 figure** signify **239 in choice** in choosing. **beguiled** self-deluded, making unaccountable choices. **240 waggish** playful, mischievous. **game** sport, jest **242 eyne** eyes. (Old form of plural.) **248 intelligence** information **249 a dear expense** i.e., a trouble worth taking on my part.
1.2. Location: Athens.
2 generally (Bottom's blunder for "individually.") **3 scrip** script. **5–6 interlude** play **10 grow to** come to **11 Marry** (A mild oath; originally the name of the Virgin Mary.) **16 Bottom** (As a weaver's term, a *bottom* was an object around which thread was wound.) **23 condole** lament, arouse pity **24 humor** inclination

25 Ercles Hercules. (The tradition of ranting came from Seneca's *Hercules Furens*.) **tear a cat** i.e., rant. **make all split** i.e., cause a stir, bring the house down. **30 Phibbus' car** Phoebus's, the sun god's, chariot **43 That's all one** It makes no difference. **44 small** high-pitched **45 An** If. (Also at line 68.) **74 aggravate** (Bottom's blunder for "moderate.") **75 roar you** i.e., roar for you. **sucking dove** (Bottom conflates *sitting dove* and *sucking lamb*, two proverbial images of innocence.) **76 an 'twere** as if it were

QUINCE You can play no part but Pyramus; for Pyramus is a sweet-faced man, a proper man as one shall see in a summer's day, a most lovely gentlemanlike man. Therefore you must needs play Pyramus.

BOTTOM Well, I will undertake it. What beard were I best to play it in?

QUINCE Why, what you will.

BOTTOM I will discharge it in either your straw-color beard, your orange-tawny beard, your purple-in-grain beard, or your French-crown-color beard, your perfect yellow.

QUINCE Some of your French crowns have no hair at all, and then you will play barefaced. But, masters, here are your parts. [*He distributes parts.*] And I am to entreat you, request you, and desire you to con them by tomorrow night, and meet me in the palace wood, a mile without the town, by moonlight. There will we rehearse; for if we meet in the city, we shall be dogged with company, and our devices known. In the meantime I will draw a bill of properties, such as our play wants. I pray you, fail me not.

BOTTOM We will meet, and there we may rehearse most obscenely and courageously. Take pains, be perfect. Adieu.

QUINCE At the Duke's oak we meet.

BOTTOM Enough. Hold, or cut bowstrings. *Exeunt.*

[2.1]

Enter a Fairy at one door, and Robin Goodfellow [Puck] at another.

PUCK
How now, spirit, whither wander you?

FAIRY
Over hill, over dale,
Thorough bush, thorough brier,
Over park, over pale,
Thorough flood, thorough fire,
I do wander everywhere,
Swifter than the moon's sphere;
And I serve the Fairy Queen,
To dew her orbs upon the green.
The cowslips tall her pensioners be.
In their gold coats spots you see;
Those be rubies, fairy favors;
In those freckles live their savors.
I must go seek some dewdrops here
And hang a pearl in every cowslip's ear.
Farewell, thou lob of spirits; I'll be gone.
Our Queen and all her elves come here anon.

PUCK
The King doth keep his revels here tonight.
Take heed the Queen come not within his sight.
For Oberon is passing fell and wrath,
Because that she as her attendant hath
A lovely boy, stolen from an Indian king;
She never had so sweet a changeling.
And jealous Oberon would have the child
Knight of his train, to trace the forests wild.
But she perforce withholds the lovèd boy,
Crowns him with flowers, and makes him all her joy.
And now they never meet in grove or green,
By fountain clear, or spangled starlight sheen,
But they do square, that all their elves for fear
Creep into acorn cups and hide them there.

FAIRY
Either I mistake your shape and making quite,
Or else you are that shrewd and knavish sprite
Called Robin Goodfellow. Are not you he
That frights the maidens of the villagery,
Skim milk, and sometimes labor in the quern,
And bootless make the breathless huswife churn,
And sometimes make the drink to bear no barm,
Mislead night wanderers, laughing at their harm?
Those that "Hobgoblin" call you, and "Sweet Puck,"
You do their work, and they shall have good luck.
Are you not he?

PUCK Thou speakest aright;
I am that merry wanderer of the night.
I jest to Oberon and make him smile
When I a fat and bean-fed horse beguile,
Neighing in likeness of a filly foal;
And sometimes lurk I in a gossip's bowl
In very likeness of a roasted crab,
And when she drinks, against her lips I bob
And on her withered dewlap pour the ale.
The wisest aunt, telling the saddest tale,

78 proper handsome **84 discharge** perform. **your** i.e., you know the kind I mean **85 purple-in-grain** dyed a very deep red. (From *grain,* the name applied to the dried insect used to make the dye.) **86 French-crown-color** i.e., color of a French crown, a gold coin **88 crowns** heads bald from syphilis, the "French disease" **91 con** memorize **95 devices** plans **96 draw a bill** draw up a list **99 obscenely** (An unintentionally funny blunder, whatever Bottom meant to say.) **perfect** i.e., letter-perfect in memorizing your parts. **102 Hold . . . bowstrings** (An archers' expression, not definitely explained, but probably meaning here "keep your promises, or give up the play.")
2.1. Location: A wood near Athens.
3 Thorough through **4 pale** enclosure **7 sphere** orbit **9 dew** sprinkle with dew. **orbs** circles, i.e., fairy rings (circular bands of grass, darker than the surrounding area, caused by fungi enriching the soil) **10 pensioners** retainers, members of the royal bodyguard **12 favors** love tokens **13 savors** sweet smells. **16 lob** country bumpkin **17 anon** at once. **20 passing fell** exceedingly angry. **wrath** wrathful **23 changeling** child exchanged for another by the fairies. **25 trace** range through **26 perforce** forcibly **29 fountain** spring. **starlight sheen** shining starlight **30 square** quarrel **33 shrewd** mischievous. **sprite** spirit **35 villagery** village population **36 Skim milk** i.e., steal the cream. **quern** hand mill (where Puck presumably hampers the grinding of grain) **37 bootless** in vain. (Puck prevents the cream from turning to butter.) **huswife** housewife **38 barm** head on the ale. (Puck prevents the barm or yeast from producing fermentation.) **39 Mislead night wanderers** i.e., mislead with false fire those who walk abroad at night (hence earning Puck his other names of Jack o' Lantern and Will o' the Wisp) **40 Those . . . Puck** i.e., Those who call you by the names you favor rather than those denoting the mischief you do **45 bean-fed** full of beans **46 a filly foal** a mare (in heat) **47 gossip's** old woman's **48 crab** crab apple **50 dewlap** loose skin on neck **51 aunt** old woman. **saddest** most serious

Sometime for three-foot stool mistaketh me;
Then slip I from her bum, down topples she,
And "Tailor" cries, and falls into a cough;
And then the whole choir hold their hips and laugh,
And waxen in their mirth, and neeze, and swear
A merrier hour was never wasted there.
But, room, fairy! Here comes Oberon.

FAIRY
And here my mistress. Would that he were gone!

Enter [*Oberon*] *the King of Fairies at one door, with his train, and* [*Titania*] *the Queen at another, with hers.*

OBERON
Ill met by moonlight, proud Titania.

TITANIA
What, jealous Oberon? Fairies, skip hence.
I have forsworn his bed and company.

OBERON
Tarry, rash wanton. Am not I thy lord?

TITANIA
Then I must be thy lady; but I know
When thou hast stolen away from Fairyland
And in the shape of Corin sat all day,
Playing on pipes of corn and versing love
To amorous Phillida. Why art thou here
Come from the farthest step of India,
But that, forsooth, the bouncing Amazon,
Your buskined mistress and your warrior love,
To Theseus must be wedded, and you come
To give their bed joy and prosperity.

OBERON
How canst thou thus for shame, Titania,
Glance at my credit with Hippolyta,
Knowing I know thy love to Theseus?
Didst not thou lead him through the glimmering night
From Perigenia, whom he ravishèd?
And make him with fair Aegles break his faith,
With Ariadne and Antiopa?

TITANIA
These are the forgeries of jealousy;
And never, since the middle summer's spring,
Met we on hill, in dale, forest, or mead,
By pavèd fountain or by rushy brook,
Or in the beachèd margent of the sea,
To dance our ringlets to the whistling wind,
But with thy brawls thou hast disturbed our sport.
Therefore the winds, piping to us in vain,
As in revenge, have sucked up from the sea
Contagious fogs which, falling in the land,
Hath every pelting river made so proud
That they have overborne their continents.
The ox hath therefore stretched his yoke in vain,
The plowman lost his sweat, and the green corn
Hath rotted ere his youth attained a beard;
The fold stands empty in the drownèd field,
And crows are fatted with the murrain flock;
The nine-men's morris is filled up with mud,
And the quaint mazes in the wanton green
For lack of tread are undistinguishable.
The human mortals want their winter here;
No night is now with hymn or carol blessed.
Therefore the moon, the governess of floods,
Pale in her anger, washes all the air,
That rheumatic diseases do abound.
And thorough this distemperature we see
The seasons alter: hoary-headed frosts
Fall in the fresh lap of the crimson rose,
And on old Hiems' thin and icy crown
An odorous chaplet of sweet summer buds
Is, as in mockery, set. The spring, the summer,
The childing autumn, angry winter, change
Their wonted liveries, and the mazèd world
By their increase now knows not which is which.
And this same progeny of evils comes
From our debate, from our dissension.
We are their parents and original.

OBERON
Do you amend it, then. It lies in you.
Why should Titania cross her Oberon?
I do but beg a little changeling boy
To be my henchman.

TITANIA
Set your heart at rest.
The fairy land buys not the child of me.
His mother was a vot'ress of my order,

54 "Tailor" (Seemingly a cry of distress or embarrassment.) **55 choir** company **56 waxen** increase. **neeze** sneeze **57 wasted** spent **58 room** stand aside, make room **63 wanton** headstrong creature. **66, 68 Corin, Phillida** (Conventional names of pastoral lovers.) **67 corn** (Here, oat stalks.) **versing love** writing love verses **69 step** farthest limit of travel, or, perhaps, *steppe,* a vast, flat, treeless tract **71 buskined** wearing half-boots called buskins **75 Glance . . . Hippolyta** make insinuations about my favored relationship with Hippolyta **78 Perigenia** i.e., Perigouna, one of Theseus's conquests. (This and the following women are named in Thomas North's translation of Plutarch's "Life of Theseus.") **79 Aegles** i.e., Aegle, for whom Theseus deserted Ariadne according to some accounts **80 Ariadne** the daughter of Minos, King of Crete, who helped Theseus to escape the labyrinth after killing the Minotaur; later she was abandoned by Theseus. **Antiopa** Queen of the Amazons and wife of Theseus; elsewhere identified with Hippolyta, but here thought of as a separate woman. **82 middle summer's spring** beginning of midsummer **83 mead** meadow

84 pavèd with pebbled bottom. **rushy** bordered with rushes **85 in** on. **margent** edge, border **86 ringlets** dances in a ring. (See *orbs* in line 9.) **to** to the sound of **90 Contagious** noxious **91 pelting** paltry **92 continents** banks that contain them. **93 stretched his yoke** i.e., pulled at his yoke in plowing **94 corn** grain of any kind **96 fold** pen for sheep or cattle **97 murrain** having died of the plague **98 nine-men's morris** i.e., portion of the village green marked out in a square for a game played with nine pebbles or pegs **99 quaint mazes** i.e., intricate paths marked out on the village green to be followed rapidly on foot as a kind of contest. **wanton** luxuriant **101 want** lack. **winter** i.e., regular winter season; or, proper observances of winter, such as the *hymn* or *carol* in the next line (?) **103 Therefore** i.e., As a result of our quarrel **104 washes** saturates with moisture **105 rheumatic diseases** colds, flu, and other respiratory infections **106 distemperature** disturbance in nature **109 Hiems'** the winter god's **112 childing** fruitful, pregnant **113 wonted liveries** usual apparel. **mazèd** bewildered **114 their increase** the increasing pace of change; or, their produce **116 debate** quarrel **117 original** origin. **121 henchman** attendant, page. **123 was . . . order** had taken a vow to serve me

And in the spicèd Indian air by night
Full often hath she gossiped by my side
And sat with me on Neptune's yellow sands,
Marking th'embarkèd traders on the flood, 127
When we have laughed to see the sails conceive
And grow big-bellied with the wanton wind; 129
Which she, with pretty and with swimming gait, 130
Following—her womb then rich with my young squire—
Would imitate, and sail upon the land
To fetch me trifles, and return again
As from a voyage, rich with merchandise.
But she, being mortal, of that boy did die;
And for her sake do I rear up her boy,
And for her sake I will not part with him.

OBERON
How long within this wood intend you stay?

TITANIA
Perchance till after Theseus' wedding day.
If you will patiently dance in our round 140
And see our moonlight revels, go with us;
If not, shun me, and I will spare your haunts. 142

OBERON
Give me that boy, and I will go with thee.

TITANIA
Not for thy fairy kingdom. Fairies, away!
We shall chide downright, if I longer stay.
Exeunt [*Titania with her train*].

OBERON
Well, go thy way. Thou shalt not from this grove 146
Till I torment thee for this injury.
My gentle Puck, come hither. Thou rememb'rest
Since once I sat upon a promontory, 149
And heard a mermaid on a dolphin's back
Uttering such dulcet and harmonious breath 151
That the rude sea grew civil at her song, 152
And certain stars shot madly from their spheres
To hear the sea-maid's music?

PUCK
I remember.

OBERON
That very time I saw, but thou couldst not,
Flying between the cold moon and the earth
Cupid, all armed. A certain aim he took 157
At a fair vestal thronèd by the west, 158
And loosed his love shaft smartly from his bow 159
As it should pierce a hundred thousand hearts; 160
But I might see young Cupid's fiery shaft 161
Quenched in the chaste beams of the wat'ry moon,
And the imperial vot'ress passèd on,
In maiden meditation, fancy-free. 164
Yet marked I where the bolt of Cupid fell: 165
It fell upon a little western flower,
Before milk-white, now purple with love's wound,
And maidens call it love-in-idleness. 168
Fetch me that flower; the herb I showed thee once.
The juice of it on sleeping eyelids laid
Will make or man or woman madly dote 171
Upon the next live creature that it sees.
Fetch me this herb, and be thou here again
Ere the leviathan can swim a league. 174

PUCK
I'll put a girdle round about the earth
In forty minutes. [*Exit*.]

OBERON
Having once this juice,
I'll watch Titania when she is asleep
And drop the liquor of it in her eyes.
The next thing then she waking looks upon,
Be it on lion, bear, or wolf, or bull,
On meddling monkey, or on busy ape,
She shall pursue it with the soul of love.
And ere I take this charm from off her sight,
As I can take it with another herb,
I'll make her render up her page to me.
But who comes here? I am invisible,
And I will overhear their conference.
[*He stands aside*.]

Enter Demetrius, Helena following him.

DEMETRIUS
I love thee not; therefore pursue me not.
Where is Lysander and fair Hermia?
The one I'll slay; the other slayeth me.
Thou told'st me they were stol'n unto this wood;
And here am I, and wood within this wood 192
Because I cannot meet my Hermia.
Hence, get thee gone, and follow me no more.

HELENA
You draw me, you hardhearted adamant! 195
But yet you draw not iron, for my heart
Is true as steel. Leave you your power to draw, 197
And I shall have no power to follow you.

DEMETRIUS
Do I entice you? Do I speak you fair? 199
Or rather do I not in plainest truth
Tell you I do not nor I cannot love you?

HELENA
And even for that do I love you the more.
I am your spaniel; and, Demetrius,
The more you beat me I will fawn on you.
Use me but as your spaniel, spurn me, strike me,
Neglect me, lose me; only give me leave,
Unworthy as I am, to follow you.
What worser place can I beg in your love—
And yet a place of high respect with me—
Than to be usèd as you use your dog?

127 traders trading vessels. **flood** flood tide **129 wanton** (1) playful (2) amorous **130 swimming** smooth, gliding **140 round** circular dance **142 spare** shun **146 from** go from **149 Since** when **151 dulcet** sweet. **breath** voice, song **152 rude** rough **157 all** fully. **certain** sure **158 vestal** vestal virgin. (Contains a complimentary allusion to Queen Elizabeth as a votaress of Diana and probably refers to an actual entertainment in her honor at Elvetham in 1591.) **by** in the region of **159 loosed** released **160 As** as if **161 might** could **164 fancy-free** free of love's spell. **165 bolt** arrow

168 love-in-idleness pansy, heartsease. **171 or man** either man **174 leviathan** sea monster, whale **192 wood . . . wood** madly frantic within these woods **195 adamant** lodestone, magnet. (With pun on *hardhearted*, since adamant was also thought to be the hardest of all stones and was confused with the diamond.) **197 Leave you** Give up **199 speak you fair** speak courteously to you.

DEMETRIUS

Tempt not too much the hatred of my spirit,
For I am sick when I do look on thee.

HELENA

And I am sick when I look not on you.

DEMETRIUS

You do impeach your modesty too much
To leave the city and commit yourself
Into the hands of one that loves you not,
To trust the opportunity of night
And the ill counsel of a desert place
With the rich worth of your virginity.

HELENA

Your virtue is my privilege. For that
It is not night when I do see your face,
Therefore I think I am not in the night;
Nor doth this wood lack worlds of company,
For you, in my respect, are all the world.
Then how can it be said I am alone
When all the world is here to look on me?

DEMETRIUS

I'll run from thee and hide me in the brakes,
And leave thee to the mercy of wild beasts.

HELENA

The wildest hath not such a heart as you.
Run when you will. The story shall be changed:
Apollo flies and Daphne holds the chase,
The dove pursues the griffin, the mild hind
Makes speed to catch the tiger—bootless speed,
When cowardice pursues and valor flies!

DEMETRIUS

I will not stay thy questions. Let me go!
Or if thou follow me, do not believe
But I shall do thee mischief in the wood.

HELENA

Ay, in the temple, in the town, the field,
You do me mischief. Fie, Demetrius!
Your wrongs do set a scandal on my sex.
We cannot fight for love, as men may do;
We should be wooed and were not made to woo.
[Exit Demetrius.]
I'll follow thee and make a heaven of hell,
To die upon the hand I love so well. *[Exit.]*

OBERON

Fare thee well, nymph. Ere he do leave this grove
Thou shalt fly him, and he shall seek thy love.

Enter Puck.

Hast thou the flower there? Welcome, wanderer.

PUCK

Ay, there it is. *[He offers the flower.]*

OBERON I pray thee, give it me.
I know a bank where the wild thyme blows,
Where oxlips and the nodding violet grows,
Quite overcanopied with luscious woodbine,
With sweet muskroses and with eglantine.
There sleeps Titania sometime of the night,
Lulled in these flowers with dances and delight;
And there the snake throws her enameled skin,
Weed wide enough to wrap a fairy in.
And with the juice of this I'll streak her eyes
And make her full of hateful fantasies.
Take thou some of it, and seek through this grove.
[He gives some love juice.]
A sweet Athenian lady is in love
With a disdainful youth. Anoint his eyes,
But do it when the next thing he espies
May be the lady. Thou shalt know the man
By the Athenian garments he hath on.
Effect it with some care, that he may prove
More fond on her than she upon her love;
And look thou meet me ere the first cock crow.

PUCK

Fear not, my lord, your servant shall do so.
Exeunt [separately].

✤

[2.2]

Enter Titania, Queen of Fairies, with her train.

TITANIA

Come, now a roundel and a fairy song;
Then, for the third part of a minute, hence—
Some to kill cankers in the muskrose buds,
Some war with reremice for their leathern wings
To make my small elves coats, and some keep back
The clamorous owl, that nightly hoots and wonders
At our quaint spirits. Sing me now asleep.
Then to your offices, and let me rest.

Fairies sing.

FIRST FAIRY

You spotted snakes with double tongue,
Thorny hedgehogs, be not seen;
Newts and blindworms, do no wrong;
Come not near our Fairy Queen.

214 impeach call into question **215 To leave** by leaving **218 desert** deserted **220 privilege** safeguard, warrant. **For that** Because **224 in my respect** as far as I am concerned, in my esteem **227 brakes** thickets **231 Apollo . . . chase** (In the ancient myth, Daphne fled from Apollo and was saved from rape by being transformed into a laurel tree; here it is the female who *holds the chase,* or pursues, instead of the male.) **232 griffin** a fabulous monster with the head and wings of an eagle and the body of a lion. **hind** female deer **233 bootless** fruitless **235 stay** wait for, put up with. **questions** talk or argument. **240 Your . . . sex** i.e., The wrongs that you do me cause me to act in a manner that disgraces my sex. **244 upon** by

249 blows blooms **250 oxlips** flowers resembling cowslip and primrose **251 woodbine** honeysuckle **252 muskroses** a kind of large, sweet-scented rose. **eglantine** sweetbrier, another kind of rose. **253 sometime of** for part of **255 throws** sloughs off, sheds **256 Weed** garment **257 streak** anoint, touch gently **266 fond on** doting on
2.2. Location: The wood.
1 roundel dance in a ring **3 cankers** cankerworms (i.e., caterpillars or grubs) **4 reremice** bats **7 quaint** dainty **9 double** forked **11 Newts** water lizards. (Considered poisonous, as were *blindworms*—small snakes with tiny eyes—and spiders.)

CHORUS [*dancing*]
Philomel, with melody 13
Sing in our sweet lullaby;
Lulla, lulla, lullaby, lulla, lulla, lullaby.
Never harm
Nor spell nor charm
Come our lovely lady nigh.
So good night, with lullaby.

FIRST FAIRY
Weaving spiders, come not here;
Hence, you long-legged spinners, hence!
Beetles black, approach not near;
Worm nor snail, do no offense. 23

CHORUS [*dancing*]
Philomel, with melody
Sing in our sweet lullaby;
Lulla, lulla, lullaby, lulla, lulla, lullaby.
Never harm
Nor spell nor charm
Come our lovely lady nigh.
So good night, with lullaby. [*Titania sleeps.*]

SECOND FAIRY
Hence, away! Now all is well.
One aloof stand sentinel. 32
[*Exeunt Fairies, leaving one sentinel.*]

Enter Oberon [*and squeezes the flower on Titania's eyelids*].

OBERON
What thou see'st when thou dost wake,
Do it for thy true love take;
Love and languish for his sake.
Be it ounce, or cat, or bear, 36
Pard, or boar with bristled hair, 37
In thy eye that shall appear
When thou wak'st, it is thy dear.
Wake when some vile thing is near. [*Exit.*]

Enter Lysander and Hermia.

LYSANDER
Fair love, you faint with wand'ring in the wood;
And to speak truth, I have forgot our way.
We'll rest us, Hermia, if you think it good,
And tarry for the comfort of the day.

HERMIA
Be it so, Lysander. Find you out a bed,
For I upon this bank will rest my head.

LYSANDER
One turf shall serve as pillow for us both;
One heart, one bed, two bosoms, and one troth. 48

HERMIA
Nay, good Lysander, for my sake, my dear,
Lie further off yet. Do not lie so near.

LYSANDER
Oh, take the sense, sweet, of my innocence! 51
Love takes the meaning in love's conference. 52
I mean that my heart unto yours is knit,
So that but one heart we can make of it;
Two bosoms interchainèd with an oath—
So then two bosoms and a single troth.
Then by your side no bed-room me deny,
For lying so, Hermia, I do not lie. 58

HERMIA
Lysander riddles very prettily.
Now much beshrew my manners and my pride 60
If Hermia meant to say Lysander lied.
But, gentle friend, for love and courtesy
Lie further off, in human modesty.
Such separation as may well be said
Becomes a virtuous bachelor and a maid,
So far be distant; and, good night, sweet friend.
Thy love ne'er alter till thy sweet life end!

LYSANDER
Amen, amen, to that fair prayer, say I,
And then end life when I end loyalty!
Here is my bed. Sleep give thee all his rest!

HERMIA
With half that wish the wisher's eyes be pressed! 71
[*They sleep, separated by a short distance.*]

Enter Puck.

PUCK
Through the forest have I gone,
But Athenian found I none
On whose eyes I might approve 74
This flower's force in stirring love.
Night and silence.—Who is here?
Weeds of Athens he doth wear.
This is he, my master said,
Despisèd the Athenian maid;
And here the maiden, sleeping sound,
On the dank and dirty ground.
Pretty soul, she durst not lie
Near this lack-love, this kill-courtesy.
Churl, upon thy eyes I throw
All the power this charm doth owe. 85
[*He applies the love juice.*]
When thou wak'st, let love forbid 86
Sleep his seat on thy eyelid. 87
So awake when I am gone,
For I must now to Oberon. *Exit.*

Enter Demetrius and Helena, running.

HELENA
Stay, though thou kill me, sweet Demetrius!

13 Philomel the nightingale. (Philomela, daughter of King Pandion, was transformed into a nightingale, according to Ovid's *Metamorphoses* 6, after she had been raped by her sister Procne's husband, Tereus.) **23 offense** harm. **32 sentinel** (Presumably Oberon is able to outwit or intimidate this guard.) **36 ounce** lynx **37 Pard** leopard **48 troth** faith, trothplight.

51–2 take . . . conference take my meaning in an innocent sense, with generosity and sympathy! True lovers do so when they converse. **58 lie** tell a falsehood. (With a riddling pun on *lie,* "recline.") **60 beshrew** (A mild oath.) **71 With . . . pressed!** i.e., I return half that wish, so that you, the wisher, may sleep well too (instead of Sleep giving all his rest to me)! **74 approve** test **85 owe** own. **86–7 let . . . eyelid** may love, heretofore denied, be enthroned in your eyes.

DEMETRIUS
I charge thee, hence, and do not haunt me thus.

HELENA
Oh, wilt thou darkling leave me? Do not so.

DEMETRIUS
Stay, on thy peril! I alone will go. [*Exit*.]

HELENA
Oh, I am out of breath in this fond chase!
The more my prayer, the lesser is my grace.
Happy is Hermia, wheresoe'er she lies,
For she hath blessèd and attractive eyes.
How came her eyes so bright? Not with salt tears;
If so, my eyes are oft'ner washed than hers.
No, no, I am as ugly as a bear,
For beasts that meet me run away for fear.
Therefore no marvel though Demetrius
Do, as a monster, fly my presence thus.
What wicked and dissembling glass of mine
Made me compare with Hermia's sphery eyne?
But who is here? Lysander, on the ground?
Dead, or asleep? I see no blood, no wound.
Lysander, if you live, good sir, awake.

LYSANDER [*awaking*]
And run through fire I will for thy sweet sake.
Transparent Helena! Nature shows art,
That through thy bosom makes me see thy heart.
Where is Demetrius? Oh, how fit a word
Is that vile name to perish on my sword!

HELENA
Do not say so, Lysander; say not so.
What though he love your Hermia? Lord, what though?
Yet Hermia still loves you. Then be content.

LYSANDER
Content with Hermia? No! I do repent
The tedious minutes I with her have spent.
Not Hermia but Helena I love.
Who will not change a raven for a dove?
The will of man is by his reason swayed,
And reason says you are the worthier maid.
Things growing are not ripe until their season;
So I, being young, till now ripe not to reason.
And, touching now the point of human skill,
Reason becomes the marshal to my will
And leads me to your eyes, where I o'erlook
Love's stories written in love's richest book.

HELENA
Wherefore was I to this keen mockery born?
When at your hands did I deserve this scorn?
Is't not enough, is't not enough, young man,
That I did never—no, nor never can—
Deserve a sweet look from Demetrius' eye,
But you must flout my insufficiency?
Good troth, you do me wrong, good sooth, you do,
In such disdainful manner me to woo.
But fare you well. Perforce I must confess
I thought you lord of more true gentleness.
Oh, that a lady, of one man refused,
Should of another therefore be abused! *Exit.*

LYSANDER
She sees not Hermia. Hermia, sleep thou there,
And never mayst thou come Lysander near!
For as a surfeit of the sweetest things
The deepest loathing to the stomach brings,
Or as the heresies that men do leave
Are hated most of those they did deceive,
So thou, my surfeit and my heresy,
Of all be hated, but the most of me!
And, all my powers, address your love and might
To honor Helen and to be her knight! *Exit.*

HERMIA [*awaking*]
Help me, Lysander, help me! Do thy best
To pluck this crawling serpent from my breast!
Ay me, for pity! What a dream was here!
Lysander, look how I do quake with fear.
Methought a serpent ate my heart away,
And you sat smiling at his cruel prey.
Lysander! What, removed? Lysander! Lord!
What, out of hearing? Gone? No sound, no word?
Alack, where are you? Speak, an if you hear;
Speak, of all loves! I swoon almost with fear.
No? Then I well perceive you are not nigh.
Either death, or you, I'll find immediately.
Exit. [*The sleeping Titania remains.*]

✤

3.1

Enter the clowns [*Quince, Snug, Bottom, Flute, Snout, and Starveling*].

BOTTOM Are we all met?

QUINCE Pat, pat; and here's a marvelous convenient place for our rehearsal. This green plot shall be our stage, this hawthorn brake our tiring-house, and we will do it in action as we will do it before the Duke.

BOTTOM Peter Quince?

QUINCE What sayest thou, bully Bottom?

BOTTOM There are things in this comedy of Pyramus and Thisbe that will never please. First, Pyramus must draw a sword to kill himself, which the ladies cannot abide. How answer you that?

SNOUT By'r lakin, a parlous fear.

92 darkling in the dark **93 on thy peril** i.e., on pain of reprisal if you don't obey me and stay. **94 fond** doting **95 my grace** the favor I obtain. **96 lies** dwells **102–3 no marvel . . . thus** i.e., no wonder that Demetrius flies from me as from a monster. **104 glass** mirror **105 compare** compare myself. **sphery eyne** eyes as bright as stars in their spheres. **110 Transparent** Radiant, pure. **art** skill, magic power **121 will** desire **124 ripe not** have not ripened **125 touching . . . skill** reaching now the age of mature judgment **127 o'erlook** read over **129 Wherefore** Why

135 Good troth, good sooth i.e., Indeed, truly **138 lord of** i.e., possessor of. **gentleness** courtesy. **139 of** by **140 abused** ill treated. **145–6 as . . . deceive** as renounced heresies are hated most by those persons who formerly were deceived by them **148 Of . . . of** by . . . by **149 address** direct, apply **156 prey** act of preying. **159 an if** if **160 of all loves** for love's sake.

3.1. Location: The action is continuous.

0.1 *clowns* rustics **2 Pat** On the dot, punctually **4 brake** thicket. **tiring-house** attiring area, hence backstage **7 bully** i.e., worthy, jolly, fine fellow **12 By'r lakin** By our ladykin, i.e., the Virgin Mary. **parlous** perilous, alarming

STARVELING I believe we must leave the killing out, when all is done.

BOTTOM Not a whit. I have a device to make all well. Write me a prologue, and let the prologue seem to say, we will do no harm with our swords, and that Pyramus is not killed indeed; and for the more better assurance, tell them that I, Pyramus, am not Pyramus but Bottom the weaver. This will put them out of fear.

QUINCE Well, we will have such a prologue, and it shall be written in eight and six.

BOTTOM No, make it two more: let it be written in eight and eight.

SNOUT Will not the ladies be afeard of the lion?

STARVELING I fear it, I promise you.

BOTTOM Masters, you ought to consider with yourself, to bring in—God shield us!—a lion among ladies is a most dreadful thing. For there is not a more fearful wildfowl than your lion living, and we ought to look to 't.

SNOUT Therefore another prologue must tell he is not a lion.

BOTTOM Nay, you must name his name, and half his face must be seen through the lion's neck, and he himself must speak through, saying thus or to the same defect: "Ladies," or "Fair ladies, I would wish you," or "I would request you," or "I would entreat you, not to fear, not to tremble; my life for yours. If you think I come hither as a lion, it were pity of my life. No, I am no such thing; I am a man as other men are." And there indeed let him name his name, and tell them plainly he is Snug the joiner.

QUINCE Well, it shall be so. But there is two hard things: that is, to bring the moonlight into a chamber; for, you know, Pyramus and Thisbe meet by moonlight.

SNOUT Doth the moon shine that night we play our play?

BOTTOM A calendar, a calendar! Look in the almanac. Find out moonshine, find out moonshine.

[They consult an almanac.]

QUINCE Yes, it doth shine that night.

BOTTOM Why then may you leave a casement of the great chamber window where we play open, and the moon may shine in at the casement.

QUINCE Ay; or else one must come in with a bush of thorns and a lantern and say he comes to disfigure, or to present, the person of Moonshine. Then there is another thing: we must have a wall in the great chamber; for Pyramus and Thisbe, says the story, did talk through the chink of a wall.

SNOUT You can never bring in a wall. What say you, Bottom?

BOTTOM Some man or other must present Wall. And let him have some plaster, or some loam, or some roughcast about him, to signify wall; or let him hold his fingers thus, and through that cranny shall Pyramus and Thisbe whisper.

QUINCE If that may be, then all is well. Come, sit down, every mother's son, and rehearse your parts. Pyramus, you begin. When you have spoken your speech, enter into that brake, and so everyone according to his cue.

Enter Robin [Puck].

PUCK *[aside]*
What hempen homespuns have we swagg'ring here
So near the cradle of the Fairy Queen?
What, a play toward? I'll be an auditor;
An actor, too, perhaps, if I see cause.

QUINCE Speak, Pyramus. Thisbe, stand forth.

BOTTOM *[as Pyramus]*
"Thisbe, the flowers of odious savors sweet—"

QUINCE Odors, odors.

BOTTOM "—Odors savors sweet;
So hath thy breath, my dearest Thisbe dear.
But hark, a voice! Stay thou but here awhile,
And by and by I will to thee appear." *Exit.*

PUCK A stranger Pyramus than e'er played here. *[Exit.]*

FLUTE Must I speak now?

QUINCE Ay, marry, must you; for you must understand he goes but to see a noise that he heard, and is to come again.

FLUTE *[as Thisbe]*
"Most radiant Pyramus, most lily-white of hue,
Of color like the red rose on triumphant brier,
Most brisky juvenal and eke most lovely Jew,
As true as truest horse that yet would never tire.
I'll meet thee, Pyramus, at Ninny's tomb."

QUINCE "Ninus' tomb," man. Why, you must not speak that yet. That you answer to Pyramus. You speak all your part at once, cues and all. Pyramus, enter. Your cue is past; it is "never tire."

FLUTE
Oh—"As true as truest horse that yet would never tire."

[Enter Puck, and Bottom as Pyramus with the ass head.]

14 when all is done i.e., when all is said and done. **16 Write me** i.e., Write at my suggestion. (*Me* is used colloquially.) **22 eight and six** alternate lines of eight and six syllables, a common ballad measure. **28 lion among ladies** (A contemporary pamphlet tells how, at the christening in 1594 of Prince Henry, eldest son of King James VI of Scotland, later James I of England, a "blackamoor" instead of a lion drew the triumphal chariot, since the lion's presence might have "brought some fear to the nearest.") **29 fearful** fear-inspiring **37 defect** (Bottom's blunder for "effect.") **39 my life for yours** i.e., I pledge my life to make your lives safe. **40 it were . . . life** i.e., I should be sorry, by my life; or, my life would be endangered. **55–6 bush of thorns** bundle of thornbush fagots. (Part of the accoutrements of the man in the moon, according to the popular notions of the time, along with his lantern and his dog.) **56 disfigure** (Quince's blunder for "figure," "represent.")

64–5 roughcast a mixture of lime and gravel used to plaster the outside of buildings **72 hempen homespuns** i.e., rustics dressed in homespun fabric made from hemp **73 cradle** i.e., Titania's bower **74 toward** about to take place. **83 A stranger . . . here** The strangest Pyramus you ever saw. **89 triumphant** magnificent **90 brisky juvenal** lively youth. **eke** also. **Jew** (A desperate attempt to rhyme with *hue*, inspired perhaps by the first syllable of *juvenal*.) **93 Ninus** mythical founder of Nineveh (whose wife, Semiramis, was supposed to have built the walls of Babylon where the story of Pyramus and Thisbe takes place) **95 part** (An actor's *part* was a script consisting only of his speeches and their cues.) ***97.1–2 with the ass head*** (This stage direction, taken from the Folio, presumably refers to a standard stage property.)

BOTTOM
"If I were fair, Thisbe, I were only thine."

QUINCE Oh, monstrous! Oh, strange! We are haunted.
Pray, masters! Fly, masters! Help!
[*Exeunt Quince, Snug, Flute, Snout, and Starveling.*]

PUCK
I'll follow you: I'll lead you about a round,
Through bog, through bush, through brake, through brier.
Sometimes a horse I'll be, sometimes a hound,
A hog, a headless bear, sometimes a fire;
And neigh, and bark, and grunt, and roar, and burn,
Like horse, hound, hog, bear, fire, at every turn. *Exit.*

BOTTOM Why do they run away? This is a knavery of them to make me afeard.

Enter Snout.

SNOUT Oh, Bottom, thou art changed! What do I see on thee?

BOTTOM What do you see? You see an ass head of your own, do you? [*Exit Snout.*]

Enter Quince.

QUINCE Bless thee, Bottom, bless thee! Thou art translated. *Exit.*

BOTTOM I see their knavery. This is to make an ass of me, to fright me, if they could. But I will not stir from this place, do what they can. I will walk up and down here, and I will sing, that they shall hear I am not afraid. [*He sings.*]
The ouzel cock so black of hue,
With orange-tawny bill,
The throstle with his note so true,
The wren with little quill—

TITANIA [*awaking*]
What angel wakes me from my flow'ry bed?

BOTTOM [*sings*]
The finch, the sparrow, and the lark,
The plainsong cuckoo gray,
Whose note full many a man doth mark,
And dares not answer nay—
For indeed, who would set his wit to so foolish a bird? Who would give a bird the lie, though he cry "cuckoo" never so?

TITANIA
I pray thee, gentle mortal, sing again.
Mine ear is much enamored of thy note;
So is mine eye enthrallèd to thy shape;
And thy fair virtue's force perforce doth move me
On the first view to say, to swear, I love thee.

BOTTOM Methinks, mistress, you should have little reason for that. And yet, to say the truth, reason and love keep little company together nowadays—the more the pity that some honest neighbors will not make them friends. Nay, I can gleek upon occasion.

TITANIA
Thou art as wise as thou art beautiful.

BOTTOM Not so, neither. But if I had wit enough to get out of this wood, I have enough to serve mine own turn.

TITANIA
Out of this wood do not desire to go.
Thou shalt remain here, whether thou wilt or no.
I am a spirit of no common rate.
The summer still doth tend upon my state,
And I do love thee. Therefore, go with me.
I'll give thee fairies to attend on thee,
And they shall fetch thee jewels from the deep,
And sing while thou on pressèd flowers dost sleep.
And I will purge thy mortal grossness so
That thou shalt like an airy spirit go.—
Peaseblossom, Cobweb, Mote, and Mustardseed!

Enter four Fairies [*Peaseblossom, Cobweb, Mote, and Mustardseed*].

PEASEBLOSSOM Ready.

COBWEB
And I.

MOTE And I.

MUSTARDSEED And I.

ALL Where shall we go?

TITANIA
Be kind and courteous to this gentleman.
Hop in his walks and gambol in his eyes;
Feed him with apricots and dewberries,
With purple grapes, green figs, and mulberries;
The honey bags steal from the humble-bees,
And for night tapers crop their waxen thighs,
And light them at the fiery glowworms' eyes,
To have my love to bed and to arise;
And pluck the wings from painted butterflies
To fan the moonbeams from his sleeping eyes.
Nod to him, elves, and do him courtesies.

PEASEBLOSSOM Hail, mortal!

COBWEB Hail!

MOTE Hail!

MUSTARDSEED Hail!

BOTTOM I cry Your Worships mercy, heartily. I beseech Your Worship's name.

COBWEB Cobweb.

98 If Even if. **fair** handsome. **were** would be **101 about a round** roundabout **104 fire** will-o'-the-wisp **113–14 translated** transformed. **120 ouzel cock** male blackbird **122 throstle** song thrush **123 with little quill** with small pipe, i.e., high-pitched note; or else with small feathers **126 plainsong** singing a melody without variations **128 dares . . . nay** i.e., cannot deny that he is a cuckold **129 set his wit to** employ his intelligence to answer **130 give . . . lie** call the bird a liar **131 never so** ever so much. **135 thy . . . force** the power of your unblemished excellence

141 gleek jest **144–5 serve . . . turn** answer my purpose. **148 rate** rank, value. **149 still . . . state** always waits upon me as a part of my royal retinue **156 Mote** i.e., speck. (The two words *moth* and *mote* were pronounced alike, and both meanings may be present.) **160 in his eyes** in his sight (i.e., before him) **161 dewberries** blackberries **164 night . . . thighs** (The waxen thighs of the bumble-bee are to be fashioned into wax candles to light Bottom's way in the dark.) **165 eyes** (In fact, the light is emitted by the abdomen. *Eyes* may be metaphorical.) **174 I cry . . . mercy** I beg pardon of Your Worships (for presuming to ask a question)

BOTTOM I shall desire you of more acquaintance, good 177
Master Cobweb. If I cut my finger, I shall make bold 178
with you.—Your name, honest gentleman? 179

PEASEBLOSSOM Peaseblossom.

BOTTOM I pray you, commend me to Mistress Squash, 181
your mother, and to Master Peascod, your father. 182
Good Master Peaseblossom, I shall desire you of more
acquaintance too.—Your name, I beseech you, sir?

MUSTARDSEED Mustardseed.

BOTTOM Good Master Mustardseed, I know your 186
patience well. That same cowardly, giantlike ox-beef 187
hath devoured many a gentleman of your house. I
promise you, your kindred hath made my eyes water 189
ere now. I desire you of more acquaintance, good
Master Mustardseed.

TITANIA
Come wait upon him; lead him to my bower.
The moon methinks looks with a wat'ry eye;
And when she weeps, weeps every little flower, 194
Lamenting some enforcèd chastity. 195
Tie up my lover's tongue; bring him silently. 196
Exeunt.

✤

[3.2]

Enter [Oberon,] King of Fairies.

OBERON
I wonder if Titania be awaked;
Then, what it was that next came in her eye,
Which she must dote on in extremity.

[Enter] Robin Goodfellow [Puck].

Here comes my messenger. How now, mad spirit?
What night-rule now about this haunted grove? 5

PUCK
My mistress with a monster is in love.
Near to her close and consecrated bower, 7
While she was in her dull and sleeping hour, 8
A crew of patches, rude mechanicals, 9
That work for bread upon Athenian stalls, 10
Were met together to rehearse a play
Intended for great Theseus' nuptial day.
The shallowest thickskin of that barren sort, 13
Who Pyramus presented, in their sport 14
Forsook his scene and entered in a brake. 15
When I did him at this advantage take,
An ass's noll I fixèd on his head. 17
Anon his Thisbe must be answerèd,
And forth my mimic comes. When they him spy, 19
As wild geese that the creeping fowler eye, 20
Or russet-pated choughs, many in sort, 21
Rising and cawing at the gun's report,
Sever themselves and madly sweep the sky, 23
So, at his sight, away his fellows fly;
And, at our stamp, here o'er and o'er one falls;
He "Murder!" cries and help from Athens calls.
Their sense thus weak, lost with their fears thus strong, 27
Made senseless things begin to do them wrong, 28
For briers and thorns at their apparel snatch;
Some, sleeves—some, hats; from yielders all things catch. 30
I led them on in this distracted fear
And left sweet Pyramus translated there,
When in that moment, so it came to pass,
Titania waked and straightway loved an ass.

OBERON
This falls out better than I could devise.
But hast thou yet latched the Athenian's eyes 36
With the love juice, as I did bid thee do?

PUCK
I took him sleeping—that is finished too—
And the Athenian woman by his side,
That, when he waked, of force she must be eyed. 40

Enter Demetrius and Hermia.

OBERON
Stand close. This is the same Athenian.

PUCK
This is the woman, but not this the man.
[They stand aside.]

DEMETRIUS
Oh, why rebuke you him that loves you so?
Lay breath so bitter on your bitter foe.

HERMIA
Now I but chide; but I should use thee worse,
For thou, I fear, hast given me cause to curse.
If thou hast slain Lysander in his sleep,
Being o'er shoes in blood, plunge in the deep, 48
And kill me too.
The sun was not so true unto the day
As he to me. Would he have stolen away
From sleeping Hermia? I'll believe as soon
This whole earth may be bored, and that the moon 53
May through the center creep, and so displease
Her brother's noontide with th'Antipodes. 55

177 I . . . acquaintance I crave to be better acquainted with you **178–9 If . . . you** (Cobwebs were used to stanch bleeding.) **181 Squash** unripe pea pod **182 Peascod** ripe pea pod **186–7 your patience** what you have endured. (Mustard is eaten with beef.) **189 water** (1) weep for sympathy (2) smart, sting **194 And . . . flower** (Dew was thought to fall from the heavens in greater proportion as the moon shown fully.) **195 enforcèd** violated. (The moon is associated throughout the play with the goddess Diana and chastity.) **196 Tie . . . tongue** (Presumably Bottom is braying like an ass.)
3.2. Location: The wood.
5 night-rule diversion or misrule for the night **7 close** secret **8 dull** drowsy **9 patches** clowns, fools. **rude mechanicals** ignorant artisans **10 stalls** market booths **13 barren sort** stupid company or crew **14 presented** acted **15 scene** playing area

17 noll noddle, head **19 mimic** actor **20 fowler** hunter of game birds **21 russet-pated choughs** reddish brown or gray-headed jackdaws. **in sort** in a flock **23 Sever themselves** i.e., scatter **27–8 Their . . . wrong** Their weakened physical senses, disabled by their strong fears, made it seem to them as though inanimate things in the forest were attacking them **30 from . . . catch** the forest snatches away everything from those who yield to it. **36 latched** snared, taken prisoner **40 of force** perforce **48 Being o'er shoes** having waded in so far **53 whole** solid **55 Her . . . Antipodes** i.e., the sun's noontime on the opposite side of the earth, among the people who live there, the Antipodes.

It cannot be but thou hast murdered him;
So should a murderer look, so dead, so grim. 57

DEMETRIUS
So should the murdered look, and so should I,
Pierced through the heart with your stern cruelty.
Yet you, the murderer, look as bright, as clear
As yonder Venus in her glimmering sphere.

HERMIA
What's this to my Lysander? Where is he? 62
Ah, good Demetrius, wilt thou give him me?

DEMETRIUS
I had rather give his carcass to my hounds.

HERMIA
Out, dog! Out, cur! Thou driv'st me past the bounds
Of maiden's patience. Hast thou slain him, then?
Henceforth be never numbered among men.
Oh, once tell true, tell true, even for my sake: 68
Durst thou have looked upon him being awake? 69
And hast thou killed him sleeping? Oh, brave touch! 70
Could not a worm, an adder, do so much? 71
An adder did it; for with doubler tongue 72
Than thine, thou serpent, never adder stung.

DEMETRIUS
You spend your passion on a misprised mood. 74
I am not guilty of Lysander's blood,
Nor is he dead, for aught that I can tell.

HERMIA
I pray thee, tell me then that he is well.

DEMETRIUS
And if I could, what should I get therefor? 78

HERMIA
A privilege never to see me more.
And from thy hated presence part I so.
See me no more, whether he be dead or no. *Exit.*

DEMETRIUS
There is no following her in this fierce vein.
Here therefore for a while I will remain.
So sorrow's heaviness doth heavier grow 84
For debt that bankrupt sleep doth sorrow owe, 85
Which now in some slight measure it will pay, 86
If for his tender here I make some stay. 87
[*He*] *lie*[*s*] *down* [*and sleeps*].

OBERON
What hast thou done? Thou hast mistaken quite
And laid the love juice on some true love's sight.
Of thy misprision must perforce ensue 90
Some true love turned, and not a false turned true.

PUCK
Then fate o'errules, that, one man holding troth, 92
A million fail, confounding oath on oath. 93

OBERON
About the wood go swifter than the wind,
And Helena of Athens look thou find.
All fancy-sick she is and pale of cheer 96
With sighs of love, that cost the fresh blood dear. 97
By some illusion see thou bring her here.
I'll charm his eyes against she do appear. 99

PUCK
I go, I go, look how I go,
Swifter than arrow from the Tartar's bow. [*Exit.*] 101

OBERON [*applying love juice to Demetrius's eyes*]
Flower of this purple dye,
Hit with Cupid's archery,
Sink in apple of his eye. 104
When his love he doth espy,
Let her shine as gloriously
As the Venus of the sky.
When thou wak'st, if she be by,
Beg of her for remedy.

Enter Puck.

PUCK
Captain of our fairy band,
Helena is here at hand,
And the youth, mistook by me,
Pleading for a lover's fee. 113
Shall we their fond pageant see? 114
Lord, what fools these mortals be!

OBERON
Stand aside. The noise they make
Will cause Demetrius to awake.

PUCK
Then will two at once woo one;
That must needs be sport alone. 119
And those things do best please me
That befall preposterously. 121
[*They stand aside.*]

Enter Lysander and Helena.

LYSANDER
Why should you think that I should woo in scorn?
Scorn and derision never come in tears.
Look when I vow, I weep; and vows so born, 124
In their nativity all truth appears. 125
How can these things in me seem scorn to you,
Bearing the badge of faith to prove them true?

HELENA
You do advance your cunning more and more. 128
When truth kills truth, oh, devilish-holy fray! 129
These vows are Hermia's. Will you give her o'er?
Weigh oath with oath, and you will nothing weigh;

57 dead deadly, or deathly pale **62 to** to do with **68 once** once and for all **69 being awake** when he was awake. **70 brave touch!** fine stroke! (Said ironically.) **71 worm** serpent **72 doubler** (1) more forked (2) more deceitful **74 You . . . mood** Your anger is misdirected. **78 therefor** in return for that. **84–7 So . . . stay** The heaviness of sorrow grows still heavier when sleepiness adds to the weariness caused by sorrow, which debt to sleepiness I will now repay in part if I can stop here and accept what sleep has to offer. **90 misprision** mistake **92–3 Then . . . oath** If so, then fate prevails; for each male who is able to keep true faith in love, a million will fail, breaking oath on oath.

96 fancy-sick lovesick. **cheer** face **97 sighs . . . dear** (Each sigh was supposed to cost the heart a drop of blood.) **99 against . . . appear** in anticipation of her coming. **101 Tartar's bow** (Tartars were famed for their skill with the bow.) **104 apple** pupil **113 fee** privilege, reward. **114 fond pageant** foolish spectacle **119 alone** unequaled. **121 preposterously** out of the natural order. **124 Look when** Whenever **124–5 vows . . . appears** i.e., vows made by one who is weeping give evidence thereby of their sincerity. **128 advance** carry forward, display **129 When . . . truth** i.e., When one of your vows cancels the other

Your vows to her and me, put in two scales,
Will even weigh, and both as light as tales. 133

LYSANDER
I had no judgment when to her I swore.

HELENA
Nor none, in my mind, now you give her o'er.

LYSANDER
Demetrius loves her, and he loves not you.

DEMETRIUS [*awaking*]
O Helen, goddess, nymph, perfect, divine!
To what, my love, shall I compare thine eyne?
Crystal is muddy. Oh, how ripe in show 139
Thy lips, those kissing cherries, tempting grow!
That pure congealèd white, high Taurus' snow, 141
Fanned with the eastern wind, turns to a crow 142
When thou hold'st up thy hand. Oh, let me kiss
This princess of pure white, this seal of bliss! 144

HELENA
Oh, spite! Oh, hell! I see you all are bent
To set against me for your merriment. 146
If you were civil and knew courtesy,
You would not do me thus much injury.
Can you not hate me, as I know you do,
But you must join in souls to mock me too? 150
If you were men, as men you are in show,
You would not use a gentle lady so—
To vow, and swear, and superpraise my parts, 153
When I am sure you hate me with your hearts.
You both are rivals, and love Hermia,
And now both rivals to mock Helena.
A trim exploit, a manly enterprise, 157
To conjure tears up in a poor maid's eyes
With your derision! None of noble sort 159
Would so offend a virgin and extort 160
A poor soul's patience, all to make you sport.

LYSANDER
You are unkind, Demetrius. Be not so.
For you love Hermia; this you know I know.
And here, with all good will, with all my heart,
In Hermia's love I yield you up my part;
And yours of Helena to me bequeath,
Whom I do love, and will do till my death.

HELENA
Never did mockers waste more idle breath.

DEMETRIUS
Lysander, keep thy Hermia; I will none. 169
If e'er I loved her, all that love is gone.
My heart to her but as guestwise sojourned, 171
And now to Helen is it home returned,
There to remain.

LYSANDER Helen, it is not so.

DEMETRIUS
Disparage not the faith thou dost not know,
Lest, to thy peril, thou aby it dear. 175
Look where thy love comes; yonder is thy dear.

Enter Hermia.

HERMIA
Dark night, that from the eye his function takes, 177
The ear more quick of apprehension makes;
Wherein it doth impair the seeing sense,
It pays the hearing double recompense.
Thou art not by mine eye, Lysander, found;
Mine ear, I thank it, brought me to thy sound.
But why unkindly didst thou leave me so?

LYSANDER
Why should he stay, whom love doth press to go?

HERMIA
What love could press Lysander from my side?

LYSANDER
Lysander's love, that would not let him bide—
Fair Helena, who more engilds the night
Than all yon fiery oes and eyes of light. 188
Why seek'st thou me? Could not this make thee
know
The hate I bear thee made me leave thee so?

HERMIA
You speak not as you think. It cannot be.

HELENA
Lo, she is one of this confederacy!
Now I perceive they have conjoined all three
To fashion this false sport, in spite of me. 194
Injurious Hermia, most ungrateful maid!
Have you conspired, have you with these contrived
To bait me with this foul derision? 197
Is all the counsel that we two have shared— 198
The sisters' vows, the hours that we have spent
When we have chid the hasty-footed time
For parting us—oh, is all forgot?
All schooldays' friendship, childhood innocence?
We, Hermia, like two artificial gods 203
Have with our needles created both one flower,
Both on one sampler, sitting on one cushion,
Both warbling of one song, both in one key,
As if our hands, our sides, voices, and minds
Had been incorporate. So we grew together, 208
Like to a double cherry, seeming parted,
But yet an union in partition,
Two lovely berries molded on one stem;
So, with two seeming bodies but one heart,
Two of the first, like coats in heraldry, 213
Due but to one and crownèd with one crest. 214
And will you rend our ancient love asunder,
To join with men in scorning your poor friend?
It is not friendly, 'tis not maidenly.

133 tales lies. **139 show** appearance **141 Taurus** a lofty mountain range in Asia Minor **142 turns to a crow** i.e., seems black by contrast **144 seal** pledge **146 set against** attack **150 in souls** i.e., heart and soul **153 superpraise** overpraise. **parts** qualities **157 trim** pretty, fine. (Said ironically.) **159 sort** character, quality **160 extort** twist, torture **169 will none** i.e., want no part of her. **171 to . . . sojourned** only visited with her

175 aby pay for **177 his** its **188 oes** spangles (here, stars) **194 in spite of me** to vex me. **197 bait** torment, as one sets on dogs to bait a bear **198 counsel** confidential talk **203 artificial** skilled in art or creation **208 incorporate** of one body. **213–14 Two . . . crest** i.e., we have two separate bodies, just as a coat of arms in heraldry can be represented twice on a shield but surmounted by a single crest.

Our sex, as well as I, may chide you for it,
Though I alone do feel the injury.

HERMIA
I am amazèd at your passionate words.
I scorn you not. It seems that you scorn me.

HELENA
Have you not set Lysander, as in scorn,
To follow me and praise my eyes and face?
And made your other love, Demetrius,
Who even but now did spurn me with his foot,
To call me goddess, nymph, divine, and rare,
Precious, celestial? Wherefore speaks he this
To her he hates? And wherefore doth Lysander
Deny your love, so rich within his soul,
And tender me, forsooth, affection,
But by your setting on, by your consent?
What though I be not so in grace as you,
So hung upon with love, so fortunate,
But miserable most, to love unloved?
This you should pity rather than despise.

HERMIA
I understand not what you mean by this.

HELENA
Ay, do! Persever, counterfeit sad looks,
Make mouths upon me when I turn my back,
Wink each at other, hold the sweet jest up.
This sport, well carried, shall be chronicled.
If you have any pity, grace, or manners,
You would not make me such an argument.
But fare ye well. 'Tis partly my own fault,
Which death, or absence, soon shall remedy.

LYSANDER
Stay, gentle Helena; hear my excuse,
My love, my life, my soul, fair Helena!

HELENA
Oh, excellent!

HERMIA [*to Lysander*] Sweet, do not scorn her so.

DEMETRIUS [*to Lysander*]
If she cannot entreat, I can compel.

LYSANDER
Thou canst compel no more than she entreat.
Thy threats have no more strength than her weak
prayers.—
Helen, I love thee, by my life, I do!
I swear by that which I will lose for thee,
To prove him false that says I love thee not.

DEMETRIUS [*to Helena*]
I say I love thee more than he can do.

LYSANDER
If thou say so, withdraw, and prove it too.

DEMETRIUS
Quick, come!

HERMIA Lysander, whereto tends all this?

LYSANDER
Away, you Ethiope!
[*He tries to break away from Hermia.*]

DEMETRIUS No, no; he'll
Seem to break loose; take on as you would follow,
But yet come not. You are a tame man. Go!

LYSANDER [*to Hermia*]
Hang off, thou cat, thou burr! Vile thing, let loose,
Or I will shake thee from me like a serpent!

HERMIA
Why are you grown so rude? What change is this,
Sweet love?

LYSANDER Thy love? Out, tawny Tartar, out!
Out, loathèd med'cine! O hated potion, hence!

HERMIA
Do you not jest?

HELENA Yes, sooth, and so do you.

LYSANDER
Demetrius, I will keep my word with thee.

DEMETRIUS
I would I had your bond, for I perceive
A weak bond holds you. I'll not trust your word.

LYSANDER
What, should I hurt her, strike her, kill her dead?
Although I hate her, I'll not harm her so.

HERMIA
What, can you do me greater harm than hate?
Hate me? Wherefore? Oh, me, what news, my love?
Am not I Hermia? Are not you Lysander?
I am as fair now as I was erewhile.
Since night you loved me; yet since night you left me.
Why, then you left me—oh, the gods forbid!—
In earnest, shall I say?

LYSANDER Ay, by my life!
And never did desire to see thee more.
Therefore be out of hope, of question, of doubt;
Be certain, nothing truer. 'Tis no jest
That I do hate thee and love Helena.

HERMIA [*to Helena*]
Oh, me! You juggler! You cankerblossom!
You thief of love! What, have you come by night
And stol'n my love's heart from him?

HELENA Fine, i'faith!
Have you no modesty, no maiden shame,
No touch of bashfulness? What, will you tear
Impatient answers from my gentle tongue?
Fie, fie! You counterfeit, you puppet, you!

HERMIA
"Puppet"? Why, so! Ay, that way goes the game.
Now I perceive that she hath made compare
Between our statures; she hath urged her height,
And with her personage, her tall personage,

230 tender offer **232 grace** favor **237 sad** grave, serious **238 mouths** i.e., mows, faces, grimaces. **upon** at **239 hold . . . up** keep up the joke. **240 carried** carried out, brought off **242 argument** subject for a jest. **248 entreat** i.e., succeed by entreaty **255 withdraw . . . too** i.e., withdraw with me and prove your claim in a duel. (The two gentlemen are armed.)

257 Ethiope (Referring to Hermia's relatively dark hair and complexion; see also *tawny Tartar* six lines later.) **258 take on as** act as if, make a fuss as if **260 Hang off** Let go **264 med'cine** i.e., poison **265 sooth** truly **268 weak bond** i.e., Hermia's arm. (With a pun on *bond,* "oath," in the previous line.) **272 what news** what is the matter **274 erewhile** just now. **282 cankerblossom** worm that destroys the flower bud, or wild rose. **288 puppet** (1) counterfeit (2) dwarfish woman (in reference to Hermia's smaller stature)

Her height, forsooth, she hath prevailed with him.
And are you grown so high in his esteem
Because I am so dwarfish and so low?
How low am I, thou painted maypole? Speak!
How low am I? I am not yet so low
But that my nails can reach unto thine eyes.
[She flails at Helena but is restrained.]

HELENA
I pray you, though you mock me, gentlemen,
Let her not hurt me. I was never curst;
I have no gift at all in shrewishness;
I am a right maid for my cowardice.
Let her not strike me. You perhaps may think,
Because she is something lower than myself,
That I can match her.

HERMIA
Lower? Hark, again!

HELENA
Good Hermia, do not be so bitter with me.
I evermore did love you, Hermia,
Did ever keep your counsels, never wronged you,
Save that, in love unto Demetrius,
I told him of your stealth unto this wood.
He followed you; for love I followed him.
But he hath chid me hence and threatened me
To strike me, spurn me, nay, to kill me too.
And now, so you will let me quiet go,
To Athens will I bear my folly back
And follow you no further. Let me go.
You see how simple and how fond I am.

HERMIA
Why, get you gone. Who is't that hinders you?

HELENA
A foolish heart, that I leave here behind.

HERMIA
What, with Lysander?

HELENA
With Demetrius.

LYSANDER
Be not afraid; she shall not harm thee, Helena.

DEMETRIUS
No, sir, she shall not, though you take her part.

HELENA
Oh, when she is angry, she is keen and shrewd.
She was a vixen when she went to school;
And though she be but little, she is fierce.

HERMIA
"Little" again? Nothing but "low" and "little"?—
Why will you suffer her to flout me thus?
Let me come to her.

LYSANDER
Get you gone, you dwarf!
You minimus, of hind'ring knotgrass made!
You bead, you acorn!

DEMETRIUS
You are too officious
In her behalf that scorns your services.
Let her alone. Speak not of Helena;
Take not her part. For, if thou dost intend
Never so little show of love to her,
Thou shalt aby it.

LYSANDER
Now she holds me not.
Now follow, if thou dar'st, to try whose right,
Of thine or mine, is most in Helena. *[Exit.]*

DEMETRIUS
Follow? Nay, I'll go with thee, cheek by jowl.
[Exit, following Lysander.]

HERMIA
You, mistress, all this coil is 'long of you.
Nay, go not back.

HELENA
I will not trust you, I,
Nor longer stay in your curst company.
Your hands than mine are quicker for a fray;
My legs are longer, though, to run away. *[Exit.]*

HERMIA
I am amazed and know not what to say. *Exit.*

[Oberon and Puck come forward.]

OBERON
This is thy negligence. Still thou mistak'st,
Or else commit'st thy knaveries willfully.

PUCK
Believe me, king of shadows, I mistook.
Did not you tell me I should know the man
By the Athenian garments he had on?
And so far blameless proves my enterprise
That I have 'nointed an Athenian's eyes;
And so far am I glad it so did sort,
As this their jangling I esteem a sport.

OBERON
Thou see'st these lovers seek a place to fight.
Hie therefore, Robin, overcast the night;
The starry welkin cover thou anon
With drooping fog as black as Acheron,
And lead these testy rivals so astray
As one come not within another's way.
Like to Lysander sometimes frame thy tongue,
Then stir Demetrius up with bitter wrong;
And sometimes rail thou like Demetrius.
And from each other look thou lead them thus,
Till o'er their brows death-counterfeiting sleep
With leaden legs and batty wings doth creep.
Then crush this herb into Lysander's eye,
[giving herb]
Whose liquor hath this virtuous property,
To take from thence all error with his might
And make his eyeballs roll with wonted sight.
When they next wake, all this derision
Shall seem a dream and fruitless vision,

300 curst shrewish **302 right** true. **for** for all **304 something** somewhat **310 stealth** stealing away **312 chid me hence** driven me away with his scolding **313 spurn** kick **314 so** if only **317 fond** foolish **323 keen and shrewd** fierce and shrewish. **329 minimus** diminutive creature. **knotgrass** a weed, an infusion of which was thought to stunt the growth

333 intend give sign of **335 aby** pay for **338 cheek by jowl** i.e., side by side. **339 coil** turmoil, dissension. **'long of** on account of **340 go not back** i.e., don't retreat. (Hermia is again proposing a fight.) **352 so far** at least to this extent. **sort** turn out **353 As** in that **355 Hie** Hasten **356 welkin** sky **357 Acheron** river of Hades (here representing Hades itself) **359 As** that **360 frame thy tongue** fashion your speech **361 wrong** insults **365 batty** batlike **366 this herb** i.e., the antidote (mentioned in 2.1.184) to love-in-idleness **367 virtuous** efficacious **368 his** its **369 wonted** accustomed **370 derision** laughable business

And back to Athens shall the lovers wend
With league whose date till death shall never end. 373
Whiles I in this affair do thee employ,
I'll to my queen and beg her Indian boy;
And then I will her charmèd eye release
From monster's view, and all things shall be peace.

PUCK
My fairy lord, this must be done with haste,
For night's swift dragons cut the clouds full fast, 379
And yonder shines Aurora's harbinger, 380
At whose approach ghosts, wand'ring here and there,
Troop home to churchyards. Damnèd spirits all,
That in crossways and floods have burial, 383
Already to their wormy beds are gone.
For fear lest day should look their shames upon,
They willfully themselves exile from light
And must for aye consort with black-browed night. 387

OBERON
But we are spirits of another sort.
I with the Morning's love have oft made sport, 389
And, like a forester, the groves may tread 390
Even till the eastern gate, all fiery red,
Opening on Neptune with fair blessèd beams,
Turns into yellow gold his salt green streams.
But notwithstanding, haste, make no delay.
We may effect this business yet ere day. [*Exit.*]

PUCK
Up and down, up and down,
I will lead them up and down.
I am feared in field and town.
Goblin, lead them up and down. 399
Here comes one.

Enter Lysander.

LYSANDER
Where art thou, proud Demetrius? Speak thou now.

PUCK [*mimicking Demetrius*]
Here, villain, drawn and ready. Where art thou? 402

LYSANDER
I will be with thee straight.

PUCK Follow me, then, 403
To plainer ground.
[*Lysander wanders about, following the voice.*]

Enter Demetrius.

DEMETRIUS Lysander! Speak again! 404
Thou runaway, thou coward, art thou fled?
Speak! In some bush? Where dost thou hide thy head?

PUCK [*mimicking Lysander*]
Thou coward, art thou bragging to the stars,
Telling the bushes that thou look'st for wars,
And wilt not come? Come, recreant; come, thou child, 409
I'll whip thee with a rod. He is defiled
That draws a sword on thee.

DEMETRIUS Yea, art thou there?

PUCK
Follow my voice. We'll try no manhood here. 412
Exeunt.

[*Lysander returns.*]

LYSANDER
He goes before me and still dares me on.
When I come where he calls, then he is gone.
The villain is much lighter-heeled than I.
I followed fast, but faster he did fly,
That fallen am I in dark uneven way,
And here will rest me. [*He lies down.*] Come, thou gentle day!
For if but once thou show me thy gray light,
I'll find Demetrius and revenge this spite. [*He sleeps.*]

[*Enter*] *Robin* [*Puck*] *and Demetrius.*

PUCK
Ho, ho, ho! Coward, why com'st thou not?

DEMETRIUS
Abide me, if thou dar'st; for well I wot 422
Thou runn'st before me, shifting every place,
And dar'st not stand nor look me in the face.
Where art thou now?

PUCK Come hither. I am here.

DEMETRIUS
Nay, then, thou mock'st me. Thou shalt buy this dear, 426
If ever I thy face by daylight see.
Now go thy way. Faintness constraineth me
To measure out my length on this cold bed.
By day's approach look to be visited.
[*He lies down and sleeps.*]

Enter Helena.

HELENA
O weary night, O long and tedious night,
Abate thy hours! Shine comforts from the east, 432
That I may back to Athens by daylight
From these that my poor company detest;
And sleep, that sometimes shuts up sorrow's eye,
Steal me awhile from mine own company!
[*She lies down and*] *sleep*[*s*].

PUCK
Yet but three? Come one more;
Two of both kinds makes up four.
Here she comes, curst and sad. 439
Cupid is a knavish lad,
Thus to make poor females mad.

[*Enter Hermia.*]

373 date term of existence **379 dragons** (Supposed here to be yoked to the car of the goddess of night or the moon.) **380 Aurora's harbinger** the morning star, precursor of dawn **383 crossways . . . burial** (Those who had committed suicide were buried at crossways, with a stake driven through them; those who intentionally or accidentally drowned [in *floods* or deep water] would be condemned to wander disconsolately for lack of burial rites.) **387 for aye** forever **389 the Morning's love** Cephalus, a beautiful youth beloved by Aurora; or perhaps the goddess of the dawn herself **390 forester** keeper of a royal forest **399 Goblin** Hobgoblin. (Puck refers to himself.) **402 drawn** with drawn sword **403 straight** immediately. **404 plainer** more open. **s.d.** ***Lysander wanders about*** (Lysander may exit here, but perhaps not; neither exit nor reentrance is indicated in the early texts.)

409 recreant cowardly wretch **412 try** test **422 Abide** Confront, face. **wot** know **426 buy this dear** pay for this dearly **432 Abate** lessen, shorten **439 curst** ill-tempered

HERMIA
Never so weary, never so in woe,
Bedabbled with the dew and torn with briers,
I can no further crawl, no further go;
My legs can keep no pace with my desires.
Here will I rest me till the break of day.
Heavens shield Lysander, if they mean a fray!
[*She lies down and sleeps.*]

PUCK
On the ground
Sleep sound.
I'll apply
To your eye,
Gentle lover, remedy.
[*He squeezes the juice on Lysander's eyes.*]
When thou wak'st,
Thou tak'st
True delight
In the sight
Of thy former lady's eye;
And the country proverb known,
That every man should take his own,
In your waking shall be shown:
Jack shall have Jill; 461
Naught shall go ill;
The man shall have his mare again, and all shall
be well. [*Exit. The four sleeping lovers remain.*]

✤

[4.1]

Enter [*Titania,*] *Queen of Fairies, and* [*Bottom the*] *clown, and Fairies; and* [*Oberon,*] *the King, behind them.*

TITANIA
Come, sit thee down upon this flow'ry bed,
While I thy amiable cheeks do coy, 2
And stick muskroses in thy sleek smooth head,
And kiss thy fair large ears, my gentle joy.
[*They recline.*]

BOTTOM Where's Peaseblossom?
PEASEBLOSSOM Ready.
BOTTOM Scratch my head, Peaseblossom. Where's
Monsieur Cobweb?
COBWEB Ready.
BOTTOM Monsieur Cobweb, good monsieur, get you
your weapons in your hand, and kill me a red-hipped
humble-bee on the top of a thistle; and, good mon-
sieur, bring me the honey bag. Do not fret yourself too
much in the action, monsieur; and, good monsieur,
have a care the honey bag break not. I would be loath
to have you overflown with a honey bag, signor.
[*Exit Cobweb.*]
Where's Monsieur Mustardseed?
MUSTARDSEED Ready.
BOTTOM Give me your neaf, Monsieur Mustardseed. 19
Pray you, leave your courtesy, good monsieur. 20
MUSTARDSEED What's your will?
BOTTOM Nothing, good monsieur, but to help Cavalery 22
Cobweb to scratch. I must to the barber's, monsieur, 23
for methinks I am marvelous hairy about the face; and
I am such a tender ass, if my hair do but tickle me I
must scratch.

TITANIA
What, wilt thou hear some music, my sweet love?
BOTTOM I have a reasonable good ear in music. Let's
have the tongs and the bones. 29
[*Music: tongs, rural music.*]

TITANIA
Or say, sweet love, what thou desirest to eat.
BOTTOM Truly, a peck of provender. I could munch 31
your good dry oats. Methinks I have a great desire to
a bottle of hay. Good hay, sweet hay, hath no fellow. 33

TITANIA
I have a venturous fairy that shall seek
The squirrel's hoard, and fetch thee new nuts.
BOTTOM I had rather have a handful or two of dried
peas. But, I pray you, let none of your people stir me. 37
I have an exposition of sleep come upon me. 38

TITANIA
Sleep thou, and I will wind thee in my arms.—
Fairies, begone, and be all ways away. 40
[*Exeunt Fairies.*]
So doth the woodbine the sweet honeysuckle 41
Gently entwist; the female ivy so
Enrings the barky fingers of the elm.
Oh, how I love thee! How I dote on thee!
[*They sleep.*]

Enter Robin Goodfellow [*Puck*].

OBERON [*coming forward*]
Welcome, good Robin. See'st thou this sweet sight?
Her dotage now I do begin to pity.
For, meeting her of late behind the wood
Seeking sweet favors for this hateful fool, 48
I did upbraid her and fall out with her.
For she his hairy temples then had rounded
With coronet of fresh and fragrant flowers;
And that same dew, which sometime on the buds 52
Was wont to swell like round and orient pearls, 53
Stood now within the pretty flowerets' eyes
Like tears that did their own disgrace bewail.
When I had at my pleasure taunted her,

461 Jack shall have Jill (Proverbial for "boy gets girl.")
4.1. Location: The action is continuous. The four lovers are still asleep onstage. (Compare with the Folio stage direction: "*They sleep all the act.*")
2 amiable lovely. **coy** caress

19 neaf fist **20 leave your courtesy** i.e., stop bowing, or put on your hat **22 Cavalery** Cavalier. (Form of address for a gentleman.)
23 Cobweb (Seemingly an error, since Cobweb has been sent to bring honey, while Peaseblossom has been asked to scratch.) **29 tongs . . . bones** instruments for rustic music. (The tongs were played like a triangle, whereas the bones were held between the fingers and used as clappers.) **29.1 *Music . . . music*** (This stage direction is added from the Folio.) **31 peck of provender** one-quarter bushel of grain.
33 bottle bundle. **fellow** equal. **37 stir** disturb **38 exposition of** (Bottom's phrase for "disposition to.") **40 all ways** in all directions
41 woodbine bindweed, a climbing plant **48 favors** i.e., gifts of flowers **52 sometime** formerly **53 orient** lustrous

And she in mild terms begged my patience,
I then did ask of her her changeling child,
Which straight she gave me, and her fairy sent
To bear him to my bower in Fairyland.
And, now I have the boy, I will undo
This hateful imperfection of her eyes.
And, gentle Puck, take this transformèd scalp
From off the head of this Athenian swain,
That he, awaking when the other do, 65
May all to Athens back again repair, 66
And think no more of this night's accidents
But as the fierce vexation of a dream.
But first I will release the Fairy Queen.
[*He squeezes an herb on her eyes.*]
Be as thou wast wont to be;
See as thou wast wont to see.
Dian's bud o'er Cupid's flower 72
Hath such force and blessèd power.
Now, my Titania, wake you, my sweet queen.

TITANIA [*awaking*]
My Oberon! What visions have I seen!
Methought I was enamored of an ass.

OBERON
There lies your love.

TITANIA How came these things to pass?
Oh, how mine eyes do loathe his visage now!

OBERON
Silence awhile. Robin, take off this head.
Titania, music call, and strike more dead
Than common sleep of all these five the sense. 81

TITANIA
Music, ho! Music, such as charmeth sleep! [*Music.*] 82

PUCK [*removing the ass head*]
Now, when thou wak'st, with thine own fool's eyes peep.

OBERON
Sound, music! Come, my queen, take hands with me,
And rock the ground whereon these sleepers be.
[*They dance.*]
Now thou and I are new in amity,
And will tomorrow midnight solemnly 87
Dance in Duke Theseus' house triumphantly,
And bless it to all fair prosperity.
There shall the pairs of faithful lovers be
Wedded, with Theseus, all in jollity.

PUCK
Fairy King, attend, and mark:
I do hear the morning lark.

OBERON
Then, my queen, in silence sad, 94
Trip we after night's shade.
We the globe can compass soon,
Swifter than the wand'ring moon.

TITANIA
Come, my lord, and in our flight
Tell me how it came this night
That I sleeping here was found
With these mortals on the ground.
Exeunt [*Oberon, Titania, and Puck*].
Wind horn [*within*].

Enter Theseus and all his train; [*Hippolyta, Egeus*].

THESEUS
Go, one of you, find out the forester,
For now our observation is performed; 103
And since we have the vaward of the day, 104
My love shall hear the music of my hounds.
Uncouple in the western valley; let them go. 106
Dispatch, I say, and find the forester.
[*Exit an Attendant.*]
We will, fair queen, up to the mountain's top
And mark the musical confusion
Of hounds and echo in conjunction.

HIPPOLYTA
I was with Hercules and Cadmus once 111
When in a wood of Crete they bayed the bear 112
With hounds of Sparta. Never did I hear 113
Such gallant chiding; for, besides the groves, 114
The skies, the fountains, every region near
Seemed all one mutual cry. I never heard
So musical a discord, such sweet thunder.

THESEUS
My hounds are bred out of the Spartan kind, 118
So flewed, so sanded; and their heads are hung 119
With ears that sweep away the morning dew;
Crook-kneed, and dewlapped like Thessalian bulls; 121
Slow in pursuit, but matched in mouth like bells, 122
Each under each. A cry more tunable 123
Was never holloed to nor cheered with horn 124
In Crete, in Sparta, nor in Thessaly.
Judge when you hear. [*He sees the sleepers.*] But soft!
What nymphs are these? 126

EGEUS
My lord, this is my daughter here asleep,
And this Lysander; this Demetrius is;
This Helena, old Nedar's Helena.
I wonder of their being here together. 130

THESEUS
No doubt they rose up early to observe
The rite of May, and hearing our intent,

65 other others **66 repair** return **72 Dian's bud** (Perhaps the flower of the *agnus castus* or chaste-tree, supposed to preserve chastity; or perhaps referring simply to Oberon's herb by which he can undo the effects of "Cupid's flower," the love-in-idleness of 2.1.166–8.) **81 these five** i.e., the four lovers and Bottom **82 charmeth** brings about, as though by a charm **87 solemnly** ceremoniously **94 sad** solemn

103 observation i.e., observance to a morn of May (1.1.167) **104 vaward** vanguard, i.e., earliest part **106 Uncouple** Set free for the hunt **111 Cadmus** mythical founder of Thebes. (This story about him is unknown.) **112 bayed** brought to bay **113 hounds of Sparta** (A breed famous in antiquity for their hunting skill.) **114 chiding** i.e., yelping **118 kind** strain, breed **119 So flewed** similarly having large hanging chaps or fleshy covering of the jaw. **sanded** of sandy color **121 dewlapped** having pendulous folds of skin under the neck. **Thessalian** from Thessaly, in Greece **122–3 matched . . . each** i.e., harmoniously matched in their various cries like a set of bells, from treble down to bass. **123 cry** pack of hounds. **tunable** well tuned, melodious **124 cheered** encouraged **126 soft** i.e., gently, wait a minute. **130 of** at

Came here in grace of our solemnity. 133
But speak, Egeus. Is not this the day
That Hermia should give answer of her choice?

EGEUS It is, my lord.

THESEUS
Go bid the huntsmen wake them with their horns.
[*Exit an Attendant.*]

Shout within. Wind horns. They all start up.

Good morrow, friends. Saint Valentine is past. 138
Begin these woodbirds but to couple now?

LYSANDER
Pardon, my lord. [*They kneel.*]

THESEUS I pray you all, stand up.
[*They stand.*]
I know you two are rival enemies;
How comes this gentle concord in the world,
That hatred is so far from jealousy
To sleep by hate and fear no enmity?

LYSANDER
My lord, I shall reply amazedly,
Half sleep, half waking; but as yet, I swear,
I cannot truly say how I came here.
But, as I think—for truly would I speak,
And now I do bethink me, so it is—
I came with Hermia hither. Our intent
Was to be gone from Athens, where we might,
Without the peril of the Athenian law—

EGEUS
Enough, enough, my lord; you have enough.
I beg the law, the law, upon his head.
They would have stol'n away; they would, Demetrius,
Thereby to have defeated you and me,
You of your wife and me of my consent,
Of my consent that she should be your wife.

DEMETRIUS
My lord, fair Helen told me of their stealth,
Of this their purpose hither to this wood,
And I in fury hither followed them,
Fair Helena in fancy following me. 162
But, my good lord, I wot not by what power—
But by some power it is—my love to Hermia,
Melted as the snow, seems to me now
As the remembrance of an idle gaud 166
Which in my childhood I did dote upon;
And all the faith, the virtue of my heart,
The object and the pleasure of mine eye,
Is only Helena. To her, my lord,
Was I betrothed ere I saw Hermia,
But like a sickness did I loathe this food;
But, as in health, come to my natural taste,
Now I do wish it, love it, long for it,
And will forevermore be true to it.

THESEUS
Fair lovers, you are fortunately met.
Of this discourse we more will hear anon.
Egeus, I will overbear your will;
For in the temple, by and by, with us
These couples shall eternally be knit.
And, for the morning now is something worn, 181
Our purposed hunting shall be set aside.
Away with us to Athens. Three and three,
We'll hold a feast in great solemnity. 184
Come, Hippolyta.
[*Exeunt Theseus, Hippolyta, Egeus, and train.*]

DEMETRIUS
These things seem small and undistinguishable,
Like far-off mountains turnèd into clouds.

HERMIA
Methinks I see these things with parted eye, 188
When everything seems double.

HELENA So methinks;
And I have found Demetrius like a jewel, 190
Mine own, and not mine own.

DEMETRIUS Are you sure 191
That we are awake? It seems to me
That yet we sleep, we dream. Do not you think
The Duke was here, and bid us follow him?

HERMIA
Yea, and my father.

HELENA And Hippolyta.

LYSANDER
And he did bid us follow to the temple.

DEMETRIUS
Why, then, we are awake. Let's follow him,
And by the way let us recount our dreams.
[*Exeunt the lovers.*]

BOTTOM [*awaking*] When my cue comes, call me, and I
will answer. My next is "Most fair Pyramus." Heigh-
ho! Peter Quince! Flute, the bellows mender! Snout,
the tinker! Starveling! God's my life, stolen hence and 202
left me asleep! I have had a most rare vision. I have
had a dream, past the wit of man to say what dream
it was. Man is but an ass if he go about to expound this 205
dream. Methought I was—there is no man can tell
what. Methought I was—and methought I had—but
man is but a patched fool if he will offer to say what 208
methought I had. The eye of man hath not heard, the 209
ear of man hath not seen, man's hand is not able to 210
taste, his tongue to conceive, nor his heart to report, 211
what my dream was. I will get Peter Quince to write
a ballad of this dream. It shall be called "Bottom's 213
Dream," because it hath no bottom; and I will sing it 214
in the latter end of a play, before the Duke. Peradventure, to make it the more gracious, I shall sing it at her 216
death. [*Exit.*]

133 in . . . solemnity in honor of our wedding ceremony. **138 Saint Valentine** (Birds were supposed to choose their mates on Saint Valentine's Day.) **162 in fancy** driven by love **166 idle gaud** worthless trinket

181 for since. **something** somewhat **184 in great solemnity** with great ceremony. **188 parted** i.e., improperly focused **190–1 like . . . own** i.e., something precious that seems mine and yet so mysteriously found that I can hardly believe it is mine. **202 God's** May God save **205 go about** attempt **208 patched** wearing motley, i.e., a dress of various colors. **offer** venture **209–11 The eye . . . report** (Bottom garbles 1 Corinthians 2:9.) **213 ballad** (The proper medium for relating sensational stories and preposterous events.) **214 hath no bottom** is unfathomable **216 her** Thisbe's (?)

[4.2]

Enter Quince, Flute, [Snout, and Starveling].

QUINCE Have you sent to Bottom's house? Is he come home yet?

STARVELING He cannot be heard of. Out of doubt he is transported.

FLUTE If he come not, then the play is marred. It goes not forward. Doth it?

QUINCE It is not possible. You have not a man in all Athens able to discharge Pyramus but he.

FLUTE No, he hath simply the best wit of any handicraft man in Athens.

QUINCE Yea, and the best person too, and he is a very paramour for a sweet voice.

FLUTE You must say "paragon." A paramour is, God bless us, a thing of naught.

Enter Snug the joiner.

SNUG Masters, the Duke is coming from the temple, and there is two or three lords and ladies more married. If our sport had gone forward, we had all been made men.

FLUTE Oh, sweet bully Bottom! Thus hath he lost sixpence a day during his life; he could not have scaped sixpence a day. An the Duke had not given him sixpence a day for playing Pyramus, I'll be hanged. He would have deserved it. Sixpence a day in Pyramus, or nothing.

Enter Bottom.

BOTTOM Where are these lads? Where are these hearts?

QUINCE Bottom! Oh, most courageous day! Oh, most happy hour!

BOTTOM Masters, I am to discourse wonders. But ask me not what; for if I tell you, I am no true Athenian. I will tell you everything, right as it fell out.

QUINCE Let us hear, sweet Bottom.

BOTTOM Not a word of me. All that I will tell you is that the Duke hath dined. Get your apparel together, good strings to your beards, new ribbons to your pumps; meet presently at the palace; every man look o'er his part; for the short and the long is, our play is preferred. In any case, let Thisbe have clean linen; and let not him that plays the lion pare his nails, for they shall hang out for the lion's claws. And, most dear actors, eat no onions nor garlic, for we are to utter sweet breath; and I do not doubt but to hear them say it is a sweet comedy. No more words. Away! Go, away!
[*Exeunt.*]

✤

4.2. Location: Athens.
4 transported carried off by fairies; or, transformed. **8 discharge** perform **9 wit** intellect **11 person** appearance **14 a . . . naught** a shameful thing. **17–18 we . . . men** i.e., we would have had our fortunes made. **20 sixpence a day** i.e., as a royal pension **25 hearts** good fellows. **28 am . . . wonders** have wonders to relate. **32 of** out of **34 strings** (to attach the beards) **35 pumps** light shoes or slippers **37 preferred** selected for consideration.

[5.1]

Enter Theseus, Hippolyta, and Philostrate, [lords, and attendants].

HIPPOLYTA
'Tis strange, my Theseus, that these lovers speak of.

THESEUS
More strange than true. I never may believe
These antique fables nor these fairy toys.
Lovers and madmen have such seething brains,
Such shaping fantasies, that apprehend
More than cool reason ever comprehends.
The lunatic, the lover, and the poet
Are of imagination all compact.
One sees more devils than vast hell can hold;
That is the madman. The lover, all as frantic,
Sees Helen's beauty in a brow of Egypt.
The poet's eye, in a fine frenzy rolling,
Doth glance from heaven to earth, from earth to heaven;
And as imagination bodies forth
The forms of things unknown, the poet's pen
Turns them to shapes and gives to airy nothing
A local habitation and a name.
Such tricks hath strong imagination
That, if it would but apprehend some joy,
It comprehends some bringer of that joy;
Or in the night, imagining some fear,
How easy is a bush supposed a bear!

HIPPOLYTA
But all the story of the night told over,
And all their minds transfigured so together,
More witnesseth than fancy's images
And grows to something of great constancy;
But, howsoever, strange and admirable.

Enter lovers: Lysander, Demetrius, Hermia, and Helena.

THESEUS
Here come the lovers, full of joy and mirth.
Joy, gentle friends! Joy and fresh days of love
Accompany your hearts!

LYSANDER More than to us
Wait in your royal walks, your board, your bed!

THESEUS
Come now, what masques, what dances shall we have,
To wear away this long age of three hours
Between our after-supper and bedtime?
Where is our usual manager of mirth?

5.1. Location: Athens. The palace of Theseus.
1 that that which **2 may** can **3 antique** old-fashioned. (Punning, too, on *antic*, "strange," "grotesque.") **fairy toys** trifling stories about fairies. **5 fantasies** imaginations. **apprehend** conceive, imagine **6 comprehends** understands. **8 compact** formed, composed. **11 Helen's** i.e., of Helen of Troy, pattern of beauty. **brow of Egypt** i.e., face of a gypsy. **20 bringer** i.e., source **21 fear** object of fear **25 More . . . images** testifies to something more substantial than mere imaginings **26 constancy** certainty **27 howsoever** in any case. **admirable** a source of wonder. **32 masques** courtly entertainments

What revels are in hand? Is there no play
To ease the anguish of a torturing hour?
Call Philostrate.

PHILOSTRATE Here, mighty Theseus.

THESEUS
Say, what abridgment have you for this evening?
What masque? What music? How shall we beguile
The lazy time, if not with some delight?

PHILOSTRATE [*giving him a paper*]
There is a brief how many sports are ripe.
Make choice of which Your Highness will see first.

THESEUS [*reads*]
"The battle with the Centaurs, to be sung
By an Athenian eunuch to the harp"?
We'll none of that. That have I told my love,
In glory of my kinsman Hercules.
[*He reads.*] "The riot of the tipsy Bacchanals,
Tearing the Thracian singer in their rage"?
That is an old device; and it was played
When I from Thebes came last a conqueror.
[*He reads.*] "The thrice three Muses mourning for the death
Of Learning, late deceased in beggary"?
That is some satire, keen and critical,
Not sorting with a nuptial ceremony.
[*He reads.*] "A tedious brief scene of young Pyramus
And his love Thisbe; very tragical mirth"?
Merry and tragical? Tedious and brief?
That is, hot ice and wondrous strange snow.
How shall we find the concord of this discord?

PHILOSTRATE
A play there is, my lord, some ten words long,
Which is as brief as I have known a play;
But by ten words, my lord, it is too long,
Which makes it tedious. For in all the play
There is not one word apt, one player fitted.
And tragical, my noble lord, it is,
For Pyramus therein doth kill himself.
Which, when I saw rehearsed, I must confess,
Made mine eyes water; but more merry tears
The passion of loud laughter never shed.

THESEUS What are they that do play it?

PHILOSTRATE
Hardhanded men that work in Athens here,
Which never labored in their minds till now,
And now have toiled their unbreathed memories
With this same play, against your nuptial.

THESEUS
And we will hear it.

PHILOSTRATE No, my noble lord,
It is not for you. I have heard it over,
And it is nothing, nothing in the world;
Unless you can find sport in their intents,
Extremely stretched and conned with cruel pain
To do you service.

THESEUS I will hear that play;
For never anything can be amiss
When simpleness and duty tender it.
Go, bring them in; and take your places, ladies.
[*Philostrate goes to summon the players.*]

HIPPOLYTA
I love not to see wretchedness o'ercharged,
And duty in his service perishing.

THESEUS
Why, gentle sweet, you shall see no such thing.

HIPPOLYTA
He says they can do nothing in this kind.

THESEUS
The kinder we, to give them thanks for nothing.
Our sport shall be to take what they mistake;
And what poor duty cannot do, noble respect
Takes it in might, not merit.
Where I have come, great clerks have purposèd
To greet me with premeditated welcomes;
Where I have seen them shiver and look pale,
Make periods in the midst of sentences,
Throttle their practiced accent in their fears,
And in conclusion dumbly have broke off,
Not paying me a welcome. Trust me, sweet,
Out of this silence yet I picked a welcome;
And in the modesty of fearful duty
I read as much as from the rattling tongue
Of saucy and audacious eloquence.
Love, therefore, and tongue-tied simplicity
In least speak most, to my capacity.

[*Philostrate returns.*]

PHILOSTRATE
So please Your Grace, the Prologue is addressed.

THESEUS Let him approach. [*A flourish of trumpets.*]

Enter the Prologue [*Quince*].

PROLOGUE
If we offend, it is with our good will.
That you should think, we come not to offend,
But with good will. To show our simple skill,
That is the true beginning of our end.

39 abridgment pastime (to abridge or shorten the evening) **42 brief** summary **44 battle . . . Centaurs** (Probably refers to the battle of the Centaurs and the Lapithae, when the Centaurs attempted to carry off Hippodamia, bride of Theseus's friend Pirothous. The story is told in Ovid's *Metamorphoses* 12.) **47 kinsman** (Plutarch's "Life of Theseus" states that Hercules and Theseus were near kinsmen. Theseus is referring to a version of the battle of the Centaurs in which Hercules was said to be present.) **48–9 The riot . . . rage** (This was the story of the death of Orpheus, as told in *Metamorphoses* 11.) **50 device** show, performance **52–3 The thrice . . . beggary** (Possibly an allusion to Spenser's *Teares of the Muses*, 1591, though "satires" deploring the neglect of learning and the creative arts were commonplace.) **55 sorting with** befitting **59 strange** (Sometimes emended to an adjective that would contrast with *snow*, just as *hot* contrasts with *ice*.) **74 toiled** taxed. **unbreathed** unexercised

75 against in preparation for **80 conned** memorized **85 wretchedness o'ercharged** social or intellectual inferiority overburdened **86 his service** its attempt to serve **88 kind** kind of thing. **91–2 noble . . . merit** noble consideration values it for the effort made rather than for the actual worth. **93 clerks** learned men **97 practiced accent** i.e., rehearsed speech; or, usual way of speaking **105 least** i.e., saying least. **to my capacity** in my judgment and understanding. **106 Prologue** speaker of the prologue. **addressed** ready.

Consider, then, we come but in despite.
We do not come, as minding to content you,
Our true intent is. All for your delight
We are not here. That you should here repent you,
The actors are at hand; and, by their show,
You shall know all that you are like to know.

THESEUS This fellow doth not stand upon points.

LYSANDER He hath rid his prologue like a rough colt; he knows not the stop. A good moral, my lord: it is not enough to speak, but to speak true.

HIPPOLYTA Indeed, he hath played on his prologue like a child on a recorder: a sound, but not in government.

THESEUS His speech was like a tangled chain: nothing impaired, but all disordered. Who is next?

Enter Pyramus [*Bottom*], *and Thisbe* [*Flute*], *and Wall* [*Snout*], *and Moonshine* [*Starveling*], *and Lion* [*Snug*].

PROLOGUE
Gentles, perchance you wonder at this show;
But wonder on, till truth make all things plain.
This man is Pyramus, if you would know;
This beauteous lady Thisbe is, certain.
This man with lime and roughcast doth present
Wall, that vile wall which did these lovers sunder;
And through Wall's chink, poor souls, they are content
To whisper. At the which let no man wonder.
This man with lantern dog and bush of thorn
Presenteth Moonshine; for, if you will know,
By moonshine did these lovers think no scorn
To meet at Ninus' tomb, there, there to woo.
This grisly beast, which Lion hight by name,
The trusty Thisbe coming first by night
Did scare away, or rather did affright;
And as she fled, her mantle she did fall,
Which Lion vile with bloody mouth did stain.
Anon comes Pyramus, sweet youth and tall,
And finds his trusty Thisbe's mantle slain;
Whereat, with blade, with bloody, blameful blade,
He bravely broached his boiling bloody breast.
And Thisbe, tarrying in mulberry shade,
His dagger drew, and died. For all the rest,
Let Lion, Moonshine, Wall, and lovers twain
At large discourse, while here they do remain.
Exeunt Lion, Thisbe, and Moonshine.

THESEUS I wonder if the lion be to speak.

DEMETRIUS No wonder, my lord. One lion may, when many asses do.

WALL
In this same interlude it doth befall
That I, one Snout by name, present a wall;
And such a wall as I would have you think
That had in it a crannied hole or chink,
Through which the lovers, Pyramus and Thisbe,
Did whisper often, very secretly.
This loam, this roughcast, and this stone doth show
That I am that same wall; the truth is so.
And this the cranny is, right and sinister,
Through which the fearful lovers are to whisper.

THESEUS Would you desire lime and hair to speak better?

DEMETRIUS It is the wittiest partition that ever I heard discourse, my lord.

[*Pyramus comes forward.*]

THESEUS Pyramus draws near the wall. Silence!

PYRAMUS
O grim-looked night! O night with hue so black!
O night, which ever art when day is not!
O night, O night! Alack, alack, alack,
I fear my Thisbe's promise is forgot.
And thou, O wall, O sweet, O lovely wall,
That stand'st between her father's ground and mine,
Thou wall, O wall, O sweet and lovely wall,
Show me thy chink, to blink through with mine eyne. [*Wall makes a chink with his fingers.*]
Thanks, courteous wall. Jove shield thee well for this.
But what see I? No Thisbe do I see.
O wicked wall, through whom I see no bliss!
Cursed be thy stones for thus deceiving me!

THESEUS The wall, methinks, being sensible, should curse again.

PYRAMUS No, in truth, sir, he should not. "Deceiving me" is Thisbe's cue: she is to enter now, and I am to spy her through the wall. You shall see, it will fall pat as I told you. Yonder she comes.

Enter Thisbe.

THISBE
O wall, full often hast thou heard my moans
For parting my fair Pyramus and me.
My cherry lips have often kissed thy stones,
Thy stones with lime and hair knit up in thee.

PYRAMUS
I see a voice. Now will I to the chink,
To spy an I can hear my Thisbe's face.
Thisbe!

THISBE My love! Thou art my love, I think.

PYRAMUS
Think what thou wilt, I am thy lover's grace,
And like Limander am I trusty still.

THISBE
And I like Helen, till the Fates me kill.

113 minding intending **118 stand upon points** (1) heed niceties or small points (2) pay attention to punctuation in his reading. (The humor of Quince's speech is in the blunders of its punctuation.) **119 rid** ridden. **rough** unbroken **120 stop** (1) stopping of a colt by reining it in (2) punctuation mark. **123 recorder** wind instrument like a flute. **government** control. **124 nothing** not at all **136 think no scorn** think it no disgraceful matter **138 hight** is called **141 fall** let fall **143 tall** courageous **146 broached** stabbed **150 At large** in full, at length **154 interlude** play

162 right and sinister from right to left **166 partition** (1) wall (2) section of a learned treatise or oration **169 grim-looked** grim-looking **181 sensible** capable of feeling **182 again** in return. **185 pat** exactly **192 an** if **194 lover's grace** i.e., gracious lover **195, 196 Limander, Helen** (Blunders for "Leander" and "Hero.")

PYRAMUS
Not Shafalus to Procrus was so true.

THISBE
As Shafalus to Procrus, I to you.

PYRAMUS
Oh, kiss me through the hole of this vile wall!

THISBE
I kiss the wall's hole, not your lips at all.

PYRAMUS
Wilt thou at Ninny's tomb meet me straightway?

THISBE
'Tide life, 'tide death, I come without delay.
[*Exeunt Pyramus and Thisbe.*]

WALL
Thus have I, Wall, my part dischargèd so;
And, being done, thus Wall away doth go. [*Exit.*]

THESEUS Now is the mural down between the two neighbors.

DEMETRIUS No remedy, my lord, when walls are so willful to hear without warning.

HIPPOLYTA This is the silliest stuff that ever I heard.

THESEUS The best in this kind are but shadows; and the worst are no worse, if imagination amend them.

HIPPOLYTA It must be your imagination then, and not theirs.

THESEUS If we imagine no worse of them than they of themselves, they may pass for excellent men. Here come two noble beasts in, a man and a lion.

Enter Lion and Moonshine.

LION
You, ladies, you, whose gentle hearts do fear
The smallest monstrous mouse that creeps on floor,
May now perchance both quake and tremble here,
When lion rough in wildest rage doth roar.
Then know that I, as Snug the joiner, am
A lion fell, nor else no lion's dam;
For, if I should as lion come in strife
Into this place, 'twere pity on my life.

THESEUS A very gentle beast, and of a good conscience.

DEMETRIUS The very best at a beast, my lord, that e'er I saw.

LYSANDER This lion is a very fox for his valor.

THESEUS True; and a goose for his discretion.

DEMETRIUS Not so, my lord, for his valor cannot carry his discretion, and the fox carries the goose.

THESEUS His discretion, I am sure, cannot carry his valor; for the goose carries not the fox. It is well. Leave it to his discretion, and let us listen to the moon.

MOON
This lanthorn doth the hornèd moon present—

DEMETRIUS He should have worn the horns on his head.

THESEUS He is no crescent, and his horns are invisible within the circumference.

MOON
This lanthorn doth the hornèd moon present;
Myself the man i'th' moon do seem to be.

THESEUS This is the greatest error of all the rest. The man should be put into the lanthorn. How is it else the man i'th' moon?

DEMETRIUS He dares not come there for the candle, for you see it is already in snuff.

HIPPOLYTA I am aweary of this moon. Would he would change!

THESEUS It appears, by his small light of discretion, that he is in the wane; but yet, in courtesy, in all reason, we must stay the time.

LYSANDER Proceed, Moon.

MOON All that I have to say is to tell you that the lanthorn is the moon, I, the man i'th' moon, this thornbush my thornbush, and this dog my dog.

DEMETRIUS Why, all these should be in the lanthorn, for all these are in the moon. But silence! Here comes Thisbe.

Enter Thisbe.

THISBE
This is old Ninny's tomb. Where is my love?

LION [*roaring*] Oh!

DEMETRIUS Well roared, Lion.
[*Thisbe runs off, dropping her mantle.*]

THESEUS Well run, Thisbe.

HIPPOLYTA Well shone, Moon. Truly, the moon shines with a good grace.
[*The Lion worries Thisbe's mantle.*]

THESEUS Well moused, Lion.

Enter Pyramus. [*Exit Lion.*]

DEMETRIUS And then came Pyramus.

LYSANDER And so the lion vanished.

PYRAMUS
Sweet Moon, I thank thee for thy sunny beams;
I thank thee, Moon, for shining now so bright;
For, by thy gracious, golden, glittering gleams,
I trust to take of truest Thisbe sight.
But stay, oh, spite!
But mark, poor knight,
What dreadful dole is here?
Eyes, do you see?
How can it be?

197 Shafalus, Procrus (Blunders for "Cephalus" and "Procris," also famous lovers.) **202 'Tide** Betide, come **208 willful** willing. **without warning** i.e., without warning the parents. (Demetrius makes a joke on the proverb "Walls have ears.") **210 in this kind** of this sort. **shadows** likenesses, representations **221–2 am . . . dam** enact the part of a fierce lion, but otherwise am not really a lion. (*Dam* means "mother"; in Shakespeare's source the beast is a lioness.) **228 is . . . valor** i.e., his valor consists of craftiness and discretion. **229 a goose . . . discretion** i.e., as discreet as a goose, that is, more foolish than discreet.

235 lanthorn (This original spelling, "lanthorne," may suggest a play on the *horn* of which lanterns were made and also on a cuckold's horns; however, the spelling "lanthorne" is not used consistently for comic effect in this play or elsewhere. At 5.1.134, for example, the word is "lanterne" in the original.) **236–7 on his head** (As a sign of cuckoldry.) **238 crescent** a waxing moon **245 for** because of, for fear of **246 in snuff** (1) offended (2) in need of snuffing or trimming. **265 moused** shaken, torn, bitten **274 dole** grievous event

Oh, dainty duck! Oh, dear!
Thy mantle good,
What, stained with blood?
Approach, ye Furies fell!
O Fates, come, come,
Cut thread and thrum;
Quail, crush, conclude, and quell!

THESEUS This passion, and the death of a dear friend, would go near to make a man look sad.

HIPPOLYTA Beshrew my heart, but I pity the man.

PYRAMUS
Oh, wherefore, Nature, didst thou lions frame?
Since lion vile hath here deflowered my dear,
Which is—no, no, which was—the fairest dame
That lived, that loved, that liked, that looked with cheer.
Come, tears, confound,
Out, sword, and wound
The pap of Pyramus;
Ay, that left pap,
Where heart doth hop. [*He stabs himself.*]
Thus die I, thus, thus, thus.
Now am I dead,
Now am I fled;
My soul is in the sky.
Tongue, lose thy light;
Moon, take thy flight. [*Exit Moonshine.*]
Now die, die, die, die, die. [*Pyramus dies.*]

DEMETRIUS No die, but an ace, for him; for he is but one.

LYSANDER Less than an ace, man; for he is dead, he is nothing.

THESEUS With the help of a surgeon he might yet recover, and yet prove an ass.

HIPPOLYTA How chance Moonshine is gone before Thisbe comes back and finds her lover?

THESEUS She will find him by starlight.

[*Enter Thisbe.*]

Here she comes; and her passion ends the play.

HIPPOLYTA Methinks she should not use a long one for such a Pyramus. I hope she will be brief.

DEMETRIUS A mote will turn the balance, which Pyramus which Thisbe, is the better: he for a man, God warrant us; she for a woman, God bless us.

LYSANDER She hath spied him already with those sweet eyes.

DEMETRIUS And thus she means, videlicet:

THISBE
Asleep, my love?
What, dead, my dove?
O Pyramus, arise!
Speak, speak. Quite dumb?
Dead, dead? A tomb
Must cover thy sweet eyes.
These lily lips,
This cherry nose,
These yellow cowslip cheeks,
Are gone, are gone!
Lovers, make moan.
His eyes were green as leeks.
O Sisters Three,
Come, come to me,
With hands as pale as milk;
Lay them in gore,
Since you have shore
With shears his thread of silk.
Tongue, not a word.
Come, trusty sword,
Come, blade, my breast imbrue!
[*She stabs herself.*]
And farewell, friends.
Thus Thisbe ends.
Adieu, adieu, adieu. [*She dies.*]

THESEUS Moonshine and Lion are left to bury the dead.

DEMETRIUS Ay, and Wall too.

BOTTOM [*starting up, as Flute does also*] No, I assure you, the wall is down that parted their fathers. Will it please you to see the epilogue, or to hear a Bergomask dance between two of our company?

[*The other players enter.*]

THESEUS No epilogue, I pray you; for your play needs no excuse. Never excuse; for when the players are all dead, there need none to be blamed. Marry, if he that writ it had played Pyramus and hanged himself in Thisbe's garter, it would have been a fine tragedy; and so it is, truly, and very notably discharged. But, come, your Bergomask. Let your epilogue alone. [*A dance.*]
The iron tongue of midnight hath told twelve.
Lovers, to bed, 'tis almost fairy time.
I fear we shall outsleep the coming morn
As much as we this night have overwatched.
This palpable-gross play hath well beguiled
The heavy gait of night. Sweet friends, to bed.
A fortnight hold we this solemnity,
In nightly revels and new jollity. [*Exeunt.*]

Enter Puck [*carrying a broom*].

280 Furies fell fierce avenging goddesses of Greek myth. **281 Fates** the three goddesses (Clotho, Lachesis, Atropos) of Greek myth who spun, drew, and cut the thread of human life **282 thread and thrum** i.e., everything—the good and bad alike; literally, the warp in weaving and the loose end of the warp **283 Quail** overpower. **quell** kill, destroy. **284–5 This . . . sad** i.e., If one had other reason to grieve, one might be sad, but not from this absurd portrayal of passion. **286 Beshrew** Curse. (A mild curse.) **287 frame** create. **290 cheer** countenance. **293 pap** breast **303 ace** the side of the die featuring the single pip, or spot. (The pun is on *die* as a singular of *dice;* Bottom's performance is not worth a whole *die* but rather one single face of it, one small portion.) **304 one** (1) an individual person (2) unique. **308 ass** (With a pun on *ace.*) **315 mote** small particle **315–16 which . . . which** whether . . . or

320 means moans, laments. (With a pun on the meaning, "lodge a formal complaint.") **videlicet** to wit **333 Sisters Three** the Fates **337 shore** shorn **341 imbrue** stain with blood. **349 Bergomask dance** a rustic dance named from Bergamo, a province in the state of Venice **358 iron tongue** i.e., of a bell. **told** counted, struck ("tolled") **361 overwatched** stayed up too late. **362 palpable-gross** palpably gross, obviously crude **363 heavy** drowsy, dull

PUCK

Now the hungry lion roars,
And the wolf behowls the moon,
Whilst the heavy plowman snores,
All with weary task fordone.
Now the wasted brands do glow,
Whilst the screech owl, screeching loud,
Puts the wretch that lies in woe
In remembrance of a shroud.
Now it is the time of night
That the graves, all gaping wide,
Every one lets forth his sprite,
In the churchway paths to glide.
And we fairies, that do run
By the triple Hecate's team.
From the presence of the sun,
Following darkness like a dream,
Now are frolic. Not a mouse
Shall disturb this hallowed house.
I am sent with broom before,
To sweep the dust behind the door.

Enter [Oberon and Titania,] King and Queen of Fairies, with all their train.

OBERON

Through the house give glimmering light,
By the dead and drowsy fire;
Every elf and fairy sprite
Hop as light as bird from brier;
And this ditty, after me,
Sing, and dance it trippingly.

TITANIA

First, rehearse your song by rote,
To each word a warbling note.
Hand in hand, with fairy grace,
Will we sing, and bless this place.
[*Song and dance.*]

OBERON

Now, until the break of day,
Through this house each fairy stray.
To the best bride-bed will we,
Which by us shall blessèd be;
And the issue there create
Ever shall be fortunate.
So shall all the couples three
Ever true in loving be;
And the blots of Nature's hand
Shall not in their issue stand;
Never mole, harelip, nor scar,
Nor mark prodigious, such as are
Despisèd in nativity,
Shall upon their children be.
With this field dew consecrate,
Every fairy take his gait,
And each several chamber bless,
Through this palace, with sweet peace;
And the owner of it blest
Ever shall in safety rest.
Trip away; make no stay;
Meet me all by break of day.
Exeunt [*Oberon, Titania, and train*].

PUCK [*to the audience*]

If we shadows have offended,
Think but this, and all is mended,
That you have but slumbered here
While these visions did appear.
And this weak and idle theme,
No more yielding but a dream,
Gentles, do not reprehend.
If you pardon, we will mend.
And, as I am an honest Puck,
If we have unearnèd luck
Now to scape the serpent's tongue,
We will make amends ere long;
Else the Puck a liar call.
So, good night unto you all.
Give me your hands, if we be friends,
And Robin shall restore amends. [*Exit.*]

368 heavy tired **369 fordone** exhausted. **370 wasted brands** burned-out logs **376 Every . . . sprite** every grave lets forth its ghost **379 triple Hecate's** (Hecate ruled in three capacities: as Luna or Cynthia in heaven, as Diana on earth, and as Proserpina in hell.) **382 frolic** merry. **385 behind** from behind, or else like sweeping the dirt under the carpet. (Robin Goodfellow was a household spirit who helped good housemaids and punished lazy ones, but he could, of course, be mischievous.) **392 rehearse** recite

400 issue offspring. **create** created **407 prodigious** monstrous, unnatural **410 consecrate** consecrated **411 take his gait** go his way **412 several** separate **420 That . . . here** i.e., that it is a "midsummer night's dream" **423 No . . . but** yielding no more than **425 mend** improve. **428 serpent's tongue** i.e., hissing **432 Give . . . hands** Applaud **433 restore amends** give satisfaction in return.

The Merchant of Venice

Although Shylock is the most prominent character in *The Merchant of Venice*, he takes part in neither the beginning nor the ending of the play. And, although the play's title might seem to suggest that he is the "merchant" of Venice, Shylock is, strictly speaking, a moneylender whose usury is portrayed as the very opposite of true commerce. His vengeful struggle to obtain a pound of flesh from Antonio contrasts with the various romantic episodes woven together in this play: Bassanio's choosing of Portia by means of the caskets, Gratiano's wooing of Nerissa, Jessica's elopement with Lorenzo, Lancelot Gobbo's changing of masters, and the episode of the rings. In all these stories, a Christian ethic of generosity, love, and risk-taking friendship is set in pointed contrast with a non-Christian ethic that is seen, from a Christian point of view, as grudging, resentful, and self-calculating. Yet this contrasting vision is made problematic by the deplorable behavior of some Christians. In stage productions today, Belmont and its inhabitants are apt to seem frivolous, pleasure-loving, hedonistic, and above all racist in their insular preference for their own economically and culturally privileged position. The play invites us to question the motives of Shylock's enemies. It makes us (today, at least, after the terrors of the German Holocaust) uncomfortable at the insularity of a Venetian ethic that has no genuine place for non-Christians or cultural outsiders. The most painful question of all, for us, is to wonder whether the play assumes for its own dramatic purposes a Christian point of view, however much it sees a genuine and understandable motive in Shylock's desire for revenge. The problem of divided sympathies is exacerbated because Shylock's structural function in the play is essentially that of the villain in a love comedy. His remorseless pursuit of Antonio darkens the mood of the play, and his overthrow signals the providential triumph of love and friendship, even though that triumph is not without its undercurrent of wry melancholy. Before we examine the painful issue of anti-Semitism more closely, we need to establish the structural context of this love comedy as a whole.

Like many of Shakespeare's philosophical and festive comedies, *The Merchant of Venice* presents two contrasting worlds—one fantasy-like and the other marked by conflict and anxiety. To an extent, these contrasting worlds can be identified with the locations of Belmont and Venice. Belmont, to which the various happy lovers and their friends eventually retire, is a place of magic and romance. As its name implies, it is on a mountain, and it is reached by a journey across water. As often happens in fairy stories, on this mountain dwells a princess who must be won by means of a riddling contest. We usually see Belmont at night. Music surrounds it, and women preside over it. Even its caskets, houses, and rings are essentially feminine symbols. Venice, on the other hand, is a place of bustle and economic competition, seen most characteristically in the heat of the day. It lies low and flat, at a point where rivers reach the sea. Men preside over its contentious marketplace and its haggling law courts. Actually, the opposition of Venice and Belmont is not quite so clear-cut: Venice contains much compassionate friendship, whereas Belmont is subject to the arbitrary command of Portia's dead father. (Portia somewhat resembles Jessica in being imprisoned by her father's will.) Even though Portia descends to Venice in the angelic role of mercy giver, she also remains very human: sharp-tongued and even venomous in caricaturing her unwelcome wooers, crafty in her legal maneuvering, saucily prankish in her torturing of Bassanio about the rings. For all its warmth and generosity, Belmont is also the embodiment of an insular Christian culture that makes room for outsiders only when they convert to Christian mores. The traits that Shylock carries to an unpleasant extreme are needed in moderation by the Venetians, notably thrift, promise-keeping, and prudent self-interest; only when the Christians temper their penchant for reckless extravagance, legal sophistry or even theft, and risk-taking is a happy resolution possible. Nevertheless, the polarity of two contrasting localities and two groups of characters is vividly real in this play.

The play's opening scene, from which Shylock is excluded, sets forth the interrelated themes of friendship, romantic love, and risk or "hazard." The merchant who seemingly fulfills the title role, Antonio, is the victim of a mysterious melancholy. He is wealthy enough and surrounded by friends, but something is missing from his life. He assures his solicitous companions that he has no financial worries, for he has been too careful to trust all his cargoes to one sea vessel. Antonio, in fact, has no idea why he is so sad. The question is haunting. What is the matter? Perhaps the answer is to be found in a paradox: those who strive to prosper in the world's terms are doomed to frustration, not because prosperity will necessarily elude them, but because it will not satisfy the spirit. "You have too much respect upon the world," argues the carefree Gratiano. "They lose it that do buy it with much care" (1.1.74–5). Portia and Jessica, too, are at first afflicted by a melancholy that stems from the incompleteness of living isolated lives, with insufficient opportunities for love and sacrifice. They must learn, as Antonio learns with the help of his dear friend Bassanio, to seek happiness by daring to risk everything for friendship. Antonio's risk is most extreme: only when he has thrown away concern for his life can he discover what there is to live for.

At first, Bassanio's request for assistance seems just as materialistic as the worldliness from which Antonio suffers. Bassanio proposes to marry a rich young lady, Portia, in order to recoup his fortune lost through prodigality, and he needs money from Antonio so that he may woo Portia in proper fashion. She is "richly left," the heiress of a dead father, a golden fleece for whom this new Jason will make a quest. Bassanio's adventure is partly commercial. Yet his pilgrimage for Portia is magnanimous as well. The occasional modern practice of playing Bassanio and Portia as cynical antiheroes of a "black" comedy points up the problematic character of their materialism and calculation, but it gives only one aspect of the portrayal. Bassanio has lost his previous fortune through the amiable faults of reckless generosity and a lack of concern for financial prudence. The money he must now borrow, and the fortune he hopes to acquire, are to him no more than a means to carefree happiness. Although Portia's rich dowry is a strong consideration, he describes her also as "fair and, fairer than that word,/Of wondrous virtues" (1.1.162–3). Moreover, he enjoys the element of risk in wooing her. It is like shooting a second arrow in order to recover one that has been lost—double or nothing. This gamble, or "hazard," involves risk for Antonio as well as for Bassanio, and it ultimately brings a double reward to them both—spiritual as well as financial. Unless one recognizes these aspects of Bassanio's quest, as well as the clear fairy-tale quality with which Shakespeare deliberately invests this part of the plot, one cannot properly assess Bassanio's role in this romantic comedy.

Bassanio's quest for Portia can, in fact, never succeed until he disavows the very financial considerations that brought him to Belmont in the first place. This is the paradox of the riddle of the three caskets, an ancient parable stressing the need for choosing by true substance rather than by outward show. To choose "what many men desire," as the Prince of Morocco does, is to pin one's hopes on worldly wealth; to believe that one "deserves" good fortune, as the Prince of Aragon does, is to reveal a fatal pride in one's own merit. Bassanio perceives that, in order to win true love, he must "give and hazard all he hath" (2.7.9). He is not "deceived with ornament" (3.2.74). Just as Antonio must risk all for friendship, and just as Bassanio himself must later be willing to risk losing Portia for the sake of true friendship (in the episode of the rings), Bassanio must renounce worldly ambition and beauty before he can be rewarded with success. Paradoxically, only those who learn to subdue such worldly desires may then legitimately enjoy the world's pleasures. Only they have acknowledged the hierarchical subservience of the flesh to the spirit. These are the philosophical truisms of Renaissance Neoplatonism, depicting love as a chain or ladder from the basest carnality to the supreme love of God for humanity. On this ladder, perfect friendship and spiritual union are more sublimely Godlike than sexual fulfillment. This idealism may seem a strange doctrine for Bassanio the fortune hunter, but, actually, its conventional wisdom simply confirms his role as romantic hero. He and Portia are not denied worldly happiness or erotic pleasure; they are merely asked to give first thought to their Christian duty in marriage.

For Portia, marriage represents both a gain and a loss. She can choose only by her dead father's will; the patriarchal system, according to which a woman is given in marriage by her father to a younger man, is seemingly able to extend its control even beyond the grave. The prospect of marrying the Prince of Morocco or the Prince of Aragon dismays her, and yet she persists in her vow of obedience and is eventually rewarded by the man of her choice. It is as though the benign father knew how to set the terms of choice in such a way that the "lottery" of the caskets would turn out right for her. When she accepts Bassanio, too, she must make a difficult choice, for in legal terms she makes Bassanio master over everything she owns. Portia is at once spirited and submissive, able to straighten out Venice's legal tangles when all the men have failed and yet ready to call Bassanio her lord. Her teasing him about the ring is a sign that she will make demands of him in marriage, but it is a testing that cannot produce lasting disharmony so long as Bassanio is truly loyal. Portia is, from Bassanio's male point of view, the perfect woman: humanly attainable and yet never seriously threatening. Guided by her, Bassanio makes the potentially hazardous transition from the male-oriented friendships of Venice (especially with Antonio) to heterosexual union. Portia is more fortunate than Jessica, who must break with her faith and her father in order to find marital happiness. The two women are alike, however, in that they experience the play's central paradox of losing the world in order to gain the world. Through them, we see that this paradox illuminates the casket episode, the struggle for the pound of flesh, the elopement of Jessica, the ring episode, and even the comic foolery of Lancelot Gobbo.

Shylock, in his quest for the pound of flesh, represents, as seen from a Christian point of view, a denial of all the paradoxical truths just described. As a usurer, he refuses to lend money interest-free in the name of friendship. Instead of taking risks, he insists on his bond. He spurns mercy and demands strict justice. By calculating all his chances too craftily, he appears to win at first but must eventually lose all. He has "too much respect upon the world" (1.1.74). His God is the Old Testament God of Moses, the God of wrath, the God of the Ten Commandments, with their forbidding emphasis on "Thou shalt not." (This oversimplified contrast between Judaism and Christianity was commonplace in Shakespeare's time.) Shylock abhors stealing but admires equivocation as a means of out-maneuvering a competitor; he approvingly cites Jacob's ruse to deprive Laban of his sheep (1.3.69–88). Any tactic is permissible so long as it falls within the realm of legality and contract.

Shylock's ethical outlook, then, justifies both usury and the old dispensation of the Jewish law. The two are philosophically combined, just as usury and Judaism had become equated in the popular imagination of Renaissance Europe. Even though lending at interest was becoming increasingly necessary and common, old prejudices against it still persisted. Angry moralists pointed out that the New Testament had condemned usury and that Aristotle had described money as barren. To breed money was therefore regarded as unnatural. Usury was considered sinful because it did not involve the usual risks of commerce; the lender was assured against loss of his principal by the posting of collateral and, at the same time, was sure to earn a handsome interest. The usurer seemed to be getting something for nothing. For these reasons, usury was sometimes declared illegal. Its practitioners were viewed as corrupt and grasping, hated as misers. In some European countries, Jews were permitted to practice this un-Christian living (and permitted to do very little else) and then, hypocritically, were detested for performing un-Christian deeds. Ironically, the moneylenders of England were Christians, and few Jews were to be found in any professions. Nominally excluded since Edward I's reign, the Jews had returned in small numbers to London but did not practice their Judaism openly. They attended Anglican services as required by law and then worshiped in private, relatively undisturbed by the authorities. Shylock may not be based on observation from London life. He is derived from continental tradition and reflects a widespread conviction that Jews and usurers were alike in being un-Christian and sinister.

Shylock is unquestionably sinister, even if he also invites sympathy. He bears an "ancient grudge" against Antonio simply because Antonio is "a Christian." We recognize in Shylock the archetype of the supposed Jew who wishes to kill a Christian and obtain his flesh. In early medieval anti-Semitic legends of this sort, the flesh thus obtained was imagined to be eaten ritually during Passover. Because some Jews had once persecuted Christ, all were unfairly presumed to be implacable enemies of all Christians. These anti-Semitic superstitions were likely to erupt into hysteria at any time, as in 1594 when Dr. Roderigo Lopez, a Portuguese Jewish physician, was accused of having plotted against the life of Queen Elizabeth and of Don Antonio, pretender to the Portuguese throne. Christopher Marlowe's *The Jew of Malta* was revived for this occasion, enjoying an unusually successful run of fifteen performances, and scholars have often wondered if Shakespeare's play was not written under the same impetus. On this score, the evidence is inconclusive, and the play might have been written any time between 1594 and 1598 (when it is mentioned by Francis Meres), but, in any case, Shakespeare has made no attempt to avoid the anti-Semitic nature of his story.

To offset the portrayal of Jewish villainy, however, the play also dramatizes the possibility of conversion to Christianity, suggesting that Judaism is more a matter of benighted faith than of ethnic origin. Converted Jews were not new on the stage: they had appeared in medieval cycle drama, in the Croxton *Play of the Sacrament* (late fifteenth century), and more recently in *The Jew of Malta*, in which Barabas' daughter Abigail falls in love with a Christian and eventually becomes a nun. Shylock's daughter Jessica similarly embraces Christianity as Lorenzo's wife and is received into the happy comradeship of Belmont. Shylock is forced to accept Christianity, presumably for the benefit of his eternal soul (though today we find this deeply offensive, and it is sometimes cut from stage productions). Earlier in the play, Antonio repeatedly indicates his willingness to befriend Shylock if the latter will only give up usury, and he is even cautiously hopeful when Shylock offers him an interest-free loan: "The Hebrew will turn Christian; he grows kind" (1.3.177). To be sure, Antonio's denunciation of Shylock's usurious Judaism has been vehement and personal; we learn that he has spat on Shylock's gaberdine and kicked him as one would kick a dog. This violent disapproval offers no opportunity for the toleration of cultural and religious differences that we expect today from people of good will, but at least Antonio is prepared to accept Shylock if Shylock will embrace the Christian faith and its ethical responsibilities. Whether the play itself endorses Antonio's Christian point of view as normative or insists on a darker reading by making us uneasy with intolerance is a matter of unceasing critical debate. Quite possibly, the play's power to disturb emanates—at least in part—from the dramatic conflict of irreconcilable sets of values.

To Antonio, then, as well as to other Venetians, true Christianity is both an absolute good from which no deviation is possible without evil and a state of faith to which aliens may turn by abjuring the benighted creeds of their ancestors. By this token, the Prince of Morocco is condemned to failure in his quest for Portia, not so much because he is black as because he is an infidel, one who worships "blind fortune" and therefore chooses a worldly rather than a spiritual reward. Although Portia pertly dismisses him with "Let all of his complexion choose me so" (2.7.79), she professes earlier to find him handsome and agrees that he should not be judged by his complexion (2.1.13–22). Unless she is merely being hypocritical, she means by her later remark that black-skinned people are generally infidels, just as Jews are as a group un-Christian. Such pejorative thinking about persons as types is no doubt distressing and suggests—at least to a modern audience—the cultural limitation of Portia's view, but, in any case, it shows her to be no less well disposed toward black suitors than toward others who are also alien. She is glad not to be won by the Prince of Aragon because he, too, though nominally a Christian, is too self-satisfied and proud. All persons, therefore, may aspire to truly virtuous conduct, and those who choose virtue are equally blessed; however, the terms of defining that ideal in this play are essentially Christian. Jews and Blacks may rise spiritually only by abandoning their pagan creeds for the new dispensation of charity and forgiveness.

The superiority of Christian teaching to the older Jewish dispensation was, of course, a widely accepted notion of Shakespeare's time. After all, these were the years when people fought and died to maintain their religious beliefs. Today, the notion of a single true church is less widely held, and we have difficulty understanding why anyone would wish to force conversion on Shylock. Modern productions find it tempting to portray Shylock as a victim of bigotry and to put great stress on his heartrending assertions of his humanity: "Hath not a Jew eyes? . . . If you prick us, do we not bleed?" (3.1.56–62). Shylock does indeed suffer from his enemies, and his sufferings add a tortured complexity to this play—even, one suspects, for an Elizabethan audience. Those who profess Christianity must surely examine their own motives and conduct. Is it right to steal treasure from Shylock's house along with his eloped daughter? Is it considerate of Jessica and Lorenzo to squander Shylock's turquoise ring, the gift of his wife Leah, on a monkey? Does Shylock's vengeful insistence on law justify the quibbling countermeasures devised by Portia even as she piously declaims about mercy? Do Shylock's misfortunes deserve the mirthful parodies of Solanio ("My daughter! Oh, my ducats!") or the hostile jeering of Gratiano at the conclusion of the trial? Because he stands outside Christian faith, Shylock can provide a perspective whereby we see the hypocrisies of those who profess a higher ethical code. Nevertheless, Shylock's compulsive desire for vengeance according to an Old Testament code of an eye for an eye cannot be justified by the wrongdoings of any particular Christian. In the play's control of an ethical point of view, such deeds condemn the doer rather than undermine the Christian standards of true virtue as ideally expressed. Shakespeare humanizes Shylock by portraying him as a believable and sensitive man, and he shows much that is to be regretted in Shylock's Christian antagonists, but he also allows Shylock to place himself in the wrong by his refusal to forgive his enemies.

Shylock thus loses everything through his effort to win everything on his own terms. His daughter, Jessica, by her elopement, follows an opposite course. She characterizes her father's home as "hell," and she resents being locked up behind closed windows. Shylock detests music and the sounds of merriment; Jessica's new life in Belmont is immersed in music. He is old, suspicious, miserly; she is young, loving, adventurous. Most important, she seems to be at least part Christian when we first see her. As Lancelot jests half in earnest, "If a Christian did not play the knave and get thee, I am much deceived" (2.3.11–12). Her removal from Shylock's house involves theft, and her running from Venice is, she confesses, an "unthrift love." Paradoxically, however, she sees this recklessness as of more blessed effect than her father's legalistic caution. As she says, "I shall be saved by my husband. He hath made me a Christian" (3.5.17–18).

Lancelot Gobbo's clowning offers a similarly paradoxical comment on the tragedy of Shylock. Lancelot debates whether or not to leave Shylock's service in terms of a soul struggle between his conscience and the devil (2.2.1–29). Conscience bids him stay, for service is a debt, a bond, an obligation, whereas abandonment of one's indenture is a kind of rebellion or stealing away. Yet Shylock's house is "hell" to Lancelot as it is to Jessica. Comparing his new master with his old, Lancelot observes to Bassanio, "You have the grace of God, sir, and he hath enough." Service with Bassanio involves imprudent risks, since Bassanio is a spendthrift. The miserly Shylock rejoices to see the ever hungry Lancelot, this "huge feeder," wasting the substance of a hated Christian. Once again, however, Shylock will lose everything in his grasping quest for security. Another spiritual renewal occurs when Lancelot encounters his old and nearly blind father (2.2). In a scene echoing the biblical stories of the Prodigal Son and of Jacob and Esau, Lancelot teases the old man with false rumors of Lancelot's own death in order to make their reunion seem all the more unexpected and precious. The illusion of loss gives way to joy: Lancelot is, in language adapted from the liturgy, "your boy that was, your son that is, your child that shall be."

In the episode of the rings, we encounter a final playful variation on the paradox of winning through losing. Portia and Nerissa cleverly present their new husbands with a cruel choice: disguised as a doctor of law and his clerk, who have just saved the life of Antonio from Shylock's wrath, the two wives ask nothing more for their services than the rings they see on the fingers of Bassanio and Gratiano. The two husbands, who have vowed never to part with these wedding rings, must therefore choose between love and friendship. Portia knows well enough that Bassanio's obedience to the Neoplatonic ideal of disinterested friendship is an essential part of his virtue. Just as he previously renounced beauty and riches before he could deserve Portia, he must now risk losing her for friendship's sake. The testing of the husbands' constancy does border at times on gratuitous harshness and exercise of power, for it deals with the oldest of masculine nightmares: cuckoldry. Wives are not without weapons in the struggle for control in marriage, and Portia and Nerissa enjoy trapping their new husbands in a no-win situation. Still, the threat is easily resolved by the dispelling of farcically mistaken identities. The young men have been tricked into bestowing their rings on their wives for a second time in the name of perfect friendship, thereby confirming a relationship that is both platonic and fleshly. As Gratiano bawdily points out in the play's last line, the ring is both a spiritual and a sexual symbol of marriage. The resolution of this illusory quarrel also brings to an end the merry battle of the sexes between wives and husbands. Having hinted at the sorts of misunderstandings that afflict even the best of human relationships and having proved themselves wittily able to torture and deceive their husbands, Portia and Nerissa submit at last to the patriarchal norms of their age and to the authority of Bassanio and Gratiano.

Bassanio's marriage to Portia represents a heterosexual fulfillment of their courtship that leaves Antonio without a partner at the play's end. He is, to be sure, included in the camaraderie of Belmont, but a part of the sacrifice he has made for Bassanio is to give that young man the freedom and means to marry as he chooses. Antonio's attachment for Bassanio is a deeply loving one, and is sometimes portrayed as homosexual in modern productions. The force of Antonio's attachment to Bassanio should not be underestimated. At the same time, he does appear to be truly willing for the young man to marry. In this sense, the marriage represents a completion in which friendship and love are fully complementary. Heterosexual union is, in this play and in Shakespearean comedy generally, a dominant and theatrically conventional resolution; but it is so without denying that there are other forms of human happiness. Whether or not Antonio is entirely content with his final role as a kind of benign older friend we cannot be sure, but his pronouncements in the final act are all aimed at encouraging the harmony between husband and wife that he has risked his life to enable.

As defined by the accepted notions of gender relations in Shakespeare's time, then, all appears to be in harmony in Belmont. The disorders of Venice have been left far behind, however imperfectly they may have been resolved. Jessica and Lorenzo contrast their present happiness with the sufferings of less fortunate lovers of long ago: Troilus and Cressida, Pyramus and Thisbe, Aeneas and Dido, Jason and Medea. The tranquil joy found in Belmont is attuned to the music of the spheres, the singing of the "young-eyed cherubins" (5.1.62), although with a proper Christian humility the lovers also realize that the harmony of immortal souls is infinitely beyond their comprehension. Bound in by the grossness of the flesh, "this muddy vesture of decay" (5.1.64), they can only reach toward the bliss of eternity through music and the perfect friendship of true love. Even in their final joy, accordingly, the lovers find an incompleteness that lends a wistful and slightly melancholy reflective tone to the play's ending. That sense of imperfection is accentuated for us by our awareness that the play's serious problems of gender relations, friendship, and anti-Semitism have by no means been fully resolved; the final concord is one that arises out of discord. Even so, this concluding sense of the unavoidable incompleteness of all human life is of a very different order from that earlier melancholy of isolation and lack of commitment experienced by Portia, Jessica, Antonio, and others.

In performance, the play has prompted both hostile and genuinely sympathetic responses for Shylock. The traditional anti-Semitic interpretation in early stage history manifested itself, for instance, in the performance of George Frederick Cooke in 1803–1804, "bent with age and ugly with mental deformity, grinning with deadly malice, with the venom of his heart congealed in the expression of his countenance, sullen, morose, gloomy, inflexible" (these are William Hazlitt's words). Still other renditions made use of the red wig and hooked nose of the stereotypical stage Jew that associated Shylock with Judas Iscariot. Conversely, Edmund Kean, in 1814, evoked such sympathy as to make the Christians in the play seem hypocrites by comparison. Henry Irving in 1879, and Beerbohm Tree in 1908, combined a kind of ancient dignity with pathos. George C. Scott, at the New York Shakespeare Festival in 1962, acted Shylock as a persecuted and desperate man surrounded by powerful enemies. Laurence Olivier's anguished Shylock (1970, subsequently televised) showed up the Christians as complacent members of a bigoted Venetian social world of privilege and exclusivity. A production in Weimar, Germany, in 1995, commemorating the fiftieth anniversary of the liberation of the concentration camp at nearby Buchenwald, captured what is so horrendously problematic in the play by imagining what it would be like if enacted by German officers and guards amusing themselves with amateur theatricals during wartime and assigning three Jewish inmates to the roles of Shylock, Tubal, and Jessica. Perhaps no Shakespeare play raises more painful issues today for us to think hard about than *The Merchant of Venice*.

The Merchant of Venice

[*Dramatis Personae*

THE DUKE OF VENICE
ANTONIO, *a merchant of Venice*
BASSANIO, *his friend, suitor to Portia*
GRATIANO, *a follower of Bassanio, in love with Nerissa*
SOLANIO, } *friends to Antonio*
SALERIO, } *and Bassanio*
LORENZO, *in love with Jessica*
LEONARDO, *servant to Bassanio*

PORTIA, *a rich heiress of Belmont*
NERISSA, *her waiting-gentlewoman*
BALTHASAR, *servant to Portia*
STEPHANO, *servant to Portia*

THE PRINCE OF MOROCCO, *suitor to Portia*
THE PRINCE OF ARAGON, *suitor to Portia*
A MESSENGER *to Portia*

SHYLOCK, *a rich Jew*
JESSICA, *his daughter*
TUBAL, *a Jew, Shylock's friend*
LANCELOT GOBBO, *a clown, servant to Shylock and then to Bassanio*
OLD GOBBO, *Lancelot's father*

Magnificoes of Venice, Officers of the Court of Justice, Jailor, Servants to Portia, and other Attendants

SCENE: *Partly at Venice and partly at Belmont, the seat of Portia*]

[1.1]

Enter Antonio, Salerio, and Solanio.

ANTONIO
In sooth, I know not why I am so sad.
It wearies me, you say it wearies you;
But how I caught it, found it, or came by it,
What stuff 'tis made of, whereof it is born,
I am to learn;
And such a want-wit sadness makes of me
That I have much ado to know myself.

SALERIO
Your mind is tossing on the ocean,
There where your argosies with portly sail,
Like signors and rich burghers on the flood,
Or as it were the pageants of the sea,
Do overpeer the petty traffickers
That curtsy to them, do them reverence,
As they fly by them with their woven wings.

SOLANIO
Believe me, sir, had I such venture forth,
The better part of my affections would

1.1. Location: A street in Venice.
1 In sooth Truly. **sad** morose, dismal-looking. **5 am to learn** have yet to learn **6 such . . . of me** such sadness makes me so distracted, lacking in good sense

9 argosies large merchant ships. (So named from *Ragusa*, the modern city of Dubrovnik.) **portly** majestic **10 signors** gentlemen. **flood** sea **11 pageants** mobile stages used in plays or processions **12 overpeer** look down upon **13 curtsy** i.e., bob up and down, or lower topsails in token of respect (*reverence*) **14 woven wings** canvas sails. **15 venture forth** investment at risk

Be with my hopes abroad. I should be still 17
Plucking the grass to know where sits the wind,
Peering in maps for ports and piers and roads; 19
And every object that might make me fear
Misfortune to my ventures, out of doubt
Would make me sad.

SALERIO
My wind cooling my broth
Would blow me to an ague when I thought 23
What harm a wind too great might do at sea.
I should not see the sandy hourglass run
But I should think of shallows and of flats, 26
And see my wealthy *Andrew* docked in sand, 27
Vailing her high-top lower than her ribs 28
To kiss her burial. Should I go to church 29
And see the holy edifice of stone
And not bethink me straight of dangerous rocks 31
Which, touching but my gentle vessel's side,
Would scatter all her spices on the stream,
Enrobe the roaring waters with my silks,
And, in a word, but even now worth this, 35
And now worth nothing? Shall I have the thought
To think on this, and shall I lack the thought
That such a thing bechanced would make me sad? 38
But tell not me. I know Antonio
Is sad to think upon his merchandise.

ANTONIO
Believe me, no. I thank my fortune for it,
My ventures are not in one bottom trusted, 42
Nor to one place; nor is my whole estate
Upon the fortune of this present year. 44
Therefore my merchandise makes me not sad.

SOLANIO
Why then, you are in love.

ANTONIO
Fie, fie!

SOLANIO
Not in love neither? Then let us say you are sad
Because you are not merry; and 'twere as easy
For you to laugh and leap, and say you are merry
Because you are not sad. Now, by two-headed
Janus, 50
Nature hath framed strange fellows in her time: 51
Some that will evermore peep through their eyes 52
And laugh like parrots at a bagpiper, 53
And other of such vinegar aspect 54
That they'll not show their teeth in way of smile
Though Nestor swear the jest be laughable. 56

Enter Bassanio, Lorenzo, and Gratiano.

Here comes Bassanio, your most noble kinsman,
Gratiano, and Lorenzo. Fare ye well.
We leave you now with better company.

SALERIO
I would have stayed till I had made you merry,
If worthier friends had not prevented me. 61

ANTONIO
Your worth is very dear in my regard.
I take it your own business calls on you,
And you embrace th'occasion to depart. 64

SALERIO Good morrow, my good lords.

BASSANIO
Good signors both, when shall we laugh? Say,
when? 66
You grow exceeding strange. Must it be so? 67

SALERIO
We'll make our leisures to attend on yours. 68

Exeunt Salerio and Solanio.

LORENZO
My lord Bassanio, since you have found Antonio,
We two will leave you, but at dinnertime,
I pray you, have in mind where we must meet.

BASSANIO I will not fail you.

GRATIANO
You look not well, Signor Antonio.
You have too much respect upon the world. 74
They lose it that do buy it with much care.
Believe me, you are marvelously changed.

ANTONIO
I hold the world but as the world, Gratiano—
A stage where every man must play a part,
And mine a sad one.

GRATIANO
Let me play the fool.
With mirth and laughter let old wrinkles come,
And let my liver rather heat with wine 81
Than my heart cool with mortifying groans. 82
Why should a man whose blood is warm within
Sit like his grandsire cut in alabaster? 84
Sleep when he wakes, and creep into the jaundice 85
By being peevish? I tell thee what, Antonio—
I love thee, and 'tis my love that speaks—
There are a sort of men whose visages
Do cream and mantle like a standing pond, 89
And do a willful stillness entertain 90
With purpose to be dressed in an opinion 91
Of wisdom, gravity, profound conceit, 92
As who should say, "I am Sir Oracle, 93

17 still continually **19 roads** anchorages, open harbors **23 blow . . . ague** i.e., start me shivering **26 flats** shoals **27 *Andrew*** name of a ship. (Perhaps after the *St. Andrew*, a Spanish galleon captured at Cadiz in 1596.) **28 Vailing** lowering. (Usually as a sign of submission.) **high-top** topmast **29 burial** burial place. **31 bethink me straight** be put in mind immediately **35 even now** a short while ago. **this** i.e., the cargo of spices and silks **38 bechanced** having happened **42 bottom** ship's hold **44 Upon . . . year** i.e., risked upon the chance of the present year. **50 two-headed Janus** a Roman god of all beginnings, represented by a figure with two faces **51 framed** fashioned **52 peep . . . eyes** i.e., look with eyes narrowed by laughter **53 at a bagpiper** i.e., even at a bagpiper, whose music was regarded as melancholic **54 other** others. **vinegar aspect** sour, sullen looks **56 Nestor** venerable senior officer in the *Iliad*, noted for gravity

61 prevented forestalled **64 th'occasion** the opportunity **66 laugh** i.e., be merry together. **67 strange** distant. **Must it be so**? Must you go? or, Must you show reserve? **68 We'll . . . yours** We'll adjust our spare time to accommodate your schedule. **74 respect . . . world** concern for worldly affairs of business. **81 heat with wine** (The liver was regarded as the seat of the passions and wine as an agency for inflaming them.) **82 mortifying** penitential and deadly. (Sighs were thought to cost the heart a drop of blood.) **84 in alabaster** i.e., in a stone effigy upon a tomb. **85 jaundice** (Regarded as arising from the effects of too much choler or yellow bile, one of the four humors, in the blood.) **89 cream and mantle** become covered with scum, i.e., acquire a lifeless, stiff expression. **standing** stagnant **90–2 And . . . conceit** and who maintain a willful silence in order to acquire a reputation for gravity and deep thought **93 As . . . say** as if to say

And when I ope my lips let no dog bark!"
Oh, my Antonio, I do know of these
That therefore only are reputed wise
For saying nothing, when, I am very sure,
If they should speak, would almost damn those ears
Which, hearing them, would call their brothers fools.
I'll tell thee more of this another time.
But fish not with this melancholy bait
For this fool gudgeon, this opinion.—
Come, good Lorenzo.—Fare ye well awhile.
I'll end my exhortation after dinner.

LORENZO [*to Antonio and Bassanio*]
Well, we will leave you then till dinnertime.
I must be one of these same dumb wise men,
For Gratiano never lets me speak.

GRATIANO
Well, keep me company but two years more,
Thou shalt not know the sound of thine own tongue.

ANTONIO
Fare you well. I'll grow a talker for this gear.

GRATIANO
Thanks, i'faith, for silence is only commendable
In a neat's tongue dried and a maid not vendible.
Exeunt [*Gratiano and Lorenzo*].

ANTONIO Is that anything now?

BASSANIO Gratiano speaks an infinite deal of nothing, more than any man in all Venice. His reasons are as two grains of wheat hid in two bushels of chaff; you shall seek all day ere you find them, and when you have them they are not worth the search.

ANTONIO
Well, tell me now what lady is the same
To whom you swore a secret pilgrimage,
That you today promised to tell me of.

BASSANIO
'Tis not unknown to you, Antonio,
How much I have disabled mine estate
By something showing a more swelling port
Than my faint means would grant continuance.
Nor do I now make moan to be abridged
From such a noble rate; but my chief care
Is to come fairly off from the great debts
Wherein my time, something too prodigal,
Hath left me gaged. To you, Antonio,
I owe the most, in money and in love,
And from your love I have a warranty
To unburden all my plots and purposes
How to get clear of all the debts I owe.

ANTONIO
I pray you, good Bassanio, let me know it;
And if it stand, as you yourself still do,
Within the eye of honor, be assured
My purse, my person, my extremest means
Lie all unlocked to your occasions.

BASSANIO
In my schooldays, when I had lost one shaft,
I shot his fellow of the selfsame flight
The selfsame way with more advisèd watch
To find the other forth, and by adventuring both
I oft found both. I urge this childhood proof
Because what follows is pure innocence.
I owe you much, and, like a willful youth,
That which I owe is lost; but if you please
To shoot another arrow that self way
Which you did shoot the first, I do not doubt,
As I will watch the aim, or to find both
Or bring your latter hazard back again
And thankfully rest debtor for the first.

ANTONIO
You know me well, and herein spend but time
To wind about my love with circumstance;
And out of doubt you do me now more wrong
In making question of my uttermost
Than if you had made waste of all I have.
Then do but say to me what I should do
That in your knowledge may by me be done,
And I am prest unto it. Therefore speak.

BASSANIO
In Belmont is a lady richly left;
And she is fair and, fairer than that word,
Of wondrous virtues. Sometimes from her eyes
I did receive fair speechless messages.
Her name is Portia, nothing undervalued
To Cato's daughter, Brutus' Portia.
Nor is the wide world ignorant of her worth,
For the four winds blow in from every coast
Renownèd suitors, and her sunny locks
Hang on her temples like a golden fleece,
Which makes her seat of Belmont Colchis' strand,
And many Jasons come in quest of her.
Oh, my Antonio, had I but the means
To hold a rival place with one of them,

94 let . . . bark i.e., let no creature dare to interrupt me. **98–9 would . . . fools** i.e., would virtually condemn their hearers into calling them fools. (Compare Matthew 5:22, in which anyone calling another a fool is threatened with damnation.) **101–2 fish . . . opinion** i.e., don't go fishing for a reputation of being wise, using your melancholy silence as the bait to fool people. (*Gudgeon*, a small fish, was thought of as a type of gullibility.) **106 dumb** mute, speechless **108 keep** if you keep **110 for this gear** in view of what you say. **112 neat's** ox's. **not vendible** i.e., not yet salable in the marriage market. **113 Is . . . now?** i.e., Was all that talk about anything? **115 reasons** reasonable ideas **119 the same** i.e., the one **124 By . . . port** by showing a somewhat more lavish style of living **125 grant continuance** allow to continue. **126–7 make . . . rate** complain at being cut back from such a high style of living **128 to . . . off** honorably to extricate myself **129 time** youthful lifetime **130 gaged** pledged, in pawn.

132 warranty authorization **133 unburden** disclose **136–7 if . . . honor** if it looks honorable, as your conduct has always done **140 shaft** arrow **141 his** its. **selfsame flight** same kind and range **142 advisèd** careful **143 forth** out. **adventuring** risking **145 innocence** ingenuousness, sincerity. **148 self** same **150 or** either **151 hazard** that which was risked **152 rest** remain **153 spend but time** only waste time **154 To . . . circumstance** i.e., in not asking plainly what you want. (*Circumstance* here means "circumlocution.") **156 In . . . uttermost** in showing any doubt of my intention to do all I can **160 prest** ready **161 richly left** left a large fortune (by her father's will) **163 Sometimes** Once **165–6 nothing undervalued To** of no less worth than **166 Portia** (The same Portia as in Shakespeare's *Julius Caesar*.) **171 Colchis'** (Jason adventured for the golden fleece in the land of Colchis, on the Black Sea.) **strand** shore

I have a mind presages me such thrift
That I should questionless be fortunate.

ANTONIO
Thou know'st that all my fortunes are at sea;
Neither have I money nor commodity
To raise a present sum. Therefore go forth.
Try what my credit can in Venice do;
That shall be racked even to the uttermost
To furnish thee to Belmont, to fair Portia.
Go presently inquire, and so will I,
Where money is, and I no question make
To have it of my trust or for my sake. *Exeunt.*

✤

[1.2]

Enter Portia with her waiting woman, Nerissa.

PORTIA By my troth, Nerissa, my little body is aweary of this great world.

NERISSA You would be, sweet madam, if your miseries were in the same abundance as your good fortunes are; and yet, for aught I see, they are as sick that surfeit with too much as they that starve with nothing. It is no mean happiness, therefore, to be seated in the mean. Superfluity comes sooner by white hairs, but competency lives longer.

PORTIA Good sentences, and well pronounced.

NERISSA They would be better if well followed.

PORTIA If to do were as easy as to know what were good to do, chapels had been churches and poor men's cottages princes' palaces. It is a good divine that follows his own instructions. I can easier teach twenty what were good to be done than to be one of the twenty to follow mine own teaching. The brain may devise laws for the blood, but a hot temper leaps o'er a cold decree; such a hare is madness, the youth, to skip o'er the meshes of good counsel, the cripple. But this reasoning is not in the fashion to choose me a husband. Oh, me, the word "choose"! I may neither choose who I would nor refuse who I dislike; so is the will of a living daughter curbed by the will of a dead father. Is it not hard, Nerissa, that I cannot choose one nor refuse none?

NERISSA Your father was ever virtuous, and holy men at their death have good inspirations; therefore the lottery that he hath devised in these three chests of gold, silver, and lead, whereof who chooses his meaning chooses you, will no doubt never be chosen by any rightly but one who you shall rightly love. But what warmth is there in your affection towards any of these princely suitors that are already come?

PORTIA I pray thee, overname them, and as thou namest them I will describe them; and according to my description level at my affection.

NERISSA First, there is the Neapolitan prince.

PORTIA Ay, that's a colt indeed, for he doth nothing but talk of his horse, and he makes it a great appropriation to his own good parts that he can shoe him himself. I am much afeard my lady his mother played false with a smith.

NERISSA Then is there the County Palatine.

PORTIA He doth nothing but frown, as who should say, "An you will not have me, choose." He hears merry tales and smiles not. I fear he will prove the weeping philosopher when he grows old, being so full of unmannerly sadness in his youth. I had rather be married to a death's-head with a bone in his mouth than to either of these. God defend me from these two!

NERISSA How say you by the French lord, Monsieur Le Bon?

PORTIA God made him, and therefore let him pass for a man. In truth, I know it is a sin to be a mocker, but he! Why, he hath a horse better than the Neapolitan's, a better bad habit of frowning than the Count Palatine; he is every man in no man. If a throstle sing, he falls straight a-capering. He will fence with his own shadow. If I should marry him, I should marry twenty husbands. If he would despise me, I would forgive him, for if he love me to madness, I shall never requite him.

NERISSA What say you, then, to Falconbridge, the young baron of England?

PORTIA You know I say nothing to him, for he understands not me, nor I him. He hath neither Latin, French, nor Italian, and you will come into the court and swear that I have a poor pennyworth in the English. He is a proper man's picture, but alas, who can converse with a dumb show? How oddly he is suited! I think he bought his doublet in Italy, his round hose

175 presages i.e., that presages. **thrift** profit and good fortune **178 commodity** merchandise **179 a present sum** ready money. **181 racked** stretched **183 presently** immediately **184 no question make** have no doubt **185 of my trust** on the basis of my credit as a merchant. **sake** i.e., personal sake.
1.2. Location: Belmont. Portia's house.
1 troth faith **3 would be** would have reason to be (weary) **5 surfeit** overindulge **7 mean** small. (With a pun; see next note.) **7–8 in the mean** having neither too much nor too little. **8 comes sooner by** acquires sooner **9 competency** modest means **10 sentences** maxims. **pronounced** delivered. **14 divine** clergyman **18 blood** (Thought of as a chief agent of the passions, which in turn were regarded as the enemies of reason.) **20 meshes** nets. (Used here for hunting hares.) **good counsel, the cripple** (Wisdom is portrayed as old and no longer agile.) **20–2 But . . . husband** But this talk is not the way to help me choose a husband. **24 will . . . will** volition . . . testament

30 who whoever. **his** i.e., the father's **32 rightly . . . rightly** correctly . . . truly **35 overname them** name them over **37 level** aim, guess **39 colt** i.e., wanton and foolish young man. (With a punning appropriateness to his interest in horses.) **40 appropriation** addition **41 good parts** accomplishments **44 County Palatine** a count entitled to supreme jurisdiction in his province. **45 as who should say** as one might say **46 An** If. **choose** i.e., do as you please. **47–8 the weeping philosopher** i.e., Heraclitus of Ephesus, a melancholic and retiring philosopher of about 500 B.C., often contrasted with Democritus, the "laughing philosopher" **49 sadness** melancholy **52 How . . . by** What do you have to say about **58 he is . . . no man** i.e., he borrows aspects from everyone but has no character of his own. **throstle** thrush **59 straight** at once **62 if** even if **64 say you . . . to** do you say about. (But Portia wittily puns, in her reply, on the literal sense of "speak to.") **68–70 come . . . English** i.e., bear witness that I can speak very little English. **70 He . . . picture** i.e., He looks handsome **71 dumb show** pantomime. **suited** dressed. **72 doublet** upper garment corresponding to a jacket. **round hose** short, puffed-out breeches

in France, his bonnet in Germany, and his behavior everywhere.

NERISSA What think you of the Scottish lord, his neighbor?

PORTIA That he hath a neighborly charity in him, for he borrowed a box of the ear of the Englishman and swore he would pay him again when he was able. I think the Frenchman became his surety and sealed under for another.

NERISSA How like you the young German, the Duke of Saxony's nephew?

PORTIA Very vilely in the morning, when he is sober, and most vilely in the afternoon, when he is drunk. When he is best he is a little worse than a man, and when he is worst he is little better than a beast. An the worst fall that ever fell, I hope I shall make shift to go without him.

NERISSA If he should offer to choose, and choose the right casket, you should refuse to perform your father's will if you should refuse to accept him.

PORTIA Therefore, for fear of the worst, I pray thee, set a deep glass of Rhenish wine on the contrary casket, for if the devil be within and that temptation without, I know he will choose it. I will do anything, Nerissa, ere I will be married to a sponge.

NERISSA You need not fear, lady, the having any of these lords. They have acquainted me with their determinations, which is indeed to return to their home and to trouble you with no more suit, unless you may be won by some other sort than your father's imposition depending on the caskets.

PORTIA If I live to be as old as Sibylla, I will die as chaste as Diana, unless I be obtained by the manner of my father's will. I am glad this parcel of wooers are so reasonable, for there is not one among them but I dote on his very absence, and I pray God grant them a fair departure.

NERISSA Do you not remember, lady, in your father's time, a Venetian, a scholar and a soldier, that came hither in company of the Marquess of Montferrat?

PORTIA Yes, yes, it was Bassanio—as I think, so was he called.

NERISSA True, madam. He, of all the men that ever my foolish eyes looked upon was the best deserving a fair lady.

PORTIA I remember him well, and I remember him worthy of thy praise.

Enter a Servingman.

How now, what news?

SERVINGMAN The four strangers seek for you, madam, to take their leave; and there is a forerunner come from a fifth, the Prince of Morocco, who brings word the Prince his master will be here tonight.

PORTIA If I could bid the fifth welcome with so good heart as I can bid the other four farewell, I should be glad of his approach. If he have the condition of a saint and the complexion of a devil, I had rather he should shrive me than wive me.
Come, Nerissa. [*To Servingman*] Sirrah, go before.
Whiles we shut the gate upon one wooer, another
knocks at the door. *Exeunt.*

[1.3]

Enter Bassanio with Shylock the Jew.

SHYLOCK Three thousand ducats, well.

BASSANIO Ay, sir, for three months.

SHYLOCK For three months, well.

BASSANIO For the which, as I told you, Antonio shall be bound.

SHYLOCK Antonio shall become bound, well.

BASSANIO May you stead me? Will you pleasure me? Shall I know your answer?

SHYLOCK Three thousand ducats for three months and Antonio bound.

BASSANIO Your answer to that.

SHYLOCK Antonio is a good man.

BASSANIO Have you heard any imputation to the contrary?

SHYLOCK Ho, no, no, no, no! My meaning in saying he is a good man is to have you understand me that he is sufficient. Yet his means are in supposition. He hath an argosy bound to Tripolis, another to the Indies. I understand, moreover, upon the Rialto, he hath a third at Mexico, a fourth for England, and other ventures he hath squandered abroad. But ships are but boards, sailors but men. There be land rats and water rats, water thieves and land thieves—I mean pirates—and then there is the peril of waters, winds, and rocks. The man is, notwithstanding, sufficient. Three thousand ducats. I think I may take his bond.

BASSANIO Be assured you may.

SHYLOCK I will be assured I may; and that I may be assured, I will bethink me. May I speak with Antonio?

73 bonnet hat **78 borrowed** received. (But with a play on the idea of something that must be repaid.) **80–1 became . . . another** offered to back up the Scottish lord and promised (with as solemn a vow as if he were signing and sealing a document) to add a blow of his own. (An allusion to the age-old alliance of the French and the Scots against the English.) **87 An** If **88 fall** befall. **make shift** manage **90 offer** undertake **94 Rhenish wine** a German white wine from the Rhine Valley. **contrary** i.e., wrong **95 if** even if **96 it** i.e., the tempting red wine. **102 sort** means. (With perhaps a suggestion too of "casting or drawing of lots.") **102–3 imposition** command, charge **104 Sibylla** the Cumaean Sibyl, to whom Apollo gave as many years as there were grains in her handful of sand **105 Diana** goddess of chastity and of the hunt **106 parcel** assembly, group

121 four (Nerissa actually names six suitors; possibly a sign of revision or the author's early draft.) **122 forerunner** herald **127 condition** disposition, character **128 complexion of a devil** (Devils were thought to be black; but *complexion* can also mean "temperament," "disposition.") **129 shrive me** pardon me, excuse me from having to be wooed. (Literally, act as my confessor and give absolution.) **130 Sirrah** (Form of address to social inferior.)
1.3. Location: Venice. A public place.
1 ducats gold coins **7 stead** supply, assist. **pleasure** oblige **12 good** (Shylock means "solvent," a good credit risk; Bassanio interprets it in the moral sense.) **17 sufficient** i.e., a good security. **in supposition** doubtful, uncertain. **19 the Rialto** the merchants' exchange in Venice and the center of commercial activity **21 squandered** scattered **27, 28 assured** (Bassanio means that Shylock may trust Antonio, whereas Shylock means that he will obtain legal assurances.)

BASSANIO If it please you to dine with us.

SHYLOCK Yes, to smell pork, to eat of the habitation which your prophet the Nazarite conjured the devil into. I will buy with you, sell with you, talk with you, walk with you, and so following, but I will not eat with you, drink with you, nor pray with you. What news on the Rialto? Who is he comes here?

Enter Antonio.

BASSANIO This is Signor Antonio.

SHYLOCK [*aside*]
How like a fawning publican he looks!
I hate him for he is a Christian,
But more for that in low simplicity
He lends out money gratis and brings down
The rate of usance here with us in Venice.
If I can catch him once upon the hip,
I will feed fat the ancient grudge I bear him.
He hates our sacred nation, and he rails,
Even there where merchants most do congregate,
On me, my bargains, and my well-won thrift,
Which he calls interest. Cursèd be my tribe
If I forgive him!

BASSANIO Shylock, do you hear?

SHYLOCK I am debating of my present store,
And, by the near guess of my memory,
I cannot instantly raise up the gross
Of full three thousand ducats. What of that?
Tubal, a wealthy Hebrew of my tribe,
Will furnish me. But soft, how many months
Do you desire? [*To Antonio*] Rest you fair, good signor!
Your Worship was the last man in our mouths.

ANTONIO
Shylock, albeit I neither lend nor borrow
By taking nor by giving of excess,
Yet, to supply the ripe wants of my friend,
I'll break a custom. [*To Bassanio*] Is he yet possessed
How much ye would?

SHYLOCK Ay, ay, three thousand ducats.

ANTONIO And for three months.

SHYLOCK
I had forgot—three months, you told me so.
Well then, your bond. And let me see—but hear you,
Methought you said you neither lend nor borrow
Upon advantage.

ANTONIO I do never use it.

SHYLOCK
When Jacob grazed his uncle Laban's sheep—
This Jacob from our holy Abram was,
As his wise mother wrought in his behalf,
The third possessor; ay, he was the third—

ANTONIO
And what of him? Did he take interest?

SHYLOCK
No, not take interest, not as you would say
Directly interest. Mark what Jacob did.
When Laban and himself were compromised
That all the eanlings which were streaked and pied
Should fall as Jacob's hire, the ewes, being rank,
In end of autumn turnèd to the rams,
And when the work of generation was
Between these woolly breeders in the act,
The skillful shepherd peeled me certain wands,
And in the doing of the deed of kind
He stuck them up before the fulsome ewes,
Who then conceiving did in eaning time
Fall parti-colored lambs, and those were Jacob's.
This was a way to thrive, and he was blest;
And thrift is blessing, if men steal it not.

ANTONIO
This was a venture, sir, that Jacob served for,
A thing not in his power to bring to pass,
But swayed and fashioned by the hand of heaven.
Was this inserted to make interest good?
Or is your gold and silver ewes and rams?

SHYLOCK
I cannot tell. I make it breed as fast.
But note me, signor—

ANTONIO Mark you this, Bassanio,
The devil can cite Scripture for his purpose.
An evil soul producing holy witness
Is like a villain with a smiling cheek,
A goodly apple rotten at the heart.
Oh, what a goodly outside falsehood hath!

SHYLOCK
Three thousand ducats. 'Tis a good round sum.
Three months from twelve, then let me see, the rate—

ANTONIO
Well, Shylock, shall we be beholding to you?

SHYLOCK
Signor Antonio, many a time and oft
In the Rialto you have rated me
About my moneys and my usances.
Still have I borne it with a patient shrug,

32 Nazarite Nazarene. (For the reference to Christ's casting evil spirits into a herd of swine, see Matthew 8:30–2, Mark 5:1–13, and Luke 8:32–3.) **34 so following** so forth **38 publican** Roman tax gatherer (a term of opprobrium; see Luke 18:9–14); or, innkeeper **39 for** because **40 low simplicity** humble foolishness **41 gratis** without charging interest **42 usance** usury, interest **43 upon the hip** i.e., at my mercy. (A figure of speech from wrestling; see Genesis 32:24–9.) **44 fat** until fatted for the kill **45 our sacred nation** i.e., the Hebrew people **50 I am . . . store** I am considering my current supply of money **52 gross** total **55 soft** i.e., wait a minute **57 Your . . . mouths** i.e., We were just speaking of you. (But with ominous connotation of devouring; compare line 44.) **59 excess** interest **60 ripe wants** pressing needs **61 possessed** informed **62 ye would** you want. **68 advantage** interest.

69 Jacob (See Genesis 27, 30:25–43.) **70 Abram** Abraham **72 third** i.e., after Abraham and Isaac. **possessor** i.e., of the birthright of which, with the help of Rebecca, he was able to cheat Esau, his elder brother **76 compromised** agreed **77 eanlings** young lambs or kids. **pied** spotted **78 hire** wages, share. **rank** in heat **80 work of generation** mating **82 peeled . . . wands** i.e., partly stripped the bark of some sticks. (*Me* is used colloquially.) **83 deed of kind** i.e., copulation **84 fulsome** lustful, well-fed **85 eaning** lambing **86 Fall** give birth to **88 thrift** thriving, profit **89 venture . . . for** uncertain commercial venture on which Jacob risked his wages **92 inserted . . . good** brought in to justify the practice of usury. **94 I cannot tell** i.e., I don't know about that. **96 devil . . . Scripture** (See Matthew 4:6.) **103 beholding** beholden, indebted **105 rated** berated, rebuked

For sufferance is the badge of all our tribe.
You call me misbeliever, cutthroat dog,
And spit upon my Jewish gaberdine,
And all for use of that which is mine own.
Well then, it now appears you need my help.
Go to, then. You come to me and you say,
"Shylock, we would have moneys"—you say so,
You, that did void your rheum upon my beard
And foot me as you spurn a stranger cur
Over your threshold. Moneys is your suit.
What should I say to you? Should I not say,
"Hath a dog money? Is it possible
A cur can lend three thousand ducats?" Or
Shall I bend low, and in a bondman's key,
With bated breath and whispering humbleness,
Say this:
"Fair sir, you spit on me on Wednesday last,
You spurned me such a day, another time
You called me dog, and for these courtesies
I'll lend you thus much moneys"?

ANTONIO
I am as like to call thee so again,
To spit on thee again, to spurn thee too.
If thou wilt lend this money, lend it not
As to thy friends, for when did friendship take
A breed for barren metal of his friend?
But lend it rather to thine enemy,
Who, if he break, thou mayst with better face
Exact the penalty.

SHYLOCK Why, look you how you storm!
I would be friends with you and have your love,
Forget the shames that you have stained me with,
Supply your present wants, and take no doit
Of usance for my moneys, and you'll not hear me.
This is kind I offer.

BASSANIO This were kindness.

SHYLOCK This kindness will I show.
Go with me to a notary, seal me there
Your single bond; and, in a merry sport,
If you repay me not on such a day,
In such a place, such sum or sums as are
Expressed in the condition, let the forfeit
Be nominated for an equal pound
Of your fair flesh, to be cut off and taken
In what part of your body pleaseth me.

ANTONIO
Content, in faith. I'll seal to such a bond
And say there is much kindness in the Jew.

BASSANIO
You shall not seal to such a bond for me!
I'll rather dwell in my necessity.

ANTONIO
Why, fear not, man, I will not forfeit it.
Within these two months—that's a month before
This bond expires—I do expect return
Of thrice three times the value of this bond.

SHYLOCK
O father Abram, what these Christians are,
Whose own hard dealings teaches them suspect
The thoughts of others! Pray you, tell me this:
If he should break his day, what should I gain
By the exaction of the forfeiture?
A pound of man's flesh taken from a man
Is not so estimable, profitable neither,
As flesh of muttons, beefs, or goats. I say
To buy his favor I extend this friendship.
If he will take it, so; if not, adieu.
And for my love, I pray you, wrong me not.

ANTONIO
Yes, Shylock, I will seal unto this bond.

SHYLOCK
Then meet me forthwith at the notary's.
Give him direction for this merry bond,
And I will go and purse the ducats straight,
See to my house, left in the fearful guard
Of an unthrifty knave, and presently
I'll be with you. *Exit.*

ANTONIO Hie thee, gentle Jew.—
The Hebrew will turn Christian; he grows kind.

BASSANIO
I like not fair terms and a villain's mind.

ANTONIO
Come on. In this there can be no dismay;
My ships come home a month before the day.
[Exeunt.]

✤

[2.1]

[Flourish of cornets.] Enter [the Prince of] Morocco, a tawny Moor all in white, and three or four followers accordingly, with Portia, Nerissa, and their train.

MOROCCO
Mislike me not for my complexion,
The shadowed livery of the burnished sun,
To whom I am a neighbor and near bred.
Bring me the fairest creature northward born,
Where Phoebus' fire scarce thaws the icicles,
And let us make incision for your love

108 sufferance endurance **110 gaberdine** loose outer garment like a cape or mantle **113 Go to** (An exclamation of impatience or annoyance.) **115 rheum** spittle **116 spurn** kick **117 suit** request. **121 bondman's key** serf's tone of voice **122 bated** subdued **128 like** likely **132 A breed . . . metal** offspring from money, which cannot naturally breed. (One of the oldest arguments against usury was that it was thereby "unnatural.") **of** from **133 to** as if to **134 Who** from whom. **break** fail to pay on time **138 doit** a Dutch coin of very small value **140 kind** kindly **141 were** would be (if seriously offered) **144 single bond** bond signed alone without other security; unconditional. (Shylock pretends the *condition*, line 147, is only a joke.) **148 nominated for** named, specified as. **equal** exact

154 dwell remain **165 estimable** valuable **168 so** well and good **169 wrong me not** do not think evil of me. **174 fearful** to be mistrusted **176 gentle** gracious, courteous. (With a play on "gentile.")
2.1. Location: Belmont. Portia's house.
0.3 *accordingly* similarly (i.e., dressed in white and dark-skinned like Morocco) **2 shadowed livery** i.e., dark complexion, worn as though it were a costume of the sun's servants **3 near bred** closely related.
5 Phoebus' i.e., the sun's

To prove whose blood is reddest, his or mine.
I tell thee, lady, this aspect of mine
Hath feared the valiant. By my love I swear,
The best-regarded virgins of our clime
Have loved it too. I would not change this hue,
Except to steal your thoughts, my gentle queen.

PORTIA
In terms of choice I am not solely led
By nice direction of a maiden's eyes;
Besides, the lott'ry of my destiny
Bars me the right of voluntary choosing.
But if my father had not scanted me,
And hedged me by his wit to yield myself
His wife who wins me by that means I told you,
Yourself, renownèd prince, then stood as fair
As any comer I have looked on yet
For my affection.

MOROCCO Even for that I thank you.
Therefore, I pray you, lead me to the caskets
To try my fortune. By this scimitar
That slew the Sophy and a Persian prince,
That won three fields of Sultan Solyman,
I would o'erstare the sternest eyes that look,
Outbrave the heart most daring on the earth,
Pluck the young sucking cubs from the she-bear,
Yea, mock the lion when 'a roars for prey,
To win thee, lady. But alas the while!
If Hercules and Lichas play at dice
Which is the better man, the greater throw
May turn by fortune from the weaker hand.
So is Alcides beaten by his page,
And so may I, blind Fortune leading me,
Miss that which one unworthier may attain,
And die with grieving.

PORTIA You must take your chance,
And either not attempt to choose at all
Or swear before you choose, if you choose wrong
Never to speak to lady afterward
In way of marriage. Therefore be advised.

MOROCCO
Nor will not. Come, bring me unto my chance.

PORTIA
First, forward to the temple. After dinner
Your hazard shall be made.

MOROCCO Good fortune then!
To make me blest or cursed'st among men.
[Cornets, and] exeunt.

[2.2]

Enter [Lancelot] the clown, alone.

LANCELOT Certainly my conscience will serve me to run from this Jew my master. The fiend is at mine elbow and tempts me, saying to me, "Gobbo, Lancelot Gobbo, good Lancelot," or "Good Gobbo," or "Good Lancelot Gobbo, use your legs, take the start, run away." My conscience says, "No, take heed, honest Lancelot, take heed, honest Gobbo," or, as aforesaid, "Honest Lancelot Gobbo, do not run; scorn running with thy heels." Well, the most courageous fiend bids me pack. "Fia!" says the fiend. "Away!" says the fiend. "For the heavens, rouse up a brave mind," says the fiend, "and run." Well, my conscience, hanging about the neck of my heart, says very wisely to me, "My honest friend Lancelot, being an honest man's son," or rather an honest woman's son—for indeed my father did something smack, something grow to, he had a kind of taste—well, my conscience says, "Lancelot, budge not." "Budge," says the fiend "Budge not," says my conscience. "Conscience," say I, "you counsel well." "Fiend," say I, "you counsel well." To be ruled by my conscience, I should stay with the Jew my master, who, God bless the mark, is a kind of devil; and to run away from the Jew, I should be ruled by the fiend, who, saving your reverence, is the devil himself. Certainly the Jew is the very devil incarnation; and, in my conscience, my conscience is but a kind of hard conscience to offer to counsel me to stay with the Jew. The fiend gives the more friendly counsel. I will run, fiend. My heels are at your commandment. I will run.

Enter Old Gobbo, with a basket.

GOBBO Master young man, you, I pray you, which is the way to master Jew's?

LANCELOT *[aside]* Oh, heavens, this is my true-begotten father, who, being more than sand-blind, high-gravel-blind, knows me not. I will try confusions with him.

GOBBO Master young gentleman, I pray you, which is the way to master Jew's?

LANCELOT Turn up on your right hand at the next turning, but at the next turning of all on your left; marry, at the very next turning, turn of no hand, but turn down indirectly to the Jew's house.

7 reddest (Red blood was regarded as a sign of courage.) **8 aspect** visage **9 feared** frightened **14 nice direction** careful guidance **17 scanted** limited **18 wit** wisdom **18–19 yield . . . who** give myself to be the wife of him who **20 then . . . fair** would then have looked as attractive and stood as fair a chance. (With a play on "fair-skinned.") **22 For my** of gaining my **25 Sophy** Shah of Persia **26 fields** battles. **Solyman** a Turkish sultan ruling from 1520 to 1566 **27 o'erstare** outstare **30 'a** he **32 Lichas** a page of Hercules (Alcides). See the note for 3.2.55. **42 be advised** take warning, consider. **43 Nor will not** i.e., Nor indeed will I violate the oath. **44 to the temple** i.e., in order to take the oaths.

2.2. Location: Venice. A street.
0.1 *clown* (1) country bumpkin (2) comic type in an Elizabethan acting company **1 serve** permit **9 with thy heels** i.e., emphatically. (With a pun on the literal sense.) **10 pack** begone. **Fia!** i.e., Via, away! **11 For the heavens** i.e., In heaven's name **12–13 hanging . . . heart** i.e., timidly **16–17 did something . . . taste** i.e., had a tendency to lechery **22 God . . . mark** (An expression by way of apology for introducing something potentially offensive, as also in *saving your reverence* in line 24.) **25 incarnation** (Lancelot means "incarnate.") **30 you** (Gobbo uses the formal *you* but switches to the familiar *thou*, line 88, when he accepts Lancelot as his son.) **33 sand-blind** dim-sighted **34 high-gravel-blind** blinder than sand-blind. (A term seemingly invented by Lancelot.) **try confusions** (Lancelot's blunder for "try conclusions," i.e., experiment, though his error is comically apt.) **40 marry** i.e., by the Virgin Mary, indeed. (A mild interjection.) **of no hand** neither right nor left

GOBBO By God's sonties, 'twill be a hard way to hit. Can you tell me whether one Lancelot, that dwells with him, dwell with him or no?

LANCELOT Talk you of young Master Lancelot? [*Aside*] Mark me now; now will I raise the waters.—Talk you of young Master Lancelot?

GOBBO No master, sir, but a poor man's son. His father, though I say't, is an honest exceeding poor man and, God be thanked, well to live.

LANCELOT Well, let his father be what 'a will, we talk of young Master Lancelot.

GOBBO Your Worship's friend, and Lancelot, sir.

LANCELOT But I pray you, ergo, old man, ergo, I beseech you, talk you of young Master Lancelot?

GOBBO Of Lancelot, an't please Your Mastership.

LANCELOT Ergo, Master Lancelot. Talk not of Master Lancelot, father, for the young gentleman, according to Fates and Destinies and such odd sayings, the Sisters Three and such branches of learning, is indeed deceased, or, as you would say in plain terms, gone to heaven.

GOBBO Marry, God forbid! The boy was the very staff of my age, my very prop.

LANCELOT Do I look like a cudgel or a hovel post, a staff, or a prop? Do you know me, father?

GOBBO Alack the day, I know you not, young gentleman. But I pray you, tell me, is my boy, God rest his soul, alive or dead?

LANCELOT Do you not know me, father?

GOBBO Alack, sir, I am sand-blind. I know you not.

LANCELOT Nay, indeed, if you had your eyes you might fail of the knowing me; it is a wise father that knows his own child. Well, old man, I will tell you news of your son. [*He kneels.*] Give me your blessing. Truth will come to light; murder cannot be hid long; a man's son may, but in the end truth will out.

GOBBO Pray you, sir, stand up. I am sure you are not Lancelot, my boy.

LANCELOT Pray you, let's have no more fooling about it, but give me your blessing. I am Lancelot, your boy that was, your son that is, your child that shall be.

GOBBO I cannot think you are my son.

LANCELOT I know not what I shall think of that; but I am Lancelot, the Jew's man, and I am sure Margery your wife is my mother.

GOBBO Her name is Margery indeed. I'll be sworn, if thou be Lancelot, thou art mine own flesh and blood. Lord worshiped might he be, what a beard hast thou got! Thou hast got more hair on thy chin than Dobbin my fill horse has on his tail.

LANCELOT [*rising*] It should seem then that Dobbin's tail grows backward. I am sure he had more hair of his tail than I have of my face when I last saw him.

GOBBO Lord, how art thou changed! How dost thou and thy master agree? I have brought him a present. How 'gree you now?

LANCELOT Well, well; but for mine own part, as I have set up my rest to run away, so I will not rest till I have run some ground. My master's a very Jew. Give him a present? Give him a halter! I am famished in his service; you may tell every finger I have with my ribs. Father, I am glad you are come. Give me your present to one Master Bassanio, who indeed gives rare new liveries. If I serve not him, I will run as far as God has any ground. Oh, rare fortune! Here comes the man. To him, father, for I am a Jew if I serve the Jew any longer.

Enter Bassanio, with [*Leonardo and*] *a follower or two.*

BASSANIO You may do so, but let it be so hasted that supper be ready at the farthest by five of the clock. See these letters delivered, put the liveries to making, and desire Gratiano to come anon to my lodging.

[*Exit a Servant.*]

LANCELOT To him, father.

GOBBO [*advancing*] God bless Your Worship!

BASSANIO Gramercy. Wouldst thou aught with me?

GOBBO Here's my son, sir, a poor boy—

LANCELOT Not a poor boy, sir, but the rich Jew's man, that would, sir, as my father shall specify—

GOBBO He hath a great infection, sir, as one would say, to serve—

LANCELOT Indeed, the short and the long is, I serve the Jew, and have a desire, as my father shall specify—

GOBBO His master and he, saving Your Worship's reverence, are scarce cater-cousins—

LANCELOT To be brief, the very truth is that the Jew, having done me wrong, doth cause me, as my father, being, I hope, an old man, shall frutify unto you—

GOBBO I have here a dish of doves that I would bestow upon Your Worship, and my suit is—

LANCELOT In very brief, the suit is impertinent to myself, as Your Worship shall know by this honest old man, and, though I say it, though old man, yet poor man, my father.

42 sonties little saints **46 raise the waters** i.e., start tears. **48 master** (The title was applied to gentlefolk only.) **50 well to live** prospering, in good health. **51 'a** he **53 Your . . . Lancelot** (Again, Old Gobbo denies that Lancelot is entitled to be called "Master.") **54 ergo** therefore. (But Lancelot may use this Latin word with no particular meaning in mind.) **58 father** (1) old man (2) father **59–60 the Sisters Three** the three Fates **65 hovel post** post holding up a hovel or open shed **73–4 it is . . . child** (Reverses the proverb "It is a wise child that knows his own father.") **81–2 your . . . shall be** (Echoes the *Gloria* from the Book of Common Prayer: "As it was in the beginning, is now, and ever shall be.") **89 beard** (Stage tradition has Old Gobbo mistaking Lancelot's long hair for a beard.) **91 fill horse** cart horse

93 grows backward grows at the wrong end. **94 of** on **99 set up my rest** determined, risked all. (A metaphor from the card game *primero*, in which a final wager is made, with a pun also on *rest* as "place of residence.") **not rest** i.e., not stop running. (More punning on *rest*.) **100 very** veritable. **Jew** (1) Hebrew (2) grasping old usurer. **101 halter** hangman's noose. **102 tell** count. **tell . . . ribs** (Comically reverses the usual saying of counting one's ribs with one's fingers.) **103 Give me** Give. (*Me* suggests "on my behalf.") **104 rare** splendid **105 liveries** uniforms or costumes for servants. **107 a Jew** i.e., a villain. (Punning on the literal sense in *the Jew*. Compare with line 100.) **108 hasted** hastened, hurried **109 farthest** latest **114 Gramercy** Many thanks. **aught** anything **115 poor** (1) unfortunate (2) penniless (contrasted with *rich* in the next line) **118 infection** (Blunder for "affection" or "inclination.") **123 cater-cousins** good friends **126 frutify** (Lancelot may be trying to say "fructify," but he means "certify" or "notify.") **129 impertinent** (Blunder for "pertinent.")

BASSANIO One speak for both. What would you?
LANCELOT Serve you, sir.
GOBBO That is the very defect of the matter, sir. 135
BASSANIO
I know thee well; thou hast obtained thy suit.
Shylock thy master spoke with me this day,
And hath preferred thee, if it be preferment 138
To leave a rich Jew's service to become
The follower of so poor a gentleman.

LANCELOT The old proverb is very well parted be- 141
tween my master Shylock and you, sir: you have the
grace of God, sir, and he hath enough.

BASSANIO
Thou speak'st it well. Go, father, with thy son.
Take leave of thy old master, and inquire
My lodging out. [*To a Servant*] Give him a livery
More guarded than his fellows'. See it done. 147

LANCELOT Father, in. I cannot get a service, no! I have
ne'er a tongue in my head, well! [*He looks at his palm.*]
If any man in Italy have a fairer table which doth offer 150
to swear upon a book, I shall have good fortune. Go 151
to, here's a simple line of life. Here's a small trifle of 152
wives! Alas, fifteen wives is nothing. Eleven widows
and nine maids is a simple coming-in for one man. 154
And then to scape drowning thrice, and to be in peril
of my life with the edge of a feather bed! Here are 156
simple scapes. Well, if Fortune be a woman, she's a 157
good wench for this gear. Father, come. I'll take my 158
leave of the Jew in the twinkling.

Exit clown [*Lancelot, with Old Gobbo*].

BASSANIO [*giving Leonardo a list*]
I pray thee, good Leonardo, think on this:
These things being bought and orderly bestowed, 161
Return in haste, for I do feast tonight 162
My best-esteemed acquaintance. Hie thee, go.

LEONARDO
My best endeavors shall be done herein.
[*He starts to leave.*]

Enter Gratiano.

GRATIANO [*to Leonardo*]
Where's your master?
LEONARDO Yonder, sir, he walks.
Exit Leonardo.

GRATIANO Signor Bassanio!
BASSANIO Gratiano!
GRATIANO
I have a suit to you.
BASSANIO You have obtained it.
GRATIANO You must not deny me. I must go with you
to Belmont.

BASSANIO
Why, then you must. But hear thee, Gratiano;
Thou art too wild, too rude and bold of voice—
Parts that become thee happily enough, 173
And in such eyes as ours appear not faults,
But where thou art not known, why, there they show
Something too liberal. Pray thee, take pain 176
To allay with some cold drops of modesty 177
Thy skipping spirit, lest through thy wild behavior
I be misconstered in the place I go to 179
And lose my hopes.

GRATIANO Signor Bassanio, hear me:
If I do not put on a sober habit, 181
Talk with respect and swear but now and then,
Wear prayer books in my pocket, look demurely,
Nay more, while grace is saying, hood mine eyes 184
Thus with my hat, and sigh and say "amen,"
Use all the observance of civility,
Like one well studied in a sad ostent 187
To please his grandam, never trust me more. 188

BASSANIO Well, we shall see your bearing.
GRATIANO
Nay, but I bar tonight. You shall not gauge me
By what we do tonight.
BASSANIO No, that were pity.
I would entreat you rather to put on
Your boldest suit of mirth, for we have friends
That purpose merriment. But fare you well;
I have some business.

GRATIANO
And I must to Lorenzo and the rest,
But we will visit you at suppertime. *Exeunt.*

✤

[2.3]

Enter Jessica and [*Lancelot*] *the clown.*

JESSICA
I am sorry thou wilt leave my father so.
Our house is hell, and thou, a merry devil,
Didst rob it of some taste of tediousness.
But fare thee well. There is a ducat for thee.
[*Giving money.*]
And, Lancelot, soon at supper shalt thou see
Lorenzo, who is thy new master's guest.
Give him this letter; do it secretly. [*Giving a letter.*]
And so farewell. I would not have my father
See me in talk with thee.

135 defect (Blunder for "effect," i.e., "purport.") **138 preferred** recommended **141 proverb** i.e., "He who has the grace of God has enough." **parted** divided **147 guarded** trimmed with braided ornament **150 table** palm of the hand. (Lancelot now reads the lines of his palm.) **151 book** i.e., Bible. (The image is of a hand being laid on the Bible to take an oath.) **151–2 Go to** (An expression of impatience.) **152 simple** unremarkable. (Said ironically.) **line of life** curved line at the base of the thumb. **154 simple coming-in** modest beginning or income. (With sexual suggestion.) **156 feather bed** (Suggesting marriage bed or love bed; Lancelot sees sexual adventure and the dangers of marriage in his palm reading.) **157 scapes** 1) adventures (2) transgressions. **Fortune . . . woman** (Fortune was personified as a goddess.) **158 gear** matter. **161 bestowed** i.e., stowed on board ship **162 feast** give a feast for

173 Parts qualities **176 liberal** free of manner. (Often with sexual connotation.) **177 allay** temper, moderate. **modesty** decorum **179 misconstered** misconstrued **181 habit** demeanor. (With a suggestion of "clothes.") **184 saying** being said **187 sad ostent** grave appearance **188 grandam** grandmother
2.3. Location: Venice. Shylock's house.

LANCELOT Adieu! Tears exhibit my tongue. Most beautiful pagan, most sweet Jew! If a Christian did not play the knave and get thee, I am much deceived. But, adieu! These foolish drops do something drown my manly spirit. Adieu!

JESSICA Farewell, good Lancelot. *[Exit Lancelot.]*
Alack, what heinous sin is it in me
To be ashamed to be my father's child!
But though I am a daughter to his blood,
I am not to his manners. O Lorenzo,
If thou keep promise, I shall end this strife,
Become a Christian and thy loving wife. *Exit.*

✤

[2.4]

Enter Gratiano, Lorenzo, Salerio, and Solanio.

LORENZO
Nay, we will slink away in suppertime,
Disguise us at my lodging, and return
All in an hour.

GRATIANO
We have not made good preparation.

SALERIO
We have not spoke us yet of torchbearers.

SOLANIO
'Tis vile, unless it may be quaintly ordered,
And better in my mind not undertook.

LORENZO
'Tis now but four o'clock. We have two hours
To furnish us.

Enter Lancelot [with a letter].

Friend Lancelot, what's the news?

LANCELOT An it shall please you to break up this, it shall seem to signify. *[Giving the letter.]*

LORENZO
I know the hand. In faith, 'tis a fair hand,
And whiter than the paper it writ on
Is the fair hand that writ.

GRATIANO Love news, in faith.

LANCELOT By your leave, sir. *[He starts to leave.]*

LORENZO Whither goest thou?

LANCELOT Marry, sir, to bid my old master the Jew to sup tonight with my new master the Christian.

LORENZO
Hold here, take this. *[He gives money.]* Tell gentle
Jessica
I will not fail her. Speak it privately.
Exit clown [Lancelot].
Go, gentlemen,
Will you prepare you for this masque tonight?
I am provided of a torchbearer.

SALERIO
Ay, marry, I'll be gone about it straight.

SOLANIO
And so will I.

LORENZO Meet me and Gratiano.
At Gratiano's lodging some hour hence.

SALERIO 'Tis good we do so. *Exit [with Solanio].*

GRATIANO
Was not that letter from fair Jessica?

LORENZO
I must needs tell thee all. She hath directed
How I shall take her from her father's house,
What gold and jewels she is furnished with,
What page's suit she hath in readiness.
If e'er the Jew her father come to heaven,
It will be for his gentle daughter's sake;
And never dare misfortune cross her foot,
Unless she do it under this excuse,
That she is issue to a faithless Jew.
Come, go with me. Peruse this as thou goest.
[He gives Gratiano the letter.]
Fair Jessica shall be my torchbearer. *Exeunt.*

✤

[2.5]

Enter [Shylock the] Jew and [Lancelot,] his man that was, the clown.

SHYLOCK
Well, thou shalt see, thy eyes shall be thy judge,
The difference of old Shylock and Bassanio.—
What, Jessica!—Thou shalt not gormandize,
As thou hast done with me—What, Jessica!—
And sleep and snore, and rend apparel out—
Why, Jessica, I say!

LANCELOT Why, Jessica!

SHYLOCK
Who bids thee call? I do not bid thee call.

LANCELOT Your Worship was wont to tell me I could do nothing without bidding.

Enter Jessica.

JESSICA Call you? What is your will?

SHYLOCK
I am bid forth to supper, Jessica.
There are my keys. But wherefore should I go?
I am not bid for love—they flatter me—
But yet I'll go in hate, to feed upon
The prodigal Christian. Jessica, my girl,
Look to my house. I am right loath to go.
There is some ill a-brewing towards my rest,
For I did dream of moneybags tonight.

LANCELOT I beseech you, sir, go. My young master doth expect your reproach.

10 exhibit (Blunder for "inhibit," "restrain.") **12 get** beget
2.4. Location: Venice. A street.
1 in during **5 spoke . . . of** yet bespoken, ordered **6 quaintly ordered** skillfully and tastefully managed **10 An** If. **break up this** unseal the letter **24 straight** at once.

26 some hour about an hour **29 must needs** must **34 gentle** (With pun on "gentile"?) **35 foot** footpath **36 she** i.e., Misfortune **37 she is issue** i.e., Jessica is daughter. **faithless** pagan
2.5. Location: Venice. Before Shylock's house.
2 of between **3 gormandize** eat gluttonously **5 rend apparel out** i.e., wear out your clothes **13 wherefore** why **17 right loath** reluctant **19 tonight** last night. **21 reproach** (Lancelot's blunder for "approach." Shylock takes it in grim humor.)

SHYLOCK So do I his.

LANCELOT And they have conspired together. I will
not say you shall see a masque, but if you do, then it
was not for nothing that my nose fell a-bleeding on
Black Monday last at six o'clock i'th' morning, falling 26
out that year on Ash Wednesday was four year in
th'afternoon.

SHYLOCK
What, are there masques? Hear you me, Jessica:
Lock up my doors, and when you hear the drum
And the vile squealing of the wry-necked fife, 31
Clamber not you up to the casements then,
Nor thrust your head into the public street
To gaze on Christian fools with varnished faces, 34
But stop my house's ears—I mean my casements.
Let not the sound of shallow fopp'ry enter
My sober house. By Jacob's staff I swear 37
I have no mind of feasting forth tonight.
But I will go.—Go you before me, sirrah.
Say I will come.

LANCELOT I will go before, sir. [*Aside to Jessica*] Mistress, look out at window, for all this;
There will come a Christian by,
Will be worth a Jewess' eye. [*Exit.*]

SHYLOCK
What says that fool of Hagar's offspring, ha? 45

JESSICA
His words were "Farewell, mistress," nothing else.

SHYLOCK
The patch is kind enough, but a huge feeder, 47
Snail-slow in profit, and he sleeps by day 48
More than the wildcat. Drones hive not with me;
Therefore I part with him, and part with him
To one that I would have him help to waste
His borrowed purse. Well, Jessica, go in.
Perhaps I will return immediately.
Do as I bid you. Shut doors after you.
Fast bind, fast find— 55
A proverb never stale in thrifty mind. *Exit.*

JESSICA
Farewell, and if my fortune be not crossed,
I have a father, you a daughter, lost. *Exit.*

✤

[2.6]

Enter the masquers, Gratiano and Salerio.

GRATIANO
This is the penthouse under which Lorenzo 1
Desired us to make stand.

SALERIO His hour is almost past.

GRATIANO
And it is marvel he outdwells his hour, 4
For lovers ever run before the clock.

SALERIO
Oh, ten times faster Venus' pigeons fly 6
To seal love's bonds new-made than they are wont 7
To keep obligèd faith unforfeited. 8

GRATIANO
That ever holds. Who riseth from a feast 9
With that keen appetite that he sits down?
Where is the horse that doth untread again 11
His tedious measures with the unbated fire 12
That he did pace them first? All things that are
Are with more spirit chasèd than enjoyed.
How like a younger or a prodigal 15
The scarfèd bark puts from her native bay, 16
Hugged and embracèd by the strumpet wind! 17
How like the prodigal doth she return,
With overweathered ribs and ragged sails, 19
Lean, rent, and beggared by the strumpet wind! 20

Enter Lorenzo.

SALERIO
Here comes Lorenzo. More of this hereafter.

LORENZO
Sweet friends, your patience for my long abode; 22
Not I, but my affairs, have made you wait.
When you shall please to play the thieves for wives,
I'll watch as long for you then. Approach; 25
Here dwells my father Jew.—Ho! Who's within? 26

[*Enter*] *Jessica, above* [*in boy's clothes*].

JESSICA
Who are you? Tell me for more certainty,
Albeit I'll swear that I do know your tongue.

LORENZO Lorenzo, and thy love.

JESSICA
Lorenzo, certain, and my love indeed,
For who love I so much? And now who knows
But you, Lorenzo, whether I am yours? 32

LORENZO
Heaven and thy thoughts are witness that thou art.

JESSICA [*throwing down a casket*]
Here, catch this casket. It is worth the pains.
I am glad 'tis night, you do not look on me,

26 Black Monday Easter Monday. (Lancelot's talk of omens is perhaps intentional gibberish, a parody of Shylock's fears.) **31 wry-necked** i.e., played with the musician's head awry; or possibly comparing the fife's *vile squealing* to the call of the wryneck, a bird with a high-pitched call and a writhing movement of head and neck **34 varnished faces** i.e., painted masks **37 Jacob's staff** (See Genesis 32:10 and Hebrews 11:21.) **45 Hagar's offspring** (Hagar, a gentile and Abraham's servant, gave birth to Ishmael; both mother and son were cast out after the birth of Isaac.) **47 patch** fool **48 profit** profitable labor **55 Fast . . . find** i.e., Keep your property secure and you will always know where it is. (Proverbial.)
2.6. Location: Before Shylock's house, as in 2.5.
1 penthouse projecting roof or upper story of a house

4 it . . . hour i.e., it is surprising that he is late **6–8 Oh, ten . . . unforfeited** i.e., Oh, lovers are ten times more alacritous in their first pledge of love than in keeping faith in a long-term commitment. (*Venus' pigeons* are the doves that draw her chariot.) **9 ever holds** always holds true. **11 untread** retrace **12 measures** paces **15 younger** i.e., younger son, as in the parable of the Prodigal Son (Luke 15). (Often emended to *younker*, youth.) **16 scarfèd bark** sailing vessel festooned with flags or streamers **17 strumpet** i.e., inconsistent, variable. (Likened metaphorically to the harlots with whom the Prodigal Son wasted his fortune.) **19 overweathered ribs** i.e., weather-beaten and leaking timbers **20 rent** torn **22 your patience** i.e., I beg your patience. **abode** delay **25 watch** keep watch **26 father** i.e., father-in-law **32 But you** better than you

For I am much ashamed of my exchange.
But love is blind, and lovers cannot see
The pretty follies that themselves commit,
For if they could, Cupid himself would blush
To see me thus transformèd to a boy.

LORENZO
Descend, for you must be my torchbearer.

JESSICA
What, must I hold a candle to my shames?
They in themselves, good sooth, are too too light.
Why, 'tis an office of discovery, love,
And I should be obscured.

LORENZO
So are you, sweet,
Even in the lovely garnish of a boy.
But come at once,
For the close night doth play the runaway,
And we are stayed for at Bassanio's feast.

JESSICA
I will make fast the doors, and gild myself
With some more ducats, and be with you straight.
[Exit above.]

GRATIANO
Now, by my hood, a gentle and no Jew.

LORENZO
Beshrew me but I love her heartily,
For she is wise, if I can judge of her,
And fair she is, if that mine eyes be true,
And true she is, as she hath proved herself;
And therefore, like herself, wise, fair, and true,
Shall she be placèd in my constant soul.

Enter Jessica [below].

What, art thou come? On, gentlemen, away!
Our masquing mates by this time for us stay.
Exit [with Jessica and Salerio; Gratiano is about to follow them].

Enter Antonio.

ANTONIO Who's there?
GRATIANO Signor Antonio?

ANTONIO
Fie, fie, Gratiano! Where are all the rest?
'Tis nine o'clock; our friends all stay for you.
No masque tonight. The wind is come about;
Bassanio presently will go aboard.
I have sent twenty out to seek for you.

GRATIANO
I am glad on 't. I desire no more delight
Than to be under sail and gone tonight. *Exeunt.*

✤

[2.7]

[Flourish of cornets.] Enter Portia, with [the Prince of] Morocco, and both their trains.

PORTIA
Go, draw aside the curtains and discover
The several caskets to this noble prince.
Now make your choice. *[The curtains are drawn.]*

MOROCCO
The first, of gold, who this inscription bears,
"Who chooseth me shall gain what many men desire";
The second, silver, which this promise carries,
"Who chooseth me shall get as much as he deserves";
This third, dull lead, with warning all as blunt,
"Who chooseth me must give and hazard all he hath."
How shall I know if I do choose the right?

PORTIA
The one of them contains my picture, Prince.
If you choose that, then I am yours withal.

MOROCCO
Some god direct my judgment! Let me see,
I will survey th'inscriptions back again.
What says this leaden casket?
"Who chooseth me must give and hazard all he hath."
Must give—for what? For lead? Hazard for lead?
This casket threatens. Men that hazard all
Do it in hope of fair advantages.
A golden mind stoops not to shows of dross.
I'll then nor give nor hazard aught for lead.
What says the silver with her virgin hue?
"Who chooseth me shall get as much as he deserves."
As much as he deserves! Pause there, Morocco,
And weigh thy value with an even hand.
If thou be'st rated by thy estimation,
Thou dost deserve enough; and yet enough
May not extend so far as to the lady;
And yet to be afeard of my deserving
Were but a weak disabling of myself.
As much as I deserve? Why, that's the lady.
I do in birth deserve her, and in fortunes,
In graces, and in qualities of breeding;
But more than these, in love I do deserve.
What if I strayed no farther, but chose here?
Let's see once more this saying graved in gold:
"Who chooseth me shall gain what many men desire."
Why, that's the lady; all the world desires her.
From the four corners of the earth they come
To kiss this shrine, this mortal breathing saint.
The Hyrcanian deserts and the vasty wilds
Of wide Arabia are as throughfares now
For princes to come view fair Portia.

36 exchange change of clothes. **38 pretty** ingenious, artful **42 hold a candle** i.e., stand by and witness. (With a play on the idea of acting as torchbearer.) **43 light** (1) immodest (2) illuminated. **44 'tis . . . discovery** i.e., torchbearing is intended to shed light on matters **46 garnish** outfit, trimmings **48 close** dark, secretive. **doth . . . runaway** i.e., is quickly passing **49 stayed** waited **50 gild** adorn. (Literally, cover with gold.) **52 by my hood** (An asseveration.) **gentle** gracious person. (With pun on "gentile," as at 2.4.34.) **53 Beshrew** i.e., A mischief on. (A mild oath.) **60 stay** wait. (Also in line 64.)

2.7. Location: Belmont. Portia's house.
0.2 *trains* followers **1 discover** reveal **2 several** different, various **4 who** which **8 dull** (1) dull-colored (2) blunt. **all as blunt** as blunt as lead **12 withal** with it. **20 dross** worthless matter. (Literally, the impurities cast off in the melting down of metals.) **21 nor give** neither give **25 even** impartial **26 estimation** worth **30 disabling** underrating **36 graved** engraved **40 mortal breathing** living **41 Hyrcanian** (Hyrcania was the country south of the Caspian Sea celebrated for its wildness.) **vasty** vast

The watery kingdom, whose ambitious head
Spits in the face of heaven, is no bar
To stop the foreign spirits, but they come,
As o'er a brook, to see fair Portia.
One of these three contains her heavenly picture.
Is't like that lead contains her? 'Twere damnation
To think so base a thought; it were too gross
To rib her cerecloth in the obscure grave.
Or shall I think in silver she's immured,
Being ten times undervalued to tried gold?
Oh, sinful thought! Never so rich a gem
Was set in worse than gold. They have in England
A coin that bears the figure of an angel
Stamped in gold, but that's insculped upon;
But here an angel in a golden bed
Lies all within. Deliver me the key.
Here do I choose, and thrive I as I may!

PORTIA
There, take it, Prince; and if my form lie there,
Then I am yours.
[He unlocks the golden casket.]

MOROCCO
Oh, hell! What have we here?
A carrion Death, within whose empty eye
There is a written scroll! I'll read the writing.
[He reads.]
"All that glisters is not gold;
Often have you heard that told.
Many a man his life hath sold
But my outside to behold.
Gilded tombs do worms infold.
Had you been as wise as bold,
Young in limbs, in judgment old,
Your answer had not been inscrolled.
Fare you well; your suit is cold."
Cold, indeed, and labor lost.
Then, farewell, heat, and welcome, frost!
Portia, adieu. I have too grieved a heart
To take a tedious leave. Thus losers part.
Exit [with his train. Flourish of cornets.]

PORTIA
A gentle riddance. Draw the curtains, go.
Let all of his complexion choose me so.
[The curtains are closed, and] exeunt.

✤

45 Spits (The image is of huge waves breaking at sea.) **46 spirits** i.e., men of courage **49 like** likely **50 base** (1) ignoble (2) low in the natural scale, as with lead, a *base* metal **50–1 it were . . . grave** i.e., it would be too gross an insult to inter her, as it were, wrapped in a waxed cloth, in a lead casket. **52 immured** enclosed, confined **53 Being . . . gold** which has only one-tenth the value of assayed and purified gold. **55 set** fixed, as a precious stone, in a border of metal **56 coin** i.e., the gold coin known as the *angel*, which bore the device of the archangel Michael treading on the dragon **57 insculped upon** merely engraved upon the surface **61 form** image **63 carrion Death** death's-head **68 But** only **72 inscrolled** i.e., written on this scroll. **77 part** depart. **79 complexion** temperament (not merely skin color)

[2.8]

Enter Salerio and Solanio.

SALERIO
Why, man, I saw Bassanio under sail.
With him is Gratiano gone along,
And in their ship I am sure Lorenzo is not.

SOLANIO
The villain Jew with outcries raised the Duke,
Who went with him to search Bassanio's ship.

SALERIO
He came too late. The ship was under sail.
But there the Duke was given to understand
That in a gondola were seen together
Lorenzo and his amorous Jessica.
Besides, Antonio certified the Duke
They were not with Bassanio in his ship.

SOLANIO
I never heard a passion so confused,
So strange, outrageous, and so variable
As the dog Jew did utter in the streets:
"My daughter! Oh, my ducats! Oh, my daughter!
Fled with a Christian! Oh, my Christian ducats!
Justice! The law! My ducats, and my daughter!
A sealèd bag, two sealèd bags of ducats,
Of double ducats, stol'n from me by my daughter!
And jewels, two stones, two rich and precious stones,
Stol'n by my daughter! Justice! Find the girl!
She hath the stones upon her, and the ducats."

SALERIO
Why, all the boys in Venice follow him,
Crying his stones, his daughter, and his ducats.

SOLANIO
Let good Antonio look he keep his day,
Or he shall pay for this.

SALERIO
Marry, well remembered.
I reasoned with a Frenchman yesterday,
Who told me, in the narrow seas that part
The French and English, there miscarrièd
A vessel of our country richly fraught.
I thought upon Antonio when he told me,
And wished in silence that it were not his.

SOLANIO
You were best to tell Antonio what you hear.
Yet do not suddenly, for it may grieve him.

SALERIO
A kinder gentleman treads not the earth.
I saw Bassanio and Antonio part.
Bassanio told him he would make some speed
Of his return; he answered, "Do not so.
Slubber not business for my sake, Bassanio,
But stay the very riping of the time;

2.8. Location: Venice. A street.
4 raised roused **12 passion** passionate outburst **24 stones** (In the boys' jeering cry, the *two stones* suggest testicles; see line 20.) **25 look . . . day** see to it that he repays his loan on time **27 reasoned** talked **28 narrow seas** English Channel **30 fraught** freighted. **39 Slubber not business** Don't do the business hastily and badly **40 But . . . time** i.e., pursue your business at Belmont until it is brought to completion

And for the Jew's bond which he hath of me, 41
Let it not enter in your mind of love. 42
Be merry, and employ your chiefest thoughts
To courtship and such fair ostents of love 44
As shall conveniently become you there."
And even there, his eye being big with tears, 46
Turning his face, he put his hand behind him, 47
And with affection wondrous sensible 48
He wrung Bassanio's hand; and so they parted.

SOLANIO
I think he only loves the world for him. 50
I pray thee, let us go and find him out
And quicken his embracèd heaviness 52
With some delight or other.

SALERIO
Do we so. *Exeunt.*

✣

[2.9]

Enter Nerissa and a Servitor.

NERISSA
Quick, quick, I pray thee, draw the curtain straight. 1
The Prince of Aragon hath ta'en his oath,
And comes to his election presently. 3
[*The curtains are drawn back.*]

[*Flourish of cornets.*] *Enter* [*the Prince of*] *Aragon, his train, and Portia.*

PORTIA
Behold, there stand the caskets, noble Prince.
If you choose that wherein I am contained,
Straight shall our nuptial rites be solemnized;
But if you fail, without more speech, my lord,
You must be gone from hence immediately.

ARAGON
I am enjoined by oath to observe three things:
First, never to unfold to anyone 10
Which casket 'twas I chose; next, if I fail
Of the right casket, never in my life
To woo a maid in way of marriage;
Lastly,
If I do fail in fortune of my choice,
Immediately to leave you and be gone.

PORTIA
To these injunctions everyone doth swear
That comes to hazard for my worthless self.

ARAGON
And so have I addressed me. Fortune now 19
To my heart's hope! Gold, silver, and base lead.
"Who chooseth me must give and hazard all he hath."
You shall look fairer ere I give or hazard.
What says the golden chest? Ha, let me see:
"Who chooseth me shall gain what many men desire."
What many men desire! That "many" may be meant
By the fool multitude, that choose by show, 26
Not learning more than the fond eye doth teach, 27
Which pries not to th'interior, but like the martlet 28
Builds in the weather on the outward wall, 29
Even in the force and road of casualty. 30
I will not choose what many men desire,
Because I will not jump with common spirits 32
And rank me with the barbarous multitudes.
Why then, to thee, thou silver treasure-house!
Tell me once more what title thou dost bear:
"Who chooseth me shall get as much as he deserves."
And well said too; for who shall go about
To cozen fortune, and be honorable 38
Without the stamp of merit? Let none presume 39
To wear an undeservèd dignity.
Oh, that estates, degrees, and offices 41
Were not derived corruptly, and that clear honor
Were purchased by the merit of the wearer!
How many then should cover that stand bare? 44
How many be commanded that command? 45
How much low peasantry would then be gleaned 46
From the true seed of honor, and how much honor 47
Picked from the chaff and ruin of the times
To be new-varnished? Well, but to my choice: 49
"Who chooseth me shall get as much as he deserves."
I will assume desert. Give me a key for this,
And instantly unlock my fortunes here.
[*He opens the silver casket.*]

PORTIA
Too long a pause for that which you find there.

ARAGON
What's here? The portrait of a blinking idiot,
Presenting me a schedule! I will read it. 55
How much unlike art thou to Portia!
How much unlike my hopes and my deservings!
"Who chooseth me shall have as much as he deserves."
Did I deserve no more than a fool's head?
Is that my prize? Are my deserts no better?

PORTIA
To offend and judge are distinct offices 61
And of opposèd natures.

ARAGON
What is here? 62

41 for as for **42 of** preoccupied with **44 ostents** expressions, shows **46 there** thereupon, then **47 behind him** (Antonio turns away in tears while extending his hand back to Bassanio.) **48 affection wondrous sensible** wondrously sensitive and keen emotion **50 he . . . him** i.e., Bassanio is all he lives for. **52 quicken . . . heaviness** lighten the sorrow he has embraced

2.9. Location: Belmont. Portia's house.

0.1 *Servitor* servant **1 straight** at once. **3 election presently** choice immediately. **10 unfold** disclose **19 addressed me** prepared myself (by this swearing).

26 By for, to signify **27 fond** foolish **28 martlet** swift **29 in** exposed to **30 force . . . casualty** power and path of mischance. **32 jump** agree **38 cozen** cheat **39 stamp** seal of approval **41 estates, degrees** status, social rank **44 cover . . . bare** i.e., wear hats (of authority) who now stand bareheaded. **45 How . . . command?** How many then should be servants that are now masters? **46 gleaned** culled out and discarded **47 the true seed of honor** i.e., persons of noble descent **49 new-varnished** i.e., having the luster of their true nobility restored to them. **55 schedule** written paper. **61–2 To offend . . . natures** i.e., You have no right, having submitted your case to judgment, to attempt to judge your own case; or, it is not for me to say, since I've been the indirect cause of your discomfiture.

[*He reads.*]"The fire seven times tried this;
Seven times tried that judgment is
That did never choose amiss.
Some there be that shadows kiss;
Such have but a shadow's bliss.
There be fools alive, iwis,
Silvered o'er, and so was this.
Take what wife you will to bed;
I will ever be your head.
So begone; you are sped."

Still more fool I shall appear
By the time I linger here.
With one fool's head I came to woo,
But I go away with two.
Sweet, adieu. I'll keep my oath,
Patiently to bear my wroth.
[*Exeunt Aragon and train.*]

PORTIA
Thus hath the candle singed the moth.
Oh, these deliberate fools! When they do choose,
They have the wisdom by their wit to lose.

NERISSA
The ancient saying is no heresy:
Hanging and wiving goes by destiny.

PORTIA Come, draw the curtain, Nerissa.
[*The curtains are closed.*]

Enter Messenger.

MESSENGER
Where is my lady?

PORTIA Here. What would my lord?

MESSENGER
Madam, there is alighted at your gate
A young Venetian, one that comes before
To signify th'approaching of his lord,
From whom he bringeth sensible regreets,
To wit, besides commends and courteous breath,
Gifts of rich value. Yet I have not seen
So likely an ambassador of love.
A day in April never came so sweet,
To show how costly summer was at hand,
As this fore-spurrer comes before his lord.

PORTIA
No more, I pray thee. I am half afeard
Thou wilt say anon he is some kin to thee,
Thou spend'st such high-day wit in praising him.
Come, come, Nerissa, for I long to see
Quick Cupid's post that comes so mannerly.

NERISSA
Bassanio, Lord Love, if thy will it be! *Exeunt.*

✤

[3.1]

[*Enter*] *Solanio and Salerio.*

SOLANIO Now, what news on the Rialto?

SALERIO Why, yet it lives there unchecked that Antonio hath a ship of rich lading wrecked on the narrow seas—the Goodwins, I think they call the place, a very dangerous flat, and fatal, where the carcasses of many a tall ship lie buried, as they say, if my gossip Report be an honest woman of her word.

SOLANIO I would she were as lying a gossip in that as ever knapped ginger or made her neighbors believe she wept for the death of a third husband. But it is true, without any slips of prolixity or crossing the plain highway of talk, that the good Antonio, the honest Antonio—oh, that I had a title good enough to keep his name company!—

SALERIO Come, the full stop.

SOLANIO Ha, what sayest thou? Why, the end is, he hath lost a ship.

SALERIO I would it might prove the end of his losses.

SOLANIO Let me say "amen" betimes, lest the devil cross my prayer, for here he comes in the likeness of a Jew.

Enter Shylock.

How now, Shylock, what news among the merchants?

SHYLOCK You knew, none so well, none so well as you, of my daughter's flight.

SALERIO That's certain. I for my part knew the tailor that made the wings she flew withal.

SOLANIO And Shylock for his own part knew the bird was fledge, and then it is the complexion of them all to leave the dam.

SHYLOCK She is damned for it.

SALERIO That's certain, if the devil may be her judge.

SHYLOCK My own flesh and blood to rebel!

SOLANIO Out upon it, old carrion! Rebels it at these years?

SHYLOCK I say my daughter is my flesh and my blood.

63 The fire . . . this This silver has been seven times tested and purified **66 shadows** illusions **68 iwis** certainly **69 Silvered o'er** i.e., with silver hair and so apparently wise **71 I . . . head** i.e., you will always have a fool's head, be a fool. **72 sped** done for. **73–4 Still . . . here** i.e., I shall seem all the greater fool for wasting any more time here. **78 wroth** sorrow, unhappy lot (a variant of *ruth*); or, anger. **80 deliberate** reasoning, calculating **85 my lord** (A jesting response to "my lady.") **89 sensible regreets** tangible gifts, greetings **90 commends** greetings. **breath** speech **91 Yet** Heretofore **94 costly** lavish, rich **95 fore-spurrer** herald, harbinger **98 high-day** holiday (i.e., extravagant) **100 post** messenger

3.1. Location: Venice. A street.
2 yet . . . unchecked i.e., a rumor is spreading undenied **3–4 the narrow seas** the English Channel, as at 2.8.28 **4 Goodwins** Goodwin Sands, off the Kentish coast near the Thames estuary **5 flat** shoal, sandbank **6 tall** gallant **6-7 gossip Report** i.e., Dame Rumor **9 knapped** nibbled **11 slips of prolixity** lapses into long-windedness; or, long-winded lies. *Slips* may be the cuttings or offshoots of tediousness. **11–12 crossing . . . talk** deviating from honest, plain speech **15 Come . . . stop** Finish your sentence; rein in your tongue as a horse is checked in its manage. **19 betimes** while there is yet time **20 cross** thwart; make the sign of the cross following **26 the wings . . . withal** i.e., the disguise she escaped in. (With a play on *wings* or ornamented shoulder flaps sewn on garments.) **28 fledge** ready to fly. **complexion** natural disposition, as at 2.7.79 **29 dam** mother. **33–4 Rebels . . . years?** (Solanio pretends to interpret Shylock's cry about the rebellion of his own flesh and blood as referring to his own carnal desires, his own erection.)

SALERIO There is more difference between thy flesh and hers than between jet and ivory, more between your bloods than there is between red wine and Rhenish. But tell us, do you hear whether Antonio have had any loss at sea or no?

SHYLOCK There I have another bad match! A bankrupt, a prodigal, who dare scarce show his head on the Rialto; a beggar, that was used to come so smug upon the mart! Let him look to his bond. He was wont to call me usurer. Let him look to his bond. He was wont to lend money for a Christian courtesy. Let him look to his bond.

SALERIO Why, I am sure, if he forfeit, thou wilt not take his flesh. What's that good for?

SHYLOCK To bait fish withal. If it will feed nothing else, it will feed my revenge. He hath disgraced me, and hindered me half a million, laughed at my losses, mocked at my gains, scorned my nation, thwarted my bargains, cooled my friends, heated mine enemies; and what's his reason? I am a Jew. Hath not a Jew eyes? Hath not a Jew hands, organs, dimensions, senses, affections, passions? Fed with the same food, hurt with the same weapons, subject to the same diseases, healed by the same means, warmed and cooled by the same winter and summer, as a Christian is? If you prick us, do we not bleed? If you tickle us, do we not laugh? If you poison us, do we not die? And if you wrong us, shall we not revenge? If we are like you in the rest, we will resemble you in that. If a Jew wrong a Christian, what is his humility? Revenge. If a Christian wrong a Jew, what should his sufferance be by Christian example? Why, revenge. The villainy you teach me I will execute, and it shall go hard but I will better the instruction.

Enter a Man from Antonio.

MAN Gentlemen, my master Antonio is at his house and desires to speak with you both.

SALERIO We have been up and down to seek him.

Enter Tubal.

SOLANIO Here comes another of the tribe. A third cannot be matched, unless the devil himself turn Jew.

Exeunt gentlemen [*Solanio, Salerio, with Man*].

SHYLOCK How now, Tubal, what news from Genoa? Hast thou found my daughter?

TUBAL I often came where I did hear of her, but cannot find her.

SHYLOCK Why, there, there, there, there! A diamond gone, cost me two thousand ducats in Frankfort! The curse never fell upon our nation till now; I never felt it till now. Two thousand ducats in that, and other precious, precious jewels. I would my daughter were dead at my foot, and the jewels in her ear! Would she were hearsed at my foot, and the ducats in her coffin! No news of them? Why, so—and I know not what's spent in the search. Why, thou loss upon loss! The thief gone with so much, and so much to find the thief, and no satisfaction, no revenge! Nor no ill luck stirring but what lights o' my shoulders, no sighs but o' my breathing, no tears but o' my shedding.

TUBAL Yes, other men have ill luck too. Antonio, as I heard in Genoa—

SHYLOCK What, what, what? Ill luck, ill luck?

TUBAL Hath an argosy cast away, coming from Tripolis.

SHYLCOK I thank God, I thank God. Is it true, is it true?

TUBAL I spoke with some of the sailors that escaped the wreck.

SHYLOCK I thank thee, good Tubal. Good news, good news! Ha, ha! Heard in Genoa?

TUBAL Your daughter spent in Genoa, as I heard, one night fourscore ducats.

SHYLOCK Thou stick'st a dagger in me. I shall never see my gold again. Fourscore ducats at a sitting? Fourscore ducats?

TUBAL There came divers of Antonio's creditors in my company to Venice that swear he cannot choose but break.

SHYLOCK I am very glad of it. I'll plague him, I'll torture him. I am glad of it.

TUBAL One of them showed me a ring that he had of your daughter for a monkey.

SHYLOCK Out upon her! Thou torturest me, Tubal. It was my turquoise; I had it of Leah when I was a bachelor. I would not have given it for a wilderness of monkeys.

TUBAL But Antonio is certainly undone.

SHYLOCK Nay, that's true, that's very true. Go, Tubal, fee me an officer; bespeak him a fortnight before. I will have the heart of him if he forfeit, for were he out of Venice I can make what merchandise I will. Go, Tubal, and meet me at our synagogue. Go, good Tubal; at our synagogue, Tubal. *Exeunt* [*separately*].

✤

[3.2]

Enter Bassanio, Portia, Gratiano, [*Nerissa,*]
and all their trains.

PORTIA
I pray you, tarry. Pause a day or two
Before you hazard, for in choosing wrong
I lose your company. Therefore forbear awhile.
There's something tells me—but it is not love—
I would not lose you; and you know yourself
Hate counsels not in such a quality.

37 jet a black, hard mineral, here contrasted with the whiteness of ivory and Jessica's fair complexion **38 Rhenish** i.e., a German white wine from the Rhine valley. (Salerio seems to prefer the white wine as more refined than the red.) **41 match** bargain. **44 mart** marketplace, Rialto. **65 what . . . Revenge** i.e., in what spirit does the Christian receive the injury, that of Christian humility? No, he seeks revenge. **66 his sufferance** the Jew's patient endurance **68 it shall . . . but** i.e., assuredly; unless difficulties intervene **72 up and down** i.e., everywhere **74 matched** i.e., found to match them **80–1 The curse** God's curse (such as the plagues visited upon Egypt in Exodus 7–12)

85 hearsed coffined **95 cast away** shipwrecked **108 break** go bankrupt. **114 Leah** Shylock's wife **119 fee** hire. **officer** bailiff. **bespeak** engage **121 make . . . I will** drive whatever bargains I please.

3.2. Location: Belmont. Portia's house.

2 in choosing if you choose **6 quality** way, manner.

But lest you should not understand me well—
And yet a maiden hath no tongue but thought—
I would detain you here some month or two
Before you venture for me. I could teach you
How to choose right, but then I am forsworn.
So will I never be. So may you miss me. 12
But if you do, you'll make me wish a sin,
That I had been forsworn. Beshrew your eyes,
They have o'erlooked me and divided me! 15
One half of me is yours, the other half yours—
Mine own, I would say; but if mine, then yours,
And so all yours. Oh, these naughty times 18
Puts bars between the owners and their rights! 19
And so, though yours, not yours. Prove it so, 20
Let Fortune go to hell for it, not I. 21
I speak too long, but 'tis to peise the time, 22
To eke it and to draw it out in length, 23
To stay you from election.

BASSANIO
Let me choose, 24
For as I am, I live upon the rack.

PORTIA
Upon the rack, Bassanio? Then confess 26
What treason there is mingled with your love. 27

BASSANIO
None but that ugly treason of mistrust, 28
Which makes me fear th'enjoying of my love. 29
There may as well be amity and life
'Tween snow and fire, as treason and my love. 31

PORTIA
Ay, but I fear you speak upon the rack,
Where men enforcèd do speak anything.

BASSANIO
Promise me life, and I'll confess the truth.

PORTIA
Well then, confess and live.

BASSANIO
"Confess and love"
Had been the very sum of my confession.
Oh, happy torment, when my torturer
Doth teach me answers for deliverance!
But let me to my fortune and the caskets. 39

PORTIA
Away, then! I am locked in one of them.
If you do love me, you will find me out.
Nerissa and the rest, stand all aloof. 42
Let music sound while he doth make his choice;
Then, if he lose, he makes a swanlike end, 44
Fading in music. That the comparison
May stand more proper, my eye shall be the stream
And wat'ry deathbed for him. He may win;
And what is music then? Then music is
Even as the flourish when true subjects bow 49
To a new-crownèd monarch. Such it is
As are those dulcet sounds in break of day
That creep into the dreaming bridegroom's ear
And summon him to marriage. Now he goes,
With no less presence, but with much more love, 54
Than young Alcides when he did redeem 55
The virgin tribute paid by howling Troy 56
To the sea monster. I stand for sacrifice; 57
The rest aloof are the Dardanian wives, 58
With bleared visages, come forth to view 59
The issue of th'exploit. Go, Hercules! 60
Live thou, I live. With much, much more dismay 61
I view the fight than thou that mak'st the fray.

A song, the whilst Bassanio comments on the caskets to himself.

Tell me where is fancy bred, 63
Or in the heart or in the head? 64
How begot, how nourishèd?
Reply, reply.
It is engendered in the eyes, 67
With gazing fed, and fancy dies
In the cradle where it lies. 69
Let us all ring fancy's knell.
I'll begin it—Ding, dong, bell.

ALL Ding, dong, bell.

BASSANIO
So may the outward shows be least themselves; 73
The world is still deceived with ornament. 74
In law, what plea so tainted and corrupt
But, being seasoned with a gracious voice,
Obscures the show of evil? In religion,
What damnèd error but some sober brow 78
Will bless it and approve it with a text, 79
Hiding the grossness with fair ornament?
There is no vice so simple but assumes 81
Some mark of virtue on his outward parts. 82
How many cowards, whose hearts are all as false
As stairs of sand, wear yet upon their chins 84
The beards of Hercules and frowning Mars,
Who, inward searched, have livers white as milk? 86
And these assume but valor's excrement 87

12 So i.e., Forsworn. **So may . . . me** That being the case, you may fail to win me. **15 o'erlooked** bewitched **18 naughty** wicked **19 bars** barriers **20 though yours, not yours** (I am) yours by right but not by actual possession. **20–1 Prove . . . not I** i.e., If it turn out thus (that you are cheated of what is justly yours, i.e., of me), let Fortune be blamed for it, not I, for I will not be forsworn. **22 peise** retard (by hanging on of weights) **23 eke it** stretch it out, make it last **24 election** choice. **26–7 confess What treason** (The rack was used to force traitors to confess.) **28 mistrust** misapprehension **29 fear** fearful about **31 as** as between **39 fortune . . . caskets** (Presumably the curtains are drawn at about this point, as in the previous "casket" scenes, revealing the three caskets.) **42 aloof** apart, at a distance. **44 swanlike** (Swans were believed to sing when they came to die.)

49 flourish sounding of trumpets **54 presence** noble bearing **55 Alcides** Hercules (called *Alcides*, as at 2.1.32–5, because he was the grandson of Alcaeus) rescued Hesione, daughter of the Trojan king Laomedon, from a monster to which, by command of Neptune, she was about to be sacrificed. Hercules was rewarded, however, not with the lady's love, but with a famous pair of horses. **56 howling** lamenting **57 stand for sacrifice** represent the sacrificial victim **58 Dardanian** Trojan **59 blearèd** tear-stained **60 issue** outcome **61 Live thou** If you live **63 fancy** love **64 Or** either **67 eyes** (Love entered the heart especially through the eyes.) **69 In the cradle** i.e., in its infancy, in the eyes **73 be least themselves** least represent the inner reality **74 still** ever **78 sober brow** i.e., solemn-faced clergyman **79 approve** confirm **81 simple** unadulterated **82 his** its **84 stairs** steps **86 searched** surgically probed. **livers** (The liver was thought to be the seat of courage; for it to be deserted by the blood would be the condition of cowardice.) **87 excrement** outgrowth, here a beard

To render them redoubted. Look on beauty,
And you shall see 'tis purchased by the weight,
Which therein works a miracle in nature,
Making them lightest that wear most of it.
So are those crispèd, snaky, golden locks,
Which maketh such wanton gambols with the wind
Upon supposèd fairness, often known
To be the dowry of a second head,
The skull that bred them in the sepulcher.
Thus ornament is but the guilèd shore
To a most dangerous sea, the beauteous scarf
Veiling an Indian beauty; in a word,
The seeming truth which cunning times put on
To entrap the wisest. Therefore, thou gaudy gold,
Hard food for Midas, I will none of thee;
Nor none of thee, thou pale and common drudge
'Tween man and man. But thou, thou meager lead,
Which rather threaten'st than dost promise aught,
Thy paleness moves me more than eloquence;
And here choose I. Joy be the consequence!

PORTIA [*aside*]

How all the other passions fleet to air,
As doubtful thoughts, and rash-embraced despair,
And shuddering fear, and green-eyed jealousy!
O love, be moderate, allay thy ecstasy,
In measure rain thy joy, scant this excess!
I feel too much thy blessing. Make it less,
For fear I surfeit.

BASSANIO [*opening the leaden casket*]

What find I here?
Fair Portia's counterfeit! What demigod
Hath come so near creation? Move these eyes?
Or whether, riding on the balls of mine,
Seem they in motion? Here are severed lips,
Parted with sugar breath; so sweet a bar
Should sunder such sweet friends. Here in her hairs
The painter plays the spider, and hath woven
A golden mesh t'entrap the hearts of men
Faster than gnats in cobwebs. But her eyes—
How could he see to do them? Having made one,
Methinks it should have power to steal both his
And leave itself unfurnished. Yet look how far
The substance of my praise doth wrong this shadow
In underprizing it, so far this shadow
Doth limp behind the substance. Here's the scroll,
The continent and summary of my fortune.
[*He reads.*] "You that choose not by the view
Chance as fair, and choose as true.
Since this fortune falls to you,
Be content and seek no new.
If you be well pleased with this,
And hold your fortune for your bliss,
Turn you where your lady is
And claim her with a loving kiss."
A gentle scroll. Fair lady, by your leave,
I come by note, to give and to receive.
Like one of two contending in a prize,
That thinks he hath done well in people's eyes,
Hearing applause and universal shout,
Giddy in spirit, still gazing in a doubt
Whether those peals of praise be his or no,
So, thrice-fair lady, stand I, even so,
As doubtful whether what I see be true,
Until confirmed, signed, ratified by you.

PORTIA

You see me, Lord Bassanio, where I stand,
Such as I am. Though for myself alone
I would not be ambitious in my wish
To wish myself much better, yet for you
I would be trebled twenty times myself,
A thousand times more fair, ten thousand times
more rich,
That only to stand high in your account
I might in virtues, beauties, livings, friends,
Exceed account. But the full sum of me
Is sum of something, which, to term in gross,
Is an unlessoned girl, unschooled, unpracticèd;
Happy in this, she is not yet so old
But she may learn; happier than this,
She is not bred so dull but she can learn;
Happiest of all is that her gentle spirit
Commits itself to yours to be directed
As from her lord, her governor, her king.
Myself and what is mine to you and yours
Is now converted. But now I was the lord
Of this fair mansion, master of my servants,
Queen o'er myself; and even now, but now,
This house, these servants, and this same myself
Are yours, my lord's. I give them with this ring,
Which when you part from, lose, or give away,
Let it presage the ruin of your love
And be my vantage to exclaim on you.
[*She puts a ring on his finger.*]

BASSANIO

Madam, you have bereft me of all words.
Only my blood speaks to you in my veins,

88 redoubted feared. **89 purchased by the weight** bought (as cosmetics) at so much per ounce **91 lightest** most frivolous or lascivious. (With pun on the sense of "least heavy.") **92 crispèd** curly **94 Upon supposèd fairness** i.e., on a woman supposed beautiful and fair-haired **95–6 To . . . sepulcher** i.e., to be a wig of hair taken from a woman now dead. **97 guilèd** treacherous **99 Indian** i.e., swarthy, not fair **102 Midas** the Phrygian king whose touch turned everything to gold, including his food **103–4 pale . . . man** i.e., silver, used in commerce. **104 meager** wanting in richness **109 As** such as **112 rain** rain down, or perhaps "rein." **scant** lessen **115 counterfeit** portrait. **demigod** i.e., the painter as creator **119–20 so . . . friends** i.e., only so sweet a barrier as her mouth and breath should be allowed to part such sweet friends as her two lips. **123 Faster** (1) more tightly (2) quicker **126 unfurnished** i.e., without a companion. **look how far** however far **127 shadow** painting, semblance **128 underprizing it** failing to do it justice. **so far** to a similar extent **129 the substance** the subject, i.e., Portia.

130 continent container **132 Chance as fair** take your chances fortunately **140 by note** by a bill of dues (i.e., the scroll). The commercial metaphor continues in *confirmed, signed, ratified* (line 148), *account* (155), *sum* (157), *term in gross* (158), etc. **141 prize** competition **145 his** for him **155 account** estimation **156 livings** possessions **157 account** calculation. (Playing on *account*, estimation, in line 155.) **157–8 But . . . something** i.e., But the full sum of my worth can only be the sum of whatever I am **158 term in gross** denote in full **167 But now** A moment ago **174 vantage to exclaim on** opportunity to reproach

And there is such confusion in my powers
As, after some oration fairly spoke
By a belovèd prince, there doth appear
Among the buzzing pleasèd multitude,
Where every something being blent together
Turns to a wild of nothing save of joy
Expressed and not expressed. But when this ring
Parts from this finger, then parts life from hence.
Oh, then be bold to say Bassanio's dead!

NERISSA
My lord and lady, it is now our time,
That have stood by and seen our wishes prosper,
To cry, "good joy." Good joy, my lord and lady!

GRATIANO
My lord Bassanio and my gentle lady,
I wish you all the joy that you can wish—
For I am sure you can wish none from me.
And when Your Honors mean to solemnize
The bargain of your faith, I do beseech you
Even at that time I may be married too.

BASSANIO
With all my heart, so thou canst get a wife.

GRATIANO
I thank Your Lordship, you have got me one.
My eyes, my lord, can look as swift as yours.
You saw the mistress, I beheld the maid;
You loved, I loved; for intermission
No more pertains to me, my lord, than you.
Your fortune stood upon the caskets there,
And so did mine too, as the matter falls;
For wooing here until I sweat again,
And swearing till my very roof was dry
With oaths of love, at last, if promise last,
I got a promise of this fair one here
To have her love, provided that your fortune
Achieved her mistress.

PORTIA Is this true, Nerissa?

NERISSA
Madam, it is, so you stand pleased withal.

BASSANIO
And do you, Gratiano, mean good faith?

GRATIANO Yes, faith, my lord.

BASSANIO
Our feast shall be much honored in your marriage.

GRATIANO We'll play with them the first boy for a thousand ducats.

NERISSA What, and stake down?

GRATIANO No, we shall ne'er win at that sport, and stake down.

Enter Lorenzo, Jessica, and Salerio, a messenger from Venice.

But who comes here? Lorenzo and his infidel?
What, and my old Venetian friend Salerio?

BASSANIO
Lorenzo and Salerio, welcome hither,
If that the youth of my new interest here
Have power to bid you welcome.—By your leave,
I bid my very friends and countrymen,
Sweet Portia, welcome.

PORTIA So do I, my lord.
They are entirely welcome.

LORENZO
I thank Your Honor. For my part, my lord,
My purpose was not to have seen you here,
But, meeting with Salerio by the way,
He did entreat me, past all saying nay,
To come with him along.

SALERIO I did, my lord,
And I have reason for it. Signor Antonio
Commends him to you. [*He gives Bassanio a letter.*]

BASSANIO Ere I ope his letter,
I pray you tell me how my good friend doth.

SALERIO
Not sick, my lord, unless it be in mind,
Nor well, unless in mind. His letter there
Will show you his estate. [*Bassanio*] *open*[*s*] *the letter.*

GRATIANO [*indicating Jessica*]
Nerissa, cheer yond stranger, bid her welcome.
Your hand, Salerio. What's the news from Venice?
How doth that royal merchant, good Antonio?
I know he will be glad of our success.
We are the Jasons; we have won the fleece.

SALERIO
I would you had won the fleece that he hath lost.

PORTIA
There are some shrewd contents in yond same paper
That steals the color from Bassanio's cheek—
Some dear friend dead, else nothing in the world
Could turn so much the constitution
Of any constant man. What, worse and worse?
With leave, Bassanio; I am half yourself,
And I must freely have the half of anything
That this same paper brings you.

BASSANIO O sweet Portia,
Here are a few of the unpleasant'st words
That ever blotted paper! Gentle lady,
When I did first impart my love to you,
I freely told you all the wealth I had
Ran in my veins, I was a gentleman;
And then I told you true. And yet, dear lady,

177 powers faculties **181–3 Where . . . expressed** i.e., in which every individual utterance, being blended and confused, turns into a hubbub of joy. **187 That** we who **191 For . . . me** i.e., I'm sure I can't wish you any more joy than you could wish for yourselves, or, I'm sure your wishes for happiness cannot take away from my happiness. **195 so** provided **198 maid** (Nerissa is a lady-in-waiting, not a house servant.) **199 intermission** delay (in loving) **202 falls** falls out, happens **203 sweat again** sweated repeatedly **204 roof** roof of my mouth **205 if promise last** i.e., if Nerissa's promise should last, hold out. (With a play on *last* and *at last*, "finally.") **209 so** provided **213 We'll . . . boy** We'll wager with them to see who has the first male heir **215 stake down** cash placed in advance. (But Gratiano, in his reply, turns the phrase into a bawdy joke; *stake down* to him suggests a non-erect phallus.)

221 youth . . . interest i.e., newness of my household authority **223 very** true **232 Commends him** desires to be remembered **236 estate** situation. **237 stranger** alien **239 royal merchant** i.e., chief among merchants **241 Jasons . . . fleece** (Compare with 1.1.170–2.) **243 shrewd** cursed, grievous **247 constant** settled, not swayed by passion **248 With leave** With your permission

Rating myself at nothing, you shall see
How much I was a braggart. When I told you
My state was nothing, I should then have told you 259
That I was worse than nothing; for indeed
I have engaged myself to a dear friend,
Engaged my friend to his mere enemy, 262
To feed my means. Here is a letter, lady,
The paper as the body of my friend,
And every word in it a gaping wound
Issuing lifeblood. But is it true, Salerio?
Hath all his ventures failed? What, not one hit? 267
From Tripolis, from Mexico, and England,
From Lisbon, Barbary, and India,
And not one vessel scape the dreadful touch
Of merchant-marring rocks?

SALERIO Not one, my lord. 271
Besides, it should appear that if he had
The present money to discharge the Jew 273
He would not take it. Never did I know 274
A creature that did bear the shape of man
So keen and greedy to confound a man. 276
He plies the Duke at morning and at night,
And doth impeach the freedom of the state 278
If they deny him justice. Twenty merchants,
The Duke himself, and the magnificoes 280
Of greatest port have all persuaded with him, 281
But none can drive him from the envious plea 282
Of forfeiture, of justice, and his bond.

JESSICA
When I was with him I have heard him swear
To Tubal and to Chus, his countrymen, 285
That he would rather have Antonio's flesh
Than twenty times the value of the sum
That he did owe him; and I know, my lord,
If law, authority, and power deny not,
It will go hard with poor Antonio.

PORTIA [*to Bassanio*]
Is it your dear friend that is thus in trouble?

BASSANIO
The dearest friend to me, the kindest man,
The best-conditioned and unwearied spirit 293
In doing courtesies, and one in whom
The ancient Roman honor more appears
Than any that draws breath in Italy.

PORTIA What sum owes he the Jew?

BASSANIO
For me, three thousand ducats.

PORTIA What, no more?
Pay him six thousand, and deface the bond; 299
Double six thousand, and then treble that,
Before a friend of this description
Shall lose a hair through Bassanio's fault.
First go with me to church and call me wife,
And then away to Venice to your friend;
For never shall you lie by Portia's side
With an unquiet soul. You shall have gold
To pay the petty debt twenty times over.
When it is paid, bring your true friend along.
My maid Nerissa and myself meantime
Will live as maids and widows. Come, away!
For you shall hence upon your wedding day.
Bid your friends welcome, show a merry cheer; 312
Since you are dear bought, I will love you dear. 313
But let me hear the letter of your friend.

BASSANIO [*reads*] "Sweet Bassanio, my ships have all miscarried, my creditors grow cruel, my estate is very low, my bond to the Jew is forfeit; and since in paying it, it is impossible I should live, all debts are cleared between you and I if I might but see you at my death. Notwithstanding, use your pleasure. If your love do not persuade you to come, let not my letter."

PORTIA
O love, dispatch all business, and begone!

BASSANIO
Since I have your good leave to go away,
I will make haste; but till I come again
No bed shall e'er be guilty of my stay,
Nor rest be interposer twixt us twain. *Exeunt.*

✤

[3.3]

Enter [*Shylock*] *the Jew and Solanio and Antonio and the Jailer.*

SHYLOCK
Jailer, look to him. Tell not me of mercy.
This is the fool that lent out money gratis. 2
Jailer, look to him.

ANTONIO Hear me yet, good Shylock.

SHYLOCK
I'll have my bond. Speak not against my bond.
I have sworn an oath that I will have my bond.
Thou called'st me dog before thou hadst a cause,
But since I am a dog, beware my fangs.
The Duke shall grant me justice. I do wonder,
Thou naughty jailer, that thou art so fond 9
To come abroad with him at his request. 10

ANTONIO I pray thee, hear me speak.

SHYLOCK
I'll have my bond. I will not hear thee speak.
I'll have my bond, and therefore speak no more.
I'll not be made a soft and dull-eyed fool, 14
To shake the head, relent, and sigh, and yield
To Christian intercessors. Follow not.
I'll have no speaking. I will have my bond. *Exit Jew.*

259 state estate **262 mere** absolute **267 hit** success. **271 merchant-marring** capable of damaging a merchant ship **273 present** available. **discharge** pay off **274 He** i.e., Shylock **276 confound** destroy **278 doth . . . state** i.e., calls in question the ability of Venice to defend legally the freedom of commerce of its citizens **280 magnificoes** chief men of Venice **281 port** dignity. **persuaded** argued **282 envious** malicious **285 Chus** the Bishops' Bible spelling of *Cush*, son of Ham and grandson of Noah. *Tubal* was son of Japheth and grandson of Noah (Genesis 10:2, 6). **293 best-conditioned** best-natured **299 deface** erase

312 cheer countenance **313 dear . . . dear** at great cost . . . dearly.
3.3. Location: Venice. A street.
2 gratis free (of interest). **9 naughty** worthless, wicked. **fond** foolish **10 abroad** outside **14 dull-eyed** easily duped

SOLANIO
It is the most impenetrable cur
That ever kept with men.
ANTONIO Let him alone.
I'll follow him no more with bootless prayers.
He seeks my life. His reason well I know:
I oft delivered from his forfeitures
Many that have at times made moan to me;
Therefore he hates me.
SOLANIO I am sure the Duke
Will never grant this forfeiture to hold.
ANTONIO
The Duke cannot deny the course of law;
For the commodity that strangers have
With us in Venice, if it be denied,
Will much impeach the justice of the state,
Since that the trade and profit of the city
Consisteth of all nations. Therefore go.
These griefs and losses have so bated me
That I shall hardly spare a pound of flesh
Tomorrow to my bloody creditor.—
Well, jailer, on. Pray God Bassanio come
To see me pay his debt, and then I care not. *Exeunt.*

✤

[3.4]

Enter Portia, Nerissa, Lorenzo, Jessica, and [Balthasar,] a man of Portia's.

LORENZO
Madam, although I speak it in your presence,
You have a noble and a true conceit
Of godlike amity, which appears most strongly
In bearing thus the absence of your lord.
But if you knew to whom you show this honor,
How true a gentleman you send relief,
How dear a lover of my lord your husband,
I know you would be prouder of the work
Than customary bounty can enforce you.
PORTIA
I never did repent for doing good,
Nor shall not now; for in companions
That do converse and waste the time together,
Whose souls do bear an equal yoke of love,
There must be needs a like proportion
Of lineaments, of manners, and of spirit;
Which makes me think that this Antonio,
Being the bosom lover of my lord,
Must needs be like my lord. If it be so,
How little is the cost I have bestowed
In purchasing the semblance of my soul
From out the state of hellish cruelty!
This comes too near the praising of myself;
Therefore no more of it. Hear other things:
Lorenzo, I commit into your hands
The husbandry and manage of my house
Until my lord's return. For mine own part,
I have toward heaven breathed a secret vow
To live in prayer and contemplation,
Only attended by Nerissa here,
Until her husband and my lord's return.
There is a monastery two miles off,
And there we will abide. I do desire you
Not to deny this imposition,
The which my love and some necessity
Now lays upon you.
LORENZO Madam, with all my heart,
I shall obey you in all fair commands.
PORTIA
My people do already know my mind,
And will acknowledge you and Jessica
In place of Lord Bassanio and myself.
So fare you well till we shall meet again.
LORENZO
Fair thoughts and happy hours attend on you!
JESSICA
I wish Your Ladyship all heart's content.
PORTIA
I thank you for your wish and am well pleased
To wish it back on you. Fare you well, Jessica.
Exeunt [Jessica and Lorenzo].
Now, Balthasar,
As I have ever found thee honest-true,
So let me find thee still. Take this same letter,
[*giving a letter*]
And use thou all th'endeavor of a man
In speed to Padua. See thou render this
Into my cousin's hands, Doctor Bellario;
And look what notes and garments he doth give thee,
Bring them, I pray thee, with imagined speed
Unto the traject, to the common ferry
Which trades to Venice. Waste no time in words,
But get thee gone. I shall be there before thee.
BALTHASAR
Madam, I go with all convenient speed. [*Exit.*]
PORTIA
Come on, Nerissa, I have work in hand
That you yet know not of. We'll see our husbands
Before they think of us.
NERISSA Shall they see us?
PORTIA
They shall, Nerissa, but in such a habit
That they shall think we are accomplishèd
With that we lack. I'll hold thee any wager,

19 kept associated, dwelt **20 bootless** unavailing **27 commodity** facilities or privileges for trading. **strangers** noncitizens, including Jews **30 Since that** since **32 bated** reduced

3.4. Location: Belmont. Portia's house.
2 conceit understanding **3 amity** friendship and love **5 to whom . . . honor** i.e., Antonio, who you honor by sending money to relieve him **7 lover** friend **9 Than . . . you** than ordinary benevolence can make you. **12 waste** spend **14 must be needs** must be **15 lineaments** physical features **17 bosom lover** dear friend **20 the semblance of my soul** i.e., Antonio, so like my Bassanio

21 From . . . cruelty from the cruel state in which he presently stands. **25 husbandry and manage** care and management **33 deny this imposition** refuse this charge imposed **37 people** servants **51 look what** whatever **52 imagined** all imaginable **53 traject** ferry. (Italian *traghetto*.) **common** public **54 trades** plies back and forth **60 habit** apparel, garb **61 accomplishèd** supplied **62 that** that which. (With a bawdy suggestion.)

When we are both accoutered like young men
I'll prove the prettier fellow of the two,
And wear my dagger with the braver grace,
And speak between the change of man and boy
With a reed voice, and turn two mincing steps
Into a manly stride, and speak of frays
Like a fine bragging youth, and tell quaint lies,
How honorable ladies sought my love,
Which I denying, they fell sick and died—
I could not do withal! Then I'll repent,
And wish, for all that, that I had not killed them;
And twenty of these puny lies I'll tell,
That men shall swear I have discontinued school
Above a twelvemonth. I have within my mind
A thousand raw tricks of these bragging Jacks,
Which I will practice.

NERISSA Why, shall we turn to men?

PORTIA Fie, what a question's that,
If thou wert near a lewd interpreter!
But come, I'll tell thee all my whole device
When I am in my coach, which stays for us
At the park gate; and therefore haste away,
For we must measure twenty miles today. *Exeunt.*

✤

[3.5]

Enter [*Lancelot the*] *clown and Jessica.*

LANCELOT Yes, truly, for look you, the sins of the father are to be laid upon the children; therefore, I promise you, I fear you. I was always plain with you, and so now I speak my agitation of the matter. Therefore be o' good cheer, for truly I think you are damned. There is but one hope in it that can do you any good, and that is but a kind of bastard hope, neither.

JESSICA And what hope is that, I pray thee?

LANCELOT Marry, you may partly hope that your father got you not, that you are not the Jew's daughter.

JESSICA That were a kind of bastard hope, indeed! So the sins of my mother should be visited upon me.

LANCELOT Truly, then, I fear you are damned both by father and mother. Thus when I shun Scylla, your father, I fall into Charybdis, your mother. Well, you are gone both ways.

JESSICA I shall be saved by my husband. He hath made me a Christian.

LANCELOT Truly, the more to blame he! We were Christians enough before, e'en as many as could well live one by another. This making of Christians will raise the price of hogs. If we grow all to be pork eaters, we shall not shortly have a rasher on the coals for money.

Enter Lorenzo.

JESSICA I'll tell my husband, Lancelot, what you say. Here he comes.

LORENZO I shall grow jealous of you shortly, Lancelot, if you thus get my wife into corners.

JESSICA Nay, you need not fear us, Lorenzo. Lancelot and I are out. He tells me flatly there's no mercy for me in heaven because I am a Jew's daughter; and he says you are no good member of the commonwealth, for in converting Jews to Christians you raise the price of pork.

LORENZO [*to Lancelot*] I shall answer that better to the commonwealth than you can the getting up of the Negro's belly. The Moor is with child by you, Lancelot.

LANCELOT It is much that the Moor should be more than reason; but if she be less than an honest woman, she is indeed more than I took her for.

LORENZO How every fool can play upon the word! I think the best grace of wit will shortly turn into silence, and discourse grow commendable in none only but parrots. Go in, sirrah, bid them prepare for dinner.

LANCELOT That is done, sir. They have all stomachs.

LORENZO Goodly Lord, what a wit-snapper are you! Then bid them prepare dinner.

LANCELOT That is done too, sir, only "cover" is the word.

LORENZO Will you cover then, sir?

LANCELOT Not so, sir, neither. I know my duty.

LORENZO Yet more quarreling with occasion! Wilt thou show the whole wealth of thy wit in an instant? I pray thee, understand a plain man in his plain meaning: go to thy fellows, bid them cover the table, serve in the meat, and we will come in to dinner.

LANCELOT For the table, sir, it shall be served in; for the meat, sir, it shall be covered; for your coming in to

69 quaint elaborate, clever **72 do withal** help it. **74 puny** childish **75–6 I . . . twelvemonth** i.e., that I am no mere schoolboy. **76 Above** more than **77 Jacks** fellows **78 turn to** turn into. (But Portia sees the occasion for a bawdy quibble on the idea of "turning toward, lying next to.") **81 device** plan **84 measure** traverse
3.5. Location: Belmont. Outside Portia's house.
2–3 promise assure **3 fear you** fear for you. **4 my agitation of** my sense of agitation about **7 bastard** i.e., unfounded. (But also anticipating the usual meaning in lines 9–10.) **neither** i.e., to be sure. **10 got** begot **14, 15 Scylla, Charybdis** twin dangers of the *Odyssey*, 12.255, a monster and a whirlpool guarding the straits presumably between Italy and Sicily. (*Fall into* plays on the idea of entering the female sexual anatomy.) **16 gone** done for **17 I . . . husband** (Compare 1 Corinthians 7:14: "the unbelieving wife is sanctified by the husband.")

19–20 We . . . enough There were enough of us Christians **21 one by another** (1) as neighbors (2) off one another. **23 rasher** i.e., of bacon **23–4 for money** even for ready money, at any price. **30 are out** have fallen out. **37 The Moor** (Lancelot has evidently impregnated some woman of the household, who, being of African heritage, is referred to as both "Negro" and "Moor.") **38–40 It is . . . for** i.e., It is a matter of concern that the Moor is larger (being pregnant) than usual, larger than she should be; but if it turns out that she is less than perfectly chaste, she is something more than I originally supposed. (Lancelot professes to be surprised by what has happened. With wordplay on *less/more* and *more/Moor.*) **42 the best . . . wit** true wittiness **46 They . . . stomachs** The guests all have appetites, and are prepared in that sense. (Lancelot quibbles with Lorenzo's meaning that the cooks and servants should be told to get dinner ready.) **49, 51 cover** spread the table for the meal. (But in line 52 Lancelot uses the word to mean "put on one's hat.") **52 my duty** i.e., my duty to remain bareheaded. **53 Yet . . . occasion!** i.e., Still quibbling at every opportunity! **57 meat** food **58 For** As for. **table** (Here Lancelot quibblingly takes the word to mean the food itself.) **59 covered** (Here used in the sense of providing a cover for each separate dish.)

dinner, sir, why, let it be as humors and conceits shall govern. *Exit* [*Lancelot the*] *clown.*

LORENZO
Oh, dear discretion, how his words are suited!
The fool hath planted in his memory
An army of good words; and I do know
A many fools, that stand in better place,
Garnished like him, that for a tricksy word
Defy the matter. How cheer'st thou, Jessica?
And now, good sweet, say thy opinion:
How dost thou like the Lord Bassanio's wife?

JESSICA
Past all expressing. It is very meet
The Lord Bassanio live an upright life,
For, having such a blessing in his lady,
He finds the joys of heaven here on earth;
And if on earth he do not merit it,
In reason he should never come to heaven.
Why, if two gods should play some heavenly match
And on the wager lay two earthly women,
And Portia one, there must be something else
Pawned with the other, for the poor rude world
Hath not her fellow.

LORENZO Even such a husband
Hast thou of me as she is for a wife.

JESSICA
Nay, but ask my opinion too of that!

LORENZO
I will anon. First let us go to dinner.

JESSICA
Nay, let me praise you while I have a stomach.

LORENZO
No, pray thee, let it serve for table talk;
Then, howsome'er thou speak'st, 'mong other things
I shall digest it.

JESSICA Well, I'll set you forth. *Exeunt.*

✤

[4.1]

Enter the Duke, the Magnificoes, Antonio, Bassanio, [*Salerio,*] *and Gratiano* [*with others. The judges take their places.*]

DUKE What, is Antonio here?

ANTONIO Ready, so please Your Grace.

DUKE
I am sorry for thee. Thou art come to answer
A stony adversary, an inhuman wretch
Uncapable of pity, void and empty
From any dram of mercy.

ANTONIO I have heard
Your Grace hath ta'en great pains to qualify
His rigorous course; but since he stands obdurate
And that no lawful means can carry me
Out of his envy's reach, I do oppose
My patience to his fury and am armed
To suffer with a quietness of spirit
The very tyranny and rage of his.

DUKE
Go one, and call the Jew into the court.

SALERIO
He is ready at the door. He comes, my lord.

Enter Shylock.

DUKE
Make room, and let him stand before our face.—
Shylock, the world thinks, and I think so too,
That thou but leadest this fashion of thy malice
To the last hour of act, and then 'tis thought
Thou'lt show thy mercy and remorse more strange
Than is thy strange apparent cruelty;
And where thou now exacts the penalty,
Which is a pound of this poor merchant's flesh,
Thou wilt not only loose the forfeiture,
But, touched with human gentleness and love,
Forgive a moiety of the principal,
Glancing an eye of pity on his losses
That have of late so huddled on his back—
Enough to press a royal merchant down
And pluck commiseration of his state
From brassy bosoms and rough hearts of flint,
From stubborn Turks and Tartars never trained
To offices of tender courtesy.
We all expect a gentle answer, Jew.

SHYLOCK
I have possessed Your Grace of what I purpose,
And by our holy Sabaoth have I sworn
To have the due and forfeit of my bond.
If you deny it, let the danger light
Upon your charter and your city's freedom!
You'll ask me why I rather choose to have
A weight of carrion flesh than to receive
Three thousand ducats. I'll not answer that,
But say it is my humor. Is it answered?
What if my house be troubled with a rat
And I be pleased to give ten thousand ducats

60 humors and conceits whims and fancies **62 Oh, dear discretion** Oh, what precious discrimination. **suited** suited to the occasion **65 A many** many. **better place** higher social station **66 Garnished** i.e., furnished with words, or with garments **66–7 that . . . matter** who for the sake of ingenious wordplay torture the plain meaning. **67 How cheer'st thou** i.e., What cheer, how are you doing **70 meet** fitting **75 In reason** it stands to reason. (Jessica jokes that for Bassanio to receive unmerited bliss on earth—unmerited because no person can earn bliss through his or her own deserving—is to run the risk of eternal damnation.) **77 lay** stake **78 else** more **79 Pawned** staked, wagered **80 fellow** equal. **84 stomach** (1) appetite (2) inclination. **87 digest** (1) ponder, analyze (2) "swallow," put up with. (With a play also on the gastronomic sense.) **set you forth** (1) serve you up, as at a feast (2) set forth your praises.
4.1. Location: Venice. A court of justice. Benches, etc., are provided for the justices.

3 answer defend yourself against. (A legal term.) **6 dram** sixty grains apothecaries' weight, a tiny quantity **7 qualify** moderate **10 envy's** malice's **13 tyranny** cruelty **16 our** (The royal plural.) **18 That . . . fashion** that you only maintain this pretense or form **19 the last . . . act** the brink of action **20 remorse** pity. **strange** remarkable **21 strange** unnatural, foreign. **apparent** (1) manifest, overt (2) seeming **24 loose** release, waive **26 moiety** part, portion **30 of** for **31 brassy** unfeeling, hard like brass **35 possessed** informed **36 Sabaoth** Lord of Hosts **38 danger** injury **39 Upon . . . freedom** (See 3.2.278.) **43 humor** whim.

To have it baned? What, are you answered yet?
Some men there are love not a gaping pig,
Some that are mad if they behold a cat,
And others, when the bagpipe sings i'th' nose,
Cannot contain their urine; for affection,
Mistress of passion, sways it to the mood
Of what it likes or loathes. Now, for your answer:
As there is no firm reason to be rendered
Why he cannot abide a gaping pig,
Why he a harmless necessary cat,
Why he a woolen bagpipe, but of force
Must yield to such inevitable shame
As to offend, himself being offended,
So can I give no reason, nor I will not,
More than a lodged hate and a certain loathing
I bear Antonio, that I follow thus
A losing suit against him. Are you answered?

BASSANIO
This is no answer, thou unfeeling man,
To excuse the current of thy cruelty.

SHYLOCK
I am not bound to please thee with my answers.

BASSANIO
Do all men kill the things they do not love?

SHYLOCK
Hates any man the thing he would not kill?

BASSANIO
Every offense is not a hate at first.

SHYLOCK
What, wouldst thou have a serpent sting thee twice?

ANTONIO
I pray you, think you question with the Jew.
You may as well go stand upon the beach
And bid the main flood bate his usual height;
You may as well use question with the wolf
Why he hath made the ewe bleat for the lamb;
You may as well forbid the mountain pines
To wag their high tops and to make no noise
When they are fretten with the gusts of heaven;
You may as well do anything most hard
As seek to soften that—than which what's harder?—
His Jewish heart. Therefore, I do beseech you,
Make no more offers, use no farther means,
But with all brief and plain conveniency
Let me have judgment, and the Jew his will.

BASSANIO [*to Shylock*]
For thy three thousand ducats here is six.

SHYLOCK
If every ducat in six thousand ducats
Were in six parts, and every part a ducat,
I would not draw them. I would have my bond.

DUKE
How shalt thou hope for mercy, rendering none?

SHYLOCK
What judgment shall I dread, doing no wrong?
You have among you many a purchased slave,
Which, like your asses and your dogs and mules,
You use in abject and in slavish parts,
Because you bought them. Shall I say to you,
"Let them be free, marry them to your heirs!
Why sweat they under burdens? Let their beds
Be made as soft as yours, and let their palates
Be seasoned with such viands"? You will answer
"The slaves are ours." So do I answer you:
The pound of flesh which I demand of him
Is dearly bought, is mine, and I will have it.
If you deny me, fie upon your law!
There is no force in the decrees of Venice.
I stand for judgment. Answer: shall I have it?

DUKE
Upon my power I may dismiss this court,
Unless Bellario, a learnèd doctor,
Whom I have sent for to determine this,
Come here today.

SALERIO
My lord, here stays without
A messenger with letters from the doctor,
New come from Padua.

DUKE
Bring us the letters. Call the messenger. [*Exit one.*]

BASSANIO
Good cheer, Antonio. What, man, courage yet!
The Jew shall have my flesh, blood, bones, and all,
Ere thou shalt lose for me one drop of blood.

ANTONIO
I am a tainted wether of the flock,
Meetest for death. The weakest kind of fruit
Drops earliest to the ground, and so let me.
You cannot better be employed, Bassanio,
Than to live still and write mine epitaph.

Enter Nerissa [*dressed like a lawyer's clerk*].

DUKE
Came you from Padua, from Bellario?

NERISSA
From both, my lord. Bellario greets Your Grace.
[*She presents a letter. Shylock whets his knife on his shoe.*]

BASSANIO
Why dost thou whet thy knife so earnestly?

SHYLOCK
To cut the forfeiture from that bankrupt there.

GRATIANO
Not on thy sole, but on thy soul, harsh Jew,
Thou mak'st thy knife keen; but no metal can,
No, not the hangman's ax, bear half the keenness
Of thy sharp envy. Can no prayers pierce thee?

46 baned poisoned. **47 love** who love. **gaping pig** pig roasted whole with its mouth open **50 affection** feeling, desire **54, 55, 56 he, he, he** one person, another, yet another **55 necessary** i.e., useful for catching rats and mice **56 woolen** i.e., with flannel-covered bag **60 lodged** settled, steadfast. **certain** unwavering, fixed **62 losing** unprofitable **64 current** flow, tendency **70 think** bear in mind. **question** argue **72 And . . . height** and bid the ocean put an end to its usual high tide **73 use question with** interrogate **77 fretten** fretted, i.e., disturbed, ruffled **87 draw** receive

89 wrong legal wrong. **92 parts** duties, capacities **97 such viands** food such as you eat. **104 Upon** In accordance with **105 doctor** person of learning. (Here, of law.) **106 determine this** resolve this legal dispute **107 stays without** waits outside **114 wether** ram, especially a castrated ram **115 Meetest** fittest **125 hangman's** executioner's. **keenness** (1) sharpness (2) savagery **126 envy** malice.

SHYLOCK
No, none that thou hast wit enough to make.
GRATIANO
Oh, be thou damned, inexecrable dog, 128
And for thy life let Justice be accused! 129
Thou almost mak'st me waver in my faith
To hold opinion with Pythagoras 131
That souls of animals infuse themselves
Into the trunks of men. Thy currish spirit
Governed a wolf who, hanged for human slaughter, 134
Even from the gallows did his fell soul fleet, 135
And, whilst thou layest in thy unhallowed dam, 136
Infused itself in thee; for thy desires
Are wolvish, bloody, starved, and ravenous.
SHYLOCK
Till thou canst rail the seal from off my bond, 139
Thou but offend'st thy lungs to speak so loud. 140
Repair thy wit, good youth, or it will fall
To cureless ruin. I stand here for law. 142
DUKE
This letter from Bellario doth commend
A young and learnèd doctor to our court.
Where is he?
NERISSA He attendeth here hard by
To know your answer, whether you'll admit him.
DUKE
With all my heart. Some three or four of you
Go give him courteous conduct to this place.
[*Exeunt some.*]
Meantime the court shall hear Bellario's letter.
[*He reads.*] "Your Grace shall understand that at the 150
receipt of your letter I am very sick; but in the instant
that your messenger came, in loving visitation was
with me a young doctor of Rome. His name is Balthasar. I acquainted him with the cause in controversy
between the Jew and Antonio the merchant. We
turned o'er many books together. He is furnished with
my opinion, which, bettered with his own learning,
the greatness whereof I cannot enough commend,
comes with him, at my importunity, to fill up Your 159
Grace's request in my stead. I beseech you, let his lack
of years be no impediment to let him lack a reverend 161
estimation, for I never knew so young a body with so
old a head. I leave him to your gracious acceptance,
whose trial shall better publish his commendation." 164

Enter Portia for Balthasar [*dressed like a doctor of laws, escorted*].

You hear the learn'd Bellario, what he writes;
And here, I take it, is the doctor come.—
Give me your hand. Come you from old Bellario?
PORTIA
I did, my lord.
DUKE You are welcome. Take your place.
[*Portia takes her place.*]
Are you acquainted with the difference 169
That holds this present question in the court?
PORTIA
I am informèd throughly of the cause. 171
Which is the merchant here, and which the Jew?
DUKE
Antonio and old Shylock, both stand forth.
[*Antonio and Shylock stand forth.*]
PORTIA
Is your name Shylock?
SHYLOCK Shylock is my name.
PORTIA
Of a strange nature is the suit you follow,
Yet in such rule that the Venetian law 176
Cannot impugn you as you do proceed.— 177
You stand within his danger, do you not?
ANTONIO
Ay, so he says.
PORTIA Do you confess the bond?
ANTONIO
I do.
PORTIA Then must the Jew be merciful.
SHYLOCK
On what compulsion must I? Tell me that.
PORTIA
The quality of mercy is not strained. 182
It droppeth as the gentle rain from heaven
Upon the place beneath. It is twice blest: 184
It blesseth him that gives and him that takes.
'Tis mightiest in the mightiest; it becomes
The thronèd monarch better than his crown.
His scepter shows the force of temporal power, 188
The attribute to awe and majesty, 189
Wherein doth sit the dread and fear of kings.
But mercy is above this sceptered sway;
It is enthronèd in the hearts of kings;
It is an attribute to God himself;
And earthly power doth then show likest God's
When mercy seasons justice. Therefore, Jew,
Though justice be thy plea, consider this,
That in the course of justice none of us 197
Should see salvation. We do pray for mercy,
And that same prayer doth teach us all to render
The deeds of mercy. I have spoke thus much
To mitigate the justice of thy plea, 201
Which if thou follow, this strict court of Venice
Must needs give sentence 'gainst the merchant there.

128 inexecrable thoroughly execrable **129 And . . . accused!** and may Justice herself be accused for allowing you to live! **131 Pythagoras** ancient Greek philosopher who argued for the transmigration of souls **134 hanged for human slaughter** (A possible allusion to the Elizabethan practice of trying and punishing animals for various crimes.) **135 fell** fierce, cruel. **fleet** flit, i.e., pass from the body **136 dam** mother. (Usually used of animals.) **139 rail** remove by your abusive language **140 Thou but offend'st** you merely injure **142 cureless** incurable **150 [*He reads.*]** (In many modern editions, the reading of the letter is assigned to a clerk, but the original text gives no such indication.) **159 comes with him** accompanies him in the form of my learned opinion. **importunity** insistence **161 to let him lack** such as would deprive him of **164 whose . . . commendation** the demonstration of whose excellence will proclaim what is commendable in him better than my letter can. **164.1 *for*** i.e., disguised as

169 difference argument **171 throughly** thoroughly. **cause** case. **176 rule** order **177 impugn** find fault with **182 strained** forced, constrained. **184 is twice blest** grants a double blessing **188 His** i.e., The monarch's **189 attribute to** symbol of **197 justice** divine justice **201 To . . . plea** i.e., to show the way in which your call for justice needs to be mitigated or reduced in severity

SHYLOCK
My deeds upon my head! I crave the law,
The penalty and forfeit of my bond.

PORTIA
Is he not able to discharge the money?

BASSANIO
Yes, here I tender it for him in the court,
Yea, twice the sum. If that will not suffice,
I will be bound to pay it ten times o'er,
On forfeit of my hands, my head, my heart.
If this will not suffice, it must appear
That malice bears down truth. And I beseech you,
Wrest once the law to your authority.
To do a great right, do a little wrong,
And curb this cruel devil of his will.

PORTIA
It must not be. There is no power in Venice
Can alter a decree establishèd.
'Twill be recorded for a precedent,
And many an error by the same example
Will rush into the state. It cannot be.

SHYLOCK
A Daniel come to judgment! Yea, a Daniel!
O wise young judge, how I do honor thee!

PORTIA
I pray you, let me look upon the bond.

SHYLOCK [*giving the bond*]
Here 'tis, most reverend doctor, here it is.

PORTIA
Shylock, there's thrice thy money offered thee.

SHYLOCK
An oath, an oath! I have an oath in heaven.
Shall I lay perjury upon my soul?
No, not for Venice.

PORTIA Why, this bond is forfeit,
And lawfully by this the Jew may claim
A pound of flesh, to be by him cut off
Nearest the merchant's heart.—Be merciful.
Take thrice thy money; bid me tear the bond.

SHYLOCK
When it is paid according to the tenor.
It doth appear you are a worthy judge.
You know the law. Your exposition
Hath been most sound. I charge you by the law,
Whereof you are a well-deserving pillar,
Proceed to judgment. By my soul I swear
There is no power in the tongue of man
To alter me. I stay here on my bond.

ANTONIO
Most heartily I do beseech the court
To give the judgment.

PORTIA Why then, thus it is:
You must prepare your bosom for his knife.

SHYLOCK
O noble judge! O excellent young man!

PORTIA
For the intent and purpose of the law
Hath full relation to the penalty
Which here appeareth due upon the bond.

SHYLOCK
'Tis very true. O wise and upright judge!
How much more elder art thou than thy looks!

PORTIA
Therefore lay bare your bosom.

SHYLOCK Ay, his breast.
So says the bond, doth it not, noble judge?
"Nearest his heart," those are the very words.

PORTIA
It is so. Are there balance here
To weigh the flesh?

SHYLOCK I have them ready.

PORTIA
Have by some surgeon, Shylock, on your charge,
To stop his wounds, lest he do bleed to death.

SHYLOCK
Is it so nominated in the bond?

PORTIA
It is not so expressed, but what of that?
'Twere good you do so much for charity.

SHYLOCK
I cannot find it. 'Tis not in the bond.

PORTIA
You, merchant, have you anything to say?

ANTONIO
But little. I am armed and well prepared.—
Give me your hand, Bassanio; fare you well!
Grieve not that I am fall'n to this for you,
For herein Fortune shows herself more kind
Than is her custom. It is still her use
To let the wretched man outlive his wealth
To view with hollow eye and wrinkled brow
An age of poverty; from which ling'ring penance
Of such misery doth she cut me off.
Commend me to your honorable wife.
Tell her the process of Antonio's end,
Say how I loved you, speak me fair in death;
And, when the tale is told, bid her be judge
Whether Bassanio had not once a love.
Repent but you that you shall lose your friend,
And he repents not that he pays your debt.
For if the Jew do cut but deep enough,
I'll pay it instantly with all my heart.

BASSANIO
Antonio, I am married to a wife,
Which is as dear to me as life itself;
But life itself, my wife, and all the world

204 My . . . head! (Compare the cry of the crowd at Jesus' crucifixion: "His blood be on us, and on our children," Matthew 27:25.) **212 bears down truth** overwhelms righteousness. **213 Wrest once** for once, forcibly subject **221 Daniel** (In the Apocrypha's story of Susannah and the Elders, Daniel is the young man who rescues Susannah from her false accusers.) **233 tenor** conditions. **240 stay** stand, insist

246 Hath . . . to is fully in accord with **253 balance** scales **255 Have by** Have ready at hand. **on your charge** at your personal expense **262 armed** i.e., fortified in spirit **266 still her use** i.e., commonly Fortune's practice **272 process** story, manner **273 speak me fair** speak well of me **275 a love** a friend's love. **276 Repent but you** Grieve only **279 with . . . heart** (1) wholeheartedly (2) literally, with my heart's blood.

Are not with me esteemed above thy life.
I would lose all, ay, sacrifice them all
Here to this devil, to deliver you.

PORTIA
Your wife would give you little thanks for that,
If she were by to hear you make the offer. 287

GRATIANO
I have a wife who, I protest, I love;
I would she were in heaven, so she could
Entreat some power to change this currish Jew.

NERISSA
'Tis well you offer it behind her back;
The wish would make else an unquiet house.

SHYLOCK
These be the Christian husbands. I have a daughter;
Would any of the stock of Barabbas 294
Had been her husband rather than a Christian!—
We trifle time. I pray thee, pursue sentence. 296

PORTIA
A pound of that same merchant's flesh is thine.
The court awards it, and the law doth give it.

SHYLOCK Most rightful judge!

PORTIA
And you must cut this flesh from off his breast.
The law allows it, and the court awards it.

SHYLOCK
Most learnèd judge! A sentence!—Come, prepare.

PORTIA
Tarry a little; there is something else.
This bond doth give thee here no jot of blood;
The words expressly are "a pound of flesh."
Take then thy bond, take thou thy pound of flesh,
But in the cutting it if thou dost shed
One drop of Christian blood, thy lands and goods
Are by the laws of Venice confiscate
Unto the state of Venice.

GRATIANO
O upright judge! Mark, Jew. O learnèd judge!

SHYLOCK
Is that the law?

PORTIA Thyself shalt see the act;
For, as thou urgest justice, be assured
Thou shalt have justice, more than thou desir'st.

GRATIANO
O learnèd judge! Mark, Jew, a learnèd judge!

SHYLOCK
I take this offer, then. Pay the bond thrice
And let the Christian go.

BASSANIO Here is the money.

PORTIA Soft! 318
The Jew shall have all justice. Soft, no haste. 319
He shall have nothing but the penalty.

GRATIANO
O Jew! An upright judge, a learnèd judge!

PORTIA
Therefore prepare thee to cut off the flesh.
Shed thou no blood, nor cut thou less nor more
But just a pound of flesh. If thou tak'st more
Or less than a just pound, be it but so much
As makes it light or heavy in the substance 326
Or the division of the twentieth part 327
Of one poor scruple, nay, if the scale do turn 328
But in the estimation of a hair,
Thou diest, and all thy goods are confiscate.

GRATIANO
A second Daniel, a Daniel, Jew! 331
Now, infidel, I have you on the hip. 332

PORTIA
Why doth the Jew pause? Take thy forfeiture.

SHYLOCK
Give me my principal, and let me go.

BASSANIO
I have it ready for thee. Here it is.

PORTIA
He hath refused it in the open court.
He shall have merely justice and his bond.

GRATIANO
A Daniel, still say I, a second Daniel!
I thank thee, Jew, for teaching me that word.

SHYLOCK
Shall I not have barely my principal?

PORTIA
Thou shalt have nothing but the forfeiture,
To be so taken at thy peril, Jew.

SHYLOCK
Why, then the devil give him good of it!
I'll stay no longer question. [*He starts to go.*]

PORTIA Tarry, Jew! 344
The law hath yet another hold on you.
It is enacted in the laws of Venice,
If it be proved against an alien
That by direct or indirect attempts
He seek the life of any citizen,
The party 'gainst the which he doth contrive
Shall seize one half his goods; the other half
Comes to the privy coffer of the state, 352
And the offender's life lies in the mercy 353
Of the Duke only, 'gainst all other voice. 354
In which predicament, I say, thou stand'st;
For it appears, by manifest proceeding,
That indirectly and directly too
Thou hast contrived against the very life
Of the defendant; and thou hast incurred
The danger formerly by me rehearsed. 360
Down therefore, and beg mercy of the Duke. 361

287 by nearby **294 Barabbas** a thief whom Pontius Pilate set free instead of Christ in response to the people's demand (see Mark 15); also, the villainous protagonist of Marlowe's *The Jew of Malta*
296 trifle waste. **pursue** proceed with **318 Soft!** i.e., Not so fast!
319 all justice precisely what the law provides.

326 substance mass or gross weight **327 division** fraction
328 scruple twenty grains apothecaries' weight, a small quantity
331 Daniel (See line 221 above and note.) **332 on the hip** i.e., at a disadvantage. (A phrase from wrestling.) **344 I'll . . . question** I'll stay no further pursuing of the case. **352 privy coffer** private treasury **353 lies in** lies at **354 'gainst . . . voice** without appeal
360 The danger . . . rehearsed the penalty already cited by me.
361 Down Down on your knees

GRATIANO
Beg that thou mayst have leave to hang thyself!
And yet, thy wealth being forfeit to the state,
Thou hast not left the value of a cord;
Therefore thou must be hanged at the state's charge.

DUKE
That thou shalt see the difference of our spirit,
I pardon thee thy life before thou ask it.
For half thy wealth, it is Antonio's;
The other half comes to the general state,
Which humbleness may drive unto a fine.

PORTIA
Ay, for the state, not for Antonio.

SHYLOCK
Nay, take my life and all! Pardon not that!
You take my house when you do take the prop
That doth sustain my house. You take my life
When you do take the means whereby I live.

PORTIA
What mercy can you render him, Antonio?

GRATIANO
A halter gratis! Nothing else, for God's sake.

ANTONIO
So please my lord the Duke and all the court
To quit the fine for one half of his goods,
I am content, so he will let me have
The other half in use, to render it,
Upon his death, unto the gentleman
That lately stole his daughter.
Two things provided more: that for this favor
He presently become a Christian;
The other, that he do record a gift
Here in the court of all he dies possessed
Unto his son Lorenzo and his daughter.

DUKE
He shall do this, or else I do recant
The pardon that I late pronouncèd here.

PORTIA
Art thou contented, Jew? What dost thou say?

SHYLOCK
I am content.

PORTIA Clerk, draw a deed of gift.

SHYLOCK
I pray you, give me leave to go from hence;
I am not well. Send the deed after me,
And I will sign it.

DUKE Get thee gone, but do it.

GRATIANO
In christening shalt thou have two godfathers.
Had I been judge, thou shouldst have had ten more,
To bring thee to the gallows, not the font.
Exit [*Shylock*].

DUKE [*to Portia*]
Sir, I entreat you home with me to dinner.

PORTIA
I humbly do desire Your Grace of pardon.
I must away this night toward Padua,
And it is meet I presently set forth.

DUKE
I am sorry that your leisure serves you not.
Antonio, gratify this gentleman,
For in my mind you are much bound to him.
Exeunt Duke and his train.

BASSANIO [*to Portia*]
Most worthy gentleman, I and my friend
Have by your wisdom been this day acquitted
Of grievous penalties, in lieu whereof,
Three thousand ducats due unto the Jew
We freely cope your courteous pains withal.
[*He offers money.*]

ANTONIO
And stand indebted over and above
In love and service to you evermore.

PORTIA
He is well paid that is well satisfied,
And I, delivering you, am satisfied,
And therein do account myself well paid.
My mind was never yet more mercenary.
I pray you, know me when we meet again.
I wish you well, and so I take my leave.
[*She starts to leave.*]

BASSANIO
Dear sir, of force I must attempt you further.
Take some remembrance of us as a tribute,
Not as fee. Grant me two things, I pray you:
Not to deny me, and to pardon me.

PORTIA
You press me far, and therefore I will yield.
Give me your gloves, I'll wear them for your sake.
And, for your love, I'll take this ring from you.
Do not draw back your hand; I'll take no more,
And you in love shall not deny me this.

BASSANIO
This ring, good sir? Alas, it is a trifle!
I will not shame myself to give you this.

PORTIA
I will have nothing else but only this;
And now, methinks, I have a mind to it.

BASSANIO
There's more depends on this than on the value.

365 charge expense. **368 For** As for **370 Which . . . fine** i.e., which penitence on your part may persuade me to reduce to a fine. **371 Ay . . . Antonio** i.e., Yes, the state's half may be reduced to a fine, but not Antonio's half. **377 halter** hangman's noose **379 To . . . goods** i.e., to cancel the fine of one-half of Shylock's estate owed to the state of Venice (line 352) **380 so** provided that **381 in use** in trust (until Shylock's death) **385 presently** at once **387 of . . . possessed** i.e., what remains of the portion not placed under Antonio's trust (which will also go to Lorenzo and Jessica) **389 late** lately **397 ten more** i.e., to make up a jury of twelve. (Jurors were colloquially termed *godfathers*.)

402 meet necessary, suitable **404 gratify** reward **408 in lieu whereof** in return for which **410 cope** requite **417 know . . . again** i.e., consider our acquaintance well established. (But punning on *know* in the sense of "recognize" and "have sexual relations with"—meanings that are hidden from Bassanio by Portia's disguise.) **419 of force** of necessity. **attempt** urge **422 pardon me** i.e., pardon my presumption in pressing the matter. **424 gloves** (Perhaps Bassanio removes his gloves, thereby revealing the ring that "Balthasar" asks of him.) **425 for your love** i.e., for friendship's sake—a polite phrase, but with ironic double meaning as applied to husband and wife

The dearest ring in Venice will I give you, 433
And find it out by proclamation.
Only for this, I pray you, pardon me.

PORTIA
I see, sir, you are liberal in offers. 436
You taught me first to beg, and now, methinks,
You teach me how a beggar should be answered.

BASSANIO
Good sir, this ring was given me by my wife,
And when she put it on she made me vow
That I should neither sell nor give nor lose it.

PORTIA
That 'scuse serves many men to save their gifts.
An if your wife be not a madwoman, 443
And know how well I have deserved this ring,
She would not hold out enemy forever
For giving it to me. Well, peace be with you!
Exeunt [Portia and Nerissa].

ANTONIO
My lord Bassanio, let him have the ring.
Let his deservings and my love withal
Be valued 'gainst your wife's commandement. 449

BASSANIO
Go, Gratiano, run and overtake him;
Give him the ring, and bring him, if thou canst,
Unto Antonio's house. Away, make haste!
Exit Gratiano [with the ring].
Come, you and I will thither presently,
And in the morning early will we both
Fly toward Belmont. Come, Antonio. *Exeunt.*

✤

[4.2]

Enter [Portia and] Nerissa [still disguised].

PORTIA [*giving a deed to Nerissa*]
Inquire the Jew's house out; give him this deed 1
And let him sign it. We'll away tonight
And be a day before our husbands home.
This deed will be well welcome to Lorenzo.

Enter Gratiano.

GRATIANO Fair sir, you are well o'erta'en. 5
My lord Bassanio upon more advice 6
Hath sent you here this ring and doth entreat
Your company at dinner. [*He gives a ring.*]

PORTIA That cannot be.
His ring I do accept most thankfully,
And so, I pray you, tell him. Furthermore,
I pray you, show my youth old Shylock's house.

GRATIANO
That will I do.

NERISSA Sir, I would speak with you.
[*Aside to Portia*] I'll see if I can get my husband's ring,
Which I did make him swear to keep forever.

PORTIA [*aside to Nerissa*]
Thou mayst, I warrant. We shall have old swearing 15
That they did give the rings away to men;
But we'll outface them, and outswear them too.— 17
Away, make haste! Thou know'st where I will tarry.

NERISSA [*to Gratiano*]
Come, good sir, will you show me to this house?
[*Exeunt, Portia separately from the others.*]

✤

[5.1]

Enter Lorenzo and Jessica.

LORENZO
The moon shines bright. In such a night as this,
When the sweet wind did gently kiss the trees
And they did make no noise, in such a night
Troilus methinks mounted the Trojan walls 4
And sighed his soul toward the Grecian tents
Where Cressid lay that night.

JESSICA In such a night
Did Thisbe fearfully o'ertrip the dew, 7
And saw the lion's shadow ere himself,
And ran dismayed away.

LORENZO In such a night
Stood Dido with a willow in her hand 10
Upon the wild sea banks, and waft her love 11
To come again to Carthage.

JESSICA In such a night
Medea gathered the enchanted herbs 13
That did renew old Aeson.

LORENZO In such a night
Did Jessica steal from the wealthy Jew 15
And with an unthrift love did run from Venice 16
As far as Belmont.

JESSICA In such a night
Did young Lorenzo swear he loved her well,
Stealing her soul with many vows of faith,
And ne'er a true one.

LORENZO In such a night
Did pretty Jessica, like a little shrew,
Slander her love, and he forgave it her.

JESSICA
I would out-night you, did nobody come. 23
But hark, I hear the footing of a man. 24

Enter [Stephano,] a messenger.

LORENZO
Who comes so fast in silence of the night?

433 dearest most expensive **436 liberal** generous **443 An if** If
449 commandement (Pronounced in four syllables.)
4.2. Location: Venice. A street.
1 this deed i.e., the deed of gift **5 you . . . o'erta'en** I'm happy to have caught up with you. **6 advice** consideration

15 old plenty of **17 outface** boldly contradict
5.1. Location: Belmont. Outside Portia's house.
4 Troilus Trojan prince deserted by his beloved, Cressida, after she had been transferred to the Greek camp **7 Thisbe** beloved of Pyramus who, arranging to meet him by night, was frightened by a lion and fled; the tragic misunderstanding of her absence led to the suicides of both lovers. (See *A Midsummer Night's Dream*, Act 5.) **10 Dido** Queen of Carthage, deserted by Aeneas. **willow** (A symbol of forsaken love.)
11 waft wafted, beckoned **13 Medea** famous sorceress of Colchis who, after falling in love with Jason and helping him to gain the Golden Fleece, used her magic to restore youth to Aeson, Jason's father
15 steal (1) escape (2) rob **16 unthrift** prodigal **23 out-night** i.e., outdo in the verbal games we've been playing **24 footing** footsteps

STEPHANO A friend.

LORENZO
A friend? What friend? Your name, I pray you, friend?

STEPHANO
Stephano is my name, and I bring word
My mistress will before the break of day
Be here at Belmont. She doth stray about
By holy crosses, where she kneels and prays
For happy wedlock hours.

LORENZO Who comes with her?

STEPHANO
None but a holy hermit and her maid.
I pray you, is my master yet returned?

LORENZO
He is not, nor we have not heard from him.
But go we in, I pray thee, Jessica,
And ceremoniously let us prepare
Some welcome for the mistress of the house.

Enter [*Lancelot, the*] *clown.*

LANCELOT Sola, sola! Wo ha, ho! Sola, sola!

LORENZO Who calls?

LANCELOT Sola! Did you see Master Lorenzo? Master Lorenzo, sola, sola!

LORENZO Leave holloing, man! Here.

LANCELOT Sola! Where, where?

LORENZO Here.

LANCELOT Tell him there's a post come from my master, with his horn full of good news: my master will be here ere morning. [*Exit.*]

LORENZO
Sweet soul, let's in, and there expect their coming.
And yet no matter. Why should we go in?
My friend Stephano, signify, I pray you,
Within the house, your mistress is at hand,
And bring your music forth into the air.
[*Exit Stephano.*]
How sweet the moonlight sleeps upon this bank!
Here will we sit and let the sounds of music
Creep in our ears. Soft stillness and the night
Become the touches of sweet harmony.
Sit, Jessica. [*They sit.*] Look how the floor of heaven
Is thick inlaid with patens of bright gold.
There's not the smallest orb which thou behold'st
But in his motion like an angel sings,
Still choiring to the young-eyed cherubins.
Such harmony is in immortal souls,
But whilst this muddy vesture of decay
Doth grossly close it in, we cannot hear it.

[*Enter musicians.*]

Come, ho, and wake Diana with a hymn!
With sweetest touches pierce your mistress' ear
And draw her home with music. *Play music.*

JESSICA
I am never merry when I hear sweet music.

LORENZO
The reason is, your spirits are attentive.
For do but note a wild and wanton herd,
Or race of youthful and unhandled colts,
Fetching mad bounds, bellowing and neighing loud,
Which is the hot condition of their blood;
If they but hear perchance a trumpet sound,
Or any air of music touch their ears,
You shall perceive them make a mutual stand,
Their savage eyes turned to a modest gaze
By the sweet power of music. Therefore the poet
Did feign that Orpheus drew trees, stones, and floods,
Since naught so stockish, hard, and full of rage
But music for the time doth change his nature.
The man that hath no music in himself,
Nor is not moved with concord of sweet sounds,
Is fit for treasons, stratagems, and spoils;
The motions of his spirit are dull as night
And his affections dark as Erebus.
Let no such man be trusted. Mark the music.

Enter Portia and Nerissa.

PORTIA
That light we see is burning in my hall.
How far that little candle throws his beams!
So shines a good deed in a naughty world.

NERISSA
When the moon shone, we did not see the candle.

PORTIA
So doth the greater glory dim the less.
A substitute shines brightly as a king
Until a king be by, and then his state
Empties itself, as doth an inland brook
Into the main of waters. Music! Hark!

NERISSA
It is your music, madam, of the house.

PORTIA
Nothing is good, I see, without respect.
Methinks it sounds much sweeter than by day.

NERISSA
Silence bestows that virtue on it, madam.

PORTIA
The crow doth sing as sweetly as the lark
When neither is attended; and I think
The nightingale, if she should sing by day,

31 holy crosses wayside shrines **39 Sola** (Imitation of a post horn.) **46 post** courier **47 horn** (Lancelot jestingly compares the courier's post horn to a cornucopia; perhaps too with a glance at the frayed jest about cuckolds' horns.) **49 expect** await **51 signify** make known **57 Become** suit. **touches** strains, notes (produced by the fingering of an instrument) **59 patens** thin, circular plates of metal **62 Still choiring** continually singing. **young-eyed** eternally clear-sighted. (In Ezekiel 10:12, the bodies and wings of cherubim are "full of eyes round about.") **64 muddy . . . decay** i.e., mortal flesh **65 close it in** i.e., enclose the soul. **hear it** i.e., hear the music of the spheres.

66 Diana (Here, goddess of the moon; compare with 1.2.105.) **70 spirits are attentive** (The spirits would be in motion within the body in merriment, whereas in sadness they would be drawn to the heart and, as it were, busy listening.) **72 race** herd **77 mutual** common or simultaneous **79 poet** perhaps Ovid, with whom the story of Orpheus was a favorite theme **80 Orpheus** legendary musician. **drew** attracted, charmed. **floods** rivers **81 stockish** unfeeling **82 his** its (a tree, a stone, etc.) **85 spoils** acts of pillage **87 Erebus** a place of primeval darkness on the way to Hades. **91 naughty** wicked **95 his** i.e., the substitute's **97 main of waters** sea. **99 respect** comparison, context. **103 attended** listened to

When every goose is cackling, would be thought
No better a musician than the wren.
How many things by season seasoned are 107
To their right praise and true perfection!
Peace, ho! The moon sleeps with Endymion 109
And would not be awaked. [*The music ceases.*]

LORENZO That is the voice,
Or I am much deceived, of Portia.

PORTIA
He knows me as the blind man knows the cuckoo,
By the bad voice.

LORENZO Dear lady, welcome home.

PORTIA
We have been praying for our husbands' welfare,
Which speed, we hope, the better for our words. 115
Are they returned?

LORENZO Madam, they are not yet;
But there is come a messenger before,
To signify their coming.

PORTIA Go in, Nerissa.
Give order to my servants that they take
No note at all of our being absent hence;
Nor you, Lorenzo; Jessica, nor you. [*A tucket sounds.*] 121

LORENZO
Your husband is at hand. I hear his trumpet.
We are no telltales, madam, fear you not.

PORTIA
This night, methinks, is but the daylight sick; 124
It looks a little paler. 'Tis a day
Such as the day is when the sun is hid.

Enter Bassanio, Antonio, Gratiano, and their followers.

BASSANIO
We should hold day with the Antipodes, 127
If you would walk in absence of the sun. 128

PORTIA
Let me give light, but let me not be light; 129
For a light wife doth make a heavy husband, 130
And never be Bassanio so for me.
But God sort all! You are welcome home, my lord. 132

BASSANIO
I thank you, madam. Give welcome to my friend.
This is the man, this is Antonio,
To whom I am so infinitely bound.

PORTIA
You should in all sense be much bound to him, 136
For, as I hear, he was much bound for you. 137

ANTONIO
No more than I am well acquitted of. 138

PORTIA
Sir, you are very welcome to our house.
It must appear in other ways than words;
Therefore I scant this breathing courtesy. 141

GRATIANO [*to Nerissa*]
By yonder moon I swear you do me wrong!
In faith, I gave it to the judge's clerk.
Would he were gelt that had it, for my part, 144
Since you do take it, love, so much at heart.

PORTIA
A quarrel, ho, already? What's the matter?

GRATIANO
About a hoop of gold, a paltry ring
That she did give me, whose posy was 148
For all the world like cutler's poetry
Upon a knife, "Love me, and leave me not."

NERISSA
What talk you of the posy or the value?
You swore to me, when I did give it you,
That you would wear it till your hour of death
And that it should lie with you in your grave.
Though not for me, yet for your vehement oaths
You should have been respective and have kept it. 156
Gave it a judge's clerk! No, God's my judge,
The clerk will ne'er wear hair on 's face that had it.

GRATIANO
He will, an if he live to be a man. 159

NERISSA
Ay, if a woman live to be a man.

GRATIANO
Now, by this hand, I gave it to a youth,
A kind of boy, a little scrubbèd boy 162
No higher than thyself, the judge's clerk,
A prating boy, that begged it as a fee. 164
I could not for my heart deny it him.

PORTIA
You were to blame—I must be plain with you—
To part so slightly with your wife's first gift,
A thing stuck on with oaths upon your finger,
And so riveted with faith unto your flesh.
I gave my love a ring and made him swear
Never to part with it; and here he stands.
I dare be sworn for him he would not leave it,
Nor pluck it from his finger, for the wealth
That the world masters. Now, in faith, Gratiano, 174
You give your wife too unkind a cause of grief.
An 'twere to me, I should be mad at it. 176

BASSANIO [*aside*]
Why, I were best to cut my left hand off
And swear I lost the ring defending it.

GRATIANO
My lord Bassanio gave his ring away

107 season fit occasion. (But playing on the idea of seasoning, spices.) **109 Endymion** a shepherd loved by the moon goddess, who caused him to sleep a perennial sleep in a cave on Mount Latmos where she could visit him **115 Which . . . words** who prosper and return speedily, we hope, because we prayed for them. **121 s.d. *tucket*** flourish on a trumpet **124 sick** i.e., made pale by the approach of dawn **127–8 We . . . sun** i.e., If you, Portia, like a second sun, would always walk about during the sun's absence, we should never have night but would enjoy daylight even when the Antipodes, those who dwell on the opposite side of the globe, enjoy daylight. **129 be light** be wanton, unchaste **130 heavy** sad. (With wordplay on the antithesis of *light* and *heavy*.) **132 sort** decide, dispose **136 in all sense** in every way, with every reason **136–7 bound . . . bound** Portia plays on (1) obligated (2) indebted and imprisoned.

138 acquitted of freed from and amply repaid (by thanks and love). **141 scant . . . courtesy** make brief these empty (i.e., merely verbal) compliments. **144 gelt** gelded, castrated. **for my part** as far as I'm concerned **148 posy** a motto on a ring **156 respective** mindful, careful **159 an if** if **162 scrubbèd** diminutive **164 prating** chattering **174 masters** owns. **176 An** If. **mad** beside myself

Unto the judge that begged it and indeed
Deserved it too; and then the boy, his clerk,
That took some pains in writing, he begged mine;
And neither man nor master would take aught
But the two rings.

PORTIA [*to Bassanio*] What ring gave you, my lord?
Not that, I hope, which you received of me.

BASSANIO
If I could add a lie unto a fault,
I would deny it; but you see my finger
Hath not the ring upon it. It is gone.

PORTIA
Even so void is your false heart of truth.
By heaven, I will ne'er come in your bed
Until I see the ring!

NERISSA [*to Gratiano*] Nor I in yours
Till I again see mine.

BASSANIO Sweet Portia,
If you did know to whom I gave the ring,
If you did know for whom I gave the ring,
And would conceive for what I gave the ring,
And how unwillingly I left the ring,
When naught would be accepted but the ring,
You would abate the strength of your displeasure.

PORTIA
If you had known the virtue of the ring,
Or half her worthiness that gave the ring,
Or your own honor to contain the ring,
You would not then have parted with the ring.
What man is there so much unreasonable,
If you had pleased to have defended it
With any terms of zeal, wanted the modesty
To urge the thing held as a ceremony?
Nerissa teaches me what to believe:
I'll die for't but some woman had the ring.

BASSANIO
No, by my honor, madam! By my soul,
No woman had it, but a civil doctor,
Which did refuse three thousand ducats of me
And begged the ring, the which I did deny him
And suffered him to go displeased away—
Even he that had held up the very life
Of my dear friend. What should I say, sweet lady?
I was enforced to send it after him.
I was beset with shame and courtesy.
My honor would not let ingratitude
So much besmear it. Pardon me, good lady!
For by these blessèd candles of the night,
Had you been there, I think you would have begged
The ring of me to give the worthy doctor.

PORTIA
Let not that doctor e'er come near my house.
Since he hath got the jewel that I loved,
And that which you did swear to keep for me,
I will become as liberal as you:
I'll not deny him anything I have,
No, not my body nor my husband's bed.
Know him I shall, I am well sure of it.
Lie not a night from home. Watch me like Argus;
If you do not, if I be left alone,
Now, by mine honor, which is yet mine own,
I'll have that doctor for my bedfellow.

NERISSA
And I his clerk; therefore be well advised
How you do leave me to mine own protection.

GRATIANO
Well, do you so. Let not me take him, then!
For if I do, I'll mar the young clerk's pen.

ANTONIO
I am th'unhappy subject of these quarrels.

PORTIA
Sir, grieve not you; you are welcome notwithstanding.

BASSANIO
Portia, forgive me this enforcèd wrong,
And in the hearing of these many friends
I swear to thee, even by thine own fair eyes
Wherein I see myself—

PORTIA Mark you but that!
In both my eyes he doubly sees himself;
In each eye, one. Swear by your double self,
And there's an oath of credit.

BASSANIO Nay, but hear me.
Pardon this fault, and by my soul I swear
I never more will break an oath with thee.

ANTONIO
I once did lend my body for his wealth,
Which, but for him that had your husband's ring,
Had quite miscarried. I dare be bound again,
My soul upon the forfeit, that your lord
Will nevermore break faith advisedly.

PORTIA
Then you shall be his surety. Give him this,
And bid him keep it better than the other.
[*She gives the ring to Antonio, who gives it to Bassanio.*]

ANTONIO
Here, Lord Bassanio. Swear to keep this ring.

BASSANIO
By heaven, it is the same I gave the doctor!

PORTIA
I had it of him. Pardon me, Bassanio,
For by this ring the doctor lay with me.

NERISSA
And pardon me, my gentle Gratiano,
For that same scrubbèd boy, the doctor's clerk,
In lieu of this last night did lie with me.
[*Presenting her ring.*]

183 aught anything **199 virtue** moral efficacy **201 contain** keep safe **205 wanted the modesty** who would have been so lacking in consideration as **206 urge** insist upon receiving. **ceremony** something sacred. **210 civil doctor** i.e., doctor of civil law **213 suffered** allowed **219 it** i.e., my honor. **220 blessèd . . . night** i.e., stars **226 liberal** generous (sexually as well as otherwise)

229 Know (With the suggestion of carnal knowledge.) **230 from** away from. **Argus** mythological monster with a hundred eyes **232 honor** (1) honorable name (2) chastity **234 be well advised** take care **236 take** apprehend **237 pen** (With sexual double meaning.) **245 double** i.e., deceitful **246 of credit** worthy to be believed. (Said ironically.) **249 wealth** welfare **252 My . . . forfeit** at the risk of eternal damnation **253 advisedly** intentionally. **254 surety** guarantor. **262 In lieu of** in return for

GRATIANO
Why, this is like the mending of highways
In summer, where the ways are fair enough.
What, are we cuckolds ere we have deserved it?

PORTIA
Speak not so grossly. You are all amazed.
Here is a letter; read it at your leisure.
[*She gives a letter.*]
It comes from Padua, from Bellario.
There you shall find that Portia was the doctor,
Nerissa there her clerk. Lorenzo here
Shall witness I set forth as soon as you,
And even but now returned; I have not yet
Entered my house. Antonio, you are welcome,
And I have better news in store for you
Than you expect. Unseal this letter soon.
[*She gives him a letter.*]
There you shall find three of your argosies
Are richly come to harbor suddenly.
You shall not know by what strange accident
I chancèd on this letter.

ANTONIO
I am dumb.

BASSANIO [*to Portia*]
Were you the doctor and I knew you not?

GRATIANO [*to Nerissa*]
Were you the clerk that is to make me cuckold?

NERISSA
Ay, but the clerk that never means to do it,
Unless he live until he be a man.

BASSANIO
Sweet doctor, you shall be my bedfellow.
When I am absent, then lie with my wife.

ANTONIO
Sweet lady, you have given me life and living;
For here I read for certain that my ships
Are safely come to road.

PORTIA
How now, Lorenzo?
My clerk hath some good comforts too for you.

NERISSA
Ay, and I'll give them him without a fee.
[*She gives a deed.*]
There do I give to you and Jessica,
From the rich Jew, a special deed of gift,
After his death, of all he dies possessed of.

LORENZO
Fair ladies, you drop manna in the way
Of starved people.

PORTIA
It is almost morning,
And yet I am sure you are not satisfied
Of these events at full. Let us go in;
And charge us there upon inter'gatories,
And we will answer all things faithfully.

GRATIANO
Let it be so. The first inter'gatory
That my Nerissa shall be sworn on is
Whether till the next night she had rather stay
Or go to bed now, being two hours to day.
But were the day come, I should wish it dark
Till I were couching with the doctor's clerk.
Well, while I live I'll fear no other thing
So sore as keeping safe Nerissa's ring. *Exeunt.*

264 are fair enough i.e., are not in need of repair. **265 cuckolds** husbands whose wives are unfaithful **279 dumb** at a loss for words.

288 road anchorage. **294 manna** the food from heaven that was miraculously supplied to the Israelites in the wilderness (Exodus 16) **298 And . . . inter'gatories** and put questions to us (as in a court of law) **302 stay** wait **305 couching** going to bed **307 ring** (With sexual suggestion.)

Much Ado About Nothing

Much Ado about Nothing belongs to a group of Shakespeare's most mature romantic comedies, linked by similar titles, that also includes *As You Like It* and *Twelfth Night* (subtitled *What You Will*). All date from the period 1598 to 1600. These plays are the culmination of Shakespeare's exuberant, philosophical, and festive vein in comedy, with only an occasional anticipation of the darker problem comedies of the early 1600s. They also parallel the culmination of Shakespeare's writing of history plays, in *Henry IV* and *V*.

Much Ado excels in combative wit and in swift, colloquial prose. It differs, too, from several other comedies (including *A Midsummer Night's Dream* and *The Merchant of Venice*) in that it features no journey of the lovers, no heroine disguised as a man, no envious court or city contrasted with an idealized landscape of the artist's imagination. Instead, the prevailing motif is that of the mask. Prominent scenes include a masked ball (2.1), a charade offstage in which the villainous Borachio misrepresents himself as the lover of Hero (actually Margaret in disguise), and a marriage ceremony with the supposedly dead bride masking as her own cousin (5.3). The word *Nothing* in the play's title, pronounced rather like *noting* in the English of Elizabethan London and vicinity, suggests a pun on the idea of overhearing as well as of musical notation; it also has a bawdy connotation, as when Hamlet wryly suggests to Ophelia that "Nothing" is "a fair thought to lie between maids' legs" (*Hamlet*, 3.2.116–18; see also *Othello*, 3.3.317, where Iago responds to his wife's "I have a thing for you" with a degrading sexual insult). Overhearings are constant and are essential to the process of both misunderstanding (as in the false rumor of Don Pedro's wooing Hero for himself) and clarification (as in the discovery by the night watch of the slander done to Hero's reputation, or in the revelation to Beatrice and Benedick of each other's true state of mind). The masks, or roles, that the characters incessantly assume are, for the most part, defensive and inimical to mutual understanding. How can they be dispelled? It is the search for candor and self-awareness in relationships with others, the quest for honesty and respect beneath conventional outward appearances, that provides the journey in this play.

Structurally, the play contrasts two pairs of lovers. The ladies, Beatrice and Hero, are cousins and close friends. The gentlemen, Benedick and Claudio, Italian gentlemen and fellow officers under the command of Don Pedro, have returned from the war, in which they have fought bravely. These similarities chiefly serve, however, to accentuate the differences between the two couples. Hero is modest, retiring, usually silent, and obedient to her father's will. Claudio appears ideally suited to her, since he is also respectful and decorous. They are conventional lovers in the roles of romantic hero and naive heroine. Beatrice and Benedick, on the other hand, are renowned for "a kind of merry war" between them. Although obviously destined to come together, they are seemingly too independent and skeptical of convention to be tolerant and accepting in love. They scoff so at romantic sentimentality that they cannot permit themselves to drop their satirical masks. Yet, paradoxically, their relationship is ultimately more surefooted because of their refusal to settle for the illusory cliches of many young wooers.

As in some of his other comic double plots (*The Taming of the Shrew*, for example), Shakespeare has linked together two stories of diverse origins and contrasting tones in order to set off one against the other. The Hero-Claudio plot is Italianate in flavor and origin, sensational, melodramatic, and potentially tragic. In fact, the often told story of the maiden falsely slandered did frequently end in disaster—as, for example, in Edmund Spenser's *Faerie Queene*, 2.4 (1590). Spenser was apparently indebted to Ariosto's *Orlando Furioso* (translated into English by Sir John Harington, 1591), as were Peter Beverly in *The Historie of Ariodanto and Ieneura* (1566) and Richard Mulcaster in his play *Ariodante and Genevora* (1583).

Shakespeare seems to have relied more on the Italian version by Matteo Bandello (Lucca, 1554) and its French translation by Belleforest, *Histoires Tragiques* (1569). Still other versions have been discovered, both nondramatic and dramatic, although it cannot be established that Shakespeare was reworking an old play. Various factual inconsistencies in Shakespeare's text (such as Leonato's wife Innogen and a "kinsman" who are named briefly in both Quarto and Folio but have no roles in the play) can perhaps be explained by Shakespeare's having worked quickly from more than one source.

Shakespeare's other plot, of Benedick and Beatrice, is much more English and his own. The battle of the sexes is a staple of English medieval humor (Chaucer's Wife of Bath, the Wakefield play of *Noah*) and of Shakespeare's own early comedy: Berowne and Rosaline in *Love's Labor's Lost*, Petruchio and Katharina in *The Taming of the Shrew*. The merry war of Benedick and Beatrice is Shakespeare's finest achievement in this vein and was to become a rich legacy in the later English comedy of William Congreve, Oscar Wilde, and George Bernard Shaw. The tone is lighthearted, bantering, and reassuring, in contrast with the Italianate mood of vengeance and duplicity in the Claudio-Hero plot. No less English are the clownish antics of Dogberry and his crew, representing still another group of characters although not a separate plot. Like Constable Dull in *Love's Labor's Lost* or the tradesmen of *A Midsummer Night's Dream*, the buffoons of *Much Ado* function in a nominally Mediterranean setting but are nonetheless recognizable London types. Their preposterous antics not only puncture the ominous mood threatening our enjoyment of the main plot but also, absurdly enough, even help to abort a potential crime. When Dogberry comes, laughter cannot be far behind.

The two plots provide contrasting perspectives on the nature of love. Because it is sensational and melodramatic, the Claudio-Hero plot stresses situation at the expense of character. The conspiracy that nearly overwhelms the lovers is an engrossing story, but they themselves remain one-dimensional. They interest us more as conventional types, and hence as foils to Benedick and Beatrice, than as lovers in their own right. Benedick and Beatrice, on the other hand, are psychologically complex. Clearly, they are fascinated with each other. Beatrice's questions in the first scene, although abusive in tone, betray her concern for Benedick's welfare. Has he safely returned from the wars? How did he bear himself in battle? Who are his companions? She tests his moral character by high standards, suspecting that he will fail because she demands so much. We are not surprised when she lectures her docile cousin, Hero, on the folly of submitting to parental choice in marriage: "It is my cousin's duty to make curtsy and say, 'Father, as it please you.' But yet for all that, cousin, let him be a handsome fellow, or else make another curtsy and say, 'Father, as it please me' " (2.1.49–52). Beatrice remains single not from love of spinsterhood but from insistence on a nearly perfect mate. Paradoxically, she who is the inveterate scoffer is the true idealist. And we know from her unceasing fascination with Benedick that he, of all the men in her acquaintance, comes closest to her mark. The only fear preventing the revelation of her love—a not unnatural fear, in view of the insults she and Benedick exchange—is that he will prove faithless and jest at her weakness.

Benedick is similarly hemmed in by his posturing as "a professed tyrant to their sex." Despite his reputation as a perennial bachelor and his wry amusement at Claudio's newfound passion, Benedick confesses in soliloquy (2.3.8–34) that he could be won to affection by the ideal woman. Again, his criteria are chiefly those of temperament and moral character, although he by no means spurns wealth, beauty, and social position; the happiest couples are those well matched in fortune's gifts. "Rich she shall be, that's certain; wise, or I'll none; virtuous, or I'll never cheapen her; fair, or I'll never look on her; mild, or come not near me; noble, or not I for an angel; of good discourse, an excellent musician, and her hair shall be of what color it please God." This last self-mocking concession indicates that Benedick is aware of how impossibly much he is asking. Still, there is one woman, Beatrice, who may well possess all of these qualities except mildness. Even her sharp wit is part of her admirable intelligence. She is a match for Benedick, and he is a man who would never tolerate the submissive conventionality of someone like Hero. All that appears to be lacking, in fact, is any sign of fondness on Beatrice's part. For him to make overtures would be to invite her withering scorn—not to mention the I-told-you-so mockery of his friends.

Benedick and Beatrice have been playing the game of verbal abuse for so long that they scarcely remember how it started—perhaps as a squaring-off between the only two intelligences worthy of contending with each other, perhaps as a more profoundly defensive reaction of two sensitive persons not willing to part lightly with their independence. They seem to have had a prior relationsip with each other that ended unhappily. They know that intimate involvement with another person is a complex matter—one that can cause heartache. Yet the masks they wear with each other are scarcely satisfactory. At the masked ball (2.1), we see how hurtful the "merry war" has become. Benedick, attempting to pass himself off as a stranger in a mask, abuses Beatrice by telling her of her reputation for disdain; but she, perceiving who he is, retaliates by telling him as a purported stranger what she "really" thinks of Benedick. These devices cut deeply and confirm the worst fears of each. Ironically, these fears can be dispelled only by the virtuous deceptions practiced on them by their friends. Once Benedick is assured that Beatrice secretly loves him, masking her affection with scorn, he acquires the confidence he needs to make a commitment, and vice versa in her case. The beauty of the virtuous deceptions, moreover, is that they are so plausible—because, indeed, they are essentially true. Benedick overhears himself described as a person so satirical that Beatrice dare not reveal her affection, for fear of being repulsed (2.3). Beatrice learns that she is indeed called disdainful by her friends (3.1). Both lovers respond generously to these revelations, accepting the accusations as richly deserved and placing no blame on the other. As Beatrice proclaims to herself, "Contempt, farewell, and maiden pride, adieu!" The relief afforded by this honesty is genuine and lasting.

Because Claudio knows so little about Hero and is content with superficial expectations, he is vulnerable to a far uglier sort of deception. Claudio's first questions about Hero betray his romantically stereotyped attitudes and his willingness to let Don Pedro and Hero's father, Leonato, arrange a financially advantageous match. Claudio treasures Hero's outward reputation for modesty, an appearance easily besmirched. When a false rumor suggests that Don Pedro is wooing the lady for himself, Claudio's response is predictably cliché-ridden: all's fair in love and war, you can't trust friends in an affair of the heart, and so farewell Hero. The rumor has a superficial plausibility about it, especially when the villainous Don John steps into the situation. Motivated in part by pure malice and the sport of ruining others' happiness, Don John speaks to the masked Claudio at the ball (2.1) as though he were speaking to Benedick and, in this guise, pretends to reveal the secret "fact" of Don Pedro's duplicity in love. (The device is precisely that used by Beatrice to put down Benedick in the same scene.) With this specious confirmation, Claudio leaps to a wrong conclusion, thereby judging both his friend and mistress to be false. He gives them no chance to speak in their own defense. To be sure, Hero's father and uncle have also believed in the false report and have welcomed the prospect of Don Pedro as Hero's husband. She herself raises no objection to the prospect of marriage with the older man. Don Pedro is, after all, a prince of presumably enormous wealth, power, and social status, well above that of Leonato and his well-to-do but bourgeois family; when he asks (perhaps as a pleasantry) if Beatrice will have him as her husband, her polite refusal seems tinged with a note of regret (2.1.303–21). These attractive features in Don Pedro tend to excuse the general willingness to accept the idea of him as a splendidly suitable husband for Hero. Even so, Claudio has revealed a lack of faith resulting from his slender knowledge of Hero and of himself.

The nearly tragic "demonstration" of Hero's infidelity follows the same course, because Claudio has not learned from his first experience. Once again, the villainous Don John first implants the insidious suggestion in Claudio's mind, then creates an illusion entirely plausible to the senses, and finally confirms it with Borachio's testimony. What Claudio and Don Pedro have actually seen is Margaret wooed at Hero's window, shrouded in the dark of night and seen from "afar off in the orchard." The power of suggestion is enough to do the rest. Don John's method, and his pleasure in evil, are much like those of his later counterparts, Iago in *Othello* and Edmund in *King Lear*. Indeed, John is compared with the devil, who has power over mortals' frail senses but must rely on their complicity and acquiescence in evil. Claudio is once again led to denounce faithlessly the virtuous woman whose loyalty he no longer deserves. Yet his fault is typically human and is shared by Don Pedro. Providence gives him a second chance, through the ludicrous and bumbling intervention of Dogberry's night watch. These men overhear the plot of Don John as soon as it is announced to us, so that we know justice will eventually prevail, even though it will also be farcically delayed. Once again, misunderstanding has become "much ado about nothing," an escalating of recriminations based on a purely chimerical assumption that must eventually be deflated. The painful experience is not without value, for it tests the characters' spiritual worth in a crisis. Beatrice, like Friar Francis, shows herself to be a person of unshakable faith in goodness. Benedick, though puzzled and torn in his loyalties, also passes the test and proves himself worthy of Beatrice. Claudio is found wanting, and indeed is judged by many modern readers and audiences to be wholly inadequate, but Hero forgives and accepts him anyway. In her role as the granter of a merciful second chance, she foreshadows the beatifically symbolic nature of many of Shakespeare's later heroines.

Much Ado comes perhaps closer to potentially tragic action than Shakespeare's other festive comedies, though *The Merchant of Venice* is another, and so are late romances like *Cymbeline* and *The Winter's Tale* that *Much Ado* can be said to anticipate in the serious matter of slander against a virtuous heroine. Most strikingly, Claudio's failure is unnervingly like that of Othello. The fact that both men are too easily persuaded to reject and humiliate the innocent women they love suggests a deep inadequacy in each. The tempters (Don John, Iago) cannot alone be blamed; the male lovers themselves are too prone to believe the worst of women. In Claudio we can see a vulnerability in the very way he looks at courtship and marriage. As Benedick jests, Claudio talks almost as though he wants to buy Hero (1.1.172). Certainly his attitude is acquisitive and superficial; as the conquering hero returned from the wars, he is ready to settle down into married respectability, and he needs a socially eligible wife. He desires Hero for her beauty, for her wealth and family connections, and above all for her modesty and her reputation for virginal purity. These are attributes easily impugned by false apearances, and in his too-quick rejection of Hero we see in Claudio a deep cynicism about women. He fears the betrayal and loss of masculine self-esteem that a woman can inflict on him by sexual infidelity. To Claudio, Hero is a saint one moment and a whore the next.

Nor is he the only man to demean her (and women) thus. Don Pedro, his patron and older friend, is no less ready to believe Don John's lies, even though Don Pedro has been deceived by his brother before and should know better. Hero's father collapses in shame when he hears his daughter publicly accused of promiscuity, for Leonato's own reputation is on the line: as a father in a patriarchal society, his responsibility is to guarantee the chastity of his daughter to the younger man who proposes to receive her. Leonato's first assumption is that she must be guilty if other men say so; even he is altogether ready to believe the worst of women. Virtually the whole male world of Messina is victimized by its own fear of womanly perfidy—a fear that seems to arise from male lack of self-assurance and a deep inner conviction of being unloved. Benedick is much to be commended for his skepticism about the slanderous attacks on Hero; in no way does he better prove his worthiness of being Beatrice's husband than in his defense of a traduced and innocent woman. Yet Benedick, too, suffers to such a degree from his own male insecurity that he nearly gives up Beatrice at the very end of the play, even as she is nearly ready to give up him. Despite their self-awareness, these lovers must be rescued from their autonomous self-defensiveness by one more intervention on the part of their friends. Benedick and Beatrice are not wholly unlike Claudio and Hero after all. Both pairs of lovers are saved from their own worst selves by a harmonizing force that works its will through strange and improbable means—even through Constable Dogberry and his watch.

Performance history has abundantly illustrated the durable quality of this remarkable play. Perhaps no other comedy by Shakespeare has been as influential as *Much Ado*, providing as it does a model for wit combat and comedy of manners in William Congreve's *The Way of the World*, Oscar Wilde's *The Importance of Being Earnest*, George Bernard Shaw's *Man and Superman*, Noel Coward's *Private Lives*, Tom Stoppard's *The Real Thing*, and many others. Onstage the play has always been a favorite in the repertory, featuring such couples as Hannah Pritchard and David Garrick, Ellen Terry and Henry Irving, Peggy Ashcroft and John Gielgud, Diana Wynyard and Anthony Quayle, Janet Suzman and Alan Howard, Maggie Smith and Robert Stephens, Judi Dench and Donald Sinden, Sinead Cusack and Derek Jacobi, and many more. A commercial television production by A. J. Antoon, originating in New York's Delacorte Theater in 1972, was witnessed by more viewers on that occasion than had seen the play in its entire stage history. Kenneth Branagh's 1993 film, with Emma Thompson and Branagh in the leading roles, along with Denzel Washington as Don Pedro and Michael Keaton as Dogberry, capitalized on a gorgeous Italian villa and its star-laden cast to produce one of the most popular of Shakespeare cinemas. Emma Thompson shows us a Beatrice who is strong, independent, not easily fooled, undaunted by men, and willing to marry Benedick (Branagh) only after she has tested him and made clear the mutuality of respect that she demands. In recent years the play has been located in a wide variety of updated settings: frontier Texas, small-town America right after the Spanish-American War, Victorian India of the British Raj, Regency England, the Edwardian era, mafiosa Sicily, and still more. The incessant updating testifies paradoxically to the play's engaging timelessness; it works anywhere and any time. The play continues to succeed because it is so genuinely open to such interpretations.

Much Ado About Nothing

[*Dramatis Personae*

DON PEDRO, *Prince of Aragon*
LEONATO, *Governor of Messina*
ANTONIO, *his brother*

BENEDICK, *a young lord of Padua*
BEATRICE, *Leonato's niece*
CLAUDIO, *a young lord of Florence*
HERO, *Leonato's daughter*
MARGARET, } *gentlewomen attending Hero*
URSULA, }

DON JOHN, *Don Pedro's bastard brother*
BORACHIO, } *followers of Don John*
CONRADE, }

DOGBERRY, *Constable in charge of the Watch*
VERGES, *the Headborough, or parish constable, Dogberry's partner*
A SEXTON (FRANCIS SEACOAL)
FIRST WATCHMAN
SECOND WATCHMAN (GEORGE SEACOAL)

BALTHASAR, *a singer attending Don Pedro*
FRIAR FRANCIS
A BOY
MESSENGER *to Leonato*
Another MESSENGER

Attendants, Musicians, Members of the Watch, Antonio's Son, and other Kinsmen

SCENE: *Messina*]

[1.1]

Enter Leonato, Governor of Messina, Hero his daughter, and Beatrice his niece, with a Messenger.

LEONATO [*holding a letter*] I learn in this letter that Don Pedro of Aragon comes this night to Messina.

MESSENGER He is very near by this. He was not three leagues off when I left him.

LEONATO How many gentlemen have you lost in this action?

MESSENGER But few of any sort and none of name.

LEONATO A victory is twice itself when the achiever brings home full numbers. I find here that Don Pedro hath bestowed much honor on a young Florentine called Claudio.

MESSENGER Much deserved on his part and equally remembered by Don Pedro. He hath borne himself beyond the promise of his age, doing in the figure of a lamb the feats of a lion. He hath indeed better bettered expectation than you must expect of me to tell you how.

LEONATO He hath an uncle here in Messina will be very much glad of it.

MESSENGER I have already delivered him letters, and there appears much joy in him, even so much that joy could not show itself modest enough without a badge of bitterness.

LEONATO Did he break out into tears?

MESSENGER In great measure.

LEONATO A kind overflow of kindness. There are no faces truer than those that are so washed. How much better is it to weep at joy than to joy at weeping!

BEATRICE I pray you, is Signor Mountanto returned from the wars or no?

MESSENGER I know none of that name, lady. There was none such in the army of any sort.

LEONATO What is he that you ask for, niece?

1.1. Location: Messina. Before Leonato's house.
4 leagues units of about three miles **6 action** battle. **7 sort** rank. **name** reputation, or noble name. **13 remembered** rewarded

16 bettered surpassed **18 will** who will **21–3 joy . . . bitterness** joy could show a decorous moderation only by weeping at the same time. **26 kind** natural **29 Mountanto** montanto, an upward blow or thrust in fencing

HERO My cousin means Signor Benedick of Padua.

MESSENGER Oh, he's returned, and as pleasant as ever he was.

BEATRICE He set up his bills here in Messina and challenged Cupid at the flight; and my uncle's fool, reading the challenge, subscribed for Cupid and challenged him at the bird-bolt. I pray you, how many hath he killed and eaten in these wars? But how many hath he killed? For indeed I promised to eat all of his killing.

LEONATO Faith, niece, you tax Signor Benedick too much, but he'll be meet with you, I doubt it not.

MESSENGER He hath done good service, lady, in these wars.

BEATRICE You had musty victual, and he hath holp to eat it. He is a very valiant trencherman; he hath an excellent stomach.

MESSENGER And a good soldier too, lady.

BEATRICE And a good soldier to a lady, but what is he to a lord?

MESSENGER A lord to a lord, a man to a man, stuffed with all honorable virtues.

BEATRICE It is so, indeed, he is no less than a stuffed man. But for the stuffing—well, we are all mortal.

LEONATO You must not, sir, mistake my niece. There is a kind of merry war betwixt Signor Benedick and her. They never meet but there's a skirmish of wit between them.

BEATRICE Alas! He gets nothing by that. In our last conflict, four of his five wits went halting off, and now is the whole man governed with one; so that if he have wit enough to keep himself warm, let him bear it for a difference between himself and his horse, for it is all the wealth that he hath left to be known a reasonable creature. Who is his companion now? He hath every month a new sworn brother.

MESSENGER Is't possible?

BEATRICE Very easily possible. He wears his faith but as the fashion of his hat; it ever changes with the next block.

MESSENGER I see, lady, the gentleman is not in your books.

BEATRICE No. An he were, I would burn my study. But I pray you, who is his companion? Is there no young squarer now that will make a voyage with him to the devil?

MESSENGER He is most in the company of the right noble Claudio.

BEATRICE Oh, Lord, he will hang upon him like a disease! He is sooner caught than the pestilence, and the taker runs presently mad. God help the noble Claudio! If he have caught the Benedick, it will cost him a thousand pound ere 'a be cured.

MESSENGER I will hold friends with you, lady.

BEATRICE Do, good friend.

LEONATO You will never run mad, niece.

BEATRICE No, not till a hot January.

MESSENGER Don Pedro is approached.

Enter Don Pedro, Claudio, Benedick, Balthasar, and [*Don*] *John the Bastard.*

DON PEDRO Good Signor Leonato, are you come to meet your trouble? The fashion of the world is to avoid cost, and you encounter it.

LEONATO Never came trouble to my house in the likeness of Your Grace. For trouble being gone, comfort should remain; but when you depart from me, sorrow abides and happiness takes his leave.

DON PEDRO You embrace your charge too willingly.—I think this is your daughter.

[*Presenting himself to Hero.*]

LEONATO Her mother hath many times told me so.

BENEDICK Were you in doubt, sir, that you asked her?

LEONATO Signor Benedick, no; for then were you a child.

DON PEDRO You have it full, Benedick. We may guess by this what you are, being a man. Truly, the lady fathers herself. Be happy, lady, for you are like an honorable father.

BENEDICK If Signor Leonato be her father, she would not have his head on her shoulders for all Messina, as like him as she is. [*Don Pedro and Leonato talk aside.*]

BEATRICE I wonder that you will still be talking, Signor Benedick. Nobody marks you.

BENEDICK What, my dear Lady Disdain! Are you yet living?

BEATRICE Is it possible disdain should die while she hath such meet food to feed it as Signor Benedick?

35 pleasant jocular **37 bills** placards, advertisements **38 at the flight** to a long-distance archery contest. (Beatrice mocks Benedick's pretentions as a lady killer.) **my uncle's fool** (Perhaps a professional fool in her uncle's service.) **39 subscribed for** accepted on behalf of **40 bird-bolt** a blunt-headed arrow used for fowling. (Sometimes used by children because of its relative harmlessness and thus conventionally appropriate to Cupid.) **43 tax** disparage **44 meet** even, quits **47 musty victual** stale food. **holp** helped **48 valiant trencherman** great eater **49 stomach** appetite. (With a mocking suggestion also of "courage.") **51 soldier to a lady** lady killer. (With a play on *to/too.*) **52 to** compared to **53 stuffed** amply supplied **55–6 a stuffed man** i.e., a figure stuffed to resemble a man. **56 the stuffing** i.e., what he's truly made of. **well . . . mortal** i.e., well, we all have our faults. **62 five wits** i.e., not the five senses, but the five faculties: memory, imagination, judgment, fantasy, common sense. **halting** limping **65 difference** heraldic feature distinguishing a junior member or branch of a family. (With a play on the usual sense.) **65–7 it is . . . creature** i.e., his feeble wit is all he has left to identify him as rationally human. **68 sworn brother** brother in arms (*frater juratus,* an allusion to the ancient practice of swearing brotherhood). **70 faith** allegiance, or fidelity **72 block** mold for shaping hats.

73–4 in your books in favor with you, in your good books. (But Beatrice, in her reply, takes *books* in the literal sense of something to be found in a library.) **75 An** If. (Also in line 131.) **77 squarer** quarreler **81 he** i.e., Benedick **83 presently** immediately **84 the Benedick** i.e., as if this were a disease **85 'a** he **86 hold friends** keep on friendly terms (so as not to earn your enmity) **88 run mad** i.e., "catch the Benedick" **89 not . . . January** i.e., not any time soon. **92 your trouble** i.e., the expense of entertaining me and my retinue. **93 encounter** go to meet **98 charge** social responsibility and expense **104 have it full** are well answered **106 fathers herself** shows by appearance who her father is. **109 his head** i.e., with Leonato's white beard and signs of age **116 meet** suitable. (With a pun on "meat.")

Courtesy itself must convert to disdain, if you come in her presence.

BENEDICK Then is courtesy a turncoat. But it is certain I am loved of all ladies, only you excepted; and I would I could find in my heart that I had not a hard heart, for truly I love none.

BEATRICE A dear happiness to women! They would else have been troubled with a pernicious suitor. I thank God and my cold blood I am of your humor for that. I had rather hear my dog bark at a crow than a man swear he loves me.

BENEDICK God keep Your Ladyship still in that mind! So some gentleman or other shall scape a predestinate scratched face.

BEATRICE Scratching could not make it worse, an 'twere such a face as yours were.

BENEDICK Well, you are a rare parrot-teacher.

BEATRICE A bird of my tongue is better than a beast of yours.

BENEDICK I would my horse had the speed of your tongue and so good a continuer. But keep your way, i'God's name; I have done.

BEATRICE You always end with a jade's trick. I know you of old.

DON PEDRO That is the sum of all, Leonato. Signor Claudio and Signor Benedick, my dear friend Leonato hath invited you all. I tell him we shall stay here at the least a month, and he heartily prays some occasion may detain us longer. I dare swear he is no hypocrite, but prays from his heart.

LEONATO If you swear, my lord, you shall not be forsworn. [*To Don John*] Let me bid you welcome, my lord, being reconciled to the Prince your brother. I owe you all duty.

DON JOHN I thank you. I am not of many words, but I thank you.

LEONATO Please it Your Grace lead on?

DON PEDRO Your hand, Leonato. We will go together.

Exeunt. Manent Benedick and Claudio.

CLAUDIO Benedick, didst thou note the daughter of Signor Leonato?

BENEDICK I noted her not, but I looked on her.

CLAUDIO Is she not a modest young lady?

BENEDICK Do you question me as an honest man should do, for my simple true judgment? Or would you have me speak after my custom, as being a professed tyrant to their sex?

CLAUDIO No, I pray thee, speak in sober judgment.

BENEDICK Why, i'faith, methinks she's too low for a high praise, too brown for a fair praise, and too little for a great praise. Only this commendation I can afford her, that were she other than she is, she were unhandsome, and being no other but as she is, I do not like her.

CLAUDIO Thou thinkest I am in sport. I pray thee, tell me truly how thou lik'st her.

BENEDICK Would you buy her, that you inquire after her?

CLAUDIO Can the world buy such a jewel?

BENEDICK Yea, and a case to put it into. But speak you this with a sad brow? Or do you play the flouting Jack, to tell us Cupid is a good hare-finder and Vulcan a rare carpenter? Come, in what key shall a man take you, to go in the song?

CLAUDIO In mine eye she is the sweetest lady that ever I looked on.

BENEDICK I can see yet without spectacles, and I see no such matter. There's her cousin, an she were not possessed with a fury, exceeds her as much in beauty as the first of May doth the last of December. But I hope you have no intent to turn husband, have you?

CLAUDIO I would scarce trust myself, though I had sworn the contrary, if Hero would be my wife.

BENEDICK Is't come to this? In faith, hath not the world one man but he will wear his cap with suspicion? Shall I never see a bachelor of threescore again? Go to, i'faith; an thou wilt needs thrust thy neck into a yoke, wear the print of it and sigh away Sundays. Look, Don Pedro is returned to seek you.

Enter Don Pedro.

DON PEDRO What secret hath held you here, that you followed not to Leonato's?

BENEDICK I would Your Grace would constrain me to tell.

DON PEDRO I charge thee on thy allegiance.

BENEDICK You hear, Count Claudio. I can be secret as a dumb man—I would have you think so—but on my allegiance, mark you this, on my allegiance! He is in love. With who? Now that is Your Grace's part. Mark how short his answer is: with Hero, Leonato's short daughter.

117 convert change **123 dear happiness** precious piece of luck **125–6 I am . . . that** I am of the same disposition in that matter, i.e., of loving no one. **129 scape** escape. **predestinate** inevitable (for any man who should woo Beatrice) **132 were** i.e., is. **133 rare** outstanding. **parrot-teacher** i.e., one who would teach a parrot well, because you merely "parrot" my lines. **134 of my tongue** taught to speak like me, i.e., incessantly **134–5 of yours** taught to speak like you. **137 and . . . continuer** i.e., and as much staying power in running as you have in talking. **139 a jade's trick** i.e., an ill-tempered horse's habit of slipping its head out of the collar or stopping suddenly (just as Benedick proposes to abandon this exchange of witticisms when he thinks he has had the last word). **141 sum of all** (Don Pedro and Leonato have been conversing apart on other matters.) **149 being** since you are **153 Please it** May it please **154 go together** i.e., go arm in arm (thus avoiding the question of precedence in order of leaving). **154.1** ***Manent*** They remain onstage **157 noted her not** gave her no special attention

162 tyrant one cruel or pitiless in attitude **164 low** short **175 case** (1) jewel case (2) clothing, outer garments. (There is also a bawdy play on the meaning "female pudenda.") **176 sad** serious. **flouting Jack** i.e., mocking rascal **177–8 to tell . . . carpenter?** i.e., are you mocking us with nonsense? (Cupid was blind, not sharp-eyed like a hunter, and Vulcan was a blacksmith, not a carpenter.) **178–9 to . . . song** as the song expresses it. (Alluding perhaps to some popular song.) **184 with a fury** by an avenging, infernal spirit **189–90 hath . . . suspicion?** i.e., isn't there a man left alive who will regard marriage with a jaundiced eye? (A cap might be used, unsuccessfully perhaps, in an attempt to hide a cuckold's horns.) **191 Go to** (An expression of impatience.) **193 wear . . . Sundays** i.e., display the marks of your domestic enslavement resignedly. **197 constrain** order **203 part** speaking part. (I.e., to say, "With who?")

CLAUDIO If this were so, so were it uttered.

BENEDICK Like the old tale, my lord: "It is not so, nor 'twas not so, but indeed, God forbid it should be so."

CLAUDIO If my passion change not shortly, God forbid it should be otherwise.

DON PEDRO Amen, if you love her, for the lady is very well worthy.

CLAUDIO You speak this to fetch me in, my lord.

DON PEDRO By my troth, I speak my thought.

CLAUDIO And in faith, my lord, I spoke mine.

BENEDICK And by my two faiths and troths, my lord, I spoke mine.

CLAUDIO That I love her, I feel.

DON PEDRO That she is worthy, I know.

BENEDICK That I neither feel how she should be loved nor know how she should be worthy is the opinion that fire cannot melt out of me. I will die in it at the stake.

DON PEDRO Thou wast ever an obstinate heretic in the despite of beauty.

CLAUDIO And never could maintain his part but in the force of his will.

BENEDICK That a woman conceived me, I thank her; that she brought me up, I likewise give her most humble thanks. But that I will have a recheat winded in my forehead or hang my bugle in an invisible baldrick, all women shall pardon me. Because I will not do them the wrong to mistrust any, I will do myself the right to trust none; and the fine is, for the which I may go the finer, I will live a bachelor.

DON PEDRO I shall see thee, ere I die, look pale with love.

BENEDICK With anger, with sickness, or with hunger, my lord, not with love. Prove that ever I lose more blood with love than I will get again with drinking, pick out mine eyes with a ballad-maker's pen and hang me up at the door of a brothel house for the sign of blind Cupid.

DON PEDRO Well, if ever thou dost fall from this faith, thou wilt prove a notable argument.

BENEDICK If I do, hang me in a bottle like a cat and shoot at me, and he that hits me, let him be clapped on the shoulder and called Adam.

DON PEDRO Well, as time shall try:
"In time the savage bull doth bear the yoke."

BENEDICK The savage bull may; but if ever the sensible Benedick bear it, pluck off the bull's horns and set them in my forehead, and let me be vilely painted, and in such great letters as they write, "Here is good horse to hire," let them signify under my sign, "Here you may see Benedick the married man."

CLAUDIO If this should ever happen, thou wouldst be horn-mad.

DON PEDRO Nay, if Cupid have not spent all his quiver in Venice, thou wilt quake for this shortly.

BENEDICK I look for an earthquake too, then.

DON PEDRO Well, you will temporize with the hours. In the meantime, good Signor Benedick, repair to Leonato's. Commend me to him, and tell him I will not fail him at supper, for indeed he hath made great preparation.

BENEDICK I have almost matter enough in me for such an embassage; and so I commit you—

CLAUDIO To the tuition of God. From my house, if I had it—

DON PEDRO The sixth of July. Your loving friend, Benedick.

BENEDICK Nay, mock not, mock not. The body of your discourse is sometime guarded with fragments, and the guards are but slightly basted on neither. Ere you flout old ends any further, examine your conscience. And so I leave you. *Exit.*

CLAUDIO
My liege, Your Highness now may do me good.

DON PEDRO
My love is thine to teach. Teach it but how,
And thou shalt see how apt it is to learn
Any hard lesson that may do thee good.

CLAUDIO
Hath Leonato any son, my lord?

DON PEDRO
No child but Hero; she's his only heir.
Dost thou affect her, Claudio?

CLAUDIO O my lord,

206 If . . . uttered If this were true, it might be told in words to this effect. **207 old tale** (In the English fairy tale known as "Mr. Fox," a murderous wooer, discovered in his crimes by the lady he seeks to marry and victimize, repeatedly disclaims her recital of what she has seen by the refrain here set in quotations. The story is a variant of the theme known as "the Robber Bridegroom." Benedick uses it mockingly here to characterize Claudio's reluctance to admit his "crime" of falling in love.) **213 fetch me in** get me to confess **214 By my troth** By my faith, upon my word. (A mild oath.) **216 by . . . troths** as it were, by my loyalty to you both **225 despite** contempt **226–7 in . . . will** by mere obstinacy (which, as defined by the Schoolmen, was the state of the heretic). **230–2 But that . . . me** i.e., Women must pardon me for refusing to have a horn placed on my head as if I were a cuckold. (A *recheat* is a hunting call sounded [*winded*] on a horn to assemble the hounds; a *baldrick* is a strap that supports the horn, here *invisible* because the horn is the metaphorical one of cuckoldry.)
234 fine conclusion **234–5 go the finer** be more finely dressed (since without a wife I will have more money to spend on clothing)
239 Prove If you can prove **239–40 lose . . . drinking** (According to Elizabethan theory, each sigh cost the heart a drop of blood, whereas blood was replenished by wine.) **241 ballad-maker's pen** i.e., such as would be used to write love ballads or satires **242 sign** painted sign, such as hung over inns and shops **245 notable argument** notorious subject for conversation, example.

246 bottle wicker or leather basket (to hold the cat sometimes used as an archery target) **248 Adam** (Probably refers to Adam Bell, archer outlaw of the ballads.) **250 In . . . yoke** (Proverbial.) **258 horn-mad** stark mad. (From the fury of horned beasts; with allusion to cuckoldry.) **260 Venice** (A city noted for licentiousness.) **quake** (With a pun on *quiver* in the previous line.) **261 I . . . then** i.e., My falling in love will be at least as rare as an earthquake. **262 temporize . . . hours** come to terms, or become milder, in time. (With perhaps a bawdy pun on *hours,* "whores," pronounced something like "hoors.")
267 matter wit, intelligence **268 embassage** mission. **and so . . . you** (A conventional close, which Claudio and Don Pedro mockingly play with as though it were the complimentary close of a letter.)
269 tuition protection **274 guarded** ornamented, trimmed
275 guards . . . neither trimmings are tenuously stitched on at best, have only the flimsiest connection. **276 flout old ends** quote or recite mockingly proverbial tags of wisdom (as well as fragments of cloth, or the *ends* of letters that Claudio and Don Pedro have been parodying). **examine your conscience** look to your own behavior or speech.
278 do me good do me some good, help me. **284 affect** love

When you went onward on this ended action,
I looked upon her with a soldier's eye,
That liked, but had a rougher task in hand
Than to drive liking to the name of love.
But now I am returned and that war thoughts
Have left their places vacant, in their rooms
Come thronging soft and delicate desires,
All prompting me how fair young Hero is,
Saying, I liked her ere I went to wars.

DON PEDRO
Thou wilt be like a lover presently
And tire the hearer with a book of words.
If thou dost love fair Hero, cherish it,
And I will break with her and with her father,
And thou shalt have her. Was't not to this end
That thou began'st to twist so fine a story?

CLAUDIO
How sweetly you do minister to love,
That know love's grief by his complexion!
But lest my liking might too sudden seem,
I would have salved it with a longer treatise.

DON PEDRO
What need the bridge much broader than the flood?
The fairest grant is the necessity.
Look what will serve is fit. 'Tis once: thou lovest,
And I will fit thee with the remedy.
I know we shall have reveling tonight;
I will assume thy part in some disguise
And tell fair Hero I am Claudio,
And in her bosom I'll unclasp my heart
And take her hearing prisoner with the force
And strong encounter of my amorous tale.
Then after to her father will I break,
And the conclusion is, she shall be thine.
In practice let us put it presently. *Exeunt.*

✤

[1.2]

Enter Leonato and an old man [*Antonio*], *brother to Leonato,* [*meeting*].

LEONATO How now, brother, where is my cousin, your son? Hath he provided this music?

ANTONIO He is very busy about it. But brother, I can tell you strange news that you yet dreamt not of.

LEONATO Are they good?

ANTONIO As the event stamps them, but they have a good cover; they show well outward. The Prince and Count Claudio, walking in a thick-pleached alley in mine orchard, were thus much overheard by a man of mine: the Prince discovered to Claudio that he loved my niece your daughter and meant to acknowledge it this night in a dance, and if he found her accordant, he meant to take the present time by the top and instantly break with you of it.

LEONATO Hath the fellow any wit that told you this?

ANTONIO A good sharp fellow. I will send for him, and question him yourself.

LEONATO No, no; we will hold it as a dream till it appear itself. But I will acquaint my daughter withal, that she may be the better prepared for an answer, if peradventure this be true. Go you and tell her of it.

[*Enter Antonio's Son, with a musician and others.*]

Cousins, you know what you have to do.—Oh, I cry you mercy, friend; go you with me, and I will use your skill.—Good cousin, have a care this busy time. *Exeunt.*

✤

[1.3]

Enter Sir [*Don*] *John the Bastard and Conrade, his companion.*

CONRADE What the goodyear, my lord! Why are you thus out of measure sad?

DON JOHN There is no measure in the occasion that breeds; therefore the sadness is without limit.

CONRADE You should hear reason.

DON JOHN And when I have heard it, what blessing brings it?

CONRADE If not a present remedy, at least a patient sufferance.

DON JOHN I wonder that thou, being, as thou say'st thou art, born under Saturn, goest about to apply a moral medicine to a mortifying mischief. I cannot hide what I am: I must be sad when I have cause and smile at no man's jests, eat when I have stomach and wait for no man's leisure, sleep when I am drowsy and tend on no man's business, laugh when I am merry and claw no man in his humor.

CONRADE Yea, but you must not make the full show of this till you may do it without controlment. You have of late stood out against your brother, and he hath ta'en you newly into his grace, where it is impossible you should take true root but by the fair weather that

285 ended action military action now ended **289 now** now that **297 break** open the subject. (As also in line 314.) **299 twist** draw out the thread of **301 his complexion** its outward appearance. **303 salved** soothed, eased the way for **304 What need** Why need be. **flood** river. **305 The fairest . . . necessity** The best thing to do is simply what is necessary. **306 Look what** Whatever. **'Tis once** In short, once and for all. (This speech of Don Pedro's is overheard by a servant of Antonio's, as we learn in the next scene.)

1.2 Location: Leonato's house.

1 cousin kinsman **5 they** i.e., the news. (Often treated as a plural noun, as at 2.1.167.) **6 event** outcome **6–7 they . . . cover** (The image is of a printed book, promising well by its cover.)

8 thick-pleached alley walk lined with dense hedges of intertwined shrubs **9 orchard** garden. **man** servant **10 discovered** disclosed **12 accordant** agreeing, consenting **13 take . . . top** i.e., seize the opportunity. (Proverbially, Occasion was imagined bald in the back of the head but with a forelock hair in the front that opportunistically could be grabbed.) **15 wit** sense, intelligence **22–3 cry you mercy** beg your pardon **23 friend** (Addressed perhaps to the musician.)

1.3. Location: Leonato's house.

1 What the goodyear i.e., What the deuce **2 out of measure** immoderately **5 hear** listen to **9 sufferance** endurance. **11 under Saturn** (Hence, of a morose disposition.) **11–12 goest . . . mischief** endeavor to cure with moral commonplaces a deadly disease. **14 stomach** appetite **16 tend on** attend to **17 claw** flatter. **humor** whim. **19 controlment** restraint. **20 stood out** rebelled **21 grace** favor

you make yourself. It is needful that you frame the season for your own harvest.

DON JOHN I had rather be a canker in a hedge than a rose in his grace, and it better fits my blood to be disdained of all than to fashion a carriage to rob love from any. In this, though I cannot be said to be a flattering honest man, it must not be denied but I am a plain-dealing villain. I am trusted with a muzzle and enfranchised with a clog; therefore I have decreed not to sing in my cage. If I had my mouth, I would bite; if I had my liberty, I would do my liking. In the meantime let me be that I am, and seek not to alter me.

CONRADE Can you make no use of your discontent?

DON JOHN I make all use of it, for I use it only. Who comes here?

Enter Borachio.

What news, Borachio?

BORACHIO I came yonder from a great supper. The Prince your brother is royally entertained by Leonato, and I can give you intelligence of an intended marriage.

DON JOHN Will it serve for any model to build mischief on? What is he for a fool that betroths himself to unquietness?

BORACHIO Marry, it is your brother's right hand.

DON JOHN Who, the most exquisite Claudio?

BORACHIO Even he.

DON JOHN A proper squire! And who, and who? Which way looks he?

BORACHIO Marry, one Hero, the daughter and heir of Leonato.

DON JOHN A very forward March chick! How came you to this?

BORACHIO Being entertained for a perfumer, as I was smoking a musty room, comes me the Prince and Claudio, hand in hand, in sad conference. I whipped me behind the arras, and there heard it agreed upon that the Prince should woo Hero for himself and, having obtained her, give her to Count Claudio.

DON JOHN Come, come, let us thither. This may prove food to my displeasure. That young start-up hath all the glory of my overthrow. If I can cross him any way, I bless myself every way. You are both sure, and will assist me?

CONRADE To the death, my lord.

DON JOHN Let us to the great supper. Their cheer is the greater that I am subdued. Would the cook were o' my mind! Shall we go prove what's to be done?

BORACHIO We'll wait upon Your Lordship. *Exeunt.*

[2.1]

Enter Leonato, his brother [Antonio], Hero his daughter, and Beatrice his niece [with Margaret and Ursula].

LEONATO Was not Count John here at supper?

ANTONIO I saw him not.

BEATRICE How tartly that gentleman looks! I never can see him but I am heartburned an hour after.

HERO He is of a very melancholy disposition.

BEATRICE He were an excellent man that were made just in the midway between him and Benedick. The one is too like an image and says nothing, and the other too like my lady's eldest son, evermore tattling.

LEONATO Then half Signor Benedick's tongue in Count John's mouth, and half Count John's melancholy in Signor Benedick's face—

BEATRICE With a good leg and a good foot, uncle, and money enough in his purse, such a man would win any woman in the world, if 'a could get her good will.

LEONATO By my troth, niece, thou wilt never get thee a husband if thou be so shrewd of thy tongue.

ANTONIO In faith, she's too curst.

BEATRICE Too curst is more than curst. I shall lessen God's sending that way; for it is said, "God sends a curst cow short horns," but to a cow too curst he sends none.

LEONATO So, by being too curst, God will send you no horns.

BEATRICE Just, if he send me no husband, for the which blessing I am at him upon my knees every morning and evening. Lord, I could not endure a husband with a beard on his face! I had rather lie in the woolen.

LEONATO You may light on a husband that hath no beard.

BEATRICE What should I do with him? Dress him in my apparel and make him my waiting-gentlewoman? He that hath a beard is more than a youth, and he that hath no beard is less than a man; and he that is more than a youth is not for me, and he that is less than a man, I am not for him. Therefore I will even take

23 frame fashion **25 canker** dog rose, one that grows wild rather than being cultivated in formal gardens **26 blood** mood, disposition **27 fashion . . . love** counterfeit a behavior to gain undeserved attention **30–1 I . . . clog** I am trusted only with my muzzle on and am allowed freedom only to the extent of being hampered by a heavy wooden block **31 decreed** determined **36 I . . . only** Discontent is my only resource, and I cultivate it alone. **41 intelligence** news **44 What . . . fool** What kind of fool is he **46 Marry** By the Virgin Mary, i.e., indeed **49 proper squire** fine young man. (Said contemptuously.) **53 forward March chick** precocious young thing (like a chick hatched early). **55 entertained for** hired as **56 smoking** sweetening the air (with aromatic smoke). **comes me** comes. (*Me* is used colloquially, as also in line 58.) **57 sad** serious **58 arras** tapestry, wall hanging **62 start-up** upstart **63 cross** thwart **64 sure** trustworthy

68–9 o' my mind i.e., of a mind to poison the food. **69 prove** try out
2.1. Location: Leonato's house.
3 tartly sour of disposition **4 heartburned** afflicted with heartburn or indigestion **6 He were** A man would be **8 image** statue **9 my . . . son** i.e., a spoiled child. **tattling** chattering. **15 'a** he **17 shrewd** sharp **18 curst** shrewish. **20 that way** in that respect **21 curst** i.e., savage, vicious. (God proverbially takes care that the vicious are limited in their ability to do harm.) **25 Just** Right, exactly so. **no husband** If Beatrice has no husband, there can be no prospect of cuckold's horns. (She may also be jesting about a short penis here and in lines 20–2.) **28 in the woolen** between blankets, without sheets.

sixpence in earnest of the bearward, and lead his apes into hell.

LEONATO Well, then, go you into hell?

BEATRICE No, but to the gate; and there will the devil meet me, like an old cuckold, with horns on his head, and say, "Get you to heaven, Beatrice, get you to heaven, here's no place for you maids." So deliver I up my apes, and away to Saint Peter, for the heavens; he shows me where the bachelors sit, and there live we as merry as the day is long.

ANTONIO [*to Hero*] Well, niece, I trust you will be ruled by your father.

BEATRICE Yes, faith, it is my cousin's duty to make curtsy and say, "Father, as it please you." But yet for all that, cousin, let him be a handsome fellow, or else make another curtsy and say, "Father, as it please me."

LEONATO Well, niece, I hope to see you one day fitted with a husband.

BEATRICE Not till God make men of some other metal than earth. Would it not grieve a woman to be overmastered with a piece of valiant dust? To make an account of her life to a clod of wayward marl? No, uncle, I'll none. Adam's sons are my brethren, and truly I hold it a sin to match in my kindred.

LEONATO [*to Hero*] Daughter, remember what I told you. If the Prince do solicit you in that kind, you know your answer.

BEATRICE The fault will be in the music, cousin, if you be not wooed in good time. If the Prince be too important, tell him there is measure in everything, and so dance out the answer. For, hear me, Hero: wooing, wedding, and repenting is as a Scotch jig, a measure, and a cinquepace. The first suit is hot and hasty, like a Scotch jig, and full as fantastical; the wedding, mannerly-modest, as a measure, full of state and ancientry; and then comes Repentance, and with his bad legs falls into the cinquepace faster and faster till he sink into his grave.

LEONATO Cousin, you apprehend passing shrewdly.

BEATRICE I have a good eye, uncle; I can see a church by daylight.

LEONATO The revelers are entering, brother. Make good room. [*The men put on their masks.*]

Enter [*as maskers*] *Prince* [*Don*] *Pedro, Claudio, and Benedick, and Balthasar,* [*Borachio,*] *and Don John.*

DON PEDRO Lady, will you walk a bout with your friend? [*The couples pair off for the dance.*]

HERO So you walk softly and look sweetly and say nothing, I am yours for the walk, and especially when I walk away.

DON PEDRO With me in your company?

HERO I may say so, when I please.

DON PEDRO And when please you to say so?

HERO When I like your favor, for God defend the lute should be like the case!

DON PEDRO My visor is Philemon's roof; within the house is Jove.

HERO Why, then, your visor should be thatched.

DON PEDRO Speak low, if you speak love.
[*They dance to one side.*]

BALTHASAR Well, I would you did like me.

MARGARET So would not I for your own sake, for I have many ill qualities.

BALTHASAR Which is one?

MARGARET I say my prayers aloud.

BALTHASAR I love you the better. The hearers may cry Amen.

MARGARET God match me with a good dancer!

BALTHASAR Amen.

MARGARET And God keep him out of my sight when the dance is done! Answer, clerk.

BALTHASAR No more words. The clerk is answered.
[*They dance to one side.*]

URSULA I know you well enough. You are Signor Antonio.

ANTONIO At a word, I am not.

URSULA I know you by the waggling of your head.

ANTONIO To tell you true, I counterfeit him.

URSULA You could never do him so ill-well unless you were the very man. Here's his dry hand up and down. You are he, you are he.

ANTONIO At a word, I am not.

URSULA Come, come, do you think I do not know you by your excellent wit? Can virtue hide itself? Go to, mum, you are he. Graces will appear, and there's an end. [*They dance to one side.*]

37 in earnest in token advance payment for. **bearward** one who keeps and exhibits a bear (and sometimes apes) **37–8 lead . . . hell** (An ancient proverb says, "Such as die maids do all lead apes in hell.") **44 for the heavens** (A common interjection, like "Good heavens!" but here also carrying its literal meaning, i.e., bound for heaven.) **45 bachelors** unmarried persons of either sex **55 metal** substance. (With play on "mettle.") **58 marl** clay, earth (such as was used by God to make Adam in Genesis 2). **59–60 Adam's . . . kindred** (Beatrice jests that since men and women are all descended from Adam, it would be incestuous for her to marry a man.) **62 in that kind** to that effect (i.e., to marriage) **65 in good time** (1) soon (2) in time to the music, rhythmically. **66 important** importunate, urgent. **measure** (1) moderation (2) rhythm, dance **68–9 a measure** a formal dance **69 cinquepace** five-step lively dance, galliard. (The pun on "sink apace," as it was pronounced, is evident in lines 72–4: repentance will *sink faster and faster,* with a suggestion of detumescence.) **71–2 state and ancientry** dignity and traditional stateliness **75 apprehend passing shrewdly** understand with unusual perspicacity. **76–7 see . . . daylight** i.e., see something as plain as the nose on your face.

80 walk a bout take a turn, join in a section of a dance. (Here probably a slow, stately pavane.) **81 friend** wooer. **88 favor** face **88–9 God . . . case!** i.e., God forbid the face within should be as unhandsome as its cover, your visor! **90–3 My . . . love** (A fourteen-syllable rhymed couplet, the verse form of Arthur Golding's translation of the *Metamorphoses,* 1567.) **90 Philemon's roof** i.e., the humble cottage in which the peasants Philemon and Baucis entertained Jove, or Jupiter, unawares. (See Ovid, *Metamorphoses,* 8.) **92 visor** mask. **thatched** i.e., whiskered, to resemble the thatch of a humble cottage. **94–105 BALTHASAR** (The speech prefixes in the Quarto text for Balthasar's lines read *Bene.* and *Balth.* Some editors speculate that *Borachio* is intended.) **104 clerk** (So addressed because of Balthasar's repeatedly answering "Amen" like the parish clerk saying the responses.) **108 At a word** In short **111 do . . . ill-well** imitate his imperfections so perfectly **112 dry hand** (A sign of age.) **up and down up** exactly. **117 mum** be silent **117–18 an end** no more to be said.

BEATRICE Will you not tell me who told you so?

BENEDICK No, you shall pardon me.

BEATRICE Nor will you not tell me who you are?

BENEDICK Not now.

BEATRICE That I was disdainful and that I had my good wit out of the *Hundred Merry Tales*—well, this was Signor Benedick that said so.

BENEDICK What's he?

BEATRICE I am sure you know him well enough.

BENEDICK Not I, believe me.

BEATRICE Did he never make you laugh?

BENEDICK I pray you, what is he?

BEATRICE Why, he is the Prince's jester, a very dull fool. Only his gift is in devising impossible slanders. None but libertines delight in him, and the commendation is not in his wit but in his villainy, for he both pleases men and angers them, and then they laugh at him and beat him. I am sure he is in the fleet. I would he had boarded me.

BENEDICK When I know the gentleman, I'll tell him what you say.

BEATRICE Do, do. He'll but break a comparison or two on me, which peradventure not marked or not laughed at strikes him into melancholy; and then there's a partridge wing saved, for the fool will eat no supper that night. [*Music.*] We must follow the leaders.

BENEDICK In every good thing.

BEATRICE Nay, if they lead to any ill, I will leave them at the next turning.

Dance. Exeunt [*all except Don John, Borachio, and Claudio. Don John and Borachio are unmasked.*]

DON JOHN [*to Borachio*] Sure my brother is amorous on Hero and hath withdrawn her father to break with him about it. The ladies follow her, and but one visor remains.

BORACHIO And that is Claudio. I know him by his bearing.

DON JOHN [*advancing to Claudio*] Are not you Signor Benedick?

CLAUDIO You know me well. I am he.

DON JOHN Signor, you are very near my brother in his love. He is enamored on Hero. I pray you, dissuade him from her; she is no equal for his birth. You may do the part of an honest man in it.

CLAUDIO How know you he loves her?

DON JOHN I heard him swear his affection.

BORACHIO So did I, too, and he swore he would marry her tonight.

DON JOHN Come, let us to the banquet.

Exeunt. Manet Claudio.

CLAUDIO

Thus answer I in name of Benedick,
But hear these ill news with the ears of Claudio.
'Tis certain so. The Prince woos for himself.
Friendship is constant in all other things
Save in the office and affairs of love;
Therefore all hearts in love use their own tongues.
Let every eye negotiate for itself
And trust no agent; for beauty is a witch
Against whose charms faith melteth into blood.
This is an accident of hourly proof,
Which I mistrusted not. Farewell therefore Hero!

Enter Benedick [*unmasked*].

BENEDICK Count Claudio?

CLAUDIO Yea, the same.

BENEDICK Come, will you go with me?

CLAUDIO Whither?

BENEDICK Even to the next willow, about your own business, County. What fashion will you wear the garland of? About your neck, like an usurer's chain? Or under your arm, like a lieutenant's scarf? You must wear it one way, for the Prince hath got your Hero.

CLAUDIO I wish him joy of her.

BENEDICK Why, that's spoken like an honest drover; so they sell bullocks. But did you think the Prince would have served you thus?

CLAUDIO I pray you, leave me.

BENEDICK Ho, now you strike like the blind man. 'Twas the boy that stole your meat, and you'll beat the post.

CLAUDIO If it will not be, I'll leave you. *Exit.*

BENEDICK Alas, poor hurt fowl! Now will he creep into sedges. But that my Lady Beatrice should know me, and not know me! The Prince's fool! Ha? It may be I go under that title because I am merry. Yea, but so I am apt to do myself wrong. I am not so reputed. It is the base, though bitter, disposition of Beatrice that puts the world into her person and so gives me out. Well, I'll be revenged as I may.

Enter the Prince [*Don Pedro*], *Hero,* [*and*] *Leonato.* [*All are unmasked.*]

124 ***Hundred Merry Tales*** (A popular collection of anecdotes first published by John Rastell in 1526.) **132 Only his gift** His only talent. **impossible** incredible **133 libertines** i.e., those who disregard conventional moral laws **134 villainy** i.e., mocking, raillery; also, clownishness **134–5 pleases . . . angers them** i.e., amuses some with his rudeness and angers others with his slanders **136 fleet** i.e., crowd, company sailing past in the dance. **137 boarded** i.e., accosted. (Continuing the nautical metaphor begun in *fleet*.) **138 know** become acquainted with **140 break a comparison** i.e., make a scornful simile (as in a tilting or breaking of lances) **141 peradventure** if it is **144 leaders** i.e., of the dance. **147 turning** turning figure in the dance. **157–8 near . . . love** close to my brother. **159 birth** aristocratic rank.

165 banquet light repast of fruit, wine, and dessert. **165.1** ***Manet*** He remains onstage **174 faith . . . blood** loyalty gives way to passion. **175 accident** occurrence **176 mistrusted** suspected **181 willow** (An emblem of disappointed love.) **182 County** count. **182–3 garland** i.e., of willow **183 usurer's chain** heavy gold chain, worn by rich men as if it were a badge of office. **184 scarf** sling. **185 one way** one way or the other **187 drover** cattle dealer **188 bullocks** oxen. **191 strike . . . man** lash out blindly in every direction. **191–2 'Twas . . . post** i.e., You're ready to blame anything but the true cause of your distress. (Benedick seemingly alludes to some fable about a boy and an innocent postman that demonstrates this object lesson.) **193 If . . . be** i.e., If you won't leave me as I asked **194–5 creep into sedges** i.e., hide himself away, as wounded fowl creep into rushes along the river. **195–6 know me, and not know me** i.e., be of my long acquaintance, and yet misjudge me so cruelly. **198–200 It is . . . out** It is Beatrice's low and harsh disposition to assume that she speaks for everyone when she characterizes me this way.

DON PEDRO Now, signor, where's the Count? Did you see him?

BENEDICK Troth, my lord, I have played the part of Lady Fame. I found him here as melancholy as a lodge in a warren. I told him, and I think I told him true, that Your Grace had got the good will of this young lady, and I offered him my company to a willow tree, either to make him a garland, as being forsaken, or to bind him up a rod, as being worthy to be whipped.

DON PEDRO To be whipped! What's his fault?

BENEDICK The flat transgression of a schoolboy, who, being overjoyed with finding a bird's nest, shows it his companion, and he steals it.

DON PEDRO Wilt thou make a trust a transgression? The transgression is in the stealer.

BENEDICK Yet it had not been amiss the rod had been made, and the garland too; for the garland he might have worn himself, and the rod he might have bestowed on you, who, as I take it, have stolen his bird's nest.

DON PEDRO I will but teach them to sing and restore them to the owner.

BENEDICK If their singing answer your saying, by my faith, you say honestly.

DON PEDRO The Lady Beatrice hath a quarrel to you. The gentleman that danced with her told her she is much wronged by you.

BENEDICK Oh, she misused me past the endurance of a block! An oak but with one green leaf on it would have answered her. My very visor began to assume life and scold with her. She told me, not thinking I had been myself, that I was the Prince's jester, that I was duller than a great thaw; huddling jest upon jest with such impossible conveyance upon me that I stood like a man at a mark, with a whole army shooting at me. She speaks poniards, and every word stabs. If her breath were as terrible as her terminations, there were no living near her; she would infect to the North Star. I would not marry her, though she were endowed with all that Adam had left him before he transgressed. She would have made Hercules have turned spit, yea, and have cleft his club to make the fire, too. Come, talk not of her. You shall find her the infernal Ate in good apparel. I would to God some scholar would conjure her, for certainly, while she is here, a man may live as quiet in hell as in a sanctuary, and people sin upon purpose because they would go thither; so indeed all disquiet, horror, and perturbation follows her.

Enter Claudio and Beatrice.

DON PEDRO Look, here she comes.

BENEDICK Will Your Grace command me any service to the world's end? I will go on the slightest errand now to the Antipodes that you can devise to send me on; I will fetch you a toothpicker now from the furthest inch of Asia, bring you the length of Prester John's foot, fetch you a hair off the great Cham's beard, do you any embassage to the Pygmies, rather than hold three words' conference with this harpy. You have no employment for me?

DON PEDRO None but to desire your good company.

BENEDICK Oh, God, sir, here's a dish I love not! I cannot endure my Lady Tongue. *Exit.*

DON PEDRO Come, lady, come, you have lost the heart of Signor Benedick.

BEATRICE Indeed, my lord, he lent it me awhile, and I gave him use for it, a double heart for his single one. Marry, once before he won it of me with false dice; therefore Your Grace may well say I have lost it.

DON PEDRO You have put him down, lady, you have put him down.

BEATRICE So I would not he should do me, my lord, lest I should prove the mother of fools. I have brought Count Claudio, whom you sent me to seek.

DON PEDRO Why, how now, Count? Wherefore are you sad?

CLAUDIO Not sad, my lord.

DON PEDRO How then? Sick?

CLAUDIO Neither, my lord.

BEATRICE The Count is neither sad, nor sick, nor merry, nor well; but civil count, civil as an orange, and something of that jealous complexion.

DON PEDRO I'faith, lady, I think your blazon to be true, though I'll be sworn, if he be so, his conceit is false. Here, Claudio, I have wooed in thy name, and fair

204 Troth By my faith **204–5 Lady Fame** Dame Rumor. **205–6 lodge in a warren** isolated gamekeeper's hut in a large game preserve. **208 offered . . . to** offered to accompany him to **209–10 bind . . . rod** tie several willow switches into a scourge for him **212 flat** plain **215 a trust** a trusted assignment (here, the Prince's having taken in trust the wooing of Hero for Claudio, not himself) **222 them** i.e., the young birds in the nest **224 answer your saying** correspond to what you say **226 to** with **230 block** (of wood). **234 great thaw** i.e., time when roads are muddy and impassable, obliging one to stay dully at home. **huddling** piling, heaping up **235 impossible conveyance** incredible dexterity **236 at a mark** at the target, marking where the arrows hit **237 poniards** daggers **238 terminations** terms, expressions **239 North Star** (Popularly supposed to be the most remote of stars.) **241 all . . . him** i.e., Paradise before the fall of man **242 Hercules . . . spit** (The Amazon Omphale forced the captive Hercules to wear women's clothing and spin; turning the spit would be an even more menial kitchen duty.) **243 cleft** split **244 Ate** goddess of discord

245 scholar . . . conjure (Scholars were supposed to be able to conjure evil spirits back into hell by addressing them in Latin.) **246 here** i.e., on earth. (As long as Beatrice is on earth, hell will seem like a place of refuge.) **253 Antipodes** people and region on the opposite side of the earth **254 toothpicker** toothpick **255 Prester John** a legendary Christian king of the Far East **256 great Cham** the Khan of Tartary, ruler of the Mongols **257 Pygmies** legendary small race thought to live in India **258 harpy** legendary creature with a woman's face and body and a bird's wings and claws. **265–7 he . . . dice** (Beatrice refers seemingly to a previous courtship in which she feels that Benedick prevailed over her unfairly, in return for which she now has paid him back with *use* or interest, two to one.) **269 put him down** got the better of him. (But Beatrice plays with the phrase in its literal and sexual sense.) **280 civil** serious, grave. (Punning on *Seville* for the city in Spain whence came bitter-tasting oranges.) **280–1 something** somewhat **281 jealous complexion**, i.e., yellow, associated with melancholy and symbolic of jealousy. **282 blazon** description. (A heraldic term.) **283 conceit** (1) notion, idea (2) heraldic device. (Continuing the metaphor of *blazon*.)

Hero is won. I have broke with her father and his good will obtained. Name the day of marriage, and God give thee joy!

LEONATO Count, take of me my daughter and with her my fortunes. His Grace hath made the match, and all grace say Amen to it.

BEATRICE Speak, Count, 'tis your cue.

CLAUDIO Silence is the perfectest herald of joy. I were but little happy if I could say how much!—Lady, as you are mine, I am yours. I give away myself for you and dote upon the exchange.

BEATRICE Speak, cousin, or if you cannot, stop his mouth with a kiss, and let not him speak neither.

[*Claudio and Hero kiss.*]

DON PEDRO In faith, lady, you have a merry heart.

BEATRICE Yea, my lord; I thank it, poor fool, it keeps on the windy side of care. My cousin tells him in his ear that he is in her heart.

CLAUDIO And so she doth, cousin.

BEATRICE Good Lord, for alliance! Thus goes everyone to the world but I, and I am sunburnt. I may sit in a corner and cry, "Heigh-ho for a husband!"

DON PEDRO Lady Beatrice, I will get you one.

BEATRICE I would rather have one of your father's getting. Hath Your Grace ne'er a brother like you? Your father got excellent husbands, if a maid could come by them.

DON PEDRO Will you have me, lady?

BEATRICE No, my lord, unless I might have another for working days. Your Grace is too costly to wear every day. But I beseech Your Grace, pardon me. I was born to speak all mirth and no matter.

DON PEDRO Your silence most offends me, and to be merry best becomes you, for out o' question you were born in a merry hour.

BEATRICE No, sure, my lord, my mother cried; but then there was a star danced, and under that was I born. Cousins, God give you joy!

LEONATO Niece, will you look to those things I told you of?

BEATRICE I cry you mercy, uncle. [*To Don Pedro*] By Your Grace's pardon. *Exit Beatrice.*

DON PEDRO By my troth, a pleasant-spirited lady.

LEONATO There's little of the melancholy element in her, my lord. She is never sad but when she sleeps, and not ever sad then; for I have heard my daughter say she hath often dreamt of unhappiness and waked herself with laughing.

DON PEDRO She cannot endure to hear tell of a husband.

LEONATO Oh, by no means. She mocks all her wooers out of suit.

DON PEDRO She were an excellent wife for Benedick.

LEONATO Oh, Lord, my lord, if they were but a week married they would talk themselves mad.

DON PEDRO County Claudio, when mean you to go to church?

CLAUDIO Tomorrow, my lord. Time goes on crutches till Love have all his rites.

LEONATO Not till Monday, my dear son, which is hence a just sevennight and a time too brief, too, to have all things answer my mind.

DON PEDRO Come, you shake the head at so long a breathing, but I warrant thee, Claudio, the time shall not go dully by us. I will in the interim undertake one of Hercules' labors, which is to bring Signor Benedick and the Lady Beatrice into a mountain of affection th'one with th'other. I would fain have it a match, and I doubt not but to fashion it, if you three will but minister such assistance as I shall give you direction.

LEONATO My lord, I am for you, though it cost me ten nights' watchings.

CLAUDIO And I, my lord.

DON PEDRO And you too, gentle Hero?

HERO I will do any modest office, my lord, to help my cousin to a good husband.

DON PEDRO And Benedick is not the unhopefullest husband that I know. Thus far can I praise him: he is of a noble strain, of approved valor and confirmed honesty. I will teach you how to humor your cousin, that she shall fall in love with Benedick; and I, with your two helps, will so practice on Benedick that, in despite of his quick wit and his queasy stomach, he shall fall in love with Beatrice. If we can do this, Cupid is no longer an archer; his glory shall be ours, for we are the only love gods. Go in with me, and I will tell you my drift. *Exeunt.*

[2.2]

Enter [*Don*] *John and Borachio.*

DON JOHN It is so. The Count Claudio shall marry the daughter of Leonato.

BORACHIO Yea, my lord, but I can cross it.

DON JOHN Any bar, any cross, any impediment will be medicinable to me. I am sick in displeasure to him,

285 broke spoken **289–90 all . . . to it** i.e., we thank God for this union. **300 windy** windward, safe. (In sailing, the ship to windward has the advantage.) **303 alliance** relationship by marriage. (Claudio has just called her "cousin.") **303–4 goes . . . world** i.e., gets married **304 sunburnt** (The Renaissance considered dark complexions unattractive.) **305 Heigh-ho . . . husband!** (The title of a ballad.) **308 getting** begetting. (Playing on *get,* "procure," in the previous speech.) **315 matter** substance. **324 cry you mercy** beg your pardon (for not having obeyed earlier) **324–5 By . . . pardon** i.e., I beg you to excuse my departure. **327 melancholy element** i.e., earth, associated with the humor of melancholy in the old physiology **329 ever** always **330 unhappiness** misfortune

333–4 She . . . suit She discomfits and discourages all her wooers. **343 a just sevennight** exactly a week **344 answer my mind** suit my wishes. **346 breathing** pause, interval **350 fain** gladly **352 minister** furnish, supply **354 watchings** staying awake. **357 do . . . office** play any seemly role **359 unhopefullest** most unpromising **361 strain** ancestry. **approved** tested. **honesty** honor. **365 queasy** squeamish, delicate (about marriage) **369 drift** purpose.
2.2. Location: Leonato's house.
1 shall is going to **3 cross** thwart. (Also in line 7.) **4 bar** obstacle **5 medicinable** medicinal. **in displeasure to** with dislike of

and whatsoever comes athwart his affection ranges evenly with mine. How canst thou cross this marriage?

BORACHIO Not honestly, my lord, but so covertly that no dishonesty shall appear in me.

DON JOHN Show me briefly how.

BORACHIO I think I told Your Lordship, a year since, how much I am in the favor of Margaret, the waiting gentlewoman to Hero.

DON JOHN I remember.

BORACHIO I can, at any unseasonable instant of the night, appoint her to look out at her lady's chamber window.

DON JOHN What life is in that, to be the death of this marriage?

BORACHIO The poison of that lies in you to temper. Go you to the Prince your brother; spare not to tell him that he hath wronged his honor in marrying the renowned Claudio—whose estimation do you mightily hold up—to a contaminated stale, such a one as Hero.

DON JOHN What proof shall I make of that?

BORACHIO Proof enough to misuse the Prince, to vex Claudio, to undo Hero, and kill Leonato. Look you for any other issue?

DON JOHN Only to despite them I will endeavor anything.

BORACHIO Go, then, find me a meet hour to draw Don Pedro and the Count Claudio alone. Tell them that you know that Hero loves me. Intend a kind of zeal both to the Prince and Claudio, as—in love of your brother's honor, who hath made this match, and his friend's reputation, who is thus like to be cozened with the semblance of a maid—that you have discovered thus. They will scarcely believe this without trial. Offer them instances, which shall bear no less likelihood than to see me at her chamber window, hear me call Margaret Hero, hear Margaret term me Claudio; and bring them to see this the very night before the intended wedding—for in the meantime I will so fashion the matter that Hero shall be absent—and there shall appear such seeming truth of Hero's disloyalty that jealousy shall be called assurance and all the preparation overthrown.

DON JOHN Grow this to what adverse issue it can, I will put it in practice. Be cunning in the working this, and thy fee is a thousand ducats.

BORACHIO Be you constant in the accusation, and my cunning shall not shame me.

DON JOHN I will presently go learn their day of marriage. *Exit [with Borachio].*

✤

[2.3]

Enter Benedick alone.

BENEDICK Boy!

[Enter Boy.]

BOY Signor?

BENEDICK In my chamber window lies a book. Bring it hither to me in the orchard.

BOY I am here already, sir.

BENEDICK I know that, but I would have thee hence and here again. *Exit [Boy].*
I do much wonder that one man, seeing how much another man is a fool when he dedicates his behaviors to love, will, after he hath laughed at such shallow follies in others, become the argument of his own scorn by falling in love; and such a man is Claudio. I have known when there was no music with him but the drum and the fife, and now had he rather hear the tabor and the pipe. I have known when he would have walked ten mile afoot to see a good armor, and now will he lie ten nights awake carving the fashion of a new doublet. He was wont to speak plain and to the purpose, like an honest man and a soldier, and now is he turned orthography—his words are a very fantastical banquet, just so many strange dishes. May I be so converted and see with these eyes? I cannot tell; I think not. I will not be sworn but Love may transform me to an oyster, but I'll take my oath on it, till he have made an oyster of me, he shall never make me such a fool. One woman is fair, yet I am well; another is wise, yet I am well; another virtuous, yet I am well; but till all graces be in one woman, one woman shall not come in my grace. Rich she shall be, that's certain; wise, or I'll none; virtuous, or I'll never cheapen her; fair, or I'll never look on her; mild, or come not near me; noble, or not I for an angel; of good discourse, an excellent musician, and her hair shall be of what color it please God. Ha! The Prince and Monsieur Love. I will hide me in the arbor. *[He hides.]*

Enter Prince [Don Pedro], Leonato, Claudio.

DON PEDRO Come, shall we hear this music?

6–7 whatsoever . . . mine whatever crosses his inclination runs parallel with mine. **12 since** ago **16 unseasonable** unsuitable, unseemly **21 lies in** rests with. **temper** mix, compound. **24–5 whose . . . up** and emphasize how much you admire his reputation **25 stale** prostitute **27 misuse** abuse, deceive **29 issue** outcome. (With a pun on children as the product of marriage; cf. 4.1.132.) **30 despite** torture, injure **32 meet** suitable **34 Intend** Pretend **35 as** i.e., saying as follows. (The words between the dashes are to be understood as instructions to Don John as to what he is to say.) **37 like** likely. **cozened** deceived, cheated **38 semblance** semblance only, outward appearance. **discovered** revealed **40 instances** proofs **42 hear . . . Claudio** (Many editors read *Borachio* for *Claudio*. The present reading may be defended if one imagines that, by arrangement with Margaret, Borachio is playing the part of Claudio, but the reading may also be an inconsistency.) **47 jealousy** suspicion. **assurance** certainty **48 preparation** i.e., for marriage **49 Grow this** Let this ripen **51 ducats** gold coins.

54 presently immediately
2.3. Location: Leonato's garden.
4 orchard garden. **5 I . . . already** i.e., I will be so quick as to use no time at all. (But Benedick quibbles on the literal sense.) **11 argument** subject **13-14 there was . . . fife** i.e., his only commitment was to soldiering **15 tabor . . . pipe** (Symbols of peaceful merriment and wooing.) **16 armor** suit of armor **17 carving** planning **18 doublet** jacket. **20 turned orthography** become fastidious and fashionable in his choice of language **30 I'll none** I'll have none of her. **cheapen** make a bid for. (The idea of lessening her value by using her may also be suggested, though historically it is a later meaning.) **31, 32 noble, angel** (Each of these words involves a pun on the meaning "a coin," a noble being worth six shillings eightpence and an angel, ten shillings.)

CLAUDIO
Yea, my good lord. How still the evening is,
As hushed on purpose to grace harmony!
DON PEDRO [*apart to them*]
See you where Benedick hath hid himself?
CLAUDIO [*apart in reply*]
Oh, very well, my lord. The music ended,
We'll fit the kid-fox with a pennyworth.

Enter Balthasar with music.

DON PEDRO
Come, Balthasar, we'll hear that song again.
BALTHASAR
Oh, good my lord, tax not so bad a voice
To slander music any more than once.
DON PEDRO
It is the witness still of excellency
To put a strange face on his own perfection.
I pray thee, sing, and let me woo no more.
BALTHASAR
Because you talk of wooing, I will sing,
Since many a wooer doth commence his suit
To her he thinks not worthy, yet he woos,
Yet will he swear he loves.
DON PEDRO Nay, pray thee, come,
Or if thou wilt hold longer argument,
Do it in notes.
BALTHASAR Note this before my notes:
There's not a note of mine that's worth the noting.
DON PEDRO
Why, these are very crotchets that he speaks!
Note, notes, forsooth, and nothing. [*Music.*]

BENEDICK [*aside*] Now, divine air! Now is his soul ravished! Is it not strange that sheeps' guts should hale souls out of men's bodies? Well, a horn for my money, when all's done.

The Song.

BALTHASAR
Sigh no more, ladies, sigh no more.
Men were deceivers ever,
One foot in sea and one on shore,
To one thing constant never.
Then sigh not so, but let them go,
And be you blithe and bonny,
Converting all your sounds of woe
Into Hey nonny, nonny.

Sing no more ditties, sing no moe,
Of dumps so dull and heavy;
The fraud of men was ever so,
Since summer first was leavy.
Then sigh not so, but let them go,
And be you blithe and bonny,
Converting all your sounds of woe
Into Hey nonny, nonny.

DON PEDRO By my troth, a good song.

BALTHASAR And an ill singer, my lord.

DON PEDRO Ha, no, no, faith, thou sing'st well enough for a shift.

BENEDICK [*aside*] An he had been a dog that should have howled thus, they would have hanged him, and I pray God his bad voice bode no mischief. I has as lief have heard the night raven, come what plague could have come after it.

DON PEDRO Yea, marry, dost thou hear, Balthasar? I pray thee, get us some excellent music, for tomorrow night we would have it at the Lady Hero's chamber window.

BALTHASAR The best I can, my lord.

DON PEDRO Do so. Farewell. *Exit Balthasar.* Come hither, Leonato. What was it you told me of today, that your niece Beatrice was in love with Signor Benedick?

CLAUDIO Oh, ay! [*Aside to Pedro*] Stalk on, stalk on; the fowl sits.—I did never think that lady would have loved any man.

LEONATO No, nor I neither, but most wonderful that she should so dote on Signor Benedick, whom she hath in all outward behaviors seemed ever to abhor.

BENEDICK [*aside*] Is't possible? Sits the wind in that corner?

LEONATO By my troth, my lord, I cannot tell what to think of it but that she loves him with an enraged affection; it is past the infinite of thought.

DON PEDRO Maybe she doth but counterfeit.

CLAUDIO Faith, like enough.

LEONATO Oh, God, counterfeit? There was never counterfeit of passion came so near the life of passion as she discovers it.

DON PEDRO Why, what effects of passion shows she?

CLAUDIO [*aside to them*] Bait the hook well; this fish will bite.

38 As as if. **grace harmony** do honor to music. **40 The music ended** When the music is over **41 We'll . . . pennyworth** i.e., we'll give our sly victim more than he bargained for. (A *kid-fox* is presumably a young fox, as in beast fable; *kid*, i.e., young goat, also suggests one whom they are stalking as their quarry. Claudio may be referring to some children's game.) **43 tax** task **45–6 It . . . perfection** It is always characteristic of excellence to pretend not to know its own skill. **47 woo** entreat **48–51 Because . . . he loves** (Balthasar modestly claims to be unworthy of being *wooed*, i.e., entreated, but will comply, since he knows Don Pedro speaks with the hyperbole all wooers use in addressing women they actually consider unworthy.) **53 notes** music. **55 crotchets** (1) whims, fancies (2) musical notes of brief duration **56 nothing** (With a pun on *noting;* the two words were pronounced alike. Compare the same pun in the title of the play, where *Nothing* suggests "noting," or eavesdropping.) **57 air** melody. **58 sheeps' guts** strings on musical instruments. **hale** draw **59 a horn** a hunting horn, a more masculine instrument than a lute. (But with a perhaps unconscious allusion to a cuckold's horns.)

66 blithe and bonny cheerful and carefree **68 Hey nonny, nonny** (A nonsense refrain.) **69 moe** more **70 dumps** mournful songs; also, dances **72 leavy** leafy. **80 for a shift** in a pinch. **81 An** If. (Also in line 161.) **84 lief** willingly. **night raven** a bird of night, portending disaster **86 Yea, marry** (A continuation of Don Pedro's speech preceding Benedick's aside.) **95–6 Stalk . . . sits** i.e., Proceed stealthily; the hunted bird is hiding in the bush. **101–2 Sits . . . corner?** Is that the way the wind is blowing? **104 enraged** maddened with passion **105 infinite** farthest reach. (It's unbelievable but true.) **107 like** likely **110 discovers** betrays

LEONATO What effects, my lord? She will sit you—you heard my daughter tell you how.

CLAUDIO She did indeed.

DON PEDRO How, how, I pray you? You amaze me. I would have thought her spirit had been invincible against all assaults of affection.

LEONATO I would have sworn it had, my lord—especially against Benedick.

BENEDICK [*aside*] I should think this a gull but that the white-bearded fellow speaks it. Knavery cannot, sure, hide himself in such reverence.

CLAUDIO [*apart to them*] He hath ta'en th'infection. Hold it up.

DON PEDRO Hath she made her affection known to Benedick?

LEONATO No, and swears she never will. That's her torment.

CLAUDIO 'Tis true, indeed. So your daughter says. "Shall I," says she, "that have so oft encountered him with scorn, write to him that I love him?"

LEONATO This says she now when she is beginning to write to him, for she'll be up twenty times a night, and there will she sit in her smock till she have writ a sheet of paper. My daughter tells us all.

CLAUDIO Now you talk of a sheet of paper, I remember a pretty jest your daughter told us of.

LEONATO Oh, when she had writ it and was reading it over, she found "Benedick" and "Beatrice" between the sheet?

CLAUDIO That.

LEONATO Oh, she tore the letter into a thousand halfpence; railed at herself, that she should be so immodest to write to one that she knew would flout her. "I measure him," says she, "by my own spirit, for I should flout him if he writ to me. Yea, though I love him, I should."

CLAUDIO Then down upon her knees she falls, weeps, sobs, beats her heart, tears her hair, prays, curses: "O sweet Benedick! God give me patience!"

LEONATO She doth indeed; my daughter says so. And the ecstasy hath so much overborne her that my daughter is sometime afeard she will do a desperate outrage to herself. It is very true.

DON PEDRO It were good that Benedick knew of it by some other, if she will not discover it.

CLAUDIO To what end? He would make but a sport of it and torment the poor lady worse.

DON PEDRO An he should, it were an alms to hang him. She's an excellent sweet lady, and, out of all suspicion, she is virtuous.

CLAUDIO And she is exceeding wise.

DON PEDRO In everything but in loving Benedick.

LEONATO O my lord, wisdom and blood combating in so tender a body, we have ten proofs to one that blood hath the victory. I am sorry for her, as I have just cause, being her uncle and her guardian.

DON PEDRO I would she had bestowed this dotage on me. I would have doffed all other respects and made her half myself. I pray you, tell Benedick of it, and hear what 'a will say.

LEONATO Were it good, think you?

CLAUDIO Hero thinks surely she will die; for she says she will die if he love her not, and she will die ere she make her love known, and she will die if he woo her, rather than she will bate one breath of her accustomed crossness.

DON PEDRO She doth well. If she should make tender of her love, 'tis very possible he'll scorn it; for the man, as you know all, hath a contemptible spirit.

CLAUDIO He is a very proper man.

DON PEDRO He hath indeed a good outward happiness.

CLAUDIO Before God, and in my mind, very wise.

DON PEDRO He doth indeed show some sparks that are like wit.

CLAUDIO And I take him to be valiant.

DON PEDRO As Hector, I assure you; and in the managing of quarrels you may say he is wise, for either he avoids them with great discretion or undertakes them with a most Christian-like fear.

LEONATO If he do fear God, 'a must necessarily keep peace. If he break the peace, he ought to enter into a quarrel with fear and trembling.

DON PEDRO And so will he do, for the man doth fear God, howsoever it seems not in him by some large jests he will make. Well, I am sorry for your niece. Shall we go seek Benedick and tell him of her love?

CLAUDIO Never tell him, my lord. Let her wear it out with good counsel.

LEONATO Nay, that's impossible. She may wear her heart out first.

DON PEDRO Well, we will hear further of it by your daughter. Let it cool the while. I love Benedick well, and I could wish he would modestly examine himself, to see how much he is unworthy so good a lady.

LEONATO My lord, will you walk? Dinner is ready.

[*They walk aside.*]

CLAUDIO If he do not dote on her upon this, I will never trust my expectation.

DON PEDRO Let there be the same net spread for her; and that must your daughter and her gentlewomen carry. The sport will be when they hold one an opinion of another's dotage, and no such matter; that's the

114 sit you i.e., sit. (*You* is used idiomatically.) **122 gull** trick, deception. **but** except for the fact **126 Hold it up** Keep up the jest. **132 she** i.e., Beatrice **136 smock** chemise **143 That** i.e., That's it. **144–5 halfpence** i.e., small pieces **146 flout** mock **154 overborne** overwhelmed **158 discover** reveal **161 alms** good deed. (Hanging would be too good for him.) **162 out of** beyond **166 blood** natural feeling

170 dotage doting affection **171 doffed** put or turned aside. **respects** considerations **172 half myself** i.e., my wife. **178 bate** abate **179 crossness** perversity, contrariety. **180 tender** offer **182 contemptible** contemptuous **183 proper** handsome **184 outward happiness** fortune in his good looks. **185 Before God** i.e., By God, you're absolutely right **189 Hector** the mightiest of the Trojans **197 by** to judge by. **large** broad, indelicate **200 wear it out** eradicate it **201 counsel** reflection, deliberation. **209 upon** as a result of, after **213 carry** carry out. **213–14 they . . . dotage** each believes the other to be in love **214 no such matter** the reality is quite otherwise

scene that I would see, which will be merely a dumb show. Let us send her to call him in to dinner.

[Exeunt Don Pedro, Claudio, and Leonato.]

BENEDICK *[coming forward]* This can be no trick. The conference was sadly borne. They have the truth of this from Hero. They seem to pity the lady. It seems her affections have their full bent. Love me? Why, it must be requited. I hear how I am censured. They say I will bear myself proudly if I perceive the love come from her; they say too that she will rather die than give any sign of affection. I did never think to marry. I must not seem proud; happy are they that hear their detractions and can put them to mending. They say the lady is fair; 'tis a truth, I can bear them witness; and virtuous; 'tis so, I cannot reprove it; and wise but for loving me; by my troth, it is no addition to her wit, nor no great argument of her folly, for I will be horribly in love with her. I may chance have some odd quirks and remnants of wit broken on me, because I have railed so long against marriage. But doth not the appetite alter? A man loves the meat in his youth that he cannot endure in his age. Shall quips and sentences and these paper bullets of the brain awe a man from the career of his humor? No, the world must be peopled. When I said I would die a bachelor, I did not think I should live till I were married. Here comes Beatrice. By this day, she's a fair lady! I do spy some marks of love in her.

Enter Beatrice.

BEATRICE Against my will I am sent to bid you come in to dinner.

BENEDICK Fair Beatrice, I thank you for your pains.

BEATRICE I took no more pains for those thanks than you take pains to thank me. If it had been painful I would not have come.

BENEDICK You take pleasure then in the message?

BEATRICE Yea, just so much as you may take upon a knife's point and choke a daw withal. You have no stomach, signor. Fare you well. *Exit.*

BENEDICK Ha! "Against my will I am sent to bid you come in to dinner." There's a double meaning in that. "I took no more pains for those thanks than you took pains to thank me." That's as much as to say, "Any pains that I take for you is as easy as thanks." If I do not take pity of her, I am a villain; if I do not love her, I am a Jew. I will go get her picture. *Exit.*

[3.1]

Enter Hero and two gentlewomen, Margaret and Ursula.

HERO
Good Margaret, run thee to the parlor.
There shalt thou find my cousin Beatrice
Proposing with the Prince and Claudio.
Whisper her ear and tell her I and Ursley
Walk in the orchard, and our whole discourse
Is all of her. Say that thou overheard'st us,
And bid her steal into the pleachèd bower,
Where honeysuckles, ripened by the sun,
Forbid the sun to enter, like favorites,
Made proud by princes, that advance their pride
Against that power that bred it. There will she hide
her,
To listen our propose. This is thy office.
Bear thee well in it and leave us alone.

MARGARET
I'll make her come, I warrant you, presently. *[Exit.]*

HERO
Now, Ursula, when Beatrice doth come,
As we do trace this alley up and down,
Our talk must only be of Benedick.
When I do name him, let it be thy part
To praise him more than ever man did merit.
My talk to thee must be how Benedick
Is sick in love with Beatrice. Of this matter
Is little Cupid's crafty arrow made,
That only wounds by hearsay.

Enter Beatrice [behind].

Now begin,
For look where Beatrice, like a lapwing, runs
Close by the ground, to hear our conference.

URSULA *[to Hero]*
The pleasant'st angling is to see the fish
Cut with her golden oars the silver stream
And greedily devour the treacherous bait.
So angle we for Beatrice, who even now
Is couchèd in the woodbine coverture.
Fear you not my part of the dialogue.

HERO *[to Ursula]*
Then go we near her, that her ear lose nothing
Of the false sweet bait that we lay for it.
[They approach the bower.]
No, truly, Ursula, she is too disdainful;
I know her spirits are as coy and wild
As haggards of the rock.

URSULA
But are you sure

215–16 dumb show pantomime (lacking their usual banter)
218 sadly borne soberly conducted. **220 have . . . bent** i.e., are fully engaged. (The image is of a bow pulled taut.) **225–6 that . . . mending** that can hear themselves criticized and undertake to remedy the defect. **228 reprove** refute **231 quirks** witty conceits or jokes
235 sentences saws, maxims **236 paper bullets** i.e., words
237 career of his humor pursuit of his inclination. (In horsemanship, a *career* is a short gallop.) **249–50 just . . . withal** i.e., very little. (A daw or jackdaw is a common blackbird, smaller than a crow.)
251 stomach appetite

3.1 Location: Leonato's garden.
3 Proposing conversing **4 Ursley** (A nickname for *Ursula*.)
7 pleachèd formed by densely interwoven branches **10–11 that . . . it** i.e., who dare set themselves up against the very princes who advanced them. **12 listen our propose** listen to our conversation. **office** responsibility. **13 leave us alone** leave the rest to us. **14 presently** immediately. **16 trace** walk **23 only . . . hearsay** wounds by mere report.
24 lapwing bird of the plover family **27 oars** i.e., fins **30 Is . . . coverture** is hid in the honeysuckle bower. **31 Fear . . . dialogue** Don't worry about my not holding up my part in the conversation. **35 coy** disdainful **36 As . . . rock** as untamed female hawks in mountainous terrain.

That Benedick loves Beatrice so entirely?

HERO
So says the Prince and my new-trothèd lord.

URSULA
And did they bid you tell her of it, madam?

HERO
They did entreat me to acquaint her of it;
But I persuaded them, if they loved Benedick,
To wish him wrestle with affection
And never to let Beatrice know of it.

URSULA
Why did you so? Doth not the gentleman
Deserve as full as fortunate a bed
As ever Beatrice shall couch upon?

HERO
O god of love! I know he doth deserve
As much as may be yielded to a man;
But Nature never framed a woman's heart
Of prouder stuff than that of Beatrice.
Disdain and scorn ride sparkling in her eyes,
Misprizing what they look on, and her wit
Values itself so highly that to her
All matter else seems weak. She cannot love,
Nor take no shape nor project of affection,
She is so self-endearèd.

URSULA Sure I think so,
And therefore certainly it were not good
She knew his love, lest she'll make sport at it.

HERO
Why, you speak truth. I never yet saw man,
How wise, how noble, young, how rarely featured,
But she would spell him backward. If fair-faced,
She would swear the gentleman should be her
sister;
If black, why, Nature, drawing of an antic,
Made a foul blot; if tall, a lance ill-headed;
If low, an agate very vilely cut;
If speaking, why, a vane blown with all winds;
If silent, why, a block movèd with none.
So turns she every man the wrong side out
And never gives to truth and virtue that
Which simpleness and merit purchaseth.

URSULA
Sure, sure, such carping is not commendable.

HERO
No, not to be so odd and from all fashions
As Beatrice is cannot be commendable.
But who dare tell her so? If I should speak,
She would mock me into air; oh, she would laugh me
Out of myself, press me to death with wit.
Therefore let Benedick, like covered fire,
Consume away in sighs, waste inwardly.
It were a better death than die with mocks,
Which is as bad as die with tickling.

URSULA
Yet tell her of it. Hear what she will say.

HERO
No, rather I will go to Benedick
And counsel him to fight against his passion.
And truly, I'll devise some honest slanders
To stain my cousin with. One doth not know
How much an ill word may empoison liking.

URSULA
Oh, do not do your cousin such a wrong!
She cannot be so much without true judgment—
Having so swift and excellent a wit
As she is prized to have—as to refuse
So rare a gentleman as Signor Benedick.

HERO
He is the only man of Italy,
Always excepted my dear Claudio.

URSULA
I pray you, be not angry with me, madam,
Speaking my fancy: Signor Benedick,
For shape, for bearing, argument, and valor,
Goes foremost in report through Italy.

HERO
Indeed, he hath an excellent good name.

URSULA
His excellence did earn it ere he had it.
When are you married, madam?

HERO
Why, every day, tomorrow. Come, go in.
I'll show thee some attires and have thy counsel
Which is the best to furnish me tomorrow.
[They walk away.]

URSULA *[to Hero]*
She's limed, I warrant you. We have caught her,
madam.

HERO *[to Ursula]*
If it prove so, then loving goes by haps;
Some Cupid kills with arrows, some with traps.
[Exeunt Hero and Ursula.]

BEATRICE *[coming forward]*
What fire is in mine ears? Can this be true?
Stand I condemned for pride and scorn so much?
Contempt, farewell, and maiden pride, adieu!
No glory lives behind the back of such.
And Benedick, love on; I will requite thee,
Taming my wild heart to thy loving hand.

45–6 as full . . . upon i.e., as good a wife as Beatrice. **52 Misprizing** undervaluing, despising **54 weak** unimportant. **55 project** conception, idea **56 self-endearèd** full of self-love. **60 How** however. **rarely** excellently **61 spell him backward** i.e., speak contrarily of him by characterizing his virtues as vices. **63 black** dark. **antic** buffoon, grotesque figure **65 agate** i.e., diminutive person. (Alluding to the small figures cut in agate for rings.) **70 simpleness** integrity, plainness. **purchaseth** earn, deserve. **72 from** contrary to **75–6 she . . . myself** she would mockingly put me down **76 press me to death** (Pressing to death with weights was the usual punishment for those accused of crimes who refused to plead either guilty or not guilty.)

78 Consume . . . sighs (An allusion to the belief that each sigh cost the heart a drop of blood.) **84 honest slanders** i.e., slanders that do not involve her virtue **90 prized** esteemed **96 argument** skill in discourse **101 every day, tomorrow** tomorrow and every day thereafter. **104 limed** caught, like a bird in birdlime, a sticky substance spread on branches to trap the birds that perch on them **105 by haps** by chance **106 Some Cupid kills** Cupid kills some **107 What . . . ears?** (An allusion to the old saying that a person's ears burn when one is being discussed in one's absence.) **110 No . . . such** Nothing is gained by hiding behind such defenses. **112 Taming . . . hand** (A figure derived from the taming of the hawk by the hand of the falconer.)

If thou dost love, my kindness shall incite thee
To bind our loves up in a holy band;
For others say thou dost deserve, and I
Believe it better than reportingly. *Exit.*

✤

[3.2]

Enter Prince [Don Pedro], Claudio, Benedick, and Leonato.

DON PEDRO I do but stay till your marriage be consummate, and then go I toward Aragon.

CLAUDIO I'll bring you thither, my lord, if you'll vouchsafe me.

DON PEDRO Nay, that would be as great a soil in the new gloss of your marriage as to show a child his new coat and forbid him to wear it. I will only be bold with Benedick for his company, for from the crown of his head to the sole of his foot he is all mirth. He hath twice or thrice cut Cupid's bowstring, and the little hangman dare not shoot at him. He hath a heart as sound as a bell, and his tongue is the clapper, for what his heart thinks his tongue speaks.

BENEDICK Gallants, I am not as I have been.

LEONATO So say I. Methinks you are sadder.

CLAUDIO I hope he be in love.

DON PEDRO Hang him, truant! There's no true drop of blood in him, to be truly touched with love. If he be sad, he wants money.

BENEDICK I have the toothache.

DON PEDRO Draw it.

BENEDICK Hang it!

CLAUDIO You must hang it first and draw it afterwards.

DON PEDRO What, sigh for the toothache?

LEONATO Where is but a humor or a worm.

BENEDICK Well, everyone can master a grief but he that has it.

CLAUDIO Yet say I, he is in love.

DON PEDRO There is no appearance of fancy in him, unless it be a fancy that he hath to strange disguises; as, to be a Dutchman today, a Frenchman tomorrow, or in the shape of two countries at once, as, a German from the waist downward, all slops, and a Spaniard from the hip upward, no doublet. Unless he have a fancy to this foolery, as it appears he hath, he is no fool for fancy, as you would have it appear he is.

CLAUDIO If he be not in love with some woman, there is no believing old signs. 'A brushes his hat o' mornings. What should that bode?

DON PEDRO Hath any man seen him at the barber's?

CLAUDIO No, but the barber's man hath been seen with him, and the old ornament of his cheek hath already stuffed tennis balls.

LEONATO Indeed he looks younger than he did by the loss of a beard.

DON PEDRO Nay, 'a rubs himself with civet. Can you smell him out by that?

CLAUDIO That's as much as to say the sweet youth's in love.

DON PEDRO The greatest note of it is his melancholy.

CLAUDIO And when was he wont to wash his face?

DON PEDRO Yea, or to paint himself? For the which I hear what they say of him.

CLAUDIO Nay, but his jesting spirit, which is now crept into a lute string and now governed by stops.

DON PEDRO Indeed, that tells a heavy tale for him. Conclude, conclude he is in love.

CLAUDIO Nay, but I know who loves him.

DON PEDRO That would I know too. I warrant, one that knows him not.

CLAUDIO Yes, and his ill conditions; and, in despite of all, dies for him.

DON PEDRO She shall be buried with her face upwards.

BENEDICK Yet is this no charm for the toothache. Old signor, walk aside with me. I have studied eight or nine wise words to speak to you, which these hobbyhorses must not hear. *[Exeunt Benedick and Leonato.]*

DON PEDRO For my life, to break with him about Beatrice.

CLAUDIO 'Tis even so. Hero and Margaret have by this played their parts with Beatrice, and then the two bears will not bite one another when they meet.

Enter [Don] John the Bastard.

DON JOHN My lord and brother, God save you!

DON PEDRO Good e'en, brother.

DON JOHN If your leisure served, I would speak with you.

DON PEDRO In private?

114 band bond **116 better than reportingly** on better evidence than mere report.
3.2. Location: Leonato's house.
1–2 consummate consummated **3 bring** escort **4 vouchsafe** allow **5 soil** stain **7 be bold with** ask **11 hangman** executioner; rogue. (Playfully applied to Cupid.) **15 sadder** more serious. **17 truant** i.e., from love. **19 wants** lacks **20 toothache** (Thought to be a common ailment of lovers.) **21 Draw** Extract. (But Claudio jokes on the method of executing traitors, who were hanged first and then cut down alive and drawn, i.e., disemboweled, and finally quartered.) **22 Hang it**! Confound it! **26 Where** Where there. **humor or a worm** (A toothache was ascribed to "humors," or unhealthy secretions, and to actual worms in the teeth.) **27 grief** pain. **but** except **30 fancy** love **31 fancy** whim, liking **34 slops** loose breeches **35 no doublet** i.e., with a hip-length cloak in place of, or covering, the close-fitting doublet.

36–7 fool for fancy i.e., lover **43–4 the old . . . tennis balls** i.e., Benedick's beard has gone to stuff tennis balls. (He appears onstage beardless in this scene for the first time.) **47 civet** perfume derived from the civet cat. **48 smell him out** (1) discern his secret (2) smell him coming **51 note** mark **52 wont** accustomed. **wash** i.e., with cosmetics; similarly with *paint* in the next line **53–4 For . . . him** That's what I hear people saying about him. **56 stops** (1) frets on the fingerboard (2) restraints. **62 ill conditions** bad qualities **64 buried . . . upwards** i.e., as the faithful, not as a suicide, who were sometimes buried face downwards (?). (There is also a sexual suggestion of her being smothered under Benedick, continuing the joke on *dies for him,* meaning to have an orgasm.) **67–8 hobbyhorses** i.e., buffoons. (Originally, figures in a morris dance made to resemble a horse and rider.) **69 For** Upon. **break** speak **71 Margaret** (Ursula joined Hero in playing the trick on Beatrice, but Margaret has been in on it.) **75 e'en** evening, i.e., afternoon

DON JOHN If it please you. Yet Count Claudio may hear,
for what I would speak of concerns him.
DON PEDRO What's the matter?
DON JOHN [*to Claudio*] Means Your Lordship to be married tomorrow?
DON PEDRO You know he does.
DON JOHN I know not that, when he knows what I
know.
CLAUDIO If there be any impediment, I pray you
discover it. 88
DON JOHN You may think I love you not. Let that
appear hereafter, and aim better at me by that I now 90
will manifest. For my brother, I think he holds you 91
well and in dearness of heart hath holp to effect your 92
ensuing marriage—surely suit ill spent and labor ill
bestowed.
DON PEDRO Why, what's the matter?
DON JOHN I came hither to tell you, and, circumstances 96
shortened—for she has been too long a-talking of— 97
the lady is disloyal. 98
CLAUDIO Who, Hero?
DON JOHN Even she—Leonato's Hero, your Hero,
every man's Hero.
CLAUDIO Disloyal?
DON JOHN The word is too good to paint out her 103
wickedness. I could say she were worse; think you of
a worse title, and I will fit her to it. Wonder not till fur- 105
ther warrant. Go but with me tonight, you shall see her 106
chamber window entered, even the night before her
wedding day. If you love her then, tomorrow wed her;
but it would better fit your honor to change your
mind.
CLAUDIO May this be so?
DON PEDRO I will not think it.
DON JOHN If you dare not trust that you see, confess not 113
that you know. If you will follow me, I will show you 114
enough; and when you have seen more and heard
more, proceed accordingly.
CLAUDIO If I see anything tonight why I should not
marry her, tomorrow in the congregation, where I
should wed, there will I shame her.
DON PEDRO And, as I wooed for thee to obtain her, I
will join with thee to disgrace her.
DON JOHN I will disparage her no farther till you are my
witnesses. Bear it coldly but till midnight, and let the 123
issue show itself. 124
DON PEDRO O day untowardly turned! 125
CLAUDIO O mischief strangely thwarting!
DON JOHN O plague right well prevented! So will you
say when you have seen the sequel. [*Exeunt.*]

88 discover reveal **90 aim better at** judge better of. **that** that which **91–2 holds you well** thinks well of you **92 holp** helped **96–7 circumstances shortened** without unnecessary details **97 a-talking of** under discussion (by us) **98 disloyal** unfaithful. **103 paint out** portray in full **105–6 till further warrant** till further proof appears. **113–14 If . . . know** i.e., If you are unwilling to believe what you see, then don't claim to know the truth. **123 coldly** calmly **124 issue** outcome **125 untowardly turned** wretchedly altered.

[3.3]

Enter Dogberry and his compartner [*Verges*] *with the Watch.*

DOGBERRY Are you good men and true?
VERGES Yea, or else it were pity but they should suffer
salvation, body and soul. 3
DOGBERRY Nay, that were a punishment too good for
them, if they should have any allegiance in them, 5
being chosen for the Prince's watch.
VERGES Well, give them their charge, neighbor Dog- 7
berry.
DOGBERRY First, who think you the most desartless 9
man to be constable?
FIRST WATCH Hugh Oatcake, sir, or George Seacoal, for
they can write and read.
DOGBERRY Come hither, neighbor Seacoal. [*Seacoal, or Second Watch, steps forward.*] God hath blessed you
with a good name. To be a well-favored man is the gift 15
of fortune, but to write and read comes by nature.
SEACOAL Both which, Master Constable—
DOGBERRY You have. I knew it would be your answer.
Well, for your favor, sir, why, give God thanks, and
make no boast of it; and for your writing and reading,
let that appear when there is no need of such vanity.
You are thought here to be the most senseless and fit 22
man for the constable of the watch; therefore bear you
the lantern. This is your charge: you shall comprehend 24
all vagrom men; you are to bid any man stand, in the 25
Prince's name.
SEACOAL How if 'a will not stand?
DOGBERRY Why, then, take no note of him, but let him
go, and presently call the rest of the watch together
and thank God you are rid of a knave.
VERGES If he will not stand when he is bidden, he is
none of the Prince's subjects.
DOGBERRY True, and they are to meddle with none but
the Prince's subjects. You shall also make no noise in
the streets; for, for the watch to babble and to talk is
most tolerable and not to be endured. 36
WATCH We will rather sleep than talk. We know what
belongs to a watch. 38
DOGBERRY Why, you speak like an ancient and most 39
quiet watchman, for I cannot see how sleeping should
offend. Only have a care that your bills be not stolen. 41
Well, you are to call at all the alehouses and bid those
that are drunk get them to bed.
WATCH How if they will not?

3.3. Location: A street.
3 salvation (A blunder for "damnation.") **5 allegiance** (For "treachery.") **7 charge** instructions **9 desartless** (For "deserving.")
15 a good name (Sea coal was high-grade coal shipped from Newcastle, not the charcoal usually sold by London colliers.) **well-favored** good-looking **22 senseless** (For "sensible.") **24 comprehend** (For "apprehend.") **25 vagrom** vagrant. **stand** stand still, stop **36 tolerable** (For "intolerable.") **37 WATCH** (Here and at lines 44, 48, 53, and 66 Shakespeare's text does not specify which watchman speaks. These lines are sometimes assigned to the Second Watch, Seacoal, but could be spoken by others of the watch.) **38 belongs to** are the duties of **39 ancient** venerable, experienced **41 bills** pikes, with axes fixed to long poles

DOGBERRY Why, then, let them alone till they are sober. If they make you not then the better answer, you may say they are not the men you took them for.

WATCH Well, sir.

DOGBERRY If you meet a thief, you may suspect him, by virtue of your office, to be no true man; and for such kind of men, the less you meddle or make with them, why, the more is for your honesty.

WATCH If we know him to be a thief, shall we not lay hands on him?

DOGBERRY Truly, by your office you may, but I think they that touch pitch will be defiled. The most peaceable way for you, if you do take a thief, is to let him show himself what he is and steal out of your company.

VERGES You have been always called a merciful man, partner.

DOGBERRY Truly, I would not hang a dog by my will, much more a man who hath any honesty in him.

VERGES If you hear a child cry in the night, you must call to the nurse and bid her still it.

WATCH How if the nurse be asleep and will not hear us?

DOGBERRY Why, then, depart in peace and let the child wake her with crying, for the ewe that will not hear her lamb when it baas will never answer a calf when he bleats.

VERGES 'Tis very true.

DOGBERRY This is the end of the charge: you, Constable, are to present the Prince's own person. If you meet the Prince in the night, you may stay him.

VERGES Nay, by'r Lady, that I think 'a cannot.

DOGBERRY Five shillings to one on't, with any man that knows the statutes, he may stay him; marry, not without the Prince be willing, for indeed the watch ought to offend no man, and it is an offense to stay a man against his will.

VERGES By'r Lady, I think it be so.

DOGBERRY Ha, ah ha! Well, masters, good night. An there be any matter of weight chances, call up me. Keep your fellows' counsels and your own, and good night. Come, neighbor. [*He starts to leave with Verges.*]

SEACOAL Well, masters, we hear our charge. Let us go sit here upon the church bench till two, and then all to bed.

DOGBERRY One word more, honest neighbors. I pray you, watch about Signor Leonato's door, for the wedding being there tomorrow, there is a great coil tonight. Adieu. Be vigitant, I beseech you.

Exeunt [*Dogberry and Verges*].

Enter Borachio and Conrade.

BORACHIO What, Conrade!

SEACOAL [*aside*] Peace! Stir not.

BORACHIO Conrade, I say!

CONRADE Here, man. I am at thy elbow.

BORACHIO Mass, and my elbow itched; I thought there would a scab follow.

CONRADE I will owe thee an answer for that. And now, forward with thy tale.

BORACHIO Stand thee close, then, under this penthouse, for it drizzles rain, and I will, like a true drunkard, utter all to thee.

SEACOAL [*aside*] Some treason, masters. Yet stand close.

BORACHIO Therefore know I have earned of Don John a thousand ducats.

CONRADE Is it possible that any villainy should be so dear?

BORACHIO Thou shouldst rather ask if it were possible any villainy should be so rich; for when rich villains have need of poor ones, poor ones may make what price they will.

CONRADE I wonder at it.

BORACHIO That shows thou art unconfirmed. Thou knowest that the fashion of a doublet, or a hat, or a cloak, is nothing to a man.

CONRADE Yes, it is apparel.

BORACHIO I mean, the fashion.

CONRADE Yes, the fashion is the fashion.

BORACHIO Tush, I may as well say the fool's the fool. But see'st thou not what a deformed thief this fashion is?

SEACOAL [*aside*] I know that Deformed. 'A has been a vile thief this seven year; 'a goes up and down like a gentleman. I remember his name.

BORACHIO Didst thou not hear somebody?

CONRADE No, 'twas the vane on the house.

BORACHIO See'st thou not, I say, what a deformed thief this fashion is, how giddily 'a turns about all the hot bloods between fourteen and five-and-thirty, sometimes fashioning them like Pharaoh's soldiers in the reechy painting, sometime like god Bel's priests in the old church-window, sometime like the shaven Hercules in the smirched worm-eaten tapestry, where his codpiece seems as massy as his club?

50 true honest **51 meddle or make** have to do **52 is** it is **56 they . . . defiled** (A commonplace, derived from Ecclesiasticus 13:1.)
74 present represent **76 by'r Lady** i.e., by Our Lady. (A mild oath.)
92 coil to-do **93 vigitant** (For "vigilant.")

98 Mass i.e., By the Mass. **my elbow itched** (Proverbially, a warning against questionable companions.) **99 scab** i.e., scoundrel. (With play on literal meaning.) **100 owe thee an answer** answer later
102 penthouse overhanging structure **103 true drunkard** (Alludes to the commonplace that the drunkard tells all; Borachio's name in Spanish means "drunkard.") **105–6 stand close** stay hidden.
110 dear expensive. **112 rich** well-paid **116 unconfirmed** inexperienced. **118 is . . . man** does not make the man. (But Conrade plays on the phrase in the sense of "means nothing to a man.") **120 I . . . fashion** i.e., My emphasis was on the mere fashion, not on the apparel itself. (But Conrade wittily refuses to allow the difference.)
123 deformed thief i.e., so called because fashion takes such varied and extreme shapes and because it impoverishes those who follow fashion **126 up and down** about, here and there **134 reechy** dirty, grimy. (Perhaps this painting is of the Israelites passing through the Red Sea.) **god Bel's priests** (Probably alludes to the story of Bel and the Dragon, from the apocryphal Book of Daniel, depicted in a stained-glass window.) **135–6 shaven Hercules** (A reference either to young Hercules at the crossroads, choosing between virtue and vice, or in the service of Omphale—see 2.1.242, note—or, confusedly, to the story of Samson.) **137 codpiece** decorative pouch at the front of a man's breeches (indelicately conspicuous in this tapestry)

CONRADE All this I see, and I see that the fashion wears out more apparel than the man. But art not thou thyself giddy with the fashion, too, that thou hast shifted out of thy tale into telling me of the fashion?

BORACHIO Not so, neither. But know that I have tonight wooed Margaret, the Lady Hero's gentlewoman, by the name of Hero. She leans me out at her mistress' chamber window, bids me a thousand times good night—I tell this tale vilely; I should first tell thee how the Prince, Claudio, and my master, planted and placed and possessed by my master Don John, saw afar off in the orchard this amiable encounter.

CONRADE And thought they Margaret was Hero?

BORACHIO Two of them did, the Prince and Claudio, but the devil my master knew she was Margaret; and partly by his oaths, which first possessed them, partly by the dark night, which did deceive them, but chiefly by my villainy, which did confirm any slander that Don John had made, away went Claudio enraged; swore he would meet her, as he was appointed, next morning at the temple, and there, before the whole congregation, shame her with what he saw o'ernight and send her home again without a husband.

SEACOAL We charge you, in the Prince's name, stand!

FIRST WATCH Call up the Right Master Constable. We have here recovered the most dangerous piece of lechery that ever was known in the commonwealth.

SEACOAL And one Deformed is one of them. I know him; 'a wears a lock.

CONRADE Masters, masters—

FIRST WATCH You'll be made bring Deformed forth, I warrant you.

CONRADE Masters—

SEACOAL Never speak, we charge you. Let us obey you to go with us.

BORACHIO We are like to prove a goodly commodity, being taken up of these men's bills.

CONRADE A commodity in question, I warrant you. Come, we'll obey you. *Exeunt.*

✤

[3.4]

Enter Hero, and Margaret and Ursula.

HERO Good Ursula, wake my cousin Beatrice, and desire her to rise.

URSULA I will, lady.

HERO And bid her come hither.

URSULA Well. *[Exit.]*

MARGARET Troth, I think your other rabato were better.

HERO No, pray thee, good Meg, I'll wear this.

MARGARET By my troth, 's not so good, and I warrant your cousin will say so.

HERO My cousin's a fool, and thou art another. I'll wear none but this.

MARGARET I like the new tire within excellently, if the hair were a thought browner; and your gown's a most rare fashion, i'faith. I saw the Duchess of Milan's gown that they praise so.

HERO Oh, that exceeds, they say.

MARGARET By my troth, 's but a nightgown in respect of yours: cloth o' gold, and cuts, and laced with silver, set with pearls, down sleeves, side sleeves, and skirts, round underborne with a bluish tinsel. But for a fine, quaint, graceful, and excellent fashion, yours is worth ten on't.

HERO God give me joy to wear it! For my heart is exceeding heavy.

MARGARET 'Twill be heavier soon by the weight of a man.

HERO Fie upon thee! Art not ashamed?

MARGARET Of what, lady? Of speaking honorably? Is not marriage honorable in a beggar? Is not your lord honorable without marriage? I think you would have me say, "saving your reverence, a husband." An bad thinking do not wrest true speaking, I'll offend nobody. Is there any harm in "the heavier for a husband"? None, I think, an it be the right husband and the right wife; otherwise 'tis light, and not heavy. Ask my Lady Beatrice else. Here she comes.

Enter Beatrice.

HERO Good morrow, coz.

BEATRICE Good morrow, sweet Hero.

HERO Why, how now? Do you speak in the sick tune?

BEATRICE I am out of all other tune, methinks.

MARGARET Clap 's into "Light o 'love." That goes without a burden; do you sing it, and I'll dance it.

BEATRICE Ye light o' love with your heels! Then, if your husband have stables enough, you'll see he shall lack no barns.

MARGARET Oh, illegitimate construction! I scorn that with my heels.

138–9 fashion . . . man i.e., fashion prompts the discarding of clothes faster than honest use. **144 leans me** leans. (*Me* is an emphatic marker.) **148 possessed** (misleadingly) informed; also, perhaps, possessed, as by the devil **149 amiable** amorous **162 Right Master Constable** (A comic title on the pattern of "Right Worshipful," etc.) **163 recovered** (For "discovered.") **164 lechery** (For "treachery.") **166 lock** lock of hair hanging down on the left shoulder; the lovelock. **171 obey** (For "oblige," "command.") **173 commodity** goods acquired **174 taken up** (1) arrested (2) obtained on credit. **bills** (1) pikes (2) bonds given as security. **175 in question** (1) subject to judicial examination (2) of doubtful value
3.4. Location: Leonato's house.
5 Well Very well, as you wish.

6 rabato tall collar supporting a ruff, stiffened with wire or starch
8 troth, 's faith, it is **12 tire within** headdress in the inner room
13 hair hairpiece attached to the *tire* (line 12) **16 exceeds** i.e., exceeds comparison **17 nightgown** dressing gown **17–18 in respect of** compared to **18 cuts . . . silver** slashes in a garment revealing the underlying fabic, and laced with silver thread **19 down sleeves** tight-fitting sleeves to the wrist. **side sleeves** secondary ornamental sleeves hanging from the shoulder **20 round underborne** with a lining around the edge of the skirt. **tinsel** cloth, usually silk, interwoven with threads of silver or gold. **21 quaint** elegant **22 on't** of it. **29 in** even in
31 saving . . . husband (By this apologetic formula, Margaret suggests that Hero is too prudish even to hear the word *husband* mentioned.)
An bad If bawdy **32 wrest** misinterpret **35 light** harmless. (With a play on the meaning "wanton.") **39 tune** i.e., mood. **41 Clap 's** Let's shift. **Light o' love** (A popular song.) **42 burden** bass accompaniment. (With play on the idea of "the weight of a man.") **43 Ye . . . heels!** i.e., You're light-heeled, wanton! **45 barns** (With pun on "bairns," children.) **46 illegitimate construction** false inference. (But with a play on the idea of bastard "bairns.") **47 with my heels** (A proverbial expression of scorn.)

BEATRICE 'Tis almost five o'clock, cousin; 'tis time you were ready. By my troth, I am exceeding ill. Heigh-ho!

MARGARET For a hawk, a horse, or a husband?

BEATRICE For the letter that begins them all, H.

MARGARET Well, an you be not turned Turk, there's no more sailing by the star.

BEATRICE What means the fool, trow?

MARGARET Nothing, I; but God send everyone their heart's desire!

HERO These gloves the Count sent me, they are an excellent perfume.

BEATRICE I am stuffed, cousin. I cannot smell.

MARGARET A maid, and stuffed! There's goodly catching of cold.

BEATRICE Oh, God help me, God help me! How long have you professed apprehension?

MARGARET Ever since you left it. Doth not my wit become me rarely?

BEATRICE It is not seen enough; you should wear it in your cap. By my troth, I am sick.

MARGARET Get you some of this distilled *carduus benedictus*, and lay it to your heart. It is the only thing for a qualm.

HERO There thou prick'st her with a thistle.

BEATRICE *Benedictus!* Why *benedictus?* You have some moral in this *benedictus*.

MARGARET Moral? No, by my troth, I have no moral meaning, I meant plain holy thistle. You may think perchance that I think you are in love. Nay, by'r Lady, I am not such a fool to think what I list, nor I list not to think what I can, nor indeed I cannot think, if I would think my heart out of thinking, that you are in love or that you will be in love or that you can be in love. Yet Benedick was such another, and now is he become a man. He swore he would never marry, and yet now, in despite of his heart, he eats his meat without grudging; and how you may be converted I know not, but methinks you look with your eyes as other women do.

BEATRICE What pace is this that thy tongue keeps?

MARGARET Not a false gallop.

Enter Ursula.

URSULA Madam, withdraw. The Prince, the Count, Signor Benedick, Don John, and all the gallants of the town are come to fetch you to church.

HERO Help to dress me, good coz, good Meg, good Ursula. [*Exeunt*.]

✤

[3.5]

Enter Leonato and the Constable [*Dogberry*] *and the Headborough* [*Verges*].

LEONATO What would you with me, honest neighbor?

DOGBERRY Marry, sir, I would have some confidence with you that decerns you nearly.

LEONATO Brief, I pray you, for you see it is a busy time with me.

DOGBERRY Marry, this it is, sir.

VERGES Yes, in truth it is, sir.

LEONATO What is it, my good friends?

DOGBERRY Goodman Verges, sir, speaks a little off the matter—an old man, sir, and his wits are not so blunt as, God help, I would desire they were, but, in faith, honest as the skin between his brows.

VERGES Yes, I thank God I am as honest as any man living that is an old man and no honester than I.

DOGBERRY Comparisons are odorous. *Palabras*, neighbor Verges.

LEONATO Neighbors, you are tedious.

DOGBERRY It pleases Your Worship to say so, but we are the poor Duke's officers. But truly, for mine own part, if I were as tedious as a king, I could find in my heart to bestow it all of Your Worship.

LEONATO All thy tediousness on me, ah?

DOGBERRY Yea, an 'twere a thousand pound more than 'tis; for I hear as good exclamation on Your Worship as of any man in the city, and though I be but a poor man, I am glad to hear it.

VERGES And so am I.

LEONATO I would fain know what you have to say.

VERGES Marry, sir, our watch tonight, excepting Your Worship's presence, ha' ta'en a couple of as arrant knaves as any in Messina.

DOGBERRY A good old man, sir; he will be talking. As they say, when the age is in, the wit is out. God help us, it is a world to see! Well said, i'faith, neighbor

50 For . . . husband? (*Heigh-ho* might be a cry of encouragement in the hunt or else "Heigh-ho for a husband!" as at 2.1.305.) **51 H** (With a pun on "ache," pronounced "aitch." Beatrice complains of aching with a cold.) **52 turned Turk** i.e., turned apostate to the true faith (by violating your oath not to become a lover) **52–3 no . . . star** no more navigating by the North Star, i.e., no certain truth in which to trust. **54 trow** I wonder. **58 perfume** (Gloves were often perfumed.) **59 stuffed** i.e., stuffed up with a cold. (But Margaret takes it in a bawdy sense.) **63 professed apprehension** made claim to be witty. **64 left it** gave it up. (Margaret gibes at Beatrice's pretending not to know what the joking is all about.) **66–7 wear . . . cap** i.e., wear it prominently visible, as a fool wears his coxcomb. (Beatrice jokes that Margaret's supposed wit is imperceptible.) **68–9 *carduus benedictus*** the blessed thistle, noted for medicinal properties. (With a pun on "Benedick.") **70 a qualm** an attack of nausea (or misgiving). **73 moral** hidden meaning **75 holy thistle** the blessed thistle or *carduus benedictus* of 68–9. **77 list** please **79 think . . . thinking** i.e., rack my brains **81 such another** i.e., seemingly proof against love **81–2 a man** i.e., like other men. **83–4 eats . . . grudging** i.e., is content to be like other men, to be in love **87 Not . . . gallop**. i.e., I'm not speaking at a false pace, at a canter; I speak the truth.

3.5. Location: Leonato's house.
0.2 *Headborough* local constable **2 confidence** (A blunder for "conference.") **3 decerns** (For "concerns.") **9 Goodman** (Title of a person under the social rank of gentleman.) **10 blunt** (He means "sharp.") **12 honest . . . brows** (Proverbial expression of honesty.) **15 odorous** (For "odious.") ***Palabras*** (For *pocas palabras,* "few words" in Spanish.) **19 poor Duke's officers** (For "Duke's poor officers.") **20 tedious** (Dogberry evidently thinks *tedious* means "rich.") **21 of** on **24 exclamation** (Possibly for "acclamation.") **29 tonight** last night **29–30 excepting . . . presence** (The normal meaning, "with the exception of your honored self," comically implies that Leonato is an even more arrant knave than the men arrested. Verges probably means, "begging Your Worship's pardon.") **30 ha' ta'en** have taken **33 when . . . out** (An adaptation of the proverb, "When ale is in, wit is out.") **34 a world** i.e., wonderful. (Proverbial.)

Verges. Well, God's a good man. An two men ride of a horse, one must ride behind. An honest soul, i'faith, sir, by my troth he is, as ever broke bread. But, God is to be worshiped, all men are not alike, alas, good neighbor!

LEONATO Indeed, neighbor, he comes too short of you.

DOGBERRY Gifts that God gives.

LEONATO I must leave you.

DOGBERRY One word, sir. Our watch, sir, have indeed comprehended two aspicious persons, and we would have them this morning examined before Your Worship.

LEONATO Take their examination yourself and bring it me. I am now in great haste, as it may appear unto you.

DOGBERRY It shall be suffigance.

LEONATO Drink some wine ere you go. Fare you well.

[Enter a Messenger.]

MESSENGER My lord, they stay for you to give your daughter to her husband.

LEONATO I'll wait upon them. I am ready.

[Exeunt Leonato and Messenger.]

DOGBERRY Go, good partner, go, get you to Francis Seacoal. Bid him bring his pen and inkhorn to the jail. We are now to examination these men.

VERGES And we must do it wisely.

DOGBERRY We will spare for no wit, I warrant you. Here's that shall drive some of them to a noncome. Only get the learned writer to set down our excommunication, and meet me at the jail. *[Exeunt.]*

✤

[4.1]

Enter Prince [Don Pedro], [Don John the] Bastard, Leonato, Friar [Francis], Claudio, Benedick, Hero, and Beatrice [with attendants].

LEONATO Come, Friar Francis, be brief—only to the plain form of marriage, and you shall recount their particular duties afterwards.

FRIAR You come hither, my lord, to marry this lady?

CLAUDIO No.

LEONATO To be married to her. Friar, you come to marry her.

FRIAR Lady, you come hither to be married to this Count?

HERO I do.

FRIAR If either of you know any inward impediment why you should not be conjoined, I charge you on your souls to utter it.

CLAUDIO Know you any, Hero?

HERO None, my lord.

FRIAR Know you any, Count?

LEONATO I dare make his answer: none.

CLAUDIO Oh, what men dare do! What men may do!
What men daily do, not knowing what they do!

BENEDICK How now? Interjections? Why, then, some be of laughing, as, ah, ha, he!

CLAUDIO
Stand thee by, Friar.—Father, by your leave,
Will you with free and unconstrainèd soul
Give me this maid, your daughter?

LEONATO
As freely, son, as God did give her me.

CLAUDIO
And what have I to give you back, whose worth
May counterpoise this rich and precious gift?

DON PEDRO
Nothing, unless you render her again.

CLAUDIO
Sweet Prince, you learn me noble thankfulness.
[He hands Hero to Leonato.]
There, Leonato, take her back again.
Give not this rotten orange to your friend;
She's but the sign and semblance of her honor.
Behold how like a maid she blushes here!
Oh, what authority and show of truth
Can cunning sin cover itself withal!
Comes not that blood as modest evidence
To witness simple virtue? Would you not swear,
All you that see her, that she were a maid,
By these exterior shows? But she is none:
She knows the heat of a luxurious bed.
Her blush is guiltiness, not modesty.

LEONATO
What do you mean, my lord?

CLAUDIO
Not to be married,
Not to knit my soul to an approvèd wanton.

LEONATO
Dear my lord, if you, in your own proof,
Have vanquished the resistance of her youth,
And made defeat of her virginity—

CLAUDIO
I know what you would say: if I have known her,
You will say, she did embrace me as a husband,
And so extenuate the forehand sin.
No, Leonato,
I never tempted her with word too large,

35 God's . . . man i.e., God is good. (A proverbial saying.) **36 of** on **44 comprehended** (For "apprehended.") **aspicious** (For "suspicious.") **50 suffigance** (For "sufficient.") **54 wait upon** attend **55–6 Francis Seacoal** i.e., the Sexton of 4.2, not George, the member of the watch in 3.3. **57 examination** (For "examine.") **60 noncome** (Probably an unintended contraction for *non compos mentis*, "not of sound mind," but Dogberry may have intended "nonplus.") **61–2 excommunication** (For "examination" or "communication.")
4.1. Location: A church.
11 inward secret

20–1 some . . . he (Benedick quotes from Lilly's Latin grammar on the subject of interjections; according to Lilly, these are to be classified as laughing interjections.) **22 Stand thee by** Stand aside **27 counterpoise** balance, be equivalent to **29 learn** teach **32 sign and semblance** pretense and outward show **36 blood** i.e., blush. **modest evidence** evidence of modesty **37 witness** bear witness to **40 luxurious** lascivious, lustful **42 mean** imply, suggest. (But Claudio bitterly replies in the sense of "intend.") **43 approvèd** proved **44 in . . . proof** in making trial of her yourself **47 known her** i.e., known her sexually **49 extenuate** excuse, lessen. **forehand sin** sin of anticipating (marriage). **51 large** broad, immodest

But, as a brother to his sister, showed
Bashful sincerity and comely love.

HERO
And seemed I ever otherwise to you?

CLAUDIO
Out on thee, seeming! I will write against it. 55
You seem to me as Dian in her orb, 56
As chaste as is the bud ere it be blown; 57
But you are more intemperate in your blood
Than Venus, or those pampered animals
That rage in savage sensuality.

HERO
Is my lord well, that he doth speak so wide? 61

LEONATO
Sweet Prince, why speak not you?

DON PEDRO What should I speak?
I stand dishonored, that have gone about 63
To link my dear friend to a common stale. 64

LEONATO
Are these things spoken, or do I but dream?

DON JOHN
Sir, they are spoken, and these things are true.

BENEDICK This looks not like a nuptial.

HERO "True"! Oh, God! 68

CLAUDIO Leonato, stand I here?
Is this the Prince? Is this the Prince's brother?
Is this face Hero's? Are our eyes our own?

LEONATO
All this is so. But what of this, my lord?

CLAUDIO
Let me but move one question to your daughter, 73
And by that fatherly and kindly power 74
That you have in her, bid her answer truly.

LEONATO [*to Hero*]
I charge thee do so, as thou art my child.

HERO
Oh, God defend me, how am I beset!
What kind of catechizing call you this? 78

CLAUDIO
To make you answer truly to your name.

HERO
Is it not Hero? Who can blot that name
With any just reproach?

CLAUDIO Marry, that can Hero!
Hero itself can blot out Hero's virtue. 82
What man was he talked with you yesternight
Out at your window betwixt twelve and one?
Now, if you are a maid, answer to this.

HERO
I talked with no man at that hour, my lord.

DON PEDRO
Why, then are you no maiden. Leonato,
I am sorry you must hear. Upon mine honor,
Myself, my brother, and this grievèd Count 89
Did see her, hear her, at that hour last night
Talk with a ruffian at her chamber window,
Who hath indeed, most like a liberal villain, 92
Confessed the vile encounters they have had
A thousand times in secret.

DON JOHN
Fie, fie, they are not to be named, my lord,
Not to be spoke of!
There is not chastity enough in language
Without offense to utter them. Thus, pretty lady,
I am sorry for thy much misgovernment. 99

CLAUDIO
O Hero, what a Hero hadst thou been
If half thy outward graces had been placed
About thy thoughts and counsels of thy heart!
But fare thee well, most foul, most fair! Farewell,
Thou pure impiety and impious purity!
For thee I'll lock up all the gates of love, 105
And on my eyelids shall conjecture hang, 106
To turn all beauty into thoughts of harm,
And never shall it more be gracious. 108

LEONATO
Hath no man's dagger here a point for me?
[*Hero swoons.*]

BEATRICE
Why, how now, cousin, wherefore sink you down? 110

DON JOHN
Come, let us go. These things, come thus to light,
Smother her spirits up.
[*Exeunt Don Pedro, Don John, and Claudio.*]

BENEDICK
How doth the lady?

BEATRICE Dead, I think. Help, uncle!
Hero, why, Hero! Uncle! Signor Benedick! Friar!

LEONATO
O Fate, take not away thy heavy hand!
Death is the fairest cover for her shame
That may be wished for.

BEATRICE How now, cousin Hero?

FRIAR Have comfort, lady.

LEONATO
Dost thou look up?

FRIAR Yea, wherefore should she not? 119

LEONATO
Wherefore? Why, doth not every earthly thing
Cry shame upon her? Could she here deny
The story that is printed in her blood? 122
Do not live, Hero, do not ope thine eyes;
For, did I think thou wouldst not quickly die,
Thought I thy spirits were stronger than thy shames, 125

55 Out . . . seeming! i.e., Shame on you, a mere semblance of good! **56 Dian . . . orb** i.e., Diana, goddess of chastity, enthroned in the moon **57 be blown** open, flowering **61 wide** wide of the mark. **63 gone about** undertaken **64 stale** whore. **68 True** (A response to Don John's use of the term.) **73 move** put **74 kindly** natural **78 catechizing** formal questioning used by the Church to teach the principles of faith. The first question in the Church of England's catechism is, "What is your name?" **82 Hero itself** The very name of Hero (who, in the story of Hero and Leander, is the faithful tragic heroine)

89 grievèd (1) aggrieved, wronged (2) struck with grief **92 liberal** licentious **99 much misgovernment** gross misconduct. **105 For thee** Because of you **106 conjecture** evil suspicion **108 be gracious** seem attractive, graceful. **110, 119 wherefore** why **122 blood** i.e., blushes. **125 spirits** life-giving energies, vital powers

Myself would, on the rearward of reproaches,
Strike at thy life. Grieved I I had but one?
Chid I for that at frugal nature's frame?
Oh, one too much by thee! Why had I one?
Why ever wast thou lovely in my eyes?
Why had I not with charitable hand
Took up a beggar's issue at my gates,
Who, smirchèd thus and mired with infamy,
I might have said, "No part of it is mine;
This shame derives itself from unknown loins"?
But mine, and mine I loved, and mine I praised,
And mine that I was proud on, mine so much
That I myself was to myself not mine,
Valuing of her—why, she, oh, she, is fallen
Into a pit of ink, that the wide sea
Hath drops too few to wash her clean again
And salt too little which may season give
To her foul-tainted flesh!

BENEDICK Sir, sir, be patient.
For my part, I am so attired in wonder,
I know not what to say.

BEATRICE
Oh, on my soul, my cousin is belied!

BENEDICK
Lady, were you her bedfellow last night?

BEATRICE
No, truly, not; although, until last night,
I have this twelvemonth been her bedfellow.

LEONATO
Confirmed, confirmed! Oh, that is stronger made
Which was before barred up with ribs of iron!
Would the two princes lie and Claudio lie,
Who loved her so that, speaking of her foulness,
Washed it with tears? Hence from her! Let her die.

FRIAR Hear me a little;
For I have only been silent so long
And given way unto this course of fortune
By noting of the lady. I have marked
A thousand blushing apparitions
To start into her face, a thousand innocent shames
In angel whiteness beat away those blushes,
And in her eye there hath appeared a fire
To burn the errors that these princes hold
Against her maiden truth. Call me a fool;
Trust not my reading nor my observations,
Which with experimental seal doth warrant
The tenor of my book; trust not my age,
My reverence, calling, nor divinity,
If this sweet lady lie not guiltless here
Under some biting error.

LEONATO Friar, it cannot be.
Thou see'st that all the grace that she hath left
Is that she will not add to her damnation
A sin of perjury; she not denies it.
Why seek'st thou then to cover with excuse
That which appears in proper nakedness?

FRIAR
Lady, what man is he you are accused of?

HERO
They know that do accuse me; I know none.
If I know more of any man alive
Than that which maiden modesty doth warrant,
Let all my sins lack mercy! O my father,
Prove you that any man with me conversed
At hours unmeet or that I yesternight
Maintained the change of words with any creature,
Refuse me, hate me, torture me to death!

FRIAR
There is some strange misprision in the princes.

BENEDICK
Two of them have the very bent of honor;
And if their wisdoms be misled in this,
The practice of it lives in John the Bastard,
Whose spirits toil in frame of villainies.

LEONATO
I know not. If they speak but truth of her,
These hands shall tear her; if they wrong her honor,
The proudest of them shall well hear of it.
Time hath not yet so dried this blood of mine,
Nor age so eat up my invention,
Nor fortune made such havoc of my means,
Nor my bad life reft me so much of friends,
But they shall find, awaked in such a kind,
Both strength of limb and policy of mind,
Ability in means, and choice of friends,
To quit me of them throughly.

FRIAR Pause awhile,
And let my counsel sway you in this case.
Your daughter here the princes left for dead,
Let her awhile be secretly kept in,
And publish it that she is dead indeed.
Maintain a mourning ostentation,
And on your family's old monument
Hang mournful epitaphs, and do all rites
That appertain unto a burial.

LEONATO
What shall become of this? What will this do?

FRIAR
Marry, this, well carried, shall on her behalf
Change slander to remorse. That is some good.
But not for that dream I on this strange course,

126 on . . . reproaches following this public disgrace **128 Chid** Chided. **frame** plan, order. **132 Took . . . issue** taken up a beggar's child **136 mine** i.e., my own daughter **138–9 That . . . her** i.e., that I set no value on myself in caring so much for her **140 that** such that **142 season** preservative **151 before** already **157 given . . . fortune** yielded to this turn of events **166–7 Which . . . book** i.e., by means of which observations and experience I have confirmed what I learned from books

175 proper true **179 warrant** sanction, permit **181 Prove you** if you prove **182 unmeet** improper **183 Maintained the change** held exchange **184 Refuse** disown **185 misprision** mistake, misunderstanding **186 Two . . . honor** i.e., Don Pedro and Claudio are wholly honorable **188 practice** scheming **189 frame** contriving **194 eat** eaten. (Pronounced "et.") **invention** power to plan (vengeance) **196 reft** robbed **197 kind** manner **198 policy** shrewdness **200 quit . . . throughly** settle accounts with them thoroughly. **202 the princes** i.e., (whom) Don Pedro and Claudio **203 in** in hiding, at home **205 Maintain . . . ostentation** Perform all the outward signs of mourning **206 monument** burial vault **209 become of** result from **210 carried** managed **212 not for that** not for that reason alone

But on this travail look for greater birth.
She—dying, as it must be so maintained,
Upon the instant that she was accused—
Shall be lamented, pitied, and excused
Of every hearer; for it so falls out
That what we have we prize not to the worth
Whiles we enjoy it, but, being lacked and lost,
Why then we rack the value, then we find
The virtue that possession would not show us
Whiles it was ours. So will it fare with Claudio.
When he shall hear she died upon his words,
Th'idea of her life shall sweetly creep
Into his study of imagination,
And every lovely organ of her life
Shall come appareled in more precious habit,
More moving-delicate, and full of life,
Into the eye and prospect of his soul,
Than when she lived indeed. Then shall he mourn,
If ever love had interest in his liver,
And wish he had not so accusèd her,
No, though he thought his accusation true.
Let this be so, and doubt not but success
Will fashion the event in better shape
Than I can lay it down in likelihood.
But if all aim but this be leveled false,
The supposition of the lady's death
Will quench the wonder of her infamy.
And if it sort not well, you may conceal her,
As best befits her wounded reputation,
In some reclusive and religious life,
Out of all eyes, tongues, minds, and injuries.

BENEDICK
Signor Leonato, let the Friar advise you.
And though you know my inwardness and love
Is very much unto the Prince and Claudio,
Yet, by mine honor, I will deal in this
As secretly and justly as your soul
Should with your body.

LEONATO Being that I flow in grief,
The smallest twine may lead me.

FRIAR
'Tis well consented. Presently away;
For to strange sores strangely they strain the cure.
Come, lady, die to live. This wedding day
Perhaps is but prolonged. Have patience, and
endure.

Exit [with all but Benedick and Beatrice].

BENDICK Lady Beatrice, have you wept all this while?

BEATRICE Yea, and I will weep a while longer.

BENEDICK I will not desire that.

BEATRICE You have no reason. I do it freely.

BENEDICK Surely I do believe your fair cousin is wronged.

BEATRICE Ah, how much might the man deserve of me that would right her!

BENEDICK Is there any way to show such friendship?

BEATRICE A very even way, but no such friend.

BENEDICK May a man do it?

BEATRICE It is a man's office, but not yours.

BENEDICK I do love nothing in the world so well as you. Is not that strange?

BEATRICE As strange as the thing I know not. It were as possible for me to say I loved nothing so well as you. But believe me not; and yet I lie not. I confess nothing, nor I deny nothing. I am sorry for my cousin.

BENEDICK By my sword, Beatrice, thou lovest me.

BEATRICE Do not swear and eat it.

BENEDICK I will swear by it that you love me, and I will make him eat it that says I love not you.

BEATRICE Will you not eat your word?

BENEDICK With no sauce that can be devised to it. I protest I love thee.

BEATRICE Why, then, God forgive me!

BENEDICK What offense, sweet Beatrice?

BEATRICE You have stayed me in a happy hour. I was about to protest I loved you.

BENEDICK And do it with all thy heart.

BEATRICE I love you with so much of my heart that none is left to protest.

BENEDICK Come, bid me do anything for thee.

BEATRICE Kill Claudio.

BENEDICK Ha! Not for the wide world.

BEATRICE You kill me to deny it. Farewell. [*Going.*]

BENEDICK Tarry, sweet Beatrice.

BEATRICE I am gone, though I am here. There is no love in you. Nay, I pray you, let me go.

BENEDICK Beatrice—

BEATRICE In faith, I will go.

BENEDICK We'll be friends first.

BEATRICE You dare easier be friends with me than fight with mine enemy.

BENEDICK Is Claudio thine enemy?

BEATRICE Is 'a not approved in the height a villain, that hath slandered, scorned, dishonored my kinswoman? Oh, that I were a man! What, bear her in hand until they come to take hands, and then, with public accusation, uncovered slander, unmitigated rancor—Oh, God, that I were a man! I would eat his heart in the marketplace.

213 on this travail from this effort (which is metaphorically like the *travail,* or labor, of childbirth) **218 to the worth** as fully as it deserves **220 rack** stretch, extend **223 upon** in consequence of **225 Into . . . imagination** into his thoughts **226 organ . . . life** aspect of her when she was alive **227 habit** apparel **229 prospect** range of vision **231 interest in** claim upon. **liver** (The supposed seat of the passion of love.) **234 success** i.e., what succeeds or happens in time as my plan unfolds **235 event** outcome **236 lay . . . likelihood** anticipate its probable course. **237 if . . . false** i.e., if every other aim miscarry **240 sort** turn out **242 reclusive** cloistered **243 injuries** insults. **245 inwardness and love** close friendship **249 Being . . . grief** Since I overflow in grief **251 Presently** Immediately **252 For . . . cure** for strange diseases require strange and desperate cures. **254 prolonged** deferred.

258 You . . . reason (Beatrice twists Benedick's "I wish you weren't so unhappy," line 257, into "There's no need for you to bid me stop weeping.") **264 even** direct, straightforward **266 office** duty **274 eat it** i.e., eat your words. **276 eat it** i.e., eat my sword, be stabbed by it **279 protest** affirm. (Also in line 283.) **282 stayed** stopped. **in . . . hour** at an appropriate moment. **286 protest** object. (With a play on the sense of "affirm" in 279 and 283.) **292 gone** i.e., in spirit **300 approved in the height** proved in the highest degree **302 bear her in hand** delude Hero with false hopes **304 uncovered** open, unconcealed

BENEDICK Hear me, Beatrice—

BEATRICE Talk with a man out at a window! A proper saying!

BENEDICK Nay, but Beatrice—

BEATRICE Sweet Hero! She is wronged, she is slandered, she is undone.

BENEDICK Beat—

BEATRICE Princes and counties! Surely, a princely testimony, a goodly count, Count Comfect; a sweet gallant, surely! Oh, that I were a man for his sake! Or that I had any friend would be a man for my sake! But manhood is melted into curtsies, valor into compliment, and men are only turned into tongue, and trim ones too. He is now as valiant as Hercules that only tells a lie and swears it. I cannot be a man with wishing, therefore I will die a woman with grieving.

BENEDICK Tarry, good Beatrice. By this hand, I love thee.

BEATRICE Use it for my love some other way than swearing by it.

BENEDICK Think you in your soul the Count Claudio hath wronged Hero?

BEATRICE Yea, as sure as I have a thought or a soul.

BENEDICK Enough, I am engaged. I will challenge him. I will kiss your hand, and so I leave you. By this hand, Claudio shall render me a dear account. As you hear of me, so think of me. Go comfort your cousin. I must say she is dead. And so, farewell. [*Exeunt separately.*]

[4.2]

Enter the Constables [*Dogberry and Verges*] *and the Town Clerk* [*Sexton*] *in gowns, Borachio,* [*Conrade, and Watch*].

DOGBERRY Is our whole dissembly appeared?

VERGES Oh, a stool and a cushion for the sexton.

[*Stool and cushion are brought. The Sexton sits.*]

SEXTON Which be the malefactors?

DOGBERRY Marry, that am I and my partner.

VERGES Nay, that's certain; we have the exhibition to examine.

SEXTON But which are the offenders that are to be examined? Let them come before Master Constable.

DOGBERRY Yea, marry, let them come before me. [*The prisoners are brought forward.*] What is your name, friend?

BORACHIO Borachio.

DOGBERRY Pray, write down Borachio.—Yours, sirrah?

CONRADE I am a gentleman, sir, and my name is Conrade.

DOGBERRY Write down Master Gentleman Conrade. Masters, do you serve God?

CONRADE, BORACHIO Yea, sir, we hope.

DOGBERRY Write down that they hope they serve God; and write God first, for God defend but God should go before such villains! Masters, it is proved already that you are little better than false knaves, and it will go near to be thought so shortly. How answer you for yourselves?

CONRADE Marry, sir, we say we are none.

DOGBERRY A marvelous witty fellow, I assure you, but I will go about with him. [*To Borachio*] Come you hither, sirrah. A word in your ear. Sir, I say to you, it is thought you are false knaves.

BORACHIO Sir, I say to you we are none.

DOGBERRY Well, stand aside. 'Fore God, they are both in a tale. Have you writ down that they are none?

SEXTON Master Constable, you go not the way to examine. You must call forth the watch that are their accusers.

DOGBERRY Yea, marry, that's the eftest way. Let the watch come forth.—Masters, I charge you in the Prince's name accuse these men.

SEACOAL This man said, sir, that Don John, the Prince's brother, was a villain.

DOGBERRY Write down Prince John a villain. Why, this is flat perjury, to call a prince's brother villain.

BORACHIO Master Constable—

DOGBERRY Pray thee, fellow, peace. I do not like thy look, I promise thee.

SEXTON What heard you him say else?

FIRST WATCH Marry, that he had received a thousand ducats of Don John for accusing the Lady Hero wrongfully.

DOGBERRY Flat burglary as ever was committed.

VERGES Yea, by Mass, that it is.

SEXTON What else, fellow?

SEACOAL And that Count Claudio did mean, upon his words, to disgrace Hero before the whole assembly, and not marry her.

DOGBERRY Oh, villain! Thou wilt be condemned into everlasting redemption for this.

SEXTON What else?

WATCH This is all.

SEXTON And this is more, masters, than you can deny: Prince John is this morning secretly stolen away. Hero was in this manner accused, in this very manner refused, and upon the grief of this suddenly died.—Master Constable, let these men be bound and brought to Leonato's. I will go before and show him their examination. [*Exit.*]

308–9 proper saying likely story. **314 counties** counts. **315 count** (1) the title (2) declaration of complaint in an indictment (3) account. **Comfect** candy or sweetmeat **319 are . . . tongue** have become mere (flattering) voices. **trim** nice, elegant, fine. (Used ironically.) **320–1 He . . . swears it** A man need only tell lies and swear they are true to gain a reputation for bravery nowadays. **330 I am engaged** I pledge myself. **332 dear** costly

4.2. Location: The jail.

1 dissembly (A blunder for "assembly.") **4 that am I** (Dogberry evidently understands *malefactors* to mean "factors," agents.) **5 exhibition** (Possibly for "commission.") **13 sirrah** (Used to address inferiors; Conrade objects.)

20 defend forbid **26 witty** clever, cunning **27 go about with** get the better of, deal with **32 in a tale** in agreement. **36 eftest** (Some sort of invention for "easiest" or "deftest.") **42 perjury** (Dogberry means "slander.") **51 by Mass** by the Mass **53–4 upon his words** on the basis of Borachio's testimony **57 redemption** (Dogberry means "damnation.") **59 WATCH** (Perhaps both Seacoal and his partner speak.)

DOGBERRY Come, let them be opinioned. 67
VERGES Let them be in the hands—
CONRADE Off, coxcomb!
DOGBERRY God's my life, where's the sexton? Let him 70
write down the Prince's officer coxcomb. Come, bind
them. Thou naughty varlet! 72
CONRADE Away! You are an ass, you are an ass.
DOGBERRY Dost thou not suspect my place? Dost thou 74
not suspect my years? Oh, that he were here to write 75
me down an ass! But masters, remember that I am an
ass; though it be not written down, yet forget not that
I am an ass. No, thou villain, thou art full of piety, as 78
shall be proved upon thee by good witness. I am a
wise fellow, and, which is more, an officer, and, which
is more, a householder, and, which is more, as pretty
a piece of flesh as any is in Messina, and one that
knows the law, go to, and a rich fellow enough, go to,
and a fellow that hath had losses, and one that hath
two gowns and everything handsome about him.—
Bring him away. Oh, that I had been writ down an ass!
Exeunt.

✤

5.1

Enter Leonato and his brother [*Antonio*].

ANTONIO
If you go on thus, you will kill yourself;
And 'tis not wisdom thus to second grief 2
Against yourself.
LEONATO I pray thee, cease thy counsel,
Which falls into mine ears as profitless
As water in a sieve. Give not me counsel,
Nor let no comforter delight mine ear
But such a one whose wrongs do suit with mine. 7
Bring me a father that so loved his child,
Whose joy of her is overwhelmed like mine,
And bid him speak of patience;
Measure his woe the length and breadth of mine, 11
And let it answer every strain for strain, 12
As thus for thus, and such a grief for such,
In every lineament, branch, shape, and form;
If such a one will smile and stroke his beard,
Bid sorrow wag, cry "hem!" when he should groan, 16
Patch grief with proverbs, make misfortune drunk 17
With candle wasters, bring him yet to me, 18
And I of him will gather patience.
But there is no such man. For, brother, men
Can counsel and speak comfort to that grief
Which they themselves not feel; but tasting it,
Their counsel turns to passion, which before
Would give preceptial medicine to rage, 24
Fetter strong madness in a silken thread,
Charm ache with air and agony with words. 26
No, no, 'tis all men's office to speak patience 27
To those that wring under the load of sorrow, 28
But no man's virtue nor sufficiency 29
To be so moral when he shall endure 30
The like himself. Therefore give me no counsel.
My griefs cry louder than advertisement. 32
ANTONIO
Therein do men from children nothing differ. 33
LEONATO
I pray thee, peace. I will be flesh and blood;
For there was never yet philosopher
That could endure the toothache patiently,
However they have writ the style of gods 37
And made a push at chance and sufferance. 38
ANTONIO
Yet bend not all the harm upon yourself.
Make those that do offend you suffer, too.
LEONATO
There thou speak'st reason. Nay, I will do so.
My soul doth tell me Hero is belied,
And that shall Claudio know; so shall the Prince
And all of them that thus dishonor her.

Enter Prince [*Don Pedro*] *and Claudio.*

ANTONIO
Here comes the Prince and Claudio hastily.
DON PEDRO
Good e'en, good e'en.
CLAUDIO Good day to both of you.
LEONATO
Hear you, my lords—
DON PEDRO We have some haste, Leonato.
LEONATO
Some haste, my lord! Well, fare you well, my lord.
Are you so hasty now? Well, all is one. 49
DON PEDRO
Nay, do not quarrel with us, good old man.
ANTONIO
If he could right himself with quarreling, 51
Some of us would lie low.
CLAUDIO Who wrongs him? 52
LEONATO
Marry, thou dost wrong me, thou dissembler, thou! 53
Nay, never lay thy hand upon thy sword;
I fear thee not.
CLAUDIO Marry, beshrew my hand 55
If it should give your age such cause of fear.
57

67 opinioned (For "pinioned.") **70 God's** May God save
72 naughty wicked **74 suspect** (For "respect.") **75 my years** (With an unconscious suggestion of "my ears," i.e., ass's ears.) **78 piety** (For "impiety.")
5.1. Location: Near Leonato's house.
2 second assist, encourage **7 suit with** match **11 Measure his woe** let his woe equal in scope **12 answer . . . for strain** correspond, pang for pang. (With a musical sense also of echoing a refrain.) **16 wag** be off. **cry "hem"** i.e., clear the throat as before some wordy speech
17 drunk i.e., insensible to pain **18 candle wasters** those who waste candles by late study, bookworms, moral philosophers

24 preceptial consisting of precepts **26 air** mere breath, words
27 office duty **28 wring** writhe **29 sufficiency** ability, power
30 moral prone to moralizing **32 advertisement** advice, counsel.
33 Therein . . . differ i.e., It is childish to be so inconsolable. **37 writ . . . gods** uttered godlike wisdom **38 made . . . sufferance** scoffed at misfortune and suffering. **49 all is one** it makes no difference. **51 he** i.e., Leonato **52 Some of us** i.e., Don Pedro and Claudio **53 thou** (Used contemptuously instead of the more polite *you*.) **55 beshrew** curse
57 my . . . sword I had no intention of using my sword.

In faith, my hand meant nothing to my sword.

LEONATO
Tush, tush, man, never fleer and jest at me.
I speak not like a dotard nor a fool,
As under privilege of age to brag
What I have done being young or what would do
Were I not old. Know, Claudio, to thy head,
Thou hast so wronged mine innocent child and me
That I am forced to lay my reverence by,
And with gray hairs and bruise of many days
Do challenge thee to trial of a man.
I say thou hast belied mine innocent child.
Thy slander hath gone through and through her heart,
And she lies buried with her ancestors—
Oh, in a tomb where never scandal slept,
Save this of hers, framed by thy villainy!

CLAUDIO
My villainy?

LEONATO Thine, Claudio, thine, I say.

DON PEDRO
You say not right, old man.

LEONATO My lord, my lord,
I'll prove it on his body if he dare,
Despite his nice fence and his active practice,
His May of youth and bloom of lustihood.

CLAUDIO
Away! I will not have to do with you.

LEONATO
Canst thou so daff me? Thou hast killed my child.
If thou kill'st me, boy, thou shalt kill a man.

ANTONIO
He shall kill two of us, and men indeed.
But that's no matter; let him kill one first.
Win me and wear me! Let him answer me.
Come follow me, boy. Come, sir boy, come follow me,
Sir boy, I'll whip you from your foining fence!
Nay, as I am a gentleman, I will.

LEONATO Brother—

ANTONIO
Content yourself. God knows I loved my niece,
And she is dead, slandered to death by villains
That dare as well answer a man indeed
As I dare take a serpent by the tongue.
Boys, apes, braggarts, jacks, milksops!

LEONATO Brother Antony—

ANTONIO
Hold you content. What, man! I know them, yea,
And what they weigh, even to the utmost scruple—
Scambling, outfacing, fashionmonging boys,
That lie and cog and flout, deprave and slander,
Go anticly, show outward hideousness,
And speak off half a dozen dangerous words
How they might hurt their enemies, if they durst,
And this is all.

LEONATO
But brother Antony—

ANTONIO Come, 'tis no matter.
Do not you meddle; let me deal in this.

DON PEDRO
Gentlemen both, we will not wake your patience.
My heart is sorry for your daughter's death;
But, on my honor, she was charged with nothing
But what was true and very full of proof.

LEONATO My lord, my lord—

DON PEDRO I will not hear you.

LEONATO
No? Come, brother, away! I will be heard.

ANTONIO
And shall, or some of us will smart for it.
Exeunt ambo [*Leonato and Antonio*].

Enter Benedick.

DON PEDRO
See, see, here comes the man we went to seek.

CLAUDIO Now, signor, what news?

BENEDICK Good day, my lord.

DON PEDRO Welcome, signor. You are almost come to part almost a fray.

CLAUDIO We had like to have had our two noses snapped off with two old men without teeth.

DON PEDRO Leonato and his brother. What think'st thou? Had we fought, I doubt we should have been too young for them.

BENEDICK In a false quarrel there is no true valor. I came to seek you both.

CLAUDIO We have been up and down to seek thee, for we are high-proof melancholy and would fain have it beaten away. Wilt thou use thy wit?

BENEDICK It is in my scabbard. Shall I draw it?

DON PEDRO Dost thou wear thy wit by thy side?

CLAUDIO Never any did so, though very many have been beside their wit. I will bid thee draw as we do the minstrels, draw to pleasure us.

DON PEDRO As I am an honest man, he looks pale. Art thou sick, or angry?

CLAUDIO What, courage, man! What though care killed a cat, thou hast mettle enough in thee to kill care.

BENEDICK Sir, I shall meet your wit in the career, an you charge it against me. I pray you, choose another subject.

58 fleer sneer, jeer **62 head** i.e., face **64 my reverence** i.e., the reverence due old age **66 trial of a man** manly contest, i.e., duel. **71 framed** devised **75 nice fence** dexterous swordsmanship. (Said contemptuously.) **76 lustihood** bodily vigor. **78 daff** doff, brush aside **82 Win . . . me!** (A proverbial expression, used as a challenge, meaning he'll have to overcome me before he can claim me as a prize.) **answer me** i.e., in a duel. **84 foining** thrusting **87 Content yourself** i.e., Don't try to stop me. **94 scruple** small measure of weight **95 Scambling . . . boys** contentious, swaggering, dandified boys **96 cog** cheat. **deprave** defame, traduce

97 anticly fantastically dressed. **hideousness** frightening appearance **98 dangerous** threatening, haughty **103 wake your patience** put your patience to any further test. **110.1 *ambo*** both **116 We had . . . had** We almost had **117 with** by **119 doubt** fear, suspect. (Said ironically.) **124 high-proof** to the highest degree. **fain** gladly **129 beside their wit** out of their wits. (Playing on *by thy side* in line 127.) **130 draw** (1) draw your weapon (2) draw a bow across a musical instrument **135 career** short gallop at full speed (as in a tourney). **an** if **136 charge** level (as a weapon)

CLAUDIO Nay, then, give him another staff. This last was broke cross.

DON PEDRO By this light, he changes more and more. I think he be angry indeed.

CLAUDIO If he be, he knows how to turn his girdle.

BENEDICK Shall I speak a word in your ear?

CLAUDIO God bless me from a challenge!

BENEDICK [*aside to Claudio*] You are a villain. I jest not. I will make it good how you dare, with what you dare, and when you dare. Do me right, or I will protest your cowardice. You have killed a sweet lady, and her death shall fall heavy on you. Let me hear from you.

CLAUDIO Well, I will meet you, so I may have good cheer.

DON PEDRO What, a feast, a feast?

CLAUDIO I'faith, I thank him, he hath bid me to a calf's head and a capon, the which if I do not carve most curiously, say my knife's naught. Shall I not find a woodcock too?

BENEDICK Sir, your wit ambles well; it goes easily.

DON PEDRO I'll tell thee how Beatrice praised thy wit the other day. I said thou hadst a fine wit. "True," said she, "a fine little one." "No," said I, "a great wit." "Right," says she, "a great gross one." "Nay," said I, "a good wit." "Just," said she, "it hurts nobody." "Nay," said I, "the gentleman is wise." "Certain," said she, "a wise gentleman." "Nay," said I, "he hath the tongues." "That I believe," said she, "for he swore a thing to me on Monday night which he forswore on Tuesday morning. There's a double tongue; there's two tongues." Thus did she, an hour together, transshape thy particular virtues. Yet at last she concluded with a sigh, thou wast the proper'st man in Italy.

CLAUDIO For the which she wept heartily and said she cared not.

DON PEDRO Yea, that she did. But yet for all that, an if she did not hate him deadly, she would love him dearly. The old man's daughter told us all.

CLAUDIO All, all. And, moreover, God saw him when he was hid in the garden.

DON PEDRO But when shall we set the savage bull's horns on the sensible Benedick's head?

CLAUDIO Yea, and text underneath, "Here dwells Benedick, the married man"?

BENEDICK Fare you well, boy. You know my mind. I will leave you now to your gossiplike humor. You break jests as braggarts do their blades, which, God be thanked, hurt not.—My lord, for your many courtesies I thank you. I must discontinue your company. Your brother the bastard is fled from Messina. You have among you killed a sweet and innocent lady. For my Lord Lackbeard there, he and I shall meet, and till then peace be with him. [*Exit.*]

DON PEDRO He is in earnest.

CLAUDIO In most profound earnest, and, I'll warrant you, for the love of Beatrice.

DON PEDRO And hath challenged thee?

CLAUDIO Most sincerely.

DON PEDRO What a pretty thing man is when he goes in his doublet and hose and leaves off his wit!

CLAUDIO He is then a giant to an ape; but then is an ape a doctor to such a man.

DON PEDRO But, soft you, let me be. Pluck up, my heart, and be sad. Did he not say my brother was fled?

Enter Constables, [Dogberry and Verges, and the Watch, with] Conrade and Borachio.

DOGBERRY Come you, sir. If Justice cannot tame you, she shall ne'er weigh more reasons in her balance. Nay, an you be a cursing hypocrite once, you must be looked to.

DON PEDRO How now, two of my brother's men bound? Borachio one!

CLAUDIO Hearken after their offense, my lord.

DON PEDRO Officers, what offense have these men done?

DOGBERRY Marry, sir, they have committed false report; moreover, they have spoken untruths; secondarily, they are slanders; sixth and lastly, they have belied a lady; thirdly, they have verified unjust things; and to conclude, they are lying knaves.

DON PEDRO First, I ask thee what they have done; thirdly, I ask thee what's their offense; sixth and lastly, why they are committed; and to conclude, what you lay to their charge.

CLAUDIO Rightly reasoned, and in his own division; and, by my troth, there's one meaning well suited.

DON PEDRO Who have you offended, masters, that you are thus bound to your answer? This learned constable is too cunning to be understood. What's your offense?

138 staff spear shaft. **139 broke cross** i.e., broken by clumsily allowing the spear to break crosswise against the opponent's shield. (In other words, Claudio accuses Benedick of having failed in his sally of wit.) **142 turn his girdle** i.e., turn his sword belt around so that he's ready to fight. (A proverbial expression of uncertain meaning.)
147 Do me right Give me satisfaction. **protest** proclaim before witnesses **151 cheer** entertainment. (Claudio is ready to fight, he says, for the pleasant diversion it should offer.) **153–6 calf's head, capon, woodcock** (In the proposed feast of dueling, Claudio plans to carve various dishes connoting foolishness, effeminate cowardice, and stupidity.) **155 curiously** daintily. **naught** good for nothing.
157 ambles i.e., minces along **162 good** (1) keen (2) harmless. **Just** Exactly **164 a wise gentleman** i.e., an old fool. **164–5 hath the tongues** masters several languages. **168–9 trans-shape** distort, turn the wrong side out **170 proper'st** handsomest **175 old man's daughter** i.e., Hero **176–7 God . . . garden** (Alluding to the trick played on Benedick to love Beatrice, and also to Genesis 3:8.)
180 text (In 1.1.251–6, Benedick vowed that, if he were ever to fall in love, his friends might set a bull's horns on his head and label him "Benedick the married man.")

184 as . . . blades i.e., as braggarts furtively damage their blades to make it appear they have been fighting fiercely **196–7 goes . . . wit** goes about fully dressed like a rational creature but forgets to equip himself with good sense. **198–9 He . . . man** i.e., Such a man looks like a hero in a fool's eyes, but actually the fool is a wise man compared to him. **200–1 soft . . . be sad** wait a minute, not so fast; let me think. Rouse yourself, my heart, and be serious. **201.1–2** (The quarto placement of this stage direction after line 197 suggests that Dogberry is visible, strutting and fussing with his prisoners, before he speaks.) **203 ne'er . . . balance** never again weigh arguments of reason in her scales. (But the pronunciation of *reason* as "raisin" invokes the comic image of a shopkeeper weighing produce.) **204 cursing** accursed. **once** in a word **208 Hearken after** Inquire into **213 slanders** (For "slanderers.") **220 his own division** its own partition in a logical arrangement. (Said ironically.) **221 well suited** nicely dressed up in the trappings of language. **223 bound** (Playing on the meanings "pinioned" and "headed for a destination.") **answer** trial, account.

BORACHIO Sweet Prince, let me go no farther to mine answer. Do you hear me, and let this count kill me. I have deceived even your very eyes. What your wisdoms could not discover, these shallow fools have brought to light, who in the night overheard me confessing to this man how Don John your brother incensed me to slander the Lady Hero, how you were brought into the orchard and saw me court Margaret in Hero's garments, how you disgraced her when you should marry her. My villainy they have upon record, which I had rather seal with my death than repeat over to my shame. The lady is dead upon mine and my master's false accusation; and, briefly, I desire nothing but the reward of a villain.

DON PEDRO [*to Claudio*]
Runs not this speech like iron through your blood?

CLAUDIO
I have drunk poison whiles he uttered it.

DON PEDRO [*to Borachio*]
But did my brother set thee on to this?

BORACHIO Yea, and paid me richly for the practice of it.

DON PEDRO
He is composed and framed of treachery,
And fled he is upon this villainy.

CLAUDIO
Sweet Hero! Now thy image doth appear
In the rare semblance that I loved it first.

DOGBERRY Come, bring away the plaintiffs. By this time our sexton hath reformed Signor Leonato of the matter. And masters, do not forget to specify, when time and place shall serve, that I am an ass.

VERGES Here, here comes Master Signor Leonato, and the sexton, too.

Enter Leonato, his brother [*Antonio*], *and the Sexton.*

LEONATO
Which is the villain? Let me see his eyes,
That when I note another man like him,
I may avoid him. Which of these is he?

BORACHIO
If you would know your wronger, look on me.

LEONATO
Art thou the slave that with thy breath hast killed
Mine innocent child?

BORACHIO Yea, even I alone.

LEONATO
No, not so, villain, thou beliest thyself.
Here stand a pair of honorable men—
A third is fled—that had a hand in it.
I thank you, princes, for my daughter's death.
Record it with your high and worthy deeds.
'Twas bravely done, if you bethink you of it.

CLAUDIO
I know not how to pray your patience,
Yet I must speak. Choose your revenge yourself;
Impose me to what penance your invention
Can lay upon my sin. Yet sinned I not
But in mistaking.

DON PEDRO By my soul, nor I.
And yet, to satisfy this good old man,
I would bend under any heavy weight
That he'll enjoin me to.

LEONATO
I cannot bid you bid my daughter live—
That were impossible—but, I pray you both,
Possess the people in Messina here
How innocent she died; and if your love
Can labor aught in sad invention,
Hang her an epitaph upon her tomb,
And sing it to her bones; sing it tonight.
Tomorrow morning come you to my house,
And since you could not be my son-in-law,
Be yet my nephew. My brother hath a daughter,
Almost the copy of my child that's dead,
And she alone is heir to both of us.
Give her the right you should have giv'n her cousin,
And so dies my revenge.

CLAUDIO O noble sir,
Your overkindness doth wring tears from me!
I do embrace your offer; and dispose
For henceforth of poor Claudio.

LEONATO
Tomorrow then I will expect your coming;
Tonight I take my leave. This naughty man
Shall face to face be brought to Margaret,
Who I believe was packed in all this wrong,
Hired to it by your brother.

BORACHIO No, by my soul, she was not,
Nor knew not what she did when she spoke to me,
But always hath been just and virtuous
In anything that I do know by her.

DOGBERRY Moreover, sir, which indeed is not under white and black, this plaintiff here, the offender, did call me ass. I beseech you, let it be remembered in his punishment. And also the watch heard them talk of one Deformed. They say he wears a key in his ear and a lock hanging by it and borrows money in God's name, the which he hath used so long and never paid that now men grow hardhearted and will lend nothing for God's sake. Pray you, examine him upon that point.

LEONATO I thank thee for thy care and honest pains.

DOGBERRY Your Worship speaks like a most thankful and reverend youth, and I praise God for you.

LEONATO There's for thy pains. [*He gives money.*]

DOGBERRY God save the foundation!

232 incensed incited **237 upon** in consequence of **243 practice** cunning execution **245 upon** i.e., having committed **247 rare semblance** splendid likeness **248 plaintiffs** (For "defendants.") **249 reformed** (For "informed.") **250 specify** (For "testify"?) **261 honorable men** i.e., Don Pedro and Claudio, men of rank

268 Impose me to Impose on me **276 Possess** inform **278 aught** to any extent **285 heir to both** (Leonato overlooks Antonio's son mentioned in 1.2.2.) **286 right** equitable treatment. (Quibbling on "rite," "ceremony.") **289 dispose** you may dispose **290 For henceforth** for the future **292 naughty** wicked **294 packed** involved as an accomplice **299 by** concerning **300–1 under . . . black** written down in black and white **304–5 key . . . by it** (This is what Dogberry has made out of the lovelock mentioned in 3.3.166.) **305–6 in God's name** (A phrase of the professional beggar.) **314 God . . . foundation!** (A formula of those who received alms at religious houses or charitable foundations.)

LEONATO Go, I discharge thee of thy prisoner, and I thank thee.

DOGBERRY I leave an arrant knave with Your Worship, which I beseech Your Worship to correct yourself, for the example of others. God keep Your Worship! I wish Your Worship well. God restore you to health! I humbly give you leave to depart; and if a merry meeting may be wished, God prohibit it! Come, neighbor.

[Exeunt Dogberry and Verges.]

LEONATO
Until tomorrow morning, lords, farewell.

ANTONIO
Farewell, my lords. We look for you tomorrow.

DON PEDRO
We will not fail.

CLAUDIO Tonight I'll mourn with Hero.

LEONATO *[to the Watch]*
Bring you these fellows on.—We'll talk with Margaret,
How her acquaintance grew with this lewd fellow.

Exeunt [separately].

[5.2]

Enter Benedick and Margaret, [meeting].

BENEDICK Pray thee, sweet Mistress Margaret, deserve well at my hands by helping me to the speech of Beatrice.

MARGARET Will you then write me a sonnet in praise of my beauty?

BENEDICK In so high a style, Margaret, that no man living shall come over it, for in most comely truth thou deservest it.

MARGARET To have no man come over me! Why, shall I always keep below stairs?

BENEDICK Thy wit is as quick as the greyhound's mouth; it catches.

MARGARET And yours as blunt as the fencer's foils, which hit but hurt not.

BENEDICK A most manly wit, Margaret; it will not hurt a woman. And so, I pray thee, call Beatrice. I give thee the bucklers.

MARGARET Give us the swords. We have bucklers of our own.

BENEDICK If you use them, Margaret, you must put in the pikes with a vice, and they are dangerous weapons for maids.

MARGARET Well, I will call Beatrice to you, who I think hath legs. *Exit Margaret.*

BENEDICK And therefore will come.
[He sings.] "The god of love,
That sits above,
And knows me, and knows me,
How pitiful I deserve—"

I mean in singing; but in loving, Leander the good swimmer, Troilus the first employer of panders, and a whole bookful of these quondam carpetmongers, whose names yet run smoothly in the even road of a blank verse, why, they were never so truly turned over and over as my poor self in love. Marry, I cannot show it in rhyme. I have tried. I can find out no rhyme to "lady" but "baby," an innocent rhyme; for "scorn," "horn," a hard rhyme; for "school," "fool," a babbling rhyme; very ominous endings. No, I was not born under a rhyming planet, nor I cannot woo in festival terms.

Enter Beatrice.

Sweet Beatrice, wouldst thou come when I called thee?

BEATRICE Yea, signor, and depart when you bid me.

BENEDICK Oh, stay but till then! *[She starts to leave.]*

BEATRICE "Then" is spoken; fare you well now. And yet, ere I go, let me go with that I came, which is, with knowing what hath passed between you and Claudio.

BENEDICK Only foul words; and thereupon I will kiss thee.

BEATRICE Foul words is but foul wind, and foul wind is but foul breath, and foul breath is noisome; therefore I will depart unkissed.

BENEDICK Thou hast frighted the word out of his right sense, so forcible is thy wit. But I must tell thee plainly, Claudio undergoes my challenge; and either I must shortly hear from him, or I will subscribe him a coward. And I pray thee now tell me, for which of my bad parts didst thou first fall in love with me?

BEATRICE For them all together, which maintained so politic a state of evil that they will not admit any good part to intermingle with them. But for which of my good parts did you first suffer love for me?

BENEDICK Suffer love! A good epithet. I do suffer love indeed, for I love thee against my will.

BEATRICE In spite of your heart, I think. Alas, poor heart, if you spite it for my sake I will spite it for yours, for I will never love that which my friend hates.

BENEDICK Thou and I are too wise to woo peaceably.

321 give you leave (For "ask your leave.") **322 prohibit** (For "permit.") **327 lewd** wicked, worthless

5.2. Location: Leonato's garden (? At the scene's end, Leonato's house is some distance away.)

2 to the speech of to speak with **6 style** (1) poetic style (2) stile, stairs over a fence **7 come over** (1) excel beyond (2) traverse, as one would cross a stile (3) in Margaret's next speech, the phrase is taken to mean "mount sexually." **comely** good. (With an allusion to Margaret's beauty.) **10 keep below stairs** dwell in the servants' quarters. **16–17 I . . . bucklers** i.e., I acknowledge myself beaten (in repartee). (Bucklers are shields with spikes [pikes] in their centers. Margaret uses the word in a bawdy sense in her reply.) **21 pikes** spikes in the center of a shield. **vice** screw. (Benedick's bawdy sense continues Margaret's jest.)

26–9 The god . . . deserve (The beginning of an old song by William Elderton.) **29 How . . . deserve** how I deserve pity. (But Benedick uses the phrase to mean "how little I deserve.") **30 Leander** lover of Hero of Sestos; he swam the Hellespont nightly to see her until he drowned **31 Troilus** lover of Cressida, whose affair was assisted by her uncle Pandarus **32 quondam carpetmongers** ladies' men of old, such as one might find in the carpeted boudoirs of the women they woo **34-5 over and over** i.e., head over heels **37 innocent** childish **38 hard** (1) exact (2) unpleasant, because of the association with cuckold's horns **46 that I came** what I came for **51 noisome** noxious **53 his** its **56 subscribe** formally proclaim in writing **60 politic** prudently governed **62 suffer** (1) experience (2) feel the pain of **63 epithet** expression.

BEATRICE It appears not in this confession. There's not one wise man among twenty that will praise himself.

BENEDICK An old, an old instance, Beatrice, that lived in the time of good neighbors. If a man do not erect in this age his own tomb ere he dies, he shall live no longer in monument than the bell rings and the widow weeps.

BEATRICE And how long is that, think you?

BENEDICK Question: why, an hour in clamor and a quarter in rheum. Therefore is it most expedient for the wise, if Don Worm, his conscience, find no impediment to the contrary, to be the trumpet of his own virtues, as I am to myself. So much for praising myself, who, I myself will bear witness, is praiseworthy. And now tell me, how doth your cousin?

BEATRICE Very ill.

BENEDICK And how do you?

BEATRICE Very ill too.

BENEDICK Serve God, love me, and mend. There will I leave you too, for here comes one in haste.

Enter Ursula.

URSULA Madam, you must come to your uncle. Yonder's old coil at home. It is proved my lady Hero hath been falsely accused, the Prince and Claudio mightily abused, and Don John is the author of all, who is fled and gone. Will you come presently?

BEATRICE Will you go hear this news, signor?

BENEDICK I will live in thy heart, die in thy lap, and be buried in thy eyes; and moreover I will go with thee to thy uncle's. *Exeunt.*

✤

[5.3]

Enter Claudio, Prince [Don Pedro, Balthasar], and three or four with tapers.

CLAUDIO Is this the monument of Leonato?

A LORD It is, my lord.

CLAUDIO [*reading from a scroll*]

Epitaph.

"Done to death by slanderous tongues
Was the Hero that here lies.
Death, in guerdon of her wrongs,
Gives her fame which never dies.
So the life that died with shame
Lives in death with glorious fame."
Hang thou there upon the tomb,
Praising her when I am dumb.
[*He hangs up the scroll.*]
Now, music, sound, and sing your solemn hymn.

Song.

BALTHASAR
Pardon, goddess of the night,
Those that slew thy virgin knight;
For the which, with songs of woe,
Round about her tomb they go.
Midnight, assist our moan;
Help us to sigh and groan,
Heavily, heavily.
Graves, yawn and yield your dead,
Till death be utterèd,
Heavily, heavily.

CLAUDIO
Now, unto thy bones good night!
Yearly will I do this rite.

DON PEDRO
Good morrow, masters. Put your torches out.
The wolves have preyed; and look, the gentle day,
Before the wheels of Phoebus, round about
Dapples the drowsy east with spots of gray.
Thanks to you all, and leave us. Fare you well.

CLAUDIO
Good morrow, masters. Each his several way.

DON PEDRO
Come, let us hence, and put on other weeds,
And then to Leonato's we will go.

CLAUDIO
And Hymen now with luckier issue speed's
Than this for whom we rendered up this woe.
Exeunt.

✤

[5.4]

Enter Leonato, Benedick, [Beatrice], Margaret, Ursula, old man [Antonio], Friar [Francis, and] Hero.

FRIAR
Did I not tell you she was innocent?

LEONATO
So are the Prince and Claudio, who accused her
Upon the error that you heard debated.
But Margaret was in some fault for this,
Although against her will, as it appears

69 It . . . confession i.e., You don't show your wisdom in praising yourself for being wise. **71 instance** proverb (i.e., "He has ill neighbors that is fain to praise himself") **72 time . . . neighbors** good old times (when one's neighbors spoke well of one). **73–5 he shall . . . weeps** i.e., he will be memorialized only during the (brief) time of the funeral service and the official mourning. **77 Question** i.e., An easy question, which I will answer as follows. **clamor** noise (of the bell) **78 rheum** tears (of the widow). **79 Don . . . conscience** (The action of the conscience was traditionally described as the gnawing of a worm; compare with Mark 9:44–8.) **90 old coil** great confusion **92 abused** deceived **93 presently** immediately. **95 die** (With the common connotation of "experience sexual climax.")
5.3. Location: A churchyard.
5 guerdon recompense

12 goddess of the night i.e., Diana, moon goddess, patroness of chastity **13 knight** i.e., follower **20 utterèd** fully expressed **25 have preyed** i.e., have done their preying **26 wheels of Phoebus** i.e., chariot of the sun god **29 several** separate **30 weeds** garments **32 And . . . speed's** And may the god of marriage favor us with better fortune
5.4. Location: Leonato's house.
3 Upon on the basis of **5 against her will** unintentionally **6 question** investigation.

In the true course of all the question.
ANTONIO 7
Well, I am glad that all things sorts so well.
BENEDICK 8
And so am I, being else by faith enforced
To call young Claudio to a reckoning for it.
LEONATO
Well, daughter, and you gentlewomen all,
Withdraw into a chamber by yourselves,
And when I send for you, come hither masked.
The Prince and Claudio promised by this hour
To visit me. You know your office, brother:
You must be father to your brother's daughter,
And give her to young Claudio. *Exeunt ladies.*
ANTONIO 17
Which I will do with confirmed countenance.
BENEDICK 18
Friar, I must entreat your pains, I think.
FRIAR To do what, signor?
BENEDICK 20
To bind me or undo me—one of them.
Signor Leonato, truth it is, good signor,
Your niece regards me with an eye of favor.
LEONATO 23
That eye my daughter lent her. 'Tis most true.
BENEDICK
And I do with an eye of love requite her.
LEONATO 25
The sight whereof I think you had from me, 26
From Claudio, and the Prince. But what's your will?
BENEDICK
Your answer, sir, is enigmatical. 28
But, for my will, my will is your good will
May stand with ours, this day to be conjoined
In the state of honorable marriage,
In which, good Friar, I shall desire your help.
LEONATO
My heart is with your liking.
FRIAR And my help.
Here comes the Prince and Claudio.

Enter Prince [*Don Pedro*] *and Claudio, and two or three other.*

DON PEDRO
Good morrow to this fair assembly.
LEONATO
Good morrow, Prince. Good morrow, Claudio. 36
We here attend you. Are you yet determined
Today to marry with my brother's daughter?
CLAUDIO
I'll hold my mind, were she an Ethiope.
LEONATO
Call her forth, brother. Here's the Friar ready.

[*Exit Antonio.*]

DON PEDRO
Good morrow, Benedick. Why, what's the matter,
That you have such a February face,
So full of frost, of storm, and cloudiness?
CLAUDIO 43
I think he thinks upon the savage bull.
Tush, fear not, man! We'll tip thy horns with gold, 45
And all Europa shall rejoice at thee, 46
As once Europa did at lusty Jove
When he would play the noble beast in love.
BENEDICK
Bull Jove, sir, had an amiable low,
And some such strange bull leapt your father's cow
And got a calf in that same noble feat
Much like to you, for you have just his bleat.

Enter [*Leonato's*] *brother* [*Antonio*], *Hero, Beatrice, Margaret,* [*and*] *Ursula,* [*the ladies masked*].

CLAUDIO 52
For this I owe you. Here comes other reckonings.
Which is the lady I must seize upon?
ANTONIO
This same is she, and I do give you her.
CLAUDIO
Why then, she's mine. Sweet, let me see your face.
LEONATO
No, that you shall not, till you take her hand
Before this friar and swear to marry her.
CLAUDIO
Give me your hand before this holy friar. 59
I am your husband, if you like of me.
HERO [*unmasking*]
And when I lived, I was your other wife;
And when you loved, you were my other husband.
CLAUDIO
Another Hero!
HERO Nothing certainer.
One Hero died defiled, but I do live,
And surely as I live, I am a maid.
DON PEDRO
The former Hero! Hero that is dead!
LEONATO 66
She died, my lord, but whiles her slander lived.
FRIAR 67
All this amazement can I qualify,
When, after that the holy rites are ended, 69
I'll tell you largely of fair Hero's death. 70
Meantime let wonder seem familiar, 71
And to the chapel let us presently.
72

7 sorts turn out **8 being . . . enforced** since otherwise I would be enforced by my promise to Beatrice **17 confirmed countenance** straight face. **18 entreat your pains** beg your help **20 undo** (1) ruin (2) untie, unbind **23 That . . . her** (Alludes to Hero's role in tricking Beatrice into confessing her love for Benedick.) **25–6 The sight . . . Prince** (Alludes to their role in tricking Benedick into confessing his love for Beatrice.) **28 for** as for. **is** is that **36 yet** still

43 I . . . bull (A jocular reminiscence of the conversation in 1.1.250 ff.) **45 Europa** Europe **46 Europa** a princess whom Jove approached in the form of a white bull and bore on his back through the sea to Crete **52 I owe you** i.e., I'll pay you back later (for calling me a calf and a bastard). **other reckonings** i.e., other matters to be settled first. **59 like of** care for **66 but whiles** only while **67 qualify** moderate **69 largely** at large, in full **70 let . . . familiar** treat these marvels as ordinary matters **71 let us presently** let us go at once. **72 Soft and fair** i.e., Wait a minute

BENEDICK
Soft and fair, Friar. Which is Beatrice?
BEATRICE [*unmasking*]
I answer to that name. What is your will?
BENEDICK
Do not you love me?
BEATRICE Why, no, no more than reason.
BENEDICK
Why, then your uncle and the Prince and Claudio
Have been deceived. They swore you did.
BEATRICE
Do not you love me?
BENEDICK Troth, no, no more than reason. 78
BEATRICE
Why, then my cousin, Margaret, and Ursula
Are much deceived, for they did swear you did.
BENEDICK
They swore that you were almost sick for me.
BEATRICE
They swore that you were well-nigh dead for me.
BENEDICK
'Tis no such matter. Then you do not love me?
BEATRICE
No, truly, but in friendly recompense. 84
LEONATO
Come, cousin, I am sure you love the gentleman.
CLAUDIO
And I'll be sworn upon't that he loves her; 87
For here's a paper written in his hand,
A halting sonnet of his own pure brain,
Fashioned to Beatrice. [*He shows a paper.*]
HERO And here's another
Writ in my cousin's hand, stol'n from her pocket,
Containing her affection unto Benedick. 91
[*She shows another paper.*] 92
BENEDICK A miracle! Here's our own hands against our
hearts. Come, I will have thee, but by this light I take
thee for pity.
96
BEATRICE I would not deny you, but by this good day,
I yield upon great persuasion, and partly to save your
life, for I was told you were in a consumption.
BENEDICK Peace! I will stop your mouth. [*Kissing her.*] 100
DON PEDRO How dost thou, Benedick, the married
man? 102
BENEDICK I'll tell thee what, Prince: a college of wit- 103
crackers cannot flout me out of my humor. Dost thou 104
think I care for a satire or an epigram? No. If a man
will be beaten with brains, 'a shall wear nothing hand- 106
some about him. In brief, since I do purpose to marry,
I will think nothing to any purpose that the world can
say against it; and therefore never flout at me for what 109
I have said against it; for man is a giddy thing, and this
is my conclusion. For thy part, Claudio, I did think to
have beaten thee, but in that thou art like to be my
kinsman, live unbruised, and love my cousin. 113
CLAUDIO I had well hoped thou wouldst have denied 114
Beatrice, that I might have cudgeled thee out of thy 115
single life, to make thee a double-dealer, which out of
question thou wilt be, if my cousin do not look
exceeding narrowly to thee.
BENEDICK Come, come, we are friends. Let's have a
dance ere we are married, that we may lighten our 120
own hearts and our wives' heels.
LEONATO We'll have dancing afterward. 122
BENEDICK First, of my word! Therefore play, music. 123
Prince, thou art sad. Get thee a wife, get thee a wife.
There is no staff more reverend than one tipped with
horn.

Enter Messenger.

MESSENGER
My lord, your brother John is ta'en in flight 127
And brought with armèd men back to Messina.
BENEDICK Think not on him till tomorrow. I'll devise
thee brave punishments for him. Strike up, pipers!
Dance. [*Exeunt.*]

78 my cousin i.e., Hero **84 cousin** i.e., niece **87 halting** limping. **his own pure** purely his own **91–2 against our hearts** i.e., to prove our hearts guilty as charged. **96 in a consumption** i.e., wasting away in sighs.

100 college assembly **102–4 If . . . him** i.e., If a man allows himself to be cowed by ridicule, he'll never dare dress handsomely or do anything conspicuous that will draw attention. **106 flout** mock **109 in that** in view of the fact that. **like** likely **113 a double-dealer** (1) a married man (2) a deceiver, adulterer **114–15 look . . . narrowly to** keep close watch over **120 of** on **122–3 tipped with horn** (Alludes to the usual joke about cuckolds, as at line 44). **127 brave** fine

The Merry Wives of Windsor

According to an early eighteenth-century tradition, Shakespeare composed *The Merry Wives of Windsor* at the behest of Queen Elizabeth. John Dennis, a critic and dramatist, asserted in 1702 that the Queen "was so eager to see it acted, that she commanded it to be finished in fourteen days." The editor Nicholas Rowe added in 1709 that the Queen, having been so pleased with Falstaff in the *Henry IV* plays, wished to see him in love. Such legends, emerging more than a century after the event, must be regarded with caution. Whether true or not, however, they do point to a passage of courtly flattery in the play that strongly suggests the presence of the court at some performance. The fairy blessing bestowed on Windsor Castle in Act 5 is unquestionably intended to celebrate the famous Order of the Garter. Mistress Quickly, disguised as leader of the fairies, orders her charges to sing nightly "Like to the Garter's compass, in a ring," to write "*Honi soit qui mal y pense*," the motto of the Garter, and to tend carefully the "several chairs of order"—those decorated stalls in the Chapel of St. George belonging to the illustrious lords who made up the Order of the Garter. Every such "installment" receives her blessing, along with each knight's "coat," "crest," and "blazon" (5.5.36–75). The topical nature of this passage is stressed by its apparent lack of relevance to the plot.

Other extraneous bits of action may allude to courtly matters or to Windsor gossip. The business about the purported three German horse thieves and their Duke (4.3, 5), which makes little sense in the play as it stands, can perhaps be explained as an in-group joke on Frederick of Würtemburg, Count Mömpelgard, a German nobleman obsessively intent on joining the Garter. He was the object of much anti-German scorn. His name, Mömpelgard or Mömpelgart, is possibly scrambled into "garmombles" in the corrupt 1602 Quarto text, where the Folio text reads "cozen-germans" (4.5.74). Also, the geography of Windsor is rendered with loving and accurate attention to detail, as though for an audience familiar with its environs.

Such topical flourishes do not rob the drama of its general appeal; it has had great success, both as a stage play and in Verdi's and Nicolai's operatic versions, and was presumably popular with Shakespeare's London audience. Shakespeare never composed exclusively for special audiences, so far as we know, and indeed the blessing of Windsor Castle could have been added to a commercial play in order to render it particularly suitable for royal performance. The allusion to "the fat woman of Brentford," a notorious tavern keeper of Brentford (halfway between London and Windsor), would have been as meaningful to Shakespeare's London audience as to the court. The same may be true of the "luces" in the coat of arms of Justice Shallow (1.1.14), sometimes thought to ridicule Shakespeare's Stratford neighbor Sir Thomas Lucy, but believed by scholar-critic Leslie Hotson to be a dig at William Gardiner, a Justice of the Peace in Surrey near London. The dig at the Brooke family, the lords of Cobham, in the disguise name (Brook) of the jealous Ford (as recorded in the unauthorized quarto of 1602), must have amused knowledgeable Londoners; indeed, the satirical hit was evidently so offensive that the name had to be changed to "Broome" (as in the Folio text). Nevertheless, *The Merry Wives* could have been originally planned as entertainment to please Queen Elizabeth. A Feast of St. George in honor of the Garter was held at Westminster on April 23, 1597, in the Queen's presence. Among those elected to the Order was George Carey, Lord Hunsdon, the patron of Shakespeare's company and the new Lord Chamberlain. He was actually installed in the Order at Windsor in May. This date is early for a play that appears to borrow several comic figures from the *Henry IV* plays and perhaps from *Henry V* (usually dated 1599) as well. Recently, however, it has been argued persuasively that *The Merry Wives* may have been written while 2 *Henry IV* was in the process of composition, making use of its comic types, but before they had actually appeared on the London stage. According to this theory, Nym was created first for *The Merry Wives* and was then reintroduced into *Henry V*. The dating and order of composition of these plays are still controversial, so that the dating of *The Merry Wives* must remain uncertain from 1597 to 1601.

Despite this uncertainty, Shakespeare's comic strategy in *The Merry Wives* seems reasonably clear: to translate highly popular comic figures, such as Falstaff, Bardolph, Pistol, and Slender, from the history plays into a ludicrously different kind of situation. Falstaff, the once resourceful and self-aware companion of Prince Hal, becomes the buffoonish wooer of two virtuously married women who thoroughly best him and subject him to a series of amusingly humiliating punishments. Prince Hal, too, of course, treats Falstaff as a scapegoat in the *Henry IV* plays and ultimately rejects him, but the farcical nature of the action in *The Merry Wives* exposes Falstaff to more openly satirical laughter and discomfiture than in the history plays. Some admirers of Falstaff have been dismayed by the falling off and dismiss the play as an insult to his greatness, but surely to view the play thus is to create false expectations and thereby miss the point of Shakespeare's comic intent. Falstaff and his companions should not be judged against their counterparts in the history plays, even though an awareness of their existence in that different context is an essential part of the jest. To see Falstaff in love as a wooer of women much younger than himself—this tour de force required that Shakespeare devise a multiple plot as unlike that of the history plays as possible, in order to stress the comic discrepancy.

The result is a structurally complex comic plot that appropriately bears more resemblance to Shakespeare's other comedies than to the history plays. At the center of *The Merry Wives* is a familiar plot of romantic intrigue, featuring a young heroine (Anne Page) whose parents object to her attachment to young Fenton. They pester her with unwelcome rival wooers (Slender and Dr. Caius), obliging her finally to dupe her parents by a cleverly engineered elopement. This plot to outwit parents and rivals in the name of young love has its ancestry in the classical comedy of Plautus and in neoclassical comedy, though Shakespeare uses no particular recognizable source. To this plot he adds a second and parallel story of a lover (Falstaff) caught in the act of wooing two women. Italian *novelle* provide many situations of this sort, including that in which the husband is deceived by concealment of the lover in a clothes basket; see especially "Of Two Brethren and Their Wives" from *Riche His Farewell to Military Profession*, 1581, "Two Lovers of Pisa" from *Tarlton's News Out of Purgatory*, 1590, and the second story of the first day from Ser Giovanni Fiorentino's *Il Pecorone*, 1558. The effect of the combined plots is often farcelike, especially in the emphasis on swift, hilarious action and comic physical abuse at the expense of consistency in character. For example, we must accept as a given the preference of wise Master Page for Slender as his son-in-law and the inexplicable preference of Mistress Page for the suit of Dr. Caius. Reasons are stated, but symmetry of the design is paramount.

In addition, Shakespeare enriches these two plot situations with minor characters, such as the rival wooers, go-betweens, and informers, who inevitably come in conflict with one another and thereby reveal their "humors" or idiosyncrasies. Only tangentially connected with the plot, these characters are prized for their eccentricity. The Welsh Parson Evans and the French Dr. Caius nearly come to blows over Caius's courtship of Anne Page. They are safely kept apart by the genial Host of the Garter Inn and are reconciled to the extent of plotting against the Host for having deceived them both. (Perhaps they carry out their threat in the guise of the mysterious Germans who purportedly steal the Host's horses, though the text is murky on this point.) Justice Shallow, a humorous character in *2 Henry IV*, is given nominal justification in this play as cousin of Anne's second unwanted suitor, Slender, but Shallow's essential function is to quarrel with Falstaff about the latter's poaching and riotous behavior. This plot goes nowhere and indeed is little more than a means for the revelation of humorous characters. Shallow's is a cameo role, like many others, enabling him to assume the fatuous postures we also encounter in *2 Henry IV*. Pistol and Nym, similarly requiring some pretext for being on hand, avenge their dismissal from Falstaff's service by informing the two husbands of Falstaff's designs on the two merry wives. Bardolph finds suitable employment as a bartender. Mistress Quickly's transformation is perhaps the most gloriously improbable of all: she becomes confidante of all three wooers of Anne Page (offering equal encouragement to each and receiving payment from each), as well as go-between for Falstaff and the two wives. She is no longer a married and then widowed hostess of a London tavern, but an unmarried housekeeper of Windsor. She triumphs over Falstaff in a way not possible in the history plays, joining the entire cast as they jeer at the discomfited horn-browed knight.

By providing occasion for the exhibition of idiosyncratic character for its own sake, side by side with his fast-moving farcical action, Shakespeare seems to have been responding to the newest dramatic genre of the late 1590s: the humors comedy. George Chapman's *The Blind Beggar of Alexandria* (1596) had done much to establish the new fashion. Ben Jonson's *Every Man in His Humor* (1598) either influenced Shakespeare or was influenced by him, depending upon the dates. Jonson's plot, like Shakespeare's, is chiefly a vehicle for displaying various humors or comically obsessed types: the overly watchful father, the jealous husband, the braggart soldier, the country simpleton intent on learning to quarrel like a gentleman, the waspishly impatient man. Similar types appear in *The Merry Wives*, although Shakespeare characteristically does not satirize affectation so much as cherish it.

Shakespeare's comic types endear themselves chiefly through their verbal traits: Nym with his use of the word "humor"; Pistol with his anachronistic terms, recondite allusions, stilted poetic inversions, and hyperboles ("O base Hungarian wight! Wilt thou the spigot wield?", 1.3.19–20); Mistress Quickly with her pungent homely metaphors (comparing a beard to "a glover's paring knife," 1.4.19–20) and her pat phrases ("But let that pass," line 14); Shallow with his legal jargon; and the French Caius and the Welsh Evans with their ability to "keep their limbs whole and hack our English" (3.1.73). Shakespeare also caricatures these humorous types by distinctive physical traits, such as Bardolph's "tinderbox" nose (1.3.23) or Slender's unappealing face and little yellow beard that so aptly suit his passion for bearbaiting and his idiotic deference to his superiors. We laugh at these deformities and yet see that no one is incorrigible. The characters amiably poke fun at one another, and every discomfiture leads ultimately to a reconciliation. Few escape laughter, even those we might regard as normative characters if this were a satire; the Host, for example, loses his horses, and Mistress Page is tricked at last by her daughter's elopement.

Nevertheless, the merry wives of the play's title come as close as any to representing the normative vision of the play, functioning as witty manipulators in a plot to expose hypocrisy and lechery. The devices they invent for Falstaff are rather like Maria's schemes for Malvolio in *Twelfth Night*, since all depend upon the complicity of the self-blinded victim. Falstaff is the dominant humors character of the play, obsessed both with lust and greed, amusing to us because the greed is predominant. His hypocritical reasons for wooing deserve comic reprisal, or "vengeance." His greed and his fatuous belief in his own charm overwhelm his natural sagacity and leave him vulnerable. He credulously accepts the bribes of the jealous Ford, disguised as Brook, and is deceived by the wives on no less than three occasions. For their part, the wives are delighted with their "sport," for they must devise increasingly clever schemes to offset Falstaff's growing suspicions. The more unlikely he is to return for more punishment, the greater must be their ingenuity in order to fool him once again. Mistress Ford enjoys the added pleasure of teaching her husband a lesson about jealousy. The wives' humorous plotting derives its sharpness from their potential to be faithless, if they choose, and hence from the power they enjoy over men like Ford and Falstaff, who are obsessed with groundless fantasies of betrayal or are compulsively in need of validating their masculinity through conquest of the female. The cleverness of the wives' sport is justified by its moral intent, and, conversely, the moral point is deprived of any tedious didacticism by the good humor of the jest. In his final humiliation, plagued by virtually all the play's characters, reduced to an absurd belief in fairies, Falstaff becomes a scapegoat in the truest sense of that term: a horned figure who embodies the faults of an entire society and whose chastisement brings about purification. Yet, as Mistress Quickly observes, "nobody but has his fault" (1.4.13–14), and this comic rejection of Falstaff leads not to banishment but to a reconciling feast at the Pages' house. Without intending it, Falstaff has cured Ford's jealousy and has helped show that "Wives may be merry, and yet honest too." (4.2.97).

The Merry Wives is a remarkable play in terms of its relationship to comedy and history, the two genres most evident in Shakespeare's dramatic writing of the 1590s. The romantic plot of love's triumph, though nominally at the center of the plot, is decidedly secondary in importance. The more dominant motif of scapegoating and renewal gives the central roles to married women rather than the young lovers of romantic comedy. Falstaff's claim to wit and vitality in *1 Henry IV* and *2 Henry IV* gives place here to the ascendancy of domestic women; the comic principle shifts to them. Mistress Quickly, translated like Falstaff and his crew from the history plays into comedy, shares in this vindication of women's wit and virtue; no longer a tavern keeper or widow enduring Falstaff's broken promises or patiently supplying him with women, Quickly becomes a go-between in a comic plot of exposure of male philandering. Women are no longer on the periphery of a male-dominated world, as in the history plays, but in their element. At the same time, the women of this play embody married virtues for the most part, rather than the youthful companionship (Portia, Beatrice, Rosalind, Viola) of the romantic comedies. The location of the play in a part of England not far from where Shakespeare grew up, the inclusion of place names familiar from his youth, the fond portrait of a schoolboy's terror in coping with Latin paradigms, all suggest a kind of tribute to the world in which Shakespeare's own family affairs remained while he sought professional advancement in London. The mildly satiric celebration of bourgeois life, found nowhere else to such an extent in Shakespeare, gives a meaningful insight into an author who profited from the limited but increasing social mobility of his age.

The Merry Wives of Windsor

[*Dramatis Personae*

MISTRESS MARGARET PAGE, *a wife of Windsor*
MASTER GEORGE PAGE, *her husband*
ANNE PAGE, *their daughter*
WILLIAM PAGE, *a schoolboy, their son*

MISTRESS ALICE FORD, *a wife of Windsor*
MASTER FRANK FORD, *her husband*
JOHN, ROBERT, } *their servants*

SIR JOHN FALSTAFF
ROBIN, *his page*
BARDOLPH, PISTOL, NYM, } *his followers*

SIR HUGH EVANS, *a Welsh parson*

DOCTOR CAIUS, *a French physician*
MISTRESS QUICKLY, *his housekeeper*
JOHN RUGBY, *his servant*

ROBERT SHALLOW, *a country justice of the peace*
ABRAHAM SLENDER, *his nephew*
PETER SIMPLE, *Slender's servant*

HOST *of the Garter Inn*
FENTON, *a gentleman in love with Anne Page*

Children of Windsor, disguised as fairies

SCENE: *Windsor, and the neighborhood*]

1.1

Enter Justice Shallow, Slender, [*and*] *Sir Hugh Evans.*

SHALLOW Sir Hugh, persuade me not. I will make a Star Chamber matter of it. If he were twenty Sir John Falstaffs, he shall not abuse Robert Shallow, Esquire.

SLENDER In the county of Gloucester, Justice of Peace and Coram.

SHALLOW Ay, cousin Slender, and Custalorum.

SLENDER Ay, and Ratolorum too. And a gentleman born, Master Parson, who writes himself "Armigero" in any bill, warrant, quittance, or obligation: "Armigero."

SHALLOW Ay, that I do, and have done any time these three hundred years.

SLENDER All his successors gone before him hath done't, and all his ancestors that come after him may. They may give the dozen white luces in their coat.

SHALLOW It is an old coat.

EVANS The dozen white louses do become an old coat well. It agrees well, passant. It is a familiar beast to man, and signifies love.

SHALLOW The luce is the fresh fish. The salt fish is an old coat.

SLENDER I may quarter, coz

SHALLOW You may, by marrying.

EVANS It is marring indeed, if he quarter it.

SHALLOW Not a whit.

1.1. Location: Windsor. Before Master Page's house.
0.1 *Sir* courtesy title for a priest. **1 persuade** argue with **1–2 Star Chamber matter** (The court of Star Chamber, composed chiefly of the King's Privy Council, was the highest and most powerful court in the realm.) **5 Coram** i.e., quorum, a title of certain justices whose presence was necessary to constitute a bench. **6 cousin** kinsman. **Custalorum** A corruption of Latin *custos rotulorum,* "keeper of the rolls." **7 Ratolorum** (For *rotulorum.*) **8 Armigero** Esquire, one entitled to bear arms. (A heraldic term.) **9 bill** bill of financial exchange. **quittance** discharge from legal agreement. **obligation** contract

12–13 successors . . . ancestors (Slender comically gets these words backwards.) **14 give** display heraldically. **luces** pikes, fresh-water fish. **coat** coat of arms. **17 passant** (1) walking (in heraldic language) (2) passing, exceeding. **familiar** (1) well-known and part of the family (2) overfamiliar (taking *louse* in the sense of a tiny biting insect) **19–20 The luce . . . coat** (The meaning is unclear, though Shallow is seemingly joking about Evans's pronunciation of *coat* as "cod.") **21 quarter** combine the arms of two families by adding to one's own coat the arms of another family in one quarter of the escutcheon. **coz** cousin, kinsman.

EVANS Yes, py'r Lady. If he has a quarter of your coat, there is but three skirts for yourself, in my simple conjectures. But that is all one. If Sir John Falstaff have committed disparagements unto you, I am of the Church, and will be glad to do my benevolence to make atonements and compromises between you.

SHALLOW The Council shall hear it. It is a riot.

EVANS It is not meet the Council hear a riot. There is no fear of Got in a riot. The Council, look you, shall desire to hear the fear of Got, and not to hear a riot. Take your visaments in that.

SHALLOW Ha! O' my life, if I were young again, the sword should end it.

EVANS It is petter that friends is the sword, and end it. And there is also another device in my prain, which peradventure prings goot discretions with it: there is Anne Page, which is daughter to Master George Page, which is pretty virginity.

SLENDER Mistress Anne Page? She has brown hair and speaks small like a woman?

EVANS It is that fery person for all the 'orld, as just as you will desire. And seven hundred pounds of moneys, and gold, and silver, is her grandsire upon his death's-bed—Got deliver to a joyful resurrections!—give, when she is able to overtake seventeen years old. It were a goot motion if we leave our pribbles and prabbles, and desire a marriage between Master Abraham and Mistress Anne Page.

SLENDER Did her grandsire leave her seven hundred pound?

EVANS Ay, and her father is make her a petter penny.

SHALLOW I know the young gentlewoman. She has good gifts.

EVANS Seven hundred pounds and possibilities is goot gifts.

SHALLOW Well, let us see honest Master Page. Is Falstaff there?

EVANS Shall I tell you a lie? I do despise a liar as I do despise one that is false, or as I despise one that is not true. The knight Sir John is there, and I beseech you be ruled by your well-willers. I will peat the door for Master Page. [*He knocks.*] What ho! Got pless your house here!

PAGE [*within*] Who's there?

EVANS Here is Got's plessing, and your friend, and Justice Shallow, and here young Master Slender, that peradventures shall tell you another tale, if matters grow to your likings.

[*Enter*] *Master Page.*

PAGE I am glad to see Your Worships well. I thank you for my venison, Master Shallow.

SHALLOW Master Page, I am glad to see you. Much good do it your good heart! I wished your venison better; it was ill killed. How doth good Mistress Page?—And I thank you always with my heart, la, with my heart.

PAGE Sir, I thank you.

SHALLOW Sir, I thank you. By yea and no I do.

PAGE I am glad to see you, good Master Slender.

SLENDER How does your fallow greyhound, sir? I heard say he was outrun on Cotswold.

PAGE It could not be judged, sir.

SLENDER You'll not confess, you'll not confess.

SHALLOW That he will not. 'Tis your fault, 'tis your fault. 'Tis a good dog.

PAGE A cur, sir.

SHALLOW Sir, he's a good dog, and a fair dog. Can there be more said? He is good and fair. Is Sir John Falstaff here?

PAGE Sir, he is within; and I would I could do a good office between you.

EVANS It is spoke as a Christians ought to speak.

SHALLOW He hath wronged me, Master Page.

PAGE Sir, he doth in some sort confess it.

SHALLOW If it be confessed, it is not redressed. Is not that so, Master Page? He hath wronged me, indeed he hath; at a word, he hath. Believe me, Robert Shallow, Esquire, saith he is wronged.

[*Enter Sir John*] *Falstaff, Bardolph, Nym,* [*and*] *Pistol.*

PAGE Here comes Sir John.

FALSTAFF Now, Master Shallow, you'll complain of me to the King?

SHALLOW Knight, you have beaten my men, killed my deer, and broke open my lodge.

FALSTAFF But not kissed your keeper's daughter?

SHALLOW Tut, a pin! This shall be answered.

FALSTAFF I will answer it straight: I have done all this. That is now answered.

SHALLOW The Council shall know this.

25 py'r Lady by Our Lady. (Evans' Welsh dialect often substitutes "p" for "b" at the start of words, as in *petter, prain,* and *prings,* lines 38–40; substitutes "f" for "v" and "t" for "d," as in *Fery goot,* line 133; leaves out initial "w," as in *'orld* and *'oman,* lines 45, 210; etc.) **26 skirts** the tails of a long doublet or coat. (Evans is still thinking of a literal coat that would be marred by quartering, i.e., cutting into quarters.) **30 atonements** reconciliations. **compromises** i.e., settlement by arbitration **31 The Council . . . riot**. (The King's Privy Council, sitting in Star Chamber, frequently concerned itself with riots. Evans, however, understands *Council* to refer to an ecclesiastical council.) **32 meet** fitting **34–5 Take . . . that** Take that into consideration. (*Visaments* means "advisements.") **38 that friends is the sword** i.e., that the quarrel be ended by friendly motions **43 Mistress** (Used of married or unmarried women.) **44 small** with a gentle, high voice **45 as just** exactly **47–9 is . . . give** has . . . given (her) **50 motion** plan **50–1 pribbles and prabbles** i.e., petty disputes **55 is make . . . penny** will provide her a pretty penny more. **57 gifts** natural endowments. **58 possibilities** pecuniary prospects **60 honest** worthy **65 well-willers** well-wishers. **peat** beat, knock

71 tell . . . tale i.e., have something more to say to you **77 ill** i.e., illegally, by Falstaff. (See below, lines 105–6.) **83 fallow** fawn-colored **84 on Cotswold** i.e., in games held in the Cotswold hills in Gloucestershire. **85 judged** fairly decided **86 confess** admit (that your dog lost) **87 That . . . fault** i.e., He (Page) certainly won't admit that. You (Slender) are in the wrong. (*Fault* also suggests "loss of scent.") **93 within** i.e., at dinner in Page's house; see lines 179–80 below **97 in some sort** to some extent **100 at a word** in a word **106 lodge** forest keeper's dwelling. **108 pin** trifle. **answered** accounted for. (But Falstaff plays on the meaning "replied to.") **109 straight** (1) at once (2) straightforwardly

FALSTAFF 'Twere better for you if it were known in counsel. You'll be laughed at.

EVANS *Pauca verba,* Sir John, good worts.

FALSTAFF Good worts? Good cabbage!—Slender, I broke your head. What matter have you against me?

SLENDER Marry, sir, I have matter in my head against you, and against your coney-catching rascals, Bardolph, Nym, and Pistol.

BARDOLPH You Banbury cheese!

SLENDER Ay, it is no matter.

PISTOL How now, Mephistopheles?

SLENDER Ay, it is no matter.

NYM Slice, I say! *Pauca, pauca.* Slice, that's my humor.

SLENDER Where's Simple, my man? Can you tell, cousin?

EVANS Peace, I pray you. Now let us understand. There is three umpires in this matter, as I understand; that is, Master Page, fidelicet Master Page; and there is myself, fidelicet myself; and the three party is, lastly and finally, mine Host of the Garter.

PAGE We three to hear it, and end it between them.

EVANS Fery goot. I will make a prief of it in my notebook, and we will afterwards 'ork upon the cause with as great discreetly as we can.

FALSTAFF Pistol!

PISTOL He hears with ears.

EVANS The tevil and his tam! What phrase is this, "He hears with ear"? Why, it is affectations.

FALSTAFF Pistol, did you pick Master Slender's purse?

SLENDER Ay, by these gloves, did he—or I would I might never come in mine own great chamber again else—of seven groats in mill-sixpences, and two Edward shovelboards, that cost me two shilling and twopence apiece of Yed Miller, by these gloves.

FALSTAFF Is this true, Pistol?

EVANS No, it is false, if it is a pickpurse.

PISTOL
Ha, thou mountain-foreigner!—Sir John and master mine,
I combat challenge of this latten bilbo.
Word of denial in thy *labras* here!
Word of denial! Froth and scum, thou liest!

SLENDER [*indicating Nym*] By these gloves, then 'twas he.

NYM Be advised, sir, and pass good humors. I will say "marry, trap with you" if you run the nuthook's humor on me. That is the very note of it.

SLENDER By this hat, then, he in the red face had it. For though I cannot remember what I did when you made me drunk, yet I am not altogether an ass.

FALSTAFF [*to Bardolph*] What say you, Scarlet and John?

BARDOLPH Why, sir, for my part, I say the gentleman had drunk himself out of his five sentences.

EVANS It is his five "senses." Fie, what the ignorance is!

BARDOLPH And being fap, sir, was, as they say, cashiered. And so conclusions passed the careers.

SLENDER Ay, you spake in Latin then, too. But 'tis no matter. I'll ne'er be drunk whilst I live again, but in honest, civil, godly company, for this trick. If I be drunk, I'll be drunk with those that have the fear of God, and not with drunken knaves.

EVANS So Got 'udge me, that is a virtuous mind.

FALSTAFF You hear all these matters denied, gentlemen. You hear it.

[*Enter*] *Anne Page* [*with wine*]; *Mistress Ford* [*and*] *Mistress Page* [*following*].

PAGE Nay, daughter, carry the wine in; we'll drink within. [*Exit Anne Page.*]

SLENDER Oh, heaven! This is Mistress Anne Page.

PAGE How now, Mistress Ford?

FALSTAFF Mistress Ford, by my troth, you are very well met. By your leave, good mistress. [*He kisses her.*]

PAGE Wife, bid these gentlemen welcome.—Come, we have a hot venison pasty to dinner. Come, gentlemen, I hope we shall drink down all unkindness.

[*Exeunt all except Shallow, Slender, and Evans.*]

SLENDER I had rather than forty shillings I had my book of songs and sonnets here.

[*Enter*] *Simple.*

How now, Simple, where have you been? I must wait on myself, must I? You have not the book of riddles about you, have you?

112–13 in counsel secretly. (Playing on *Council.*) **114** *Pauca verba* (Let's have) few words **115 worts** vegetables, cabbages. (A quibble on Sir Hugh's pronunciation of *words.*) **116 broke your head** made a slight bleeding wound on your head. **116, 117 matter** (1) cause of complaint (2) matter of consequence; pus **118 coney-catching** cheating. (A *coney* is literally a rabbit, a proverbially gullible animal.) **120 Banbury cheese** (Banbury cheeses were noted for their thinness; a reference to Slender's name and physique.) **122 Mephistopheles** name of the devil in Marlowe's *Doctor Faustus.* **124 Slice** (1) Speak briefly (2) I will slice with my sword (3) a reference to Bardolph's calling Slender a cheese (?) *Pauca* Speak briefly. **humor** mood. **129 fidelicet** i.e., *videlicet,* namely **130 three** third **131 Garter** the name of an inn in Windsor. **133 prief** brief, summary **135 discreetly** discretion **138 tam** dam, mother. **142 great chamber** hall **143 groats** coins equal to four pence. **mill-sixpences** coins stamped by means of the mill and press **144 Edward shovelboards** shillings coined in the reign of Edward VI. (So called from their use in the gambling game of shovelboard.) **145 Yed** Ed, Edward **147 it is false** i.e., Pistol is false, not *true* ("honest"). **if it** if he **148 mountain-foreigner** i.e., Welshman. **149 combat challenge** (A flowery way of issuing a challenge to a duel.) **latten bilbo** *Latten* (literally, a yellow brasslike alloy) refers to the inferior color and *bilbo* (from Bilbao in Spain) to the thinness of a Spanish sword. Both make fun of Slender.

150 *labras* lips, i.e., face **153 Be . . . humors** i.e., Be careful what you say and don't say anything to rile me up. **154 marry, trap with you** (An insulting phrase meaning something like "run off," "beat it.") **154–5 run . . . me** threaten me with a constable, or behave like one. (A *nuthook* literally is a hooked stick used to pull nuts from trees; applied to a constable.) **155 very note of it** truth of the matter. **156 he . . . face** (as in *1* and *2 Henry IV* and *Henry V,* Bardolph's face is flushed and inflamed from habitual drinking.) **it** Slender's purse. **159 Scarlet and John** (Names of Robin Hood's companions, Will Scarlet and Little John. *Scarlet* is humorously applied to Bardolph's red face.) **163 fap** drunk **164 cashiered** deprived (of his senses; but perhaps suggesting, too, that he was fleeced). **164 conclusions . . . careers** i.e., they got out of control. (*Careers* means "short gallops at full speed.") **170 'udge** (For "judge.") **mind** intent. **180 pasty to** meat pie for **183 book of songs and sonnets** (Probably refers to Tottel's *Miscellany,* published in 1557 and quite old-fashioned by the late 1590s.) **185 book of riddles** (Such a book is mentioned as in the library of Captain Cox in *Laneham's Letter,* 1575. No copy is extant earlier than 1629.)

SIMPLE Book of riddles? Why, did you not lend it to Alice Shortcake upon Allhallowmas last, a fortnight afore Michaelmas?

SHALLOW Come, coz, come, coz, we stay for you. A word with you, coz—marry, this, coz: there is as 'twere a tender, a kind of tender, made afar off by Sir Hugh here. Do you understand me?

SLENDER Ay, sir, you shall find me reasonable. If it be so, I shall do that that is reason.

SHALLOW Nay, but understand me.

SLENDER So I do, sir.

EVANS Give ear to his motions. Master Slender, I will description the matter to you, if you be capacity of it.

SLENDER Nay, I will do as my cousin Shallow says. I pray you, pardon me. He's a Justice of Peace in his country, simple though I stand here.

EVANS But that is not the question. The question is concerning your marriage.

SHALLOW Ay, there's the point, sir.

EVANS Marry, is it, the very point of it—to Mistress Anne Page.

SLENDER Why, if it be so, I will marry her upon any reasonable demands.

EVANS But can you affection the 'oman? Let us command to know that of your mouth or of your lips; for divers philosophers hold that the lips is parcel of the mouth. Therefore, precisely, can you carry your good will to the maid?

SHALLOW Cousin Abraham Slender, can you love her?

SLENDER I hope, sir, I will do as it shall become one that would do reason.

EVANS Nay, Got's lords and his ladies! You must speak positable, if you can carry her your desires towards her.

SHALLOW That you must. Will you, upon good dowry, marry her?

SLENDER I will do a greater thing than that upon your request, cousin, in any reason.

SHALLOW Nay, conceive me, conceive me, sweet coz. What I do is to pleasure you, coz. Can you love the maid?

SLENDER I will marry her, sir, at your request. But if there be no great love in the beginning, yet heaven may decrease it upon better acquaintance, when we are married and have more occasion to know one another. I hope upon familiarity will grow more content. But if you say, "Marry her," I will marry her. That I am freely dissolved, and dissolutely.

EVANS It is a fery discretion answer; save the faul is in the 'ort "dissolutely." The 'ort is, according to our meaning, "resolutely." His meaning is good.

SHALLOW Ay, I think my cousin meant well.

SLENDER Ay, or else I would I might be hanged, la!

[*Enter Anne Page.*]

SHALLOW Here comes fair Mistress Anne.—Would I were young for your sake, Mistress Anne!

ANNE The dinner is on the table. My father desires Your Worships' company.

SHALLOW I will wait on him, fair Mistress Anne.

EVANS 'Od's plessed will! I will not be absence at the grace. [*Exeunt Shallow and Evans.*]

ANNE Will 't please Your Worship to come in, sir?

SLENDER No, I thank you, forsooth, heartily. I am very well.

ANNE The dinner attends you, sir.

SLENDER I am not ahungry, I thank you, forsooth. [*To Simple*] Go, sirrah, for all you are my man, go wait upon my cousin Shallow. [*Exit Simple.*] A Justice of Peace sometime may be beholding to his friend for a man. I keep but three men and a boy yet, till my mother be dead. But what though? Yet I live like a poor gentleman born.

ANNE I may not go in without Your Worship. They will not sit till you come.

SLENDER I'faith, I'll eat nothing. I thank you as much as though I did.

ANNE I pray you, sir, walk in.

SLENDER I had rather walk here, I thank you. I bruised my shin th'other day with playing at sword and dagger with a master of fence—three veneys for a dish of stewed prunes—and, by my troth, I cannot abide the smell of hot meat since. Why do your dogs bark so? Be there bears i'th' town?

ANNE I think there are, sir. I heard them talked of.

SLENDER I love the sport well, but I shall as soon quarrel at it as any man in England. You are afraid if you see the bear loose, are you not?

ANNE Ay, indeed, sir.

SLENDER That's meat and drink to me, now. I have seen Sackerson loose twenty times, and have taken him by the chain. But, I warrant you, the women have so cried and shrieked at it that it passed. But women,

188–9 Allhallowmas . . . Michaelmas (Simple's blunder. Michaelmas occurs on September 29; Allhallowmas or All Saints' Day is November 1.) **190 stay** wait **191 marry** (A mild oath, originally "by the Virgin Mary.") **192 tender** offer (of marriage). **afar off** indirectly **198 motions** proposal. **199 description** describe. **be . . . of it** have the capacity to understand. **202 country** district. **simple though** as sure as. (But also suggesting "however humble I, his kinsman, may appear to be.") **209 demands** requests, terms. **212 parcel** part **219 positable** (For "positively.") **221 upon good dowry** if a suitable dowry is arranged **225 conceive** understand **226 pleasure** please **230 decrease** (For "increase." But with unintended comic meaning; the proverb "Marry first and love will after" contends with "Familiarity breeds contempt" in line 232.) **232 hope** hope that. **content** (Unwittingly suggesting "contempt," as in the proverb cited in note 230 above.)

234 dissolved (For "resolved.") **dissolutely** (For "resolutely.") **235 faul** i.e., fault **236 'ort** word **244 wait on him** join him **245 'Od's** God's **250 attends** waits for **252 sirrah** (Usual form of address to a social inferior.) **for all** even though **252–3 wait upon** attend **254 beholding** beholden **256 till . . . dead** (Slender's widowed mother evidently controls a sizable portion of the family estate until she dies.) **what though?** what of it? **256–7 Yet . . . born** (Slender lives like a gentleman, but one without much income at present.) **264 playing at** practicing with **265 fence** fencing. **veneys** bouts in fencing **266 stewed prunes** (A comically homespun sort of prize for fencing, and one also associated with the "stews" or brothel houses, where they might be served.) **270–1 quarrel at it** i.e., become involved in altercations or competition with other men at the bearbaiting arena **275 Sackerson** a famous bear at the Paris Garden near the theaters on the Bankside **277 passed** i.e., surpassed description.

indeed, cannot abide 'em—they are very ill-favored, rough things.

[*Enter Page.*]

PAGE Come, gentle Master Slender, come. We stay for you.

SLENDER I'll eat nothing, I thank you, sir.

PAGE By cock and pie, you shall not choose, sir. Come, come.

SLENDER Nay, pray you, lead the way.

PAGE Come on, sir.

SLENDER Mistress Anne, yourself shall go first.

ANNE Not I, sir. Pray you, keep on.

SLENDER Truly, I will not go first, truly, la! I will not do you that wrong.

ANNE I pray you, sir.

SLENDER I'll rather be unmannerly than troublesome. You do yourself wrong, indeed, la! *Exeunt.*

1.2

Enter Evans [*from dinner*] *and Simple.*

EVANS Go your ways, and ask of Doctor Caius' house which is the way. And there dwells one Mistress Quickly, which is in the manner of his nurse, or his dry nurse, or his cook, or his laundry, his washer, and his wringer.

SIMPLE Well, sir.

EVANS Nay, it is petter yet. Give her this letter. [*He gives a letter.*] For it is a 'oman that altogether's acquaintance with Mistress Anne Page. And the letter is to desire and require her to solicit your master's desires to Mistress Anne Page. I pray you, begone. I will make an end of my dinner; there's pippins and cheese to come. *Exeunt* [*separately*].

1.3

Enter Falstaff, Host, Bardolph, Nym, Pistol, [*and Robin, Falstaff's*] *Page.*

FALSTAFF Mine Host of the Garter!

HOST What says my bully rook? Speak scholarly and wisely.

FALSTAFF Truly, mine Host, I must turn away some of my followers.

HOST Discard, bully Hercules, cashier. Let them wag; trot, trot.

FALSTAFF I sit at ten pounds a week.

HOST Thou'rt an emperor—Caesar, Kaiser, and Pheezer. I will entertain Bardolph; he shall draw, he shall tap. Said I well, bully Hector?

FALSTAFF Do so, good mine Host.

HOST I have spoke; let him follow. [*To Bardolph*] Let me see thee froth and lime. I am at a word. Follow. [*Exit.*]

FALSTAFF Bardolph, follow him. A tapster is a good trade. An old cloak makes a new jerkin; a withered servingman a fresh tapster. Go; adieu.

BARDOLPH It is a life that I have desired. I will thrive. [*Exit Bardolph.*]

PISTOL O base Hungarian wight! Wilt thou the spigot wield?

NYM He was gotten in drink. Is not the humor conceited?

FALSTAFF I am glad I am so acquit of this tinderbox. His thefts were too open. His filching was like an unskillful singer: he kept not time.

NYM The good humor is to steal at a minute's rest.

PISTOL "Convey," the wise it call. "Steal"? Foh! A fico for the phrase!

FALSTAFF Well, sirs, I am almost out at heels.

PISTOL Why then, let kibes ensue.

FALSTAFF There is no remedy; I must coney-catch, I must shift.

PISTOL Young ravens must have food.

FALSTAFF Which of you know Ford of this town?

PISTOL I ken the wight. He is of substance good.

FALSTAFF My honest lads, I will tell you what I am about.

PISTOL Two yards, and more.

FALSTAFF No quips now, Pistol. Indeed, I am in the waist two yards about. But I am now about no waste; I am about thrift. Briefly, I do mean to make love to

278 ill-favored ugly **283 By cock and pie** (A popular oath, combining *cock,* a euphemism for "God," with *pie,* a dig at the service book for the pre-Reformation church.) **shall not choose** must **288 keep on** go ahead.

1.2. Location: The same scene, a short time later, essentially continuous.

1 ask of inquire concerning **4 dry nurse** i.e., attendant to an adult, not a child; a housekeeper. **laundry** laundress **8–9 altogether's acquaintance** is well acquainted **10 solicit your master's** plead the case for Master Slender's **12 pippins** a kind of apple

1.3. Location: The Garter Inn.

2 bully rook i.e., fine fellow. (An abusive epithet, used jocularly here as an endearment; a *rook* is often a slang term for a swindler or a gull.)

6 cashier dismiss. **wag** move on **8 I sit at** My expenses are **9 Kaiser** emperor **9–10 Pheezer** i.e., Vizier. (Another extravagant epithet, like *Kaiser.*) **10 entertain** employ. **draw** draw liquor **11 tap** serve as tapster. **bully Hector** the hero of Troy, and a type of manliness, like *Hercules* in line 6. (*Bully* means "worthy," "gallant.") **14 froth** draw liquor in such a way as to make it frothy, filling the glass with less beer. **lime** adulterate wine by putting lime into it to mask the sour taste. **I am at a word** I say no more. **16 jerkin** jacket **19 Hungarian wight** i.e., beggarly person. **21 gotten** begotten **21–2 conceited** ingenious. **23 acquit** rid. **tinderbox** (Alluding to Bardolph's fiery complexion.) **25 he . . . time** i.e., he moved too slowly and didn't know when to stop. **26 The good . . . rest** i.e., The smart thing is to steal quickly, within a minute's time. **27 "Convey . . . call** i.e., *Convey* is the cant phrase for stealing used by those in the know. **fico** Italian for *fig,* an insulting phrase and obscene gesture of putting the thumb between the second and third fingers **29 out at heels** i.e., out of money. (Literally, with stockings or shoes worn through at the heel.) **30 kibes** chilblains. (Pistol interprets *out at heels* literally.) **31 coney-catch** catch rabbits, i.e., cheat victims in a con game **32 shift** devise a stratagem. **33 Young . . . food** (Young ravens are always hungry.) **35 I ken . . . good** I know the chap. He is a person of means. **36–7 what I am about** what I am up to. (But Pistol plays with the meaning "what I measure round about the waist.") **40 waste** (With wordplay on *waist* and on the antithesis of *waste* and *thrift.*)

Ford's wife. I spy entertainment in her. She discourses, she carves, she gives the leer of invitation. I can construe the action of her familiar style; and the hardest voice of her behavior, to be Englished rightly, is, "I am Sir John Falstaff's."

PISTOL [*to Nym*] He hath studied her well and translated her will—out of honesty into English.

NYM The anchor is deep. Will that humor pass?

FALSTAFF Now, the report goes she has all the rule of her husband's purse. He hath a legion of angels.

PISTOL As many devils entertain; and "To her, boy!" say I.

NYM The humor rises; it is good. Humor me the angels.

FALSTAFF [*showing letters*] I have writ me here a letter to her; and here another to Page's wife, who even now gave me good eyes too, examined my parts with most judicious oeillades. Sometimes the beam of her view gilded my foot, sometimes my portly belly.

PISTOL [*to Nym*] Then did the sun on dunghill shine.

NYM [*to Pistol*] I thank thee for that humor.

FALSTAFF Oh, she did so course o'er my exteriors, with such a greedy intention that the appetite of her eye did seem to scorch me up like a burning glass! Here's another letter to her. She bears the purse too; she is a region in Guiana, all gold and bounty. I will be cheaters to them both, and they shall be exchequers to me. They shall be my East and West Indies, and I will trade to them both. [*To Pistol*] Go bear thou this letter to Mistress Page. [*To Nym*] And thou this to Mistress Ford. We will thrive, lads, we will thrive.

PISTOL [*giving the letter back*]
Shall I Sir Pandarus of Troy become,
And by my side wear steel? Then Lucifer take all!

NYM I will run no base humor. Here, take the humor-letter. [*He gives the letter back.*] I will keep the havior of reputation.

FALSTAFF [*to Robin*]
Hold, sirrah, bear you these letters tightly.
[*He gives the letters.*]
Sail like my pinnace to these golden shores.—
Rogues, hence, avaunt! Vanish like hailstones, go!
Trudge, plod away o'th' hoof! Seek shelter, pack!
Falstaff will learn the humor of the age:
French thrift, you rogues—myself and skirted page.
[*Exeunt Falstaff and Robin.*]

PISTOL
Let vultures gripe thy guts! For gourd and fullam holds,
And high and low beguiles the rich and poor.
Tester I'll have in pouch when thou shalt lack,
Base Phrygian Turk!

NYM I have operations which be humors of revenge.

PISTOL Wilt thou revenge?

NYM By welkin and her star!

PISTOL With wit or steel?

NYM
With both the humors, I.
I will discuss the humor of this love to Page.

PISTOL And I to Ford shall eke unfold
How Falstaff, varlet vile,
His dove will prove, his gold will hold,
And his soft couch defile.

NYM My humor shall not cool. I will incense Page to deal with poison; I will possess him with yellowness, for the revolt of mine is dangerous. That is my true humor.

PISTOL Thou art the Mars of malcontents. I second thee. Troop on. *Exeunt.*

1.4

Enter Mistress Quickly [*and*] *Simple.*

QUICKLY [*calling*] What, John Rugby!

[*Enter Rugby.*]

42 entertainment (1) readiness to receive me (2) a source of supply **43 carves** i.e., is welcoming and affable. **leer** come-hither glance **44 construe** interpret. (Introducing an extended grammatical pun, continued in *style, voice,* and *Englished.*) **44–5 the hardest . . . rightly** the most severe construction that could be placed on her behavior toward me, if translated into English speech **48 will** (1) intent (2) sexual desire. **honesty** chastity **49 The anchor . . . pass?** The plan is well anchored and secure. Will it work? Or, Will my newly coined expression pass muster? **51 angels** coins stamped with the figure of the archangel Michael, worth about ten shillings. **52 As . . . entertain** (Pistol, taking *legion of angels* in the sense of "heavenly host," plays on the idea of a battle between them and a legion of devils. Falstaff, with his devilish devices, is to take on the angels and *entertain* them to his own use.) **To her, boy!** (A cry of encouragement to a hunting hound.) **54–5 Humor me the angels** i.e., Yes, take the money by this device. (Nym is seconding Pistol's advice; the *humor* of the enterprise takes shape.) **56 writ me** written. (*Me* is used colloquially.) **57 even now** just now **59 oeillades** amorous glances. **the beam . . . view** her eyebeam. (Eyes were thought to emit rays toward the object being looked at.) **63 course o'er** run her eyes over **64 intention** intentness of gaze **65 burning glass** magnifying glass to focus rays of the sun. **67 region in Guiana** (A possible reference to Sir Walter Ralegh's *Discovery of the Large, Rich, and Beautiful Empire of Guiana,* published 1596.) **67–8 cheaters** escheaters, officers appointed to look after the King's escheats, i.e., land reverted to the crown. (With a quibble on the ordinary sense of "those who cheat.") **68 exchequers** treasuries **73 Sir Pandarus** uncle of Cressida, and go-between in the story of Troilus and Cressida. (From his name originated the word *pander.*) **74 And . . . steel**? i.e., even though I am a soldier?

76–7 I . . . reputation I will guard my reputation (as one who refuses to pimp). **78 tightly** deftly, securely. **79 pinnace** a small, swift sailing vessel **81 pack!** be off! **82 humor** fashion **83 French thrift** (Alludes to the current practice of economizing with one French page instead of a more numerous retinue.) **skirted** wearing a doublet with long skirts or tails **84 gourd and fullam** two kinds of false dice. **holds** hold good, can still be used as a means of livelihood **85 high and low** i.e., false dice weighted so as to produce high and low numbers **86 Tester** Sixpence. **pouch** purse **87 Phrygian Turk** (A term of opprobrium.) **88 operations** plans **90 welkin** sky **91 wit or steel** i.e., cunning or violence. **92 both the humors** i.e., wit and sword **93 discuss** declare **94 eke** also **96 His . . . prove** will test the virtue of Ford's wife. **hold** seize **99 possess** fill. **yellowness** i.e., jealousy. (In the Folio text, Nym plans to incense *Ford* with jealousy, which seems more appropriate to Ford's jealous temperament, while in line 94 Pistol plans to speak to Page; however, in 2.1.104 ff., Nym speaks to Page, trying to make him jealous, and Pistol to Ford, and so it seems best to follow the Quarto assignments here in lines 93–4 and 98. See Textual Notes.) **100 the revolt . . . dangerous** i.e., my turning against Falstaff will harm him. **102 the Mars** i.e., the most warlike and mighty
1.4. Location: Doctor Caius' house.

I pray thee, go to the casement and see if you can see my master, Master Doctor Caius, coming. If he do, i'faith, and find anybody in the house, here will be an old abusing of God's patience and the King's English.

RUGBY I'll go watch.

QUICKLY Go; and we'll have a posset for't soon at night, in faith, at the latter end of a sea-coal fire. [*Rugby goes to look out the window.*] An honest, willing, kind fellow as ever servant shall come in house withal, and, I warrant you, no telltale nor no breed-bate. His worst fault is that he is given to prayer. He is something peevish that way, but nobody but has his fault. But let that pass. Peter Simple you say your name is?

SIMPLE Ay, for fault of a better.

QUICKLY And Master Slender's your master?

SIMPLE Ay, forsooth.

QUICKLY Does he not wear a great round beard, like a glover's paring knife?

SIMPLE No, forsooth. He hath but a little whey face, with a little yellow beard, a Cain-colored beard.

QUICKLY A softly spirited man, is he not?

SIMPLE Ay, forsooth. But he is as tall a man of his hands as any is between this and his head. He hath fought with a warrener.

QUICKLY How say you? Oh, I should remember him. Does he not hold up his head, as it were, and strut in his gait?

SIMPLE Yes indeed does he.

QUICKLY Well, heaven send Anne Page no worse fortune! Tell Master Parson Evans I will do what I can for your master. Anne is a good girl, and I wish—

[*Rugby returns.*]

RUGBY Out, alas! Here comes my master.

QUICKLY We shall all be shent. Run in here, good young man; go into this closet. He will not stay long. [*She shuts Simple in.*] What, John Rugby! John! What, John, I say! Go, John, go inquire for my master. I doubt he be not well, that he comes not home.

[*Exit Rugby.*]

[*Singing*] "And down, down, adown-a," etc.

[*Enter*] *Doctor Caius.*

CAIUS Vat is you sing? I do not like dese toys. Pray you, go and vetch me in my closet *un boîtier vert*, a box, a green-a box. Do intend vat I speak? A green-a box.

QUICKLY Ay, forsooth, I'll fetch it you. [*Aside*] I am glad he went not in himself. If he had found the young man, he would have been horn-mad.

[*She goes to the door.*]

CAIUS *Fe, fe, fe, fe! Ma foi, il fait fort chaud. Je m'en vais à la cour—la grande affaire.*

QUICKLY Is it this, sir? [*She offers him a box.*]

CAIUS *Oui; mets-le à ma* pocket. *Dépêche,* quickly! Vere is dat knave Rugby?

QUICKLY What, John Rugby! John!

[*Enter Rugby.*]

RUGBY Here, sir.

CAIUS You are John Rugby, and you are Jack Rugby. Come, take-a your rapier, and come after my heel to the court.

RUGBY 'Tis ready, sir, here in the porch.

CAIUS By my trot, I tarry too long. 'Od's me, *qu'ai-j'oublié?* Dere is some simples in my closet dat I vill not for the varld I shall leave behind.

QUICKLY [*aside*] Ay me, he'll find the young man there, and be mad!

CAIUS [*going to the room*] O *diable, diable!* Vat is in my closet? Villainy! *Larron!* [*Pulling Simple out.*] Rugby, my rapier!

QUICKLY Good master, be content.

CAIUS Wherefore shall I be content-a?

QUICKLY The young man is an honest man.

CAIUS What shall de honest man do in my closet? Dere is no honest man dat shall come in my closet.

QUICKLY I beseech you, be not so phlegmatic. Hear the truth of it: he came of an errand to me from Parson Hugh.

CAIUS Vell?

SIMPLE Ay, forsooth, to desire her to—

QUICKLY Peace, I pray you.

CAIUS Peace-a your tongue.—Speak-a your tale.

SIMPLE To desire this honest gentlewoman, your maid, to speak a good word to Mistress Anne Page for my master in the way of marriage.

QUICKLY This is all, indeed, la! But I'll ne'er put my finger in the fire, and need not.

CAIUS Sir Hugh send-a you? Rugby, *baille* me some paper. [*To Simple*] Tarry you a little-a while. [*Rugby fetches paper, and Dr. Caius writes.*]

QUICKLY [*aside to Simple*] I am glad he is so quiet. If he had been throughly moved, you should have heard him so loud and so melancholy. But notwithstanding,

1 casement window **5 old** plentiful, great **7 a posset** a drink of hot milk curdled with ale or wine **7–8 soon at night** as soon as night comes **8 sea-coal** mineral coal brought by sea (as distinguished from charcoal) **9 s.d.** *window* (Rugby perhaps looks offstage.) **10–11 as ever . . . withal** i.e., as good a servant as ever served in a household **11–12 breed-bate** mischief maker. **13 something peevish** somewhat whimsical, fussy **16 for fault of** for lack of **21 whey** i.e., pallid **22 Cain-colored** (Cain is often pictured in old tapestries with a yellow or reddish beard.) **23 softly spirited** gentle **24 as tall . . . hands** as valiant a man, as stout of arms **25 between . . . head** i.e., in these parts, anywhere. (Proverbial.) **26 warrener** gamekeeper **33 Out** (A cry of dismay.) **34 shent** blamed, disgraced. **35 closet** closet or private room. **38 doubt** fear **39 And . . . adown-a** (A balled refrain.) **40 toys** trifles, i.e., songs. **41** ***un boîtier vert*** a green box **42 Do intend** Do you understand. (French *entendre.*)

45 horn-mad (1) enraged, like a horned beast (2) enraged like a jealous cuckold. **46–7** ***Ma foi . . . affaire*** By my faith, it is very hot; I am going to court—the great affair. **49** ***Oui . . . Dépêche*** Yes, put it in my pocket; be quick **54 your rapier** i.e., your master's rapier **57 trot** truth, faith. **'Od's me** God save me. ***qu'ai-j'oublié?*** what have I forgotten? **58 simples** medicinal herbs **62** ***diable*** devil **63** ***Larron!*** Robber! **65 content** calm. **70 phlegmatic** (Probably a blunder for "choleric," hot-tempered; *phlegmatic* is the very opposite in the physiology of humors.) **71 of an** on an **80–1 I'll . . . not** i.e., I'll never meddle and risk hurting myself if I don't need to. **82** ***baille*** fetch **85 throughly moved** thoroughly angered **86 melancholy** (Perhaps a blunder again, like ***phlegmatic***, above.)

man, I'll do you your master what good I can. And the very yea and the no is, the French doctor, my master—I may call him my master, look you, for I keep his house, and I wash, wring, brew, bake, scour, dress meat and drink, make the beds, and do all myself—

SIMPLE [*aside to Quickly*] 'Tis a great charge to come under one body's hand.

QUICKLY [*aside to Simple*] Are you advised o' that? You shall find it a great charge. And to be up early and down late. But notwithstanding—to tell you in your ear; I would have no words of it—my master himself is in love with Mistress Anne Page. But notwithstanding that, I know Anne's mind: that's neither here nor there.

CAIUS [*giving Simple a letter*] You jack'nape, give-a this letter to Sir Hugh. By gar, it is a shallenge. I will cut his troat in de park, and I will teach a scurvy jackanape priest to meddle or make. You may be gone; it is not good you tarry here. [*Exit Simple.*] By gar, I will cut all his two stones. By gar, he shall not have a stone to throw at his dog.

QUICKLY Alas, he speaks but for his friend.

CAIUS It is no matter-a ver dat. Do not you tell-a me dat I shall have Anne Page for myself? By gar, I vill kill de jack priest; and I have appointed mine Host of de Jarteer to measure our weapon. By gar, I will myself have Anne Page.

QUICKLY Sir, the maid loves you, and all shall be well. We must give folks leave to prate. What the goodyear!

CAIUS Rugby, come to the court with me. [*To Mistress Quickly*] By gar, if I have not Anne Page, I shall turn your head out of my door.—Follow my heels, Rugby. [*Exeunt Caius and Rugby.*]

QUICKLY You shall have An fool's head of your own. No, I know Anne's mind for that. Never a woman in Windsor knows more of Anne's mind than I do, nor can do more than I do with her, I thank heaven.

FENTON [*within*] Who's within there, ho?

QUICKLY Who's there, I trow? Come near the house, I pray you.

[*Enter*] *Fenton.*

FENTON How now, good woman, how dost thou?

QUICKLY The better that it pleases Your good Worship to ask.

FENTON What news? How does pretty Mistress Anne?

QUICKLY In truth, sir, and she is pretty, and honest, and gentle, and one that is your friend, I can tell you that by the way, I praise heaven for it.

FENTON Shall I do any good, think'st thou? Shall I not lose my suit?

QUICKLY Troth, sir, all is in His hands above. But notwithstanding, Master Fenton, I'll be sworn on a book she loves you. Have not Your Worship a wart above your eye?

FENTON Yes, marry, have I. What of that?

QUICKLY Well, thereby hangs a tale. Good faith, it is such another Nan! But, I detest, an honest maid as ever broke bread. We had an hour's talk of that wart. I shall never laugh but in that maid's company! But indeed she is given too much to allicholy and musing. But for you—well, go to.

FENTON Well, I shall see her today. Hold, there's money for thee. [*He gives money.*] Let me have thy voice in my behalf. If thou see'st her before me, commend me.

QUICKLY Will I? I'faith, that I will. And I will tell Your Worship more of the wart the next time we have confidence, and of other wooers.

FENTON Well, farewell. I am in great haste now.

QUICKLY Farewell to Your Worship. [*Exit Fenton.*] Truly, an honest gentleman. But Anne loves him not, for I know Anne's mind as well as another does.—Out upon't! What have I forgot? *Exit.*

2.1

Enter Mistress Page [*with a letter*].

MRS. PAGE What, have I scaped love letters in the holiday time of my beauty, and am I now a subject for them? Let me see. [*She reads.*]

"Ask me no reason why I love you, for though Love use Reason for his precision, he admits him not for his counselor. You are not young; no more am I. Go to, then, there's sympathy. You are merry; so am I. Ha, ha! Then there's more sympathy. You love sack, and so do I. Would you desire better sympathy? Let it suffice thee, Mistress Page—at the least, if the love of soldier can suffice—that I love thee. I will not say, 'pity me'—'tis not a soldierlike phrase—but I say, 'love me.' By me,

Thine own true knight,
By day or night
Or any kind of light,
With all his might
For thee to fight,

John Falstaff."

87 you for you, since you ask me **87–8 the very yea and the no** the long and short of it **90–1 scour . . . meat** scrub, prepare food **92 charge** responsibility **94 Are . . . that?** i.e., Do you understand that? You can say that again. **97 I would . . . of it** I wouldn't want the word to get out **101 jack'nape** i.e., coxcomb, conceited fop. (A contemptuous epithet; literally, Jack of Naples, an ape or tame monkey.) **102 gar** i.e., God **104 meddle or make** meddle. **106 cut . . . stones** castrate him. **109 ver** for **111 jack** (A contemptuous epithet.) **112 Jarteer** Garter. **measure our weapon** i.e., act as second or referee. (Literally, to make sure that the swords are of equal length.) **115 What the goodyear!** i.e., What the deuce! **119 An** (The Folio uses the same spelling, *An,* for *Anne,* in lines 120 and 121, suggesting a pun on *Anne Page;* Caius is to have a fool's head for wooing Anne.) **124 trow** wonder. **Come near** Enter

130 honest chaste **131 gentle** well-bred. **your friend** friendly disposed toward you. **136–7 a book** i.e., a Bible **140–1 it is . . . Nan** ie., you wouldn't believe it if I told you about Ann; she's a wonder. **141 detest** (For "protest.") **143 but** except **144 allicholy** (For "melancholy.") **145 go to** i.e., enough; come, come. **147 voice** word of support **151 confidence** (For "conference," blurred here with the notion of confiding.) **156 Out upon't!** i.e., Deuce take it!
2.1. Location: Before Page's house.
5 precisian strict adviser **6 counselor** personal guide. **7 sympathy** congeniality. **8 sack** a Spanish wine

What a Herod of Jewry is this! Oh, wicked, wicked world! One that is well-nigh worn to pieces with age, to show himself a young gallant! What an unweighed behavior hath this Flemish drunkard picked, i'th' devil's name, out of my conversation, that he dares in this manner assay me? Why, he hath not been thrice in my company. What should I say to him? I was then frugal of my mirth. Heaven forgive me! Why, I'll exhibit a bill in the Parliament for the putting down of men. How shall I be revenged on him? For revenged I will be, as sure as his guts are made of puddings.

[Enter] Mistress Ford.

MRS. FORD Mistress Page! Trust me, I was going to your house.

MRS. PAGE And, trust me, I was coming to you. You look very ill.

MRS. FORD Nay, I'll ne'er believe that. I have to show to the contrary.

MRS. PAGE Faith, but you do, in my mind.

MRS. FORD Well, I do, then. Yet I say I could show you to the contrary. Oh, Mistress Page, give me some counsel!

MRS. PAGE What's the matter, woman?

MRS. FORD Oh, woman, if it were not for one trifling respect, I could come to such honor!

MRS. PAGE Hang the trifle, woman, take the honor. What is it? Dispense with trifles. What is it?

MRS. FORD If I would but go to hell for an eternal moment or so, I could be knighted.

MRS. PAGE What? Thou liest! Sir Alice Ford? These knights will hack, and so thou shouldst not alter the article of thy gentry.

MRS. FORD We burn daylight. Here, read, read. Perceive how I might be knighted. [*She gives a letter.*] I shall think the worse of fat men as long as I have an eye to make difference of men's liking. And yet he would not swear, praised women's modesty, and gave such orderly and well-behaved reproof to all uncomeliness that I would have sworn his disposition would have gone to the truth of his words. But they do no more adhere and keep place together than the Hundredth Psalm to the tune of "Greensleeves." What tempest, I trow, threw this whale, with so many tuns of oil in his belly, ashore at Windsor? How shall I be revenged on him? I think the best way were to entertain him with hope, till the wicked fire of lust have melted him in his own grease. Did you ever hear the like?

MRS. PAGE Letter for letter, but that the name of Page and Ford differs! To thy great comfort in this mystery of ill opinions, here's the twin brother of thy letter. [*She shows her letter.*] But let thine inherit first, for I protest mine never shall. I warrant he hath a thousand of these letters, writ with blank space for different names—sure, more—and these are of the second edition. He will print them, out of doubt; for he cares not what he puts into the press, when he would put us two. I had rather be a giantess and lie under Mount Pelion. Well, I will find you twenty lascivious turtles ere one chaste man.

MRS. FORD [*comparing the letters*] Why, this is the very same: the very hand, the very words. What doth he think of us?

MRS. PAGE Nay, I know not. It makes me almost ready to wrangle with mine own honesty. I'll entertain myself like one that I am not acquainted withal; for, sure, unless he know some strain in me that I know not myself, he would never have boarded me in this fury.

MRS. FORD "Boarding," call you it? I'll be sure to keep him above deck.

MRS. PAGE So will I. If he come under my hatches, I'll never to sea again. Let's be revenged on him. Let's appoint him a meeting, give him a show of comfort in his suit, and lead him on with a fine-baited delay till he hath pawned his horses to mine Host of the Garter.

MRS. FORD Nay, I will consent to act any villainy against him that may not sully the chariness of our honesty. Oh, that my husband saw this letter! It would give eternal food to his jealousy.

MRS. PAGE Why, look where he comes, and my goodman too. He's as far from jealousy as I am from giving him cause, and that, I hope, is an unmeasurable distance.

MRS. FORD You are the happier woman.

MRS. PAGE Let's consult together against this greasy knight. Come hither. [*They retire.*]

[Enter] Master Page [with] Nym, Master Ford [with] Pistol.

20 Herod of Jewry bombastic ranter, like the comic villain of the Corpus Christi plays **22 unweighed** unconsidered, inadvertent **23 Flemish drunkard** (The Flemish were proverbially heavy drinkers.) **24 conversation** conduct **25 assay** accost, address (with proposals of love) **26 should I say** was I to say **27 exhibit** introduce **28 putting down** suppression. (But with bawdy suggestion.) **30 puddings** mixture of meat, herbs, etc., stuffed into intestines of animals, as sausage. **31 Trust me** Believe me **34 ill** unhappy, out of sorts. (But Mistress Ford, in replying, plays on the sense of "ugly.") **35 have** have something, i.e., the letter **43 respect** matter, consideration **48–50 These . . . gentry** i.e., These knights are a quarrelsome and promiscuous lot, and so you should not risk your social respectability for the dubious honor of being a knight's lover. **51 burn daylight** i.e., waste time. **53–4 to make . . . liking** to discriminate among men. **54–5 he . . . swear** he would not use profanity in my presence **56 uncomeliness** unseemly behavior **58 gone . . . words** matched his language. **60 Greensleeves** (A popular tune, to which many sets of words have been sung, some of them erotic and thus wholly unlike the Hundredth Psalm; compare 5.5.19.) **61 trow** wonder. **tuns** (1) large casks (2) tons

63–4 entertain . . . hope lead him on **67–8 mystery . . . opinions** i.e., revelation of the low opinion Falstaff has of us, and thus of our low opinion of Falstaff **69 inherit** come into possession, as of a legacy **73 out of** without **74 into the press** (1) into the printing press (2) under his weight **76 Pelion** mountain in Thessaly. (The giants, according to Greek mythology, heaped it on a neighboring mountain, Ossa, and Ossa on Olympus, in their attempts to overthrow the gods.) **turtles** turtledoves, proverbially faithful to their mates and therefore not likely to be promiscuous **79 hand** handwriting **82 wrangle with** quarrel with, doubt. **honesty** chastity. **entertain** treat **83 withal** with **84 strain** quality **85 boarded** accosted, made advances to. (A term of naval warfare.) **91 fine-baited** with the hook well baited **91–2 till . . . Garter** i.e., until Falstaff is even more in debt than he is now. **93 Nay** i.e., Indeed **94–5 the chariness . . . honesty** the integrity of our chaste virtue. **95 that** if only **97–8 goodman** husband **99 unmeasurable** infinite **101 happier** more fortunate (than I)

FORD Well, I hope it be not so.

PISTOL
Hope is a curtal dog in some affairs.
Sir John affects thy wife.

FORD Why, sir, my wife is not young.

PISTOL
He woos both high and low, both rich and poor
Both young and old, one with another, Ford.
He loves the gallimaufry. Ford, perpend.

FORD Love my wife?

PISTOL
With liver burning hot. Prevent, or go thou,
Like Sir Actaeon, he, with Ringwood at thy heels.—
Oh, odious is the name!

FORD What name, sir?

PISTOL The horn, I say. Farewell.
Take heed, have open eye, for thieves do foot by night.
Take heed, ere summer comes or cuckoo birds do sing.
Away, Sir Corporal Nym!
Believe it, Page, he speaks sense. [*Exit.*]

FORD [*aside*] I will be patient. I will find out this.

NYM [*to Page*] And this is true. I like not the humor of lying. He hath wronged me in some humors. I should have borne the humored letter to her; but I have a sword, and it shall bite upon my necessity. He loves your wife; there's the short and the long. My name is Corporal Nym. I speak and I avouch 'tis true. My name is Nym, and Falstaff loves your wife. Adieu. I love not the humor of bread and cheese, and there's the humor of it. Adieu.

PAGE [*aside*] "The humor of it," quoth 'a! Here's a fellow frights English out of his wits.

FORD [*aside*] I will seek out Falstaff.

PAGE [*aside*] I never heard such a drawling, affecting rogue.

FORD [*aside*] If I do find it—well.

PAGE [*aside*] I will not believe such a Cathayan, though the priest o'th' town commended him for a true man.

FORD [*aside*] 'Twas a good sensible fellow. Well.

[*Mistress Page and Mistress Ford come forward.*]

PAGE How now, Meg?

MRS. PAGE Whither go you, George? Hark you. [*They converse apart.*]

MRS. FORD How now, sweet Frank, why art thou melancholy?

FORD I melancholy? I am not melancholy. Get you home, go.

MRS. FORD Faith, thou hast some crotchets in thy head now.—Will you go, Mistress Page?

MRS. PAGE Have with you. You'll come to dinner, George?

[*Enter Mistress*] *Quickly.*

[*Aside to Mistress Ford*] Look who comes yonder. She shall be our messenger to this paltry knight.

MRS. FORD [*aside to Mistress Page*] Trust me, I thought on her. She'll fit it.

MRS. PAGE [*to Mistress Quickly*] You are come to see my daughter Anne?

QUICKLY Ay, forsooth; and, I pray, how does good Mistress Anne?

MRS. PAGE Go in with us and see. We have an hour's talk with you.

[*Exeunt Mistress Page, Mistress Ford, and Mistress Quickly.*]

PAGE How now, Master Ford?

FORD You heard what this knave told me, did you not?

PAGE Yes, and you heard what the other told me?

FORD Do you think there is truth in them?

PAGE Hang 'em, slaves! I do not think the knight would offer it. But these that accuse him in his intent towards our wives are a yoke of his discarded men—very rogues, now they be out of service.

FORD Were they his men?

PAGE Marry, were they.

FORD I like it never the better for that. Does he lie at the Garter?

PAGE Ay, marry, does he. If he should intend this voyage toward my wife, I would turn her loose to him; and what he gets more of her than sharp words, let it lie on my head.

FORD I do not misdoubt my wife, but I would be loath to turn them together. A man may be too confident. I would have nothing lie on my head. I cannot be thus satisfied.

[*Enter*] *Host.*

PAGE Look where my ranting Host of the Garter comes. There is either liquor in his pate or money in his purse when he looks so merrily.—How now, mine Host?

HOST How now, bully rook? Thou'rt a gentleman. [*He turns and calls.*] Cavaleiro Justice, I say!

[*Enter*] *Shallow.*

105 Hope . . . affairs i.e., Hope is not to be trusted. (A *curtal dog* is one with docked tail, often used to run a treadwheel, perhaps likened here to a creature turning Fortune's wheel.) **106 affects** loves, aims at **110 gallimaufry** a dish of miscellaneous ingredients; hence, the whole lot. **perpend** consider. **112 liver burning hot** (The liver was considered the seat of the passions.) **113 Actaeon** huntsman who was changed into a stag by Diana as punishment for watching her and her nymphs at their bath and was torn to pieces by his own hounds. (Pistol urges Ford to avoid the fate of the horned beast: that of wearing a cuckold's horns.) **Ringwood** one of Actaeon's hounds. (Mentioned in Golding's translation of Ovid.) **114 the name** i.e., the name of Actaeon or cuckold. **117 foot** walk **118 cuckoo birds** (Associated with cuckoldry because of their call, "cuckoo," and because they lay eggs in other birds' nests.) **119 Away** Come away **123–4 I . . . borne** i.e., He wanted me to carry **125 upon my necessity** when I have need. **129 humor . . . cheese** (Alludes to the scant rations Nym received as Falstaff's retainer.) **132 his** its **134 affecting** affected **136 If . . . well** If I find it's true, well, I'll take steps. **137 Cathayan** person from Cathay, i.e., China, and therefore assumed by Page to be a scoundrel. **though** even if

146 crotchets whims, fancies **148 Have with you** I'll go along with you. **152 She'll fit it** She is just the person for the part. **164 offer** venture **165 yoke** pair **169 lie** lodge **171 intend** propose making **174 lie on my head** be my responsibility. (But Ford, in his reply, sees a reference to cuckold's horns.) **175 misdoubt** mistrust **176 turn them together** i.e., let them loose together in the same pasture, as in line 172 above. **179 ranting** speaking in a high-flown, bombastic style **182 bully rook** i.e., fine fellow. (See 1.3.2 and note. Similarly in lines 187 and 191 below.) **183 Cavaleiro Justice** Gallant Justice Shallow. (Put here in the form of an honorific title. The Spanish *caballero* is a gentleman trained in arms; the Italian *cavaliere* is a knight.)

SHALLOW I follow, mine Host, I follow.—Good even and twenty, good Master Page! Master Page, will you go with us? We have sport in hand.

HOST Tell him, Cavaleiro Justice. Tell him, bully rook.

SHALLOW Sir, there is a fray to be fought between Sir Hugh the Welsh priest and Caius the French doctor.

FORD Good mine Host o'th' Garter, a word with you.

HOST What say'st thou, my bully rook?

[*They converse apart.*]

SHALLOW [*to Page*] Will you go with us to behold it? My merry Host hath had the measuring of their weapons, and, I think, hath appointed them contrary places; for, believe me, I hear the parson is no jester. Hark, I will tell you what our sport shall be.

[*They converse apart.*]

HOST [*to Ford*] Hast thou no suit against my knight, my guest cavalier?

FORD None, I protest. But I'll give you a pottle of burnt sack to give me recourse to him and tell him my name is Brook—only for a jest.

HOST My hand, bully. Thou shalt have egress and regress—said I well?—and thy name shall be Brook. It is a merry knight.—Will you go, mynheers?

SHALLOW Have with you, mine Host.

PAGE I have heard the Frenchman hath good skill in his rapier.

SHALLOW Tut, sir, I could have told you more. In these times you stand on distance—your passes, stoccados, and I know not what. 'Tis the heart, Master Page; 'tis here, 'tis here. I have seen the time, with my long sword I would have made you four tall fellows skip like rats.

HOST Here, boys, here, here! Shall we wag?

PAGE Have with you. I had rather hear them scold than fight. *Exeunt* [*Host, Shallow, and Page*].

FORD Though Page be a secure fool, and stands so firmly on his wife's frailty, yet I cannot put off my opinion so easily. She was in his company at Page's house, and what they made there I know not. Well, I will look further into't, and I have a disguise to sound Falstaff. If I find her honest, I lose not my labor; if she be otherwise, 'tis labor well bestowed. [*Exit.*]

2.2

Enter Falstaff [*and*] *Pistol.*

FALSTAFF I will not lend thee a penny.

PISTOL
Why, then the world's mine oyster,
Which I with sword will open.
I will retort the sum in equipage.

FALSTAFF Not a penny. I have been content, sir, you should lay my countenance to pawn. I have grated upon my good friends for three reprieves for you and your coach-fellow Nym, or else you had looked through the grate like a gemini of baboons. I am damned in hell for swearing to gentlemen my friends you were good soldiers and tall fellows. And when Mistress Bridget lost the handle of her fan, I took't upon mine honor thou hadst it not.

PISTOL
Didst not thou share? Hadst thou not fifteen pence?

FALSTAFF Reason, you rogue, reason. Think'st thou I'll endanger my soul gratis? At a word, hang no more about me. I am no gibbet for you. Go. A short knife and a throng! To your manor of Pickt-hatch, go. You'll not bear a letter for me, you rogue? You stand upon your honor? Why, thou unconfinable baseness, it is as much as I can do to keep the terms of my honor precise. Ay, ay, I myself sometimes, leaving the fear of God on the left hand and hiding mine honor in my necessity, am fain to shuffle, to hedge, and to lurch; and yet you, you rogue, will ensconce your rags, your cat-a-mountain looks, your red-lattice phrases, and your bold-beating oaths, under the shelter of your honor! You will not do it? You?

PISTOL I do relent. What would thou more of man?

[*Enter*] *Robin.*

ROBIN Sir, here's a woman would speak with you.

FALSTAFF Let her approach.

[*Enter Mistress*] *Quickly.*

184–5 Good . . . twenty i.e., Good afternoon, many times over **193–4 hath had . . . weapons** i.e., has been appointed referee **194–5 contrary places** different meeting places **195 the parson . . . jester** i.e., Parson Evans is serious about this challenge to a duel, and is a swordsman to be reckoned with. (Earlier, Evans played peacemaker with Falstaff and Shallow, but the present quarrel is, for him, a matter of honor in defending his candidate for Anne Page's hand, Slender, against Doctor Caius.) **197–8 my . . . cavalier** Falstaff, residing in the Host's inn. **199 protest** insist. **pottle** two-quart measure. **burnt** heated **200 recourse** access **201 Brook** (Ford's alias, usually spelled *Brooke* in the 1602 Quarto, was changed to *Broome* in the Folio because Brooke was the family name of Lord Cobham. See Introduction.) **202–3 egress and regresss** i.e., free access to come and go **204 mynheers** gentlemen. (Dutch.) **205 Have with you** I'll come with you. (Also in line 215.) **209 you stand on distance** one attaches great importance to prescribed space between fencers. **passes** lunges. **stoccados** thrusts **210–11 'Tis . . . 'tis here** i.e., Real fencing, Master Page, is a matter of the heart, not of this affected modern etiquette. (Shallow perhaps taps his chest as he says, "'Tis here.") **211–12 long sword** an old-fashioned, heavy weapon **212 tall** valiant **214 wag** go. (See 1.3.6.) **217 secure** overconfident **219 She** i.e., Mistress Ford. **his** i.e., Falstaff's **220 made** did **221 sound** test, plumb the depths of

2.2. Location: The Garter Inn.
4 retort . . . equipage i.e., pay back the whole amount in military equipment. **6 lay . . . pawn** i.e., borrow money on the strength of my patronage. **6–7 grated upon** i.e., persistently and irritatingly begged **8 coach-fellow** partner (like a fellow horse in harness) **9 grate** i.e., of a debtors' prison window. **gemini** pair **10 gentlemen my friends** my gentlemen friends **11 tall** brave **12–13 took't upon** swore by **15 Reason** With good reason **16 gratis** for free. **At a word** In short. **hang** loiter. (With pun on hanging from a *gibbet* in line 17.) **17–18 A short . . . throng!** i.e., With a short knife you might cut purses in a crowd! **18 Pickt-hatch** (A quarter in London, notorious in Elizabethan times for criminal types and prostitutes, the houses having hatches, or half-doors, the lower half-door surmounted with spikes.) **20 unconfinable** infinite **21–2 to keep . . . precise** i.e., to keep my reputation unsullied by associating with you. (*Precise* is a term often associated with puritanism.) **22–3 leaving . . . hand** i.e., disregarding a proper fear of God **24 fain . . . lurch** obliged to practice trickery, to dodge, and to steal **26 cat-a-mountain** catamount, leopard or panther, wildcat. **red-lattice phrases** alehouse talk. (Lattices painted red identified an alehouse.) **27 bold-beating oaths** the oaths of a rowdy braggart, oaths as violent as blows

QUICKLY Give Your Worship good morrow.

FALSTAFF Good morrow, goodwife.

QUICKLY Not so, an't please Your Worship.

FALSTAFF Good maid, then.

QUICKLY I'll be sworn: as my mother was, the first hour I was born.

FALSTAFF I do believe the swearer. What with me?

QUICKLY Shall I vouchsafe Your Worship a word or two?

FALSTAFF Two thousand, fair woman, and I'll vouchsafe thee the hearing.

QUICKLY There is one Mistress Ford, sir—I pray, come a little nearer this ways. I myself dwell with Master Doctor Caius—

FALSTAFF Well, on. Mistress Ford, you say—

QUICKLY Your Worship says very true. I pray Your Worship, come a little nearer this ways.

FALSTAFF I warrant thee, nobody hears. Mine own people, mine own people.

QUICKLY Are they so? God bless them and make them His servants!

FALSTAFF Well; Mistress Ford: what of her?

QUICKLY Why, sir, she's a good creature. Lord, Lord, Your Worship's a wanton! Well, heaven forgive you and all of us, I pray!

FALSTAFF Mistress Ford; come, Mistress Ford—

QUICKLY Marry, this is the short and the long of it: you have brought her into such a canaries as 'tis wonderful. The best courtier of them all, when the court lay at Windsor, could never have brought her to such a canary. Yet there has been knights, and lords, and gentlemen, with their coaches, I warrant you, coach after coach, letter after letter, gift after gift, smelling so sweetly, all musk, and so rushling, I warrant you, in silk and gold, and in such alligant terms, and in such wine and sugar of the best and the fairest, that would have won any woman's heart; and, I warrant you, they could never get an eye-wink of her. I had myself twenty angels given me this morning; but I defy all angels, in any such sort, as they say, but in the way of honesty; and, I warrant you, they could never get her so much as sip on a cup with the proudest of them all. And yet there has been earls, nay, which is more, pensioners, but I warrant you all is one with her.

FALSTAFF But what says she to me? Be brief, my good she-Mercury.

QUICKLY Marry, she hath received your letter, for the which she thanks you a thousand times, and she gives you to notify that her husband will be absence from his house between ten and eleven.

FALSTAFF Ten and eleven?

QUICKLY Ay, forsooth; and then you may come and see the picture, she says, that you wot of. Master Ford, her husband, will be from home. Alas, the sweet woman leads an ill life with him. He's a very jealousy man. She leads a very frampold life with him, good heart.

FALSTAFF Ten and eleven. Woman, commend me to her. I will not fail her.

QUICKLY Why, you say well. But I have another messenger to Your Worship. Mistress Page hath her hearty commendations to you, too; and let me tell you in your ear, she's as fartuous a civil modest wife, and one, I tell you, that will not miss you morning nor evening prayer, as any is in Windsor, whoe'er be the other. And she bade me tell Your Worship that her husband is seldom from home, but she hopes there will come a time. I never knew a woman so dote upon a man. Surely I think you have charms, la! Yes, in truth.

FALSTAFF Not I, I assure thee. Setting the attraction of my good parts aside, I have no other charms.

QUICKLY Blessing on your heart for't!

FALSTAFF But, I pray thee, tell me this: has Ford's wife and Page's wife acquainted each other how they love me?

QUICKLY That were a jest indeed! They have not so little grace, I hope. That were a trick indeed! But Mistress Page would desire you to send her your little page, of all loves. Her husband has a marvelous infection to the little page; and truly Master Page is an honest man. Never a wife in Windsor leads a better life than she does. Do what she will, say what she will, take all, pay all, go to bed when she list, rise when she list—all is as she will. And truly she deserves it, for if there be a kind woman in Windsor, she is one. You must send her your page, no remedy.

FALSTAFF Why, I will.

QUICKLY Nay, but do so, then. And, look you, he may come and go between you both. And in any case have a nayword, that you may know one another's mind, and the boy never need to understand anything; for 'tis not good that children should know any wickedness. Old folks, you know, have discretion, as they say, and know the world.

FALSTAFF Fare thee well. Commend me to them both. There's my purse; I am yet thy debtor. [*He gives money.*] Boy, go along with this woman.

[*Exeunt Mistress Quickly and Robin.*]

This news distracts me!

34 Not so i.e., I am not a wife. **an't** if it **36 I'll be sworn** I'll swear to that **36–7 as . . . born** (Mistress Quickly probably means "as much a maid as when I was born, just like my mother before me," but manages instead to allege the impossible, that her mother was a virgin when Mistress Quickly was born.) **39 vouchsafe** deign to grant. (The comic pompousness of *vouchsafe* prompts Falstaff to use it in his reply.) **58 canaries** state of excitement. (Confusing "quandary" with the dance called the canary?) **59 lay** resided **64 rushling** i.e., rustling **65 alligant** i.e., elegant, or eloquent (?) **69 twenty angels** i.e., as a bribe to act as go-between. *Angels* are gold coins. **defy** reject, spurn **70 sort** manner **71 they** the supposed admirers of Mistress Ford **74 pensioners** crown pensioners, who were required to pray twice a day for the monarch in return for their pension. (In elevating them above earls in the social order, Mistress Quickly is either confused or exaggerating in order to flatter Falstaff.) **all is one** it's a matter of indifference **76 she-Mercury** woman messenger.

78–9 gives you to notify bids you take notice **79 absence** (For "absent.") **83 wot** know **86 frampold** disagreeable **89–90 messenger** (For "message.") **92 fartuous** (For "virtuous.") **modest** decent, proper **93 miss you** miss. (*You* is used colloquially.) **98 have charms** use magic. **100 parts** qualities **107–8 of all loves** for love's sake. **108 infection to** (For "affection for.") **109 an honest** a worthy **112 list** wishes **115 no remedy** no two ways about it. **119 nayword** watchword **127 distracts** bewilders (with ecstasy)

PISTOL [*aside*]
This punk is one of Cupid's carriers.
Clap on more sails! Pursue! Up with your fights!
Give fire! She is my prize, or ocean whelm them all!
[*Exit.*]

FALSTAFF Say'st thou so, old Jack? Go thy ways. I'll make more of thy old body than I have done. Will they yet look after thee? Wilt thou, after the expense of so much money, be now a gainer? Good body, I thank thee. Let them say 'tis grossly done; so it be fairly done, no matter.

[*Enter*] *Bardolph* [*with wine*].

BARDOLPH Sir John, there's one Master Brook below would fain speak with you and be acquainted with you, and hath sent Your Worship a morning's draft of sack.

FALSTAFF Brook is his name?

BARDOLPH Ay, sir.

FALSTAFF Call him in. Such Brooks are welcome to me, that o'erflows such liquor. [*Exit Bardolph.*] Aha! Mistress Ford and Mistress Page, have I encompassed you? Go to. *Via!*

[*Enter Bardolph, with*] *Ford* [*disguised*].

FORD Bless you, sir.

FALSTAFF And you, sir. Would you speak with me?

FORD I make bold to press with so little preparation upon you.

FALSTAFF You're welcome. What's your will? [*To Bardolph*] Give us leave, drawer. [*Exit Bardolph.*]

FORD Sir, I am a gentleman that have spent much. My name is Brook.

FALSTAFF Good Master Brook, I desire more acquaintance of you.

FORD Good Sir John, I sue for yours—not to charge you, for I must let you understand I think myself in better plight for a lender than you are, the which hath something emboldened me to this unseasoned intrusion; for they say if money go before, all ways do lie open.

FALSTAFF Money is a good soldier, sir, and will on.

FORD Troth, and I have a bag of money here troubles me. If you will help to bear it, Sir John, take all, or half, for easing me of the carriage.

FALSTAFF Sir, I know not how I may deserve to be your porter.

FORD I will tell you, sir, if you will give me the hearing.

FALSTAFF Speak, good Master Brook. I shall be glad to be your servant.

FORD Sir, I hear you are a scholar—I will be brief with you—and you have been a man long known to me, though I had never so good means as desire to make myself acquainted with you. I shall discover a thing to you wherein I must very much lay open mine own imperfection. But, good Sir John, as you have one eye upon my follies, as you hear them unfolded, turn another into the register of your own, that I may pass with a reproof the easier, sith you yourself know how easy it is to be such an offender.

FALSTAFF Very well, sir. Proceed.

FORD There is a gentlewoman in this town; her husband's name is Ford.

FALSTAFF Well, sir.

FORD I have long loved her, and, I protest to you, bestowed much on her, followed her with a doting observance, engrossed opportunities to meet her, fee'd every slight occasion that could but niggardly give me sight of her, not only bought many presents to give her but have given largely to many to know what she would have given. Briefly, I have pursued her as love hath pursued me, which hath been on the wing of all occasions. But whatsoever I have merited—either in my mind or in my means—meed I am sure I have received none, unless experience be a jewel. That I have purchased at an infinite rate, and that hath taught me to say this:
"Love like a shadow flies when substance love
pursues,
Pursuing that that flies, and flying what pursues."

FALSTAFF Have you received no promise of satisfaction at her hands?

FORD Never.

FALSTAFF Have you importuned her to such a purpose?

FORD Never.

FALSTAFF Of what quality was your love, then?

FORD Like a fair house built on another man's ground, so that I have lost my edifice by mistaking the place where I erected it.

FALSTAFF To what purpose have you unfolded this to me?

FORD When I have told you that, I have told you all. Some say that though she appear honest to me, yet in other places she enlargeth her mirth so far that there is shrewd construction made of her. Now, Sir John, here is the heart of my purpose. You are a gentleman of excellent breeding, admirable discourse, of great admittance, authentic in your place and person, gener-

128 punk whore. **carriers** messengers. **129 Clap** Put. **fights** fighting sails, i.e., screens raised during naval engagements to conceal and protect the crew. **130 prize** booty. **ocean whelm** let the ocean overwhelm. (Pistol, having refused to carry Falstaff's love notes, sees Mistress Quickly as an adversary.) **131 Say'st . . . ways** i.e., What do you think of that, Jack, my boy? Not bad. **133 look after** i.e., lust after **135–6 Let . . . matter** i.e., My enemies can criticize me all they want for indelicacy (and fatness), but so long as my plan succeeds, that is all that matters. **145–6 encompassed you** achieved you. **146 Go to** i.e., Well, then. *Via!* Go on! (A shout of encouragement.)
149 preparation advance notice **152 Give . . . drawer** Leave us alone, tapster. **157–8 charge you** put you to expense **160 something** somewhat. **unseasoned** unseasonable **166 the carriage** the carrying of it.

175 discover reveal **179 register** record **180 sith** since
187–8 observance attentiveness **188 engrossed** seized. **fee'd** purchased **191 largely** generously **191–2 what . . . given** what she would like to have given to her. **195 meed** reward **199–200 Love . . . pursues** i.e., Love runs away when pursued but pursues when run away from, just as a shadow seems to run away from a body (a *substance*) running in its direction but follows a body running the other way. (Proverbial.) **213 honest** chaste **214 enlargeth** gives free scope to **215 shrewd construction** malicious interpretation **217–18 of great admittance** i.e., widely received in society **218 authentic** entitled to respect

ally allowed for your many warlike, courtlike, and 219
learned preparations. 220

FALSTAFF Oh, sir!

FORD Believe it, for you know it. There is money. Spend
it, spend it; spend more; spend all I have. [*He offers
money.*] Only give me so much of your time in exchange of it as to lay an amiable siege to the honesty of 225
this Ford's wife. Use your art of wooing; win her to
consent to you. If any man may, you may as soon as
any.

FALSTAFF Would it apply well to the vehemency of your
affection that I should win what you would enjoy?
Methinks you prescribe to yourself very prepester-
ously.

FORD Oh, understand my drift. She dwells so securely
on the excellency of her honor that the folly of my soul
dares not present itself; she is too bright to be looked
against. Now, could I come to her with any detection 236
in my hand, my desires had instance and argument to 237
commend themselves. I could drive her then from the
ward of her purity, her reputation, her marriage vow, 239
and a thousand other her defenses, which now are too 240
too strongly embattled against me. What say you to't,
Sir John?

FALSTAFF Master Brook, I will first make bold with your
money; next, give me your hand; and last, as I am a
gentleman, you shall, if you will, enjoy Ford's wife.

[*He accepts the money and takes Ford's hand.*]

FORD Oh, good sir!

FALSTAFF I say you shall.

FORD Want no money, Sir John, you shall want none. 248

FALSTAFF Want no Mistress Ford, Master Brook, you
shall want none. I shall be with her, I may tell you, by
her own appointment. Even as you came in to me, her
assistant or go-between parted from me. I say I shall
be with her between ten and eleven, for at that time
the jealous rascally knave her husband will be forth. 254
Come you to me at night; you shall know how I
speed. 256

FORD I am blest in your acquaintance. Do you know
Ford, sir?

FALSTAFF Hang him, poor cuckoldly knave! I know him
not. Yet I wrong him to call him poor. They say the
jealous wittolly knave hath masses of money, for the 261
which his wife seems to me well-favored. I will use her 262
as the key of the cuckoldly rogue's coffer, and there's
my harvest home. 264

FORD I would you knew Ford, sir, that you might avoid
him if you saw him.

FALSTAFF Hang him, mechanical salt-butter rogue! I 267
will stare him out of his wits. I will awe him with my
cudgel; it shall hang like a meteor o'er the cuckold's 269
horns. Master Brook, thou shalt know I will predomi- 270
nate over the peasant, and thou shalt lie with his wife. 271
Come to me soon at night. Ford's a knave, and I will
aggravate his style: thou, Master Brook, shalt know 273
him for knave and cuckold. Come to me soon at night.

[*Exit.*]

FORD What a damned Epicurean rascal is this! My heart 275
is ready to crack with impatience. Who says this is
improvident jealousy? My wife hath sent to him, the
hour is fixed, the match is made. Would any man
have thought this? See the hell of having a false
woman! My bed shall be abused, my coffers ransacked, my reputation gnawn at; and I shall not only
receive this villainous wrong but stand under the 282
adoption of abominable terms, and by him that does 283
me this wrong. Terms! Names! "Amaimon" sounds 284
well, "Lucifer" well, "Barbason" well, yet they are 285
devils' additions, the names of fiends. But "Cuckold!" 286
"Wittol!"—"Cuckold!" The devil himself hath not
such a name. Page is an ass, a secure ass. He will trust 288
his wife; he will not be jealous. I will rather trust a
Fleming with my butter, Parson Hugh the Welshman
with my cheese, an Irishman with my aqua vitae 291
bottle, or a thief to walk my ambling gelding, than my 292
wife with herself. Then she plots, then she ruminates,
then she devises; and what they think in their hearts 294
they may effect, they will break their hearts but they
will effect. Heaven be praised for my jealousy! Eleven
o'clock the hour. I will prevent this, detect my wife, be 297
revenged on Falstaff, and laugh at Page. I will about it;
better three hours too soon than a minute too late. Fie,
fie, fie! Cuckold, cuckold, cuckold! *Exit.*

✤

2.3

Enter Caius [and] Rugby.

CAIUS Jack Rugby!

RUGBY Sir?

CAIUS Vat is de clock, Jack?

RUGBY 'Tis past the hour, sir, that Sir Hugh promised to meet.

CAIUS By gar, he has save his soul dat he is no come; he has pray his Pible well dat he is no come. By gar, Jack Rugby, he is dead already if he be come.

RUGBY He is wise, sir. He knew Your Worship would kill him if he came.

219 allowed acknowledged and approved **220 preparations** accomplishments. **225 of it** for it. **amiable** amorous **236 against** directly toward (like looking at the sun). **237 had instance** would have proof and precedent **239 ward** defensive posture in fencing **240 other her defenses** other defenses of hers **248 Want** Lack **254 forth** away from home. **256 speed** succeed. **261 wittolly** willingly cuckolded **261–2 for the which** for which reason **262 well-favored** attractive. **264 harvest home** occasion for reaping a profit. **267 mechanical** i.e., base. (Literally, one engaged in manual occupation). **salt-butter** butter preserved with salt, often old and of inferior quality

269 meteor (An ominous sign.) **270–1 predominate** be in the ascendancy. (An astrological term.) **273 aggravate his style** increase or add to his title (by adding *cuckold*) **275 Epicurean** pleasure-loving **282–3 stand . . . terms** have to put up with being called names **284, 285 Amaimon, Lucifer, Barbason** (Names of devils; they occur in Scot's *Discovery of Witchcraft,* 1584.) **286 additions** titles **288 a secure ass** an overconfident fool. **291 aqua vitae** any strong spirit like brandy. (Irish were known for their drinking, just as Welshmen for eating of cheese and Flemish for love of butter.) **292 to walk . . . gelding** i.e., to exercise my good riding horse. (*Geldings,* or castrated male horses, are gentle and well suited to going at a comfortable pace.) **294 they** i.e., scheming wives **297 prevent** come there before **2.3. Location: A field near Windsor.**

CAIUS By gar, de herring is no dead so as I vill kill him. Take your rapier, Jack. I vill tell you how I vill kill him.

RUGBY Alas, sir, I cannot fence.

CAIUS Villainy, take your rapier.

RUGBY Forbear. Here's company.

[Enter] Page, Shallow, Slender, [and] Host.

HOST Bless thee, bully Doctor!

SHALLOW Save you, Master Doctor Caius!

PAGE Now, good Master Doctor!

SLENDER Give you good morrow, sir.

CAIUS Vat be all you, one, two, tree, four, come for?

HOST To see thee fight, to see thee foin, to see thee traverse; to see thee here, to see thee there; to see thee pass thy punto, thy stock, thy reverse, thy distance, thy montant. Is he dead, my Ethiopian? Is he dead, my Francisco? Ha, bully? What says my Aesculapius, my Galen, my heart of elder, ha? Is he dead, bully stale? Is he dead?

CAIUS By gar, he is de coward jack priest of de vorld. He is not show his face.

HOST Thou art a Castilian King-Urinal. Hector of Greece, my boy!

CAIUS I pray you, bear witness that me have stay six or seven, two, tree hours for him, and he is no come.

SHALLOW He is the wiser man, Master Doctor. He is a curer of souls, and you a curer of bodies. If you should fight, you go against the hair of your professions. Is it not true, Master Page?

PAGE Master Shallow, you have yourself been a great fighter, though now a man of peace.

SHALLOW Bodykins, Master Page, though I now be old and of the peace, if I see a sword out, my finger itches to make one. Though we are justices and doctors and churchmen, Master Page, we have some salt of our youth in us. We are the sons of women, Master Page.

PAGE 'Tis true, Master Shallow.

SHALLOW It will be found so, Master Page.—Master Doctor Caius, I am come to fetch you home. I am sworn of the peace. You have showed yourself a wise physician, and Sir Hugh hath shown himself a wise and patient churchman. You must go with me, Master Doctor.

HOST Pardon, guest Justice. A word, Monsieur Mockwater.

CAIUS Mockvater? Vat is dat?

HOST "Mockwater," in our English tongue, is "valor," bully.

CAIUS By gar, den, I have as mush mockvater as de Englishman. Scurvy jack-dog priest! By gar, me vill cut his ears.

HOST He will clapper-claw thee tightly, bully.

CAIUS Clapper-de-claw? Vat is dat?

HOST That is, he will make thee amends.

CAIUS By gar, me do look he shall clapper-de-claw me, for, by gar, me vill have it.

HOST And I will provoke him to't, or let him wag.

CAIUS Me tank you for dat.

HOST And, moreover, bully—*[aside to the others]* but first, master guest and Master Page, and eke Cavaleiro Slender, go you through the town to Frogmore.

PAGE Sir Hugh is there, is he?

HOST He is there. See what humor he is in, and I will bring the Doctor about by the fields. Will it do well?

SHALLOW We will do it.

PAGE, SHALLOW, AND SLENDER Adieu, good Master Doctor. *[Exeunt Page, Shallow, and Slender.]*

CAIUS *[drawing his rapier]* By gar, me vill kill de priest, for he speak for a jackanape to Anne Page.

HOST Let him die. But first, sheathe thy impatience; throw cold water on thy choler. Go about the fields with me through Frogmore. I will bring thee where Mistress Anne Page is, at a farmhouse a-feasting; and thou shalt woo her. Cried game? Said I well?

CAIUS *[sheathing his rapier]* By gar, me dank you vor dat. By gar, I love you; and I shall procure-a you de good guest: de earl, de knight, de lords, de gentlemen, my patients.

HOST For the which I will be thy adversary toward Anne Page. Said I well?

CAIUS By gar, 'tis good. Vell said.

HOST Let us wag, then.

CAIUS Come at my heels, Jack Rugby. *Exeunt.*

✤

3.1

Enter Evans [and] Simple.

EVANS I pray you now, good Master Slender's servingman, and friend Simple by your name, which way have you looked for Master Caius, that calls himself doctor of physic?

11 no dead so not so dead. (Compare with "dead as a herring.") **14 Villainy** i.e., Villain **17 Save** God save **21 foin** thrust. (A fencing term, like those that follow here.) **22 traverse** move from side to side. **23–4 pass . . . montant** employ your stroke or thrust with the point of the sword, your stoccado or thrust, your backhand stroke, your keeping of the prescribed distance between contestants, your upright thrust. **24 Ethiopian** (An extravagant epithet applied to Doctor Caius, perhaps in acknowledgment of a dark complexion.) **25 Francisco** i.e., Frenchman. **Aesculapius** i.e., doctor. (Literally, Greek god of medicine.) **26 Galen** famous Greek physician. **heart of elder** i.e., opposite of "heart of oak." (The elder has no heart, though Caius, with his halting English, presumably is unaware of the insult.) **27 stale** i.e., doctor. (Literally, "urine," which is used to make medical diagnosis; see also *urinal* in Host's next speech, and *Mockwater,* lines 51–2. A *stale* is also a dupe.) **30 Castilian** i.e., Spanish. (An insulting term in a time of war with Spain, though Caius, with his imperfect English, is presumably oblivious of this. The term also suggests *Castalian* [Folio: Castalion], relating to the sacred spring on Mount Parnassus.) **Urinal** (Comically appropriate to a doctor, who uses urine for diagnosis.) **Hector** chief warrior of ancient Troy (not Greece) **32 me have stay** I have stayed **36 go . . . of** i.e., act contrary to. (Literally, rub hair the wrong way.) **40 Bodykins** i.e., By God's little body **42 make one** join in. **43 salt** savor **44 We . . . women** i.e., We are men. (Proverbial.)

51 guest Justice i.e., a justice of the peace who is a paying guest in my inn. (Said to Shallow.) **51–2 Mockwater** (See the note to line 27, above; said to Caius.) **57 jack-dog** mongrel **59 clapper-claw** thrash. **tightly** soundly **64 wag** go on his way, run for his life. **68 Frogmore** small village near Windsor. **76 for a jackanape** on behalf of an ape, i.e., Slender **81 Cried game?** Have I announced good sport? (A hunting cry.) **86 adversary** (The Host again takes advantage of Caius' poor English; the expected word is "emissary" or "advocate.")
3.1. Location: A field near Frogmore.

SIMPLE Marry, sir, the Petty-ward, the Park-ward, every way; Old Windsor way, and every way but the town way.

EVANS I most fehemently desire you you will also look that way.

SIMPLE I will, sir. *[Going aside.]*

EVANS Pless my soul, how full of cholers I am, and trempling of mind! I shall be glad if he have deceived me. How melancholies I am! I will knog his urinals about his knave's costard when I have good opportunities for the 'ork. Pless my soul! *[He sings.]*

"To shallow rivers, to whose falls
Melodious birds sings madrigals;
There will we make our peds of roses,
And a thousand fragrant posies.
To shallow—"

Mercy on me! I have a great dispositions to cry. *[He sings.]*

"Melodious birds sing madrigals—
Whenas I sat in Pabylon—
And a thousand vagram posies.
To shallow," etc.

[Simple returns.]

SIMPLE Yonder he is, coming this way, Sir Hugh.

EVANS He's welcome. *[He sings.]*

"To shallow rivers, to whose falls—"

God prosper the right! What weapons is he?

SIMPLE No weapons, sir. There comes my master, Master Shallow, and another gentleman, from Frogmore, over the stile, this way.

EVANS Pray you, give me my gown; or else keep it in your arms. *[He reads in a book.]*

[Enter] Page, Shallow, [and] Slender.

SHALLOW How now, Master Parson? Good morrow, good Sir Hugh. Keep a gamester from the dice and a good student from his book, and it is wonderful.

SLENDER *[aside]* Ah, sweet Anne Page!

PAGE God save you, good Sir Hugh!

EVANS God pless you from His mercy sake, all of you!

SHALLOW What, the sword and the Word? Do you study them both, Master Parson?

PAGE And youthful still—in your doublet and hose this raw rheumatic day?

EVANS There is reasons and causes for it.

PAGE We are come to you to do a good office, Master Parson.

EVANS Fery well. What is it?

PAGE Yonder is a most reverend gentleman, who, belike having received wrong by some person, is at most odds with his own gravity and patience that ever you saw.

SHALLOW I have lived fourscore years and upward; I never heard a man of his place, gravity, and learning so wide of his own respect.

EVANS What is he?

PAGE I think you know him: Master Doctor Caius, the renowned French physician.

EVANS Got's will and His passion of my heart! I had as lief you would tell me of a mess of porridge.

PAGE Why?

EVANS He has no more knowledge in Hibbocrates and Galen—and he is a knave besides, a cowardly knave as you would desires to be acquainted withal.

PAGE *[to Shallow]* I warrant you, he's the man should fight with him.

SLENDER *[aside]* Oh, sweet Anne Page!

SHALLOW *[to Page]* It appears so by his weapons. Keep them asunder; here comes Doctor Caius.

[Enter] Host, Caius, [and] Rugby. [Evans and Caius offer to fight.]

PAGE Nay, good Master Parson, keep in your weapon.

SHALLOW So do you, good Master Doctor.

HOST Disarm them and let them question. Let them keep their limbs whole and hack our English. *[Caius and Evans are disarmed.]*

CAIUS *[to Evans]* I pray you, let-a me speak a word with your ear. Vherefore vill you not meet-a me?

EVANS *[aside to Caius]* Pray you, use your patience. *[Aloud]* In good time.

CAIUS By gar, you are de coward, de jack dog, john ape.

EVANS *[aside to Caius]* Pray you, let us not be laughingstocks to other men's humors; I desire you in friendship, and I will one way or other make you amends. *[Aloud]* I will knog your urinal about your knave's cogscomb for missing your meetings and appointments.

CAIUS *Diable!* Jack Rugby—mine Host de Jarteer—have I not stay for him to kill him? Have I not, at de place I did appoint?

EVANS As I am a Christians soul now, look you, this is the place appointed. I'll be judgment by mine Host of the Garter.

HOST Peace, I say, Gallia and Gaul, French and Welsh, soul curer and body curer!

CAIUS Ay, dat is very good, *excellent.*

HOST Peace, I say! Hear mine Host of the Garter. Am I

5 the Petty-ward toward Windsor Petty (or Little) Park. **the Park-ward** toward Windsor Great Park **13 knog** knock **14 costard** i.e., head. (Literally, apple.) **16–25 To shallow rivers,** etc. (Lines from Marlowe's "Come live with me and be my love.") **23 Whenas . . . Pabylon** (An insertion of a line from the metrical Psalms, number 137.) **24 vagram** i.e., vagrant. (But Evans means "fragrant.") **29 is he** is he carrying. **36–7 Keep . . . wonderful** i.e., It's as hard to keep a true student from his book as to keep a gamester from dice. **40 from His mercy sake** (The correct phrase is "for His mercy's sake.") **41 the Word** i.e., the Bible. **43 in . . . hose** i.e., without a cloak, in close-fitting jacket and breeches

50 belike it would seem **55 so . . . respect** i.e., so out of keeping with the gravity and patience that he is respected for (see lines 50–2), having lost control. **59–60 had as lief** would just as soon **62 Hibbocrates** Hippocrates, ancient Greek physician **65 he's** i.e., Evans is. **should** who is supposed to **69.2 *offer*** make as if, prepare. (The stage direction is substantially from the Quarto.) **72 question** talk, discuss. **77 In good time** All in good time. **87 stay** waited **90 judgment** judged **92 Gallia and Gaul** Wales and France

politic? Am I subtle? Am I a Machiavel? Shall I lose my 96
doctor? No, he gives me the potions and the motions. 97
Shall I lose my parson, my priest, my Sir Hugh? No,
he gives me the proverbs and the no-verbs. Give me 99
thy hand, terrestrial; so. Give me thy hand, celestial; 100
so. [*He joins their hands.*] Boys of art, I have deceived 101
you both; I have directed you to wrong places. Your
hearts are mighty, your skins are whole, and let burnt 103
sack be the issue. Come, lay their swords to pawn. 104
Follow me, lads of peace, follow, follow, follow.

SHALLOW Trust me, a mad host. Follow, gentlemen, 106
follow.

SLENDER [*aside*] Oh, sweet Anne Page!

[*Exeunt Shallow, Slender, Page, and Host.*]

CAIUS Ha, do I perceive dat? Have you make-a de sot 109
of us, ha, ha?

EVANS This is well! He has made us his vloutingstog. I 111
desire you that we may be friends; and let us knog our
prains together to be revenge on this same scall, 113
scurvy, cogging companion, the Host of the Garter. 114

CAIUS By gar, with all my heart. He promise to bring
me where is Anne Page. By gar, he deceive me too.

EVANS Well, I will smite his noddles. Pray you, follow. 117

[*Exeunt.*]

3.2

[*Enter*] *Mistress Page* [*and*] *Robin.*

MRS. PAGE Nay, keep your way, little gallant. You were 1
wont to be a follower, but now you are a leader.
Whether had you rather, lead mine eyes or eye your 3
master's heels?

ROBIN I had rather, forsooth, go before you like a man
than follow him like a dwarf.

MRS. PAGE Oh, you are a flattering boy. Now I see you'll
be a courtier.

[*Enter*] *Ford.*

FORD Well met, Mistress Page. Whither go you?

MRS. PAGE Truly, sir, to see your wife. Is she at home?

FORD Ay, and as idle as she may hang together, for 11
want of company. I think if your husbands were dead 12
you two would marry.

MRS. PAGE Be sure of that—two other husbands.

FORD Where had you this pretty weathercock? 15

MRS. PAGE I cannot tell what the dickens his name is
my husband had him of.—What do you call your 17
knight's name, sirrah?

ROBIN Sir John Falstaff.

FORD Sir John Falstaff!

MRS. PAGE He, he. I can never hit on 's name. There is
such a league between my goodman and he! Is your 22
wife at home indeed?

FORD Indeed she is.

MRS. PAGE By your leave, sir. I am sick till I see her.

[*Exeunt Mistress Page and Robin.*]

FORD Has Page any brains? Hath he any eyes? Hath he
any thinking? Sure they sleep; he hath no use of them.
Why, this boy will carry a letter twenty mile as easy as
a cannon will shoot point-blank twelve score. He 29
pieces out his wife's inclination; he gives her folly 30
motion and advantage. And now she's going to my 31
wife, and Falstaff's boy with her. A man may hear this 32
shower sing in the wind. And Falstaff's boy with her! 33
Good plots! They are laid; and our revolted wives share
damnation together. Well, I will take him, then torture 35
my wife, pluck the borrowed veil of modesty from the
so-seeming Mistress Page, divulge Page himself for a
secure and willful Actaeon; and to these violent pro- 38
ceedings all my neighbors shall cry aim. [*A clock* 39
strikes.] The clock gives me my cue, and my assurance 40
bids me search. There I shall find Falstaff. I shall be
rather praised for this than mocked, for it is as positive
as the earth is firm that Falstaff is there. I will go.

[*Enter*] *Page, Shallow, Slender, Host, Evans, Caius,* [*and Rugby*].

SHALLOW, PAGE, ETC Well met, Master Ford.

FORD [*aside*] Trust me, a good knot. [*To them*] I have 45
good cheer at home, and I pray you all go with me. 46

SHALLOW I must excuse myself, Master Ford.

SLENDER And so must I, sir. We have appointed to dine
with Mistress Anne, and I would not break with her 49
for more money than I'll speak of.

SHALLOW We have lingered about a match between
Anne Page and my cousin Slender, and this day we 52
shall have our answer.

SLENDER I hope I have your good will, father Page.

PAGE You have, Master Slender; I stand wholly for you.
But my wife, Master Doctor, is for you altogether.

CAIUS Ay, by gar, and de maid is love-a me. My
nursh-a Quickly tell me so mush.

96 Machiavel i.e., an intriguer, modeled on Niccolò Machiavelli, the Italian political philosopher who symbolized crafty and ruthless ambition to Elizabethans. **97 motions** purges. **99 proverbs . . . no-verbs** i.e., proverbial wisdom and Thou-shalt-not's. **100 terrestrial** i.e., the Doctor, who treats the body **101 art** learning **103–4 burnt sack** heated and mulled wine, as at 2.1.199–200 **104 issue** outcome. **to pawn** as a pledge or surety. **106 Trust me** Believe me. **mad** madcap **109 you** i.e., the Host. **sot** fool **111 vloutingstog** flouting-stock, i.e., laughingstock. **113–14 scall . . . companion** scurvy cheating rascal **117 noddles** head.

3.2. Location: A street in Windsor.

1 keep your way keep on your way (in front of me) **3 Whether** Which of the two **11–12 as idle . . . company** i.e., women as idle as my wife (and you, Mistress Page) may band together for lack of better company.

15 Where . . . weathercock? i.e., Where did you find this sprucely dressed little fellow? (A *weathercock,* literally a weathervane in the shape of rooster, shifts direction quickly, as a young lad might in fashion of dress.) **17 had him of** got him from. **22 league** friendship. **goodman** husband **29 point-blank** in a straight trajectory. **twelve score** i.e., 240 paces. **29–30 He pieces out** Page positively encourages **30 folly** wantonness **31 motion and advantage** encouragement and opportunity. **32–3 hear . . . wind** tell from the rising wind that a storm is coming up, i.e., that trouble is brewing. **35 take him** take him by surprise **38 secure** overconfident. **Actaeon** i.e., horned man, cuckold. (See the note for 2.1.113.) **39 cry aim** applaud. (A term from archery.) **40 assurance** foreknowledge **45 knot** group, company. **46 cheer** fare **49 break with** break my promise to **52 cousin** kinsman, i.e., nephew

HOST What say you to young Master Fenton? He capers, he dances, he has eyes of youth, he writes verses, he speaks holiday, he smells April and May. He will carry't, he will carry't. 'Tis in his buttons he will carry't.

PAGE Not by my consent, I promise you. The gentleman is of no having. He kept company with the wild Prince and Poins. He is of too high a region; he knows too much. No, he shall not knit a knot in his fortunes with the finger of my substance. If he take her, let him take her simply. The wealth I have waits on my consent, and my consent goes not that way.

FORD I beseech you heartily, some of you go home with me to dinner. Besides your cheer, you shall have sport: I will show you a monster. Master Doctor, you shall go. So shall you, Master Page, and you, Sir Hugh.

SHALLOW Well, fare you well. We shall have the freer wooing at Master Page's.

[*Exeunt Shallow and Slender.*]

CAIUS Go home, John Rugby. I come anon.

[*Exit Rugby.*]

HOST Farewell, my hearts. I will to my honest knight Falstaff, and drink canary with him. [*Exit.*]

FORD [*aside*] I think I shall drink in pipe-wine first with him; I'll make him dance.—Will you go, gentles?

ALL Have with you to see this monster. *Exeunt.*

3.3

Enter Mistress Ford [*and*] *Mistress Page.*

MRS. FORD What, John! What, Robert!

MRS. PAGE Quickly, quickly! Is the buck basket—

MRS. FORD I warrant. What, Robert, I say!

[*Enter*] *Servants* [*with a great basket*].

MRS. PAGE Come, come, come.

MRS. FORD Here, set it down.

MRS. PAGE Give your men the charge. We must be brief.

MRS. FORD Marry, as I told you before, John and Robert, be ready here hard by in the brewhouse; and when I suddenly call you, come forth, and without any pause or staggering take this basket on your shoulders. That done, trudge with it in all haste, and carry it among the whitsters in Datchet Mead, and there empty it in the muddy ditch close by the Thames' side.

MRS. PAGE You will do it?

MRS. FORD I ha' told them over and over; they lack no direction.—Begone, and come when you are called.

[*Exeunt Servants.*]

MRS. PAGE Here comes little Robin.

[*Enter*] *Robin.*

MRS. FORD How now, my eyas musket, what news with you?

ROBIN My master, Sir John, is come in at your back door, Mistress Ford, and requests your company.

MRS. PAGE You little Jack-a-Lent, have you been true to us?

ROBIN Ay, I'll be sworn. My master knows not of your being here and hath threatened to put me into everlasting liberty if I tell you of it; for he swears he'll turn me away.

MRS. PAGE Thou'rt a good boy. This secrecy of thine shall be a tailor to thee and shall make thee a new doublet and hose.—I'll go hide me.

MRS. FORD Do so.—Go tell thy master I am alone.

[*Exit Robin.*]

Mistress Page, remember you your cue.

MRS. PAGE I warrant thee. If I do not act it, hiss me.

[*Exit.*]

MRS. FORD Go to, then. We'll use this unwholesome humidity, this gross watery pumpkin. We'll teach him to know turtles from jays.

[*Enter*] *Falstaff.*

FALSTAFF "Have I caught thee, my heavenly jewel?" Why, now let me die, for I have lived long enough. This is the period of my ambition. Oh, this blessed hour!

MRS. FORD O sweet Sir John!

FALSTAFF Mistress Ford, I cannot cog, I cannot prate, Mistress Ford. Now shall I sin in my wish: I would thy husband were dead. I'll speak it before the best lord: I would make thee my lady.

MRS. FORD I your lady, Sir John? Alas, I should be a pitiful lady!

FALSTAFF Let the court of France show me such another. I see how thine eye would emulate the diamond. Thou hast the right arched beauty of the brow that becomes the ship-tire, the tire-valiant, or any tire of Venetian admittance.

MRS. FORD A plain kerchief, Sir John. My brows become nothing else, nor that well neither.

61 holiday in a fashion appropriate to a holiday, elegantly **62 carry't** carry it off **62–3 'Tis . . . carry't** i.e., He's sure to succeed. **65 having** estate. **65–6 wild . . . Poins** i.e., Prince Hal and Poins of *1 Henry IV* and *2 Henry IV.* **66 region** social status **67 knit a knot in** mend **69 simply** i.e., by herself, without a dowry. **waits on** is subject to **75–6 We shall . . . Page's** i.e., Slender's wooing of Anne will be less constrained if Caius, Evans, and Anne's father are not there. **78 my hearts** my hearties. **79 canary** a sweet wine from the Canary Islands. (*Canary* is also a dance, and this sense of the word may inspire Ford's metaphor of dancing in the next line.) **80 pipe-wine** wine from the cask, or wood. (With a pun on *pipe* as a musical instrument played for the *dance,* line 81. See next note.) **81 I'll . . . dance** i.e., I'll make Falstaff jump, make it hot for him. **gentles** gentlemen. **82 Have with you** We'll go with you

3.3. Location: Ford's house.

1 What i.e., Move quickly **2 buck basket** basket for soiled clothes. (*Bucking* means "washing.") **6 charge** instructions. **8 hard by** close at hand

12 whitsters bleachers of linen. **Datchet Mead** a meadow along the Thames, near Windsor Park **18 eyas musket** young male sparrow hawk **22 Jack-a-Lent** figure of a man set up during Lent to be pelted by boys, a puppet **26 liberty** i.e., unemployment **27 turn me away** dismiss me. **34 use** trick **36 turtles** turtledoves, models of constancy in love. **jays** i.e., loose women. **37 Have . . . jewel?** (From Sir Philip Sidney's *Astrophel and Stella.*) **39 period** goal **41 cog** deceive, flatter. (Also in line 63.) **43 I'll speak . . . lord** I will proclaim this publicly in the presence of the most distinguished lord in England **49–50 that . . . ship-tire** that suits the elaborate woman's headdress shaped to resemble a ship **50 tire-valiant** (An invented word seemingly describing a headdress of daunting proportions.) **51 admittance** fashion. **52–3 become** suit

FALSTAFF By the Lord, thou art a tyrant to say so. Thou wouldst make an absolute courtier, and the firm fixture of thy foot would give an excellent motion to thy gait in a semicircled farthingale. I see what thou wert, if Fortune thy foe were not, Nature thy friend. Come, thou canst not hide it.

MRS. FORD Believe me, there's no such thing in me.

FALSTAFF What made me love thee? Let that persuade thee there's something extraordinary in thee. Come, I cannot cog and say thou art this and that, like a many of these lisping hawthorn buds, that come like women in men's apparel and smell like Bucklersbury in simple time. I cannot. But I love thee, none but thee; and thou deserv'st it.

MRS. FORD Do not betray me, sir. I fear you love Mistress Page.

FALSTAFF Thou mightst as well say I love to walk by the Counter gate, which is as hateful to me as the reek of a limekiln.

MRS. FORD Well, heaven knows how I love you, and you shall one day find it.

FALSTAFF Keep in that mind. I'll deserve it.

MRS. FORD Nay, I must tell you, so you do, or else I could not be in that mind.

[*Enter Robin.*]

ROBIN Mistress Ford, Mistress Ford! Here's Mistress Page at the door, sweating and blowing and looking wildly, and would needs speak with you presently.

FALSTAFF She shall not see me. I will ensconce me behind the arras.

MRS. FORD Pray you, do so. She's a very tattling woman. [*Falstaff hides himself behind the arras.*]

[*Enter Mistress Page.*]

What's the matter? How now!

MRS. PAGE Oh, Mistress Ford, what have you done? You're shamed, you're overthrown, you're undone forever!

MRS. FORD What's the matter, good Mistress Page?

MRS. PAGE Oh, welladay, Mistress Ford, having an honest man to your husband, to give him such cause of suspicion!

MRS. FORD What cause of suspicion?

MRS. PAGE What cause of suspicion? Out upon you! How am I mistook in you!

MRS. FORD Why, alas, what's the matter?

MRS. PAGE Your husband's coming hither, woman, with all the officers in Windsor, to search for a gentleman that he says is here now in the house, by your consent, to take an ill advantage of his absence. You are undone.

MRS. FORD 'Tis not so, I hope.

MRS. PAGE Pray heaven it be not so, that you have such a man here! But 'tis most certain your husband's coming, with half Windsor at his heels, to search for such a one. I come before to tell you. If you know yourself clear, why, I am glad of it. But if you have a friend here, convey, convey him out. Be not amazed! Call all your senses to you; defend your reputation, or bid farewell to your good life forever.

MRS. FORD What shall I do? There is a gentleman, my dear friend; and I fear not mine own shame so much as his peril. I had rather than a thousand pound he were out of the house.

MRS. PAGE For shame! Never stand "you had rather" and "you had rather." Your husband's here at hand! Bethink you of some conveyance. In the house you cannot hide him. Oh, how have you deceived me! Look, here is a basket. If he be of any reasonable stature, he may creep in here; and throw foul linen upon him, as if it were going to bucking. Or—it is whiting time—send him by your two men to Datchet Mead.

MRS. FORD He's too big to go in there. What shall I do?

FALSTAFF [*coming forward*] Let me see't, let me see't, oh, let me see't! I'll in, I'll in. Follow your friend's counsel. I'll in.

MRS. PAGE What, Sir John Falstaff? [*Aside to him*] Are these your letters, knight?

FALSTAFF [*aside to her*] I love thee. Help me away. Let me creep in here. I'll never—

[*He gets into the basket; they cover him with foul linen.*]

MRS. PAGE Help to cover your master, boy.—Call your men, Mistress Ford.—You dissembling knight!

MRS. FORD What, John! Robert! John!

[*Enter Servants.*]

Go take up these clothes here quickly. Where's the cowlstaff? Look how you drumble! Carry them to the laundress in Datchet Mead. Quickly! Come.

[*The Servants lift the basket and start to leave.*]

[*Enter*] *Ford, Page, Caius,* [*and*] *Evans.*

FORD Pray you, come near. If I suspect without cause, why then make sport at me. Then let me be your jest; I deserve it.—How now? Whither bear you this?

SERVANT To the laundress, forsooth.

MRS. FORD Why, what have you to do whither they bear it? You were best meddle with buck washing.

55 absolute perfect **55–6 the firm . . . foot** your firm and assured way of putting your feet on the ground **57 semicircled farthingale** petticoat with hoops at the sides and back but not extending in front. **57–8 I see . . . friend** i.e., I can imagine how impressive you would be at court if Fortune had not cast you in a lowly lot with only your natural beauty to assist you. ("Fortune My Foe" is the name of a popular ballad tune.) **64 hawthorn buds** i.e., young fops **65 Bucklersbury** a London street inhabited by herbalists **65–6 simple time** midsummer, the time when apothecaries were supplied with simples or herbs. **68 betray** deceive **71 Counter gate** gate of the Counter or debtors' prison in London **79 blowing** puffing **80 presently** at once. **81 ensconce me** hide myself **82 arras** tapestry wall hanging. **90 welladay** alas **91 to** as **94 Out upon you!** i.e., For shame!

107 clear clear of blame **108 friend** lover. **amazed** stunned, bewildered. **110 your good life** your respectability **115 stand** lose time over **117 conveyance** means of conveying him. **121 bucking** washing. **whiting time** bleaching time **135 cowlstaff** pole on which a "cowl" or basket is carried between two persons. **drumble** are sluggish. **142 buck washing** washing clothes. (But Ford puns on *buck* in the sense of "horned male deer," resembling the cuckold, and also of "copulating.")

FORD Buck? I would I could wash myself of the buck! Buck, buck, buck! Ay, buck! I warrant you, buck—and of the season too, it shall appear.

[*Exeunt Servants with the basket.*]

Gentlemen, I have dreamed tonight; I'll tell you my dream. Here, here, here be my keys. Ascend my chambers. Search, seek, find out. I'll warrant we'll unkennel the fox. Let me stop this way first. [*He locks the door.*] So, now uncape.

PAGE Good Master Ford, be contented. You wrong yourself too much.

FORD True, Master Page. Up, gentlemen, you shall see sport anon. Follow me, gentlemen. [*Exit.*]

EVANS This is fery fantastical humors and jealousies.

CAIUS By gar, 'tis no the fashion of France. It is not jealous in France.

PAGE Nay, follow him, gentlemen. See the issue of his search. [*Exeunt Page, Caius, and Evans.*]

MRS. PAGE Is there not a double excellency in this?

MRS. FORD I know not which pleases me better, that my husband is deceived, or Sir John.

MRS. PAGE What a taking was he in when your husband asked who was in the basket!

MRS. FORD I am half afraid he will have need of washing, so throwing him into the water will do him a benefit.

MRS. PAGE Hang him, dishonest rascal! I would all of the same strain were in the same distress.

MRS. FORD I think my husband hath some special suspicion of Falstaff's being here, for I never saw him so gross in his jealousy till now.

MRS. PAGE I will lay a plot to try that, and we will yet have more tricks with Falstaff. His dissolute disease will scarce obey this medicine.

MRS. FORD Shall we send that foolish carrion Mistress Quickly to him, and excuse his throwing into the water, and give him another hope, to betray him to another punishment?

MRS. PAGE We will do it. Let him be sent for tomorrow eight o'clock, to have amends.

[*Enter Ford, Page, Caius, and Evans.*]

FORD I cannot find him. Maybe the knave bragged of that he could not compass.

MRS. PAGE [*aside to Mistress Ford*] Heard you that?

MRS. FORD You use me well, Master Ford, do you?

FORD Ay, I do so.

MRS. FORD Heaven make you better than your thoughts!

FORD Amen!

MRS. PAGE You do yourself mighty wrong, Master Ford.

FORD Ay, ay, I must bear it.

EVANS If there be anybody in the house, and in the chambers, and in the coffers, and in the presses, heaven forgive my sins at the day of judgment!

CAIUS By gar, nor I too. There is nobodies.

PAGE Fie, fie, Master Ford, are you not ashamed? What spirit, what devil suggests this imagination? I would not ha' your distemper in this kind for the wealth of Windsor Castle.

FORD 'Tis my fault, Master Page. I suffer for it.

EVANS You suffer for a pad conscience. Your wife is as honest a 'omans as I will desires among five thousand, and five hundred too.

CAIUS By gar, I see 'tis an honest woman.

FORD Well, I promised you a dinner. Come, come, walk in the park. I pray you, pardon me. I will hereafter make known to you why I have done this.—Come, wife, come, Mistress Page, I pray you, pardon me. Pray, heartily, pardon me.

PAGE Let's go in, gentlemen; but, trust me, we'll mock him. I do invite you tomorrow morning to my house to breakfast. After, we'll a-birding together. I have a fine hawk for the bush. Shall it be so?

FORD Anything.

EVANS If there is one, I shall make two in the company.

CAIUS If there be one or two, I shall make-a the turd.

FORD Pray you, go, Master Page.

[*Exeunt Ford and Page.*]

EVANS [*to Caius*] I pray you now, remembrance tomorrow on the lousy knave, mine Host.

CAIUS Dat is good, by gar; with all my heart!

EVANS A lousy knave, to have his gibes and his mockeries! *Exeunt.*

3.4

Enter Fenton [*and*] *Anne Page.*

FENTON
I see I cannot get thy father's love;
Therefore no more turn me to him, sweet Nan.

ANNE
Alas, how then?

FENTON Why, thou must be thyself.
He doth object I am too great of birth,
And that, my state being galled with my expense,
I seek to heal it only by his wealth.
Besides these, other bars he lays before me—
My riots past, my wild societies;

145 of the season in the rutting season **146 tonight** last night **149 unkennel** dislodge, unearth **150 uncape** unkennel (as in line 149), dislodge, uncase (?). **151–2 wrong yourself** put yourself in the wrong **153 True** (Ford may mean that he is indeed too much wronged, or else placates Page by seeming to agree with him.) **158 issue** outcome **163 taking** fright **165–6 will . . . washing** i.e., will have befouled himself in fright **169 strain** character, kind **173 try** test **175 obey this medicine** i.e., yield to this first dose. **176 carrion** rotten old flesh, bawd (?) **177 excuse** make excuses for **183 that** that which. **compass** accomplish.

192 presses cupboards, clothes presses **196 suggests** incites, prompts you to. **imagination** wild suspicion. **197 distemper . . . kind** mental disorder of this sort **205 walk . . . park** i.e., stroll till dinnertime. **209 go in** i.e., go in to dinner at the proper time **211 a-birding** go hunting small birds of the bush with a hawk and guns **212 for the bush** for driving the small birds into the bush (where they can be shot). **217–18 remembrance . . . Host** (A seeming allusion to the conversation at the end of 3.1 and to the plot carried out in 4.5.)
3.4. Location: Before Page's house.
1 love good will **2 turn** direct **3 be thyself** be your own mistress. **5 my state . . . expense** my estate being wasted away by my extravagance **8 societies** companionships

And tells me 'tis a thing impossible
I should love thee but as a property.

ANNE Maybe he tells you true.

FENTON
No, heaven so speed me in my time to come!
Albeit I will confess thy father's wealth
Was the first motive that I wooed thee, Anne,
Yet, wooing thee, I found thee of more value
Than stamps in gold or sums in sealèd bags;
And 'tis the very riches of thyself
That now I aim at.

ANNE Gentle Master Fenton,
Yet seek my father's love; still seek it, sir.
If opportunity and humblest suit
Cannot attain it, why, then—hark you hither.
[*They converse apart.*]

[*Enter*] *Shallow, Slender,* [*and Mistress*] *Quickly.*

SHALLOW Break their talk, Mistress Quickly. My kinsman shall speak for himself.

SLENDER I'll make a shaft or a bolt on't. 'Slid, 'tis but venturing.

SHALLOW Be not dismayed.

SLENDER No, she shall not dismay me. I care not for that, but that I am afeard.

QUICKLY [*to Anne*] Hark ye, Master Slender would speak a word with you.

ANNE
I come to him. [*Aside*] This is my father's choice.
Oh, what a world of vile ill-favored faults
Looks handsome in three hundred pounds a year!

QUICKLY And how does good Master Fenton? Pray you, a word with you. [*She draws him aside.*]

SHALLOW She's coming. To her, coz! O boy, thou hadst a father!

SLENDER I had a father, Mistress Anne; my uncle can tell you good jests of him.—Pray you, uncle, tell Mistress Anne the jest how my father stole two geese out of a pen, good uncle.

SHALLOW Mistress Anne, my cousin loves you.

SLENDER Ay, that I do, as well as I love any woman in Gloucestershire.

SHALLOW He will maintain you like a gentlewoman.

SLENDER Ay, that I will, come cut and longtail, under the degree of a squire.

SHALLOW He will make you a hundred and fifty pounds jointure.

ANNE Good Master Shallow, let him woo for himself.

SHALLOW Marry, I thank you for it; I thank you for that good comfort.—She calls you, coz. I'll leave you. [*He moves aside.*]

ANNE Now, Master Slender—

SLENDER Now, good Mistress Anne—

ANNE What is your will?

SLENDER My will? 'Od's heartlings, that's a pretty jest indeed! I ne'er made my will yet, I thank heaven; I am not such a sickly creature, I give heaven praise.

ANNE I mean, Master Slender, what would you with me?

SLENDER Truly, for mine own part, I would little or nothing with you. Your father and my uncle hath made motions. If it be my luck, so; if not, happy man be his dole! They can tell you how things go better than I can. You may ask your father. Here he comes.

[*Enter*] *Page* [*and*] *Mistress Page.*

PAGE
Now, Master Slender. Love him, daughter Anne.—
Why, how now? What does Master Fenton here?
You wrong me, sir, thus still to haunt my house.
I told you, sir, my daughter is disposed of.

FENTON
Nay, Master Page, be not impatient.

MRS. PAGE
Good Master Fenton, come not to my child.

PAGE She is no match for you.

FENTON Sir, will you hear me?

PAGE No, good Master Fenton.
Come, Master Shallow; come, son Slender, in.—
Knowing my mind, you wrong me, Master Fenton.
[*Exeunt Page, Shallow, and Slender.*]

QUICKLY [*to Fenton*] Speak to Mistress Page.

FENTON
Good Mistress Page, for that I love your daughter
In such a righteous fashion as I do,
Perforce, against all checks, rebukes, and manners
I must advance the colors of my love
And not retire. Let me have your good will.

ANNE Good mother, do not marry me to yond fool.

MRS. PAGE I mean it not; I seek you a better husband.

QUICKLY [*aside to Anne*] That's my master, Master Doctor.

ANNE
Alas, I had rather be set quick i'th' earth
And bowled to death with turnips!

MRS. PAGE
Come, trouble not yourself. Good Master Fenton,
I will not be your friend nor enemy.
My daughter will I question how she loves you,
And, as I find her, so am I affected.

12 heaven . . . come i.e., as I hope to be saved. **speed** prosper **13 Albeit** Although **16 stamps in gold** gold coins **22 Break** Interrupt **24 I'll . . . on't** i.e., I'll try it one way or another. (A *shaft* is a slender arrow; a *bolt,* a thick and blunt one.) **'Slid** By his (God's) eyelid **28 but . . . afeard** except that I am afraid. (Slender evidently doesn't understand what *dismayed* means.) **32 ill-favored** unattractive **36–7 thou hadst a father** i.e., remember that your father wooed a woman; be like him. (But Slender misses the point.) **42 cousin** i.e., kinsman **46 come . . . longtail** i.e., come what may. (Literally, horses or dogs with docked and long tails, i.e., all sorts.) **46–7 under . . . squire** (Slender promises to provide Anne with the lifestyle to which squires are entitled. A squire is here a landed gentleman, often a Justice of the Peace.) **48 make** give, assure **49 jointure** settlement in the marriage contract providing for the wife's widowhood.

56 'Od's heartlings By God's little heart **63 motions** proposals. **so** well and good. **63–4 happy . . . dole** i.e., may whoever succeeds with you be happy. (Literally, may his lot in life be that of a happy man.) **78 for that** because **80 checks** reproofs. **manners** usage, (hostile) behavior **81 advance the colors** raise high the standard (as in anticipation of battle) **84 mean** intend **86 quick** alive **87 bowled** i.e., pelted with turnips as bowling balls **91 affected** inclined.

Till then farewell, sir. She must needs go in;
Her father will be angry.

FENTON
Farewell, gentle mistress. Farewell, Nan.
[Exeunt Mistress Page and Anne.]

QUICKLY This is my doing, now. "Nay," said I, "will you cast away your child on a fool, and a physician? Look on Master Fenton." This is my doing.

FENTON
I thank thee; and I pray thee, once tonight
Give my sweet Nan this ring. There's for thy pains.
[He gives a ring and money.]

QUICKLY Now heaven send thee good fortune!
[Exit Fenton.]
A kind heart he hath. A woman would run through fire and water for such a kind heart. But yet I would my master had Mistress Anne; or I would Master Slender had her; or, in sooth, I would Master Fenton had her. I will do what I can for them all three; for so I have promised, and I'll be as good as my word—but speciously for Master Fenton. Well, I must of another errand to Sir John Falstaff from my two mistresses. What a beast am I to slack it! *Exit.*

3.5

Enter Falstaff.

FALSTAFF Bardolph, I say!

[Enter] Bardolph.

BARDOLPH Here, sir.

FALSTAFF Go fetch me a quart of sack; put a toast in't.
[Exit Bardolph.]
Have I lived to be carried in a basket, like a barrow of butcher's offal, and to be thrown in the Thames? Well, if I be served such another trick, I'll have my brains ta'en out and buttered, and give them to a dog for a New Year's gift. The rogues slighted me into the river with as little remorse as they would have drowned a blind bitch's puppies, fifteen i'th' litter! And you may know by my size that I have a kind of alacrity in sinking; if the bottom were as deep as hell, I should down. I had been drowned, but that the shore was shelvy and shallow—a death that I abhor; for the water swells a man, and what a thing should I have been when I had been swelled! I should have been a mountain of mummy.

[Enter Bardolph with sack.]

BARDOLPH Here's Mistress Quickly, sir, to speak with you.

FALSTAFF Come, let me pour in some sack to the Thames water, for my belly's as cold as if I had swallowed snowballs for pills to cool the reins. *[He drinks.]* Call her in.

BARDOLPH Come in, woman!

[Enter Mistress] Quickly.

QUICKLY By your leave; I cry you mercy. Give Your Worship good morrow.

FALSTAFF *[to Bardolph]* Take away these chalices. Go brew me a pottle of sack finely.

BARDOLPH With eggs, sir?

FALSTAFF Simple of itself. I'll no pullet sperm in my brewage. *[Exit Bardolph.]*
How now?

QUICKLY Marry, sir, I come to Your Worship from Mistress Ford.

FALSTAFF Mistress Ford? I have had ford enough. I was thrown into the ford. I have my belly full of ford.

QUICKLY Alas the day, good heart, that was not her fault. She does so take on with her men; they mistook their erection.

FALSTAFF So did I mine, to build upon a foolish woman's promise.

QUICKLY Well, she laments, sir, for it, that it would yearn your heart to see it. Her husband goes this morning a-birding. She desires you once more to come to her, between eight and nine. I must carry her word quickly. She'll make you amends, I warrant you.

FALSTAFF Well, I will visit her; tell her so. And bid her think what a man is. Let her consider his frailty, and then judge of my merit.

QUICKLY I will tell her.

FALSTAFF Do so. Between nine and ten, say'st thou?

QUICKLY Eight and nine, sir.

FALSTAFF Well, begone. I will not miss her.

QUICKLY Peace be with you, sir. *[Exit.]*

FALSTAFF I marvel I hear not of Master Brook; he sent me word to stay within. I like his money well. Oh, here he comes.

[Enter] Ford [disguised].

FORD Bless you, sir!

FALSTAFF Now, Master Brook, you come to know what hath passed between me and Ford's wife?

FORD That, indeed, Sir John, is my business.

FALSTAFF Master Brook, I will not lie to you. I was at her house the hour she appointed me.

FORD And sped you, sir?

FALSTAFF Very ill-favoredly, Master Brook.

98 once sometime **107 speciously** (For "specially.") **107–8 must of** must undertake
3.5. Location: The Garter Inn.
3 toast piece of toast **5 barrow** wheelbarrowful **8 slighted me** dumped me heedlessly **9 remorse** compunction **10 a blind bitch's puppies** a bitch's puppies, blind at birth **13 down** sink. **14 shore** bottom near the edge. **17 mummy** dead flesh.

22 reins kidneys. **25 cry you mercy** beg your pardon. **27 chalices** (A lofty name for drinking cups.) **27–8 Go . . . finely** Go fix me a two-quart measure of sack (a sweet white wine) tastefully brewed. (*Brew* and *brewage*, lines 28 and 31, signify that such a drink might well have been heated and spiced, perhaps with ginger and with other possible ingredients as well, though on this occasion Falstaff declines the offer of eggs.) **30 Simple of itself** Unadulterated. **I'll** I'll have **35 ford** i.e., river, stream. (Literally, a shallow place in the river where one may cross.) **38 take on with** berate, scold **39 erection** (Blunder for "direction"; Falstaff plays bawdily on her malapropism.) **42 that** so that **43 yearn** grieve **48 his** i.e., man's **53 miss** fail **64 sped you** did you succeed **65 ill-favoredly** badly

FORD How so, sir? Did she change her determination?

FALSTAFF No, Master Brook, but the peaking cornuto her husband, Master Brook, dwelling in a continual larum of jealousy, comes me in the instant of our encounter, after we had embraced, kissed, protested, and, as it were, spoke the prologue of our comedy; and at his heels a rabble of his companions, thither provoked and instigated by his distemper, and, forsooth, to search his house for his wife's love.

FORD What, while you were there?

FALSTAFF While I was there.

FORD And did he search for you, and could not find you?

FALSTAFF You shall hear. As good luck would have it, comes in one Mistress Page, gives intelligence of Ford's approach, and, in her invention and Ford's wife's distraction, they conveyed me into a buck basket.

FORD A buck basket?

FALSTAFF By the Lord, a buck basket! Rammed me in with foul shirts and smocks, socks, foul stockings, greasy napkins, that, Master Brook, there was the rankest compound of villainous smell that ever offended nostril.

FORD And how long lay you there?

FALSTAFF Nay, you shall hear, Master Brook, what I have suffered to bring this woman to evil for your good. Being thus crammed in the basket, a couple of Ford's knaves, his hinds, were called forth by their mistress to carry me in the name of foul clothes to Datchet Lane. They took me on their shoulders, met the jealous knave their master in the door, who asked them once or twice what they had in their basket. I quaked for fear lest the lunatic knave would have searched it; but fate, ordaining he should be a cuckold, held his hand. Well, on went he for a search, and away went I for foul clothes. But mark the sequel, Master Brook. I suffered the pangs of three several deaths: first, an intolerable fright to be detected with a jealous rotten bellwether; next, to be compassed, like a good bilbo, in the circumference of a peck, hilt to point, heel to head; and then, to be stopped in, like a strong distillation, with stinking clothes that fretted in their own grease. Think of that—a man of my kidney. Think of that—that am as subject to heat as butter; a man of continual dissolution and thaw. It was a miracle to scape suffocation. And in the height of this bath, when I was more than half stewed in grease, like a Dutch dish, to be thrown into the Thames and cooled, glowing hot, in that surge, like a horseshoe! Think of that—hissing hot—think of that, Master Brook!

FORD In good sadness, sir, I am sorry that for my sake you have suffered all this. My suit then is desperate; you'll undertake her no more?

FALSTAFF Master Brook, I will be thrown into Etna, as I have been into Thames, ere I will leave her thus. Her husband is this morning gone a-birding. I have received from her another embassy of meeting. Twixt eight and nine is the hour, Master Brook.

FORD 'Tis past eight already, sir.

FALSTAFF Is it? I will then address me to my appointment. Come to me at your convenient leisure, and you shall know how I speed; and the conclusion shall be crowned with your enjoying her. Adieu. You shall have her, Master Brook; Master Brook, you shall cuckold Ford. [*Exit.*]

FORD Hum! Ha! Is this a vision? Is this a dream? Do I sleep? Master Ford, awake! Awake, Master Ford! There's a hole made in your best coat, Master Ford. This 'tis to be married! This 'tis to have linen and buck baskets! Well, I will proclaim myself what I am. I will now take the lecher. He is at my house. He cannot scape me. 'Tis impossible he should. He cannot creep into a halfpenny purse, nor into a pepperbox. But, lest the devil that guides him should aid him, I will search impossible places. Though what I am I cannot avoid, yet to be what I would not shall not make me tame. If I have horns to make one mad, let the proverb go with me: I'll be horn-mad. *Exit.*

4.1

Enter Mistress Page, [*Mistress*] *Quickly,* [*and*] *William.*

MRS. PAGE Is he at Master Ford's already, think'st thou?

QUICKLY Sure he is by this, or will be presently. But truly he is very courageous mad about his throwing into the water. Mistress Ford desires you to come suddenly.

MRS. PAGE I'll be with her by and by. I'll but bring my young man here to school.

[*Enter Sir Hugh*] *Evans.*

Look where his master comes. 'Tis a playing day, I see.—How now, Sir Hugh, no school today?

66 change her determination change her mind. **67 peaking cornuto** sneaking horned person, i.e., cuckold **69 larum** i.e., state of surprise and fear. **comes me** comes. (*Me* is used colloquially.) **70 protested** i.e., solemnly swore our vows of love **85 that** so that **92 hinds** servants **94 took . . . shoulders** i.e., shouldered the heavy basket by means of a cowlstaff. (See 3.3.135.) **101 several** distinct **102 with** by **103 bellwether** castrated or old ram, leader of a flock (provided with a noisy bell and horned like a cuckold). **compassed** (1) encompassed, surrounded (2) bent into a circle **104 bilbo** finely tempered and flexible sword of Bilbao in Spain. **peck** container holding a quarter of a bushel; i.e., a very small space. **hilt to point** (Falstaff is bent over, head to toes, like a fine Spanish sword that could be bent thus without breaking.) **105 stopped** shut, stoppered **106 fretted** fermented, stewed **107 kidney** temperament, constitution. **109 dissolution** liquefaction

115 good sadness all seriousness. **118 Etna** volcano in Sicily **121 embassy** message **124 address me to** prepare myself for, betake myself to **132 There's . . . coat** (A proverb warning of unseen dangers and of hidden faults that may come to light.) **134 what I am** i.e., a cuckold. **135 take** apprehend **137 halfpenny purse** small purse for small coins **139–41 Though . . . tame** i.e., Though I cannot avoid being a cuckold, I will not be so complacently; I won't take it lying down. **142 horn-mad** frenzied like a horned animal in rutting season. (As at 1.4.45.)
4.1. Location: A street in Windsor.
3 courageous (For "outrageously" or "ragingly"?) **5 suddenly** at once. **8 playing day** holiday

EVANS No. Master Slender is let the boys leave to play.

QUICKLY Blessing of his heart!

MRS. PAGE Sir Hugh, my husband says my son profits nothing in the world at his book. I pray you, ask him some questions in his accidence.

EVANS Come hither, William. Hold up your head. Come.

MRS. PAGE Come on, sirrah, hold up your head. Answer your master. Be not afraid.

EVANS William, how many numbers is in nouns?

WILLIAM Two.

QUICKLY Truly, I thought there had been one number more, because they say "'Od's nouns."

EVANS Peace your tattlings!—What is "fair," William?

WILLIAM *Pulcher.*

QUICKLY Polecats? There are fairer things than polecats, sure.

EVANS You are a very simplicity 'oman. I pray you, peace.—What is *lapis,* William?

WILLIAM A stone.

EVANS And what is "a stone," William?

WILLIAM A pebble.

EVANS No, it is *lapis.* I pray you, remember in your prain.

WILLIAM *Lapis.*

EVANS That is a good William. What is he, William, that does lend articles?

WILLIAM Articles are borrowed of the pronoun, and be thus declined, *singulariter, nominativo, hic, haec, hoc.*

EVANS *Nominativo, hig, hag, hog.* Pray you, mark: *genitivo, huius.* Well, what is your accusative case?

WILLIAM *Accusativo, hinc.*

EVANS I pray you, have your remembrance, child. *Accusativo, hung, hang, hog.*

QUICKLY "Hang-hog" is Latin for bacon, I warrant you.

EVANS Leave you prabbles, 'oman.—What is the focative case, William?

WILLIAM O—*vocativo,* O.

EVANS Remember, William, focative is *caret.*

QUICKLY And that's a good root.

EVANS 'Oman, forbear.

MRS. PAGE [*to Mistress Quickly*] Peace!

EVANS What is your genitive case plural, William?

WILLIAM Genitive case?

EVANS Ay.

WILLIAM *Genitivo—horum, harum, horum.*

QUICKLY Vengeance of Jenny's case! Fie on her! Never name her, child, if she be a whore.

EVANS For shame, 'oman!

QUICKLY You do ill to teach the child such words. He teaches him to hick and to hack, which they'll do fast enough of themselves, and to call "whorum." Fie upon you!

EVANS 'Oman, art thou lunatics? Hast thou no understandings for thy cases and the numbers of the genders? Thou art as foolish Christian creatures as I would desires.

MRS. PAGE [*to Mistress Quickly*] Prithee, hold thy peace.

EVANS Show me now, William, some declensions of your pronouns.

WILLIAM Forsooth, I have forgot.

EVANS It is *qui, quae, quod.* If you forget your *qui's,* your *quae's,* and your *quod's,* you must be preeches. Go your ways and play, go.

MRS. PAGE He is a better scholar than I thought he was.

EVANS He is a good sprag memory. Farewell, Mistress Page.

MRS. PAGE Adieu, good Sir Hugh. [*Exit Sir Hugh.*]
Get you home, boy. [*Exit William.*]
Come, we stay too long. *Exeunt.*

✤

4.2

Enter Falstaff [*and*] *Mistress Ford.*

FALSTAFF Mistress Ford, your sorrow hath eaten up my sufferance. I see you are obsequious in your love, and I profess requital to a hair's breadth, not only, Mistress Ford, in the simple office of love, but in all the accoutrement, complement, and ceremony of it. But are you sure of your husband now?

MRS. FORD He's a-birding, sweet Sir John.

MRS. PAGE [*within*] What ho, gossip Ford! What ho!

MRS. FORD Step into the chamber, Sir John.

[*Exit Falstaff.*]

[*Enter*] *Mistress Page.*

MRS. PAGE How now, sweetheart, who's at home besides yourself?

MRS. FORD Why, none but mine own people.

MRS. PAGE Indeed?

10 Master . . . play (As nephew of Robert Shallow, Justice of the Peace, Slender has the authority to interrupt the school calendar; the schoolmaster serves at the pleasure of the county's first family. Presumably Slender wants Evans free of his teaching duties so that he can work to further the marriage of Slender to Anne.) **11 of** on **12–13 profits . . . book** isn't making any progress in his studies. **14 accidence** rudiments of Latin grammar. **19 numbers** i.e., singular and plural **22 'Od's nouns** by God's wounds. (Confused with *odd* numbers, e.g., three.) **23 Peace your tattlings!** Cease your prattle! **25 Polecats** (Many of Quickly's misconstruings are bawdy: *polecats,* "prostitutes"; *horum,* "whores"; *harum,* "hare," "prostitute"; *Jenny's case,* "a whore's pudendum," or, "her pregnancy"; etc.) **37 Articles . . . pronoun** (William is reciting uncomprehendingly from William Lilly's widely used Latin grammar, which followed the ancient stoic grammarians in regarding demonstrative pronouns—*hic, haec, hoc*—as a sort of article, like *the.*) **38 *singulariter*** in the singular. ***nominativo*** in the nominative. (Similarly with *genitivo, accusativo,* and *vocativo.*) **44 Hang-hog** (Bacon is made by hanging up a hog.) **49 *caret*** is lacking. (But Quickly interprets it as "carrot.")

57 Vengeance of i.e., A plague on **61 to hick and to hack** i.e., to drink and engage in sex; see 2.1.49 **74 preeches** breeched, i.e., whipped on the bare buttocks. **77 sprag** sprack, lively, alert
4.2. Location: Ford's house.
1–2 your . . . sufferance i.e., your sorrow for what I have suffered has taken away my distress. **2 obsequious** zealously devoted **3 I profess . . . breadth** I declare that I return your love in full measure **3–5 not only . . . of it** i.e., not only in the simple fact of my loving you, but in the outward ceremonies and flourishes that embellish that love. **8 gossip** i.e., friend, neighbor. (Literally, fellow godparent.) **12 people** household servants.

MRS. FORD No, certainly. [*Aside to her*] Speak louder.

MRS. PAGE Truly, I am so glad you have nobody here.

MRS. FORD Why?

MRS. PAGE Why, woman, your husband is in his old lines again. He so takes on yonder with my husband, so rails against all married mankind, so curses all Eve's daughters, of what complexion soever, and so buffets himself on the forehead, crying, "Peer out, peer out!", that any madness I ever yet beheld seemed but tameness, civility, and patience to this his distemper he is in now. I am glad the fat knight is not here.

MRS. FORD Why, does he talk of him?

MRS. PAGE Of none but him, and swears he was carried out, the last time he searched for him, in a basket; protests to my husband he is now here, and hath drawn him and the rest of their company from their sport, to make another experiment of his suspicion. But I am glad the knight is not here. Now he shall see his own foolery.

MRS. FORD How near is he, Mistress Page?

MRS. PAGE Hard by, at street end. He will be here anon.

MRS. FORD I am undone! The knight is here.

MRS. PAGE Why, then, you are utterly shamed, and he's but a dead man. What a woman are you! Away with him, away with him! Better shame than murder.

MRS. FORD Which way should he go? How should I bestow him? Shall I put him into the basket again?

[*Enter Falstaff.*]

FALSTAFF No, I'll come no more i'th' basket. May I not go out ere he come?

MRS. PAGE Alas, three of Master Ford's brothers watch the door with pistols, that none shall issue out; otherwise you might slip away ere he came. But what make you here?

FALSTAFF What shall I do? I'll creep up into the chimney.

MRS. FORD There they always use to discharge their birding pieces.

MRS. PAGE Creep into the kilnhole.

FALSTAFF Where is it?

MRS. FORD He will seek there, on my word. Neither press, coffer, chest, trunk, well, vault, but he hath an abstract for the remembrance of such places, and goes to them by his note. There is no hiding you in the house.

FALSTAFF I'll go out, then.

MRS. PAGE If you go out in your own semblance, you die, Sir John—unless you go out disguised.

MRS. FORD How might we disguise him?

MRS. PAGE Alas the day, I know not! There is no woman's gown big enough for him; otherwise he might put on a hat, a muffler, and a kerchief, and so escape.

FALSTAFF Good hearts, devise something. Any extremity rather than a mischief.

MRS. FORD My maid's aunt, the fat woman of Brentford, has a gown above.

MRS. PAGE On my word, it will serve him; she's as big as he is. And there's her thrummed hat and her muffler too. Run up, Sir John.

MRS. FORD Go, go, sweet Sir John. Mistress Page and I will look some linen for your head.

MRS. PAGE Quick, quick! We'll come dress you straight. Put on the gown the while. [*Exit Falstaff.*]

MRS. FORD I would my husband would meet him in this shape. He cannot abide the old woman of Brentford. He swears she's a witch, forbade her my house, and hath threatened to beat her.

MRS. PAGE Heaven guide him to thy husband's cudgel, and the devil guide his cudgel afterwards!

MRS. FORD But is my husband coming?

MRS. PAGE Ay, in good sadness, is he, and talks of the basket too, howsoever he hath had intelligence.

MRS. FORD We'll try that; for I'll appoint my men to carry the basket again, to meet him at the door with it, as they did last time.

MRS. PAGE Nay, but he'll be here presently. Let's go dress him like the witch of Brentford.

MRS. FORD I'll first direct my men what they shall do with the basket. Go up. I'll bring linen for him straight. [*Exit.*]

MRS. PAGE Hang him, dishonest varlet! We cannot misuse him enough.
We'll leave a proof, by that which we will do,
Wives may be merry, and yet honest too.
We do not act that often jest and laugh;
'Tis old, but true, "Still swine eats all the draff."
[*Exit.*]

[*Enter Mistress Ford with two*] *Servants.*

MRS. FORD Go, sirs, take the basket again on your shoulders. Your master is hard at door. If he bid you set it down, obey him. Quickly, dispatch! [*Exit.*]

FIRST SERVANT Come, come, take it up.

SECOND SERVANT Pray heaven it be not full of knight again.

FIRST SERVANT I hope not. I had as lief bear so much lead. [*They take up the basket.*]

[*Enter*] *Ford, Page, Caius, Evans,* [*and*] *Shallow.*

18 lines fits of temper or madness. **He . . . with** He argues with, harangues **21 Peer out** i.e., Let my cuckold's horns come forth and be visible **23 to** compared to **30 experiment** trial **32 his** Ford's **45–6 what . . . here?** what are you doing here? **49–50 There . . . pieces** (After the hunt, the hunters fire off any gun that is still loaded, using the chimney as a convenient place to do so and also as a way of scouring the chimney; removing the bullet, powder, etc., is too cumbersome.) **51 kilnhole** oven. **54 press** clothes cupboard **55 abstract** inventory

67 mischief calamity. **68–9 Brentford** a nearby village **69 above** upstairs. **71 thrummed** made of or fringed with the unwoven ends of the warp threads **74 look** look for **75 straight** at once. **84 in good sadness** in all seriousness **86 try** test **89 presently** right away. **90 him** Falstaff **94 dishonest** lecherous **97 honest** chaste **98–9 We . . . draff** i.e., We wives are often merry, but that does not mean we act unchastely; as the proverb says, "It is the quiet ones whom you have to watch for licentious conduct." **101 hard at door** right at the door. **102 dispatch** get it done, hurry. **106 I had as lief** I would just as soon

FORD Ay, but if it prove true, Master Page, have you any way then to unfool me again?—Set down the basket, villain! Somebody call my wife. Youth in a basket! Oh, you panderly rascals! There's a knot, a ging, a pack, a conspiracy against me. Now shall the devil be shamed.—What, wife, I say! Come, come forth! Behold what honest clothes you send forth to bleaching!

PAGE Why, this passes, Master Ford. You are not to go loose any longer; you must be pinioned.

EVANS Why, this is lunatics. This is mad as a mad dog.

SHALLOW Indeed, Master Ford, this is not well, indeed.

FORD So say I, too, sir.

[*Enter Mistress Ford.*]

Come hither, Mistress Ford—Mistress Ford, the honest woman, the modest wife, the virtuous creature, that hath the jealous fool to her husband! I suspect without cause, mistress, do I?

MRS. FORD Heaven be my witness you do, if you suspect me in any dishonesty.

FORD Well said, brazenface! Hold it out.—Come forth, sirrah! [*He pulls clothes out of the basket.*]

PAGE This passes!

MRS. FORD Are you not ashamed? Let the clothes alone.

FORD I shall find you anon.

EVANS 'Tis unreasonable. Will you take up your wife's clothes? Come, away.

FORD Empty the basket, I say!

MRS. FORD Why, man, why?

FORD Master Page, as I am a man, there was one conveyed out of my house yesterday in this basket. Why may not he be there again? In my house I am sure he is. My intelligence is true; my jealousy is reasonable.—Pluck me out all the linen.

MRS. FORD If you find a man there, he shall die a flea's death.

PAGE Here's no man.

SHALLOW By my fidelity, this is not well, Master Ford. This wrongs you.

EVANS Master Ford, you must pray, and not follow the imaginations of your own heart. This is jealousies.

FORD Well, he's not here I seek for.

PAGE No, nor nowhere else but in your brain.

FORD Help to search my house this one time. If I find not what I seek, show no color for my extremity; let me forever be your table sport. Let them say of me, "As jealous as Ford, that searched a hollow walnut for his wife's leman." Satisfy me once more; once more search with me. [*Exeunt Servants with basket.*]

MRS. FORD [*calling upstairs*] What ho, Mistress Page! Come you and the old woman down. My husband will come into the chamber.

FORD Old woman? What old woman's that?

MRS. FORD Why, it is my maid's aunt of Brentford.

FORD A witch, a quean, an old, cozening quean! Have I not forbid her my house? She comes of errands, does she? We are simple men; we do not know what's brought to pass under the profession of fortunetelling. She works by charms, by spells, by th' figure, and such daubery as this is, beyond our element; we know nothing.—Come down, you witch, you hag, you! Come down, I say!

MRS. FORD Nay, good sweet husband!—Good gentlemen, let him not strike the old woman.

[*Enter Falstaff in woman's clothes, and Mistress Page.*]

MRS. PAGE Come, Mother Prat, come, give me your hand.

FORD I'll prat her. [*Beating him.*] Out of my door, you witch, you rag, you baggage, you polecat, you ronyon! Out, out! I'll conjure you, I'll fortune-tell you. [*Exit Falstaff.*]

MRS. PAGE Are you not ashamed? I think you have killed the poor woman.

MRS. FORD Nay, he will do it.—'Tis a goodly credit for you.

FORD Hang her, witch!

EVANS By Jeshu, I think the 'oman is a witch indeed. I like not when a 'oman has a great peard. I spy a great peard under his muffler.

FORD Will you follow, gentlemen? I beseech you, follow. See but the issue of my jealousy. If I cry out thus upon no trail, never trust me when I open again.

PAGE Let's obey his humor a little further. Come, gentlemen.

[*Exeunt Ford, Page, Shallow, Caius, and Evans.*]

MRS. PAGE Trust me, he beat him most pitifully.

MRS. FORD Nay, by th' Mass, that he did not; he beat him most unpitifully, methought.

MRS. PAGE I'll have the cudgel hallowed and hung o'er the altar. It hath done meritorious service.

MRS. FORD What think you? May we, with the warrant of womanhood and the witness of a good conscience, pursue him with any further revenge?

109 unfool me disburden me of a reputation for folly **111 a knot . . . pack** a company, a gang, a confederacy **112–13 Now . . . shamed** i.e., Now truth will out. (From the proverb "Tell the truth and shame the devil.") **115 passes** surpasses, goes beyond all bounds **116 be pinioned** (Such restraint was standard procedure in treating insanity.) **119 So say I, too** (Ford means that something is amiss; not, as Shallow intended to say, that Ford's behavior is deplorable.) **126 Hold it out** i.e., Continue to maintain your falsehood. **131 take up** pick up. (But with unintended bawdy suggestion of lifting his wife's dress.) **138 intelligence** information **139 Pluck me out** Pluck out for me **140–1 he . . . death** i.e., he will die an ignominious death, squashed like a flea. **143 By my fidelity** Upon my word **144 wrongs you** does you dishonor. **150 show . . . extremity** make no attempt to excuse my extreme behavior **151 your table sport** butt or laughingstock of the company.

153 leman lover. **160 quean** slut, hussy. **cozening** deceiving **161 of** on **164 by the figure** i.e., by making wax figures and sticking pins in them, or, by astrological charts **165 daubery** false show. **beyond our element** beyond our comprehension, belonging to another world **172 prat** beat, teach a lesson, practice tricks on (?) **173–4 you rag . . . ronyon!** i.e., you worthless wretch, you slut, you whore, you bitch! **177–8 'Tis . . . you** It does you great credit. (Said ironically.) **184 issue** conclusion **184–5 cry . . . trail** bay like a hunting dog despite the absence of a scent **185 open** give voice (like a hunting dog) **186 obey his humor** humor him

MRS. PAGE The spirit of wantonness is, sure, scared out of him. If the devil have him not in fee simple, with fine and recovery, he will never, I think, in the way of waste, attempt us again.

MRS. FORD Shall we tell our husbands how we have served him?

MRS. PAGE Yes, by all means, if it be but to scrape the figures out of your husband's brains. If they can find in their hearts the poor, unvirtuous, fat knight shall be any further afflicted, we two will still be the ministers.

MRS. FORD I'll warrant they'll have him publicly shamed, and methinks there would be no period to the jest, should he not be publicly shamed.

MRS. PAGE Come, to the forge with it, then shape it. I would not have things cool. *Exeunt.*

✤

4.3

Enter Host and Bardolph.

BARDOLPH Sir, the Germans desire to have three of your horses. The Duke himself will be tomorrow at court, and they are going to meet him.

HOST What duke should that be comes so secretly? I hear not of him in the court. Let me speak with the gentlemen. They speak English?

BARDOLPH Ay, sir. I'll call them to you.

HOST They shall have my horses, but I'll make them pay; I'll sauce them. They have had my house a week at command. I have turned away my other guests. They must come off. I'll sauce them. Come. *Exeunt.*

4.4

Enter Page, Ford, Mistress Page, Mistress Ford, and Evans.

EVANS 'Tis one of the best discretions of a 'oman as ever I did look upon.

PAGE And did he send you both these letters at an instant?

MRS. PAGE Within a quarter of an hour.

FORD
Pardon me, wife. Henceforth do what thou wilt;
I rather will suspect the sun with cold
Than thee with wantonness. Now doth thy honor stand,
In him that was of late an heretic,
As firm as faith.

PAGE 'Tis well, 'tis well. No more.
Be not as extreme in submission as in offense.
But let our plot go forward. Let our wives
Yet once again, to make us public sport,
Appoint a meeting with this old fat fellow,
Where we may take him and disgrace him for it.

FORD
There is no better way than that they spoke of.

PAGE How? To send him word they'll meet him in the park at midnight? Fie, fie, he'll never come.

EVANS You say he has been thrown in the rivers and has been grievously peaten as an old 'oman. Methinks there should be terrors in him that he should not come. Methinks his flesh is punished; he shall have no desires.

PAGE So think I too.

MRS. FORD
Devise but how you'll use him when he comes,
And let us two devise to bring him thither.

MRS. PAGE
There is an old tale goes that Herne the hunter,
Sometime a keeper here in Windsor Forest,
Doth all the wintertime, at still midnight,
Walk round about an oak, with great ragg'd horns;
And there he blasts the tree, and takes the cattle,
And makes milch kine yield blood, and shakes a chain
In a most hideous and dreadful manner.
You have heard of such a spirit, and well you know
The superstitious idle-headed eld
Received and did deliver to our age
This tale of Herne the hunter for a truth.

PAGE
Why, yet there want not many that do fear
In deep of night to walk by this Herne's oak.
But what of this?

MRS. FORD Marry, this is our device:
That Falstaff at that oak shall meet with us,
Disguised like Herne, with huge horns on his head.

PAGE
Well, let it not be doubted but he'll come.
And in this shape when you have brought him thither,
What shall be done with him? What is your plot?

MRS. PAGE
That likewise have we thought upon, and thus:
Nan Page my daughter, and my little son,
And three or four more of their growth, we'll dress
Like urchins, aufs, and fairies, green and white,
With rounds of waxen tapers on their heads,
And rattles in their hands. Upon a sudden,

196 wantonness lust **197 fee simple** estate belonging to an owner and his heirs forever; hence, absolute possession **198 fine and recovery** procedures by which an entailed estate was converted into fee simple. (Unless Falstaff already belongs to the devil outright, says Mistress Page, he won't try us again.) **199 waste** spoliation, despoiling. (Another legal term.) **203 figures** fantasies, conceits **205 ministers** agents. **207 period** suitable conclusion **209 Come . . . shape it** i.e., Strike while the iron is hot.

4.3. Location: The Garter Inn.

9 sauce them i.e., make them pay dearly. **10 at command** retained for their use upon their expected arrival. **11 come off** pay up.

4.4. Location: Page's house.

1–2 'Tis . . . upon i.e., This joke played on Falstaff by the merry wives is one of the best instances of feminine wit and adroit management I have ever seen. **3–4 at an instant** at the same time. **7 with** with being

20–2 Methinks . . . come I should think he'd be too afraid to come. **25 use** treat **28 Sometime** formerly **30 ragg'd** shaggy, pronged **31 blasts** blights, or blasts with lightning. **takes** bewitches **32 milch kine** dairy cattle **35 idle-headed eld** ignorant folk of olden time **38 yet . . . many** even today there are many **40 device** plan **48 growth** size, age **49 urchins, aufs** (Terms for goblins or elves.) **50 rounds** circlets, coronets

As Falstaff, she, and I are newly met,
Let them from forth a sawpit rush at once 53
With some diffusèd song. Upon their sight, 54
We two in great amazedness will fly.
Then let them all encircle him about,
And, fairylike, to pinch the unclean knight,
And ask him why, that hour of fairy revel,
In their so sacred paths he dares to tread
In shape profane.

MRS. FORD And till he tell the truth,
Let the supposèd fairies pinch him sound 61
And burn him with their tapers.

MRS. PAGE The truth being known,
We'll all present ourselves, dis-horn the spirit,
And mock him home to Windsor.

FORD The children must
Be practiced well to this, or they'll ne'er do't.

EVANS I will teach the children their behaviors, and I
will be like a jackanapes also, to burn the knight with 67
my taber. 68

FORD
That will be excellent. I'll go buy them vizards. 69

MRS. PAGE
My Nan shall be the queen of all the fairies,
Finely attirèd in a robe of white.

PAGE
That silk will I go buy. [*Aside*] And in that tire 72
Shall Master Slender steal my Nan away
And marry her at Eton. [*To Mistress Page*] Go,
send to Falstaff straight. 74

FORD
Nay, I'll to him again in name of Brook.
He'll tell me all his purpose. Sure he'll come.

MRS. PAGE
Fear not you that. Go get us properties 77
And tricking for our fairies. 78

EVANS Let us about it. It is admirable pleasures and fery honest knaveries. [*Exeunt Page, Ford, and Evans.*]

MRS. PAGE Go, Mistress Ford,
Send quickly to Sir John, to know his mind.
[*Exit Mistress Ford.*]
I'll to the Doctor. He hath my good will,
And none but he, to marry with Nan Page.
That Slender, though well landed, is an idiot; 85
And he my husband best of all affects. 86
The Doctor is well moneyed, and his friends
Potent at court. He, none but he, shall have her,
Though twenty thousand worthier come to crave her.
[*Exit.*]

53 **sawpit** a pit over which wood was sawed 54 **diffusèd** confused, disorderly 61 **sound** soundly 67 **like a jackanapes** disguised as an ape or monkey. (Evans actually disguises himself as a satyr.) 68 **taber** taper, candle. 69 **vizards** visors, masks. 72 **tire** attire 74 **Eton** town across the Thames from Windsor. 77 **properties** theatrical props 78 **tricking** adornment, costumes 85 **well landed** rich in land 86 **he** i.e., him. **affects** prefers.

4.5

Enter Host [and] Simple.

HOST What wouldst thou have, boor? What, thickskin? 1
Speak, breathe, discuss; brief, short, quick, snap. 2

SIMPLE Marry, sir, I come to speak with Sir John Falstaff from Master Slender.

HOST There's his chamber, his house, his castle, his
standing bed and truckle bed. 'Tis painted about with 6
the story of the Prodigal, fresh and new. Go knock and 7
call. He'll speak like an Anthropophaginian unto thee. 8
Knock, I say.

SIMPLE There's an old woman, a fat woman, gone up into his chamber. I'll be so bold as stay, sir, till she come down. I come to speak with her, indeed.

HOST Ha, a fat woman? The knight may be robbed. I'll 13
call.—Bully knight! Bully Sir John! Speak from thy
lungs military. Art thou there? It is thine Host, thine
Ephesian, calls. 16

FALSTAFF [*within*] How now, mine Host?

HOST Here's a Bohemian Tartar tarries the coming 18
down of thy fat woman. Let her descend, bully, let
her descend. My chambers are honorable. Fie, pri- 20
vacy? Fie!

[*Enter*] *Falstaff.*

FALSTAFF There was, mine Host, an old fat woman even now with me, but she's gone.

SIMPLE Pray you, sir, was't not the wise woman of 24
Brentford?

FALSTAFF Ay, marry, was it, mussel shell. What would 26
you with her?

SIMPLE My master, sir, my Master Slender, sent to her, seeing her go through the streets, to know, sir, whether one Nym, sir, that beguiled him of a chain, had the chain or no.

FALSTAFF I spake with the old woman about it.

SIMPLE And what says she, I pray, sir?

FALSTAFF Marry, she says that the very same man that be- 34
guiled Master Slender of his chain cozened him of it. 35

SIMPLE I would I could have spoken with the woman herself. I had other things to have spoken with her too from him.

FALSTAFF What are they? Let us know.

HOST Ay, come. Quick.

4.5. Location: The Garter Inn.
1 thickskin one slow or dull of feeling. **2 discuss** declare **6 truckle bed** trundle bed, low bed stored under the *standing bed* or regular bed. **7 the Prodigal** (Compare *1 Henry IV*, 4.2.34 and *2 Henry IV*, 2.1.143, where this story from Luke 15:11–32 is again associated with Falstaff.) **8 Anthropophaginian** (One of the Host's extravagant epithets, perhaps intended to frighten Simple. Literally, a cannibal.) **13 The knight . . . robbed** (The Host is worried that an unaccompanied woman going up to man's chambers is likely to be a prostitute and a thief.) **16 Ephesian** i.e., boon companion **18 Bohemian Tartar** i.e., barbarian, wild man. **tarries** (who) awaits **20 My . . . honorable** i.e., I won't have any whores in my inn. **24 wise woman** i.e., fortune-teller **26 mussel shell** i.e., one who gapes. **34–5 Marry . . . of it** (Falstaff wittily answers Simple as a soothsayer might, with a seeming profundity that merely restates the obvious: the beguiler was the cozener or cheater.)

SIMPLE I may not conceal them, sir.

HOST Conceal them or thou diest.

SIMPLE Why, sir, they were nothing but about Mistress Anne Page, to know if it were my master's fortune to have her or no.

FALSTAFF 'Tis, 'tis his fortune.

SIMPLE What, sir?

FALSTAFF To have her, or no. Go, say the woman told me so.

SIMPLE May I be bold to say so, sir?

FALSTAFF Ay, sir; like who more bold.

SIMPLE I thank Your Worship. I shall make my master glad with these tidings. *[Exit.]*

HOST Thou art clerkly, thou art clerkly, Sir John. Was there a wise woman with thee?

FALSTAFF Ay, that there was, mine Host, one that hath taught me more wit than ever I learned before in my life. And I paid nothing for it, neither, but was paid for my learning.

[Enter] Bardolph.

BARDOLPH Out, alas, sir! Cozenage, mere cozenage!

HOST Where be my horses? Speak well of them, varletto.

BARDOLPH Run away with the cozeners. For so soon as I came beyond Eton, they threw me off from behind one of them, in a slough of mire, and set spurs and away, like three German devils, three Doctor Faustuses.

HOST They are gone but to meet the Duke, villain. Do not say they be fled. Germans are honest men.

[Enter] Evans.

EVANS Where is mine Host?

HOST What is the matter, sir?

EVANS Have a care of your entertainments. There is a friend of mine come to town tells me there is three cozen-germans that has cozened all the hosts of Reading, of Maidenhead, of Colnbrook, of horses and money. I tell you for good will, look you. You are wise, and full of gibes and vloutingstocks, and 'tis not convenient you should be cozened. Fare you well. *[Exit.]*

[Enter] Caius.

CAIUS Vere is mine Host de Jarteer?

HOST Here, Master Doctor, in perplexity and doubtful dilemma.

CAIUS I cannot tell vat is dat. But it is tell-a me dat you make grand preparation for a duke de Jamany. By my trot, dere is no duke that the court is know to come. I tell you for good will. Adieu. *[Exit.]*

HOST Hue and cry, villain, go!—Assist me, knight. I am undone!—Fly, run, hue and cry, villain! I am undone! *[Exeunt Host and Bardolph.]*

FALSTAFF I would all the world might be cozened, for I have been cozened and beaten too. If it should come to the ear of the court how I have been transformed, and how my transformation hath been washed and cudgeled, they would melt me out of my fat drop by drop and liquor fishermen's boots with me. I warrant they would whip me with their fine wits till I were as crestfallen as a dried pear. I never prospered since I forswore myself at primero. Well, if my wind were but long enough to say my prayers, I would repent.

[Enter Mistress] Quickly.

Now, whence come you?

QUICKLY From the two parties, forsooth.

FALSTAFF The devil take one party and his dam the other! And so they shall be both bestowed. I have suffered more for their sakes, more than the villainous inconstancy of man's disposition is able to bear.

QUICKLY And have not they suffered? Yes, I warrant, speciously one of them. Mistress Ford, good heart, is beaten black and blue, that you cannot see a white spot about her.

FALSTAFF What tell'st thou me of black and blue? I was beaten myself into all the colors of the rainbow, and I was like to be apprehended for the witch of Brentford. But that my admirable dexterity of wit, my counterfeiting the action of an old woman, delivered me, the knave constable had set me i'the stocks, i'th' common stocks, for a witch.

QUICKLY Sir, let me speak with you in your chamber, you shall hear how things go, and, I warrant, to your content. Here is a letter will say somewhat. *[She gives a letter.]* Good hearts, what ado is here to bring you together! Sure, one of you does not serve heaven well, that you are so crossed.

FALSTAFF Come up into my chamber. *Exeunt.*

41 conceal (For "reveal." The Host answers ironically with the same misused word.) **48 To have . . . no** (As in lines 34-5, Falstaff again speaks in oracular ambiguities that say nothing: either Slender will succeed or he won't.) **51 like . . . bold** i.e., who could possibly have a right to be bolder than you? (Said with mock politeness.) **54 clerkly** scholarly, wise, clever. (The Host admires Falstaff's wit at Simple's expense.) **58 was paid** i.e., with a beating **60 Cozenage** Double-dealing. **mere** absolute **61–2 Speak . . . varletto** i.e., Tell me good news of them, you rascal. **65 one of them** one of the horses **66–7 Doctor Faustuses** (Named for the German scholar-magician who practices devilish arts in Marlowe's play.) **72 your entertainments** i.e., your guests. **74 cozen-germans** (1) first cousins (2) cozening or cheating Germans; see note 83 below for a topical reference **75 Reading** a town not far from Windsor. (Also true of *Maidenhead* and *Colnbrook.*) **77 vloutingstocks** i.e., taunts **78 convenient** fitting

80 doubtful full of doubts **83 duke de Jamany** duke of Germany. (Seemingly a satirical reference to Count Mömpelgard, later Duke of Württemberg, who offended many observers by his self-serving maneuvering to be elected Knight of the Garter in 1592 and afterwards. The Quarto's "cosen garmombles" in place of the Folio's "three Cozen-Iermans" in lines 73–4 hints topically at Mömpelgard.) **84 trot** troth. **that . . . to come** whose arrival is expected at court. **86 Hue and cry, villain** (The Host bids Bardolph go raise the cry for pursuit of a felon.) **93 liquor** saturate with oil to make waterproof **95 crestfallen** i.e., shriveled **96 forswore . . . primero** i.e., swore a false oath that I had never cheated at primero, a gambling card game, and was detected in the lie. **100 dam** mother **101 bestowed** i.e., lodged where they deserve. **105 speciously** (For "specially.") **110 like** likely, about **111 But that** Were it not that **115 let** if you will let **120 crossed** thwarted.

4.6

Enter Fenton [*and*] *Host.*

HOST Master Fenton, talk not to me. My mind is
heavy. I will give over all. 2

FENTON
Yet hear me speak. Assist me in my purpose,
And, as I am a gentleman, I'll give thee
A hundred pound in gold more than your loss.

HOST I will hear you, Master Fenton, and I will at the
least keep your counsel. 7

FENTON
From time to time I have acquainted you
With the dear love I bear to fair Anne Page,
Who mutually hath answered my affection,
So far forth as herself might be her chooser, 11
Even to my wish. I have a letter from her 12
Of such contents as you will wonder at,
The mirth whereof so larded with my matter 14
That neither singly can be manifested
Without the show of both. Fat Falstaff
Hath a great scene; the image of the jest 17
I'll show you here at large. [*He shows a letter.*] Hark,
good mine Host. 18
Tonight at Herne's oak, just twixt twelve and one,
Must my sweet Nan present the Fairy Queen— 20
The purpose why is here—in which disguise,
While other jests are something rank on foot, 22
Her father hath commanded her to slip
Away with Slender, and with him at Eton
Immediately to marry. She hath consented.
Now, sir,
Her mother, even strong against that match 27
And firm for Doctor Caius, hath appointed
That he shall likewise shuffle her away, 29
While other sports are tasking of their minds, 30
And at the deanery, where a priest attends,
Straight marry her. To this her mother's plot
She, seemingly obedient, likewise hath
Made promise to the Doctor. Now, thus it rests: 34
Her father means she shall be all in white,
And in that habit, when Slender sees his time 36
To take her by the hand and bid her go,
She shall go with him. Her mother hath intended, 38
The better to denote her to the Doctor—
For they must all be masked and vizarded—
That quaint in green she shall be loose enrobed, 41
With ribbons pendent, flaring 'bout her head;
And when the Doctor spies his vantage ripe,
To pinch her by the hand, and on that token
The maid hath given consent to go with him.

HOST
Which means she to deceive, father or mother?

FENTON
Both, my good Host, to go along with me.
And here it rests: that you'll procure the vicar
To stay for me at church twixt twelve and one,
And, in the lawful name of marrying,
To give our hearts united ceremony.

HOST
Well, husband your device. I'll to the vicar. 52
Bring you the maid, you shall not lack a priest. 53

FENTON
So shall I evermore be bound to thee.
Besides, I'll make a present recompense. *Exeunt.* 55

✤

5.1

Enter Falstaff [*and Mistress*] *Quickly.*

FALSTAFF Prithee, no more prattling; go. I'll hold. This 1
is the third time; I hope good luck lies in odd numbers. Away, go. They say there is divinity in odd 3
numbers, either in nativity, chance, or death. Away!

QUICKLY I'll provide you a chain, and I'll do what I can
to get you a pair of horns.

FALSTAFF Away, I say! Time wears. Hold up your 7
head, and mince. [*Exit Mistress Quickly.*] 8

[*Enter*] *Ford* [*disguised*].

How now, Master Brook? Master Brook, the matter
will be known tonight or never. Be you in the park
about midnight, at Herne's oak, and you shall see
wonders.

FORD Went you not to her yesterday, sir, as you told 13
me you had appointed?

FALSTAFF I went to her, Master Brook, as you see, like
a poor old man, but I came from her, Master Brook,
like a poor old woman. That same knave Ford, her
husband, hath the finest mad devil of jealousy in him,
Master Brook, that ever governed frenzy. I will tell you:
he beat me grievously, in the shape of a woman; for
in the shape of man, Master Brook, I fear not Goliath 21
with a weaver's beam, because I know also life is a 22
shuttle. I am in haste. Go along with me; I'll tell you 23
all, Master Brook. Since I plucked geese, played 24
truant, and whipped top, I knew not what 'twas to be 25
beaten till lately. Follow me. I'll tell you strange things
of this knave Ford, on whom tonight I will be

4.6. Location: The Garter Inn, as before.
2 give over abandon **7 keep your counsel** keep your secret. **11 So far forth** insofar **12 to** according to **14 larded . . . matter** intermingled with what concerns me **17 image** form, idea **18 at large** at length. **20 present** represent **22 something . . . foot** abundantly being devised **27 even** equally **29 shuffle** smuggle, steal **30 tasking of** busily occupying **34 it rests** matters stand **36 habit** dress **38 intended** arranged **41 quaint** decorously

52 husband manage prudently **53 Bring you** If you bring **55 present** immediate
5.1. Location: The Garter Inn, as before.
1 hold persevere, keep the appointment. **3 divinity** mysterious power **7–8 Hold . . . mince** Hold your head proudly erect as you trip away. **13 yesterday** (Actually, the meeting appears to have been earlier this same day.) **21–2 Goliath . . . beam** (See 1 Samuel 17:7: "The staff of his [Goliath's] spear was like a weaver's beam." See also 2 Samuel 21:19. A weaver's beam is a wooden cylinder in a loom.) **22–3 life is a shuttle** (See Job 7:6: "My days are swifter than a weaver's shuttle.") **24–5 plucked . . . top** i.e., committed various boyhood pranks. To whip a top is to set it spinning.

revenged, and I will deliver his wife into your hand. Follow. Strange things in hand, Master Brook! Follow.
Exeunt.

✤

5.2

Enter Page, Shallow, [*and*] *Slender.*

PAGE Come, come. We'll couch i'th' castle ditch till we see the light of our fairies. Remember, son Slender, my daughter.

SLENDER Ay, forsooth. I have spoke with her, and we have a nayword how to know one another. I come to her in white and cry "mum," she cries "budget," and by that we know one another.

SHALLOW That's good too. But what needs either your "mum" or her "budget"? The white will decipher her well enough.—It hath struck ten o'clock.

PAGE The night is dark; light and spirits will become it well. Heaven prosper our sport! No man means evil but the devil, and we shall know him by his horns. Let's away. Follow me. *Exeunt.*

✤

5.3

Enter Mistress Page, Mistress Ford, [*and*] *Caius.*

MRS. PAGE Master Doctor, my daughter is in green. When you see your time, take her by the hand, away with her to the deanery, and dispatch it quickly. Go before into the park. We two must go together.

CAIUS I know vat I have to do. Adieu.

MRS. PAGE Fare you well, sir. [*Exit Caius.*]
My husband will not rejoice so much at the abuse of Falstaff as he will chafe at the Doctor's marrying my daughter. But'tis no matter. Better a little chiding than a great deal of heartbreak.

MRS. FORD Where is Nan now, and her troop of fairies, and the Welsh devil Hugh?

MRS. PAGE They are all couched in a pit hard by Herne's Oak, with obscured lights, which, at the very instant of Falstaff's and our meeting, they will at once display to the night.

MRS. FORD That cannot choose but amaze him.

MRS. PAGE If he be not amazed, he will be mocked. If he be amazed, he will every way be mocked.

MRS. FORD We'll betray him finely.

MRS. PAGE
Against such lewdsters and their lechery,
Those that betray them do no treachery.

MRS. FORD The hour draws on. To the oak, to the oak!
Exeunt.

5.2. Location: On the way to Windsor Park.
1 couch hide **5 nayword** password, watchword **6 mum, budget** (*Mumbudget* connotes silence, as in a children's game by that name.) **8 what needs** what need is there for **9 decipher** identify **11 become** suit
5.3. Location: Somewhere in Windsor.
3 dispatch conclude **17 cannot choose but amaze** is certain to astound and terrify **18–19 mocked . . . mocked** deceived . . . ridiculed.

5.4

Enter Evans [*as a satyr*] *and* [*children disguised as*] *fairies.*

EVANS Trib, trib, fairies. Come, and remember your parts. Be pold, I pray you. Follow me into the pit, and when I give the watch'ords, do as I pid you. Come, come; trib, trib. *Exeunt.*

5.5

Enter Falstaff [*disguised as Herne, wearing a buck's head*].

FALSTAFF The Windsor bell hath struck twelve; the minute draws on. Now, the hot-blooded gods assist me! Remember, Jove, thou wast a bull for thy Europa; love set on thy horns. O powerful Love, that in some respects makes a beast a man, in some other a man a beast! You were also, Jupiter, a swan for the love of Leda. O omnipotent Love, how near the god drew to the complexion of a goose! A fault done first in the form of a beast—O Jove, a beastly fault!—and then another fault in the semblance of a fowl; think on't, Jove, a foul fault! When gods have hot backs, what shall poor men do? For me, I am here a Windsor stag, and the fattest, I think, i'th' forest. Send me a cool rut-time, Jove, or who can blame me to piss my tallow? Who comes here? My doe?

[*Enter*] *Mistress Page* [*and*] *Mistress Ford.*

MRS. FORD Sir John? Art thou there, my deer, my male deer?

FALSTAFF My doe with the black scut! Let the sky rain potatoes; let it thunder to the tune of "Greensleeves," hail kissing-comfits, and snow eringoes; let there come a tempest of provocation, I will shelter me here.
[*He embraces her.*]

MRS. FORD Mistress Page is come with me, sweetheart.

FALSTAFF Divide me like a bribed buck, each a haunch. I will keep my sides to myself, my shoulders for the fellow of this walk, and my horns I bequeath your husbands. Am I a woodman, ha? Speak I like Herne

5.4. Location: Windsor Park, as before.
1 Trib Trip, move nimbly
5.5. Location: Windsor Park, as before.
3, 6–7 bull . . . Europa, swan . . . Leda (References to legends of Jupiter's animal disguises when engaged in various amours.)
14 rut-time mating season **14–15 piss my tallow** i.e., sweat off and excrete excess fat during mating season, like a stag. **16 deer** (With a pun on "dear.") **18 scut** tail, pudendum. **19 potatoes** i.e., sweet potatoes. (Regarded by Elizabethans as aphrodisiac.) **Greensleeves** (A popular tune; see the note for 2.1.60.) **20 kissing-comfits** perfumed sweetmeats for sweetening the breath. **eringoes** candied root of a plant called sea holly. (Regarded as aphrodisiac.) **21 provocation** i.e., sexual stimulation **23 bribed** stolen (and then quickly cut up and divided by the poachers) **25 fellow . . . walk** i.e., keeper of the forest. (Traditionally, the forester received the shoulders of slaughtered beasts as his fee.) **25-6 my horns . . . husbands** (Falstaff will make the husbands wear cuckold's horns.) **26 woodman** (1) hunter (2) woman chaser

the hunter? Why, now is Cupid a child of conscience; he makes restitution. As I am a true spirit, welcome!
[*A noise within.*]

MRS. PAGE Alas, what noise?
MRS. FORD Heaven forgive our sins!
FALSTAFF What should this be?
MRS. FORD, MRS. PAGE Away, away! [*They run off.*]
FALSTAFF I think the devil will not have me damned, lest the oil that's in me should set hell on fire. He would never else cross me thus.

[*Enter*] *Evans,* [*disguised as a satyr, Mistress*] *Quickly* [*as the Fairy Queen*], *Anne Page* [*and children as*] *fairies,* [*with tapers, and*] *Pistol* [*as Hobgoblin*].

QUICKLY [*as Fairy Queen*]
Fairies, black, gray, green, and white,
You moonshine revelers, and shades of night,
You orphan heirs of fixèd destiny,
Attend your office and your quality.
Crier Hobgoblin, make the fairy oyes.
PISTOL [*as Hobgoblin*]
Elves, list your names. Silence, you airy toys!
Cricket, to Windsor chimneys shalt thou leap.
Where fires thou find'st unraked and hearths
unswept,
There pinch the maids as blue as bilberry.
Our radiant Queen hates sluts and sluttery.
FALSTAFF
They are fairies. He that speaks to them shall die.
I'll wink and couch; no man their works must eye.
[*He lies face downward.*]
EVANS [*as a satyr*]
Where's Bead? Go you, and where you find a maid
That, ere she sleep, has thrice her prayers said,
Raise up the organs of her fantasy;
Sleep she as sound as careless infancy.
But those as sleep and think not on their sins,
Pinch them, arms, legs, backs, shoulders, sides, and
shins.
QUICKLY About, about!
Search Windsor Castle, elves, within and out.
Strew good luck, aufs, on every sacred room,
That it may stand till the perpetual doom
In state as wholesome as in state 'tis fit,
Worthy the owner, and the owner it.
The several chairs of order look you scour
With juice of balm and every precious flower.
Each fair installment, coat, and several crest
With loyal blazon evermore be blest!
And nightly, meadow fairies, look you sing,
Like to the Garter's compass, in a ring.
Th'expressure that it bears, green let it be,
More fertile-fresh than all the field to see;
And "*Honi soit qui mal y pense*" write
In em'rald tufts, flow'rs purple, blue, and white,
Like sapphire, pearl, and rich embroidery,
Buckled below fair knighthood's bending knee;
Fairies use flowers for their charactery.
Away, disperse! But till 'tis one o'clock,
Our dance of custom, round about the oak
Of Herne the hunter, let us not forget.
EVANS Pray you,
Lock hand in hand. Yourselves in order set;
And twenty glowworms shall our lanterns be
To guide our measure round about the tree.
But stay! I smell a man of middle-earth.
FALSTAFF Heavens defend me from that Welsh fairy, lest he transform me to a piece of cheese!
[*They discover Falstaff hiding.*]
PISTOL
Vile worm, thou wast o'erlooked even in thy birth.
QUICKLY [*to Fairies*]
With trial-fire touch me his finger end.
If he be chaste, the flame will back descend
And turn him to no pain; but if he start,
It is the flesh of a corrupted heart.
PISTOL
A trial, come.
EVANS
Come, will this wood take fire?
[*They put the tapers to his fingers, and he starts.*]
FALSTAFF Oh, Oh, Oh!
QUICKLY
Corrupt, corrupt, and tainted in desire!
About him, fairies. Sing a scornful rhyme,
And, as you trip, still pinch him to your time.

The Song.

FAIRIES
Fie on sinful fantasy!
Fie on lust and luxury!

27 is Cupid . . . conscience i.e., Cupid is keeping faith with me **35 cross** thwart **37 shades** spirits **38 orphan** i.e., parentless. (Fairies were thought to be not of human parentage.) **heirs . . . destiny** i.e., inheritors of commissions to specific fairy assignments **39 Attend . . . quality** attend to your duties and particular functions. **40 oyes** oyez, hear ye. (The call of the public crier.) **41 list** listen for. **toys** substanceless beings. **43 unraked** not raked together to last through the night **44 bilberry** a kind of blueberry. **45 sluttery** sluttishness. **46 He . . . die** (A widespread tradition about fairies.) **47 wink and couch** close my eyes and lie hidden **50 Raise . . . fantasy** i.e., give her pleasant dreams **51 Sleep she** let her sleep. **careless** free of care **52 as** who **54 About** i.e., Get to work **56 aufs** elves **57 perpetual doom** Day of Judgment **58 In . . . fit** i.e., in a healthy condition, as befits its dignity

60 The several . . . order i.e., The individual stalls of the Garter knights (in Saint George's chapel at Windsor) **62 Each . . . crest** Each place in which a knight is installed, coat of arms, and separate heraldic device **63 loyal blazon** coat of arms, armorial bearings of a loyal knight. **65 compass** circle. (The garter was worn below the left knee by knights of the order.) **66 Th'expressure** the image, picture **68 *Honi . . . pense*** Evil to him who evil thinks. (The motto of the Order of the Garter.) **72 charactery** writing. **74 dance of custom** customary dance **79 measure** stately dance **80 middle-earth** i.e., the earth, the center of the universe, conceived of as between the heavens and the underworld. **82 cheese** (The Welshman's favorite food; compare 2.2.290–1.) **83 o'erlooked** bewitched, looked on with an evil eye **86 turn** put **88.1 *fingers*** fingertips. (The stage direction is from the Quarto.) **92 still** continually **94 luxury** lechery.

Lust is but a bloody fire,
Kindled with unchaste desire,
Fed in heart, whose flames aspire,
As thoughts do blow them, higher and higher.
Pinch him, fairies, mutually!
Pinch him for his villainy.
Pinch him, and burn him, and turn him about,
Till candles and starlight and moonshine be out.

[During this song they pinch Falstaff. Doctor] Caius *[enters one way, and steals away a fairy in green]*; Slender, *[another way, and takes off a fairy in white; and]* Fenton *[enters, and steals away Mistress Anne page. A noise of hunting is heard within. Mistress Quickly, Evans, Pistol, and all the Fairies run away. Falstaff pulls off his buck's head, and rises.]*

[Enter] Page, Ford, *[Mistress Page, and Mistress Ford].*

PAGE
Nay, do not fly. I think we have watched you now.
Will none but Herne the hunter serve your turn?

MRS. PAGE
I pray you, come, hold up the jest no higher.
Now, good Sir John, how like you Windsor wives?
[She points to Falstaff's horns.]
See you these, husband? Do not these fair yokes
Become the forest better than the town?

FORD Now, sir, who's a cuckold now? Master Brook, Falstaff's a knave, a cuckoldly knave; here are his horns, Master Brook. And, Master Brook, he hath enjoyed nothing of Ford's but his buck basket, his cudgel, and twenty pounds of money, which must be paid to Master Brook. His horses are arrested for it, Master Brook.

MRS. FORD Sir John, we have had ill luck; we could never meet. I will never take you for my love again, but I will always count you my deer.

FALSTAFF I do begin to perceive that I am made an ass.

FORD Ay, and an ox too. Both the proofs are extant.

FALSTAFF And these are not fairies? I was three or four times in the thought they were not fairies; and yet the guiltiness of my mind, the sudden surprise of my powers, drove the grossness of the foppery into a received belief, in despite of the teeth of all rhyme and reason, that they were fairies. See now how wit may be made a Jack-a-Lent when 'tis upon ill employment!

EVANS Sir John Falstaff, serve Got, and leave your desires, and fairies will not pinse you.

FORD Well said, fairy Hugh.

EVANS And leave you your jealousies too, I pray you.

FORD I will never mistrust my wife again till thou art able to woo her in good English.

FALSTAFF Have I laid my brain in the sun and dried it, that it wants matter to prevent so gross o'erreaching as this? Am I ridden with a Welsh goat too? Shall I have a coxcomb of frieze? 'Tis time I were choked with a piece of toasted cheese.

EVANS Seese is not good to give putter. Your belly is all putter.

FALSTAFF "Seese" and "putter"! Have I lived to stand at the taunt of one that makes fritters of English? This is enough to be the decay of lust and late walking through the realm.

MRS. PAGE Why, Sir John, do you think, though we would have thrust virtue out of our hearts by the head and shoulders, and have given ourselves without scruple to hell, that ever the devil could have made you our delight?

FORD What, a hodge pudding? A bag of flax?

MRS. PAGE A puffed man?

PAGE Old, cold, withered and of intolerable entrails?

FORD And one that is as slanderous as Satan?

PAGE And as poor as Job?

FORD And as wicked as his wife?

EVANS And given to fornications, and to taverns, and sack, and wine, and metheglins, and to drinkings, and swearings, and starings, pribbles and prabbles?

FALSTAFF Well, I am your theme. You have the start of me. I am dejected. I am not able to answer the Welsh flannel. Ignorance itself is a plummet o'er me. Use me as you will.

FORD Marry, sir, we'll bring you to Windsor, to one Master Brook, that you have cozened of money, to whom you should have been a pander. Over and above that you have suffered, I think to repay that money will be a biting affliction.

PAGE Yet be cheerful, knight. Thou shalt eat a posset tonight at my house, where I will desire thee to laugh at my wife that now laughs at thee. Tell her Master Slender hath married her daughter.

MRS. PAGE *[aside]* Doctors doubt that. If Anne Page be my daughter, she is, by this, Doctor Caius' wife.

[Enter Slender.]

95 bloody fire fire in the blood **99 mutually** jointly, in unison. **103 watched you** caught you in the act **104 serve your turn** do for you. (Addressed to Falstaff in the disguise of Herne or in mock reproof to Mistress Page—part of "the jest" of line 105.) **105 hold . . . higher** maintain the jest no longer. **107 these fair yokes** i.e., the horns **114 arrested** seized by warrant as a security for paying **117 meet** (With a pun on "mate.") **118 deer** (With a pun on "dear.") **120 ox** i.e., fool. (With reference to the ox's horns, the *proofs* that are *extant,* i.e., still in existence and also protuberant.) **124 powers** faculties. **foppery** deceit **125 received** accepted. **in despite of the teeth of** in the teeth of, in defiance of **127 Jack-a-Lent** butt. (See the note for 3.3.22.)

135 wants matter lacks means **136 ridden with** mastered by **137 coxcomb of frieze** fool's cap of coarse woolen cloth, common in Wales. **143 decay** ruin. **late walking** keeping late hours (in pursuit of women) **150 hodge pudding** large "pudding," or sausage, made with a medley of ingredients. **bag of flax** i.e., a large, shapeless bag of flax. **151 puffed** dropsied, corpulent **152 intolerable** excessive **154 Job** (See Job 1 for Job's sudden descent into poverty.) **155 his wife** i.e., Job's wife, who advised him to curse God (Job 2:9). **157 metheglins** spiced drink made from wort and honey, Welsh in origin **158 starings** glaring, madly raving **159 theme** i.e., subject of mirth. **start** advantage **160 dejected** (1) overthrown (2) disheartened. **161 flannel** a Welsh cloth. **plummet** (A quibble on *plumbet,* a woolen fabric, suggested by *flannel,* and *plummet,* "a line for fathoming." Falstaff laments that he has been fathomed even by an ignorant Welshman.) **165 should have been** were to have been **166 above that** above that which **168 eat a posset** imbibe a nightcap of curdled ale or wine **172 Doctors doubt that** i.e., The wise are skeptical; things may turn out differently from what you expected. (Proverbial.) **173 this** this time

SLENDER Whoa, ho, ho, father Page!

PAGE Son, how now? How now, son? Have you dispatched?

SLENDER Dispatched? I'll make the best in Gloucestershire know on't. Would I were hanged, la, else!

PAGE Of what, son?

SLENDER I came yonder at Eton to marry Mistress Anne Page, and she's a great lubberly boy. If it had not been i' th' church, I would have swinged him, or he should have swinged me. If I did not think it had been Anne Page, would I might never stir! And 'tis a postmaster's boy.

PAGE Upon my life, then, you took the wrong.

SLENDER What need you tell me that? I think so, when I took a boy for a girl. If I had been married to him, for all he was in woman's apparel, I would not have had him.

PAGE Why, this is your own folly. Did not I tell you how you should know my daughter by her garments?

SLENDER I went to her in white and cried "mum," and she cried "budget," as Anne and I had appointed. And yet it was not Anne, but a postmaster's boy.

MRS. PAGE Good George, be not angry. I knew of your purpose, turned my daughter into green, and indeed she is now with the Doctor at the deanery, and there married.

[*Enter Caius.*]

CAIUS Vere is Mistress Page? By gar, I am cozened! I ha' married *un garçon,* a boy; *un paysan,* by gar, a boy. It is not Anne Page. By gar, I am cozened.

MRS. PAGE Why, did you take her in green?

CAIUS Ay, by gar, and 'tis a boy. By gar, I'll raise all Windsor.

FORD This is strange. Who hath got the right Anne?

PAGE My heart misgives me. Here comes Master Fenton.

[*Enter Fenton and Anne Page.*]

How now, Master Fenton?

ANNE
Pardon, good father! Good my mother, pardon!

PAGE Now, mistress, how chance you went not with Master Slender?

MRS. PAGE Why went you not with Master Doctor, maid?

FENTON
You do amaze her. Hear the truth of it.
You would have married her most shamefully,
Where there was no proportion held in love.
The truth is, she and I, long since contracted,
Are now so sure that nothing can dissolve us.
Th'offense is holy that she hath committed,
And this deceit loses the name of craft,
Of disobedience, or unduteous title,
Since therein she doth evitate and shun
A thousand irreligious cursèd hours
Which forcèd marriage would have brought upon her.

FORD
Stand not amazed. Here is no remedy.
In love the heavens themselves do guide the state;
Money buys lands, and wives are sold by fate.

FALSTAFF I am glad, though you have ta'en a special stand to strike at me, that your arrow hath glanced.

PAGE
Well, what remedy? Fenton, heaven give thee joy!
What cannot be eschewed must be embraced.

FALSTAFF
When night dogs run, all sorts of deer are chased.

MRS. PAGE
Well, I will muse no further. Master Fenton,
Heaven give you many, many merry days!
Good husband, let us every one go home
And laugh this sport o'er by a country fire—
Sir John and all.

FORD Let it be so.—Sir John,
To Master Brook you yet shall hold your word,
For he tonight shall lie with Mistress Ford. *Exeunt.*

176 dispatched finished the business. **178 on't** of it. **else** if I don't **182 swinged** thrashed **184–5 postmaster's boy** boy of the master of the post-horses. **201** ***paysan*** peasant, i.e., yokel

214 amaze bewilder **216 proportion** equality **217 contracted** betrothed **218 sure** fast knit **221 unduteous title** title of undutifulness **222 evitate** avoid **227 Money . . . fate** (A variant of the proverb "Marriage and hanging go by destiny.") **229 stand** concealed place for shooting. **glanced** (Falstaff takes comfort in the fact that, though he was the main target of the plot of exposure, others have suffered mild humiliation as well.) **233 muse** grumble, complain

As You Like It

As You Like It represents, together with *Much Ado About Nothing* and *Twelfth Night,* the summation of Shakespeare's achievement in festive, happy comedy during the years 1598–1601. *As You Like It* contains several motifs found in other Shakespearean comedies: the journey from a jaded court into a transforming sylvan environment and back to a revitalized court (as in *A Midsummer Night's Dream*); hence, a contrasting of two worlds in the play—one presided over by a virtuous but exiled older brother and the other, by a usurping younger brother (as in *The Tempest*); the heroine disguised as a man (as in *The Merchant of Venice, The Two Gentlemen of Verona, Cymbeline,* and *Twelfth Night*); and a structure of multiple plotting in which numerous groups of characters are thematically played off against one another (as in several of Shakespeare's comedies). What chiefly distinguishes this play from the others, however, is the nature and function of its pastoral setting—the Forest of Arden.

The Forest of Arden is seen in many perspectives. As a natural wilderness, it is probably most like the real forest Shakespeare knew near Stratford-upon-Avon in Warwickshire—a place capable of producing the vulgarity of an Audrey or the bumptuous clowning of a William. The forest bears the name of Shakespeare's mother, Mary Arden, the daughter of a prosperous Warwickshire farmer. Its name also owes something to the forest in Shakespeare's source, *Rosalynde,* based in turn on the forest of Ardennes in France. No less vividly, the place recalls for us Nottinghamshire and the Sherwood Forest of Robin Hood, where persons in retreat from a society seemingly beyond repair find refuge in a mythic folk world purged of social injustice. As the "golden world" (1.1.114), the forest evokes an even deeper longing for a mythological past age of innocence and plenty, when humans shared some attributes of the giants and the gods. This myth has its parallel in the biblical Garden of Eden, before the human race experienced "the penalty of Adam" (2.1.5). Finally, in another of its aspects, the forest is Arcadia, a pastoral landscape embodied in an ancient and sophisticated literary tradition and peopled by the likes of Corin, Silvius, and Phoebe.

All but the first of these Ardens, compared and contrasted with one another, involve some idealization, not only of nature and the natural landscape, but also of the human condition. These various Ardens place our real life in a complex perspective and force us to a fresh appraisal of our own ordinary existence. Duke Senior, for example, describes the forest environment as a corrective for the evils of society. He addresses his followers in the forest as "my co-mates and brothers in exile" (2.1.1), suggesting a kind of social equality that he could never know in the cramped formality of his previous official existence. The banished Duke Senior and his followers have had to leave behind their lands and revenues in the grip of the usurping Duke Frederick. No longer rich, though adequately provided with life's necessities, the Duke and his "merry men" live "like the old Robin Hood of England" and "fleet the time carelessly as they did in the golden world" (1.1.111–14). In this friendly society, a strong communal sense replaces the necessity for individual proprietorship. All comers are welcome, with food for all.

There are no luxuries in the forest, to be sure, but even this spare existence affords relief from the decadence of courtly life. "Sweet are the uses of adversity" (2.1.12), insists Duke Senior. He welcomes the cold of winter because it teaches him the true condition of humanity and of himself. The forest is serenely impartial: neither malicious nor compassionate. Death, and even killing for food, are an inevitable part of forest existence. The Duke concedes that his presence in the forest means the slaughter of deer, who were the original inhabitants; Orlando and Adam find that death through starvation in the forest is all too real a possibility. The forest is never guilty of the degrading perversity of humans at their worst, but it is also incapable of charity and forgiveness.

Shakespeare's sources reflect the complexity of his vision of Arden. The original of the Orlando story, which Shakespeare may not have used directly, is *The Cook's Tale of Gamelyn,* found in a number of manuscripts of *The Canterbury Tales* and wrongly attributed to Chaucer. This hearty English romance glorifies the rebellious and even violent spirit of its Robin Hood hero, the neglected youngest son Gamelyn, who, aided by faithful old Adam the Spencer, evades his wicked eldest brother in a cunning and bloody escape. As king of the outlaws in Sherwood Forest, Gamelyn eventually triumphs over his eldest brother (now the sheriff) and sees him hanged. Here, then, originates the motif of refuge from social injustice in Arden, even though most of the actual violence has been omitted from Shakespeare's version. (A trio of Robin Hood plays on a similar theme, beginning in 1598 with Anthony Munday's *The Downfall of Robert Earl of Huntingdon After Called Robin Hood,* was being performed with great success by the Admiral's company, chief rivals of the Lord Chamberlain's company to which Shakespeare belonged.)

As You Like It is clearly indebted to Thomas Lodge's *Rosalynde: Euphues' Golden Legacy* (published in 1590), a prose narrative version of the Gamelyn story in the ornate Euphuistic style of the 1580s. (Lodge's Epistle to the Gentleman Readers, casually inviting them to be pleased with this story if they are so inclined—"*If you like it, so*"—probably gave Shakespeare a hint for the name of his play.) Lodge accentuated the love story with its courtship in masquerade, provided some charming songs, and introduced the pastoral love motif involving Corin, Silvius, Phoebe, and Ganymede. Shakespeare's ordering of episode is generally close to that of Lodge. Pastoral literature, which had become a literary rage in the 1580s and early 1590s, owing particularly to Edmund Spenser's *Shepheardes Calendar* (1579) and Philip Sidney's *Arcadia* (1590), traced its ancestry through such Renaissance continental writers as Jorge de Montemayor, Jacopo Sannazaro, and Giovanni Battista Guarini to the so-called Greek romances, and finally back to the eclogues of Virgil, Theocritus, and Bion. A literary mode that had begun originally as a realistic evocation of difficult country life had become, in the Renaissance, an elegant vehicle for the loftiest and most patrician sentiments in love, for philosophic debate, and even for extensive political analysis and satire of the clergy.

Shakespeare's alterations and additions give us insight into his method of construction and his thematic focus. Whereas Lodge cheerfully accepts the pastoral conventions of his day, Shakespeare exposes those conventions to some criticism and considerable irony. Alongside the mannered and literary Silvius and Phoebe, he places William and Audrey, as peasantlike a couple as ever drew milk from a cow's teat. The juxtaposition holds up to critical perspective the rival claims of the literary and natural worlds by examining the defects of each in relation to the strengths of the other. William and Audrey are Shakespeare's own creation, based presumably on observation and also on the dramatic convention of the rustic clown and wench, as exemplified earlier in his Costard and Jaquenetta *(Love's Labor's Lost).*

Equally original, and essential to the many-sided debate concerning the virtues of the court versus those of the country, are Touchstone and Jaques. Touchstone is a professional court fool, dressed in motley, a new comic type in Shakespeare, created apparently in response to the recent addition to the Lord Chamberlain's company of the brilliant actor Robert Armin. Jaques is also a new type, the malcontent satirist, reflecting the very latest literary vogue in the nondramatic poetry and in drama of George Chapman, John Marston, and Ben Jonson. (The so-called private theaters, featuring boy actors, reopened in 1598–1599 after nearly a decade of enforced silence and proceeded at once to specialize in satirical drama; the public theaters like the Globe, the Rose, and the Swan sometimes joined in.) Touchstone and Jaques complement one another as critics and observers—one laughing at human folly with quizzical comic detachment and the other satirizing it with self-righteous scorn. Once we have been exposed to this assortment of newly created characters, we can no longer view either pastoral life or pastoral love as simply as Lodge and some other writers of the period portray them.

When *As You Like It* is compared with its chief source, Shakespeare can also be seen to have altered and considerably softened the characters of the wicked brothers Oliver and Frederick. Whereas Lodge's Saladyne is motivated by a greedy desire to seize his younger brother Rosader's property, Shakespeare's Oliver is envious of Orlando's natural goodness and popularity. As he confesses in soliloquy, Orlando is "so much in the heart of the world and especially of my own people . . . that I am altogether misprized" (1.1.159–61). In his warped way, Oliver desires to be more like Orlando, and in the enchanted forest of Arden he eventually becomes so. Duke Frederick, too, is plainly envious of goodness. Trying to persuade his daughter Celia of the need for banishing Rosalind, he argues, "thou wilt show more bright and seem more virtuous / When she is gone" (1.3.79–80). In spite of his obsession with the mere "seeming" of virtue, Duke Frederick acknowledges the power of a goodness that will eventually convert him along with the rest. Penitence and conciliation replace the vengeful conclusion of Lodge's novel, in which the nobles of France finally overthrow and execute the usurping king. Although Shakespeare's resolutions are sudden, like all miracles they attest to the inexplicable power of goodness.

The court of Duke Frederick is "the envious court," identified by this fixed epithet. In it, brothers turn unnaturally against brothers: the younger Frederick usurps his older brother's throne, whereas the older Oliver denies the younger Orlando his birthright of education. In still another parallel, both Rosalind and Orlando find themselves mistrusted as the children of Frederick's political enemies, Duke Senior and Sir Rowland de Boys. A daughter and a son are held to be guilty by association. "Thou art thy father's daughter. There's enough" (1.3.56), Frederick curtly retorts in explaining Rosalind's exile. And to Orlando, triumphant in wrestling with Charles, Frederick asserts, "I would thou hadst been son to some man else" (1.2.214). Here again, Frederick plaintively reveals his envy of goodness, even if at present any potential for goodness in him is thwarted by tyrannous whim. Many of Frederick's entourage might also be better persons if they only knew how to escape the insincerities of their courtly life. Charles the wrestler, for example, places himself at Oliver's service, and yet he would happily avoid breaking Orlando's neck if to do so were consistent with self-interest. Even Le Beau, the giddy fop so delighted at first with the cruel sport of wrestling, takes Orlando aside at some personal risk to warn him of Duke Frederick's foul humor. Ideally, Le Beau would prefer to be a companion of Orlando's "in a better world than this" (1.2.275). The vision of a regenerative Utopia secretly abides in the heart of this courtly creature.

It is easier to anatomize the defects of a social order than to propound solutions. As have other creators of visionary landscapes (including Thomas More in his *Utopia*), Shakespeare uses playful debate to elicit complicated responses on the part of his audience. Which is preferable, the court or the country? Jaques and Touchstone are adept gadflies, incessantly pointing out contradictions and ironies. Jaques, the malcontent railer derived from literary satire, takes delight in being out of step with everyone. Seemingly, his chief reason for having joined the others in the forest is to jibe at their motives for being there. To their song about the rejection of courtly ambition he mockingly supplies another verse, charging them with having left their wealth and ease out of mere willfulness (2.5.46–54). With ironic appropriateness, Jaques eventually decides to remain in the forest in the company of Frederick; Jaques cannot thrive on resolution and harmony. His humor is "melancholy," from which, as he observes, he draws consolation as a weasel sucks eggs (2.5.11–12). The others treat him as a sort of profane jester whose soured conceits add relish to their enjoyment of the forest life.

Despite his affectation, however, Jaques is serious and even excited in his defense of satire as a curative form of laughter (2.7.47–87). The appearance of Touchstone in the forest has reaffirmed in Jaques his profound commitment to a view of life as an absurd process of decay governed by inexorable time. His function in such a life is to be mordant, unsparing. As literary satirist, he must be free to awaken people's minds to their own folly. To Duke Senior's protestation that the satirist is merely self-indulgent and licentious, Jaques counters with a thoughtful and classically Horatian defense of satire as an art form devoted not to libelous attacks on individuals but to exposing types of folly. Any observer who feels individually portrayed merely condemns himself or herself by confessing his or her resemblance to the type. This particular debate between Duke Senior and Jaques ends, appropriately, in a draw. The Duke's point is well taken, for Jaques's famous "Seven Ages of Man" speech, so often read out of context, occurs in a scene that also witnesses the sacrifices and brave deeds that Orlando and Adam are prepared to undertake for each other. The feeling bond between the generations that they share refutes Jaques's wry narrative of isolated self-interest. As though in answer to Jaques's acid depiction of covetous old age, we see old Adam's self-sacrifice and trust in Providence. Instead of "mere oblivion," we see charitable compassion prompting Duke Senior to aid Orlando and Orlando to aid Adam. Perhaps this vision seems of a higher spiritual order than that of Jaques. Nonetheless, without him the forest would lack a satirical perspective that continually requires us to reexamine our romantic assumptions about human happiness.

Touchstone's name suggests that he similarly offers a multiplicity of viewpoints. (A touchstone is a kind of stone used to test for gold and silver.) He shares with Jaques a skeptical view of life, but for Touchstone the inconsistency and absurdity of life are occasions for wit and humor rather than melancholy and cynicism. As a professional fool, he observes that many supposedly sane men are more foolish than he—as, for example, in their elaborate dueling code of the Retort Courteous and the Reply Churlish, leading finally to the Lie Circumstantial and the Lie Direct. He is fascinated by the games people make of their lives and is amused by their inability to be content with what they already have. Of the shepherd's life, he comments, "In respect that it is solitary, I like it very well; but in respect that it is private, it is a very vile life" (3.2.15–16). This paradox, though nonsensical, captures the restlessness of human striving for a life that can somehow combine the peaceful solitude of nature with the convenience and excitement of city life. Although Touchstone marries, even his marriage is a spoof of the institution rather than a serious attempt at commitment. Like all fools, who in Renaissance times were regarded as a breed apart, Touchstone exists outside the realm of ordinary human responses. There he can comment disinterestedly on human folly. He is prevented, however, from sharing fully in the human love and conciliation with which the play ends. He and Jaques are not touched by the play's regenerative magic; Jaques will remain in the forest, and Touchstone will remain forever a childlike entertainer.

The regenerative power of Arden, as we have seen, is not the forest's alone. What saves Orlando is the human charity practiced by him and by Duke Senior, who, for all his love of the forest, longs to rejoin that human society where he has "with holy bell been knolled to church" (2.7.120). Civilization at its best is no less necessary to the human spirit than is the natural order of the forest. In love, also, perception and wisdom must be combined with nature's gifts. Orlando, when we first see him, is a young man of the finest natural qualities but admittedly lacking experience in the nuances of complex human relationships. Nowhere does his lack of sophistication betray him more unhappily than in his first encounter with Rosalind, following the wrestling match. In response to her unmistakable hints of favor, he stands ox-like, tongue-tied. Later, in the forest, his first attempts at self-education in love lead him into an opposite danger: an excess of platitudinous manners parading in the guise of Petrarchism. (The Italian sonneteer Francis Petrarch has given to the language a name for the stereotypical literary mannerisms we associate with courtly love: the sighing and self-abasement of the young man, the chaste denial of love by the woman whom he worships, and the like.) Orlando's newfound self-abasement and idealization of his absent mistress are as unsatisfactory as his former naiveté. The sonnets he hangs on trees are deserving of the delicious parody they get from Touchstone. Orlando must learn from Rosalind that a quest for true understanding in love avoids the extreme of pretentious mannerism as well as that of mere artlessness. Orlando as Petrarchan lover too much resembles Silvius, the lovesick young man, cowering before the imperious will of his coy mistress Phoebe. This stereotyped relationship, taken from the pages of fashionable pastoral romance, represents a posturing that Rosalind hopes to cure in Silvius and Phoebe even as she will also cure Orlando.

Rosalind is, above all, the realistic one, the plucky Shakespearean heroine showing her mettle in the world of men, emotionally more mature than her lover. Her concern is with a working and clear-sighted relationship in love, and to that end she daringly insists that Orlando learn something of woman's changeable mood. Above all, she must disabuse him of the dangerously misleading clichés of the Petrarchan love myth. When he protests he would die for love of Rosalind, she lectures him mockingly in her guise of Ganymede: "No, faith, die by attorney. The poor world is almost six thousand years old, and in all this time there was not any man died in his own person, videlicet, in a love cause." She debunks the legends of Troilus and Leander, youths supposed to have died for love who, if they had ever really existed, would no doubt have met with more prosaic ends. "But these are all lies. Men have died from time to time, and worms have eaten them, but not for love" (4.1.89–102). Rosalind wants Orlando to know that women are not goddesses but frail human beings who can be giddy, jealous, infatuated with novelty, irritatingly talkative, peremptory, and hysterical (4.1.142–9), though she is circumspect as to whether women can also be unfaithful. Orlando must be taught that love is a madness (3.2.390), and he must be cured, not of loving Rosalind, but of worshiping her with unrealistic expectations that can lead only to disillusionment. Rosalind teases him, as Portia does Bassanio in *The Merchant of Venice,* but she does not seriously threaten him with wantonness. Her disguise as Ganymede provides for her the perfect role in Orlando's approach to sexual manhood: he can learn to love "Ganymede" as a friend and then make the transition to heterosexual union in his blessed discovery that the friend is also the lover. Rosalind's own rite of passage is easier; for all her reliance on her loving friendship with Celia, or "Aliena," she is ready to exclaim, "But what talk we of fathers, when there is such a man as Orlando?" (3.4.36–7). She is spiritedly independent, even more so than Portia; whereas Portia's choice of husband is controlled by her father from his grave, Rosalind picks for herself. To be sure, Duke Senior is certainly happy that she marries Orlando, and she is glad to be reunited with her father, but her choice in marriage is very much her own. The forest is indeed a place where she can encounter her father "man to man," as it were, and be liberated from him while coming to terms with a patriarchal world. She is ready to give herself to Orlando, but she must educate him first. When Orlando has been sufficiently tested as to patience, loyalty, and understanding, she unmasks herself to him and simultaneously unravels the plot of ridiculous love we have come to associate with Silvius and Phoebe.

Rosalind's disguise name, Ganymede, has connotations that suggest ways in which human sexuality can be partly understood as socially constructed. If Rosalind in disguise as Ganymede wins the affection and eventually the love of Orlando, while her father and the other forest dwellers are equally taken in by the disguise, are maleness and femaleness chiefly matters of sartorial convention and superficial appearance? When Phoebe falls in love with Ganymede, is not her infatuation a way of showing that the roles of the sexes can be put on and off? Theatrically, the device of having a young male actor play Rosalind who then disguises him/herself as a young man adds to the witty confusion of sexual identities by introducing homoerotic possibilities. Not only can the roles of the sexes be put on and off, sexual desire itself is unstable, attaching itself to effeminate or sexually indeterminate young men like Ganymede, who is described as being "Of female favor" and "Like a ripe sister" (4.3.87–8; compare *Twelfth Night*, 1.4.31–4, where Orsino says of "Cesario" that "all is semblative a woman's part"). Both Phoebe and Orlando are in some ways attracted to Ganymede; when Rosalind says of Orlando that "his kissing is as full of sanctity as the touch of holy bread" (3.4.13–14), she seems to suggest that Orlando has kissed her in her male disguise. Mythologically Ganymede is Zeus's or Jupiter's young male lover as well as cupbearer. The very role of boy actors in an all-male acting company must have struck some viewers as homoerotically suggestive.

At the same time, the motif of disguise enables the play to pursue a serious point about love and friendship. Orlando can speak frankly and personally to "Ganymede" as a perfect friend, one who can enable him as a young man still faced with the uncertainties and hazards of courtship to traverse the potentially difficult transition from male-to-male friendship into adult heterosexuality. The relationship closely anticipates that of "Cesario" and Orsino in *Twelfth Night*, where once again a powerful and loving attraction to a sexually ambiguous young man/woman ripens into mature love when the older man has been educated by the experience of loving friendship. Both plays depict heterosexual courtship as full of dangers for the male. In *As You Like It*, Rosalind is at pains to coach Orlando in what to expect from unruly women; and indeed, Rosalind's very readiness to wear male apparel bespeaks her daring intrusion into a man's world, even if Shakespeare carefully hedges this threat by insisting on Rosalind's hesitancy in being so bold. Rosalind is thus, like Portia in *The Merchant of Venice*, both spirited and eventually ready to comply with the mores of a male-dominated world.

By becoming Orlando's teacher, Rosalind is able to claim a strong position in their friendship and in our estimate of her remarkable worthiness. Posing as Ganymede, Rosalind can observe and test Orlando and thereby learn the truth about his capability for lifelong fidelity as only another man would have the opportunity to do. Once a loving friendship has grown strong between them, the unmasking of Rosalind's sexual identity makes possible a physical union between them to confirm and express the spiritual. In these terms, the play's happy ending affirms marriage as an institution, not simply as the expected denouement. The procession to the altar is synchronous with the return to civilization's other institutions, made whole again not solely by the forest but by the power of goodness embodied in Rosalind, Orlando, Duke Senior, and the others who persevere.

As You Like It

[*Dramatis Personae*

DUKE SENIOR, *a banished duke*
DUKE FREDERICK, *his usurping brother*
ROSALIND, *daughter of Duke Senior, later disguised as* GANYMEDE
CELIA, *daughter of Duke Frederick, later disguised as* ALIENA

OLIVER, JAQUES, ORLANDO, *sons of Sir Rowland de Boys*

AMIENS, JAQUES, *lords attending Duke Senior*

LE BEAU, *a courtier attending Duke Frederick*
CHARLES, *a wrestler in the court of Duke Frederick*

ADAM, *an aged servant of Oliver and then Orlando*
DENNIS, *a servant of Oliver*

TOUCHSTONE, *the* CLOWN *or* FOOL

CORIN, *an old shepherd*
SILVIUS, *a young shepherd, in love with Phoebe*
PHOEBE, *a shepherdess*
WILLIAM, *a country youth, in love with Audrey*
AUDREY, *a country wench*
SIR OLIVER MAR-TEXT, *a country vicar*

HYMEN, *god of marriage*

Lords and Attendants waiting on Duke Frederick and Duke Senior

SCENE: *Oliver's house; Duke Frederick's court; and the Forest of Arden*]

1.1

Enter Orlando and Adam.

ORLANDO As I remember, Adam, it was upon this fashion bequeathed me by will but poor a thousand crowns and, as thou say'st, charged my brother on his blessing to breed me well; and there begins my sadness. My brother Jaques he keeps at school, and report speaks goldenly of his profit. For my part, he keeps me rustically at home—or, to speak more properly, stays me here at home unkept; for call you that "keeping" for a gentleman of my birth, that differs not from the stalling of an ox? His horses are bred better, for besides that they are fair with their feeding, they are taught their manage, and to that end riders dearly hired. But I, his brother, gain nothing under him but growth, for the which his animals on his dunghills are as much bound to him as I. Besides this nothing that he so plentifully gives me, the something that nature gave me his countenance seems to take from me. He lets me feed with his hinds, bars me the place of a brother, and as much as in him lies, mines my gentility with my education. This is it, Adam, that grieves me; and the spirit of my father, which I think is within me, begins to mutiny against this servitude. I will no longer endure it, though yet I know no wise remedy how to avoid it.

Enter Oliver.

ADAM Yonder comes my master, your brother.
ORLANDO Go apart, Adam, and thou shalt hear how he will shake me up. [*Adam stands aside.*]
OLIVER Now, sir, what make you here?

1.1 Location: The garden of Oliver's house.
1–3 it was . . . crowns it was in this way that I was left, by the terms of my father's will, a mere thousand crowns or £250 **3 crowns** coins worth five shillings. **3–4 charged . . . well** my brother was instructed as a condition of my father's blessing to educate me well **5 My . . . school** My oldest brother Oliver maintains my other brother, Jaques, at university **6 profit** progress. **8 stays** detains. **unkept** poorly supported **11–12 fair . . . feeding** kept well groomed with good diet **12 manage** manège, paces and maneuvers in the art of horsemanship

13 riders trainers. **dearly** expensively **17 countenance** behavior; (neglectful) patronage **19 hinds** farm hands. **bars me** excludes me from **19–20 as much . . . education** with all the power at his disposal, undermines my right to be educated as a gentleman. **26 Go apart** Stand aside **27 shake me up** abuse me. **28 make** do. (But Orlando takes it in the more usual sense.)

ORLANDO Nothing. I am not taught to make anything.

OLIVER What mar you then, sir?

ORLANDO Marry, sir, I am helping you to mar that which God made, a poor unworthy brother of yours, with idleness.

OLIVER Marry, sir, be better employed, and be naught awhile.

ORLANDO Shall I keep your hogs and eat husks with them? What prodigal portion have I spent, that I should come to such penury?

OLIVER Know you where you are, sir?

ORLANDO Oh, sir, very well: here in your orchard.

OLIVER Know you before whom, sir?

ORLANDO Ay, better than him I am before knows me. I know you are my eldest brother, and in the gentle condition of blood you should so know me. The courtesy of nations allows you my better, in that you are the firstborn, but the same tradition takes not away my blood, were there twenty brothers betwixt us. I have as much of my father in me as you, albeit I confess your coming before me is nearer to his reverence.

OLIVER What, boy! *[He strikes Orlando.]*

ORLANDO Come, come, elder brother, you are too young in this. *[He seizes Oliver by the throat.]*

OLIVER Wilt thou lay hands on me, villain?

ORLANDO I am no villain. I am the youngest son of Sir Rowland de Boys. He was my father, and he is thrice a villain that says such a father begot villains. Wert thou not my brother, I would not take this hand from thy throat till this other had pulled out thy tongue for saying so. Thou hast railed on thyself.

ADAM Sweet masters, be patient! For your father's remembrance, be at accord.

OLIVER Let me go, I say.

ORLANDO I will not till I please. You shall hear me. My father charged you in his will to give me good education. You have trained me like a peasant, obscuring and hiding from me all gentlemanlike qualities. The spirit of my father grows strong in me, and I will no longer endure it; therefore allow me such exercises as may become a gentleman, or give me the poor allotery my father left me by testament. With that I will go buy my fortunes. *[He releases Oliver.]*

OLIVER And what wilt thou do? Beg when that is spent? Well, sir, get you in. I will not long be troubled with you; you shall have some part of your will. I pray you, leave me.

ORLANDO I will no further offend you than becomes me for my good.

OLIVER *[to Adam]* Get you with him, you old dog.

ADAM Is "old dog" my reward? Most true, I have lost my teeth in your service. God be with my old master! He would not have spoke such a word.

Exeunt Orlando [and] Adam.

OLIVER Is it even so? Begin you to grow upon me? I will physic your rankness and yet give no thousand crowns neither.—Holla, Dennis!

Enter Dennis.

DENNIS Calls Your Worship?

OLIVER Was not Charles, the Duke's wrestler, here to speak with me?

DENNIS So please you, he is here at the door and importunes access to you.

OLIVER Call him in. *[Exit Dennis.]*
'Twill be a good way; and tomorrow the wrestling is.

Enter Charles.

CHARLES Good morrow to Your Worship.

OLIVER Good Monsieur Charles, what's the new news at the new court?

CHARLES There's no news at the court, sir, but the old news: that is, the old Duke is banished by his younger brother the new Duke, and three or four loving lords have put themselves into voluntary exile with him, whose lands and revenues enrich the new Duke; therefore he gives them good leave to wander.

OLIVER Can you tell if Rosalind, the Duke's daughter, be banished with her father?

CHARLES Oh, no; for the Duke's daughter, her cousin, so loves her, being ever from their cradles bred together, that she would have followed her exile or have died to stay behind her. She is at the court and no less beloved of her uncle than his own daughter, and never two ladies loved as they do.

OLIVER Where will the old Duke live?

CHARLES They say he is already in the Forest of Arden, and a many merry men with him; and there they live like the old Robin Hood of England. They say many young gentlemen flock to him every day and fleet the time carelessly as they did in the golden world.

OLIVER What, you wrestle tomorrow before the new Duke?

30 mar ("To make or mar" is a commonplace antithesis.) **31 Marry** i.e., Indeed. (Originally an oath by the Virgin Mary.) **34–5 be naught awhile** i.e., stay in your place, don't grumble. **36–8 Shall . . . penury?** (Alluding to the story of the Prodigal Son, in Luke 15:11–32, who, having wasted his "portion" or inheritance, had to tend swine and eat with them.) **39 where** in whose presence. (But Orlando sarcastically takes the more literal meaning.) **40 orchard** garden. **43–4 in . . . blood** acknowledging the bond of our being of gentle birth **44–5 courtesy of nations** recognized custom (of primogeniture, whereby the eldest son inherits all the land) **47 blood** (1) gentlemanly lineage (2) spirit **49 is nearer . . . reverence** is closer to his position of authority (as head of family). **52 young** inexperienced (at fighting) **53 villain** i.e., wicked fellow. (But Orlando plays on the literal meaning of "bondman" or "serf," as well as Oliver's meaning.) **55 he** anyone **59 railed on thyself** insulted your own blood. **60–1 your father's remembrance** the sake of your father's memory **66 qualities** (1) characteristics (2) accomplishments. **68 exercises** employments **69 allottery** portion

74 will (1) desire (2) portion from your father's will (3) willfulness (i.e., you'll get what is coming to you). **82 grow upon me** take liberties with me; grow too big for your breeches. **83 physic your rankness** apply medicine to your overweening **84 neither** either. **88 So please you** If you please **92 Good morrow** Good morning **99 whose** all of whose **100 good leave** full permission **104 being** they being **105–6 died to stay** died from being forced to stay **113 fleet** pass **114 carelessly** free from care. **golden world** the primal age of innocence and ease from which humankind was thought to have degenerated. (See Ovid, *Metamorphoses* 1.)

CHARLES Marry, do I, sir; and I came to acquaint you with a matter. I am given, sir, secretly to understand that your younger brother Orlando hath a disposition to come in disguised against me to try a fall. Tomorrow, sir, I wrestle for my credit, and he that escapes me without some broken limb shall acquit him well. Your brother is but young and tender, and for your love I would be loath to foil him, as I must for my own honor if he come in. Therefore, out of my love to you, I came hither to acquaint you withal, that either you might stay him from his intendment or brook such disgrace well as he shall run into, in that it is a thing of his own search and altogether against my will.

OLIVER Charles, I thank thee for thy love to me, which thou shalt find I will most kindly requite. I had myself notice of my brother's purpose herein and have by underhand means labored to dissuade him from it, but he is resolute. I'll tell thee, Charles, it is the stubbornest young fellow of France, full of ambition, an envious emulator of every man's good parts, a secret and villainous contriver against me his natural brother. Therefore use thy discretion. I had as lief thou didst break his neck as his finger. And thou wert best look to't; for if thou dost him any slight disgrace, or if he do not mightily grace himself on thee, he will practice against thee by poison, entrap thee by some treacherous device, and never leave thee till he hath ta'en thy life by some indirect means or other; for I assure thee, and almost with tears I speak it, there is not one so young and so villainous this day living. I speak but brotherly of him, but should I anatomize him to thee as he is, I must blush and weep, and thou must look pale and wonder.

CHARLES I am heartily glad I came hither to you. If he come tomorrow, I'll give him his payment. If ever he go alone again, I'll never wrestle for prize more. And so God keep Your Worship!

OLIVER Farewell, good Charles. *Exit* [*Charles*].
Now will I stir this gamester. I hope I shall see an end of him; for my soul, yet I know not why, hates nothing more than he. Yet he's gentle, never schooled and yet learned, full of noble device, of all sorts enchantingly beloved, and indeed so much in the heart of the world and especially of my own people, who best know him, that I am altogether misprized. But it shall not be so long; this wrestler shall clear all. Nothing remains but that I kindle the boy thither, which now I'll go about. *Exit.*

1.2

Enter Rosalind and Celia.

CELIA I pray thee, Rosalind, sweet my coz, be merry.

ROSALIND Dear Celia, I show more mirth than I am mistress of, and would you yet I were merrier? Unless you could teach me to forget a banished father, you must not learn me how to remember any extraordinary pleasure.

CELIA Herein I see thou lov'st me not with the full weight that I love thee. If my uncle, thy banished father, had banished thy uncle, the Duke my father, so thou hadst been still with me, I could have taught my love to take thy father for mine. So wouldst thou, if the truth of thy love to me were so righteously tempered as mine is to thee.

ROSALIND Well, I will forget the condition of my estate to rejoice in yours.

CELIA You know my father hath no child but I, nor none is like to have. And truly, when he dies thou shalt be his heir, for what he hath taken away from thy father perforce I will render thee again in affection. By mine honor, I will, and when I break that oath, let me turn monster. Therefore, my sweet Rose, my dear Rose, be merry.

ROSALIND From henceforth I will, coz, and devise sports. Let me see, what think you of falling in love?

CELIA Marry, I prithee, do, to make sport withal. But love no man in good earnest, nor no further in sport neither than with safety of a pure blush thou mayst in honor come off again.

ROSALIND What shall be our sport, then?

CELIA Let us sit and mock the good huswife Fortune from her wheel, that her gifts may henceforth be bestowed equally.

ROSALIND I would we could do so, for her benefits are mightily misplaced, and the bountiful blind woman doth most mistake in her gifts to women.

CELIA 'Tis true, for those that she makes fair she scarce makes honest, and those that she makes honest she makes very ill-favoredly.

120 a fall a bout of wrestling. **121 credit** reputation **122 shall . . . well** (1) must exert himself very skillfully (2) will be lucky indeed. **124 foil** defeat **126 withal** with this **127 stay . . . intendment** restrain him from his intent. **brook** endure **129 search** seeking **133 underhand** unobtrusive **135–6 envious emulator** malicious disparager **136 parts** qualities **137 contriver** plotter. **natural** blood **138 lief** willingly **139–40 thou . . . to't** you'd better beware **140–1 if he . . . on thee** if he fails to distinguish himself at your expense **141 practice** plot **147 brotherly** as a brother should. **anatomize** analyze **152 go alone** walk unassisted **155 gamester** sportsman. (Said sardonically.) **157 gentle** gentlemanly **158 noble device** lofty aspiration. **sorts** classes of people. **enchantingly** as if they were under his spell **160 people** servants **161 misprized** undervalued, scorned.

162 clear all solve everything. **163 kindle . . . thither** inflame Orlando with desire to go to the wrestling match
1.2 Location: Duke Frederick's court. A place suitable for wrestling.
1 sweet my coz my sweet cousin **5 learn** teach **8 that** with which **10 so** provided that **12–13 righteously tempered** harmoniously composed **14 condition of my estate** state of my fortunes **17 like** likely **19 perforce** by force **25 sport** pastimes **27 pure** (1) mere (2) innocent **28 come off** retire, leave **30 huswife** one who manages household affairs and operates the spinning wheel. (Shakespeare conflates this wheel with the commonplace wheel of Fortune.) *Huswife* is used derogatorily here, with a suggestion of "hussy." **34 bountiful blind woman** i.e., Fortune **36 scarce** rarely **37 honest** chaste **38 ill-favoredly** ugly.

ROSALIND Nay, now thou goest from Fortune's office to Nature's. Fortune reigns in gifts of the world, not in the lineaments of Nature.

Enter [*Touchstone the*] *Clown.*

CELIA No; when Nature hath made a fair creature, may she not by Fortune fall into the fire? Though Nature hath given us wit to flout at Fortune, hath not Fortune sent in this fool to cut off the argument?

ROSALIND Indeed, there is Fortune too hard for Nature, when Fortune makes Nature's natural the cutter-off of Nature's wit.

CELIA Peradventure this is not Fortune's work neither but Nature's, who perceiveth our natural wits too dull to reason of such goddesses and hath sent this natural for our whetstone; for always the dullness of the fool is the whetstone of the wits.—How now, wit, whither wander you?

TOUCHSTONE Mistress, you must come away to your father.

CELIA Were you made the messenger?

TOUCHSTONE No, by mine honor, but I was bid to come for you.

ROSALIND Where learned you that oath, Fool?

TOUCHSTONE Of a certain knight that swore by his honor they were good pancakes and swore by his honor the mustard was naught. Now I'll stand to it the pancakes were naught and the mustard was good, and yet was not the knight forsworn.

CELIA How prove you that in the great heap of your knowledge?

ROSALIND Ay, marry, now unmuzzle your wisdom.

TOUCHSTONE Stand you both forth now. Stroke your chins, and swear by your beards that I am a knave.

CELIA By our beards, if we had them, thou art.

TOUCHSTONE By my knavery, if I had it, then I were; but if you swear by that that is not, you are not forsworn. No more was this knight, swearing by his honor, for he never had any; or if he had, he had sworn it away before ever he saw those pancakes or that mustard.

CELIA Prithee, who is't that thou mean'st?

TOUCHSTONE One that old Frederick, your father, loves.

CELIA My father's love is enough to honor him enough. Speak no more of him; you'll be whipped for taxation one of these days.

TOUCHSTONE The more pity that fools may not speak wisely what wise men do foolishly.

CELIA By my troth, thou sayest true; for since the little wit that fools have was silenced, the little foolery that wise men have makes a great show. Here comes Monsieur Le Beau.

Enter Le Beau.

ROSALIND With his mouth full of news.

CELIA Which he will put on us as pigeons feed their young.

ROSALIND Then shall we be news-crammed.

CELIA All the better; we shall be the more marketable.—*Bonjour,* Monsieur Le Beau. What's the news?

LE BEAU Fair princess, you have lost much good sport.

CELIA Sport? Of what color?

LE BEAU What color, madam? How shall I answer you?

ROSALIND As wit and fortune will.

TOUCHSTONE Or as the Destinies decrees.

CELIA Well said. That was laid on with a trowel.

TOUCHSTONE Nay, if I keep not my rank—

ROSALIND Thou loosest thy old smell.

LE BEAU You amaze me, ladies. I would have told you of good wrestling, which you have lost the sight of.

ROSALIND Yet tell us the manner of the wrestling.

LE BEAU I will tell you the beginning, and if it please Your Ladyships you may see the end, for the best is yet to do, and here, where you are, they are coming to perform it.

CELIA Well, the beginning, that is dead and buried.

LE BEAU There comes an old man and his three sons—

CELIA I could match this beginning with an old tale.

LE BEAU Three proper young men, of excellent growth and presence—

ROSALIND With bills on their necks, "Be it known unto all men by these presents."

LE BEAU The eldest of the three wrestled with Charles, the Duke's wrestler, which Charles in a moment threw him and broke three of his ribs, that there is little hope of life in him. So he served the second, and so the third. Yonder they lie, the poor old man their father making such pitiful dole over them that all the beholders take his part with weeping.

ROSALIND Alas!

TOUCHSTONE But what is the sport, monsieur, that the ladies have lost?

LE BEAU Why, this that I speak of.

40 gifts of the world e.g., riches and power **41 the lineaments of Nature** the features that Nature provides (like beauty or ugliness). **41.1 *Touchstone*** a stone used to test for gold and silver **43 she** the woman whom Nature has made beautiful **44 flout** scoff **46 there** in that instance **47–8 when . . . wit** i.e., when Fortune makes this natural half-wit (Touchstone) the cutter-off of witty dialogue that our natural gifts enable us to engage in. (A *natural* here means a born idiot; also in line 51.) **49 Peradventure** Perhaps **51 to reason . . . goddesses** to engage in debate about Reason and Nature **52 whetstone** grinding stone against which to sharpen things (in this case, wit) **52–3 the dullness . . . wits** i.e., the mindless things said by an idiot serve as material on which to sharpen our wits. **53–4 whither wander you** (An allusion to the expression "wandering wits.") **62 pancakes** fritters (which might be made of meat and so require mustard) **63 naught** worthless. **stand to it** maintain, argue **65 forsworn** perjured. **81 taxation** censure, slander

85–6 since . . . silenced (Perhaps refers specifically to the Bishops' order of June 1599 banning satirical books.) **90 put on** force upon **93–4 marketable** i.e., like animals that have been crammed with food before being sent to market. **97 color** kind. **101 with a trowel** i.e., thick. **102 rank** i.e., status as a wit. (But Rosalind plays on the sense of "stench.") **104 amaze** bewilder **108–9 yet to do** still to come **111 the beginning** tell us what has already occurred **114 proper** handsome **116 bills** proclamations **117 these presents** the present document. (Rosalind uses this legal phrase to pun on *presence* in line 115.) **121 So** Similarly **123 dole** lamentation

TOUCHSTONE Thus men may grow wiser every day. It is the first time that ever I heard breaking of ribs was sport for ladies.

CELIA Or I, I promise thee.

ROSALIND But is there any else longs to see this broken music in his sides? Is there yet another dotes upon rib breaking?—Shall we see this wrestling, cousin?

LE BEAU You must if you stay here, for here is the place appointed for the wrestling, and they are ready to perform it.

CELIA Yonder, sure, they are coming. Let us now stay and see it.

Flourish. Enter Duke [Frederick], Lords, Orlando, Charles, and attendants.

DUKE FREDERICK Come on. Since the youth will not be entreated, his own peril on his forwardness.

ROSALIND [*to Le Beau*] Is yonder the man?

LE BEAU Even he, madam.

CELIA Alas, he is too young! Yet he looks successfully.

DUKE FREDERICK How now, daughter and cousin? Are you crept hither to see the wrestling?

ROSALIND Ay, my liege, so please you give us leave.

DUKE FREDERICK You will take little delight in it, I can tell you, there is such odds in the man. In pity of the challenger's youth I would fain dissuade him, but he will not be entreated. Speak to him, ladies; see if you can move him.

CELIA Call him hither, good Monsieur Le Beau.

DUKE FREDERICK Do so. I'll not be by. [*He steps aside.*]

LE BEAU [*to Orlando*] Monsieur the challenger, the princess calls for you.

ORLANDO [*approaching the ladies*] I attend them with all respect and duty.

ROSALIND Young man, have you challenged Charles the wrestler?

ORLANDO No, fair princess. He is the general challenger. I come but in, as others do, to try with him the strength of my youth.

CELIA Young gentleman, your spirits are too bold for your years. You have seen cruel proof of this man's strength. If you saw yourself with your eyes or knew yourself with your judgment, the fear of your adventure would counsel you to a more equal enterprise. We pray you, for your own sake, to embrace your own safety and give over this attempt.

ROSALIND Do, young sir. Your reputation shall not therefore be misprized. We will make it our suit to the Duke that the wrestling might not go forward.

ORLANDO I beseech you, punish me not with your hard thoughts, wherein I confess me much guilty to deny so fair and excellent ladies anything. But let your fair eyes and gentle wishes go with me to my trial, wherein if I be foiled, there is but one shamed that was never gracious, if killed, but one dead that is willing to be so. I shall do my friends no wrong, for I have none to lament me; the world no injury, for in it I have nothing. Only in the world I fill up a place which may be better supplied when I have made it empty.

ROSALIND The little strength that I have, I would it were with you.

CELIA And mine, to eke out hers.

ROSALIND Fare you well. Pray heaven I be deceived in you!

CELIA Your heart's desires be with you!

CHARLES Come, where is this young gallant that is so desirous to lie with his mother earth?

ORLANDO Ready, sir, but his will hath in it a more modest working.

DUKE FREDERICK You shall try but one fall.

CHARLES No, I warrant Your Grace, you shall not entreat him to a second, that have so mightily persuaded him from a first.

ORLANDO You mean to mock me after; you should not have mocked me before. But come your ways.

ROSALIND Now Hercules be thy speed, young man!

CELIA I would I were invisible, to catch the strong fellow by the leg. [*Orlando and Charles*] *wrestle.*

ROSALIND Oh, excellent young man!

CELIA If I had a thunderbolt in mine eye, I can tell who should down. *Shout.* [*Charles is thrown.*]

DUKE FREDERICK No more, no more.

ORLANDO Yes, I beseech Your Grace. I am not yet well breathed.

DUKE FREDERICK
How dost thou, Charles?

LE BEAU He cannot speak, my lord.

DUKE FREDERICK
Bear him away.—What is thy name, young man?
[*Charles is borne out.*]

ORLANDO Orlando, my liege, the youngest son of Sir Rowland de Boys.

DUKE FREDERICK
I would thou hadst been son to some man else.
The world esteemed thy father honorable,
But I did find him still mine enemy.
Thou shouldst have better pleased me with this deed
Hadst thou descended from another house.
But fare thee well; thou art a gallant youth.
I would thou hadst told me of another father.
Exit Duke [with train, and others. Rosalind and Celia remain; Orlando stands apart from them.]

132 promise assure **133 any else** anyone else who **133–4 broken music** literally, music arranged in parts for different instruments; here applied to the breaking of ribs **134 another** another who
142 entreated . . . forwardness i.e., entreated to desist, let the risk be blamed upon his own rashness. **145 successfully** i.e., as if he would be successful. **146 cousin** i.e., niece. **148 so . . . leave** if you will permit us. **150 there . . . man** Charles is such an odds-on favorite to win. **151 fain** willingly **162–3 the general challenger** the one who is ready to take on all comers. (Orlando is the challenger in a more limited sense.) **167–8 If . . . judgment** If you saw yourself objectively **169 equal** i.e., where the odds are more equal **173 misprized** despised, undervalued.

176 wherein though. **to deny** in denying **180 gracious** looked upon with favor **183 Only . . . I** In the world I merely
188–9 deceived in you i.e., mistaken in fearing you will lose.
194 modest working decorous endeavor (than to lie with one's mother earth. For a man to lie with his mother is to commit incest.)
200 come your ways come on. **201 Hercules be thy speed** may Hercules help you **205 If . . . eye** i.e., If I were Zeus or Jupiter
206 down fall. **208–9 well breathed** warmed up.

CELIA [*to Rosalind*]
Were I my father, coz, would I do this?

ORLANDO [*to no one in particular*]
I am more proud to be Sir Rowland's son,
His youngest son, and would not change that calling
To be adopted heir to Frederick.

ROSALIND [*to Celia*]
My father loved Sir Rowland as his soul,
And all the world was of my father's mind.
Had I before known this young man his son,
I should have given him tears unto entreaties
Ere he should thus have ventured.

CELIA [*to Rosalind*] Gentle cousin,
Let us go thank him and encourage him.
My father's rough and envious disposition
Sticks me at heart.—Sir, you have well deserved.
If you do keep your promises in love
But justly as you have exceeded all promise,
Your mistress shall be happy.

ROSALIND [*giving him a chain from her neck*] Gentleman,
Wear this for me, one out of suits with fortune,
That could give more, but that her hand lacks means.
[*To Celia*] Shall we go, coz?

CELIA Ay.—Fare you well, fair gentleman.
[*Rosalind and Celia start to leave.*]

ORLANDO [*aside*]
Can I not say, "I thank you"? My better parts
Are all thrown down, and that which here stands up
Is but a quintain, a mere lifeless block.

ROSALIND [*to Celia*]
He calls us back. My pride fell with my fortunes;
I'll ask him what he would.—Did you call, sir?
Sir, you have wrestled well and overthrown
More than your enemies.

CELIA Will you go, coz?

ROSALIND Have with you.—Fare you well.
Exit [*with Celia*].

ORLANDO
What passion hangs these weights upon my tongue?
I cannot speak to her, yet she urged conference.
O poor Orlando, thou art overthrown!
Or Charles or something weaker masters thee.

Enter Le Beau.

LE BEAU
Good sir, I do in friendship counsel you
To leave this place. Albeit you have deserved
High commendation, true applause, and love,
Yet such is now the Duke's condition
That he misconsters all that you have done.
The Duke is humorous. What he is indeed
More suits you to conceive than I to speak of.

ORLANDO
I thank you, sir. And, pray you, tell me this:
Which of the two was daughter of the Duke
That here was at the wrestling?

LE BEAU
Neither his daughter, if we judge by manners,
But yet indeed the taller is his daughter.
The other is daughter to the banished Duke,
And here detained by her usurping uncle
To keep his daughter company, whose loves
Are dearer than the natural bond of sisters.
But I can tell you that of late this Duke
Hath ta'en displeasure gainst his gentle niece,
Grounded upon no other argument
But that the people praise her for her virtues
And pity her for her good father's sake;
And, on my life, his malice gainst the lady
Will suddenly break forth. Sir, fare you well.
Hereafter, in a better world than this,
I shall desire more love and knowledge of you.

ORLANDO
I rest much bounden to you. Fare you well.
[*Exit Le Beau.*]
Thus must I from the smoke into the smother,
From tyrant Duke unto a tyrant brother.
But heavenly Rosalind! *Exit.*

✤

1.3

Enter Celia and Rosalind.

CELIA Why, cousin, why, Rosalind! Cupid have mercy! Not a word?

ROSALIND Not one to throw at a dog.

CELIA No, thy words are too precious to be cast away upon curs. Throw some of them at me. Come, lame me with reasons.

ROSALIND Then there were two cousins laid up, when the one should be lamed with reasons and the other mad without any.

CELIA But is all this for your father?

ROSALIND No, some of it is for my child's father. Oh, how full of briers is this working-day world!

CELIA They are but burrs, cousin, thrown upon thee in holiday foolery. If we walk not in the trodden paths, our very petticoats will catch them.

ROSALIND I could shake them off my coat. These burs are in my heart.

223 change that calling exchange that name and vocation **228 unto** in addition to **232 Sticks** stabs **234 But justly** exactly **235 s.d. *chain*** (See 3.2.178, where Celia speaks of a chain given to Orlando by Rosalind.) **236 out . . . fortune** (1) whose petitions to Fortune are rejected (2) not wearing the livery of Fortune, not in her service **237 could** would **241 quintain** wooden figure used as a target in tilting **243 would** wants. **247 Have with you** I'll go with you. **249 urged conference** invited conversation. **251 Or** Either **255 condition** disposition **256 misconsters** misconstrues **257 humorous** capricious. **258 conceive** imagine, understand

263 taller (Perhaps a textual error for *smaller* or *lesser,* or else an inconsistency on Shakespeare's part; at 1.3.113, Rosalind is shown to be the taller.) **270 argument** reason **274 suddenly** very soon **275 in . . . world** in better times **277 bounden** indebted **278 from . . . smother** i.e., out of the frying pan into the fire. (*Smother* means "a dense suffocating smoke.")

1.3 Location: Duke Frederick's court.

5–6 lame . . . reasons throw some explanations (for your silence) at me. **11 my child's father** one who might father my children, i.e., Orlando. **13–15 They . . . them** i.e., You are making too much of minor difficulties; one catches such burrs on one's clothes constantly if one strays from the path of propriety (by falling into the folly of love). (*Holiday* and *working-day*, lines 12 and 14, form a crucial comic binary in this play.)

CELIA Hem them away.

ROSALIND I would try, if I could cry "hem" and have him.

CELIA Come, come, wrestle with thy affections.

ROSALIND Oh, they take the part of a better wrestler than myself.

CELIA Oh, a good wish upon you! You will try in time, in despite of a fall. But, turning these jests out of service, let us talk in good earnest. Is it possible, on such a sudden, you should fall into so strong a liking with old Sir Rowland's youngest son?

ROSALIND The Duke my father loved his father dearly.

CELIA Doth it therefore ensue that you should love his son dearly? By this kind of chase, I should hate him, for my father hated his father dearly; yet I hate not Orlando.

ROSALIND No, faith, hate him not, for my sake.

CELIA Why should I not? Doth he not deserve well?

Enter Duke [*Frederick*], *with Lords.*

ROSALIND Let me love him for that, and do you love him because I do.—Look, here comes the Duke.

CELIA With his eyes full of anger.

DUKE FREDERICK [*to Rosalind*]
Mistress, dispatch you with your safest haste
And get you from our court.

ROSALIND Me, uncle?

DUKE FREDERICK You, cousin.
Within these ten days if that thou be'st found
So near our public court as twenty miles,
Thou diest for it.

ROSALIND I do beseech Your Grace
Let me the knowledge of my fault bear with me.
If with myself I hold intelligence
Or have acquaintance with mine own desires,
If that I do not dream or be not frantic—
As I do trust I am not—then, dear uncle,
Never so much as in a thought unborn
Did I offend Your Highness.

DUKE FREDERICK Thus do all traitors.
If their purgation did consist in words,
They are as innocent as grace itself.
Let it suffice thee that I trust thee not.

ROSALIND
Yet your mistrust cannot make me a traitor.
Tell me whereon the likelihood depends.

DUKE FREDERICK
Thou art thy father's daughter. There's enough.

ROSALIND
So was I when Your Highness took his dukedom;
So was I when Your Highness banished him.
Treason is not inherited, my lord;
Or, if we did derive it from our friends,
What's that to me? My father was no traitor.
Then, good my liege, mistake me not so much
To think my poverty is treacherous.

CELIA Dear sovereign, hear me speak.

DUKE FREDERICK
Ay, Celia, we stayed her for your sake,
Else had she with her father ranged along.

CELIA
I did not then entreat to have her stay;
It was your pleasure and your own remorse.
I was too young that time to value her,
But now I know her. If she be a traitor,
Why, so am I. We still have slept together,
Rose at an instant, learned, played, eat together,
And wheresoe'er we went, like Juno's swans
Still we went coupled and inseparable.

DUKE FREDERICK
She is too subtle for thee; and her smoothness,
Her very silence, and her patience
Speak to the people, and they pity her.
Thou art a fool. She robs thee of thy name,
And thou wilt show more bright and seem more virtuous
When she is gone. Then open not thy lips.
Firm and irrevocable is my doom
Which I have passed upon her; she is banished.

CELIA
Pronounce that sentence then on me, my liege!
I cannot live out of her company.

DUKE FREDERICK
You are a fool.—You, niece, provide yourself.
If you outstay the time, upon mine honor,
And in the greatness of my word, you die.
Exit Duke [*with Lords*].

CELIA
O my poor Rosalind, whither wilt thou go?
Wilt thou change fathers? I will give thee mine.
I charge thee, be not thou more grieved than I am.

ROSALIND
I have more cause.

CELIA Thou hast not, cousin.
Prithee, be cheerful. Know'st thou not the Duke
Hath banished me, his daughter?

ROSALIND That he hath not.

18 Hem (1) Tuck (2) Cough (since you say they are in the chest.) A *bur* can be something that sticks in the throat. **19 cry "hem"** attract Orlando's attention by coughing. (But with the suggestion too of a bawd's warning cry to the lovers whose secrecy is being guarded. With a pun on *"hem"* and *him*.) **24–5 Oh . . . fall** i.e., Good luck to you; you'll undertake to wrestle with Orlando sooner or later, despite the danger of your being thrown down. (With sexual suggestion.) **25–6 turning . . . service** i.e., dismissing this banter **31 By . . . chase** To pursue this line of reasoning **32 dearly** intensely **34 faith** in truth **35 Why . . . not?** Why shouldn't I hate him, i.e., love him? (Celia has just argued by chop-logic, in lines 30-2, that to love is to hate and vice versa.) **40 cousin** i.e., niece. **45 if . . . intelligence** If I understand my own feelings **47 If that** if. **frantic** insane **51 purgation** clearing of guilt. (A medical, legal, and theological metaphor.)

56 There's enough That's reason enough. **60 friends** relatives **63 To think** as to think **65 stayed** kept **66 ranged** roamed **68 remorse** compassion. **69 that time** at that time **71 still** continually **72 at an instant** at the same time. **eat** ate **73 Juno's swans** i.e., yoked together. (Though according to Ovid it was Venus, not Juno, who used swans to draw her chariot.) **78 name** reputation **81 doom** sentence **85 provide yourself** get ready. **87 in . . . word** upon my authority as Duke **89 change** exchange

CELIA
No, hath not? Rosalind lacks then the love
Which teacheth thee that thou and I am one.
Shall we be sundered? Shall we part, sweet girl?
No, let my father seek another heir.
Therefore devise with me how we may fly,
Whither to go, and what to bear with us.
And do not seek to take your change upon you,
To bear your griefs yourself and leave me out;
For, by this heaven, now at our sorrows pale,
Say what thou canst, I'll go along with thee.

ROSALIND Why, whither shall we go?

CELIA
To seek my uncle in the Forest of Arden.

ROSALIND
Alas, what danger will it be to us,
Maids as we are, to travel forth so far!
Beauty provoketh thieves sooner than gold.

CELIA
I'll put myself in poor and mean attire
And with a kind of umber smirch my face;
The like do you. So shall we pass along
And never stir assailants.

ROSALIND Were it not better,
Because that I am more than common tall,
That I did suit me all points like a man?
A gallant curtal ax upon my thigh,
A boar spear in my hand, and—in my heart
Lie there what hidden woman's fear there will—
We'll have a swashing and a martial outside,
As many other mannish cowards have
That do outface it with their semblances.

CELIA
What shall I call thee when thou art a man?

ROSALIND
I'll have no worse a name than Jove's own page,
And therefore look you call me Ganymede.
But what will you be called?

CELIA
Something that hath a reference to my state:
No longer Celia, but Aliena.

ROSALIND
But, cousin, what if we assayed to steal
The clownish fool out of your father's court?
Would he not be a comfort to our travel?

CELIA
He'll go along o'er the wide world with me.
Leave me alone to woo him. Let's away,
And get our jewels and our wealth together,
Devise the fittest time and safest way
To hide us from pursuit that will be made
After my flight. Now go we in content
To liberty, and not to banishment. *Exeunt.*

✤

2.1

Enter Duke Senior, Amiens, and two or three Lords, [dressed] like foresters.

DUKE SENIOR
Now, my co-mates and brothers in exile,
Hath not old custom made this life more sweet
Than that of painted pomp? Are not these woods
More free from peril than the envious court?
Here feel we not the penalty of Adam,
The seasons' difference, as the icy fang
And churlish chiding of the winter's wind,
Which when it bites and blows upon my body
Even till I shrink with cold, I smile and say
"This is no flattery; these are counselors
That feelingly persuade me what I am."
Sweet are the uses of adversity,
Which, like the toad, ugly and venomous,
Wears yet a precious jewel in his head;
And this our life, exempt from public haunt,
Finds tongues in trees, books in the running brooks,
Sermons in stones, and good in everything.

AMIENS
I would not change it. Happy is Your Grace
That can translate the stubbornness of fortune
Into so quiet and so sweet a style.

DUKE SENIOR
Come, shall we go and kill us venison?
And yet it irks me the poor dappled fools,
Being native burghers of this desert city,
Should in their own confines with forkèd heads
Have their round haunches gored.

FIRST LORD Indeed, my lord,
The melancholy Jaques grieves at that,
And in that kind swears you do more usurp
Than doth your brother that hath banished you.
Today my lord of Amiens and myself
Did steal behind him as he lay along
Under an oak whose antique root peeps out
Upon the brook that brawls along this wood,
To the which place a poor sequestered stag
That from the hunter's aim had ta'en a hurt
Did come to languish. And indeed, my lord,
The wretched animal heaved forth such groans

100 change change of fortune **102 pale** (Heaven is pale in sympathy with their plight.) **109 mean** lowly **110 umber** yellow-brown pigment (to give a tanned appearance appropriate to countrywomen) **114 suit me all points** outfit myself in all ways **115 curtal ax** broad cutting sword **118 swashing** swaggering **120 outface . . . semblances** bluff their way through with mere appearances. **123 Ganymede** Jupiter's cupbearer. (The name used for disguise also in Lodge's *Rosalynde*.) **126 Aliena** the estranged one. **127 assayed** undertook **129 travel** (1) movement from place to place (2) labor, hardship (*travail*) **131 Leave . . . him** Leave it to me to persuade him.

135 content contentment
2.1 Location: The Forest of Arden.
2 old custom long experience **5–6 feel . . . difference** we don't mind the consequences of Adam's original sin—the hardship of the seasons. (*Not* is often emended to *but*.) **6 as** such as **13–14 like . . . head** (Alludes to the widespread belief that the toad was a poisonous creature but with a jewel embedded in its head that worked as an antidote.) **15 exempt** cut off. **haunt** society **22 fools** innocents **23 burghers** citizens. **desert city** uninhabited place **24 forkèd heads** barbed hunting arrows, but also suggesting antlers **27 kind** regard **30 along** stretched out **31 antique** (1) ancient or (2) *antic*, "gnarled" **32 brawls** noisily flows **33 sequestered** separated (from the herd)

That their discharge did stretch his leathern coat
Almost to bursting, and the big round tears
Coursed one another down his innocent nose
In piteous chase. And thus the hairy fool,
Much markèd of the melancholy Jaques,
Stood on th'extremest verge of the swift brook,
Augmenting it with tears.

DUKE SENIOR But what said Jaques?
Did he not moralize this spectacle?

FIRST LORD
Oh, yes, into a thousand similes.
First, for his weeping into the needless stream:
"Poor deer," quoth he, "thou mak'st a testament
As worldings do, giving thy sum of more
To that which had too much." Then, being there alone,
Left and abandoned of his velvet friends:
"'Tis right," quoth he, "thus misery doth part
The flux of company." Anon a careless herd,
Full of the pasture, jumps along by him
And never stays to greet him. "Ay," quoth Jaques,
"Sweep on, you fat and greasy citizens;
'Tis just the fashion. Wherefore do you look
Upon that poor and broken bankrupt there?"
Thus most invectively he pierceth through
The body of the country, city, court,
Yea, and of this our life, swearing that we
Are mere usurpers, tyrants, and what's worse,
To fright the animals and to kill them up
In their assigned and native dwelling place.

DUKE SENIOR
And did you leave him in this contemplation?

SECOND LORD
We did, my lord, weeping and commenting
Upon the sobbing deer.

DUKE SENIOR Show me the place.
I love to cope him in these sullen fits,
For then he's full of matter.

FIRST LORD I'll bring you to him straight. *Exeunt.*

✤

2.2

Enter Duke [*Frederick*], *with Lords.*

DUKE FREDERICK
Can it be possible that no man saw them?
It cannot be. Some villains of my court
Are of consent and sufferance in this.

FIRST LORD
I cannot hear of any that did see her.
The ladies, her attendants of her chamber,
Saw her abed, and in the morning early
They found the bed untreasured of their mistress.

SECOND LORD
My lord, the roynish clown, at whom so oft
Your Grace was wont to laugh, is also missing.
Hisperia, the princess' gentlewoman,
Confesses that she secretly o'erheard
Your daughter and her cousin much commend
The parts and graces of the wrestler
That did but lately foil the sinewy Charles,
And she believes wherever they are gone
That youth is surely in their company.

DUKE FREDERICK
Send to his brother. Fetch that gallant hither.
If he be absent, bring his brother to me;
I'll make him find him. Do this suddenly,
And let not search and inquisition quail
To bring again these foolish runaways. *Exeunt.*

✤

2.3

Enter Orlando and Adam, [*meeting*].

ORLANDO Who's there?

ADAM
What, my young master? Oh, my gentle master,
Oh, my sweet master, oh, you memory
Of old Sir Rowland! Why, what make you here?
Why are you virtuous? Why do people love you?
And wherefore are you gentle, strong, and valiant?
Why would you be so fond to overcome
The bonny prizer of the humorous Duke?
Your praise is come too swiftly home before you.
Know you not, master, to some kind of men
Their graces serve them but as enemies?
No more do yours. Your virtues, gentle master,
Are sanctified and holy traitors to you.

39 Coursed chased **41 markèd of** observed by **42 th'extremest verge** the very edge **44 moralize** draw out the hidden meaning of **46 needless** having no need of more water. (Weeping deer are common in literature.) **47 testament** will **48 worldings** worldly men **48–9 giving . . . much** bequeathing your superabundance of wealth to heirs who are already too wealthy. **49 being** the deer being **50 of** by. **velvet** i.e., prosperous. (Velvet was an appropriately rich dress for a courtier; the term also alludes here to the deers' velvety coat or to the covering of their antlers during rapid growth.) **51 'Tis right** i.e., That's how it goes **51–2 thus . . . company** thus the miserable are separated from and forgotten by the herd. **52 careless** (1) carefree (2) uncaring **53 the pasture** i.e., good food **55 greasy** fat and unctuously prosperous, like rich burghers or *citizens* **56–7 Wherefore . . . there?** Why do you even bother to glance at that poor physically shattered deer there? (*Broken* also hints at a financial ruin appropriate to *citizens* in line 55.) **58 invectively** in the most bitter terms **61 what's worse** whatever is worse than these **62 up** off, utterly **67 cope** encounter **68 matter** substance. **69 straight** at once.

2.2 Location: Duke Frederick's court.
3 Are . . . this have conspired in and permitted this. **4 her** Celia. **8 roynish** scurvy, rascally. (Literally, covered with scale or scurf.) **13 parts** good qualities **17 Send . . . hither** i.e., Send word to Oliver to bring Orlando here. **18 he** i.e., Orlando. **his brother** i.e., Oliver. (Or possibly referring to Jaques de Boys, the other brother.) **19 suddenly** speedily **20 inquisition quail** investigation fail **21 again** back

2.3 Location: Before Oliver's house.
3 memory likeness, reminder **4 what make you** what are you doing **7 fond to** foolish as to **8 bonny prizer** sturdy prizefighter. **humorous** temperamental **12 No . . . yours** Your fine qualities serve you no better than that.

Oh, what a world is this, when what is comely
Envenoms him that bears it!

ORLANDO
Why, what's the matter?

ADAM
O unhappy youth,
Come not within these doors! Within this roof
The enemy of all your graces lives.
Your brother—no, no brother; yet the son—
Yet not the son, I will not call him son
Of him I was about to call his father—
Hath heard your praises, and this night he means 22
To burn the lodging where you use to lie 23
And you within it. If he fail of that,
He will have other means to cut you off.
I overheard him and his practices. 26
This is no place, this house is but a butchery. 27
Abhor it, fear it, do not enter it.

ORLANDO
Why, whither, Adam, wouldst thou have me go?

ADAM
No matter whither, so you come not here. 30

ORLANDO
What, wouldst thou have me go and beg my food?
Or with a base and boist'rous sword enforce 32
A thievish living on the common road?
This I must do or know not what to do;
Yet this I will not do, do how I can.
I rather will subject me to the malice
Of a diverted blood and bloody brother. 37

ADAM
But do not so. I have five hundred crowns,
The thrifty hire I saved under your father, 39
Which I did store to be my foster nurse
When service should in my old limbs lie lame 41
And unregarded age in corners thrown. 42
Take that, and He that doth the ravens feed, 43
Yea, providently caters for the sparrow, 44
Be comfort to my age! Here is the gold; [*offering gold*]
All this I give you. Let me be your servant.
Though I look old, yet I am strong and lusty, 47
For in my youth I never did apply
Hot and rebellious liquors in my blood,
Nor did not with unbashful forehead woo 50
The means of weakness and debility; 51
Therefore my age is as a lusty winter,
Frosty but kindly. Let me go with you. 53
I'll do the service of a younger man
In all your business and necessities.

ORLANDO
Oh, good old man, how well in thee appears
The constant service of the antique world, 57
When service sweat for duty, not for meed! 58
Thou art not for the fashion of these times,
Where none will sweat but for promotion,
And having that do choke their service up 61
Even with the having. It is not so with thee. 62
But, poor old man, thou prun'st a rotten tree,
That cannot so much as a blossom yield
In lieu of all thy pains and husbandry. 65
But come thy ways. We'll go along together,
And ere we have thy youthful wages spent,
We'll light upon some settled low content. 68

ADAM
Master, go on, and I will follow thee
To the last gasp, with truth and loyalty.
From seventeen years till now almost fourscore
Here livèd I, but now live here no more.
At seventeen years many their fortunes seek,
But at fourscore it is too late a week; 74
Yet fortune cannot recompense me better
Than to die well and not my master's debtor.
Exeunt.

✣

2.4

Enter Rosalind for Ganymede, Celia for Aliena, and Clown, alias Touchstone.

ROSALIND Oh, Jupiter, how weary are my spirits!

TOUCHSTONE I care not for my spirits, if my legs were not weary.

ROSALIND I could find in my heart to disgrace my man's
apparel and to cry like a woman; but I must comfort 5
the weaker vessel, as doublet and hose ought to show 6
itself courageous to petticoat. Therefore courage, good
Aliena!

CELIA I pray you, bear with me. I cannot go no further.

TOUCHSTONE For my part, I had rather bear with you
than bear you; yet I should bear no cross if I did bear 11
you, for I think you have no money in your purse.

ROSALIND Well, this is the Forest of Arden.

TOUCHSTONE Ay, now am I in Arden; the more fool I. When I was at home I was in a better place, but travelers must be content.

Enter Corin and Silvius.

22 your praises people's praise of you **23 use** are accustomed **26 practices** plots. **27 place** place for you **30 so** provided that **32 boist'rous** rough **37 diverted blood** kinship diverted from the natural source **39 thrifty . . . saved** wages I thriftily saved **41 lie lame** i.e., be performed only lamely **42 And . . . thrown** and when I will be neglected and thrown aside because of my old age. **43–4 and He . . . sparrow** i.e., and may God, who guards over all His creatures (see Luke 12:6, 22-4, Psalms 147:9, etc.) **47 lusty** vigorous **50–1 Nor . . . debility** nor did I with shameless countenance chase after pleasures that would have weakened and disabled me **53 Frosty** i.e., white-haired

57 constant faithful. **antique** ancient (as in the Golden Age) **58 sweat** sweated. **meed** reward. **61–2 do choke . . . having** i.e., cease serving once they have gained promotion. **65 lieu of** return for **68 low content** lowly contented state. **74 too . . . week** i.e., too late in life

2.4 Location: The Forest of Arden.

0.1. *for* i.e., disguised as **5–6 comfort the weaker vessel** (The First Epistle of Peter, 3:7, bids husbands give honor to their wives "as unto the weaker vessel.") **6 doublet and hose** close-fitting jacket and breeches; typical male attire **11 cross** (1) burden (2) coin having on it a figure of a cross

ROSALIND Ay, be so, good Touchstone.—Look you who comes here, a young man and an old in solemn talk. [*They stand aside and listen.*]

CORIN
That is the way to make her scorn you still.

SILVIUS
Oh, Corin, that thou knew'st how I do love her!

CORIN
I partly guess, for I have loved ere now.

SILVIUS
No, Corin, being old, thou canst not guess,
Though in thy youth thou wast as true a lover
As ever sighed upon a midnight pillow.
But if thy love were ever like to mine—
As sure I think did never man love so—
How many actions most ridiculous
Hast thou been drawn to by thy fantasy?

CORIN
Into a thousand that I have forgotten.

SILVIUS
Oh, thou didst then never love so heartily!
If thou remember'st not the slightest folly
That ever love did make thee run into,
Thou hast not loved.
Or if thou hast not sat as I do now,
Wearing thy hearer in thy mistress' praise,
Thou hast not loved.
Or if thou hast not broke from company
Abruptly, as my passion now makes me,
Thou has not loved.
O Phoebe, Phoebe, Phoebe! *Exit.*

ROSALIND
Alas, poor shepherd! Searching of thy wound,
I have by hard adventure found mine own.

TOUCHSTONE And I mine. I remember, when I was in love I broke my sword upon a stone and bid him take that for coming a-night to Jane Smile; and I remember the kissing of her batler and the cow's dugs that her pretty chapped hands had milked; and I remember the wooing of a peascod instead of her, from whom I took two cods and, giving her them again, said with weeping tears, "Wear these for my sake." We that are true lovers run into strange capers; but as all is mortal in nature, so is all nature in love mortal in folly.

ROSALIND Thou speak'st wiser than thou art ware of.

TOUCHSTONE Nay, I shall ne'er be ware of mine own wit till I break my shins against it.

ROSALIND
Jove, Jove! This shepherd's passion
Is much upon my fashion.

TOUCHSTONE
And mine, but it grows something stale with me.

CELIA
I pray you, one of you question yond man
If he for gold will give us any food.
I faint almost to death.

TOUCHSTONE [*to Corin*] Holla: you, clown!

ROSALIND
Peace, Fool! He's not thy kinsman.

CORIN Who calls?

TOUCHSTONE
Your betters, sir.

CORIN Else are they very wretched.

ROSALIND
Peace, I say.—Good even to you, friend.

CORIN
And to you, gentle sir, and to you all.

ROSALIND
I prithee, shepherd, if that love or gold
Can in this desert place buy entertainment,
Bring us where we may rest ourselves and feed.
Here's a young maid with travel much oppressed,
And faints for succor.

CORIN Fair sir, I pity her
And wish, for her sake more than for mine own,
My fortunes were more able to relieve her;
But I am shepherd to another man
And do not shear the fleeces that I graze.
My master is of churlish disposition,
And little recks to find the way to heaven
By doing deeds of hospitality.
Besides, his cote, his flocks, and bounds of feed
Are now on sale, and at our sheepcote now,
By reason of his absence, there is nothing
That you will feed on. But what is, come see,
And in my voice most welcome shall you be.

ROSALIND
What is he that shall buy his flock and pasture?

CORIN
That young swain that you saw here but erewhile,
That little cares for buying anything.

ROSALIND
I pray thee, if it stand with honesty,
Buy thou the cottage, pasture, and the flock,
And thou shalt have to pay for it of us.

29 fantasy love imaginings. **36 Wearing** wearing out **42 Searching of** Probing **43 hard adventure** painful experience **45–6 I broke . . . Smile** (In his parody of a distraught lover, Touchstone imagines himself attacking a stone as if it were his rival for a country maiden named Jane Smile. *A-night* means "by night.") **47 batler** club for beating clothes in process of washing. **dugs** udder **48–51 and I . . . sake** (Touchstone absurdly imagines himself courting a pea plant as though it were Jane Smile and exchanging pea pods with her by way of love tokens.) **52 mortal** subject to death **53 mortal** typically human, frail **54 ware** aware **55–6 Nay . . . against it** (Touchstone, as a professional fool, laughs at the idea of stumbling on or discovering his own capacity for saying something wise. His use of *ware* plays on [1] aware [2] wary.)

58 upon after, according to **59 something** somewhat **62 clown** yokel. (But Rosalind then alludes to the word as it applies to Touchstone as a court fool or clown.) **65 even** evening, i.e., afternoon **67 if that** if **68 desert** uninhabited. **entertainment** hospitality, provision **71 for succor** for lack of food. **75 do . . . fleeces** i.e., do not obtain the profits from the flock **76 churlish** miserly **77 recks** reckons **79 cote** cottage. **bounds of feed** range of pasture **82 That . . . feed on** suitable for your refined tastes. **83 in my voice** insofar as I have authority to speak **84 What** Who **85 but erewhile** just now **87 stand** be consistent **89 have to pay** have the money

CELIA
And we will mend thy wages. I like this place
And willingly could waste my time in it.

CORIN
Assuredly the thing is to be sold.
Go with me. If you like upon report
The soil, the profit, and this kind of life,
I will your very faithful feeder be
And buy it with your gold right suddenly. *Exeunt.*

✤

2.5

Enter Amiens, Jaques, and others. [*A table is set out.*]

Song.

AMIENS [*sings*]
Under the greenwood tree
Who loves to lie with me,
And turn his merry note
Unto the sweet bird's throat,
Come hither, come hither, come hither.
Here shall he see
No enemy
But winter and rough weather.

JAQUES More, more, I prithee, more.

AMIENS It will make you melancholy, Monsieur Jaques.

JAQUES I thank it. More, I prithee, more. I can suck melancholy out of a song as a weasel sucks eggs. More, I prithee, more.

AMIENS My voice is ragged. I know I cannot please you.

JAQUES I do not desire you to please me, I do desire you to sing. Come, more, another stanzo. Call you 'em "stanzos"?

AMIENS What you will, Monsieur Jaques.

JAQUES Nay, I care not for their names; they owe me nothing. Will you sing?

AMIENS More at your request than to please myself.

JAQUES Well then, if ever I thank any man, I'll thank you; but that they call "compliment" is like th'encounter of two dog-apes, and when a man thanks me heartily, methinks I have given him a penny and he renders me the beggarly thanks. Come, sing; and you that will not, hold your tongues.

AMIENS Well, I'll end the song.—Sirs, cover the while; the Duke will drink under this tree.—He hath been all this day to look you. [*Food and drink are set out.*]

JAQUES And I have been all this day to avoid him. He is too disputable for my company. I think of as many matters as he, but I give heaven thanks and make no boast of them. Come, warble, come.

Song.

AMIENS [*sings*]
Who doth ambition shun
And loves to live i'th' sun,
Seeking the food he eats
And pleased with what he gets,
All together here.
Come hither, come hither, come hither.
Here shall he see
No enemy
But winter and rough weather.

JAQUES I'll give you a verse to this note that I made yesterday in despite of my invention.

AMIENS And I'll sing it.

JAQUES Thus it goes:

If it do come to pass
That any man turn ass,
Leaving his wealth and ease,
A stubborn will to please,
Ducdame, ducdame, ducdame.
Here shall he see
Gross fools as he,
An if he will come to me.

AMIENS What's that "ducdame"?

JAQUES 'Tis a Greek invocation, to call fools into a circle. I'll go sleep, if I can; if I cannot, I'll rail against all the firstborn of Egypt.

AMIENS And I'll go seek the Duke. His banquet is prepared. *Exeunt* [*separately*].

✤

2.6

Enter Orlando and Adam.

ADAM Dear master, I can go no further. Oh, I die for food! Here lie I down and measure out my grave. Farewell, kind master. [*He lies down.*]

90 mend improve **91 waste** spend **95 feeder** dependent, servant **96 right suddenly** without delay.

2.5 Location: The forest.

2 Who anyone who. **lie** dwell **3–4 And . . . throat** and tune his song to the bird's voice **14 ragged** hoarse. **16 stanzo** (The word *stanza*, variously spelled, was newfangled and therefore of ironic interest to Jaques.) **19–20 they owe me nothing** (Jaques speaks of names as of something valuable only when written as signatures to a bond of indebtedness.) **23 that** what. **"compliment"** courtesy **24 dog-apes** dog-faced baboons **26 beggarly** effusive, like the thanks of a beggar **28 cover the while** set the table for a meal meanwhile **30 to look** looking for

32 disputable inclined to dispute **36 live i'th' sun** dwell in the open air, without the cares of the court **37 Seeking** hunting for **43 note** tune **44 in . . . invention** i.e., without needing to make use of my powerful rhetorical skills. (The nonsense that follows will make a mockery of true invention.) **51 Ducdame** (Probably a nonsense term devised to puzzle Jaques's hearers, although with intriguing resemblances to phrases in Romany, *dukrà me*, "I foretell," or Welsh *Dewch da mi*, "Come with (or to) me," or dog-Latin *Duc ad me*, "Lead him to me," or simply "Duke damn me.") **58 firstborn of Egypt** (In Exodus 12:28–33, the firstborn of Egypt are slain by the Lord as the enemies of Moses and the Israelites, who, like the Duke and his followers, are in exile.) **59 banquet** wine and dessert after dinner. (This repast, now prepared on stage, seemingly is to remain there during the short following scene.)

2.6. Location: The forest. The scene is continuous. By convention we understand that Adam and Orlando are in a different part of the forest and do not "see" the table remaining onstage.

ORLANDO Why, how now, Adam? No greater heart in thee? Live a little, comfort a little, cheer thyself a little. If this uncouth forest yield anything savage, I will either be food for it or bring it for food to thee. Thy conceit is nearer death than thy powers. For my sake be comfortable; hold death awhile at the arm's end. I will here be with thee presently, and if I bring thee not something to eat, I will give thee leave to die; but if thou diest before I come, thou art a mocker of my labor. Well said! Thou look'st cheerly, and I'll be with thee quickly. Yet thou liest in the bleak air. Come, I will bear thee to some shelter; and thou shalt not die for lack of a dinner, if there live anything in this desert. [*He picks up Adam.*] Cheerly, good Adam! *Exeunt.*

2.7

Enter Duke Senior and Lords, like outlaws.

DUKE SENIOR
I think he be transformed into a beast,
For I can nowhere find him like a man.

FIRST LORD
My lord, he is but even now gone hence.
Here was he merry, hearing of a song.

DUKE SENIOR
If he, compact of jars, grow musical,
We shall have shortly discord in the spheres.
Go seek him. Tell him I would speak with him.

Enter Jaques.

FIRST LORD
He saves my labor by his own approach.

DUKE SENIOR
Why, how now, monsieur, what a life is this,
That your poor friends must woo your company!
What, you look merrily.

JAQUES
A fool, a fool! I met a fool i'th' forest,
A motley fool. A miserable world!
As I do live by food, I met a fool,
Who laid him down and basked him in the sun,
And railed on Lady Fortune in good terms,
In good set terms, and yet a motley fool.
"Good morrow, Fool," quoth I. "No, sir," quoth he,
"Call me not fool till heaven hath sent me fortune."
And then he drew a dial from his poke
And, looking on it with lackluster eye,
Says very wisely, "It is ten o'clock.
Thus we may see," quoth he, "how the world wags.
'Tis but an hour ago since it was nine,
And after one hour more 'twill be eleven;
And so from hour to hour we ripe and ripe,
And then from hour to hour we rot and rot,
And thereby hangs a tale." When I did hear
The motley fool thus moral on the time,
My lungs began to crow like Chanticleer,
That fools should be so deep-contemplative,
And I did laugh sans intermission
An hour by his dial. Oh, noble fool!
A worthy fool! Motley's the only wear.

DUKE SENIOR What fool is this?

JAQUES
Oh, worthy fool! One that hath been a courtier,
And says, if ladies be but young and fair,
They have the gift to know it. And in his brain,
Which is as dry as the remainder biscuit
After a voyage, he hath strange places crammed
With observation, the which he vents
In mangled forms. Oh, that I were a fool!
I am ambitious for a motley coat.

DUKE SENIOR
Thou shalt have one.

JAQUES It is my only suit,
Provided that you weed your better judgments
Of all opinion that grows rank in them
That I am wise. I must have liberty
Withal, as large a charter as the wind,
To blow on whom I please, for so fools have.
And they that are most gallèd with my folly,
They most must laugh. And why, sir, must they so?
The "why" is plain as way to parish church:
He that a fool doth very wisely hit
Doth very foolishly, although he smart,
Not to seem senseless of the bob. If not,
The wise man's folly is anatomized
Even by the squand'ring glances of the fool.
Invest me in my motley; give me leave
To speak my mind, and I will through and through
Cleanse the foul body of th'infected world,
If they will patiently receive my medicine.

DUKE SENIOR
Fie on thee! I can tell what thou wouldst do.

JAQUES
What, for a counter, would I do but good?

5 comfort comfort yourself **6 uncouth** strange, wild **7–8 Thy conceit . . . powers** You imagine you are nearer death than you really are. **9 comfortable** comforted **13 Well said!** Well done!

2.7. Location: The forest; the scene is continuous. (A repast, set out for the Duke in 2.5, has remained onstage during 2.6.)

5 compact of jars composed of discords **6 the spheres** the concentric spheres of the old Ptolemaic solar system (which, by their movement, were thought to produce harmonious music). **13 motley** wearing motley, the parti-colored dress of the professional jester **17 set** carefully composed **19 Call . . . fortune** (An allusion to the proverb "Fortune favors fools.") **20 dial** pocket sundial or watch. **poke** pouch or pocket

23 wags goes. **29 moral** moralize **30 crow** i.e., laugh merrily. **Chanticleer** a rooster **32 sans** without **34 only wear** only thing worth wearing. **38 know it** i.e., put their beauty to advantage. **39 dry** (According to Elizabethan physiology, a dry brain was marked by a strong memory but a slowness of apprehension.) **remainder** left over **40 places** (1) nooks and corners (2) rhetorical topics **41 vents** utters **44 suit** (1) request (2) suit of clothes **46 rank** wildly, coarsely **48 Withal** in addition. **charter** license, privilege **50 gallèd** rubbed sore **53–5 He . . . bob** He whom a fool wittily attacks behaves very foolishly, no matter how much he feels the sting, unless he pretends to be unaware of the taunt. **55–7 If not . . . fool** Otherwise, the folly of even a wise person is dissected and laid open even by the variously directed shots of wit made by the fool. **58 Invest** Array **60 Cleanse** purge. (A medical metaphor.) **63 counter** (1) thing of no intrinsic value, a metal disk used in counting (2) parry

DUKE SENIOR
Most mischievous foul sin, in chiding sin.
For thou thyself hast been a libertine,
As sensual as the brutish sting itself;
And all th'embossèd sores and headed evils
That thou with license of free foot hast caught
Wouldst thou disgorge into the general world.

JAQUES Why, who cries out on pride
That can therein tax any private party?
Doth it not flow as hugely as the sea,
Till that the weary very means do ebb?
What woman in the city do I name,
When that I say the city woman bears
The cost of princes on unworthy shoulders?
Who can come in and say that I mean her,
When such a one as she, such is her neighbor?
Or what is he of basest function
That says his bravery is not on my cost,
Thinking that I mean him, but therein suits
His folly to the mettle of my speech?
There then, how then? What then? Let me see wherein
My tongue hath wronged him. If it do him right,
Then he hath wronged himself. If he be free,
Why then my taxing like a wild goose flies,
Unclaimed of any man.—But who comes here?

Enter Orlando [with his sword drawn].

ORLANDO
Forbear, and eat no more!

JAQUES Why, I have eat none yet.

ORLANDO
Nor shalt not, till necessity be served.

JAQUES
Of what kind should this cock come of?

DUKE SENIOR
Art thou thus boldened, man, by thy distress,
Or else a rude despiser of good manners,
That in civility thou seem'st so empty?

ORLANDO
You touched my vein at first. The thorny point
Of bare distress hath ta'en from me the show
Of smooth civility; yet am I inland bred
And know some nurture. But forbear, I say.
He dies that touches any of this fruit
Till I and my affairs are answerèd.

JAQUES
An you will not be answered with reason, I must die.

DUKE SENIOR
What would you have? Your gentleness shall force
More than your force move us to gentleness.

ORLANDO
I almost die for food, and let me have it!

DUKE SENIOR
Sit down and feed, and welcome to our table.

ORLANDO
Speak you so gently? Pardon me, I pray you.
I thought that all things had been savage here,
And therefore put I on the countenance
Of stern commandment. But whate'er you are
That in this desert inaccessible,
Under the shade of melancholy boughs,
Lose and neglect the creeping hours of time;
If ever you have looked on better days,
If ever been where bells have knolled to church,
If ever sat at any good man's feast,
If ever from your eyelids wiped a tear
And know what 'tis to pity and be pitied,
Let gentleness my strong enforcement be,
In the which hope I blush and hide my sword.
[*He sheathes his sword.*]

DUKE SENIOR
True is it that we have seen better days,
And have with holy bell been knolled to church,
And sat at good men's feasts, and wiped our eyes
Of drops that sacred pity hath engendered.
And therefore sit you down in gentleness,
And take upon command what help we have
That to your wanting may be ministered.

ORLANDO
Then but forbear your food a little while,
Whiles, like a doe, I go to find my fawn
And give it food. There is an old poor man
Who after me hath many a weary step
Limped in pure love. Till he be first sufficed,
Oppressed with two weak evils, age and hunger,
I will not touch a bit.

DUKE SENIOR Go find him out,
And we will nothing waste till you return.

ORLANDO
I thank ye; and be blest for your good comfort!
[*Exit.*]

DUKE SENIOR
Thou see'st we are not all alone unhappy.
This wide and universal theater
Presents more woeful pageants than the scene
Wherein we play in.

JAQUES All the world's a stage,

66 brutish sting carnal impulse **67 th'embossèd** the swollen. **headed evils** sores that have come to a head **68 license . . . foot** the licentious freedom of a libertine **69 disgorge** vomit **70–1 who . . . party?** what true satirist inveighs against extravagance in dress with only some private individual in mind? **72–3 Doth . . . ebb?** Is not pride as universal as the sea, overflowing everywhere until it finally ebbs like the tide, having exhausted what it fed upon? **75–6 When . . . shoulders?** when I characterize the typical citizen's wife as dressing herself in finery that is costly enough to adorn a prince? **77 come in** i.e., come into court as a complainant **79–82 Or . . . speech?** Or who is he of even the lowest social standing that does not object to my saying that sartorial finery is a fit subject for my satirical spleen, thinking I am satirizing him when his own folly shows how well he fits the contents of my speech? **84–7 If . . . man** If my satirical sketch fits him, then he condemns himself by resembling my portrait of folly. If he does not resemble my sketch, my criticism does him no harm. **88 have eat** have eaten. (Pronounced "et.") **90 Of . . . of?** What sort of fighting cock is this? **94 You . . . first** Your first supposition is correct. **96 inland bred** i.e., raised in the center of civilization rather than on the outskirts

97 nurture education, training. **99 answerèd** satisfied. **100 An** If. **reason** (A pun on "raisin" plays upon *fruit* in line 98.) **110 melancholy** dark, shadowy **113 knolled** knelled, rung **124 upon command** for the asking **125 wanting** need **131 weak evils** disabilities causing weakness **133 waste** consume

And all the men and women merely players.
They have their exits and their entrances,
And one man in his time plays many parts,
His acts being seven ages. At first the infant,
Mewling and puking in the nurse's arms.
Then the whining schoolboy, with his satchel
And shining morning face, creeping like snail
Unwillingly to school. And then the lover,
Sighing like furnace, with a woeful ballad
Made to his mistress' eyebrow. Then a soldier,
Full of strange oaths and bearded like the pard,
Jealous in honor, sudden, and quick in quarrel,
Seeking the bubble reputation
Even in the cannon's mouth. And then the justice,
In fair round belly with good capon lined,
With eyes severe and beard of formal cut,
Full of wise saws and modern instances;
And so he plays his part. The sixth age shifts
Into the lean and slippered pantaloon,
With spectacles on nose and pouch on side,
His youthful hose, well saved, a world too wide
For his shrunk shank; and his big manly voice,
Turning again toward childish treble, pipes
And whistles in his sound. Last scene of all,
That ends this strange, eventful history,
Is second childishness and mere oblivion,
Sans teeth, sans eyes, sans taste, sans everything.

Enter Orlando, with Adam.

DUKE SENIOR
Welcome. Set down your venerable burden
And let him feed.

ORLANDO I thank you most for him.
[*He sets down Adam.*]

ADAM So had you need.
I scarce can speak to thank you for myself.

DUKE SENIOR
Welcome. Fall to. I will not trouble you
As yet to question you about your fortunes.—
Give us some music, and, good cousin, sing.
[*They eat, while Orlando and Duke Senior converse apart.*]

Song.

AMIENS [*sings*]
Blow, blow, thou winter wind.
Thou art not so unkind
As man's ingratitude.
Thy tooth is not so keen,
Because thou art not seen,
Although thy breath be rude.
Heigh-ho, sing heigh-ho, unto the green holly.
Most friendship is feigning, most loving mere folly.
Then heigh-ho, the holly!
This life is most jolly.
Freeze, freeze, thou bitter sky,
That dost not bite so nigh
As benefits forgot.
Though thou the waters warp,
Thy sting is not so sharp
As friend remembered not.
Heigh-ho, sing heigh-ho, unto the green holly.
Most friendship is feigning, most loving mere folly.
Then heigh-ho, the holly!
This life is most jolly.

DUKE SENIOR [*to Orlando*]
If that you were the good Sir Rowland's son,
As you have whispered faithfully you were
And as mine eye doth his effigies witness
Most truly limned and living in your face,
Be truly welcome hither. I am the Duke
That loved your father. The residue of your fortune,
Go to my cave and tell me.—Good old man,
Thou art right welcome as thy master is.—
Support him by the arm. Give me your hand,
And let me all your fortunes understand. *Exeunt.*

✣

3.1

Enter Duke [*Frederick*], *Lords, and Oliver.*

DUKE FREDERICK
Not see him since? Sir, sir, that cannot be.
But were I not the better part made mercy,
I should not seek an absent argument
Of my revenge, thou present. But look to it:
Find out thy brother, wheresoe'er he is.
Seek him with candle. Bring him dead or living
Within this twelvemonth, or turn thou no more
To seek a living in our territory.
Thy lands and all things that thou dost call thine
Worth seizure do we seize into our hands,
Till thou canst quit thee by thy brother's mouth
Of what we think against thee.

143 Mewling crying with a catlike noise **149 bearded . . . pard** having bristling mustaches like the leopard's **150 Jealous in honor** quick to anger in matters of honor **153 capon** rooster castrated to make the flesh more tender for eating (and often presented to judges as a bribe) **155 saws** sayings. **modern instances** commonplace illustrations **157 pantaloon** ridiculous, enfeebled old man. (A stock type in Italian *commedia dell'arte*.) **160 shank** calf **162 his** its **164 mere oblivion** total forgetfulness **165 Sans** without **173 cousin** (A term used by sovereigns to address their nobility.) **179 rude** rough.

180 holly (An emblem of Christmastime and holiday cheer, as in "the holly and the ivy.") **185 nigh** deeply, near (to the heart) **187 warp** freeze so that the surface of the ice cracks and forces up ridges **194 If that** If **195 faithfully** persuasively and honestly **196 doth . . . witness** witnesses the likeness of the dead Sir Rowland **197 limned** painted **199 The . . . fortune** The rest of your adventure **203 s.d. *Exeunt*** (The table must be removed at this point.)
3.1. Location: Duke Frederick's court.
1 Not . . . since? i.e., You mean to tell me you claim not to have seen Orlando since the disappearance of Celia and Rosalind? **2 were . . . mercy** i.e., if I were not a merciful man. (Literally, if I were not composed mostly of mercy.) **3–4 I . . . present** i.e., I would seek revenge not on the absent Orlando, but on you, who are right here. **6 Seek . . . candle** i.e., Look for him everywhere, even in the darkest corners. (See Luke 15:8.) **7 turn** return **10 we . . . our** (The royal plural.) **11 quit . . . mouth** acquit yourself by the direct testimony of Orlando. (The Duke suspects that Oliver has murdered Orlando.)

OLIVER
Oh, that Your Highness knew my heart in this!
I never loved my brother in my life.

DUKE FREDERICK
More villain thou.—Well, push him out of doors,
And let my officers of such a nature
Make an extent upon his house and lands.
Do this expediently, and turn him going. *Exeunt.*

✤

3.2

Enter Orlando [with a paper].

ORLANDO
Hang there, my verse, in witness of my love;
And thou, thrice-crownèd queen of night, survey
With thy chaste eye, from thy pale sphere above,
Thy huntress' name that my full life doth sway.
O Rosalind! These trees shall be my books,
And in their barks my thoughts I'll character,
That every eye which in this forest looks
Shall see thy virtue witnessed everywhere.
Run, run, Orlando, carve on every tree
The fair, the chaste, and unexpressive she. *Exit.*

Enter Corin and [Touchstone the] Clown.

CORIN And how like you this shepherd's life, Master Touchstone?

TOUCHSTONE Truly, shepherd, in respect of itself, it is a good life; but in respect that it is a shepherd's life, it is naught. In respect that it is solitary, I like it very well; but in respect that it is private, it is a very vile life. Now in respect it is in the fields, it pleaseth me well; but in respect it is not in the court, it is tedious. As it is a spare life, look you, it fits my humor well; but as there is no more plenty in it, it goes much against my stomach. Hast any philosophy in thee, shepherd?

CORIN No more but that I know the more one sickens the worse at ease he is; and that he that wants money, means, and content is without three good friends; that the property of rain is to wet and fire to burn; that good pasture makes fat sheep and that a great cause of the night is lack of the sun; that he that hath learned no wit by nature nor art may complain of good breeding or comes of a very dull kindred.

TOUCHSTONE Such a one is a natural philosopher. Wast ever in court, shepherd?

CORIN No, truly.

TOUCHSTONE Then thou art damned.

CORIN Nay, I hope.

TOUCHSTONE Truly, thou art damned, like an ill-roasted egg, all on one side.

CORIN For not being at court? Your reason.

TOUCHSTONE Why, if thou never wast at court, thou never saw'st good manners; if thou never saw'st good manners, then thy manners must be wicked; and wickedness is sin, and sin is damnation. Thou art in a parlous state, shepherd.

CORIN Not a whit, Touchstone. Those that are good manners at the court are as ridiculous in the country as the behavior of the country is most mockable at the court. You told me you salute not at the court but you kiss your hands; that courtesy would be uncleanly, if courtiers were shepherds.

TOUCHSTONE Instance, briefly; come, instance.

CORIN Why, we are still handling our ewes, and their fells you know are greasy.

TOUCHSTONE Why, do not your courtier's hands sweat? And is not the grease of a mutton as wholesome as the sweat of a man? Shallow, shallow. A better instance, I say. Come.

CORIN Besides, our hands are hard.

TOUCHSTONE Your lips will feel them the sooner. Shallow again. A more sounder instance. Come.

CORIN And they are often tarred over with the surgery of our sheep; and would you have us kiss tar? The courtier's hands are perfumed with civet.

TOUCHSTONE Most shallow man! Thou worms'meat, in respect of a good piece of flesh indeed! Learn of the wise, and perpend: civet is of a baser birth than tar, the very uncleanly flux of a cat. Mend the instance, shepherd.

CORIN You have too courtly a wit for me. I'll rest.

TOUCHSTONE Wilt thou rest damned? God help thee, shallow man! God make incision in thee! Thou art raw.

CORIN Sir, I am a true laborer: I earn that I eat, get that I wear, owe no man hate, envy no man's happiness, glad of other men's good, content with my harm, and the greatest of my pride is to see my ewes graze and my lambs suck.

TOUCHSTONE That is another simple sin in you, to bring the ewes and the rams together and to offer to get your

16 of such a nature who attend to such duties **17 extent** writ of seizure **18 expediently** expeditiously. **turn him going** send him packing.
3.2. Location: The forest.
2 thrice-crownèd . . . night i.e., Diana in the three aspects of her divinity: as Luna or Cynthia, goddess of the moon; as Diana, goddess on earth; and as Hecate or Proserpina, goddess in the lower world
4 Thy huntress' i.e., Rosalind's, who is here thought of as accompanying Diana, patroness of the hunt and of chastity. **sway** control.
6 character inscribe **10 unexpressive** inexpressible **13 in respect of itself** considered in and for itself **15 naught** vile, of no social consequence. **19 spare** frugal. **humor** temperament **23 wants** lacks
28 wit wisdom. **art** study. **complain of** lament the lack of

34 hope i.e., hope not. **39 manners** etiquette **40 manners** morals
42 parlous perilous **46 salute** greet **46–7 but . . . hands** without kissing the other person's hands **49 Instance** Proof **50 still** constantly **51 fells** skins with the wool, or fleeces **52 your courtier's** your typical courtier's **53–4 And . . . man?** (Human sweat was thought to be fat oozing from the pores.) **59 tarred over** anointed with tar on their cuts and sores **61 civet** a musky perfume derived from glands in the anal pouch of the civet cat. (As Touchstone points out.) **62–3 Thou . . . indeed!** You miserable creature (literally, you food for worms, subject to the decay of death), if we compare you with any worthy sample of humankind! **64 perpend** consider
65 flux secretion. **Mend** Improve **69 incision** a cut, perhaps for the purpose of letting blood (here, to let out folly); or for seasoning as raw meat is scored and salted before cooking **70 raw** (1) wet behind the ears (2) uncooked (3) afflicted with a raw wound. **71 earn . . . eat** earn my living **73 content . . . harm** patient with my ill fortune
76 simple sin sin arising from simplicity **77 offer** undertake

living by the copulation of cattle; to be bawd to a bellwether, and to betray a she-lamb of a twelvemonth to a crooked-pated old cuckoldly ram, out of all reasonable match. If thou be'st not damned for this, the devil himself will have no shepherds; I cannot see else how thou shouldst scape.

CORIN Here comes young Master Ganymede, my new mistress's brother.

Enter Rosalind [*with a paper, reading*].

ROSALIND
"From the east to western Ind,
No jewel is like Rosalind.
Her worth, being mounted on the wind,
Through all the world bears Rosalind.
All the pictures fairest lined
Are but black to Rosalind.
Let no face be kept in mind
But the fair of Rosalind."

TOUCHSTONE I'll rhyme you so eight years together, dinners and suppers and sleeping hours excepted. It is the right butter-women's rank to market.

ROSALIND Out, fool!

TOUCHSTONE For a taste:
If a hart do lack a hind,
Let him seek out Rosalind.
If the cat will after kind,
So, be sure, will Rosalind.
Wintered garments must be lined,
So must slender Rosalind.
They that reap must sheaf and bind;
Then to cart with Rosalind.
Sweetest nut hath sourest rind;
Such a nut is Rosalind.
He that sweetest rose will find
Must find love's prick and Rosalind.

This is the very false gallop of verses. Why do you infect yourself with them?

ROSALIND Peace, you dull fool! I found them on a tree.

TOUCHSTONE Truly, the tree yields bad fruit.

ROSALIND I'll graft it with you, and then I shall graft it with a medlar. Then it will be the earliest fruit i'th' country; for you'll be rotten ere you be half ripe, and that's the right virtue of the medlar.

TOUCHSTONE You have said; but whether wisely or no, let the forest judge.

Enter Celia, with a writing.

ROSALIND Peace! Here comes my sister, reading. Stand aside.

CELIA [*reads*]
"Why should this a desert be?
For it is unpeopled? No.
Tongues I'll hang on every tree,
That shall civil sayings show:
Some, how brief the life of man
Runs his erring pilgrimage,
That the stretching of a span
Buckles in his sum of age;
Some, of violated vows
Twixt the souls of friend and friend;
But upon the fairest boughs,
Or at every sentence end,
Will I 'Rosalinda' write,
Teaching all that read to know
The quintessence of every sprite
Heaven would in little show.
Therefore heaven Nature charged
That one body should be filled
With all graces wide-enlarged.
Nature presently distilled
Helen's cheek, but not her heart,
Cleopatra's majesty,
Atalanta's better part,
Sad Lucretia's modesty.
Thus Rosalind of many parts
By heavenly synod was devised
Of many faces, eyes, and hearts
To have the touches dearest prized.
Heaven would that she these gifts should have,
And I to live and die her slave."

78 cattle livestock **78–9 bellwether** the leading male sheep of a flock, wearing a bell **80 crooked-pated** with crooked horns. **cuckoldly** i.e., horned like a cuckold (husband of an unfaithful wife). **out of** contrary to **81–2 If . . . shepherds** i.e., Your only possible escape from damnation would be if the devil should find shepherds too objectionable to have in hell under any circumstances **83 scape** escape. **86 Ind** Indies **90 lined** drawn **91 black to** dark-complexioned and hence ugly compared to **93 fair** beauty **94 together** without stop **95–6 It is . . . market** i.e., The rhymes, all alike, follow each other precisely like a line of butter women or dairy women jogging along to market. **97 Out** (An exclamation here denoting comic indignation.) **99 If . . . hind** If a male deer longs for a female deer. (Touchstone wryly suggests in his verses that Rosalind is the responsive object of male desire.) **101 after kind** follow its natural instinct **103 Wintered** Old, worn; used in winter. **lined** (1) given a winter lining (2) stuffed. (The term was sometimes used for the copulating of dogs.) **105 sheaf and bind** tie in a bundle **106 to cart** (1) onto the harvest cart (2) onto the cart used to carry prostitutes through the streets, exposing them to public ridicule **110 prick** thorn. (With bawdy suggestion.) **111 false gallop** canter

115 you (With a pun on "yew.") **116 medlar** a fruit like a small brown-skinned apple that is eaten when it starts to decay. (With a pun on "meddler.") **118 right virtue** true quality **124 For** Because **126 civil sayings** maxims of civilized life **128 his erring** its wandering **129–30 That . . . age** i.e., so that a very brief span encompasses his whole life. (A *span* is a handbreadth. See Psalm 39:5.) **137 quintessence** highest perfection. (Literally, the fifth essence or element of the medieval alchemists, purer even than fire.) **sprite** spirit **138 Heaven . . . show** that heaven wishes to show in one small person, Rosalind (who, in microcosm, embodies the supreme essence of the heavens, or macrocosm). **139 heaven . . . charged** heaven commanded Nature **141 wide-enlarged** all-encompassing. **143 Helen's . . . heart** i.e., the beauty of Helen of Troy but not her false heart **145 Atalanta's better part** i.e., her beauty or her fleetness of foot, not her scornfulness and greed. (She refused to marry any man who was unable to defeat her in a foot race and, when challenged by Hippomenes, lost to him because Hippomenes dropped in her way three golden apples of the Hesperides.) **146 Lucretia** an honorable Roman lady raped by Tarquin (whose story Shakespeare tells in *The Rape of Lucrece*). **148 synod** assembly **150 touches** traits **151 would** decreed **152 And I to** and that I should

ROSALIND Oh, most gentle Jupiter, what tedious homily of love have you wearied your parishioners withal, and never cried, "Have patience, good people!"

CELIA How now? Back, friends. Shepherd, go off a little. [*To Touchstone*] Go with him, sirrah.

TOUCHSTONE Come, shepherd, let us make an honorable retreat, though not with bag and baggage, yet with scrip and scrippage. *Exit* [*with Corin*].

CELIA Didst thou hear these verses?

ROSALIND Oh, yes, I heard them all, and more, too, for some of them had in them more feet than the verses would bear.

CELIA That's no matter. The feet might bear the verses.

ROSALIND Ay, but the feet were lame and could not bear themselves without the verse and therefore stood lamely in the verse.

CELIA But didst thou hear without wondering how thy name should be hanged and carved upon these trees?

ROSALIND I was seven of the nine days out of the wonder before you came; for look here what I found on a palm tree. I was never so berhymed since Pythagoras' time, that I was an Irish rat, which I can hardly remember.

CELIA Trow you who hath done this?

ROSALIND Is it a man?

CELIA And a chain that you once wore about his neck. Change you color?

ROSALIND I prithee, who?

CELIA Oh, Lord, Lord, it is a hard matter for friends to meet; but mountains may be removed with earthquakes and so encounter.

ROSALIND Nay, but who is it?

CELIA Is it possible?

ROSALIND Nay, I prithee now with most petitionary vehemence, tell me who it is.

CELIA Oh, wonderful, wonderful, and most wonderful-wonderful! And yet again wonderful, and after that, out of all whooping!

ROSALIND Good my complexion! Dost thou think, though I am caparisoned like a man, I have a doublet and hose in my disposition? One inch of delay more is a South Sea of discovery. I prithee, tell me who is it quickly, and speak apace. I would thou couldst stammer, that thou mightst pour this concealed man out of thy mouth as wine comes out of a narrow-mouthed bottle, either too much at once or none at all. I prithee, take the cork out of thy mouth that I may drink thy tidings.

CELIA So you may put a man in your belly.

ROSALIND Is he of God's making? What manner of man? Is his head worth a hat, or his chin worth a beard?

CELIA Nay, he hath but a little beard.

ROSALIND Why, God will send more, if the man will be thankful. Let me stay the growth of his beard, if thou delay me not the knowledge of his chin.

CELIA It is young Orlando, that tripped up the wrestler's heels and your heart both in an instant.

ROSALIND Nay, but the devil take mocking. Speak sad brow and true maid.

CELIA I'faith, coz, 'tis he.

ROSALIND Orlando?

CELIA Orlando.

ROSALIND Alas the day, what shall I do with my doublet and hose? What did he when thou saw'st him? What said he? How looked he? Wherein went he? What makes he here? Did he ask for me? Where remains he? How parted he with thee? And when shalt thou see him again? Answer me in one word.

CELIA You must borrow me Gargantua's mouth first; 'tis a word too great for any mouth of this age's size. To say ay and no to these particulars is more than to answer in a catechism.

ROSALIND But doth he know that I am in this forest and in man's apparel? Looks he as freshly as he did the day he wrestled?

CELIA It is as easy to count atomies as to resolve the propositions of a lover. But take a taste of my finding him, and relish it with good observance. I found him under a tree, like a dropped acorn.

ROSALIND It may well be called Jove's tree, when it drops forth such fruit.

CELIA Give me audience, good madam.

ROSALIND Proceed.

CELIA There lay he, stretched along, like a wounded knight.

ROSALIND Though it be pity to see such a sight, it well becomes the ground.

CELIA Cry "holla" to thy tongue, I prithee; it curvets unseasonably. He was furnished like a hunter.

153 Jupiter (Often emended to "pulpiter.") **156 Back** i.e., Move back, away. (Addressed to Corin and Touchstone.) **157 sirrah** a form of address to inferiors (here, Touchstone). **159 bag and baggage** i.e., equipment appropriate to a retreating army **160 scrip and scrippage** shepherd's pouch and its contents. **167 without** (1) without the help of (2) outside **171–2 seven . . . wonder** (A reference to the common phrase "a nine days' wonder.") **174 Pythagoras** Greek philosopher credited with the doctrine of the transmigration of souls. **that** when. **Irish rat** (Refers to a current belief that Irish enchanters could rhyme rats and other animals to death.) **which** a thing which **176 Trow you** Have you any idea **178 And a chain** And with a chain **181–3 it is . . . encounter** (A playful inversion of the proverb, "Friends may meet, but mountains never greet." Celia appears to be teasing Rosalind's eagerness to meet Orlando.) **removed with** moved by **185 possible** i.e., possible you don't know. **190 out . . . whooping** beyond all power to utter. **191 Good my complexion!** Oh, my (feminine) temperament, my woman's curiosity! **192 caparisoned** bedecked. (Usually said of a horse.) **192–3 I have . . . disposition?** i.e., that I have a man's patience? **194 a South Sea of discovery** i.e., as tedious as a long exploratory voyage to the South Pacific Ocean.

201 belly (1) stomach (2) womb. **202 of God's making** i.e., a real man, not of a tailor's making. **207 stay** wait for **211–12 sad . . . maid** i.e., seriously and truthfully. **218 Wherein went he?** In what clothes was he dressed? **219 makes** does **220 remains** dwells **222 Gargantua's mouth** (Gargantua is the giant of popular literature who, in Rabelais' novel, swallowed five pilgrims in a salad.) **224–5 To . . . catechism** To give even yes and no answers to these questions would take longer than to go through the catechism (i.e., the formal questioning used in the Church to teach the principles of faith). **229 atomies** motes, specks of dirt **230 propositions** questions **231 relish it** heighten its pleasant taste. **observance** attention. **233 Jove's tree** the oak **235 Give me audience** Listen to me **240 becomes** adorns **241 holla** stop. **curvets** prances **242 furnished** equipped, dressed

ROSALIND Oh, ominous! He comes to kill my heart.

CELIA I would sing my song without a burden. Thou bring'st me out of tune.

ROSALIND Do you not know I am a woman? When I think, I must speak. Sweet, say on.

Enter Orlando and Jaques.

CELIA You bring me out.—Soft, comes he not here?

ROSALIND 'Tis he. Slink by, and note him.

[*They stand aside and listen.*]

JAQUES [*to Orlando*] I thank you for your company, but, good faith, I had as lief have been myself alone.

ORLANDO And so had I; but yet, for fashion sake, I thank you too for your society.

JAQUES God b'wi'you. Let's meet as little as we can.

ORLANDO I do desire we may be better strangers.

JAQUES I pray you, mar no more trees with writing love songs in their barks.

ORLANDO I pray you, mar no more of my verses with reading them ill-favoredly.

JAQUES Rosalind is your love's name?

ORLANDO Yes, just.

JAQUES I do not like her name.

ORLANDO There was no thought of pleasing you when she was christened.

JAQUES What stature is she of?

ORLANDO Just as high as my heart.

JAQUES You are full of pretty answers. Have you not been acquainted with goldsmiths' wives, and conned them out of rings?

ORLANDO Not so; but I answer you right painted cloth, from whence you have studied your questions.

JAQUES You have a nimble wit; I think 'twas made of Atalanta's heels. Will you sit down with me? And we two will rail against our mistress the world and all our misery.

ORLANDO I will chide no breather in the world but myself, against whom I know most faults.

JAQUES The worst fault you have is to be in love.

ORLANDO 'Tis a fault I will not change for your best virtue. I am weary of you.

JAQUES By my troth, I was seeking for a fool when I found you.

ORLANDO He is drowned in the brook. Look but in, and you shall see him.

JAQUES There I shall see mine own figure.

ORLANDO Which I take to be either a fool or a cipher.

JAQUES I'll tarry no longer with you. Farewell, good Seigneur Love.

ORLANDO I am glad of your departure. Adieu, good Monsieur Melancholy. [*Exit Jaques.*]

ROSALIND [*aside to Celia*] I will speak to him like a saucy lackey and under that habit play the knave with him.—Do you hear, forester?

ORLANDO Very well. What would you?

ROSALIND I pray you, what is't o'clock?

ORLANDO You should ask me what time o' day. There's no clock in the forest.

ROSALIND Then there is no true lover in the forest, else sighing every minute and groaning every hour would detect the lazy foot of Time as well as a clock.

ORLANDO And why not the swift foot of Time? Had not that been as proper?

ROSALIND By no means, sir. Time travels in divers paces with divers persons. I'll tell you who Time ambles withal, who Time trots withal, who Time gallops withal, and who he stands still withal.

ORLANDO I prithee, who doth he trot withal?

ROSALIND Marry, he trots hard with a young maid between the contract of her marriage and the day it is solemnized. If the interim be but a se'nnight, Time's pace is so hard that it seems the length of seven year.

ORLANDO Who ambles Time withal?

ROSALIND With a priest that lacks Latin and a rich man that hath not the gout, for the one sleeps easily because he cannot study and the other lives merrily because he feels no pain, the one lacking the burden of lean and wasteful learning, the other knowing no burden of heavy tedious penury. These Time ambles withal.

ORLANDO Who doth he gallop withal?

ROSALIND With a thief to the gallows, for though he go as softly as foot can fall, he thinks himself too soon there.

ORLANDO Who stays it still withal?

ROSALIND With lawyers in the vacation; for they sleep between term and term, and then they perceive not how Time moves.

ORLANDO Where dwell you, pretty youth?

ROSALIND With this shepherdess, my sister, here in the skirts of the forest, like fringe upon a petticoat.

ORLANDO Are you native of this place?

ROSALIND As the coney that you see dwell where she is kindled.

ORLANDO Your accent is something finer than you could purchase in so removed a dwelling.

ROSALIND I have been told so of many. But indeed an old religious uncle of mine taught me to speak, who was in his youth an inland man, one that knew courtship too well, for there he fell in love. I have

243 heart (With pun on "hart.") **244 burden** refrain, or bass part. **244–5 Thou bring'st** You put **248 Soft** i.e., Wait a minute, or, stop talking **252 fashion** fashion's **254 God b'wi'you** God be with you, good-bye **259 ill-favoredly** unsympathetically. **261 just** just so. **268 conned** memorized **269 rings** (Verses or "posies" were often inscribed in rings.) **270 right painted cloth** in the true spirit of a painted cloth decorated with commonplace pictures and cliché mottoes (frequently mythological or scriptural) **273 Atalanta's heels** (See above, the note for line 145.) **276 breather** living being **285 figure** reflection. (Narcissus fell in love with his own reflection in a pool.) **286 cipher** nonentity, zero.

292 and under . . . knave and in that disguise (1) pose as a boy (2) deal mischievously **300 detect** reveal **305 withal** with **310 se'nnight** week **317 lean** unremunerative. **wasteful** making one waste away **326 term** court session **332 coney** rabbit **333 kindled** littered, born. **334 something** somewhat **335 purchase** acquire. **removed** remote **337 religious** i.e., belonging to a religious order **338 inland** from a center of civilization **339 courtship** (1) wooing (2) knowledge of courtly manners

heard him read many lectures against it, and I thank God I am not a woman, to be touched with so many giddy offenses as he hath generally taxed their whole sex withal.

ORLANDO Can you remember any of the principal evils that he laid to the charge of women?

ROSALIND There were none principal; they were all like one another as halfpence are, every one fault seeming monstrous till his fellow fault came to match it.

ORLANDO I prithee, recount some of them.

ROSALIND No, I will not cast away my physic but on those that are sick. There is a man haunts the forest that abuses our young plants with carving "Rosalind" on their barks, hangs odes upon hawthorns and elegies on brambles, all, forsooth, deifying the name of Rosalind. If I could meet that fancy-monger, I would give him some good counsel, for he seems to have the quotidian of love upon him.

ORLANDO I am he that is so love-shaked. I pray you, tell me your remedy.

ROSALIND There is none of my uncle's marks upon you. He taught me how to know a man in love, in which cage of rushes I am sure you are not prisoner.

ORLANDO What were his marks?

ROSALIND A lean cheek, which you have not; a blue eye and sunken, which you have not; an unquestionable spirit, which you have not; a beard neglected, which you have not—but I pardon you for that, for simply your having in beard is a younger brother's revenue. Then your hose should be ungartered, your bonnet unbanded, your sleeve unbuttoned, your shoe untied, and everything about you demonstrating a careless desolation. But you are no such man. You are rather point-device in your accoutrements, as loving yourself, than seeming the lover of any other.

ORLANDO Fair youth, I would I could make thee believe I love.

ROSALIND Me believe it? You may as soon make her that you love believe it, which I warrant she is apter to do than to confess she does. That is one of the points in the which women still give the lie to their consciences. But in good sooth, are you he that hangs the verses on the trees, wherein Rosalind is so admired?

ORLANDO I swear to thee, youth, by the white hand of Rosalind, I am that he, that unfortunate he.

ROSALIND But are you so much in love as your rhymes speak?

ORLANDO Neither rhyme nor reason can express how much.

ROSALIND Love is merely a madness and, I tell you, deserves as well a dark house and a whip as madmen do; and the reason why they are not so punished and cured is that the lunacy is so ordinary that the whippers are in love too. Yet I profess curing it by counsel.

ORLANDO Did you ever cure any so?

ROSALIND Yes, one, and in this manner. He was to imagine me his love, his mistress; and I set him every day to woo me. At which time would I, being but a moonish youth, grieve, be effeminate, changeable, longing and liking, proud, fantastical, apish, shallow, inconstant, full of tears, full of smiles; for every passion something and for no passion truly anything, as boys and women are for the most part cattle of this color; would now like him, now loathe him; then entertain him, then forswear him; now weep for him, then spit at him; that I drave my suitor from his mad humor of love to a living humor of madness, which was to forswear the full stream of the world and to live in a nook merely monastic. And thus I cured him; and this way will I take upon me to wash your liver as clean as a sound sheep's heart, that there shall not be one spot of love in't.

ORLANDO I would not be cured, youth.

ROSALIND I would cure you, if you would but call me Rosalind and come every day to my cote and woo me.

ORLANDO Now by the faith of my love, I will. Tell me where it is.

ROSALIND Go with me to it, and I'll show it you; and by the way you shall tell me where in the forest you live. Will you go?

ORLANDO With all my heart, good youth.

ROSALIND Nay, you must call me Rosalind.—Come, sister, will you go? *Exeunt.*

✣

3.3

Enter [*Touchstone the*] *Clown, Audrey; and Jaques* [*apart*].

TOUCHSTONE Come apace, good Audrey. I will fetch up your goats, Audrey. And how, Audrey, am I the man yet? Doth my simple feature content you?

AUDREY Your features, Lord warrant us! What features?

TOUCHSTONE I am here with thee and thy goats, as the most capricious poet, honest Ovid, was among the Goths.

340 read many lectures deliver many admonitory speeches **341 touched** tainted **348 his** its **350 physic** medicine **355 fancy-monger** love peddler **357 quotidian** fever recurring daily. (See *love-shaked*, line 358.) **362 cage of rushes** i.e., flimsy prison **364 blue eye** i.e., having dark circles **365 unquestionable** unwilling to be conversed with **367–8 simply . . . revenue** what beard you have is like a younger brother's inheritance (i.e., small). **369–70 bonnet unbanded** hat lacking a band around the crown **373 point-device** faultless
380 still continually **381 good sooth** honest truth

390 merely utterly **391 dark . . . whip** (The common treatment of lunatics.) **394 profess** am expert in **400 moonish** changeable
405 entertain receive cordially **407 that** with the result that. **drave** drove **407–8 mad . . . madness** mad fancy of love to a real madness
410 merely utterly **411 liver** (Supposed seat of the emotions, especially love.) **416 cote** cottage **420 by** on
3.3 Location: The forest.
1 apace quickly **2 And how** i.e., What do you say **3 simple feature** plain appearance. (But Audrey, in her answer, may have her mind on *features* as "parts of the body.") **4 warrant** protect **6 capricious** witty, fanciful. (Derived from the Latin *caper,* "male goat"; hence, "goatish, lascivious.") **7 Goths** (With pun on "goats"; the two words were pronounced alike.)

JAQUES [*aside*] Oh, knowledge ill-inhabited, worse than Jove in a thatched house!

TOUCHSTONE When a man's verses cannot be understood, nor a man's good wit seconded with the forward child, understanding, it strikes a man more dead than a great reckoning in a little room. Truly, I would the gods had made thee poetical.

AUDREY I do not know what "poetical" is. Is it honest in deed and word? Is it a true thing?

TOUCHSTONE No, truly; for the truest poetry is the most feigning, and lovers are given to poetry, and what they swear in poetry may be said as lovers they do feign.

AUDREY Do you wish then that the gods had made me poetical?

TOUCHSTONE I do, truly; for thou swear'st to me thou art honest. Now, if thou wert a poet, I might have some hope thou didst feign.

AUDREY Would you not have me honest?

TOUCHSTONE No, truly, unless thou wert hard-favored; for honesty coupled to beauty is to have honey a sauce to sugar.

JAQUES [*aside*] A material fool!

AUDREY Well, I am not fair, and therefore I pray the gods make me honest.

TOUCHSTONE Truly, and to cast away honesty upon a foul slut were to put good meat into an unclean dish.

AUDREY I am not a slut, though I thank the gods I am foul.

TOUCHSTONE Well, praised be the gods for thy foulness! Sluttishness may come hereafter. But be it as it may be, I will marry thee, and to that end I have been with Sir Oliver Mar-text, the vicar of the next village, who hath promised to meet me in this place of the forest and to couple us.

JAQUES [*aside*] I would fain see this meeting.

AUDREY Well, the gods give us joy!

TOUCHSTONE Amen. A man may, if he were of a fearful heart, stagger in this attempt; for here we have no temple but the wood, no assembly but horn-beasts. But what though? Courage! As horns are odious, they are necessary. It is said, "Many a man knows no end of his goods." Right! Many a man has good horns and knows no end of them. Well, that is the dowry of his wife; 'tis none of his own getting. Horns? Even so. Poor men alone? No, no, the noblest deer hath them as huge as the rascal. Is the single man therefore blessed? No. As a walled town is more worthier than a village, so is the forehead of a married man more honorable than the bare brow of a bachelor; and by how much defense is better than no skill, by so much is a horn more precious than to want.

Enter Sir Oliver Mar-text.

Here comes Sir Oliver.—Sir Oliver Mar-text, you are well met. Will you dispatch us here under this tree, or shall we go with you to your chapel?

SIR OLIVER Is there none here to give the woman?

TOUCHSTONE I will not take her on gift of any man.

SIR OLIVER Truly, she must be given, or the marriage is not lawful.

JAQUES [*advancing*] Proceed, proceed. I'll give her.

TOUCHSTONE Good even, good Master What-ye-call-'t. How do you, sir? You are very well met. God 'ild you for your last company. I am very glad to see you. Even a toy in hand here, sir.—Nay, pray be covered.

JAQUES Will you be married, motley?

TOUCHSTONE As the ox hath his bow, sir, the horse his curb, and the falcon her bells, so man hath his desires; and as pigeons bill, so wedlock would be nibbling.

JAQUES And will you, being a man of your breeding, be married under a bush like a beggar? Get you to church, and have a good priest that can tell you what marriage is. This fellow will but join you together as they join wainscot; then one of you will prove a shrunk panel and, like green timber, warp, warp.

8 ill-inhabited ill-lodged **9 Jove . . . house!** (An allusion to Ovid's *Metamorphoses* 8, containing the story of Jupiter and Mercury lodging disguised in the humble cottage of Baucis and Philemon.) **10–11 verses . . . understood** (Ovid's verses were misunderstood by the barbaric Goths, among whom he lived in exile, just as Touchstone's wit is misunderstood by Audrey.) **11–12 nor . . . understanding** (Wisdom, understanding, and memory were thought to occupy three main ventricles in the brain, and to be interconnected in the process of thought. *Forward* means "precocious.") **13 great . . . room** exorbitant charge for refreshment or lodging in a cramped tavern room. (Some scholars see in this passage an allusion to the death of Christopher Marlowe, who was stabbed by Ingram Frysar at an inn in Deptford in a quarrel over a tavern reckoning, May 30, 1593.) **18 feigning** inventive, imaginative. (But Touchstone plays on the sense of "false, lying.") **19 may be said** i.e., it may be said **20 feign** (With a further play on "desire.") **24 honest** chaste. **25 feign** (1) pretend (2) desire. **27–8 hard-favored** ugly **28 honesty** chastity **30 material** full of pithy matter **34 foul** ugly **35–6 I thank . . . foul** i.e., my unattractive looks are what destiny has allotted to me. **40 Sir** (Courtesy title for a clergyman.) **43 fain** gladly **46 stagger** hesitate **47 horn-beasts** antlered animals like deer and cattle, and therefore resembling cuckolded men with their cuckolds' horns.

48 what though what though it be so. **As** Though **49 necessary** (1) useful to horned animals (2) unavoidable to cuckolds. **49–50 knows . . . goods** is endlessly well provided. **51 knows . . . them** i.e., is endlessly supplied with cuckold's horns. (A sardonic interpretation of the proverb in lines 49–50.) **dowry** marriage gift **52 getting** (1) obtaining (2) begetting (in the sense that his wife's children will not be his). **Even so** That's just how it is. **53 deer** (1) horned animal (2) dear husband **54 rascal** (1) young deer that are lean and out of season (2) poor ordinary husband. **single** unmarried **58 defense** (1) fortifications (including a type known as "hornwork") (2) the art of self-defense **59 than to want** i.e., than to be without a horn. (Recalling the "horn of plenty," which is indeed precious.) **61 dispatch us** finish off our business **63 give the woman** give away the bride; conventionally, the bride's father answered the question, "Who giveth this woman to be married to this man?" **68 What-ye-call-'t** (Probably joking on *Jakes* as "outhouse.") **69 'ild you** yield you, reward you **70 last** most recent **71 a toy in hand** a trifle to be attended to, or literally by the hand. **be covered** put on your hat, i.e., no need to show respect; or, cover up your bosom. (Said to Audrey, or perhaps to Jaques, who may have removed his hat in sardonic deference to the ceremony.) **73 bow** yoke **74 curb** chain or strap attached to the horse's bit and used to control it. **bells** (Attached to a falcon's leg during training.) **75 bill** stroke bill with bill **77 under a bush** i.e., by a "hedge-priest," an uneducated clergyman **78–9 tell . . . is** expound the obligations of marriage. **81 warp** (1) shrivel and fit badly together (2) stray from the true path.

TOUCHSTONE I am not in the mind but I were better to be married of him than of another, for he is not like to marry me well; and not being well married, it will be a good excuse for me hereafter to leave my wife.

JAQUES Go thou with me, and let me counsel thee.

TOUCHSTONE
Come, sweet Audrey.
We must be married, or we must live in bawdry.
Farewell, good Master Oliver; not
"O sweet Oliver,
O brave Oliver,
Leave me not behind thee";
but
"Wind away,
Begone, I say,
I will not to wedding with thee."
[Exeunt Jaques, Touchstone, and Audrey.]

SIR OLIVER 'Tis no matter. Ne'er a fantastical knave of them all shall flout me out of my calling. *Exit.*

3.4

Enter Rosalind and Celia.

ROSALIND Never talk to me. I will weep.

CELIA Do, I prithee, but yet have the grace to consider that tears do not become a man.

ROSALIND But have I not cause to weep?

CELIA As good cause as one would desire; therefore weep.

ROSALIND His very hair is of the dissembling color.

CELIA Something browner than Judas's. Marry, his kisses are Judas's own children.

ROSALIND I'faith, his hair is of a good color.

CELIA An excellent color. Your chestnut was ever the only color.

ROSALIND And his kissing is as full of sanctity as the touch of holy bread.

CELIA He hath bought a pair of cast lips of Diana. A nun of winter's sisterhood kisses not more religiously; the very ice of chastity is in them.

ROSALIND But why did he swear he would come this morning, and comes not?

CELIA Nay, certainly, there is no truth in him.

ROSALIND Do you think so?

CELIA Yes. I think he is not a pickpurse nor a horse-stealer, but for his verity in love, I do think him as concave as a covered goblet or a worm-eaten nut.

ROSALIND Not true in love?

CELIA Yes, when he is in, but I think he is not in.

ROSALIND You have heard him swear downright he was.

CELIA "Was" is not "is." Besides, the oath of a lover is no stronger than the word of a tapster; they are both the confirmer of false reckonings. He attends here in the forest on the Duke your father.

ROSALIND I met the Duke yesterday and had much question with him. He asked me of what parentage I was. I told him, of as good as he; so he laughed and let me go. But what talk we of fathers, when there is such a man as Orlando?

CELIA Oh, that's a brave man! He writes brave verses, speaks brave words, swears brave oaths, and breaks them bravely, quite traverse, athwart the heart of his lover, as a puny tilter, that spurs his horse but on one side, breaks his staff like a noble goose. But all's brave that youth mounts and folly guides. Who comes here?

Enter Corin.

CORIN
Mistress and master, you have oft inquired
After the shepherd that complained of love,
Who you saw sitting by me on the turf,
Praising the proud disdainful shepherdess
That was his mistress.

CELIA Well, and what of him?

CORIN
If you will see a pageant truly played
Between the pale complexion of true love
And the red glow of scorn and proud disdain,
Go hence a little, and I shall conduct you,
If you will mark it.

ROSALIND Oh, come, let us remove!
The sight of lovers feedeth those in love.
Bring us to this sight, and you shall say
I'll prove a busy actor in their play. *Exeunt.*

82 I am . . . better I do not know but that it would be better for me. (Touchstone may be speaking aside here to Jaques.) **83 of** by **84 like** likely. **well** (1) suitably (2) legally **89 married** i.e., properly married, as Jaques suggests, not by a hedge-priest. (Having been found out, Touchstone wryly defers matters for the present.) **91–7 "O . . . thee."** (Phrases from a current ballad.) **92 brave** worthy **95 Wind** Wend, go **98 fantastical** affected

3.4 Location: The forest.

7 the dissembling color i.e., reddish, traditionally the color of Judas's hair. **8 Something** Somewhat **9 Judas's own children** i.e., as false and betraying as the kiss given by Judas to Jesus when he betrayed him to the high priests. **11 Your chestnut** i.e., This chestnut color that people talk about **12 only** only fashionable **14 holy bread** either the unleavened bread of the Eucharist or ordinary leavened bread that was blessed after the Eucharist and distributed to those who had not received communion. **15 cast** (1) chaste, cold (2) molded (3) cast off. **Diana** goddess of chastity. **16 of winter's sisterhood** i.e., devoted to barrenness and cold

24 concave hollow, i.e., insincere **31 false reckonings** (Tapsters, or barkeeps, were notorious for inflating bills.) **34 question** conversation **36 what** why **38 brave** fine, excellent **40 traverse** across, awry. (A term from medieval jousting or tilting; hence *tilter*, line 41.) **41 puny** inexperienced. (Literally, junior.) **but** only **42 a noble goose** i.e., a goose-headed young gallent. **42–3 But . . . guides** But everything is admirable that youth undertakes under the influence of folly. (Said sardonically.) **46 complained of** uttered a lament against **51 pale complexion** (Sighing was believed to draw the blood from the heart.) **54 will mark** wish to observe. **remove** leave here and go.

3.5

Enter Silvius and Phoebe.

SILVIUS
Sweet Phoebe, do not scorn me, do not, Phoebe!
Say that you love me not, but say not so
In bitterness. The common executioner,
Whose heart th'accustomed sight of death makes hard,
Falls not the ax upon the humbled neck 5
But first begs pardon. Will you sterner be 6
Than he that dies and lives by bloody drops? 7

Enter Rosalind, Celia, and Corin [behind].

PHOEBE
I would not be thy executioner;
I fly thee, for I would not injure thee.
Thou tell'st me there is murder in mine eye.
'Tis pretty, sure, and very probable, 11
That eyes, that are the frail'st and softest things,
Who shut their coward gates on atomies, 13
Should be called tyrants, butchers, murderers!
Now I do frown on thee with all my heart,
And if mine eyes can wound, now let them kill thee.
Now counterfeit to swoon; why, now fall down,
Or if thou canst not, oh, for shame, for shame,
Lie not, to say mine eyes are murderers! 19
Now show the wound mine eye hath made in thee.
Scratch thee but with a pin, and there remains
Some scar of it; lean upon a rush, 22
The cicatrice and capable impressure 23
Thy palm some moment keeps; but now mine eyes, 24
Which I have darted at thee, hurt thee not,
Nor, I am sure, there is no force in eyes
That can do hurt.

SILVIUS O dear Phoebe,
If ever—as that "ever" may be near—
You meet in some fresh cheek the power of fancy, 29
Then shall you know the wounds invisible
That love's keen arrows make.

PHOEBE But till that time
Come not thou near me; and when that time comes,
Afflict me with thy mocks; pity me not,
As till that time I shall not pity thee. 34

ROSALIND [*advancing*]
And why, I pray you? Who might be your mother, 35
That you insult, exult, and all at once, 36
Over the wretched? What though you have no beauty— 37
As, by my faith, I see no more in you 38
Than without candle may go dark to bed— 39
Must you be therefore proud and pitiless?
Why, what means this? Why do you look on me?
I see no more in you than in the ordinary 42
Of nature's sale-work. 'Od's my little life, 43
I think she means to tangle my eyes too! 44
No, faith, proud mistress, hope not after it.
'Tis not your inky brows, your black silk hair,
Your bugle eyeballs, nor your cheek of cream 47
That can entame my spirits to your worship. 48
[*To Silvius*] You foolish shepherd, wherefore do you follow her,
Like foggy south, puffing with wind and rain? 50
You are a thousand times a properer man 51
Than she a woman. 'Tis such fools as you
That makes the world full of ill-favored children. 53
'Tis not her glass, but you, that flatters her, 54
And out of you she sees herself more proper 55
Than any of her lineaments can show her.— 56
But, mistress, know yourself. Down on your knees,
And thank heaven, fasting, for a good man's love!
For I must tell you friendly in your ear,
Sell when you can. You are not for all markets.
Cry the man mercy, love him, take his offer; 61
Foul is most foul, being foul to be a scoffer.— 62
So take her to thee, shepherd. Fare you well.

PHOEBE
Sweet youth, I pray you, chide a year together. 64
I had rather hear you chide than this man woo.

ROSALIND [*to Phoebe*] He's fallen in love with your foulness, [*to Silvius*] and she'll fall in love with my anger. If it be so, as fast as she answers thee with frowning looks, I'll sauce her with bitter words. [*To* 69
Phoebe] Why look you so upon me?

PHOEBE For no ill will I bear you.

ROSALIND
I pray you, do not fall in love with me,
For I am falser than vows made in wine. 73
Besides, I like you not. [*To Silvius*] If you will know my house,
'Tis at the tuft of olives here hard by.—
Will you go, sister?—Shepherd, ply her hard.— 76

3.5 Location: The forest.
5 Falls lets fall **6 But first begs pardon** without first begging pardon (as executioners did in Elizabethan times). **7 dies . . . drops** makes his living by the deaths of others. (Stated as an oxymoron.) **11 sure** to be sure **13 coward gates on atomies** i.e., sensitive eyelids to protect against specks of dirt **19 to say** by saying **22 a rush** a reed **23–4 The cicatrice . . . keeps** the scarlike and perceptible impression is retained by one's palm for a moment **29 You . . . fancy** you yourself feel the powerful spell of love for some new face **34 As** since **35 Who . . . mother** (1) What human mother could have produced so inhuman a daughter (2) From what sort of a mother did you learn such scorn **36 insult** exult scornfully. **all at once** all at the same time

37 have no beauty are not particularly beautiful **38–9 I see . . . bed** i.e., I see nothing in your beauty that might not go entirely unnoticed, nothing to distinguish you from other young women **42 ordinary** common run **43 sale-work** ready-made products, not of the best quality, not distinctive. **'Od's** May God save **44 tangle** ensnare **47 bugle** beadlike, black and glassy **48 to your worship** (1) to the worship of you (2) to adore Your Worship (as such beauty deserved an honorific title). **50 south** south wind (from which came fog and rain; hence, Silvius's sighs and tears) **51 properer** better-looking (since handsome is as handsome does) **53 ill-favored** ugly **54 glass** mirror **55 out of you** i.e., with you as her mirror **56 lineaments** features **61 Cry . . . mercy** Beg the man's pardon **62 Foul . . . scoffer** i.e., unattractive behavior like yours is at its most foul when it consists of scoffing. (Plays on two meanings of *foul*.) **64 together** without intermission. **69 sauce** rebuke **73 in wine** while drunk. **76 ply her hard** woo her energetically.

Come, sister.—Shepherdess, look on him better,
And be not proud. Though all the world could see,
None could be so abused in sight as he.—
Come, to our flock. *Exit [with Celia and Corin].*

PHOEBE
Dead shepherd, now I find thy saw of might,
"Who ever loved that loved not at first sight?"

SILVIUS
Sweet Phoebe—

PHOEBE Ha, what say'st thou, Silvius?

SILVIUS Sweet Phoebe, pity me.

PHOEBE
Why, I am sorry for thee, gentle Silvius.

SILVIUS
Wherever sorrow is, relief would be.
If you do sorrow at my grief in love,
By giving love, your sorrow and my grief
Were both extermined.

PHOEBE
Thou hast my love. Is not that neighborly?

SILVIUS
I would have you.

PHOEBE Why, that were covetousness.
Silvius, the time was that I hated thee,
And yet it is not that I bear thee love;
But since that thou canst talk of love so well,
Thy company, which erst was irksome to me,
I will endure, and I'll employ thee too.
But do not look for further recompense
Than thine own gladness that thou art employed.

SILVIUS
So holy and so perfect is my love,
And I in such a poverty of grace,
That I shall think it a most plenteous crop
To glean the broken ears after the man
That the main harvest reaps. Loose now and then
A scattered smile, and that I'll live upon.

PHOEBE
Know'st thou the youth that spoke to me erewhile?

SILVIUS
Not very well, but I have met him oft,
And he hath bought the cottage and the bounds
That the old carlot once was master of.

PHOEBE
Think not I love him, though I ask for him.
'Tis but a peevish boy—yet he talks well—
But what care I for words? Yet words do well
When he that speaks them pleases those that hear.
It is a pretty youth—not very pretty—
But sure he's proud—and yet his pride becomes him.
He'll make a proper man. The best thing in him
Is his complexion; and faster than his tongue
Did make offense, his eye did heal it up.
He is not very tall—yet for his years he's tall.
His leg is but so-so—and yet 'tis well.
There was a pretty redness in his lip,
A little riper and more lusty red
Than that mixed in his cheek; 'twas just the difference
Betwixt the constant red and mingled damask.
There be some women, Silvius, had they marked him
In parcels as I did, would have gone near
To fall in love with him; but for my part,
I love him not nor hate him not; and yet
I have more cause to hate him than to love him.
For what had he to do to chide at me?
He said mine eyes were black and my hair black,
And, now I am remembered, scorned at me.
I marvel why I answered not again.
But that's all one; omittance is no quittance.
I'll write to him a very taunting letter,
And thou shalt bear it. Wilt thou, Silvius?

SILVIUS
Phoebe, with all my heart.

PHOEBE I'll write it straight;
The matter's in my head and in my heart.
I will be bitter with him and passing short.
Go with me, Silvius. *Exeunt.*

✤

4.1

Enter Rosalind and Celia, and Jaques.

JAQUES I prithee, pretty youth, let me be better acquainted with thee.

ROSALIND They say you are a melancholy fellow.

JAQUES I am so. I do love it better than laughing.

ROSALIND Those that are in extremity of either are abominable fellows and betray themselves to every modern censure worse than drunkards.

JAQUES Why, 'tis good to be sad and say nothing.

ROSALIND Why then, 'tis good to be a post.

JAQUES I have neither the scholar's melancholy, which is emulation, nor the musician's, which is fantastical, nor the courtier's, which is proud, nor the soldier's, which is ambitious, nor the lawyer's, which is politic, nor the lady's, which is nice, nor the lover's, which is

78 could see could look at you **79 abused in sight** deceived through the eyes **81 Dead shepherd** i.e., Christopher Marlowe, who died in 1593. **saw** saying. **of might** forceful, convincing **82 Who . . . sight?** (From Marlowe's *Hero and Leander,* Sestiad 1, 176, first published in 1598.) **86 Wherever . . . be** Sorrow cries out for relief. **89 Were both extermined** would both be exterminated, ended. **90 Is . . . neighborly?** i.e., May not I love you in the sense of loving one's neighbor as oneself? **91 covetousness** (The tenth commandment forbids coveting anything that is one's neighbor's.) **93 yet it is not** the time has not yet come **94 since that** since **95 erst** formerly **100 poverty of grace** lack of reciprocated affection **104 scattered** thrown negligently, as in the gleanings of the harvest **105 erewhile** just now. **107 bounds** pastures **108 carlot** churl, countryman. (Perhaps a proper name.)

115 proper handsome **123 mingled damask** mingled red and white, the color of the damask rose. **125 In parcels** bit by bit **125–6 gone . . . fall** been on the point of falling **129 what . . . do** what business had he **131 am remembered** remember **132 again** back. **133 But . . . quittance** i.e., But just the same, my failure to answer him doesn't mean I won't do so later. **136 straight** immediately **138 passing short** exceedingly curt.

4.1. Location: The forest.

5 are . . . of go to extremes in **7 modern censure** common judgment **11 emulation** envy (of the fellow scholar). **fantastical** extravagantly fanciful **13 politic** grave and diplomatic, calculated **14 nice** fastidious

all these; but it is a melancholy of mine own, compounded of many simples, extracted from many objects, and indeed the sundry contemplation of my travels, in which my often rumination wraps me in a most humorous sadness.

ROSALIND A traveler! By my faith, you have great reason to be sad. I fear you have sold your own lands to see other men's. Then to have seen much and to have nothing is to have rich eyes and poor hands.

JAQUES Yes, I have gained my experience.

Enter Orlando.

ROSALIND And your experience makes you sad. I had rather have a fool to make me merry than experience to make me sad—and to travel for it too!

ORLANDO Good day and happiness, dear Rosalind!

JAQUES Nay, then, God b'wi'you, an you talk in blank verse.

ROSALIND Farewell, Monsieur Traveler. Look you lisp and wear strange suits, disable all the benefits of your own country, be out of love with your nativity, and almost chide God for making you that countenance you are, or I will scarce think you have swam in a gondola. [*Exit Jaques.*] Why, how now, Orlando, where have you been all this while? You a lover? An you serve me such another trick, never come in my sight more.

ORLANDO My fair Rosalind, I come within an hour of my promise.

ROSALIND Break an hour's promise in love? He that will divide a minute into a thousand parts and break but a part of the thousandth part of a minute in the affairs of love, it may be said of him that Cupid hath clapped him o'th' shoulder, but I'll warrant him heart-whole.

ORLANDO Pardon me, dear Rosalind.

ROSALIND Nay, an you be so tardy, come no more in my sight. I had as lief be wooed of a snail.

ORLANDO Of a snail?

ROSALIND Ay, of a snail; for though he comes slowly, he carries his house on his head—a better jointure, I think, than you make a woman. Besides, he brings his destiny with him.

ORLANDO What's that?

ROSALIND Why, horns, which such as you are fain to be beholding to your wives for. But he comes armed in his fortune and prevents the slander of his wife.

ORLANDO Virtue is no horn-maker, and my Rosalind is virtuous.

ROSALIND And I am your Rosalind.

CELIA It pleases him to call you so; but he hath a Rosalind of a better leer than you.

ROSALIND Come, woo me, woo me, for now I am in a holiday humor and like enough to consent. What would you say to me now, an I were your very, very Rosalind?

ORLANDO I would kiss before I spoke.

ROSALIND Nay, you were better speak first, and when you were graveled for lack of matter, you might take occasion to kiss. Very good orators, when they are out, they will spit; and for lovers lacking—God warrant us!—matter, the cleanliest shift is to kiss.

ORLANDO How if the kiss be denied?

ROSALIND Then she puts you to entreaty, and there begins new matter.

ORLANDO Who could be out, being before his beloved mistress?

ROSALIND Marry, that should you, if I were your mistress, or I should think my honesty ranker than my wit.

ORLANDO What, of my suit?

ROSALIND Not out of your apparel, and yet out of your suit. Am not I your Rosalind?

ORLANDO I take some joy to say you are, because I would be talking of her.

ROSALIND Well, in her person I say I will not have you.

ORLANDO Then in mine own person, I die.

ROSALIND No, faith, die by attorney. The poor world is almost six thousand years old, and in all this time there was not any man died in his own person, videlicet, in a love cause. Troilus had his brains dashed out with a Grecian club, yet he did what he could to die before, and he is one of the patterns of love. Leander, he would have lived many a fair year though Hero had turned nun, if it had not been for a hot midsummer night; for, good youth, he went but forth to wash him in the Hellespont and being taken with the cramp was drowned; and the foolish chron-

15–19 compounded . . . sadness made up of many ingredients, extracted from the many objects of my observation and, indeed, from the diversified considerations of my travels, my frequent rumination upon which wraps me in a most whimsical and moody sadness.
27 travel (Meaning also "travail," labor.) **29 an** if **31 Look** Be sure. (Said ironically.) **lisp** i.e., affect a foreign accent **32 disable** disparage **33 nativity** country of birth **35 are** i.e., have **35–6 swam . . . gondola** floated in a gondola, i.e., been in Venice, where almost all travelers go. **45–6 Cupid . . . heart-whole** Cupid may have tried to arrest him, but I'm sure his heart remains unengaged. (Arresting officers customarily grasped the culprit by the shoulder.) **49 lief** willingly. **of** by **52 jointure** marriage settlement **53 than . . . woman** than you, Orlando, are able to settle on your prospective wife.
56 horns (1) snails' horns (2) cuckold's horns, signs of an unfaithful wife. **fain** obliged **57 beholding** beholden, indebted

57–8 But . . . fortune The snail comes already provided with the horns that are his nature and his destiny, thereby forestalling the scandal that would otherwise attach to his wife. (Since a snail is naturally horned, no scandal can be adduced from them.) **63 leer** appearance, color **70 graveled** stuck. (Literally, run aground on a shoal.) **71 out** at a loss through forgetfulness or confusion **72 warrant** defend **73 shift** tactic **80 honesty ranker** chastity more corrupt. (Rosalind would rely on her wit to keep her lover off balance and thus defend her chastity. She may use Orlando's *out*, line 77, in a sexual sense of not being admitted.) **82 of my suit** (Orlando means "out of my suit," at a loss for words in my wooing; but Rosalind puns on the meaning "suit of clothes"; to be out of apparel would be to be undressed.) **89 attorney** proxy. **90 six . . . old** (A common figure in biblical calculation.) **91 died** who died **92 videlicet** namely. **Troilus** hero of the story of Troilus and Cressida, in which he remains faithful to her, but she is faithless to him **92–3 had . . . club** (Troilus was slain by Achilles with sword or spear in more traditional accounts. Rosalind's version is calculatedly unromantic.) **95 Leander** the hero of the story of Hero and Leander, who lost his life swimming the Hellespont to visit his sweetheart. (Rosalind's account of the cramp again undercuts romantic idealism.)

iclers of that age found it was—Hero of Sestos. But these are all lies. Men have died from time to time, and worms have eaten them, but not for love.

ORLANDO I would not have my right Rosalind of this mind, for I protest her frown might kill me.

ROSALIND By this hand, it will not kill a fly. But come, now I will be your Rosalind in a more coming-on disposition; and ask me what you will, I will grant it.

ORLANDO Then love me, Rosalind.

ROSALIND Yes, faith, will I, Fridays and Saturdays and all.

ORLANDO And wilt thou have me?

ROSALIND Ay, and twenty such.

ORLANDO What sayest thou?

ROSALIND Are you not good?

ORLANDO I hope so.

ROSALIND Why then, can one desire too much of a good thing?—Come, sister, you shall be the priest and marry us.—Give me your hand, Orlando.—What do you say, sister?

ORLANDO Pray thee, marry us.

CELIA I cannot say the words.

ROSALIND You must begin, "Will you,Orlando—"

CELIA Go to. Will you, Orlando, have to wife this Rosalind?

ORLANDO I will.

ROSALIND Ay, but when?

ORLANDO Why now, as fast as she can marry us.

ROSALIND Then you must say, "I take thee, Rosalind, for wife."

ORLANDO I take thee, Rosalind, for wife.

ROSALIND I might ask you for your commission; but I do take thee, Orlando, for my husband. There's a girl goes before the priest, and certainly a woman's thought runs before her actions.

ORLANDO So do all thoughts; they are winged.

ROSALIND Now tell me how long you would have her after you have possessed her.

ORLANDO For ever and a day.

ROSALIND Say "a day," without the "ever." No, no, Orlando, men are April when they woo, December when they wed. Maids are May when they are maids, but the sky changes when they are wives. I will be more jealous of thee than a Barbary cock-pigeon over his hen, more clamorous than a parrot against rain, more newfangled than an ape, more giddy in my desires than a monkey. I will weep for nothing, like Diana in the fountain, and I will do that when you are disposed to be merry; I will laugh like a hyena, and that when thou art inclined to sleep.

ORLANDO But will my Rosalind do so?

ROSALIND By my life, she will do as I do.

ORLANDO Oh, but she is wise.

ROSALIND Or else she could not have the wit to do this. The wiser, the waywarder. Make the doors upon a woman's wit, and it will out at the casement; shut that, and 'twill out at the keyhole; stop that, 'twill fly with the smoke out at the chimney.

ORLANDO A man that had a wife with such a wit, he might say, "Wit, whither wilt?"

ROSALIND Nay, you might keep that check for it till you met your wife's wit going to your neighbor's bed.

ORLANDO And what wit could wit have to excuse that?

ROSALIND Marry, to say she came to seek you there. You shall never take her without her answer unless you take her without her tongue. Oh, that woman that cannot make her fault her husband's occasion, let her never nurse her child herself, for she will breed it like a fool!

ORLANDO For these two hours, Rosalind, I will leave thee.

ROSALIND Alas, dear love, I cannot lack thee two hours!

ORLANDO I must attend the Duke at dinner. By two o'clock I will be with thee again.

ROSALIND Ay, go your ways, go your ways. I knew what you would prove. My friends told me as much, and I thought no less. That flattering tongue of yours won me. 'Tis but one cast away, and so, come, death! Two o'clock is your hour?

ORLANDO Ay, sweet Rosalind.

ROSALIND By my troth, and in good earnest, and so God mend me, and by all pretty oaths that are not dangerous, if you break one jot of your promise or come one minute behind your hour, I will think you the most pathetical break-promise, and the most hollow lover, and the most unworthy of her you call Rosalind, that may be chosen out of the gross band of the unfaithful. Therefore beware my censure, and keep your promise.

ORLANDO With no less religion than if thou wert indeed my Rosalind. So adieu.

100 found it was arrived at the verdict that the cause (of his death) was **103 right** real **104 protest** insist, proclaim **106 coming-on** compliant **123 Go to** (An exclamation of mild impatience.) **131 ask . . . commission** ask you what authority you have for taking her (since no one is here to give the bride away and since she herself has not yet consented) **133 goes . . . priest** who anticipates before the "priest" has even asked the question **134 runs . . . actions** i.e., goes flightily on, outstripping sane conduct. **143 Barbary cock-pigeon** an ornamental pigeon actually from the orient, not the Barbary (north) coast of Africa. (Following Pliny, the cock-pigeon's jealousy was often contrasted with the mildness of the hen.) **144 against** in expectation of **145 newfangled** infatuated with novelty **146 for nothing** for no apparent reason

146-7 Diana in the fountain (Diana frequently appeared as the centerpiece of fountains. Stow's *Survey of London* describes the setting up of a fountain with a Diana in green marble in the year 1596.) **154 The wiser, the waywarder** i.e., The more experienced in the war of the sexes, the more insisting on her own way. **Make** Make fast, shut **155 casement** hinged window **159 Wit, whither wilt?** Wit, where are you going? (A common Elizabethan expression implying that one is talking fantastically, with a wildly wandering wit.) **160 check** retort **166 make . . . occasion** i.e., turn a defense of her own conduct into an accusation against her husband **167 breed it** bring it up **177 but one cast away** only one woman jilted **182 dangerous** i.e., blasphemous. (Rosalind's oaths are decorous.) **184 pathetical** awful, miserable **186 gross band** whole troop **189 religion** strict fidelity

ROSALIND Well, Time is the old justice that examines all such offenders, and let Time try. Adieu.

Exit [*Orlando*].

CELIA You have simply misused our sex in your love prate. We must have your doublet and hose plucked over your head and show the world what the bird hath done to her own nest.

ROSALIND Oh, coz, coz, coz, my pretty little coz, that thou didst know how many fathom deep I am in love! But it cannot be sounded; my affection hath an unknown bottom, like the Bay of Portugal.

CELIA Or rather, bottomless, that as fast as you pour affection in, it runs out.

ROSALIND No, that same wicked bastard of Venus, that was begot of thought, conceived of spleen, and born of madness, that blind rascally boy that abuses every-one's eyes because his own are out, let him be judge how deep I am in love. I'll tell thee, Aliena, I cannot be out of the sight of Orlando. I'll go find a shadow and sigh till he come.

CELIA And I'll sleep. *Exeunt.*

✤

4.2

Enter Jaques and Lords [*dressed as*] *foresters.*

JAQUES Which is he that killed the deer?

FIRST LORD Sir, it was I.

JAQUES Let's present him to the Duke, like a Roman conqueror, and it would do well to set the deer's horns upon his head for a branch of victory. Have you no song, Forester, for this purpose?

SECOND LORD Yes, sir.

JAQUES Sing it. 'Tis no matter how it be in tune, so it make noise enough. *Music.*

Song.

SECOND LORD [*sings*]
What shall he have that killed the deer?
His leather skin and horns to wear.
Then sing him home; the rest shall bear
This burden.
Take thou no scorn to wear the horn;
It was a crest ere thou wast born.
Thy father's father wore it,
And thy father bore it.
The horn, the horn, the lusty horn
Is not a thing to laugh to scorn. *Exeunt.*

4.3

Enter Rosalind and Celia.

ROSALIND How say you now? Is it not past two o'clock?
And here much Orlando!

CELIA I warrant you, with pure love and troubled brain he hath ta'en his bow and arrows and is gone forth—to sleep.

Enter Silvius [*with a letter*].

Look who comes here.

SILVIUS [*to Rosalind*]
My errand is to you, fair youth.
My gentle Phoebe bid me give you this.
[*He gives the letter.*]
I know not the contents, but as I guess,
By the stern brow and waspish action
Which she did use as she was writing of it,
It bears an angry tenor. Pardon me;
I am but as a guiltless messenger.

ROSALIND [*examining the letter*]
Patience herself would startle at this letter
And play the swaggerer. Bear this, bear all!
She says I am not fair, that I lack manners;
She calls me proud, and that she could not love me
Were man as rare as phoenix. 'Od's my will!
Her love is not the hare that I do hunt.
Why writes she so to me? Well, shepherd, well,
This is a letter of your own device.

SILVIUS
No, I protest, I know not the contents.
Phoebe did write it.

ROSALIND Come, come, you are a fool,
And turned into the extremity of love.
I saw her hand; she has a leathern hand,
A freestone-colored hand. I verily did think
That her old gloves were on, but 'twas her hands;
She has a huswife's hand—but that's no matter.
I say she never did invent this letter;
This is a man's invention and his hand.

SILVIUS Sure it is hers.

ROSALIND
Why, 'tis a boisterous and a cruel style,
A style for challengers. Why, she defies me,
Like Turk to Christian. Women's gentle brain
Could not drop forth such giant-rude invention,

192 try determine, judge. **193 simply misused** absolutely slandered **194–6 We . . . nest** i.e., We must expose you for what you are, a woman, and show everyone how a woman has defamed her own kind just as a foul bird proverbially fouls its own nest. **199 sounded** measured for depth **201 that** so that **203 bastard of Venus** i.e., Cupid, son of Venus and Mercury (or Zeus) rather than Vulcan, Venus's husband **204 thought** fancy. **spleen** i.e., impulse **205 abuses** deceives **206 out** blinded **208 shadow** shady spot

4.2 Location: The forest.

5 branch wreath **8 so** provided that **12–13 bear This burden** (1) sing this refrain (2) wear the horns that all cuckolds must wear. **14 Take . . . scorn** Be not ashamed. (Alludes to joke about cuckold's horns.)

4.3 Location: The forest.

2 much (Said ironically: A fat lot we see of Orlando!) **3 warrant** assure **14–15 Patience . . . all!** Patience herself would be startled into a violent display by this letter. If one were to put up with such a missive, one would have to accept any insult! **18 phoenix** a fabulous bird of Arabia, the only one of its kind, which lived five hundred years, died in flames, and was reborn of its own ashes. **'Od's my will!** (An oath: "May God's will be done!") **24 turned** transformed **25 leathern** leathery **26 freestone-colored** sandstone-colored, brownish-yellow **28 hand** handwriting. (With play on "dishpan hands.")

Such Ethiop words, blacker in their effect
Than in their countenance. Will you hear the letter?

SILVIUS
So please you, for I never heard it yet;
Yet, heard too much of Phoebe's cruelty.

ROSALIND
She Phoebes me. Mark how the tyrant writes.
(*Read*) "Art thou god to shepherd turned,
That a maiden's heart hath burned?"
Can a woman rail thus?

SILVIUS Call you this railing?

ROSALIND
(*Read*) "Why, thy godhead laid apart,
War'st thou with a woman's heart?"
Did you ever hear such railing?
"Whiles the eye of man did woo me,
That could do no vengeance to me."—
Meaning me a beast.
"If the scorn of your bright eyne
Have power to raise such love in mine,
Alack, in me what strange effect
Would they work in mild aspect!
Whiles you chid me, I did love;
How then might your prayers move!
He that brings this love to thee
Little knows this love in me;
And by him seal up thy mind,
Whether that thy youth and kind
Will the faithful offer take
Of me and all that I can make,
Or else by him my love deny,
And then I'll study how to die."

SILVIUS Call you this chiding?

CELIA Alas, poor shepherd!

ROSALIND Do you pity him? No, he deserves no pity.— Wilt thou love such a woman? What, to make thee an instrument and play false strains upon thee? Not to be endured! Well, go your way to her, for I see love hath made thee a tame snake, and say this to her: that if she love me, I charge her to love thee; if she will not, I will never have her unless thou entreat for her. If you be a true lover, hence, and not a word; for here comes more company. *Exit Silvius.*

Enter Oliver.

OLIVER
Good morrow, fair ones. Pray you, if you know,
Where in the purlieus of this forest stands
A sheepcote fenced about with olive trees?

CELIA
West of this place, down in the neighbor bottom;
The rank of osiers by the murmuring stream
Left on your right hand brings you to the place.
But at this hour the house doth keep itself;
There's none within.

OLIVER
If that an eye may profit by a tongue,
Then should I know you by description,
Such garments and such years: "The boy is fair,
Of female favor, and bestows himself
Like a ripe sister; the woman, low
And browner than her brother." Are not you
The owner of the house I did inquire for?

CELIA
It is no boast, being asked, to say we are.

OLIVER
Orlando doth commend him to you both,
And to that youth he calls his Rosalind
He sends this bloody napkin. Are you he?
[*He produces a bloody handkerchief.*]

ROSALIND
I am. What must we understand by this?

OLIVER
Some of my shame, if you will know of me
What man I am, and how, and why, and where
This handkerchief was stained.

CELIA I pray you, tell it.

OLIVER
When last the young Orlando parted from you
He left a promise to return again
Within an hour, and, pacing through the forest,
Chewing the food of sweet and bitter fancy,
Lo, what befell! He threw his eye aside,
And mark what object did present itself:
Under an old oak, whose boughs were mossed with age
And high top bald with dry antiquity,
A wretched, ragged man, o'ergrown with hair,
Lay sleeping on his back. About his neck
A green and gilded snake had wreathed itself,
Who with her head, nimble in threats, approached
The opening of his mouth; but suddenly,
Seeing Orlando, it unlinked itself
And with indented glides did slip away
Into a bush, under which bush's shade
A lioness, with udders all drawn dry,
Lay couching, head on ground, with catlike watch,
When that the sleeping man should stir; for 'tis

36 Ethiop i.e., black **36–7 blacker . . . countenance** even blacker in what they say than in their black appearance on the page. **40 Phoebes me** i.e., addresses me in her cruel style. **45 thy . . . apart** having laid aside your godhead (for human shape) **49 vengeance** mischief, harm **50 Meaning me** i.e., Implying that I am **51 eyne** eyes **54 in mild aspect** i.e., if they looked on me mildly. (Suggests also astrological influence.) **55 chid** chided **59 by . . . mind** i.e., send your thoughts in a letter via Silvius **60 Whether . . . kind** if your youthful nature **62 make** make offer of **68–9 to make . . . instrument** to make an instrument (i.e., messenger) of you. (With a suggestion of making a person into a musical instrument; cf. *Hamlet*, 3.2.363, "You would play upon me," etc.) **69 strains** parts of a piece of music **71 tame snake** i.e., pathetic wretch

77 purlieus borders, boundaries **79 neighbor bottom** neighboring dell **80 rank of osiers** row of willows **81 Left** left behind, passed **87 favor** features. **bestows** comports **88 ripe** mature or elder **92 doth commend him** sends his greetings **94 napkin** handkerchief. **102 Chewing . . . fancy** ruminating on the bittersweet nature of love **112 unlinked** uncoiled **113 indented** zigzag **115 with . . . dry** (It would therefore be fierce with hunger.) **117 When** for the moment

The royal disposition of that beast
To prey on nothing that doth seem as dead.
This seen, Orlando did approach the man
And found it was his brother, his elder brother.

CELIA
Oh, I have heard him speak of that same brother,
And he did render him the most unnatural 123
That lived amongst men.

OLIVER And well he might so do,
For well I know he was unnatural.

ROSALIND
But to Orlando: did he leave him there,
Food to the sucked and hungry lioness?

OLIVER
Twice did he turn his back and purposed so;
But kindness, nobler ever than revenge,
And nature, stronger than his just occasion, 130
Made him give battle to the lioness,
Who quickly fell before him; in which hurtling 132
From miserable slumber I awaked.

CELIA
Are you his brother?

ROSALIND Was't you he rescued?

CELIA
Was't you that did so oft contrive to kill him?

OLIVER
'Twas I, but 'tis not I. I do not shame 136
To tell you what I was, since my conversion
So sweetly tastes, being the thing I am.

ROSALIND
But for the bloody napkin?

OLIVER By and by. 139
When from the first to last betwixt us two
Tears our recountments had most kindly bathed, 141
As how I came into that desert place,
In brief, he led me to the gentle Duke,
Who gave me fresh array and entertainment, 144
Committing me unto my brother's love;
Who led me instantly unto his cave,
There stripped himself, and here upon his arm
The lioness had torn some flesh away,
Which all this while had bled; and now he fainted
And cried, in fainting, upon Rosalind.
Brief, I recovered him, bound up his wound, 151
And after some small space, being strong at heart,
He sent me hither, stranger as I am,
To tell this story, that you might excuse
His broken promise, and to give this napkin
Dyed in his blood unto the shepherd youth
That he in sport doth call his Rosalind.
[*Rosalind swoons.*]

CELIA
Why, how now, Ganymede, sweet Ganymede!

OLIVER
Many will swoon when they do look on blood.

CELIA
There is more in it.—Cousin Ganymede!

OLIVER Look, he recovers.

ROSALIND I would I were at home.

CELIA We'll lead you thither.—
I pray you, will you take him by the arm?
[*They help Rosalind up.*]

OLIVER Be of good cheer, youth. You a man? You lack a man's heart.

ROSALIND I do so, I confess it. Ah, sirrah, a body would 167
think this was well counterfeited. I pray you, tell your brother how well I counterfeited. Heigh-ho!

OLIVER This was not counterfeit. There is too great testimony in your complexion that it was a passion of 171
earnest. 172

ROSALIND Counterfeit, I assure you.

OLIVER Well then, take a good heart and counterfeit to be a man.

ROSALIND So I do; but, i'faith, I should have been a woman by right.

CELIA Come, you look paler and paler. Pray you, draw homewards.—Good sir, go with us.

OLIVER
That will I, for I must bear answer back
How you excuse my brother, Rosalind.

ROSALIND I shall devise something. But, I pray you, commend my counterfeiting to him. Will you go?
Exeunt.

✤

5.1

Enter [*Touchstone the*] *Clown and Audrey.*

TOUCHSTONE We shall find a time, Audrey. Patience, gentle Audrey.

AUDREY Faith, the priest was good enough, for all the 3
old gentleman's saying. 4

TOUCHSTONE A most wicked Sir Oliver, Audrey, a most vile Mar-text. But Audrey, there is a youth here in the forest lays claim to you.

AUDREY Ay, I know who 'tis. He hath no interest in me 8
in the world. Here comes the man you mean.

Enter William.

TOUCHSTONE It is meat and drink to me to see a clown. 10
By my troth, we that have good wits have much to 11
answer for. We shall be flouting; we cannot hold. 12

WILLIAM Good even, Audrey.

AUDREY God gi' good even, William. 14

WILLIAM And good even to you, sir.
[*He removes his hat.*]

123 render him describe him as **130 just occasion** just opportunity and motive (for revenge) **132 hurtling** conflict, tumult **136 do not shame** am not ashamed **139 for** as regards **141 recountments** relating of events (to one another) **144 array** attire. **entertainment** hospitality, provision **151 Brief** In brief. **recovered** revived

167 a body anybody **171–2 a passion of earnest** a genuine swoon.
5.1 Location: The forest.
3–4 the old gentleman's i.e., Jaques's **8 interest in** claim to **10 clown** i.e., country yokel. **11–12 we . . . hold** i.e., we professional fools have much to answer for in providing a model of folly that yokels like William are too apt to imitate. We fools are always scoffing; we can't restrain ourselves. **14 God gi' good even** God give you good evening. (Here, afternoon.)

TOUCHSTONE Good even, gentle friend. Cover thy head, cover thy head. Nay, prithee be covered. How old are you, friend?

WILLIAM Five-and-twenty, sir.

TOUCHSTONE A ripe age. Is thy name William?

WILLIAM William, sir.

TOUCHSTONE A fair name. Wast born i'th' forest here?

WILLIAM Ay, sir, I thank God.

TOUCHSTONE "Thank God"—a good answer. Art rich?

WILLIAM Faith, sir, so-so.

TOUCHSTONE "So-so" is good, very good, very excellent good; and yet it is not, it is but so-so. Art thou wise?

WILLIAM Ay, sir, I have a pretty wit.

TOUCHSTONE Why, thou say'st well. I do now remember a saying, "The fool doth think he is wise, but the wise man knows himself to be a fool." The heathen philosopher, when he had a desire to eat a grape, would open his lips when he put it into his mouth, meaning thereby that grapes were made to eat and lips to open. You do love this maid?

WILLIAM I do, sir.

TOUCHSTONE Give me your hand. Art thou learned?

WILLIAM No, sir.

TOUCHSTONE Then learn this of me: to have is to have. For it is a figure in rhetoric that drink, being poured out of a cup into a glass, by filling the one doth empty the other. For all your writers do consent that *ipse* is he. Now, you are not *ipse*, for I am he.

WILLIAM Which he, sir?

TOUCHSTONE He, sir, that must marry this woman. Therefore, you clown, abandon—which is in the vulgar "leave"—the society—which in the boorish is "company"—of this female—which in the common is "woman"; which together is, abandon the society of this female, or, clown, thou perishest; or, to thy better understanding, diest; or, to wit, I kill thee, make thee away, translate thy life into death, thy liberty into bondage. I will deal in poison with thee, or in bastinado, or in steel; I will bandy with thee in faction, I will o'errun thee with policy; I will kill thee a hundred and fifty ways. Therefore tremble, and depart.

AUDREY Do, good William.

WILLIAM God rest you merry, sir. *Exit.*

Enter Corin.

CORIN Our master and mistress seeks you. Come, away, away!

TOUCHSTONE Trip, Audrey, trip, Audrey!—I attend, I attend. *Exeunt.*

✤

5.2

Enter Orlando [with his wounded arm in a sling] and Oliver.

ORLANDO Is't possible that on so little acquaintance you should like her? That but seeing, you should love her? And loving, woo? And, wooing, she should grant? And will you persevere to enjoy her?

OLIVER Neither call the giddiness of it in question, the poverty of her, the small acquaintance, my sudden wooing, nor her sudden consenting; but say with me, "I love Aliena"; say with her that she loves me; consent with both that we may enjoy each other. It shall be to your good; for my father's house and all the revenue that was old Sir Rowland's will I estate upon you, and here live and die a shepherd.

Enter Rosalind.

ORLANDO You have my consent. Let your wedding be tomorrow. Thither will I invite the Duke and all 's contented followers. Go you and prepare Aliena; for look you, here comes my Rosalind.

ROSALIND God save you, brother.

OLIVER And you, fair sister. *[Exit.]*

ROSALIND O my dear Orlando, how it grieves me to see thee wear thy heart in a scarf!

ORLANDO It is my arm.

ROSALIND I thought thy heart had been wounded with the claws of a lion.

ORLANDO Wounded it is, but with the eyes of a lady.

ROSALIND Did your brother tell you how I countefeited to swoon when he showed me your handkerchief?

ORLANDO Ay, and greater wonders than that.

ROSALIND Oh, I know where you are. Nay, 'tis true. There was never anything so sudden but the fight of two rams and Caesar's thrasonical brag of "I came, saw, and overcame." For your brother and my sister no sooner met but they looked, no sooner looked but they loved, no sooner loved but they sighed, no sooner sighed but they asked one another the reason, no sooner knew the reason but they sought the remedy; and in these degrees have they made a pair of

32–6 The heathen . . . open (This bit of fatuously self-evident wisdom parodies the logical proofs of the ancient philosophers. William, whose mouth is no doubt gaping like a rustic's, is invited to consider the consequences of his desire.) **41 figure** figure of speech, trope **41–3 drink . . . other** i.e., both Touchstone and William cannot possess Audrey. **43–4 For . . . am he** For all the ancient authorities concur that the word *ipse* in Latin means "he." But you are not *ipse*, i.e., the man of the hour, the one destined to win Audrey, for I am that man. **54–5 bastinado** beating with a cudgel **55 bandy** contend. **in faction** factiously **56 o'errun . . . policy** overwhelm you with craft, cunning **59 God . . . merry** (A common salutation at parting.)

62 Trip Go nimbly
5.2 Location: The forest.
5 giddiness sudden speed **11 estate** settle as an estate, bestow **14 all 's** all his **17 brother** i.e., brother-in-law to be. **18 sister** (Rosalind is still dressed as a man, but Oliver evidently adopts the fiction that "Ganymede" is Orlando's Rosalind. See 4.3.92 ff.) **20 scarf** sling. **28 where you are** i.e., what you mean. **30 thrasonical** boastful. (From Thraso, the boaster in Terence's *Eunuchus*.) **30–1 "I came . . . overcame"** (Julius Caesar's famous pronouncement, *Veni, vidi, vici*, on the occasion of his victory over Pharnaces at Zela in 47 B.C.) **36 degrees** (Plays on the original meaning, "steps," and also on the rhetorical figure of climax illustrated by Rosalind's sentence as it moves from one step to the next by linked words, *looked, loved, sighed*, etc.) **pair** flight

stairs to marriage which they will climb incontinent, or else be incontinent before marriage. They are in the very wrath of love, and they will together. Clubs cannot part them.

ORLANDO They shall be married tomorrow, and I will bid the Duke to the nuptial. But oh, how bitter a thing it is to look into happiness through another man's eyes! By so much the more shall I tomorrow be at the height of heart-heaviness, by how much I shall think my brother happy in having what he wishes for.

ROSALIND Why, then, tomorrow I cannot serve your turn for Rosalind?

ORLANDO I can live no longer by thinking.

ROSALIND I will weary you then no longer with idle talking. Know of me then—for now I speak to some purpose—that I know you are a gentleman of good conceit. I speak not this that you should bear a good opinion of my knowledge, insomuch I say I know you are; neither do I labor for a greater esteem than may in some little measure draw a belief from you to do yourself good, and not to grace me. Believe then, if you please, that I can do strange things. I have, since I was three year old, conversed with a magician, most profound in his art and yet not damnable. If you do love Rosalind so near the heart as your gesture cries it out, when your brother marries Aliena shall you marry her. I know into what straits of fortune she is driven; and it is not impossible to me, if it appear not inconvenient to you, to set her before your eyes tomorrow, human as she is, and without any danger.

ORLANDO Speak'st thou in sober meanings?

ROSALIND By my life, I do, which I tender dearly, though I say I am a magician. Therefore, put you in your best array; bid your friends; for if you will be married tomorrow, you shall, and to Rosalind, if you will.

Enter Silvius and Phoebe.

Look, here comes a lover of mine and a lover of hers.

PHOEBE [*to Rosalind*]
Youth, you have done me much ungentleness,
To show the letter that I writ to you.

ROSALIND
I care not if I have. It is my study
To seem despiteful and ungentle to you.
You are there followed by a faithful shepherd.
Look upon him; love him. He worships you.

PHOEBE [*to Silvius*]
Good shepherd, tell this youth what 'tis to love.

SILVIUS
It is to be all made of sighs and tears;
And so am I for Phoebe.

PHOEBE And I for Ganymede.

ORLANDO And I for Rosalind.

ROSALIND And I for no woman.

SILVIUS
It is to be all made of faith and service;
And so am I for Phoebe.

PHOEBE And I for Ganymede.

ORLANDO And I for Rosalind.

ROSALIND And I for no woman.

SILVIUS
It is to be all made of fantasy,
All made of passion and all made of wishes,
All adoration, duty, and observance,
All humbleness, all patience and impatience,
All purity, all trial, all observance;
And so am I for Phoebe.

PHOEBE And so am I for Ganymede.

ORLANDO And so am I for Rosalind.

ROSALIND And so am I for no woman.

PHOEBE [*to Rosalind*]
If this be so, why blame you me to love you?

SILVIUS [*to Phoebe*]
If this be so, why blame you me to love you?

ORLANDO
If this be so, why blame you me to love you?

ROSALIND Why do you speak too, "Why blame you me to love you?"

ORLANDO To her that is not here, nor doth not hear.

ROSALIND Pray you, no more of this; 'tis like the howling of Irish wolves against the moon. [*To Silvius*] I will help you, if I can. [*To Phoebe*] I would love you, if I could.—Tomorrow meet me all together. [*To Phoebe*] I will marry you, if ever I marry woman, and I'll be married tomorrow. [*To Orlando*] I will satisfy you, if ever I satisfied man, and you shall be married tomorrow. [*To Silvius*] I will content you, if what pleases you contents you, and you shall be married tomorrow. [*To Orlando*] As you love Rosalind, meet. [*To Silvius*] As you love Phoebe, meet. And as I love no woman, I'll meet. So fare you well. I have left you commands.

SILVIUS I'll not fail, if I live.

PHOEBE Nor I.

ORLANDO Nor I. *Exeunt* [*separately*].

37 incontinent immediately. (Followed by a pun on the meaning "unchaste or sexually unrestrained.") **39 wrath** impetuosity, ardor. **Clubs** i.e., Physical force, such as that employed by nightwatchmen armed with clubs **52–3 conceit** intelligence, understanding. **53 that** in order that **54 insomuch . . . are** from my saying I know you to be intelligent **55–7 neither . . . grace me** nor am I interested in winning approval except insofar as it may, by inspiring your confidence in my ability, prompt you to do something for your own benefit; it is not intended to bring favor on myself. **59 conversed** associated **60 not damnable** not a practicer of forbidden or black magic, worthy of execution and damnation. **61 gesture** bearing **61–2 cries it out** proclaims **63 she** Rosalind **65 inconvenient** inappropriate **66 human** i.e., the real Rosalind, not a phantom. **danger** i.e., the danger to the soul from one's involvement in magic or witchcraft. **67 in sober meanings** seriously. **68 tender dearly** value highly **69 though . . . magician** (According to Elizabethan antiwitchcraft statutes, some forms of witchcraft were punishable by death; Rosalind thus endangers her life by what she has said.) **70 bid** invite. **friends** family and friends **74 ungentleness** discourtesy

76 study conscious endeavor **91 fantasy** fancy, imagination **93 observance** devotion, respect **95 observance** (Perhaps a compositor's error, repeated from two lines previous; many editors emend it to *obedience*.) **100 to love you** for loving you.

5.3

Enter [Touchstone the] Clown and Audrey.

TOUCHSTONE Tomorrow is the joyful day, Audrey; tomorrow will we be married.

AUDREY I do desire it with all my heart; and I hope it is no dishonest desire to desire to be a woman of the world. Here come two of the banished Duke's pages.

Enter two Pages.

FIRST PAGE Well met, honest gentleman.

TOUCHSTONE By my troth, well met. Come, sit, sit, and a song. *[They sit.]*

SECOND PAGE We are for you. Sit i'th' middle.

FIRST PAGE Shall we clap into't roundly, without hawking or spitting or saying we are hoarse, which are the only prologues to a bad voice?

SECOND PAGE I'faith, i'faith, and both in a tune, like two gypsies on a horse.

Song.

BOTH PAGES

It was a lover and his lass,
With a hey, and a ho, and a hey-nonny-no,
That o'er the green cornfield did pass
In springtime, the only pretty ring time,
When birds do sing, hey ding a ding, ding,
Sweet lovers love the spring.

Between the acres of the rye,
With a hey, and a ho, and a hey-nonny-no,
These pretty country folks would lie
In springtime, the only pretty ring time,
When birds do sing, hey ding a ding, ding,
Sweet lovers love the spring.

This carol they began that hour,
With a hey, and a ho, and hey-nonny-no,
How that a life was but a flower
In springtime, the only pretty ring time,
When birds do sing, hey ding a ding, ding,
Sweet lovers love the spring.

And therefore take the present time,
With a hey, and a ho, and a hey-nonny-no,
For love is crownèd with the prime
In springtime, the only pretty ring time,
When birds do sing, hey ding a ding, ding,
Sweet lovers love the spring.

TOUCHSTONE Truly, young gentlemen, though there was no great matter in the ditty, yet the note was very untunable.

FIRST PAGE You are deceived, sir. We kept time, we lost not our time.

TOUCHSTONE By my troth, yes; I count it but time lost to hear such a foolish song. God b'wi'you, and God mend your voices! Come, Audrey. *Exeunt [separately].*

✣

5.4

Enter Duke Senior, Amiens, Jaques, Orlando, Oliver, [and] Celia.

DUKE SENIOR
Dost thou believe, Orlando, that the boy
Can do all this that he hath promisèd?

ORLANDO
I sometimes do believe, and sometimes do not,
As those that fear they hope and know they fear.

Enter Rosalind, Silvius, and Phoebe.

ROSALIND
Patience once more, whiles our compact is urged.
[To the Duke] You say, if I bring in your Rosalind
You will bestow her on Orlando here?

DUKE SENIOR
That would I, had I kingdoms to give with her.

ROSALIND *[to Orlando]*
And you say you will have her when I bring her?

ORLANDO
That would I, were I of all kingdoms king.

ROSALIND *[to Phoebe]*
You say you'll marry me if I be willing?

PHOEBE
That will I, should I die the hour after.

ROSALIND
But if you do refuse to marry me
You'll give yourself to this most faithful shepherd?

PHOEBE So is the bargain.

ROSALIND *[to Silvius]*
You say that you'll have Phoebe if she will?

SILVIUS
Though to have her and death were both one thing.

ROSALIND
I have promised to make all this matter even.
Keep you your word, O Duke, to give your daughter;
You yours, Orlando, to receive his daughter;
Keep you your word, Phoebe, that you'll marry me,
Or else, refusing me, to wed this shepherd;
Keep your word, Silvius, that you'll marry her
If she refuse me; and from hence I go,
To make these doubts all even.
Exeunt Rosalind and Celia.

DUKE SENIOR
I do remember in this shepherd boy
Some lively touches of my daughter's favor.

5.3 Location: The forest.
4 dishonest immodest **4–5 woman of the world** married woman; also, one who advances herself socially. **6 honest** worthy **9 We are for you** i.e., Fine, we're ready. **10 clap . . . roundly** begin briskly and with spirit **10–11 hawking** clearing the throat **12 only** customary **13 in a tune** (1) in unison (2) keeping time **14 on a** on one **17 cornfield** field of grain **18 ring time** time most apt for marriage
21 Between the acres On unplowed strips between the fields
35 prime (1) height of perfection (2) spring **40 matter** sense, meaning. **note** music **41 untunable** discordant.

42 deceived mistaken
5.4 Location: The forest.
4 they hope i.e., that they merely hope **5 urged** put forward.
18 make . . . even set all this to rights, square accounts. **27 lively** lifelike. **favor** appearance.

ORLANDO
My lord, the first time that I ever saw him
Methought he was a brother to your daughter.
But, my good lord, this boy is forest-born
And hath been tutored in the rudiments
Of many desperate studies by his uncle,
Whom he reports to be a great magician,
Obscurèd in the circle of this forest.

Enter [*Touchstone the*] *Clown and Audrey.*

JAQUES There is, sure, another flood toward, and these couples are coming to the ark. Here comes a pair of very strange beasts, which in all tongues are called fools.

TOUCHSTONE Salutation and greeting to you all!

JAQUES [*to the Duke*] Good my lord, bid him welcome. This is the motley-minded gentleman that I have so often met in the forest. He hath been a courtier, he swears.

TOUCHSTONE If any man doubt that, let him put me to my purgation. I have trod a measure; I have flattered a lady; I have been politic with my friend, smooth with mine enemy; I have undone three tailors; I have had four quarrels and like to have fought one.

JAQUES And how was that ta'en up?

TOUCHSTONE Faith, we met and found the quarrel was upon the seventh cause.

JAQUES How seventh cause?—Good my lord, like this fellow.

DUKE SENIOR I like him very well.

TOUCHSTONE God 'ild you, sir, I desire you of the like. I press in here, sir, amongst the rest of the country copulatives, to swear and to forswear, according as marriage binds and blood breaks. A poor virgin, sir, an ill-favored thing, sir, but mine own; a poor humor of mine, sir, to take that that no man else will. Rich honesty dwells like a miser, sir, in a poor house, as your pearl in your foul oyster.

DUKE SENIOR By my faith, he is very swift and sententious.

TOUCHSTONE According to the fool's bolt, sir, and such dulcet diseases.

JAQUES But for the seventh cause. How did you find the quarrel on the seventh cause?

TOUCHSTONE Upon a lie seven times removed—bear your body more seeming, Audrey—as thus, sir. I did dislike the cut of a certain courtier's beard. He sent me word if I said his beard was not cut well, he was in the mind it was: this is called the Retort Courteous. If I sent him word again it was not well cut, he would send me word he cut it to please himself: this is called the Quip Modest. If again it was not well cut, he disabled my judgment: this is called the Reply Churlish. If again it was not well cut, he would answer I spake not true: this is called the Reproof Valiant. If again it was not well cut, he would say I lie: this is called the Countercheck Quarrelsome. And so to the Lie Circumstantial and the Lie Direct.

JAQUES And how oft did you say his beard was not well cut?

TOUCHSTONE I durst go no further than the Lie Circumstantial, nor he durst not give me the Lie Direct; and so we measured swords and parted.

JAQUES Can you nominate in order now the degrees of the lie?

TOUCHSTONE Oh, sir, we quarrel in print, by the book, as you have books for good manners. I will name you the degrees. The first, the Retort Courteous; the second, the Quip Modest; the third, the Reply Churlish; the fourth, the Reproof Valiant; the fifth, the Countercheck Quarrelsome; the sixth, the Lie with Circumstance; the seventh, the Lie Direct. All these you may avoid but the Lie Direct; and you may avoid that, too, with an If. I knew when seven justices could not take up a quarrel, but when the parties were met themselves, one of them thought but of an If, as, "If you said so, then I said so"; and they shook hands and swore brothers. Your If is the only peacemaker; much virtue in If.

JAQUES Is not this a rare fellow, my lord? He's as good at anything and yet a fool.

DUKE SENIOR He uses his folly like a stalking-horse, and under the presentation of that he shoots his wit.

Enter Hymen, Rosalind, and Celia. Still music.
[*Rosalind and Celia are no longer disguised.*]

HYMEN
Then is there mirth in heaven,
When earthly things made even
Atone together.
Good Duke, receive thy daughter;
Hymen from heaven brought her,
Yea, brought her hither,

32 desperate dangerous **34 Obscurèd** hidden. **circle** compass, boundaries. (With a possible allusion to the magic circle that protected the magician from the devil during incantation.) **35 toward** coming on **36 a pair** (In Genesis 7:2, God commands Noah to take on board every "clean" beast by sevens, but those that are not clean, by twos.) **44 purgation** proof, trial. **measure** slow, stately dance **45 politic** cunning, Machiavellian. **smooth** insinuating **46 undone** bankrupted (by refusing to pay debts owed them) **47 like** came close **48 ta'en up** settled, made up. **54 'ild** yield, reward. **I . . . like** I wish the same to you. (A polite phrase used to reply to a compliment.) **55–6 country copulatives** country couples about to marry and with sex on their minds **57 blood breaks** as desire bursts forth. **58 humor** whim **60 honesty** chastity **61 your pearl** i.e., the pearl that one hears about **62–3 swift and sententious** quick-witted and good at aphorisms. **64 fool's bolt** (Alluding to the proverb "A fool's bolt [arrow] is soon shot.") **65 dulcet diseases** pleasant afflictions, entertaining yet sharp. (Touchstone wryly agrees with the Duke's assessment of the Fool as swift and sententious.)

69 seeming seemly **70 dislike** express dislike of **75–6 disabled** disparaged **80 Countercheck** Rebuff **86 measured swords** i.e., as in the mere preliminary to a duel **89 in . . . book** in a precise way. (Touchstone is travestying books on the general subject of honor and arms, which dealt with occasions and circumstances of the duel.) **97–8 take up** settle **101 swore brothers** became sworn brothers. **105 stalking-horse** a real or artificial horse under cover of which the hunter approached his game **106 presentation** semblance **106.1 *Hymen*** Roman god of faithful marriage. ***Still*** Soft **107 mirth** joy **108 made even** set straight **109 Atone** are at one

That thou mightst join her hand with his
Whose heart within his bosom is.

ROSALIND [*to the Duke*]
To you I give myself, for I am yours.
[*To Orlando*] To you I give myself, for I am yours.

DUKE SENIOR
If there be truth in sight, you are my daughter.

ORLANDO
If there be truth in sight, you are my Rosalind.

PHOEBE
If sight and shape be true,
Why then, my love adieu!

ROSALIND [*to the Duke*]
I'll have no father, if you be not he.
[*To Orlando*] I'll have no husband, if you be not he.
[*To Phoebe*] Nor ne'er wed woman, if you be not she.

HYMEN
Peace, ho! I bar confusion.
'Tis I must make conclusion
Of these most strange events.
Here's eight that must take hands
To join in Hymen's bands,
If truth holds true contents.
[*To Orlando and Rosalind*]
You and you no cross shall part.
[*To Oliver and Celia*]
You and you are heart in heart.
[*To Phoebe*]
You to his love must accord
Or have a woman to your lord.
[*To Touchstone and Audrey*]
You and you are sure together,
As the winter to foul weather.
[*To all*]
Whiles a wedlock hymn we sing,
Feed yourselves with questioning,
That reason wonder may diminish
How thus we met, and these things finish.

Song.

Wedding is great Juno's crown,
O blessèd bond of board and bed!
'Tis Hymen peoples every town;
High wedlock then be honorèd.
Honor, high honor and renown
To Hymen, god of every town!

DUKE SENIOR [*to Celia*]
O my dear niece, welcome thou art to me!
Even daughter, welcome, in no less degree.

PHOEBE [*to Silvius*]
I will not eat my word, now thou art mine;
Thy faith my fancy to thee doth combine.

Enter Second Brother [Jaques de Boys].

JAQUES DE BOYS
Let me have audience for a word or two.
I am the second son of old Sir Rowland,
That bring these tidings to this fair assembly.
Duke Frederick, hearing how that every day
Men of great worth resorted to this forest,
Addressed a mighty power, which were on foot
In his own conduct, purposely to take
His brother here and put him to the sword;
And to the skirts of this wild wood he came,
Where, meeting with an old religious man,
After some question with him, was converted
Both from his enterprise and from the world,
His crown bequeathing to his banished brother,
And all their lands restored to them again
That were with him exiled. This to be true
I do engage my life.

DUKE SENIOR Welcome, young man.
Thou offer'st fairly to thy brothers' wedding:
To one his lands withheld and to the other
A land itself at large, a potent dukedom.
First, in this forest let us do those ends
That here were well begun and well begot;
And after, every of this happy number
That have endured shrewd days and nights with us
Shall share the good of our returnèd fortune
According to the measure of their states.
Meantime, forget this new-fall'n dignity,
And fall into our rustic revelry.
Play, music! And you, brides and bridegrooms all,
With measure heaped in joy, to th' measures fall.

JAQUES
Sir, by your patience.—If I heard you rightly,
The Duke hath put on a religious life
And thrown into neglect the pompous court.

JAQUES DE BOYS He hath.

JAQUES
To him will I. Out of these convertites
There is much matter to be heard and learned.
[*To the Duke*] You to your former honor I bequeath;
Your patience and your virtue well deserves it.
[*To Orlando*] You to a love that your true faith doth merit;

114 Whose (Refers to Rosalind.) **129 If . . . contents** if the newly revealed truths are indeed true and bring true contentment. **130 cross** vexation, mischance **132 his** i.e., Silvius's. **accord** agree **133 to your lord** for your husband. **134 sure** closely united **137 Feed** satisfy **138 That . . . diminish** that understanding may lessen your wonder **140 Juno's** (Juno was the Roman queen of the gods, presiding, in the Renaissance view, over faithful wedlock.) **141 board and bed** sustenance and lodging; the household. **143 High** solemn **147 Even . . . degree** You are as welcome as a daughter.

149 Thy faith . . . combine your faithful love for me ties my love to you. **155 Addressed** prepared. **power** army **156 In . . . conduct** under his own command **160 question** conversation **165 engage** pledge **166 Thou offer'st fairly** You contribute handsomely **167 To one** to Oliver **167–8 to the other . . . large** to Orlando an entire dukedom (since, as husband of Rosalind, Orlando will eventually inherit as duke). **169 do those ends** accomplish those purposes **170 begot** conceived **171 every** every one **172 shrewd** hard, trying **174 According . . . states** according to their degrees. **175 new-fall'n** newly acquired **178 With . . . fall** with an overflowing measure of joy, fall to dancing. (With wordplay on *measure* and *measures,* "dances.") **179 by your patience** by your leave, i.e., let the music wait a moment. **181 pompous** ceremonious **183 convertites** converts **184 matter** sound sense

[*To Oliver*] You to your land and love and great allies;
[*To Silvius*] You to a long and well-deservèd bed;
[*To Touchstone*] And you to wrangling, for thy loving voyage
Is but for two months victualed. So, to your pleasures.
I am for other than for dancing measures.

DUKE SENIOR Stay, Jaques, stay.

JAQUES
To see no pastime I. What you would have
I'll stay to know at your abandoned cave. *Exit.*

DUKE SENIOR
Proceed, proceed. We'll begin these rites,
As we do trust they'll end, in true delights.
[*They dance.*] *Exeunt* [*all but Rosalind*].

✤

[Epilogue]

ROSALIND
It is not the fashion to see the lady the epilogue; but it is no more unhandsome than to see the lord the prologue. If it be true that good wine needs no bush, 'tis true that a good play needs no epilogue. Yet to good wine they do use good bushes, and good plays prove the better by the help of good epilogues. What a case am I in then, that am neither a good epilogue nor cannot insinuate with you in the behalf of a good play! I am not furnished like a beggar; therefore to beg will not become me. My way is to conjure you, and I'll begin with the women. I charge you, O women, for the love you bear to men, to like as much of this play as please you; and I charge you, O men, for the love you bear to women—as I perceive by your simpering, none of you hates them—that between you and the women the play may please. If I were a woman I would kiss as many of you as had beards that pleased me, complexions that liked me, and breaths that I defied not; and I am sure as many as have good beards or good faces or sweet breaths will, for my kind offer, when I make curtsy, bid me farewell. *Exit.*

188 allies kinfolk **191 victualed** provisioned.

Epilogue

2 unhandsome in bad taste

3–4 good . . . bush (A proverb derived from the custom of displaying a piece of ivy or holly at the tavern door to denote that wine was for sale there.) **8 insinuate** ingratiate myself **9 furnished** equipped, decked out **10 conjure** adjure, earnestly charge **16–17 If . . . woman** (Womens's parts on the Elizabethan stage were played by boys in feminine costume.) **18 liked** pleased **19 defied** rejected, disdained **21–2 bid me farewell** i.e., applaud me.

Twelfth Night; or, What You Will

Twelfth Night is possibly the latest of the three festive comedies, including *Much Ado About Nothing* and *As You Like It*, with which Shakespeare climaxed his distinctively philosophical and joyous vein of comic writing. Performed on February 2, 1602, at the Middle Temple and written possibly as early as 1599, *Twelfth Night* is usually dated 1600 or 1601. This play is indeed the most festive of the lot. Its keynote is Saturnalian release and the carnival pursuit of love and mirth. Along with such familiar motifs as the plucky heroine disguised as a man (found earlier in *The Two Gentlemen of Verona, As You Like It,* and *The Merchant of Venice*), *Twelfth Night* also returns to the more farcical routines of mistaken identity found in Shakespeare's early comedy. As a witness of the 1602 performance, John Manningham, observes, the play is "much like the *Comedy of Errors*, or *Menaechmi* in Plautus, but most like and near to that in Italian called *Inganni.*"

The carnival atmosphere is appropriate to the season designated in the play's title: the twelfth night of Christmas, January 6, the Feast of Epiphany. (The prologue to *Gl'Ingannati,* perhaps the Italian play referred to by Manningham, speaks of "La Notte di Beffania," Epiphany night.) Along with its primary Christian significance as the Feast of the Magi, Epiphany was also in Renaissance times the last day of the Christmas revels. Over a twelve-day period, from Christmas until January 6, noble households sponsored numerous performances of plays, masques, banquets, and every kind of festivity. (Leslie Hotson argues, in fact, that *Twelfth Night* was first performed on twelfth night in early 1601, in the presence of Queen Elizabeth.) Students left schools for vacations, celebrating release from study with plays and revels of their own. The stern rigors of a rule-bound society gave way temporarily to playful inversions of authority. The reign of the Boy Bishop and the Feast of Fools, for example, gave choristers and minor church functionaries the cherished opportunity to boss the hierarchy around, mock the liturgy with outrageous lampooning, and generally let off steam. Although such customs occasionally got out of hand, the idea was to channel potentially destructive insubordination into playacting and thereby promote harmony. Behind these Elizabethan midwinter customs lies the Roman Saturnalia, with its pagan spirit of gift giving, sensual indulgence, and satirical hostility to those who would curb merriment. Shakespeare's play captures the medieval and Renaissance spirit of Epiphany by its often playful allusions to religious practice: Feste's disguise as "Sir Topas," the priest, Feste's joke about living by the church (3.1.3–7), Sir Toby's defense of "cakes and ale," Feste's swearing by Saint Anne, mother of the Virgin Mary (2.3.116), Feste's joking about "clerestories" (4.2.38), and the like. Shakespeare lovingly evokes a tradition of festivals and ceremonies that incorporates self-mockery into its celebration of renewal at Christmas time.

Shakespeare's choice of sources for *Twelfth Night* underscores his commitment to mirth. Renaissance literature offered numerous instances of mistaken identity among twins and of the disguised heroine serving as page to her beloved. Among those in English were the anonymous play *Sir Clyomon and Sir Clamydes* (c. 1570–1583), Sir Philip Sidney's *Arcadia* (1590), and the prose romance *Parismus* by Emmanuel Forde (1598), featuring both a shipwreck and two characters with the names of Olivia and Violetta. Of particular significance, though partly for negative reasons, is Barnabe Riche's tale of "Apollonius and Silla" in *Riche His Farewell to Military Profession* (1581), which was based on François de Belleforest's 1571 French version of Matteo Bandello's *Novelle* (1554). Here we find most of the requisite plot elements: the shipwreck; Silla's disguise as a page in Duke Apollonius' court; her office as ambassador of love from Apollonius to the lady Julina, who thereupon falls in love with Silla; and the arrival of Silla's twin brother Silvio and his consequent success in winning Julina's affection. To Riche, however, this tale is merely a long warning against the enervating power of infatuation. Silvio gets Julina with child and disappears forthwith, making his belated reappearance almost too late to save the wrongly accused Silla. Riche's moralizing puts the blame on the gross and drunken appetite of carnal love. The total mismatching of affection with which the story begins, and the sudden realignments of desire based on mere outward resemblances, are seen as proofs of love's unreasonableness. Shakespeare, of course, retains and capitalizes on the irrational quality of love, as in *A Midsummer Night's Dream,* but in doing so he minimizes the harm done (Olivia is not made pregnant) and repudiates any negative moral judgments. The added subplot, with its rebuking of Malvolio's censoriousness, may have been conceived as a further answer to Riche, Fenton, and their sober school.

Shakespeare's festive spirit owes much, as Manningham observed, to Plautus and the neoclassical Italian comic writers. At least three Italian comedies called *Gl'Inganni* ("The Frauds") employ the motif of mistaken identity, and one of them, by Curzio Gonzaga (1592), supplies Viola's assumed name of "Cesare," or Cesario. Another play with the same title appeared in 1562. More useful is *Gl'Ingannati* ("The Deceived"), performed in 1531 and translated into French in 1543. Besides a plot line generally similar to *Twelfth Night* and the reference to La Notte di Beffania (Epiphany), this play offers the suggestive name *Malevolti,* "evil-faced," and *Fabio* (which resembles "Fabian"). It also contains possible hints for Malvolio, Sir Toby, and company, although the plot of the counterfeit letter is original with Shakespeare. Essentially, Shakespeare combines his own plot with an Italianate novella plot, as he did in *The Taming of the Shrew* and *Much Ado About Nothing*. And it is in the Malvolio story that Shakespeare most pointedly defends merriment. Feste the professional fool, an original stage type for Shakespeare in *Twelfth Night* and in *As You Like It,* also reinforces the theme of seizing the moment of mirth.

This great lesson, of savoring life's pleasures while one is still young, is something that Orsino and Olivia have not yet learned when the play commences. Although suited to one another in rank, wealth, and attractiveness, they are unable to overcome their own willful posturing in the elaborate charade of courtship. Like Silvius in *As You Like It,* Orsino is the conventional wooer trapped in the courtly artifice of love's rules. He opens the play on a cloying note of self-pity. He is fascinated with his own degradation as a rejected suitor and bores his listeners with his changeable moods and fondness for poetical "conceits." He sees himself as a hart pursued by his desires "like fell and cruel hounds," reminding us that enervating lovesickness has, in fact, robbed him of his manly occupation, hunting. He sends ornately contrived messages to Olivia but has not seen her in so long that his passion has become unreal and fantastical, feeding on itself.

Olivia plays the opposite role of chaste, denying womanhood. She explains her retirement from the world as mourning for a dead brother (whose name we never learn), but this withdrawal from life is another unreal vision. Olivia's practice of mourning, whereby she will "water once a day her chamber round / With eye-offending brine" (1.1.28–9), is a lifeless ritual. As others view the matter, she is senselessly wasting her beauty and affection on the dead. "What a plague means my niece to take the death of her brother thus?" Sir Toby expostulates (1.3.1–2). Viola, though she, too, has seemingly lost a brother, is an important foil in this regard, for she continues to hope for her brother's safety, trusts his soul is in heaven if he is dead, and refuses to give up her commitment to life in any case. We suspect that Olivia takes a willful pleasure in self-denial not unlike Orsino's self-congratulatory suffering. She appears to derive satisfaction from the power she holds over Orsino, a power of refusal. And she must know that she looks stunning in black.

Olivia's household reflects, in part, her mood of self-denial. She keeps Malvolio as steward because he, too, dresses somberly, insists on quiet as befits a house in mourning, and maintains order. Yet Olivia also retains a fool, Feste, who is Malvolio's opposite in every way. Hard-pressed to defend his mirthful function in a household so given over to melancholy, Feste must find some way of persuading his mistress that her very gravity is itself the essence of folly. This is a paradox, because sobriety and order appeal to the conventional wisdom of the world. Malvolio, sensing that his devotion to propriety is being challenged by the fool's prating, chides Olivia for taking "delight in such a barren rascal" (1.5.80–1).

Feste must argue for an inversion of appearance and reality whereby many of the world's ordinary pursuits can be seen to be ridiculous. As he observes, in his habitually elliptical manner of speech, "*Cucullus non facit monachum* [the cowl doesn't make the monk]; that's as much to say as I wear not motley in my brain" (1.5.52–4). Feste wins his case by making Olivia laugh at her own illogic in grieving for a brother whose soul she assumes to be in heaven. By extension, Olivia has indeed been a fool for allowing herself to be deprived of happiness in love by her brother's death ("there is no true cuckold but calamity") and for failing to consider the brevity of youth ("beauty's a flower"). Yet, paradoxically, only one who professes to be a fool can point this out, enabled by his detachment and innocence to perceive simple but profound truths denied to supposedly rational persons. This vision of the fool as naturally wise, and of society as self-indulgently insane, fascinated Renaissance writers, from Erasmus's *In Praise of Folly* and Cervantes's *Don Quixote* to Shakespeare's *King Lear.*

Viola, although not dressed in motley, aligns herself with Feste's rejection of self-denial. Refreshingly, even comically, she challenges the staid artifice of Orsino's and Olivia's lives. She is an ocean traveler, like many of Shakespeare's later heroines (Marina in *Pericles,* Perdita in *The Winter's Tale),* arriving on Illyria's shore plucky and determined. On her first embassy to Olivia from Orsino, she exposes with disarming candor the willfully ritualistic quality of Olivia's existence. Viola discards the flowery set speech she had prepared and memorized at Orsino's behest; despite her charmingly conceited assertion that the speech has been "excellently well penned," she senses that its elegant but empty rhetoric is all too familiar to the disdainful Olivia. Instead, Viola departs from her text to urge seizing the moment of happiness. "You do usurp yourself," she lectures Olivia, "for what is yours to bestow is not yours to reserve" (1.5.183–4). Beauty is a gift of nature, and failure to use it is a sin against nature. Or, again, "Lady, you are the cruel'st she alive / If you will lead these graces [Olivia's beauty] to the grave / And leave the world no copy" (lines 236–8). An essential argument in favor of love, as in Shakespeare's sonnets, is the necessity of marriage and childbearing in order to perpetuate beauty. This approach is new to Olivia and catches her wholly by surprise. In part, she reacts, like Phoebe in *As You Like It,* with perverse logic, rejecting a too-willing wooer for one who is hard to get. Yet Olivia is also attracted by a new note of sincerity, prompting her to reenter life and accept maturely both the risks and rewards of romantic involvement. Her longing for "Cesario" is, of course, sexually misdirected, but the appearance of Viola's identical twin, Sebastian, soon puts all to rights.

The motifs of Olivia's attraction for another woman (both actors would have been boys) and of Orsino's deep fondness for a seeming young man ("Cesario"), which matures into sexual love, raise delicate suggestions of love between members of the same sex, as in *As You Like It.* Once again, the ambiguities of disguise point toward the socially constructed nature of sexual difference. Viola as "Cesario" strikes those who meet her as almost sexually indeterminate. Orsino puts the matter well, in conversing with "Cesario," when he observes, "they shall yet belie thy happy years / That say thou art a man. Diana's lip / Is not more smooth and rubious; thy small pipe / Is as the maiden's organ, shrill and sound, / And all is semblative a woman's part" (1.4.30–4). Male adolescence and femininity are seen as virtually indistinguishable—a point that is wittily reinforced in the theater by the fact that a boy actor is playing Viola disguised as "Cesario."

At the same time, this playful confusion of sexual difference becomes the vehicle for a serious exploration of love and friendship. Like Rosalind in *As You Like It,* Viola uses her male attire to win Orsino's pure affection in a friendship nominally devoid of sexual interest, since both seemingly are men. Friendship must come first; the Renaissance generally accorded a higher value to friendship than to erotic passion. Yet Shakespeare also insists, as did many of his contemporaries (including Montaigne), that friendship is not only possible between men and women but also that such a relationship, formalized in marriage, offers the best of all worlds; hence, the importance of Viola's male disguise. As "Cesario," she can teach Orsino about the conventions of love in relaxed and frank conversations that would not be possible if she were known to be a woman. She teaches him to avoid the beguiling but misleading myths of Petrarchan love (named after the Italian sonneteer Francis Petrarch, whose poems embody the idealization of courtly love) and so prepares him for the realities of marriage. Comparing men and women in love, she confides, "We men may say more, swear more, but indeed / Our shows are more than will; for still we prove / Much in our vows, but little in our love" (2.4.116–18). Once she and Orsino have achieved an instinctive rapport—all the more remarkable for their talking so often at cross-purposes—Viola's unmasking can make possible a physical communion as well. Orsino, no longer trapped in the futile worship of a seemingly unapproachable goddess, can come to terms with his sexuality as part of a unified and loving human relationship.

The friendship of Sebastian and Antonio, meanwhile, sorely tested by the mix-ups of the mistaken identity plot, similarly places Sebastian in a love-and-friendship triangle like that involving Bassanio, Portia, and Antonio in *The Merchant of Venice.* Sebastian and Antonio are loving friends, so much so that Antonio willingly risks his life to be with Sebastian in a country where Antonio has many enemies. Antonio's expressions of fondness for Sebastian are extraordinarily warm. "If you will not murder me for my love, let me be your servant," he pleads. "I do adore thee so / That danger shall seem sport, and I will go" (2.1.33–4, 45–6). A desire "More sharp than filèd steel" spurs Antonio to seek out his friend, despite the manifest danger (3.3.4–5). "A witchcraft" draws him to Sebastian (5.1.72). Whether the attachment is homosexual, as it is often played on the modern stage, is debatable; expressions of warmth between men seem to have been more common in Elizabethan times than today, and centuries of intervening time have no doubt altered our understanding of same-sex relationships; the term *homosexual* is of much later date. What remains true for the play is that this portrayal of emotional and loving closeness between two men gives way to the marriage of one of them to a woman (as in *The Merchant of Venice*). The depiction of love and friendship between two men is a repeated motif in the play, embodied most of all in the loving relationship of Orsino and "Cesario." Shakespeare chooses to resolve his plot by defining heterosexual marriage as the completion of relationships begun in friendship and incorporating that friendship in a union that finally offers heterosexual fulfillment as well.

The below-stairs characters of the subplot, Sir Toby and the rest, share with Feste and Viola a commitment to joy. As Sir Toby proclaims in his first speech, "care's an enemy to life" (1.3.2–3). Even the simpleton Sir Andrew, although gulled by Sir Toby into spending his money on a hopeless pursuit of Olivia, seems none the worse for his treatment; he loves to drink in Sir Toby's company and can afford to pay for his entertainment. Sir Toby gives us some of the richly inventive humor of Falstaff, another lovable fat roguish knight. In this subplot, however, the confrontations between merriment and sobriety are more harshly drawn than in the main plot. Whereas the gracious Olivia is won away from her folly, the obdurate Malvolio can only be exposed to ridicule. He is chiefly to blame for the polarization of attitudes, for he insists on rebuking the mirth of others. His name (*Mal-volio,* the "ill-wisher") implies a self-satisfied determination to impose his rigid moral code on others. As Sir Toby taunts him, "Dost thou think, because thou art virtuous, there shall be no more cakes and ale?" (2.3.114–15). Malvolio's inflexible hostility provokes a desire for comic vengeance. The method is satiric: the clever manipulators, Maria and Sir Toby, invent a scheme to entrap Malvolio in his own self-deceit. The punishment fits the crime, for he has long dreamed of himself as "Count Malvolio," rich, powerful, and in a position to demolish Sir Toby and the rest. Without Malvolio's infatuated predisposition to believe that Olivia could actually love him and write such a letter as he finds, Maria's scheme would have no hope of success. He tortures the text to make it yield a suitable meaning, much in the style of Puritan theologizing. His conviction that Jove is with him (2.5.169) reminds us of the Puritan belief that prosperity of the "elect" is a sign of God's grace.

Indeed, Malvolio in some ways does resemble a Puritan, as Maria observes (2.3.139–47), even though she qualifies the assertion by saying that he is not a religious fanatic but a "time-pleaser." She directs her observation not at a religious group but at all who would be killjoys; if the Puritans are like that, she intimates, so much the worse for them. This uncharacteristic lack of charity gives a sharp tone to the vengeance practiced on Malvolio, evoking from Olivia a protest that "he hath been most notoriously abused" (5.1.379). The belated attempt to make a reconciliation with him seems, however, doomed to failure, in light of his grim resolve to "be revenged on the whole pack of you." At the height of his discomfiture, he has been tricked into doing the two things he hates most: smiling affably and wearing sportive attire. The appearance of merriment is so grossly unsuited to him that he is declared mad and put into safekeeping. The apostle of sobriety in this play thus comes before us as a declared madman, while the fool Feste offers him sage comment in the guise of a priest. Wisdom and folly have changed places. The upside-down character of the play is epitomized in Malvolio's plaintive remark to Feste (no longer posing as the priest): "I am as well in my wits, Fool, as thou art" (4.2.88). Malvolio's comeuppance is richly deserved, but the severity of vengeance and countervengeance suggests that the triumph of festival will not last long. This brevity is, of course, inherent in the nature of such holiday release from responsibility. As Feste sings, "What's to come is still unsure. / In delay there lies no plenty."

Twelfth Night; or, What You Will

[*Dramatis Personae*

ORSINO, *Duke (sometimes called Count) of Illyria*
VALENTINE, *gentleman attending on Orsino*
CURIO, *gentleman attending on Orsino*

VIOLA, *a shipwrecked lady, later disguised as Cesario*
SEBASTIAN, *twin brother of Viola*
ANTONIO, *a sea captain, friend to Sebastian*
CAPTAIN *of the shipwrecked vessel*

OLIVIA, *a rich countess of Illyria*
MARIA, *gentlewoman in Olivia's household*

SIR TOBY BELCH, *Olivia's uncle*
SIR ANDREW AGUECHEEK, *a companion of Sir Toby*
MALVOLIO, *steward of Olivia's household*
FABIAN, *a member of Olivia's household*
FESTE, *a clown, also called* FOOL, *Olivia's jester*

A PRIEST
FIRST OFFICER
SECOND OFFICER

Lords, Sailors, Musicians, and other Attendants

SCENE: *Illyria*]

1.1

Enter Orsino Duke of Illyria, Curio, and other lords [*with musicians*].

ORSINO
If music be the food of love, play on;
Give me excess of it, that surfeiting,
The appetite may sicken and so die.
That strain again! It had a dying fall;
Oh, it came o'er my ear like the sweet sound
That breathes upon a bank of violets,
Stealing and giving odor. Enough, no more.
'Tis not so sweet now as it was before.
O spirit of love, how quick and fresh art thou,
That, notwithstanding thy capacity
Receiveth as the sea, naught enters there,
Of what validity and pitch soe'er,
But falls into abatement and low price
Even in a minute! So full of shapes is fancy
That it alone is high fantastical.

CURIO
Will you go hunt, my lord?

ORSINO
What, Curio?

CURIO
The hart.

ORSINO
Why, so I do, the noblest that I have.
Oh, when mine eyes did see Olivia first,
Methought she purged the air of pestilence.
That instant was I turned into a hart,
And my desires, like fell and cruel hounds,
E'er since pursue me.

Enter Valentine.

How now, what news from her?

VALENTINE
So please my lord, I might not be admitted,
But from her handmaid do return this answer:
The element itself, till seven years' heat,
Shall not behold her face at ample view;
But like a cloistress she will veilèd walk,
And water once a day her chamber round
With eye-offending brine—all this to season

1.1 Location: Orsino's court.
0.1 ***Illyria*** Nominally on the east coast of the Adriatic Sea, but with a suggestion also of "illusion" and "delirium." **4 fall** cadence **9 quick and fresh** keen and hungry **12 validity** value. **pitch** superiority. (Literally, the highest point of a falcon's flight.) **13 abatement** depreciation. (The lover's brain entertains innumerable fantasies but soon tires of them all.) **14 shapes** imagined forms. **fancy** love **15 it . . . fantastical** it surpasses everything else in imaginative power.

17 the noblest . . . have i.e., my noblest part, my heart. (Punning on *hart.*) **21 fell** fierce **22 pursue me** (Alludes to the story in Ovid of Actaeon, who, having seen Diana bathing, was transformed into a stag and killed by his own hounds.) **25 element** sky. **seven years' heat** seven summers **27 cloistress** nun secluded in a religious community **29 season** keep fresh. (Playing on the idea of the salt in her tears.)

A brother's dead love, which she would keep fresh 30
And lasting in her sad remembrance.

ORSINO
Oh, she that hath a heart of that fine frame 32
To pay this debt of love but to a brother,
How will she love, when the rich golden shaft 34
Hath killed the flock of all affections else 35
That live in her; when liver, brain, and heart, 36
These sovereign thrones, are all supplied, and filled 37
Her sweet perfections, with one self king! 38
Away before me to sweet beds of flowers.
Love-thoughts lie rich when canopied with bowers.
Exeunt.

✤

1.2

Enter Viola, a Captain, and sailors.

VIOLA What country, friends, is this?
CAPTAIN This is Illyria, lady.
VIOLA
And what should I do in Illyria?
My brother he is in Elysium. 4
Perchance he is not drowned. What think you, sailors? 5
CAPTAIN
It is perchance that you yourself were saved. 6
VIOLA
Oh, my poor brother! And so perchance may he be.
CAPTAIN
True, madam, and to comfort you with chance, 8
Assure yourself, after our ship did split,
When you and those poor number saved with you
Hung on our driving boat, I saw your brother, 11
Most provident in peril, bind himself,
Courage and hope both teaching him the practice,
To a strong mast that lived upon the sea; 14
Where, like Arion on the dolphin's back, 15
I saw him hold acquaintance with the waves
So long as I could see.
VIOLA For saying so, there's gold. [*She gives money.*]
Mine own escape unfoldeth to my hope, 19
Whereto thy speech serves for authority, 20
The like of him. Know'st thou this country? 21
CAPTAIN
Ay, madam, well, for I was bred and born
Not three hours' travel from this very place.
VIOLA Who governs here?
CAPTAIN A noble duke, in nature as in name.
VIOLA What is his name?
CAPTAIN Orsino.
VIOLA
Orsino! I have heard my father name him.
He was a bachelor then.
CAPTAIN
And so is now, or was so very late; 30
For but a month ago I went from hence,
And then 'twas fresh in murmur—as, you know, 32
What great ones do the less will prattle of— 33
That he did seek the love of fair Olivia.
VIOLA What's she?
CAPTAIN
A virtuous maid, the daughter of a count
That died some twelvemonth since, then leaving her
In the protection of his son, her brother,
Who shortly also died; for whose dear love,
They say, she hath abjured the sight
And company of men.
VIOLA Oh, that I served that lady,
And might not be delivered to the world 42
Till I had made mine own occasion mellow, 43
What my estate is!
CAPTAIN That were hard to compass, 44
Because she will admit no kind of suit,
No, not the Duke's. 46
VIOLA
There is a fair behavior in thee, Captain,
And though that nature with a beauteous wall 48
Doth oft close in pollution, yet of thee
I will believe thou hast a mind that suits
With this thy fair and outward character. 51
I prithee, and I'll pay thee bounteously,
Conceal me what I am, and be my aid
For such disguise as haply shall become 54
The form of my intent. I'll serve this duke. 55
Thou shalt present me as an eunuch to him. 56
It may be worth thy pains, for I can sing
And speak to him in many sorts of music
That will allow me very worth his service. 59
What else may hap, to time I will commit;
Only shape thou thy silence to my wit. 61
CAPTAIN
Be you his eunuch, and your mute I'll be; 62
When my tongue blabs, then let mine eyes not see.
VIOLA I thank thee. Lead me on. *Exeunt.*

30 A brother's dead love her love for her dead brother and the memory of his love for her **32 frame** construction **34 golden shaft** Cupid's golden-tipped arrow, causing love. (His lead-tipped arrow causes aversion.) **35 affections else** other feelings **36–8 when . . . king** i.e., when passion, thought, and feeling all sit in majesty in their proper thrones (liver, brain, and heart), and her sweet perfections are brought to completion by her union with a single lord and husband.
1.2 Location: The seacoast.
4 Elysium classical abode of the blessed dead. **5-6 Perchance . . . perchance** Perhaps . . . by mere chance **8 chance** i.e., what one may hope that chance will bring about **11 driving** drifting, driven by the seas **14 lived** i.e., kept afloat **15 Arion** a Greek poet who so charmed the dolphins with his lyre that they saved him when he leaped into the sea to escape murderous sailors **19-21 unfoldeth . . . him** offers a hopeful example that he may have escaped similarly, to which hope your speech provides support.

30 late lately **32 murmur** rumor **33 less** social inferiors **42 delivered** revealed, made known. (With suggestion of "born.") **43 Till . . . mellow** until the time is ripe for my purpose **44 estate** social rank. **compass** encompass, bring about **46 not** not even **48 though that** though **51 character** face or features as indicating moral qualities. **54–5 as haply . . . intent** as may suit the nature of my purpose. **56 eunuch** castrato, high-voiced singer **59 allow** prove **61 wit** plan, invention. **62 mute** silent attendant. (Sometimes used of non-speaking actors.)

1.3

Enter Sir Toby [Belch] and Maria.

SIR TOBY What a plague means my niece to take the death of her brother thus? I am sure care's an enemy to life.

MARIA By my troth, Sir Toby, you must come in earlier o'nights. Your cousin, my lady, takes great exceptions to your ill hours.

SIR TOBY Why, let her except before excepted.

MARIA Ay, but you must confine yourself within the modest limits of order.

SIR TOBY Confine? I'll confine myself no finer than I am. These clothes are good enough to drink in, and so be these boots too. An they be not, let them hang themselves in their own straps.

MARIA That quaffing and drinking will undo you. I heard my lady talk of it yesterday, and of a foolish knight that you brought in one night here to be her wooer.

SIR TOBY Who, Sir Andrew Aguecheek?

MARIA Ay, he.

SIR TOBY He's as tall a man as any's in Illyria.

MARIA What's that to the purpose?

SIR TOBY Why, he has three thousand ducats a year.

MARIA Ay, but he'll have but a year in all these ducats. He's a very fool and a prodigal.

SIR TOBY Fie, that you'll say so! He plays o'th' viol-de-gamboys, and speaks three or four languages word for word without book, and hath all the good gifts of nature.

MARIA He hath indeed, almost natural, for, besides that he's a fool, he's a great quarreler, and but that he hath the gift of a coward to allay the gust he hath in quarreling, 'tis thought among the prudent he would quickly have the gift of a grave.

SIR TOBY By this hand, they are scoundrels and substractors that say so of him. Who are they?

MARIA They that add, moreover, he's drunk nightly in your company.

SIR TOBY With drinking healths to my niece. I'll drink to her as long as there is a passage in my throat and drink in Illyria. He's a coward and a coistrel that will not drink to my niece till his brains turn o'th' toe like a parish top. What, wench? *Castiliano vulgo!* For here comes Sir Andrew Agueface.

Enter Sir Andrew [Aguecheek].

SIR ANDREW Sir Toby Belch! How now, Sir Toby Belch?

SIR TOBY Sweet Sir Andrew!

SIR ANDREW [*to Maria*] Bless you, fair shrew.

MARIA And you too, sir.

SIR TOBY Accost, Sir Andrew, accost.

SIR ANDREW What's that?

SIR TOBY My niece's chambermaid.

SIR ANDREW Good Mistress Accost, I desire better acquaintance.

MARIA My name is Mary, sir.

SIR ANDREW Good Mistress Mary Accost—

SIR TOBY You mistake, knight. "Accost" is front her, board her, woo her, assail her.

SIR ANDREW By my troth, I would not undertake her in this company. Is that the meaning of "accost"?

MARIA Fare you well, gentlemen. [*Going.*]

SIR TOBY An thou let part so, Sir Andrew, would thou mightst never draw sword again.

SIR ANDREW An you part so, mistress, I would I might never draw sword again. Fair lady, do you think you have fools in hand?

MARIA Sir, I have not you by the hand.

SIR ANDREW Marry, but you shall have, and here's my hand. [*He gives her his hand.*]

MARIA Now, sir, thought is free. I pray you, bring your hand to th' buttery-bar, and let it drink.

SIR ANDREW Wherefore, sweetheart? What's your metaphor?

MARIA It's dry, sir.

SIR ANDREW Why, I think so. I am not such an ass but I can keep my hand dry. But what's your jest?

MARIA A dry jest, sir.

SIR ANDREW Are you full of them?

MARIA Ay, sir, I have them at my fingers' ends. Marry, now I let go your hand, I am barren.

[*She lets go his hand.*] *Exit Maria.*

1.3 Location: Olivia's house.
5 cousin kinswoman **7 let . . . excepted** i.e., let her take exception to my conduct all she wants; I don't care. (Plays on the legal phrase *exceptis excipiendis,* "with the exceptions before named.") **9 modest** moderate **10 I'll . . . finer** (1) I'll constrain myself no more rigorously (2) I'll dress myself no more finely **12 An** If **20 tall** brave. (But Maria pretends to take the word in the common sense.)
22 ducats coins worth about four or five shillings **23 he'll . . . ducats** he'll spend all his money within a year. **25–6 viol-de-gamboys** viola da gamba, leg-viol, bass viol **27 without book** by heart
29 natural (With a play on the sense "born idiot.") **31 gift** natural ability. (But shifted to mean "present" in line 33.) **allay the gust** moderate the taste **34–5 substractors** detractors **40 coistrel** horse-groom, base fellow

42 parish top a large top provided by the parish to be spun by whipping, apparently for exercise. ***Castiliano vulgo!*** (Of uncertain meaning. Possibly Sir Toby is saying "Speak of the devil!" Castiliano is the name adopted by a devil in Haughton's *Grim the Collier of Croydon.*)
43 Agueface (Like *Aguecheek,* this name betokens the thin, pale countenance of one suffering from an ague or fever.) **46 shrew** i.e., diminutive creature. (But with probably unintended suggestion of shrewishness.) **48 Accost** Go alongside (a nautical term), i.e., greet her, address her **50 chambermaid** lady-in-waiting (a gentlewoman, not one who would do menial tasks). **55 front** confront, come alongside **56 board** greet, approach (as though preparing to board in a naval encounter) **57 undertake** have to do with. (Here with unintended sexual suggestion, to which Maria mirthfully replies with her jokes about *dry jests, barren,* and *buttery-bar*.) **60 An . . . part** If you let her leave **64 have . . . hand** i.e., have to deal with fools. (But Maria puns on the literal sense.) **66 Marry** i.e., Indeed. (Originally, "By the Virgin Mary.") **68 thought is free** i.e., I may think what I like. (Proverbial; replying to *do you think . . . in hand,* above.) **69 buttery-bar** ledge on top of the half-door to the buttery or the wine cellar. (Maria's language is sexually suggestive, though Sir Andrew seems oblivious to that.) **72 dry** thirsty; also dried up, a sign of age and sexual debility **75 dry** (1) ironic (2) dull, barren. (Referring to Sir Andrew.) **77 at my fingers' ends** (1) at the ready (2) by the hand.
78 barren i.e., empty of jests and of Sir Andrew's hand.

SIR TOBY Oh, knight, thou lack'st a cup of canary! When did I see thee so put down?

SIR ANDREW Never in your life, I think, unless you see canary put me down. Methinks sometimes I have no more wit than a Christian or an ordinary man has. But I am a great eater of beef, and I believe that does harm to my wit.

SIR TOBY No question.

SIR ANDREW An I thought that, I'd forswear it. I'll ride home tomorrow, Sir Toby.

SIR TOBY *Pourquoi,* my dear knight?

SIR ANDREW What is *"pourquoi"*? Do or not do? I would I had bestowed that time in the tongues that I have in fencing, dancing, and bearbaiting. Oh, had I but followed the arts!

SIR TOBY Then hadst thou had an excellent head of hair.

SIR ANDREW Why, would that have mended my hair?

SIR TOBY Past question, for thou see'st it will not curl by nature.

SIR ANDREW But it becomes me well enough, does't not?

SIR TOBY Excellent. It hangs like flax on a distaff; and I hope to see a huswife take thee between her legs and spin it off.

SIR ANDREW Faith, I'll home tomorrow, Sir Toby. Your niece will not be seen, or if she be, it's four to one she'll none of me. The Count himself here hard by woos her.

SIR TOBY She'll none o'th' Count. She'll not match above her degree, neither in estate, years, nor wit; I have heard her swear't. Tut, there's life in't, man.

SIR ANDREW I'll stay a month longer. I am a fellow o'th' strangest mind i'th' world; I delight in masques and revels sometimes altogether.

SIR TOBY Art thou good at these kickshawses, knight?

SIR ANDREW As any man in Illyria, whatsoever he be, under the degree of my betters, and yet I will not compare with an old man.

SIR TOBY What is thy excellence in a galliard, knight?

SIR ANDREW Faith, I can cut a caper.

SIR TOBY And I can cut the mutton to't.

SIR ANDREW And I think I have the back-trick simply as strong as any man in Illyria.

SIR TOBY Wherefore are these things hid? Wherefore have these gifts a curtain before 'em? Are they like to take dust, like Mistress Mall's picture? Why dost thou not go to church in a galliard and come home in a coranto? My very walk should be a jig; I would not so much as make water but in a sink-a-pace. What dost thou mean? Is it a world to hide virtues in? I did think, by the excellent constitution of thy leg, it was formed under the star of a galliard.

SIR ANDREW Ay, 'tis strong, and it does indifferent well in a dun-colored stock. Shall we set about some revels?

SIR TOBY What shall we do else? Were we not born under Taurus?

SIR ANDREW Taurus? That's sides and heart.

SIR TOBY No, sir, it is legs and thighs. Let me see thee caper. [*Sir Andrew capers.*] Ha, higher! Ha, ha, excellent! *Exeunt.*

✤

1.4

Enter Valentine, and Viola in man's attire.

VALENTINE If the Duke continue these favors towards you, Cesario, you are like to be much advanced. He hath known you but three days, and already you are no stranger.

VIOLA You either fear his humor or my negligence, that you call in question the continuance of his love. Is he inconstant, sir, in his favors?

VALENTINE No, believe me.

Enter Duke [Orsino], Curio, and attendants.

VIOLA I thank you. Here comes the Count.

ORSINO Who saw Cesario, ho?

VIOLA On your attendance, my lord, here.

ORSINO
Stand you awhile aloof. [*The others stand aside.*]
Cesario,
Thou know'st no less but all. I have unclasped
To thee the book even of my secret soul.
Therefore, good youth, address thy gait unto her;
Be not denied access, stand at her doors,

79 thou . . . canary i.e., you look as if you need a drink. (*Canary* is a sweet wine from the Canary Islands.) **82 put me down** (1) baffle my wits (2) lay me out flat. **89 *Pourquoi*** Why **91 tongues** languages. (Sir Toby then puns on "tongs," curling irons.) **92 bearbaiting** the sport of setting dogs on a chained bear. **93 the arts** the liberal arts, learning. (But Sir Toby plays on the phrase as meaning "artifice," the antithesis of *nature.*) **95 mended** improved **100 distaff** a staff for holding the flax, tow, or wool in spinning **102 spin it off** i.e., (1) treat your flaxen hair as though it were flax on a distaff to be spun (2) cause you to lose hair as a result of venereal disease (3) make you ejaculate. (*Huswife* suggests "hussy," "whore.") **105 Count** i.e., Duke Orsino, sometimes referred to as Count. **hard** near **108 degree** social position. **estate** fortune, social position **109 there's life in't** i.e., while there's life there's hope **113 kickshawses** delicacies, fancy trifles. (From the French, *quelque chose.*) **115 under . . . betters** excepting those who are above me **116 old man** i.e., one experienced through age. **117 galliard** lively dance in triple time **118 cut a caper** make a lively leap. (But Sir Toby puns on the *caper* used to make a sauce served with mutton. *Mutton,* in turn, suggests "whore.")

120 back-trick backward step in the galliard. (With sexual innuendo; the back was associated with sexual vigor.) **123–4 like to take** likely to collect **124 Mistress Mall's picture** i.e., perhaps the portrait of some woman protected from light and dust, as many pictures were, by curtains. (*Mall* is a diminutive of *Mary.*) **126 coranto** lively running dance. **127 sink-a-pace** dance like the galliard. (French *cinquepace. Sink* also suggests a cesspool into which one might urinate.) **128 virtues** talents **130 under . . . galliard** i.e., under a star favorable to dancing. **131 indifferent well** well enough. (Said complacently.) **132 dun-colored stock** mouse-colored stocking.
135 Taurus zodiacal sign. (Sir Andrew is mistaken, since Leo governed sides and hearts in medical astrology. Taurus governed legs and thighs, or, more commonly, neck and throat.)
1.4 Location: Orsino's court.
2 like likely **5 humor** changeableness **11 On your attendance** Ready to do you service **12 aloof** aside. **15 address thy gait** go

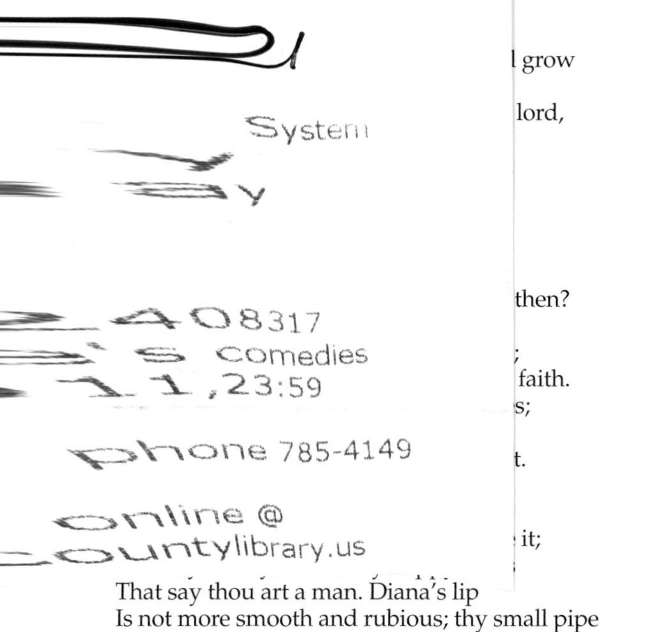

l grow
lord,

then?
;
faith.
s;
t.

it;

That say thou art a man. Diana's lip
Is not more smooth and rubious; thy small pipe
Is as the maiden's organ, shrill and sound,
And all is semblative a woman's part.
I know thy constellation is right apt
For this affair.—Some four or five attend him.
All, if you will, for I myself am best
When least in company.—Prosper well in this,
And thou shalt live as freely as thy lord,
To call his fortunes thine.

VIOLA I'll do my best
To woo your lady. [*Aside*] Yet a barful strife!
Whoe'er I woo, myself would be his wife. *Exeunt.*

✤

1.5

Enter Maria and Clown [*Feste*].

MARIA Nay, either tell me where thou hast been, or I will not open my lips so wide as a bristle may enter in way of thy excuse. My lady will hang thee for thy absence.

FESTE Let her hang me. He that is well hanged in this world needs to fear no colors.

MARIA Make that good.

FESTE He shall see none to fear.

MARIA A good Lenten answer. I can tell thee where that saying was born, of "I fear no colors."

FESTE Where, good Mistress Mary?

MARIA In the wars, and that may you be bold to say in your foolery.

FESTE Well, God give them wisdom that have it; and those that are fools, let them use their talents.

MARIA Yet you will be hanged for being so long absent; or to be turned away, is not that as good as a hanging to you?

FESTE Many a good hanging prevents a bad marriage; and for turning away, let summer bear it out.

MARIA You are resolute, then?

FESTE Not so, neither, but I am resolved on two points.

MARIA That if one break, the other will hold; or if both break, your gaskins fall.

FESTE Apt, in good faith, very apt. Well, go thy way. If Sir Toby would leave drinking, thou wert as witty a piece of Eve's flesh as any in Illyria.

MARIA Peace, you rogue, no more o' that. Here comes my lady. Make your excuse wisely, you were best. [*Exit.*]

Enter Lady Olivia with Malvolio, [*and attendants*].

FESTE [*aside*] Wit, an't be thy will, put me into good fooling! Those wits that think they have thee do very oft prove fools, and I that am sure I lack thee may pass for a wise man. For what says Quinapalus? "Better a witty fool than a foolish wit."—God bless thee, lady!

OLIVIA [*to attendants*] Take the fool away.

FESTE Do you not hear, fellows? Take away the lady.

OLIVIA Go to, you're a dry fool. I'll no more of you. Besides, you grow dishonest.

FESTE Two faults, madonna, that drink and good counsel will amend. For give the dry fool drink, then is the fool not dry. Bid the dishonest man mend himself; if he mend, he is no longer dishonest; if he cannot, let the botcher mend him. Anything that's mended is but patched; virtue that transgresses is but patched with sin, and sin that amends is but patched with virtue. If that this simple syllogism will serve, so; if it will not, what remedy? As there is no true cuckold but calamity, so beauty's a flower. The lady bade take

17 them i.e., Olivia's servants **21 civil bounds** bounds of civility **25 Surprise** Take by storm. (A military term.) **dear** heartfelt **26 become** suit **28 nuncio's** messenger's **32 rubious** ruby red. **pipe** voice, throat **33 shrill and sound** high and clear, uncracked **34 semblative** resembling, like **35 constellation** i.e., nature as determined by your horoscope **41 barful strife** endeavor full of impediments.

1.5 Location: Olivia's house.

6 fear no colors i.e., fear no foe, fear nothing. (With pun on *colors,* worldly deceptions, and "collars," halters or nooses.) **7 Make that good** Explain that. **8 He . . . fear** i.e., The hanged man will be dead and unable to see anything. **9 Lenten** meager, scanty (like Lenten fare), and morbid

12 In the wars (Where *colors* would mean "military standards, enemy flags"—the literal meaning of the proverb.) **12–13 that . . . foolery** that's an answer you may be bold to use in your fool's conundrums. (*Colors* here refer to military banners and insignia used to align rows of fighting men in battle.) **15 talents** abilities. (Also alluding to the parable of the talents, Matthew 25:14–29, and to "talons," claws.) **17 turned away** dismissed. (Possibly also meaning "turned off," "hanged.") **19 good hanging** (With possible bawdy pun on "being well hung.") **20 for** as for. **let . . . out** i.e., let mild weather make dismissal endurable. **23 points** (Maria plays on the meaning "laces used to hold up hose or breeches.") **25 gaskins** wide breeches **27–8 thou . . . Illyria** (Feste may be hinting ironically that Maria would be a suitable mate for Sir Toby.) **30 you were best** it would be best for you. **31 an't** if it **34 Quinapalus** (Feste's invented authority.) **38 Go to** (An expression of annoyance or expostulation.) **dry** dull **40 madonna** my lady **44 botcher** mender of old clothes and shoes. (Playing on two senses of *mend:* "reform" and "repair.") **44–5 Anything . . . patched** i.e., Life is patched or parti-colored like the Fool's garment, a mix of good and bad **47 so** well and good **48–9 As . . . flower** (Nonsense, yet with a suggestion that Olivia has wedded calamity but should not be faithful to it, for the natural course is to seize the moment of youth and beauty before we lose it.)

away the fool; therefore I say again, take her away.

OLIVIA Sir, I bade them take away you.

FESTE Misprision in the highest degree! Lady, *cucullus non facit monachum;* that's as much to say as I wear not motley in my brain. Good madonna, give me leave to prove you a fool.

OLIVIA Can you do it?

FESTE Dexteriously, good madonna.

OLIVIA Make your proof.

FESTE I must catechize you for it, madonna. Good my mouse of virtue, answer me.

OLIVIA Well, sir, for want of other idleness, I'll bide your proof.

FESTE Good madonna, why mourn'st thou?

OLIVIA Good fool, for my brother's death.

FESTE I think his soul is in hell, madonna.

OLIVIA I know his soul is in heaven, fool.

FESTE The more fool, madonna, to mourn for your brother's soul, being in heaven.—Take away the fool, gentlemen.

OLIVIA What think you of this fool, Malvolio? Doth he not mend?

MALVOLIO Yes, and shall do till the pangs of death shake him. Infirmity, that decays the wise, doth ever make the better fool.

FESTE God send you, sir, a speedy infirmity for the better increasing your folly! Sir Toby will be sworn that I am no fox, but he will not pass his word for twopence that you are no fool.

OLIVIA How say you to that, Malvolio?

MALVOLIO I marvel Your Ladyship takes delight in such a barren rascal. I saw him put down the other day with an ordinary fool that has no more brain than a stone. Look you now, he's out of his guard already. Unless you laugh and minister occasion to him, he is gagged. I protest I take these wise men that crow so at these set kind of fools no better than the fools' zanies.

OLIVIA Oh, you are sick of self-love, Malvolio, and taste with a distempered appetite. To be generous, guiltless, and of free disposition is to take those things for bird-bolts that you deem cannon bullets. There is no slander in an allowed fool, though he do nothing but rail; nor no railing in a known discreet man, though he do nothing but reprove.

FESTE Now Mercury endue thee with leasing, for thou speak'st well of fools!

Enter Maria.

MARIA Madam, there is at the gate a young gentleman much desires to speak with you.

OLIVIA From the Count Orsino, is it?

MARIA I know not, madam. 'Tis a fair young man, and well attended.

OLIVIA Who of my people hold him in delay?

MARIA Sir Toby, madam, your kinsman.

OLIVIA Fetch him off, I pray you. He speaks nothing but madman. Fie on him! [*Exit Maria.*] Go you, Malvolio. If it be a suit from the Count, I am sick or not at home; what you will, to dismiss it.

Exit Malvolio.

Now you see, sir, how your fooling grows old, and people dislike it.

FESTE Thou hast spoke for us, madonna, as if thy eldest son should be a fool; whose skull Jove cram with brains, for—here he comes—

Enter Sir Toby.

one of thy kin has a most weak *pia mater.*

OLIVIA By mine honor, half drunk.—What is he at the gate, cousin?

SIR TOBY A gentleman.

OLIVIA A gentleman? What gentleman?

SIR TOBY 'Tis a gentleman here—[*He belches.*] A plague o' these pickle-herring! [*To Feste*] How now, sot?

FESTE Good Sir Toby.

OLIVIA Cousin, cousin, how have you come so early by this lethargy?

SIR TOBY Lechery? I defy lechery. There's one at the gate.

OLIVIA Ay, marry, what is he?

SIR TOBY Let him be the devil an he will, I care not. Give me faith, say I. Well, it's all one. *Exit.*

OLIVIA What's a drunken man like, Fool?

FESTE Like a drowned man, a fool, and a madman. One draft above heat makes him a fool, the second mads him, and a third drowns him.

OLIVIA Go thou and seek the crowner, and let him sit o' my coz; for he's in the third degree of drink, he's drowned. Go, look after him.

FESTE He is but mad yet, madonna; and the fool shall look to the madman. [*Exit.*]

Enter Malvolio.

MALVOLIO Madam, yond young fellow swears he will speak with you. I told him you were sick; he takes on him to understand so much, and therefore comes to speak with you. I told him you were asleep; he seems

52 Misprision Mistake, misunderstanding. (A legal term meaning a wrongful action or misdemeanor.) **52–3 *cucullus . . . monachum*** the cowl does not make the monk **54 motley** the many-colored garment of jesters **59–60 Good . . . virtue** My good, virtuous mouse. (A term of endearment.) **61 idleness** pastime. **bide** endure **71 mend** i.e., improve, grow more amusing. (But Malvolio uses the word to mean "grow more like a fool.") **77 pass** give **82 with** by **83 out of his guard** defenseless, unprovided with a witty answer **84 minister occasion** provide opportunity (for his fooling) **85 protest** avow, declare. **crow** laugh stridently **86 set** artificial, stereotyped. **zanies** assistants, aping attendants. **88 distempered** diseased. **generous** noble-minded **89 free** magnanimous **89–90 bird-bolts** blunt arrows for shooting small birds **90–3 There . . . reprove** Both a licensed fool and a man known for discretion can criticize freely without being accused of slander in the first instance or railing in the second. (In rebuking Malvolio here, Olivia implies that he is not behaving like a "known discreet man.") **91 allowed** licensed (to speak freely)

94 Now . . . leasing i.e., May Mercury, the god of deception, make you a skillful liar **104 madman** i.e., the words of madness. **107 old** stale **112 *pia mater*** i.e., brain. (Actually the soft membrane enclosing the brain.) **118 sot** (1) fool (2) drunkard. **120 Cousin** Kinsman. (Here, uncle.) **126 Give me faith** i.e., to resist the devil. **it's all one** it doesn't matter. **129 draft above heat** helping of drink raising his temperature above normal bodily warmth **131 crowner** coroner **131–2 sit o' my coz** hold an inquest on my kinsman (Sir Toby)

to have a foreknowledge of that too, and therefore comes to speak with you. What is to be said to him, lady? He's fortified against any denial.

OLIVIA Tell him he shall not speak with me.

MALVOLIO He's been told so; and he says he'll stand at your door like a sheriff's post, and be the supporter to a bench, but he'll speak with you.

OLIVIA What kind o' man is he?

MALVOLIO Why, of mankind.

OLIVIA What manner of man?

MALVOLIO Of very ill manner. He'll speak with you, will you or no.

OLIVIA Of what personage and years is he?

MALVOLIO Not yet old enough for a man, nor young enough for a boy; as a squash is before 'tis a peascod, or a codling when 'tis almost an apple. 'Tis with him in standing water between boy and man. He is very well-favored, and he speaks very shrewishly. One would think his mother's milk were scarce out of him.

OLIVIA Let him approach. Call in my gentlewoman.

MALVOLIO Gentlewoman, my lady calls. *Exit.*

Enter Maria.

OLIVIA
Give me my veil. Come, throw it o'er my face.
We'll once more hear Orsino's embassy. [*Olivia veils.*]

Enter Viola.

VIOLA The honorable lady of the house, which is she?

OLIVIA Speak to me; I shall answer for her. Your will?

VIOLA Most radiant, exquisite, and unmatchable beauty—I pray you, tell me if this be the lady of the house, for I never saw her. I would be loath to cast away my speech; for besides that it is excellently well penned, I have taken great pains to con it. Good beauties, let me sustain no scorn; I am very comptible, even to the least sinister usage.

OLIVIA Whence came you, sir?

VIOLA I can say little more than I have studied, and that question's out of my part. Good gentle one, give me modest assurance if you be the lady of the house, that I may proceed in my speech.

OLIVIA Are you a comedian?

VIOLA No, my profound heart; and yet, by the very fangs of malice, I swear I am not that I play. Are you the lady of the house?

OLIVIA If I do not usurp myself, I am.

VIOLA Most certain, if you are she, you do usurp yourself; for what is yours to bestow is not yours to reserve. But this is from my commiss[...] speech in your praise, and then[...] my message.

OLIVIA Come to what is importa[...] the praise.

VIOLA Alas, I took great pains to[...] poetical.

OLIVIA It is the more like to be feig[...] keep it in. I heard you were saucy a[...] allowed your approach rather to won[...] to hear you. If you be not mad, begon[...] reason, be brief. 'Tis not that time of mo[...] make one in so skipping a dialogue.

MARIA Will you hoist sail, sir? Here lies yo[...]

VIOLA No, good swabber, I am to hull h[...] longer.—Some mollification for your gi[...] lady. Tell me your mind; I am a messenger.

OLIVIA Sure you have some hideous matter to[...] when the courtesy of it is so fearful. Speak you[...]

VIOLA It alone concerns your ear. I bring no over[...] war, no taxation of homage. I hold the olive [...] hand; my words are as full of peace as matter.

OLIVIA Yet you began rudely. What are you? W[...] would you?

VIOLA The rudeness that hath appeared in me have I learned from my entertainment. What I am and what I would are as secret as maidenhead—to your ears, divinity; to any other's, profanation.

OLIVIA [*to the others*] Give us the place here alone. We will hear this divinity. [*Exeunt Maria and attendants.*] Now, sir, what is your text?

VIOLA Most sweet lady—

OLIVIA A comfortable doctrine, and much may be said of it. Where lies your text?

VIOLA In Orsino's bosom.

OLIVIA In his bosom? In what chapter of his bosom?

VIOLA To answer by the method, in the first of his heart.

OLIVIA Oh, I have read it. It is heresy. Have you no more to say?

VIOLA Good madam, let me see your face.

OLIVIA Have you any commission from your lord to negotiate with my face? You are now out of your text. But we will draw the curtain and show you the

145 sheriff's post post before the sheriff's door to mark a residence of authority, often elaborately carved and decorated. **supporter** prop **154 squash** unripe pea pod. **peascod** ripe pea pod. (The image suggests that the boy's testicles have not yet dropped.) **155 codling** unripe apple **155–6 in standing water** at the turn of the tide **157 well-favored** good-looking. **shrewishly** sharply. **170 con** memorize **171 comptible** susceptible, sensitive **172 least sinister** slightest discourteous **176 modest** reasonable **178 comedian** actor. **179 my profound heart** my most wise lady; or, in all sincerity **179–80 by . . . I play** (Viola hints at her true identity, which malice itself might not detect.) **182 do . . . myself** am not an impostor **183–4 usurp yourself** i.e., misappropriate yourself, by withholding yourself from love and marriage

185 from outside of **188 forgive you** excuse you from repeating **195 not mad** i.e., not altogether mad **196 reason** sanity. **moon** (The moon was thought to affect lunatics according to its changing phases.) **197 make one** take part **199 swabber** one in charge of washing the decks. (A nautical retort to *hoist sail.*) **hull** lie with sails furled **200 Some . . . for** i.e., Please mollify, pacify. **giant** i.e., the diminutive Maria who, like many giants in medieval romances, is guarding the lady **203 courtesy** i.e., complimentary, "poetical" introduction. (Or Olivia may refer to Cesario's importunate manner at her gate, as reported by Malvolio.) **office** commission, business. **204 overture** declaration. (Literally, opening.) **205 taxation of homage** demand for tribute. **olive** olive-branch (signifying peace) **207 Yet . . . rudely** i.e., Yet you were saucy at my gates. **210 entertainment** reception. **211 maidenhead** virginity **212 divinity** sacred discourse **217 comfortable** comforting **221 To . . . method** i.e., To continue the metaphor of delivering a sermon, begun with *divinity* and *what is your text* and continued in *doctrine, heresy,* etc. **227 out of** straying from

picture. [*Unveiling.*] Look you, sir, such a one I was this present. Is't not well done?

VIOLA Excellently done, if God did all.

OLIVIA 'Tis in grain, sir; 'twill endure wind and weather.

VIOLA
'Tis beauty truly blent, whose red and white
Nature's own sweet and cunning hand laid on.
Lady, you are the cruel'st she alive
If you will lead these graces to the grave
And leave the world no copy.

OLIVIA Oh, sir, I will not be so hardhearted. I will give out divers schedules of my beauty. It shall be inventoried, and every particle and utensil labeled to my will: as, item, two lips, indifferent red; item, two gray eyes, with lids to them; item, one neck, one chin, and so forth. Were you sent hither to praise me?

VIOLA
I see you what you are: you are too proud.
But, if you were the devil, you are fair.
My lord and master loves you. Oh, such love
Could be but recompensed, though you were
 crowned
The nonpareil of beauty!

OLIVIA How does he love me?

VIOLA
With adorations, fertile tears,
With groans that thunder love, with sighs of fire.

OLIVIA
Your lord does know my mind; I cannot love him.
Yet I suppose him virtuous, know him noble,
Of great estate, of fresh and stainless youth,
In voices well divulged, free, learned, and valiant,
And in dimension and the shape of nature
A gracious person. But yet I cannot love him.
He might have took his answer long ago.

VIOLA
If I did love you in my master's flame,
With such a suff'ring, such a deadly life,
In your denial I would find no sense;
I would not understand it.

OLIVIA Why, what would you?

VIOLA
Make me a willow cabin at your gate
And call upon my soul within the house;
Write loyal cantons of contemnèd love
And sing them loud even in the dead of night;
Hallow your name to the reverberate hills,
And make the babbling gossip of the air
Cry out "Olivia!" Oh, you should not rest
Between the elements of air and earth
But you should pity me!

OLIVIA You might do much.
What is your parentage?

VIOLA
Above my fortunes, yet my state is well:
I am a gentleman.

OLIVIA Get you to your lord.
I cannot love him. Let him send no more—
Unless, perchance, you come to me again
To tell me how he takes it. Fare you well.
I thank you for your pains. Spend this for me.
[*She offers a purse.*]

VIOLA
I am no fee'd post, lady. Keep your purse.
My master, not myself, lacks recompense.
Love make his heart of flint that you shall love,
And let your fervor, like my master's, be
Placed in contempt! Farewell, fair cruelty. *Exit.*

OLIVIA "What is your parentage?"
"Above my fortunes, yet my state is well:
I am a gentleman." I'll be sworn thou art!
Thy tongue, thy face, thy limbs, actions, and spirit
Do give thee fivefold blazon. Not too fast! Soft, soft!
Unless the master were the man. How now?
Even so quickly may one catch the plague?
Methinks I feel this youth's perfections
With an invisible and subtle stealth
To creep in at mine eyes. Well, let it be.—
What ho, Malvolio!

Enter Malvolio.

MALVOLIO Here, madam, at your service.

OLIVIA
Run after that same peevish messenger,
The County's man. He left this ring behind him,
[*giving a ring*]
Would I or not. Tell him I'll none of it.
Desire him not to flatter with his lord,
Nor hold him up with hopes; I am not for him.
If that the youth will come this way tomorrow,
I'll give him reasons for't. Hie thee, Malvolio.

MALVOLIO Madam, I will. *Exit.*

OLIVIA
I do I know not what, and fear to find
Mine eye too great a flatterer for my mind.

229–30 such . . . present this is a recent portrait of me. (Since it was customary to hang curtains in front of pictures, Olivia in unveiling speaks as if she were displaying a picture of herself.) **232 in grain** fast dyed **234 blent** blended **235 cunning** skillful **238 copy** i.e., a child. (But Olivia uses the word to mean "transcript.") **240 schedules** inventories **241 utensil** article, item. **labeled** added as a codicil **242 indifferent** somewhat **244 praise** (With pun on "appraise.") **246 if** even if **247–9 Oh . . . beauty!** i.e., Even if you were the most beautiful woman alive, that beauty could do no more than repay my master's love for you! **250 fertile** copious **255 In . . . divulged** well spoken of. **free** generous **256 in . . . nature** in his physical form **257 gracious** graceful, attractive **259 flame** passion **260 deadly** deathlike **263 willow cabin** shelter, hut. (Willow was a symbol of unrequited love.) **264 my soul** i.e., Olivia **265 cantons** songs. **contemnèd** rejected

267 Hallow (1) halloo (2) bless **268 babbling . . . air** echo **270 Between . . . air** i.e., anywhere **273 state** social standing **279 fee'd post** messenger to be tipped **281 Love . . . love** May Cupid make the heart of the man you love as hard as flint **288 blazon** heraldic description. **Soft** Wait a minute **289 Unless . . . man** i.e., Unless Cesario and Orsino changed places. **296 County's** Count's, i.e., Duke's **297 Would I or not** whether I wanted it or not. **298 flatter with** encourage **301 Hie thee** Hasten **304 Mine . . . mind** i.e., that my eyes (through which love enters the soul) have deceived my reason.

Fate, show thy force. Ourselves we do not owe.
What is decreed must be; and be this so. [*Exit.*]

✤

2.1

Enter Antonio and Sebastian.

ANTONIO Will you stay no longer? Nor will you not that I go with you?

SEBASTIAN By your patience, no. My stars shine darkly over me. The malignancy of my fate might perhaps distemper yours; therefore I shall crave of you your leave that I may bear my evils alone. It were a bad recompense for your love to lay any of them on you.

ANTONIO Let me yet know of you whither you are bound.

SEBASTIAN No, sooth, sir; my determinate voyage is mere extravagancy. But I perceive in you so excellent a touch of modesty that you will not extort from me what I am willing to keep in; therefore it charges me in manners the rather to express myself. You must know of me then, Antonio, my name is Sebastian, which I called Roderigo. My father was that Sebastian of Messaline whom I know you have heard of. He left behind him myself and a sister, both born in an hour. If the heavens had been pleased, would we had so ended! But you, sir, altered that, for some hour before you took me from the breach of the sea was my sister drowned.

ANTONIO Alas the day!

SEBASTIAN A lady, sir, though it was said she much resembled me, was yet of many accounted beautiful. But though I could not with such estimable wonder overfar believe that, yet thus far I will boldly publish her: she bore a mind that envy could not but call fair. She is drowned already, sir, with salt water, though I seem to drown her remembrance again with more.

ANTONIO Pardon me, sir, your bad entertainment.

SEBASTIAN O good Antonio, forgive me your trouble.

ANTONIO If you will not murder me for my love, let me be your servant.

SEBASTIAN If you will not undo what you have done, that is, kill him whom you have recovered, desire it not. Fare ye well at once. My bosom is full of kindness, and I am yet so near the manners of my mother that upon the least occasion more mine eyes will tell tales of me. I am bound to the Count Orsino's court. Farewell. *Exit.*

ANTONIO
The gentleness of all the gods go with thee!
I have many enemies in Orsino's court,
Else would I very shortly see thee there.
But come what may, I do adore thee so
That danger shall seem sport, and I will go. *Exit.*

✤

2.2

Enter Viola and Malvolio, at several doors.

MALVOLIO Were not you even now with the Countess Olivia?

VIOLA Even now, sir. On a moderate pace I have since arrived but hither.

MALVOLIO She returns this ring to you, sir. You might have saved me my pains, to have taken it away yourself. She adds, moreover, that you should put your lord into a desperate assurance she will none of him. And one thing more: that you be never so hardy to come again in his affairs, unless it be to report your lord's taking of this. Receive it so.

VIOLA She took the ring of me. I'll none of it.

MALVOLIO Come, sir, you peevishly threw it to her, and her will is it should be so returned. [*He throws down the ring.*] If it be worth stooping for, there it lies, in your eye; if not, be it his that finds it. *Exit.*

VIOLA [*picking up the ring*]
I left no ring with her. What means this lady?
Fortune forbid my outside have not charmed her!
She made good view of me, indeed so much
That sure methought her eyes had lost her tongue,
For she did speak in starts, distractedly.
She loves me, sure! The cunning of her passion
Invites me in this churlish messenger.
None of my lord's ring? Why, he sent her none.
I am the man. If it be so—as 'tis—
Poor lady, she were better love a dream.
Disguise, I see, thou art a wickedness
Wherein the pregnant enemy does much.
How easy is it for the proper false
In women's waxen hearts to set their forms!
Alas, our frailty is the cause, not we,
For such as we are made of, such we be.

305 owe own, control.
2.1 Location: Somewhere in Illyria.
1 Nor will you not Do you not wish **3 patience** leave **4 malignancy** malevolence (of the stars; also in a medical sense) **5 distemper** infect **10 sooth** truly. **determinate** intended, determined upon **11 extravagancy** aimless wandering. **13 am willing . . . in** wish to keep secret **13–14 it . . . manners** it is incumbent upon me in all courtesy **14 express** reveal **17 Messaline** possibly Messina, or, more likely, Massila (the modern Marseilles). In Plautus's *Menaechmi,* Massilians and Illyrians are mentioned together. **18 in an hour** in the same hour. **20 some hour** about an hour **21 breach of the sea** surf **26 estimable wonder** admiring judgment **27 publish** proclaim **28 envy** even malice **31 Pardon . . . entertainment** i.e., I'm sorry I cannot offer you better hospitality and comfort. **32 your trouble** the trouble I put you to. **33 murder . . . love** i.e., cause me to die from lacking your love **36 recovered** rescued, restored

38 kindness emotion, affection **38–9 manners of my mother** i.e., womanly inclination to weep
2.2 Location: Near Olivia's house.
0.1 *several* different **6 to have taken** by taking **8 desperate** without hope **9–10 so hardy to come** so bold as to come **12 She . . . it** (Viola tells a quick and friendly lie to shield Olivia.) **16 in your eye** in plain sight **18 charmed** enchanted **20 her eyes . . . tongue** i.e., the sight of me had deprived her of speech **23 in** in the person of **25 the man** the man of her choice. **28 the pregnant enemy** the resourceful enemy (either Satan or Cupid) **29 the proper false** deceptively handsome men **30 waxen** i.e., malleable, impressionable. **set their forms** stamp their images (as of a seal). **31–2 our . . . be** i.e., the fault lies not in us as individuals, but in the frailty of female nature.

How will this fadge? My master loves her dearly,
And I, poor monster, fond as much on him;
And she, mistaken, seems to dote on me.
What will become of this? As I am man,
My state is desperate for my master's love;
As I am woman—now, alas the day!—
What thriftless sighs shall poor Olivia breathe!
O Time, thou must untangle this, not I;
It is too hard a knot for me t'untie. [*Exit.*]

✤

2.3

Enter Sir Toby and Sir Andrew.

SIR TOBY Approach, Sir Andrew. Not to be abed after midnight is to be up betimes; and *diluculo surgere,* thou know'st—

SIR ANDREW Nay, by my troth, I know not, but I know to be up late is to be up late.

SIR TOBY A false conclusion. I hate it as an unfilled can. To be up after midnight and to go to bed then, is early; so that to go to bed after midnight is to go to bed betimes. Does not our lives consist of the four elements?

SIR ANDREW Faith, so they say, but I think it rather consists of eating and drinking.

SIR TOBY Thou'rt a scholar; let us therefore eat and drink.—Marian, I say, a stoup of wine!

Enter Clown [*Feste*].

SIR ANDREW Here comes the Fool, i'faith.

FESTE How now, my hearts! Did you never see the picture of "we three"?

SIR TOBY Welcome, ass. Now let's have a catch.

SIR ANDREW By my troth, the Fool has an excellent breast. I had rather than forty shillings I had such a leg, and so sweet a breath to sing, as the Fool has. In sooth, thou wast in very gracious fooling last night, when thou spok'st of Pigrogromitus, of the Vapians passing the equinoctial of Queubus. 'Twas very good, i'faith. I sent thee sixpence for thy leman. Hadst it?

FESTE I did impeticos thy gratillity; for Malvolio's nose is no whipstock. My lady has a white hand, and the Myrmidons are no bottle-ale houses.

SIR ANDREW Excellent! Why, this is the best fooling, when all is done. Now, a song.

SIR TOBY Come on, there is sixpence for you. [*He gives money.*] Let's have a song.

SIR ANDREW There's a testril of me too. [*He gives money.*] If one knight give a—

FESTE Would you have a love song, or a song of good life?

SIR TOBY A love song, a love song.

SIR ANDREW Ay, ay, I care not for good life.

FESTE (*sings*)

O mistress mine, where are you roaming?
Oh, stay and hear, your true love 's coming,
That can sing both high and low.
Trip no further, pretty sweeting;
Journeys end in lovers' meeting,
Every wise man's son doth know.

SIR ANDREW Excellent good, i'faith.

SIR TOBY Good, good.

FESTE [*sings*]

What is love? 'Tis not hereafter;
Present mirth hath present laughter;
What's to come is still unsure.
In delay there lies no plenty.
Then come kiss me, sweet and twenty;
Youth's a stuff will not endure.

SIR ANDREW A mellifluous voice, as I am true knight.

SIR TOBY A contagious breath.

SIR ANDREW Very sweet and contagious, i'faith.

SIR TOBY To hear by the nose, it is dulcet in contagion. But shall we make the welkin dance indeed? Shall we rouse the night owl in a catch that will draw three souls out of one weaver? Shall we do that?

SIR ANDREW An you love me, let's do't. I am dog at a catch.

FESTE By'r Lady, sir, and some dogs will catch well.

SIR ANDREW Most certain. Let our catch be "Thou knave."

FESTE "Hold thy peace, thou knave," knight? I shall be constrained in't to call thee knave, knight.

SIR ANDREW 'Tis not the first time I have constrained one to call me knave. Begin, Fool. It begins, "Hold thy peace."

33 fadge turn out **34 monster** i.e., being both man and woman. **fond** dote **39 thriftless** unprofitable
2.3. Location: Olivia's house.
2 betimes early. ***diluculo surgere*** (***saluberrimum est***) to rise early is most healthful. (A sentence from Lilly's *Latin Grammar.*) **6 can** tankard. **9-10 four elements** i.e., fire, air, water, and earth, the elements that were thought to make up all matter. **14 stoup** drinking vessel **17 picture of "we three"** picture of two fools or asses inscribed "we three," the spectator being the third. **18 catch** round. **20 breast** voice. **21 leg** (for dancing) **23-4 Pigrogromitus . . . Queubus** (Feste's mock erudition.) **25 leman** sweetheart.
26 impeticos thy gratillity (Suggests "impetticoat, or pocket up, thy gratuity.") **27 is no whipstock** is no whip-handle. (More nonsense, but perhaps suggesting that Malvolio's nose for smelling out faults does not give him the right to punish, so that he need not be feared.) **has a white hand** i.e., is lady-like. (But Feste's speech may be mere nonsense.) **28 Myrmidons** followers of Achilles. **bottle-ale houses** (Used contemptuously of taverns because they sold low-class drink.)

33 testril tester, a coin worth sixpence **35-6 good life** virtuous living. (Or perhaps Feste means simply "life's pleasures," but is misunderstood by Sir Andrew to mean "virtuous living.") **49 still** always **51 sweet and twenty** i.e., sweet and twenty times sweet, or twenty years old **54 contagious** infectiously delightful **56 To . . . contagion** i.e., If we were to describe hearing in olfactory terms, we could say it is sweet in stench. **57 make . . . dance** i.e., drink till the sky seems to turn around **58–9 draw three souls** (Refers to the threefold nature of the soul—vegetal, sensible, and intellectual—or to the three singers of the three-part catch; or, just a comic exaggeration.)
59 weaver (Weavers were often associated with psalm singing.)
60 dog at very clever at. (But Feste uses the word literally.) **61 catch** round. (But Feste uses it to mean "seize.") **62 By 'r Lady** (An oath, originally, "by the Virgin Mary.") **63–4 "Thou knave"** (This popular round is arranged so that the three singers repeatedly accost one another with "Thou knave.") **65–6 "Hold . . . knight** ("Knight and knave" is a common antithesis, like "rich and poor.")

FESTE I shall never begin if I hold my peace.
SIR ANDREW Good, i'faith. Come, begin. *Catch sung.*

Enter Maria.

MARIA What a caterwauling do you keep here! If my 72
lady have not called up her steward Malvolio and bid
him turn you out of doors, never trust me.
SIR TOBY My lady's a Cataian, we are politicians, 75
Malvolio's a Peg-o'-Ramsey, and [*he sings*] "Three 76
merry men be we." Am not I consanguineous? Am I 77
not of her blood? Tillyvally! Lady! [*He sings.*] "There 78
dwelt a man in Babylon, lady, lady." 79
FESTE Beshrew me, the knight's in admirable fooling. 80
SIR ANDREW Ay, he does well enough if he be disposed,
and so do I too. He does it with a better grace,
but I do it more natural. 83
SIR TOBY [*sings*]
"O' the twelfth day of December"— 84
MARIA For the love o' God, peace!

Enter Malvolio.

MALVOLIO My masters, are you mad? Or what are you?
Have you no wit, manners, nor honesty but to gabble 87
like tinkers at this time of night? Do ye make an alehouse of my lady's house, that ye squeak out your coz- 89
iers' catches without any mitigation or remorse of 90
voice? Is there no respect of place, persons, nor time in
you?
SIR TOBY We did keep time, sir, in our catches. Sneck 93
up! 94
MALVOLIO Sir Toby, I must be round with you. My 95
lady bade me tell you that though she harbors you as
her kinsman, she's nothing allied to your disorders. If
you can separate yourself and your misdemeanors,
you are welcome to the house; if not, an it would
please you to take leave of her, she is very willing to
bid you farewell.
SIR TOBY [*sings*]
"Farewell, dear heart, since I must needs be gone." 102
MARIA Nay, good Sir Toby.
FESTE [*sings*]
"His eyes do show his days are almost done."
MALVOLIO Is't even so?
SIR TOBY [*sings*]
"But I will never die."
FESTE
"Sir Toby, there you lie."
MALVOLIO This is much credit to you.
SIR TOBY [*sings*]
"Shall I bid him go?"
FESTE [*sings*]
"What an if you do?"
SIR TOBY [*sings*]
"Shall I bid him go, and spare not?"
FESTE [*sings*]
"Oh, no, no, no, no, you dare not."
SIR TOBY Out o' tune, sir? Ye lie. Art any more than a 113
steward? Dost thou think, because thou art virtuous,
there shall be no more cakes and ale?
FESTE Yes, by Saint Anne, and ginger shall be hot i'th' 116
mouth, too.
SIR TOBY Thou'rt i'the right.—Go, sir, rub your chain 118
with crumbs.—A stoup of wine, Maria! 119
MALVOLIO Mistress Mary, if you prized my lady's
favor at anything more than contempt, you would not
give means for this uncivil rule. She shall know of it, 122
by this hand. *Exit.*
MARIA Go shake your ears. 124
SIR ANDREW 'Twere as good a deed as to drink when a
man's a-hungry to challenge him the field and then to 126
break promise with him and make a fool of him.
SIR TOBY Do't, knight. I'll write thee a challenge, or I'll
deliver thy indignation to him by word of mouth.
MARIA Sweet Sir Toby, be patient for tonight. Since the
youth of the Count's was today with my lady, she is
much out of quiet. For Monsieur Malvolio, let me 132
alone with him. If I do not gull him into a nayword 133
and make him a common recreation, do not think I 134
have wit enough to lie straight in my bed. I know I can
do it.
SIR TOBY Possess us, possess us. Tell us something of 137
him.
MARIA Marry, sir, sometimes he is a kind of puritan. 139
SIR ANDREW Oh, if I thought that, I'd beat him like a
dog.
SIR TOBY What, for being a puritan? Thy exquisite
reason, dear knight?
SIR ANDREW I have no exquisite reason for't, but I
have reason good enough.

72 keep keep up **75 Cataian** Cathayan, i.e., Chinese, a trickster or inscrutable; or, just nonsense. **politicians** schemers, intriguers **76 Peg-o'-Ramsey** character in a popular song. (Used here contemptuously.) **76–7 "Three . . . we"** (A snatch of an old song.) **77 consanguineous** i.e., a blood relative of Olivia. **78 Tillyvally!** Nonsense, fiddle-faddle! **78–9 "There . . . lady"** (The first line of a ballad, "The Constancy of Susanna," together with the refrain, "Lady, lady.") **80 Beshrew** i.e., The devil take. (A mild curse.) **83 natural** naturally. (But unconsciously suggesting idiocy.) **84 "O' . . . December"** (Possibly part of a ballad about the Battle of Musselburgh Field, or Toby's error for the "twelfth day of Christmas," i.e., Twelfth Night.) **87 wit** common sense. **honesty** decency **89–90 coziers'** cobblers' **90 mitigation or remorse** i.e., considerate lowering **93–4 Sneck up!** Go hang! **95 round** blunt **102 "Farewell . . . gone"** (From the ballad "Corydon's Farewell to Phyllis.")

113 Out o' tune (Perhaps a quibbling reply—"We did too keep time in our tune"—to Malvolio's accusation of having no respect for place or time, line 91. Often emended to *Out o' time,* easily misread in secretary hand.) **116 Saint Anne** mother of the Virgin Mary. (Her cult was derided in the Reformation, much as Puritan reformers also derided the tradition of *cakes and ale* at church feasts.) **ginger** (Commonly used to spice ale.) **118–19 rub . . . crumbs** i.e., scour or polish your steward's chain; attend to your own business and remember your station. **122 give means** i.e., supply drink. **rule** conduct. **124 your ears** i.e., your ass's ears. **126 the field** i.e., to a duel **132 For** As for **132–3 let . . . him** leave him to me. **133 gull** trick. **nayword** byword. (His name will be synonymous with "dupe.") **134 recreation** sport **137 Possess** Inform **139 puritan** (Maria's point is that Malvolio is sometimes a *kind* of puritan, insofar as he is precise about moral conduct and censorious of others for immoral conduct, but that he is nothing consistently except a time-server. He is not, then, simply a satirical type of the Puritan sect. The extent of the resemblance is left unstated.)

MARIA The devil a puritan that he is, or anything constantly, but a time-pleaser; an affectioned ass, that cons state without book and utters it by great swaths; the best persuaded of himself, so crammed, as he thinks, with excellencies, that it is his grounds of faith that all that look on him love him; and on that vice in him will my revenge find notable cause to work.

SIR TOBY What wilt thou do?

MARIA I will drop in his way some obscure epistles of love, wherein by the color of his beard, the shape of his leg, the manner of his gait, the expressure of his eye, forehead, and complexion, he shall find himself most feelingly personated. I can write very like my lady your niece; on a forgotten matter we can hardly make distinction of our hands.

SIR TOBY Excellent! I smell a device.

SIR ANDREW I have't in my nose too.

SIR TOBY He shall think, by the letters that thou wilt drop, that they come from my niece, and that she's in love with him.

MARIA My purpose is indeed a horse of that color.

SIR ANDREW And your horse now would make him an ass.

MARIA Ass, I doubt not.

SIR ANDREW Oh, 'twill be admirable!

MARIA Sport royal, I warrant you. I know my physic will work with him. I will plant you two, and let the Fool make a third, where he shall find the letter. Observe his construction of it. For this night, to bed, and dream on the event. Farewell. *Exit.*

SIR TOBY Good night, Penthesilea.

SIR ANDREW Before me, she's a good wench.

SIR TOBY She's a beagle true-bred and one that adores me. What o'that?

SIR ANDREW I was adored once, too.

SIR TOBY Let's to bed, knight. Thou hadst need send for more money.

SIR ANDREW If I cannot recover your niece, I am a foul way out.

SIR TOBY Send for money, knight. If thou hast her not i'th' end, call me cut.

SIR ANDREW If I do not, never trust me, take it how you will.

SIR TOBY Come, come, I'll go burn some sack. 'Tis too late to go to bed now. Come, knight; come, knight. *Exeunt.*

2.4

Enter Duke [Orsino], Viola, Curio, and others.

ORSINO
Give me some music. Now, good morrow, friends.
Now, good Cesario, but that piece of song,
That old and antique song we heard last night.
Methought it did relieve my passion much,
More than light airs and recollected terms
Of these most brisk and giddy-pacèd times.
Come, but one verse.

CURIO He is not here, so please Your Lordship, that should sing it.

ORSINO Who was it?

CURIO Feste the jester, my lord, a fool that the Lady Olivia's father took much delight in. He is about the house.

ORSINO
Seek him out, and play the tune the while.
[Exit Curio.] Music plays.
[To Viola] Come hither, boy. If ever thou shalt love,
In the sweet pangs of it remember me;
For such as I am, all true lovers are,
Unstaid and skittish in all motions else
Save in the constant image of the creature
That is beloved. How dost thou like this tune?

VIOLA
It gives a very echo to the seat
Where Love is throned.

ORSINO Thou dost speak masterly.
My life upon't, young though thou art, thine eye
Hath stayed upon some favor that it loves.
Hath it not, boy?

VIOLA A little, by your favor.

ORSINO
What kind of woman is't?

VIOLA Of your complexion.

ORSINO
She is not worth thee, then. What years, i'faith?

VIOLA About your years, my lord.

ORSINO
Too old, by heaven. Let still the woman take
An elder than herself. So wears she to him;
So sways she level in her husband's heart.
For, boy, however we do praise ourselves,

146–7 constantly consistently **147 time-pleaser** time-server, sycophant. **affectioned** affected **147–8 cons . . . book** learns by heart the phrases and mannerisms of the great **148 by great swaths** in great sweeps, like rows of mown grain **148–9 the best persuaded** having the best opinion **150 grounds of faith** creed, belief
154 some obscure epistles an ambigiously worded letter
156 expressure expression **158 personated** represented. **159 on a forgotten matter** when we've forgotten which of us wrote something or what it was about **160 hands** handwriting. **169 Ass, I** (With a pun on "as I.") **171 physic** medicine **174 construction** interpretation **175 event** outcome. **176 Penthesilea** Queen of the Amazons. (Another ironical allusion to Maria's diminutive stature.)
177 Before me i.e., On my soul. (A mild oath.) **178 beagle** a small, intelligent hunting dog **183 recover** win **183–4 foul way out** i.e., miserably out of pocket. (Literally, out of my way and in the mire.)
186 cut A proverbial term of abuse: literally, a horse with a docked tail; also, a gelding, or the female genital organ.

189 burn some sack warm some Spanish wine. **190.1 *Exeunt*** (Feste may have left earlier; he says nothing after line 117 and is perhaps referred to without his being present at 172–3.)
2.4 Location: Orsino's court.
1 morrow morning **2 but** i.e., I ask only **3 antique** old, quaint, fantastic **5 recollected terms** studied and artificial expressions **18 all motions else** all other thoughts and emotions **21 the seat** i.e., the heart **24 stayed . . . favor** rested upon some face **25 by your favor** if you please. (But also hinting at "like you in feature.") **29 still** always **30 wears she** she adapts herself **31 sways she level** she keeps a perfect equipoise and steady affection

Our fancies are more giddy and unfirm,
More longing, wavering, sooner lost and worn,
Than women's are.

VIOLA I think it well, my lord.

ORSINO
Then let thy love be younger than thyself,
Or thy affection cannot hold the bent;
For women are as roses, whose fair flower
Being once displayed, doth fall that very hour.

VIOLA
And so they are. Alas that they are so,
To die even when they to perfection grow!

Enter Curio and Clown [*Feste*].

ORSINO
Oh, fellow, come, the song we had last night.
Mark it, Cesario, it is old and plain;
The spinsters and the knitters in the sun,
And the free maids that weave their thread with
bones,
Do use to chant it. It is silly sooth,
And dallies with the innocence of love,
Like the old age.

FESTE Are you ready, sir?

ORSINO Ay, prithee, sing. *Music.*

The Song.

FESTE [*sings*]
Come away, come away, death,
And in sad cypress let me be laid.
Fly away, fly away, breath;
I am slain by a fair cruel maid.
My shroud of white, stuck all with yew,
Oh, prepare it!
My part of death, no one so true
Did share it.

Not a flower, not a flower sweet
On my black coffin let there be strown;
Not a friend, not a friend greet
My poor corpse, where my bones shall be
thrown.
A thousand thousand sighs to save,
Lay me, oh, where
Sad true lover never find my grave,
To weep there!

ORSINO [*offering money*] There's for thy pains.

FESTE No pains, sir. I take pleasure in singing, sir.

ORSINO I'll pay thy pleasure then.

FESTE Truly, sir, and pleasure will be paid, one time or another.

ORSINO Give me now leave to leave thee.

FESTE Now, the melancholy god protect thee, and the tailor make thy doublet of changeable taffeta, for thy mind is a very opal. I would have men of such constancy put to sea, that their business might be everything and their intent everywhere, for that's it that always makes a good voyage of nothing. Farewell. *Exit.*

ORSINO
Let all the rest give place.
[*Curio and attendants withdraw.*]
Once more, Cesario,
Get thee to yond same sovereign cruelty.
Tell her, my love, more noble than the world,
Prizes not quantity of dirty lands;
The parts that fortune hath bestowed upon her,
Tell her, I hold as giddily as fortune;
But 'tis that miracle and queen of gems
That nature pranks her in attracts my soul.

VIOLA But if she cannot love you, sir?

ORSINO
I cannot be so answered.

VIOLA Sooth, but you must.
Say that some lady—as perhaps there is—
Hath for your love as great a pang of heart
As you have for Olivia. You cannot love her;
You tell her so. Must she not then be answered?

ORSINO There is no woman's sides
Can bide the beating of so strong a passion
As love doth give my heart; no woman's heart
So big, to hold so much. They lack retention.
Alas, their love may be called appetite,
No motion of the liver, but the palate,
That suffer surfeit, cloyment, and revolt;
But mine is all as hungry as the sea,
And can digest as much. Make no compare
Between that love a woman can bear me
And that I owe Olivia.

VIOLA Ay, but I know—

ORSINO What dost thou know?

34 worn exhausted. (Sometimes emended to *won.*) **37 hold the bent** hold steady, keep the intensity (like the tension of a bow) **39 displayed** full blown **41 even when** just as **44 spinsters** spinners **45 free** carefree, innocent. **bones** bobbins on which bone-lace was made **46 Do use** are accustomed. **silly sooth** simple truth **47 dallies with** dwells lovingly on, sports with **48 Like . . . age** as in the good old times. **51 Come away** Come hither **52 cypress** i.e., a coffin of cypress wood, or bier strewn with sprigs of cypress **55 yew** yew sprigs. (Emblematic of mourning, like cypress.) **57–8 My . . . it** No one died for love so true to love as I. **60 strown** strewn

70–1 pleasure . . . another sooner or later one must pay for indulgence. **72 leave to leave** permission to take leave of, dismiss **73 the melancholy god** i.e., Saturn, whose planet was thought to control the melancholy temperament **74 doublet** close-fitting jacket. **changeable taffeta** a silk so woven of various-colored threads that its color shifts with changing perspective **75 opal** an iridescent precious stone that changes color when seen from various angles or in different lights. **76–7 that . . . everywhere** i.e., so that in the changeableness of the sea their inconstancy could always be exercised **77–8 for . . . nothing** because that's the quality that is satisfied with an aimless voyage. **79 give place** withdraw. **83 parts** attributes such as wealth or rank **84 I . . . fortune** I esteem as carelessly as I do fortune, that fickle goddess **85 that miracle . . . gems** i.e., her beauty **86 pranks** adorns. **attracts** that attracts **88 Sooth** In truth **92 be answered** be satisfied with your answer. **94 bide** withstand **96 to hold** as to contain. **retention** constancy, the power of retaining. **98 motion** impulse. **liver . . . palate** (Real love is a passion of the liver, whereas fancy, light love, is born in the eye and nourished in the palate.) **99 cloyment** satiety. **revolt** revulsion **101 compare** comparison **103 owe** have for

VIOLA
Too well what love women to men may owe.
In faith, they are as true of heart as we.
My father had a daughter loved a man
As it might be, perhaps, were I a woman,
I should Your Lordship.

ORSINO
And what's her history?

VIOLA
A blank, my lord. She never told her love,
But let concealment, like a worm i'th' bud,
Feed on her damask cheek. She pined in thought,
And with a green and yellow melancholy;
She sat like Patience on a monument,
Smiling at grief. Was not this love indeed?
We men may say more, swear more, but indeed
Our shows are more than will; for still we prove
Much in our vows, but little in our love.

ORSINO
But died thy sister of her love, my boy?

VIOLA
I am all the daughters of my father's house,
And all the brothers too—and yet I know not.
Sir, shall I to this lady?

ORSINO
Ay, that's the theme.
To her in haste; give her this jewel. [*He gives a jewel.*]
Say
My love can give no place, bide no denay.

Exeunt [*separately*].

✤

2.5

Enter Sir Toby, Sir Andrew, and Fabian.

SIR TOBY Come thy ways, Signor Fabian.

FABIAN Nay, I'll come. If I lose a scruple of this sport, let me be boiled to death with melancholy.

SIR TOBY Wouldst thou not be glad to have the niggardly rascally sheep-biter come by some notable shame?

FABIAN I would exult, man. You know he brought me out o'favor with my lady about a bearbaiting here.

SIR TOBY To anger him we'll have the bear again, and we will fool him black and blue. Shall we not, Sir Andrew?

SIR ANDREW An we do not, it is pity of our lives.

Enter Maria [*with a letter*].

SIR TOBY Here comes the little villain.—How now, my metal of India!

MARIA Get ye all three into the boxtree. Malvolio's coming down this walk. He has been yonder i'the sun practicing behavior to his own shadow this half hour. Observe him, for the love of mockery, for I know this letter will make a contemplative idiot of him. Close, in the name of jesting! [*The others hide.*] Lie thou there [*throwing down a letter*]; for here comes the trout that must be caught with tickling. *Exit.*

Enter Malvolio.

MALVOLIO 'Tis but fortune; all is fortune. Maria once told me she did affect me; and I have heard herself come thus near, that should she fancy, it should be one of my complexion. Besides, she uses me with a more exalted respect than anyone else that follows her. What should I think on't?

SIR TOBY Here's an overweening rogue!

FABIAN Oh, peace! Contemplation makes a rare turkeycock of him. How he jets under his advanced plumes!

SIR ANDREW 'Slight, I could so beat the rogue!

SIR TOBY Peace, I say.

MALVOLIO To be Count Malvolio.

SIR TOBY Ah, rogue!

SIR ANDREW Pistol him, pistol him.

SIR TOBY Peace, peace!

MALVOLIO There is example for't. The lady of the Strachy married the yeoman of the wardrobe.

SIR ANDREW Fie on him, Jezebel!

FABIAN Oh, peace! Now he's deeply in. Look how imagination blows him.

MALVOLIO Having been three months married to her, sitting in my state—

SIR TOBY Oh, for a stone-bow, to hit him in the eye!

MALVOLIO Calling my officers about me, in my branched velvet gown; having come from a daybed, where I have left Olivia sleeping—

SIR TOBY Fire and brimstone!

FABIAN Oh, peace, peace!

MALVOLIO And then to have the humor of state; and after a demure travel of regard, telling them I know my place as I would they should do theirs, to ask for my kinsman Toby.

SIR TOBY Bolts and shackles!

FABIAN Oh, peace, peace, peace! Now, now.

112 damask pink and white like the damask rose **113 green and yellow** pale and sallow **114 on a monument** carved in statuary on a tomb **117 shows** displays of passion. **more than will** greater than our determination. **still** always **124 can . . . denay** cannot yield or endure denial.

2.5 Location: Olivia's garden.

1 Come thy ways Come along **2 a scruple** the least bit **3 boiled** (With a pun on "biled"; black bile was the "humor" of melancholy and was thought to be a cold humor.) **5 sheep-biter** a dog that bites sheep, i.e., a scoundrel **8 bearbaiting** (A special target of Puritan disapproval.) **10 fool . . . blue** mock him until he is figuratively black and blue. **12 An** If. **pity of our lives** a pity we should live.

13 villain (Here, a term of endearment.) **14 metal** gold, i.e., priceless one **15 boxtree** an evergreen shrub. **19 contemplative** i.e., from his musings. **Close** i.e., Keep close, stay hidden **22 tickling** (1) stroking gently about the gills—an actual method of fishing (2) deception. **24 she** Olivia. **affect** have fondness for **25 fancy** fall in love **27 follows** serves **30 rare** extraordinary **31 jets** struts. **advanced** prominent **32 'Slight** By His (God's) light **38 example** precedent **38–9 lady of the Strachy** (Apparently a lady who had married below her station; no certain identification.) **40 Jezebel** the proud queen of Ahab, King of Israel. **42 blows** puffs up **44 state** chair of state **45 stone-bow** crossbow that shoots stones **47 branched** adorned with a figured pattern suggesting branched leaves or flowers. **daybed** sofa, couch **51 have . . . state** adopt the imperious manner of authority **52 demure . . . regard** grave survey of the company **54 Toby** (Malvolio omits the title *Sir.*)

MALVOLIO Seven of my people, with an obedient start, make out for him. I frown the while, and perchance wind up my watch, or play with my—some rich jewel. Toby approaches; curtsies there to me—

SIR TOBY Shall this fellow live?

FABIAN Though our silence be drawn from us with cars, yet peace.

MALVOLIO I extend my hand to him thus, quenching my familiar smile with an austere regard of control—

SIR TOBY And does not Toby take you a blow o'the lips then?

MALVOLIO Saying, "Cousin Toby, my fortunes having cast me on your niece give me this prerogative of speech—"

SIR TOBY What, what?

MALVOLIO "You must amend your drunkenness."

SIR TOBY Out, scab!

FABIAN Nay, patience, or we break the sinews of our plot.

MALVOLIO "Besides, you waste the treasure of your time with a foolish knight—"

SIR ANDREW That's me, I warrant you.

MALVOLIO "One Sir Andrew."

SIR ANDREW I knew 'twas I, for many do call me fool.

MALVOLIO What employment have we here?

[*Taking up the letter.*]

FABIAN Now is the woodcock near the gin.

SIR TOBY Oh, peace, and the spirit of humors intimate reading aloud to him!

MALVOLIO By my life, this is my lady's hand. These be her very c's, her u's, and her t's; and thus makes she her great P's. It is in contempt of question her hand.

SIR ANDREW Her c's, her u's, and her t's. Why that?

MALVOLIO [*reads*] "To the unknown beloved, this, and my good wishes."—Her very phrases! By your leave, wax. Soft! And the impressure her Lucrece, with which she uses to seal. 'Tis my lady. To whom should this be? [*He opens the letter.*]

FABIAN This wins him, liver and all.

MALVOLIO [*reads*]

"Jove knows I love,
  But who?
Lips, do not move;
  No man must know."

"No man must know." What follows? The numbers altered! "No man must know." If this should be thee, Malvolio?

SIR TOBY Marry, hang thee, brock!

MALVOLIO [*reads*]

"I may command where I adore,
  But silence, like a Lucrece knife,
With bloodless stroke my heart doth gore;
  M.O.A.I. doth sway my life."

FABIAN A fustian riddle!

SIR TOBY Excellent wench, say I.

MALVOLIO "M.O.A.I. doth sway my life." Nay, but first, let me see, let me see, let me see.

FABIAN What dish o'poison has she dressed him!

SIR TOBY And with what wing the staniel checks at it!

MALVOLIO "I may command where I adore." Why, she may command me; I serve her, she is my lady. Why, this is evident to any formal capacity. There is no obstruction in this. And the end—what should that alphabetical position portend? If I could make that resemble something in me! Softly! "M.O.A.I."—

SIR TOBY Oh, ay, make up that. He is now at a cold scent.

FABIAN Sowter will cry upon't for all this, though it be as rank as a fox.

MALVOLIO "M"—Malvolio. "M"! Why, that begins my name!

FABIAN Did not I say he would work it out? The cur is excellent at faults.

MALVOLIO "M"—But then there is no consonancy in the sequel that suffers under probation: "A" should follow, but "O" does.

FABIAN And "O" shall end, I hope.

SIR TOBY Ay, or I'll cudgel him, and make him cry "Oh!"

MALVOLIO And then "I" comes behind.

FABIAN Ay, an you had any eye behind you, you might see more detraction at your heels than fortunes before you.

MALVOLIO "M.O.A.I." This simulation is not as the former. And yet, to crush this a little, it would bow to me, for every one of these letters are in my name. Soft! Here follows prose.

59 play with my (Malvolio perhaps means his steward's chain but checks himself in time; as "Count Malvolio," he would not be wearing it. A bawdy meaning of playing with himself is also suggested.) **60 curtsies** bows **62–3 with cars** with chariots, i.e., pulling apart by force **65 familiar** (1) customary (2) friendly. **regard of control** look of authority **66 take** deliver **73 scab** scurvy fellow. **74 break . . . of** hamstring, disable **81 employment** business **82 woodcock** (A bird proverbial for its stupidity.) **gin** snare. **83 humors** whim, caprice **86 c's . . . t's** i.e., *cut,* slang for the female pudenda **87 great** (1) uppercase (2) copious. (*P* suggests "pee.") **in contempt of** beyond **90–1 By . . . wax** (Addressed to the seal on the letter.) **91 Soft** Softly, not so fast. **impressure** device imprinted on the seal. **Lucrece** Lucretia, chaste matron who, ravished by Tarquin, committed suicide **92 uses** is accustomed **94 liver** i.e., the seat of passion **99–100 The numbers altered!** More verses, in a different meter!

102 brock badger. (Used contemptuously.) **107 fustian** bombastic, ridiculously pompous **111 What** What a. **dressed** prepared for **112 wing** speed. **staniel** kestrel, a sparrow hawk. (The word is used contemptuously because of the uselessness of the staniel for falconry.) **112–13 checks at it** turns to fly at it. **116 formal capacity** normal understanding. **118 position** arrangement **120 Oh, ay** (Playing on *O.I.* of *M.O.A.I.*) **make up** work out **121–2 Sowter . . . fox** The hound Sowter (literally, "Cobbler") will bay triumphantly at picking up this false scent, even though the smell is as rank as a fox. ("M.O.A.I." is a false lead that reeks.) **126 at faults** i.e., at maneuvering his way past breaks in the line of scent—in this case, on a false trail. **127–8 no consonancy . . . probation** no pattern in the following letters that stands up under examination. (In fact, the letters "M.O.A.I." represent the first, last, second, and next to last letters of Malvolio's name.) **130 "O" shall end** (1) "O" ends Malvolio's name (2) *omega* ends the Greek alphabet and is thus a symbol for the ending of the world, *alpha* to *omega* (3) Malvolio's cry of pain will end the matter, as Sir Toby suggests in the next line. **133 eye** (punning on the "I" of "Oh, ay" and "M.O.A.I.") **134 detraction . . . heels** defamation pursuing you **136 simulation** disguise, puzzle

[*He reads.*] "If this fall into thy hand, revolve. In my stars I am above thee, but be not afraid of greatness. Some are born great, some achieve greatness, and some have greatness thrust upon 'em. Thy Fates open their hands; let thy blood and spirit embrace them; and, to inure thyself to what thou art like to be, cast thy humble slough and appear fresh. Be opposite with a kinsman, surly with servants. Let thy tongue tang arguments of state; put thyself into the trick of singularity. She thus advises thee that sighs for thee. Remember who commended thy yellow stockings, and wished to see thee ever cross-gartered. I say, remember. Go to, thou art made, if thou desir'st to be so. If not, let me see thee a steward still, the fellow of servants, and not worthy to touch Fortune's fingers. Farewell. She that would alter services with thee,

The Fortunate-Unhappy."

Daylight and champaign discovers not more! This is open. I will be proud, I will read politic authors, I will baffle Sir Toby, I will wash off gross acquaintance, I will be point-devise the very man. I do not now fool myself, to let imagination jade me; for every reason excites to this, that my lady loves me. She did commend my yellow stockings of late, she did praise my leg being cross-gartered; and in this she manifests herself to my love, and with a kind of injunction drives me to these habits of her liking. I thank my stars, I am happy. I will be strange, stout, in yellow stockings and cross-gartered, even with the swiftness of putting on. Jove and my stars be praised! Here is yet a postscript. [*He reads.*] "Thou canst not choose but know who I am. If thou entertain'st my love, let it appear in thy smiling; thy smiles become thee well. Therefore in my presence still smile, dear my sweet, I prithee." Jove, I thank thee. I will smile; I will do everything that thou wilt have me. *Exit.*

[*Sir Toby, Sir Andrew, and Fabian come from hiding.*]

FABIAN I will not give my part of this sport for a pension of thousands to be paid from the Sophy.

SIR TOBY I could marry this wench for this device.

SIR ANDREW So could I too.

SIR TOBY And ask no other dowry with her but such another jest.

Enter Maria.

SIR ANDREW Nor I neither.

FABIAN Here comes my noble gull-catcher.

SIR TOBY Wilt thou set thy foot o' my neck?

SIR ANDREW Or o' mine either?

SIR TOBY Shall I play my freedom at tray-trip, and become thy bondslave?

SIR ANDREW I'faith, or I either?

SIR TOBY Why, thou hast put him in such a dream that when the image of it leaves him he must run mad.

MARIA Nay, but say true, does it work upon him?

SIR TOBY Like aqua vitae with a midwife.

MARIA If you will then see the fruits of the sport, mark his first approach before my lady. He will come to her in yellow stockings, and 'tis a color she abhors, and cross-gartered, a fashion she detests; and he will smile upon her, which will now be so unsuitable to her disposition, being addicted to a melancholy as she is, that it cannot but turn him into a notable contempt. If you will see it, follow me.

SIR TOBY To the gates of Tartar, thou most excellent devil of wit!

SIR ANDREW I'll make one too. *Exeunt.*

3.1

Enter Viola, and Clown [*Feste, playing his pipe and tabor*].

VIOLA Save thee, friend, and thy music. Dost thou live by thy tabor?

FESTE No, sir, I live by the church.

VIOLA Art thou a churchman?

FESTE No such matter, sir. I do live by the church, for I do live at my house, and my house doth stand by the church.

VIOLA So thou mayst say the king lies by a beggar if a beggar dwell near him, or the church stands by thy tabor if thy tabor stand by the church.

FESTE You have said, sir. To see this age! A sentence is but a cheveril glove to a good wit. How quickly the wrong side may be turned outward!

VIOLA Nay, that's certain. They that dally nicely with words may quickly make them wanton.

FESTE I would therefore my sister had had no name, sir.

VIOLA Why, man?

140 revolve consider. **141 stars** fortune **143–4 open their hands** offer their bounty **145 inure** accustom. **like** likely. **cast** cast off **146 slough** skin of a snake; hence, former demeanor of humbleness. **opposite** contradictory **147 tang** sound loud with **148 state** politics, statecraft **148–9 trick of singularity** eccentricity of manner. **151 cross-gartered** wearing garters above and below the knee so as to cross behind it. **152 Go to** (An expression of remonstrance.) **155 alter services** i.e., exchange place of mistress and servant **157 champaign** open country. **discovers** discloses **158 politic** dealing with state affairs **159 baffle** deride, degrade. (A technical chivalric term used to describe the disgrace of a perjured knight.) **gross** base **160 point-devise** correct to the letter **161 to let** by letting. **jade me** trick me, make me look ridiculous (as an unruly horse might do) **162 excites to this** prompts this conclusion **164 this** this letter **166 these habits** this attire **167 happy** fortunate. **strange, stout** aloof, haughty **171 thou entertain'st** you accept **173 still** continually **177 Sophy** Shah of Persia.

183 gull-catcher tricker of *gulls* or dupes. **186 play** gamble. **tray-trip** a game of dice, success in which depended on throwing a three (*tray*) **192 aqua vitae** brandy or other distilled liquor **199 notable contempt** notorious object of contempt. **201 Tartar** Tartarus, the infernal regions **203 make one** i.e., tag along

3.1 Location: Olivia's garden.

1 Save God save **1–2 live by** earn your living with. (But Feste uses the phrase to mean "dwell near.") **2 tabor** small drum. **8 lies by** (1) lies sexually with (2) dwells near **9–10 stands by . . . stand by** (1) is maintained by (2) is placed near **11 You have said** You've expressed your opinion. **sentence** maxim, judgment, opinion **12 cheveril** kidskin **14 dally nicely** (1) play subtly (2) toy amorously **15 wanton** (1) equivocal (2) licentious, unchaste. (Feste then "dallies" with the word in its sexual sense; see line 20.)

FESTE Why, sir, her name's a word, and to dally with that word might make my sister wanton. But indeed, words are very rascals since bonds disgraced them.

VIOLA Thy reason, man?

FESTE Troth, sir, I can yield you none without words, and words are grown so false I am loath to prove reason with them.

VIOLA I warrant thou art a merry fellow and car'st for nothing.

FESTE Not so, sir, I do care for something; but in my conscience, sir, I do not care for you. If that be to care for nothing, sir, I would it would make you invisible.

VIOLA Art not thou the Lady Olivia's fool?

FESTE No indeed, sir. The Lady Olivia has no folly. She will keep no fool, sir, till she be married, and fools are as like husbands as pilchers are to herrings—the husband's the bigger. I am indeed not her fool but her corrupter of words.

VIOLA I saw thee late at the Count Orsino's.

FESTE Foolery, sir, does walk about the orb like the sun; it shines everywhere. I would be sorry, sir, but the fool should be as oft with your master as with my mistress. I think I saw Your Wisdom there.

VIOLA Nay, an thou pass upon me, I'll no more with thee. Hold, there's expenses for thee.

[*She gives a coin.*]

FESTE Now Jove, in his next commodity of hair, send thee a beard!

VIOLA By my troth, I'll tell thee, I am almost sick for one—[*aside*] though I would not have it grow on my chin.—Is thy lady within?

FESTE Would not a pair of these have bred, sir?

VIOLA Yes, being kept together and put to use.

FESTE I would play Lord Pandarus of Phrygia, sir, to bring a Cressida to this Troilus.

VIOLA I understand you, sir. 'Tis well begged.

[*She gives another coin.*]

FESTE The matter, I hope, is not great, sir, begging but a beggar; Cressida was a beggar. My lady is within, sir. I will conster to them whence you come. Who you are and what you would are out of my welkin—I might say "element," but the word is overworn. *Exit.*

VIOLA
This fellow is wise enough to play the fool,
And to do that well craves a kind of wit.
He must observe their mood on whom he jests,
The quality of persons, and the time,
Not, like the haggard, check at every feather
That comes before his eye. This is a practice
As full of labor as a wise man's art;
For folly that he wisely shows is fit,
But wise men, folly-fall'n, quite taint their wit.

Enter Sir Toby and [Sir] Andrew.

SIR TOBY Save you, gentleman.

VIOLA And you, sir.

SIR ANDREW *Dieu vous garde, monsieur.*

VIOLA *Et vous aussi; votre serviteur.*

SIR ANDREW I hope, sir, you are, and I am yours.

SIR TOBY Will you encounter the house? My niece is desirous you should enter, if your trade be to her.

VIOLA I am bound to your niece, sir; I mean, she is the list of my voyage.

SIR TOBY Taste your legs, sir. Put them to motion.

VIOLA My legs do better understand me, sir, than I understand what you mean by bidding me taste my legs.

SIR TOBY I mean, to go, sir, to enter.

VIOLA I will answer you with gait and entrance.—But we are prevented.

Enter Olivia and gentlewoman [Maria].

Most excellent accomplished lady, the heavens rain odors on you!

SIR ANDREW [*to Sir Toby*] That youth's a rare courtier. "Rain odors"—well.

VIOLA [*to Olivia*] My matter hath no voice, lady, but to your own most pregnant and vouchsafed ear.

SIR ANDREW [*to Sir Toby*] "Odors," "pregnant," and "vouchsafed." I'll get 'em all three all ready.

OLIVIA Let the garden door be shut, and leave me to my hearing. [*Exeunt Sir Toby, Sir Andrew, and Maria.*] Give me your hand, sir.

VIOLA
My duty, madam, and most humble service.

OLIVIA What is your name?

VIOLA
Cesario is your servant's name, fair princess.

21 since . . . them i.e., since bonds have been needed to make sworn statements good. (Words cannot be relied on since not even contractual promises are reliable.) **26–7 car'st for nothing** are without any worries. (But Feste puns on *care for* in lines 29–30 in the sense of "like.") **30 invisible** i.e., nothing; absent. **34 pilchers** pilchards, fish resembling herring but smaller **35 the bigger** (1) the larger (2) the bigger fool. **37 late** recently **38 orb** earth **39–41 I would . . . mistress** (1) I should be sorry not to visit Orsino's house often (2) It would be a shame if folly were no less common there than in Olivia's household. **41 Your Wisdom** i.e., you. (A title of mock courtesy.) **42 an . . . me** if you fence (verbally) with me, pass judgment on me **44 commodity** supply **46–7 sick for one** (1) eager to have a beard (2) in love with a bearded man **50 put to use** put out at interest. **51 Pandarus** the go-between in the love story of Troilus and Cressida; uncle to Cressida **54–5 begging . . . was a beggar** (A reference to Henryson's *Testament of Cresseid* in which Cressida became a leper and a beggar. Feste desires another coin to be the mate of the one he has, just as Cressida, the beggar, was mate to Troilus.) **56 conster** construe, explain **58 welkin** sky. **element** (The word can be synonymous with *welkin,* but the common phrase *out of my element* means "beyond my scope.")

63 quality character, rank **64 haggard** untrained adult hawk, hence unmanageable **64–5 check . . . eye** strike at every bird it sees, i.e., dart from subject to subject. **65 practice** exercise of skill **67–8 For . . . wit** for the folly he judiciously displays is appropriate and clever, whereas when wise men fall into folly they utterly infect their own intelligence. **71 *Dieu . . . monsieur*** God keep you, sir. **72 *Et . . . serviteur*** And you, too; (I am) your servant. (Sir Andrew is not quite up to a reply in French.) **74 encounter** (High-sounding word to express "approach.") **75 trade** business. (Suggesting also a commercial venture.) **76 I am bound** (1) I am on a journey. (Continuing Sir Toby's metaphor in *trade.*) (2) I am confined, obligated **77 list** limit, destination **78 Taste** Try **79 understand** stand under, support **82 gait and entrance** going and entering. (With a pun on *gate:* [1] stride [2] entryway.) **83 prevented** anticipated. **88 hath no voice** cannot be uttered **89 pregnant and vouchsafed** receptive and attentive **91 all ready** committed to memory for future use.

OLIVIA
My servant, sir? 'Twas never merry world
Since lowly feigning was called compliment.
You're servant to the Count Orsino, youth.

VIOLA
And he is yours, and his must needs be yours;
Your servant's servant is your servant, madam.

OLIVIA
For him, I think not on him. For his thoughts,
Would they were blanks, rather than filled with me!

VIOLA
Madam, I come to whet your gentle thoughts
On his behalf.

OLIVIA Oh, by your leave, I pray you.
I bade you never speak again of him.
But, would you undertake another suit,
I had rather hear you to solicit that
Than music from the spheres.

VIOLA Dear lady—

OLIVIA
Give me leave, beseech you. I did send,
After the last enchantment you did here,
A ring in chase of you; so did I abuse
Myself, my servant, and, I fear me, you.
Under your hard construction must I sit,
To force that on you in a shameful cunning
Which you knew none of yours. What might you think?
Have you not set mine honor at the stake
And baited it with all th'unmuzzled thoughts
That tyrannous heart can think? To one of your receiving
Enough is shown; a cypress, not a bosom,
Hides my heart. So, let me hear you speak.

VIOLA
I pity you.

OLIVIA That's a degree to love.

VIOLA
No, not a grece; for 'tis a vulgar proof
That very oft we pity enemies.

OLIVIA
Why then, methinks 'tis time to smile again.
Oh, world, how apt the poor are to be proud!
If one should be a prey, how much the better
To fall before the lion than the wolf! *Clock strikes.*
The clock upbraids me with the waste of time.
Be not afraid, good youth, I will not have you;
And yet, when wit and youth is come to harvest
Your wife is like to reap a proper man.
There lies your way, due west.

VIOLA Then westward ho!
Grace and good disposition attend Your Ladyship.
You'll nothing, madam, to my lord by me?

OLIVIA Stay.
I prithee, tell me what thou think'st of me.

VIOLA
That you do think you are not what you are.

OLIVIA
If I think so, I think the same of you.

VIOLA
Then think you right. I am not what I am.

OLIVIA
I would you were as I would have you be!

VIOLA
Would it be better, madam, than I am?
I wish it might, for now I am your fool.

OLIVIA [*aside*]
Oh, what a deal of scorn looks beautiful
In the contempt and anger of his lip!
A murderous guilt shows not itself more soon
Than love that would seem hid; love's night is noon.—
Cesario, by the roses of the spring,
By maidhood, honor, truth, and everything,
I love thee so that, maugre all thy pride,
Nor wit nor reason can my passion hide.
Do not extort thy reasons from this clause,
For that I woo, thou therefore hast no cause.
But rather reason thus with reason fetter:
Love sought is good, but given unsought is better.

VIOLA
By innocence I swear, and by my youth,
I have one heart, one bosom, and one truth,
And that no woman has, nor never none
Shall mistress be of it save I alone.
And so adieu, good madam. Nevermore
Will I my master's tears to you deplore.

OLIVIA
Yet come again, for thou perhaps mayst move
That heart, which now abhors, to like his love.
Exeunt [*separately*].

98–9 'Twas . . . compliment Things have never been the same since affected humility (like calling oneself another's servant) began to be mistaken for courtesy. **101 is yours** is your servant. **his** those belonging to him **103 For** As for **104 blanks** blank coins ready to be stamped or empty sheets of paper **106 by your leave** i.e., allow me to interrupt **110 music from the spheres** (The heavenly bodies were thought to be fixed in hollow concentric spheres that revolved one about the other, producing a harmony too exquisite to be heard by human ears.) **113 abuse** wrong, mislead **115 hard construction** harsh interpretation **116 To force that** for forcing the ring **118 at the stake** (The figure is from bearbaiting.) **119 baited** harassed. (Literally, set the unmuzzled dogs on to bite the bear.) **120 receiving** capacity, intelligence **121–2 a cypress . . . heart** i.e., I have shown my heart to you, veiled only with thin, gauzelike cypress cloth rather than the opaque flesh of my bosom. **124 grece** step. (Synonymous with *degree* in the preceding line.) **vulgar proof** common experience **126 smile** i.e., cast off love's melancholy **127 how . . . proud!** how ready the unfortunate and rejected (like myself) are to find something to be proud of in their distress! Or, how apt are persons of comparatively low social station like yourself to show pride in rejecting love!

129 To fall . . . wolf! i.e., to fall before a noble adversary rather than to a person like you who attacks me thus! **133 like** likely. **proper** handsome, worthy **134 westward ho** (The cry of Thames watermen to attract westward-bound passengers.) **135 Grace . . . Ladyship** May you enjoy God's blessing and a happy frame of mind. **139 That . . . are** i.e., That you think you are in love with a man, and you are mistaken. **140 If . . . you** (Olivia may interpret Viola's cryptic statement as suggesting that Olivia "does not know herself," i.e., is distracted with passion; she may also hint at her suspicion that "Cesario" is higher born than he admits.) **144 fool** butt. **148 love's . . . noon** i.e., love, despite its attempt to be secret, reveals itself as plain as day. **151 maugre** in spite of **152 Nor** neither **153–4 Do . . . cause** Do not rationalize your indifference along these lines, that because I am the wooer you have no cause to reciprocate. **155 But . . . fetter** But instead control your reasoning with the following reason **162 deplore** beweep.

3.2

Enter Sir Toby, Sir Andrew, and Fabian.

SIR ANDREW No, faith, I'll not stay a jot longer.

SIR TOBY Thy reason, dear venom, give thy reason.

FABIAN You must needs yield your reason, Sir Andrew.

SIR ANDREW Marry, I saw your niece do more favors to the Count's servingman than ever she bestowed upon me. I saw't i'th' orchard.

SIR TOBY Did she see thee the while, old boy? Tell me that.

SIR ANDREW As plain as I see you now.

FABIAN This was a great argument of love in her toward you.

SIR ANDREW 'Slight, will you make an ass o'me?

FABIAN I will prove it legitimate, sir, upon the oaths of judgment and reason.

SIR TOBY And they have been grand-jurymen since before Noah was a sailor.

FABIAN She did show favor to the youth in your sight only to exasperate you, to awake your dormouse valor, to put fire in your heart and brimstone in your liver. You should then have accosted her, and with some excellent jests, fire-new from the mint, you should have banged the youth into dumbness. This was looked for at your hand, and this was balked. The double gilt of this opportunity you let time wash off, and you are now sailed into the north of my lady's opinion, where you will hang like an icicle on a Dutchman's beard unless you do redeem it by some laudable attempt either of valor or policy.

SIR ANDREW An't be any way, it must be with valor, for policy I hate. I had as lief be a Brownist as a politician.

SIR TOBY Why, then, build me thy fortunes upon the basis of valor. Challenge me the Count's youth to fight with him; hurt him in eleven places. My niece shall take note of it; and assure thyself, there is no love-broker in the world can more prevail in man's commendation with woman than report of valor.

FABIAN There is no way but this, Sir Andrew.

SIR ANDREW Will either of you bear me a challenge to him?

SIR TOBY Go, write it in a martial hand. Be curst and brief; it is no matter how witty, so it be eloquent and full of invention. Taunt him with the license of ink. If thou "thou"-est him some thrice, it shall not be amiss; and as many lies as will lie in thy sheet of paper, although the sheet were big enough for the bed of Ware in England, set 'em down. Go, about it. Let there be gall enough in thy ink, though thou write with a goose pen, no matter. About it.

SIR ANDREW Where shall I find you?

SIR TOBY We'll call thee at the cubiculo. Go.

Exit Sir Andrew.

FABIAN This is a dear manikin to you, Sir Toby.

SIR TOBY I have been dear to him, lad, some two thousand strong or so.

FABIAN We shall have a rare letter from him; but you'll not deliver't?

SIR TOBY Never trust me, then; and by all means stir on the youth to an answer. I think oxen and wainropes cannot hale them together. For Andrew, if he were opened and you find so much blood in his liver as will clog the foot of a flea, I'll eat the rest of th'anatomy.

FABIAN And his opposite, the youth, bears in his visage no great presage of cruelty.

Enter Maria.

SIR TOBY Look where the youngest wren of nine comes.

MARIA If you desire the spleen, and will laugh yourselves into stitches, follow me. Yond gull Malvolio is turned heathen, a very renegado; for there is no Christian that means to be saved by believing rightly can ever believe such impossible passages of grossness. He's in yellow stockings.

SIR TOBY And cross-gartered?

MARIA Most villainously, like a pedant that keeps a school i'th' church. I have dogged him like his murderer. He does obey every point of the letter that I dropped to betray him. He does smile his face into more lines than is in the new map with the augmentation of the Indies. You have not seen such a thing as 'tis. I can hardly forbear hurling things at him. I know my lady will strike him. If she do, he'll smile and take't for a great favor.

SIR TOBY Come, bring us, bring us where he is.

Exeunt omnes.

3.2. Location: Olivia's house.
2 venom i.e., person filled with venomous anger **6 orchard** garden. **10 argument** proof **12 'Slight** By his (God's) light **13 it** my contention. **oaths** i.e., testimony under oath **18 dormouse** i.e., sleepy and timid **21 fire-new . . . mint** newly coined **22 banged** struck **23 balked** missed, neglected. **23–4 double gilt** thick layer of gold, i.e., rare worth **25 into . . . opinion** i.e., out of the warmth and sunshine of Olivia's favor **26–7 icicle . . . beard** (Alludes to the arctic voyage of William Barents in 1596–1597.) **28 policy** stratagem.
30 Brownist (An early name of the Congregationalists, from the name of the founder, Robert Browne.) **30–1 politician** intriguer. (Sir Andrew misinterprets Fabian's more neutral use of *policy,* "clever stratagem.") **32–3 build me . . . Challenge me** build . . . Challenge. ("Me" is idiomatic.) **36 love-broker** agent between lovers **41 curst** fierce **43 with . . . ink** i.e., with all the unfettered eloquence at your disposal as a writer.

44 "thou"-est ("Thou" was used only between friends or to inferiors.) **45 lies** charges of lying **46–7 bed of Ware** a famous bedstead capable of holding twelve persons, about eleven feet square, said to have been at the Stag Inn in Ware, Hertfordshire **48 gall** (1) bitterness, rancor (2) a growth found on certain oaks, used as an ingredient of ink
49 goose pen (1) goose quill (2) foolish style **51 call thee** call for you. **cubiculo** little chamber, bedchamber. **52 manikin** puppet **53 dear** expensive. (Playing on *dear,* "fond," in the previous speech.) **55 rare** extraordinary **58 wainropes** wagon ropes **59 hale** haul. **For** As for **60 liver** (A pale and bloodless liver was a sign of cowardice.)
61 th'anatomy the cadaver. **62 opposite** adversary **64 youngest . . . nine** the last hatched and smallest of a nest of wrens **66 the spleen** a laughing fit. (The spleen was thought to be the seat of immoderate laughter.) **68 renegado** renegade, deserter of his religion
70–1 impossible . . . grossness gross impossibilities (i.e., in the letter). **73 villainously** i.e., abominably. **pedant** schoolmaster **77–8 the new . . . Indies** (Probably a reference to a map made by Emmeric Mollineux in 1599–1600 to be printed in Hakluyt's *Voyages,* showing more of the East indies, including Japan, than had ever been mapped before.)

3.3

Enter Sebastian and Antonio.

SEBASTIAN
I would not by my will have troubled you,
But since you make your pleasure of your pains,
I will no further chide you.

ANTONIO
I could not stay behind you. My desire,
More sharp than filèd steel, did spur me forth,
And not all love to see you—though so much
As might have drawn one to a longer voyage—
But jealousy what might befall your travel,
Being skilless in these parts, which to a stranger,
Unguided and unfriended, often prove
Rough and unhospitable. My willing love,
The rather by these arguments of fear,
Set forth in your pursuit.

SEBASTIAN My kind Antonio,
I can no other answer make but thanks,
And thanks; and ever oft good turns
Are shuffled off with such uncurrent pay.
But were my worth, as is my conscience, firm,
You should find better dealing. What's to do?
Shall we go see the relics of this town?

ANTONIO
Tomorrow, sir. Best first go see your lodging.

SEBASTIAN
I am not weary, and 'tis long to night.
I pray you, let us satisfy our eyes
With the memorials and the things of fame
That do renown this city.

ANTONIO Would you'd pardon me.
I do not without danger walk these streets.
Once in a sea fight 'gainst the Count his galleys
I did some service, of such note indeed
That were I ta'en here it would scarce be answered.

SEBASTIAN
Belike you slew great number of his people?

ANTONIO
Th'offense is not of such a bloody nature,
Albeit the quality of the time and quarrel
Might well have given us bloody argument.
It might have since been answered in repaying
What we took from them, which for traffic's sake
Most of our city did. Only myself stood out,
For which, if I be lapsèd in this place,
I shall pay dear.

SEBASTIAN Do not then walk too open.

ANTONIO
It doth not fit me. Hold, sir, here's my purse.
[*He gives his purse.*]
In the south suburbs, at the Elephant,
Is best to lodge. I will bespeak our diet,
Whiles you beguile the time and feed your knowl-
edge
With viewing of the town. There shall you have me.

SEBASTIAN Why I your purse?

ANTONIO
Haply your eye shall light upon some toy
You have desire to purchase; and your store
I think is not for idle markets, sir.

SEBASTIAN
I'll be your purse-bearer and leave you
For an hour.

ANTONIO To th'Elephant.

SEBASTIAN I do remember.
Exeunt [*separately*].

✤

3.4

Enter Olivia and Maria.

OLIVIA [*aside*]
I have sent after him; he says he'll come.
How shall I feast him? What bestow of him?
For youth is bought more oft than begged or
borrowed.
I speak too loud.—
Where's Malvolio? He is sad and civil,
And suits well for a servant with my fortunes.
Where is Malvolio?

MARIA He's coming, madam, but in very strange manner. He is, sure, possessed, madam.

OLIVIA Why, what's the matter? Does he rave?

MARIA No, madam, he does nothing but smile. Your Ladyship were best to have some guard about you if he come, for sure the man is tainted in's wits.

OLIVIA
Go call him hither. [*Maria summons Malvolio.*] I am as
mad as he,
If sad and merry madness equal be.

Enter Malvolio, [*cross-gartered and in yellow stockings*].

How now, Malvolio?

MALVOLIO Sweet lady, ho, ho!

OLIVIA Smil'st thou? I sent for thee upon a sad occasion.

3.3. Location: A Street.
6 all only, merely. **so much** i.e., that was great enough **8 jealousy** anxiety **9 skilless in** unacquainted with **12 The rather** made all the more willing **15 And . . . turns** (This probably corrupt line is usually made to read, "And thanks and ever thanks; and oft good turns.") **16 shuffled off** turned aside. **uncurrent** worthless (such as mere thanks) **17 worth** wealth. **conscience** i.e., moral inclination to assist **18 dealing** treatment, payment. **19 relics** antiquities **24 renown** make famous **26 Count his** Count's, i.e., Duke's **28 it . . . answered** I'd be hard put to offer a defense. **29 Belike** Perhaps **32 bloody argument** cause for bloodshed. **33 answered** compensated **34 traffic's** trade's **36 lapsèd** caught off guard, surprised

39 Elephant the name of an inn **40 bespeak our diet** order our food **42 have** find **44 Haply** Perhaps. **toy** trifle **45 store** store of money **46 is not . . . markets** cannot afford luxuries
3.4. Location: Olivia's garden.
1 he . . . come i.e., suppose he says he'll come. **2 of** on **5 sad and civil** sober and decorous **9 possessed** (1) possessed with an evil spirit (2) mad **13 in's** in his **15 If . . . equal be** i.e., if love melancholy and smiling madness are essentially alike. (Love melancholy was regarded as a kind of madness.) **18 sad** serious

MALVOLIO Sad, lady? I could be sad. This does make some obstruction in the blood, this cross-gartering, but what of that? If it please the eye of one, it is with me as the very true sonnet is, "Please one and please all."

OLIVIA Why, how dost thou, man? What is the matter with thee?

MALVOLIO Not black in my mind, though yellow in my legs. It did come to his hands, and commands shall be executed. I think we do know the sweet roman hand.

OLIVIA Wilt thou go to bed, Malvolio?

MALVOLIO To bed! "Ay, sweetheart, and I'll come to thee."

OLIVIA God comfort thee! Why dost thou smile so and kiss thy hand so oft?

MARIA How do you, Malvolio?

MALVOLIO At your request? Yes, nightingales answer daws.

MARIA Why appear you with this ridiculous boldness before my lady?

MALVOLIO "Be not afraid of greatness." 'Twas well writ.

OLIVIA What mean'st thou by that, Malvolio?

MALVOLIO "Some are born great—"

OLIVIA Ha?

MALVOLIO "Some achieve greatness—"

OLIVIA What say'st thou?

MALVOLIO "And some have greatness thrust upon them."

OLIVIA Heaven restore thee!

MALVOLIO "Remember who commended thy yellow stockings—"

OLIVIA Thy yellow stockings?

MALVOLIO "And wished to see thee cross-gartered."

OLIVIA Cross-gartered?

MALVOLIO "Go to, thou art made, if thou desir'st to be so—"

OLIVIA Am I made?

MALVOLIO "If not, let me see thee a servant still."

OLIVIA Why, this is very midsummer madness.

Enter Servant.

SERVANT Madam, the young gentleman of the Count Orsino's is returned. I could hardly entreat him back. He attends Your Ladyship's pleasure.

OLIVIA I'll come to him. [*Exit Servant.*] Good Maria, let this fellow be looked to. Where's my cousin Toby? Let some of my people have a special care of him. I would not have him miscarry for the half of my dowry.

Exeunt [Olivia and Maria, different ways].

MALVOLIO Oho, do you come near me now? No worse man than Sir Toby to look to me! This concurs directly with the letter. She sends him on purpose that I may appear stubborn to him, for she incites me to that in the letter. "Cast thy humble slough," says she; "be opposite with a kinsman, surly with servants; let thy tongue tang with arguments of state; put thyself into the trick of singularity." And consequently sets down the manner how: as, a sad face, a reverend carriage, a slow tongue, in the habit of some sir of note, and so forth. I have limed her, but it is Jove's doing, and Jove make me thankful! And when she went away now, "Let this fellow be looked to." "Fellow!" Not "Malvolio," nor after my degree, but "fellow." Why, everything adheres together, that no dram of a scruple, no scruple of a scruple, no obstacle, no incredulous or unsafe circumstance—what can be said?—nothing that can be can come between me and the full prospect of my hopes. Well, Jove, not I, is the doer of this, and he is to be thanked.

Enter [Sir] Toby, Fabian, and Maria.

SIR TOBY Which way is he, in the name of sanctity? If all the devils of hell be drawn in little, and Legion himself possessed him, yet I'll speak to him.

FABIAN Here he is, here he is.—How is't with you, sir? How is't with you, man?

MALVOLIO Go off. I discard you. Let me enjoy my private. Go off.

MARIA Lo, how hollow the fiend speaks within him! Did not I tell you? Sir Toby, my lady prays you to have a care of him.

MALVOLIO Aha, does she so?

SIR TOBY Go to, go to! Peace, peace, we must deal gently with him. Let me alone.—How do you, Malvolio? How is't with you? What, man, defy the devil! Consider, he's an enemy to mankind.

MALVOLIO Do you know what you say?

MARIA La you, an you speak ill of the devil, how he takes it at heart! Pray God he be not bewitched!

FABIAN Carry his water to th' wise woman.

MARIA Marry, and it shall be done tomorrow morning, if I live. My lady would not lose him for more than I'll say.

MALVOLIO How now, mistress?

20 sad (1) serious (2) melancholy. **23 sonnet** song, ballad **23–4 "Please . . . all"** "To please one special person is as good as to please everybody." (The refain of a ballad.) **27 black** i.e., melancholic **28 It** i.e., The letter. **his** Malvolio's **29 roman hand** fashionable italic or Italian style of handwriting rather than English "secretary" handwriting. **30 go to bed** i.e., try to sleep off your mental distress. (But Malvolio misinterprets as a sexual invitation.) **31–2 "Ay . . . thee"** (Malvolio quotes from a popular song of the day.) **36–7 nightingales answer daws** i.e. (to Maria), do you suppose a fine fellow like me would answer a lowly creature (a *daw*, a "jackdaw") like you? **57 midsummer madness** (A proverbial phrase; the midsummer moon was supposed to cause madness.)

64 miscarry come to harm **66 come near** understand, appreciate **73 consequently** thereafter **74 sad** serious **75 habit . . . note** attire suited to a man of distinction **76 limed** caught like a bird with birdlime (a sticky substance spread on branches) **78 Fellow** (Malvolio takes the basic meaning, "companion.") **79 after my degree** according to my position **80 dram** (Literally, one-eighth of a fluid ounce.) **scruple** (Literally, one-third of a dram.) **81 incredulous** incredible **81–2 unsafe** uncertain, unreliable **87 drawn in little** (1) portrayed in miniature (2) gathered into a small space. **Legion** an unclean spirit. ("My name is Legion, for we are many," Mark 5:9.) **92 private** privacy. **98 Let me alone** Leave him to me. **99 defy** renounce **102 La you** Look you **104 water** urine (for medical analysis). **wise woman** sorceress.

MARIA Oh, Lord!

SIR TOBY Prithee, hold thy peace; this is not the way. Do you not see you move him? Let me alone with him.

FABIAN No way but gentleness, gently, gently. The fiend is rough, and will not be roughly used.

SIR TOBY Why, how now, my bawcock! How dost thou, chuck?

MALVOLIO Sir!

SIR TOBY Ay, biddy, come with me. What, man, 'tis not for gravity to play at cherry-pit with Satan. Hang him, foul collier!

MARIA Get him to say his prayers, good Sir Toby, get him to pray.

MALVOLIO My prayers, minx?

MARIA No, I warrant you, he will not hear of godliness.

MALVOLIO Go hang yourselves all! You are idle, shallow things; I am not of your element. You shall know more hereafter. *Exit.*

SIR TOBY Is't possible?

FABIAN If this were played upon a stage, now, I could condemn it as an improbable fiction.

SIR TOBY His very genius hath taken the infection of the device, man.

MARIA Nay, pursue him now, lest the device take air and taint.

FABIAN Why, we shall make him mad indeed.

MARIA The house will be the quieter.

SIR TOBY Come, we'll have him in a dark room and bound. My niece is already in the belief that he's mad. We may carry it thus for our pleasure and his penance till our very pastime, tired out of breath, prompt us to have mercy on him, at which time we will bring the device to the bar and crown thee for a finder of madmen. But see, but see!

Enter Sir Andrew [with a letter].

FABIAN More matter for a May morning.

SIR ANDREW Here's the challenge. Read it. I warrant there's vinegar and pepper in't.

FABIAN Is't so saucy?

SIR ANDREW Ay, is't, I warrant him. Do but read.

SIR TOBY Give me. [*He reads.*] "Youth, whatsoever thou art, thou art but a scurvy fellow."

FABIAN Good, and valiant.

SIR TOBY [*reads*] "Wonder not, nor admire not in thy mind, why I do call thee so, for I will show thee no reason for't."

FABIAN A good note, that keeps you from the blow of the law.

SIR TOBY [*reads*] "Thou com'st to the Lady Olivia, and in my sight she uses thee kindly. But thou liest in thy throat; that is not the matter I challenge thee for."

FABIAN Very brief, and to exceeding good sense—less.

SIR TOBY [*reads*] "I will waylay thee going home, where if it be thy chance to kill me—"

FABIAN Good.

SIR TOBY [*reads*] "Thou kill'st me like a rogue and a villain."

FABIAN Still you keep o' th' windy side of the law. Good.

SIR TOBY [*reads*] "Fare thee well, and God have mercy upon one of our souls! He may have mercy upon mine, but my hope is better, and so look to thyself. Thy friend, as thou usest him, and thy sworn enemy,
Andrew Aguecheek."
If this letter move him not, his legs cannot. I'll give't him.

MARIA You may have very fit occasion for't. He is now in some commerce with my lady, and will by and by depart.

SIR TOBY Go, Sir Andrew. Scout me for him at the corner of the orchard like a bum-baily. So soon as ever thou see'st him, draw, and as thou draw'st, swear horrible; for it comes to pass oft that a terrible oath, with a swaggering accent sharply twanged off, gives manhood more approbation than ever proof itself would have earned him. Away!

SIR ANDREW Nay, let me alone for swearing. *Exit.*

SIR TOBY Now will not I deliver his letter, for the behavior of the young gentleman gives him out to be of good capacity and breeding; his employment between his lord and my niece confirms no less. Therefore this letter, being so excellently ignorant, will breed no terror in the youth. He will find it comes from a clodpoll. But, sir, I will deliver his challenge by word of mouth, set upon Aguecheek a notable report of valor, and drive the gentleman—as I know his youth will aptly receive it—into a most hideous opinion of his rage, skill, fury, and impetuosity. This will so fright them both that they will kill one another by the look, like cockatrices.

Enter Olivia and Viola.

FABIAN Here he comes with your niece. Give them way till he take leave, and presently after him.

111 move upset, excite **115 bawcock** fine fellow. (From the French *beau-coq.*) **116 chuck** (A form of "chick," term of endearment.) **118 biddy** chicken **119 for gravity** suitable for a man of your dignity. **cherry-pit** a children's game consisting of throwing cherry stones into a little hole **120 collier** i.e., Satan. (Literally, a coal vendor.) **125 idle** foolish **126 element** sphere. **126–7 know more** i.e., hear about this **131 genius** i.e., soul, spirit **133–4 take . . . taint** become exposed to air (i.e., become known) and thus spoil. **137–8 have . . . bound** (The standard treatment for insanity at this time.) **139 carry** manage **142 bar** i.e., bar of judgment **142–3 finder of madmen** member of a jury changed with "finding" if the accused is insane. **144 matter . . . morning** sport for Mayday plays or games. **147 saucy** (1) spicy (2) insolent. **148 him** it. **152 admire** marvel

155 note observation, remark **166 windy** windward, i.e., safe, where one is less likely to be driven onto legal rocks and shoals **170 my hope is better** (Sir Andrew's comically inept way of saying he hopes to be the survivor; instead, he seems to say, "May I be damned.") **173 move** (1) stir up (2) set in motion **176 commerce** transaction **178 Scout me** Keep watch **179 bum-baily** minor sheriff's officer employed in making arrests. **180–1 horrible** horribly **183 approbation** reputation (for courage). **proof** performance **185 let . . . swearing** don't worry about my ability in swearing. **191 clodpoll** blockhead. **194–5 his . . . it** his inexperience will make him all the more ready to believe it **198 cockatrices** basilisks, fabulous serpents reputed to be able to kill by a mere look. **199 Give them way** Stay out of their way **200 presently** immediately

SIR TOBY I will meditate the while upon some horrid message for a challenge.

[Exeunt Sir Toby, Fabian, and Maria.]

OLIVIA
I have said too much unto a heart of stone
And laid mine honor too unchary on't.
There's something in me that reproves my fault,
But such a headstrong potent fault it is
That it but mocks reproof.

VIOLA
With the same havior that your passion bears
Goes on my master's griefs.

OLIVIA *[giving a locket]*
Here, wear this jewel for me. 'Tis my picture.
Refuse it not; it hath no tongue to vex you.
And I beseech you come again tomorrow.
What shall you ask of me that I'll deny,
That honor, saved, may upon asking give?

VIOLA
Nothing but this: your true love for my master.

OLIVIA
How with mine honor may I give him that
Which I have given to you?

VIOLA
I will acquit you.

OLIVIA
Well, come again tomorrow. Fare thee well.
A fiend like thee might bear my soul to hell. *[Exit.]*

Enter [Sir] Toby and Fabian.

SIR TOBY Gentleman, God save thee.

VIOLA And you, sir.

SIR TOBY That defense thou hast, betake thee to't. Of what nature the wrongs are thou hast done him, I know not, but thy intercepter, full of despite, bloody as the hunter, attends thee at the orchard end. Dismount thy tuck, be yare in thy preparation, for thy assailant is quick, skillful, and deadly.

VIOLA You mistake sir. I am sure no man hath any quarrel to me. My remembrance is very free and clear from any image of offense done to any man.

SIR TOBY You'll find it otherwise, I assure you. Therefore, if you hold your life at any price, betake you to your guard, for your opposite hath in him what youth, strength, skill, and wrath can furnish man withal.

VIOLA I pray you, sir, what is he?

SIR TOBY He is knight, dubbed with unhatched rapier and on carpet consideration, but he is a devil in private brawl. Souls and bodies hath he divorced three, and his incensement at this moment is so implacable that satisfaction can be none but by pangs of death and sepulchre. Hob, nob is his word; give't or take't.

VIOLA I will return again into the house and desire some conduct of the lady. I am no fighter. I have heard of some kind of men that put quarrels purposely on others, to taste their valor. Belike this is a man of that quirk.

SIR TOBY Sir, no. His indignation derives itself out of a very competent injury; therefore, get you on and give him his desire. Back you shall not to the house unless you undertake that with me which with as much safety you might answer him. Therefore, on, or strip your sword stark naked; for meddle you must, that's certain, or forswear to wear iron about you.

VIOLA This is as uncivil as strange. I beseech you, do me this courteous office as to know of the knight what my offense to him is. It is something of my negligence, nothing of my purpose.

SIR TOBY I will do so.—Signor Fabian, stay you by this gentleman till my return. *Exit [Sir] Toby.*

VIOLA Pray you, sir, do you know of this matter?

FABIAN I know the knight is incensed against you, even to a mortal arbitrament, but nothing of the circumstance more.

VIOLA I beseech you, what manner of man is he?

FABIAN Nothing of that wonderful promise, to read him by his form, as you are like to find him in the proof of his valor. He is, indeed, sir, the most skillful, bloody, and fatal opposite that you could possibly have found in any part of Illyria. Will you walk towards him, I will make your peace with him if I can.

VIOLA I shall be much bound to you for't. I am one that had rather go with Sir Priest than Sir Knight. I care not who knows so much of my mettle. *Exeunt.*

Enter [Sir] Toby and [Sir] Andrew.

SIR TOBY Why, man, he's a very devil; I have not seen such a firago. I had a pass with him, rapier, scabbard, and all, and he gives me the stuck-in with such a mortal motion that it is inevitable; and on the answer, he pays you as surely as your feet hits the ground they step on. They say he has been fencer to the Sophy.

SIR ANDREW Pox on't, I'll not meddle with him.

201 horrid terrifying. (Literally, "bristling.") **204 laid** hazarded. **unchary on't** recklessly on it. **208–9 With . . . griefs** i.e., Orsino's sufferings in love are as reckless and uncontrollable as your feelings. **214 That . . . give?** that can be granted without compromising my honor? **217 acquit you** release you of your promise. **219 A fiend . . . hell** i.e., You are my torment. (*Like thee* means "in your likeness.") **222 That . . . to't** Get ready to deploy whatever skill you have in fencing. **224 intercepter** he who lies in wait. **despite** defiance, ill will **224–5 bloody as the hunter** bloodthirsty as a hunting dog **226 Dismount thy tuck** Draw your rapier. **yare** ready, nimble **229 to** with **233 opposite** opponent. **what** whatsoever **234 withal** with. **236 unhatched** unhacked, unused in battle

237 carpet consideration (A carpet knight was one whose title was obtained, not in battle, but through connections at court.) **241 Hob, nob** Have or have not, i.e., give it or take it, kill or be killed. **word** motto **244 conduct** safe-conduct, escort **246 taste** test, prove **Belike** Probably **247 quirk** peculiar humor. **249 competent** sufficient **252–3 strip . . . naked** draw your sword from its sheath **253 meddle** engage (in conflict) **254 forswear . . . iron** give up your right to wear a sword **256 know of** inquire from **257–8 It is . . . purpose** It is the result of some oversight, not anything I intended. **263 mortal arbitrament** trial to the death **266–7 read . . . form** judge him by his appearance **267 like** likely **270 Will you** If you will **273 go with** associate with. **Sir Priest** (*Sir* was a courtesy title for priests.) **276 firago** virago. **pass** bout **277 stuck-in** stoccado, a thrust in fencing **278 answer** return hit **280 to** in the service of

SIR TOBY Ay, but he will not now be pacified. Fabian can scarce hold him yonder.

SIR ANDREW Plague on't, an I thought he had been valiant and so cunning in fence, I'd have seen him damned ere I'd have challenged him. Let him let the matter slip and I'll give him my horse, gray Capilet.

SIR TOBY I'll make the motion. Stand here, make a good show on't. This shall end without the perdition of souls. [*Aside, as he crosses to meet Fabian*] Marry, I'll ride your horse as well as I ride you.

Enter Fabian and Viola.

[*Aside to Fabian*] I have his horse to take up the quarrel. I have persuaded him the youth's a devil.

FABIAN He is as horribly conceited of him, and pants and looks pale as if a bear were at his heels.

SIR TOBY [*to Viola*] There's no remedy, sir, he will fight with you for's oath's sake. Marry, he hath better bethought him of his quarrel, and he finds that now scarce to be worth talking of. Therefore draw, for the supportance of his vow; he protests he will not hurt you.

VIOLA [*aside*] Pray God defend me! A little thing would make me tell them how much I lack of a man.

FABIAN Give ground, if you see him furious.

SIR TOBY [*crossing to Sir Andrew*] Come, Sir Andrew, there's no remedy. The gentleman will, for his honor's sake, have one bout with you. He cannot by the *duello* avoid it. But he has promised me, as he is a gentleman and a soldier, he will not hurt you. Come on, to't.

SIR ANDREW Pray God he keep his oath!

Enter Antonio.

VIOLA [*to Fabian*] I do assure you, 'tis against my will.
[*They draw.*]

ANTONIO [*drawing, to Sir Andrew*]
Put up your sword. If this young gentleman
Have done offense, I take the fault on me;
If you offend him, I for him defy you.

SIR TOBY You, sir? Why, what are you?

ANTONIO
One, sir, that for his love dares yet do more
Than you have heard him brag to you he will.

SIR TOBY [*drawing*]
Nay, if you be an undertaker, I am for you.

Enter Officers.

FABIAN Oh, good Sir Toby, hold! Here come the officers.

SIR TOBY [*to Antonio*] I'll be with you anon.

VIOLA [*to Sir Andrew*] Pray, sir, put your sword up, if you please.

SIR ANDREW Marry, will I, sir; and for that I promised you, I'll be as good as my word. He will bear you easily, and reins well.

FIRST OFFICER This is the man. Do thy office.

SECOND OFFICER
Antonio, I arrest thee at the suit
Of Count Orsino.

ANTONIO You do mistake me, sir.

FIRST OFFICER
No, sir, no jot. I know your favor well,
Though now you have no sea-cap on your head.—
Take him away. He knows I know him well.

ANTONIO
I must obey. [*To Viola*] This comes with seeking you.
But there's no remedy; I shall answer it.
What will you do, now my necessity
Makes me to ask you for my purse? It grieves me
Much more for what I cannot do for you
Than what befalls myself. You stand amazed,
But be of comfort.

SECOND OFFICER Come, sir, away.

ANTONIO [*to Viola*]
I must entreat of you some of that money.

VIOLA What money, sir?
For the fair kindness you have showed me here,
And part being prompted by your present trouble,
Out of my lean and low ability
I'll lend you something. My having is not much;
I'll make division of my present with you.
Hold, there's half my coffer. [*She offers money.*]

ANTONIO Will you deny me now?
Is't possible that my deserts to you
Can lack persuasion? Do not tempt my misery,
Lest that it make me so unsound a man
As to upbraid you with those kindnesses
That I have done for you.

VIOLA I know of none,
Nor know I you by voice or any feature.
I hate ingratitude more in a man
Than lying, vainness, babbling drunkenness,
Or any taint of vice whose strong corruption
Inhabits our frail blood.

ANTONIO Oh, heavens themselves!

SECOND OFFICER Come, sir, I pray you, go.

ANTONIO
Let me speak a little. This youth that you see here
I snatched one half out of the jaws of death,
Relieved him with such sanctity of love,
And to his image, which methought did promise
Most venerable worth, did I devotion.

287 Capilet i.e., "little horse." (From "capel," a nag.) **288 motion** offer. **289–90 perdition of souls** i.e., loss of lives. **292 take up** settle, make up **294 He . . . him** i.e., Cesario has as horrible a conception of Sir Andrew **300 supportance** upholding **302–3 A little . . . man** (With bawdy suggestion of the penis.) **308 *duello*** dueling code **319 undertaker** one who takes upon himself a task or business; here, a challenger. **for you** ready for you.

324 for that as for what **325 He** i.e., The horse **330 favor** face **334 answer it** stand trial and make reparation for it. **343 part** partly **345 having** wealth **346 present** present store **347 coffer** purse. (Literally, strongbox.) **349–50 deserts . . . persuasion** claims on you can fail to persuade you to help me. **350 tempt** try too severely **351 unsound** morally weak, lacking in self-control **356 vainness** vaingloriousness **363 such . . . love** i.e., such veneration as is due to a sacred relic **364 image** what he appeared to be. (Playing on the idea of a religious icon to be venerated.) **365 venerable worth** worthiness of being venerated

FIRST OFFICER
What's that to us? The time goes by. Away!

ANTONIO
But, oh, how vile an idol proves this god!
Thou hast, Sebastian, done good feature shame. 368
In nature there's no blemish but the mind;
None can be called deformed but the unkind. 370
Virtue is beauty, but the beauteous evil 371
Are empty trunks o'erflourished by the devil. 372

FIRST OFFICER
The man grows mad. Away with him! Come, come, sir.

ANTONIO Lead me on. *Exit* [*with Officers*].

VIOLA [*aside*]
Methinks his words do from such passion fly
That he believes himself. So do not I. 376
Prove true, imagination, oh, prove true,
That I, dear brother, be now ta'en for you!

SIR TOBY Come hither, knight. Come hither, Fabian.
We'll whisper o'er a couplet or two of most sage saws. 380
[*They gather apart from Viola.*]

VIOLA
He named Sebastian. I my brother know 381
Yet living in my glass; even such and so 382
In favor was my brother, and he went 383
Still in this fashion, color, ornament, 384
For him I imitate. Oh, if it prove, 385
Tempests are kind, and salt waves fresh in love!
[*Exit.*]

SIR TOBY A very dishonest paltry boy, and more a 387
coward than a hare. His dishonesty appears in leaving 388
his friend here in necessity and denying him; and for 389
his cowardship, ask Fabian.

FABIAN A coward, a most devout coward, religious in it. 391

SIR ANDREW 'Slid, I'll after him again and beat him. 392

SIR TOBY Do, cuff him soundly, but never draw thy sword.

SIR ANDREW An I do not— [*Exit.*]

FABIAN Come, let's see the event. 396

SIR TOBY I dare lay any money 'twill be nothing yet. 397
Exeunt.

4.1

Enter Sebastian and Clown [*Feste*].

FESTE Will you make me believe that I am not sent for you?

SEBASTIAN Go to, go to, thou art a foolish fellow. Let me be clear of thee.

FESTE Well held out, i'faith! No, I do not know you, 5
nor I am not sent to you by my lady to bid you come
speak with her, nor your name is not Master Cesario,
nor this is not my nose, neither. Nothing that is so is so.

SEBASTIAN I prithee, vent thy folly somewhere else. 9
Thou know'st not me.

FESTE Vent my folly! He has heard that word of some 11
great man, and now applies it to a fool. Vent my folly!
I am afraid this great lubber, the world, will prove a 13
cockney. I prithee now, ungird thy strangeness and 14
tell me what I shall vent to my lady. Shall I vent to her
that thou art coming?

SEBASTIAN I prithee, foolish Greek, depart from me. 17
There's money for thee. [*He gives money.*] If you tarry
longer, I shall give worse payment.

FESTE By my troth, thou hast an open hand. These 20
wise men that give fools money get themselves a good
report—after fourteen years' purchase. 22

Enter [*Sir*] *Andrew,* [*Sir*] *Toby, and Fabian.*

SIR ANDREW Now, sir, have I met you again? There's for you! [*He strikes Sebastian.*]

SEBASTIAN Why, there's for thee, and there, and there!
[*He beats Sir Andrew with the hilt of his dagger.*]
Are all the people mad?

SIR TOBY Hold, sir, or I'll throw your dagger o'er the house.

FESTE This will I tell my lady straight. I would not be in 29
some of your coats for twopence. [*Exit.*] 30

SIR TOBY Come on, sir, hold! [*He grips Sebastian.*]

SIR ANDREW Nay, let him alone. I'll go another way to
work with him. I'll have an action of battery against 33
him, if there be any law in Illyria. Though I struck him
first, yet it's no matter for that.

SEBASTIAN Let go thy hand!

SIR TOBY Come, sir, I will not let you go. Come, my
young soldier, put up your iron. You are well fleshed. 38
Come on.

SEBASTIAN
I will be free from thee. [*He breaks free and draws his sword.*] What wouldst thou now?
If thou dar'st tempt me further, draw thy sword. 41

SIR TOBY What, what? Nay, then I must have an ounce
or two of this malapert blood from you. [*He draws.*] 43

Enter Olivia.

368 Thou . . . shame i.e., You have shamed physical beauty by showing that it does not always reflect inner beauty. **370 unkind** ungrateful, unnatural. **371 beauteous evil** those who are outwardly beautiful but evil within **372 trunks** (1) chests (2) bodies. **o'erflourished** (1) covered with ornamental carvings (2) made outwardly beautiful **376 So . . . I** i.e., I do not believe myself (in the hope that has arisen in me). **380 We'll . . . saws** i.e., Let's converse privately. (*Saws* are sayings.) **381–2 I . . . glass** i.e., I know that my brother's likeness lives in me **383 favor** appearance **384 Still** always **385 prove** prove true **387 dishonest** dishonorable **388 dishonesty** dishonor **389 denying** refusing to acknowledge **391 religious in it** making a religion of cowardice. **392 'Slid** By his (God's) eyelid **396 event** outcome. **397 lay** wager. **yet** nevertheless, after all.
4.1. Location: Before Olivia's house.

5 held out kept up **9 vent** (1) utter (2) void, excrete, get rid of **11 of** from, suited to the diction of; or, with reference to **13 lubber** lout **14 cockney** effeminate or foppish fellow. (Feste comically despairs of finding common sense anywhere if people start using affected phrases like those Sebastian uses.) **ungird thy strangeness** put off your affectation of being a stranger. (Feste apes the kind of high-flown speech he has just deplored.) **17 Greek** (1) one who speaks gibberish (as in "It's all Greek to me") (2) buffoon (as in "merry Greek") **20 open** generous. (With money or with blows.) **22 report** reputation. **after . . . purchase** i.e., at great cost and after long delays. (Land was ordinarily valued at the price of twelve years' rental; the Fool adds two years to this figure.) **29 straight** at once. **29–30 in . . . coats** i.e., in your shoes **33 action of battery** lawsuit for physical assault **38 fleshed** initiated into battle. **41 tempt** make trial of **43 malapert** saucy, impudent

OLIVIA
Hold, Toby! On thy life I charge thee, hold!
SIR TOBY Madam—
OLIVIA
Will it be ever thus? Ungracious wretch,
Fit for the mountains and the barbarous caves,
Where manners ne'er were preached! Out of my sight!—
Be not offended, dear Cesario.—
Rudesby, begone!
[Exeunt Sir Toby, Sir Andrew, and Fabian.]
I prithee, gentle friend,
Let thy fair wisdom, not thy passion, sway
In this uncivil and unjust extent
Against thy peace. Go with me to my house,
And hear thou there how many fruitless pranks
This ruffian hath botched up, that thou thereby
Mayst smile at this. Thou shalt not choose but go.
Do not deny. Beshrew his soul for me!
He started one poor heart of mine, in thee.
SEBASTIAN *[aside]*
What relish is in this? How runs the stream?
Or I am mad, or else this is a dream.
Let fancy still my sense in Lethe steep;
If it be thus to dream, still let me sleep!
OLIVIA
Nay, come, I prithee. Would thou'dst be ruled by me!
SEBASTIAN
Madam, I will.
OLIVIA Oh, say so, and so be! *Exeunt.*

✤

4.2

Enter Maria [carrying a gown and a false beard], and Clown [Feste].

MARIA Nay, I prithee, put on this gown and this beard; make him believe thou art Sir Topas the curate. Do it quickly. I'll call Sir Toby the whilst. *[Exit.]*

FESTE Well, I'll put it on, and I will dissemble myself in't, and I would I were the first that ever dissembled in such a gown. *[He disguises himself in gown and beard.]* I am not tall enough to become the function well, nor lean enough to be thought a good student; but to be said an honest man and a good housekeeper goes as fairly as to say a careful man and a great scholar. The competitors enter.

Enter [Sir] Toby [and Maria].

SIR TOBY Jove bless thee, Master Parson.

FESTE *Bonos dies,* Sir Toby. For, as the old hermit of Prague, that never saw pen and ink, very wittily said to a niece of King Gorboduc, "That that is, is"; so I, being Master Parson, am Master Parson; for what is "that" but "that," and "is" but "is"?

SIR TOBY To him, Sir Topas.

FESTE What, ho, I say! Peace in this prison!
[He approaches the door behind which Malvolio is confined.]

SIR TOBY The knave counterfeits well; a good knave.

MALVOLIO *(within)* Who calls there?

FESTE Sir Topas the curate, who comes to visit Malvolio the lunatic.

MALVOLIO Sir Topas, Sir Topas, good Sir Topas, go to my lady—

FESTE Out, hyperbolical fiend! How vexest thou this man! Talkest thou nothing but of ladies?

SIR TOBY Well said, Master Parson.

MALVOLIO Sir Topas, never was man thus wronged. Good Sir Topas, do not think I am mad. They have laid me here in hideous darkness.

FESTE Fie, thou dishonest Satan! I call thee by the most modest terms, for I am one of those gentle ones that will use the devil himself with courtesy. Say'st thou that house is dark?

MALVOLIO As hell, Sir Topas.

FESTE Why, it hath bay windows transparent as barricadoes, and the clerestories toward the south north are as lustrous as ebony; and yet complainest thou of obstruction?

MALVOLIO I am not mad, Sir Topas. I say to you this house is dark.

FESTE Madman, thou errest. I say there is no darkness but ignorance, in which thou art more puzzled than the Egyptians in their fog.

MALVOLIO I say this house is as dark as ignorance, though ignorance were as dark as hell; and I say there was never man thus abused. I am no more mad than you are. Make the trial of it in any constant question.

50 Rudesby Ruffian **52 extent** attack **55 botched up** clumsily contrived **56 Thou . . . go** I insist on your going with me. **57 deny** refuse. **Beshrew** Curse. (A mild oath.) **for me** for my part. **58 He . . . thee** i.e., He alarmed that part of my heart which lies in your bosom. (To *start* is also to drive an animal such as a *hart* [*heart*] from its cover.) **59 What . . . this?** i.e., What am I to make of this? (*Relish* means "taste.") **60 Or** Either **61 Let . . . steep** i.e., Let this fantasy continue to steep my senses in forgetfulness. (*Lethe* is the river of forgetfulness in the underworld.)
4.2. Location: Olivia's house.
2 Sir (An honorific title for priests.) **Topas** (A name perhaps derived from Chaucer's comic knight in the "Rime of Sir Thopas" or from a similar character in Lyly's *Endymion.* Topaz, a semiprecious stone, was believed to be a cure for lunacy.) **3 the whilst** in the meantime. **4 dissemble** disguise. (With a play on "feign.") **7 become the function** adorn the priestly office **8 lean** (Scholars were proverbially sparing of diet.) **student** scholar (in divinity)

9–11 to be . . . scholar to be accounted honest and hospitable is as good as being known as a painstaking scholar. (Feste suggests that honesty and charity are found as often in ordinary men as in clerics.) **11 competitors** associates, partners (in this plot) **13 *Bonos dies*** Good day **13–14 hermit of Prague** (Probably another invented authority.) **15 King Gorboduc** a legendary king of ancient Britain, protagonist in the English tragedy *Gorboduc* (1562) **26 hyperbolical** vehement, boisterous. **fiend** i.e., the devil supposedly possessing Malvolio. **33 modest** moderate **35 house** i.e., room **37–8 barricadoes** barricades. (Which are opaque. Feste speaks comically in impossible paradoxes, but Malvolio seems not to notice.) **38 clerestories** windows in an upper wall **45 Egyptians . . . fog** (Alluding to the darkness brought upon Egypt by Moses; see Exodus 10:21–3.) **49 constant question** problem that requires consecutive reasoning.

FESTE What is the opinion of Pythagoras concerning wildfowl?

MALVOLIO That the soul of our grandam might haply inhabit a bird.

FESTE What think'st thou of his opinion?

MALVOLIO I think nobly of the soul, and no way approve his opinion.

FESTE Fare thee well. Remain thou still in darkness. Thou shalt hold th'opinion of Pythagoras ere I will allow of thy wits, and fear to kill a woodcock lest thou dispossess the soul of thy grandam. Fare thee well.

[*He moves away from Malvolio's prison.*]

MALVOLIO Sir Topas, Sir Topas!

SIR TOBY My most exquisite Sir Topas!

FESTE Nay, I am for all waters.

MARIA Thou mightst have done this without thy beard and gown. He sees thee not.

SIR TOBY To him in thine own voice, and bring me word how thou find'st him.—I would we were well rid of this knavery. If he may be conveniently delivered, I would he were, for I am now so far in offense with my niece that I cannot pursue with any safety this sport to the upshot. Come by and by to my chamber.

Exit [*with Maria*].

FESTE [*singing as he approaches Malvolio's prison*]

"Hey, Robin, jolly Robin,
Tell me how thy lady does."

MALVOLIO Fool!

FESTE "My lady is unkind, pardie."

MALVOLIO Fool!

FESTE "Alas, why is she so?"

MALVOLIO Fool, I say!

FESTE "She loves another—" Who calls, ha?

MALVOLIO Good Fool, as ever thou wilt deserve well at my hand, help me to a candle, and pen, ink, and paper. As I am a gentleman, I will live to be thankful to thee for't.

FESTE Master Malvolio?

MALVOLIO Ay, good Fool.

FESTE Alas, sir, how fell you besides your five wits?

MALVOLIO Fool, there was never man so notoriously abused. I am as well in my wits, Fool, as thou art.

FESTE But as well? Then you are mad indeed, if you be no better in your wits than a fool.

MALVOLIO They have here propertied me, keep me in darkness, send ministers to me—asses—and do all they can to face me out of my wits.

FESTE Advise you what you say. The minister is here. [*He speaks as Sir Topas.*] Malvolio, Malvolio, thy wits the heavens restore! Endeavor thyself to sleep, and leave thy vain bibble-babble.

MALVOLIO Sir Topas!

FESTE [*in Sir Topas's voice*] Maintain no words with him, good fellow. [*In his own voice*] Who, I, sir? Not I, sir. God b'wi'you, good Sir Topas. [*In Sir Topas's voice*] Marry, amen. [*In his own voice*] I will, sir, I will.

MALVOLIO Fool! Fool! Fool, I say!

FESTE Alas, sir, be patient. What say you, sir? I am shent for speaking to you.

MALVOLIO Good Fool, help me to some light and some paper. I tell thee I am as well in my wits as any man in Illyria.

FESTE Welladay that you were, sir!

MALVOLIO By this hand, I am. Good Fool, some ink, paper, and light; and convey what I will set down to my lady. It shall advantage thee more than ever the bearing of letter did.

FESTE I will help you to't. But tell me true, are you not mad indeed, or do you but counterfeit?

MALVOLIO Believe me, I am not. I tell thee true.

FESTE Nay, I'll ne'er believe a madman till I see his brains. I will fetch you light and paper and ink.

MALVOLIO Fool, I'll requite it in the highest degree. I prithee, begone.

FESTE [*sings*]

I am gone, sir,
And anon, sir,
I'll be with you again,
In a trice,
Like to the old Vice,
Your need to sustain;

Who, with dagger of lath,
In his rage and his wrath,
Cries, "Aha!" to the devil;
Like a mad lad,
"Pare thy nails, dad?
Adieu, goodman devil!" *Exit.*

✤

4.3

Enter Sebastian [*with a pearl*].

SEBASTIAN

This is the air; that is the glorious sun;

50–1 Pythagoras . . . wildfowl (An opening for the discussion of transmigration of souls, a doctrine held by Pythagoras.) **52 haply** perhaps **59 allow of thy wits** certify your sanity. **woodcock** (A proverbially stupid bird, easily caught.) **63 Nay . . . waters** i.e., Indeed, I can turn my hand to anything. **68 delivered** i.e., delivered from prison **71 upshot** conclusion. **72–3 "Hey, Robin . . . does"** (Another fragment of an old song, a version of which is attributed to Sir Thomas Wyatt.) **75 pardie** i.e., by God, certainly. **86 besides** out of. **five wits** The intellectual faculties, usually listed as common wit, imagination, fantasy, judgment, and memory. **87–8 notoriously abused** egregiously ill treated. **89 But** Only **91 propertied me** i.e., treated me as property and thrown me into the lumber-room **93 face . . . wits** brazenly represent me as having lost my wits.

94 Advise you Take care **105 shent** scolded, rebuked **109 Welladay** Alas, would that **125 Vice** comic tempter of the "old" morality plays **127 dagger of lath** comic weapon of the Vice in at least some morality plays **131 Pare thy nails** (This may allude to the belief that evil spirits could use nail parings to get control of their victims; cf. Dromio of Syracuse in *The Comedy of Errors*, 4.3.69, "Some devils ask but the parings of one's nail," and the Boy's characterization of Pistol in *Henry V*, 4.4.72–3, as "this roaring devil i'th' old play, that everyone may pare his nails with a wooden dagger.") **132 goodman** title for a person of substance but not of gentle birth. (This line could be Feste's farewell to Malvolio and his "devil.")
4.3. Location: Olivia's garden.

This pearl she gave me, I do feel't and see't;
And though 'tis wonder that enwraps me thus,
Yet 'tis not madness. Where's Antonio, then?
I could not find him at the Elephant;
Yet there he was, and there I found this credit, 6
That he did range the town to seek me out.
His counsel now might do me golden service;
For though my soul disputes well with my sense 9
That this may be some error, but no madness,
Yet doth this accident and flood of fortune 11
So far exceed all instance, all discourse, 12
That I am ready to distrust mine eyes
And wrangle with my reason that persuades me
To any other trust but that I am mad, 15
Or else the lady's mad. Yet if 'twere so,
She could not sway her house, command her followers, 17
Take and give back affairs and their dispatch 18
With such a smooth, discreet, and stable bearing
As I perceive she does. There's something in't
That is deceivable. But here the lady comes. 21

Enter Olivia and Priest.

OLIVIA
Blame not this haste of mine. If you mean well,
Now go with me and with this holy man
Into the chantry by. There, before him, 24
And underneath that consecrated roof,
Plight me the full assurance of your faith,
That my most jealous and too doubtful soul 27
May live at peace. He shall conceal it
Whiles you are willing it shall come to note, 29
What time we will our celebration keep 30
According to my birth. What do you say? 31

SEBASTIAN
I'll follow this good man, and go with you,
And having sworn truth, ever will be true.

OLIVIA
Then lead the way, good father, and heavens so shine
That they may fairly note this act of mine! *Exeunt.* 35

5.1

Enter Clown [Feste] and Fabian.

FABIAN Now, as thou lov'st me, let me see his letter.
FESTE Good Master Fabian, grant me another request.
FABIAN Anything.
FESTE Do not desire to see this letter.
FABIAN This is to give a dog and in recompense desire 5
my dog again. 6

Enter Duke [Orsino], Viola, Curio, and lords.

ORSINO Belong you to the Lady Olivia, friends?
FESTE Ay, sir, we are some of her trappings. 8
ORSINO I know thee well. How dost thou, my good fellow?
FESTE Truly, sir, the better for my foes and the worse 10
for my friends.
ORSINO Just the contrary—the better for thy friends.
FESTE No, sir, the worse.
ORSINO How can that be?
FESTE Marry, sir, they praise me, and make an ass of 15
me. Now my foes tell me plainly I am an ass, so that 16
by my foes, sir, I profit in the knowledge of myself,
and by my friends I am abused; so that, conclusions to 18
be as kisses, if your four negatives make your two 19
affirmatives, why then the worse for my friends and 20
the better for my foes.
ORSINO Why, this is excellent.
FESTE By my troth, sir, no, though it please you to be 23
one of my friends. 24
ORSINO Thou shalt not be the worse for me. There's gold.
[*He gives a coin.*]
FESTE But that it would be double-dealing, sir, I would 26
you could make it another.
ORSINO Oh, you give me ill counsel.
FESTE Put your grace in your pocket, sir, for this once, 29
and let your flesh and blood obey it. 30
ORSINO Well, I will be so much a sinner to be a 31
double-dealer. There's another. [*He gives another coin.*]
FESTE *Primo, secundo, tertio,* is a good play, and the old 33
saying is, the third pays for all. The triplex, sir, is a 34
good tripping measure; or the bells of Saint Bennet, 35
sir, may put you in mind—one, two, three.
ORSINO You can fool no more money out of me at this
throw. If you will let your lady know I am here to 38
speak with her, and bring her along with you, it may
awake my bounty further.
FESTE Marry, sir, lullaby to your bounty till I come
again. I go, sir, but I would not have you to think that

6 was was previously. **credit** report **9 my soul . . . sense** i.e., both my rational faculties and my physical senses come to the conclusion **11 accident** unexpected event **12 instance** precedent. **discourse** reason **15 trust** belief **17 sway** rule **18 Take . . . dispatch** receive reports on matters of household business and see to their execution **21 deceivable** deceptive. **24 chantry by** private endowed chapel nearby (where mass would be said for the souls of the dead, including Olivia's brother). **27 jealous** anxious, mistrustful. **doubtful** full of doubts **29 Whiles** until. **come to note** become known **30 What time** at which time. **our celebration** i.e., the actual marriage. (What they are about to perform is a binding betrothal.) **31 birth** social position. **35 fairly note** look upon with favor
5.1. Location: Before Olivia's house.

5–6 This . . . again (Apparently a reference to a well-known reply of Dr. Bulleyn when Queen Elizabeth asked for his dog and promised a gift of his choosing in return; he asked to have his dog back.) **8 trappings** ornaments, decorations. **10 for** because of **15–16 make an ass of me** i.e., flatter me into foolishly thinking well of myself. **18 abused** flatteringly deceived **18–20 conclusions . . . affirmatives** i.e., as when a young lady, asked for a kiss, says "no, no" really meaning "yes"; or, as in grammar, two negatives make an affirmative **23 though** even though **24 friends** i.e., those who, according to Feste's syllogism, flatter him. **26 But** Except for the fact. **double-dealing** (1) giving twice (2) deceit, duplicity **29 Put . . . pocket** (1) Pay no attention to your honor, put it away (2) Reach in your pocket or purse and show your customary grace or munificence. (*Your Grace* is also the formal way of addressing a duke.) **30 it** i.e., my "ill counsel." **31 to be** as to be **33 *Primo . . . tertio*** Latin ordinals: first, second, third. **play** (Perhaps a mathematical game or game of dice.) **34 the third . . . all** the third time is lucky. (Proverbial.) **triplex** triple time in music **35 Saint Bennet** church of St. Benedict **38 throw** (1) time (2) throw of the dice.

my desire of having is the sin of covetousness. But as you say, sir, let your bounty take a nap. I will awake it anon. *Exit.*

Enter Antonio and Officers.

VIOLA
Here comes the man, sir, that did rescue me.

ORSINO
That face of his I do remember well,
Yet when I saw it last it was besmeared
As black as Vulcan in the smoke of war.
A baubling vessel was he captain of,
For shallow draft and bulk unprizable,
With which such scatheful grapple did he make
With the most noble bottom of our fleet
That very envy and the tongue of loss
Cried fame and honor on him. What's the matter?

FIRST OFFICER
Orsino, this is that Antonio
That took the *Phoenix* and her freight from Candy,
And this is he that did the *Tiger* board
When your young nephew Titus lost his leg.
Here in the streets, desperate of shame and state,
In private brabble did we apprehend him.

VIOLA
He did me kindness, sir, drew on my side,
But in conclusion put strange speech upon me.
I know not what 'twas but distraction.

ORSINO
Notable pirate, thou saltwater thief,
What foolish boldness brought thee to their mercies
Whom thou in terms so bloody and so dear
Hast made thine enemies?

ANTONIO Orsino, noble sir,
Be pleased that I shake off these names you give me.
Antonio never yet was thief or pirate,
Though, I confess, on base and ground enough
Orsino's enemy. A witchcraft drew me hither.
That most ingrateful boy there by your side
From the rude sea's enraged and foamy mouth
Did I redeem; a wreck past hope he was.
His life I gave him, and did thereto add
My love, without retention or restraint,
All his in dedication. For his sake
Did I expose myself—pure for his love—
Into the danger of this adverse town,
Drew to defend him when he was beset;
Where being apprehended, his false cunning,
Not meaning to partake with me in danger,
Taught him to face me out of his acquaintance
And grew a twenty years' removèd thing
While one would wink; denied me mine own purse,
Which I had recommended to his use
Not half an hour before.

VIOLA How can this be?

ORSINO When came he to this town?

ANTONIO
Today, my lord; and for three months before,
No interim, not a minute's vacancy,
Both day and night did we keep company.

Enter Olivia and attendants.

ORSINO
Here comes the Countess. Now heaven walks on earth.
But for thee, fellow—fellow, thy words are madness.
Three months this youth hath tended upon me;
But more of that anon.—Take him aside.

OLIVIA [*to Orsino*]
What would my lord—but that he may not have—
Wherein Olivia may seem serviceable?—
Cesario, you do not keep promise with me.

VIOLA Madam?

ORSINO Gracious Olivia—

OLIVIA
What do you say, Cesario?—Good my lord—

VIOLA
My lord would speak. My duty hushes me.

OLIVIA
If it be aught to the old tune, my lord,
It is as fat and fulsome to mine ear
As howling after music.

ORSINO Still so cruel?

OLIVIA Still so constant, lord.

ORSINO
What, to perverseness? You uncivil lady,
To whose ingrate and unauspicious altars
My soul the faithfull'st off'rings have breathed out
That e'er devotion tendered! What shall I do?

OLIVIA
Even what it please my lord that shall become him.

ORSINO
Why should I not, had I the heart to do it,
Like to th'Egyptian thief at point of death
Kill what I love?—a savage jealousy
That sometime savors nobly. But hear me this:

49 Vulcan Roman god of fire and smith to the other gods; his face was blackened by the fire **50 baubling** insignificant, trifling **51 For** because of. **draft** depth of water a ship draws. **unprizable** of value too slight to be estimated, not worth taking as a "prize" **52 scatheful** destructive **53 bottom** ship **54 very envy** i.e., even those who had most reason to hate him, his enemies. **loss** i.e., the losers **57 from Candy** on her return from Candia, or Crete **60 desperate . . . state** recklessly disregarding the disgrace and danger to himself **61 brabble** brawl **63 put . . . me** spoke to me strangely. **64 but distraction** unless (it was) madness. **65 Notable** Notorious **67 in terms . . . dear** in so bloodthirsty and costly a manner **69 Be pleased that I** Allow me to **71 base and ground** solid grounds **75 wreck** shipwrecked person **77 retention** reservation **78 All . . . dedication** devoted wholly to him. **79 pure** entirely, purely **80 Into** unto. **adverse** hostile

84 face . . . acquaintance brazenly deny he knew me **85–6 grew . . . wink** in the twinkling of an eye acted as though we had been estranged for twenty years **87 recommended** consigned **95 for** as for **98 but . . . have** except that which he may not have—i.e., my love **103 Good my lord** (Olivia urges Orsino to listen to Cesario.) **106 fat and fulsome** gross and offensive **111 ingrate and unauspicious** thankless and unpropitious **114 become** suit **116 th'Egyptian thief** (An allusion to the story of Theagenes and Chariclea in the *Ethiopica,* a Greek romance by Heliodorus. The robber chief, Thyamis of Memphis, having captured Chariclea and fallen in love with her, is attacked by a larger band of robbers; threatened with death, he attempts to slay her first.) **118 savors nobly** is not without nobility.

Since you to nonregardance cast my faith,
And that I partly know the instrument
That screws me from my true place in your favor,
Live you the marble-breasted tyrant still.
But this your minion, whom I know you love,
And whom, by heaven I swear, I tender dearly,
Him will I tear out of that cruel eye
Where he sits crownèd in his master's spite.—
Come, boy, with me. My thoughts are ripe in
mischief.
I'll sacrifice the lamb that I do love,
To spite a raven's heart within a dove. [*Going*.]

VIOLA
And I, most jocund, apt, and willingly,
To do you rest, a thousand deaths would die.
[*Going*.]

OLIVIA
Where goes Cesario?

VIOLA After him I love
More than I love these eyes, more than my life,
More by all mores than e'er I shall love wife.
If I do feign, you witnesses above
Punish my life for tainting of my love!

OLIVIA
Ay me, detested! How am I beguiled!

VIOLA
Who does beguile you? Who does do you wrong?

OLIVIA
Hast thou forgot thyself? Is it so long?
Call forth the holy father. [*Exit an attendant*.]

ORSINO [*to Viola*] Come, away!

OLIVIA
Whither, my lord?—Cesario, husband, stay.

ORSINO
Husband?

OLIVIA Ay, husband. Can he that deny?

ORSINO [*to Viola*]
Her husband, sirrah?

VIOLA No, my lord, not I.

OLIVIA
Alas, it is the baseness of thy fear
That makes thee strangle thy propriety.
Fear not, Cesario, take thy fortunes up;
Be that thou know'st thou art, and then thou art
As great as that thou fear'st.

Enter Priest.

Oh, welcome, father!
Father, I charge thee by thy reverence
Here to unfold—though lately we intended
To keep in darkness what occasion now
Reveals before 'tis ripe—what thou dost know
Hath newly passed between this youth and me.

PRIEST
A contract of eternal bond of love,
Confirmed by mutual joinder of your hands,
Attested by the holy close of lips,
Strengthened by interchangement of your rings,
And all the ceremony of this compact
Sealed in my function, by my testimony;
Since when, my watch hath told me, toward my
grave
I have traveled but two hours.

ORSINO [*to Viola*]
Oh, thou dissembling cub! What wilt thou be
When time hath sowed a grizzle on thy case?
Or will not else thy craft so quickly grow
That thine own trip shall be thine overthrow?
Farewell, and take her, but direct thy feet
Where thou and I henceforth may never meet.

VIOLA
My Lord, I do protest—

OLIVIA Oh, do not swear!
Hold little faith, though thou hast too much fear.

Enter Sir Andrew.

SIR ANDREW For the love of God, a surgeon! Send one presently to Sir Toby.

OLIVIA What's the matter?

SIR ANDREW He's broke my head across, and has given Sir Toby a bloody coxcomb too. For the love of God, your help! I had rather than forty pound I were at home.

OLIVIA Who has done this, Sir Andrew?

SIR ANDREW The Count's gentleman, one Cesario. We took him for a coward, but he's the very devil incardinate.

ORSINO My gentleman, Cesario?

SIR ANDREW 'Od's lifelings, here he is!—You broke my head for nothing, and that that I did I was set on to do't by Sir Toby.

VIOLA
Why do you speak to me? I never hurt you.
You drew your sword upon me without cause,
But I bespake you fair, and hurt you not.

SIR ANDREW If a bloody coxcomb be a hurt, you have hurt me. I think you set nothing by a bloody coxcomb.

Enter [*Sir*] *Toby and Clown* [*Feste*].

119 nonregardance neglect **120 that** since **121 screws** pries, forces **123 minion** darling, favorite **124 tender** regard **125–6 Him . . . spite** I will tear Cesario away from Olivia, in whose cruel eye he sits like a king to spite me, his true master. **128–9 I'll . . . dove** i.e., I'll kill Cesario, whom I love, to revenge myself on this seemingly gracious but black-hearted lady. **130 apt** readily **131 do you rest** give you ease **134 by all mores** by all such comparisons **136 Punish . . . love!** punish me with death for being disloyal to the love I feel! **137 detested** hated and denounced by another. **143 sirrah** (The normal way of addressing an inferior.) **145 strangle thy propriety** i.e., deny what is properly yours, disavow your marriage to me. **147 that** that which **148 as that thou fear'st** as him you fear, i.e., Orsino.

151 occasion necessity **155 joinder** joining **156 close** meeting **159 Sealed . . . function** ratified through my carrying out of my priestly office **163 grizzle** scattering of gray hair. **case** skin. **165 trip** wrestling trick used to throw an opponent. (You'll get overclever and trip yourself up.) **169 Hold . . . fear** Keep to your oath as well as you can, even if you are frightened by Orsino's threats. **171 presently** immediately **173 broke** broken the skin, cut **174 coxcomb** fool's cap resembling the crest of a cock; here, head **180 incardinate** (For "incarnate.") **182 'Od's lifelings** By God's little lives **187 bespake you fair** addressed you courteously **189 set nothing by** regard as insignificant

Here comes Sir Toby, halting. You shall hear more. But if he had not been in drink, he would have tickled you othergates than he did.

ORSINO How now, gentleman? How is't with you?

SIR TOBY That's all one. He's hurt me, and there's th'end on't.—Sot, didst see Dick surgeon, sot?

FESTE Oh, he's drunk, Sir Toby, an hour agone; his eyes were set at eight i'th' morning.

SIR TOBY Then he's a rogue, and a passy measures pavane. I hate a drunken rogue.

OLIVIA Away with him! Who hath made this havoc with them?

SIR ANDREW I'll help you, Sir Toby, because we'll be dressed together.

SIR TOBY Will you help? An ass-head and a coxcomb and a knave, a thin-faced knave, a gull!

OLIVIA
Get him to bed, and let his hurt be looked to.
[*Exeunt Feste, Fabian, Sir Toby, and Sir Andrew.*]

Enter Sebastian.

SEBASTIAN
I am sorry, madam, I have hurt your kinsman;
But, had it been the brother of my blood,
I must have done no less with wit and safety.—
You throw a strange regard upon me, and by that
I do perceive it hath offended you.
Pardon me, sweet one, even for the vows
We made each other but so late ago.

ORSINO
One face, one voice, one habit, and two persons,
A natural perspective, that is and is not!

SEBASTIAN
Antonio, O my dear Antonio!
How have the hours racked and tortured me
Since I have lost thee!

ANTONIO Sebastian are you?

SEBASTIAN Fear'st thou that, Antonio?

ANTONIO
How have you made division of yourself?
An apple cleft in two is not more twin
Than these two creatures. Which is Sebastian?

OLIVIA Most wonderful!

SEBASTIAN [*seeing Viola*]
Do I stand there? I never had a brother;
Nor can there be that deity in my nature
Of here and everywhere. I had a sister,
Whom the blind waves and surges have devoured.
Of charity, what kin are you to me?
What countryman? What name? What parentage?

VIOLA
Of Messaline. Sebastian was my father.
Such a Sebastian was my brother, too.
So went he suited to his watery tomb.
If spirits can assume both form and suit,
You come to fright us.

SEBASTIAN A spirit I am indeed,
But am in that dimension grossly clad
Which from the womb I did participate.
Were you a woman, as the rest goes even,
I should my tears let fall upon your cheek
And say, "Thrice welcome, drownèd Viola!"

VIOLA
My father had a mole upon his brow.

SEBASTIAN And so had mine.

VIOLA
And died that day when Viola from her birth
Had numbered thirteen years.

SEBASTIAN
Oh, that record is lively in my soul!
He finishèd indeed his mortal act
That day that made my sister thirteen years.

VIOLA
If nothing lets to make us happy both
But this my masculine usurped attire,
Do not embrace me till each circumstance
Of place, time, fortune, do cohere and jump
That I am Viola—which to confirm
I'll bring you to a captain in this town
Where lie my maiden weeds, by whose gentle help
I was preserved to serve this noble count.
All the occurrence of my fortune since
Hath been between this lady and this lord.

SEBASTIAN [*to Olivia*]
So comes it, lady, you have been mistook.
But nature to her bias drew in that.
You would have been contracted to a maid,
Nor are you therein, by my life, deceived.
You are betrothed both to a maid and man.

ORSINO [*to Olivia*]
Be not amazed; right noble is his blood.
If this be so, as yet the glass seems true,
I shall have share in this most happy wreck.
[*To Viola*] Boy, thou hast said to me a thousand times
Thou never shouldst love woman like to me.

VIOLA
And all those sayings will I over swear,
And all those swearings keep as true in soul

191 halting limping. **193 othergates** otherwise **195 That's all one** It doesn't matter; never mind. **195–6 there's . . . on't** that's all there is to it. **196 Sot** (1) Fool (2) Drunkard **197 agone** ago **198 set** fixed or closed **199–200 passy measures pavane** passe-measure pavane, a slow-moving, stately dance. (Suggesting Sir Toby's impatience to have his wounds dressed.) **203–4 be dressed** have our wounds surgically dressed **209 the brother . . . blood** my own brother **210 with wit and safety** with intelligent concern for my own safety. **211 You . . . me** You look strangely at me **215 habit** dress **216 A natural perspective** an optical device or illusion created in this instance by nature **218 racked** tortured **221 Fear'st thou that** Do you doubt that **228 here and everywhere** omnipresence. **229 blind** heedless, indiscriminate **230 Of charity** (Tell me) in kindness

234 suited dressed; clad in human form **235 form and suit** physical appearance and dress **237 in . . . clad** clothed in that fleshly shape **238 participate** possess in common with all humanity. **239 as . . . even** since everything else agrees **246 record** recollection **249 lets** hinders **252 jump** coincide, fit exactly **255 weeds** clothes **260 nature . . . that** nature followed her bent in that. (The metaphor is from the game of bowls.) **263 a maid** i.e., a virgin man **265 the glass** i.e., the *natural perspective* of line 216 **266 wreck** shipwreck, accident. **268 like to me** as well as you love me. **269 over swear** swear again

As doth that orbèd continent the fire 271
That severs day from night.

ORSINO Give me thy hand,
And let me see thee in thy woman's weeds.

VIOLA
The captain that did bring me first on shore
Hath my maid's garments. He upon some action 275
Is now in durance, at Malvolio's suit, 276
A gentleman and follower of my lady's.

OLIVIA
He shall enlarge him. Fetch Malvolio hither. 278
And yet, alas, now I remember me,
They say, poor gentleman, he's much distract.

Enter Clown [Feste] with a letter, and Fabian.

A most extracting frenzy of mine own 281
From my remembrance clearly banished his. 282
How does he, sirrah?

FESTE Truly, madam, he holds Beelzebub at the stave's 284
end as well as a man in his case may do. He's here 285
writ a letter to you; I should have given't you today
morning. But as a madman's epistles are no gospels, 287
so it skills not much when they are delivered. 288

OLIVIA Open't and read it.

FESTE Look then to be well edified when the fool
delivers the madman. [*He reads loudly.*] "By the Lord, 291
madam—"

OLIVIA How now, art thou mad?

FESTE No, madam, I do but read madness. An Your
Ladyship will have it as it ought to be, you must allow
vox. 296

OLIVIA Prithee, read i'thy right wits.

FESTE So I do, madonna; but to read his right wits is to 298
read thus. Therefore perpend, my princess, and give 299
ear.

OLIVIA [*to Fabian*] Read it you, sirrah.

FABIAN (*reads*) "By the Lord, madam, you wrong me,
and the world shall know it. Though you have put me
into darkness and given your drunken cousin rule
over me, yet have I the benefit of my senses as well
as Your Ladyship. I have your own letter that induced
me to the semblance I put on, with the which I 307
doubt not but to do myself much right or you much
shame. Think of me as you please. I leave my duty 309
a little unthought of, and speak out of my injury. 310
The madly used Malvolio."

OLIVIA Did he write this?

FESTE Ay, madam.

ORSINO This savors not much of distraction.

OLIVIA
See him delivered, Fabian. Bring him hither. 315
[*Exit Fabian.*]
My lord, so please you, these things further thought
on, 316
To think me as well a sister as a wife, 317
One day shall crown th'alliance on't, so please you, 318
Here at my house and at my proper cost. 319

ORSINO
Madam, I am most apt t'embrace your offer. 320
[*To Viola*] Your master quits you; and for your
service done him, 321
So much against the mettle of your sex, 322
So far beneath your soft and tender breeding,
And since you called me master for so long,
Here is my hand. You shall from this time be
Your master's mistress.

OLIVIA A sister! You are she.

Enter [Fabian, with] Malvolio.

ORSINO
Is this the madman?

OLIVIA Ay, my lord, this same.
How now, Malvolio?

MALVOLIO Madam, you have done me wrong,
Notorious wrong.

OLIVIA Have I, Malvolio? No.

MALVOLIO [*showing a letter*]
Lady, you have. Pray you, peruse that letter.
You must not now deny it is your hand.
Write from it, if you can, in hand or phrase, 332
Or say 'tis not your seal, not your invention. 333
You can say none of this. Well, grant it then,
And tell me, in the modesty of honor, 335
Why you have given me such clear lights of favor, 336
Bade me come smiling and cross-gartered to you,
To put on yellow stockings, and to frown
Upon Sir Toby and the lighter people? 339
And, acting this in an obedient hope, 340
Why have you suffered me to be imprisoned,
Kept in a dark house, visited by the priest, 342
And made the most notorious geck and gull 343
That e'er invention played on? Tell me why? 344

OLIVIA
Alas, Malvolio, this is not my writing,
Though, I confess, much like the character; 346

271 As . . . fire i.e., as the sphere of the sun keeps the fire **275 action** legal charge **276 in durance** imprisoned **278 enlarge** release **281 extracting** i.e., that obsessed me and drew all thoughts except of Cesario from my mind **282 his** i.e., his madness. **284–5 holds . . . end** i.e., keeps the devil at a safe distance. (The metaphor is of fighting with quarterstaffs or long poles.) **287 a madman's . . . gospels** i.e., there is no truth in a madman's letters. (An allusion to readings in the church service of selected passages from the epistles and the gospels.) **288 skills** matters. **delivered** (1) delivered to their recipient (2) read aloud. **291 delivers** speaks the words of **296 *vox*** voice, i.e., an appropriately loud voice. **298 to read . . . wits** to express his true state of mind **299 perpend** consider, attend. (A deliberately lofty word.) **307 the which** i.e., the letter **309–10 I leave . . . injury** I leave unsaid the expressions of duty with which I would normally conclude, and convey instead my sense of having been wronged.

315 delivered released **316 so . . . on** if you are pleased on further consideration of all that has happened **317 To . . . wife** to regard me as favorably as a sister-in-law as you had hoped to regard me as a wife **318 crown . . . on't** i.e., serve as occasion for two marriages confirming our new relationships **319 proper** own **320 apt** ready **321 quits** releases **322 mettle** natural disposition **332 from it** differently **333 invention** composition. **335 in . . . honor** in the name of all that is decent and honorable **336 clear lights** evident signs **339 lighter** lesser **340 acting . . . hope** when I acted thus out of obedience to you and in hope of your favor **342 priest** i.e., Feste **343 geck** dupe **344 invention played on** contrivance sported with. **346 the character** my handwriting

But out of question 'tis Maria's hand. 347
And now I do bethink me, it was she
First told me thou wast mad; then cam'st in smiling, 349
And in such forms which here were presupposed 350
Upon thee in the letter. Prithee, be content.
This practice hath most shrewdly passed upon thee; 352
But when we know the grounds and authors of it,
Thou shalt be both the plaintiff and the judge
Of thine own cause.

FABIAN Good madam, hear me speak,
And let no quarrel nor no brawl to come 356
Taint the condition of this present hour, 357
Which I have wondered at. In hope it shall not,
Most freely I confess, myself and Toby
Set this device against Malvolio here,
Upon some stubborn and uncourteous parts 361
We had conceived against him. Maria writ 362
The letter at Sir Toby's great importance, 363
In recompense whereof he hath married her.
How with a sportful malice it was followed 365
May rather pluck on laughter than revenge, 366
If that the injuries be justly weighed 367
That have on both sides passed.

OLIVIA [*to Malvolio*]
Alas, poor fool, how have they baffled thee! 369

FESTE Why, "Some are born great, some achieve
greatness, and some have greatness thrown upon
them." I was one, sir, in this interlude, one Sir Topas, 372
sir, but that's all one. "By the Lord, fool, I am not 373
mad." But do you remember? "Madam, why laugh
you at such a barren rascal? An you smile not, he's
gagged." And thus the whirligig of time brings in his 376
revenges.

MALVOLIO I'll be revenged on the whole pack of you!
[*Exit.*]

OLIVIA
He hath been most notoriously abused.

ORSINO
Pursue him, and entreat him to a peace.
He hath not told us of the captain yet.
When that is known, and golden time convents, 382
A solemn combination shall be made
Of our dear souls. Meantime, sweet sister,
We will not part from hence. Cesario, come—
For so you shall be, while you are a man;
But when in other habits you are seen, 387
Orsino's mistress and his fancy's queen. 388
Exeunt [*all, except Feste*].

FESTE (*sings*)
When that I was and a little tiny boy, 389
With hey, ho, the wind and the rain,
A foolish thing was but a toy, 391
For the rain it raineth every day.

But when I came to man's estate,
With hey, ho, the wind and the rain,
'Gainst knaves and thieves men shut their gate,
For the rain it raineth every day.

But when I came, alas, to wive,
With hey, ho, the wind and the rain,
By swaggering could I never thrive,
For the rain it raineth every day.

But when I came unto my beds, 401
With hey, ho, the wind and the rain,
With tosspots still had drunken heads, 403
For the rain it raineth every day.

A great while ago the world begun,
With hey, ho, the wind and the rain,
But that's all one, our play is done,
And we'll strive to please you every day.
[*Exit.*]

347 out of beyond **349 cam'st** you came **350 presupposed** specified beforehand **352 practice** plot. **shrewdly passed** mischievously been perpetrated **356 to come** in the future **357 condition** (happy) nature **361 Upon** on account of. **parts** qualities, deeds **362 conceived against him** seen and resented in him. **363 importance** importunity **365 followed** carried out **366 pluck on** induce **367 If that** if **369 baffled** disgraced, quelled **372 interlude** little play **373 that's all one** no matter for that. **376 whirligig** spinning top

382 convents (1) summons, calls together (2) suits **387 habits** attire **388 fancy's** love's **389 and a little** a little **391 toy** trifle **401 unto my beds** i.e., (1) drunk to bed, or, perhaps, (2) in the evening of life **403 tosspots** drunkards

All's Well That Ends Well

All's Well That Ends Well belongs to that period of Shakespeare's creative life when he concentrated on his great tragedies and wrote little comedy. The few apparent exceptions do not fit readily into conventional dramatic genres. *Measure for Measure* (1603–1604), usually called a problem play, is darkly preoccupied with human carnality and injustice. *Troilus and Cressida* (c. 1601–1602), printed between the histories and the tragedies in the Folio of 1623, is a disillusioning satire of love and war somewhat akin to the black comedy of our modern theater. *All's Well* shares, to an extent, the satiric and brooding spirit of these two plays. Its "bed trick," in which one woman is substituted for another in an assignation with the protagonist, Bertram, poses ethical problems for the audience (as does a similar trick in *Measure for Measure*). Helena, in arranging the substitution, may seem too much of a schemer. The relations between the sexes are problematic in this play, written, as it seemingly was, at a time when Shakespeare was preoccupied with tragedies that are haunted by images of destructive femaleness and of debasing sexuality. The action of *All's Well* is, to a large extent, controlled by an admirable and attractive woman, and yet the play dwells more than do earlier comedies on the potential hazards of sexuality. For these and other reasons, *All's Well* is often grouped with the problem plays.

At the same time, the play also looks forward to Shakespeare's late romances, *Pericles, Cymbeline, The Winter's Tale*, and *The Tempest*. Here the mode of comedy turns toward the miraculous and tragicomic, with journeys of separation ending in tearful reunion, and sinful error ending in spiritual rebirth. This mode was not unknown in Shakespeare's comedies of the late 1590s: *As You Like it* ends with the sudden and implausible conversion of its villains, and *Much Ado About Nothing* offers forgiveness to the undeserving Claudio while restoring his traduced fiancée, Hero, to a new life. *Measure for Measure* follows a similar pattern of redemptive pardon for the corrupted Angelo and providential deliverance for Isabella. Both *All's Well* and *Measure for Measure* contain features of this comedy of forgiveness, even if admittedly the ironies surrounding the gesture of forgiving are far less controlled than in the late romances.

Certainly, in any case, *All's Well* occupies a central position in the line of development from the early comedies to the late romances. Helena points back to earlier comic women in her role as engineer of the love plot and points forward to women of the late romances in her role as daughter, victim, and savior (though early comedy and late romance are, to be sure, not as neatly distinguishable as this antithesis suggests). Bertram, who is virtually without precedent in earlier comedies, anticipates, to a degree, Posthumus in *Cymbeline*, Florizel in *The Winter's Tale*, and Ferdinand in *The Tempest* in that he takes part in a marriage sanctioned and defined largely by paternal intervention. *All's Well*, like the romances and unlike the earlier comedies, affords a remarkably prominent role to the older generation.

The probable date of *All's Well* is consistent with such a transitional function. Its dates are hard to fix by external evidence, for it was neither registered nor printed until 1623, and allusions to it are scarce. Some scholars think that it is the *Love's Labor's Won* intriguingly mentioned by Francis Meres in *Palladis Tamia* in 1598, which Shakespeare might then have revised some time around 1601–1604. Portions of the play do feature the rhymed couplets, letters in sonnet form, and witty conceits that we normally associate with Shakespeare's early style. These old-fashioned effects may have been deliberate on Shakespeare's part, however, not unlike the anachronisms he later introduces in *Pericles* and *Cymbeline*. Certainly, a major portion of the play dates stylistically from 1601–1604 or even later. Here the language is elliptical and compact, the images complexly interwoven, the verse rhythms free.

In any event, with its two contrasting styles poised between romance and satire, *All's Well* juxtaposes the reassurances of comedy with the pessimistic ironies of Shakespeare's tragic period. It lacks many of the felicities we associate with the festive comedies of the 1590s: the love songs, the innocently hedonistic joy, and the well-mated young lovers escaping from stern parents or an envious court. *All's Well* has too often been judged negatively for its failure to achieve a festive mood that Shakespeare probably did not intend it to have. Both of its central figures are flawed, to the extent that they seem oddly cast in the roles normally demanded by romantic comedy of young men and women who fall in love and eventually marry. Bertram as nominal hero quickly loses our sympathy when he runs away from his marriage vows to pursue warmongering, male camaraderie, and the attempted seduction of a virgin; Helena as nominal heroine complicates our response by the ethically dubious ways in which she tricks Bertram into marrying her and then becoming her partner in bed when he has sworn he will never do so. As the undeserving hero, forgiven in spite of his waywardness, however, Bertram plays an essential role in the play's problematic resolution—or failure to achieve complete resolution. He is, in the common Renaissance view of all humanity, unworthy of the forgiveness he receives, whereas Helena's generosity in forgiving him suggests at least a capability in humanity for decency and compassion. We are left, as in *Measure for Measure*, with a sense of the perennially unbridgeable gap between human ideals and their achievement, and yet we view this dilemma in a comic context where second chances and hope are bestowed even on those who appear to deserve them least.

The satiric mode in *All's Well* is conveyed chiefly through Lavatch the clown and through Parolles, the boastful, cowardly knave who accompanies Bertram to the wars. Lavatch, with the bitter and riddling wit of the professional fool, gives expression to many of the satirical themes that are also illustrated by the exposure of Parolles. Lavatch jests about cuckoldry and the other marital difficulties that cause men to flee from women; he pokes fun at court manners and apes the prodigal disobedience of his master Bertram. He is, like Parolles, called a "foulmouthed and calumnious knave" (1.3.56–7), although the inversion of appearance and reality is evident here, as with all Shakespearean fools: Parolles is truly more fool and knave than his mocking counterpart. Parolles is all pretense. Full of sound, but hollow like the drum to which he is compared, he is a swaggerer and a fashionmonger whose clothes conceal his lack of inner substance. He is a recognizable satiric type that goes back to the Latin dramatists Plautus and Terence: the braggart soldier. He is, to be sure, endearing in his outrageousness; Shakespeare endows him with that vitality we find also in those earlier braggart soldiers, Falstaff and Pistol. He enlists sympathy and fellow-feeling from an audience when, having been exposed and humiliated by his military comrades for his cowardice, he rejoins, "Who cannot be crushed with a plot?", and goes on to insist in soliloquy that "Simply the thing I am / Shall make me live" (4.3.326–36). Ultimately, his ebullient vitality leads to his being forgiven even by old Lafew, who has long been on to Parolles's tricks but finds him irresistible nonetheless. Because Parolles lacks the self-awareness of Falstaff, we merely laugh at him rather than with him. To the impressionable young Bertram, hungry for fame, Parolles represents smartness and military style. Bertram rejects the true worth of Helena because she lacks family position and, ironically, embraces the false worth of a parvenu. Parolles and Helena are foils from their first encounter, when the braggart sardonically derides virginity as unnatural and out of fashion. Parolles stands opposite also to Lafew, the Countess, and the King—those dignified embodiments of a traditional chivalrous order, whose generous teachings Bertram rejects for the company of Parolles and of women he hopes to seduce. By disguising his slick insolence in the guise of fashionable manliness, Parolles is able to win Bertram's friendship for a time. Parolles is not really a tempter, for we never see him bending Bertram from his true inclination; rather, Bertram is himself too much in love with sham reputation, too rebellious against the civilized decencies of his elders. He is the Prodigal Son, or Youth in the old morality play, perversely eager to prove his own worst enemy.

Yet Bertram is not without a redeeming nobleness—he bears himself bravely in the Florentine wars—and cannot be fooled indefinitely by his roguish companion. The exposure of Parolles is one of satiric humiliation, even if he is eventually forgiven and reconciled in a way that Mavolio in *Twelfth Night* or many of Ben Jonson's humorous gulls are not. The engineers of Parolles's exposure use the language of Jonsonian satire in their devices to outwit him: their game is a "sport" done "for the love of laughter," employing a snare whereby the "fox" or the "woodcock" will entrap himself (3.6.34–102 and 4.1.92). The device of public humiliation is particularly appropriate, because Parolles is himself a railing slanderer, like Lucio in *Measure for Measure*, caustically brilliant in his invective but nonetheless a slayer of men's reputations. The punishment of ridicule fits his particular crime. His callous disregard for the good name of various French military commanders is parallel to Bertram's indifference to the public shame he has heaped upon his virtuous wife. Once Parolles's bluff has been called, Bertram is, in part, disabused of his folly; but other means are needed to convince him of the wrong he has done to Helena. Indeed, Bertram's very coldness in turning away from Parolles shows a lack of humility. Bertram must learn to know himself better by being tricked, exposed, and humiliated.

The fabulous romancelike aspect of *All's Well* is conveyed chiefly through its folktale plot and through the character of Helena. The story is derived from the third "day" of Giovanni Boccaccio's *Decameron*, a day devoted to tales of lovers obliged to overcome seemingly impossible obstacles in order to achieve love's happiness. The story was translated into English by William Painter in *The Palace of Pleasure* (1566). To win the nobly born Beltramo, Giletta of Narbona must cure the French king with her physician-father's secret remedy and then must perform the riddling tasks assigned her by Beltramo as his means of being rid of her. Both these motifs have ancient antecedents in folklore, and, as in his late romances, Shakespeare puts great stress on the wondrous and improbable nature of these events.

All common sense warns against the likelihood of Helena's success. She is vastly below Bertram in social station or in "blood," even though she excels in "virtue." (This low station is unique among Shakespeare's comic heroines, and it contributes to what is so unusual about this play.) Her only hope is a desperate gamble: to cure the ailing King and so win Bertram as her reward. No one supposes at first she will even be admitted to the King, who has given up all hope of living; his "congregated college" of learned doctors "have concluded / That laboring art can never ransom nature / From her inaidible estate" (2.1.119–21). Helena transcends these rational doubts through resourcefulness and, above all, through a faith in help from above. She is willing to "hazard" all for love. She senses that her father's legacy will "be sanctified / By th' luckiest stars in heaven" (1.3.243–4), and she manages to convince not only the Countess and Lafew (persons who do not appear in Boccaccio) but also the King himself. Believing, like George Bernard Shaw's Saint Joan, that God will perform his greatest works through the humblest of his creatures, Helena inspires her listeners with faith in the impossible. Lafew is so moved by her simple eloquence that he proclaims to the King, "I have seen a medicine / That's able to breathe life into a stone" (2.1.73–4). Soon the King, too, is persuaded that in Helena "some blessèd spirit doth speak / His powerful sound within an organ weak" (lines 177–8). Once the King's cure has been effected, even Parolles and Bertram must agree with Lafew that the age of miracles, long thought to have passed, is with them again. The King's cure by the "Very hand of heaven," through the agency of a "weak—/And debile minister," is matter for a pious ballad or an old tale (2.3.31–4). At the same time, Helena is very determined and is willing to use whatever means are necessary to get what she wants.

Helena's assuming the role of wooer is a problem for Bertram—as indeed it was for many a male reader in Victorian times, who found her worrisomely guilty of transgressing the boundaries between acceptable and unacceptable female behavior. Bertram nominally objects to her lower social station, but that is a matter the King can remedy. Evidently, Bertram is daunted by something else: by the very prospect of marriage with a virtuous and attractive young woman who unmistakably wants him. He reacts with subterfuge and flight, subscribing to Parolles's notion that it is better to be a soldier than to be one who "hugs his kicky-wicky here at home, / Spending his manly marrow in her arms" (2.3:281–2). War gives Bertram his excuse to evade the responsibilities of marriage. In Italy, to be sure, he finds the prospect of sexual encounter with Diana irresistible, since he thinks he can obtain and then discard her when the affair is done. He is prepared to cheapen "available" women this way but not to commit himself to the complex and mutual commitment that marriage requires. In these terms, Helena's task is to bring Bertram to the point of understanding that sexuality and deep friendship can and should exist in a single relationship, and that women must not be bifurcated by his imagination into those who are respectable but untouchable (like his mother) or cheap and violable. Bertram's unself-knowing friendship with Parolles is symptomatic of his immaturity, and hence the exposure of Parolles is a necessary part of Bertram's education, but Helena must also find a way to help Bertram get over his mistrust of her sexuality.

In so doing, she resembles other Shakespeare heroines, such as Desdemona in *Othello*, Rosalind in *As You Like It*, and Silvia in *The Two Gentlemen of Verona*, who take the initiative in wooing. Helena is fully aware that her intrepidity offends Bertram. Yet she is abundantly admired by the King, Lafew, the Countess, and other rightminded persons in the play, all of whom find Bertram's reluctance immature and virtually incomprehensible. Moreover, her enterprising spirit (see 1.1.216–29) finds its reward in marital success at the end. Throughout his romantic comedies, Shakespeare invites us to admire women who take the lead in wooing, even if he problematizes the issue in *All's Well* by emphasizing Bertram's hostility and Helena's consequent need for deceptive stratagems, and even if he also sees how such a story can end tragically in *Romeo and Juliet* and *Othello*.

The impossible tasks Helena must perform are stated as riddles, as is usual in a folktale, and must be solved by riddling or paradoxical means. Bertram writes that she must "get the ring upon my finger, which never shall come off, and show me a child begotten of thy body that I am father to" (3.2.57–9). Such a challenge invites ingenuity, as in Boccaccio, but in Shakespeare the solution also requires providential aid. Helena's first sad response is to set Bertram free and renounce her audacious pretentions. Her pilgrimage of grief takes her to Florence, where Bertram happens to be serving in the wars. This cannot be mere coincidence, and yet we do not accuse her of scheming in any opprobrious sense. Throughout, her motives are at once virtuous and deceitful, lawful and sinful, just as her very sexuality is wholesome and yet is seen by us in a context of debased human nature (as is generally not the case with Shakespeare's earlier heroines). Her acts are prompted at once by providence and by shrewd calculation. Even if providence must be credited with introducing her to Diana, the very lady whom Bertram is importuning in love, Helena makes the most of such opportunities afforded her, never doubting that "heaven" has "fated" her both to help Diana and simultaneously to serve her own turn (4.4.18–20). The bed trick is a "plot," but a virtuous one, a "deceit" that is "lawful," a deed that is "not sin, and yet a sinful fact" (3.7.38–47). Diana repeatedly plays upon these same riddles in accusing Bertram before the King: he is "guilty, and he is not guilty" (5.3.290).

These conundrums, although playful and entertaining in Shakespeare's highly complicated denouement (not found in Boccaccio), also hint at paradoxes in the nature of humanity. Bertram's typically human waywardness justifies a cunning response. "I think't no sin," argues Diana, "To cozen him that would unjustly win" (4.2.75–6). Justice on earth, as in *Measure for Measure*, must take forms only roughly approximating those of heavenly justice, for human depravity sometimes requires a harsh remedy in kind. Yet, by a providential paradox, humanity's thwarted and evil nature, seemingly so fatal, leads instead to regeneration: by being humbled, humanity is enabled to rise: "The web of our life is of a mingled yarn, good and ill together," says a sympathetic observer of Bertram. "Our virtues would be proud if our faults whipped them not, and our crimes would despair if they were not cherished by our virtues" (4.3.70–3). Human perversity accentuates the need for divine grace.

Helena is a romantic heroine, only metaphorically the "angel" who must "Bless this unworthy husband," reprieving him by her "prayers" from "the wrath / Of greatest justice" (3.4.25–9). Indeed, she is capable of being quite threatening to Bertram. If Bertram typifies the "Natural rebellion" of all youth and Helena, the "herb of grace" whom he has willfully rejected (5.3.6 and 4.5.17), Helena is also an aggressive woman whose clever plans to win Bertram against his will produce an understandable reluctance in the young man. Still, the spiritual overtones are not extraneous to this bittersweet comedy. However much we may sympathize with his desire to choose in love for himself, Bertram's revolt is incomprehensible to every witness except Parolles. Bertram himself concedes, too late it seems, that he has recognized Helena's precious worth. This note of "love that comes too late," wherein the penitent sinner confesses "That's good that's gone," hovers over the play with its tragicomic mood (5.3.58–61). Helena is a "jewel" thrown away and seemingly forever lost (5.3.1). The semblance of her death is, in fact, only another one of her inventive schemes, along with the bewildering contretemps of the final scene. Yet, when she reappears, setting all to rights, she comes as "one that's dead" but is now "quick," alive again, merely a "shadow" of her former self (5.3.304–8). Bertram has not actually committed the evil he intended; by a providential sophistry, he is innocent, like Claudio in *Much Ado* or Angelo in *Measure for Measure*, and so is reconciled to the goodness he has failed to merit. Even Parolles is given a second chance by the magnanimous Lafew. As the play's title implies, all might have miscarried through humanity's "rash faults" that "Make trivial price of serious things we have" (5.3.61–2), were it not for a forgiving power that can make people's worst failings an instrument of their penitence and recovery. This resolution fleetingly comforts us in the final scene, even though it must do battle with such manifest imbalances as the prolonged shaming of Bertram and the scant attention paid to his reunion with Helena. The web of human life remains a mingled yarn.

The balance in this remarkable play between comedy and tragedy is very much subject to decisions made in performance. For many years after it was written and presumably performed in London, the theatrical decision was to avoid the play entirely or to transform it into something else. An operatic version in 1832 attempted to compensate for the play's purported ethical dubieties with a medley of songs from other plays. Not until the twentieth century did the play begin to come into its own. Even then, Helena remained troublesome for some directors and audiences. In a 1955 production at Stratford-upon-Avon by Noel Willman, Helena was persistent and even aggressive in her pursuit of a Bertram whose responses were plainly triggered by male anxieties about female dominance. In Michael Benthall's Old Vic production of 1953, on the other hand, Helena (Claire Bloom) was a Cinderella fairy princess eventually reunited with her truculent Prince Charming (John Neville). In Trevor Nunn's production for the Royal Shakespeare Company in 1981, Bertram's caddish behavior was made distinctly unsympathetic, to the extent that he was allowed no opportunity to redeem himself at the end. The military action of the play has lent itself to disenchantment engendered by the Vietnam War, as in John Barton's 1967 production for the Royal Shakespeare Company. War becomes a gentleman's game, or (as in Nunn's version) a reminiscence of the Crimea or the trenches of World War I. David Jones's highly successful production at Stratford, Canada, in 1977 was autumnal in mood. Yet the play can succeed also as hilarious comedy throughout. Performance history demonstrates how fluid interpretation can be: there are many Helenas, many Bertrams, many Parolles.

All's Well That Ends Well

[*Dramatis Personae*

COUNTESS OF ROSSILLION, *Bertram's mother and Helena's guardian*
BERTRAM, *Count of Rossillion*
HELENA (*or* HELEN), *orphaned daughter of the Countess's physician*
PAROLLES, *a follower of Bertram*
RINALDO, *a steward,* LAVATCH, *a clown or fool,* PAGE, } *servants of the Countess of Rossillion*

KING OF FRANCE
LAFEW, *an old lord*

Two FRENCH LORDS, *the brothers Dumain, later captains in the Florentine army*
Other LORDS
Two FRENCH SOLDIERS
A GENTLEMAN
A MESSENGER

DUKE OF FLORENCE
WIDOW CAPILET *of Florence*
DIANA, *her daughter*
MARIANA, *neighbor and friend of the Widow*

Lords, Attendants, Soldiers, Citizens

SCENE: *Rossillion; Paris; Florence; Marseilles*]

1.1

Enter young Bertram, Count of Rossillion, his mother [*the Countess*]*, and Helena,* [*with*] *Lord Lafew, all in black.*

COUNTESS In delivering my son from me, I bury a second husband.

BERTRAM And I in going, madam, weep o'er my father's death anew. But I must attend His Majesty's command, to whom I am now in ward, evermore in subjection.

LAFEW You shall find of the King a husband, madam; you, sir, a father. He that so generally is at all times good must of necessity hold his virtue to you, whose worthiness would stir it up where it wanted rather than lack it where there is such abundance.

COUNTESS What hope is there of His Majesty's amendment?

LAFEW He hath abandoned his physicians, madam, under whose practices he hath persecuted time with hope, and finds no other advantage in the process but only the losing of hope by time.

COUNTESS This young gentlewoman had a father—oh, that "had," how sad a passage 'tis!—whose skill was almost as great as his honesty; had it stretched so far, would have made nature immortal, and death should have play for lack of work. Would for the King's sake he were living! I think it would be the death of the King's disease.

LAFEW How called you the man you speak of, madam?

1.1. Location: Rossillion, i.e., Roussillon, in southern France, on the Spanish border near the Mediterranean. The Count's residence.
1 delivering sending. (With play on "giving birth to" and "freeing.") **4 attend** obey **5 in ward** (According to a feudal custom, the King became the guardian of orphaned heirs to estates, who remained "in ward" so long as they were minors. The King's jurisdiction extended even so far as the bestowal of his ward in marriage, but only to someone of equal rank.) **7 of** in the person of. **husband** i.e., protector **8 generally** to all people

9 hold continue to devote **9–11 whose . . . abundance** you whose virtue is such that it would inspire generosity even in those who normally lack it, and who therefore cannot fail to find it in a king who is so abundantly generous. **10 wanted** is lacking **12–13 amendment** recovery. **15–16 hath . . . hope** has tormented his time with painful treatments in vain hope of cure **19 passage** (1) phrase, expression (2) passing away **20 honesty** integrity of character **22 Would** Would that

COUNTESS He was famous, sir, in his profession, and it was his great right to be so: Gerard de Narbonne.

LAFEW He was excellent indeed, madam. The King very lately spoke of him admiringly and mourningly. He was skillful enough to have lived still, if knowledge could be set up against mortality.

BERTRAM What is it, my good lord, the King languishes of?

LAFEW A fistula, my lord.

BERTRAM I heard not of it before.

LAFEW I would it were not notorious.—Was this gentlewoman the daughter of Gerard de Narbonne?

COUNTESS His sole child, my lord, and bequeathed to my overlooking. I have those hopes of her good that her education promises her dispositions she inherits, which makes fair gifts fairer; for where an unclean mind carries virtuous qualities, there commendations go with pity—they are virtues and traitors too. In her they are the better for their simpleness. She derives her honesty and achieves her goodness.

LAFEW Your commendations, madam, get from her tears.

COUNTESS 'Tis the best brine a maiden can season her praise in. The remembrance of her father never approaches her heart but the tyranny of her sorrows takes all livelihood from her cheek.—No more of this, Helena. Go to, no more, lest it be rather thought you affect a sorrow than to have—

HELENA I do affect a sorrow indeed, but I have it too.

LAFEW Moderate lamentation is the right of the dead, excessive grief the enemy to the living.

COUNTESS If the living be enemy to the grief, the excess makes it soon mortal.

BERTRAM Madam, I desire your holy wishes.

LAFEW How understand we that?

COUNTESS
Be thou blest, Bertram, and succeed thy father
In manners as in shape! Thy blood and virtue
Contend for empire in thee, and thy goodness
Share with thy birthright! Love all, trust a few,
Do wrong to none. Be able for thine enemy
Rather in power than use, and keep thy friend
Under thy own life's key. Be checked for silence
But never taxed for speech. What heaven more will,
That thee may furnish and my prayers pluck down,
Fall on thy head! Farewell. [*To Lafew*] My lord,
'Tis an unseasoned courtier; good my lord,
Advise him.

LAFEW He cannot want the best
That shall attend his love.

COUNTESS Heaven bless him!—Farewell, Bertram.

BERTRAM The best wishes that can be forged in your thoughts be servants to you! [*Exit Countess.*] [*To Helena*] Be comfortable to my mother, your mistress, and make much of her.

LAFEW Farewell, pretty lady. You must hold the credit of your father. [*Exeunt Bertram and Lafew.*]

HELENA Oh, were that all! I think not on my father,
And these great tears grace his remembrance more
Than those I shed for him. What was he like?
I have forgot him. My imagination
Carries no favor in't but Bertram's.
I am undone. There is no living, none,
If Bertram be away. 'Twere all one
That I should love a bright particular star
And think to wed it, he is so above me.
In his bright radiance and collateral light
Must I be comforted, not in his sphere.
Th'ambition in my love thus plagues itself;
The hind that would be mated by the lion
Must die for love. 'Twas pretty, though a plague,
To see him every hour, to sit and draw
His archèd brows, his hawking eye, his curls,
In our heart's table—heart too capable
Of every line and trick of his sweet favor.
But now he's gone, and my idolatrous fancy
Must sanctify his relics. Who comes here?

Enter Parolles.

[*Aside*] One that goes with him. I love him for his sake;
And yet I know him a notorious liar,

30 still (1) now as before (2) forever **34 fistula** ulcerous sore **39 overlooking** supervision. **39–45 I have . . . goodness** I have those high hopes for her future well-being which her education will further, nurturing the goodness which she was born with, and enhancing her innate gifts; for where a corrupted mind carries a veneer of learned goodness, praise is mingled with regret for good qualities betrayed by their opposite. In her there is no such division: she inherits a pure heart and nourishes it with good deeds. **48 season** (1) add flavor to (2) preserve (as with salt) **51 livelihood** animation **52 Go to** i.e., Come, come **53 affect** are enamored of, make an exaggerated show of. **than** rather than **54 I do . . . too** I do put on an outward show of sorrow, but I feel it as well. **55 right** rightful due **57–8 If . . . mortal** i.e., If grief is by its nature injurious to human happiness, excess of it soon proves fatal. **60 How . . . that?** What do you mean? (Spoken perhaps in response to the Countess in lines 57–8, simultaneously with Bertram's speech in line 59.) **62 manners** conduct. **Thy blood** May your noble birth **63–4 thy goodness . . . birthright** may the good qualities you achieve share with your inherited qualities in ruling your life.

65–7 Be able . . . key Be powerful enough to resist your enemy without having to use that power, and hold your friend's life as dearly as your own. **67 checked** reproved **68–70 What . . . head!** May such blessings heaven intends for you, such as will assist you and that my prayers can draw down from heaven, bestow their goodness upon you! **71 unseasoned** inexperienced **72–3 He . . . love** He will not be without the best advice that my love can provide him with. **75–6 The best . . . you!** May the best wishes you can imagine always assist you! **77 comfortable** comforting, serviceable **78 make much of** be devoted to **79 hold the credit** uphold the reputation **82 his** Bertram's **83 for him** i.e., for my father when he died. **85 favor** (1) image, face (2) preference **87–8 'Twere . . . That** It would be all the same if **90 collateral** distant and parallel, shed from a different sphere. (The different Ptolemaic spheres were said to move collaterally, the implication here being that the distance cannot be closed.) **93 hind** (1) female deer (2) servant **94 pretty** pleasing **96 hawking** keen **97 table** drawing board or tablet **97–8 capable Of** susceptible to **98 trick** characteristic expression. **favor** face. **99 fancy** (1) imagination, fantasy (2) love **101 his** Bertram's

Think him a great way fool, solely a coward.
Yet these fixed evils sit so fit in him
That they take place when virtue's steely bones
Looks bleak i'th' cold wind. Withal, full oft we see
Cold wisdom waiting on superfluous folly.

PAROLLES Save you, fair queen!

HELENA And you, monarch!

PAROLLES No.

HELENA And no.

PAROLLES Are you meditating on virginity?

HELENA Ay. You have some stain of soldier in you; let me ask you a question. Man is enemy to virginity; how may we barricado it against him?

PAROLLES Keep him out.

HELENA But he assails, and our virginity, though valiant, in the defense yet is weak. Unfold to us some warlike resistance.

PAROLLES There is none. Man setting down before you will undermine you and blow you up.

HELENA Bless our poor virginity from underminers and blowers-up! Is there no military policy how virgins might blow up men?

PAROLLES Virginity being blown down, man will quicklier be blown up. Marry, in blowing him down again, with the breach yourselves made you lose your city. It is not politic in the commonwealth of nature to preserve virginity. Loss of virginity is rational increase, and there was never virgin got till virginity was first lost. That you were made of is metal to make virgins. Virginity by being once lost may be ten times found; by being ever kept, it is ever lost. 'Tis too cold a companion. Away with't!

HELENA I will stand for't a little, though therefore I die a virgin.

PAROLLES There's little can be said in't; 'tis against the rule of nature. To speak on the part of virginity is to accuse your mothers, which is most infallible disobedience. He that hangs himself is a virgin; virginity murders itself, and should be buried in highways out of all sanctified limit, as a desperate offendress against nature. Virginity breeds mites, much like a cheese, consumes itself to the very paring, and so dies with feeding his own stomach. Besides, virginity is peevish, proud, idle, made of self-love, which is the most inhibited sin in the canon. Keep it not; you cannot choose but lose by't. Out with't! Within th'one year it will make itself two, which is a goodly increase, and the principal itself not much the worse. Away with't!

HELENA How might one do, sir, to lose it to her own liking?

PAROLLES Let me see. Marry, ill, to like him that ne'er it likes. 'Tis a commodity will lose the gloss with lying; the longer kept, the less worth. Off with't while 'tis vendible; answer the time of request. Virginity, like an old courtier, wears her cap out of fashion, richly suited, but unsuitable, just like the brooch and the toothpick, which wear not now. Your date is better in your pie and your porridge than in your cheek; and your virginity, your old virginity, is like one of our French withered pears—it looks ill, it eats drily. Marry, 'tis a withered pear; it was formerly better; marry, yet 'tis a withered pear. Will you anything with it?

HELENA
Not my virginity, yet . . .
There shall your master have a thousand loves,
A mother, and a mistress, and a friend,
A phoenix, captain, and an enemy,
A guide, a goddess, and a sovereign,
A counselor, a traitress, and a dear;
His humble ambition, proud humility,
His jarring concord, and his discord dulcet,
His faith, his sweet disaster, with a world

103 a great way in large measure a. **solely** completely **104 fixed** ineradicable, firmly established. **sit so fit** are so natural and plausible (in him) **105–6 take . . . wind** find acceptance and take precedence, while virtue, in its uncompromising severity, is left out in the cold. **106 Withal** Consequently **107 Cold . . . folly** wisdom lacking warmth obliged to dance attendance on a useless display of comfortable foolishness. **108 Save** i.e., God save. **queen** (A hyperbolical compliment, which Helena answers in kind, whereupon they both deny their titles.) **113 stain** tinge **115 barricado** barricade
118 Unfold Reveal **120 setting . . . you** laying siege (as though to a town, but with bawdy quibbling that is elaborated in the following lines. To *undermine* in 121 is to tunnel under and into [in both a military and sexual sense]; to *blow up* is to explode with mines and impregnate.) **123 policy** stratagem **125–8 Virginity . . . city** Continuing the metaphor of siege warfare, Parolles argues that virginity's attempts to defend itself against male assault are doomed to self-defeat, just as a defending city, by digging countermines, opens up more breaches through which the defenses can be undermined. Virginal resistance will only sharpen a man's appetite and blow him up—i.e., make him erect. (*Marry* is a mild oath derived from "by the Virgin Mary.") **128 politic** expedient **129 rational increase** (1) an increase by the law of nature (2) an increase of rational beings
130 got begotten **131 That** That which. **metal** substance, as in minting of coins or compounding of interest. (With idea also of *mettle,* "spirit," "temperament.") **132–3 may . . . found** i.e., may reproduce itself tenfold **135 stand** fight, stand up. (With a sexual quibble.) **die** (With probable quibble on "experience orgasm.") **137 in't** in its behalf **138 on the part of** in behalf of

140 is a virgin i.e., is like a virgin, since virginity is a kind of suicide **141–2 buried . . . limit** (Suicides were customarily buried at crossroads of highways, not in consecrated ground.) **144 paring** covering rind **145 his** its. **stomach** (1) maw (2) pride. **147 inhibited** prohibited. **canon** catalogue of sins. (Pride is the first of the Deadly Sins.) **147–8 Keep . . . by't** (With a play on the idea of losing one's virginity.) **148 Out with't!** (1) Away with it! (2) Put it out at interest!
150 the principal the original investment **151 How** What
153–4 ill . . . likes i.e., one must do ill, by liking a man that dislikes virginity. **154 will . . . lying** that will lose the gloss of newness with being unused. (With a quibble on "lying down.") **156 vendible** marketable. **the time of request** when there is still demand.
158 unsuitable unfashionable **159 wear not** are not in fashion. (Brooches in hats and the affectation of using toothpicks, once fashionable, are no longer so.) **159–60 Your . . . cheek** i.e., The date does better as an ingredient in cooking than as an emblem of withering in your cheek. (*Date* also suggests age.) **162 withered pears** poppering pears, a variety that are not edible until partly decayed (and that physically resemble the aging female genitalia, as does the *date,* line 159) **eats drily** is dry to eat. **165 Not . . . yet** The moment for surrendering my virginity has not yet arrived (?) (There may be a textual omission here.) **166 There** i.e., At court **167–73 A mother . . . disaster** (Helena here provides a catalogue of the various emotional relationships and paradoxical emotional attitudes found in Elizabethan courtly love poetry.) **168 phoenix** i.e., nonpareil. (Literally, a fabulous bird of which only one exists at any given time.) **173 disaster** unlucky star

Of pretty, fond, adoptious christendoms
That blinking Cupid gossips. Now shall he—
I know not what he shall. God send him well!
The court's a learning place, and he is one—

PAROLLES What one, i'faith?

HELENA That I wish well. 'Tis pity—

PAROLLES What's pity?

HELENA
That wishing well had not a body in't
Which might be felt, that we, the poorer born,
Whose baser stars do shut us up in wishes,
Might with effects of them follow our friends
And show what we alone must think, which never
Returns us thanks.

Enter Page.

PAGE Monsieur Parolles, my lord calls for you. [*Exit.*]

PAROLLES Little Helen, farewell. If I can remember thee, I will think of thee at court.

HELENA Monsieur Parolles, you were born under a charitable star.

PAROLLES Under Mars, I.

HELENA I especially think under Mars.

PAROLLES Why under Mars?

HELENA The wars hath so kept you under that you must needs be born under Mars.

PAROLLES When he was predominant.

HELENA When he was retrograde, I think rather.

PAROLLES Why think you so?

HELENA You go so much backward when you fight.

PAROLLES That's for advantage.

HELENA So is running away, when fear proposes the safety. But the composition that your valor and fear makes in you is a virtue of a good wing, and I like the wear well.

PAROLLES I am so full of businesses I cannot answer thee acutely. I will return perfect courtier, in the which my instruction shall serve to naturalize thee, so thou wilt be capable of a courtier's counsel and understand what advice shall thrust upon thee; else thou diest in thine unthankfulness, and thine ignorance makes thee away. Farewell. When thou hast leisure, say thy prayers; when thou hast none, remember thy friends. Get thee a good husband, and use him as he uses thee. So, farewell. [*Exit.*]

HELENA
Our remedies oft in ourselves do lie
Which we ascribe to heaven. The fated sky
Gives us free scope, only doth backward pull
Our slow designs when we ourselves are dull.
What power is it which mounts my love so high,
That makes me see and cannot feed mine eye?
The mightiest space in fortune nature brings
To join like likes and kiss like native things.
Impossible be strange attempts to those
That weigh their pains in sense and do suppose
What hath been cannot be. Who ever strove
To show her merit that did miss her love?
The King's disease—my project may deceive me,
But my intents are fixed and will not leave me. *Exit.*

[1.2]

Flourish cornets. Enter the King of France, with letters, and [two Lords and] divers attendants.

KING
The Florentines and Senoys are by th' ears,
Have fought with equal fortune and continue
A braving war.

FIRST LORD So 'tis reported, sir.

KING
Nay, 'tis most credible. We here receive it
A certainty, vouched from our cousin Austria,
With caution that the Florentine will move us
For speedy aid, wherein our dearest friend
Prejudicates the business, and would seem
To have us make denial.

FIRST LORD His love and wisdom,
Approved so to Your Majesty, may plead
For amplest credence.

KING He hath armed our answer,
And Florence is denied before he comes.
Yet for our gentlemen that mean to see

174–5 Of . . . gossips of pretty, foolish lovers who give pet names to their mistresses and at whose love-christenings Cupid acts as godfather. **181–6 That . . . thanks** It is a pity that wishing good fortune to someone does not command a tangible reality enabling us of humble station, whose lesser fortune confines us to mere wishing, to be able instead to bestow positive effects of that wishing on those whom we love, thereby yielding a benefit which, as things now stand, we can only ponder in our private thoughts without receiving any thanks. **195 under** down, in an inferior position. (Playing on Parolles's *Under*, line 192, in the sense of "governed by.") **197 predominant** in the ascendant, ruling. **198 retrograde** moving backward (i.e., in a direction from east to west relative to the fixed positions of the signs of the zodiac) **201 for advantage** to gain tactical advantage. (But Helena caustically interprets it as "craven self-protection.") **203 composition** mixture **204 of a good wing** strong in flight (and hence useful in rapid retreat; with a quibble on a sartorial sense of *wing*, meaning "an ornamental shoulder flap") **205 wear** fashion **207 perfect** complete. **in the which** i.e., in which courtly behavior **208 naturalize** familiarize; also, deflower. **so** provided that **209 capable** receptive. (With bawdy double meaning, continued in *understand, thrust*, and *diest*.) **211–12 makes thee away** destroys, puts an end to you.

212–213 When . . . friends i.e., (patronizingly) Don't forget to say your prayers, but remember you have friends who can help you out. **217 fated** invested with the power of destiny **219 dull** slow, sluggish. **220 so high** to so exalted an object, i.e., to Bertram **221 That . . . eye?** that puts Bertram before me as an object of desire but gives my gazing no fulfillment? **222–3 The . . . things** i.e., Natural affection can cause even those separated by the widest diversity in social status to come together as if they belonged together. **224–6 Impossible . . . be** Extraordinary attempts (at surmounting social barriers) seem impossible to those who calculate too carefully the extent and cost of their difficulties and suppose something to be impossible even though it has been done before. **227 miss** fail to achieve

1.2. Location: Paris. The royal court.

1 Senoys natives of Siena. **by th' ears** at variance, quarreling. (The King plans to deny Florence help [see 3.1], though allowing his lords free choice in what they do.) **3 braving war** war of mutual defiance. **5 our cousin** my fellow sovereign of **6 move** petition **7 friend** i.e., the Duke of Austria **8 Prejudicates** prejudges **8–9 would . . . denial** appears to wish that we deny aid (to the Florentines). **10 Approved** demonstrated, proved **11 credence** belief. **armed** fortified (against denial) **13 for** as for. **see** i.e., participate in

The Tuscan service, freely have they leave
To stand on either part.

SECOND LORD It well may serve
A nursery to our gentry, who are sick
For breathing and exploit.

KING What's he comes here?

Enter Bertram, Lafew, and Parolles.

FIRST LORD
It is the Count Rossillion, my good lord,
Young Bertram.

KING [*to Bertram*] Youth, thou bear'st thy father's face.
Frank nature, rather curious than in haste,
Hath well composed thee. Thy father's moral parts
Mayst thou inherit too! Welcome to Paris.

BERTRAM
My thanks and duty are Your Majesty's.

KING
I would I had that corporal soundness now
As when thy father and myself in friendship
First tried our soldiership! He did look far
Into the service of the time, and was
Discipled of the bravest. He lasted long,
But on us both did haggish age steal on,
And wore us out of act. It much repairs me
To talk of your good father. In his youth
He had the wit which I can well observe
Today in our young lords; but they may jest
Till their own scorn return to them unnoted
Ere they can hide their levity in honor.
So like a courtier, contempt nor bitterness
Were in his pride or sharpness; if they were,
His equal had awaked them, and his honor,
Clock to itself, knew the true minute when
Exception bid him speak, and at this time
His tongue obeyed his hand. Who were below him
He used as creatures of another place
And bowed his eminent top to their low ranks,
Making them proud of his humility
In their poor praise he humbled. Such a man
Might be a copy to these younger times,
Which, followed well, would demonstrate them now
But goers backward.

BERTRAM His good remembrance, sir,
Lies richer in your thoughts than on his tomb.
So in approof lives not his epitaph
As in your royal speech.

KING
Would I were with him! He would always say—
Methinks I hear him now; his plausive words
He scattered not in ears, but grafted them
To grow there and to bear—"Let me not live—"
This his good melancholy oft began
On the catastrophe and heel of pastime,
When it was out—"Let me not live," quoth he,
"After my flame lacks oil, to be the snuff
Of younger spirits, whose apprehensive senses
All but new things disdain, whose judgments are
Mere fathers of their garments, whose constancies
Expire before their fashions." This he wished.
I, after him, do after him wish too,
Since I nor wax nor honey can bring home,
I quickly were dissolvèd from my hive
To give some laborers room.

SECOND LORD You're lovèd, sir.
They that least lend it you shall lack you first.

KING
I fill a place, I know't.—How long is't, Count,
Since the physician at your father's died?
He was much famed.

BERTRAM Some six months since, my lord.

KING
If he were living, I would try him yet.—
Lend me an arm.—The rest have worn me out
With several applications. Nature and sickness
Debate it at their leisure. Welcome, Count;
My son's no dearer.

BERTRAM Thank Your Majesty.
Exeunt. Flourish.

✣

[1.3]

Enter Countess, Steward [*Rinaldo*], *and Clown* [*Lavatch*].

15 stand serve, fight. **part** side. **serve** serve as **16 nursery** training school **16–17 sick . . . exploit** longing for, or sick for lack of, action. **18 Rossillion** (The Folio *"Rosignoll"* suggests a nightingale: French *rossignol*.) **20 Frank** Generous, bountiful. **curious** careful, skillful **21 parts** qualities **24 corporal soundness** physical health **26 tried** tested **26–7 He did . . . time** He had a deep understanding of the affairs of war **27–8 was Discipled of** had as his pupils (or, perhaps, "was taught by") **29 haggish** like a hag, malevolent **30 wore . . . act** wore us down into inactivity. **repairs** restores **33–5 but . . . honor** but the young men of today may jest until their witty scorn goes scornfully unheeded sooner than they can hide the effects of their frivolous jesting with truly honorable action. **36–45 So . . . humbled** True courtier that he was, he allowed neither contempt nor asperity to darken his proper self-esteem and sharpness of wit; if he ever showed contempt or asperity, it was to a social equal who had done something to deserve such a response; and his honor, self-governing, knew the exact minute when unacceptable behavior (such as an insult) bade him speak, at which time he did exactly what he said he would do and no more. Those who were below him in social station he treated as though they were not in fact his inferiors, bowing his head graciously to their humbleness, making them proud that he should humble his own eminence in acknowledgment of them.

46 copy model **47–8 demonstrate . . . backward** show today's young men to be inferior to him. **50 So . . . epitaph** The epitaph on his tomb is nowhere so amply confirmed **53 plausive** praiseworthy **54 scattered not** did not strew haphazardly **55 bear** bear fruit **57–8 On . . . out** at the drawing to a close of some sport (such as hunting), when the sport was over **59 snuff** burned wick that interferes with proper burning of the candle, hence, hindrance **60 apprehensive** quick to perceive, keen but impatient **61–2 whose . . . garments** i.e., whose wisdom produces nothing but new fashions **62 constancies** loyalties **63 before** even before **64 I . . . too** I, surviving him, wish as he did. (With a suggestion also of wishing to follow him in death.) **65 nor wax** neither wax **68 lend it you** give love to you. **lack** miss **73 The rest** i.e., My physicians **74 several applications** various medical treatments. **75 Debate . . . leisure** i.e., contend over my condition at length.
1.3. Location: Rossillion.

COUNTESS I will now hear. What say you of this gentlewoman?

RINALDO Madam, the care I have had to even your content I wish might be found in the calendar of my past endeavors; for then we wound our modesty, and make foul the clearness of our deservings, when of ourselves we publish them.

COUNTESS What does this knave here?—Get you gone, sirrah. The complaints I have heard of you I do not all believe. 'Tis my slowness that I do not, for I know you lack not folly to commit them and have ability enough to make such knaveries yours.

LAVATCH 'Tis not unknown to you, madam, I am a poor fellow.

COUNTESS Well, sir.

LAVATCH No, madam, 'tis not so well that I am poor, though many of the rich are damned; but if I may have Your Ladyship's good will to go to the world, Isbel the woman and I will do as we may.

COUNTESS Wilt thou needs be a beggar?

LAVATCH I do beg your good will in this case.

COUNTESS In what case?

LAVATCH In Isbel's case and mine own. Service is no heritage, and I think I shall never have the blessing of God till I have issue o' my body; for they say bairns are blessings.

COUNTESS Tell me thy reason why thou wilt marry.

LAVATCH My poor body, madam, requires it. I am driven on by the flesh, and he must needs go that the devil drives.

COUNTESS Is this all Your Worship's reason?

LAVATCH Faith, madam, I have other holy reasons, such as they are.

COUNTESS May the world know them?

LAVATCH I have been, madam, a wicked creature, as you and all flesh and blood are, and indeed I do marry that I may repent.

COUNTESS Thy marriage, sooner than thy wickedness.

LAVATCH I am out o' friends, madam, and I hope to have friends for my wife's sake.

COUNTESS Such friends are thine enemies, knave.

LAVATCH You're shallow, madam, in great friends, for the knaves come to do that for me which I am aweary of. He that ears my land spares my team and gives me leave to in the crop. If I be his cuckold, he's my drudge. He that comforts my wife is the cherisher of my flesh and blood; he that cherishes my flesh and blood loves my flesh and blood; he that loves my flesh and blood is my friend. Ergo, he that kisses my wife is my friend. If men could be contented to be what they are, there were no fear in marriage; for young Charbon the puritan and old Poysam the papist, howsome'er their hearts are severed in religion, their heads are both one—they may jowl horns together like any deer i'th' herd.

COUNTESS Wilt thou ever be a foulmouthed and calumnious knave?

LAVATCH A prophet I, madam, and I speak the truth the next way:

For I the ballad will repeat
 Which men full true shall find:
Your marriage comes by destiny,
 Your cuckoo sings by kind.

COUNTESS Get you gone, sir. I'll talk with you more anon.

RINALDO May it please you, madam, that he bid Helen come to you. Of her I am to speak.

COUNTESS [*to Lavatch*] Sirrah, tell my gentlewoman I would speak with her—Helen, I mean.

LAVATCH [*sings*]

"Was this fair face the cause," quoth she,
 "Why the Grecians sackèd Troy?
Fond done, done fond,
 Was this King Priam's joy?"
With that she sighèd as she stood,
With that she sighèd as she stood,
 And gave this sentence then:
"Among nine bad if one be good,
Among nine bad if one be good,
 There's yet one good in ten."

COUNTESS What, one good in ten? You corrupt the song, sirrah.

1–2 this gentlewoman Helena. **3–4 to . . . content** to meet your expectations **4 calendar** record. (Rinaldo hopes that his blameless record will clear him of blame in what he is about to say to the Countess about Helena.) **5–7 and make . . . them** (Rinaldo expresses an unwillingness to insist on his own deservings or reliability as a witness, for fear of protesting too much.) **7 publish** make known **9 sirrah** (Form of address to a social inferior.) **16 well** (The Clown plays on the Countess's "Well" in line 15, i.e., "Well, go ahead"; he means "satisfactory." He also plays on *poor* in lines 14 and 16: [1] wretched [2] impoverished.) **18 go . . . world** i.e., marry **18–19 Isbel the woman** Lavatch appears to be interested amorously in Isbel or Isabel, a woman presumably serving in the Countess's household. She does not appear onstage in the play. **19 do** (1) get along (2) copulate **23 case** (With a bawdy pun on "female pudenda.") **23–4 Service is no heritage** i.e., Being a servant gives me little to bequeath to my posterity **25 bairns** children **29 needs** necessarily **31 Your Worship's** (The Countess uses a mock title.) **32 holy reasons** i.e., reasons sanctioned by the marriage service. (With obscene puns on "holey" and "raisings.") **37 repent** i.e., (1) atone for my carnal ways by making them legitimate (2) regret marrying. **38 Thy marriage** i.e., You'll repent your marriage (since proverbially hasty marriage leads to regret) **40 for . . . sake** to keep my wife company. (With a suggestion of sexual activity as a result.)

42 shallow . . . in a superficial judge of **44–5 He . . . crop** i.e., He that plows (*ears*) my wife sexually takes the load off my *team*, my sexual organs, and provides me with a *crop* of children. **45 in** bring in, harvest. **cuckold** a man whose wife is unfaithful **46 drudge** menial laborer. **50–1 what they are** i.e., cuckolds **52 Charbon . . . papist** the meat-eating Puritan and the fish-eating Catholic. (Corruptions of *chairbonne*, good meat, and *poisson*, fish, the fast-day diets of Puritans and Catholics, respectively.) **54 both one** alike (in having cuckolds' horns). **jowl** dash, knock **56 ever** always **56–7 calumnious** slandering **59 next** nearest, most direct **63 kind** nature (since cuckoldry is natural). **70 fair face** i.e., Helen of Troy's face. **she** i.e., Hecuba, wife of Priam, or Helen, or the singer of the ballad **72 Fond** Foolishly **73 Was . . . joy?** i.e., Was the taking of Helen, that led to the Trojan War and the eventual sacking of Priam's palace, his joy? **76 sentence** maxim **77 Among** along with **80–1 You . . . song** (The song must have had "nine good in ten," or "one bad in ten.")

LAVATCH One good woman in ten, madam, which is a purifying o'th' song. Would God would serve the world so all the year! We'd find no fault with the tithe-woman if I were the parson. One in ten, quoth 'a? An we might have a good woman born but ere every blazing star, or at an earthquake, 'twould mend the lottery well. A man may draw his heart out ere 'a pluck one.

COUNTESS You'll be gone, sir knave, and do as I command you?

LAVATCH That man should be at woman's command, and yet no hurt done! Though honesty be no Puritan, yet it will do no hurt; it will wear the surplice of humility over the black gown of a big heart. I am going, forsooth. The business is for Helen to come hither.

Exit.

COUNTESS Well, now.

RINALDO I know, madam, you love your gentlewoman entirely.

COUNTESS Faith, I do. Her father bequeathed her to me, and she herself, without other advantage, may lawfully make title to as much love as she finds. There is more owing her than is paid, and more shall be paid her than she'll demand.

RINALDO Madam, I was very late more near her than I think she wished me. Alone she was, and did communicate to herself her own words to her own ears; she thought, I dare vow for her, they touched not any stranger sense. Her matter was, she loved your son. Fortune, she said, was no goddess, that had put such difference betwixt their two estates; Love no god, that would not extend his might only where qualities were level; Dian no queen of virgins, that would suffer her poor knight surprised without rescue in the first assault or ransom afterward. This she delivered in the most bitter touch of sorrow that e'er I heard virgin exclaim in, which I held my duty speedily to acquaint you withal, sithence, in the loss that may happen, it concerns you something to know it.

COUNTESS You have discharged this honestly. Keep it to yourself. Many likelihoods informed me of this before, which hung so tottering in the balance that I could neither believe nor misdoubt. Pray you, leave me. Stall this in your bosom, and I thank you for your honest care. I will speak with you further anon.

Exit Steward [*Rinaldo*].

Enter Helena.

Even so it was with me when I was young.
If ever we are nature's, these are ours. This thorn
Doth to our rose of youth rightly belong;
Our blood to us, this to our blood is born.
It is the show and seal of nature's truth,
Where love's strong passion is impressed in youth.
By our remembrances of days forgone,
Such were our faults, or then we thought them
none.
Her eye is sick on't. I observe her now.

HELENA What is your pleasure, madam?

COUNTESS
You know, Helen, I am a mother to you.

HELENA
Mine honorable mistress.

COUNTESS Nay, a mother.
Why not a mother? When I said "a mother,"
Methought you saw a serpent. What's in "mother"
That you start at it? I say I am your mother,
And put you in the catalogue of those
That were enwombèd mine. 'Tis often seen
Adoption strives with nature, and choice breeds
A native slip to us from foreign seeds.
You ne'er oppressed me with a mother's groan,
Yet I express to you a mother's care.
God's mercy, maiden, does it curd thy blood
To say I am thy mother? What's the matter,
That this distempered messenger of wet,
The many-colored Iris, rounds thine eye?
Why? That you are my daughter?

HELENA That I am not.

COUNTESS
I say I am your mother.

HELENA Pardon, madam;

82–3 which . . . song which corrects the song's incorrect statistics. **83–8 Would . . . one** If only God would give us one good woman in ten as a regular thing! I'd settle for that. (Literally, if I were the parson, I'd settle for that tithing, or payment to the church of one-tenth of one's income.) If only we could find one good woman born on the occasion of rare events like comets or earthquakes, it would improve the odds. A man might just as easily pull his own heart out of his chest as draw one good woman by lottery. **91–2 That . . . done!** Lavatch sardonically professes to be horrified at the idea of a man being at a woman's command, in disregard of the Saint Paul's insistence that the man should be the head of the woman. (*That* means "To think that.") **92–4 Though . . . heart** i.e., Though my outspokenness has no desire to be hypocritical, it will, like the Puritan, hide its proud spirit (*big heart*) beneath the guise of humble obedience. (Many Puritans who demurred at the rubrics and canons of the Established Church, in order to *do no hurt,* conformed outwardly by wearing the prescribed surplice while still wearing underneath that surplice the black gown customarily worn by Calvinists.) **100–1 may . . . finds** i.e., may claim love of me, which she will find in abundance. (The Countess's metaphor is of the inheritance of a valuable property that is entitled to high regard in its own right.) **104 late** recently **108 any stranger sense** any other person's sense of hearing. **matter** theme **109 was no goddess** i.e., was a thing of accident only, not divine **110–14 Love . . . afterward** Cupid, she said, was capricious and unworthy of being worshiped as a god, in that Cupid would give his blessing and assistance only to couples who were socially equal; and Diana unworthy of being called the patron goddess of virgins, in that she would allow her hapless devotee, her *poor knight,* to be captured and left unransomed in the war of the sexes. **114 delivered** spoke **115 touch** note, pang

117 withal with. **sithence . . . happen** since in view of the harm that may come of this **118 something** somewhat **119 discharged** performed **120 likelihoods** indications **122 misdoubt** doubt. **123 Stall** Lodge **125 Even so** (The Countess speaks without being heard by Helena, who has entered.) **126 these** i.e., these pangs of love (signs of which the Countess sees manifested in Helena) **128–9 Our . . . truth** sexual passion is an inborn part of us, and these pangs of love are born of that passion. It is the sign and guarantee of nature's authority **130 impressed** imprinted (as by a seal in wax, or a thorn) **132 or . . . none** or rather things we didn't consider faults at the time. **133 on't** with it. **142 strives** vies (in strength of attachment) **142–3 choice . . . seeds** grafting from an unrelated stock makes wholly ours what was originally foreign. **144 with a mother's groan** i.e., in childbirth **148–9 That . . . eye?** that the many-colored rainbow, representing Juno's messenger Iris as the bringer of sad news and rain, is refracted in your tearful eyes? **150 not** i.e., not daughter-in-law.

The Count Rossillion cannot be my brother.
I am from humble, he from honored name;
No note upon my parents, his all noble.
My master, my dear lord he is, and I
His servant live and will his vassal die.
He must not be my brother.

COUNTESS Nor I your mother?

HELENA
You are my mother, madam. Would you were—
So that my lord your son were not my brother—
Indeed my mother! Or were you both our mothers,
I care no more for than I do for heaven,
So I were not his sister. Can't no other
But, I your daughter, he must be my brother?

COUNTESS
Yes, Helen, you might be my daughter-in-law.
God shield you mean it not! "Daughter" and
"mother"
So strive upon your pulse. What, pale again?
My fear hath catched your fondness. Now I see
The mystery of your loneliness and find
Your salt tears' head. Now to all sense 'tis gross:
You love my son. Invention is ashamed,
Against the proclamation of thy passion,
To say thou dost not. Therefore tell me true,
But tell me then 'tis so, for look, thy cheeks
Confess it th'one to th'other, and thine eyes
See it so grossly shown in thy behaviors
That in their kind they speak it. Only sin
And hellish obstinacy tie thy tongue,
That truth should be suspected. Speak, is't so?
If it be so, you have wound a goodly clew;
If it be not, forswear't. Howe'er, I charge thee,
As heaven shall work in me for thine avail,
To tell me truly.

HELENA Good madam, pardon me!

COUNTESS
Do you love my son?

HELENA Your pardon, noble mistress!

COUNTESS
Love you my son?

HELENA Do not you love him, madam?

COUNTESS
Go not about. My love hath in't a bond
Whereof the world takes note. Come, come, disclose
The state of your affection, for your passions
Have to the full appeached.

HELENA [*kneeling*] Then I confess
Here on my knee, before high heaven and you,
That before you, and next unto high heaven,
I love your son.
My friends were poor but honest, so's my love.
Be not offended, for it hurts not him
That he is loved of me. I follow him not
By any token of presumptuous suit,
Nor would I have him till I do deserve him,
Yet never know how that desert should be.
I know I love in vain, strive against hope;
Yet in this captious and intenible sieve
I still pour in the waters of my love
And lack not to lose still. Thus, Indian-like,
Religious in mine error, I adore
The sun, that looks upon his worshiper
But knows of him no more. My dearest madam,
Let not your hate encounter with my love
For loving where you do; but if yourself,
Whose agèd honor cites a virtuous youth,
Did ever in so true a flame of liking
Wish chastely and love dearly, that your Dian
Was both herself and Love, oh, then, give pity
To her whose state is such that cannot choose
But lend and give where she is sure to lose;
That seeks not to find that her search implies,
But riddle-like lives sweetly where she dies.

COUNTESS
Had you not lately an intent—speak truly—
To go to Paris?

HELENA Madam, I had.

COUNTESS Wherefore?
Tell true.

HELENA
I will tell truth, by grace itself I swear.
You know my father left me some prescriptions
Of rare and proved effects, such as his reading
And manifest experience had collected
For general sovereignty; and that he willed me
In heedfull'st reservation to bestow them,
As notes whose faculties inclusive were
More than they were in note. Amongst the rest
There is a remedy, approved, set down,

154 note mark of distinction. **parents** ancestors **159 So** provided **160 both our mothers** mother of us both **161 I . . . heaven** (Helena ambiguously suggests [1] she wouldn't care much for this [2] she would care for it as much as she longs for heaven.) **162 So** so long as **162–3 Can't . . . daughter** Must it be that if I'm your daughter **165 shield** forbid. (But the construction with *not* is ambiguous.) **167 catched** caught. **fondness** love (of Bertram); or foolishness. (The Countess speaks ambiguously while she tests Helena.) **169 head** source. **sense** perception. **gross** palpable, apparent **170 Invention** i.e., Your ability to invent excuses **171 Against** in the face of **176 in their kind** according to their nature, i.e., by weeping **178 suspected** surmised (by me) rather than openly declared; or, rendered suspect, brought into disrepute. **179 wound . . . clew** wound up a fine ball of twine, i.e., snarled things up beautifully **180 forswear't** deny it under oath. **Howe'er** In any case **181 avail** benefit **185 Go not about** Don't evade me. **bond** i.e., maternal bond **186 Whereof . . . note** which society acknowledges.

188 appeached informed against (you). **190 before you** even more than (I love) you: or, even more than you love him **192 friends** kinfolk **195 By . . . suit** with any indication of my presumptuous love **199 captious** deceptive; also, capacious. **intenible** incapable of holding **201 lack . . . still** still have enough to keep pouring without diminishing my supply; also, continually lose. **Indian-like** idolatrously, like the savage (who worships the sun) **204 no more** nothing else. **205 encounter with** oppose **207 agèd honor cites** honorable old age bespeaks, gives evidence of **208 liking** love **209 that** so that **210 both . . . Love** i.e., both Diana and Venus, chaste and passionate **213 that . . . implies** what her search is for **214 riddle-like** paradoxically, with an unguessed mystery **216 Wherefore?** Why? **221 manifest experience** i.e., the practice, in antithesis to the theory (*reading*) **222 general sovereignty** universal efficacy and use **222–5 he . . . note** he exhorted me to take great care in making use of them, as prescriptions whose comprehensive powers were greater than recognized. **226 approved** tested

To cure the desperate languishings whereof
The King is rendered lost. 228

COUNTESS
This was your motive for Paris, was it? Speak.

HELENA
My lord your son made me to think of this,
Else Paris and the medicine and the King
Had from the conversation of my thoughts 232
Haply been absent then.

COUNTESS But think you, Helen, 133
If you should tender your supposèd aid, 234
He would receive it? He and his physicians
Are of a mind: he, that they cannot help him,
They, that they cannot help. How shall they credit 237
A poor unlearnèd virgin, when the schools,
Emboweled of their doctrine, have left off 239
The danger to itself?

HELENA There's something in't
More than my father's skill—which was the great'st
Of his profession—that his good receipt 242
Shall for my legacy be sanctified
By th' luckiest stars in heaven; and would your honor 244
But give me leave to try success, I'd venture 245
The well-lost life of mine on His Grace's cure 246
By such a day and hour. 247

COUNTESS Dost thou believe't?

HELENA Ay, madam, knowingly. 249

COUNTESS
Why, Helen, thou shalt have my leave and love,
Means and attendants, and my loving greetings
To those of mine in court. I'll stay at home
And pray God's blessing into thy attempt. 253
Be gone tomorrow, and be sure of this:
What I can help thee to thou shalt not miss. *Exeunt.* 255

✣

2.1

Enter the King [*in his chair*] *with divers young Lords taking leave for the Florentine war,* [*Bertram*] *Count Rossillion, and Parolles. Flourish cornets.*

KING
Farewell, young lords. These warlike principles 1
Do not throw from you. And you, my lords, farewell. 2
Share the advice betwixt you; if both gain all, 3
The gift doth stretch itself as 'tis received, 4
And is enough for both.

FIRST LORD 'Tis our hope, sir,
After well-entered soldiers, to return 6
And find Your Grace in health.

KING
No, no, it cannot be; and yet my heart
Will not confess he owes the malady 9
That doth my life besiege. Farewell, young lords.
Whether I live or die, be you the sons
Of worthy Frenchmen. Let higher Italy— 12
Those bated that inherit but the fall 13
Of the last monarchy—see that you come 14
Not to woo honor, but to wed it. When 15
The bravest questant shrinks, find what you seek, 16
That fame may cry you loud. I say, farewell. 17

SECOND LORD
Health at your bidding serve Your Majesty!

KING
Those girls of Italy, take heed of them.
They say our French lack language to deny 20
If they demand. Beware of being captives 21
Before you serve.

BOTH Our hearts receive your warnings. 22

KING
Farewell.—Come hither to me. [*The King converses privately with various lords; Bertram, Parolles, and their companions move apart.*]

FIRST LORD [*to Bertram*]
Oh my sweet lord, that you will stay behind us!

PAROLLES
'Tis not his fault, the spark.

SECOND LORD Oh, 'tis brave wars! 25

PAROLLES Most admirable. I have seen those wars.

BERTRAM I am commanded here and kept a coil with 27
"Too young" and "The next year" and "'Tis too early."

PAROLLES An thy mind stand to't, boy, steal away 29
bravely. 30

BERTRAM
I shall stay here the forehorse to a smock, 31
Creaking my shoes on the plain masonry, 32
Till honor be bought up, and no sword worn 33
But one to dance with. By heaven, I'll steal away! 34

FIRST LORD
There's honor in the theft.

PAROLLES Commit it, Count.

228 rendered lost reckoned to be incurable. **232 conversation** movement, train **233 Haply** perhaps **234 tender** offer **237 credit** trust **239 Emboweled** emptied. **left off** abandoned **242 that** whereby. **receipt** prescription **244 th' luckiest** i.e., the most able to confer luck **245 venture** risk, wager **246 well-lost** i.e., well lost in such a cause, worthless otherwise **247 such a** i.e., a specific **249 knowingly** with confidence. **253 into** upon **255 miss** be lacking.

2.1. Location: Paris. The royal court.

1–2 These . . . you i.e., Remember this military advice. **3–4 if . . . received** if both groups wish to profit fully from my advice, it will stretch to the extent that it is accepted

6 After . . . soldiers after having become seasoned soldiers; or, in the manner of experienced soldiers **9 he owes** it owns **12 higher Italy** (1) the knightly class of Italy, corresponding to *worthy Frenchmen*, or (2) Tuscany, of which Florence and Siena are cities **13–14 Those . . . monarchy** i.e., except those who inherit unworthily the poor remains of the Holy Roman Empire. (Such undeserving knights are not to be taken into account.) **15 woo** flirt with. **wed** possess as your own **16 questant** seeker (after honor) **17 cry you loud** proclaim you loudly. **20–2 They . . . serve** People say we French have low resistance to the sexual blandishments of women. Beware of being captive to their charms even before you enter into military action. **25 spark** elegant young man. **brave** splendid **27 here** i.e., to remain here. **kept a coil** pestered, fussed over **29 An** If **30 bravely** (1) worthily (2) valiantly. **31 the forehorse . . . smock** the lead horse of a team driven by a woman **32 plain masonry** smooth masonry floor (instead of a battlefield) **33 Till . . . up** till opportunity for winning honor in the wars is past, all consumed **34 one . . . with** i.e., a light ornamental weapon.

SECOND LORD
I am your accessory. And so, farewell.

BERTRAM I grow to you, and our parting is a tortured body.

FIRST LORD Farewell, Captain.

SECOND LORD Sweet Monsieur Parolles!

PAROLLES Noble heroes, my sword and yours are kin. Good sparks and lustrous, a word, good metals: you shall find in the regiment of the Spinii one Captain Spurio, with his cicatrice, an emblem of war, here on his sinister cheek; it was this very sword entrenched it. Say to him I live, and observe his reports for me.

FIRST LORD We shall, noble Captain.

PAROLLES Mars dote on you for his novices!
[*Exeunt Lords.*]
[*To Bertram*] What will ye do?

BERTRAM Stay the King.

PAROLLES Use a more spacious ceremony to the noble lords; you have restrained yourself within the list of too cold an adieu. Be more expressive to them, for they wear themselves in the cap of the time; there do muster true gait, eat, speak, and move under the influence of the most received star; and, though the devil lead the measure, such are to be followed. After them, and take a more dilated farewell.

BERTRAM And I will do so.

PAROLLES Worthy fellows, and like to prove most sinewy swordmen. *Exeunt* [*Bertram and Parolles*].

Enter Lafew [*and approaches the King*].

LAFEW [*kneeling*]
Pardon, my lord, for me and for my tidings.

KING I'll fee thee to stand up.

LAFEW [*rising*]
Then here's a man stands that has brought his pardon.
I would you had kneeled, my lord, to ask me mercy,
And that at my bidding you could so stand up.

KING
I would I had, so I had broke thy pate
And asked thee mercy for't.

LAFEW Good faith, across!
But, my good lord, 'tis thus: will you be cured
Of your infirmity?

KING No.

LAFEW Oh, will you eat
No grapes, my royal fox? Yes, but you will
My noble grapes, an if my royal fox
Could reach them. I have seen a medicine
That's able to breathe life into a stone,
Quicken a rock, and make you dance canary
With sprightly fire and motion, whose simple touch
Is powerful to araise King Pepin, nay,
To give great Charlemain a pen in's hand
And write to her a love line.

KING What "her" is this?

LAFEW
Why, Doctor She! My lord, there's one arrived,
If you will see her. Now by my faith and honor,
If seriously I may convey my thoughts
In this my light deliverance, I have spoke
With one that in her sex, her years, profession,
Wisdom, and constancy hath amazed me more
Than I dare blame my weakness. Will you see her,
For that is her demand, and know her business?
That done, laugh well at me.

KING Now, good Lafew,
Bring in the admiration, that we with thee
May spend our wonder too, or take off thine
By wondering how thou took'st it.

LAFEW Nay, I'll fit you,
And not be all day neither. [*He goes to the door.*]

KING
Thus he his special nothing ever prologues.

LAFEW [*to Helena*] Nay, come your ways.

Enter Helena.

KING This haste hath wings indeed.

LAFEW Nay, come your ways.
This is His Majesty. Say your mind to him.
A traitor you do look like, but such traitors
His Majesty seldom fears. I am Cressid's uncle,
That dare leave two together. Fare you well. *Exit.*

KING
Now, fair one, does your business follow us?

37 grow to grow deeply attached to, become as one with **37–8 a tortured body** i.e., as painful as a body being torn apart by torture. **42 metals** i.e., "blades"; spirits of mettle **44 Spurio** (This name suggests "spurious," "counterfeit.") **cicatrice** scar **45 sinister** left. **it was . . . entrenched it** mine was the sword that dug that trench-like scar. **46 reports** reply **48 Mars** May Mars. **novices** devotees. **50 Stay the King** Support or wait on the King. (But also interpreted, with different punctuation, as "Stay; the King wills it" or "Stay; the King approaches.") **51 spacious ceremony** effusive courtesy **53 list** boundary. (Literally, the selvage or finished edge of cloth.) **54 wear . . . time** stand out as ornaments of the fashionable world **55 muster true gait** set the right pace, move gracefully **56 received** fashionable **57 measure** dance **58 dilated** protracted; expansive **60 like** likely **60–1 sinewy** energetic, forceful **62 tidings** news, information. **63 I'll . . . up** i.e., I bid you rise; or, I will rather reward you for rising. **64 pardon** i.e., something to win the King's indulgence. **65–8 I would . . . for't** (Lafew hyperbolically suggests that he and the King really ought to change places, turning the King into the petitioner, since Lafew has brought something worth begging for. The King, not knowing what is in store, jests that he might be willing to beg forgiveness of Lafew if he could first give Lafew a sharp blow to the head for his seeming insolence, thus providing the King an occasion for begging pardon.) **68 across** i.e., well parried.

70–1 will . . . fox? i.e., will you be like the fox in Aesop's fable and call the grapes sour because they are beyond your reach? **72 an if** if **73 medicine** i.e., physician **75 Quicken** bring to life. **canary** a lively Spanish dance **76 simple** (1) mere (2) medicinal, making use of "simples" or herbs **77 to araise . . . Pepin** to raise from the dead King Pepin, a French king of the eighth century and father of Charlemagne. (The name has a folklorish ring.) **79 love line** (Some of Lafew's terms, such as *stone, quicken, fire and motion, touch, araise*, and *pen in's hand*, have possible erotic undertones that link recovery to restored potency.) **83 deliverance** manner of speaking **84 profession** what she professes to be able to do **85–6 more . . . weakness** more than I can attribute to my feebleness or susceptibility as an old man. **89 admiration** wonder **90 spend** expend. **take off** dispel, end **91 took'st** conceived. (With a play on *take* in the previous line.) **fit** satisfy **93 special nothing** particular trifles. **prologues** introduces. **94 come your ways** come along. **98 traitor** (Lafew's joke depends on the idea that it is dangerous to leave an unknown person alone with a king, for fear of a plot.) **99 Cressid's uncle** Pandarus, go-between for the lovers Troilus and Cressida **101 follow** concern

HELENA Ay, my good lord.
Gerard de Narbonne was my father;
In what he did profess, well found.
KING I knew him.
HELENA
The rather will I spare my praises towards him;
Knowing him is enough. On 's bed of death
Many receipts he gave me, chiefly one
Which, as the dearest issue of his practice,
And of his old experience th'only darling,
He bade me store up as a triple eye
Safer than mine own two, more dear. I have so;
And hearing Your High Majesty is touched
With that malignant cause wherein the honor
Of my dear father's gift stands chief in power,
I come to tender it and my appliance
With all bound humbleness.
KING We thank you, maiden,
But may not be so credulous of cure
When our most learnèd doctors leave us and
The congregated college have concluded
That laboring art can never ransom nature
From her inaidible estate. I say we must not
So stain our judgment, or corrupt our hope,
To prostitute our past-cure malady
To empirics, or to dissever so
Our great self and our credit, to esteem
A senseless help when help past sense we deem.
HELENA
My duty then shall pay me for my pains.
I will no more enforce mine office on you,
Humbly entreating from your royal thoughts
A modest one to bear me back again.
KING
I cannot give thee less, to be called grateful.
Thou thought'st to help me, and such thanks I give
As one near death to those that wish him live.
But what at full I know, thou know'st no part,
I knowing all my peril, thou no art.
HELENA
What I can do can do no hurt to try,
Since you set up your rest 'gainst remedy.
He that of greatest works is finisher
Oft does them by the weakest minister.
So holy writ in babes hath judgment shown,
When judges have been babes; great floods have
flown
From simple sources; and great seas have dried
When miracles have by the great'st been denied.
Oft expectation fails, and most oft there
Where most it promises, and oft it hits
Where hope is coldest and despair most fits.
KING
I must not hear thee. Fare thee well, kind maid.
Thy pains, not used, must by thyself be paid;
Proffers not took reap thanks for their reward.
HELENA
Inspirèd merit so by breath is barred.
It is not so with Him that all things knows
As 'tis with us that square our guess by shows;
But most it is presumption in us when
The help of heaven we count the act of men.
Dear sir, to my endeavors give consent;
Of heaven, not me, make an experiment.
I am not an impostor that proclaim
Myself against the level of mine aim;
But know I think, and think I know most sure,
My art is not past power, nor you past cure.
KING
Art thou so confident? Within what space
Hop'st thou my cure?
HELENA The great'st grace lending grace,
Ere twice the horses of the sun shall bring
Their fiery torcher his diurnal ring,
Ere twice in murk and occidental damp
Moist Hesperus hath quenched her sleepy lamp,
Or four-and-twenty times the pilot's glass
Hath told the thievish minutes how they pass,
What is infirm from your sound parts shall fly,
Health shall live free, and sickness freely die.
KING
Upon thy certainty and confidence
What dar'st thou venture?
HELENA Tax of impudence,
A strumpet's boldness, a divulgèd shame

104 In . . . found in his medical practice he was reputed to be skilled. **107 receipts** remedies **108–9 the dearest . . . darling** the favorite child or product of his many years of practice **110 triple** third **111 Safer** more safely **113–14 With . . . power** with that malignant disease over which my father's medical skill has chief power to effect a cure **115 tender** offer. **appliance** treatment **116 bound** dutiful **117 credulous of** ready to believe in **119 congregated college** college of physicians **120 art** skill, i.e., medicine **122 stain** sully **123–6 To . . . deem** by basely submitting my past-cure illness to quack doctors, or by divorcing my kingly greatness from my reputation to such an extent as to put credulous faith in a cure too improbable to be believed when the disease exceeds all reasonable hope. **127 My . . . pains** My thanks then must be that I have dutifully offered my aid. **128 office** dutiful service **130 A modest . . . again** i.e., a favorable regard commensurate with my humble station and with my maidenly modesty to take back with me. **134 no part** not at all **135 thou no art** i.e., you having no medical skill capable of saving my life. **137 set . . . rest** stake your all. (A figure from the gambling game of primero.) **138 He** God

140–1 So . . . babes (See, for example, Matthew 11:25 and 1 Corinthians 1:27.) **141 babes** i.e., babyish, foolish. (The inversion of babes and wise men appears often in the Bible.) **142 simple** small, insignificant. **great seas** (Probably the Red Sea; *the great'st* in line 143 is presumably Pharaoh.) **145 hits** succeeds, is confirmed **148 by . . . paid** i.e., be their own reward **149 Proffers . . . thanks** offers not accepted reap thanks (and only thanks) **150 Inspirèd . . . barred** Divinely inspired virtue is thus denied by mere spoken words. **152 square . . . shows** support our conjectures on the basis of appearances **154 count** account **156 experiment** trial. **157–8 that . . . aim** who claims to be more of a marksman than my ability to aim would warrant **159–60 But . . . power** but I have every confidence, given the uncertainty of all human knowing, that what I claim to be able to do is not beyond my power to perform **161 space** period of time **162 Hop'st thou** do you hope for. **The great'st . . . grace** i.e., With God's help **164 Their . . . ring** i.e., the fiery sun-god on his daily round **165 occidental** western, sunset **166 Hesperus** evening star (actually Venus) **167 glass** hour-glass **172 venture** risk, wager. **Tax** Accusation

Traduced by odious ballads; my maiden's name
Seared otherwise; nay, worse of worst, extended
With vilest torture let my life be ended.

KING
Methinks in thee some blessèd spirit doth speak
His powerful sound within an organ weak;
And what impossibility would slay
In common sense, sense saves another way.
Thy life is dear, for all that life can rate
Worth name of life in thee hath estimate:
Youth, beauty, wisdom, courage, all
That happiness and prime can happy call.
Thou this to hazard needs must intimate
Skill infinite, or monstrous desperate.
Sweet practicer, thy physic I will try,
That ministers thine own death if I die.

HELENA
If I break time or flinch in property
Of what I spoke, unpitied let me die,
And well deserved. Not helping, death's my fee;
But, if I help, what do you promise me?

KING
Make thy demand.

HELENA
But will you make it even?

KING
Ay, by my scepter and my hopes of heaven.

HELENA
Then shalt thou give me with thy kingly hand
What husband in thy power I will command.
Exempted be from me the arrogance
To choose from forth the royal blood of France,
My low and humble name to propagate
With any branch or image of thy state;
But such a one, thy vassal, whom I know
Is free for me to ask, thee to bestow.

KING
Here is my hand. The premises observed,
Thy will by my performance shall be served.
So make the choice of thy own time, for I,
Thy resolved patient, on thee still rely.
More should I question thee, and more I must—
Though more to know could not be more to trust—
From whence thou cam'st, how tended on; but rest
Unquestioned welcome and undoubted blest.—
Give me some help here, ho!—If thou proceed
As high as word, my deed shall match thy meed.

Flourish. Exeunt, [*the King carried in*].

[2.2]

Enter Countess and Clown [*Lavatch*].

COUNTESS Come on, sir. I shall now put you to the height of your breeding.

LAVATCH I will show myself highly fed and lowly taught. I know my business is but to the court.

COUNTESS "To the court"? Why, what place make you special, when you put off that with such contempt? "But to the court"!

LAVATCH Truly, madam, if God have lent a man any manners, he may easily put it off at court. He that cannot make a leg, put off's cap, kiss his hand, and say nothing has neither leg, hands, lip, nor cap; and indeed such a fellow, to say precisely, were not for the court. But for me, I have an answer will serve all men.

COUNTESS Marry, that's a bountiful answer that fits all questions.

LAVATCH It is like a barber's chair that fits all buttocks: the pin-buttock, the quatch-buttock, the brawn-buttock, or any buttock.

COUNTESS Will your answer serve fit to all questions?

LAVATCH As fit as ten groats is for the hand of an attorney, as your French crown for your taffety punk, as Tib's rush for Tom's forefinger, as a pancake for Shrove Tuesday, a morris for May Day, as the nail to his hole, the cuckold to his horn, as a scolding quean to a wrangling knave, as the nun's lip to the friar's mouth, nay, as the pudding to his skin.

COUNTESS Have you, I say, an answer of such fitness for all questions?

LAVATCH From below your duke to beneath your constable, it will fit any question.

COUNTESS It must be an answer of most monstrous size that must fit all demands.

LAVATCH But a trifle neither, in good faith, if the learned should speak truth of it. Here it is, and all that belongs to't. Ask me if I am a courtier. It shall do you no harm to learn.

174 Traduced slandered **175 Seared otherwise** branded in other ways as well. **extended** stretched out on the rack; or, drawn out in time **179–80 what . . . way** what common sense would regard as impossible, a higher sense (faith) can regard as possible. **181–2 for . . . estimate** for everything that life can consider worthy the name of life is to be found and esteemed in you. **181 rate** value **184 That . . . call** that good fortune and the "springtime" of youth can call happy. **185–6 Thou . . . desperate** The fact that you are prepared to hazard all this argues infinite skill or desperation. **187 physic** medicine **188 ministers** administers **189 If . . . property** If I fail to meet my deadline or fall short in any respect **191 Not helping** If I do not help **193 make it even** carry it out. **203 The premises observed** The conditions of the agreement having been fulfilled **206 still** continually **209 tended on** attended **210 Unquestioned** (1) without being questioned (2) unquestionably

212 As high as word as fully as you have promised. **meed** merit, worth.

2.2. Location: Rossillion.

1–2 put . . . breeding test your good manners. **3–4 highly . . . taught** overfed and underdisciplined. ("Better fed than taught" was proverbial for a spoiled child.) **5–6 make you special** do you consider special **6 put off** dismiss **9 put it off** carry it off. (With a play on *put off* in line 6 and anticipating the meaning "doff" in line 10.) **10 leg** respectful bow or curtsy **17 pin** narrow, pointed. **quatch** fat, wide. **brawn** hefty, fleshy **20 ten groats** forty pence **21 French crown** (1) coin (2) *corona veneris*, a scab on the head symptomatic of syphilis, the "French disease." **taffety punk** finely dressed prostitute **22 Tib's rush** (Refers to a folk custom of exchanging rings made of reed in a marriage without benefit of clergy.) **pancake** (Traditionally eaten as a last feast on the final day before Lent, Shrove Tuesday.) **23 morris** morris dance, country dance common at May Day celebrations **24 his** its. **quean** wench **26 pudding** sausage. **his hole** its hole **33 But . . . neither** On the contrary, it's only a trifle

COUNTESS To be young again, if we could! I will be a fool in question, hoping to be the wiser by your answer. I pray you, sir, are you a courtier?

LAVATCH Oh, Lord, sir!—There's a simple putting off. More, more, a hundred of them.

COUNTESS Sir, I am a poor friend of yours, that loves you.

LAVATCH Oh, Lord, sir!—Thick, thick, spare not me.

COUNTESS I think, sir, you can eat none of this homely meat.

LAVATCH Oh, Lord, sir!—Nay, put me to't, I warrant you.

COUNTESS You were lately whipped, sir, as I think.

LAVATCH Oh, Lord, sir!—Spare not me.

COUNTESS Do you cry, "Oh, Lord, sir!" at your whipping, and "spare not me"? Indeed your "Oh, Lord, sir!" is very sequent to your whipping. You would answer very well to a whipping, if you were but bound to't.

LAVATCH I ne'er had worse luck in my life in my "Oh, Lord, sir!" I see things may serve long, but not serve ever.

COUNTESS
I play the noble huswife with the time,
To entertain it so merrily with a fool.

LAVATCH Oh, Lord, sir!—Why, there't serves well again.

COUNTESS
An end, sir! To your business. Give Helen this,
[*giving a letter*]
And urge her to a present answer back.
Commend me to my kinsmen and my son.
This is not much.

LAVATCH Not much commendation to them?

COUNTESS Not much employment for you. You understand me?

LAVATCH Most fruitfully. I am there before my legs.

COUNTESS Haste you again. *Exeunt* [*separately*].

✤

[2.3]

Enter Count [*Bertram*], *Lafew, and Parolles.*

LAFEW They say miracles are past, and we have our philosophical persons to make modern and familiar things supernatural and causeless. Hence is it that we make trifles of terrors, ensconcing ourselves into seeming knowledge when we should submit ourselves to an unknown fear.

PAROLLES Why, 'tis the rarest argument of wonder that hath shot out in our latter times.

BERTRAM And so 'tis.

LAFEW To be relinquished of the artists—

PAROLLES So I say, both of Galen and Paracelsus.

LAFEW Of all the learned and authentic fellows—

PAROLLES Right, so I say.

LAFEW That gave him out incurable—

PAROLLES Why, there 'tis; so say I too.

LAFEW Not to be helped.

PAROLLES Right! As 'twere a man assured of a—

LAFEW Uncertain life and sure death.

PAROLLES Just, you say well; so would I have said.

LAFEW I may truly say it is a novelty to the world.

PAROLLES It is, indeed. If you will have it in showing, you shall read it in—what-do-ye-call there?
[*He points to a ballad in Lafew's hand.*]

LAFEW [*reading*] "A showing of a heavenly effect in an earthly actor."

PAROLLES That's it, I would have said the very same.

LAFEW Why, your dolphin is not lustier. 'Fore me, I speak in respect—

PAROLLES Nay, 'tis strange, 'tis very strange, that is the brief and the tedious of it; and he's of a most facinorous spirit that will not acknowledge it to be the—

LAFEW Very hand of heaven.

PAROLLES Ay, so I say.

LAFEW In a most weak—

PAROLLES And debile minister, great power, great transcendence, which should indeed give us a further use to be made than alone the recovery of the King, as to be—

LAFEW Generally thankful.

Enter King, Helena, and attendants. [*The King sits.*]

PAROLLES I would have said it; you say well. Here comes the King.

LAFEW Lustig, as the Dutchman says. I'll like a maid the better whilst I have a tooth in my head. Why, he's able to lead her a coranto.

PAROLLES *Mort du vinaigre!* Is not this Helen?

40 Oh, Lord, sir (A foppish phrase currently in vogue at court. Here it suggests, "I do indeed presume to be a courtier; isn't that plain enough from my appearance?") **putting off** evasion. **44 Thick** Quickly **45–6 homely meat** plain fare. **52 is very sequent to** is a pertinent response to (because it would be a plea for mercy)
52–3 answer . . . to (1) reply cleverly to (2) serve as a suitable subject for **53 bound to't** (1) obliged to reply (2) tied up for it. **61 present** immediate **62 Commend me** Give my greetings **67 before my legs** (A comically absurd hyperbole suggesting incredible speed.)
68 again back again.
2.3 Location: Paris. The royal court.
1 They . . . past (It was commonplace wisdom that the miracles described in the Bible and other early religious writings were somehow unique to an era long past.) **2–3 philsophical . . . causeless** scientists who can cause happenings that strike us as supernatural and inexplicable seem commonplace and familiar. (*Modern* means ordinary or commonplace.) **4 ensconcing** taking refuge, fortifying

6 unknown fear awe of the unknown. **7–8 'tis . . . times** it is the most remarkable demonstration of the extraordinary that has suddenly appeared in recent times. **10 relinquished . . . artists** abandoned by the physicians **11 Galen** Greek physician of the second century; the traditional authority. **Paracelsus** Swiss physician of the sixteenth century; the new and more radical authority. **12 authentic fellows** those properly licensed to practice **14 gave him out** proclaimed him **19 Just** Exactly **21 in showing** i.e., in print **26 dolphin** (A sportive and vigorous sea animal; with a pun perhaps on *dauphin*, "French crown prince.") **'Fore me** i.e., Upon my soul **27 in respect** intending no disrespect **28–9 the brief . . . it** i.e., the short and the long of it **29–30 facinorous** infamous, wicked **34 debile minister** weak agent **38 Generally** universally **41 Lustig** Lusty, sportive. **Dutchman** i.e., from any Germanic country **42 have a tooth** (With a play on the meaning "have a sweet tooth, a taste for the pleasures of the senses.") **43 coranto** lively dance. **44 *Mort du vinaigre!*** (An oath, perhaps referring to the vinegar offered by a bystander to Christ to drink as he hung dying on the cross; see Matthew 27:48, Mark 15:36, and John 19:29; literally, "death of vinegar.")

LAFEW 'Fore God, I think so.

KING
Go, call before me all the lords in court.
[*Exit one or more attendants.*]
Sit, my preserver, by thy patient's side, [*She sits.*]
And with this healthful hand, whose banished sense
Thou hast repealed, a second time receive
The confirmation of my promised gift,
Which but attends thy naming.

Enter four Lords.

Fair maid, send forth thine eye. This youthful parcel
Of noble bachelors stand at my bestowing,
O'er whom both sovereign power and father's voice
I have to use. Thy frank election make;
Thou hast power to choose, and they none to forsake.

HELENA
To each of you one fair and virtuous mistress
Fall, when Love please! Marry, to each but one!

LAFEW [*aside*]
I'd give bay Curtal and his furniture
My mouth no more were broken than these boys',
And writ as little beard.

KING Peruse them well.
Not one of those but had a noble father.

HELENA Gentlemen,
Heaven hath through me restored the King to health.

ALL THE LORDS
We understand it, and thank heaven for you.

HELENA
I am a simple maid, and therein wealthiest
That I protest I simply am a maid.—
Please it Your Majesty, I have done already.
The blushes in my cheeks thus whisper me,
"We blush that thou shouldst choose; but, be refused,
Let the white death sit on thy cheek forever,
We'll ne'er come there again."

KING Make choice and see.
Who shuns thy love shuns all his love in me.

HELENA
Now, Dian, from thy altar do I fly,
And to imperial Love, that god most high,
Do my sighs stream. (*She addresses her to a Lord.*) Sir,
will you hear my suit?

FIRST LORD
And grant it.

HELENA Thanks, sir. All the rest is mute.

LAFEW [*aside*] I had rather be in this choice than throw ambs-ace for my life.

HELENA [*to Second Lord*]
The honor, sir, that flames in your fair eyes
Before I speak too threateningly replies.
Love make your fortunes twenty times above
Her that so wishes, and her humble love!

SECOND LORD
No better, if you please.

HELENA My wish receive,
Which great Love grant! And so I take my leave.

LAFEW [*aside*] Do all they deny her? An they were sons of mine, I'd have them whipped, or I would send them to the Turk to make eunuchs of.

HELENA [*to Third Lord*]
Be not afraid that I your hand should take;
I'll never do you wrong for your own sake.
Blessing upon your vows, and in your bed
Find fairer fortune, if you ever wed!

LAFEW [*aside*] These boys are boys of ice; they'll none have her. Sure they are bastards to the English; the French ne'er got 'em.

HELENA [*to Fourth Lord*]
You are too young, too happy, and too good
To make yourself a son out of my blood.

FOURTH LORD Fair one, I think not so.

LAFEW [*aside*] There's one grape yet; I am sure thy father drunk wine. But if thou be'st not an ass, I am a youth of fourteen; I have known thee already.

HELENA [*to Bertram*]
I dare not say I take you, but I give
Me and my service, ever whilst I live,
Into your guiding power.—This is the man.

KING
Why, then, young Bertram, take her; she's thy wife.

BERTRAM
My wife, my liege? I shall beseech Your Highness,
In such a business give me leave to use
The help of mine own eyes.

KING Know'st thou not, Bertram,
What she has done for me?

BERTRAM Yes, my good lord,
But never hope to know why I should marry her.

KING
Thou know'st she has raised me from my sickly bed.

BERTRAM
But follows it, my lord, to bring me down

45 I think so i.e., I should say it is. (Lafew knows it is Helena.) **48 banished sense** loss of feeling **49 repealed** recalled (from death) **51 attends** waits upon **52 parcel** group **53 stand . . . bestowing** i.e., are my wards, whom I may give in marriage **55 frank election** free choice **56 forsake** refuse. **58 Love** Cupid **59 bay Curtal** my bay horse, Curtal. (From the French *court,* short- or docked-tail.) **furniture** trappings **60 My . . . broken** i.e., (1) that I had lost no more teeth (2) that I, like a young horse, were no more "broken to the bit" **61 And writ** i.e., and that I laid claim to. (Lafew wishes he were young enough to be a suitor of Helena.) **67 protest** avow **70 be refused** i.e., if you are refused **71 the white death** i.e., death in its pallor **73 Who** He who **74 Dian** Diana, the goddess of chastity **75 imperial Love** i.e., the god of love, Cupid **77 All . . . mute** I have nothing more to say to you.

79 ambs-ace two aces, the lowest possible throw in dice. (To throw ambs-ace with one's life at stake is to risk all on a throw.) **82 Love make** May Love make **83 Her . . . love** her that speaks this wish—i.e., myself—and the humble love I deserve or can give. **84 No better** i.e., I wish for nothing better than your humble love. **My wish receive** i.e., Take my *wish* for your fortunate marriage, rather than me **86 Do . . . her?** (Lafew, unable to hear, misinterprets her passing from one to another.) **An** If **94 Sure** Certainly. **bastards to** illegitimate children of **95 got** begot **96 happy** fortunate **99 grape** i.e., scion of a good family. **thy** i.e., Bertram's **100 drunk wine** i.e., was red-blooded. **101 known** i.e., seen through **112 bring me down** i.e., lower me to a socially inferior wife, to the (marriage) bed. (With sexual wordplay in *bring me down,* and *raising* in line 113.)

Must answer for your raising? I know her well;
She had her breeding at my father's charge.
A poor physician's daughter my wife? Disdain
Rather corrupt me ever!

KING
'Tis only title thou disdain'st in her, the which
I can build up. Strange is it that our bloods,
Of color, weight, and heat, poured all together,
Would quite confound distinction, yet stands off
In differences so mighty. If she be
All that is virtuous save what thou dislik'st—
A poor physician's daughter—thou dislik'st
Of virtue for the name. But do not so.
From lowest place when virtuous things proceed,
The place is dignified by th' doer's deed.
Where great additions swell's, and virtue none,
It is a dropsied honor. Good alone
Is good without a name; vileness is so;
The property by what it is should go,
Not by the title. She is young, wise, fair;
In these to nature she's immediate heir,
And these breed honor. That is honor's scorn
Which challenges itself as honor's born
And is not like the sire. Honors thrive
When rather from our acts we them derive
Than our foregoers. The mere word's a slave
Debauched on every tomb, on every grave
A lying trophy, and as oft is dumb
Where dust and damned oblivion is the tomb
Of honored bones indeed. What should be said?
If thou canst like this creature as a maid,
I can create the rest. Virtue and she
Is her own dower; honor and wealth from me.

BERTRAM
I cannot love her, nor will strive to do't.

KING
Thou wrong'st thyself, if thou shouldst strive to
choose.

HELENA
That you are well restored, my lord, I'm glad.
Let the rest go.

KING
My honor's at the stake, which to defeat,
I must produce my power. Here, take her hand,
Proud, scornful boy, unworthy this good gift,
That dost in vile misprision shackle up
My love and her desert; that canst not dream,
We, poising us in her defective scale,
Shall weigh thee to the beam; that wilt not know
It is in us to plant thine honor where
We please to have it grow. Check thy contempt;
Obey our will, which travails in thy good;
Believe not thy disdain, but presently
Do thine own fortunes that obedient right
Which both thy duty owes and our power claims,
Or I will throw thee from my care forever
Into the staggers and the careless lapse
Of youth and ignorance, both my revenge and hate
Loosing upon thee in the name of justice
Without all terms of pity. Speak; thine answer.

BERTRAM
Pardon, my gracious lord, for I submit
My fancy to your eyes. When I consider
What great creation and what dole of honor
Flies where you bid it, I find that she, which late
Was in my nobler thoughts most base, is now
The praisèd of the King, who, so ennobled,
Is as 'twere born so.

KING
Take her by the hand,
And tell her she is thine, to whom I promise
A counterpoise, if not to thy estate,
A balance more replete.

BERTRAM
I take her hand.

KING
Good fortune and the favor of the King
Smile upon this contract, whose ceremony
Shall seem expedient on the now-born brief
And be performed tonight. The solemn feast
Shall more attend upon the coming space,
Expecting absent friends. As thou lov'st her,
Thy love's to me religious; else, does err.

Exeunt. Parolles and Lafew stay behind, commenting of this wedding.

114 charge cost. **115–16 Disdain . . . ever!** i.e., Rather let my disdain for her ruin me forever in your favor! (With unintentional irony; disdain does indeed corrupt Bertram.) **117 title** i.e., her lack of title **120–1 Would . . . mighty** (blood) is indistinguishable from one person to the next, yet is made the basis of such mighty differences in rank. **124 name** i.e., lack of a name (title). **125 proceed** emanate **127 great . . . swell's** pompous titles puff us up **128 dropsied** unhealthily swollen **128–9 Good . . . so** What is in itself good is so without a title; the same is true of vileness **130 property** quality. **go** i.e., be judged, be valued **132 In . . . heir** in these qualities she inherits directly from nature **133–5 That . . . sire** True honor is scornful of any claim to honor based only on birth that is not validated by behavior worthy of one's heritage. **138 Debauched** corrupted **139 trophy** memorial. **dumb** silent **141 honored bones indeed** i.e., the remains of those who were genuinely honorable. **143–4 Virtue . . . dower** i.e., Her marriage gift to you will be her virtue and herself **146 strive to choose** try to assert your own choice. **149 which** i.e., which threat to my honor

152–5 That . . . beam you who with base mistaking fetter both my love and her worth; you who cannot imagine how I, adding my royal weight to her deficiency in order to counterbalance your wealth and position, will equalize the cross-beam of the balance scales. (*We* is the royal plural, continued in lines 157–8.) **156 in us** within my royal power **157 Check** Curb, restrain **158 travails in** labors for **159 Believe not** do not place faith in or obey. **presently** at once **160 obedient right** right of obedience **163 staggers** giddy decline. (Literally, a horse disease.) **careless lapse** irresponsible fall **165 Loosing** turning loose **166 all . . . pity** pity in any form. **168 fancy** desires **169 great creation** creating of greatness. **dole** share, doling out **170 which late** who lately **175–6 A counterpoise . . . replete** i.e., an equal weight of wealth as dowry, if not an amount even exceeding your estate. **178–9 whose . . . brief** whose performing ceremoniously will seem appropriate to the present contract. (*Brief* suggests both "short" and "expeditious." The King specifies a marriage contract rather than a full wedding ceremony.) **180–2 The solemn . . . friends** The full festival of celebration must be delayed for a time until absent friends and relatives can arrive. (Following the formal betrothal just completed onstage, there is to be a wedding tonight and a celebratory feast later on when all can gather.) **182–3 As . . . err** So long as you love her truly, I will regard your love for me as holy and true; otherwise, regarding your obligations to me you are a heretic and a traitor. **183.2 *of*** on

LAFEW Do you hear, monsieur? A word with you.

PAROLLES Your pleasure, sir?

LAFEW Your lord and master did well to make his recantation.

PAROLLES Recantation? My lord? My master?

LAFEW Ay. Is it not a language I speak?

PAROLLES A most harsh one, and not to be understood without bloody succeeding. My master?

LAFEW Are you companion to the Count Rossillion?

PAROLLES To any count, to all counts, to what is man.

LAFEW To what is count's man. Count's master is of another style.

PAROLLES You are too old, sir; let it satisfy you, you are too old.

LAFEW I must tell thee, sirrah, I write man, to which title age cannot bring thee.

PAROLLES What I dare too well do, I dare not do.

LAFEW I did think thee, for two ordinaries, to be a pretty wise fellow; thou didst make tolerable vent of thy travel; it might pass. Yet the scarves and the bannerets about thee did manifoldly dissuade me from believing thee a vessel of too great a burden. I have now found thee. When I lose thee again, I care not; yet art thou good for nothing but taking up, and that thou'rt scarce worth.

PAROLLES Hadst thou not the privilege of antiquity upon thee—

LAFEW Do not plunge thyself too far in anger, lest thou hasten thy trial; which if—Lord have mercy on thee for a hen! So, my good window of lattice, fare thee well. Thy casement I need not open, for I look through thee. Give me thy hand.

PAROLLES My lord, you give me most egregious indignity.

LAFEW Ay, with all my heart, and thou art worthy of it.

PAROLLES I have not, my lord, deserved it.

LAFEW Yes, good faith, every dram of it, and I will not bate thee a scruple.

PAROLLES Well, I shall be wiser.

LAFEW Even as soon as thou canst, for thou hast to pull at a smack o'th' contrary. If ever thou be'st bound in thy scarf and beaten, thou shall find what it is to be proud of thy bondage. I have a desire to hold my acquaintance with thee, or rather my knowledge, that I may say in the default, "He is a man I know."

PAROLLES My lord, you do me most insupportable vexation.

LAFEW I would it were hell-pains for thy sake, and my poor doing eternal; for doing I am past, as I will by thee, in what motion age will give me leave. *Exit.*

PAROLLES Well, thou hast a son shall take this disgrace off me—scurvy, old, filthy, scurvy lord! Well, I must be patient; there is no fettering of authority. I'll beat him, by my life, if I can meet him with any convenience, an he were double and double a lord. I'll have no more pity of his age than I would have of—I'll beat him, an if I could but meet him again.

Enter Lafew.

LAFEW Sirrah, your lord and master's married; there's news for you. You have a new mistress.

PAROLLES I most unfeignedly beseech Your Lordship to make some reservation of your wrongs. He is my good lord; whom I serve above is my master.

LAFEW Who? God?

PAROLLES Ay, sir.

LAFEW The devil it is that's thy master. Why dost thou garter up thy arms o' this fashion? Dost make hose of thy sleeves? Do other servants so? Thou wert best set thy lower part where thy nose stands. By mine honor, if I were but two hours younger, I'd beat thee. Methink'st thou art a general offense, and every man

191 bloody succeeding outcome with bloodshed, attendant on change of faith. (Sustaining the language of religion and treachery from lines 182–3.) **192 companion** (1) comrade (2) rascally knave **193 what is man** i.e., any true man; or, what is manly. **194–5 Count's . . . style** i.e., "Man" and "master" are worlds apart, and you belong to the first. **196 too old** i.e., for me to duel with. **let . . . you** i.e., take that as a satisfaction instead of a duel **198 write man** i.e., account myself a man, lay claim to that title **200 What . . . not do** i.e., What I could too easily accomplish—thrash you—I must not do because of your age. **201 for two ordinaries** during the space of two meals **202 didst . . . of** discoursed tolerably upon **203–4 scarves, bannerets** i.e., soldiers' scarves, reminding Lafew of a ship's pennants **205 burden** cargo, capacity. **206 found** found out. **lose thee** lose your company. (With a play on the antithesis of "find" and "lose.") **207 yet . . . taking up** you are like a commodity one *takes up* in the sense of taking a loan at exorbitant rates of interest and being paid in shoddy goods not worth the amount borrowed **212 thy trial** i.e., the testing of your supposed valor **213 hen** i.e., cackling, cowardly female. **window of lattice** wooden frame with cross-hatched slats (instead of glass), often painted red and used as the sign of an alehouse; something easily seen through and common, disreputable **214 casement** window sash **216 give** offer. (But Lafew mockingly replies as though he were indeed making a valuable gift. He plays with *deserved* the same way in lines 220–1: "Oh, you *deserved* it, all right.") **egregious** outrageous, flagrant **220 dram** bit. (Literally, one-eighth of an ounce.) **221 bate** abate, remit. **scruple** smallest bit. (Literally, one-third of a dram.)

222 wiser i.e., wiser than to deal with such dotards in the future. (But Lafew jestingly answers that Parolles indeed has to learn to be wise, i.e., less foolish.) **223–4 for . . . contrary** i.e., because it's necessary for you to have a taste of your own folly before you can be called self-knowing and wise. **224–5 If . . . beaten** i.e., If even you are subjected to one of the greatest indignities an officer can suffer, to be tied up in the scarves you festoon yourself with and thrashed as a poltroon. (See note 248–50 below.) **226 bondage** i.e., the scarf, in which you would be bound and of which you are now vainly proud. **hold** continue **228 in the default** when you default, i.e., show your emptiness on being brought to trial **231–2 my poor doing** i.e., my inadequate power to teach you a lesson **232 for doing** for energetic activity. (With a sexual suggestion.) **232–3 will by thee** i.e., will pass by you. (Punning on *past,* "passed.") **233 in . . . leave** with whatever speed age will allow me. **234–5 shall . . . me** i.e., on whom I will vindicate myself for these insults. (Parolles, pretending to be unwilling to fight Lafew because of the latter's older years, asserts that only a son of Lafew would be a fit opponent for Parolles in a duel.) **236 there . . . authority** there's no use trying to bring a figure of authority like Lafew to account. **237–8 with any convenience** on a suitable occasion **238 an** even if **240 an if** if **244 make . . . wrongs** put some restraint upon your insults, qualify the insults you've given me. **245 good lord** i.e., patron (not master, as Lafew has insultingly said). **whom** i.e., he whom (God) **248–50 Why . . . sleeves?** (Parolles apparently has decorative scarves tied around the sleeves of his outfit. Lafew acidly points out that the *hose* or breeches would be a fitter place for such decorations in Parolles's case.) **249 o'** of, in **250–1 Thou . . . stands** i.e., Mixing up sleeves and breeches is turning things upside down, as if your ass were where your nose is. (With a scatological suggestion of smelling one's own excrement.)

should beat thee. I think thou wast created for men to breathe themselves upon thee.

PAROLLES This is hard and undeserved measure, my lord.

LAFEW Go to, sir. You were beaten in Italy for picking a kernel out of a pomegranate. You are a vagabond and no true traveler. You are more saucy with lords and honorable personages than the commission of your birth and virtue gives you heraldry. You are not worth another word, else I'd call you knave. I leave you. *Exit.*

PAROLLES Good, very good! It is so, then. Good, very good. Let it be concealed awhile.

Enter [*Bertram*] *Count Rossillion.*

BERTRAM Undone, and forfeited to cares forever!

PAROLLES What's the matter, sweetheart?

BERTRAM Although before the solemn priest I have sworn, I will not bed her.

PAROLLES What, what, sweetheart?

BERTRAM
Oh, my Parolles, they have married me!
I'll to the Tuscan wars, and never bed her.

PAROLLES France is a dog-hole, and it no more merits the tread of a man's foot. To th' wars!

BERTRAM There's letters from my mother. What th'import is I know not yet.

PAROLLES Ay, that would be known. To th' wars, my boy, to th' wars!
He wears his honor in a box unseen
That hugs his kicky-wicky here at home,
Spending his manly marrow in her arms,
Which should sustain the bound and high curvet
Of Mars's fiery steed. To other regions!
France is a stable, we that dwell in't jades.
Therefore, to th' war!

BERTRAM
It shall be so. I'll send her to my house,
Acquaint my mother with my hate to her
And wherefore I am fled, write to the King
That which I durst not speak. His present gift
Shall furnish me to those Italian fields
Where noble fellows strike. Wars is no strife
To the dark house and the detested wife.

PAROLLES
Will this capriccio hold in thee? Art sure?

BERTRAM
Go with me to my chamber and advise me.
I'll send her straight away. Tomorrow
I'll to the wars, she to her single sorrow.

PAROLLES
Why, these balls bound; there's noise in it. 'Tis hard!
A young man married is a man that's marred.
Therefore away, and leave her bravely. Go.
The King has done you wrong, but hush, 'tis so.
Exeunt.

✤

[2.4]

Enter Helena [*with a letter*], *and Clown* [*Lavatch*].

HELENA
My mother greets me kindly. Is she well?

LAVATCH She is not well, but yet she has her health. She's very merry, but yet she is not well. But thanks be given, she's very well and wants nothing i'th' world; but yet she is not well.

HELENA If she be very well, what does she ail that she's not very well?

LAVATCH Truly, she's very well indeed, but for two things.

HELENA What two things?

LAVATCH One, that she's not in heaven, whither God send her quickly. The other, that she's in earth, from whence God send her quickly.

Enter Parolles.

PAROLLES Bless you, my fortunate lady!

HELENA I hope, sir, I have your good will to have mine own good fortunes.

PAROLLES You had my prayers to lead them on, and to keep them on have them still.—Oh, my knave, how does my old lady?

LAVATCH So that you had her wrinkles and I her money, I would she did as you say.

PAROLLES Why, I say nothing.

LAVATCH Marry, you are the wiser man, for many a man's tongue shakes out his master's undoing. To say nothing, to do nothing, to know nothing, and to have nothing is to be a great part of your title, which is within a very little of nothing.

PAROLLES Away! Thou'rt a knave.

255 breathe exercise **258–9 for . . . pomegranate** i.e., for some petty offense, or, on a slight pretext. **259 vagabond** (A word used by the authorities to describe actors—thus inviting sympathy for Parolles, a play-actor to the core, whose business, like theirs, is words.) **260 saucy** unbecomingly familiar **261 commission** warrant **262 gives you heraldry** entitles you to be. **276 letters** i.e., a letter **281 kicky-wicky** woman. (With sexual suggestion, as also in *box* in the previous line and *Spending* and *marrow* in the following line.) **282 manly marrow** masculine essence, semen **283 curvet** leap **285 jades** worn-out horses. **291 furnish me** (Knights customarily provided themselves with trappings and armed retainers when enlisting in warlike enterprises.) **293 To . . . house** i.e., compared to the madhouse (of marriage) **294 capriccio** caprice, whim **296 straight** at once **298 Why . . . hard!** i.e., Now you're talking; that's the way! (*Balls* here are tennis balls.)

2.4. Location: Paris. The royal court.

2 not well (Referring to the Elizabethan euphemism by which the dead were spoken of as "well," i.e., well rid of this life and well off in heaven.) **15–16 I hope . . . fortunes** I hope my good fortunes need not depend on your good wishes, if you don't mind my saying so. **17 them** i.e., your good fortunes. (A plural concept.) **17–18 to . . . still** to maintain your good fortune, you have my prayers continually. **20–1 So . . . say** Provided you were old (and wise), like her, and I had her wealth, I'd be happy to have her follow your advice. **24 man's** servant's. **shakes out** i.e., brings about by talking too freely **26 your title** i.e., your reputation for being all bluster and no substance. (With wordplay on *title/tittle,* any tiny amount.)

LAVATCH You should have said, sir, "Before a knave thou'rt a knave"; that's, "Before me thou'rt a knave." This had been truth, sir.

PAROLLES Go to, thou art a witty fool. I have found thee.

LAVATCH Did you find me in yourself, sir? Or were you taught to find me? The search, sir, was profitable; and much fool may you find in you, even to the world's pleasure and the increase of laughter.

PAROLLES
A good knave, i'faith, and well fed.—
Madam, my lord will go away tonight;
A very serious business calls on him.
The great prerogative and rite of love,
Which, as your due time claims, he does
    acknowledge,
But puts if off to a compelled restraint,
Whose want and whose delays is strewed with
    sweets,
Which they distill now in the curbèd time,
To make the coming hour o'erflow with joy
And pleasure drown the brim.

HELENA What's his will else?

PAROLLES
That you will take your instant leave o'th' King
And make this haste as your own good proceeding,
Strengthened with what apology you think
May make it probable need.

HELENA What more commands he?

PAROLLES
That, having this obtained, you presently
Attend his further pleasure.

HELENA
In every thing I wait upon his will.

PAROLLES I shall report it so.

HELENA I pray you. *Exit Parolles.*
[*To Lavatch*] Come, sirrah. *Exeunt.*

✤

[2.5]

Enter Lafew and Bertram.

LAFEW But I hope Your Lordship thinks not him a soldier.

BERTRAM Yes, my lord, and of very valiant approof.

LAFEW You have it from his own deliverance.

BERTRAM And by other warranted testimony.

LAFEW Then my dial goes not true. I took this lark for a bunting.

BERTRAM I do assure you, my lord, he is very great in knowledge, and accordingly valiant.

LAFEW I have then sinned against his experience and transgressed against his valor; and my state that way is dangerous, since I cannot yet find in my heart to repent. Here he comes. I pray you, make us friends; I will pursue the amity.

Enter Parolles.

PAROLLES [*to Bertram*] These things shall be done, sir.

LAFEW [*to Bertram*] Pray you, sir, who's his tailor?

PAROLLES Sir?

LAFEW Oh, I know him well. Ay, sir, he, sir, 's a good workman, a very good tailor.

BERTRAM [*aside to Parolles*] Is she gone to the King?

PAROLLES She is.

BERTRAM Will she away tonight?

PAROLLES As you'll have her.

BERTRAM
I have writ my letters, casketed my treasure,
Given order for our horses; and tonight,
When I should take possession of the bride,
End ere I do begin.

LAFEW A good traveler is something at the latter end of a dinner; but one that lies three thirds, and uses a known truth to pass a thousand nothings with, should be once heard and thrice beaten. God save you, Captain.

BERTRAM [*to Parolles*] Is there any unkindness between my lord and you, monsieur?

PAROLLES I know not how I have deserved to run into my lord's displeasure.

LAFEW You have made shift to run into't, boots and spurs and all, like him that leapt into the custard; and out of it you'll run again, rather than suffer question for your residence.

BERTRAM It may be you have mistaken him, my lord.

LAFEW And shall do so ever, though I took him at 's prayers. Fare you well, my lord, and believe this of

29 Before In presence of **30 Before me** i.e., Upon my soul. (But, by substituting *me* for *knave*, Lavatch suggests that Parolles call himself a knave.) **32–3 found thee** found you out, found you to be a fool. **34 Did . . . sir?** i.e., Did you find folly in yourself, sir? (Since I, Lavatch, am a fool.) **38 well fed** (Referring to the proverb "better fed than taught," as at 2.2.3.) **42 Which . . . acknowledge** he does acknowledge as your due, in the fullness of time, the rite and privilege of sexual consummation **43 to** owing to **44 Whose . . . sweets** the desire for which, being delayed, is made all the sweeter by waiting, like perfume made sweeter by distillation. (*Sweets* are sweet-smelling flowers.) **45 Which . . . time** which sweet-smelling flowers of desire and delay distill their essence into this period of restraint **47 drown** overflow. **else** besides. **49 make** represent. **proceeding** course of action **51 probable need** a plausible necessity. **53 Attend** await. **pleasure** command.
2.5. Location: Paris. The royal court.
3 valiant approof proven valor.

4 deliverance testimony, word. **6 dial** clock, compass, i.e., judgment **6–7 I . . . bunting** i.e., I underestimated him. (The bunting resembles the lark but lacks the lark's beautiful song. Lafew suggests that Parolles is all show and no substance. Compare 1.2.18, where, in the Folio, Bertram is called Count *Rosignoll*, nightingale.) **9 accordingly** correspondingly **11 my state** i.e., the state of my soul. (Lafew uses an elaborate metaphor of religious penitence ironically.) **12 find in** find it in **16 who's his tailor?** i.e., what tailor made this stuffed (bombast) figure? (Lafew says this to Bertram but is taunting Parolles, who replies indignantly.) **18–19 Oh . . . tailor** (Lafew mockingly takes Parolles's *Sir* in line 17 as the name of his tailor.) **28–9 A good . . . dinner** i.e., A person with many traveling experiences is an asset as a storyteller after dinner **29 three thirds** i.e., all the time **33 unkindness** ill will **37 made shift** contrived (at our previous meeting) **38 like . . . custard** i.e., like a clown at a city entertainment jumping into a large, deep custard **39 you'll run** you will want to run **39–40 suffer . . . residence** undergo questioning about your being there, i.e., explain how your cowardice displeased me. **41 mistaken him** misjudged him. (But Lafew deliberately takes the phrase in the sense of "taken exception to his behavior.")

me: there can be no kernel in this light nut. The soul of this man is his clothes. Trust him not in matter of heavy consequence. I have kept of them tame, and know their natures.—Farewell, monsieur. I have spoken better of you than you have or will to deserve at my hand; but we must do good against evil.

[*Exit.*]

PAROLLES An idle lord, I swear.

BERTRAM I think so.

PAROLLES Why, do you not know him?

BERTRAM
Yes, I do know him well, and common speech
Gives him a worthy pass. Here comes my clog.

Enter Helena.

HELENA
I have, sir, as I was commanded from you,
Spoke with the King, and have procured his leave
For present parting; only he desires
Some private speech with you.

BERTRAM I shall obey his will.
You must not marvel, Helen, at my course,
Which holds not color with the time, nor does
The ministration and requirèd office
On my particular. Prepared I was not
For such a business; therefore am I found
So much unsettled. This drives me to entreat you
That presently you take your way for home;
And rather muse than ask why I entreat you,
For my respects are better than they seem,
And my appointments have in them a need
Greater than shows itself at the first view
To you that know them not. This to my mother.

[*He gives a letter.*]

'Twill be two days ere I shall see you, so
I leave you to your wisdom.

HELENA Sir, I can nothing say
But that I am your most obedient servant.

BERTRAM
Come, come, no more of that.

HELENA And ever shall
With true observance seek to eke out that
Wherein toward me my homely stars have failed
To equal my great fortune.

BERTRAM Let that go.
My haste is very great. Farewell. Hie home.

[*He starts to go.*]

HELENA
Pray, sir, your pardon.

BERTRAM Well, what would you say?

HELENA
I am not worthy of the wealth I owe,
Nor dare I say 'tis mine, and yet it is;
But, like a timorous thief, most fain would steal
What law does vouch mine own.

BERTRAM What would you have?

HELENA
Something, and scarce so much; nothing, indeed.
I would not tell you what I would, my lord. Faith,
yes—
Strangers and foes do sunder, and not kiss.

BERTRAM
I pray you, stay not, but in haste to horse.

HELENA
I shall not break your bidding, good my lord.

BERTRAM [*to Parolles*]
Where are my other men, monsieur?—Farewell.

Exit [*Helena.*]

Go thou toward home, where I will never come
Whilst I can shake my sword or hear the drum.
Away, and for our flight.

PAROLLES Bravely, *coraggio*! [*Exeunt.*]

✤

3.1

Flourish. Enter the Duke of Florence [*attended*]; *the two Frenchmen, with a troop of soldiers.*

DUKE
So that from point to point now have you heard
The fundamental reasons of this war,
Whose great decision hath much blood let forth,
And more thirsts after.

FIRST LORD Holy seems the quarrel
Upon Your Grace's part, black and fearful
On the opposer.

DUKE
Therefore we marvel much our cousin France
Would in so just a business shut his bosom
Against our borrowing prayers.

SECOND LORD Good my lord,
The reasons of our state I cannot yield
But like a common and an outward man
That the great figure of a council frames
By self-unable motion, therefore dare not

46 heavy serious. **I . . . tame** I have kept tame creatures of this kind (for the amusement they provide) **48 have . . . deserve** have deserved or are likely to deserve **50 idle** foolish **51 I think so** i.e., I suppose you're right. (Parolles emphasizes *know* in the next line to contrast with *think.*) **54 pass** reputation. **clog** a heavy weight attached to the leg or neck of a man or animal to prevent freedom of movement. **60–2 Which . . . particular** which does not appear to suit with the occasion (of our marriage), nor does it fulfill what is incumbent upon me as a husband. **66 muse** wonder **67 my respects** the circumstances prompting me **68 appointments** purposes **72 to your wisdom** to do what you think best. **75 observance** dutiful and reverential service. **eke out** add to **76 homely stars** i.e., lowly origin **78 Hie** Hasten

80 owe own **82 fain** gladly **83 vouch** affirm to be **86 Strangers . . . kiss** i.e, Only strangers and enemies depart from one another without a farewell kiss. **87 stay** delay **92** *coraggio!* courage, bravo!
3.1. Location: Florence.
3–4 Whose . . . after the violent deciding of which has led to much shedding of blood and a thirsting after still more. **6 the opposer** the opposer's part. **7 cousin** i.e., fellow sovereign **9 borrowing prayers** prayers for assistance. **10–13 The reasons . . . motion** I cannot explain to you the rationale of our statecraft other than as an ordinary citizen, not being privy to the workings of the state; I am one who constructs in his own imagination an imperfect idea of whatever grand schemes the King and his counsel may be devising

Say what I think of it, since I have found
Myself in my incertain grounds to fail
As often as I guessed.

DUKE Be it his pleasure.

FIRST LORD
But I am sure the younger of our nature,
That surfeit on their ease, will day by day
Come here for physic.

DUKE Welcome shall they be,
And all the honors that can fly from us
Shall on them settle. You know your places well;
When better fall, for your avails they fell.
Tomorrow to the field. *Flourish.* [*Exeunt.*]

✣

[3.2]

Enter Countess and Clown [*Lavatch*].

COUNTESS It hath happened all as I would have had it, save that he comes not along with her.

LAVATCH By my troth, I take my young lord to be a very melancholy man.

COUNTESS By what observance, I pray you?

LAVATCH Why, he will look upon his boot and sing, mend the ruff and sing, ask questions and sing, pick his teeth and sing. I know a man that had this trick of melancholy sold a goodly manor for a song.

COUNTESS Let me see what he writes and when he means to come. [*Opening a letter.*]

LAVATCH I have no mind to Isbel since I was at court. Our old lings and our Isbels o'th' country are nothing like your old ling and your Isbels o'th' court. The brains of my Cupid's knocked out, and I begin to love as an old man loves money, with no stomach.

COUNTESS What have we here?

LAVATCH E'en that you have there. *Exit.*

COUNTESS [*reads*] *a letter.* "I have sent you a daughter-in-law. She hath recovered the King and undone me. I have wedded her, not bedded her, and sworn to make the 'not' eternal. You shall hear I am run away; know it before the report come. If there be breadth enough in the world, I will hold a long distance. My duty to you.

Your unfortunate son,
Bertram."

This is not well, rash and unbridled boy,
To fly the favors of so good a king,
To pluck his indignation on thy head
By the misprizing of a maid too virtuous
For the contempt of empire.

Enter Clown [*Lavatch*].

LAVATCH O madam, yonder is heavy news within between two soldiers and my young lady!

COUNTESS What is the matter?

LAVATCH Nay, there is some comfort in the news, some comfort. Your son will not be killed so soon as I thought he would.

COUNTESS Why should he be killed?

LAVATCH So say I, madam, if he run away, as I hear he does. The danger is in standing to't; that's the loss of men, though it be the getting of children. Here they come will tell you more. For my part, I only hear your son was run away. [*Exit.*]

Enter Helena and [*the*] *two* [*French*] *Gentlemen* [*or Lords*].

SECOND LORD Save you, good madam.

HELENA
Madam, my lord is gone, forever gone!

FIRST LORD Do not say so.

COUNTESS
Think upon patience.—Pray you, gentlemen,
I have felt so many quirks of joy and grief
That the first face of neither, on the start,
Can woman me unto't. Where is my son, I pray you?

FIRST LORD
Madam, he's gone to serve the Duke of Florence.
We met him thitherward; for thence we came,
And, after some dispatch in hand at court,
Thither we bend again.

HELENA
Look on his letter, madam; here's my passport.
[*She reads.*] "When thou canst get the ring upon my finger, which never shall come off, and show me a child begotten of thy body that I am father to, then call me husband; but in such a 'then' I write a 'never.' "
This is a dreadful sentence.

COUNTESS
Brought you this letter, gentlemen?

FIRST LORD Ay, madam,
And for the contents' sake are sorry for our pains.

COUNTESS
I prithee, lady, have a better cheer.

16 Be . . . pleasure i.e., Be it as the King of France wishes. **17 nature** outlook, disposition **18 surfeit** grow sick **19 physic** i.e., cure of their surfeit (through bloodletting). **20 can fly from us** i.e., we can grant **22 When . . . fell** whenever better places fall vacant, they will have done so for you to fill.

3.2. Location: Rossillion.

3 troth faith **5 observance** observation **7 mend the ruff** adjust the loose turned-over flap at the top of his boot or his frilled collar **7–8 pick his teeth** (An affected mannerism, as at 1.1.159.) **9 sold** who sold **13 lings** cunts. Lavatch is saying that all women, both old ("old lings") and young ("Isbels"), are much better at the court than in the country. **16 stomach** appetite. **18 E'en . . . there** (The Clown is playfully literal: to the Countess's "What's this?" he replies, "It looks like a letter.") **20 recovered** cured **22 not** (With a pun on "knot.") **24 hold a long distance** stay far away.

30 pluck bring down **31 misprizing** scorning, failing to appreciate **32 of empire** of even an emperor. **33 heavy** sad **41 standing to't** standing one's ground. (With sexual pun. The Clown jests on running from a battle and running from a woman; in both cases, a soldier can avoid the *danger* of dying; with its suggestion of sexual climax.) **42 getting** begetting **44 was** has **50–1 That . . . unto't** i.e., that neither joy nor grief, no matter how suddenly either appears, can make me weep as women are supposed to do. **53 thitherward** on his way there **54 dispatch in hand** business to be taken care of **55 Thither . . . again** to Florence we will direct our steps. **56 passport** license to wander as a beggar. **61 sentence** (1) sentence of punishment (2) statement, utterance.

If thou engrossest all the griefs are thine,
Thou robb'st me of a moi'ty. He was my son,
But I do wash his name out of my blood,
And thou art all my child.—Towards Florence is he?

FIRST LORD
Ay, madam.

COUNTESS And to be a soldier?

FIRST LORD
Such is his noble purpose; and, believe't,
The Duke will lay upon him all the honor
That good convenience claims.

COUNTESS Return you thither?

SECOND LORD
Ay, madam, with the swiftest wing of speed.

HELENA [*reading*]
"Till I have no wife, I have nothing in France."
'Tis bitter.

COUNTESS Find you that there?

HELENA Ay, madam.

SECOND LORD
'Tis but the boldness of his hand, haply,
Which his heart was not consenting to.

COUNTESS
Nothing in France, until he have no wife!
There's nothing here that is too good for him
But only she, and she deserves a lord
That twenty such rude boys might tend upon
And call her, hourly, mistress. Who was with him?

SECOND LORD
A servant only, and a gentleman
Which I have sometime known.

COUNTESS Parolles, was it not?

SECOND LORD Ay, my good lady, he.

COUNTESS
A very tainted fellow, and full of wickedness.
My son corrupts a well-derivèd nature
With his inducement.

SECOND LORD Indeed, good lady,
The fellow has a deal of that too much
Which holds him much to have.

COUNTESS You're welcome, gentlemen.
I will entreat you, when you see my son,
To tell him that his sword can never win
The honor that he loses. More I'll entreat you
Written to bear along.

FIRST LORD We serve you, madam,
In that and all your worthiest affairs.

COUNTESS
Not so, but as we change our courtesies.
Will you draw near? *Exit* [*with Gentlemen*].

HELENA
"Till I have no wife, I have nothing in France."
Nothing in France, until he has no wife!
Thou shalt have none, Rossillion, none in France;
Then hast thou all again. Poor lord, is't I
That chase thee from thy country and expose
Those tender limbs of thine to the event
Of the none-sparing war? And is it I
That drive thee from the sportive court, where thou
Wast shot at with fair eyes, to be the mark
Of smoky muskets? O you leaden messengers,
That ride upon the violent speed of fire,
Fly with false aim; move the still-piecing air,
That sings with piercing; do not touch my lord!
Whoever shoots at him, I set him there;
Whoever charges on his forward breast,
I am the caitiff that do hold him to't;
And, though I kill him not, I am the cause
His death was so effected. Better 'twere
I met the ravin lion when he roared
With sharp constraint of hunger; better 'twere
That all the miseries which nature owes
Were mine at once. No, come thou home, Rossillion,
Whence honor but of danger wins a scar,
As oft it loses all. I will be gone.
My being here it is that holds thee hence.
Shall I stay here to do't? No, no, although
The air of paradise did fan the house
And angels officed all. I will be gone,
That pitiful rumor may report my flight
To consolate thine ear. Come, night; end, day!
For with the dark, poor thief, I'll steal away. *Exit.*

[3.3]

Flourish. Enter the Duke of Florence, [*Bertram, Count*] *Rossillion, drum and trumpets, soldiers, Parolles.*

DUKE
The General of our Horse thou art, and we,
Great in our hope, lay our best love and credence
Upon thy promising fortune.

BERTRAM Sir, it is
A charge too heavy for my strength, but yet

65–6 If thou . . . moi'ty If you refuse to share your griefs, you rob me of my right to half of them (in that Bertram is my son). **68 all my** my only **72 That . . . claims** that he can in propriety claim. **76 haply** perhaps **88–9 My . . . inducement** My son corrupts the fine qualities he inherited from his ancestors, owing to Parolles's corrupt influence. **90–1 The fellow . . . have** The fellow has a great supply of that "excess" which it would be beholding to him much to restrain or withhold. **96 Written . . . along** to take with you in the form of a letter. **98 but . . . courtesies** i.e., only if I can repay or exchange your courtesy with my own. **99 draw near** come with me.

102 Rossillion i.e., Bertram (whom Helena refers to by his title) **105 event** hazard, outcome **107 sportive** amorous **108 mark** target **109 leaden messengers** i.e., bullets **111–12 move . . . piercing** part the always-parting air, which appears to be still but which whistles musically when a bullet passes through it. (The Folio reading, "still-peering," is here emended to "still-piecing," always closing or repairing itself again.) **114 forward** facing forward in battle, in the van **115 caitiff** base wretch **118 ravin** ravenous **120 nature owes** human nature possesses, suffers **122–3 Whence . . . all** i.e., from war, in which honor is at best rewarded for danger with a scar, and often loses life itself. **125 do't** i.e., keep you hence. **although** even if **127 officed all** performed all domestic duties. **128 pitiful** compassionate **129 consolate** console **130 poor thief** (The night is thief of the light of day; Helen is an unwilling thief in having "stolen" the title of wife and in having to steal away.)
3.3. Location: Florence.
2 Great pregnant, expectant. **lay** wager. **credence** trust

We'll strive to bear it for your worthy sake
To th'extreme edge of hazard.

DUKE Then go thou forth,
And Fortune play upon thy prosperous helm,
As thy auspicious mistress!

BERTRAM This very day,
Great Mars, I put myself into thy file.
Make me but like my thoughts, and I shall prove
A lover of thy drum, hater of love. *Exeunt omnes.*

✤

[3.4]

Enter Countess and Steward [*Rinaldo*].

COUNTESS
Alas! And would you take the letter of her?
Might you not know she would do as she has done,
By sending me a letter? Read it again.

RINALDO [*reads the*] *letter*
"I am Saint Jaques' pilgrim, thither gone.
Ambitious love hath so in me offended
That barefoot plod I the cold ground upon,
With sainted vow my faults to have amended.
Write, write, that from the bloody course of war
My dearest master, your dear son, may hie.
Bless him at home in peace, whilst I from far
His name with zealous fervor sanctify.
His taken labors bid him me forgive;
I, his despiteful Juno, sent him forth
From courtly friends, with camping foes to live
Where death and danger dogs the heels of worth.
He is too good and fair for death and me;
Whom I myself embrace, to set him free."

COUNTESS
Ah, what sharp stings are in her mildest words!
Rinaldo, you did never lack advice so much
As letting her pass so. Had I spoke with her,
I could have well diverted her intents,
Which thus she hath prevented.

RINALDO Pardon me, madam.
If I had given you this at overnight,
She might have been o'erta'en; and yet she writes
Pursuit would be but vain.

COUNTESS What angel shall
Bless this unworthy husband? He cannot thrive,
Unless her prayers, whom heaven delights to hear
And loves to grant, reprieve him from the wrath
Of greatest justice. Write, write, Rinaldo,
To this unworthy husband of his wife.
Let every word weigh heavy of her worth
That he does weigh too light. My greatest grief,
Though little he do feel it, set down sharply.
Dispatch the most convenient messenger.
When haply he shall hear that she is gone,
He will return; and hope I may that she,
Hearing so much, will speed her foot again,
Led hither by pure love. Which of them both
Is dearest to me, I have no skill in sense
To make distinction. Provide this messenger.
My heart is heavy and mine age is weak;
Grief would have tears, and sorrow bids me speak.
Exeunt.

✤

[3.5]

A tucket afar off. Enter old Widow of Florence, her daughter [*Diana*], *and Mariana, with other citizens.*

WIDOW Nay, come, for if they do approach the city we shall lose all the sight.

DIANA They say the French count has done most honorable service.

WIDOW It is reported that he has taken their great'st commander, and that with his own hand he slew the Duke's brother. [*Tucket.*] We have lost our labor; they are gone a contrary way. Hark! You may know by their trumpets.

MARIANA Come, let's return again and suffice ourselves with the report of it.—Well, Diana, take heed of this French earl. The honor of a maid is her name, and no legacy is so rich as honesty.

WIDOW [*to Diana*] I have told my neighbor how you have been solicited by a gentleman, his companion.

MARIANA I know that knave, hang him! One Parolles, a filthy officer he is in those suggestions for the young earl. Beware of them, Diana; their promises, enticements, oaths, tokens, and all these engines of lust are not the things they go under. Many a maid hath been seduced by them; and the misery is, example, that so terrible shows in the wreck of maidenhood, cannot for all that dissuade succession, but that they are limed with the twigs that threatens them. I hope I need not

6 edge of hazard limit of peril. **7 helm** helmet **9 file** battle line; ranks, catalogue. **10 like my thoughts** i.e., as valiant as I aspire to be
3.4. Location: Rossillion.
4–17 (The letter is in the form of a sonnet.) **4 Saint Jaques' pilgrim** i.e., a pilgrim to the shrine of Saint James, presumably the famous shrine of Santiago de Compostella in Spain **4 Jaques'** (Pronounced in two syllables.) **7 sainted** (1) holy (2) offered to a saint **9 hie** hasten. **12 His taken labors** The labors he has undertaken **13 despiteful Juno** spitefully jealous queen of Olympus, who imposed on Hercules his twelve labors because he was the product of one of Jupiter's many amours. She was also partisan in the Trojan War on the Greek side because of the abduction of Helen. **14 camping** encamped, contending. (Playing on the antithesis of court and military camp.) **17 Whom** i.e., death **19 advice** judgment **22 prevented** forestalled. **23 at overnight** last night

27 her i.e., Helena's. (Helena is likened to saints who can intercede with heaven on behalf of a sinner.) **30 unworthy . . . wife** husband unworthy of his wife. **31 weigh heavy of** emphasize **39 in sense** in perception **40 this messenger** a messenger to carry this letter.
3.5. Location: Florence. Outside the walls.
0.1 *tucket* a trumpet fanfare **2 lose . . . sight** miss seeing them. **5 their** i.e., the Sienese's **10 suffice** content **12 earl** i.e., Count Bertram. **her name** her reputation (for chastity) **13 honesty** chastity. **14 my neighbor** i.e., Mariana **17 officer** agent. **suggestions for** solicitings on behalf of, or, temptations of **19 engines** artifices, devices **20 go under** pretend to be. **21–3 example . . . succession** the dreadful example of what happens with the loss of virginity nonetheless cannot dissuade another from a similar course **23–4 they . . . twigs** i.e., other maidens are caught in the same trap. (Birdlime was smeared on twigs to ensnare birds.)

to advise you further, but I hope your own grace will keep you where you are, though there were no further danger known but the modesty which is so lost.

DIANA You shall not need to fear me.

Enter Helena [disguised like a pilgrim].

WIDOW I hope so.—Look, here comes a pilgrim. I know she will lie at my house; thither they send one another. I'll question her.—God save you, pilgrim! Whither are bound?

HELENA To Saint Jaques le Grand.
Where do the palmers lodge, I do beseech you?

WIDOW
At the Saint Francis here beside the port.

HELENA Is this the way? *(A march afar.)*

WIDOW
Ay, marry, is't. Hark you, they come this way.
If you will tarry, holy pilgrim,
But till the troops come by,
I will conduct you where you shall be lodged,
The rather for I think I know your hostess
As ample as myself.

HELENA Is it yourself?

WIDOW If you shall please so, pilgrim.

HELENA
I thank you, and will stay upon your leisure.

WIDOW
You came, I think, from France?

HELENA I did so.

WIDOW
Here you shall see a countryman of yours
That has done worthy service.

HELENA His name, I pray you?

DIANA
The Count Rossillion. Know you such a one?

HELENA
But by the ear, that hears most nobly of him.
His face I know not.

DIANA Whatsome'er he is,
He's bravely taken here. He stole from France,
As 'tis reported, for the King had married him
Against his liking. Think you it is so?

HELENA
Ay, surely, mere the truth. I know his lady.

DIANA
There is a gentleman that serves the Count
Reports but coarsely of her.

HELENA What's his name?

DIANA
Monsieur Parolles.

HELENA Oh, I believe with him.
In argument of praise, or to the worth
Of the great Count himself, she is too mean
To have her name repeated. All her deserving
Is a reservèd honesty, and that
I have not heard examined.

DIANA Alas, poor lady!
'Tis a hard bondage to become the wife
Of a detesting lord.

WIDOW
I warrant, good creature, wheresoe'er she is,
Her heart weighs sadly. This young maid might do her
A shrewd turn, if she pleased.

HELENA How do you mean?
Maybe the amorous Count solicits her
In the unlawful purpose?

WIDOW He does indeed,
And brokes with all that can in such a suit
Corrupt the tender honor of a maid.
But she is armed for him and keeps her guard
In honestest defense.

Drum and colors. Enter [Bertram] Count Rossillion, Parolles, and the whole army.

MARIANA The gods forbid else!

WIDOW So, now they come.
That is Antonio, the Duke's eldest son;
That, Escalus.

HELENA Which is the Frenchman?

DIANA He,
That with the plume. 'Tis a most gallant fellow.
I would he loved his wife. If he were honester
He were much goodlier. Is't not a handsome gentleman?

HELENA I like him well.

[The warriors pass in file and exit in succession. Parolles comes last.]

DIANA 'Tis pity he is not honest. Yond's that same knave
That leads him to these places. Were I his lady
I would poison that vile rascal.

HELENA Which is he?

DIANA
That jackanapes with scarves. Why is he melancholy?

HELENA Perchance he's hurt i'th' battle.

PAROLLES Lose our drum? Well.

MARIANA He's shrewdly vexed at something. Look, he has spied us.

WIDOW [*to Parolles*] Marry, hang you!

MARIANA [*to Parolles*] And your courtesy, for a ring-carrier!

Exeunt [Bertram and the last of the army, Parolles among them].

25 grace virtuous strength of grace given by God to resist temptation **26 though** even though **26–7 further danger** i.e., pregnancy **27 modesty** chastity and chaste reputation **28 fear** worry about **30 lie** lodge **32 are** are you **34 palmers** pilgrims **35 the Saint Francis** the inn with the sign of Saint Francis. **port** city gate **42 ample** fully, completely **45 stay . . . leisure** await your convenience. **52 bravely taken** highly regarded **53 for** because **55 mere** absolutely **58 believe** agree **59 In argument of** As a subject for. **to** compared to

60 mean lowly **61–2 All . . . honesty** Her only merit is a well-guarded chastity **63 examined** doubted, questioned. **68 shrewd** crafty, cunning **71 brokes** bargains **74 honestest** most chaste **75 else** that it should be otherwise. **80 honester** more honorable (and more chaste) **86 jackanapes** monkey **89 shrewdly** sorely **92 courtesy** ceremonious bow **92–3 ring-carrier** go-between.

WIDOW
The troop is past. Come, pilgrim, I will bring you
Where you shall host. Of enjoined penitents
There's four or five, to great Saint Jaques bound,
Already at my house.

HELENA I humbly thank you.
Please it this matron and this gentle maid
To eat with us tonight, the charge and thanking
Shall be for me; and, to requite you further,
I will bestow some precepts of this virgin
Worthy the note.

BOTH We'll take your offer kindly.

Exeunt.

[3.6]

Enter [Bertram] *Count Rossillion and the* [*two*] *Frenchmen, as at first.*

FIRST LORD Nay, good my lord, put him to't. Let him have his way.

SECOND LORD If Your Lordship find him not a hilding, hold me no more in your respect.

FIRST LORD On my life, my lord, a bubble.

BERTRAM Do you think I am so far deceived in him?

FIRST LORD Believe it, my lord, in mine own direct knowledge, without any malice, but to speak of him as my kinsman, he's a most notable coward, an infinite and endless liar, an hourly promise-breaker, the owner of no one good quality worthy Your Lordship's entertainment.

SECOND LORD It were fit you knew him, lest, reposing too far in his virtue, which he hath not, he might at some great and trusty business in a main danger fail you.

BERTRAM I would I knew in what particular action to try him.

SECOND LORD None better than to let him fetch off his drum, which you hear him so confidently undertake to do.

FIRST LORD I, with a troop of Florentines, will suddenly surprise him; such I will have whom I am sure he knows not from the enemy. We will bind and hoodwink him so that he shall suppose no other but that he is carried into the leaguer of the adversary's, when we bring him to our own tents. Be but Your Lordship present at his examination. If he do not, for the promise of his life and in the highest compulsion of base fear, offer to betray you and deliver all the intelligence in his power against you, and that with the divine forfeit of his soul upon oath, never trust my judgment in anything.

SECOND LORD Oh, for the love of laughter, let him fetch his drum. He says he has a stratagem for't. When Your Lordship sees the bottom of his success in't, and to what metal this counterfeit lump of ore will be melted, if you give him not John Drum's entertainment, your inclining cannot be removed. Here he comes.

Enter Parolles.

FIRST LORD [*aside to Bertram*] Oh, for the love of laughter, hinder not the honor of his design. Let him fetch off his drum in any hand.

BERTRAM How now, monsieur? This drum sticks sorely in your disposition.

SECOND LORD A pox on't, let it go. 'Tis but a drum.

PAROLLES But a drum! Is't but a drum? A drum so lost! There was excellent command—to charge in with our horse upon our own wings and to rend our own soldiers!

SECOND LORD That was not to be blamed in the command of the service. It was a disaster of war that Caesar himself could not have prevented, if he had been there to command.

BERTRAM Well, we cannot greatly condemn our success. Some dishonor we had in the loss of that drum, but it is not to be recovered.

PAROLLES It might have been recovered.

BERTRAM It might, but it is not now.

PAROLLES It is to be recovered. But that the merit of service is seldom attributed to the true and exact performer, I would have that drum or another, or *hic jacet*.

BERTRAM Why, if you have a stomach, to't, monsieur! If you think your mystery in stratagem can bring this instrument of honor again into his native quarter, be magnanimous in the enterprise and go on. I will grace the attempt for a worthy exploit. If you speed well in it, the Duke shall both speak of it and extend to you what further becomes his greatness, even to the utmost syllable of your worthiness.

PAROLLES By the hand of a soldier, I will undertake it.

BERTRAM But you must not now slumber in it.

PAROLLES I'll about it this evening, and I will presently pen down my dilemmas, encourage myself in my certainty, put myself into my mortal preparation; and by midnight look to hear further from me.

95 host lodge. **enjoined penitents** those bound by oath to undertake a pilgrimage as penance for sin **98 Please it** If it please **99–100 the charge . . . me** i.e., I will bear the expense and be grateful at the same time **101 of** on **102 kindly** gratefully.
3.6. Location: The Florentine camp.
0.2 ***as at first*** (See 3.1.0.2.) **1 to't** i.e., to the test. **3 hilding** good-for-nothing **8–9 to speak . . . kinsman** to speak as candidly and fairly as I would even if he were my own kinsman **12 entertainment** patronage. **13 reposing** trusting **15 trusty** demanding trustworthiness **18 try** test **19 fetch off** recapture **23 surprise** capture **25 hoodwink** blindfold **26 leaguer** camp **30–1 intelligence in his power** information at his command

36 bottom extent **38 John Drum's entertainment** (Slang phrase for a thorough beating and unceremonious dismissal.) **39 inclining** partiality (for Parolles) **42 in any hand** in any case. **43–4 sticks . . . disposition** i.e., greatly troubles you. **45 A pox on't** Plague take it **48 wings** flanks. **rend** cut up, attack **50–1 in . . . service** upon the orders given for the action. **54 we . . . success** i.e., we were successful enough. **59 But that** Were it not that **61–2** ***hic jacet*** Latin for *here lies*, the beginning phrase of tomb inscriptions. Hence, Parolles means "I would die in the attempt." **63 stomach** appetite **64 mystery** skill **65 again . . . quarter** back home again **66 grace** honor **67 speed** succeed **69 becomes** does credit to **73 presently** immediately **74 pen . . . dilemmas** make note of my difficult choices **75 my mortal preparation** spiritual preparedness for my death; or, death-dealing readiness

BERTRAM May I be bold to acquaint His Grace you are gone about it?

PAROLLES I know not what the success will be, my lord, but the attempt I vow.

BERTRAM I know thou'rt valiant, and to the possibility of thy soldiership will subscribe for thee. Farewell.

PAROLLES I love not many words. *Exit.*

FIRST LORD No more than a fish loves water. Is not this a strange fellow, my lord, that so confidently seems to undertake this business, which he knows is not to be done, damns himself to do, and dares better be damned than to do't?

SECOND LORD You do not know him, my lord, as we do. Certain it is that he will steal himself into a man's favor and for a week escape a great deal of discoveries; but when you find him out, you have him ever after.

BERTRAM Why, do you think he will make no deed at all of this that so seriously he does address himself unto?

FIRST LORD None in the world, but return with an invention, and clap upon you two or three probable lies. But we have almost embossed him. You shall see his fall tonight; for indeed he is not for Your Lordship's respect.

SECOND LORD We'll make you some sport with the fox ere we case him. He was first smoked by the old lord Lafew. When his disguise and he is parted, tell me what a sprat you shall find him, which you shall see this very night.

FIRST LORD
I must go look my twigs. He shall be caught.

BERTRAM
Your brother he shall go along with me.

FIRST LORD
As't please Your Lordship. I'll leave you. [*Exit.*]

BERTRAM
Now will I lead you to the house and show you
The lass I spoke of.

SECOND LORD But you say she's honest.

BERTRAM
That's all the fault. I spoke with her but once
And found her wondrous cold; but I sent to her,
By this same coxcomb that we have i'th' wind,
Tokens and letters, which she did re-send,
And this is all I have done. She's a fair creature.
Will you go see her?

SECOND LORD With all my heart, my lord.
Exeunt.

[3.7]

Enter Helena and Widow.

HELENA
If you misdoubt me that I am not she,
I know not how I shall assure you further
But I shall lose the grounds I work upon.

WIDOW
Though my estate be fall'n, I was well born,
Nothing acquainted with these businesses,
And would not put my reputation now
In any staining act.

HELENA Nor would I wish you.
First give me trust the Count he is my husband,
And what to your sworn counsel I have spoken
Is so from word to word; and then you cannot,
By the good aid that I of you shall borrow,
Err in bestowing it.

WIDOW I should believe you,
For you have showed me that which well approves
You're great in fortune.

HELENA [*giving money*] Take this purse of gold,
And let me buy your friendly help thus far,
Which I will overpay and pay again
When I have found it. The Count he woos your
daughter,
Lays down his wanton siege before her beauty,
Resolved to carry her. Let her in fine consent,
As we'll direct her how 'tis best to bear it.
Now his important blood will naught deny
That she'll demand. A ring the County wears,
That downward hath succeeded in his house
From son to son some four or five descents
Since the first father wore it. This ring he holds
In most rich choice, yet, in his idle fire,
To buy his will it would not seem too dear,
Howe'er repented after.

WIDOW
Now I see the bottom of your purpose.

HELENA
You see it lawful, then. It is no more
But that your daughter, ere she seems as won,
Desires this ring; appoints him an encounter;
In fine, delivers me to fill the time,

81 possibility capacity **82 subscribe** vouch **87–8 damns . . . do't** i.e., swears perjured oaths to carry out the mission, but ends up damned if he does and damned if he doesn't. **91–2 escape . . . discoveries** i.e., almost get away with it **92 have him** have a true knowledge of him **94 deed** attempt **98 invention** fabrication. **probable** plausible **99 embossed** driven to exhaustion, cornered. (A hunting term.) **100 not for** not worthy of **101 respect** regard. **103 case** skin, strip, unmask. **smoked** smelled out; smoked out into the open **104 is parted** are separated **105 sprat** a small fish; a contemptible creature **107 look my twigs** i.e., see to my trap (as in catching birds with birdlime on twigs). **108 Your brother** i.e., the Second Lord **111 honest** chaste. **114 coxcomb** fool. **have i'th' wind** have to our downwind side, whom we are tracking **115 re-send** send back

3.7. Location: Florence. The Widow's house.
1 misdoubt doubt **3 But . . . upon** i.e., without abandoning my disguise and thus forfeiting the ground upon which my plans are built. **4 estate** worldly condition **8 give me trust** believe me (that) **9 to . . . counsel** to your private understanding, guarded by your oath of secrecy **10 Is so . . . to word** is true in every word **11 By** with regard to **13 approves** proves **17 found it** i.e., received your help with success. **19 carry** win. **in fine** finally, or, to sum up. (As also in line 33.) **20 bear** manage **21 important blood** importunate passion **22 That** whatever. **County** Count **26 choice** estimation, regard. **idle fire** foolish passion **27 will** sexual desire **32 appoints him an encounter** arranges a rendezvous

Herself most chastely absent. After,
To marry her, I'll add three thousand crowns
To what is passed already.

WIDOW I have yielded.
Instruct my daughter how she shall persever,
That time and place with this deceit so lawful
May prove coherent. Every night he comes
With musics of all sorts, and songs composed
To her unworthiness. It nothing steads us
To chide him from our eaves, for he persists
As if his life lay on't.

HELENA Why then tonight
Let us essay our plot, which, if it speed,
Is wicked meaning in a lawful deed,
And lawful meaning in a wicked act,
Where both not sin, and yet a sinful fact.
But let's about it. *[Exeunt.]*

✤

4.1

Enter one of the Frenchmen [the First Lord] with five or six other Soldiers, in ambush.

FIRST LORD He can come no other way but by this hedge corner. When you sally upon him, speak what terrible language you will. Though you understand it not yourselves, no matter; for we must not seem to understand him, unless someone among us whom we must produce for an interpreter.

FIRST SOLDIER Good Captain, let me be th'interpreter.

FIRST LORD Art not acquainted with him? Knows he not thy voice?

FIRST SOLDIER No, sir, I warrant you.

FIRST LORD But what linsey-woolsey hast thou to speak to us again?

FIRST SOLDIER E'en such as you speak to me.

FIRST LORD He must think us some band of strangers i'th'adversary's entertainment. Now he hath a smack of all neighboring languages. Therefore we must every one be a man of his own fancy, not to know what we speak one to another; so we seem to know is to know straight our purpose: choughs' language, gabble enough and good enough. As for you, interpreter, you must seem very politic. But couch, ho! Here he comes, to beguile two hours in a sleep, and then to return and swear the lies he forges. *[They hide.]*

Enter Parolles.

PAROLLES Ten o'clock. Within these three hours 'twill be time enough to go home. What shall I say I have done? It must be a very plausive invention that carries it. They begin to smoke me, and disgraces have of late knocked too often at my door. I find my tongue is too foolhardy; but my heart hath the fear of Mars before it, and of his creatures, not daring the reports of my tongue.

FIRST LORD *[aside]* This is the first truth that e'er thine own tongue was guilty of.

PAROLLES What the devil should move me to undertake the recovery of this drum, being not ignorant of the impossibility, and knowing I had no such purpose? I must give myself some hurts, and say I got them in exploit. Yet slight ones will not carry it—they will say, "Came you off with so little?"—and great ones I dare not give. Wherefore? What's the instance? Tongue, I must put you into a butter-woman's mouth and buy myself another of Bajazeth's mule, if you prattle me into these perils.

FIRST LORD *[aside]* Is it possible he should know what he is, and be that he is?

PAROLLES I would the cutting of my garments would serve the turn, or the breaking of my Spanish sword.

FIRST LORD *[aside]* We cannot afford you so.

PAROLLES Or the baring of my beard, and to say it was in stratagem.

FIRST LORD *[aside]* 'Twould not do.

PAROLLES Or to drown my clothes, and say I was stripped.

FIRST LORD *[aside]* Hardly serve.

PAROLLES Though I swore I leapt from the window of the citadel—

FIRST LORD *[aside]* How deep?

PAROLLES Thirty fathom.

FIRST LORD *[aside]* Three great oaths would scarce make that be believed.

PAROLLES I would I had any drum of the enemy's. I would swear I recovered it.

FIRST LORD *[aside]* You shall hear one anon.

PAROLLES A drum now of the enemy's—

Alarum within.

35 To marry her as her dowry **39 coherent** suitable. **40 musics** musicians **41 To her unworthiness** to her, my humble daughter; or, to the end of persuading her to do an unworthy deed. **nothing steads us** profits us not at all **42 chide . . . eaves** i.e., drive him away **43 lay** depended **44 essay** try. **speed** succeed **45–6 Is . . . act** i.e., is wicked intention (on Bertram's part) converted into a lawful act of sex between married partners, and lawful intent (on Helena's part) carried out in an ethically dubious way **47 fact** deed (which would have been sinful as Bertram intended it).

4.1. Location: Outside the Florentine camp.

2 sally rush out **3 terrible** terrifying **5 unless** except for **11 linsey-woolsey** a fabric woven from wool and flax; figuratively, a hodge-podge **12 again** in reply. **14 strangers** foreigners **15 entertainment** service. **smack** smattering **16–19 we . . . purpose** each of us must make up his own imaginative language, unintelligible to the others; so long as we seem to know what is said, we'll accomplish our purpose **19 choughs' language** the chattering of a small species of the crow family, the jackdaw

21 politic shrewd, cunning. **couch** take concealment **22 beguile** while away. **sleep** nap **26 plausive** plausible **26–7 carries it** carries it off. **27 smoke** suspect **29–31 hath . . . tongue** is frightened by the prospect of the god of war and his followers, and I dare not carry out my boast. **40 Wherefore . . . instance?** (Parolles may be saying "Why did I ever open my mouth?" or "Where's the evidence to be produced from?") **41 butter-woman** dairywoman, i.e., a proverbial scold and garrulous talker **42 of Bajazeth's mule** i.e., from a Turkish mule, since mules are notoriously mute (?) (Many emendations have been proposed, including *mute* for *mule*.) **47 serve the turn** suffice **48 afford you so** i.e., let you off so lightly. **49 baring** shaving **50 in stratagem** an act of cunning. **58 fathom** (A fathom is a unit of measure equal to six feet.) **63 anon** immediately. **64.1** ***Alarum*** Call to arms

FIRST LORD [*coming forward*] *Throca movousus, cargo, cargo, cargo.*
ALL *Cargo, cargo, cargo, villianda par corbo, cargo.*
[*They seize and blindfold him.*]
PAROLLES
Oh, ransom, ransom! Do not hide mine eyes.
FIRST SOLDIER *Boskos thromuldo boskos.*
PAROLLES
I know you are the Muskos' regiment, 70
And I shall lose my life for want of language. 71
If there be here German, or Dane, Low Dutch,
Italian, or French, let him speak to me,
I'll discover that which shall undo the Florentine. 74
FIRST SOLDIER *Boskos vauvado.* I understand thee and can speak thy tongue. *Kerelybonto.* Sir, betake thee to 76
thy faith, for seventeen poniards are at thy bosom. 77
PAROLLES Oh!
FIRST SOLDIER Oh, pray, pray, pray! *Manka revania dulche.*
FIRST LORD *Oscorbidulchos volivorco.*
FIRST SOLDIER
The General is content to spare thee yet,
And, hoodwinked as thou art, will lead thee on 83
To gather from thee. Haply thou mayst inform 84
Something to save thy life.
PAROLLES Oh, let me live,
And all the secrets of our camp I'll show,
Their force, their purposes; nay, I'll speak that
Which you will wonder at.
FIRST SOLDIER But wilt thou faithfully?
PAROLLES
If I do not, damn me.
FIRST SOLDIER *Acordo linta.*
Come on; thou art granted space. *Exit* [*with Parolles* 90
guarded]. *A short alarum within.*
FIRST LORD
Go tell the Count Rossillion and my brother
We have caught the woodcock and will keep him muffled 92
Till we do hear from them.
SECOND SOLDIER Captain, I will.
FIRST LORD
'A will betray us all unto ourselves. 94
Inform on that. 95
SECOND SOLDIER So I will, sir.
FIRST LORD
Till then I'll keep him dark and safely locked. *Exeunt.*

✤

[4.2]

Enter Bertram and the maid called Diana.

BERTRAM
They told me that your name was Fontibell.
DIANA
No, my good lord, Diana.
BERTRAM Titled goddess, 2
And worth it, with addition! But, fair soul, 3
In your fine frame hath love no quality? 4
If the quick fire of youth light not your mind, 5
You are no maiden, but a monument. 6
When you are dead, you should be such a one
As you are now; for you are cold and stern,
And now you should be as your mother was
When your sweet self was got. 10
DIANA
She then was honest.
BERTRAM So should you be.
DIANA No. 11
My mother did but duty—such, my lord,
As you owe to your wife.
BERTRAM No more o' that.
I prithee, do not strive against my vows. 14
I was compelled to her, but I love thee
By love's own sweet constraint and will forever
Do thee all rights of service.
DIANA Ay, so you serve us
Till we serve you; but when you have our roses, 18
You barely leave our thorns to prick ourselves 19
And mock us with our bareness.
BERTRAM How have I sworn! 20
DIANA
'Tis not the many oaths that makes the truth,
But the plain single vow that is vowed true.
What is not holy, that we swear not by, 23
But take the High'st to witness. Then pray you, tell me, 24
If I should swear by Jove's great attributes
I loved you dearly, would you believe my oaths
When I did love you ill? This has no holding, 27
To swear by Him whom I protest to love 28
That I will work against Him. Therefore your oaths 29
Are words and poor conditions but unsealed, 30
At least in my opinion.
BERTRAM Change it, change it! 31
Be not so holy-cruel. Love is holy, 32
And my integrity ne'er knew the crafts 33
That you do charge men with. Stand no more off,

70 Muskos' Muscovites' **71 want** lack **74 discover** reveal
76–7 betake . . . faith i.e., say your prayers **77 poniards** daggers
83 hoodwinked blindfolded. **on** onward, elsewhere **84 gather** get information. **Haply** Perhaps **90 space** time. **92 woodcock** (A proverbially stupid bird.) **muffled** blindfolded **94 'A** He
95 Inform on Report
4.2. Location: Florence. The Widow's house.

2–3 Titled . . . addition! You who have the name of a goddess, and who deserve that and more! **4 frame** makeup, being. **quality** position, part. **5 quick** lively **6 monument** statue, lifeless effigy. **10 got** begotten. **11 honest** chaste, true to marriage vows. (But Bertram uses it to mean "frank.") **14 vows** i.e., vows to live apart from Helena. **18 serve you** i.e., serve you sexually. (The sexual suggestion is continued in *roses* and in *prick*, line 19.) **19 You . . . thorns** you leave us with only the bare thorns (of shame and guilt) **20 our bareness** i.e., the loss of our rose of virginity. **23–4 What . . . witness** When we swear an oath, we do so not in the name of unholy things, but with God as our witness. **27 ill** perfidiously and hence contrary to the purport of an oath sworn to God. **holding** power to bind; consistency **28 protest** profess **29 work against Him** oppose His will by my sinful action. **30 Are words . . . unsealed** are mere words and invalid provisos, unratified and hence lacking in legally binding force **31 it** i.e., your opinion **32 holy-cruel** i.e., cruel to me in your holiness. **33 crafts** deceits

But give thyself unto my sick desires,
Who then recovers. Say thou art mine, and ever
My love as it begins shall so persever.

DIANA
I see that men may rope 's in such a snare
That we'll forsake ourselves. Give me that ring.

BERTRAM
I'll lend it thee, my dear, but have no power
To give it from me.

DIANA Will you not, my lord?

BERTRAM
It is an honor 'longing to our house,
Bequeathèd down from many ancestors,
Which were the greatest obloquy i'th' world
In me to lose.

DIANA Mine honor's such a ring.
My chastity's the jewel of our house,
Bequeathèd down from many ancestors,
Which were the greatest obloquy i'th' world
In me to lose. Thus your own proper wisdom
Brings in the champion Honor on my part
Against your vain assault.

BERTRAM Here, take my ring!
My house, mine honor, yea, my life, be thine,
And I'll be bid by thee. *[He gives the ring.]*

DIANA
When midnight comes, knock at my chamber
window.
I'll order take my mother shall not hear.
Now will I charge you in the bond of truth,
When you have conquered my yet maiden bed,
Remain there but an hour, nor speak to me.
My reasons are most strong, and you shall know
them
When back again this ring shall be delivered.
And on your finger in the night I'll put
Another ring, that what in time proceeds
May token to the future our past deeds.
Adieu till then; then, fail not. You have won
A wife of me, though there my hope be done.

BERTRAM
A heaven on earth I have won by wooing thee.
[Exit.]

DIANA
For which live long to thank both heaven and me!
You may so in the end.
My mother told me just how he would woo,
As if she sat in 's heart. She says all men
Have the like oaths. He had sworn to marry me
When his wife's dead; therefore I'll lie with him
When I am buried. Since Frenchmen are so braid,
Marry that will, I live and die a maid.
Only in this disguise I think't no sin
To cozen him that would unjustly win. *Exit.*

✣

[4.3]

Enter the two French Captains and some two or three Soldiers.

FIRST LORD You have not given him his mother's letter?

SECOND LORD I have delivered it an hour since. There is something in't that stings his nature, for on the reading it he changed almost into another man.

FIRST LORD He has much worthy blame laid upon him for shaking off so good a wife and so sweet a lady.

SECOND LORD Especially he hath incurred the everlasting displeasure of the King, who had even tuned his bounty to sing happiness to him. I will tell you a thing, but you shall let it dwell darkly with you.

FIRST LORD When you have spoken it, 'tis dead, and I am the grave of it.

SECOND LORD He hath perverted a young gentlewoman here in Florence, of a most chaste renown, and this night he fleshes his will in the spoil of her honor. He hath given her his monumental ring and thinks himself made in the unchaste composition.

FIRST LORD Now, God delay our rebellion! As we are ourselves, what things are we!

SECOND LORD Merely our own traitors. And as in the common course of all treasons we still see them reveal themselves till they attain to their abhorred ends, so he that in this action contrives against his own nobility, in his proper stream o'erflows himself.

35 sick i.e., unfulfilled and in need of your ministrations **36 Who then recovers** which will then recover. **38 rope 's** rope us, entrap us. (The Folio reads "make rope 's in such a scarre.") **44 obloquy** disgrace. (As also in line 48.) **49 proper** personal **50 part** side **53 bid** commanded **55 order take** make provision **59–60 you . . . delivered** (Diana hints obscurely at the eventual return of Bertram's ring, when he will understand everything; see 5.3.192 ff.) **62 Another ring** i.e., the ring the King gave Helena; see 5.3.77 ff.) **62–3 that . . . deeds** so that whatever happens and whatever we do may be known in time. **63 token** betoken, indicate **65 A wife . . . done** i.e., me as your love partner, although all hope of marriage is thereby destroyed for me.

71–3 He . . . buried i.e., Divorce being impossible, Bertram has promised under oath to marry me after Helen dies and then remain true to me until we both die and are buried together. **71 had** has (?) would have (?) **73 braid** i.e., deceitful. (A *braid* is a trick.)
74 Marry let those marry **76 cozen** cheat
4.3. Location: The Florentine camp.
2 since ago. **5 worthy** deserved **8–9 who . . . to him** i.e., who had especially tuned the instrument of his generosity in order to make Bertram happy (by bestowing Helena on him). **10 darkly** secretly **13 perverted** seduced **15 he fleshes . . . honor** he rewards and stimulates his lust, permitting his desires to triumph in the (de)spoiling of her honor. (The image may also suggest a hunter rewarding his hounds or hawks with some flesh from the animal they have hunted down, the *spoil* or quarry of the hunt.) **16 monumental** i.e., serving as a token of his identity. (With a continuation of the genital imagery, with an interesting confusion of gender identity; rings are commonly vaginal in connotation.) **17 made** a made man. (With a painful suggestion that the deed has "unmade" [un-maid] him by despoiling him of honor as much as it has "un-maid" her. He has lost his ring, as she also has, in losing her virginity.) **composition** bargain.
18 delay our rebellion make us slow to rebel, assuage our lustful appetites. **18–19 As . . . ourselves** Being as we are unregenerate and fallen **20 Merely** Absolutely, entirely **21–2 still . . . themselves** always see traitors express their true natures **23–4 he . . . himself** i.e., Bertram, who thus seduces a woman, subverts his own nobility by abusing the qualities that should channel and perpetuate it.

FIRST LORD Is it not meant damnable in us to be trumpeters of our unlawful intents? We shall not then have his company tonight?

SECOND LORD Not till after midnight, for he is dieted to his hour.

FIRST LORD That approaches apace. I would gladly have him see his company anatomized, that he might take a measure of his own judgments wherein so curiously he had set this counterfeit.

SECOND LORD We will not meddle with him till he come, for his presence must be the whip of the other.

FIRST LORD In the meantime, what hear you of these wars?

SECOND LORD I hear there is an overture of peace.

FIRST LORD Nay, I assure you, a peace concluded.

SECOND LORD What will Count Rossillion do then? Will he travel higher or return again into France?

FIRST LORD I perceive, by this demand, you are not altogether of his council.

SECOND LORD Let it be forbid, sir! So should I be a great deal of his act.

FIRST LORD Sir, his wife some two months since fled from his house. Her pretense is a pilgrimage to Saint Jaques le Grand, which holy undertaking with most austere sanctimony she accomplished. And, there residing, the tenderness of her nature became as a prey to her grief; in fine, made a groan of her last breath, and now she sings in heaven.

SECOND LORD How is this justified?

FIRST LORD The stronger part of it by her own letters, which makes her story true even to the point of her death. Her death itself, which could not be her office to say is come, was faithfully confirmed by the rector of the place.

SECOND LORD Hath the Count all this intelligence?

FIRST LORD Ay, and the particular confirmations, point from point, to the full arming of the verity.

SECOND LORD I am heartily sorry that he'll be glad of this.

FIRST LORD How mightily sometimes we make us comforts of our losses!

SECOND LORD And how mightily some other times we drown our gain in tears! The great dignity that his valor hath here acquired for him shall at home be encountered with a shame as ample.

FIRST LORD The web of our life is of a mingled yarn, good and ill together. Our virtues would be proud if our faults whipped them not, and our crimes would despair if they were not cherished by our virtues.

Enter a [Servant as] messenger.

How now? Where's your master?

SERVANT He met the Duke in the street, sir, of whom he hath taken a solemn leave. His Lordship will next morning for France. The Duke hath offered him letters of commendations to the King.

SECOND LORD They shall be no more than needful there, if they were more than they can commend.

Enter [Bertram] Count Rossillion.

FIRST LORD They cannot be too sweet for the King's tartness. Here's His Lordship now.—How now, my lord, is't not after midnight?

BERTRAM I have tonight dispatched sixteen businesses, a month's length apiece, by an abstract of success: I have congeed with the Duke, done my adieu with his nearest, buried a wife, mourned for her, writ to my lady mother I am returning, entertained my convoy, and between these main parcels of dispatch effected many nicer needs. The last was the greatest, but that I have not ended yet.

SECOND LORD If the business be of any difficulty, and this morning your departure hence, it requires haste of Your Lordship.

BERTRAM I mean, the business is not ended, as fearing to hear of it hereafter. But shall we have this dialogue between the fool and the soldier? Come, bring forth this counterfeit module; he's deceived me like a double-meaning prophesier.

SECOND LORD [*to the Soldiers*] Bring him forth. [*Exit one or more.*]

He's sat i'the stocks all night, poor gallant knave.

BERTRAM No matter; his heels have deserved it, in usurping his spurs so long. How does he carry himself?

SECOND LORD I have told Your Lordship already, the stocks carry him. But to answer you as you would be understood, he weeps like a wench that had shed her milk. He hath confessed himself to Morgan, whom he supposes to be a friar, from the time of his remembrance to this very instant disaster of his setting i'th' stocks. And what think you he hath confessed?

BERTRAM Nothing of me, has 'a?

25–6 Is it . . . intents? Is it not a sign of our fallen natures to be proud proclaimers of our sinful intents? **28–9 dieted to his hour** tied to his schedule. **31 his company** the company he keeps, his companion. **anatomized** dissected, exposed **32 curiously** carefully, elaborately **33 counterfeit** false jewel, i.e., Parolles. **34 him** Parolles. **he** Bertram **35 his . . . the other** i.e., Bertram's . . . Parolles. **41 higher** farther **42 demand** question **43 of his council** in his confidence. **45 of his act** an accessory to his misdeeds. **47 pretense** intent **49 sanctimony** holiness **51 in fine** at last **53 justified** made certain. **55 point** time, moment **61 arming** corroboration, strengthening. **verity** truth. **64–7 make . . . tears** perversely take comfort in misfortune and at other times weep when we are fortunate. (Bertram is glad to lose Helena, having previously grieved at gaining her.)

71–3 Our virtues . . . virtues Our virtues would become arrogant if they were not chastized by our faults, and our wickednesses would despair if the presence of our virtues did not comfort them. **76 will** i.e., intends to depart **79–80 They . . . commend** Even if they were stronger than any recommendation could be, they would still be no more than what is needed (to calm the King's anger at Bertram). **85 by . . . success** by a series of successful moves, as follows, or, by a series of moves that may be summarized as follows **86 congeed with** taken leave of **86–7 his nearest** those persons nearest him **88 entertained my convoy** hired my transportation **89 main . . . dispatch** major items to be settled **90 nicer** more delicate. **The last** i.e., The affair with Diana **95–6 the business . . . hereafter** Bertram fears that Diana may be pregnant, with inevitable consequences. **98 module** mere image **99 double-meaning** ambiguous, equivocating **107 shed** spilled. (With the implication of crying over spilt milk.) **109–10 the time . . . remembrance** as far back as he can recall **110 instant** present

SECOND LORD His confession is taken, and it shall be read to his face. If Your Lordship be in't, as I believe you are, you must have the patience to hear it.

Enter Parolles [guarded and blindfolded] with [First Soldier as] his interpreter.

BERTRAM A plague upon him! Muffled! He can say nothing of me.

FIRST LORD Hush, hush! Hoodman comes!—*Portotartarosa.*

FIRST SOLDIER [*to Parolles*] He calls for the tortures. What will you say without 'em?

PAROLLES I will confess what I know without constraint. If ye pinch me like a pasty, I can say no more.

FIRST SOLDIER *Bosko chimurcho.*

FIRST LORD *Boblibindo chicurmurco.*

FIRST SOLDIER You are a merciful general.—Our general bids you answer to what I shall ask you out of a note.

PAROLLES And truly, as I hope to live.

FIRST SOLDIER [*as if reading*] "First demand of him how many horse the Duke is strong." What say you to that?

PAROLLES Five or six thousand, but very weak and unserviceable. The troops are all scattered and the commanders very poor rogues, upon my reputation and credit and as I hope to live.

FIRST SOLDIER Shall I set down your answer so?

[*He makes as though to write.*]

PAROLLES Do. I'll take the sacrament on't, how and which way you will.

BERTRAM [*aside to the Lords*] All's one to him. What a past-saving slave is this!

FIRST LORD [*aside to Bertram*] You're deceived, my lord. This is Monsieur Parolles, the gallant militarist—that was his own phrase—that had the whole theoric of war in the knot of his scarf, and the practice in the chape of his dagger.

SECOND LORD [*aside*] I will never trust a man again for keeping his sword clean, nor believe he can have everything in him by wearing his apparel neatly.

FIRST SOLDIER [*to Parolles*] Well, that's set down.

PAROLLES "Five or six thousand horse," I said—I will say true—"or thereabouts," set down, for I'll speak truth.

FIRST LORD [*aside*] He's very near the truth in this.

BERTRAM [*aside*] But I con him no thanks for't, in the nature he delivers it.

PAROLLES "Poor rogues," I pray you, say.

FIRST SOLDIER Well, that's set down.

PAROLLES I humbly thank you, sir. A truth's a truth. The rogues are marvelous poor.

FIRST SOLDIER [*as if reading*] "Demand of him of what strength they are afoot." What say you to that?

PAROLLES By my troth, sir, if I were to live this present hour, I will tell true. Let me see: Spurio, a hundred and fifty; Sebastian, so many; Corambus, so many; Jaques, so many; Guiltian, Cosmo, Lodowick, and Gratii, two hundred fifty each; mine own company, Chitopher, Vaumond, Bentii, two hundred fifty each; so that the muster-file, rotten and sound, upon my life, amounts not to fifteen thousand poll, half of the which dare not shake the snow from off their cassocks, lest they shake themselves to pieces.

BERTRAM [*aside to the Lords*] What shall be done to him?

FIRST LORD [*aside*] Nothing, but let him have thanks.—Demand of him my condition and what credit I have with the Duke.

FIRST SOLDIER Well, that's set down. [*As if reading*] "You shall demand of him whether one Captain Dumain be i'th' camp, a Frenchman; what his reputation is with the Duke; what his valor, honesty, and expertness in wars; or whether he thinks it were not possible, with well-weighing sums of gold, to corrupt him to a revolt." What say you to this? What do you know of it?

PAROLLES I beseech you, let me answer to the particular of the inter'gatories. Demand them singly.

FIRST SOLDIER Do you know this Captain Dumain?

PAROLLES I know him. 'A was a botcher's prentice in Paris, from whence he was whipped for getting the sheriff's fool with child—a dumb innocent that could not say him nay.

BERTRAM [*aside to First Lord, who makes as if to strike Parolles*] Nay, by your leave, hold your hands—though I know his brains are forfeit to the next tile that falls.

FIRST SOLDIER Well, is this captain in the Duke of Florence's camp?

PAROLLES Upon my knowledge, he is, and lousy.

FIRST LORD [*aside to Bertram*] Nay, look not so upon me. We shall hear of Your Lordship anon.

FIRST SOLDIER What is his reputation with the Duke?

PAROLLES The Duke knows him for no other but a poor officer of mine, and writ to me this other day to turn him out o'th' band. I think I have his letter in my pocket.

FIRST SOLDIER Marry, we'll search.

[*They search his pockets.*]

PAROLLES In good sadness, I do not know; either it is there, or it is upon a file with the Duke's other letters in my tent.

FIRST SOLDIER Here 'tis, here's a paper. Shall I read it to you?

PAROLLES I do not know if it be it or no.

116 Muffled! Blindfolded! **118 Hoodman comes** (Customary call in the game of blindman's buff.) **123 pasty** meat pie **127 note** memorandum or list. **129 demand** ask **130 horse** horsemen, cavalry troops **139 past-saving** beyond redemption. (Referring back to "sacrament" in line 136.) **142 theoric** theory **144 chape** scabbard tip **146 clean** i.e., polished **153 con** offer. (Literally, "know.") **153–4 in . . . it** considering what sort of truth it is that he tells. **160 afoot** in numbers of foot soldiers.

161 live i.e., live only **163 so many** the same number **167 file** roll **168 poll** heads **169 cassocks** cloaks **181 well-weighing** heavy and persuasive **182 revolt** desertion. **185 inter'gatories** questions. **187 botcher's** mender's, especially a tailor or cobbler who makes "botch-job" repairs **189 sheriff's fool** feeble-minded girl in the sheriff's custody **193–4 his . . . falls** i.e., such a liar is headed straight for sudden and violent death. **197 lousy** (1) contemptible (2) infested with lice. **203 band** company, army. **206 sadness** seriousness

BERTRAM [*aside*] Our interpreter does it well.

FIRST LORD [*aside*] Excellently.

FIRST SOLDIER [*reads*]
"Dian, the Count's a fool, and full of gold—"

PAROLLES That is not the Duke's letter, sir. That is an advertisement to a proper maid in Florence, one Diana, to take heed of the allurement of one Count Rossillion, a foolish idle boy, but for all that very ruttish. I pray you, sir, put it up again.

FIRST SOLDIER Nay, I'll read it first, by your favor.

PAROLLES My meaning in 't, I protest, was very honest in the behalf of the maid, for I knew the young Count to be a dangerous and lascivious boy, who is a whale to virginity, and devours up all the fry it finds.

BERTRAM [*aside*] Damnable both-sides rogue!

FIRST SOLDIER [*reads the*] *letter*
"When he swears oaths, bid him drop gold, and take it;
After he scores, he never pays the score.
Half won is match well made; match, and well make it.
He ne'er pays after-debts; take it before.
And say a soldier, Dian, told thee this:
Men are to mell with, boys are not to kiss.
For count of this, the Count's a fool, I know it,
Who pays before, but not when he does owe it.
Thine, as he vowed to thee in thine ear,
Parolles."

BERTRAM [*aside*] He shall be whipped through the army with this rhyme in's forehead.

SECOND LORD [*aside*] This is your devoted friend, sir, the manifold linguist and the armipotent soldier.

BERTRAM [*aside*] I could endure anything before but a cat, and now he's a cat to me.

FIRST SOLDIER I perceive, sir, by our general's looks, we shall be fain to hang you.

PAROLLES My life, sir, in any case! Not that I am afraid to die, but that, my offenses being many, I would repent out the remainder of nature. Let me live, sir, in a dungeon, i'th' stocks, or anywhere, so I may live.

FIRST SOLDIER We'll see what may be done, so you confess freely. Therefore, once more to this Captain Dumain. You have answered to his reputation with the Duke, and to his valor. What is his honesty?

PAROLLES He will steal, sir, an egg out of a cloister. For rapes and ravishments he parallels Nessus. He professes not keeping of oaths; in breaking 'em he is stronger than Hercules. He will lie, sir, with such volubility that you would think truth were a fool. Drunkenness is his best virtue, for he will be swine-drunk, and in his sleep he does little harm, save to his bedclothes about him; but they know his conditions, and lay him in straw. I have but little more to say, sir, of his honesty. He has everything that an honest man should not have; what an honest man should have, he has nothing.

FIRST LORD [*aside*] I begin to love him for this.

BERTRAM [*aside*] For this description of thine honesty? A pox upon him for me, he's more and more a cat.

FIRST SOLDIER What say you to his expertness in war?

PAROLLES Faith, sir, he's led the drum before the English tragedians. To belie him I will not, and more of his soldiership I know not, except in that country he had the honor to be the officer at a place there called Mile End, to instruct for the doubling of files. I would do the man what honor I can, but of this I am not certain.

FIRST LORD [*aside*] He hath out-villained villainy so far that the rarity redeems him.

BERTRAM [*aside*] A pox on him, he's a cat still.

FIRST SOLDIER His qualities being at this poor price, I need not to ask you if gold will corrupt him to revolt.

PAROLLES Sir, for a cardecu he will sell the fee simple of his salvation, the inheritance of it, and cut th'entail from all remainders, and a perpetual succession for it perpetually.

FIRST SOLDIER What's his brother, the other Captain Dumain?

SECOND LORD [*aside*] Why does he ask him of me?

FIRST SOLDIER What's he?

PAROLLES E'en a crow o'th' same nest; not altogether so great as the first in goodness, but greater a great deal in evil. He excels his brother for a coward, yet his brother is reputed one of the best that is. In a retreat he outruns any lackey; marry, in coming on he has the cramp.

FIRST SOLDIER If your life be saved, will you undertake to betray the Florentine?

PAROLLES Ay, and the Captain of his Horse, Count Rossillion.

216 advertisement warning. **proper** respectable **219 ruttish** lecherous. **224 fry** small fish **226 drop** i.e., offer, pay. **take it** i.e., you should take it **227 scores** (1) buys on credit (2) hits the mark, scores sexually. **score** bill. **228 Half . . . make it** i.e., One is halfway to success if the *match* or bargain is well stated with clearly defined agreements, so be sure to do this. **229 after-debts** debts payable after the goods are received. **it** i.e., payment **231 Men . . . kiss** i.e., Don't fool around with mere boys (like Bertram), but with real men (like me). (*Mell with* means "mingle with in intercourse.") **232 For count of** On account of, or, therefore take note of **233 before** in advance (when he is required to do so). **does owe it** (1) owes payment for something already received (2) possesses it, i.e., her maidenhead. **239 manifold linguist** speaker of many languages. **armipotent** powerful in arms **241 cat** (A term of contempt.) **243 fain** obliged **246 the remainder of nature** what is left of my natural life.

253 Nessus a centaur who attempted to rape the wife of Hercules. **253–4 professes** makes a practice of **256 volubility** fluency, facility. **truth were a fool** i.e., truth here seems so easily put down and made to look foolish. **259 they** i.e., his servants. **conditions** habits **268–9 led . . . tragedians** (It was a custom of actors entering a village or town to parade in the street before the performance of a play.) **272 Mile End** place near London where citizen militiamen were regularly exercised. (A slur of amateurism.) **doubling of files** simple drill maneuver in which the soldiers stand in a row two deep. **275–6 He . . . him** His villainy has so surpassed ordinary villainy that its extraordinariness redeems him. **280 cardecu** quart d'écu, one-quarter of a French crown. **fee simple** total and perpetual ownership **281–3 cut . . . perpetually** prevent it from being passed on successively to subsequent heirs. **292 lackey** running footman. **coming on** moving forward **296 Captain of his Horse** cavalry commander

FIRST SOLDIER I'll whisper with the General and know his pleasure.

PAROLLES [*to himself*] I'll no more drumming. A plague of all drums! Only to seem to deserve well, and to beguile the supposition of that lascivious young boy, the Count, have I run into this danger. Yet who would have suspected an ambush where I was taken?

FIRST SOLDIER There is no remedy, sir, but you must die. The General says, you that have so traitorously discovered the secrets of your army and made such pestiferous reports of men very nobly held can serve the world for no honest use; therefore you must die.—Come, headsman, off with his head.

PAROLLES Oh, Lord, sir, let me live, or let me see my death!

FIRST SOLDIER That shall you, and take your leave of all your friends. [*Unblindfolding him.*] So, look about you. Know you any here?

BERTRAM Good morrow, noble Captain.

SECOND LORD God bless you, Captain Parolles.

FIRST LORD God save you, noble Captain.

SECOND LORD Captain, what greeting will you to my Lord Lafew? I am for France.

FIRST LORD Good Captain, will you give me a copy of the sonnet you writ to Diana in behalf of the Count Rossillion? An I were not a very coward, I'd compel it of you; but fare you well. *Exeunt* [*Bertram and Lords*].

FIRST SOLDIER You are undone, Captain, all but your scarf; that has a knot on't yet.

PAROLLES Who cannot be crushed with a plot?

FIRST SOLDIER If you could find out a country where but women were that had received so much shame, you might begin an impudent nation. Fare ye well, sir. I am for France too. We shall speak of you there.

Exit [*with Soldiers*].

PAROLLES

Yet am I thankful. If my heart were great,
'Twould burst at this. Captain I'll be no more,
But I will eat and drink, and sleep as soft
As captain shall. Simply the thing I am
Shall make me live. Who knows himself a braggart,
Let him fear this, for it will come to pass
That every braggart shall be found an ass.
Rust, sword! Cool, blushes! And, Parolles, live
Safest in shame! Being fooled, by fool'ry thrive!
There's place and means for every man alive.
I'll after them. *Exit.*

302 **supposition** judgment 307 **discovered** revealed 308 **pestiferous** malicious, pernicious. **held** regarded 311 **Oh, Lord, sir** (Unconsciously echoing Lavatch's parody of the courtier at 2.2.49–59.) 319 **will you** do you wish to send 320 **for** bound for, off to 323 **An** If 330 **impudent** shameless 332 **heart** (Thought to be the seat of courage.) 336 **Who** He who 340 **Being . . . thrive!** i.e., Since they have made a fool of me, I will now thrive by being what I am, a fool!

[4.4]

Enter Helena, Widow, and Diana.

HELENA

That you may well perceive I have not wronged you,
One of the greatest in the Christian world
Shall be my surety; 'fore whose throne 'tis needful,
Ere I can perfect mine intents, to kneel.
Time was, I did him a desirèd office,
Dear almost as his life, which gratitude
Through flinty Tartar's bosom would peep forth
And answer thanks. I duly am informed
His Grace is at Marseilles, to which place
We have convenient convoy. You must know
I am supposèd dead. The army breaking,
My husband hies him home, where, heaven aiding,
And by the leave of my good lord the King,
We'll be before our welcome.

WIDOW Gentle madam,
You never had a servant to whose trust
Your business was more welcome.

HELENA Nor you, mistress,
Ever a friend whose thoughts more truly labor
To recompense your love. Doubt not but heaven
Hath brought me up to be your daughter's dower,
As it hath fated her to be my motive
And helper to a husband. But oh, strange men,
That can such sweet use make of what they hate,
When saucy trusting of the cozened thoughts
Defiles the pitchy night! So lust doth play
With what it loathes for that which is away.
But more of this hereafter. You, Diana,
Under my poor instructions yet must suffer
Something in my behalf.

DIANA Let death and honesty
Go with your impositions, I am yours
Upon your will to suffer.

HELENA Yet, I pray you;
But with the word the time will bring on summer,
When briers shall have leaves as well as thorns,
And be as sweet as sharp. We must away;
Our wagon is prepared, and time revives us.

4.4. Location: Florence. The Widow's house.
2 **One . . . world** i.e., the French King 3 **surety** guarantee 6 **which gratitude** gratitude for which 7 **Through** even through 10 **convenient convoy** suitable transport. 11 **breaking** disbanding 12 **hies him** hastens 14 **We'll be . . . welcome** we will arrive before we are expected. 19 **Hath . . . dower** i.e., has groomed me for the role of providing a dowry for your daughter 20 **motive** means
23–4 **When . . . night** when lustful confidence in deceived fancies sullies the darkness of night. (Recalling the proverbial idea that "pitch doth defile"; here man's lust defiles pitch, i.e., night.) 24–5 **So . . . away** i.e., Thus Bertram's lust enjoys itself with Helena, the loathed wife, supposing her to be Diana. 27 **yet** for a time yet 28–30 **Let . . . suffer** Even if a chaste death were a result of what you ask of me, I am yours, ready to accede to your will. 30 **Yet** A little longer
31–2 **But . . . thorns** i.e., but soon enough, time will bring on a happier state of affairs, with rewards to compensate for our suffering
34 **revives** will revive

All's well that ends well. Still the fine's the crown;
Whate'er the course, the end is the renown. *Exeunt.*

✤

[4.5]

Enter Clown [*Lavatch*], *Old Lady* [*Countess*], *and Lafew.*

LAFEW No, no, no, your son was misled with a snipped-taffeta fellow there, whose villainous saffron would have made all the unbaked and doughy youth of a nation in his color. Your daughter-in-law had been alive at this hour, and your son here at home, more advanced by the King than by that red-tailed humble-bee I speak of.

COUNTESS I would I had not known him! It was the death of the most virtuous gentlewoman that ever nature had praise for creating. If she had partaken of my flesh, and cost me the dearest groans of a mother, I could not have owed her a more rooted love.

LAFEW 'Twas a good lady, 'twas a good lady. We may pick a thousand salads ere we light on such another herb.

LAVATCH Indeed, sir, she was the sweet marjoram of the salad, or rather the herb of grace.

LAFEW They are not herbs, you knave, they are nose-herbs.

LAVATCH I am no great Nebuchadnezzar, sir. I have not much skill in grass.

LAFEW Whether dost thou profess thyself, a knave or a fool?

LAVATCH A fool, sir, at a woman's service, and a knave at a man's.

LAFEW Your distinction?

LAVATCH I would cozen the man of his wife and do his service.

LAFEW So you were a knave at his service, indeed.

LAVATCH And I would give his wife my bauble, sir, to do her service.

LAFEW I will subscribe for thee, thou art both knave and fool.

LAVATCH At your service.

LAFEW No, no, no!

LAVATCH Why, sir, if I cannot serve you, I can serve as great a prince as you are.

LAFEW Who's that, a Frenchman?

LAVATCH Faith, sir, 'a has an English name, but his physnomy is more hotter in France than there.

LAFEW What prince is that?

LAVATCH The black prince, sir, alias the prince of darkness, alias the devil.

LAFEW Hold thee, there's my purse. [*He gives money.*] I give thee not this to suggest thee from thy master thou talk'st of; serve him still.

LAVATCH I am a woodland fellow, sir, that always loved a great fire, and the master I speak of ever keeps a good fire. But sure he is the prince of the world; let his nobility remain in 's court. I am for the house with the narrow gate, which I take to be too little for pomp to enter. Some that humble themselves may, but the many will be too chill and tender, and they'll be for the flowery way that leads to the broad gate and the great fire.

LAFEW Go thy ways. I begin to be aweary of thee; and I tell thee so before, because I would not fall out with thee. Go thy ways. Let my horses be well looked to, without any tricks.

LAVATCH If I put any tricks upon 'em, sir, they shall be jades' tricks, which are their own right by the law of nature. *Exit.*

LAFEW A shrewd knave and an unhappy.

COUNTESS So 'a is. My lord that's gone made himself much sport out of him. By his authority he remains here, which he thinks is a patent for his sauciness; and indeed he has no pace, but runs where he will.

LAFEW I like him well; 'tis not amiss. And I was about to tell you, since I heard of the good lady's death, and that my lord your son was upon his return home, I moved the King my master to speak in the behalf of my daughter, which, in the minority of them both, His Majesty, out of a self-gracious remembrance, did first propose. His Highness hath promised me to do it, and to stop up the displeasure he hath conceived against

35 the fine's the crown the end is the crown of all **36 Whate'er . . . renown** by whatever means we proceed, the conclusion is what makes for worth. (I.e., the end justifies the means.)
4.5. Location: Rossillion.
1 with by **2 snipped-taffeta** wearing taffeta silk garments with slashes to allow the under material to be visible (suggestive of Parolles' hollow flashiness). **saffron** bright yellow spice used in making pastry and also in dyeing starched ruffs and collars
3 unbaked and doughy raw and unformed **7 humble-bee** bumblebee (noisy and useless) **11 dearest** (1) direst (2) most loving. **groans of a mother** pains of childbirth **12 rooted** firm **17 herb of grace** rue for remembrance. (Also picking up on the theological theme of "grace.") **18 not herbs** i.e., not edible salad herbs or greens
18–19 nose-herbs fragrant herbs used for bouquets, not salads.
20–1 Nebuchadnezzar . . . grass In Daniel 4:28–37, King Nebuchadnezzar is reported to have gone mad and eaten grass like a grazing ox. (With a pun on *grass/grace* and also *graze*; the word in the Folio is "grace.") **22 Whether** Which of the two **27 cozen** cheat **27–8 do his service** i.e., usurp his sexual role. **30 bauble** stick carried by a court fool. (With bawdy suggestion.) **32 subscribe** vouch

35 No, no, no! i.e., Not under the terms of service you have described! **39 English name** i.e., the Black Prince, a widely known name for the eldest son of Edward III who defeated the French.
40 physnomy physiognomy. **more hotter** (1) more choleric in the fury of fighting (2) more susceptible to the "French disease," syphilis
45 suggest tempt **47 woodland** rustic **49 a good fire** i.e., hellfire.
51 narrow gate (Compare with Matthew 7:14: "Strait is the gate, and narrow is the way, which leadeth unto life.") **53 many** multitude.
chill and tender sensitive to cold and pampered. (Most people are so fond of a good fire that they are not keeping in mind the great fire [lines 54–5] of hell.) **53–5 the flowery . . . fire** (Compare with Matthew 7:13: "Wide is the gate, and broad is the way, that leadeth to destruction.") **56 Go thy ways** Get along with you. **57 before** i.e., before I grow thoroughly weary **61 jades' tricks** (1) the vicious behavior of *jades* or ill-tempered horses (2) malicious tricks that hostlers might play on horses, such as greasing their teeth or their hay **63 shrewd** sharp-tongued and witty. **unhappy** discontented.
64 gone dead **67 has no pace** observes no restraint. (A term from horse training.) **69 the good lady's** Helena's **72 in . . . both** i.e., since both my daughter and Bertram are legally minors or wards
73 self-gracious remembrance thoughtful recollection that came to him without prompting

your son there is no fitter matter. How does Your
Ladyship like it?

COUNTESS With very much content, my lord, and I
wish it happily effected.

LAFEW His Highness comes post from Marseilles, of as 80
able body as when he numbered thirty. 'A will be here 81
tomorrow, or I am deceived by him that in such 82
intelligence hath seldom failed. 83

COUNTESS It rejoices me that I hope I shall see him ere
I die. I have letters that my son will be here tonight. I
shall beseech Your Lordship to remain with me till they
meet together.

LAFEW Madam, I was thinking with what manners I
might safely be admitted. 89

COUNTESS You need but plead your honorable privi- 90
lege. 91

LAFEW Lady, of that I have made a bold charter, but I 92
thank my God it holds yet.

Enter Clown [Lavatch].

LAVATCH Oh, madam, yonder's my lord your son with a
patch of velvet on 's face. Whether there be a scar
under't or no, the velvet knows, but 'tis a goodly
patch of velvet. His left cheek is a cheek of two pile 97
and a half, but his right cheek is worn bare. 98

LAFEW A scar nobly got, or a noble scar, is a good livery 99
of honor; so belike is that. 100

LAVATCH But it is your carbonadoed face. 101

LAFEW Let us go see your son, I pray you. I long to talk
with the young noble soldier.

LAVATCH Faith, there's a dozen of 'em, with delicate
fine hats, and most courteous feathers, which bow the
head and nod at every man. *Exeunt.*

✤

5.1

Enter Helena, Widow, and Diana, with two attendants.

HELENA
But this exceeding posting day and night 1
Must wear your spirits low. We cannot help it.
But since you have made the days and nights as one
To wear your gentle limbs in my affairs, 4
Be bold you do so grow in my requital 5
As nothing can unroot you.

Enter a Gentleman.

In happy time! 6
This man may help me to His Majesty's ear,
If he would spend his power.—God save you, sir. 8

GENTLEMAN And you.

HELENA
Sir, I have seen you in the court of France.

GENTLEMAN I have been sometimes there.

HELENA
I do presume, sir, that you are not fall'n
From the report that goes upon your goodness;
And therefore, goaded with most sharp occasions 14
Which lay nice manners by, I put you to 15
The use of your own virtues, for the which
I shall continue thankful.

GENTLEMAN What's your will?

HELENA That it will please you
To give this poor petition to the King
[*showing a petition*]
And aid me with that store of power you have
To come into his presence.

GENTLEMAN
The King's not here.

HELENA Not here, sir?

GENTLEMAN Not indeed.
He hence removed last night, and with more haste 23
Than is his use.

WIDOW Lord, how we lose our pains! 24

HELENA All's well that ends well yet,
Though time seem so adverse and means unfit.
I do beseech you, whither is he gone?

GENTLEMAN
Marry, as I take it, to Rossillion,
Whither I am going.

HELENA I do beseech you, sir,
Since you are like to see the King before me,
Commend the paper to his gracious hand, 31
[*giving the petition*]
Which I presume shall render you no blame
But rather make you thank your pains for it.
I will come after you with what good speed
Our means will make us means.

GENTLEMAN This I'll do for you. 35

HELENA And you shall find yourself to be well
thanked,
Whate'er falls more. We must to horse again.— 37
Go, go, provide. [*Exeunt separately.*]

✤

[5.2]

Enter Clown [Lavatch], and Parolles.

PAROLLES Good Monsieur Lavatch, give my Lord
Lafew this letter. [*He offers a letter.*] I have ere now, sir,
been better known to you, when I have held familiarity with fresher clothes; but I am now, sir, muddied in

80 post posthaste **81 numbered thirty** was thirty years old. **82 him** i.e., a messenger **83 intelligence** news **89 admitted** i.e., allowed to be present at that meeting. **90–1 honorable privilege** privilege due your honor. **92 made . . . charter** asserted my claim as far as I dare **97–8 two . . . half** i.e., a thick velvet **98 worn bare** i.e., without a velvet patch. **99 livery** uniform **100 belike** probably **101 But** Unless. **carbonadoed** slashed or scored across with gashes, as to broil meat (here suggesting a cut made to drain a venereal ulcer and covered with a velvet patch)

5.1. Location: Marseilles. A street.

1 posting riding in haste **4 wear** wear out **5 bold** confident. **requital** i.e., debt, thankfulness **6 happy** opportune

8 spend expend **14 sharp occasions** urgent circumstances **15 nice** scrupulous. **put** urge **23 removed** departed **24 use** usual practice. **31 Commend** present as worthy of favorable consideration **35 Our . . . means** our resources will allow us. **37 falls more** else may happen.

5.2. Location: Rossillion.

Fortune's mood, and smell somewhat strong of her strong displeasure.

LAVATCH Truly, Fortune's displeasure is but sluttish if it smell so strongly as thou speak'st of. I will henceforth eat no fish of Fortune's buttering. Prithee, allow the wind.

PAROLLES Nay, you need not to stop your nose, sir. I spake but by a metaphor.

LAVATCH Indeed, sir, if your metaphor stink, I will stop my nose, or against any man's metaphor. Prithee, get thee further.

PAROLLES Pray you, sir, deliver me this paper.

LAVATCH Foh! Prithee, stand away. A paper from Fortune's close-stool to give to a nobleman! Look, here he comes himself.

Enter Lafew.

Here is a purr of Fortune's sir, or of Fortune's cat—but not a musk cat—that has fallen into the unclean fishpond of her displeasure, and, as he says, is muddied withal. Pray you, sir, use the carp as you may, for he looks like a poor, decayed, ingenious, foolish, rascally knave. I do pity his distress in my similes of comfort, and leave him to Your Lordship. [*Exit.*]

PAROLLES My lord, I am a man whom Fortune hath cruelly scratched.

LAFEW And what would you have me to do? 'Tis too late to pare her nails now. Wherein have you played the knave with Fortune that she should scratch you, who of herself is a good lady and would not have knaves thrive long under her? There's a cardecu for you. [*He gives money.*] Let the justices make you and Fortune friends; I am for other business.

[*He starts to leave.*]

PAROLLES I beseech Your Honor to hear me one single word.

LAFEW You beg a single penny more. Come, you shall ha't. Save your word.

PAROLLES My name, my good lord, is Parolles.

LAFEW You beg more than "word," then. Cox my passion! Give me your hand. How does your drum?

PAROLLES O my good lord, you were the first that found me.

LAFEW Was I, in sooth? And I was the first that lost thee.

PAROLLES It lies in you, my lord, to bring me in some grace, for you did bring me out.

LAFEW Out upon thee, knave! Dost thou put upon me at once both the office of God and the devil? One brings thee in grace and the other brings thee out. [*Trumpets sound.*] The King's coming; I know by his trumpets. Sirrah, inquire further after me. I had talk of you last night. Though you are a fool and a knave, you shall eat. Go to, follow.

PAROLLES I praise God for you. [*Exeunt.*]

[5.3]

Flourish. Enter King, Old Lady [*Countess*], *Lafew, the two French Lords, with attendants.*

KING
We lost a jewel of her, and our esteem
Was made much poorer by it; but your son,
As mad in folly, lacked the sense to know
Her estimation home.

COUNTESS 'Tis past, my liege,
And I beseech Your Majesty to make it
Natural rebellion, done i'th' blade of youth,
When oil and fire, too strong for reason's force,
O'erbears it and burns on.

KING My honored lady,
I have forgiven and forgotten all,
Though my revenges were high bent upon him
And watched the time to shoot.

LAFEW This I must say—
But first I beg my pardon—the young lord
Did to His Majesty, his mother, and his lady
Offense of mighty note, but to himself
The greatest wrong of all. He lost a wife
Whose beauty did astonish the survey
Of richest eyes, whose words all ears took captive,
Whose dear perfection hearts that scorned to serve
Humbly called mistress.

KING Praising what is lost
Makes the remembrance dear. Well, call him hither.
We are reconciled, and the first view shall kill

9 of Fortune's buttering i.e., prepared and served by Fortune. **9–10 allow the wind** stand downwind of me. (The hunter stands downwind of the deer so that that the prey won't smell him. Lavatch responds with jesting literalness to Parolles's lament that he has been befouled by evil-smelling Fortune.) **16 me** for me **18 close-stool** privy **20 purr** (The multiple pun here may include "male child," "piece of dung," "the purr of a cat," and the name given to the jack or knave in the card game post and pair. Or perhaps the word should be *paw;* Parolles is a cat's paw; he has been fishing as a cat does in Fortune's pond and has fallen in himself. Fortune's paw has scratched.) **21 musk cat** (Both the civet cat and musk deer were prized for their musk scent, used in perfumes.) **23 carp** (1) a fish often bred in sewage-rich fish ponds or moats (2) a chatterer **24 ingenious** stupid, lacking in genius or intellect (?) **25 similes of comfort** comforting or instructive similes **33 cardecu** quart d'écu, one-quarter of a French crown **34 justices** i.e., Justices of the Peace, responsible in Elizabethan England for beggars under the Elizabethan poor law **41 more than "word"** i.e., many words; *Parolles* suggests a plural of the French *parole,* "word" **41–2 Cox my passion!** i.e., By God's (Christ's) passion on the cross! **44 found me** found me out.

45 lost abandoned. (Playing on *lost* and *found,* and recalling the parable of the lost sheep.) **48 grace** favor. (With perhaps a suggesting of "graze.") **out** (1) out of favor, out of safe pasture (2) "out" in the theatrical sense of having forgotten one's lines.
5.3. Location: Rossillion.
0.2 *Lafew* (Lafew may remain onstage from the end of the previous scene.) **1 of** in. **our esteem** my own value **3–4 know . . . home** appreciate her value fully. **5 make** account, consider **6 Natural rebellion** rebellion by the passions. **blade** greenness, freshness **10 high bent** i.e., as with a fully drawn bow **11 watched** waited for **12 But . . . pardon** (Lafew ceremoniously begs pardon for expressing an opinion that may seem critical.) **16 astonish the survey** dazzle the sight **17 richest** (1) richest in experience (2) nobly born **18–19 Whose . . . mistress** whose dear perfection was such that gallants who scorned to owe service to anyone humbly did so to her.

All repetition. Let him not ask our pardon.
The nature of his great offense is dead,
And deeper than oblivion we do bury
Th'incensing relics of it. Let him approach
A stranger, no offender; and inform him
So 'tis our will he should.

GENTLEMAN I shall, my liege. [*Exit.*]

KING [*to Lafew*]
What says he to your daughter? Have you spoke?

LAFEW
All that he is hath reference to Your Highness.

KING
Then shall we have a match. I have letters sent me
That sets him high in fame.

Enter Count Bertram.

LAFEW He looks well on't.

KING I am not a day of season,
For thou mayst see a sunshine and a hail
In me at once. But to the brightest beams
Distracted clouds give way; so stand thou forth.
The time is fair again.

BERTRAM My high-repented blames,
Dear sovereign, pardon to me.

KING All is whole;
Not one word more of the consumèd time.
Let's take the instant by the forward top;
For we are old, and on our quick'st decrees
Th'inaudible and noiseless foot of Time
Steals ere we can effect them. You remember
The daughter of this lord?

BERTRAM Admiringly, my liege. At first
I stuck my choice upon her, ere my heart
Durst make too bold a herald of my tongue;
Where the impression of mine eye infixing,
Contempt his scornful perspective did lend me,
Which warped the line of every other favor,
Scorned a fair color, or expressed it stolen,
Extended or contracted all proportions
To a most hideous object. Thence it came
That she whom all men praised and whom myself,
Since I have lost, have loved, was in mine eye
The dust that did offend it.

KING Well excused.
That thou didst love her strikes some scores away
From the great compt. But love that comes too late,
Like a remorseful pardon slowly carried,
To the great sender turns a sour offense,
Crying, "That's good that's gone." Our rash faults
Make trivial price of serious things we have,
Not knowing them until we know their grave.
Oft our displeasures, to ourselves unjust,
Destroy our friends, and after weep their dust;
Our own love waking cries to see what's done,
While shameful hate sleeps out the afternoon.
Be this sweet Helen's knell, and now forget her.
Send forth your amorous token for fair Maudlin.
The main consents are had; and here we'll stay
To see our widower's second marriage day.

COUNTESS
Which better than the first, O dear heaven, bless!
Or, ere they meet, in me, O nature, cesse!

LAFEW
Come on, my son, in whom my house's name
Must be digested: give a favor from you
To sparkle in the spirits of my daughter,
That she may quickly come. [*Bertram gives a ring.*]
By my old beard,
And every hair that's on't, Helen that's dead
Was a sweet creature; such a ring as this,
The last that e'er I took her leave at court,
I saw upon her finger.

BERTRAM Hers it was not.

KING
Now, pray you, let me see it, for mine eye,
While I was speaking, oft was fastened to't.
[*The ring is given to the King.*]
This ring was mine, and when I gave it Helen
I bade her, if her fortunes ever stood
Necessitied to help, that by this token
I would relieve her. Had you that craft to reave her
Of what should stead her most?

BERTRAM My gracious sovereign,
Howe'er it pleases you to take it so,
The ring was never hers.

COUNTESS Son, on my life,
I have seen her wear it, and she reckoned it
At her life's rate.

LAFEW I am sure I saw her wear it.

22 repetition reviewing of past wrongs, with recurrence of my anger. **23 dead** i.e., forgotten **25 Th'incensing relics** reminders that kindle anger **26 A stranger** i.e., as one whose story is unknown **27 GENTLEMAN** (This could be one of the two French lords or some other person in attendance.) **29 hath reference to** defers to **33 of season** i.e., of one consistent kind of weather **36 Distracted . . . way** clouds disperse and give way **37 high-repented blames** sorely repented failings **38 whole** mended, well **39 consumèd** past **40 take . . . top** take time by the forelock **41 quick'st** most urgent **46 stuck** fixed **48 Where . . . infixing** i.e., the image of her entering first at my eye and then fixing itself in my heart. (Bertram seems to say, in lines 45-56, that he loved Lafew's daughter some time ago but dared not speak of his love, and that, on her account, he came to scorn all women, especially Helena, who was like an offending speck in his eye, though since then he has learned to love the memory of the wife he lost.) **49 perspective** an optical glass for producing distorted images **50 favor** face **51 expressed it stolen** declared it to be painted cosmetically **52–3 Extended . . . object** elongated or compressed all other forms until they made a hideous sight. **54 she** i.e., Helena

56 offend it (1) give it offense (2) blur its vision. **58 compt** account, reckoning. (With a suggestion of the Day of Judgment.) **59 remorseful** compassionate. **slowly carried** i.e., arriving too late **60 turns . . . offense** i.e., turns sour on him **62 Make trivial price of** greatly undervalue **63 knowing** i.e., appreciating. **know their grave** i.e., are aware of their irrevocable loss. **64 displeasures** offenses **65 weep their dust** mourn over their remains **67 sleeps . . . afternoon** i.e., sleeps at ease, having done its work. **69 Maudlin** i.e., Magdalen, the daughter of Lafew. **73 ere they meet** i.e., before the two marriages come to resemble one another in unhappiness. **cesse** cease. **75 digested** incorporated. **favor** token **76 To sparkle in** i.e., to cheer with its luster **80 The last** the last time. **took her leave** took leave of her **85 bade her** i.e., bade her remember **86 Necessitied to** in need of **87 reave** deprive, rob **88 stead** help **92 rate** value.

BERTRAM You are deceived, my lord; she never saw it.
In Florence was it from a casement thrown me,
Wrapped in a paper, which contained the name
Of her that threw it. Noble she was, and thought
I stood engaged; but when I had subscribed
To mine own fortune, and informed her fully
I could not answer in that course of honor
As she had made the overture, she ceased
In heavy satisfaction, and would never
Receive the ring again.

KING Plutus himself,
That knows the tinct and multiplying med'cine,
Hath not in nature's mystery more science
Than I have in this ring. 'Twas mine, 'twas Helen's,
Whoever gave it you. Then, if you know
That you are well acquainted with yourself,
Confess 'twas hers, and by what rough enforcement
You got it from her. She called the saints to surety
That she would never put it from her finger
Unless she gave it to yourself in bed,
Where you have never come, or sent it us
Upon her great disaster.

BERTRAM She never saw it.

KING
Thou speak'st it falsely, as I love mine honor,
And mak'st conjectural fears to come into me
Which I would fain shut out. If it should prove
That thou art so inhuman—'twill not prove so,
And yet I know not. Thou didst hate her deadly,
And she is dead, which nothing but to close
Her eyes myself could win me to believe,
More than to see this ring.—Take him away.
My forepast proofs, howe'er the matter fall,
Shall tax my fears of little vanity,
Having vainly feared too little. Away with him!
We'll sift this matter further.

BERTRAM If you shall prove
This ring was ever hers, you shall as easy
Prove that I husbanded her bed in Florence,
Where yet she never was. [*Exit, guarded.*]

Enter a Gentleman.

KING
I am wrapped in dismal thinkings.

GENTLEMAN Gracious sovereign,
Whether I have been to blame or no, I know not.
Here's a petition from a Florentine, [*giving petition*]
Who hath for four or five removes come short
To tender it herself. I undertook it,
Vanquished thereto by the fair grace and speech
Of the poor suppliant, who by this I know
Is here attending. Her business looks in her
With an importing visage, and she told me,
In a sweet verbal brief, it did concern
Your Highness with herself.

KING [*reads*] *a letter* "Upon his many protestations to marry me when his wife was dead, I blush to say it, he won me. Now is the Count Rossillion a widower, his vows are forfeited to me, and my honor's paid to him. He stole from Florence, taking no leave, and I follow him to his country for justice. Grant it me, O King! In you it best lies; otherwise a seducer flourishes and a poor maid is undone. Diana Capilet"

LAFEW I will buy me a son-in-law in a fair, and toll for this. I'll none of him.

KING
The heavens have thought well on thee, Lafew,
To bring forth this discovery.—Seek these suitors.
Go speedily and bring again the Count.
[*Exeunt one or more attendants.*]
I am afeard the life of Helen, lady,
Was foully snatched.

COUNTESS Now, justice on the doers!

Enter Bertram [*guarded*].

KING
I wonder, sir, since wives are monsters to you,
And that you fly them as you swear them lordship,
Yet you desire to marry.

Enter Widow [*and*] *Diana.*

What woman's that?

DIANA
I am, my lord, a wretched Florentine,
Derivèd from the ancient Capilet.
My suit, as I do understand, you know,
And therefore know how far I may be pitied.

WIDOW
I am her mother, sir, whose age and honor
Both suffer under this complaint we bring,
And both shall cease, without your remedy.

KING
Come hither, Count. Do you know these women?

97 engaged i.e., pledged to her; or, possibly, not pledged to another. (The Folio spelling, "ingag'd," may suggest a negative prefix.) **97–8 subscribed . . . fortune** i.e., explained my true situation (of my marriage) **99–100 in that . . . overture** in the same honorable way that she had followed when she proposed **101 heavy satisfaction** doleful resignation **102 Plutus** the god of wealth **103 the tinct . . . med'cine** the alchemical elixir for transmuting base metals into gold **104 science** knowledge **106–7 if . . . yourself** i.e., if you are willing to examine yourself and your motives (something that Bertram has been notoriously unable to do) **109 to surety** to witness **113 Upon . . . disaster** when a catastrophe befell her. **115 conjectural fears** fearful conjectures **116 fain** willingly **122 My forepast proofs** The evidence I already have. **fall** turn out **123–4 Shall . . . too little** will hardly censure my fears (concerning Helena) as inconsequential; indeed, I have foolishly been too little apprehensive.

132 for . . . short on account of four or five shifts of residence of the court (as it moved from Marseilles to Rossillion) come too late **133 tender** offer **134 Vanquished** won **135 by this** by this time **136 looks** manifests itself **137 importing** urgent and full of import **138 brief** summary **144 taking no leave** not even saying goodbye **148 in a fair** i.e., where stolen and disreputable merchandise are common. (Lafew says he can do better at such a place than with Bertram.) **148–9 toll for this** i.e., put Bertram up for sale. (Merchants wishing to sell at market paid a toll or fee in order to enter their goods in a register.) **151 suitors** petitioners. **156 as . . . lordship** as soon as you swear to be their lord and husband **157 Yet** still **159 Derivèd** descended **164 both** i.e., both age and honor. (I will die dishonored.)

BERTRAM
My lord, I neither can nor will deny
But that I know them. Do they charge me further?
DIANA
Why do you look so strange upon your wife?
BERTRAM
She's none of mine, my lord.
DIANA If you shall marry,
You give away this hand, and that is mine; 170
You give away heaven's vows, and those are mine;
You give away myself, which is known mine;
For I by vow am so embodied yours
That she which marries you must marry me,
Either both or none.
LAFEW [*to Bertram*] Your reputation comes too short
for my daughter; you are no husband for her.
BERTRAM
My lord, this is a fond and desp'rate creature, 178
Whom sometime I have laughed with. Let Your
Highness
Lay a more noble thought upon mine honor
Than for to think that I would sink it here.
KING
Sir for my thoughts, you have them ill to friend 182
Till your deeds gain them. Fairer prove your honor
Than in my thought it lies!
DIANA Good my lord,
Ask him upon his oath if he does think
He had not my virginity.
KING What say'st thou to her?
BERTRAM She's impudent, my lord, 188
And was a common gamester to the camp. 189
DIANA He does me wrong, my lord. If I were so,
He might have bought me at a common price.
Do not believe him. Oh, behold this ring,
[*showing a ring*]
Whose high respect and rich validity 193
Did lack a parallel; yet for all that
He gave it to a commoner o'th' camp,
If I be one.
COUNTESS He blushes, and 'tis hit. 196
Of six preceding ancestors, that gem,
Conferred by testament to th' sequent issue, 198
Hath it been owed and worn. This is his wife; 199
That ring's a thousand proofs.
KING [*to Diana*] Methought you said
You saw one here in court could witness it.
DIANA
I did, my lord, but loath am to produce
So bad an instrument. His name's Parolles.
LAFEW
I saw the man today, if man he be.
KING
Find him, and bring him hither. [*Exit an Attendant.*]
BERTRAM What of him?
He's quoted for a most perfidious slave, 206
With all the spots o'th' world taxed and debauched, 207
Whose nature sickens but to speak a truth.
Am I or that or this for what he'll utter, 209
That will speak anything?
KING She hath that ring of yours.
BERTRAM
I think she has. Certain it is I liked her,
And boarded her i'th' wanton way of youth. 212
She knew her distance and did angle for me, 213
Madding my eagerness with her restraint, 214
As all impediments in fancy's course 215
Are motives of more fancy; and, in fine, 216
Her infinite cunning, with her modern grace, 217
Subdued me to her rate. She got the ring, 218
And I had that which any inferior might
At market price have bought.
DIANA I must be patient.
You that have turned off a first so noble wife
May justly diet me. I pray you yet— 222
Since you lack virtue, I will lose a husband—
Send for your ring, I will return it home,
And give me mine again.
BERTRAM I have it not.
KING [*to Diana*] What ring was yours, I pray you?
DIANA
Sir, much like the same upon your finger.
KING
Know you this ring? This ring was his of late.
DIANA
And this was it I gave him, being abed.
KING
The story then goes false you threw it him 231
Out of a casement?
DIANA I have spoke the truth.

Enter Parolles [attended].

BERTRAM
My lord, I do confess the ring was hers.
KING
You boggle shrewdly; every feather starts you.— 234
Is this the man you speak of?
DIANA Ay, my lord.
KING [*to Parolles*]
Tell me, sirrah—but tell me true, I charge you,
Not fearing the displeasure of your master,
Which on your just proceeding I'll keep off— 238
By him and by this woman here what know you? 239

170 this hand i.e., Bertram's hand **178 fond** foolish **182 for** as for. **you . . . friend** they are not well disposed toward you **188 impudent** shameless **189 gamester** prostitute **193 validity** value **196 'tis hit** i.e., that point scored. **198 sequent issue** next heir **199 owed** owned

206 quoted for set down as **207 With . . . debauched** accused of, and corrupted by, all the stains of the world **209 Am I . . . utter** Am I to be considered either one thing or another on the evidence of what he will say **212 boarded her** accosted her sexually **213 knew her distance** i.e., knew how to keep her distance, knew her value **214 Madding** making mad, exciting **215 fancy's** love's **216 motives** causes. **in fine** in conclusion **217 modern** commonplace **218 her rate** her terms. **222 diet me** refuse me as part of your fare, as you did her. (Bertram has turned away Helena as he would a dish, and thus does the same to Diana.) **231 The story . . . false** The story then is not true that **234 boggle shrewdly** shy away violently. **starts** startles **238 on . . . proceeding** if you speak honestly **239 By** concerning

PAROLLES So please Your Majesty, my master hath been an honorable gentleman. Tricks he hath had in him, which gentlemen have.

KING Come, come, to th' purpose. Did he love this woman?

PAROLLES Faith, sir, he did love her; but how?

KING How, I pray you?

PAROLLES He did love her, sir, as a gentleman loves a woman.

KING How is that?

PAROLLES He loved her, sir, and loved her not.

KING As thou art a knave and no knave. What an equivocal companion is this!

PAROLLES I am a poor man, and at Your Majesty's command.

LAFEW He's a good drum, my lord, but a naughty orator.

DIANA Do you know he promised me marriage?

PAROLLES Faith, I know more than I'll speak.

KING But wilt thou not speak all thou know'st?

PAROLLES Yes, so please Your Majesty. I did go between them, as I said; but more than that, he loved her, for indeed he was mad for her, and talked of Satan and of Limbo and of Furies and I know not what. Yet I was in that credit with them at that time that I knew of their going to bed, and of other motions, as promising her marriage, and things which would derive me ill will to speak of. Therefore I will not speak what I know.

KING Thou hast spoken all already, unless thou canst say they are married. But thou art too fine in thy evidence; therefore stand aside.—
This ring, you say, was yours?

DIANA
Ay, my good lord.

KING
Where did you buy it? Or who gave it you?

DIANA
It was not given me, nor I did not buy it.

KING
Who lent it you?

DIANA
It was not lent me neither.

KING
Where did you find it, then?

DIANA
I found it not.

KING
If it were yours by none of all these ways,
How could you give it him?

DIANA
I never gave it him.

LAFEW This woman's an easy glove, my lord; she goes off and on at pleasure.

KING
This ring was mine. I gave it his first wife.

DIANA
It might be yours or hers, for aught I know.

KING
Take her away; I do not like her now.
To prison with her. And away with him.—
Unless thou tell'st me where thou hadst this ring,
Thou diest within this hour.

DIANA
I'll never tell you.

KING
Take her away.

DIANA
I'll put in bail, my liege.

KING
I think thee now some common customer.

DIANA
By Jove, if ever I knew man, 'twas you.

KING
Wherefore hast thou accused him all this while?

DIANA
Because he's guilty, and he is not guilty.
He knows I am no maid, and he'll swear to't;
I'll swear I am a maid, and he knows not.
Great King, I am no strumpet, by my life;
I am either maid or else this old man's wife.
[*Pointing to Lafew.*]

KING
She does abuse our ears. To prison with her!

DIANA Good mother, fetch my bail. [*Exit Widow.*]
Stay, royal sir.
The jeweler that owes the ring is sent for,
And he shall surety me. But for this lord,
Who hath abused me, as he knows himself,
Though yet he never harmed me, here I quit him.
He knows himself my bed he hath defiled,
And at that time he got his wife with child.
Dead though she be, she feels her young one kick.
So there's my riddle: one that's dead is quick—
And now behold the meaning.

Enter Helena and Widow.

KING
Is there no exorcist
Beguiles the truer office of mine eyes?
Is't real that I see?

HELENA
No, my good lord,
'Tis but the shadow of a wife you see,
The name and not the thing.

BERTRAM
Both, both. Oh, pardon!

HELENA
Oh, my good lord, when I was like this maid,
I found you wondrous kind. There is your ring,
And, look you, here's your letter. [*She produces a letter.*] This it says:
"When from my finger you can get this ring
And are by me with child," et cetera. This is done.
Will you be mine, now you are doubly won?

BERTRAM
If she, my liege, can make me know this clearly,
I'll love her dearly, ever, ever dearly.

250 loved her not i.e., desired her only sexually. **252 equivocal companion** equivocating knave **255 drum** drummer (capable of mere noise). **naughty** worthless **264 in . . . with them** so much in their confidence **265 motions** proposals **266 derive** gain **269 fine** subtle

286 put in bail make bail, i.e., produce evidence to assure my liberty **287 customer** i.e., prostitute. **288 if . . . you** i.e., I have known no man sexually any more than I have slept with Your Majesty. **289 Wherefore** Why **297 owes** owns **298 surety me** be my security. **300 quit** (1) acquit (2) repay **304 quick** alive (and pregnant) **305 exorcist** one who conjures up spirits **310 like this maid** i.e., disguised as Diana **311 There** i.e., On Diana's finger (unless Diana has returned the ring to Helena)

HELENA
If it appear not plain and prove untrue,
Deadly divorce step between me and you!— 319
O my dear mother, do I see you living?

LAFEW
Mine eyes smell onions; I shall weep anon.
[*To Parolles*] Good Tom Drum, lend me a handkerchief.
So, I thank thee. Wait on me home, I'll make sport
with thee. Let thy curtsies alone; they are scurvy ones. 324

KING
Let us from point to point this story know,
To make the even truth in pleasure flow. 326
[*To Diana*] If thou be'st yet a fresh uncroppèd flower,
Choose thou thy husband, and I'll pay thy dower; 328
For I can guess that by thy honest aid
Thou kept'st a wife herself, thyself a maid.
Of that and all the progress, more and less,
Resolvedly more leisure shall express. 332
All yet seems well, and if it end so meet, 333
The bitter past, more welcome is the sweet. *Flourish.* 334

[Epilogue]

KING [*advancing*]
The king's a beggar, now the play is done.
All is well ended, if this suit be won,
That you express content; which we will pay, 3
With strife to please you, day exceeding day. 4
Ours be your patience then, and yours our parts; 5
Your gentle hands lend us, and take our hearts. 6
Exeunt omnes.

319 Deadly divorce may divorcing death **324 curtsies** courteous bows. (A word applied to men as well as women.) **326 even** precise, plain **328 Choose . . . dower** (The king offers Diana what he offered earlier to Helena.) **332 Resolvedly** in such a way that all doubts are removed

333 meet fittingly **334 past** being past

Epilogue

3 express content i.e., applaud **3–4 which . . . day** which we will repay by striving to please you, day after day. **5 Ours . . . parts** i.e., We will patiently attend, like an audience, while you undertake the active role by applauding **6 Your . . . us** i.e., please applaud. **hearts** i.e., gratitude.

Measure for Measure

"A play Caled Mesur for Mesur" by "Shaxberd" was performed at court, for the new King James I, by "his Maiesties plaiers" on December 26, 1604. Probably it had been composed that same year or in late 1603. The play dates from the very height of Shakespeare's tragic period, three years or so after *Hamlet,* contemporary with *Othello,* shortly before *King Lear* and *Macbeth.* This period includes very little comedy of any sort, and what there is differs markedly from the festive comedy of the 1590s. *Troilus and Cressida* (c. 1601–1602), hovering between satire and tragedy, bleakly portrays a hopeless love affair caught in the toils of a pointless and stalemated war. *All's Well That Ends Well* (c. 1601–1604) resembles *Measure for Measure* in its portrayal of an undeserving protagonist who must be deceived into marriage by the ethically ambiguous trick of substituting one woman for another in the protagonist's bed. *Measure for Measure,* perhaps the last such comedy from the tragic period, illustrates most clearly of all what critics usually mean by "problem comedy" or "problem play."

Its chief concern is not with the triumphs of love, as in the happy comedies, but with moral and social problems: "filthy vices" arising from sexual desire and the abuses of judicial authority. Images of disease abound in this play. We see corruption in Vienna "boil and bubble / Till it o'errun the stew" (5.1.326–7). The protagonist, Angelo, is for most of the play a deeply torn character, abhorring his own perverse sinfulness, compulsively driven to an attempted murder in order to cover up his lust for the heroine, Isabella. His soliloquies are introspective, tortured, focused on the psychological horror of an intelligent mind succumbing to criminal desire. The disguised Duke Vincentio, witnessing this fall into depravity and despair, can offer Angelo's intended victims no better philosophical counsel than Christian renunciation of the world and all its vain hopes. Tragedy is averted only by providential intervention and by the harsh trickery of "Craft against vice" (3.2.270), in which the Duke becomes involved as chief manipulator and stage manager. Of the concluding marriages, two are foisted on the bridegrooms (Angelo and Lucio) against their wills, whereas that of the Duke and Isabella jars oddly with his stoical teachings and with her previous determination to be a nun. The ending thus seems arbitrary; both justice and romantic happiness are so perilously achieved in this play that they seem inconsistent with the injustice and lechery that have prevailed until the last.

Yet the very improbability of the ending and the sense of tragedy narrowly averted are perhaps intentional. These features are appropriate, not only for problem comedy, but also for tragicomedy or comedy of forgiveness, overlapping genres toward which Shakespeare gravitated in his late romances. Angelo is, like Leontes in *The Winter's Tale* (or like Bertram in *All's Well That Ends Well* and Claudio in *Much Ado About Nothing*), an erring protagonist forgiven in excess of his deserving, spared by a benign, overseeing providence from destroying that which is most precious to him.

That providence is partly ascribed to divine intervention, as when the disguised Duke, at a loss for a means of saving Claudio from imminent death, and learning that a prisoner named Ragozine has just died and is enough like Claudio physically that his head can be substituted for that of Claudio as proof that an execution has taken place, exclaims, "Oh, 'tis an accident that heaven provides!" (4.3.77). Yet most of the "providential" oversight in this play is essentially theatrical and humanly devised. It is engineered by "the old fantastical duke of dark corners" (4.3.156–7), the resourceful Vincentio. Indeed, this mysterious Duke becomes a kind of embodiment of the manipulations and sleights of hand through which this dark comedy achieves its improbable ends.

The play's title, *Measure for Measure,* introduces a paradox of human justice which this "problem" play cannot wholly resolve. How are fallible humans to judge the sins of their fellow mortals and still obey Christ's injunction of the Sermon on the Mount: "Judge not that ye be not judged"? Three positions emerge from the debate: absolute justice at one extreme, mercy at the other, and equity as a middle ground. Isabella speaks for mercy, and her words ring with biblical authority. Since all humanity would be condemned to eternal darkness were God not merciful as well as just, should not humans also be merciful? The difficulty, however, is that Vienna shows all too clearly the effects of leniency under the indulgent Duke. Vice is rampant; stern measures are needed. Though he has not wished to crack the whip himself, the Duke firmly endorses "strict statutes and most biting laws, / The needful bits and curbs to headstrong steeds" (1.3.19–20). To carry out necessary reform, the Duke has chosen Angelo, spokesman for absolute justice, to represent him. Angelo's position is cold but consistent. Only by a literal and impartial administering of the statutes, he maintains, can the law deter potential offenders. If the judge is found guilty, he must pay the penalty as well. One difficulty here, however, is that literal enforcement of the statute on fornication seems ironically to catch the wrong culprits. Claudio and Juliet, who are about to be married and are already joined by a "true contract" of betrothal, are sentenced to the severest limit of the law, whereas the pimps and whores of Vienna's suburbs manage at first to evade punishment entirely. Angelo's deputy, Escalus, can only shake his head in dismay at this unjust result of strict justice. Angelo has not remembered fully the terms of his commission from the Duke: to practice both "Mortality and mercy" in Vienna, to "enforce or qualify the laws / As to your soul seems good." The attributes of a ruler, like those of God, must include "terror" but also "love" (1.1.20–67).

Escalus's compassionate and pragmatic approach to law illustrates equity or the flexible application of the law to particular cases. Because Claudio is only technically guilty (though still guilty), Escalus would pronounce for him a light sentence. Pompey and Mistress Overdone, on the other hand, require vigorous prosecution. The problem of policing vice is compounded by the law's inefficiency, as well as by erring human nature, which will never be wholly tamed. Constable Elbow, like Dogberry in *Much Ado*, is a pompous user of malapropisms, less clever by far than the criminals he would arrest. His evidence against Pompey is so absurdly circumstantial that Escalus is first obliged to let off this engaging pimp with a stern warning. Yet Escalus patiently and tenaciously attends to such proceedings, unlike Angelo, whose interest in the law is too theoretical. Escalus deals with day-to-day problems effectively. He orders reforms of the system by which constables are selected, instructs Elbow in the rudiments of his office, and so proceeds, ultimately, to an effective arrest. Vice is not eliminated; as Pompey defiantly points out, unless someone plans to "geld and splay all the youth of the city," they "will to't then" (2.1.229–33). Still, vice is held in check. Law can shape the outer person and hope for some inner reform. Even Pompey is taught a trade, albeit a grisly one, as an apprentice hangman. The law must use both "correction" and "instruction."

The solutions arrived at in the comic subplot do not fit the case of Angelo, for he is powerful enough to be above the Viennese law. Indeed, he tries finally to brazen it out, pitting his authority against that of the seemingly friendless Isabella, much like the biblical Elders when justly accused of immorality by the innocent Susannah. Society is on Angelo's side—even the well-meaning Escalus; only a seeming providence can rescue the defenseless. The Duke of Vienna, hovering in the background and seeing all that happens, intervenes just at those points when tragedy threatens to become irreversible. Moreover, the Duke is testing those he observes. As he says to Friar Thomas, explaining why he has delegated his power to Angelo: "Hence shall we see, / If power change purpose, what our seemers be" (1.3.53–4). The Duke obviously expects Angelo to fall. Indeed, he has known all along that Angelo had dishonorably repudiated his solemn contract to Mariana when her marriage dowry disappeared at sea (3.1.215–25). Like an all-seeing deity who keeps a reckoning of humanity's good and evil deeds, the Duke has found out Angelo's great weakness. As Angelo confesses, "I perceive Your Grace, like power divine, / Hath looked upon my passes" (5.1.377–8). Paradoxically, this seemingly tragic story of temptation and fall yields precious benefits of remorse and humility. Angelo is rescued from his self-made nightmare of seduction, murder, and tyranny. Knowing now that he is prone like other mortals to fleshly weakness, he knows also that he needs spiritual assistance and that, as judge, he ought to use mercy. Seen in retrospect, his panic, despair, and humiliation are curative.

The Duke is no less a problematic character than Angelo, Isabella, and the rest. Vienna's deep corruption is, in part, the result of his unwillingness to bear down on vice, and yet, rather than undertake to remedy the failure himself, this strange monarch elects to leave the business to one he suspects will make matters worse. The Duke has a great deal to learn about his own dislike of crowds, his complacent tolerance of human weakness, and his naive supposition that all his subjects speak well of him. He is a highly manipulative character, the one most responsible in the play for the ethically dubious solutions through which craft must be employed against vice. The comforting words of spiritual counsel he offers Claudio, Juliet, and the rest are spoken by a secular ruler fraudulently disguised as a friar. Certainly, the Duke is no allegorized god-figure, for all his omniscience and final role as both punisher and forgiver. As *deux ex machina* of this problem comedy, the Duke is human, frail, and vulnerable—as indeed he ought to be in a play that explores with such rich complexity the ironic distance between divine and human justice.

Yet, for all his manifest and even comic weaknesses, the Duke is finally the authority figure who must attempt to bring order to the imperfect world of Vienna. The devices he employs, including the bed trick, seem morally questionable and yet are palpable comic fictions that unmistakably notify us what genre we are watching. If the Duke's role is more that of artist than ruler or diety, his being so is appropriate to the artistically contrived and theatrical world that Shakespeare presents to us. Within the world of this play, the disguised Duke's chief function is to test the other characters and to mislead them intentionally into expecting the worst, in order to try their resolve. On a comic level, he exposes the amiable but loose-tongued Lucio as a slanderer against the Duke himself and devises for Lucio a suitably satirical exposure and witty punishment. More seriously, as confessor to Juliet, he assures her that her beloved Claudio must die on the morrow. As she ought, she penitentially accepts "shame with joy" and so is cleansed (2.3.37). Because the Duke is not really a friar, he does not have the spiritual authority to do this, and the ruse strikes us as theatrical, employing devices of illusion that actors and dramatists use. Even so, it provides real comfort for Juliet. The very theatricality of the illusion, by reminding us that we are in the theater, enables us to see the Duke as a kind of morally persuasive playwright who can change the lives of his characters for the better.

Similarly, the counsel of Christian renunciation offered to Claudio by the bogus friar (3.1) is at once illusory and comforting. The Duke's poignant reflection on the vanity of human striving is made ironic but not invalid by our awareness that we are viewing a deception with a seemingly benign purpose—that of persuading Claudio to see matters in their true perspective. The Duke characterizes life as a breath, a dreamlike "after-dinner's sleep," a fever of inconstancy in which timorous humans long fretfully for what they do not have and spurn those things they have. Claudio responds as he ought, resolving to "find life" by "seeking death" (3.1.5–43). He achieves this calm, however, in the face of certain execution; ironically, what he must then learn to overmaster is the desperate hope of living by means of his sister's dishonor. Claudio is broken by this test and perversely begs for a few years of guilty life at the cost of eternal shame for himself and Isabella. From this harrowing experience, he emerges at length with a better understanding of his own weakness and a greater compassion toward the weakness of others.

The searing encounter between Claudio and Isabella puts her to the test as well, and her response seems hysterical and no doubt prudish to modern audiences. She has much to learn about the complexities of human behavior. Although she is sincere in protesting that she would lay down her life for her brother and is correct, in the play's terms, to prefer virtue to mere existence, her tone is too strident. Like other major characters, she must be humbled before she can rise. She and Claudio must heed the Duke's essential admonition: "Do not satisfy your resolution with hopes that are fallible" (3.1.170–1). Only then, paradoxically, can Isabella and Claudio go on to achieve earthly happiness.

Isabella and Angelo are paradoxically alike. Both have retreated from the world of carnal pleasure into havens they regard as safe but that turn out not to work in the way they had hoped. Isabella longs for the restraints of the sisterhood into which she is about to enter. Her suspicions about human frailty can be seen in her testing of her brother; she fears he will fail her by begging life at the cost of her eternal shame, and when he does just that, she reacts with shrill condemnation and even hatred. This is a dark moment for Isabella, and she needs the spiritual counsel of the disguised Duke to enable her to forgive not only her brother but also herself. Angelo, meanwhile, has attempted to put down the rebellion of the flesh by suppressing and denying all such feeling in himself. We see him at first as the workaholic official who is not hesitant to condemn in others what he believes he is free of personally. He cherishes restraint as much as Isabella does, and that is why he is so terrified when the apparent absence of his only superior, the Duke, opens up to him the abyss of his own licentiousness. Once his word is law, Angelo perceives that he can play the tyrant and seducer without check. He is horrified to discover not only that he has ungovernable sexual longings within him but also that they perversely direct themselves toward a woman who is virginal and saintly. Why does he yearn to "raze the sanctuary" thus (2.2.178)? The revelation to him of his own innate evil is virtually tragic in the intensity of his self-loathing, and yet, in this strange comedy, this revelation is a first step toward coming to terms with his reprobate self. Until Angelo acknowledges the carnal within, he cannot begin looking for a way to understand and accept this frailty. The Duke's test provides the means of self-discovery that Angelo cannot fashion on his own.

In her final testing, Isabella shows greatness of spirit. Here, Shakespeare significantly alters his chief sources, George Whetstone's *Promos and Cassandra* (1578), Giovanni Baptista Giraldi Cinthio's *Hecatommithi*, and Whetstone's *Heptameron of Civil Discourses*. In all these versions, the character corresponding to Angelo does actually ravish the heroine, and in the *Hecatommithi* he also murders her brother. Shakespeare, by withholding these irreversible acts, not only gives to Angelo a technical innocence, but also allows the Duke, as *deus ex machina,* to practice virtuous deception on Isabella one more time. Can she forgive the supposed murderer of her brother? Her affirmative answer confutes the Old Testament ethic of "An Angelo for Claudio, death for death" whereby "Like doth quit like, and measure still for measure" (5.1.417–19). Although Angelo concedes that he deserves to die for what he intended, the forfeit need not be paid so long as humanity can reveal itself capable of Isabella's godlike mercy.

With its apparently unsuitable marriages and its improbable plotting, *Measure for Measure* does end by dealing directly with the problems of human nature confronted in the earlier scenes. The bed trick (switching Mariana for Isabella) may seem a legalistic and contrived way to bring Angelo to terms with his own carnality, but it is instructive not only to him but also to Isabella; she, like Angelo, must learn to accept the realities of the human condition. By helping Mariana to achieve her legitimate desire to couple and marry, Isabella sees into her own need. Her begging for Angelo's life is not merely an act of forgiveness to an enemy; it is a gift of continued marriage to Mariana. This realization helps to prepare Isabella herself for a marriage that, although dramatically surprising on stage (and even rejected by her in some modern productions), may be intended to demonstrate her having given up the cloistered life for all that marriage signifies. *Measure for Measure* is thus essentially comic (unlike *Troilus and Cressida*), despite its harrowing scenes of conflict and its awareness of vice everywhere in human nature. The play celebrates the *felix culpa* of human nature, the fall from grace that is an integral part of humanity's rise to happiness and self-knowledge. Throughout, in the play's finest scenes, poignancy is tempered by a wit and humor that are ultimately gracious. The formal and substantive emphasis on marriage stresses not just the benefits of remorse and humility but also the real possibility of psychic and spiritual growth: Isabella can acknowledge that she is a woman, Angelo can be genuinely freed from repression, and Claudio can value life more intensely because he has confronted death. All these recognitions affirm the acceptance and proper use of the physical and sexual side of human nature, and yet they are achieved only through charity and forgiveness. Humanity can learn, however slowly and painfully, that the talents entrusted to it by providence are to be used wisely.

The guardedly hopeful reading of the play offered here is, to be sure, not the only way in which it can be understood. The stage history of *Measure for Measure* highlights much that is problematic and troubling about it. For virtually all of the seventeenth, eighteenth, and nineteenth centuries, after its initial production, the play disappeared from the theater, other than in a heavily rewritten adaptation of the Restoration period and an even more radically recast nineteenth-century operatic version by Richard Wagner called *Das Liebesverbot* ("Forbidden Love"). The play was, it seems, too disagreeable for audiences in those centuries, too given over to vice and moral ambiguity. Readers were sometimes warned away from it. The twentieth and twenty-first centuries, conversely, have found in *Measure for Measure* a persuasive and even devastating dramatization of human imperfection. In an age that has learned to distrust authority figures, Duke Vincentio can come across as officious and sadistic in his manipulation of human lives, rather than ultimately benign. The director Keith Hack, at Stratford-upon-Avon in 1974, saw the Duke as devious, hypocritical, deeply implicated in the corruption of his city, and bitterly resented by the characters whose lives are intrusively managed by him. Some productions have asked if Lucio is justified in his suspicions that the Duke is really a fleshmonger after all. Isabella's longing for the cloistered life of the convent is sometimes seen today as psychologically driven by a fear of sexuality more than by religious faith. Some stage productions revel in the tawdriness of the bordello world of a corrupted Vienna, as for example in Michael Bogdanov's production at Stratford, Canada, in 1985. To Keith Hack, in 1974, the play was as fable of social impression in the vein of Bertolt Brecht. The marriages with which the play ends are often held up to skeptical scrutiny. Is Angelo chastised by his searing experience into resolving to be a good husband to Mariana, or does he snarl at her when he is led off with her to be married? Most significantly, perhaps, does Isabella accept the surprising offer of marriage from the Duke who has protected her but also deceived her into believing that her brother was dead? Today, beginning with Estelle Kohler in John Barton's production at Stratford-upon-Avon in 1970, actresses and directors get to choose; since Isabella is given no lines indicating her acceptance, the actress may simply be bewildered or may decide, with a gesture of defiance or indifference, to have nothing to do with men. The range of options is extraordinary, and helps demonstrate the way in which Shakespeare provides such an unsettling challenge to actors, directors, and audiences alike.

Measure for Measure

The Names of All the Actors

VINCENTIO, *the Duke*
ANGELO, *the deputy*
ESCALUS, *an ancient lord*
CLAUDIO, *a young gentleman*
LUCIO, *a fantastic*
Two other like GENTLEMEN
PROVOST
THOMAS, } *two friars*
PETER, }
[A JUSTICE]
[VARRIUS, *a friend of the Duke*]

ELBOW, *a simple constable*
FROTH, *a foolish gentleman*
CLOWN [*POMPEY, a servant to Mistress Overdone*]

ABHORSON, *an executioner*
BARNARDINE, *a dissolute prisoner*

ISABELLA, *sister to Claudio*
MARIANA, *betrothed to Angelo*
JULIET, *beloved of Claudio*
FRANCISCA, *a nun*
MISTRESS OVERDONE, *a bawd*

[A SERVANT *of Angelo*
BOY *singer*
A MESSENGER *from Angelo*

Lords, Officers, Citizens, Servants, and other Attendants]

THE SCENE: *Vienna*

1.1

Enter Duke, Escalus, lords, [and attendants].

DUKE Escalus.
ESCALUS My lord.
DUKE
Of government the properties to unfold 3
Would seem in me t'affect speech and discourse, 4
Since I am put to know that your own science 5
Exceeds, in that, the lists of all advice 6
My strength can give you. Then no more remains 7
But that to your sufficiency 8
. . . . as your worth is able, 9
And let them work. The nature of our people,
Our city's institutions, and the terms 11
For common justice, you're as pregnant in 12
As art and practice hath enrichèd any 13
That we remember. There is our commission,
[*giving a paper*]
From which we would not have you warp.—Call hither, 15
I say, bid come before us Angelo. [*Exit one.*]
What figure of us think you he will bear? 17
For you must know, we have with special soul 18
Elected him our absence to supply, 19
Lent him our terror, dressed him with our love, 20
And given his deputation all the organs 21
Of our own power. What think you of it?
ESCALUS
If any in Vienna be of worth
To undergo such ample grace and honor, 24

1.1 Location: Vienna. The court of Duke Vincentio.
3–4 Of . . . discourse For me to deliver an oration on the qualities needed in governing well would make me seem enamored of my own pomposity **5 put to know** obliged to admit. **science** knowledge **6 that** i.e., properties of government (line 3). **lists** limits **7 strength** power of mind **8–9 But . . . able** (The passage appears in the Folio as a single line. Several attempts at emendation have been made, but the most plausible explanation is that something has been deleted or inadvertently omitted.)

11 terms terms of court; or, modes of procedure **12 pregnant** well-informed **13 art** learning, theory **15 warp** deviate. **17 What . . . bear?** i.e., How do you think he will do as my substitute? **18 special soul** all the powers of the mind; whole heart **19 Elected** chosen. **supply** fill, make up for **20 terror** power to inspire awe and fear **21 his deputation** him as deputy. **organs** instruments **24 undergo** bear the weight of

It is Lord Angelo.

Enter Angelo.

DUKE Look where he comes.

ANGELO
Always obedient to Your Grace's will,
I come to know your pleasure.

DUKE Angelo,
There is a kind of character in thy life
That to th'observer doth thy history
Fully unfold. Thyself and thy belongings
Are not thine own so proper as to waste
Thyself upon thy virtues, they on thee.
Heaven doth with us as we with torches do,
Not light them for themselves; for if our virtues
Did not go forth of us, 'twere all alike
As if we had them not. Spirits are not finely touched
But to fine issues, nor Nature never lends
The smallest scruple of her excellence
But, like a thrifty goddess, she determines
Herself the glory of a creditor,
Both thanks and use. But I do bend my speech
To one that can my part in him advertise.
Hold, therefore, Angelo:
In our remove be thou at full ourself.
Mortality and mercy in Vienna
Live in thy tongue and heart. Old Escalus,
Though first in question, is thy secondary.
Take thy commission. [*He gives a paper.*]

ANGELO Now, good my lord,
Let there be some more test made of my mettle
Before so noble and so great a figure
Be stamped upon it.

DUKE No more evasion.
We have with a leavened and preparèd choice
Proceeded to you; therefore take your honors.
Our haste from hence is of so quick condition
That it prefers itself and leaves unquestioned
Matters of needful value. We shall write to you,
As time and our concernings shall importune,
How it goes with us, and do look to know
What doth befall you here. So, fare you well.
To th' hopeful execution do I leave you
Of your commissions.

ANGELO Yet give leave, my lord,
That we may bring you something on the way.

DUKE My haste may not admit it;
Nor need you, on mine honor, have to do
With any scruple. Your scope is as mine own,
So to enforce or qualify the laws
As to your soul seems good. Give me your hand.
I'll privily away. I love the people
But do not like to stage me to their eyes;
Though it do well, I do not relish well
Their loud applause and "aves" vehement,
Nor do I think the man of safe discretion
That does affect it. Once more, fare you well.

ANGELO
The heavens give safety to your purposes!

ESCALUS
Lead forth and bring you back in happiness!

DUKE I thank you. Fare you well. *Exit.*

ESCALUS
I shall desire you, sir, to give me leave
To have free speech with you; and it concerns me
To look into the bottom of my place.
A power I have, but of what strength and nature
I am not yet instructed.

ANGELO
'Tis so with me. Let us withdraw together,
And we may soon our satisfaction have
Touching that point.

ESCALUS I'll wait upon Your Honor.
Exeunt.

✤

1.2

Enter Lucio and two other Gentlemen.

LUCIO If the Duke with the other dukes come not to composition with the King of Hungary, why then all the dukes fall upon the King.

FIRST GENTLEMAN Heaven grant us its peace, but not the King of Hungary's!

SECOND GENTLEMAN Amen.

LUCIO Thou conclud'st like the sanctimonious pirate that went to sea with the Ten Commandments but scraped one out of the table.

SECOND GENTLEMAN "Thou shalt not steal"?

LUCIO Ay, that he razed.

30 belongings attributes, endowments **31 proper** exclusively **31–2 as to . . . thee** that you can expend all your efforts developing your own talents or use them solely for your own advantage. **33 torches** (Compare Jesus' command that we not hide our light under a bushel, Matthew 5:14–16.) **35 forth of us** out of us and into the world. **'twere all alike** it would be exactly the same **36–7 Spirits . . . issues** Souls are not deeply moved unless for noble purposes **38 scruple** bit. (Literally, a small weight.) **39–41 But . . . use** unless, like a thrifty goddess, she gathers to herself the glory due to a creditor, gaining both thanks from her debtor and interest on the loan. **41 bend** direct **42 that . . . advertise** who can instruct my role as duke now vested in him, i.e., who knows already more about governing in my absence than I can tell him. **44 In . . . ourself** During my absence be in every respect my deputy. (The royal plural.) **45 Mortality** The full rigor of the law, the death sentence **47 first in question** senior and first appointed **49 mettle** substance, quality. (With play on "metal," a common variant spelling, continued in the coining imagery of lines 50–1.) **52 leavened** i.e., carefully considered (just as yeast is given time to leaven dough) **54–5 Our . . . itself** The cause for my hasty departure is so urgent that it takes precedence over all other matters **55 unquestioned** not yet considered **57 concernings** affairs. **importune** urge **58 look to know** expect to be informed

60 th' hopeful exciting hopes of success. **execution** carrying out **61 leave** permission **62 bring you something** accompany you for a short distance **63 admit** permit **64–5 have . . . scruple** have the least doubt or hesitation about what is to be done. **68 I'll privily away** I'll go away secretly. **69 stage me** make a show of myself **70 do well** i.e., serves a political purpose **71 aves** hails of acclamation **72 safe** sound **73 affect** desire, court **75 Lead** May the heavens conduct you **78 free** frank **79 the bottom of my place** the extent of my commission.
1.2. Location: A public place.
2 composition agreement **3 fall upon** attack **9 table** tablet. **11 razed** scraped out. (The word may also suggest *rased*, "erased.")

FIRST GENTLEMAN Why, 'twas a commandment to command the captain and all the rest from their function; they put forth to steal. There's not a soldier of us all that, in the thanksgiving before meat, do relish the petition well that prays for peace.

SECOND GENTLEMAN I never heard any soldier dislike it.

LUCIO I believe thee, for I think thou never wast where grace was said.

SECOND GENTLEMAN No? A dozen times at least.

FIRST GENTLEMAN What, in meter?

LUCIO In any proportion or in any language.

FIRST GENTLEMAN I think, or in any religion.

LUCIO Ay, why not? Grace is grace, despite of all controversy; as, for example, thou thyself art a wicked villain, despite of all grace.

FIRST GENTLEMAN Well, there went but a pair of shears between us.

LUCIO I grant; as there may between the lists and the velvet. Thou art the list.

FIRST GENTLEMAN And thou the velvet. Thou art good velvet; thou'rt a three-piled piece, I warrant thee. I had as lief be a list of an English kersey as be piled, as thou art piled, for a French velvet. Do I speak feelingly now?

LUCIO I think thou dost, and indeed with most painful feeling of thy speech. I will, out of thine own confession, learn to begin thy health, but, whilst I live, forget to drink after thee.

FIRST GENTLEMAN I think I have done myself wrong, have I not?

SECOND GENTLEMAN Yes, that thou hast, whether thou art tainted or free.

Enter bawd [Mistress Overdone].

LUCIO Behold, behold, where Madam Mitigation comes! I have purchased as many diseases under her roof as come to—

SECOND GENTLEMAN To what, I pray?

LUCIO Judge.

SECOND GENTLEMAN To three thousand dolors a year.

FIRST GENTLEMAN Ay, and more.

LUCIO A French crown more.

FIRST GENTLEMAN Thou art always figuring diseases in me, but thou art full of error. I am sound.

LUCIO Nay, not, as one would say, healthy, but so sound as things that are hollow. Thy bones are hollow; impiety has made a feast of thee.

FIRST GENTLEMAN [*to Mistress Overdone*] How now, which of your hips has the most profound sciatica?

MISTRESS OVERDONE Well, well; there's one yonder arrested and carried to prison was worth five thousand of you all.

SECOND GENTLEMAN Who's that, I pray thee?

MISTRESS OVERDONE Marry, sir, that's Claudio, Signor Claudio.

FIRST GENTLEMAN Claudio to prison? 'Tis not so.

MISTRESS OVERDONE Nay, but I know 'tis so. I saw him arrested, saw him carried away; and, which is more, within these three days his head to be chopped off.

LUCIO But, after all this fooling, I would not have it so. Art thou sure of this?

MISTRESS OVERDONE I am too sure of it; and it is for getting Madam Julietta with child.

LUCIO Believe me, this may be. He promised to meet me two hours since, and he was ever precise in promise-keeping.

SECOND GENTLEMAN Besides, you know, it draws something near to the speech we had to such a purpose.

FIRST GENTLEMAN But most of all agreeing with the proclamation.

LUCIO Away! Let's go learn the truth of it.

Exit [Lucio with the Gentlemen].

MISTRESS OVERDONE Thus, what with the war, what with the sweat, what with the gallows, and what with poverty, I am custom-shrunk.

Enter Clown [Pompey].

How now, what's the news with you?

POMPEY Yonder man is carried to prison.

MISTRESS OVERDONE Well, what has he done?

POMPEY A woman.

MISTRESS OVERDONE But what's his offense?

POMPEY Groping for trouts in a peculiar river.

14 put forth set out to sea **15 thanksgiving before meat** saying of grace before a meal. (As in line 19.) **22 proportion** form **24–5 Grace . . . controversy** (Refers to the Catholic-Protestant *controversy*, line 25, as to whether humanity can be saved by works or by grace alone; with punning on *grace* as "thanks for a meal," line 19, and "gracefulness" or "becomingness," line 26.) **27–8 there . . . between us** i.e., we're cut from the same cloth. **29–30 as . . . list** (Lucio jokes that the shears might also cut between, i.e., distinguish between, the mere *lists* or selvages, edges of a woven fabric, and the *velvet* betokening a true gentlemen. Lucio wittily asserts himself to be a true gentleman; the other speaker, not.) **32 three-piled** having a threefold pile or nap, the best grade. (Velvet patches might be used to conceal syphilitic sores or scars.) **33 as lief** as soon, rather. **kersey** a coarse woolen fabric. (The First Gentleman turns the joke on Lucio by saying he would rather be a plain, homespun Englishman than a Frenchified velvet gentleman in decay and threadbare. *Velvet* suggests prostitutes and venereal disease, as in the following notes.) **be piled** (1) have a cloth nap (2) suffer from hemorrhoids (3) be pilled or peeled, i.e., hairless, bald, as a result of mercury treatment for syphilis (known as the "French disease"; see *French velvet* in the next line and *French crown,* line 50) **34 feelingly** to the purpose, so as to hit home. (But Lucio's reply quibbles on "painfully," meaning the Gentleman's mouth is affected by the French disease; hence, Lucio will not drink from the same cup after him.) **37 begin thy health** drink to your health **37–8 forget . . . thee** take care not to drink from your cup. **39 done myself wrong** i.e., asked for that **42 tainted** infected **43 Mitigation** (So called because her function is to relieve desire.)

47 Judge Guess. **48 dolors** (Quibbling on *dollars;* spelled "Dollours" in the Folio.) **50 French crown** (1) gold coin (2) bald head incurred through syphilis, the "French disease" **51 figuring** (1) imagining (2) reckoning. (Recalling the monetary puns of lines 48 and 50.) **54 sound** (1) healthy (2) resounding (because of hollow bones caused by syphilis) **55 impiety** wickedness **57 sciatica** a disease affecting the sciatic nerve in the hip and thigh, thought to be a symptom of syphilis. **62 Marry** i.e., By the Virgin Mary **66 which** what **68 after** notwithstanding **73 ever** always **75–6 draws . . . near to** approaches, sounds somewhat like **76–7 to . . . purpose** on that topic. **82 sweat** sweating sickness (often fatal), or the plague; also, the sweating tub, a treatment for syphilis **83 custom-shrunk** having fewer customers. **86 done** (Pompey quibbles in line 87 on a sexual sense of the word, present also in Mistress Overdone's name.) **89 peculiar** privately owned. (With bawdy suggestion.)

MISTRESS OVERDONE What? Is there a maid with child by him?

POMPEY No, but there's a woman with maid by him. You have not heard of the proclamation, have you?

MISTRESS OVERDONE What proclamation, man?

POMPEY All houses in the suburbs of Vienna must be plucked down.

MISTRESS OVERDONE And what shall become of those in the city?

POMPEY They shall stand for seed. They had gone down too, but that a wise burgher put in for them.

MISTRESS OVERDONE But shall all our houses of resort in the suburbs be pulled down?

POMPEY To the ground, mistress.

MISTRESS OVERDONE Why, here's a change indeed in the commonwealth! What shall become of me?

POMPEY Come, fear not you. Good counselors lack no clients. Though you change your place, you need not change your trade; I'll be your tapster still. Courage! There will be pity taken on you. You that have worn your eyes almost out in the service, you will be considered.

MISTRESS OVERDONE What's to do here, Thomas Tapster? Let's withdraw.

POMPEY Here comes Signor Claudio, led by the Provost to prison; and there's Madam Juliet. *Exeunt.*

Enter Provost, Claudio, Juliet, Officers; Lucio and two Gentlemen [follow].

CLAUDIO [*to the Provost*]
Fellow, why dost thou show me thus to the world?
Bear me to prison, where I am committed.

PROVOST
I do it not in evil disposition,
But from Lord Angelo by special charge.

CLAUDIO
Thus can the demigod Authority
Make us pay down for our offense, by weight,
The words of heaven. On whom it will, it will;
On whom it will not, so; yet still 'tis just.

LUCIO
Why, how now, Claudio? Whence comes this
restraint?

CLAUDIO
From too much liberty, my Lucio, liberty.
As surfeit is the father of much fast,
So every scope, by the immoderate use,
Turns to restraint. Our natures do pursue,
Like rats that ravin down their proper bane,
A thirsty evil, and when we drink we die.

LUCIO If I could speak so wisely under an arrest, I would send for certain of my creditors. And yet, to say the truth, I had as lief have the foppery of freedom as the morality of imprisonment. What's thy offense, Claudio?

CLAUDIO
What but to speak of would offend again.

LUCIO
What, is't murder?

CLAUDIO No.

LUCIO Lechery?

CLAUDIO
Call it so.

PROVOST Away, sir, you must go.

CLAUDIO
One word, good friend.—Lucio, a word with you.

LUCIO
A hundred, if they'll do you any good.
Is lechery so looked after?

CLAUDIO
Thus stands it with me: upon a true contract
I got possession of Julietta's bed.
You know the lady; she is fast my wife,
Save that we do the denunciation lack
Of outward order. This we came not to,
Only for propagation of a dower
Remaining in the coffer of her friends,
From whom we thought it meet to hide our love
Till time had made them for us. But it chances
The stealth of our most mutual entertainment
With character too gross is writ on Juliet.

LUCIO
With child, perhaps?

CLAUDIO Unhappily, even so.
And the new deputy now for the Duke—
Whether it be the fault and glimpse of newness,
Or whether that the body public be
A horse whereon the governor doth ride,
Who, newly in the seat, that it may know
He can command, lets it straight feel the spur;

92 woman with maid (Pompey playfully corrects Mistress Overdone's use of the word "maid," joking that a pregnant woman cannot be a virgin [*maid*] though the child she carries is one.) **95 houses** i.e., brothels. **suburbs** (Location of the brothels in Shakespeare's London, as in other walled cities.) **99 for seed** to preserve the species. (With ribald pun.) **100 burgher** citizen. **put . . . them** interceded on their behalf, offered to acquire them. **106–7 Good . . . clients** Good lawyers (and, by implication, pimps and bawds) are never at a loss for clients. **108 tapster** one who draws beer in an alehouse **109–10 worn . . . out** i.e., worked so hard. (Perhaps with an ironic reference to the traditional image of the blind Cupid, often depicted on signs hung at the doors of brothels.) **114–15 Provost** officer charged with apprehension, custody, and punishment of offenders **121–2 Make . . . heaven** make us pay the full penalty for our offenses called for in the Bible. **122–3 On whom . . . 'tis just** (Compare Romans 9:18: "Therefore hath he [God] mercy on whom he will have mercy, and whom he will he hardeneth.")

126 As . . . fast Just as excessive indulgence inevitably leads to revulsion and abstinence **127 scope** liberty, license **129 ravin . . . bane** greedily devour what is poisonous to them **131–2 If . . . creditors** If imprisonment would gain me such wisdom, I would send for those to whom I owe money and thus be arrested for debt. **133 lief** willingly. **foppery** folly **141 looked after** kept under observation. **142 a true contract** i.e., one made in the presence of witnesses, though without a religious ceremony. (Such a precontract was binding but, in the eyes of the Church, did not confer the right of sexual consummation before the nuptials.) **144 fast my wife** i.e., firmly bound by precontract **145 denunciation** formal declaration **146 outward order** public ceremony. **147 propagation** increase, begetting **148 friends** relatives **149 meet** fitting, necessary **150 made . . . us** disposed them in our favor. **152 character too gross** writing too evident **155 the fault . . . newness** the faulty flashiness of novelty **159 straight** at once

Whether the tyranny be in his place,
Or in his eminence that fills it up,
I stagger in—but this new governor
Awakes me all the enrollèd penalties
Which have, like unscoured armor, hung by the wall
So long that nineteen zodiacs have gone round
And none of them been worn; and for a name
Now puts the drowsy and neglected act
Freshly on me. 'Tis surely for a name.

LUCIO I warrant it is, and thy head stands so tickle on thy shoulders that a milkmaid, if she be in love, may sigh it off. Send after the Duke and appeal to him.

CLAUDIO
I have done so, but he's not to be found.
I prithee, Lucio, do me this kind service:
This day my sister should the cloister enter
And there receive her approbation.
Acquaint her with the danger of my state;
Implore her, in my voice, that she make friends
To the strict deputy; bid herself assay him.
I have great hope in that, for in her youth
There is a prone and speechless dialect
Such as move men; beside, she hath prosperous art
When she will play with reason and discourse,
And well she can persuade.

LUCIO I pray she may, as well for the encouragement of the like, which else would stand under grievous imposition, as for the enjoying of thy life, who I would be sorry should be thus foolishly lost at a game of tick-tack. I'll to her.

CLAUDIO I thank you, good friend Lucio.
LUCIO Within two hours.
CLAUDIO Come, officer, away! *Exeunt.*

✤

1.[3]

Enter Duke and Friar Thomas.

DUKE
No, holy Father, throw away that thought;
Believe not that the dribbling dart of love
Can pierce a complete bosom. Why I desire thee
To give me secret harbor hath a purpose
More grave and wrinkled than the aims and ends
Of burning youth.
FRIAR THOMAS May Your Grace speak of it?

DUKE
My holy sir, none better knows than you
How I have ever loved the life removed
And held in idle price to haunt assemblies
Where youth and cost witless bravery keeps.
I have delivered to Lord Angelo,
A man of stricture and firm abstinence,
My absolute power and place here in Vienna,
And he supposes me traveled to Poland;
For so I have strewed it in the common ear,
And so it is received. Now, pious sir,
You will demand of me why I do this.
FRIAR THOMAS Gladly, my lord.
DUKE
We have strict statutes and most biting laws,
The needful bits and curbs to headstrong steeds,
Which for this fourteen years we have let slip,
Even like an o'ergrown lion in a cave
That goes not out to prey. Now, as fond fathers,
Having bound up the threat'ning twigs of birch
Only to stick it in their children's sight
For terror, not to use, in time the rod
Becomes more mocked than feared, so our decrees,
Dead to infliction, to themselves are dead;
And liberty plucks justice by the nose,
The baby beats the nurse, and quite athwart
Goes all decorum.
FRIAR THOMAS It rested in Your Grace
To unloose this tied-up justice when you pleased;
And it in you more dreadful would have seemed
Than in Lord Angelo.
DUKE I do fear, too dreadful.
Sith 'twas my fault to give the people scope,
'Twould be my tyranny to strike and gall them
For what I bid them do; for we bid this be done
When evil deeds have their permissive pass
And not the punishment. Therefore indeed, my father,
I have on Angelo imposed the office,
Who may in th'ambush of my name strike home,
And yet my nature never in the fight
To do in slander. And to behold his sway
I will, as 'twere a brother of your order,
Visit both prince and people. Therefore, I prithee,
Supply me with the habit, and instruct me
How I may formally in person bear

160 in his place inherent in the office **161 his eminence** the eminence of him **162 I stagger in** I am uncertain **163 Awakes me** i.e., awakes, activates. (*Me* is used colloquially.) **enrollèd** written on a roll or deed **165 zodiacs** i.e., years **166 for a name** for reputation's sake **169 tickle** uncertain, unstable **174 cloister** i.e., convent **175 approbation** novitiate, period of probation. **178 To** with. **assay** try, test **180 prone** eager, apt, supplicating. **dialect** language **181 prosperous art** skill or ability to gain favorable results **184–6 as well . . . life** both for the encouragement of similar sexual activity, which otherwise would be subject to grave charges or accusations, and for you to continue to live **187–8 tick-tack** a form of backgammon in which pegs were fitted into holes. (Here applied bawdily.)
1.3. Location: A friary.
2 dribbling falling short or wide of the mark **3 complete** perfect, whole, strong **4 harbor** shelter **5 wrinkled** i.e., mature

8 removed retired **9 in idle price** as little worth. *Idle* means "unprofitable." **10 Where . . . keeps** where youth and costly expenditure put themselves foolishly on display. **12 stricture** strictness **20 steeds** (The Folio reading, "weedes," is possible in the sense of "lawless and uncontrolled impulses.") **21 fourteen** (Claudio mentions nineteen years at 1.2.165; possibly the compositor confused *xiv* and *xix*.) **22 o'ergrown** too old and large **23 fond** doting **28 Dead to infliction** dead in that they are not executed **29 liberty** license **30 athwart** wrongly, awry **31 decorum** social order. **It rested . . . Grace** It lay in your ducal authority, was incumbent on you **35 Sith** Since **36 gall** chafe, injure **37 we . . . done** i.e., we virtually order a crime to be committed **38 pass** sanction **40 office** duty **41 Who . . . home** who may, under cover of my ducal authority, strike to the heart of the matter **42 nature** i.e., personal identity (as distinguished from official capacity) **43 do in slander** act so as to invite slander (for being too repressive). **sway** rule **46 habit** garment (of a friar) **47 formally** in outward appearance. **bear** bear myself

Like a true friar. More reasons for this action
At our more leisure shall I render you.
Only this one: Lord Angelo is precise,
Stands at a guard with envy, scarce confesses
That his blood flows or that his appetite
Is more to bread than stone. Hence shall we see,
If power change purpose, what our seemers be.
Exeunt.

✤

1.[4]

Enter Isabella and Francisca, a nun.

ISABELLA
And have you nuns no farther privileges?
FRANCISCA Are not these large enough?
ISABELLA
Yes, truly. I speak not as desiring more,
But rather wishing a more strict restraint
Upon the sisterhood, the votarists of Saint Clare.
LUCIO (*within*)
Ho! Peace be in this place!
ISABELLA Who's that which calls?
FRANCISCA
It is a man's voice. Gentle Isabella,
Turn you the key, and know his business of him.
You may, I may not; you are yet unsworn.
When you have vowed, you must not speak with men
But in the presence of the prioress;
Then if you speak you must not show your face,
Or if you show your face you must not speak.
He calls again. I pray you, answer him. [*Exit.*]
ISABELLA
Peace and prosperity! Who is 't that calls?

[*She opens the door. Enter Lucio.*]

LUCIO
Hail, virgin, if you be, as those cheek roses
Proclaim you are no less. Can you so stead me
As bring me to the sight of Isabella,
A novice of this place, and the fair sister
To her unhappy brother Claudio?
ISABELLA
Why "her unhappy brother"? Let me ask,
The rather for I now must make you know
I am that Isabella, and his sister.
LUCIO
Gentle and fair, your brother kindly greets you.
Not to be weary with you, he's in prison.
ISABELLA Woe me! For what?
LUCIO
For that which, if myself might be his judge,
He should receive his punishment in thanks:
He hath got his friend with child.
ISABELLA
Sir, make me not your story.
LUCIO 'Tis true.
I would not—though 'tis my familiar sin
With maids to seem the lapwing, and to jest,
Tongue far from heart—play with all virgins so.
I hold you as a thing enskied and sainted
By your renouncement, an immortal spirit
And to be talked with in sincerity
As with a saint.
ISABELLA
You do blaspheme the good in mocking me.
LUCIO
Do not believe it. Fewness and truth, 'tis thus:
Your brother and his lover have embraced.
As those that feed grow full, as blossoming time
That from the seedness the bare fallow brings
To teeming foison, even so her plenteous womb
Expresseth his full tilth and husbandry.
ISABELLA
Someone with child by him? My cousin Juliet?
LUCIO Is she your cousin?
ISABELLA
Adoptedly, as schoolmaids change their names
By vain though apt affection.
LUCIO She it is.
ISABELLA
Oh, let him marry her.
LUCIO This is the point.
The Duke is very strangely gone from hence;
Bore many gentlemen, myself being one,
In hand and hope of action; but we do learn,
By those that know the very nerves of state,
His givings-out were of an infinite distance
From his true-meant design. Upon his place,
And with full line of his authority,
Governs Lord Angelo, a man whose blood
Is very snow broth; one who never feels
The wanton stings and motions of the sense,
But doth rebate and blunt his natural edge

49 more greater **50 precise** strict, puritanical **51 Stands . . . envy** guards himself severely against calumny **52–3 or . . . stone** or that he has an appetite for bread (i.e., food or physical pleasure) any more than if it were stone. (See Matthew 4.3, where the devil tempts Jesus to turn stone into bread.)
1.4. Location: A convent.
5 votarists of Saint Clare An order founded in 1212 by Saint Francis of Assisi and Saint Clare; its members were enjoined to a life of poverty, service, and contemplation. **9 you . . . unsworn** i.e., you have not yet taken your formal vows to enter the convent. **16 cheek roses** i.e., blushes **17 stead** help **18 As** as to **20 unhappy** unfortunate **22 The rather for** the more so because **25 weary** wearisome

30 story subject for mirth. **31 familiar** customary **32 lapwing** peewit or plover. (The lapwing runs away from its nest in order to draw away enemies from its young, much as Lucio throws up smokescreens in his seductive talk with young women.) **34 enskied** placed in heaven **38 You . . . me** You blaspheme goodness itself when you mockingly praise me, unworthy as I am, for saintliness. **39 it** i.e., that I am mocking. **Fewness and truth** In few words and truly **41–3 As . . . foison** Just as the season of blossoming brings the sowing of the bare untilled land to teeming fruitfulness **44 Expresseth . . . husbandry** makes plainly visible Claudio's tilling of the crop, i.e., his plowing and fertilizing Juliet's body. **47 change** exchange **48 vain though apt** girlish though natural and suitable **51–2 Bore . . . action** i.e., he misleadingly kept us in expectation of some military action **54 givings-out** public statements **55 Upon** In **56 line** extent **58 snow broth** melted snow (i.e., ice water) **59 motions . . . sense** promptings of sexual desire **60 But . . . edge** but dulls and blunts the sharp desire of sexuality

With profits of the mind, study, and fast.
He—to give fear to use and liberty,
Which have for long run by the hideous law
As mice by lions—hath picked out an act,
Under whose heavy sense your brother's life
Falls into forfeit. He arrests him on it
And follows close the rigor of the statute
To make him an example. All hope is gone,
Unless you have the grace by your fair prayer
To soften Angelo. And that's my pith of business
Twixt you and your poor brother.

ISABELLA Doth he so
Seek his life?

LUCIO He's censured him already,
And, as I hear, the Provost hath a warrant
For 's execution.

ISABELLA Alas, what poor
Ability's in me to do him good?

LUCIO Assay the power you have.

ISABELLA
My power? Alas, I doubt.

LUCIO Our doubts are traitors,
And makes us lose the good we oft might win,
By fearing to attempt. Go to Lord Angelo,
And let him learn to know, when maidens sue
Men give like gods, but when they weep and kneel,
All their petitions are as freely theirs
As they themselves would owe them.

ISABELLA I'll see what I can do.

LUCIO But speedily.

ISABELLA I will about it straight,
No longer staying but to give the Mother
Notice of my affair. I humbly thank you.
Commend me to my brother. Soon at night
I'll send him certain word of my success.

LUCIO
I take my leave of you.

ISABELLA Good sir, adieu.

Exeunt [*separately*].

✤

2.1

Enter Angelo, Escalus, and servants, [*a*] *Justice.*

ANGELO
We must not make a scarecrow of the law,
Setting it up to fear the birds of prey,
And let it keep one shape till custom make it
Their perch and not their terror.

ESCALUS Ay, but yet
Let us be keen and rather cut a little
Than fall and bruise to death. Alas, this gentleman
Whom I would save had a most noble father!
Let but Your Honor know,
Whom I believe to be most strait in virtue,
That, in the working of your own affections,
Had time cohered with place, or place with wishing,
Or that the resolute acting of your blood
Could have attained th'effect of your own purpose,
Whether you had not sometime in your life
Erred in this point which now you censure him,
And pulled the law upon you.

ANGELO
'Tis one thing to be tempted, Escalus,
Another thing to fall. I not deny
The jury, passing on the prisoner's life,
May in the sworn twelve have a thief or two
Guiltier than him they try. What's open made to
justice,
That justice seizes. What knows the laws
That thieves do pass on thieves? 'Tis very pregnant,
The jewel that we find, we stoop and take't
Because we see it; but what we do not see
We tread upon and never think of it.
You may not so extenuate his offense
For I have had such faults; but rather tell me,
When I that censure him do so offend,
Let mine own judgment pattern out my death
And nothing come in partial. Sir, he must die.

Enter Provost.

ESCALUS
Be it as your wisdom will.

ANGELO Where is the Provost?

PROVOST
Here, if it like Your Honor.

ANGELO See that Claudio
Be executed by nine tomorrow morning.
Bring him his confessor; let him be prepared.
For that's the utmost of his pilgrimage.

[*Exit Provost.*]

ESCALUS
Well, heaven forgive him, and forgive us all!
Some rise by sin, and some by virtue fall;
Some run from breaks of ice and answer none,
And some condemnèd for a fault alone.

Enter Elbow, Froth, Clown [*Pompey*], *officers.*

62 use and liberty habitual licentiousness **65 heavy sense** severe interpretation **70 my pith of business** the essence of my business **72 censured** sentenced **76 Assay** Try **78 makes** make **82 their petitions** i.e., the things the maidens ask for **83 As . . . them** as they themselves would wish to have them. **87 but** than. **Mother** Mother Superior, prioress **89 Soon at night** Early tonight **90 my success** how I have succeeded.
2.1 Location: A court of justice.
2 fear frighten **5 keen** sharp

6 fall let fall heavily. **bruise** i.e., crush **8 know** consider **9 strait** strict **10 affections** desires **12 blood** passion **13 effect** realization **14 had** would have. **sometime** on some occasion **15 censure him** sentence him for **22–3 What . . . on thieves?** Who knows what laws thieves apply to their fellow thieves? **23 pregnant** clear **28 For** because **30–1 Let . . . partial** let the sentence I have imposed serve as a model in sentencing me if I commit a crime, no partiality or extenuating circumstances being admitted. **33 like** please **36 that's . . . pilgrimage** that's the furthest point of his life's journey. **39 Some . . . none** some break the ice repeatedly (i.e., commit serious infractions of the law) and yet escape punishment. (A famous crux; the Folio reads "brakes of Ice.") **40 a fault alone** one single infraction.

ELBOW Come, bring them away. If these be good people in a commonweal that do nothing but use their abuses in common houses, I know no law. Bring them away.

ANGELO How now, sir, what's your name? And what's the matter?

ELBOW If it please Your Honor, I am the poor Duke's constable, and my name is Elbow. I do lean upon justice, sir, and do bring in here before Your good Honor two notorious benefactors.

ANGELO Benefactors? Well, what benefactors are they? Are they not malefactors?

ELBOW If it please Your Honor, I know not well what they are; but precise villains they are, that I am sure of, and void of all profanation in the world that good Christians ought to have.

ESCALUS [*to Angelo*] This comes off well. Here's a wise officer.

ANGELO Go to. What quality are they of?—Elbow is your name? Why dost thou not speak, Elbow?

POMPEY He cannot, sir; he's out at elbow.

ANGELO What are you, sir?

ELBOW He, sir? A tapster, sir, parcel-bawd, one that serves a bad woman, whose house, sir, was, as they say, plucked down in the suburbs; and now she professes a hothouse, which I think is a very ill house too.

ESCALUS How know you that?

ELBOW My wife, sir, whom I detest before heaven and Your Honor—

ESCALUS How? Thy wife?

ELBOW Ay, sir; whom I thank heaven is an honest woman—

ESCALUS Dost thou detest her therefore?

ELBOW I say, sir, I will detest myself also, as well as she, that this house, if it be not a bawd's house, it is pity of her life, for it is a naughty house.

ESCALUS How dost thou know that, Constable?

ELBOW Marry, sir, by my wife, who, if she had been a woman cardinally given, might have been accused in fornication, adultery, and all uncleanliness there.

ESCALUS By the woman's means?

ELBOW Ay, sir, by Mistress Overdone's means; but as she spit in his face, so she defied him.

POMPEY Sir, if it please Your Honor, this is not so.

ELBOW Prove it before these varlets here, thou honorable man, prove it.

ESCALUS [*to Angelo*] Do you hear how he misplaces?

POMPEY Sir, she came in great with child, and longing, saving Your Honor's reverence, for stewed prunes. Sir, we had but two in the house, which at that very distant time stood, as it were, in a fruit dish, a dish of some threepence. Your Honors have seen such dishes; they are not China dishes, but very good dishes—

ESCALUS Go to, go to. No matter for the dish, sir.

POMPEY No, indeed, sir, not of a pin; you are therein in the right. But to the point. As I say, this Mistress Elbow, being, as I say, with child, and being great-bellied, and longing, as I said, for prunes; and having but two in the dish, as I said, Master Froth here, this very man, having eaten the rest, as I said, and, as I say, paying for them very honestly—for, as you know, Master Froth, I could not give you threepence again.

FROTH No, indeed.

POMPEY Very well. You being then, if you be remembered, cracking the stones of the foresaid prunes—

FROTH Ay, so I did indeed.

POMPEY Why, very well; I telling you then, if you be remembered, that such a one and such a one were past cure of the thing you wot of, unless they kept very good diet, as I told you—

FROTH All this is true.

POMPEY Why, very well, then—

ESCALUS Come, you are a tedious fool. To the purpose. What was done to Elbow's wife, that he hath cause to complain of? Come me to what was done to her.

POMPEY Sir, Your Honor cannot come to that yet.

ESCALUS No, sir, nor I mean it not.

POMPEY Sir, but you shall come to it, by Your Honor's leave. And, I beseech you, look into Master Froth here, sir, a man of fourscore pound a year, whose father died at Hallowmas.—Was 't not at Hallowmas, Master Froth?

FROTH All-hallond eve.

POMPEY Why, very well. I hope here be truths. He, sir, sitting, as I say, in a lower chair, sir—'twas in the Bunch of Grapes, where indeed you have a delight to sit, have you not?

41 away onward. **42–3 use . . . houses** practice their vices in bawdy houses **47 poor Duke's** i.e., Duke's poor **48 lean upon** rely on, appeal to. (With an unintended comic reference to the idea of leaning on one's elbow.) **54 precise** complete. (Or perhaps a blunder for "precious." *Precise* unintentionally recalls the description of Angelo as *precise,* i.e., strict or puritanical, at 1.3.50.) **55 profanation** (A blunder for "profession," or a word meaning "irreverence" where Elbow intends "reverence." Elbow already has used several malapropisms, including *lean upon, benefactors,* and *precise.*) **59 Go to** An expression of impatience or reproof. **quality** social standing, occupation **61 out at elbow** (1) impoverished, threadbare, hence without any ideas (2) missing his cue, i.e., at a loss for words after being called by his name. **63 parcel-bawd** part-time bawd (and part-time tapster) **66 professes a hothouse** professes to run a bathhouse **69 detest** (For "protest.") **77 pity of her life** a great pity. **naughty** wicked **80 cardinally** (For "carnally.") **given** inclined **84 she spit . . . face** Elbow's wife spit in the face of Pompey (who, as pimp, was acting as Mistress Overdone's *means,* line 83).

86–7 varlets . . . honorable (Elbow reverses or *misplaces* these epithets.) **90 saving . . . reverence** i.e., begging your pardon for what I'm about to say. **stewed prunes** (Commonly served in houses of prostitution, or *stews,* and therefore suggesting prostitutes. The dialogue throughout is sexually suggestive.) **92 distant** (Blunder for "instant"?) **97 a pin** i.e., an insignificant trifle **105 again** back. **108 stones** pits. (With suggestion also of "testicles.") **113 the thing . . . of** you know what I mean (i.e., venereal disease) **114 diet** strict regimen prescribed for medical treatment **119 Come me** i.e., Come. (*Me* is used colloquially. Pompey makes a vulgar joke on the words *come* and *done;* see note at line 140.) **124 of . . . year** i.e., well off **125 Hallowmas** All Saints' Day, November 1 **127 All-hallond eve** Halloween, October 31. **129 a lower chair** i.e., an easy chair (?) **130 Bunch of Grapes** (It was not uncommon to designate particular rooms in inns by such names.)

FROTH I have so, because it is an open room and good for winter.

POMPEY Why, very well, then. I hope here be truths.

ANGELO
This will last out a night in Russia,
When nights are longest there. I'll take my leave
And leave you to the hearing of the cause,
Hoping you'll find good cause to whip them all.

ESCALUS
I think no less. Good morrow to Your Lordship.
Exit [*Angelo*].
Now, sir, come on. What was done to Elbow's wife, once more?

POMPEY Once, sir? There was nothing done to her once.

ELBOW I beseech you, sir, ask him what this man did to my wife.

POMPEY I beseech Your Honor, ask me.

ESCALUS Well, sir, what did this gentleman to her?

POMPEY I beseech you, sir, look in this gentleman's face. Good Master Froth, look upon His Honor; 'tis for a good purpose. Doth Your Honor mark his face?

ESCALUS Ay, sir, very well.

POMPEY Nay, I beseech you, mark it well.

ESCALUS Well, I do so.

POMPEY Doth Your Honor see any harm in his face?

ESCALUS Why, no.

POMPEY I'll be supposed upon a book, his face is the worst thing about him. Good, then; if his face be the worst thing about him, how could Master Froth do the Constable's wife any harm? I would know that of Your Honor.

ESCALUS He's in the right, Constable. What say you to it?

ELBOW First, an it like you, the house is a respected house; next, this is a respected fellow; and his mistress is a respected woman.

POMPEY By this hand, sir, his wife is a more respected person than any of us all.

ELBOW Varlet, thou liest! Thou liest, wicked varlet! The time is yet to come that she was ever respected with man, woman, or child.

POMPEY Sir, she was respected with him before he married with her.

ESCALUS Which is the wiser here, Justice or Iniquity?— Is this true?

ELBOW O thou caitiff! O thou varlet! O thou wicked Hannibal! I respected with her before I was married to her?—If ever I was respected with her, or she with me, let not Your Worship think me the poor Duke's officer.—Prove this, thou wicked Hannibal, or I'll have mine action of battery on thee.

ESCALUS If he took you a box o'th'ear, you might have your action of slander too.

ELBOW Marry, I thank Your good Worship for it. What is't Your Worship's pleasure I shall do with this wicked caitiff?

ESCALUS Truly, officer, because he hath some offenses in him that thou wouldst discover if thou couldst, let him continue in his courses till thou know'st what they are.

ELBOW Marry, I thank Your Worship for it.—Thou see'st, thou wicked varlet, now, what's come upon thee: thou art to continue now, thou varlet, thou art to continue.

ESCALUS [*to Froth*] Where were you born, friend?

FROTH Here in Vienna, sir.

ESCALUS Are you of fourscore pounds a year?

FROTH Yes, an't please you, sir.

ESCALUS So. [*To Pompey*] What trade are you of, sir?

POMPEY A tapster, a poor widow's tapster.

ESCALUS Your mistress' name?

POMPEY Mistress Overdone.

ESCALUS Hath she had any more than one husband?

POMPEY Nine, sir. Overdone by the last.

ESCALUS Nine?—Come hither to me, Master Froth. Master Froth, I would not have you acquainted with tapsters. They will draw you, Master Froth, and you will hang them. Get you gone, and let me hear no more of you.

FROTH I thank Your Worship. For mine own part, I never come into any room in a taphouse but I am drawn in.

ESCALUS Well, no more of it, Master Froth. Farewell.
[*Exit Froth.*]
Come you hither to me, Master Tapster. What's your name, Master Tapster?

POMPEY Pompey.

ESCALUS What else?

POMPEY Bum, sir.

ESCALUS Troth, and your bum is the greatest thing about you, so that in the beastliest sense you are Pompey the Great. Pompey, you are partly a bawd, Pompey, howsoever you color it in being a tapster, are you not? Come, tell me true. It shall be the better for you.

POMPEY Truly, sir, I am a poor fellow that would live.

ESCALUS How would you live, Pompey? By being a bawd? What do you think of the trade, Pompey? Is it a lawful trade?

POMPEY If the law would allow it, sir.

132 open public **137 cause** case. (With word play on *cause,* "reason," in the next line. See also the play on *leave* in 136–7.) **139 I . . . less** I think so, too. **140 done** (Pompey, in his answer, uses *done* in a sexual sense.) **143 once** only once. (Pompey replies wittily to Escalus's *once more* in 141, meaning "once again.") **150 mark** observe **156 supposed** (A malapropism for "deposed," i.e., sworn.) **book** i.e., Bible **163 an it like** if it please. **respected** (For "suspected.") **173 Justice or Iniquity** (Personified characters in a morality play.) **175 caitiff** knave, villain. **176 Hannibal** (A blunder for "cannibal," perhaps also suggested by the fact that Hannibal and Pompey were both famous generals in the classical world.)

180 battery (An error for "slander," as Escalus amusedly points out.) **181 took** gave. **o'** on **187 discover** (1) detect (2) reveal **188 courses** courses of action **192 continue** (Elbow may confuse the word with its opposite.) **195 of** possessed of **202 Overdone . . . last** (1) Her name, Overdone, was given her by her last husband (2) She has been worn out *(overdone)* by the last one. **205 draw** (1) cheat, take in (2) empty, deplete. (With a pun on the tapster's trade of drawing liquor from a barrel, and on Froth's name.) (3) disembowel, or drag to execution **206 will hang them** will be the cause of their hanging. **209 taphouse** alehouse **210 drawn in** enticed. (Still another meaning of *draw,* line 205.) **220 color** disguise **223 live** make a living

ESCALUS But the law will not allow it, Pompey; nor it
shall not be allowed in Vienna.

POMPEY Does Your Worship mean to geld and splay all 229
the youth of the city?

ESCALUS No, Pompey.

POMPEY Truly, sir, in my poor opinion they will to't
then. If Your Worship will take order for the drabs and 233
the knaves, you need not to fear the bawds.

ESCALUS There is pretty orders beginning, I can tell
you. It is but heading and hanging. 236

POMPEY If you head and hang all that offend that way
but for ten year together, you'll be glad to give out a 238
commission for more heads. If this law hold in Vienna 239
ten year, I'll rent the fairest house in it after threepence 240
a bay. If you live to see this come to pass, say Pompey 241
told you so.

ESCALUS Thank you, good Pompey. And, in requital of 243
your prophecy, hark you: I advise you let me not find
you before me again upon any complaint whatsoever;
no, not for dwelling where you do. If I do, Pompey, I
shall beat you to your tent and prove a shrewd Caesar 247
to you; in plain dealing, Pompey, I shall have you
whipped. So for this time, Pompey, fare you well.

POMPEY I thank Your Worship for your good counsel.
[*Aside*] But I shall follow it as the flesh and fortune
shall better determine.
Whip me? No, no, let carman whip his jade. 253
The valiant heart's not whipped out of his trade.
Exit.

ESCALUS Come hither to me, Master Elbow; come
hither, Master Constable. How long have you been in
this place of constable?

ELBOW Seven year and a half, sir.

ESCALUS I thought, by the readiness in the office, you 259
had continued in it some time. You say, seven years
together?

ELBOW And a half, sir.

ESCALUS Alas, it hath been great pains to you. They do
you wrong to put you so oft upon't. Are there not
men in your ward sufficient to serve it? 265

ELBOW Faith, sir, few of any wit in such matters. As
they are chosen, they are glad to choose me for them. 267
I do it for some piece of money and go through with 268
all. 269

ESCALUS Look you bring me in the names of some six 270
or seven, the most sufficient of your parish.

ELBOW To Your Worship's house, sir?

ESCALUS To my house. Fare you well. [*Exit Elbow.*]
What's o'clock, think you?

JUSTICE Eleven, sir.

ESCALUS
I pray you home to dinner with me. 276

JUSTICE I humbly thank you.

ESCALUS
It grieves me for the death of Claudio;
But there's no remedy.

JUSTICE Lord Angelo is severe.

ESCALUS It is but needful.
Mercy is not itself, that oft looks so; 281
Pardon is still the nurse of second woe. 282
But yet—poor Claudio! There is no remedy.
Come, sir. *Exeunt.*

✤

2.2

Enter Provost [and a] Servant.

SERVANT
He's hearing of a cause; he will come straight. 1
I'll tell him of you.

PROVOST Pray you, do. [*Exit Servant.*]
I'll know
His pleasure; maybe he will relent. Alas,
He hath but as offended in a dream! 4
All sects, all ages smack of this vice—and he 5
To die for't!

Enter Angelo.

ANGELO Now, what's the matter, Provost?

PROVOST
Is it your will Claudio shall die tomorrow?

ANGELO
Did not I tell thee yea? Hadst thou not order?
Why dost thou ask again?

PROVOST Lest I might be too rash.
Under your good correction, I have seen 11
When, after execution, judgment hath
Repented o'er his doom. 13

ANGELO Go to; let that be mine. 14
Do you your office, or give up your place,
And you shall well be spared. 16

PROVOST I crave Your Honor's pardon.
What shall be done, sir, with the groaning Juliet? 18
She's very near her hour. 19

ANGELO Dispose of her
To some more fitter place, and that with speed.

[*Enter a Servant.*]

229 splay spay **233 take order** take measures. **drabs** prostitutes **236 It . . . hanging** Beheading and hanging are the order of the day. **238 year together** years at a stretch **239 commission** order. **hold** remain in force **240 after** at the rate of **241 bay** division of a house included under one gable. **243 requital of** return for **247 shrewd** harsh, severe. **Caesar** (Julius Caesar defeated Pompey at Pharsalia in 48 B.C.) **253 carman** cart driver. **jade** broken-down horse. **259 readiness** proficiency, alacrity **265 sufficient** able **267 for them** i.e., to take their place. **268–9 go . . . all** i.e., perform my duties thoroughly. **270 Look** See to it that

276 dinner (Dinner was customarily eaten just before midday.) **281 Mercy . . . so** i.e., What seems merciful may not really be so (since it may encourage crime and hence lead to more punishment) **282 Pardon . . . woe** i.e., pardon continually nurtures and encourages a repetition of offenses and hence of punishment.
2.2 Location: Adjacent to the court of justice, perhaps at Angelo's official residence.
1 hearing . . . cause listening to a case. **straight** immediately. **4 He . . . dream** i.e., Claudio offended only as if in a dream. **5 All sects . . . smack** All classes of people of all ages (and in all past history) partake **11 Under . . . correction** i.e., Allow me to say **13 doom** sentence. **14 mine** my business. **16 well be spared** easily be done without. **18 groaning** (with labor pains) **19 hour** time of delivery.

SERVANT
Here is the sister of the man condemned
Desires access to you.
ANGELO Hath he a sister? 22
PROVOST
Ay, my good lord, a very virtuous maid,
And to be shortly of a sisterhood,
If not already.
ANGELO Well, let her be admitted.
[Exit Servant.]
See you the fornicatress be removed.
Let her have needful but not lavish means.
There shall be order for't.

Enter Lucio and Isabella.

PROVOST Save Your Honor! 28
ANGELO *[to Provost]*
Stay a little while. *[To Isabella]* You're welcome.
What's your will?
ISABELLA
I am a woeful suitor to Your Honor,
Please but Your Honor hear me.
ANGELO Well, what's your suit? 31
ISABELLA
There is a vice that most I do abhor,
And most desire should meet the blow of justice,
For which I would not plead, but that I must;
For which I must not plead, but that I am
At war twixt will and will not.
ANGELO Well, the matter?
ISABELLA
I have a brother is condemned to die.
I do beseech you, let it be his fault, 38
And not my brother.
PROVOST *[aside]* Heaven give thee moving graces!
ANGELO
Condemn the fault, and not the actor of it?
Why, every fault's condemned ere it be done.
Mine were the very cipher of a function,
To fine the faults, whose fine stands in record, 43
And let go by the actor.
ISABELLA Oh, just but severe law!
I had a brother, then. Heaven keep your honor!
LUCIO *[aside to Isabella]*
Give't not o'er so. To him again, entreat him! 47
Kneel down before him; hang upon his gown.
You are too cold. If you should need a pin, 49
You could not with more tame a tongue desire it.
To him, I say!
ISABELLA *[to Angelo]*
Must he needs die?
ANGELO Maiden, no remedy.
ISABELLA
Yes, I do think that you might pardon him,
And neither heaven nor man grieve at the mercy.

ANGELO
I will not do't.
ISABELLA But can you, if you would?
ANGELO
Look what I will not, that I cannot do. 56
ISABELLA
But might you do't, and do the world no wrong,
If so your heart were touched with that remorse 58
As mine is to him?
ANGELO He's sentenced. 'Tis too late.
LUCIO *[aside to Isabella]* You are too cold.
ISABELLA
Too late? Why, no; I that do speak a word
May call it back again. Well, believe this:
No ceremony that to great ones 'longs, 64
Not the king's crown, nor the deputed sword, 65
The marshal's truncheon, nor the judge's robe 66
Become them with one half so good a grace
As mercy does.
If he had been as you, and you as he,
You would have slipped like him; but he, like you, 70
Would not have been so stern.
ANGELO Pray you, begone.
ISABELLA
I would to heaven I had your potency,
And you were Isabel. Should it then be thus?
No, I would tell what 'twere to be a judge 74
And what a prisoner.
LUCIO *[aside to Isabella]* Ay, touch him; there's the vein. 75
ANGELO
Your brother is a forfeit of the law, 76
And you but waste your words.
ISABELLA Alas, alas!
Why, all the souls that were were forfeit once, 78
And He that might the vantage best have took 79
Found out the remedy. How would you be, 80
If He, which is the top of judgment, should 81
But judge you as you are? Oh, think on that,
And mercy then will breathe within your lips,
Like man new-made.
ANGELO Be you content, fair maid. 84
It is the law, not I, condemn your brother.
Were he my kinsman, brother, or my son,
It should be thus with him. He must die tomorrow.
ISABELLA
Tomorrow! Oh, that's sudden! Spare him, spare him!
He's not prepared for death. Even for our kitchens
We kill the fowl of season. Shall we serve heaven 90
With less respect than we do minister

22 Desires who desires **28 Save** May God save **31 Please . . . me** if Your Honor will please hear me. **38 let . . . fault** i.e., let the fault die, be condemned **43 To fine . . . record** to punish only the faults, for which the penalty stands in the statute books **47 Give't . . . so** Don't give up so soon. **49 need a pin** i.e., ask for the smallest trifle

56 Look what Whatever **58 remorse** pity **64 'longs** is fitting, belongs **65 deputed sword** sword of justice entrusted to the ruler **66 truncheon** staff borne by military officers **70 like you** in your situation **74 tell** make known **75 there's the vein** i.e., that's the right approach. (*Vein* means "lode to be profitably mined," or perhaps "vein for bloodletting.") **76 a forfeit** one who must incur the penalty **78–80 Why . . . remedy** (A reference to God's redemption of sinful humanity when He would have been justified in destroying humankind.) **81 top of judgment** supreme judge **84 new-made** i.e., created new by salvation, born again. **90 of season** that is in season and properly mature.

To our gross selves? Good, good my lord, bethink
you:
Who is it that hath died for this offense?
There's many have committed it.
LUCIO [*aside to Isabella*] Ay, well said.
ANGELO
The law hath not been dead, though it hath slept.
Those many had not dared to do that evil
If the first that did th'edict infringe
Had answered for his deed. Now 'tis awake,
Takes note of what is done, and like a prophet
Looks in a glass that shows what future evils,
Either now, or by remissness new-conceived
And so in progress to be hatched and born,
Are now to have no successive degrees,
But ere they live, to end.
ISABELLA Yet show some pity.
ANGELO
I show it most of all when I show justice;
For then I pity those I do not know,
Which a dismissed offense would after gall,
And do him right that, answering one foul wrong,
Lives not to act another. Be satisfied;
Your brother dies tomorrow. Be content.
ISABELLA
So you must be the first that gives this sentence,
And he that suffers. Oh, it is excellent
To have a giant's strength, but it is tyrannous
To use it like a giant.
LUCIO [*aside to Isabella*] That's well said.
ISABELLA Could great men thunder
As Jove himself does, Jove would never be quiet,
For every pelting, petty officer
Would use his heaven for thunder,
Nothing but thunder. Merciful heaven,
Thou rather with thy sharp and sulfurous bolt
Splits the unwedgeable and gnarlèd oak
Than the soft myrtle; but man, proud man,
Dressed in a little brief authority,
Most ignorant of what he's most assured,
His glassy essence, like an angry ape
Plays such fantastic tricks before high heaven
As makes the angels weep; who, with our spleens,
Would all themselves laugh mortal.
LUCIO [*aside to Isabella*]
Oh, to him, to him, wench! He will relent.
He's coming, I perceive't.
PROVOST [*aside*] Pray heaven she win him!
ISABELLA
We cannot weigh our brother with ourself.
Great men may jest with saints; 'tis wit in them,
But in the less, foul profanation.
LUCIO [*aside to Isabella*]
Thou'rt i'th' right, girl. More o' that.
ISABELLA
That in the captain's but a choleric word
Which in the soldier is flat blasphemy.
LUCIO [*aside to Isabella*] Art advised o' that? More on't.
ANGELO
Why do you put these sayings upon me?
ISABELLA
Because authority, though it err like others,
Hath yet a kind of medicine in itself
That skins the vice o'th' top. Go to your bosom;
Knock there, and ask your heart what it doth know
That's like my brother's fault. If it confess
A natural guiltiness such as is his,
Let it not sound a thought upon your tongue
Against my brother's life.
ANGELO [*aside*] She speaks, and 'tis such sense
That my sense breeds with it.—Fare you well.
[*He starts to go.*]
ISABELLA Gentle my lord, turn back.
ANGELO
I will bethink me. Come again tomorrow.
ISABELLA
Hark how I'll bribe you. Good my lord, turn back.
ANGELO How? Bribe me?
ISABELLA
Ay, with such gifts that heaven shall share with you.
LUCIO [*aside to Isabella*] You had marred all else.
ISABELLA
Not with fond sicles of the tested gold,
Or stones whose rate are either rich or poor
As fancy values them, but with true prayers
That shall be up at heaven and enter there
Ere sunrise—prayers from preservèd souls,

100 glass magic crystal **101 Either . . . new-conceived** i.e., both evils already hatched and those that would be encouraged by continued laxity of enforcement **102 in progress** in the course of time **103 successive degrees** successors or future stages. (Future evils are to be aborted before they are born and propagate.) **104 ere they live** i.e., before they can be committed **107 Which . . . gall** whom a forgiven offense would give trouble to later on **108 do . . . answering** do justice to that person who, by paying the penalty for **116 be quiet** have any quiet **117 pelting** paltry **120 bolt** thunderbolt **121 unwedgeable** unsplittable **124–5 Most . . . essence** i.e., most ignorant of what religion teaches him to know, his spiritual nature; or, of that which is most certainly his natural frailty **125 angry ape** i.e., ludicrous buffoon **127–8 who . . . mortal** who, if they had the organs of laughter that we have, would laugh themselves mortal, becoming like us. (The *spleen* was thought to be the seat of laughter.)

130 coming coming around **131–3 We . . . profanation** We cannot judge our fellow mortals by the same standards we use in judging ourselves. Persons of great authority are allowed liberties that in lesser persons would be condemned as blasphemies. (Lines 135–6 make much the same point.) **135 That . . . word** i.e., We treat the abusive language a commanding officer uses in anger merely as an outburst; we are indulgent toward the failings of *great men.* (As in lines 131–3, Isabella's point seems to be that our judgments are biased by our inordinate regard for authority.) **137 advised** informed, aware. **on't** of it. **138 put . . . me** apply these sayings to me. **139–41 Because . . . top** Because authority, though prone to sinfulness like all of humankind, has a way of seeming to heal itself by covering over the boil with a film of skin, leaving the sore unhealed. **147–8 sense . . . sense** import . . . sensuality **149 Gentle my lord** My noble lord **150 bethink me** think it over. **153 that** as **154 else** otherwise. **155 Not . . . gold** Not with foolishly valued shekels of pure gold. (*Shekels* are Hebrew coins.) **156–7 Or . . . them** or jewels the value of which is merely subjective and transitory **159 preservèd souls** devout religious who have withdrawn from the world

From fasting maids whose minds are dedicate
To nothing temporal.

ANGELO Well, come to me tomorrow.

LUCIO [*aside to Isabella*] Go to, 'tis well. Away!

ISABELLA
Heaven keep Your Honor safe!

ANGELO [*aside*] Amen!
For I am that way going to temptation,
Where prayers cross.

ISABELLA At what hour tomorrow
Shall I attend Your Lordship?

ANGELO At any time 'fore noon.

ISABELLA Save Your Honor!

[*Exeunt Isabella, Lucio, and Provost.*]

ANGELO From thee, even from thy virtue!
What's this, what's this? Is this her fault or mine?
The tempter or the tempted, who sins most, ha?
Not she, nor doth she tempt; but it is I
That, lying by the violet in the sun,
Do, as the carrion does, not as the flower,
Corrupt with virtuous season. Can it be
That modesty may more betray our sense
Than woman's lightness? Having waste ground enough,
Shall we desire to raze the sanctuary
And pitch our evils there? Oh, fie, fie, fie!
What dost thou, or what art thou, Angelo?
Dost thou desire her foully for those things
That make her good? Oh, let her brother live!
Thieves for their robbery have authority
When judges steal themselves. What, do I love her,
That I desire to hear her speak again
And feast upon her eyes? What is't I dream on?
Oh, cunning enemy that, to catch a saint,
With saints dost bait thy hook! Most dangerous
Is that temptation that doth goad us on
To sin in loving virtue. Never could the strumpet,
With all her double vigor—art and nature—
Once stir my temper; but this virtuous maid
Subdues me quite. Ever till now,
When men were fond, I smiled and wondered how.

Exit.

✣

2.3

Enter, [*meeting,*] *Duke* [*disguised as a friar*] *and Provost.*

DUKE
Hail to you, Provost—so I think you are.

PROVOST
I am the Provost. What's your will, good Friar?

DUKE
Bound by my charity and my blest order,
I come to visit the afflicted spirits
Here in the prison. Do me the common right
To let me see them and to make me know
The nature of their crimes, that I may minister
To them accordingly.

PROVOST
I would do more than that, if more were needful.

Enter Juliet.

Look, here comes one: a gentlewoman of mine,
Who, falling in the flaws of her own youth,
Hath blistered her report. She is with child,
And he that got it, sentenced—a young man
More fit to do another such offense
Than die for this.

DUKE
When must he die?

PROVOST As I do think, tomorrow.
[*To Juliet*] I have provided for you. Stay awhile,
And you shall be conducted.

DUKE
Repent you, fair one, of the sin you carry?

JULIET
I do, and bear the shame most patiently.

DUKE
I'll teach you how you shall arraign your conscience,
And try your penitence, if it be sound
Or hollowly put on.

JULIET I'll gladly learn.

DUKE Love you the man that wronged you?

JULIET
Yes, as I love the woman that wronged him.

DUKE
So then it seems your most offenseful act
Was mutually committed?

JULIET Mutually.

DUKE
Then was your sin of heavier kind than his.

JULIET
I do confess it and repent it, Father.

DUKE
'Tis meet so, daughter. But lest you do repent
As that the sin hath brought you to this shame,
Which sorrow is always toward ourselves, not heaven,
Showing we would not spare heaven as we love it,
But as we stand in fear—

JULIET
I do repent me as it is an evil,

160 fasting maids i.e., nuns. **dedicate** dedicated **165 cross** are at cross purposes. **168 Save** May God save **174 carrion** decaying flesh **175 Corrupt . . . season** i.e., putrefy while all else flourishes. (The warmth of flowering time causes the violet, Isabella, to blossom but causes the carrion lying beside it, Angelo, to rot.) **176 modesty** virtue, chastity. **sense** sensual nature **177 lightness** immodesty, lust. **179 pitch our evils there** i.e., erect a privy, not on *waste ground* (line 177), but on sanctified ground. (*Evils* also has the more common meaning of "wickedness.") **187 enemy** i.e., Satan **191 double . . . nature** twofold power (of alluring men) through artifice and a sensuous nature **192 temper** temperament **194 fond** foolishly in love
2.3 Location: A prison.

5 common right i.e., right of all clerics **11 flaws** (1) weaknesses, fissures (2) sudden gusts (of passion) **12 blistered her report** marred her reputation. **13 got** begot **17 provided** provided a place to stay **18 conducted** taken there. **21 arraign** accuse **22 try** test **23 hollowly** falsely **31 'Tis meet so** It is fitting that you do so **32 As that** merely because **33 toward ourselves** i.e., narrowly self-concerned rather than loving virtue for its own sake **34 Showing . . . it** showing that we wish to avoid offending heaven not out of sheer love of goodness

And take the shame with joy.

DUKE There rest.
Your partner, as I hear, must die tomorrow,
And I am going with instruction to him.
Grace go with you. *Benedicite!* *Exit.*

JULIET
Must die tomorrow? O injurious love,
That respites me a life whose very comfort
Is still a dying horror!

PROVOST 'Tis pity of him. *Exeunt.*

✤

2.4

Enter Angelo.

ANGELO
When I would pray and think, I think and pray
To several subjects. Heaven hath my empty words,
Whilst my invention, hearing not my tongue,
Anchors on Isabel; Heaven in my mouth,
As if I did but only chew His name,
And in my heart the strong and swelling evil
Of my conception. The state, whereon I studied,
Is like a good thing, being often read,
Grown sere and tedious. Yea, my gravity,
Wherein—let no man hear me—I take pride,
Could I with boot change for an idle plume,
Which the air beats for vain. O place, O form,
How often dost thou with thy case, thy habit,
Wrench awe from fools and tie the wiser souls
To thy false seeming! Blood, thou art blood.
Let's write "good angel" on the devil's horn,
'Tis not the devil's crest.

Enter Servant.

How now? Who's there?

SERVANT
One Isabel, a sister, desires access to you.

ANGELO Teach her the way. [*Exit Servant.*]
Oh, heavens!
Why does my blood thus muster to my heart,
Making both it unable for itself
And dispossessing all my other parts
Of necessary fitness?
So play the foolish throngs with one that swoons,
Come all to help him, and so stop the air
By which he should revive; and even so
The general subject to a well-wished king
Quit their own part and in obsequious fondness
Crowd to his presence, where their untaught love
Must needs appear offense.

Enter Isabella.

How now, fair maid?

ISABELLA I am come to know your pleasure.

ANGELO
That you might know it would much better please me
Than to demand what 'tis. Your brother cannot live.

ISABELLA
Even so. Heaven keep Your Honor!
[*She turns to leave.*]

ANGELO
Yet may he live awhile; and, it may be,
As long as you or I. Yet he must die.

ISABELLA Under your sentence?

ANGELO Yea.

ISABELLA
When, I beseech you? That in his reprieve,
Longer or shorter, he may be so fitted
That his soul sicken not.

ANGELO
Ha? Fie, these filthy vices! It were as good
To pardon him that hath from nature stolen
A man already made, as to remit
Their saucy sweetness that do coin heaven's image
In stamps that are forbid. 'Tis all as easy
Falsely to take away a life true made
As to put metal in restrainèd means
To make a false one.

ISABELLA
'Tis set down so in heaven, but not in earth.

ANGELO
Say you so? Then I shall pose you quickly:
Which had you rather, that the most just law
Now took your brother's life, or, to redeem him,
Give up your body to such sweet uncleanness

37 There rest. Hold fast to that truth. **40 *Benedicite!*** Blessings on you! **41–3 O . . . horror!** i.e., O sinful pregnancy, that prolongs a life whose greatest comfort will always be a deadly horror! (Pregnancy could save a woman from being executed. However, *love* is sometimes emended to *law*.) **43 pity of** a pity about

2.4 Location: Angelo's official residence.

2 several separate **3 invention** imagination **5 His** i.e., heaven's, God's **7 conception** thought. **The state** Statecraft **9 sere** withered, old **11–12 Could . . . vain** I could willingly exchange (my gravity) for the frivolity of a pleasure-loving gallant, sporting a feather that seems to beat the air in its vanity (or, perhaps, is beaten by the air in reproof of its vanity). **12 O place, O form** O authority of high position, O ceremonial dignity of office **13 thy case . . . habit** your mere outward appearance and garb **14–15 Wrench . . . seeming** intimidate ordinary foolish men and subjugate even the wise to the seeming virtue of authority. **15 Blood . . . blood** i.e., No position of authority or birth, no matter how lofty, can protect a person from his own lustful appetites. **16–17 Let's . . . crest** i.e., No matter how hard we try to disguise evil under the semblance of good, it remains recognizably evil still. (In heraldic terms, the devil is known by his baleful horns; the heraldic crest on his coat of arms does not alter his true identity.) **19 Teach** Show **20 muster to** assemble like soldiers in

21 unable ineffectual **24 play** behave **27 general subject** i.e., commoners, subjects. **well-wished** attended by good wishes **28 Quit . . . part** abandon their proper function and (politely distant) place **29 untaught** ignorant, unmannerly **30 Must needs** will necessarily **32–3 That . . . 'tis** i.e., I wish you could know the nature of my desire without your asking and my having to be explicit. (*Know* suggests carnal knowledge.) **34 Even so** So be it. **40 fitted** prepared **42–6 It were . . . forbid** One might as well pardon the murderer of a man already alive as pardon the wanton pleasures of those persons who produce illegitimate offspring, like counterfeit coiners. (*Heaven's image* is humankind, made in God's likeness; Genesis 1:27.) **48 metal** i.e., the metal used in coining (lines 45–6), with a play on *mettle*, natural vigor or spirit. **restrainèd** prohibited, illicit (both in counterfeiting coinage and in begetting illegitimate children) **50 'Tis . . . earth** i.e., Equating murder and bastardizing accords with divine law but not with human law, according to which murder is more heinous. **51 pose you** put a perplexing question to you

As she that he hath stained?

ISABELLA
Sir, believe this,
I had rather give my body than my soul.

ANGELO
I talk not of your soul. Our compelled sins
Stand more for number than for account.

ISABELLA
How say you?

ANGELO
Nay, I'll not warrant that, for I can speak
Against the thing I say. Answer to this:
I, now the voice of the recorded law,
Pronounce a sentence on your brother's life;
Might there not be a charity in sin
To save this brother's life?

ISABELLA
Please you to do't,
I'll take it as a peril to my soul;
It is no sin at all, but charity.

ANGELO
Pleased you to do't at peril of your soul
Were equal poise of sin and charity.

ISABELLA
That I do beg his life, if it be sin,
Heaven let me bear it! You granting of my suit,
If that be sin, I'll make it my morn prayer
To have it added to the faults of mine,
And nothing of your answer.

ANGELO
Nay, but hear me.
Your sense pursues not mine. Either you are ignorant
Or seem so craftily; and that's not good.

ISABELLA
Let me be ignorant, and in nothing good,
But graciously to know I am no better.

ANGELO
Thus wisdom wishes to appear most bright
When it doth tax itself, as these black masks
Proclaim an enshield beauty ten times louder
Than beauty could, displayed. But mark me.
To be receivèd plain, I'll speak more gross:
Your brother is to die.

ISABELLA So.

ANGELO
And his offense is so, as it appears,
Accountant to the law upon that pain.

ISABELLA True.

ANGELO
Admit no other way to save his life—
As I subscribe not that, nor any other,
But in the loss of question—that you, his sister,
Finding yourself desired of such a person
Whose credit with the judge, or own great place,
Could fetch your brother from the manacles
Of the all-binding law; and that there were
No earthly means to save him, but that either
You must lay down the treasures of your body
To this supposed, or else to let him suffer.
What would you do?

ISABELLA
As much for my poor brother as myself:
That is, were I under the terms of death,
Th'impression of keen whips I'd wear as rubies,
And strip myself to death as to a bed
That longing have been sick for, ere I'd yield
My body up to shame.

ANGELO Then must your brother die.

ISABELLA And 'twere the cheaper way.
Better it were a brother died at once
Than that a sister, by redeeming him,
Should die forever.

ANGELO
Were not you then as cruel as the sentence
That you have slandered so?

ISABELLA
Ignomy in ransom and free pardon
Are of two houses. Lawful mercy
Is nothing kin to foul redemption.

ANGELO
You seemed of late to make the law a tyrant,
And rather proved the sliding of your brother
A merriment than a vice.

ISABELLA
Oh, pardon me, my lord. It oft falls out,
To have what we would have, we speak not what
we mean.
I something do excuse the thing I hate
For his advantage that I dearly love.

ANGELO
We are all frail.

ISABELLA
Else let my brother die,
If not a fedary but only he
Owe and succeed thy weakness.

ANGELO Nay, women are frail too.

ISABELLA
Ay, as the glasses where they view themselves,
Which are as easy broke as they make forms.

56 give i.e., give to death or punishment. (Isabella avoids or does not understand the drift of the question.) **57–8 Our . . . account** Our sins committed under compulsion are recorded but not charged to our spiritual account. **59 I'll . . . that** i.e., I'm not necessarily endorsing the view I just expressed **64 Please you** If you please **65 take** accept **67 Pleased** If it pleased **68 Were equal poise** there would be equal balance **73 of your answer** to which you will have to answer. **77 graciously** through divine grace **79 tax itself** accuse itself (of ignorance). **these** (Generically referring to any.) **80 enshield** shielded, protected from view behind the black masks **82 receivèd plain** plainly understood. **gross** (1) openly (2) offensively **86 Accountant** accountable. **pain** penalty. **88 Admit** Suppose **89–90 As . . . question** since I will admit no alternative possibility in our discussion. (*Loss of question* means "forfeiting the terms of our debate.")

91 of by **97 supposed** hypothetical person. **him** i.e., Claudio **100 terms** sentence **103 That . . . for** i.e., that I have been sick with longing for. (Isabella's images are of love, death, and flagellation.) **107 died at once** should die once for all, rather than *die forever* (line 109) in the death of the soul through sin **112–14 Ignomy . . . redemption** Being ransomed under ignominious circumstances and being released without conditions are two entirely different things. Mercy under law bears no relation to being spared under foul stipulations. **116 proved** argued **120 something** to some extent **123 fedary** confederate, companion who is equally guilty **124 Owe . . . weakness** possess and inherit the weakness you speak of, or the weakness to which all men as a class are prone. (Isabella argues that Claudio should die only if he is the only man who is frail.) **126 glasses** mirrors **127 forms** (1) images (2) copies of themselves, i.e., children

Women? Help, heaven! Men their creation mar 128
In profiting by them. Nay, call us ten times frail, 129
For we are soft as our complexions are, 130
And credulous to false prints.

ANGELO I think it well. 131
And from this testimony of your own sex— 132
Since I suppose we are made to be no stronger 133
Than faults may shake our frames—let me be bold. 134
I do arrest your words. Be that you are, 135
That is, a woman; if you be more, you're none. 136
If you be one, as you are well expressed 137
By all external warrants, show it now 138
By putting on the destined livery. 139

ISABELLA
I have no tongue but one. Gentle my lord, 140
Let me entreat you speak the former language. 141

ANGELO Plainly conceive, I love you.

ISABELLA My brother did love Juliet,
And you tell me that he shall die for't.

ANGELO
He shall not, Isabel, if you give me love.

ISABELLA
I know your virtue hath a license in't, 146
Which seems a little fouler than it is 147
To pluck on others.

ANGELO Believe me, on mine honor, 148
My words express my purpose.

ISABELLA
Ha! Little honor to be much believed,
And most pernicious purpose! Seeming, seeming!
I will proclaim thee, Angelo, look for't!
Sign me a present pardon for my brother, 153
Or with an outstretched throat I'll tell the world aloud
What man thou art.

ANGELO Who will believe thee, Isabel?
My unsoiled name, th'austereness of my life,
My vouch against you, and my place i'th' state 157
Will so your accusation overweigh
That you shall stifle in your own report
And smell of calumny. I have begun, 160
And now I give my sensual race the rein. 161
Fit thy consent to my sharp appetite;
Lay by all nicety and prolixious blushes 163
That banish what they sue for. Redeem thy brother 164
By yielding up thy body to my will,
Or else he must not only die the death, 166
But thy unkindness shall his death draw out
To ling'ring sufferance. Answer me tomorrow, 168
Or, by the affection that now guides me most, 169
I'll prove a tyrant to him. As for you,
Say what you can, my false o'erweighs your true.
Exit.

ISABELLA
To whom should I complain? Did I tell this, 172
Who would believe me? O perilous mouths, 173
That bear in them one and the selfsame tongue, 174
Either of condemnation or approof, 175
Bidding the law make curtsy to their will, 176
Hooking both right and wrong to th'appetite, 177
To follow as it draws! I'll to my brother. 178
Though he hath fall'n by prompture of the blood, 179
Yet hath he in him such a mind of honor
That, had he twenty heads to tender down 181
On twenty bloody blocks, he'd yield them up
Before his sister should her body stoop
To such abhorred pollution.
Then, Isabel, live chaste, and, brother, die;
More than our brother is our chastity.
I'll tell him yet of Angelo's request,
And fit his mind to death, for his soul's rest. *Exit.*

✣

3.1

Enter Duke [disguised as before], Claudio, and Provost.

DUKE
So then you hope of pardon from Lord Angelo?

CLAUDIO
The miserable have no other medicine
But only hope.
I have hope to live and am prepared to die.

DUKE
Be absolute for death. Either death or life
Shall thereby be the sweeter. Reason thus with life:
If I do lose thee, I do lose a thing
That none but fools would keep. A breath thou art,
Servile to all the skyey influences 9
That dost this habitation where thou keep'st 10
Hourly afflict. Merely, thou art death's fool, 11
For him thou labor'st by thy flight to shun,
And yet run'st toward him still. Thou art not noble, 13

128–9 Men . . . them Men mar their creation in God's likeness by taking advantage of women. **130 complexions** constitutions, appearance **131 credulous . . . prints** susceptible to false impressions. (The metaphor is from the stamping of coins and other metal.) **132 of** about **133 we** i.e., men and women **134 Than** than that **135 arrest your words** take what you have said and hold you to it. **that** what **136 if . . . none** i.e., if you insist on remaining a virgin and free of fleshly desire, you are no woman as we have defined the term—that is, frail and susceptible. **137–8 expressed . . . warrants** shown to be by your physical beauty **139 putting . . . livery** i.e., assuming the characteristic frailty that all women possess. **140 tongue** language **141 speak . . . language** speak to be understood, in the language I understand. **146–8 I know . . . others** i.e., I am sure that you, out of virtuous motives, are speaking licentiously (and with the license of authority) in order to put me to the test. **153 present** immediate **157 vouch** allegation **160 calumny** slander. **161 I give . . . rein** I give free rein to my sensual desires to gallop as they please. **163–4 Lay . . . sue for** Set aside all the coyness and time-wasting blushes that make a pretense of repulsing the embrace they actually beg for.

166 die the death be put to death **168 sufferance** torture. **169 affection** passion **172 Did I tell** If I told **173–8 O perilous . . . draws!** O dangerous voices of authority, able with one tongue either to condemn or approve, forcing both right and wrong to obey the willful appetite! **179 prompture** prompting, suggestion **181 tender down** lay down in payment
3.1 Location: The prison.
9 skyey influences influence of the stars **10 this habitation** i.e., the earth (and the body as well). **keep'st** dwell **11 Merely** Utterly, only **13 still** always.

For all th'accommodations that thou bear'st
Are nursed by baseness. Thou'rt by no means valiant,
For thou dost fear the soft and tender fork
Of a poor worm. Thy best of rest is sleep,
And that thou oft provok'st, yet grossly fear'st
Thy death, which is no more. Thou art not thyself,
For thou exists on many a thousand grains
That issue out of dust. Happy thou art not,
For what thou hast not, still thou striv'st to get,
And what thou hast, forget'st. Thou art not certain,
For thy complexion shifts to strange effects,
After the moon. If thou art rich, thou'rt poor,
For, like an ass whose back with ingots bows,
Thou bear'st thy heavy riches but a journey,
And death unloads thee. Friend hast thou none,
For thine own bowels which do call thee sire,
The mere effusion of thy proper loins,
Do curse the gout, serpigo, and the rheum
For ending thee no sooner. Thou hast nor youth
nor age,
But as it were an after-dinner's sleep
Dreaming on both, for all thy blessèd youth
Becomes as agèd and doth beg the alms
Of palsied eld; and, when thou art old and rich,
Thou hast neither heat, affection, limb, nor beauty
To make thy riches pleasant. What's yet in this
That bears the name of life? Yet in this life
Lie hid more thousand deaths; yet death we fear,
That makes these odds all even.

CLAUDIO I humbly thank you.
To sue to live, I find I seek to die,
And, seeking death, find life. Let it come on.

Enter Isabella.

ISABELLA
What, ho! Peace here; grace and good company!

PROVOST
Who's there? Come in. The wish deserves a welcome.
[*He goes to greet her.*]

DUKE [*to Claudio*]
Dear sir, ere long I'll visit you again.

CLAUDIO Most holy sir, I thank you.

ISABELLA
My business is a word or two with Claudio.

PROVOST
And very welcome.—Look, signor, here's your sister.

DUKE [*aside to the Provost*] Provost, a word with you.

PROVOST As many as you please.

DUKE
Bring me to hear them speak, where I may be
Concealed. [*The Duke and the Provost withdraw.*]

CLAUDIO Now, sister, what's the comfort?

ISABELLA Why,
As all comforts are: most good, most good indeed.
Lord Angelo, having affairs to heaven,
Intends you for his swift ambassador,
Where you shall be an everlasting leiger.
Therefore your best appointment make with speed;
Tomorrow you set on.

CLAUDIO Is there no remedy?

ISABELLA
None but such remedy as, to save a head,
To cleave a heart in twain.

CLAUDIO But is there any?

ISABELLA Yes, brother, you may live.
There is a devilish mercy in the judge,
If you'll implore it, that will free your life
But fetter you till death.

CLAUDIO Perpetual durance?

ISABELLA
Ay, just; perpetual durance, a restraint,
Though all the world's vastidity you had,
To a determined scope.

CLAUDIO But in what nature?

ISABELLA
In such a one as, you consenting to't,
Would bark your honor from that trunk you bear
And leave you naked.

CLAUDIO Let me know the point.

ISABELLA
Oh, I do fear thee, Claudio, and I quake
Lest thou a feverous life shouldst entertain,
And six or seven winters more respect
Than a perpetual honor. Dar'st thou die?
The sense of death is most in apprehension,
And the poor beetle that we tread upon
In corporal sufferance finds a pang as great
As when a giant dies.

CLAUDIO Why give you me this shame?
Think you I can a resolution fetch
From flow'ry tenderness? If I must die,
I will encounter darkness as a bride
And hug it in mine arms.

ISABELLA
There spake my brother! There my father's grave
Did utter forth a voice. Yes, thou must die.
Thou art too noble to conserve a life

14 accommodations conveniences, civilized comforts **15 nursed by baseness** nurtured by ignoble means. **16 fork** forked tongue **17 worm** (1) snake (2) grave worm. **18 thou oft provok'st** you often invoke, summon **23 certain** steadfast **24 complexion** constitution. **strange effects** new appearances, manifestations **25 After** in obedience to, under the influence of **29 bowels** i.e., offspring **30 mere** very. **proper** own **31 serpigo** a skin eruption. **rheum** catarrh **32 nor youth** neither youth **33 after-dinner's** i.e., afternoon's **34–6 all . . . eld** your happy youth must decline all too soon into old age and become like a beggar, pleading for the little comfort that palsied infirmity can provide. (Youth is penniless and dependent on the aged, whereas the old lack the physical capacity of youth.) **37 heat, affection** vigor, passion **41 makes . . . even** makes all equal. **42 To sue** Suing, petitioning **44 grace** God's grace

57 leiger resident ambassador. **58 appointment** preparation **59 set on** set forward. **66 durance** imprisonment. **67 just** just so **67–9 a restraint . . . scope** a confinement to fixed limits or bounds (i.e., to inescapable guilt and perpetual remorse for the sinful bargain you had struck), even if you had the entire vastness of the world to wander in. **71 bark** strip off (as one strips bark from a tree *trunk*) **73 fear** fear for **74 feverous** feverish. **entertain** maintain, desire **75 respect** value **77 apprehension** anticipation **82–3 Think . . . tenderness?** Do you think I can find the courage to face death in flowery figures of speech?

In base appliances. This outward-sainted deputy,
Whose settled visage and deliberate word
Nips youth i'th' head, and follies doth enew
As falcon doth the fowl, is yet a devil;
His filth within being cast, he would appear
A pond as deep as hell.

CLAUDIO The prenzie Angelo?

ISABELLA
Oh, 'tis the cunning livery of hell,
The damned'st body to invest and cover
In prenzie guards! Dost thou think, Claudio:
If I would yield him my virginity,
Thou mightst be freed!

CLAUDIO Oh, heavens, it cannot be.

ISABELLA
Yes, he would give't thee, from this rank offense,
So to offend him still. This night's the time
That I should do what I abhor to name,
Or else thou diest tomorrow.

CLAUDIO Thou shalt not do't.

ISABELLA Oh, were it but my life,
I'd throw it down for your deliverance
As frankly as a pin.

CLAUDIO Thanks, dear Isabel.

ISABELLA
Be ready, Claudio, for your death tomorrow.

CLAUDIO
Yes. Has he affections in him,
That thus can make him bite the law by th' nose
When he would force it? Sure it is no sin,
Or of the deadly seven it is the least.

ISABELLA Which is the least?

CLAUDIO
If it were damnable, he being so wise,
Why would he for the momentary trick
Be perdurably fined? Oh, Isabel!

ISABELLA
What says my brother?

CLAUDIO Death is a fearful thing.

ISABELLA And shamèd life a hateful.

CLAUDIO
Ay, but to die, and go we know not where,
To lie in cold obstruction and to rot,
This sensible warm motion to become
A kneaded clod, and the delighted spirit
To bathe in fiery floods, or to reside
In thrilling region of thick-ribbèd ice;
To be imprisoned in the viewless winds
And blown with restless violence round about
The pendent world; or to be worse than worst
Of those that lawless and incertain thought
Imagine howling—'tis too horrible!
The weariest and most loathèd worldly life
That age, ache, penury, and imprisonment
Can lay on nature is a paradise
To what we fear of death.

ISABELLA Alas, alas!

CLAUDIO Sweet sister, let me live.
What sin you do to save a brother's life,
Nature dispenses with the deed so far
That it becomes a virtue.

ISABELLA Oh, you beast!
Oh, faithless coward! Oh, dishonest wretch!
Wilt thou be made a man out of my vice?
Is't not a kind of incest, to take life
From thine own sister's shame? What should I think?
Heaven shield my mother played my father fair!
For such a warpèd slip of wilderness
Ne'er issued from his blood. Take my defiance,
Die, perish! Might but my bending down
Reprieve thee from thy fate, it should proceed.
I'll pray a thousand prayers for thy death,
No word to save thee.

CLAUDIO
Nay, hear me, Isabel.

ISABELLA Oh, fie, fie, fie!
Thy sin's not accidental, but a trade.
Mercy to thee would prove itself a bawd;
'Tis best that thou diest quickly.

CLAUDIO Oh, hear me, Isabella!

[*The Duke comes forward.*]

DUKE
Vouchsafe a word, young sister, but one word.

ISABELLA What is your will?

DUKE Might you dispense with your leisure, I would by and by have some speech with you. The satisfaction I would require is likewise your own benefit.

ISABELLA I have no superfluous leisure—my stay must be stolen out of other affairs—but I will attend you awhile. [*She walks apart.*]

DUKE Son, I have overheard what hath passed between you and your sister. Angelo had never the purpose to

89 In base appliances by means of ignoble devices, remedies. **89–92 This . . . fowl** This outwardly holy deputy, who with composed features and judiciously chosen words swoops down on youth like a falcon and drives his prey into covert. (To *enew* is to drive prey down into the water or into hiding.) **93 cast** dug out; diagnosed, sounded; vomited **94, 97 prenzie** (A word unknown elsewhere, perhaps meaning "princely" or "precise.") **95–7 'tis . . . guards** it is the cunning ruse of the devil to clothe and conceal the wickedest man imaginable in decorously proper trimmings. **97 Dost thou think** i.e., Would you believe **100–1 he would . . . still** he would grant you license, in return for the committing of this foul crime, to continue with your fornication. **107 frankly** freely **109 affections** passions **110 bite . . . nose** i.e., flout the law **111 force** enforce. (Claudio wonders that lust can drive Angelo to make a mockery of the law even while purporting to enforce it.) **115 trick** trifle **116 perdurably fined** everlastingly punished. **120 obstruction** cessation of vital functions **121 sensible** endowed with feeling. **motion** organism

122 kneaded clod shapeless lump of earth. **delighted spirit** spirit that is now attended with delight, or capable of being so **124 thrilling** piercingly cold **125 viewless** invisible **127 pendent** hanging in space. (A Ptolemaic concept.) **128 lawless . . . thought** i.e., wild conjecture **133 To** compared to **137 dispenses with** grants a dispensation for, excuses **139 dishonest** dishonorable **143 Heaven . . . fair!** God forbid that my mother was being faithful to my father when you were conceived! **144 warpèd . . . wilderness** perverse, licentious scion, one that reverts to the original wild stock **146 but** merely **151 accidental** casual. **trade** established habit. **152 prove . . . bawd** i.e., provide opportunity for sexual license **155 Vouchsafe** Allow **159 require** ask **161 attend** await; listen to

corrupt her; only he hath made an assay of her virtue to practice his judgment with the disposition of natures. She, having the truth of honor in her, hath made him that gracious denial which he is most glad to receive. I am confessor to Angelo, and I know this to be true; therefore prepare yourself to death. Do not satisfy your resolution with hopes that are fallible. Tomorrow you must die. Go to your knees and make ready.

CLAUDIO Let me ask my sister pardon. I am so out of love with life that I will sue to be rid of it.

DUKE Hold you there. Farewell. [*Claudio retires.*] Provost, a word with you.

[*The Provost comes forward.*]

PROVOST What's your will, Father?

DUKE That now you are come, you will be gone. Leave me awhile with the maid. My mind promises with my habit no loss shall touch her by my company.

PROVOST In good time. *Exit* [*Provost with Claudio*].

[*Isabella comes forward.*]

DUKE The hand that hath made you fair hath made you good. The goodness that is cheap in beauty makes beauty brief in goodness; but grace, being the soul of your complexion, shall keep the body of it ever fair. The assault that Angelo hath made to you, fortune hath conveyed to my understanding; and, but that frailty hath examples for his falling, I should wonder at Angelo. How will you do to content this substitute and to save your brother?

ISABELLA I am now going to resolve him. I had rather my brother die by the law than my son should be unlawfully born. But, oh, how much is the good Duke deceived in Angelo! If ever he return and I can speak to him, I will open my lips in vain, or discover his government.

DUKE That shall not be much amiss. Yet, as the matter now stands, he will avoid your accusation; he made trial of you only. Therefore fasten your ear on my advisings. To the love I have in doing good a remedy presents itself. I do make myself believe that you may most uprighteously do a poor wronged lady a merited benefit, redeem your brother from the angry law, do no stain to your own gracious person, and much please the absent Duke, if peradventure he shall ever return to have hearing of this business.

ISABELLA Let me hear you speak farther. I have spirit to do anything that appears not foul in the truth of my spirit.

DUKE Virtue is bold, and goodness never fearful. Have you not heard speak of Mariana, the sister of Frederick, the great soldier who miscarried at sea?

ISABELLA I have heard of the lady, and good words went with her name.

DUKE She should this Angelo have married, was affianced to her by oath, and the nuptial appointed; between which time of the contract and limit of the solemnity, her brother Frederick was wrecked at sea, having in that perished vessel the dowry of his sister. But mark how heavily this befell to the poor gentlewoman. There she lost a noble and renowned brother, in his love toward her ever most kind and natural; with him, the portion and sinew of her fortune, her marriage dowry; with both, her combinate husband, this well-seeming Angelo.

ISABELLA Can this be so? Did Angelo so leave her?

DUKE Left her in her tears, and dried not one of them with his comfort; swallowed his vows whole, pretending in her discoveries of dishonor; in few, bestowed her on her own lamentation, which she yet wears for his sake; and he, a marble to her tears, is washed with them but relents not.

ISABELLA What a merit were it in death to take this poor maid from the world! What corruption in this life, that it will let this man live! But how out of this can she avail?

DUKE It is a rupture that you may easily heal, and the cure of it not only saves your brother but keeps you from dishonor in doing it.

ISABELLA Show me how, good Father.

DUKE This forenamed maid hath yet in her the continuance of her first affection; his unjust unkindness, that in all reason should have quenched her love, hath, like an impediment in the current, made it more violent and unruly. Go you to Angelo; answer his requiring with a plausible obedience; agree with his demands to the point. Only refer yourself to this advantage: first, that your stay with him may not be long, that the time may have all shadow and silence in it, and the place answer to convenience. This being granted in course—and now follows all—we shall advise this wronged maid to stead up your appointment, go in your place. If the encounter acknowledge itself hereafter, it may compel him to her recompense. And here, by this, is your brother saved, your honor untainted, the poor Mariana advantaged, and the corrupt deputy scaled. The maid will I frame and make fit for his at-

165 only he hath he has only. **assay** test **166–7 his judgment . . . natures** his ability to judge people's characters. **168 gracious** virtuous **175 Hold you there** Hold fast to that resolution.
179–80 with my habit as well as my priestly garb (that) **181 In good time** i.e., Very well. **183–84 The goodness . . . in goodness** i.e., The physical attractions that come easily with beauty make beauty soon cease to be morally good **185 complexion** character and appearance **187 but that** were it not that **188 examples** precedents **189 this substitute** i.e., the deputy, Angelo **191 resolve him** set his mind at rest. **195–6 discover his government** expose Angelo's misconduct. **198 avoid** evade, refute. **he made** i.e., he will say that he made **207 spirit** courage **208 truth** righteousness **209 spirit** soul.

215 She . . . married Angelo was supposed to have married her. **was** i.e., he was **217–18 limit . . . solemnity** date set for the ceremony **223 the portion and sinew** i.e., the mainstay **224 combinate husband** i.e., betrothed **228–9 pretending . . . dishonor** falsely alleging to have found evidence of unchastity in her **229–30 in few . . . lamentation** in short, left her to her grief. (With quibble on *bestowed*, meaning "gave in marriage.") **230 wears** i.e., carries in her heart **231 a marble to** i.e., unmoved by **236 avail** benefit. **246–7 to the point** precisely. **247 refer . . . advantage** obtain these conditions **249 shadow** darkness, secrecy **252 stead . . . appointment** go in your stead **253–4 If the . . . hereafter** i.e., If she should become pregnant **257 scaled** weighed in the scales of justice (and found wanting). **frame** prepare

tempt. If you think well to carry this as you may, the doubleness of the benefit defends the deceit from reproof. What think you of it?

ISABELLA The image of it gives me content already, and I trust it will grow to a most prosperous perfection.

DUKE It lies much in your holding up. Haste you speedily to Angelo. If for this night he entreat you to his bed, give him promise of satisfaction. I will presently to Saint Luke's; there, at the moated grange, resides this dejected Mariana. At that place call upon me; and dispatch with Angelo, that it may be quickly.

ISABELLA I thank you for this comfort. Fare you well, good Father. *Exit.* [*The Duke remains.*]

[3.2]

Enter [*to the Duke*] *Elbow, Clown* [*Pompey, and*] *officers.*

ELBOW Nay, if there be no remedy for it but that you will needs buy and sell men and women like beasts, we shall have all the world drink brown and white bastard.

DUKE [*aside*] Oh, heavens, what stuff is here?

POMPEY 'Twas never merry world since, of two usuries, the merriest was put down, and the worser allowed by order of law a furred gown to keep him warm, and furred with fox on lambskins too, to signify that craft, being richer than innocency, stands for the facing.

ELBOW Come your way, sir.—Bless you, good Father Friar.

DUKE And you, good Brother Father. What offense hath this man made you, sir?

ELBOW Marry, sir, he hath offended the law; and, sir, we take him to be a thief too, sir, for we have found upon him, sir, a strange picklock, which we have sent to the deputy.

DUKE [*to Pompey*]
Fie, sirrah, a bawd, a wicked bawd!
The evil that thou causest to be done,
That is thy means to live. Do thou but think
What 'tis to cram a maw or clothe a back
From such a filthy vice; say to thyself,
From their abominable and beastly touches
I drink, I eat, array myself, and live.
Canst thou believe thy living is a life,
So stinkingly depending? Go mend, go mend.

POMPEY Indeed, it does stink in some sort, sir. But yet, sir, I would prove—

DUKE
Nay, if the devil have given thee proofs for sin,
Thou wilt prove his.—Take him to prison, officer.
Correction and instruction must both work
Ere this rude beast will profit.

ELBOW He must before the deputy, sir; he has given him warning. The deputy cannot abide a whoremaster. If he be a whoremonger and comes before him, he were as good go a mile on his errand.

DUKE
That we were all, as some would seem to be,
From our faults, as faults from seeming, free!

Enter Lucio.

ELBOW His neck will come to your waist—a cord, sir.

POMPEY I spy comfort, I cry bail. Here's a gentleman and a friend of mine.

LUCIO How now, noble Pompey? What, at the wheels of Caesar? Art thou led in triumph? What, is there none of Pygmalion's images, newly made woman, to be had now, for putting the hand in the pocket and extracting it clutched? What reply, ha? What say'st thou to this tune, matter, and method? Is 't not drowned i'th' last rain, ha? What say'st thou, trot? Is the world as it was, man? Which is the way? Is it sad, and few words? Or how? The trick of it?

DUKE Still thus, and thus; still worse!

LUCIO How doth my dear morsel, thy mistress? Procures she still, ha?

POMPEY Troth, sir, she hath eaten up all her beef, and she is herself in the tub.

LUCIO Why, 'tis good. It is the right of it, it must be so. Ever your fresh whore and your powdered bawd; an unshunned consequence, it must be so. Art going to prison, Pompey?

264 holding up ability to carry it off. **267 moated grange** country house surrounded by a ditch **269 dispatch** settle, conclude business
3.2 Location: Scene continues. The Duke remains onstage.
4 bastard sweet Spanish wine. (Used quibblingly.) **6–7 two usuries** i.e., moneylending (the *worser*) and procuring for fornication (the *merriest*), both of which yield increase **8 furred gown** (Characteristic attire of usurers.) **10–11 stands . . . facing** represents the outer covering. (Fox symbolizes *craft* or craftiness, lambskin, *innocency.*)
14 Brother Father (The Duke's retort to Elbow's *Father Friar,* i.e., Father Brother.) **18 picklock** skeleton key, or perhaps a chastity belt in Pompey's possession as pimp; it might seem *strange* to the innocent Elbow **23 cram . . . back** fill a stomach or provide clothing
25 touches sexual encounters

28 depending supported. **30 prove** i.e., argue, demonstrate
31 proofs for arguments in defense of **32 prove** turn out to be
35 must must go. **deputy** i.e., Angelo. (Though Escalus gave Pompey the warning.) **37–8 he were . . . errand** i.e., he will have a hard road to travel. **39 That** Would that **40 From . . . free** i.e., free from faults, and our faults free from dissembling. **41 His . . . cord** i.e., He is likely to hang by a cord like that around your waist. (The Duke is habited as a friar.) **45 Caesar** (Who defeated Pompey at Pharsalia and led his sons in triumph after defeating them at Munda.) **46 Pygmalion's images** i.e., prostitutes, so called because they "painted" with cosmetics like a painted statue. (Pygmalion was a sculptor, according to legend, whose female statue came to life "newly made.") **48 clutched** i.e., with money in it. (But also with sexual suggestion.) **48–50 What say'st . . . rain** i.e., What do you say now to this latest turn of events? Are our prospects a little dampened? **50 trot** old bawd. **51–2 Which . . . words?** i.e., What is the latest fashion? Is melancholy now in vogue? (A wry comment on Pompey's silence.) **52 trick** fashion **56 eaten . . . beef** (1) consumed all her salt beef, which had been prepared in a powder-tub like that also used to treat venereal disease (2) run through all her prostitutes **57 in the tub** being treated for venereal disease by the sweating-tub treatment (much as beef was salted down in a tub to preserve it). **59 Ever . . . bawd** i.e., It is always thus with young whores and old bawds, *powdered* like beef in a tub and caked with cosmetics **60 unshunned** unshunnable, unavoidable

POMPEY Yes, faith, sir.

LUCIO Why, 'tis not amiss, Pompey. Farewell. Go, say I sent thee thither. For debt, Pompey? Or how?

ELBOW For being a bawd, for being a bawd.

LUCIO Well, then, imprison him. If imprisonment be the due of a bawd, why, 'tis his right. Bawd is he doubtless, and of antiquity too; bawd-born. Farewell, good Pompey. Commend me to the prison, Pompey. You will turn good husband now, Pompey; you will keep the house.

POMPEY I hope, sir, Your good Worship will be my bail.

LUCIO No, indeed, will I not, Pompey; it is not the wear. I will pray, Pompey, to increase your bondage. If you take it not patiently, why, your mettle is the more. Adieu, trusty Pompey.—Bless you, Friar.

DUKE And you.

LUCIO Does Bridget paint still, Pompey, ha?

ELBOW [*to Pompey*] Come your ways, sir, come.

POMPEY [*to Lucio*] You will not bail me, then, sir?

LUCIO Then, Pompey, nor now.—What news abroad, Friar? What news?

ELBOW Come your ways, sir, come.

LUCIO Go to kennel, Pompey, go.

[*Exeunt Elbow, Pompey, and Officers.*]

What news, Friar, of the Duke?

DUKE I know none. Can you tell me of any?

LUCIO Some say he is with the Emperor of Russia; other some, he is in Rome. But where is he, think you?

DUKE I know not where; but wheresoever, I wish him well.

LUCIO It was a mad fantastical trick of him to steal from the state and usurp the beggary he was never born to. Lord Angelo dukes it well in his absence; he puts transgression to't.

DUKE He does well in't.

LUCIO A little more lenity to lechery would do no harm in him. Something too crabbed that way, Friar.

DUKE It is too general a vice, and severity must cure it.

LUCIO Yes, in good sooth, the vice is of a great kindred; it is well allied. But it is impossible to extirp it quite, Friar, till eating and drinking be put down. They say this Angelo was not made by man and woman after this downright way of creation. Is it true, think you?

DUKE How should he be made, then?

LUCIO Some report a sea maid spawned him; some, that he was begot between two stockfishes. But it is certain that when he makes water his urine is congealed ice; that I know to be true. And he is a motion ungenerative; that's infallible.

DUKE You are pleasant, sir, and speak apace.

LUCIO Why, what a ruthless thing is this in him, for the rebellion of a codpiece to take away the life of a man! Would the Duke that is absent have done this? Ere he would have hanged a man for the getting a hundred bastards, he would have paid for the nursing a thousand. He had some feeling of the sport; he knew the service, and that instructed him to mercy.

DUKE I never heard the absent Duke much detected for women. He was not inclined that way.

LUCIO Oh, sir, you are deceived.

DUKE 'Tis not possible.

LUCIO Who, not the Duke? Yes, your beggar of fifty; and his use was to put a ducat in her clack-dish. The Duke had crotchets in him. He would be drunk too, that let me inform you.

DUKE You do him wrong, surely.

LUCIO Sir, I was an inward of his. A shy fellow was the Duke, and I believe I know the cause of his withdrawing.

DUKE What, I prithee, might be the cause?

LUCIO No, pardon. 'Tis a secret must be locked within the teeth and the lips. But this I can let you understand: the greater file of the subject held the Duke to be wise.

DUKE Wise? Why, no question but he was.

LUCIO A very superficial, ignorant, unweighing fellow.

DUKE Either this is envy in you, folly, or mistaking. The very stream of his life and the business he hath helmed must, upon a warranted need, give him a better proclamation. Let him be but testimonied in his own bringings-forth, and he shall appear to the envious a scholar, a statesman, and a soldier. Therefore you speak unskillfully; or, if your knowledge be more, it is much darkened in your malice.

LUCIO Sir, I know him, and I love him.

DUKE Love talks with better knowledge, and knowledge with dearer love.

LUCIO Come, sir, I know what I know.

DUKE I can hardly believe that, since you know not what you speak. But if ever the Duke return, as our prayers are he may, let me desire you to make your answer before him. If it be honest you have spoke, you have courage to maintain it. I am bound to call upon you; and, I pray you, your name?

68 antiquity long continuance. **bawd-born** a born bawd and born of a bawd. **70 good husband** thrifty manager **71 keep the house** stay indoors. (With pun on the pimp's function as doorkeeper.) **74 wear** fashion. **75–6 your . . . more** (1) your spirit is revealed all the more (2) your shackles will be made heavier. (Playing on *mettle/metal.*) **78 paint** use cosmetics **79 Come your ways** Come along **81 Then** Neither then. **abroad** about town **87–8 other some** some others **91 steal** steal away **92 beggary** i.e., status of a wanderer or traveler. (With unconscious ironic appropriateness; Lucio clearly does not see through the Duke's disguise as a mendicant friar.) **93–4 puts . . . to't** puts lawbreaking under severe restraint. **97 Something too crabbed** Somewhat too harsh **99 kindred** i.e., family, numerous and well connected **100 extirp** eradicate **102 after** in accordance with **103 downright** straightforward, usual **105 sea maid** mermaid **106 stockfishes** dried codfish.

108–9 motion ungenerative masculine puppet, without sexual potency **110 pleasant** jocose. **apace** fast and idly. **112 codpiece** an appendage to the front of close-fitting hose or breeches worn by men, often ornamented and indelicately conspicuous; hence, slang for "penis" **117 the service** i.e., prostitution **118 detected** accused **123 his . . . clack-dish** his custom was to put a coin in her wooden beggar's bowl, with its lid that was "clacked" to attract attention. (Lucio hints that the Duke had sex with her.) **127 inward** intimate **133 the greater . . . subject** most of his subjects **136 unweighing** injudicious **137 envy** malice **138 helmed** steered **139 upon . . . need** if a warrant were needed **139–40 give . . . proclamation** proclaim him better (than you assert). **140–1 in . . . bringings-forth** by his own public actions **141 to the envious** even to the malicious **143 unskillfully** in ignorance

LUCIO Sir, my name is Lucio, well known to the Duke.

DUKE He shall know you better, sir, if I may live to report you.

LUCIO I fear you not.

DUKE Oh, you hope the Duke will return no more, or you imagine me too unhurtful an opposite. But indeed I can do you little harm; you'll forswear this again.

LUCIO I'll be hanged first. Thou art deceived in me, Friar. But no more of this. Canst thou tell if Claudio die tomorrow or no?

DUKE Why should he die, sir?

LUCIO Why? For filling a bottle with a tundish. I would the Duke we talk of were returned again. This ungenitured agent will unpeople the province with continency. Sparrows must not build in his house eaves, because they are lecherous. The Duke yet would have dark deeds darkly answered; he would never bring them to light. Would he were returned! Marry, this Claudio is condemned for untrussing. Farewell, good Friar. I prithee, pray for me. The Duke, I say to thee again, would eat mutton on Fridays. He's now past it, yet, and I say to thee, he would mouth with a beggar, though she smelt brown bread and garlic. Say that I said so. Farewell. *Exit.*

DUKE

No might nor greatness in mortality
Can censure scape; back-wounding calumny
The whitest virtue strikes. What king so strong
Can tie the gall up in the slanderous tongue?
But who comes here?

Enter Escalus, Provost, and [*officers with*] *bawd* [*Mistress Overdone*].

ESCALUS Go, away with her to prison.

MISTRESS OVERDONE Good my lord, be good to me. Your Honor is accounted a merciful man. Good my lord.

ESCALUS Double and treble admonition, and still forfeit in the same kind! This would make mercy swear and play the tyrant.

PROVOST A bawd of eleven years' continuance, may it please Your Honor.

MISTRESS OVERDONE My lord, this is one Lucio's information against me. Mistress Kate Keepdown was with child by him in the Duke's time; he promised her marriage. His child is a year and a quarter old, come Philip and Jacob. I have kept it myself; and see how he goes about to abuse me!

ESCALUS That fellow is a fellow of much license. Let him be called before us. Away with her to prison! Go to, no more words. [*Exeunt Officers with Mistress Overdone.*] Provost, my brother Angelo will not be altered; Claudio must die tomorrow. Let him be furnished with divines and have all charitable preparation. If my brother wrought by my pity, it should not be so with him.

PROVOST So please you, this friar hath been with him, and advised him for th'entertainment of death.

ESCALUS Good even, good Father.

DUKE Bliss and goodness on you!

ESCALUS Of whence are you?

DUKE

Not of this country, though my chance is now
To use it for my time. I am a brother
Of gracious order, late come from the See
In special business from His Holiness.

ESCALUS What news abroad i'th' world?

DUKE None but that there is so great a fever on goodness that the dissolution of it must cure it. Novelty is only in request, and, as it is, as dangerous to be aged in any kind of course as it is virtuous to be constant in any undertaking. There is scarce truth enough alive to make societies secure, but security enough to make fellowships accursed. Much upon this riddle runs the wisdom of the world. This news is old enough, yet it is every day's news. I pray you, sir, of what disposition was the Duke?

ESCALUS One that, above all other strifes, contended especially to know himself.

DUKE What pleasure was he given to?

ESCALUS Rather rejoicing to see another merry than merry at anything which professed to make him rejoice—a gentleman of all temperance. But leave we him to his events, with a prayer they may prove prosperous, and let me desire to know how you find Claudio prepared. I am made to understand that you have lent him visitation.

160 too . . . opposite too harmless an adversary. **161 forswear this again** deny another time what you have said under oath. **166 tundish** funnel. (Here representing the penis.) **167–8 ungenitured agent** sexless deputy **169 Sparrows** (Proverbially lecherous birds.) **171 darkly** secretly **173 untrussing** undressing. (Specifically, untying the points used to fasten hose to doublet.) **175 eat . . . Fridays** i.e., frequent loose women in flagrant disregard of the law. (Literally, violate religious observance by eating meat on fast days.) **past it** beyond the age for sex **176 mouth** kiss **177 smelt brown bread** smelled of coarse bran bread **179 mortality** humankind; human life **180–1 Can . . . strikes** can escape censure; backbiting slander strikes even the purest of virtues. **181 so** be he never so **188–9 forfeit . . . kind** guilty of the same offense. **189 mercy** i.e., even mercy **193–4 information** accusation

196–7 Philip and Jacob the Feast of Saint Philip and Saint James (*Jacobus* in Latin), May 1. **197–8 goes about** busies himself **202 brother** i.e., fellow officer of state **204 divines** clergymen **205 wrought . . . pity** acted in accord with my impulses of pity **208 th'entertainment** the reception, acceptance **213 To . . . time** to dwell here for my present purposes. **214 the See** Rome **218 the dissolution . . . cure it** i.e., only by dying can goodness be rid of the disease. **218–19 is only in request** is the only thing people seek **219–21 as it . . . undertaking** as things currently stand, (it is) as dangerous to be constant in any undertaking as it is virtuous to be thus constant. **221–3 There . . . accursed** i.e., There is hardly enough integrity extant to establish secure and trusting associations among men, but binding contractual obligations enough to be the curse of friendship. (The Duke thus puns on *security* [1] a sense of trust [2] financial pledge required to borrow money, and on *fellowship* [1] friendship [2] corporations formed for trading ventures.) **223 upon this riddle** in this riddling fashion **227 strifes** endeavors **231 professed** attempted **233 his events** the outcome of his affairs **236 lent him visitation** paid him a visit.

DUKE He professes to have received no sinister measure from his judge, but most willingly humbles himself to the determination of justice; yet had he framed to himself, by the instruction of his frailty, many deceiving promises of life, which I, by my good leisure, have discredited to him, and now is he resolved to die.

ESCALUS You have paid the heavens your function, and the prisoner the very debt of your calling. I have labored for the poor gentleman to the extremest shore of my modesty, but my brother justice have I found so severe that he hath forced me to tell him he is indeed Justice.

DUKE If his own life answer the straitness of his proceeding, it shall become him well; wherein if he chance to fail, he hath sentenced himself.

ESCALUS I am going to visit the prisoner. Fare you well.

DUKE Peace be with you!

[*Exeunt Escalus and Provost.*]

He who the sword of heaven will bear
Should be as holy as severe;
Pattern in himself to know,
Grace to stand, and virtue go;
More nor less to others paying
Than by self-offenses weighing.
Shame to him whose cruel striking
Kills for faults of his own liking!
Twice treble shame on Angelo,
To weed my vice and let his grow!
Oh, what may man within him hide,
Though angel on the outward side!
How may likeness made in crimes,
Making practice on the times,
To draw with idle spiders' strings
Most ponderous and substantial things!
Craft against vice I must apply.
With Angelo tonight shall lie
His old betrothèd but despisèd;
So disguise shall, by the disguisèd,
Pay with falsehood false exacting
And perform an old contracting. *Exit.*

4.1

Enter Mariana, and Boy singing.

Song.

BOY

Take, oh, take those lips away,
That so sweetly were forsworn,
And those eyes, the break of day,
Lights that do mislead the morn;
But my kisses bring again, bring again,
Seals of love, but sealed in vain, sealed in vain.

Enter Duke [*disguised as before*].

MARIANA

Break off thy song, and haste thee quick away.
Here comes a man of comfort, whose advice
Hath often stilled my brawling discontent. [*Exit Boy.*]
I cry you mercy, sir, and well could wish
You had not found me here so musical.
Let me excuse me, and believe me so,
My mirth it much displeased, but pleased my woe.

DUKE

'Tis good; though music oft hath such a charm
To make bad good, and good provoke to harm.
I pray you, tell me, hath anybody inquired for me here today? Much upon this time have I promised here to meet.

MARIANA You have not been inquired after. I have sat here all day.

Enter Isabella.

DUKE I do constantly believe you. The time is come even now. I shall crave your forbearance a little. Maybe I will call upon you anon, for some advantage to yourself.

MARIANA I am always bound to you. *Exit.*

DUKE Very well met, and welcome.
What is the news from this good deputy?

ISABELLA

He hath a garden circummured with brick,
Whose western side is with a vineyard backed;
And to that vineyard is a planchèd gate,
That makes his opening with this bigger key.
[*She shows keys.*]

237 sinister measure unfair treatment meted out to him **239–40 framed to himself** formulated in his mind **240 by . . . frailty** at the prompting of his natural human weakness **244 the prisoner . . . calling** what your calling as a friar obliges you to give the prisoner, i.e., the comforts of spiritual counsel. **245–6 shore . . . modesty** limit of propriety **249 straitness** strictness **256–9 Pattern . . . weighing** he must know himself and be a pattern for others to emulate, with the grace to stand firm and the virtue to guide himself in the straight path, judging and punishing others with neither more nor less severity than he applies to his own offenses. **263 my vice** i.e., vice in everyone except Angelo. (The Duke speaks chorically on behalf of everyone generally.) **266–9 How . . . things!** How may false seeming of a criminal sort, practicing deception on the world, make weighty and substantial matters seem as illusory and unsubstantial as spider webs! **273–5 So . . . contracting** so shall disguise, employed by those in disguise (i.e., Mariana and the Duke himself), use a kind of (virtuous) falsehood to pay back what was exacted through deception (by Angelo), and thereby fulfill an old contract.

4.1 Location: The moated grange at Saint Luke's.
4 Lights . . . morn eyes that mislead the morning (the goddess of dawn, Eos or Aurora) into taking them for the rising sun **5 again** back **6 Seals** confirmations, pledges **9 brawling** clamorous **10 cry you mercy** beg your pardon **13 My . . . woe** i.e., it suited not a merry but a melancholy mood. **15 bad good** i.e., bad seem good, attractive. (The Duke, echoing Renaissance conceptions of the psychological effects of music, warns that music can sometimes give a pleasing appearance to sin and lead virtue into harm.) **17 Much upon** Pretty nearly about **21 constantly** confidently **22 crave . . . little** i.e., ask you to withdraw briefly. **23 anon** presently **28 circummured** walled about **30 planchèd** made of boards, planks **31 his** its

This other doth command a little door
Which from the vineyard to the garden leads;
There have I made my promise, upon the
Heavy middle of the night, to call upon him.

DUKE
But shall you on your knowledge find this way?

ISABELLA
I have ta'en a due and wary note upon't.
With whispering and most guilty diligence,
In action all of precept, he did show me
The way twice o'er.

DUKE Are there no other tokens
Between you 'greed concerning her observance?

ISABELLA
No, none, but only a repair i'th' dark,
And that I have possessed him my most stay
Can be but brief; for I have made him know
I have a servant comes with me along,
That stays upon me, whose persuasion is
I come about my brother.

DUKE 'Tis well borne up.
I have not yet made known to Mariana
A word of this.—What, ho, within! Come forth!

Enter Mariana.

I pray you, be acquainted with this maid;
She comes to do you good.

ISABELLA I do desire the like.

DUKE
Do you persuade yourself that I respect you?

MARIANA
Good Friar, I know you do, and have found it.

DUKE
Take then this your companion by the hand,
Who hath a story ready for your ear.
I shall attend your leisure. But make haste;
The vaporous night approaches.

MARIANA Will't please you walk aside?
Exit [*with Isabella*].

DUKE
O place and greatness! Millions of false eyes
Are stuck upon thee. Volumes of report
Run with these false and most contrarious quests
Upon thy doings; thousand escapes of wit
Make thee the father of their idle dream
And rack thee in their fancies.

Enter Mariana and Isabella.

Welcome. How agreed?

ISABELLA
She'll take the enterprise upon her, Father,
If you advise it.

DUKE It is not my consent,
But my entreaty too.

ISABELLA Little have you to say
When you depart from him but, soft and low,
"Remember now my brother."

MARIANA Fear me not.

DUKE
Nor, gentle daughter, fear you not at all.
He is your husband on a precontract;
To bring you thus together, 'tis no sin,
Sith that the justice of your title to him
Doth flourish the deceit. Come, let us go.
Our corn's to reap, for yet our tithe's to sow. *Exeunt.*

✤

4.2

Enter Provost and Clown [*Pompey*].

PROVOST Come hither, sirrah. Can you cut off a man's head?

POMPEY If the man be a bachelor, sir, I can; but if he be a married man, he's his wife's head, and I can never cut off a woman's head.

PROVOST Come, sir, leave me your snatches, and yield me a direct answer. Tomorrow morning are to die Claudio and Barnardine. Here is in our prison a common executioner, who in his office lacks a helper. If you will take it on you to assist him, it shall redeem you from your gyves; if not, you shall have your full time of imprisonment and your deliverance with an unpitied whipping, for you have been a notorious bawd.

POMPEY Sir, I have been an unlawful bawd time out of mind, but yet I will be content to be a lawful hangman. I would be glad to receive some instruction from my fellow partner.

PROVOST [*calling*] What, ho, Abhorson! Where's Abhorson, there?

Enter Abhorson.

ABHORSON Do you call, sir?

PROVOST Sirrah, here's a fellow will help you tomorrow in your execution. If you think it meet, compound with him by the year, and let him abide here with you; if not, use him for the present and dismiss him.

34 upon during, at **39 In action . . . precept** i.e., teaching by demonstration **41 her observance** what she is supposed to do. **42 repair** act of going or coming to a place **43 possessed** informed. **my most stay** my stay at the longest **46 stays upon** waits for. **persuasion** belief **47 borne up** sustained, carried out. **52 respect you** are concerned for your welfare. **53 found it** found it to be true. **60 stuck** fastened **60–2 Volumes . . . doings** Innumerable rumors follow a false scent and hunt counter in pursuing your activities **62 escapes** sallies **63 Make . . . dream** credit you with being the source of their fantasies **64 rack** stretch as on the rack, distort

66 not not only **67 Little . . . say** Say little **69 Fear me not** i.e., Don't worry about my carrying out my part. **71 precontract** legally binding agreement entered into before any church ceremony. (Compare Claudio's and Juliet's *true contract* at 1.2.142.) **73 Sith that** since **74 flourish** adorn, make fair **75 Our corn's . . . sow** We must first sow grain before we can expect to reap a harvest; i.e., we must get started. **tithe** grain sown for tithe dues; or, an error for "tilth"
4.2 Location: The prison.
4 he's . . . head (Compare Ephesians 5:23: "The husband is the head of the wife.") **5 head** (With wordplay on "maidenhead.") **6 leave . . . snatches** leave off your quibbles **8–9 common** public **11 gyves** fetters, shackles **23 compound** make an agreement

He cannot plead his estimation with you; he hath been a bawd.

ABHORSON A bawd, sir? Fie upon him! He will discredit our mystery.

PROVOST Go to, sir, you weigh equally; a feather will turn the scale. *Exit.*

POMPEY Pray, sir, by your good favor—for surely, sir, a good favor you have, but that you have a hanging look—do you call, sir, your occupation a mystery?

ABHORSON Ay, sir, a mystery.

POMPEY Painting, sir, I have heard say, is a mystery, and your whores, sir, being members of my occupation, using painting, do prove my occupation a mystery. But what mystery there should be in hanging, if I should be hanged, I cannot imagine.

ABHORSON Sir, it is a mystery.

POMPEY Proof?

ABHORSON Every true man's apparel fits your thief. If it be too little for your thief, your true man thinks it big enough; if it be too big for your thief, your thief thinks it little enough. So every true man's apparel fits your thief.

Enter Provost.

PROVOST Are you agreed?

POMPEY Sir, I will serve him, for I do find your hangman is a more penitent trade than your bawd: he doth oftener ask forgiveness.

PROVOST You, sirrah, provide your block and your ax tomorrow four o'clock.

ABHORSON Come on, bawd. I will instruct thee in my trade. Follow!

POMPEY I do desire to learn, sir; and I hope, if you have occasion to use me for your own turn, you shall find me yare. For truly, sir, for your kindness I owe you a good turn.

PROVOST
Call hither Barnardine and Claudio.
Exit [*Pompey, with Abhorson*].
Th'one has my pity; not a jot the other,
Being a murderer, though he were my brother.

Enter Claudio.

Look, here's the warrant, Claudio, for thy death.
'Tis now dead midnight, and by eight tomorrow
Thou must be made immortal. Where's Barnardine?

CLAUDIO
As fast locked up in sleep as guiltless labor
When it lies starkly in the traveler's bones.
He will not wake.

PROVOST Who can do good on him?
Well, go, prepare yourself. [*Knocking within.*] But hark, what noise?
Heaven give your spirits comfort! [*Exit Claudio.*]
[*calling*] By and by.—
I hope it is some pardon or reprieve
For the most gentle Claudio.

Enter Duke [*disguised as before*].

Welcome, Father.

DUKE
The best and wholesom'st spirits of the night
Envelop you, good Provost! Who called here of late?

PROVOST None since the curfew rung.

DUKE
Not Isabel?

PROVOST No.

DUKE They will, then, ere't be long.

PROVOST What comfort is for Claudio?

DUKE
There's some in hope.

PROVOST It is a bitter deputy.

DUKE
Not so, not so. His life is paralleled
Even with the stroke and line of his great justice.
He doth with holy abstinence subdue
That in himself which he spurs on his power
To qualify in others. Were he mealed with that
Which he corrects, then were he tyrannous;
But this being so, he's just. [*Knocking within.*] Now are they come. [*The Provost goes to the door.*]
This is a gentle provost; seldom when
The steelèd jailer is the friend of men.
[*Knocking within.*]
How now? What noise? That spirit's possessed with haste
That wounds th'unsisting postern with these strokes.

PROVOST [*speaking at the door*]
There he must stay until the officer
Arise to let him in. He is called up.
[*He returns to the Duke.*]

DUKE
Have you no countermand for Claudio yet,
But he must die tomorrow?

PROVOST None, sir, none.

DUKE
As near the dawning, Provost, as it is,

26 plead his estimation claim any respect on account of his reputation **29 mystery** craft, occupation. **32 favor** leave, permission **33 favor** face **33–4 hanging look** (1) downcast look (2) look of a hangman **36 Painting** (1) Painting of pictures (2) Applying cosmetics **43–7 Every . . . thief** (Abhorson alludes to the custom of giving to the hangman the garments of the executed criminal. Like a thief, a hangman takes from all sorts of persons; death is the great thief. The hangman's occupation is to settle all scores.) **44–5 big enough** i.e., enough of a loss **46 little enough** little enough for his efforts. **50–1 he doth . . . forgiveness** (The executioner perfunctorily asked forgiveness of those whose lives he was about to take.) **57 for . . . turn** (1) as a pimp to provide for your sexual needs (2) as your hangman when it is your turn to be hanged or "turned off" the ladder **58 yare** ready, alacritous. **65 made immortal** i.e., executed.

66 fast firmly, soundly. **guiltless labor** (A personification of the well-earned weariness that tires the innocent laborer.) **67 starkly** stiffly. **traveler's bones** bones of one who travails or labors or journeys. **79–80 His . . . justice** His life runs parallel and in exact conformity with the straight line and precise execution of the justice he carries out. **82 spurs on** encourages, urges **83 qualify** mitigate. **mealed** spotted, stained **86 seldom when** i.e., it is seldom that **87 steelèd** hardened **89 unsisting** unyielding, unresting, or unresisting. **postern** small door

You shall hear more ere morning.
PROVOST Happily
You something know, yet I believe there comes
No countermand. No such example have we;
Besides, upon the very siege of justice
Lord Angelo hath to the public ear
Professed the contrary.

Enter a Messenger.

This is His Lordship's man.
DUKE
And here comes Claudio's pardon.

MESSENGER [*giving a paper*] My lord hath sent you this note, and by me this further charge, that you swerve not from the smallest article of it, neither in time, matter, or other circumstance. Good morrow; for, as I take it, it is almost day.

PROVOST I shall obey him. [*Exit Messenger.*]

DUKE [*aside*]
This is his pardon, purchased by such sin
For which the pardoner himself is in.
Hence hath offense his quick celerity,
When it is borne in high authority.
When vice makes mercy, mercy's so extended
That for the fault's love is th'offender friended.—
Now, sir, what news?

PROVOST I told you. Lord Angelo, belike thinking me remiss in mine office, awakens me with this unwonted putting-on—methinks strangely, for he hath not used it before.

DUKE Pray you, let's hear.

PROVOST [*reads*] *the letter* "Whatsoever you may hear to the contrary, let Claudio be executed by four of the clock, and in the afternoon Barnardine. For my better satisfaction, let me have Claudio's head sent me by five. Let this be duly performed, with a thought that more depends on it than we must yet deliver. Thus fail not to do your office, as you will answer it at your peril." What say you to this, sir?

DUKE What is that Barnardine who is to be executed in th'afternoon?

PROVOST A Bohemian born, but here nursed up and bred; one that is a prisoner nine years old.

DUKE How came it that the absent Duke had not either delivered him to his liberty or executed him? I have heard it was ever his manner to do so.

PROVOST His friends still wrought reprieves for him; and indeed his fact, till now in the government of Lord Angelo, came not to an undoubtful proof.

DUKE It is now apparent?

PROVOST Most manifest, and not denied by himself.

DUKE Hath he borne himself penitently in prison? How seems he to be touched?

PROVOST A man that apprehends death no more dreadfully but as a drunken sleep—careless, reckless, and fearless of what's past, present, or to come; insensible of mortality, and desperately mortal.

DUKE He wants advice.

PROVOST He will hear none. He hath evermore had the liberty of the prison; give him leave to escape hence, he would not. Drunk many times a day, if not many days entirely drunk. We have very oft awaked him, as if to carry him to execution, and showed him a seeming warrant for it; it hath not moved him at all.

DUKE More of him anon. There is written in your brow, Provost, honesty and constancy; if I read it not truly, my ancient skill beguiles me, but, in the boldness of my cunning, I will lay myself in hazard. Claudio, whom here you have warrant to execute, is no greater forfeit to the law than Angelo who hath sentenced him. To make you understand this in a manifested effect, I crave but four days' respite, for the which you are to do me both a present and a dangerous courtesy.

PROVOST Pray, sir, in what?

DUKE In the delaying death.

PROVOST Alack, how may I do it, having the hour limited, and an express command, under penalty, to deliver his head in the view of Angelo? I may make my case as Claudio's, to cross this in the smallest.

DUKE By the vow of mine order I warrant you, if my instructions may be your guide. Let this Barnardine be this morning executed, and his head borne to Angelo.

PROVOST Angelo hath seen them both and will discover the favor.

DUKE Oh, death's a great disguiser, and you may add to it. Shave the head, and tie the beard, and say it was the desire of the penitent to be so bared before his death. You know the course is common. If anything fall to you upon this more than thanks and good fortune, by the saint whom I profess, I will plead against it with my life.

PROVOST Pardon me, good Father, it is against my oath.

DUKE Were you sworn to the Duke or to the deputy?

PROVOST To him, and to his substitutes.

DUKE You will think you have made no offense if the Duke avouch the justice of your dealing?

PROVOST But what likelihood is in that?

DUKE Not a resemblance, but a certainty. Yet since I see you fearful, that neither my coat, integrity, nor

95 Happily Haply, perhaps **97 example** precedent **98 siege** seat **109 in** engaged. **110–11 Hence . . . authority** Hence it is that criminal behavior in high places has its (*his*) own quick way of covering its tracks. **112–13 When . . . friended** When criminality acts to save a life, as in this case, mercy is so strangely broadened in definition that the offender (here, Claudio) is spared for the fault committed by the person in authority. **115 belike** perchance **116–17 unwonted putting-on** unaccustomed urging **123 better satisfaction** greater assurance **126 deliver** make known. **131 here** i.e., in Vienna **132 a prisoner . . . old** nine years a prisoner. **137 fact** crime

142 touched affected, touched by remorse. **143–4 no more dreadfully but** with no more dread than **145–6 insensible . . . mortal** incapable of comprehending the meaning of death, and incorrigible. **147 wants advice** needs spiritual counsel. **148 evermore** constantly **148–9 the liberty . . . prison** freedom to go anywhere within the prison **156–7 in the . . . hazard** confident in my knowledge (of human character), I will put myself at risk. **160 in . . . effect** by means of concrete proof **162 present** immediate **166 limited** fixed, set **173–4 discover the favor** recognize the face. **176 tie** tie up, tidy up **178 course** practice **179 fall to** befall **180 the saint . . . profess** i.e., St. Benedict, whose example I follow **186 avouch** confirm

persuasion can with ease attempt you, I will go further than I meant, to pluck all fears out of you. Look you, sir, here is the hand and seal of the Duke. [*He shows a letter.*] You know the character, I doubt not, and the signet is not strange to you.

PROVOST I know them both.

DUKE The contents of this is the return of the Duke. You shall anon overread it at your pleasure, where you shall find within these two days he will be here. This is a thing that Angelo knows not, for he this very day receives letters of strange tenor, perchance of the Duke's death, perchance entering into some monastery, but by chance nothing of what is writ. Look, th'unfolding star calls up the shepherd. Put not yourself into amazement how these things should be; all difficulties are but easy when they are known. Call your executioner, and off with Barnardine's head. I will give him a present shrift and advise him for a better place. Yet you are amazed, but this shall absolutely resolve you. Come away; it is almost clear dawn.

Exit [*with Provost*].

✤

4.3

Enter Clown [*Pompey*].

POMPEY I am as well acquainted here as I was in our house of profession. One would think it were Mistress Overdone's own house, for here be many of her old customers. First, here's young Master Rash; he's in for a commodity of brown paper and old ginger, nine-score and seventeen pounds, of which he made five marks, ready money. Marry, then ginger was not much in request, for the old women were all dead. Then is there here one Master Caper, at the suit of Master Three-pile the mercer, for some four suits of peach-colored satin, which now peaches him a beggar. Then have we here young Dizzy, and young Master Deep-vow, and Master Copper-spur, and Master Starve-lackey the rapier and dagger man, and young Drop-heir that killed lusty Pudding, and Master Forthlight the tilter, and brave Master Shoe-tie the great traveler, and wild Half-can that stabbed Pots, and I think forty more, all great doers in our trade, and are now "for the Lord's sake."

Enter Abhorson.

ABHORSON Sirrah, bring Barnardine hither.

POMPEY [*calling*] Master Barnardine! You must rise and be hanged, Master Barnardine!

ABHORSON What, ho, Barnardine!

BARNARDINE (*within*) A pox o' your throats! Who makes that noise there? What are you?

POMPEY Your friends, sir, the hangman. You must be so good, sir, to rise and be put to death.

BARNARDINE [*within*] Away, you rogue, away! I am sleepy.

ABHORSON Tell him he must awake, and that quickly, too.

POMPEY Pray, Master Barnardine, awake till you are executed, and sleep afterwards.

ABHORSON Go in to him, and fetch him out.

POMPEY He is coming, sir, he is coming. I hear his straw rustle.

Enter Barnardine.

ABHORSON Is the ax upon the block, sirrah?

POMPEY Very ready, sir.

BARNARDINE How now, Abhorson? What's the news with you?

ABHORSON Truly, sir, I would desire you to clap into your prayers; for, look you, the warrant's come.

BARNARDINE You rogue, I have been drinking all night. I am not fitted for't.

POMPEY Oh, the better, sir, for he that drinks all night and is hanged betimes in the morning may sleep the sounder all the next day.

Enter Duke [*disguised as before*].

ABHORSON Look you, sir, here comes your ghostly father. Do we jest now, think you?

DUKE Sir, induced by my charity, and hearing how hastily you are to depart, I am come to advise you, comfort you, and pray with you.

BARNARDINE Friar, not I. I have been drinking hard all night, and I will have more time to prepare me, or

190 attempt win, tempt **193 character** handwriting **194 strange** unknown **201 entering** of his entering **202 writ** i.e., written here. **202-3 unfolding star** i.e., morning star, Venus, which bids the shepherd lead his sheep from the fold **207 present shrift** immediate absolution for sins (after confession) **207–8 advise . . . place** counsel him on the comforts of heaven. **208 Yet** Still **209 resolve you** dispel your uncertainties.

4.3 Location: The prison.

1 well widely **4 Rash** (All the names mentioned by Pompey apparently glance at contemporary social affectations and defects. *Rash* means "reckless.") **5–8 a commodity . . . dead** (To circumvent the laws against excessive rates of interest, moneylenders often advanced cheap commodities to gullible borrowers in lieu of cash. Master Rash, having agreed to a valuation of 197 pounds for such merchandise, has been able to resell it for only five marks, each mark worth about two-thirds of a pound, and has been thrown into prison for debt. The ginger has not fetched a good price, owing to lack of customers, since the old women who are proverbially fond of ginger are no longer alive.) **9 Caper** (To *caper* was to dance or leap gracefully.)

10 Three-pile the thickest nap and most expensive grade of velvet. **mercer** cloth merchant. **suits** (With a play on *suit,* line 9.)

11 peaches him denounces him as. (With a play on *peach.*) **12 Dizzy** i.e., giddy, foolish **13 Deep-vow** one who swears earnestly and often. **Copper-spur** (Copper was often used fraudulently to simulate gold.)

14 Starve-lackey (Spendthrift gallants often virtually starved their pages.) **15 Drop-heir** (Perhaps referring to those who disinherited or preyed on unsuspecting heirs; or else *Drop-hair,* losing hair from syphilis.) **lusty** vigorous. **Pudding** i.e., sausage **16 Forthlight** (Unexplained; perhaps an error for *Forthright,* referring to a style of tilting.) **tilter** jouster. **brave** showy, splendidly dressed. **Shoe-tie** (Evidently a nickname for travelers and others who affected the foreign fashion of elaborate rosettes on the tie of the shoe.) **17 Half-can** i.e., a small drinking tankard. **Pots** i.e., ale pots **19 "for . . . sake"** (The cry of prisoners from jail grates to passers-by to give them food or alms.) **22 be hanged** (With a play on the imprecation; compare "go to the devil.") **41 clap into** quickly begin **46 betimes** early **48 ghostly** spiritual

they shall beat out my brains with billets. I will not consent to die this day, that's certain.

DUKE
Oh, sir, you must, and therefore I beseech you
Look forward on the journey you shall go.

BARNARDINE I swear I will not die today for any man's persuasion.

DUKE But hear you—

BARNARDINE Not a word. If you have anything to say to me, come to my ward, for thence will not I today.
Exit.

Enter Provost.

DUKE
Unfit to live or die. Oh, gravel heart!
After him, fellows. Bring him to the block.
[*Exeunt Abhorson and Pompey.*]

PROVOST
Now, sir, how do you find the prisoner?

DUKE
A creature unprepared, unmeet for death;
And to transport him in the mind he is
Were damnable.

PROVOST Here in the prison, Father,
There died this morning of a cruel fever
One Ragozine, a most notorious pirate,
A man of Claudio's years, his beard and head
Just of his color. What if we do omit
This reprobate till he were well inclined,
And satisfy the deputy with the visage
Of Ragozine, more like to Claudio?

DUKE
Oh, 'tis an accident that heaven provides!
Dispatch it presently; the hour draws on
Prefixed by Angelo. See this be done,
And sent according to command, whiles I
Persuade this rude wretch willingly to die.

PROVOST
This shall be done, good Father, presently.
But Barnardine must die this afternoon.
And how shall we continue Claudio,
To save me from the danger that might come
If he were known alive?

DUKE Let this be done:
Put them in secret holds, both Barnardine and
Claudio.
Ere twice the sun hath made his journal greeting
To yond generation, you shall find
Your safety manifested.

PROVOST I am your free dependent.

DUKE
Quick, dispatch, and send the head to Angelo.
Exit [*Provost*].
Now will I write letters to Varrius—
The Provost, he shall bear them—whose contents
Shall witness to him I am near at home,
And that, by great injunctions, I am bound
To enter publicly. Him I'll desire
To meet me at the consecrated fount
A league below the city; and from thence,
By cold gradation and well-balanced form,
We shall proceed with Angelo.

Enter Provost [*with Ragozine's head*].

PROVOST
Here is the head. I'll carry it myself.

DUKE
Convenient is it. Make a swift return,
For I would commune with you of such things
That want no ear but yours.

PROVOST I'll make all speed. *Exit.*

ISABELLA (*within*) Peace, ho, be here!

DUKE
The tongue of Isabel. She's come to know
If yet her brother's pardon be come hither.
But I will keep her ignorant of her good,
To make her heavenly comforts of despair
When it is least expected.

Enter Isabella.

ISABELLA Ho, by your leave!

DUKE
Good morning to you, fair and gracious daughter.

ISABELLA
The better, given me by so holy a man.
Hath yet the deputy sent my brother's pardon?

DUKE
He hath released him, Isabel, from the world.
His head is off and sent to Angelo.

ISABELLA
Nay, but it is not so!

DUKE It is no other.
Show your wisdom, daughter, in your close patience.

ISABELLA
Oh, I will to him and pluck out his eyes!

DUKE
You shall not be admitted to his sight.

ISABELLA
Unhappy Claudio! Wretched Isabel!
Injurious world! Most damnèd Angelo!

55 billets cudgels, blocks of wood. **63 ward** cell **64 gravel** stony
67 unmeet unready, unfit **68 transport him** i.e., send him to his doom. **he is** he is in **73 omit** ignore, overlook **78 presently** immediately. (As also in line 82.) **79 Prefixed** appointed beforehand, stipulated **81 rude** uncivilized **84 continue** preserve
87 holds cells, dungeons **88 journal** daily **89 yond** i.e., beyond these walls, outside the perpetually dark prison (?). Sometimes it is emended to *th' under*, the people of the Antipodes, on the opposite side of the earth, or, people under the sun, the human race. **91 free dependent** willing servant.

93 to Varrius (The Folio reads "to Angelo," but see line 99 below and 4.5.12–14; evidently, the Duke's plan is to meet Varrius "a league below the city" and then proceed to the rendezvous with Angelo.)
96 by great injunctions by powerful precedent or for compelling reasons **98 fount** spring **99 league** (A measure of varying length but usually about three miles.) **100 cold . . . form** i.e., moving deliberately and with proper observance of all formalities **103 Convenient** Timely, fitting **104 commune** converse **105 want** require **110 of** from, transformed out of **118 close patience** silent enduring.

DUKE
This nor hurts him nor profits you a jot. 123
Forbear it therefore; give your cause to heaven.
Mark what I say, which you shall find
By every syllable a faithful verity. 126
The Duke comes home tomorrow. Nay, dry your eyes;
One of our convent, and his confessor,
Gives me this instance. Already he hath carried 129
Notice to Escalus and Angelo,
Who do prepare to meet him at the gates,
There to give up their pow'r. If you can, pace your
wisdom 132
In that good path that I would wish it go,
And you shall have your bosom on this wretch, 134
Grace of the Duke, revenges to your heart, 135
And general honor.

ISABELLA I am directed by you.

DUKE
This letter, then, to Friar Peter give.
[He gives her a letter.]
'Tis that he sent me of the Duke's return. 138
Say, by this token, I desire his company
At Mariana's house tonight. Her cause and yours
I'll perfect him withal, and he shall bring you 141
Before the Duke, and to the head of Angelo 142
Accuse him home and home. For my poor self, 143
I am combinèd by a sacred vow, 144
And shall be absent. Wend you with this letter.
Command these fretting waters from your eyes 146
With a light heart. Trust not my holy order
If I pervert your course. Who's here?

Enter Lucio.

LUCIO Good even. Friar, where's the Provost?

DUKE Not within, sir.

LUCIO Oh, pretty Isabella, I am pale at mine heart to see 151
thine eyes so red. Thou must be patient. I am fain to 152
dine and sup with water and bran; I dare not for my 153
head fill my belly; one fruitful meal would set me 154
to't. But they say the Duke will be here tomorrow. 155
By my troth, Isabel, I loved thy brother. If the old fantastical Duke of dark corners had been at home, he
had lived. *[Exit Isabella.]*

DUKE Sir, the Duke is marvelous little beholding to 159
your reports; but the best is, he lives not in them. 160

LUCIO Friar, thou knowest not the Duke so well as I
do. He's a better woodman than thou tak'st him for. 162

DUKE Well, you'll answer this one day. Fare ye well.
[He starts to go.]

LUCIO Nay, tarry, I'll go along with thee. I can tell thee pretty tales of the Duke.

DUKE You have told me too many of him already, sir, if they be true; if not true, none were enough.

LUCIO I was once before him for getting a wench with child.

DUKE Did you such a thing?

LUCIO Yes, marry, did I, but I was fain to forswear it.
They would else have married me to the rotten medlar. 172

DUKE Sir, your company is fairer than honest. Rest you well.

LUCIO By my troth, I'll go with thee to the lane's end. If bawdy talk offend you, we'll have very little of it. Nay, Friar, I am a kind of burr; I shall stick. *Exeunt.*

4.4

Enter Angelo and Escalus, [reading letters].

ESCALUS Every letter he hath writ hath disvouched 1
other.

ANGELO In most uneven and distracted manner. His actions show much like to madness. Pray heaven his
wisdom be not tainted! And why meet him at the 5
gates and redeliver our authorities there?

ESCALUS I guess not. 7

ANGELO And why should we proclaim it in an hour be- 8
fore his entering, that if any crave redress of injustice,
they should exhibit their petitions in the street? 10

ESCALUS He shows his reason for that: to have a
dispatch of complaints, and to deliver us from devices 12
hereafter, which shall then have no power to stand against us.

ANGELO Well, I beseech you, let it be proclaimed.
Betimes i'th' morn I'll call you at your house. Give 16
notice to such men of sort and suit as are to meet him. 17

ESCALUS I shall, sir. Fare you well.

ANGELO Good night. *Exit [Escalus].*
This deed unshapes me quite, makes me unpregnant 20
And dull to all proceedings. A deflowered maid,
And by an eminent body that enforced 22
The law against it! But that her tender shame 23
Will not proclaim against her maiden loss,
How might she tongue me! Yet reason dares her no, 25
For my authority bears of a credent bulk 26
That no particular scandal once can touch
But it confounds the breather. He should have lived, 28

123 nor hurts neither hurts **126 By** with respect to **129 instance** proof. **132 pace** teach to move in response to your will, as with a horse **134 bosom** heart's desire **135 Grace of** manifestation of favor from. **to your heart** to your heart's content **138 that** that which. **of** concerning **141 perfect** acquaint completely. **withal** with **142 head** i.e., face **143 home and home** thoroughly. **144 combinèd** bound **146 fretting** corroding **151 pale . . . heart** i.e., pale from sighing (since sighs cost the heart loss of blood) **152 fain** compelled. (As also in line 171.) **153–4 for my head** i.e., on my life **154 fruitful** abundant **154–5 set me to't** i.e., awaken my lust and thus place me in danger of Angelo's edict. **159 marvelous** marvelously. **beholding** beholden **160 he . . . them** i.e., he is not accurately described by them. **162 woodman** i.e., hunter (of women)

172 medlar a fruit that was eaten after it had begun to rot; here, signifying a prostitute.
4.4. Location: In Vienna.
1 disvouched contradicted **5 tainted** diseased. **7 guess not** cannot guess. **8 in an hour** i.e., a full hour **10 exhibit** present **12 dispatch** prompt settlement. **devices** contrived complaints **16 Betimes** Early **17 men . . . suit** men of rank with a retinue **20 unpregnant** unapt **22 body** person **23 But that** Were it not that **25 tongue** i.e., reproach, accuse. **dares her no** i.e., frightens her to say nothing **26 bears . . . bulk** bears such a huge credibility **28 But . . . breather** without its confuting the person who speaks.

Save that his riotous youth, with dangerous sense,
Might in the times to come have ta'en revenge
By so receiving a dishonored life
With ransom of such shame. Would yet he had lived!
Alack, when once our grace we have forgot,
Nothing goes right; we would, and we would not.
Exit.

✤

4.5

Enter Duke [in his own habit] and Friar Peter.

DUKE
These letters at fit time deliver me. [*Giving letters.*]
The Provost knows our purpose and our plot.
The matter being afoot, keep your instruction,
And hold you ever to our special drift,
Though sometimes you do blench from this to that
As cause doth minister. Go call at Flavius' house,
And tell him where I stay. Give the like notice
To Valencius, Rowland, and to Crassus,
And bid them bring the trumpets to the gate;
But send me Flavius first.

FRIAR PETER It shall be speeded well. [*Exit.*]

Enter Varrius.

DUKE
I thank thee, Varrius. Thou hast made good haste.
Come, we will walk. There's other of our friends
Will greet us here anon. My gentle Varrius! *Exeunt.*

✤

4.6

Enter Isabella and Mariana.

ISABELLA
To speak so indirectly I am loath.
I would say the truth, but to accuse him so,
That is your part. Yet I am advised to do it,
He says, to veil full purpose.

MARIANA Be ruled by him.

ISABELLA
Besides, he tells me that if peradventure
He speak against me on the adverse side,
I should not think it strange, for 'tis a physic
That's bitter to sweet end.

Enter [Friar] Peter.

MARIANA
I would Friar Peter—

ISABELLA Oh, peace, the Friar is come.

FRIAR PETER
Come, I have found you out a stand most fit,
Where you may have such vantage on the Duke
He shall not pass you. Twice have the trumpets sounded.
The generous and gravest citizens
Have hent the gates, and very near upon
The Duke is entering. Therefore hence, away!
Exeunt.

✤

5.1

Enter Duke, Varrius, lords, Angelo, Escalus, Lucio, [Provost, officers, and] citizens at several doors.

DUKE
My very worthy cousin, fairly met!
Our old and faithful friend, we are glad to see you.

ANGELO, ESCALUS
Happy return be to Your royal Grace!

DUKE
Many and hearty thankings to you both.
We have made inquiry of you, and we hear
Such goodness of your justice that our soul
Cannot but yield you forth to public thanks,
Forerunning more requital.

ANGELO You make my bonds still greater.

DUKE
Oh, your desert speaks loud, and I should wrong it
To lock it in the wards of covert bosom,
When it deserves with characters of brass
A forted residence 'gainst the tooth of time
And razure of oblivion. Give me your hand,
And let the subject see, to make them know
That outward courtesies would fain proclaim
Favors that keep within. Come, Escalus,
You must walk by us on our other hand,
And good supporters are you.

Enter [Friar] Peter and Isabella.

FRIAR PETER [*to Isabella*]
Now is your time. Speak loud, and kneel before him.

ISABELLA [*kneeling*]
Justice, O royal Duke! Vail your regard
Upon a wronged—I would fain have said a maid.
O worthy prince, dishonor not your eye
By throwing it on any other object
Till you have heard me in my true complaint
And given me justice, justice, justice, justice!

29 sense passion, intention **31 By** for, because of
4.5. Location: Outside the city.
1 me for me **3 keep** keep to **4 drift** plot **5 blench . . . that** swerve from one expedient to another **6 minister** prompt, provide occasion. **9 trumpets** trumpeters **11 speeded** accomplished, expedited
4.6. Location: Near the city gate. 4 veil full pupose conceal our full plan. **5 peradventure** perhaps **7 physic** remedy

10 stand place to stand **13 generous** highborn **14 hent** reached, occupied. **very near upon** almost immediately now
5.1 Location: The city gate.
0.2 ***several*** separate **1 cousin** fellow nobleman. (Addressed to Angelo.) **2 friend** i.e., Escalus **7 yield . . . to** call you forth to give you **8 more requital** further reward. **9 bonds** obligations **11 To lock . . . bosom** i.e., to keep it locked up in my heart **12 characters** writing, letters **13 forted** fortified **14 razure** effacement **15 the subject** those who are subjects **16–17 That . . . within** that public ceremonies serve as outward manifestations of the approval my heart feels for you. **21 Vail your regard** Look down

DUKE
Relate your wrongs. In what? By whom? Be brief.
Here is Lord Angelo shall give you justice.
Reveal yourself to him.

ISABELLA O worthy Duke,
You bid me seek redemption of the devil.
Hear me yourself; for that which I must speak
Must either punish me, not being believed,
Or wring redress from you.
Hear me, oh, hear me, hear!

ANGELO
My lord, her wits, I fear me, are not firm.
She hath been a suitor to me for her brother
Cut off by course of justice.

ISABELLA [*standing*] By course of justice!

ANGELO
And she will speak most bitterly and strange.

ISABELLA
Most strange, but yet most truly, will I speak.
That Angelo's forsworn, is it not strange?
That Angelo's a murderer, is 't not strange?
That Angelo is an adulterous thief,
An hypocrite, a virgin-violator,
Is it not strange, and strange?

DUKE Nay, it is ten times strange.

ISABELLA
It is not truer he is Angelo
Than this is all as true as it is strange.
Nay, it is ten times true, for truth is truth
To th'end of reck'ning.

DUKE Away with her! Poor soul,
She speaks this in th'infirmity of sense.

ISABELLA
O prince, I conjure thee, as thou believ'st
There is another comfort than this world,
That thou neglect me not with that opinion
That I am touched with madness. Make not
impossible
That which but seems unlike. 'Tis not impossible
But one, the wicked'st caitiff on the ground,
May seem as shy, as grave, as just, as absolute
As Angelo; even so may Angelo,
In all his dressings, characts, titles, forms,
Be an archvillain. Believe it, royal prince,
If he be less, he's nothing; but he's more,
Had I more name for badness.

DUKE By mine honesty,
If she be mad—as I believe no other—
Her madness hath the oddest frame of sense,
Such a dependency of thing on thing,
As e'er I heard in madness.

ISABELLA O gracious Duke,
Harp not on that, nor do not banish reason
For inequality, but let your reason serve
To make the truth appear where it seems hid,
And hide the false seems true.

DUKE Many that are not mad
Have, sure, more lack of reason. What would
you say?

ISABELLA
I am the sister of one Claudio,
Condemned upon the act of fornication
To lose his head, condemned by Angelo.
I, in probation of a sisterhood,
Was sent to by my brother; one Lucio
As then the messenger—

LUCIO That's I, an't like Your Grace.
I came to her from Claudio and desired her
To try her gracious fortune with Lord Angelo
For her poor brother's pardon.

ISABELLA That's he indeed.

DUKE [*to Lucio*]
You were not bid to speak.

LUCIO No, my good lord,
Nor wished to hold my peace.

DUKE I wish you now, then.
Pray you, take note of it. And when you have
A business for yourself, pray heaven you then
Be perfect.

LUCIO I warrant Your Honor.

DUKE
The warrant's for yourself. Take heed to 't.

ISABELLA
This gentleman told somewhat of my tale—

LUCIO Right.

DUKE
It may be right, but you are i'the wrong
To speak before your time.—Proceed.

ISABELLA I went
To this pernicious caitiff deputy—

DUKE
That's somewhat madly spoken.

ISABELLA Pardon it;
The phrase is to the matter.

DUKE Mended again. The matter; proceed.

ISABELLA
In brief, to set the needless process by,
How I persuaded, how I prayed and kneeled,
How he refelled me, and how I replied—
For this was of much length—the vile conclusion

28 shall who shall **32 not being** if I am not **38 strange** strangely. **47 Than** than that **49 To . . . reck'ning** to the end of time and Day of Judgment, always. **50 in . . . sense** out of a sick mind, out of the weakness of passion. **53 with that opinion** out of a supposition **54 Make not** Do not consider as **55 unlike** unlikely. **56 But** but that. **ground** earth **57 shy** quietly dignified. **absolute** flawless **59 dressings, characts** ceremonial robes, insignia of office **61 If . . . nothing** i.e., even if he were less than an archvillain, he would be worthless **64 frame of sense** form of reason **65 dependency . . . on thing** coherence

67–8 do . . . inequality i.e., do not assume lack of reason on my part because of the inconsistency between my story and Angelo's refutation, or because of the inequality in our reputations **70 hide** put out of sight, remove from consideration. **seems** that seems **76 in probation** i.e., a novice **78 As then** being at that time. **an't like** if it please **86 perfect** prepared. **87 warrant** assure. (The Duke, however, quibbles in line 88 on the meaning "judicial writ.") **95 to the matter** to the purpose. **96 Mended . . . proceed** That sets things right. Proceed to the main point. **97 to set . . . by** not to dwell on unnecessary details in the story **99 refelled** refuted, repelled

I now begin with grief and shame to utter.
He would not, but by gift of my chaste body
To his concupiscible intemperate lust,
Release my brother; and after much debatement
My sisterly remorse confutes mine honor,
And I did yield to him. But the next morn betimes,
His purpose surfeiting, he sends a warrant
For my poor brother's head.

DUKE This is most likely!

ISABELLA
Oh, that it were as like as it is true!

DUKE
By heaven, fond wretch, thou know'st not what thou speak'st,
Or else thou art suborned against his honor
In hateful practice. First, his integrity
Stands without blemish. Next, it imports no reason
That with such vehemency he should pursue
Faults proper to himself. If he had so offended,
He would have weighed thy brother by himself
And not have cut him off. Someone hath set you on.
Confess the truth, and say by whose advice
Thou cam'st here to complain.

ISABELLA And is this all?
Then, O you blessèd ministers above,
Keep me in patience, and with ripened time
Unfold the evil which is here wrapped up
In countenance! Heaven shield Your Grace from woe,
As I thus wronged hence unbelievèd go!
[*She starts to leave.*]

DUKE
I know you'd fain be gone.—An officer!
To prison with her. Shall we thus permit
A blasting and a scandalous breath to fall
On him so near us? This needs must be a practice.
Who knew of your intent and coming hither?

ISABELLA
One that I would were here, Friar Lodowick.

DUKE
A ghostly father, belike. Who knows that Lodowick?

LUCIO
My lord, I know him; 'tis a meddling friar.
I do not like the man. Had he been lay, my lord,
For certain words he spake against Your Grace
In your retirement, I had swinged him soundly.

DUKE
Words against me? This' a good friar, belike!
And to set on this wretched woman here
Against our substitute! Let this friar be found.
[*Exit one or more attendants.*]

LUCIO
But yesternight, my lord, she and that friar,
I saw them at the prison. A saucy friar,
A very scurvy fellow.

FRIAR PETER Blessed be Your royal Grace!
I have stood by, my lord, and I have heard
Your royal ear abused. First, hath this woman
Most wrongfully accused your substitute,
Who is as free from touch or soil with her
As she from one ungot.

DUKE We did believe no less.
Know you that Friar Lodowick that she speaks of?

FRIAR PETER
I know him for a man divine and holy,
Not scurvy, nor a temporary meddler,
As he's reported by this gentleman;
And, on my trust, a man that never yet
Did, as he vouches, misreport Your Grace.

LUCIO
My lord, most villainously, believe it.

FRIAR PETER
Well, he in time may come to clear himself;
But at this instant he is sick, my lord,
Of a strange fever. Upon his mere request,
Being come to knowledge that there was complaint
Intended 'gainst Lord Angelo, came I hither,
To speak, as from his mouth, what he doth know
Is true and false, and what he with his oath
And all probation will make up full clear,
Whensoever he's convented. First, for this woman,
To justify this worthy nobleman,
So vulgarly and personally accused,
Her shall you hear disprovèd to her eyes,
Till she herself confess it. [*Exit Isabella, guarded.*]

DUKE Good Friar, let's hear it.
[*Friar Peter goes to bring in Mariana.*]
Do you not smile at this, Lord Angelo?
Oh, heaven, the vanity of wretched fools!
Give us some seats. [*Seats are provided.*]
Come, cousin Angelo,
In this I'll be impartial. Be you judge
Of your own cause. [*The Duke and Angelo sit.*]

Enter Mariana, [*veiled, with Friar Peter*].

Is this the witness, Friar?
First, let her show her face, and after speak.

MARIANA
Pardon, my lord, I will not show my face
Until my husband bid me.

103 concupiscible lustful **104 debatement** argument, debate **105 remorse** pity. **confutes** confounds, silences **106 betimes** early **107 surfeiting** being satiated **109 like** likely **110 fond** foolish **111 suborned** induced to give false testimony **112 practice** machination, conspiracy. **113 imports no reason** i.e., makes no sense **115 proper to himself** of which he himself is guilty. **116 weighed** judged **122 Unfold** disclose **122–3 wrapped . . . countenance** concealed by the privilege of authority. **127 blasting** blighting **131 A ghostly . . . belike** A cleric, apparently. **133 lay** not a cleric **135 In your retirement** during your absence. **had swinged** would have beaten **136 This'** This is

147 ungot unbegotten. **151 temporary meddler** meddler in temporal affairs **158 Upon . . . request** Solely at his request **159 Being . . . knowledge** he having learned **163 probation** proof **164 convented** summoned. **166 vulgarly** publicly **167 to her eyes** i.e., to her face **168 s.d. *Exit Isbella, guarded*** (Isabella seemingly must leave the stage here or soon afterwards. She is described as "gone" at line 250, and is summoned at line 278. The phrase "to her eyes" in line 167 may mean "incontrovertibly.") **170 vanity** folly

DUKE What, are you married?
MARIANA No, my lord.
DUKE Are you a maid?
MARIANA No, my lord.
DUKE A widow, then?
MARIANA Neither, my lord.
DUKE Why, you are nothing then, neither maid, widow, nor wife?
LUCIO My lord, she may be a punk, for many of them are neither maid, widow, nor wife.
DUKE
Silence that fellow. I would he had some cause
To prattle for himself.
LUCIO Well, my lord.
MARIANA
My lord, I do confess I ne'er was married,
And I confess besides I am no maid.
I have known my husband, yet my husband
Knows not that ever he knew me.
LUCIO He was drunk then, my lord; it can be no better.
DUKE For the benefit of silence, would thou wert so too!
LUCIO Well, my lord.
DUKE
This is no witness for Lord Angelo.
MARIANA Now I come to 't, my lord.
She that accuses him of fornication
In selfsame manner doth accuse my husband,
And charges him, my lord, with such a time
When, I'll depose, I had him in mine arms
With all th'effect of love.
ANGELO Charges she more than me?
MARIANA Not that I know.
DUKE No? You say your husband?
MARIANA
Why, just, my lord, and that is Angelo,
Who thinks he knows that he ne'er knew my body,
But knows he thinks that he knows Isabel's.
ANGELO
This is a strange abuse. Let's see thy face.
MARIANA
My husband bids me. Now I will unmask.
[*She unveils.*]
This is that face, thou cruel Angelo,
Which once thou swor'st was worth the looking on;
This is the hand which, with a vowed contract,
Was fast belocked in thine; this is the body
That took away the match from Isabel,
And did supply thee at thy garden house
In her imagined person.
DUKE [*to Angelo*] Know you this woman?
LUCIO Carnally, she says.
DUKE Sirrah, no more!
LUCIO Enough, my lord.
ANGELO
My lord, I must confess I know this woman,
And five years since there was some speech of marriage
Betwixt myself and her, which was broke off,
Partly for that her promisèd proportions
Came short of composition, but in chief
For that her reputation was disvalued
In levity. Since which time of five years
I never spake with her, saw her, nor heard from her,
Upon my faith and honor.
MARIANA [*kneeling*] Noble prince,
As there comes light from heaven and words from breath,
As there is sense in truth and truth in virtue,
I am affianced this man's wife as strongly
As words could make up vows; and, my good lord,
But Tuesday night last gone in's garden house
He knew me as a wife. As this is true,
Let me in safety raise me from my knees,
Or else forever be confixèd here,
A marble monument!
ANGELO I did but smile till now.
Now, good my lord, give me the scope of justice.
My patience here is touched. I do perceive
These poor informal women are no more
But instruments of some more mightier member
That sets them on. Let me have way, my lord,
To find this practice out.
DUKE Ay, with my heart,
And punish them to your height of pleasure.—
Thou foolish friar, and thou pernicious woman,
Compact with her that's gone, think'st thou thy oaths,
Though they would swear down each particular saint,
Were testimonies against his worth and credit
That's sealed in approbation?—You, Lord Escalus,
Sit with my cousin; lend him your kind pains
To find out this abuse, whence 'tis derived.
There is another friar that set them on;
Let him be sent for.
[*The Duke rises; Escalus takes his chair.*]
FRIAR PETER
Would he were here, my lord! For he indeed
Hath set the women on to this complaint.
Your Provost knows the place where he abides,
And he may fetch him.
DUKE Go do it instantly.
[*Exit Provost.*]
And you, my noble and well-warranted cousin,
Whom it concerns to hear this matter forth,
Do with your injuries as seems you best,

185 punk harlot **188 To . . . himself** to speak in his own defense. (The Duke hints that there might well be charges pending against Lucio.) **192 known** had sexual intercourse with **201 with . . . time** with doing the deed at just the same time **202 depose** testify under oath **203 With . . . love** i.e., with sexual fulfillment. **204 Charges . . . me?** Does she (Isabella) bring charges against persons besides myself? **207 just** just so **210 abuse** deception. **215 fast belocked** firmly locked **216 match** assignation

226 for that because. **proportions** dowry **227 composition** agreement **228–9 disvalued In levity** discredited for lightness. **239 confixèd** firmly fixed **242 scope** full authority **243 touched** injured, affected. **244 informal** rash, distracted **245 But** than **250 Compact . . . gone** i.e., in collusion with Isabella **251 swear . . . saint** call down to witness every single saint **253 sealed in approbation** ratified by proof, like weights and measures being given a stamp or seal to attest to their genuineness. **263 forth** through **264 Do . . . best** respond to the wrongs done you as seems best to you

In any chastisement. I for a while
Will leave you; but stir not you till you have
Well determined upon these slanderers.

ESCALUS My lord, we'll do it throughly. *Exit* [*Duke*].
Signor Lucio, did not you say you knew that Friar Lodowick to be a dishonest person?

LUCIO *Cucullus non facit monachum*; honest in nothing but in his clothes, and one that hath spoke most villainous speeches of the Duke.

ESCALUS We shall entreat you to abide here till he come, and enforce them against him. We shall find this friar a notable fellow.

LUCIO As any in Vienna, on my word.

ESCALUS Call that same Isabel here once again. I would speak with her. [*Exit an Attendant.*]
Pray you, my lord, give me leave to question. You shall see how I'll handle her.

LUCIO Not better than he, by her own report.

ESCALUS Say you?

LUCIO Marry, sir, I think, if you handled her privately, she would sooner confess; perchance publicly she'll be ashamed.

ESCALUS I will go darkly to work with her.

LUCIO That's the way, for women are light at midnight.

Enter Duke [*disguised as a friar*], *Provost, Isabella,* [*and officers*].

ESCALUS Come on, mistress. Here's a gentlewoman denies all that you have said.

LUCIO My lord, here comes the rascal I spoke of, here with the Provost.

ESCALUS In very good time. Speak not you to him till we call upon you.

LUCIO Mum.

ESCALUS Come, sir, did you set these women on to slander Lord Angelo? They have confessed you did.

DUKE 'Tis false.

ESCALUS How? Know you where you are?

DUKE
Respect to your great place! And let the devil
Be sometime honored for his burning throne!
Where is the Duke? 'Tis he should hear me speak.

ESCALUS
The Duke's in us, and we will hear you speak.
Look you speak justly.

DUKE
Boldly, at least. But oh, poor souls,
Come you to seek the lamb here of the fox?
Good night to your redress! Is the Duke gone?
Then is your cause gone too. The Duke's unjust,
Thus to retort your manifest appeal,
And put your trial in the villain's mouth
Which here you come to accuse.

LUCIO
This is the rascal. This is he I spoke of.

ESCALUS
Why, thou unreverend and unhallowed friar,
Is't not enough thou hast suborned these women
To accuse this worthy man, but, in foul mouth
And in the witness of his proper ear,
To call him villain? And then to glance from him
To th'Duke himself, to tax him with injustice?—
Take him hence. To th' rack with him!—We'll touse
you
Joint by joint, but we will know his purpose.
What, "unjust"?

DUKE Be not so hot. The Duke
Dare no more stretch this finger of mine than he
Dare rack his own. His subject am I not,
Nor here provincial. My business in this state
Made me a looker-on here in Vienna,
Where I have seen corruption boil and bubble
Till it o'errun the stew; laws for all faults,
But faults so countenanced that the strong statutes
Stand like the forfeits in a barber's shop,
As much in mock as mark.

ESCALUS Slander to th' state!
Away with him to prison.

ANGELO
What can you vouch against him, Signor Lucio?
Is this the man that you did tell us of?

LUCIO 'Tis he, my lord.—Come hither, Goodman Baldpate. Do you know me?

DUKE I remember you, sir, by the sound of your voice. I met you at the prison, in the absence of the Duke.

LUCIO Oh, did you so? And do you remember what you said of the Duke?

DUKE Most notedly, sir.

LUCIO Do you so, sir? And was the Duke a fleshmonger, a fool, and a coward, as you then reported him to be?

DUKE You must, sir, change persons with me ere you make that my report. You indeed spoke so of him, and much more, much worse.

LUCIO Oh, thou damnable fellow! Did not I pluck thee by the nose for thy speeches?

DUKE I protest I love the Duke as I love myself.

ANGELO Hark how the villain would close now, after his treasonable abuses!

267 determined reached judgment **268 throughly** thoroughly.
271 *Cucullus . . . monachum* A cowl doesn't make a monk
275 enforce them forcefully urge your charges **276 notable** notorious **282 Not . . . report** (Lucio salaciously turns Escalus's *handle her* into a sexual slur: You, Escalus, will do no better at "handling" Isabella than did Angelo, according to Isabella's testimony.) **284 if . . . privately** (Lucio continues his sexual joke about "handling.") **287 darkly** subtly, slyly **288 light** wanton, unchaste **300–1 let . . . throne** i.e., may all authority be respected, even the devil's. (Said sardonically.) **309 retort** turn back. **manifest** obviously just

316 in . . . ear within his own hearing **318 tax him with** accuse him of **319 touse** tear **320 but we will** i.e., if necessary to; until we **324 provincial** subject to the religious authority of this province or state. **327 stew** (1) stewpot (2) brothel **328 countenanced** tolerated and protected by corrupt authority **329 forfeits** cautionary displays, or lists of rules and fines for handling razors, etc., which barbers (who also acted as dentists and surgeons) hung in their shops
330 As . . . mark as often flouted as observed. **334–5 Goodman Baldpate** (Lucio refers to the tonsure that he assumes the Duke must have under his hood, though the Duke is clearly hooded at this point.) **340 notedly** particularly **344 change** exchange **350 close** come to terms, compromise

ESCALUS Such a fellow is not to be talked withal. Away with him to prison! Where is the Provost? Away with him to prison! Lay bolts enough upon him. Let him speak no more. Away with those giglots too, and with the other confederate companion!

[The Provost lays hands on the Duke.]

DUKE *[to Provost]* Stay, sir, stay awhile.

ANGELO What, resists he? Help him, Lucio.

LUCIO Come, sir, come, sir, come, sir; foh, sir! Why, you bald-pated, lying rascal, you must be hooded, must you? Show your knave's visage, with a pox to you! Show your sheep-biting face, and be hanged an hour! Will't not off?

[He pulls off the friar's hood, and discovers the Duke. Angelo and Escalus rise.]

DUKE
Thou art the first knave that e'er mad'st a duke.
First, Provost, let me bail these gentle three.
[To Lucio] Sneak not away, sir, for the Friar and you
Must have a word anon.—Lay hold on him.

LUCIO This may prove worse than hanging.

DUKE *[to Escalus]*
What you have spoke I pardon. Sit you down.
We'll borrow place of him. *[To Angelo]* Sir, by your
leave. *[He takes Angelo's seat. Escalus also sits.]*
Hast thou or word, or wit, or impudence,
That yet can do thee office? If thou hast,
Rely upon it till my tale be heard,
And hold no longer out.

ANGELO *[kneeling]* O my dread lord,
I should be guiltier than my guiltiness
To think I can be undiscernible,
When I perceive Your Grace, like power divine,
Hath looked upon my passes. Then, good prince,
No longer session hold upon my shame,
But let my trial be mine own confession.
Immediate sentence then and sequent death
Is all the grace I beg.

DUKE Come hither, Mariana.—
Say, wast thou e'er contracted to this woman?

ANGELO I was, my lord.

DUKE
Go take her hence and marry her instantly.
Do you the office, Friar, which consummate,
Return him here again. Go with him, Provost.

Exit [Angelo, with Mariana, Friar Peter, and Provost].

ESCALUS
My lord, I am more amazed at his dishonor
Than at the strangeness of it.

DUKE Come hither, Isabel.
Your friar is now your prince. As I was then
Advertising and holy to your business,
Not changing heart with habit, I am still
Attorneyed at your service.

ISABELLA Oh, give me pardon,
That I, your vassal, have employed and pained
Your unknown sovereignty!

DUKE You are pardoned, Isabel.
And now, dear maid, be you as free to us.
Your brother's death, I know, sits at your heart;
And you may marvel why I obscured myself,
Laboring to save his life, and would not rather
Make rash remonstrance of my hidden power
Than let him so be lost. O most kind maid,
It was the swift celerity of his death,
Which I did think with slower foot came on,
That brained my purpose. But peace be with him!
That life is better life past fearing death
Than that which lives to fear. Make it your comfort,
So happy is your brother.

Enter Angelo, Mariana, [Friar] Peter, [and] Provost.

ISABELLA I do, my lord.

DUKE
For this new-married man approaching here,
Whose salt imagination yet hath wronged
Your well-defended honor, you must pardon
For Mariana's sake. But as he adjudged your
brother—
Being criminal, in double violation
Of sacred chastity and of promise-breach
Thereon dependent, for your brother's life—
The very mercy of the law cries out
Most audible, even from his proper tongue,
"An Angelo for Claudio, death for death!"
Haste still pays haste, and leisure answers leisure;
Like doth quit like, and measure still for measure.
Then, Angelo, thy fault's thus manifested,
Which, though thou wouldst deny, denies thee
vantage.
We do condemn thee to the very block
Where Claudio stooped to death, and with like haste.
Away with him!

MARIANA O my most gracious lord,
I hope you will not mock me with a husband!

DUKE
It is your husband mocked you with a husband.
Consenting to the safeguard of your honor,
I thought your marriage fit; else imputation,
For that he knew you, might reproach your life

354 bolts iron fetters **355 giglots** wanton women **356 confederate companion** i.e., Friar Peter. **362 sheep-biting** knavish. (From the action of wolves or dogs that prey on sheep.) **362–3 hanged an hour** (A sardonic way of saying "hanged.") **365 gentle three** i.e., Mariana, Isabella, and Friar Peter. **371 or word** either word **372 office** service. **374 hold . . . out** then persist no longer. **378 passes** actions, trespasses. **381 sequent** subsequent **386 Do . . . office** Please perform the service. **consummate** being completed

391 Advertising and holy attentive and wholly dedicated (in my priestly role) **393 Attorneyed at** serving as agent in **394 pained** put to trouble **396 as free to us** i.e., as generous in pardoning me. **400 rash remonstrance** sudden manifestation **404 brained** dashed, defeated **407 So** thus **409 salt** lecherous **413–14 promise-breach . . . dependent** i.e., breaking his promise made in return for the yielding up of chastity **415 The very . . . law** i.e., even mercy itself **416 his proper** its own **418 still** always **419 quit** requite **421 though** even if. **vantage** i.e., any advantage. (Angelo must suffer the same penalty as Claudio.) **428 fit** appropriate. **imputation** accusation, slander **429 For that he knew you** since he knew you sexually

And choke your good to come. For his possessions,
Although by confiscation they are ours,
We do instate and widow you withal,
To buy you a better husband.

MARIANA O my dear lord,
I crave no other, nor no better man.

DUKE
Never crave him; we are definitive.

MARIANA [*kneeling*]
Gentle my liege—

DUKE You do but lose your labor.—
Away with him to death! [*To Lucio*] Now, sir, to you.

MARIANA
O my good lord!—Sweet Isabel, take my part!
Lend me your knees, and all my life to come
I'll lend you all my life to do you service.

DUKE
Against all sense you do importune her.
Should she kneel down in mercy of this fact,
Her brother's ghost his pavèd bed would break,
And take her hence in horror.

MARIANA Isabel,
Sweet Isabel, do yet but kneel by me!
Hold up your hands, say nothing; I'll speak all.
They say best men are molded out of faults,
And, for the most, become much more the better
For being a little bad. So may my husband.
O Isabel, will you not lend a knee?

DUKE
He dies for Claudio's death.

ISABELLA [*kneeling*] Most bounteous sir,
Look, if it please you, on this man condemned
As if my brother lived. I partly think
A due sincerity governed his deeds,
Till he did look on me. Since it is so,
Let him not die. My brother had but justice,
In that he did the thing for which he died.
For Angelo,
His act did not o'ertake his bad intent,
And must be buried but as an intent
That perished by the way. Thoughts are no subjects,
Intents but merely thoughts.

MARIANA Merely, my lord.

DUKE
Your suit's unprofitable. Stand up, I say.
[*They stand.*]
I have bethought me of another fault.
Provost, how came it Claudio was beheaded
At an unusual hour?

PROVOST It was commanded so.

DUKE
Had you a special warrant for the deed?

PROVOST
No, my good lord, it was by private message.

DUKE
For which I do discharge you of your office.
Give up your keys.

PROVOST Pardon me, noble lord.
I thought it was a fault, but knew it not,
Yet did repent me after more advice;
For testimony whereof, one in the prison,
That should by private order else have died,
I have reserved alive.

DUKE What's he?

PROVOST His name is Barnardine.

DUKE
I would thou hadst done so by Claudio.
Go fetch him hither. Let me look upon him.
[*Exit Provost.*]

ESCALUS
I am sorry one so learnèd and so wise
As you, Lord Angelo, have still appeared,
Should slip so grossly, both in the heat of blood
And lack of tempered judgment afterward.

ANGELO
I am sorry that such sorrow I procure,
And so deep sticks it in my penitent heart
That I crave death more willingly than mercy.
'Tis my deserving, and I do entreat it.

Enter Barnardine and Provost, Claudio [*muffled*], [*and*] *Juliet.*

DUKE
Which is that Barnardine?

PROVOST This, my lord.

DUKE
There was a friar told me of this man.—
Sirrah, thou art said to have a stubborn soul
That apprehends no further than this world,
And squar'st thy life according. Thou'rt condemned;
But, for those earthly faults, I quit them all,
And pray thee take this mercy to provide
For better times to come.—Friar, advise him;
I leave him to your hand.—What muffled fellow's
that?

PROVOST
This is another prisoner that I saved,
Who should have died when Claudio lost his head,
As like almost to Claudio as himself.
[*He unmuffles Claudio.*]

DUKE [*to Isabella*]
If he be like your brother, for his sake
Is he pardoned, and for your lovely sake,
Give me your hand and say you will be mine;
He is my brother too. But fitter time for that.
By this Lord Angelo perceives he's safe;
Methinks I see a quick'ning in his eye.
Well, Angelo, your evil quits you well.
Look that you love your wife, her worth worth yours.

430 For As for **432 widow** endow with a widow's rights **435 definitive** firmly resolved. **442 in . . . fact** pleading mercy for this crime **443 pavèd bed** grave covered with a stone slab **447 best men** even the best of men **448 most** most part **460 buried** i.e., forgotten **461 no subjects** i.e., not subject to the state's authority

472 knew it not was not sure **473 advice** consideration **482 still** always **485 procure** cause, prompt **488.1 *muffled*** wrapped up so as to conceal identity. (As also in line 497.) **493 squar'st** regulates **494 for** as for. **quit** pardon **507 quits** rewards, requites **508 her . . . yours** her worthiness richly deserving your love and worthy of your estate.

I find an apt remission in myself;
And yet here's one in place I cannot pardon.
[*To Lucio*] You, sirrah, that knew me for a fool, a coward,
One all of luxury, an ass, a madman—
Wherein have I so deserved of you
That you extol me thus?

LUCIO Faith, my lord, I spoke it but according to the trick. If you will hang me for it, you may; but I had rather it would please you I might be whipped.

DUKE
Whipped first, sir, and hanged after.—
Proclaim it, Provost, round about the city,
If any woman wronged by this lewd fellow—
As I have heard him swear himself there's one
Whom he begot with child—let her appear,
And he shall marry her. The nuptial finished,
Let him be whipped and hanged.

LUCIO I beseech Your Highness, do not marry me to a whore. Your Highness said even now I made you a duke; good my lord, do not recompense me in making me a cuckold.

DUKE
Upon mine honor, thou shalt marry her.
Thy slanders I forgive and therewithal
Remit thy other forfeits.—Take him to prison,
And see our pleasure herein executed.

LUCIO Marrying a punk, my lord, is pressing to death, whipping, and hanging.

DUKE
Slandering a prince deserves it.
[*Exeunt officers with Lucio.*]
She, Claudio, that you wronged, look you restore.
Joy to you, Mariana! Love her, Angelo.
I have confessed her, and I know her virtue.
Thanks, good friend Escalus, for thy much goodness;
There's more behind that is more gratulate.
Thanks, Provost, for thy care and secrecy;
We shall employ thee in a worthier place.
Forgive him, Angelo, that brought you home
The head of Ragozine for Claudio's;
Th'offense pardons itself. Dear Isabel,
I have a motion much imports your good,
Whereto if you'll a willing ear incline,
What's mine is yours, and what is yours is mine.—
So, bring us to our palace, where we'll show
What's yet behind, that's meet you all should know.
[*Exeunt.*]

509 apt remission readiness to show mercy **510 in place** present **512 luxury** lechery **516 trick** fashion. **526 even** just **530–1 and therewithal . . . forfeits** i.e., and in addition to that I will not have you whipped and hanged.

532 see . . . executed i.e., see that my order be carried out that Lucio marry Kate Keepdown (see 3.2.194–6). **533 pressing to death** i.e., by having heavy weights placed on the chest. (A standard form of executing those who refused to plead to a felony charge.) Lucio wryly complains that marrying a whore is as bad as death by torture. **536 She . . . restore** i.e., See to it that you marry Juliet. **540 behind** in store, to come. **gratulate** gratifying. **546 motion** proposal (which) **549 bring** escort **550 What's yet behind** what is still to be told

Troilus and Cressida

Shakespeare must have had some relative failures in the theater, as well as enormous successes. *Troilus and Cressida* seems to have been a relative failure, at least onstage in its original run. As we shall see, questions arise as to whether it was produced at all. It is a bitter play about an inconclusive war and a failed love affair, quite unlike anything Shakespeare had written before in his romantic comedies and English history plays. Its bleak satire of political stalemate seems directed, in part, at the unhappy story of the abortive rebellion of the Earl of Essex in 1601; like many of the warriors in *Troilus and Cressida*, Essex was a tarnished hero whose charisma fell victim to his own egomaniacal ambitions and to the mood of anxious helplessness that hovered over Queen Elizabeth's last years. The play is unusually elliptical in its language, as though Shakespeare deliberately adopted a new, contorted style to express the unresolvable paradoxes of the political and psychological no-man's-land he wanted to describe. A major topic of the play is fame, or rather notoriety, for most of Shakespeare's major characters came to him in the story with full-blown legendary identities as antiheroes: Cressida, the faithless woman; Troilus, the rejected male; Pandarus, the go-between; and Achilles, the butcherer of Hector. Shakespeare's language has to deal with shattered identities, with the unstable subjectivity of human willfulness, and with spiritual exhaustion and neurosis. Perhaps some members of Shakespeare's audience were not quite prepared for all of this.

Today, on the other hand, the play enjoys high critical esteem and has shown itself to be theatrically powerful. What we perceive is that its mordant wit, its satirical depiction of war, and its dispiriting portrayal of sexual infidelity call for a response very different from the one required for an appreciation of *A Midsummer Night's Dream* and *As You Like It* or *1 Henry IV*. *Troilus and Cressida*, written probably in 1601–1602, shortly before the Stationers' Register entry of 1603, is attuned to a new and darker mood emerging during this period in Shakespeare's work and in the work of his contemporaries.

In the early 1600s, dramatic satire enjoyed a sudden and highly visible notoriety. Catering, in large part, to select and courtly audiences, and given new impetus by the reopening of the boys' acting companies at the indoor theaters in 1599, satirical drama quickly employed the talents of Ben Jonson, John Marston, and George Chapman, as well as other sophisticated dramatists. Jonson launched a series of plays he called comical satires, in which he rebuked the London citizenry and presumed to teach manners to the court as well. The so-called War of the Theaters among Jonson, Marston, and Thomas Dekker, although partly a personality clash of no consequence, was also a serious debate between public and more courtly or select stages on the proper uses of satire. Public dramatists complained about the libelous boldness of the new satire and were galled by the preference of some audiences for this new theatrical phenomenon; even Shakespeare fretted in *Hamlet* (2.2.353–79) about the rivalry. Yet, as an artist in search of new forms, he also responded with positive interest. He experimented with a Jonsonian type of satirical plot in the exposure of Malvolio in *Twelfth Night* (1600–1602). *Troilus and Cressida* seems to have been another and more ambitious experiment, embracing a different kind of satire, not of witty exposure, but of disillusionment.

This satiric genre is hard to classify according to the conventional definitions of tragedy, comedy, or history even though it does have its own clearly defined rationale that makes special sense in terms of our modern theater. The play is partly tragic in that it presents the fall of great Hector and adumbrates the fall of Troy, yet its love story merely dwindles into frustrated estrangement without the death of either lover. The play is comic only insofar as it is black comedy or comedy of the absurd. Its leering sexual titillation and its mood of spiritual paralysis link *Troilus and Cressida* to the problem comedies *All's Well*

That Ends Well (c. 1601–1604) and *Measure for Measure* (1603–1604). The play is called a "history" on both its early title pages and assuredly deals with the great events of history's most famous war, but history has become essentially ironic. In this, *Troilus and Cressida* represents a culmination of Shakespeare's ironic exploration of history as begun in the impasses of *Richard II* or *Henry IV* and as portrayed more fully in the sustained ambiguities of *Julius Caesar* (1599). However much Shakespeare may have been influenced by the contemporary vogue of satire in the boys' theater, his own satire of disillusion is integral to his development as an artist. *Troilus and Cressida* is a fitting companion and contemporary for *Hamlet* (c. 1599–1601). Like that play, it evokes a universal disorder that may well reflect the loss of an assured sense of philosophical reliance on the medieval hierarchies of the old Ptolemaic earth-centered cosmos.

Troilus and Cressida achieves its disillusioning effect through repeated ironic juxtaposition of heroic ideals and tarnished realities. Although it deals with the greatest war in history and a renowned love affair, we as audience know that Troy and the lovers will be overthrown by cunning and infidelity. Shakespeare partly inherited from his sources this duality of epic grandness and dispiriting conclusion. To learn of the war itself, he must have known George Chapman's translation of Homer's *Iliad* (of which seven books were published in 1598) and, of course, Virgil's account of the destruction of Troy, but he relied more particularly on medieval romances: Raoul Lefevre's *Recueil des Histoires de Troyes*, as translated and published by William Caxton, and perhaps John Lydgate's *Troy Book*, derived in part from Guido delle Colonne's *Historia Trojana*. These romances were Trojan in point of view and hence concerned with the fall of that city. For the bitter love story, Shakespeare went to Geoffrey Chaucer's *Troilus and Criseyde* (c. 1385–1386), which had been derived from the twelfth-century medieval romance of Benoit de Sainte-Maure, *Le Roman de Troie*, as amplified and retold in Boccaccio's *Il Filostrato*. Chaucer's Criseyde is an admirably self-possessed young woman, and her love for Troilus captures the spirit of the courtly love tradition upon which the story was based. After the late fourteenth century, however, Chaucer's heroine suffered a drastic decline in esteem. In Robert Henryson's *Testament of Cresseid*, for example, Cressida becomes a leper and beggar, the "lazar kite of Cressid's kind" to whom Pistol alludes in *Henry V*. Her name has become synonymous with womanly infidelity, as Shakespeare wryly points out in *Troilus and Cressida:* "Let all constant men be Troiluses, all false women Cressids, and all brokers-between Pandars" (3.2.201–3). Shakespeare is fascinated by this phenomenon of declining reputations. Just as the illustrious warrior Achilles must learn that envious time detracts from our best achievements and stigmatizes us for our worst failings, Troilus, Cressida, and Pandarus all anticipate the lasting consequences to their reputations of a failed love relationship. The passion to which they commit themselves eternally becomes not only an emblem of lost hopes and promises but also a caricature to later generations of enervating and frustrated desire, promiscuity, and pandering. Thus, Shakespeare finds in his materials both chivalric splendor and a deflation of it.

Stylistically, Shakespeare exploits this juxtaposition. He employs epic conventions more than is his custom. The narrative commences, as the Prologue informs us, *in medias res*, "beginning in the middle." Epic similes adorn the formal speeches of Ulysses, Agamemnon, and Nestor. The rhetoric of persuasion plays an important role, as in *Julius Caesar* and other Roman plays. The great names of antiquity are paraded past us in a roll call of heroes. Hector, above all, is an epic hero, although in the fashion of medieval romance he is also the prince of chivalry. He longs to resolve the war by a challenge to single combat, in tournament, with the breaking of lances and with each warrior defending the honor of his lady-fair (1.3.264–83). The Greeks respond for a time to this stirring call to arms. Yet, in the broader context of the war itself, with its unworthy causes, its frustrating irresolution, and its debilitating effect on the morale of both sides, Hector's idealism cannot prevail. On the Greek side, Ulysses's ennobling vision of "degree, priority, and place" (1.3.86), by which the heavens show to humanity the value of harmonious order, serves more to criticize and mock the present disorder of the Greek army than to offer guidance toward a restoration of that order. Epic convention becomes hollow travesty, as chivalric aspirations repeatedly dissolve into the sordid insinuations of Thersites or Pandarus. Despite the play's epic machinery, the gods are nowhere to be found.

A prevailing metaphor is that of disease (as also in *Hamlet*). Insubordinate conduct "infects" (1.3.187) the body politic. The Greek commanders hope to "physic" (1.3.378) Achilles lest his virtues, "like fair fruit in an unwholesome dish," rot untasted (2.3.119). Hector deplores the way his fellow Trojans "infectiously" enslave themselves to willful appetite (2.2.59). Elsewhere, love is described as an open ulcer and as an itch that must be scratched; Helen is "contaminated carrion" (4.1.73). Thersites, most of all, invites us to regard both love and war as disease-ridden, afflicted by boils, plagues, scabs, the "Neapolitan bone-ache" (syphilis), "lethargies, cold palsies, raw eyes, dirt-rotten livers, wheezing lungs, bladders full of imposthume [abscesses], sciaticas," and still more (2.3.18 and 5.1.19–21). Pandarus ends the play on a similarly tawdry note by jesting about prostitutes (Winchester geese, he calls them) and the "sweating" or venereal diseases.

The war is both glorious and absurd. It calls forth brave deeds and heroic sacrifices. Yet it is correctly labeled by the choric Prologue as a "quarrel," begun over an "old aunt," whom the Greeks have held captive, and Helen, whom the Trojans abducted in reprisal. No one believes the original cause to justify the bloodletting that has ensued. Menelaus's cuckoldry is the subject of obscene mirth in the Greek camp. Among the Trojans, Troilus can argue only that one does not return soiled goods; since all Troy consented to Helen's abduction, Troy must continue the war to maintain its honor. The war thus assumes a grim momentum of its own. The combatants repeatedly discover that they are trapped in the ironies of a situation they helped make but can no longer unmake. Hector's challenge to single combat falls upon Ajax, his "father's sister's son." Achilles, too, has allegiances in the enemy's camp, since he is enamored of Priam's daughter Polyxena. In the parleys between the two sides, the warriors greet one another as long-lost brothers, though they vow to slaughter one another on the morrow. With fitting oxymoron, Paris comments on the paradox of this "most despiteful gentle greeting," this "noblest hateful love" (4.1.34–5). Only a barbarian could be free of regret for a peace that seems so near and is yet so far. The war offers insidious temptations to potentially worthy men, perverting Achilles's once-honorable quest for fame into maniacal ambition and an irresistible impulse to murder Hector. History and tradition, we know, will mock Achilles for this craven deed. It will put him down as a bully rather than as a brave soldier, just as Troilus, Cressida, and Pandarus will come to be regarded in time as stereotypes of the cheated man, the whore, and the procurer. Even before the murder of Hector, Achilles sees his reputation for bravery tarnished by his inaction, while Ajax is hoisted into prominence by the machinations of Ulysses and the other generals.

Hector's tragedy is, in its own way, no less ironic. Even though he emerges as the most thoughtful and courageous man on either side and advises his fellow Trojans to let Helen go in response to the "moral laws / Of nature and of nations" (2.2.184–5), he nonetheless ends the Trojan council of war by resolving to fight on with them. This conclusion may represent, in part, a realization that the others will fight on, in any case, and that he must therefore be loyal to them, but the choice also reflects hubris. Hector is not unlike Julius Caesar in his proud repudiation of his wife Andromache's ominous dreams, his sister Cassandra's mad but oracular prophecies, and his own conviction that Troy's pursuit of honor stems from a sickened appetite. He goes to his death because "The gods have heard me swear" (5.3.15). His character is his fate. Even his humane compunctions, like Brutus's, are held against him; he spares the life of Achilles and is murdered in reward. War is no place for men of scruple, as Troilus reminds his older brother. Yet, Hector, at least, is the better man for refusing to be corrupted by the savagery of war; we honor his memory, even if we also view him as senselessly victimized by a meaningless conflict.

The lovers, as well, are caught in war's trap—not only Troilus and Cressida, but also Paris and Helen, Achilles and Polyxena. Achilles vows to Polyxena not to fight and thereby misses his cherished opportunity for fame; ironically, he is aroused to vengeful action only by the death of a male friend, Patroclus, who is whispered to be his "male varlet" or "masculine whore" (5.1.15–17). Paris is obliged to ask his brother Troilus to return Cressida to the Greeks, so that Paris may continue to enjoy Helen. What else can Paris do? "There is no help," he complains. "The bitter disposition of the time / Will have it so" (4.1.49–51). Troilus prepares his own undoing when he argues in the Trojan council of war that Helen must be kept at all cost; the cost, it turns out, is his own Cressida. He sees this irony at once: "How my achievements mock me!" (4.2.71); that is, he has no sooner achieved her sexually than he must give her up so that the war may go on with Trojan honor intact and Helen still in Paris's bed. The love of Troilus and Cressida is dwarfed by the war, which has no regard for their private concerns. Troilus wins Cressida after many months of wooing, only to lose her the next day. Yet how could Cressida's father Calchas know of her personal situation? He wishes only to have his daughter back. And, although the Trojan leaders do know of Troilus's affair, they must pay heed first to such matters of state as the exchange of prisoners.

So, too, must Troilus. Perhaps the greatest irony is that he must himself choose to send Cressida to the Greeks, placing duty above personal longing. He appears to have no real choice, but the result is surrounded by absurdities, and it is something that Cressida cannot comprehend. She has determined to stay no matter what the world may think; passionate love is more important to her. Although Cressida was first introduced to us as a sardonic and worldly young woman, urbane, mocking, self-possessed, witty, unsentimental, even scheming and opportunistic, and, above all, wary of emotional commitment, her brief involvement with Troilus does touch deep emotion. For a moment, she catches a glimpse of something precious to which she would cling, something genuine in her unstable world. Yet Troilus, caught between love and duty, consents to her departure to the Greek camp. There she reverts to her former disillusioned self, behaving as is expected of her. Who has deserted whom? Cressida gives up, hating herself for doing so. She knows she cannot be true because, like too many women in her experience, she is led by "The error of our eye" and is thus a prey to male importunity (5.2.113). Alone and friendless in the Greek camp except for her neglectful father, she turns to a self-assured and opportunistic man (Diomedes) who is perfectly cynical about women generally but who will at least protect her against the other sex-starved Greek officers. Sometimes she seems, to Ulysses at least, one of those "sluttish spoils of opportunity / And daughters of the game" (4.5.63–4). Still, this surrender to will and appetite in her is not unsympathetic, and does not happen without inner struggle. Her weakness is emblematic of a universal disorder and is partly caused by it. In the grim interplay of war and love, both men and women are powerless to assert their true selves. As the malcontent Thersites concludes, "Lechery, lechery, still wars and lechery; nothing else holds fashion."

The printing history of *Troilus and Cressida* is full of obscurities that may give some insight into the play's apparent lack of stage success. On February 7, 1603, the printer James Roberts entered his name on the Register of the Company of Stationers (i.e., publishers and booksellers) to print, "when he hath gotten sufficient authority for it, the book of Troilus and Cressida as it is acted by my Lord Chamberlain's Men." Evidently, the authority was not forthcoming, for in 1609 the play was reregistered to R. Bonian and H. Walley and published by them that year in quarto as *The History of Troilus and Cressida. As it was acted by the King's Majesty's servants at the Globe. Written by William Shakespeare*. Immediately afterward, and well before this first printing had sold out, a new title page was substituted as follows: *The Famous History of Troilus and Cresseid. Excellently expressing the beginning of their loves, with the conceited wooing of Pandarus Prince of Lycia. Written by William Shakespeare*. This second version had, moreover, a preface to the reader (something found in no other Shakespearean quarto) declaring *Troilus and Cressida* to be "a new play, never staled with the stage, never clapper-clawed with the palms of the vulgar," nor "sullied with the smoky breath of the multitude." The preface goes on to imply that the play's "grand possessors" (i.e., Shakespeare's acting company) had not wished to see the play released at all. What this substituted title page and added preface may suggest is that Bonian and Walley felt constrained to present their text as a new one—a literary rather than a theatrical text—and hence different from the version entered in the Stationers' Register "as it is acted by my Lord Chamberlain's Men." Because that version had been legally registered in the name of James Roberts, the new publishers made their case for legal possession by offering a "new" play.

Later, the editors of the First Folio edition of 1623 seemed to have had difficulty in obtaining permission to print *Troilus and Cressida*. Three pages of the play were actually printed to follow *Romeo and Juliet*, among the tragedies, but were then withdrawn to be replaced by *Timon of Athens*. Ultimately, the play appeared in the Folio almost without pagination, unlisted in the table of contents, and placed with fitting ambiguity between the histories and the tragedies.

This unusual printing history offers conflicting information about original stage performance. Against the evidence of the second version of the 1609 Quarto, with its preface proclaiming a play "never staled with the stage," we have the evidence of the first title page mentioning the King's Majesty's servants at the Globe and of the Stationers' Register entry in 1603 referring to the play "as it is acted." Since the 1609 preface may be part of a legal maneuver designed to represent the play as new, the case in favor of actual performance has some weight. We cannot be sure, however, that the performance was successful or that it reached a very large audience. Some scholars have hypothesized that Shakespeare's company mounted a special production of the play for a private audience at the Inns of Court (where young men studied law) or a similar place, even though an arrangement of this sort would have been most unusual, if not unique; Shakespeare's company often took its regular plays to court or other special audiences, but no instance is positively known in which Shakespeare wrote on commission for a private showing. More likely, *Troilus and Cressida* was performed publicly without great success. A sequel, promised in the closing lines of the play by Pandarus to be presented "some two months hence," evidently did not materialize, perhaps because public demand was insufficient. The 1609 Quarto, with its revised title page and added preface, may have attempted to capitalize on the play's public failure by touting it as sophisticated fare, to be appreciated only by discerning readers. Possibly, Shakespeare and his company took another look at *Troilus and Cressida* in 1608, after they had acquired the right to perform in their indoor theater at Blackfriars, where audiences tended to be more select, only to discover anew that the play was not a great success on the stage. Its subsequent stage history, in any case, is largely a blank until the twentieth century, except for a much changed Restoration adaptation by John Dryden (1679) in which Cressida remains true to Troilus and slays herself when accused of infidelity.

Since 1907, on the other hand, when the play was finally revived on the London stage, it has enjoyed a genuine and growing success. Its disillusionment about war seems admirably suited to an era of world conflict, superpower confrontations, and deepening cynicism about politics. Thersites and Pandarus sound positively choric today in their chortling and obscene reflections on the perversions of human sexuality. Helen as insipid sex goddess and Paris as her languid admirer strike us as boldly modern, as in Michael Macowan's antiwar production for the London Mask Theatre Company on the eve of World War II, in 1938. Most of all, perhaps, Cressida as failed heroine has come into her own. Centuries of disparaging sexist dismissal of her as a typically faithless woman have given way to nuanced interpretations in which male importunity is at least as much to blame for her desertion of Troilus as her own admitted weakness. Once Troilus has possessed her sexually, he seems less obsessively interested in her and consents, even if unwillingly, to her return to the Greeks. Her awareness that something of this sort was bound to happen provides modern actresses with a potent indictment of the male species, as in Juliet Stevenson's sympathetic portrayal of Cressida as a victim of war and male violence in Howard Davies's 1985 production for the Royal Shakespeare Company. Paradoxically, this searing play about the decay of "notorious identities" (Linda Charnes's phrase) has led to a resuscitation of reputation for the woman who was once the most notorious of them all.

The following is a complete text of the preface to the reader from the second "state" of the 1609 Quarto.

A Never Writer, to an Ever Reader. News.

Eternal reader, you have here a new play, never staled with the stage, never clapper-clawed with the palms of the vulgar, and yet passing full of the palm comical; for it is a birth of your brain that never undertook anything comical vainly. And were but the vain names of comedies changed for the titles of commodities, or of plays for pleas, you should see all those grand censors, that now style them such vanities, flock to them for the main grace of their gravities, especially this author's comedies, that are so framed to the life that they serve for the most common commentaries of all the actions of our lives, showing such a dexterity and power of wit that the most displeased with plays are pleased with his comedies. And all such dull and heavy-witted worldlings as were never capable of the wit of a comedy, coming by report of them to his representations, have found that wit there that they never found in themselves and have parted better witted than they came, feeling an edge of wit set upon them more than ever they dreamed they had brain to grind it on. So much and such savored salt of wit is in his comedies that they seem, for their height of pleasure, to be born in that sea that brought forth Venus. Amongst all there is none more witty than this; and had I time I would comment upon it, though I know it needs not, for so much as will make you think your testern well bestowed, but for so much worth as even poor I know to be stuffed in it. It deserves such a labor as well as the best comedy in Terence or Plautus. And believe this, that when he is gone and his comedies out of sale, you will scramble for them and set up a new English Inquisition. Take this for a warning, and at the peril of your pleasure's loss, and judgment's, refuse not, nor like this the less for not being sullied with the smoky breath of the multitude; but thank fortune for the scape it hath made amongst you, since by the grand possessors' wills I believe you should have prayed for them rather than been prayed. And so I leave all such to be prayed for, for the states of their wits' healths, that will not praise it. *Vale.*

Troilus and Cressida

[*Dramatis Personae*

PROLOGUE

PRIAM, *King of Troy*
HECTOR,
TROILUS,
PARIS
DEIPHOBUS,
HELENUS, *a priest,*
MARGARETON, *a bastard,* } *his sons*
AENEAS,
ANTENOR, } *Trojan commanders*
CALCHAS, *a Trojan priest, Cressida's father, and defector to the Greeks*
PANDARUS, *Cressida's uncle*
SERVANT *to Troilus*
SERVANT *to Paris*

CASSANDRA, *Priam's daughter, a prophetess*
ANDROMACHE, *Hector's wife*
HELEN, *former wife of Menelaus, now Paris's mistress*
CRESSIDA, *Calchas's daughter, loved by Troilus*
ALEXANDER, *Cressida's servant*

AGAMEMNON, *the Greek General*
MENELAUS, *brother of Agamemnon*
ACHILLES,
AJAX,
ULYSSES,
NESTOR,
DIOMEDES, } *Greek commanders*
PATROCLUS, *Achilles's friend*
THERSITES, *a scurrilous fool*
SERVANT *to Diomedes*

Trojan and Greek Soldiers, and Attendants

SCENE: *Troy, and the Greek camp before it*]

Prologue

[*Enter the Prologue, in armor.*]

PROLOGUE
In Troy, there lies the scene. From isles of Greece
The princes orgulous, their high blood chafed, 2
Have to the port of Athens sent their ships,
Fraught with the ministers and instruments 4
Of cruel war. Sixty and nine, that wore
Their crownets regal, from th'Athenian bay 6
Put forth toward Phrygia, and their vow is made 7
To ransack Troy, within whose strong immures 8
The ravished Helen, Menelaus' queen, 9
With wanton Paris sleeps; and that's the quarrel.
To Tenedos they come, 11
And the deep-drawing barks do there disgorge 12
Their warlike freightage. Now on Dardan plains 13
The fresh and yet unbruisèd Greeks do pitch
Their brave pavilions. Priam's six-gated city— 15
Dardan, and Timbria, Helias, Chetas, Troien, 16
And Antenorides—with massy staples 17
And corresponsive and fulfilling bolts, 18
Spar up the sons of Troy. 19
Now expectation, tickling skittish spirits 20
On one and other side, Trojan and Greek,

Prologue
2 orgulous proud. **chafed** heated, angered **4 Fraught** laden. **ministers** agents, i.e., soldiers **6 crownets** coronets, crowns worn by nobles **7 Phrygia** district in western Asia Minor, identified as Troy by the Roman poets, and hence in Renaissance poetry **8 immures** walls **9 ravished** abducted

11 Tenedos small island in the Aegean Sea off the coast of Asia Minor **12 deep-drawing barks** ships lying low in the water (with their heavy cargo) **13 Dardan** Trojan. (From *Dardanus*, son of Zeus and Electra, daughter of Atlas. According to legend, Dardanus was the ancestor of the Trojan race.) **15 brave pavilions** splendid tents. **16–17 Dardan . . . Antenorides** (The names of Troy's six gates.) **17–18 massy . . . bolts** i.e., massive posts fitted with sockets to receive matching and well-fitted bolts **19 Spar** close **20 skittish** lively

Sets all on hazard. And hither am I come,
A prologue armed, but not in confidence
Of author's pen or actor's voice, but suited
In like conditions as our argument,
To tell you, fair beholders, that our play
Leaps o'er the vaunt and firstlings of those broils,
Beginning in the middle, starting thence away
To what may be digested in a play.
Like or find fault; do as your pleasures are;
Now, good or bad, 'tis but the chance of war.
[*Exit.*]

✤

[1.1]

Enter Pandarus and Troilus.

TROILUS
Call here my varlet; I'll unarm again.
Why should I war without the walls of Troy,
That find such cruel battle here within?
Each Trojan that is master of his heart,
Let him to field; Troilus, alas, hath none.

PANDARUS Will this gear ne'er be mended?

TROILUS
The Greeks are strong, and skillful to their strength,
Fierce to their skill, and to their fierceness valiant;
But I am weaker than a woman's tear,
Tamer than sleep, fonder than ignorance,
Less valiant than the virgin in the night,
And skilless as unpracticed infancy.

PANDARUS Well, I have told you enough of this. For my part, I'll not meddle nor make no farther. He that will have a cake out of the wheat must tarry the grinding.

TROILUS Have I not tarried?

PANDARUS Ay, the grinding, but you must tarry the bolting.

TROILUS Have I not tarried?

PANDARUS Ay, the bolting, but you must tarry the leavening.

TROILUS Still have I tarried.

PANDARUS Ay, to the leavening, but here's yet in the word "hereafter" the kneading, the making of the cake, the heating the oven, and the baking; nay, you must stay the cooling too, or ye may chance burn your lips.

TROILUS
Patience herself, what goddess e'er she be,
Doth lesser blench at suff'rance than I do.
At Priam's royal table do I sit,
And when fair Cressid comes into my thoughts—
So, traitor! When she comes? When is she thence?

PANDARUS Well, she looked yesternight fairer than ever I saw her look, or any woman else.

TROILUS
I was about to tell thee—when my heart,
As wedgèd with a sigh, would rive in twain,
Lest Hector or my father should perceive me,
I have, as when the sun doth light a-scorn,
Buried this sigh in wrinkle of a smile;
But sorrow that is couched in seeming gladness
Is like that mirth fate turns to sudden sadness.

PANDARUS An her hair were not somewhat darker than Helen's—well, go to—there were no more comparison between the women. But, for my part, she is my kinswoman; I would not, as they term it, praise her. But I would somebody had heard her talk yesterday, as I did. I will not dispraise your sister Cassandra's wit, but—

TROILUS
Oh, Pandarus! I tell thee, Pandarus—
When I do tell thee there my hopes lie drowned,
Reply not in how many fathoms deep
They lie indrenched. I tell thee I am mad
In Cressid's love. Thou answer'st she is fair;
Pour'st in the open ulcer of my heart
Her eyes, her hair, her cheek, her gait, her voice;
Handlest in thy discourse—oh!—that her hand,
In whose comparison all whites are ink
Writing their own reproach, to whose soft seizure
The cygnet's down is harsh, and spirit of sense
Hard as the palm of plowman. This thou tell'st me,
As true thou tell'st me, when I say I love her;
But saying thus, instead of oil and balm
Thou lay'st in every gash that love hath given me
The knife that made it.

PANDARUS I speak no more than truth.

TROILUS Thou dost not speak so much.

PANDARUS Faith, I'll not meddle in it. Let her be as she is. If she be fair, 'tis the better for her; an she be not, she has the mends in her own hands.

22 Sets . . . hazard puts all at risk. **23 armed** in armor **23–4 not . . . voice i.e.,** not overconfident in the value of the play or the acting **24–5 suited . . . argument** i.e., dressed in armor to match the character of the military plot. (*Argument* means both "plot of the story" and "quarrel.") **27 vaunt and firstlings** beginnings **28 Beginning in the middle** (Alluding to the tradition of beginning epic poetry *in medias res*.)
1.1. Location: Troy.
1 varlet page or servant of a knight **5 none** i.e., no heart to fight. **6 gear** business **7, 8 to** in addition to, in proportion to **10 fonder** more foolish **14 meddle nor make** have anything more to do with it **15 tarry** wait for **19 bolting** sifting. **27 stay** wait for **29 what . . . be** however much a goddess; or, if she is a goddess

30 Doth . . . suff'rance flinches under suffering with less fortitude **33 So, traitor . . . thence?** (Troilus rebukes himself as a traitor to Love for implying that Cressida is ever out of his thoughts, as she would have to be before she could come into them.) **37 As wedgèd** as if cleft by a wedge. **rive** split **39 a-scorn** scorningly, mockingly. (Troilus compares his face to that of the sun, putting on a false look of joviality.) **41 couched** hidden **43 An** If. **darker** (A dark complexion was considered less handsome; Helen is blonde.) **44 go to** (An exclamation of impatience or irritation.) **were** would be
53 indrenched drowned. **57 Handlest . . . hand** you discourse on that wondrous hand of hers **58 In whose comparison** in comparison with which **59 to . . . seizure** in comparison with whose soft clasp **60 cygnet's** young swan's. **spirit of sense** the most delicate of all material substances. (According to Renaissance physiology, spirits were the invisible vapors that transmitted sense impressions to the soul.) **63 oil and balm** ointments, salves **67 Thou . . . much** i.e., You cannot possibly speak the whole truth about Cressida (since she is indescribable). **70 has . . . hands** i.e., can apply remedy, such as cosmetics.

TROILUS Good Pandarus, how now, Pandarus?

PANDARUS I have had my labor for my travail; ill thought on of her and ill thought on of you; gone between and between, but small thanks for my labor

TROILUS What, art thou angry, Pandarus? What, with me?

PANDARUS Because she's kin to me, therefore she's not so fair as Helen. An she were not kin to me, she would be as fair o' Friday as Helen is on Sunday. But what care I? I care not an she were a blackamoor. 'Tis all one to me.

TROILUS Say I she is not fair?

PANDARUS I do not care whether you do or no. She's a fool to stay behind her father. Let her to the Greeks, and so I'll tell her the next time I see her. For my part, I'll meddle nor make no more i'th' matter.

TROILUS Pandarus—

PANDARUS Not I.

TROILUS Sweet Pandarus—

PANDARUS Pray you, speak no more to me. I will leave all as I found it, and there an end. *Exit.*

Sound alarum.

TROILUS
Peace, you ungracious clamors! Peace, rude sounds!
Fools on both sides! Helen must needs be fair,
When with your blood you daily paint her thus.
I cannot fight upon this argument;
It is too starved a subject for my sword.
But Pandarus—O gods, how do you plague me!
I cannot come to Cressid but by Pandar,
And he's as tetchy to be wooed to woo
As she is stubborn-chaste against all suit.
Tell me, Apollo, for thy Daphne's love,
What Cressid is, what Pandar, and what we?
Her bed is India, there she lies, a pearl;
Between our Ilium and where she resides,
Let it be called the wild and wand'ring flood,
Ourself the merchant, and this sailing Pandar
Our doubtful hope, our convoy, and our bark.

Alarum. Enter Aeneas.

AENEAS
How now, Prince Troilus, wherefore not afield?

TROILUS
Because not there. This woman's answer sorts,
For womanish it is to be from thence.
What news, Aeneas, from the field today?

AENEAS
That Paris is returnèd home and hurt.

TROILUS
By whom, Aeneas?

AENEAS Troilus, by Menelaus.

TROILUS
Let Paris bleed. 'Tis but a scar to scorn;
Paris is gored with Menelaus' horn. *Alarum.*

AENEAS
Hark, what good sport is out of town today!

TROILUS
Better at home, if "would I might" were "may."
But to the sport abroad. Are you bound thither?

AENEAS
In all swift haste.

TROILUS Come, go we then together. *Exeunt.*

[1.2]

Enter Cressida and her man [Alexander].

CRESSIDA
Who were those went by?

ALEXANDER Queen Hecuba and Helen.

CRESSIDA
And whither go they?

ALEXANDER Up to the eastern tower,
Whose height commands as subject all the vale,
To see the battle. Hector, whose patience
Is as a virtue fixed, today was moved.
He chid Andromache and struck his armorer,
And, like as there were husbandry in war,
Before the sun rose he was harnessed light,
And to the field goes he, where every flower
Did as a prophet weep what it foresaw
In Hector's wrath.

CRESSIDA What was his cause of anger?

ALEXANDER
The noise goes, this: there is among the Greeks
A lord of Trojan blood, nephew to Hector;
They call him Ajax.

CRESSIDA Good; and what of him?

ALEXANDER
They say he is a very man per se
And stands alone.

72 had had only **73 of** by **78–9 An . . . Sunday** i.e., If I were free to praise her unreservedly, without appearing to be biased as her kinsman, I would pronounce her to be as attractive in her plainest attire as Helen in her Sunday best. **80 blackamoor** dark-skinned African. **84 her father** i.e., Calchas, a Trojan priest, who, advised by the oracle of Apollo that Troy would fall, fled to the Greeks. **91.1 *alarum*** trumpet signal to arms. **94 paint** (As though the blood were cosmetic, reddening her complexion.) **95 upon this argument** for this cause, theme **96 starved** empty, trivial. (Troilus would have to fight on an empty stomach, as it were.) **99 tetchy to be** irritable at being **101 Apollo** (The ardent pursuer of the nymph Daphne who, coy like Cressida, was changed into a bay tree to elude Apollo's pursuit.) **102 we** i.e., I. **104 Ilium** i.e., Troy generally, but here Priam's palace **105 flood** open sea **109 sorts** is appropriate

114 a scar to scorn (1) a wound not sufficiently serious to be regarded (2) a scar in return for Paris' scorn of Menelaus **115 horn** i.e., cuckold's horn, since Paris had stolen Helen from Menelaus. **116 out of town** outside the walls **117 Better . . . "may"** If I had my wish, I'd have better entertainment at home in amorous pursuit.
1.2. Location: Troy.
5 fixed steadfast. **moved** angry. (With wordplay on the antithesis between *fixed* and *moved*.) **7 like as** as if. **husbandry** good management (by rising early and getting to work. Hector is a stern "husband" in marriage and in war.) **8 harnessed light** dressed in light armor **10 weep** (The early morning dew on the flowers suggests tears and extends the metaphor of a husbandman or farmer going into the field.) **12 noise** rumor **13 nephew** i.e., kinsmen, first cousin **15 per se** all to himself, without peer **16 alone** without peer. (But Cressida sardonically takes it to mean literally "all by himself, without support.")

CRESSIDA So do all men, unless they are drunk, sick, or have no legs.

ALEXANDER This man, lady, hath robbed many beasts of their particular additions. He is as valiant as the lion, churlish as the bear, slow as the elephant; a man into whom nature hath so crowded humors that his valor is crushed into folly, his folly sauced with discretion. There is no man hath a virtue that he hath not a glimpse of, nor any man an attaint but he carries some stain of it. He is melancholy without cause and merry against the hair. He hath the joints of everything, but everything so out of joint that he is a gouty Briareus, many hands and no use, or purblind Argus, all eyes and no sight.

CRESSIDA But how should this man, that makes me smile, make Hector angry?

ALEXANDER They say he yesterday coped Hector in the battle and struck him down, the disdain and shame whereof hath ever since kept Hector fasting and waking.

[*Enter Pandarus.*]

CRESSIDA Who comes here?

ALEXANDER Madam, your uncle Pandarus.

CRESSIDA Hector's a gallant man.

ALEXANDER As may be in the world, lady.

PANDARUS What's that? What's that?

CRESSIDA Good morrow, uncle Pandarus.

PANDARUS Good morrow, cousin Cressid. What do you talk of?—Good morrow, Alexander.—How do you, cousin? When were you at Ilium?

CRESSIDA This morning, uncle.

PANDARUS What were you talking of when I came? Was Hector armed and gone ere ye came to Ilium? Helen was not up, was she?

CRESSIDA Hector was gone, but Helen was not up?

PANDARUS E'en so. Hector was stirring early.

CRESSIDA That were we talking of, and of his anger.

PANDARUS Was he angry?

CRESSIDA So he says here.

PANDARUS True, he was so. I know the cause too. He'll lay about him today, I can tell them that; and there's Troilus will not come far behind him. Let them take heed of Troilus, I can tell them that too.

CRESSIDA What, is he angry too?

PANDARUS Who, Troilus? Troilus is the better man of the two.

CRESSIDA O Jupiter! There's no comparison.

PANDARUS What, not between Troilus and Hector? Do you know a man if you see him?

CRESSIDA Ay, if I ever saw him before and knew him.

PANDARUS Well, I say Troilus is Troilus.

CRESSIDA Then you say as I say, for I am sure he is not Hector.

PANDARUS No, nor Hector is not Troilus in some degrees.

CRESSIDA 'Tis just to each of them; he is himself.

PANDARUS Himself? Alas, poor Troilus! I would he were.

CRESSIDA So he is.

PANDARUS Condition, I had gone barefoot to India.

CRESSIDA He is not Hector.

PANDARUS Himself? No, he's not himself. Would 'a were himself! Well, the gods are above; time must friend or end. Well, Troilus, well, I would my heart were in her body. No, Hector is not a better man than Troilus.

CRESSIDA Excuse me.

PANDARUS He is elder.

CRESSIDA Pardon me, pardon me.

PANDARUS Th'other's not come to't. You shall tell me another tale, when th'other's come to't. Hector shall not have his wit this year.

CRESSIDA He shall not need it, if he have his own.

PANDARUS Nor his qualities.

CRESSIDA No matter.

PANDARUS Nor his beauty.

CRESSIDA 'Twould not become him; his own's better.

PANDARUS You have no judgment, niece. Helen herself swore th'other day that Troilus, for a brown favor—for so 'tis, I must confess—not brown neither—

CRESSIDA No, but brown.

PANDARUS Faith, to say truth, brown and not brown.

CRESSIDA To say the truth, true and not true.

PANDARUS She praised his complexion above Paris'.

CRESSIDA Why, Paris hath color enough.

PANDARUS So he has.

CRESSIDA Then Troilus should have too much. If she praised him above, his complexion is higher than his. He having color enough, and the other higher, is too flaming a praise for a good complexion. I had as lief Helen's golden tongue had commended Troilus for a copper nose.

PANDARUS I swear to you, I think Helen loves him better than Paris.

CRESSIDA Then she's a merry Greek indeed.

20 additions qualities bestowing special distinction. **22 humors** temperamental characteristics **25 glimpse** trace. **attaint** defect, stain. **but** but that **27 against the hair** contrary to natural tendency. **28 Briareus** Greek mythological monster with fifty heads and one hundred hands; here, all those hands are gouty **29 Argus** a monster with one hundred eyes; here, all are blind (*purblind*) **33 coped** encountered, came to blows with **43 cousin** kinswoman, i.e., niece **45 Ilium** the palace. **56 lay about him** fight fiercely **64 know a man** recognize a complete man. (But Cressida, pretending to misunderstand, takes it to mean simply "recognize.")

66 is Troilus is that extraordinary individual known far and wide as Troilus. (But, again, Cressida reduces it to the literal.) **69 in some** by several **71 he** each **72 Himself** (Pandarus plays with the expression "not to be oneself," to be out of sorts.) **75 Condition . . . India** i.e., Troilus is about as likely to be himself again as I am to have walked barefoot on pilgrimage to India, which of course I haven't. **77 'a** he **79 friend** befriend **82 Excuse me** i.e., I beg to differ. (Line 84 means the same.) **85 to't** i.e., to Hector's age, to maturity. **87 his wit** i.e., Troilus's intelligence **94 for a brown favor** considering he has a dark complexion **96 No, but brown** (Cressida mocks her uncle's hairsplitting: "It isn't brown, but it's brown.") **102 should** would of necessity **103 higher than his** i.e., ruddier than Paris's. **105 flaming** (1) flamboyant (2) inflamed with pimples. **lief** willingly **107 copper** red (with drinking) **110 merry Greek** (Slang for a frivolous person, loose in morals.)

PANDARUS Nay, I am sure she does. She came to him
th'other day into the compassed window—and, you 112
know, he has not past three or four hairs on his chin—

CRESSIDA Indeed, a tapster's arithmetic may soon bring 114
his particulars therein to a total.

PANDARUS Why, he is very young; and yet will he,
within three pound, lift as much as his brother Hector.

CRESSIDA Is he so young a man and so old a lifter? 118

PANDARUS But to prove to you that Helen loves him: she
came and puts me her white hand to his cloven chin— 120

CRESSIDA Juno have mercy! How came it cloven?

PANDARUS Why, you know, 'tis dimpled. I think his
smiling becomes him better than any man in all
Phrygia.

CRESSIDA Oh, he smiles valiantly.

PANDARUS Does he not?

CRESSIDA Oh, yes, an 'twere a cloud in autumn. 127

PANDARUS Why, go to, then. But to prove to you that
Helen loves Troilus—

CRESSIDA Troilus will stand to the proof, if you'll prove 130
it so.

PANDARUS Troilus? Why, he esteems her no more than
I esteem an addle egg. 133

CRESSIDA If you love an addle egg as well as you love
an idle head, you would eat chickens i'th' shell. 135

PANDARUS I cannot choose but laugh to think how she
tickled his chin. Indeed, she has a marvelous white 137
hand, I must needs confess—

CRESSIDA Without the rack. 139

PANDARUS And she takes upon her to spy a white hair
on his chin.

CRESSIDA Alas, poor chin! Many a wart is richer.

PANDARUS But there was such laughing! Queen
Hecuba laughed that her eyes ran o'er.

CRESSIDA With millstones. 145

PANDARUS And Cassandra laughed.

CRESSIDA But there was a more temperate fire under the 147
pot of her eyes. Did her eyes run o'er too?

PANDARUS And Hector laughed.

CRESSIDA At what was all this laughing?

PANDARUS Marry, at the white hair that Helen spied
on Troilus' chin.

CRESSIDA An't had been a green hair, I should have 153
laughed too.

PANDARUS They laughed not so much at the hair as at
his pretty answer.

CRESSIDA What was his answer?

PANDARUS Quoth she, "Here's but two-and-fifty hairs 158
on your chin, and one of them is white."

CRESSIDA This is her question.

PANDARUS That's true, make no question of that. "Two-
and-fifty hairs," quoth he, "and one white. That white
hair is my father, and all the rest are his sons."
"Jupiter!" quoth she, "which of these hairs is Paris my
husband?" "The forked one," quoth he, "pluck't out, 165
and give it him." But there was such laughing! And
Helen so blushed, and Paris so chafed, and all the rest 167
so laughed, that it passed. 168

CRESSIDA So let it now, for it has been a great while 169
going by.

PANDARUS Well, cousin, I told you a thing yesterday.
Think on't.

CRESSIDA So I do.

PANDARUS I'll be sworn 'tis true. He will weep you an 174
'twere a man born in April. 175

CRESSIDA And I'll spring up in his tears an 'twere a 176
nettle against May. *Sound a retreat.* 177

PANDARUS Hark, they are coming from the field. Shall
we stand up here and see them as they pass toward
Ilium? Good niece, do, sweet niece Cressida.

CRESSIDA At your pleasure.

PANDARUS Here, here, here's an excellent place; here
we may see most bravely. I'll tell you them all by their 183
names as they pass by, but mark Troilus above the
rest.

Enter Aeneas [and passes across the stage].

CRESSIDA Speak not so loud.

PANDARUS That's Aeneas. Is not that a brave man? He's 187
one of the flowers of Troy, I can tell you. But mark
Troilus; you shall see anon.

Enter Antenor [and passes across the stage].

CRESSIDA Who's that?

PANDARUS That's Antenor. He has a shrewd wit, I can
tell you, and he's a man good enough. He's one o'th'
soundest judgments in Troy whosoever, and a proper 193
man of person. When comes Troilus? I'll show you
Troilus anon. If he see me, you shall see him nod
at me.

CRESSIDA Will he give you the nod? 197

PANDARUS You shall see.

CRESSIDA If he do, the rich shall have more. 199

Enter Hector [and passes across the stage].

112 compassed bay **114 tapster** barkeep. (Proverbially slow at simple addition.) **118 old** experienced. **lifter** (With a pun on the meaning "thief.") **120 puts me** i.e., puts. (*Me* is merely an emphatic marker implying "listen to this.") **127 an** as if. **an . . . autumn** i.e., his smile is like a dark and threatening rain cloud in autumn. (Cressida is teasing her uncle by dispraising Troilus.) **130 stand . . . proof** i.e., not shrink from the test. (With bawdy pun on *stand,* be erect.) **133 addle** spoiled **135 idle** foolish. (With wordplay on *addle.*) **you . . . shell** i.e., you would positively devour addled eggs (which are often spoiled in the sense of being several days old, so that the chick is starting to develop). **137 marvelous** marvelously **139 rack** torture device (used to elicit confessions). **145 With millstones** i.e., Mirthlessly, since nothing has been said funny enough to make the eyes weep tears of laughter. (To *weep millstones* is to be cruel and heartless.) **147 temperate** (since Cassandra was an unheeded prophetess who seldom laughed) **153 An't** If it

158 two-and-fifty (Priam had fifty sons. Perhaps the forked hair is to count for two.) **hairs** (With a pun on "heirs"; the Quarto spelling is "heires.") **165 forked** (1) bifurcated (2) bearing a cuckold's horns. (The suggestion is that Helen will cheat Paris in love as she has done Menelaus.) **167 so chafed** was so angry **168 it passed** it exceeded all description. (But Cressida puns on the sense of "passed by.") **169 it** i.e., Pandarus' story **174–5 an 'twere** as if he were **175 April** i.e., the season of showers. **176–7 an 'twere . . . May** as if I were a nettle in anticipation of May. (Cressida will "nettle" Troilus.) **177 s.d. *retreat*** trumpet signal for withdrawal. **183 bravely** excellently. **187 brave** excellent **193 proper** handsome **197 nod** nod of recognition. (With a pun on *noddy,* fool, simpleton.) **199 the rich . . . more** i.e., the fool will become more foolish as you are, will receive the *nod,* or noddy (line 197).

PANDARUS That's Hector, that, that, look you, that.
There's a fellow! Go thy way, Hector! There's a brave
man, niece. O brave Hector! Look how he looks!
There's a countenance! Is't not a brave man?

CRESSIDA Oh, a brave man!

PANDARUS Is 'a not? It does a man's heart good. Look
you what hacks are on his helmet! Look you yonder, 206
do you see? Look you there. There's no jesting; there's
laying on, take't off who will, as they say. There be 208
hacks.

CRESSIDA Be those with swords?

Enter Paris [and passes across the stage].

PANDARUS Swords, anything, he cares not; an the
devil come to him, it's all one. By God's lid, it does 212
one's heart good. Yonder comes Paris, yonder comes
Paris. Look ye yonder, niece. Is't not a gallant man,
too, is't not? Why, this is brave now. Who said he
came hurt home today? He's not hurt. Why, this will
do Helen's heart good now, ha! Would I could see
Troilus now! You shall see Troilus anon.

CRESSIDA Who's that?

Enter Helenus [and passes across the stage].

PANDARUS That's Helenus. I marvel where Troilus is.
That's Helenus. I think he went not forth today. That's 221
Helenus.

CRESSIDA Can Helenus fight, uncle?

PANDARUS Helenus? No. Yes, he'll fight indifferent 224
well. I marvel where Troilus is. Hark, do you not hear 225
the people cry "Troilus"? Helenus is a priest.

CRESSIDA What sneaking fellow comes yonder?

Enter Troilus [and passes across the stage].

PANDARUS Where? Yonder? That's Deiphobus. 'Tis
Troilus! There's a man, niece! Hem! Brave Troilus! The
prince of chivalry!

CRESSIDA Peace, for shame, peace!

PANDARUS Mark him, note him. O brave Troilus! Look
well upon him, niece. Look you how his sword is
bloodied and his helm more hacked than Hector's, 234
and how he looks, and how he goes! O admirable 235
youth! He ne'er saw three-and-twenty. Go thy way,
Troilus, go thy way! Had I a sister were a grace, or a 237
daughter a goddess, he should take his choice. O
admirable man! Paris? Paris is dirt to him; and
I warrant Helen, to change, would give an eye to 240
boot. 241

[Enter common soldiers and pass across the stage.]

CRESSIDA Here comes more.

PANDARUS Asses, fools, dolts! Chaff and bran, chaff
and bran! Porridge after meat! I could live and die 244
i'th'eyes of Troilus. Ne'er look, ne'er look. The eagles
are gone; crows and daws, crows and daws! I had 246
rather be such a man as Troilus than Agamemnon and
all Greece.

CRESSIDA There is among the Greeks Achilles, a better
man than Troilus.

PANDARUS Achilles? A drayman, a porter, a very camel. 251

CRESSIDA Well, well.

PANDARUS "Well, well"! Why, have you any discretion?
Have you any eyes? Do you know what a man is? Is
not birth, beauty, good shape, discourse, manhood,
learning, gentleness, virtue, youth, liberality, and so
forth, the spice and salt that season a man?

CRESSIDA Ay, a minced man; and then to be baked 258
with no date in the pie, for then the man's date is out. 259

PANDARUS You are such another woman! One knows
not at what ward you lie. 261

CRESSIDA Upon my back to defend my belly, upon my
wit to defend my wiles, upon my secrecy to defend 263
mine honesty, my mask to defend my beauty, and 264
you to defend all these, and at all these wards I lie, at 265
a thousand watches. 266

PANDARUS Say one of your watches.

CRESSIDA Nay, I'll watch you for that; and that's one of
the chiefest of them too. If I cannot ward what I would 269
not have hit, I can watch you for telling how I took the
blow—unless it swell past hiding, and then it's past 271
watching. 272

PANDARUS You are such another! 273

Enter [Troilus'] Boy.

BOY Sir, my lord would instantly speak with you.

PANDARUS Where?

BOY At your own house. There he unarms him.

PANDARUS Good boy, tell him I come. *[Exit Boy.]*
I doubt he be hurt. Fare ye well, good niece. 278

CRESSIDA Adieu, uncle.

PANDARUS I'll be with you, niece, by and by.

CRESSIDA To bring, uncle? 281

PANDARUS Ay, a token from Troilus.

206 hacks dents, gashes **208 laying on** i.e., evidence of blows exchanged. **take't off who will** whatever anyone may say to the contrary. (With a pun on *taking off* as contrasted with *laying on*.) **212 all one** all the same to him. **By God's lid** By God's eyelid. (An oath.) **221 he** Troilus **224 indifferent** moderately **225 marvel** wonder **234 helm** helmet **235 goes** walks. **237 a grace** one of the three Graces, the personification of loveliness **240–1 to change . . . boot** would give Paris plus one of her eyes besides to have Troilus in exchange.

244 Porridge Soup (usually eaten before the meat course; after, it would be an anticlimax) **246 daws** jackdaws (glossy, black crowlike birds) **251 drayman** one who draws a cart **258 minced** (1) chopped up fine (2) affected, effeminate **259 the man's date is out** (1) the man is like a pie without any dates, a common ingredient used for flavoring (2) the man is past his prime. (With a suggestion, too, of his being a sexual failure.) **261 at what . . . lie** what defensive postures you adopt. (*Ward* and *lie* are technical terms from fencing. Cressida picks up *lie* in a sexual sense.) **263 my secrecy** (1) my ability to keep a secret (2) my sexual anatomy **264 honesty** (1) chastity (2) reputation for chastity. **mask** (Used to protect fair skin from tanning, considered unhandsome, and also to ward against public gaze.) **265–6 at a thousand watches** i.e., guarding myself in a thousand ways. (Subsequently, in the wordplay, *watch* means "devotional exercises" or "night watches," line 267, "keep under observation," line 268, and "watch out lest you tell," line 270.) **269 ward** shield **271 swell** i.e., in pregnancy **271–2 past watching** too late to do anything about. **273 You . . . another!** i.e., What a woman you are! **278 doubt** fear **281 To bring** i.e., Are you bringing someone or something? (But Cressida's phrase also completes a colloquial expression, "be with you to bring," meaning roughly, "I'll get even with you.")

CRESSIDA By the same token, you are a bawd.
[*Exit Pandarus.*]
Words, vows, gifts, tears, and love's full sacrifice
He offers in another's enterprise;
But more in Troilus thousandfold I see
Than in the glass of Pandar's praise may be.
Yet hold I off. Women are angels, wooing;
Things won are done; joy's soul lies in the doing.
That she beloved knows naught that knows not this:
Men prize the thing ungained more than it is.
That she was never yet that ever knew
Love got so sweet as when desire did sue.
Therefore this maxim out of love I teach:
Achievement is command; ungained, beseech.
Then though my heart's contents firm love doth
bear,
Nothing of that shall from mine eyes appear.
Exit [*with Alexander*].

✤

[1.3]

[*Sennet.*] *Enter Agamemnon, Nestor, Ulysses, Diomedes, Menelaus, with others.*

AGAMEMNON Princes,
What grief hath set the jaundice on your cheeks?
The ample proposition that hope makes
In all designs begun on earth below
Fails in the promised largeness. Checks and disasters
Grow in the veins of actions highest reared,
As knots, by the conflux of meeting sap,
Infects the sound pine and diverts his grain
Tortive and errant from his course of growth.
Nor, princes, is it matter new to us
That we come short of our suppose so far
That after seven years' siege yet Troy walls stand,
Sith every action that hath gone before,
Whereof we have record, trial did draw
Bias and thwart, not answering the aim
And that unbodied figure of the thought
That gave't surmisèd shape. Why then, you princes,
Do you with cheeks abashed behold our works
And think them shames, which are indeed naught
else
But the protractive trials of great Jove
To find persistive constancy in men?
The fineness of which metal is not found
In Fortune's love; for then the bold and coward,
The wise and fool, the artist and unread,
The hard and soft, seem all affined and kin.
But in the wind and tempest of her frown,
Distinction, with a broad and powerful fan,
Puffing at all, winnows the light away,
And what hath mass or matter by itself
Lies rich in virtue and unminglèd.

NESTOR
With due observance of thy godly seat,
Great Agamemnon, Nestor shall apply
Thy latest words. In the reproof of chance
Lies the true proof of men. The sea being smooth,
How many shallow bauble boats dare sail
Upon her patient breast, making their way
With those of nobler bulk!
But let the ruffian Boreas once enrage
The gentle Thetis, and anon behold
The strong-ribbed bark through liquid mountains
cut,
Bounding between the two moist elements
Like Perseus' horse. Where's then the saucy boat
Whose weak untimbered sides but even now
Corrivaled greatness? Either to harbor fled
Or made a toast for Neptune. Even so
Doth valor's show and valor's worth divide
In storms of Fortune. For in her ray and brightness
The herd hath more annoyance by the breese
Than by the tiger; but when the splitting wind
Makes flexible the knees of knotted oaks,
And flies fled under shade, why, then the thing of
courage,
As roused with rage, with rage doth sympathize,
And with an accent tuned in selfsame key
Retorts to chiding Fortune.

ULYSSES Agamemnon,

287 glass mirror **288 wooing** being wooed **290 That she** Any woman. (Also in line 292.) **291 than it is** than its intrinsic worth. **292–3 That she . . . sue** No woman has ever lived who experienced love so sweet as when the man still desires what he has not yet obtained; the love once *got* or obtained by him is never the same. **294 out of love** as from love's book **295 Achievement . . . beseech** To achieve and win a woman is to command her; not yet won, she must be entreated. **296 though . . . bear** though I carry firm love in my heart

1.3. Location: The Greek camp. Before Agamemnon's tent.
0.1 ***Sennet*** trumpet call signaling a processional entrance or exit **2 jaundice** sallowness of complexion **3–5 The ample . . . largeness** The ample hopes and desires that we humans propose for ourselves fail to materialize fully as promised. **5–9 Checks . . . growth** i.e., Hindrances and disasters attend great enterprises, just as knots, at the points where a pine tree's sap should fully flow, adversely affect the health of the tree by twisting and diverting the proper course of its growth. (*Veins* are sap vessels in plants.) **7 conflux** flowing together **8,9 his** its **9 Tortive and errant** twisted and deviating **11 suppose** expectation, purpose **12 yet** still **13–17 Sith . . . shape** since every military action on record has gone awry in the doing of it, not corresponding to our aims and imaginings as to how it should go.

20 protractive drawn out **21 persistive** enduring **23 In Fortune's love** i.e., when Fortune smiles **24 artist** scholar **25 affined** related **26 her** Fortune's **27–8 Distinction . . . away** (Fortune is a winnowing tool, blowing away like chaff those who do not persevere and leaving behind like grain those who do.) **30 virtue** excellence. **unminglèd** unalloyed, uncontaminated. **31 observance of** respect for. **seat** throne, i.e., dignity of office **32 apply** explore the implications of **33 In . . . chance** In the harsh test of misfortune **35 bauble** toylike **38 Boreas** north wind **39 Thetis** a sea deity, mother of Achilles; here, used for the sea itself. (Probably confused with Tethys, the wife of Oceanus.) **41 moist elements** air and water **42 Perseus' horse** Pegasus, a winged horse that sprang from the blood of Medusa when Perseus cut off her head. (The horse was given to Bellerophon by the gods. It is associated, however, with Perseus, probably because Ovid relates that the latter hero was mounted on Pegasus when he rescued Andromeda from the sea monster.) **43 but even now** only a moment ago **45 toast** rich morsel to be swallowed, like toasted bread floating in liquor **46 show** mere appearance **47 storms of Fortune** trials and tests visited by misfortune. **her** Fortune's **48 breese** gadfly **51 fled** are fled. **the thing of courage** any brave heart **52 As** being. **sympathize** correspond

Thou great commander, nerves and bone of Greece,
Heart of our numbers, soul and only sprite,
In whom the tempers and the minds of all
Should be shut up, hear what Ulysses speaks.
Besides th'applause and approbation
The which, [*to Agamemnon*] most mighty for thy
place and sway,
[*To Nestor*] And thou most reverend for thy
stretched-out life,
I give to both your speeches, which were such
As Agamemnon and the hand of Greece
Should hold up high in brass, and such again
As venerable Nestor, hatched in silver,
Should with a bond of air, strong as the axletree
On which the heavens ride, knit all Greeks' ears
To his experienced tongue, yet let it please both,
Thou great, and wise, to hear Ulysses speak.

AGAMEMNON

Speak, Prince of Ithaca, and be't of less expect
That matter needless, of importless burden,
Divide thy lips, than we are confident,
When rank Thersites opes his mastic jaws,
We shall hear music, wit, and oracle.

ULYSSES

Troy, yet upon his basis, had been down,
And the great Hector's sword had lacked a master,
But for these instances.
The specialty of rule hath been neglected;
And look how many Grecian tents do stand
Hollow upon this plain, so many hollow factions.
When that the general is not like the hive
To whom the foragers shall all repair,
What honey is expected? Degree being vizarded,
Th'unworthiest shows as fairly in the mask.
The heavens themselves, the planets, and this center
Observe degree, priority, and place,
Insisture, course, proportion, season, form,
Office, and custom, in all line of order.
And therefore is the glorious planet Sol
In noble eminence enthroned and sphered
Amidst the other, whose med'cinable eye
Corrects the ill aspects of planets evil
And posts, like the commandment of a king,
Sans check, to good and bad. But when the planets
In evil mixture to disorder wander,
What plagues and what portents, what mutiny,
What raging of the sea, shaking of earth,
Commotion in the winds, frights, changes, horrors,
Divert and crack, rend and deracinate
The unity and married calm of states
Quite from their fixure! Oh, when degree is shaked,
Which is the ladder to all high designs,
The enterprise is sick. How could communities,
Degrees in schools, and brotherhoods in cities,
Peaceful commerce from dividable shores,
The primogeneity and due of birth,
Prerogative of age, crowns, scepters, laurels,
But by degree stand in authentic place?
Take but degree away, untune that string,
And hark what discord follows. Each thing meets
In mere oppugnancy. The bounded waters
Should lift their bosoms higher than the shores
And make a sop of all this solid globe;
Strength should be lord of imbecility,
And the rude son should strike his father dead;
Force should be right; or rather, right and wrong,
Between whose endless jar justice resides,
Should lose their names, and so should justice too.
Then everything includes itself in power,
Power into will, will into appetite;
And appetite, an universal wolf,
So doubly seconded with will and power,
Must make perforce an universal prey
And last eat up himself. Great Agamemnon,
This chaos, when degree is suffocate,
Follows the choking.
And this neglection of degree it is
That by a pace goes backward in a purpose
It hath to climb. The general's disdained
By him one step below, he by the next,
That next by him beneath; so every step,
Exampled by the first pace that is sick
Of his superior, grows to an envious fever
Of pale and bloodless emulation.

55 nerves sinews **56 numbers** armies. **sprite** spirit, animating principle **57 tempers** dispositions **58 shut up** gathered in, embodied **59 approbation** approval **64 Should . . . brass** should hold up for emulation, immortalized in brass inscription **65 hatched in silver** (1) adorned with silver hair, a sign of age and wisdom (2) born wise **66 bond of air** i.e., his breath or words as speech, powerful oration **66–7 axletree . . . ride** axis on which the heavens, in the Ptolemaic cosmology, revolve around the earth **70–2 be't . . . than** be it even less to be expected that matters of unimportance pass through your lips than that **73 rank** disgusting, foul-smelling. **mastic** gummy, abusive, scouring **75 yet . . . basis** still standing on its foundations **78 specialty of rule** particular rights and responsibilities of supreme authority **79 look how many** however many, just as many **80 Hollow** (1) empty, because of the present assembly (2) symbolizing faction **81 When . . . hive** i.e., When General Agamemnon, and the general state he embodies, fail to serve as the focus of activity, the command center **82 repair** return **83 Degree being vizarded** When the hierarchical function of authority is masked **84 shows as fairly** appears as attractive (as the most noble) **85 this center** the earth, center of the Ptolemaic universe **87 Insisture** steady continuance in their path **89 Sol** sun. (Regarded as a planet because of its apparent movement around the earth.) **90 sphered** placed in its sphere

91 other others. **med'cinable** healing **92 aspects** relative positions of the heavenly bodies as they appear to an observer on the earth's surface at a given time, and the influence attributed thereto **93 posts** speeds **94 Sans . . . bad** without pause, to foster the good and chastise the bad. **95 mixture** conjunction **99 deracinate** uproot **101 fixure** stability. **104 Degrees in schools** academic rank. **brotherhoods** corporations, guilds **105 from . . . shores** between countries separated by the sea **106 primogeneity** right of the eldest son to succeed to his father's estate **111 mere oppugnancy** total strife. **113 sop** piece of bread or cake floating in liquor; pulp **114 imbecility** weakness **115 rude** brutal **117 Between . . . resides** i.e., justice is arrived at only through an unceasing adjudication between right and wrong. (*Jar* means "collision.") **119 includes** subsumes **123 Must . . . prey** must inevitably prey on everything **125 suffocate** suffocated **126 choking** act of suffocation. **127 neglection** neglect **128 by a pace** step by step **128–9 in . . . climb** when it intends to climb. **132–3 Exampled . . . superior** shown a precedent by the first envious step that his superior takes

And 'tis this fever that keeps Troy on foot,
Not her own sinews. To end a tale of length,
Troy in our weakness lives, not in her strength.

NESTOR
Most wisely hath Ulysses here discovered
The fever whereof all our power is sick.

AGAMEMNON
The nature of the sickness found, Ulysses,
What is the remedy?

ULYSSES
The great Achilles, whom opinion crowns
The sinew and the forehand of our host,
Having his ear full of his airy fame,
Grows dainty of his worth and in his tent
Lies mocking our designs. With him Patroclus
Upon a lazy bed the livelong day
Breaks scurril jests,
And with ridiculous and awkward action,
Which, slanderer, he imitation calls,
He pageants us. Sometime, great Agamemnon,
Thy topless deputation he puts on,
And like a strutting player, whose conceit
Lies in his hamstring, and doth think it rich
To hear the wooden dialogue and sound
Twixt his stretched footing and the scaffoldage,
Such to-be-pitied and o'erwrested seeming
He acts thy greatness in; and when he speaks,
'Tis like a chime a-mending, with terms unsquared,
Which, from the tongue of roaring Typhon dropped,
Would seem hyperboles. At this fusty stuff
The large Achilles, on his pressed bed lolling,
From his deep chest laughs out a loud applause,
Cries, "Excellent! 'Tis Agamemnon just.
Now play me Nestor; hem, and stroke thy beard,
As he being dressed to some oration."
That's done, as near as the extremest ends
Of parallels, as like as Vulcan and his wife,
Yet god Achilles still cries, "Excellent!
'Tis Nestor right. Now play him me, Patroclus,
Arming to answer in a night alarm."
And then, forsooth, the faint defects of age
Must be the scene of mirth; to cough and spit,
And with a palsy, fumbling on his gorget,
Shake in and out the rivet. And at this sport
Sir Valor dies; cries, "Oh, enough, Patroclus,
Or give me ribs of steel! I shall split all
In pleasure of my spleen." And in this fashion,
All our abilities, gifts, natures, shapes,
Severals and generals of grace exact,
Achievements, plots, orders, preventions,
Excitements to the field, or speech for truce,
Success or loss, what is or is not, serves
As stuff for these two to make paradoxes.

NESTOR
And in the imitation of these twain—
Who, as Ulysses says, opinion crowns
With an imperial voice—many are infect.
Ajax is grown self-willed and bears his head
In such a rein, in full as proud a place
As broad Achilles; keeps his tent like him;
Makes factious feasts; rails on our state of war,
Bold as an oracle; and sets Thersites,
A slave whose gall coins slanders like a mint,
To match us in comparisons with dirt,
To weaken and discredit our exposure,
How rank soever rounded in with danger.

ULYSSES
They tax our policy and call it cowardice,
Count wisdom as no member of the war,
Forestall prescience, and esteem no act
But that of hand. The still and mental parts
That do contrive how many hands shall strike
When fitness calls them on and know by measure
Of their observant toil the enemy's weight—
Why, this hath not a finger's dignity.
They call this bed-work, mapp'ry, closet war;
So that the ram that batters down the wall,
For the great swinge and rudeness of his poise,
They place before his hand that made the engine,
Or those that with the fineness of their souls
By reason guide his execution.

NESTOR
Let this be granted, and Achilles' horse
Makes many Thetis' sons. [*Tucket.*]

138 discovered revealed **139 power** army **143 forehand** first in might. **host** army **144 airy fame** unsubstantial reputation **145 dainty** fastidious **151 pageants** mimics **152 topless deputation** supreme power **153–4 whose . . . hamstring** i.e., whose wits are in his thighs **154 rich** admirable **155–6 To hear . . . scaffoldage** i.e., to hear the echoing sound of his marching to and fro on the stage or scaffolding **157 to-be-pitied . . . seeming** pitiful and exaggerated acting **159 a-mending** being repaired or retuned. **terms unsquared** expressions unadapted to their subject, ill-fitted (like unsquared timbers or stones in architecture) **160 from** even if from. **Typhon** Greek mythological monster with a hundred heads that breathed fire; he made war against the gods and was destroyed by one of Zeus's thunderbolts **161 fusty** stale. (And suggesting *fustian,* bombastic.) **162 pressed** weighed down (by its occupant) **164 just** exactly. **165 me** for my benefit. (Also in line 170.) **166 dressed** addressed **167–8 as near . . . parallels** (Parallel lines never meet, no matter how far they are extended.) **168 Vulcan . . . wife** i.e., the ugliest god, and Venus, the most beautiful goddess **171 answer . . . alarm** respond to a nighttime military alert. **172 faint** weak **174 palsy** tremor. **gorget** piece of armor for the throat

178 spleen (Regarded as the seat of laughter.) **180 Severals . . . exact** well-ordered gifts, individual and general **181 preventions** defensive precautions **182 Excitements** exhortations **184 paradoxes** absurdities. **186–7 crowns . . . voice** i.e., regards most highly, adulates **189 In . . . rein** i.e., so haughtily **190 broad** hefty. **keeps** keeps to **191 factious** for his faction; seditious. **our state of war** our state of preparedness for war; our soldiers in their readiness **193 slave** contemptible person. **gall** the seat of bile and rancor **195 exposure** vulnerable situation **196 rank** thickly. **rounded in with** surrounded by **197 tax our policy** censure our prudent management **198 no member** no fit guide or companion **199 Forestall prescience** condemn beforehand any attempts at foresight **200 that of hand** any immediate physical response. **202 fitness** suitability of occasion **202–3 know . . . weight** figure out by laborious calculation the enemy's strength **204 hath . . . dignity** is not worth a snap of the fingers. **205 bed-work . . . war** i.e., armchair strategy, mere map-making, war planned in the study **206–10 So . . . execution** so that they put more value on the great battering ram, because of its huge impetus and roughness of impact, than they give to military planners and generals who devise the weapon, or to those who, with their superior insight, guide its operation. **211–12 Let . . . sons** If this is granted, then Achilles's horse in its brute strength outvalues many an Achilles (the son of Thetis). **212 s.d.** ***Tucket*** signal given on a trumpet

AGAMEMNON What trumpet? Look, Menelaus.
MENELAUS From Troy.

[*Enter Aeneas with a trumpeter.*]

AGAMEMNON What would you 'fore our tent?
AENEAS
Is this great Agamemnon's tent, I pray you?
AGAMEMNON Even this.
AENEAS
May one that is a herald and a prince
Do a fair message to his kingly ears?
AGAMEMNON
With surety stronger than Achilles' arm 220
'Fore all the Greekish host, which with one voice 221
Call Agamemnon head and general.
AENEAS
Fair leave and large security. How may 223
A stranger to those most imperial looks
Know them from eyes of other mortals?
AGAMEMNON How?
AENEAS
Ay. I ask, that I might waken reverence,
And bid the cheek be ready with a blush
Modest as morning when she coldly eyes 229
The youthful Phoebus. 230
Which is that god in office, guiding men?
Which is the high and mighty Agamemnon?
AGAMEMNON
This Trojan scorns us, or the men of Troy
Are ceremonious courtiers.
AENEAS
Courtiers as free, as debonair, unarmed, 235
As bending angels—that's their fame in peace. 236
But when they would seem soldiers, they have galls, 237
Good arms, strong joints, true swords, and—Jove's accord— 238
Nothing so full of heart. But peace, Aeneas, 239
Peace, Trojan; lay thy finger on thy lips!
The worthiness of praise distains his worth, 241
If that the praised himself bring the praise forth. 242
But what the repining enemy commends, 243
That breath fame blows; that praise, sole pure, transcends. 244
AGAMEMNON
Sir, you of Troy, call you yourself Aeneas?
AENEAS Ay, Greek, that is my name.
AGAMEMNON What's your affair, I pray you?
AENEAS
Sir, pardon. 'Tis for Agamemnon's ears.
AGAMEMNON
He hears naught privately that comes from Troy.
AENEAS
Nor I from Troy come not to whisper him. 250
I bring a trumpet to awake his ear, 251
To set his sense on the attentive bent, 252
And then to speak.
AGAMEMNON Speak frankly as the wind;
It is not Agamemnon's sleeping hour.
That thou shalt know, Trojan, he is awake,
He tells thee so himself.
AENEAS Trumpet, blow loud;
Send thy brass voice through all these lazy tents,
And every Greek of mettle, let him know
What Troy means fairly shall be spoke aloud.
Sound trumpet.
We have, great Agamemnon, here in Troy
A prince called Hector—Priam is his father—
Who in this dull and long-continued truce
Is resty grown. He bade me take a trumpet 263
And to this purpose speak: Kings, princes, lords!
If there be one among the fair'st of Greece
That holds his honor higher than his ease,
That seeks his praise more than he fears his peril,
That knows his valor and knows not his fear,
That loves his mistress more than in confession 269
With truant vows to her own lips he loves, 270
And dare avow her beauty and her worth
In other arms than hers—to him this challenge. 272
Hector, in view of Trojans and of Greeks,
Shall make it good, or do his best to do it,
He hath a lady, wiser, fairer, truer,
Than ever Greek did compass in his arms, 276
And will tomorrow with his trumpet call
Midway between your tents and walls of Troy
To rouse a Grecian that is true in love.
If any come, Hector shall honor him;
If none, he'll say in Troy when he retires,
The Grecian dames are sunburnt and not worth 282
The splinter of a lance. Even so much. 283
AGAMEMNON
This shall be told our lovers, Lord Aeneas.
If none of them have soul in such a kind, 285
We left them all at home. But we are soldiers;
And may that soldier a mere recreant prove 287
That means not, hath not, or is not in love! 288
If then one is, or hath, or means to be,
That one meets Hector; if none else, I am he.

220 surety security **221 'Fore . . . voice** leading into battle the entire Greek army, who with one voice **223 Fair leave** Courteous permission **229 she** i.e., Aurora, the blushing dawn goddess. **coldly** demurely **230 Phoebus** Apollo, here referred to as the sun-god. **235 free** generous. **debonair** gracious in manner **236 bending** bowing. **fame** reputation **237 galls** i.e., spirit to resent injury. (See line 193.) **238 Jove's accord** Jove being in full accord, God willing **239 Nothing . . . heart** nothing is so full of unequaled courage as they. **241 distains his** sullies its own **242 If . . . forth** if the person being praised is the one who speaks this praise. **243–4 But . . . transcends** But whenever an enemy offers praise, being naturally reluctant to do so, that praise is trumpeted by Fame herself; such praise is transcendent because it is unmixed with unworthy motives.

250 whisper whisper to **251 trumpet** trumpeter **252 set . . . bent** i.e., bend his sense of hearing attentively toward me **263 resty** sluggish, inactive, restive **269–70 That . . . loves** i.e., who shows his love for his beloved more in deeds of arms than in sweet nothings promised lip to lip **272 In . . . hers** i.e., in the arms of warfare rather than those of his mistress **276 compass** encompass, embrace **282 sunburnt** i.e., unattractive, according to Elizabethan tastes in beauty **283 Even so much** (A formulaic conclusion to a delivered message, meaning, "that is the totality of what I am bid to say.") **285 have . . . kind** i.e., have the spirit to undertake this challenge **287 mere recreant** utter coward **288 means not** intends not to be

NESTOR
Tell him of Nestor, one that was a man
When Hector's grandsire sucked. He is old now,
But if there be not in our Grecian host
One noble man that hath one spark of fire
To answer for his love, tell him from me
I'll hide my silver beard in a gold beaver, 296
And in my vambrace put this withered brawn, 297
And meeting him will tell him that my lady
Was fairer than his grandam and as chaste 299
As may be in the world. His youth in flood, 300
I'll prove this truth with my three drops of blood.

AENEAS
Now heavens forbid such scarcity of youth!

ULYSSES Amen.

AGAMEMNON
Fair Lord Aeneas, let me touch your hand;
To our pavilion shall I lead you first.
Achilles shall have word of this intent;
So shall each lord of Greece, from tent to tent.
Yourself shall feast with us before you go,
And find the welcome of a noble foe. 309
[*Exeunt. Manent Ulysses and Nestor.*]

ULYSSES Nestor!

NESTOR What says Ulysses?

ULYSSES
I have a young conception in my brain;
Be you my time to bring it to some shape. 313

NESTOR What is't?

ULYSSES This 'tis:
Blunt wedges rive hard knots; the seeded pride 316
That hath to this maturity blown up 317
In rank Achilles must or now be cropped 318
Or, shedding, breed a nursery of like evil 319
To overbulk us all.

NESTOR Well, and how? 320

ULYSSES
This challenge that the gallant Hector sends,
However it is spread in general name,
Relates in purpose only to Achilles.

NESTOR
The purpose is perspicuous even as substance, 324
Whose grossness little characters sum up; 325
And, in the publication, make no strain 326
But that Achilles, were his brain as barren
As banks of Libya—though, Apollo knows, 328
'Tis dry enough—will, with great speed of judgment, 329
Ay, with celerity, find Hector's purpose
Pointing on him.

ULYSSES And wake him to the answer, think you?

NESTOR
Yes, 'tis most meet. Who may you else oppose 333
That can from Hector bring his honor off 334
If not Achilles? Though 't be a sportful combat,
Yet in this trial much opinion dwells, 336
For here the Trojans taste our dear'st repute 337
With their fin'st palate. And trust to me, Ulysses, 338
Our imputation shall be oddly poised 339
In this wild action. For the success, 340
Although particular, shall give a scantling 341
Of good or bad unto the general; 342
And in such indices, although small pricks 343
To their subsequent volumes, there is seen 344
The baby figure of the giant mass
Of things to come at large. It is supposed
He that meets Hector issues from our choice;
And choice, being mutual act of all our souls,
Makes merit her election and doth boil, 349
As 'twere from forth us all, a man distilled
Out of our virtues; who miscarrying, 351
What heart from hence receives the conquering part, 352
To steel a strong opinion to themselves? 353
Which entertained, limbs are his instruments, 354
In no less working than are swords and bows 355
Directive by the limbs. 356

ULYSSES Give pardon to my speech:
Therefore 'tis meet Achilles meet not Hector. 358
Let us, like merchants, show our foulest wares,
And think perchance they'll sell; if not,
The luster of the better yet to show
Shall show the better. Do not consent
That ever Hector and Achilles meet;
For both our honor and our shame in this
Are dogged with two strange followers.

NESTOR
I see them not with my old eyes. What are they?

ULYSSES
What glory our Achilles shares from Hector, 367
Were he not proud, we all should wear with him.
But he already is too insolent,
And we were better parch in Afric sun

296 beaver face guard of a helmet **297 vambrace** armor for the front part of the arm. **brawn** i.e., arm **299 grandam** grandmother **300 His . . . flood** i.e., Though Hector's manhood and vigor be at their height **309.1** *Manent* They remain **313 Be . . . time** i.e., act as midwife to my newly conceived plan **316 rive** split, break apart. **seeded pride** pride that has gone to seed, overblown **317 blown up** sprouted, puffed up **318 rank** overripe, swollen. **or** either **319 shedding** if it scatters its seeds. **nursery** (1) breeding ground (2) crop **320 overbulk** overwhelm, outgrow **324–5 perspicuous . . . up** as perceivable as great wealth or matter, the size of which can be rendered in little figures **326 in . . . strain** when it is publicly announced, have no doubt **328 banks** sandbanks; shores **329 dry** dull

333 meet fitting. **else oppose** otherwise put forward as opponent **334 That . . . off** who can acquit himself honorably in doing battle with Hector **336 opinion** reputation **337 taste our dear'st repute** i.e., put to the test Achilles, our warrior of greatest reputation **338 their fin'st palate** i.e., Hector. **339 Our imputation** what is imputed to us, our reputation. **oddly poised** unequally balanced **340 wild** rash. **success** outcome **341 particular** relating to (two) particular men. **scantling** specimen, sample **342 general** army at large **343 indices** indications, table of contents **343–4 small . . . volumes** small indicators in comparison with the volumes that follow **349 election** basis of choice **351 miscarrying** i.e., if he should fail **352 What . . . part** what cheer will the conquering party, i.e., the Trojans, receive from this **353 steel** strengthen **354–6 Which . . . limbs** And in that strengthening of opinion, the limbs that direct the use of weapons are held no less effective than the weapons themselves. (The implication is that those who choose a challenger to Hector will be held as fully to account as the challenger himself.) **358 meet** fitting **367 shares from** gains at the expense of

Than in the pride and salt scorn of his eyes,
Should he scape Hector fair. If he were foiled,
Why then we did our main opinion crush
In taint of our best man. No, make a lottery,
And, by device, let blockish Ajax draw
The sort to fight with Hector. Among ourselves
Give him allowance as the worthier man;
For that will physic the great Myrmidon
Who broils in loud applause, and make him fall
His crest that prouder than blue Iris bends.
If the dull brainless Ajax come safe off,
We'll dress him up in voices; if he fail,
Yet go we under our opinion still
That we have better men. But, hit or miss,
Our project's life this shape of sense assumes:
Ajax employed plucks down Achilles' plumes.

NESTOR
Now, Ulysses, I begin to relish thy advice;
And I will give a taste of it forthwith
To Agamemnon. Go we to him straight.
Two curs shall tame each other; pride alone
Must tar the mastiffs on, as 'twere their bone.

Exeunt.

✤

[2.1]

Enter Ajax and Thersites.

AJAX Thersites!

THERSITES Agamemnon—how if he had boils, full, all over, generally?

AJAX Thersites!

THERSITES And those boils did run? Say so. Did not the General run, then? Were not that a botchy core?

AJAX Dog!

THERSITES Then there would come some matter from him. I see none now.

AJAX Thou bitch-wolf's son, canst thou not hear? [*Strikes him.*] Feel, then.

THERSITES The plague of Greece upon thee, thou mongrel beef-witted lord!

AJAX Speak then, thou vinewed'st leaven, speak. I will beat thee into handsomeness.

THERSITES I shall sooner rail thee into wit and holiness; but I think thy horse will sooner con an oration than thou learn a prayer without book. Thou canst strike, canst thou? A red murrain o' thy jade's tricks!

AJAX Toadstool, learn me the proclamation.

THERSITES Dost thou think I have no sense, thou strikest me thus?

AJAX The proclamation!

THERSITES Thou art proclaimed a fool, I think.

AJAX Do not, porcupine, do not. My fingers itch.

THERSITES I would thou didst itch from head to foot. An I had the scratching of thee, I would make thee the loathsomest scab in Greece. When thou art forth in the incursions, thou strikest as slow as another.

AJAX I say, the proclamation!

THERSITES Thou grumblest and railest every hour on Achilles, and thou art as full of envy at his greatness as Cerberus is at Proserpina's beauty, ay, that thou bark'st at him.

AJAX Mistress Thersites!

THERSITES Thou shouldst strike him—

AJAX Cobloaf!

THERSITES He would pun thee into shivers with his fist, as a sailor breaks a biscuit.

AJAX [*beating him*] You whoreson cur!

THERSITES Do, do.

AJAX Thou stool for a witch!

THERSITES Ay, do, do, thou sodden-witted lord! Thou hast no more brain than I have in mine elbows; an asinego may tutor thee. Thou scurvy-valiant ass! Thou art here but to thrash Trojans, and thou art bought and sold among those of any wit, like a barbarian slave. If thou use to beat me, I will begin at thy heel and tell what thou art by inches, thou thing of no bowels, thou!

AJAX You dog!

THERSITES You scurvy lord!

AJAX [*beating him*] You cur!

THERSITES Mars his idiot! Do, rudeness, do, camel, do, do.

[*Enter Achilles and Patroclus.*]

ACHILLES Why, how now, Ajax, wherefore do ye thus?
How now, Thersites, what's the matter, man?

THERSITES You see him there, do you?

ACHILLES Ay; what's the matter?

THERSITES Nay, look upon him.

ACHILLES So I do. What's the matter?

THERSITES Nay, but regard him well.

372 scape Hector fair come off undefeated in fighting Hector. (Ulysses's argument is that Achilles, already too proud, will be insufferable if he wins, and that, if he loses, the Greeks will undergo the humiliation of losing with their best-reputed warrior.) **373–4 we . . . taint** we would destroy the mainstay of our reputation in the dishonor **376 sort** lot **377 allowance as** acknowledgment as **378 physic** purge medically. **Myrmidon** i.e., Achilles. (So called here because accompanied by a band of Myrmidon warriors, from a tribe living in Thessaly.) **379 broils in** basks in **379–80 and make . . . bends** and cause him to lower the plumes of his helmet that now arch and wave more proudly than the rainbow. (Literally, Iris, the many-colored messenger of Juno.) **382 voices** applause **385 life** success **391 tar** provoke

2.1. Location: The Greek camp; Achilles's tent.

6 botchy core central hard mass of a boil or tumor. **8 matter** (1) sense (2) pus **12–13 mongrel** (Ajax's mother was a Trojan, the sister of Priam; compare 2.2.77 [note], 4.5.84, and 4.5.121.) **13 beef-witted** i.e., slow-witted. (Perhaps this refers to the belief that eating beef made one dull, or Thersites may merely be calling Ajax a "stupid ox.") **14 vinewed'st leaven** moldiest dough

17 con memorize **18 without book** by heart. **19 murrain** plague. **jade's tricks** i.e., ill-tempered kicking and rearing, as of a worthless horse. **20 learn me** find out for me **21 sense** feeling **25 porcupine** (A term of abuse for one who is prickly and small.) **29 incursions** i.e., attacks upon the Trojan forces **33 Cerberus** three-headed dog that guarded the entrance to Hades. **Proserpina** Queen of Hades **36 Thou** If thou **37 Cobloaf** Small round loaf; a bun. **38 pun** pound. **shivers** fragments **41 Do** i.e., Go ahead, I dare you **42 stool** privy **43 sodden-witted** boiled-brained **45 asinego** little ass **46–7 bought and sold** i.e., treated like merchandise **48 use** continue **49 by inches** methodically, inch by inch **50 bowels** sensitivity, human feeling **54 Mars his** Mars's **56 wherefore** why

ACHILLES Well, why, I do so.

THERSITES But yet you look not well upon him; for, whomsoever you take him to be, he is Ajax.

ACHILLES I know that, fool.

THERSITES Ay, but that fool knows not himself.

AJAX Therefore I beat thee.

THERSITES Lo, lo, lo, lo, what modicums of wit he utters! His evasions have ears thus long. I have bobbed his brain more than he has beat my bones. I will buy nine sparrows for a penny, and his pia mater is not worth the ninth part of a sparrow. This lord, Achilles—Ajax, who wears his wit in his belly and his guts in his head—I'll tell you what I say of him.

ACHILLES What?

THERSITES I say, this Ajax— [*Ajax threatens him.*]

ACHILLES Nay, good Ajax.

THERSITES Has not so much wit—

ACHILLES Nay, I must hold you.

THERSITES As will stop the eye of Helen's needle, for whom he comes to fight.

ACHILLES Peace, fool!

THERSITES I would have peace and quietness, but the fool will not—he there, that he. Look you there.

AJAX Oh, thou damned cur! I shall—

ACHILLES Will you set your wit to a fool's?

THERSITES No, I warrant you, for a fool's will shame it.

PATROCLUS Good words, Thersites.

ACHILLES What's the quarrel?

AJAX I bade the vile owl go learn me the tenor of the proclamation, and he rails upon me.

THERSITES I serve thee not.

AJAX Well, go to, go to.

THERSITES I serve here voluntary.

ACHILLES Your last service was suff'rance, 'twas not voluntary; no man is beaten voluntary. Ajax was here the voluntary, and you as under an impress.

THERSITES E'en so. A great deal of your wit, too, lies in your sinews, or else there be liars. Hector shall have a great catch an 'a knock out either of your brains; 'a were as good crack a fusty nut with no kernel.

ACHILLES What, with me too, Thersites?

THERSITES There's Ulysses and old Nestor, whose wit was moldy ere your grandsires had nails on their toes, yoke you like draft-oxen and make you plow up the war.

ACHILLES What? What?

THERSITES Yes, good sooth. To, Achilles! To, Ajax! To!

AJAX I shall cut out your tongue.

THERSITES 'Tis no matter. I shall speak as much wit as thou afterwards.

PATROCLUS No more words, Thersites. Peace!

THERSITES I will hold my peace when Achilles' brach bids me, shall I?

ACHILLES There's for you, Patroclus.

THERSITES I will see you hanged like clodpolls ere I come any more to your tents. I will keep where there is wit stirring and leave the faction of fools. *Exit.*

PATROCLUS A good riddance.

ACHILLES
Marry, this, sir, is proclaimed through all our host:
That Hector, by the fifth hour of the sun,
Will with a trumpet twixt our tents and Troy
Tomorrow morning call some knight to arms
That hath a stomach, and such a one that dare
Maintain—I know not what, 'tis trash. Farewell.

AJAX Farewell. Who shall answer him?

ACHILLES I know not. 'Tis put to lottery. Otherwise
He knew his man. [*Exit with Patroclus.*]

AJAX Oh, meaning you? I will go learn more of it.
Exit.

✤

[2.2]

Enter Priam, Hector, Troilus, Paris, and Helenus.

PRIAM
After so many hours, lives, speeches spent,
Thus once again says Nestor from the Greeks:
"Deliver Helen, and all damage else—
As honor, loss of time, travail, expense,
Wounds, friends, and what else dear that is consumed
In hot digestion of this cormorant war—
Shall be struck off." Hector, what say you to't?

HECTOR
Though no man lesser fears the Greeks than I
As far as toucheth my particular,
Yet, dread Priam,
There is no lady of more softer bowels,
More spongy to suck in the sense of fear,
More ready to cry out, "Who knows what follows?"
Than Hector is. The wound of peace is surety,
Surety secure; but modest doubt is called
The beacon of the wise, the tent that searches

65 Ajax (With probable pun on *a jakes,* a latrine.) **67 that fool . . . himself** (Thersites answers as though Achilles had said, "I know that fool.") **68 Therefore . . . thee** i.e., I beat you because you are the real fool, not me. (This attempt at wit draws Thersites's sarcasm in the next speech.) **69 modicums** small amounts **70 have . . . long** i.e., are those of an ass, are asinine. **bobbed** thumped **71 will** can **pia mater** (Literally, membrane cover of the brain; used here for the brain.) **81 stop** stop up, fill. (Perhaps with a bawdy sense.) **Helen's needle** (Aristocratic women customarily did needlework as an avocation.) **87 set your wit to** match wits with **88 a fool's . . . shame it** i.e., Ajax's intelligence is even less than a fool's. **89 Good words** i.e., Speak gently **95 voluntary** voluntarily. **96 suff'rance** something imposed **98 impress** (1) impressment, military draft (2) imprint (of blows). **99 E'en so** Exactly. **100 or . . . liars** unless Report is a liar. **101 an 'a** if he **101–2 'a . . . good** he might as well **102 fusty** moldy

109 To . . . To! (Thersites impersonates Nestor and Ulysses as drivers of a team, urging Achilles and Ajax to plow.) **112 afterwards** i.e., even after my tongue is cut out. **114 brach** bitch hound. (The Quarto reading, "brooch," could mean "bauble, plaything," referring to Patroclus.) **117 clodpolls** blockheads **122 fifth hour** eleven o'clock **125 stomach** appetite (for fighting) **129 knew** would know
2.2. Location: Troy. The palace.
3 Deliver Hand over **4 travail** strenuous effort **6 cormorant** voracious (like the seabird) **7 struck off** canceled. **9 my particular** me personally **11 bowels** i.e., mercy, pity **14 The . . . surety** The danger of peace is in the sense of overconfidence and security it breeds **15 secure** overconfident. **modest doubt** a reasonable estimate of danger **16 beacon** warning signal. **tent** surgical probe

To th'bottom of the worst. Let Helen go.
Since the first sword was drawn about this question,
Every tithe soul, 'mongst many thousand dismes, 19
Hath been as dear as Helen; I mean, of ours.
If we have lost so many tenths of ours 21
To guard a thing not ours—nor worth to us,
Had it our name, the value of one ten— 23
What merit's in that reason which denies 24
The yielding of her up?

TROILUS Fie, fie, my brother!
Weigh you the worth and honor of a king
So great as our dread father in a scale
Of common ounces? Will you with counters sum 28
The past-proportion of his infinite, 29
And buckle in a waist most fathomless 30
With spans and inches so diminutive 31
As fears and reasons? Fie, for godly shame! 32

HELENUS [*to Troilus*]
No marvel, though you bite so sharp at reasons, 33
You are so empty of them. Should not our father 34
Bear the great sway of his affairs with reason,
Because your speech hath none that tell him so? 36

TROILUS
You are for dreams and slumbers, brother priest;
You fur your gloves with reason. Here are your
reasons: 38
You know an enemy intends you harm;
You know a sword employed is perilous,
And reason flies the object of all harm. 41
Who marvels then, when Helenus beholds
A Grecian and his sword, if he do set
The very wings of reason to his heels
And fly like chidden Mercury from Jove 45
Or like a star disorbed? Nay, if we talk of reason, 46
Let's shut our gates and sleep. Manhood and honor
Should have hare hearts, would they but fat their
thoughts 48
With this crammed reason. Reason and respect 49
Make livers pale and lustihood deject. 50

HECTOR [*to Troilus*]
Brother, she is not worth what she doth cost
The holding.

TROILUS What's aught but as 'tis valued?

HECTOR
But value dwells not in particular will; 53
It holds his estimate and dignity 54
As well wherein 'tis precious of itself 55
As in the prizer. 'Tis mad idolatry 56
To make the service greater than the god;
And the will dotes that is inclinable 58
To what infectiously itself affects 59
Without some image of th'affected merit. 60

TROILUS
I take today a wife, and my election 61
Is led on in the conduct of my will—
My will enkindled by mine eyes and ears,
Two traded pilots twixt the dangerous shores 64
Of will and judgment. How may I avoid, 65
Although my will distaste what it elected, 66
The wife I chose? There can be no evasion
To blench from this and to stand firm by honor. 68
We turn not back the silks upon the merchant
When we have soiled them, nor the remainder viands 70
We do not throw in unrespective sieve 71
Because we now are full. It was thought meet
Paris should do some vengeance on the Greeks. 73
Your breath of full consent bellied his sails; 74
The seas and winds, old wranglers, took a truce 75
And did him service. He touched the ports desired,
And for an old aunt whom the Greeks held captive 77
He brought a Grecian queen, whose youth and
freshness
Wrinkles Apollo's and makes stale the morning. 79
Why keep we her? The Grecians keep our aunt.
Is she worth keeping? Why, she is a pearl
Whose price hath launched above a thousand ships 82
And turned crowned kings to merchants. 83
If you'll avouch 'twas wisdom Paris went—
As you must needs, for you all cried, "Go, go"—
If you'll confess he brought home noble prize—
As you must needs, for you all clapped your hands
And cried, "Inestimable!"—why do you now

19 Every . . . dismes every human life exacted by the war as a tithe or tenth, amongst many thousand such exactions **21 tenths** i.e., lives exacted by the war **23 Had . . . name** i.e., even if Helen were a Trojan. **one ten** one tithe exacted by the war, one Trojan life **24 reason** reasoning **28–32 Will . . . reasons?** Will you employ the valueless disks used by shopkeepers in their commercial bargaining to sum up Priam's infinite worth exceeding all calculation, and attempt to confine his unfathomable greatness with fears and pretexts that are as puny as the nine-inch span from hand to thumb? **33 reasons** (Pronounced like "raisins," with pun.) **34 not our father** our father not **36 Because . . . so?** i.e., simply because you unreasonably urge him to govern unreasonably? **38 fur** line with soft fur. (Troilus accuses Helenus of using reason as a justification for personal comfort, explaining cowardly flight as prudence.) **41 And . . . harm** and such cowardly "reason" flees at the sight of anything threatening. **45 chidden Mercury** (Mercury as Jove's errand boy was subject to his chiding or impatient bidding.) **46 disorbed** removed from its sphere (like a shooting star). **48–9 Should . . . reason** would have the craven hearts of hares if they would cram their thoughts with this "reason." **49 respect** caution **50 livers pale** (A bloodless liver was thought to be a sign of cowardice.) **and . . . deject** and bodily vigor overthrown.

53 particular will i.e., one person's preference merely **54 his** its. **dignity** worth **55–6 As well . . . prizer** as much in its intrinsic worth as in the opinion of the person who prizes or appraises it. **58–60 the will . . . merit** any will is mere willfulness that is derived from the will's own diseased affection without some visible appearance of merit in the thing desired. **61 I take today a wife** (Troilus, in setting up a hypothetical case that applies to Paris, is also stating his own credo about love.) **election** choice **64 traded** skillful in their trade; trafficking back and forth **65 avoid** rid myself of **66 distaste** dislike (in time) **68 blench** shrink. **and** and simultaneously **70 remainder viands** leftover food **71 unrespective sieve** undiscriminating receptacle, i.e., garbage can **73 vengeance** i.e., in return for Hesione's abduction; see line 77 and note **74 bellied** swelled **75 old wranglers** traditional enemies **77 an old aunt** i.e., Hesione, Priam's sister, rescued from the wrath of Poseidon by Hercules and bestowed by him on the Greek, Telamon, father of Ajax; we learn in 4.5.84 and 4.5.121 that she was Ajax' mother **79 Wrinkles Apollo's** makes Apollo's youthful countenance look old and ugly by comparison **82 Whose . . . ships** (Perhaps echoes the famous line from Marlowe's *Doctor Faustus:* "Was this the face that launched a thousand ships?") **83 turned . . . merchants** i.e., has made kings behave like merchants seeking a rare pearl. (Compare Matthew 13:45.)

The issue of your proper wisdoms rate
And do a deed that never Fortune did,
Beggar the estimation which you prized
Richer than sea and land? Oh, theft most base,
That we have stol'n what we do fear to keep!
But thieves unworthy of a thing so stol'n,
That in their country did them that disgrace
We fear to warrant in our native place!

Enter Cassandra, [*raving,*] *with her hair about her ears.*

CASSANDRA
Cry, Trojans, cry!
PRIAM What noise? What shriek is this?
TROILUS
'Tis our mad sister. I do know her voice.
CASSANDRA Cry, Trojans!
HECTOR It is Cassandra.
CASSANDRA
Cry, Trojans, cry! Lend me ten thousand eyes,
And I will fill them with prophetic tears.
HECTOR Peace, sister, peace!
CASSANDRA
Virgins and boys, mid-age and wrinkled old,
Soft infancy, that nothing canst but cry,
Add to my clamor! Let us pay betimes
A moiety of that mass of moan to come.
Cry, Trojans, cry! Practice your eyes with tears!
Troy must not be, nor goodly Ilium stand;
Our firebrand brother, Paris, burns us all.
Cry, Trojans, cry! A Helen and a woe!
Cry, cry! Troy burns, or else let Helen go. *Exit.*
HECTOR
Now, youthful Troilus, do not these high strains
Of divination in our sister work
Some touches of remorse? Or is your blood
So madly hot that no discourse of reason,
Nor fear of bad success in a bad cause,
Can qualify the same?
TROILUS Why, brother Hector,
We may not think the justness of each act
Such and no other than th'event doth form it,
Nor once deject the courage of our minds
Because Cassandra's mad. Her brainsick raptures
Cannot distaste the goodness of a quarrel
Which hath our several honors all engaged
To make it gracious. For my private part,
I am no more touched than all Priam's sons,
And Jove forbid there should be done amongst us
Such things as might offend the weakest spleen
To fight for and maintain!
PARIS
Else might the world convince of levity
As well my undertakings as your counsels.
But I attest the gods, your full consent
Gave wings to my propension and cut off
All fears attending on so dire a project.
For what, alas, can these my single arms?
What propugnation is in one man's valor
To stand the push and enmity of those
This quarrel would excite? Yet, I protest,
Were I alone to pass the difficulties,
And had as ample power as I have will,
Paris should ne'er retract what he hath done
Nor faint in the pursuit.
PRIAM Paris, you speak
Like one besotted on your sweet delights.
You have the honey still, but these the gall.
So to be valiant is no praise at all.
PARIS
Sir, I propose not merely to myself
The pleasures such a beauty brings with it,
But I would have the soil of her fair rape
Wiped off in honorable keeping her.
What treason were it to the ransacked queen,
Disgrace to your great worths, and shame to me,
Now to deliver her possession up
On terms of base compulsion! Can it be
That so degenerate a strain as this
Should once set footing in your generous bosoms?
There's not the meanest spirit on our party
Without a heart to dare or sword to draw
When Helen is defended, nor none so noble
Whose life were ill bestowed or death unfamed
Where Helen is the subject. Then I say,
Well may we fight for her whom we know well
The world's large spaces cannot parallel.
HECTOR
Paris and Troilus, you have both said well,
And on the cause and question now in hand

89 The issue . . . rate condemn the results of your own wise deliberation **90 do . . . did** act more capriciously than Fortune ever did **91 Beggar . . . which** consider valueless the once esteemed object that **94 But** i.e., We are but **95–6 That . . . place** who disgraced the Greeks in their own country through an act (the abducting of Helen) that we are now too cowardly to justify right here in our own native land. **96.1–2 *about her ears*** (Betokening unmarried status and also distraction. Perhaps Cassandra's wild appearance helps explain why the Trojans do not recognize her at first.) **104 old** old persons **105 nothing canst** can do nothing **106 betimes** before it is too late **107 moiety** part **108 Practice** Make use of **110 firebrand** (Paris's mother, Hecuba, dreamed when pregnant with Paris that she would be delivered of a firebrand destined to burn down Troy.) **118 qualify** moderate **119–22 We . . . mad** we must not judge the justice of our proceedings on the outcome, nor abate our courage solely because of Cassandra's mad warnings. **123 distaste** render distasteful **124 our several honors** the honor of each of us **125 gracious** righteous, dignified. (Because our honorable selves "grace" the enterprise.) **126 touched** affected **127–9 Jove . . . maintain!** Jove forbid that any act done by any of Priam's sons (such as abducting Helen) should be such that even the least courageous among us would not willingly fight to maintain! **130 convince** convict **131 As well . . . as** both . . . and **132 attest** call to witness **133 propension** propensity, inclination **135 can . . . arms?** can my arms alone accomplish? **136 propugnation** defense, might **139 pass** experience, undergo **142 faint** lose heart **143 besotted** drunk **145 So** Thus, under these circumstances. **praise** merit **148 soil** stain. **rape** abduction **150 ransacked** carried off **152 her possession** possession of her **154 strain** muddied thought **155 generous** noble **156–7 There's . . . heart** Not even the most low-born Trojan would lack the courage **159 Whose . . . unfamed** whose life would be unworthily given or whose death would be neglected by fame **162 The world's . . . spaces** all the world

Have glozed—but superficially, not much
Unlike young men, whom Aristotle thought
Unfit to hear moral philosophy.
The reasons you allege do more conduce
To the hot passion of distempered blood
Than to make up a free determination
Twixt right and wrong, for pleasure and revenge
Have ears more deaf than adders to the voice
Of any true decision. Nature craves
All dues be rendered to their owners. Now,
What nearer debt in all humanity
Than wife is to the husband? If this law
Of nature be corrupted through affection,
And that great minds, of partial indulgence
To their benumbèd wills, resist the same,
There is a law in each well-ordered nation
To curb those raging appetites that are
Most disobedient and refractory.
If Helen then be wife to Sparta's king,
As it is known she is, these moral laws
Of nature and of nations speak aloud
To have her back returned. Thus to persist
In doing wrong extenuates not wrong
But makes it much more heavy. Hector's opinion
Is this in way of truth; yet ne'ertheless,
My sprightly brethren, I propend to you
In resolution to keep Helen still,
For 'tis a cause that hath no mean dependence
Upon our joint and several dignities.

TROILUS
Why, there you touched the life of our design!
Were it not glory that we more affected
Than the performance of our heaving spleens,
I would not wish a drop of Trojan blood
Spent more in her defense. But, worthy Hector,
She is a theme of honor and renown,
A spur to valiant and magnanimous deeds,
Whose present courage may beat down our foes,
And fame in time to come canonize us;
For I presume brave Hector would not lose
So rich advantage of a promised glory
As smiles upon the forehead of this action
For the wide world's revenue.

HECTOR I am yours,
You valiant offspring of great Priamus.
I have a roisting challenge sent amongst
The dull and factious nobles of the Greeks
Will strike amazement to their drowsy spirits.
I was advertised their great general slept,
Whilst emulation in the army crept.
This, I presume, will wake him. *Exeunt.*

✤

[2.3]

Enter Thersites, solus.

THERSITES How now, Thersites? What, lost in the labyrinth of thy fury? Shall the elephant Ajax carry it thus? He beats me, and I rail at him. Oh, worthy satisfaction! Would it were otherwise, that I could beat him whilst he railed at me. 'Sfoot, I'll learn to conjure and raise devils but I'll see some issue of my spiteful execrations. Then there's Achilles, a rare engineer! If Troy be not taken till these two undermine it, the walls will stand till they fall of themselves. O thou great thunder-darter of Olympus, forget that thou art Jove, the king of gods, and, Mercury, lose all the serpentine craft of thy caduceus, if ye take not that little little less than little wit from them that they have, which short-armed ignorance itself knows is so abundant scarce it will not in circumvention deliver a fly from a spider without drawing their massy irons and cutting the web! After this, the vengeance on the whole camp! Or rather, the Neapolitan bone-ache! For that, methinks, is the curse dependent on those that war for a placket. I have said my prayers, and devil Envy say "Amen."—What ho! My lord Achilles!

[*Enter Patroclus at the door of the tent.*]

PATROCLUS Who's there? Thersites? Good Thersites, come in and rail. [*Exit.*]

THERSITES If I could ha' remembered a gilt counterfeit, thou wouldst not have slipped out of my contemplation. But it is no matter; thyself upon thyself! The common curse of mankind, folly and ignorance, be thine in great revenue! Heaven bless thee from a tutor, and discipline come not near thee! Let thy blood be

165 glozed commented on **167 moral philosophy** (Aristotle says this of political philosophy in the *Nichomachean Ethics.*) **168 conduce** lead, tend **170 free** unbiased **172 adders** (Psalms 58:4–5 speaks of adders as deaf.) **173 craves** demands **177 affection** erotic passion **178 that** if that, if. **of partial** out of self-interested **182 refractory** obstinate. **189 truth** abstract principle **190 sprightly** full of spirit. **propend** incline **192–3 'tis . . . dignities** i.e., it is a cause upon which depends our collective and individual honors, and they on it. **195 more affected** desired more **196 heaving spleens** i.e., aroused anger **201 Whose . . . foes** the ready and courageous spirit of which will enable us to beat down our foes **202 canonize** enroll among famous persons **205 forehead** i.e., prospect, beginning **208 roisting** roistering, clamorous **210 Will** that will

211 advertised informed. **their great general** i.e., Achilles; or possibly Agamemnon **212 emulation** ambitious or jealous rivalry
2.3. Location: The Greek camp. Before Achilles's tent.
2 carry it carry off the honors **5 'Sfoot** By His (God's) foot **6 but . . . issue** i.e., if it takes that to see some result **7 execrations** curses. **engineer** one who digs countermines or tunnels underneath the enemy's battlements, or devises plans for such undertakings **11–12 serpentine . . . caduceus** (Alludes to Mercury's wand, having two serpents twined round it.) **13–14 short-armed** inadequate in its reach, finding everything beyond its grasp **15 circumvention** craft, stratagem **16 massy irons** massive swords. (Used with overkill on a mere spider's web.) **18 Neapolitan bone-ache** i.e., venereal disease. **19 dependent on** hanging over. **placket** slit in a petticoat; hence (indecently) a woman. **24 ha'** have. **gilt counterfeit** counterfeit coin. (Often called a "slip"; hence the quibble in line 25.) **26 thyself upon thyself** (Thersites, after alleging that he would have cursed Patroclus along with Ajax and Achilles if he were not counterfeit and hence so easily overlooked, now undertakes to curse Patroclus with the most dire curse imaginable: may Patroclus simply be himself, be plagued by himself.) **28 great revenue** generous amounts. **bless thee from** bless you by protecting you from (so as to preserve your native ignorance) **29 discipline** instruction. **blood** violent passion

thy direction till thy death; then if she that lays thee out says thou art a fair corpse, I'll be sworn and sworn upon't she never shrouded any but lazars.

[Enter Patroclus.]

Amen.—Where's Achilles?

PATROCLUS What, art thou devout? Wast thou in prayer?

THERSITES Ay. The heavens hear me!

PATROCLUS Amen.

Enter Achilles.

ACHILLES Who's there?

PATROCLUS Thersites, my lord.

ACHILLES Where, where? Oh, where?—Art thou come? Why, my cheese, my digestion, why hast thou not served thyself in to my table so many meals? Come, what's Agamemnon?

THERSITES Thy commander, Achilles.—Then tell me, Patroclus, what's Achilles?

PATROCLUS Thy lord, Thersites. Then tell me, I pray thee, what's thyself?

THERSITES Thy knower, Patroclus. Then tell me, Patroclus, what art thou?

PATROCLUS Thou mayst tell that knowest.

ACHILLES Oh, tell, tell.

THERSITES I'll decline the whole question. Agamemnon commands Achilles, Achilles is my lord, I am Patroclus' knower, and Patroclus is a fool.

PATROCLUS You rascal!

THERSITES Peace, fool! I have not done.

ACHILLES He is a privileged man.—Proceed, Thersites.

THERSITES Agamemnon is a fool, Achilles is a fool, Thersites is a fool, and, as aforesaid, Patroclus is a fool.

ACHILLES Derive this. Come.

THERSITES Agamemnon is a fool to offer to command Achilles, Achilles is a fool to be commanded of Agamemnon, Thersites is a fool to serve such a fool, and Patroclus is a fool positive.

PATROCLUS Why am I a fool?

THERSITES Make that demand to the Creator. It suffices me thou art. Look you, who comes here?

Enter [at a distance] Agamemnon, Ulysses, Nestor, Diomedes, Ajax, and Calchas.

ACHILLES Patroclus, I'll speak with nobody.—Come in with me, Thersites. *[Exit.]*

THERSITES Here is such patchery, such juggling, and such knavery! All the argument is a whore and a cuckold, a good quarrel to draw emulous factions and bleed to death upon. Now, the dry serpigo on the subject, and war and lechery confound all! *[Exit.]*

AGAMEMNON Where is Achilles?

PATROCLUS Within his tent, but ill disposed, my lord.

AGAMEMNON Let it be known to him that we are here.
He shent our messengers, and we lay by
Our appertainments, visiting of him.
Let him be told so, lest perchance he think
We dare not move the question of our place,
Or know not what we are.

PATROCLUS I shall so say to him. *[Exit.]*

ULYSSES We saw him at the opening of his tent. He is not sick.

AJAX Yes, lion-sick, sick of proud heart. You may call it melancholy if you will favor the man, but, by my head, 'tis pride. But why, why? Let him show us the cause.—A word, my lord. *[He takes Agamemnon aside.]*

NESTOR What moves Ajax thus to bay at him?

ULYSSES Achilles hath inveigled his fool from him.

NESTOR Who, Thersites?

ULYSSES He.

NESTOR Then will Ajax lack matter, if he have lost his argument.

ULYSSES No, you see, he is his argument that has his argument—Achilles.

NESTOR All the better; their fraction is more our wish than their faction. But it was a strong council that a fool could disunite.

ULYSSES The amity that wisdom knits not, folly may easily untie.

Enter Patroclus.

Here comes Patroclus.

NESTOR No Achilles with him.

ULYSSES The elephant hath joints, but none for courtesy. His legs are legs for necessity, not for flexure.

PATROCLUS
Achilles bids me say he is much sorry
If anything more than your sport and pleasure
Did move your greatness and this noble state
To call upon him. He hopes it is no other
But for your health and your digestion sake,

30–1 she . . . out the woman who prepares your body for burial **32 lazars** lepers. **41 cheese** (Supposed, proverbially, to aid digestion.) **52 decline** go through in order from beginning to end (as when declining a noun) **57 privileged man** (Fools were permitted to speak without restraint.) **60 Derive** Explain, give the origin of. (The grammatical metaphor is continued here and also in line 64.) **61 offer** undertake **64 positive** absolute. **66 Make that demand** Ask that question **70 patchery** knavery

71–3 All . . . upon i.e., This war is nothing but a quarrel about a whore and a cuckold (Helen and Menelaus), a fine quarrelsome basis upon which to draw rival factions into bloody and fatal conflict. **73 serpigo** skin eruption **74 confound** destroy; throw into turmoil **78 shent** sent back insultingly **79 appertainments** rights, prerogatives **81 move the question** insist upon the prerogatives **85 lion-sick** i.e., sick with pride **93 matter** subject matter (to rail upon) **93–4 his argument** i.e., the subject of his railing, Thersites. **95–6 No . . . Achilles** i.e., No, Ajax has not lost something to rail on, since Achilles, who now has Thersites, has become Ajax's latest object of quarreling. **97–9 their fraction . . . disunite** i.e., this discord between Achilles and Ajax better suits our wishes than their uniting in faction against us. But the alliance between them cannot have been strong in any case if a fool like Thersites was able to undo it. **104 The elephant hath joints** (Refers to a common belief that elephants' joints did not enable them to lie down.) **108 state** council of state **110 digestion** digestion's

An after-dinner's breath.

AGAMEMNON Hear you, Patroclus:
We are too well acquainted with these answers;
But his evasion, wingèd thus swift with scorn,
Cannot outfly our apprehensions.
Much attribute he hath, and much the reason
Why we ascribe it to him. Yet all his virtues,
Not virtuously on his own part beheld,
Do in our eyes begin to lose their gloss,
Yea, like fair fruit in an unwholesome dish,
Are like to rot untasted. Go and tell him
We come to speak with him. And you shall not sin
If you do say we think him overproud
And underhonest, in self-assumption greater
Than in the note of judgment; and worthier than himself
Here tend the savage strangeness he puts on,
Disguise the holy strength of their command,
And underwrite in an observing kind
His humorous predominance—yea, watch
His pettish lunes, his ebbs, his flows, as if
The passage and whole carriage of this action
Rode on his tide. Go tell him this, and add
That if he overhold his price so much,
We'll none of him, but let him, like an engine
Not portable, lie under this report:
"Bring action hither; this cannot go to war."
A stirring dwarf we do allowance give
Before a sleeping giant. Tell him so.

PATROCLUS
I shall, and bring his answer presently.

AGAMEMNON
In second voice we'll not be satisfied.
We come to speak with him.—Ulysses, enter you.
[*Exit Ulysses with Patroclus.*]

AJAX What is he more than another?

AGAMEMNON No more than what he thinks he is.

AJAX Is he so much? Do you not think he thinks himself a better man than I am?

AGAMEMNON No question.

AJAX Will you subscribe his thought and say he is?

AGAMEMNON No, noble Ajax, you are as strong, as valiant, as wise, no less noble, much more gentle, and altogether more tractable.

AJAX Why should a man be proud? How doth pride grow? I know not what it is.

AGAMEMNON Your mind is the clearer, Ajax, and your virtues the fairer. He that is proud eats up himself. Pride is his own glass, his own trumpet, his own chronicle; and whatever praises itself but in the deed devours the deed in the praise.

Enter Ulysses.

AJAX I do hate a proud man as I hate the engend'ring of toads.

NESTOR [*aside*] Yet he loves himself. Is't not strange?

ULYSSES
Achilles will not to the field tomorrow.

AGAMEMNON
What's his excuse?

ULYSSES He doth rely on none,
But carries on the stream of his dispose
Without observance or respect of any,
In will peculiar and in self-admission.

AGAMEMNON
Why, will he not upon our fair request
Untent his person and share th' air with us?

ULYSSES
Things small as nothing, for request's sake only,
He makes important. Possessed he is with greatness,
And speaks not to himself but with a pride
That quarrels at self-breath. Imagined worth
Holds in his blood such swoll'n and hot discourse
That twixt his mental and his active parts
Kingdomed Achilles in commotion rages
And batters down himself. What should I say?
He is so plaguey proud that the death tokens of it
Cry "No recovery."

AGAMEMNON Let Ajax go to him.—
Dear lord, go you and greet him in his tent.
'Tis said he holds you well and will be led,
At your request, a little from himself.

ULYSSES
O Agamemnon, let it not be so!
We'll consecrate the steps that Ajax makes
When they go from Achilles. Shall the proud lord
That bastes his arrogance with his own seam
And never suffers matter of the world
Enter his thoughts, save such as do revolve
And ruminate himself, shall he be worshiped
Of that we hold an idol more than he?

111 breath i.e., stroll for a breath of fresh air. **114 apprehensions** (1) power of arrest (2) understanding. **115 attribute** credit, reputation **117 Not . . . beheld** not being modestly observed or kept by him **120 like** likely **121 sin** err **123 self-assumption** self-importance **124 Than . . . judgment** than men of true judgment know him to be; or, than in qualities of wise judgment **124–5 worthier . . . on** worthier persons than himself stand here in attendance while he assumes an uncivil aloofness **127–8 underwrite . . . predominance** deferentially subscribe to the humor now dominant in him—i.e., arrogant pride **129 pettish lunes** ill-humored tantrums **130 this action** the Trojan war **132 overhold** overvalue **133 engine** military machine **134 lie under** suffer under **135 "Bring . . . war"** i.e., "Let the war come to me; I am too proud to accommodate myself to it." **136 stirring** active. **allowance** approbation, praise **138 presently** right away. **139 In second voice** i.e., With a mere messenger's report **146 subscribe** concur in

154–5 Pride . . . chronicle Pride is its own mirror and proclaimer of its greatness **155 but in the deed** in any way other than in doing (praiseworthy) deeds **163 dispose** bent of mind **165 will peculiar** his own independent will. **self-admission** self-approbation. **168 for . . . only** only because they are requested **171 quarrels at self-breath** i.e., is almost too proud to speak to himself. **174 Kingdomed** i.e., like a microcosm of a state **176 death tokens** fatal symptoms **179 holds** regards **180 from himself** i.e., from his usual arrogant behavior. **182–3 We'll . . . Achilles** i.e., Let us instead venerate Ajax when he puts as much distance between himself and Achilles as possible. **184 seam** fat, grease (by means of which Achilles feeds his own pride) **185 suffers** allows **186–7 save . . . himself** other than thoughts that serve for endless self-contemplation **188 Of . . . idol** by one whom we venerate

No, this thrice worthy and right valiant lord
Must not so stale his palm, nobly acquired,
Nor, by my will, assubjugate his merit,
As amply titled as Achilles' is,
By going to Achilles.
That were to enlard his fat-already pride
And add more coals to Cancer when he burns
With entertaining great Hyperion.
This lord go to him? Jupiter forbid,
And say in thunder, "Achilles, go to him."

NESTOR [*aside to Diomedes*]
Oh, this is well. He rubs the vein of him.

DIOMEDES [*aside to Nestor*]
And how his silence drinks up this applause!

AJAX
If I go to him, with my armèd fist
I'll pash him o'er the face.

AGAMEMNON Oh, no, you shall not go.

AJAX
An 'a be proud with me, I'll feeze his pride.
Let me go to him.

ULYSSES
Not for the worth that hangs upon our quarrel.

AJAX A paltry, insolent fellow!

NESTOR [*aside*] How he describes himself!

AJAX Can he not be sociable?

ULYSSES [*aside*] The raven chides blackness.

AJAX I'll let his humor's blood.

AGAMEMNON [*aside*] He will be the physician that should be the patient.

AJAX An all men were o' my mind—

ULYSSES [*aside*] Wit would be out of fashion.

AJAX 'A should not bear it so. 'A should eat swords first. Shall pride carry it?

NESTOR [*aside*] An 'twould, you'd carry half.

ULYSSES [*aside*] 'A would have ten shares.

AJAX I will knead him; I'll make him supple.

NESTOR [*aside*] He's not yet through warm. Farce him with praises. Pour in, pour in; his ambition is dry.

ULYSSES [*to Agamemnon*]
My lord, you feed too much on this dislike.

NESTOR
Our noble general, do not do so.

DIOMEDES
You must prepare to fight without Achilles.

ULYSSES
Why, 'tis this naming of him does him harm.
Here is a man—but 'tis before his face;
I will be silent.

NESTOR Wherefore should you so?
He is not emulous, as Achilles is.

ULYSSES
Know the whole world, he is as valiant—

AJAX A whoreson dog, that shall palter thus with us!
Would he were a Trojan!

NESTOR What a vice were it in Ajax now—

ULYSSES If he were proud—

DIOMEDES Or covetous of praise—

ULYSSES Ay, or surly borne—

DIOMEDES Or strange, or self-affected!

ULYSSES [*to Ajax*]
Thank the heavens, lord, thou art of sweet composure.
Praise him that got thee, she that gave thee suck;
Famed be thy tutor, and thy parts of nature
Thrice famed, beyond, beyond all erudition;
But he that disciplined thine arms to fight,
Let Mars divide eternity in twain
And give him half; and, for thy vigor,
Bull-bearing Milo his addition yield
To sinewy Ajax. I will not praise thy wisdom,
Which, like a bourn, a pale, a shore, confines
Thy spacious and dilated parts. Here's Nestor,
Instructed by the antiquary times;
He must, he is, he cannot but be wise.
But pardon, father Nestor, were your days
As green as Ajax' and your brain so tempered,
You should not have the eminence of him,
But be as Ajax.

AJAX Shall I call you father?

ULYSSES
Ay, my good son.

DIOMEDES Be ruled by him, Lord Ajax.

ULYSSES
There is no tarrying here; the hart Achilles
Keeps thicket. Please it our great general
To call together all his state of war.
Fresh kings are come to Troy; tomorrow
We must with all our main of power stand fast.
And here's a lord—come knights from east to west,
And cull their flower, Ajax shall cope the best.

190 stale . . . acquired sully his nobly won honor. (*Palm* means "palm leaf.") **191 assubjugate** debase, reduce to subjection **192 As . . . is** having as great a name as Achilles's. (Or, if *Achilles* is not a possessive, this could mean, "granted that Achilles is also rich in titles.") **195–6 add . . . Hyperion** i.e., add a fire to the heat of summer. (Cancer is the sign of the zodiac into which the sun [Hyperion] enters at the beginning of summer.) **199 vein** humor, disposition **202 pash** smash **204 An . . . pride** i.e., If he puts on airs with me, I'll settle his hash. **206 our quarrel** i.e., with the Trojans. **211 let . . . blood** bleed him (as a physician would) to cure his excessive humors. **216 'A** He. **eat swords** swallow my sword, i.e., be beaten in fight **218 An** If **219 ten shares** i.e., the whole without sharing. **221 through** thoroughly. **Farce** Stuff **223 this dislike** i.e., Achilles's truculence. **226 this . . . harm** this continual citing of Achilles as our chief hero that creates the difficulty.

229 emulous envious, eager for glory **230 Know . . . world** Let the whole world know **231 that shall palter** who thinks he can trifle, dodge **236 surly borne** bearing himself in a surly fashion **237 strange** distant. **self-affected** in love with himself. **238 composure** temperament, constitution. **239 got** begot **240–1 thy parts . . . erudition** i.e., your natural gifts thrice exceeding what erudition can add thereto. (With an ironic double meaning, suggesting that erudition can add little.) **242 But he** but as for him **245 Bull-bearing . . . yield** let bull-bearing Milo yield up his title. (Milo, a celebrated athlete of phenomenal strength, was able to carry a bull on his shoulders.) **246 I will not** (1) I will forbear to (2) I won't **247 bourn** boundary. **pale** fence **248 dilated parts** extensive and well-known qualities. (But also hinting at Ajax's beefy build.) **249 antiquary** ancient **252 green** immature. **tempered** composed **253 have . . . of** be reckoned superior to **257 Keeps thicket** i.e., stays hidden. (A *thicket* is a dense growth of shrubs or trees.) **258 state** council **260 main** full force **262 cull their flower** choose their flower of chivalry. **cope** prove a match for

AGAMEMNON
Go we to council. Let Achilles sleep.
Light boats sail swift, though greater hulks draw deep. *Exeunt.*

✤

[3.1]

[*Music sounds within.*] *Enter Pandarus* [*and a Servant*].

PANDARUS Friend, you, pray you, a word. Do not you follow the young Lord Paris?

SERVANT Ay, sir, when he goes before me.

PANDARUS You depend upon him, I mean?

SERVANT Sir, I do depend upon the lord.

PANDARUS You depend upon a notable gentleman; I must needs praise him.

SERVANT The Lord be praised!

PANDARUS You know me, do you not?

SERVANT Faith, sir, superficially.

PANDARUS Friend, know me better. I am the Lord Pandarus.

SERVANT I hope I shall know Your Honor better.

PANDARUS I do desire it.

SERVANT You are in the state of grace?

PANDARUS Grace? Not so, friend. "Honor" and "lordship" are my titles. What music is this?

SERVANT I do but partly know, sir. It is music in parts.

PANDARUS Know you the musicians?

SERVANT Wholly, sir.

PANDARUS Who play they to?

SERVANT To the hearers, sir.

PANDARUS At whose pleasure, friend?

SERVANT At mine, sir, and theirs that love music.

PANDARUS Command, I mean, friend.

SERVANT Who shall I command, sir?

PANDARUS Friend, we understand not one another; I am too courtly and thou too cunning. At whose request do these men play?

SERVANT That's to't indeed, sir. Marry, sir, at the request of Paris my lord, who's there in person; with him, the mortal Venus, the heart-blood of beauty, love's visible soul—

PANDARUS Who, my cousin Cressida?

SERVANT No, sir, Helen. Could not you find out that by her attributes?

PANDARUS It should seem, fellow, that thou hast not seen the Lady Cressida. I come to speak with Paris from the Prince Troilus. I will make a complimental assault upon him, for my business seethes.

SERVANT Sodden business! There's a stewed phrase, indeed!

Enter Paris and Helen [*attended*].

PANDARUS Fair be to you, my lord, and to all this fair company! Fair desires, in all fair measure, fairly guide them! Especially to you, fair queen, fair thoughts be your fair pillow!

HELEN Dear lord, you are full of fair words.

PANDARUS You speak your fair pleasure, sweet queen.—Fair prince, here is good broken music.

PARIS You have broke it, cousin, and, by my life, you shall make it whole again; you shall piece it out with a piece of your performance.—Nell, he is full of harmony.

PANDARUS Truly, lady, no.

HELEN Oh, sir—

PANDARUS Rude, in sooth; in good sooth, very rude.

PARIS Well said, my lord. Well, you say so in fits.

PANDARUS I have business to my lord, dear queen.—My lord, will you vouchsafe me a word?

HELEN Nay, this shall not hedge us out. We'll hear you sing, certainly.

PANDARUS Well, sweet queen, you are pleasant with me.—But, marry, thus, my lord: my dear lord and most esteemed friend, your brother Troilus—

HELEN My lord Pandarus, honey-sweet lord—

PANDARUS Go to, sweet queen, go to—commends himself most affectionately to you—

HELEN You shall not bob us out of our melody. If you do, our melancholy upon your head!

PANDARUS Sweet queen, sweet queen, that's a sweet queen, i'faith.

HELEN And to make a sweet lady sad is a sour offense.

PANDARUS Nay, that shall not serve your turn, that shall it not, in truth, la. Nay, I care not for such words, no, no.—And, my lord, he desires you, that if the King call for him at supper you will make his excuse.

HELEN My lord Pandarus—

PANDARUS What says my sweet queen, my very very sweet queen?

PARIS What exploit's in hand? Where sups he tonight?

HELEN Nay, but, my lord—

PANDARUS What says my sweet queen? My cousin will fall out with you.

264 hulks big, unwieldy ships
3.1. Location: Troy. The palace.
2 follow serve. (But the servant takes it in the sense of "follow after.") **3 goes** walks **4 depend upon** serve as dependent to. (The servant mockingly uses a more spiritual sense.) **5 lord** (Quibbling on *lord,* referring to Paris, and "Lord" as "God.") **7 needs** necessarily **10 superficially** (1) slightly (2) as a superficial person. **13 know . . . better** (1) become better acquainted with you (2) see you become a more humble man. (*Your Honor* is a polite form of address to one of social consequence.) **15 in . . . grace** i.e., in the way of salvation because of desiring to be better. (Pandarus answers as though *grace* referred to the courtly title applicable to a duke or prince.) **18 partly** (1) partially (2) in parts **30 to't** to the point

39 complimental courteous **40 seethes** boils, requires haste. **41 Sodden, stewed** (A play on *seethes* and with quibbling reference to stews or brothels and to the sweating treatment for venereal disease.) **43 Fair** Fair wishes, good fortune. (With wordplay in subsequent uses of *fair:* attractive, pleasing, just, clean.) **44 fairly** favorably **49 broken music** music arranged for different families of instruments. **50 broke** interrupted. **cousin** (Often used at court in addressing a social equal.) **51 piece it out** mend it **56 Rude** (I am) unpolished **57 in fits** (1) by fits and starts (2) in divisions of a song, in stanzas. **59 vouchsafe** permit **60 hedge** shut **62 pleasant** jocular **66 Go to** (An expression of mild protest.) **68 bob** cheat **74 la** (An exclamation accompanying a conventional phrase.) **82–3 My . . . you** i.e., Paris will be angry with you for interrupting so.

HELEN [*to Paris*] You must not know where he sups.

PARIS I'll lay my life, with my disposer Cressida.

PANDARUS No, no, no such matter; you are wide. Come, your disposer is sick.

PARIS Well, I'll make 's excuse.

PANDARUS Ay, good my lord. Why should you say Cressida? No, your poor disposer's sick.

PARIS I spy.

PANDARUS You spy! What do you spy?—Come, give me an instrument. [*He is handed a musical instrument.*] Now, sweet queen.

HELEN Why, this is kindly done.

PANDARUS My niece is horribly in love with a thing you have, sweet queen.

HELEN She shall have it, my lord, if it be not my lord Paris.

PANDARUS He? No, she'll none of him. They two are twain.

HELEN Falling in, after falling out, may make them three.

PANDARUS Come, come, I'll hear no more of this. I'll sing you a song now.

HELEN Ay, ay, prithee. Now, by my troth, sweet lord, thou hast a fine forehead.

PANDARUS Ay, you may, you may.

HELEN Let thy song be love. This love will undo us all. Oh, Cupid, Cupid, Cupid!

PANDARUS Love? Ay, that it shall, i'faith.

PARIS Ay, good now, "Love, love, nothing but love."

PANDARUS In good truth, it begins so: [*He sings.*]

Love, love, nothing but love, still love, still more!
  For, oh, love's bow
  Shoots buck and doe.
  The shaft confounds
  Not that it wounds,
But tickles still the sore.
These lovers cry, "Oh! Oh!", they die!
  Yet that which seems the wound to kill
Doth turn "Oh! Oh!" to "ha, ha, he!"
  So dying love lives still.
"Oh! Oh!" awhile, but "ha, ha, ha!"
"Oh! Oh!" groans out for "ha! ha! ha!"—
Heigh-ho!

HELEN In love, i'faith, to the very tip of the nose.

PARIS He eats nothing but doves, love, and that breeds hot blood, and hot blood begets hot thoughts, and hot thoughts beget hot deeds, and hot deeds is love.

PANDARUS Is this the generation of love? Hot blood, hot thoughts, and hot deeds? Why, they are vipers. Is love a generation of vipers? Sweet lord, who's afield today?

PARIS Hector, Deiphobus, Helenus, Antenor, and all the gallantry of Troy. I would fain have armed today, but my Nell would not have it so. How chance my brother Troilus went not?

HELEN He hangs the lip at something.—You know all, Lord Pandarus.

PANDARUS Not I, honey-sweet queen. I long to hear how they sped today.—You'll remember your brother's excuse?

PARIS To a hair.

PANDARUS Farewell, sweet queen.

HELEN Commend me to your niece.

PANDARUS I will, sweet queen. [*Exit.*]

Sound a retreat.

PARIS
They're come from field. Let us to Priam's hall
To greet the warriors. Sweet Helen, I must woo you
To help unarm our Hector. His stubborn buckles,
With these your white enchanting fingers touched,
Shall more obey than to the edge of steel
Or force of Greekish sinews. You shall do more
Than all the island kings: disarm great Hector.

HELEN
'Twill make us proud to be his servant, Paris.
Yea, what he shall receive of us in duty
Gives us more palm in beauty than we have,
Yea, overshines ourself.

PARIS Sweet, above thought I love thee. *Exeunt.*

✤

[3.2]

Enter Pandarus and Troilus' Man, [*meeting*].

PANDARUS How now, where's thy master? At my cousin Cressida's?

MAN No, sir, he stays for you to conduct him thither.

[*Enter Troilus.*]

PANDARUS Oh, here he comes.—How now, how now?

TROILUS Sirrah, walk off. [*Exit Man.*]

PANDARUS Have you seen my cousin?

TROILUS
No, Pandarus. I stalk about her door,
Like a strange soul upon the Stygian banks
Staying for waftage. Oh, be thou my Charon,

84 You must not i.e., Pandarus does not want you to. **he** i.e., Troilus **85 lay** wager. **my disposer** i.e., one who may do what she likes (with me or Troilus) **86 wide** wide of the mark. **88 make 's excuse** make his (Troilus's) excuse (to Priam). **91 I spy** I get it. **101 twain** not in accord. **102–3 Falling . . . three** (Helen bawdily jokes that Cressida's game will result in the birth of a child, a third person.) **108 you may** go on, have your joke. **112 good now** please **116 buck and doe** i.e., male and female. **117 confounds** overwhelms **118 Not that** (1) not that which, or (2) not so much that. (The erotic suggestion is that love does its harm by penetrating and tickling.) **119 sore** (1) wound (2) buck in its fourth year. **120, 123 die, dying** (Quibbling on the idea of experiencing orgasm.) **121 wound to kill** fatal wound

131 generation genealogy **133 generation of vipers** (See Matthew 3:7, 12:34, and 23:33.) **139 He hangs the lip** Pandarus pouts, sulks **142 sped** succeeded **144 To a hair** To the last detail. **154 island kings** i.e., Greek chieftains **157 Gives . . . have** bestows more honor on me than my own beauty does. (Helen uses the royal plural.)
3.2. Location: The garden of Cressida's house (formerly her father's house until he abandoned Troy).
0.1 *Man* servant. (Probably the *varlet* referred to in 1.1.1.)
8–9 a strange . . . Charon (Refers to the Greek mythological conception of the fate of departed souls who had to wait on the banks of the Styx or Acheron until the boatman Charon ferried them across to the infernal region.)

And give me swift transportance to those fields
Where I may wallow in the lily beds
Proposed for the deserver! O gentle Pandar,
From Cupid's shoulder pluck his painted wings,
And fly with me to Cressid!

PANDARUS Walk here i'th'orchard. I'll bring her straight. [*Exit Pandarus.*]

TROILUS
I am giddy; expectation whirls me round.
Th'imaginary relish is so sweet
That it enchants my sense. What will it be
When that the wat'ry palates taste indeed
Love's thrice repurèd nectar? Death, I fear me,
Swooning destruction, or some joy too fine,
Too subtle-potent, tuned too sharp in sweetness
For the capacity of my ruder powers.
I fear it much; and I do fear besides
That I shall lose distinction in my joys,
As doth a battle, when they charge on heaps
The enemy flying.

[*Enter Pandarus.*]

PANDARUS She's making her ready; she'll come straight. You must be witty now. She does so blush, and fetches her wind so short, as if she were frayed with a spirit. I'll fetch her. It is the prettiest villain! She fetches her breath as short as a new-ta'en sparrow. *Exit Pandarus.*

TROILUS
Even such a passion doth embrace my bosom.
My heart beats thicker than a feverous pulse,
And all my powers do their bestowing lose,
Like vassalage at unawares encount'ring
The eye of majesty.

Enter Pandarus, and Cressida, [*veiled*].

PANDARUS Come, come, what need you blush? Shame's a baby.—Here she is now. Swear the oaths now to her that you have sworn to me. [*Cressida draws back.*] What, are you gone again? You must be watched ere you be made tame, must you? Come your ways, come your ways; an you draw backward, we'll put you i'th' thills.—Why do you not speak to her?—Come, draw this curtain, and let's see your picture. [*She is unveiled.*] Alas the day, how loath you are to offend daylight! An 'twere dark, you'd close sooner. So, so, rub on, and kiss the mistress. [*They kiss.*] How now, a kiss in fee-farm? Build there, carpenter, the air is sweet. Nay, you shall fight your hearts out ere I part you—the falcon as the tercel, for all the ducks i'th' river. Go to, go to.

TROILUS You have bereft me of all words, lady.

PANDARUS Words pay no debts; give her deeds. But she'll bereave you o'th' deeds too, if she call your activity in question. What, billing again? Here's "In witness whereof the parties interchangeably"—Come in, come in. I'll go get a fire. [*Exit.*]

CRESSIDA Will you walk in, my lord?

TROILUS Oh, Cressida, how often have I wished me thus!

CRESSIDA Wished, my lord? The gods grant—Oh, my lord!

TROILUS What should they grant? What makes this pretty abruption? What too curious dreg espies my sweet lady in the fountain of our love?

CRESSIDA More dregs than water, if my fears have eyes.

TROILUS Fears make devils of cherubins; they never see truly.

CRESSIDA Blind fear that seeing reason leads finds safer footing than blind reason stumbling without fear. To fear the worst oft cures the worse.

TROILUS Oh, let my lady apprehend no fear. In all Cupid's pageant there is presented no monster.

CRESSIDA Nor nothing monstrous neither?

TROILUS Nothing but our undertakings, when we vow to weep seas, live in fire, eat rocks, tame tigers, thinking it harder for our mistress to devise imposition enough than for us to undergo any difficulty imposed. This is the monstrosity in love, lady, that the will is infinite and the execution confined, that the desire is boundless and the act a slave to limit.

CRESSIDA They say all lovers swear more performance than they are able, and yet reserve an ability that they never perform, vowing more than the perfection of ten and discharging less than the tenth part of one. They that have the voice of lions and the act of hares, are they not monsters?

TROILUS Are there such? Such are not we. Praise us as we are tasted, allow us as we prove; our head shall go

10 fields the Elysian fields **12 Proposed for** promised to **15 orchard** garden. **20 wat'ry palates** i.e., sense of taste watering with anticipation **21 repurèd** refined, repurified **26 lose . . . joys** be unable to distinguish one delight from another **27 battle** army **30 witty** alert, resourceful in easy conversation **31 fetches . . . short** is short of breath **31–2 frayed . . . spirit** frightened by a ghost. **32 villain** (Used endearingly.) **35 thicker** faster **36 bestowing** proper use **37 vassalage at unawares** vassals unexpectedly **42 watched** kept awake (like a hawk that is being tamed through sleeplessness) **45 thills** shafts of a cart or wagon. (An image of domesticating the woman, as in hawking.) **46 curtain** veil. (Curtains were hung in front of pictures.) **48 close** (1) encounter (2) come to terms

49 kiss the mistress (In bowls, to touch the central target; to *rub* is to maneuver obstacles as the ball rolls; *mistress* is analogous to "master," short for "master bowl," a small bowl placed as a mark for players to aim at.) **50 in fee-farm** i.e., unending, as with land that is held in perpetuity. **50–1 Build . . . sweet** (1) Erect your house in this fresh and unspoiled location (2) Place your love here where her breath is sweet. **52–3 the falcon . . . river** i.e., I'll bet all the ducks in the river that the female hawk will be as eager as the male. **56–7 activity** virility. (Pandarus jests that Cressida will wear Troilus down in lovemaking.) **57 billing** kissing **57–8 "In . . . interchangeably"** (A legal formula used for contracts, ending "have set their hand and seals.") **59 get a fire** order a fire (for the bedroom). **65 abruption** breaking off. **curious dreg** finicky and anxiety-causing impurity **68 make . . . cherubins** i.e., make things seem worst rather than best **70 that . . . leads** that is led by clear-sighted reason **72 oft . . . worse** enables us to avoid lesser dangers. **76 undertakings** vows **78 to devise imposition** to think up tasks to impose **85 perfection of ten** accomplishment of ten perfect lovers **90 tasted** tried, proved. **allow** acknowledge, approve

bare till merit crown it. No perfection in reversion shall have a praise in present; we will not name desert before his birth, and, being born, his addition shall be humble. Few words to fair faith. Troilus shall be such to Cressid as what envy can say worst shall be a mock for his truth, and what truth can speak truest not truer than Troilus.

CRESSIDA Will you walk in, my lord?

[*Enter Pandarus.*]

PANDARUS What, blushing still? Have you not done talking yet?

CRESSIDA Well, uncle, what folly I commit, I dedicate to you.

PANDARUS I thank you for that. If my lord get a boy of you, you'll give him me. Be true to my lord. If he flinch, chide me for it.

TROILUS You know now your hostages: your uncle's word and my firm faith.

PANDARUS Nay, I'll give my word for her too. Our kindred, though they be long ere they are wooed, they are constant being won. They are burrs, I can tell you; they'll stick where they are thrown.

CRESSIDA
Boldness comes to me now and brings me heart.
Prince Troilus, I have loved you night and day
For many weary months.

TROILUS
Why was my Cressid then so hard to win?

CRESSIDA
Hard to seem won; but I was won, my lord,
With the first glance that ever—pardon me;
If I confess much, you will play the tyrant.
I love you now, but till now not so much
But I might master it. In faith, I lie;
My thoughts were like unbridled children, grown
Too headstrong for their mother. See, we fools!
Why have I blabbed? Who shall be true to us,
When we are so unsecret to ourselves?
But, though I loved you well, I wooed you not;
And yet, good faith, I wished myself a man,
Or that we women had men's privilege
Of speaking first. Sweet, bid me hold my tongue,
For in this rapture I shall surely speak
The thing I shall repent. See, see, your silence,
Cunning in dumbness, in my weakness draws
My soul of counsel from me! Stop my mouth.

TROILUS
And shall, albeit sweet music issues thence.
[*He kisses her.*]

PANDARUS Pretty, i'faith.

CRESSIDA
My lord, I do beseech you, pardon me;
'Twas not my purpose thus to beg a kiss.
I am ashamed. Oh, heavens, what have I done?
For this time will I take my leave, my lord.

TROILUS Your leave, sweet Cressid?

PANDARUS Leave? An you take leave till tomorrow morning—

CRESSIDA Pray you, content you.

TROILUS What offends you, lady?

CRESSIDA Sir, mine own company.

TROILUS You cannot shun yourself.

CRESSIDA Let me go and try.
I have a kind of self resides with you,
But an unkind self that itself will leave
To be another's fool. Where is my wit?
I would be gone. I speak I know not what.

TROILUS
Well know they what they speak that speak so wisely.

CRESSIDA
Perchance, my lord, I show more craft than love,
And fell so roundly to a large confession
To angle for your thoughts. But you are wise,
Or else you love not, for to be wise and love
Exceeds man's might; that dwells with gods above.

TROILUS
Oh, that I thought it could be in a woman—
As, if it can, I will presume in you—
To feed for aye her lamp and flames of love,
To keep her constancy in plight and youth,
Outliving beauty's outward, with a mind
That doth renew swifter than blood decays!
Or that persuasion could but thus convince me
That my integrity and truth to you
Might be affronted with the match and weight
Of such a winnowed purity in love;
How were I then uplifted! But, alas,
I am as true as truth's simplicity,
And simpler than the infancy of truth.

CRESSIDA
In that I'll war with you.

TROILUS Oh, virtuous fight,
When right with right wars who shall be most right!
True swains in love shall in the world to come
Approve their truth by Troilus. When their rhymes,

91 No . . . reversion No promise of perfection to come **93 addition** title **94 Few . . . faith** (Compare the proverb: "Where many words are, the truth goes by.") **95–6 as what . . . truth** that the worst that malice can do is to mock Troilus's loyalty **101 folly** foolishness. (Pandarus understands it to mean "lechery.") **111 thrown** (1) tossed (2) thrown down in the act of seduction. **121 unbridled** unrestrained **132 My . . . counsel** my inmost thoughts

140 An If **142 content you** don't be upset. **148 unkind** unnatural **148–9 that . . . fool** that will desert its true nature to be your dupe or plaything. **149 Where . . . wit?** What am I saying? **151 Well . . . wisely** Anyone who speaks as wisely as you do knows what he or she is saying. **152 Perchance** Perchance you think that. **craft** cunning **153 roundly** outspokenly. **large** free **154 To . . . thoughts** to draw forth a confession from you. **155–6 Or . . . might** or, to put it another way, you are too wise to be really in love, since to be wise and love at the same time is beyond human capacity **158 presume** presume that it is **160 To . . . youth** to keep her pledged constancy fresh **161 outward** appearance **162 blood decays** passions wane. **165–6 affronted . . . love** matched with an equal quantity of purified love (in you). **winnowed** separated from the chaff **168 truth's simplicity** the simple truth **169 the infancy of truth** i.e., pure, innocent truth. **173 Approve** attest. **by Troilus** i.e., using Troilus as an ideal comparison.

Full of protest, of oath and big compare,
Wants similes, truth tired with iteration—
"As true as steel, as plantage to the moon,
As sun to day, as turtle to her mate,
As iron to adamant, as earth to th' center"—
Yet, after all comparisons of truth,
As truth's authentic author to be cited,
"As true as Troilus" shall crown up the verse
And sanctify the numbers.

CRESSIDA Prophet may you be!
If I be false or swerve a hair from truth,
When time is old and hath forgot itself,
When waterdrops have worn the stones of Troy,
And blind oblivion swallowed cities up,
And mighty states characterless are grated
To dusty nothing, yet let memory,
From false to false, among false maids in love,
Upbraid my falsehood! When they've said "as false
As air, as water, wind, or sandy earth,
As fox to lamb, or wolf to heifer's calf,
Pard to the hind, or stepdame to her son,"
Yea, let them say, to stick the heart of falsehood,
"As false as Cressid."

PANDARUS Go to, a bargain made. Seal it, seal it; I'll be the witness. Here I hold your hand, here my cousin's. If ever you prove false one to another, since I have taken such pains to bring you together, let all pitiful goers-between be called to the world's end after my name: call them all Pandars. Let all constant men be Troiluses, all false women Cressids, and all brokers-between Pandars! Say "Amen."

TROILUS Amen.

CRESSIDA Amen.

PANDARUS Amen. Whereupon I will show you a chamber with a bed, which bed, because it shall not speak of your pretty encounters, press it to death. Away!

Exeunt [*Troilus and Cressida*].

And Cupid grant all tongue-tied maidens here
Bed, chamber, pander to provide this gear! *Exit.*

✣

[3.3]

Flourish. Enter Ulysses, Diomedes, Nestor, Agamemnon, [*Ajax, Menelaus,*] *and Calchas.*

CALCHAS
Now, princes, for the service I have done you,
Th'advantage of the time prompts me aloud
To call for recompense. Appear it to your mind
That, through the sight I bear in things to come,
I have abandoned Troy, left my possessions,
Incurred a traitor's name, exposed myself
From certain and possessed conveniences
To doubtful fortunes, sequest'ring from me all
That time, acquaintance, custom, and condition
Made tame and most familiar to my nature;
And here, to do you service, am become
As new into the world, strange, unacquainted.
I do beseech you, as in way of taste,
To give me now a little benefit
Out of those many registered in promise
Which, you say, live to come in my behalf.

AGAMEMNON
What wouldst thou of us, Trojan, make demand?

CALCHAS
You have a Trojan prisoner called Antenor
Yesterday took. Troy holds him very dear.
Oft have you—often have you thanks therefor—
Desired my Cressid in right great exchange,
Whom Troy hath still denied; but this Antenor,
I know, is such a wrest in their affairs
That their negotiations all must slack,
Wanting his manage, and they will almost
Give us a prince of blood, a son of Priam,
In change of him. Let him be sent, great princes,
And he shall buy my daughter; and her presence
Shall quite strike off all service I have done
In most accepted pain.

AGAMEMNON Let Diomedes bear him,
And bring us Cressid hither. Calchas shall have
What he requests of us. Good Diomed,
Furnish you fairly for this interchange.
Withal bring word if Hector will tomorrow
Be answered in his challenge. Ajax is ready.

DIOMEDES
This shall I undertake, and 'tis a burden
Which I am proud to bear. *Exit* [*with Calchas*].

Achilles and Patroclus stand in their tent.

ULYSSES
Achilles stands i'th'entrance of his tent.
Please it our general pass strangely by him,
As if he were forgot; and, princes all,
Lay negligent and loose regard upon him.

174 protest protestation (of love). **big compare** extravagant comparisons **175 Wants . . . iteration** are in need of new similes, having worn out their usual expressions of love through too much repetition **176 plantage** vegetation (waxing in growth by the moon's influence) **177 turtle** turtledove **178 adamant** lodestone (magnetic). **center** center of the earth, axis **179 comparisons** illustrative similes **180 As . . . cited** when we want to cite as our authority the very fountainhead of truth **181 crown up** give the finishing touches to **182 numbers** verses. **187 characterless** unrecorded, without a mark left. **grated** pulverized **189 From . . . love** passing from one false one to another among false-hearted young women **193 Pard** leopard or panther. **hind** doe. **stepdame** stepmother **194 stick the heart** pierce the center of the target **199 pitiful** compassionate **208 press . . . death** (Alludes to the usual punishment by weights for accused persons refusing to plead or "speak.") **209 here** i.e., in the audience **210 gear** equipment.
3.3. Location: The Greek camp. Before Achilles's tent.

2 advantage of favorable opportunity offered by **3 Appear it** Let it appear **4 bear** am endowed with **7 From** turning from **8 sequest'ring** separating, removing **10 tame** familiar, domestic **11 am** have **13 taste** foretaste **16 live to come** await fulfillment **21 right great exchange** exchange for distinguished captives **22 still** continually **23 wrest** tuning key, i.e., one producing harmony and order **25 Wanting his manage** lacking his management **27 change of** exchange for **30 In . . . pain** in pains (troubles, hardships) which I have endured most willingly. **bear** escort **34 Withal** In addition **35 Be answered in** meet the answerer of **37.1 *stand in*** i.e., enter on stage and stand in the entrance of **39 strangely** i.e., as one who pretends to be a stranger

I will come last. 'Tis like he'll question me
Why such unplausive eyes are bent, why turned, on
him.
If so, I have derision medicinable
To use between your strangeness and his pride,
Which his own will shall have desire to drink.
It may do good. Pride hath no other glass
To show itself but pride, for supple knees
Feed arrogance and are the proud man's fees.

AGAMEMNON
We'll execute your purpose and put on
A form of strangeness as we pass along.
So do each lord, and either greet him not
Or else disdainfully, which shall shake him more
Than if not looked on. I will lead the way.
[*They move in procession past Achilles' tent.*]

ACHILLES
What, comes the general to speak with me?
You know my mind. I'll fight no more 'gainst Troy.

AGAMEMNON
What says Achilles? Would he aught with us?

NESTOR
Would you, my lord, aught with the general?

ACHILLES No.

NESTOR Nothing, my lord.

AGAMEMNON The better.
[*Exeunt Agamemnon and Nestor.*]

ACHILLES [*to Menelaus*] Good day, good day.

MENELAUS How do you? How do you? [*Exit.*]

ACHILLES What, does the cuckold scorn me?

AJAX How now, Patroclus!

ACHILLES Good morrow, Ajax.

AJAX Ha?

ACHILLES Good morrow.

AJAX Ay, and good next day too.
Exit. [*Ulysses remains behind, reading.*]

ACHILLES
What mean these fellows? Know they not Achilles?

PATROCLUS
They pass by strangely. They were used to bend,
To send their smiles before them to Achilles,
To come as humbly as they use to creep
To holy altars.

ACHILLES What, am I poor of late?
'Tis certain, greatness, once fall'n out with fortune,
Must fall out with men too. What the declined is
He shall as soon read in the eyes of others
As feel in his own fall; for men, like butterflies,
Show not their mealy wings but to the summer,
And not a man, for being simply man,
Hath any honor but honor for those honors
That are without him—as place, riches, and favor,
Prizes of accident as oft as merit;
Which, when they fall, as being slippery standers,
The love that leaned on them, as slippery too,
Doth one pluck down another and together
Die in the fall. But 'tis not so with me;
Fortune and I are friends. I do enjoy
At ample point all that I did possess,
Save these men's looks, who do, methinks, find out
Something not worth in me such rich beholding
As they have often given. Here is Ulysses;
I'll interrupt his reading.—How now, Ulysses?

ULYSSES Now, great Thetis' son!

ACHILLES What are you reading?

ULYSSES A strange fellow here
Writes me that man, how dearly ever parted,
How much in having, or without or in,
Cannot make boast to have that which he hath,
Nor feels not what he owes, but by reflection;
As when his virtues, shining upon others,
Heat them, and they retort that heat again
To the first givers.

ACHILLES This is not strange, Ulysses.
The beauty that is borne here in the face
The bearer knows not, but commends itself
To others' eyes; nor doth the eye itself,
That most pure spirit of sense, behold itself,
Not going from itself, but eye to eye opposed
Salutes each other with each other's form.
For speculation turns not to itself
Till it hath traveled and is mirrored there
Where it may see itself. This is not strange at all.

ULYSSES
I do not strain at the position—
It is familiar—but at the author's drift,
Who, in his circumstance, expressly proves
That no man is the lord of anything,
Though in and of him there be much consisting,
Till he communicate his parts to others;
Nor doth he of himself know them for aught
Till he behold them formed in the applause

43 unplausive disapproving **44 derision medicinable** curative scorn **45 use** i.e., make connection. **strangeness** aloofness **46 Which . . . drink** which medicine his own pride will thirst for. **47 glass** mirror **48 To show . . . pride** in which to see its image except the pride of others **48–9 for supple . . . fees** i.e., since obsequiousness merely encourages arrogance by rewarding pride with the adulation it expects. **50 We'll** I will. (The royal "we.") **57 Would he aught** Does he want anything **61 The better** So much the better. **71 used** accustomed **73 use** are accustomed **76 the declined** the man brought low **79 mealy** powdery

80–2 not . . . him no one is honored for himself but, rather, for those marks of distinction that are external to him **82 as** such as **84 being . . . standers** standing on uncertain foundation **89 At ample point** to the full **91 Something . . . beholding** something in me not worthy of such high respect **97–8 Writes . . . or in** writes that any individual, however richly endowed with natural good qualities both external and internal **100 owes** owns. **but by reflection** i.e., except as reflected in others' opinions **102 retort** reflect **105 but** (1) unless it (2) but instead **107 most . . . sense** most exquisite of the five senses. (Compare 1.1.60.) **108–9 Not . . . form** since it cannot go out from itself; instead, two persons' eyes gazing into each other must convey to both persons a sense of what they look like from another's point of view. **110 speculation** power of sight **113 strain . . . position** find difficulty in the writer's general stance **114 drift** i.e., particular application **115 circumstance** detailed argument **117 Though . . . consisting** though he enjoys many fine qualities that cohere and harmonize **119 aught** anything of value

Where they're extended; who, like an arch,
reverb'rate 121
The voice again, or, like a gate of steel
Fronting the sun, receives and renders back 123
His figure and his heat. I was much rapt in this 124
And apprehended here immediately
Th'unknown Ajax. Heavens, what a man is there! 126
A very horse, that has he knows not what. 127
Nature, what things there are
Most abject in regard and dear in use! 129
What things again most dear in the esteem 130
And poor in worth! Now shall we see tomorrow—
An act that very chance doth throw upon him—
Ajax renowned. Oh, heavens, what some men do,
While some men leave to do! 134
How some men creep in skittish Fortune's hall, 135
Whiles others play the idiots in her eyes! 136
How one man eats into another's pride, 137
While pride is fasting in his wantonness! 138
To see these Grecian lords—why, even already
They clap the lubber Ajax on the shoulder, 140
As if his foot were on brave Hector's breast
And great Troy shrinking.

ACHILLES I do believe it,
For they passed by me as misers do by beggars,
Neither gave to me good word nor look.
What, are my deeds forgot?

ULYSSES
Time hath, my lord, a wallet at his back, 146
Wherein he puts alms for oblivion, 147
A great-sized monster of ingratitudes.
Those scraps are good deeds past, which are
devoured
As fast as they are made, forgot as soon
As done. Perseverance, dear my lord,
Keeps honor bright; to have done is to hang
Quite out of fashion, like a rusty mail 153
In monumental mock'ry. Take the instant way, 154
For honor travels in a strait so narrow
Where one but goes abreast. Keep then the path, 156
For emulation hath a thousand sons 157
That one by one pursue. If you give way, 158
Or hedge aside from the direct forthright, 159
Like to an entered tide they all rush by
And leave you hindmost;
Or, like a gallant horse fall'n in first rank,
Lie there for pavement to the abject rear, 163
O'errun and trampled on. Then what they do in
present, 164
Though less than yours in past, must o'ertop yours;
For Time is like a fashionable host
That slightly shakes his parting guest by th' hand, 167
And with his arms outstretched, as he would fly, 168
Grasps in the comer. The welcome ever smiles, 169
And farewell goes out sighing. Let not virtue seek 170
Remuneration for the thing it was; 171
For beauty, wit,
High birth, vigor of bone, desert in service,
Love, friendship, charity, are subjects all
To envious and calumniating Time. 175
One touch of nature makes the whole world kin, 176
That all with one consent praise newborn gauds,
Though they are made and molded of things past, 178
And give to dust that is a little gilt 179
More laud than gilt o'erdusted. 180
The present eye praises the present object.
Then marvel not, thou great and complete man, 182
That all the Greeks begin to worship Ajax,
Since things in motion sooner catch the eye
Than what not stirs. The cry went once on thee, 185
And still it might, and yet it may again,
If thou wouldst not entomb thyself alive
And case thy reputation in thy tent, 188
Whose glorious deeds but in these fields of late 189
Made emulous missions 'mongst the gods themselves 190
And drave great Mars to faction.

ACHILLES Of this my privacy 191
I have strong reasons.

ULYSSES But 'gainst your privacy
The reasons are more potent and heroical. 193
'Tis known, Achilles, that you are in love
With one of Priam's daughters.

ACHILLES Ha! Known? 195

ULYSSES Is that a wonder?
The providence that's in a watchful state 197
Knows almost every grain of Pluto's gold, 198
Finds bottom in th'uncomprehensive deeps, 199

121 Where they're extended of those persons to whom they are displayed. **who** i.e., the applauders **123 Fronting** facing **124 His** its, the sun's **126 unknown** as yet obscure in reputation **127 has . . . what** does not know his own strength. **129 abject . . . use** lowly esteemed and yet valuable, of practical value. **130 again** on the other hand **134 to do** undone. **135 creep** i.e., are unobtrusive, draw no attention to themselves. **skittish** fickle **136 Whiles . . . eyes** while others attract the attention of the goddess Fortune by making fools of themselves. **137–8 How . . . wantonness!** i.e., How one man, like Ajax, encroaches on another's glory, while that other man, like Achilles, starves his own glory through self-indulgence or caprice! **140 lubber** clumsy lout **146 wallet** knapsack **147 alms for oblivion** i.e., noble deeds destined to be forgotten **153 mail** suit of armor **154 In . . . mock'ry** serving as a mocking trophy of forgotten noble deeds. **instant way** way that lies immediately before you now **156 one but** only one **157 emulation** envious rivalry **158 one by one pursue** crowd after one another in single file, vying for supremacy. **159 Or . . . forthright** or veer from the straight path **163–4 for pavement . . . on** as a pavement to be trampled on by the cowardly and inferior troops who bring up the rear. **167 slightly** negligently **168 as . . . fly** as if he were about to depart **169 Grasps in** welcomes, embraces **170–1 Let . . . was** Don't be so naive as to expect reward for past achievements **175 calumniating** slandering **176 nature** i.e., natural human weakness; here, the propensity of men to praise frivolous novelty (*newborn gauds*) **178 Though . . . past** i.e., even though their apparent novelty is all derivative **179–80 And . . . o'erdusted** i.e., and give more praise to trivial things that have been made to look glittering than to objects of true worth that have been covered by the dust of oblivion. **182 complete** accomplished **185 cry** acclaim **188 case** box up, enclose **189 but . . . late** only recently on the battlefield **190–1 Made . . . faction** i.e., caused the gods themselves to join in the fighting on opposing sides, emulously, and even drove the god of war to be partisan. **193 heroical** suitable to a hero. **195 one . . . daughters** i.e., Polyxena. **197 providence** foresight **198 Pluto's** (Pluto, god of the underworld, was often confused with Plutus, god of riches.) **199 th'uncomprehensive** the unfathomable

Keeps place with thought and almost, like the gods,
Do thoughts unveil in their dumb cradles.
There is a mystery—with whom relation
Durst never meddle—in the soul of state,
Which hath an operation more divine
Than breath or pen can give expressure to.
All the commerce that you have had with Troy
As perfectly is ours as yours, my lord;
And better would it fit Achilles much
To throw down Hector than Polyxena.
But it must grieve young Pyrrhus now at home,
When Fame shall in our islands sound her trump,
And all the Greekish girls shall tripping sing,
"Great Hector's sister did Achilles win,
But our great Ajax bravely beat down him."
Farewell, my lord. I as your lover speak.
The fool slides o'er the ice that you should break.
[*Exit.*]

PATROCLUS
To this effect, Achilles, have I moved you.
A woman impudent and mannish grown
Is not more loathed than an effeminate man
In time of action. I stand condemned for this;
They think my little stomach to the war
And your great love to me restrains you thus.
Sweet, rouse yourself, and the weak wanton Cupid
Shall from your neck unloose his amorous fold
And, like a dewdrop from the lion's mane,
Be shook to air.

ACHILLES Shall Ajax fight with Hector?

PATROCLUS
Ay, and perhaps receive much honor by him.

ACHILLES
I see my reputation is at stake;
My fame is shrewdly gored.

PATROCLUS Oh, then, beware!
Those wounds heal ill that men do give themselves.
Omission to do what is necessary
Seals a commission to a blank of danger;
And danger, like an ague, subtly taints
Even then when we sit idly in the sun.

ACHILLES
Go call Thersites hither, sweet Patroclus.
I'll send the fool to Ajax and desire him
T'invite the Trojan lords after the combat
To see us here unarmed. I have a woman's longing,
An appetite that I am sick withal,
To see great Hector in his weeds of peace,
To talk with him and to behold his visage,
Even to my full of view.

Enter Thersites.

A labor saved.

THERSITES A wonder!

ACHILLES What?

THERSITES Ajax goes up and down the field, asking for himself.

ACHILLES How so?

THERSITES He must fight singly tomorrow with Hector and is so prophetically proud of an heroical cudgeling that he raves in saying nothing.

ACHILLES How can that be?

THERSITES Why, 'a stalks up and down like a peacock—a stride and a stand; ruminates like an hostess that hath no arithmetic but her brain to set down her reckoning; bites his lip with a politic regard, as who should say, "There were wit in this head, an 'twould out"—and so there is, but it lies as coldly in him as fire in a flint, which will not show without knocking. The man's undone forever, for if Hector break not his neck i'th' combat, he'll break't himself in vainglory. He knows not me. I said, "Good morrow, Ajax," and he replies, "Thanks, Agamemnon." What think you of this man, that takes me for the general? He's grown a very land-fish, languageless, a monster. A plague of opinion! A man may wear it on both sides, like a leather jerkin.

ACHILLES Thou must be my ambassador to him, Thersites.

THERSITES Who, I? Why, he'll answer nobody; he professes not answering. Speaking is for beggars; he wears his tongue in 's arms. I will put on his presence. Let Patroclus make demands to me; you shall see the pageant of Ajax.

ACHILLES To him, Patroclus. Tell him I humbly desire the valiant Ajax to invite the most valorous Hector to come unarmed to my tent, and to procure safe-conduct for his person of the magnanimous and most illustrious six-or-seven-times-honored Captain-General of the Grecian army, Agamemnon, et cetera. Do this.

PATROCLUS Jove bless great Ajax!

THERSITES Hum!

PATROCLUS I come from the worthy Achilles—

THERSITES Ha?

PATROCLUS Who most humbly desires you to invite Hector to his tent—

THERSITES Hum!

200 Keeps . . . thought keeps up with what is being thought **201 Do . . . cradles** uncover thoughts as they are conceived in the mind and before they are spoken. **202–3 with . . . meddle** that can never be talked about **205 expressure** expression **206 commerce** dealings (i.e., with Polyxena) **207 As perfectly . . . as yours** is known to us of the Greek council as completely as to you **210 Pyrrhus** Achilles's son, also called Neoptolemus **211 trump** trumpet **214 him** i.e., Hector. **215 lover** friend **216 The fool . . . break** i.e., The fool easily escapes dangers that to a man of your dignity would be fatal. **218 impudent** shameless **221 little stomach to** lack of enthusiasm for **224 fold** embrace **229 shrewdly gored** severely wounded. **232 Seals . . . danger** i.e., gives danger unlimited license, a blank check. (Literally, a warrant with blank spaces.) **233 ague** fever. **taints** infects. (Meat spoils when left lying in the sun.)

239 withal with **240 weeds** garments **242 to . . . view** to the fullest satisfaction of my eyes. **246 himself** i.e., "Ajax." (With a quibble on "a jakes" or latrine.) **253–4 hostess . . . arithmetic** (Tavern keepers were proverbially poor at addition; compare 1.2.114.) **255–6 with a . . . say** with an assumption of a knowing manner, as if one should say **264 land-fish** i.e., monstrous creature **264–6 A plague . . . jerkin** A curse on the way men flirt with reputation! It can be turned inside out, like a man's close-fitting jacket. **270 professes** i.e., makes a point of **271 arms** weapons. **put . . . presence** assume his demeanor.

PATROCLUS And to procure safe-conduct from Agamemnon.
THERSITES Agamemnon?
PATROCLUS Ay, my lord.
THERSITES Ha!
PATROCLUS What say you to't?
THERSITES God b'wi'you, with all my heart.
PATROCLUS Your answer, sir.
THERSITES If tomorrow be a fair day, by eleven o'clock it will go one way or other. Howsoever, he shall pay for me ere he has me.
PATROCLUS Your answer, sir.
THERSITES Fare ye well, with all my heart.
ACHILLES Why, but he is not in this tune, is he?
THERSITES No, but he's out o' tune thus. What music will be in him when Hector has knocked out his brains, I know not; but, I am sure, none, unless the fiddler Apollo get his sinews to make catlings on.
ACHILLES
Come, thou shalt bear a letter to him straight.
THERSITES Let me carry another to his horse, for that's the more capable creature.
ACHILLES
My mind is troubled, like a fountain stirred,
And I myself see not the bottom of it.
[*Exeunt Achilles and Patroclus.*]
THERSITES Would the fountain of your mind were clear again, that I might water an ass at it! I had rather be a tick in a sheep than such a valiant ignorance. [*Exit.*]

✤

[4.1]

Enter, at one door, Aeneas, [*with a torch;*] *at another, Paris, Deiphobus, Antenor, Diomedes the Grecian* [*and others*], *with torches.*

PARIS See, ho! Who is that there?
DEIPHOBUS It is the Lord Aeneas.
AENEAS Is the prince there in person?
Had I so good occasion to lie long
As you, Prince Paris, nothing but heavenly business
Should rob my bedmate of my company.
DIOMEDES
That's my mind too. Good morrow, Lord Aeneas.
PARIS
A valiant Greek, Aeneas; take his hand.
Witness the process of your speech, wherein
You told how Diomed, a whole week by days,
Did haunt you in the field.
AENEAS Health to you, valiant sir,
During all question of the gentle truce;
But when I meet you armed, as black defiance
As heart can think or courage execute.
DIOMEDES
The one and other Diomed embraces.
Our bloods are now in calm; and so long, health!
But when contention and occasion meet,
By Jove, I'll play the hunter for thy life
With all my force, pursuit, and policy.
AENEAS And thou shalt hunt a lion that will fly
With his face backward. In humane gentleness,
Welcome to Troy! Now, by Anchises' life,
Welcome, indeed! By Venus' hand I swear,
No man alive can love in such a sort
The thing he means to kill more excellently.
DIOMEDES
We sympathize. Jove, let Aeneas live,
If to my sword his fate be not the glory,
A thousand complete courses of the sun!
But, in mine emulous honor, let him die
With every joint a wound, and that tomorrow!
AENEAS We know each other well.
DIOMEDES
We do, and long to know each other worse.
PARIS
This is the most despiteful gentle greeting,
The noblest hateful love, that e'er I heard of.
What business, lord, so early?
AENEAS
I was sent for to the King, but why, I know not.
PARIS
His purpose meets you. 'Twas to bring this Greek
To Calchas' house, and there to render him,
For the enfreed Antenor, the fair Cressid.
Let's have your company, or, if you please,
Haste there before us. [*Aside to Aeneas*] I constantly do think—
Or rather, call my thought a certain knowledge—
My brother Troilus lodges there tonight.
Rouse him and give him note of our approach,
With the whole quality whereof. I fear
We shall be much unwelcome.
AENEAS That I assure you.
Troilus had rather Troy were borne to Greece
Than Cressid borne from Troy.
PARIS There is no help.
The bitter disposition of the time
Will have it so. On, lord; we'll follow you.
AENEAS Good morrow, all. [*Exit Aeneas.*]
PARIS
And tell me, noble Diomed, faith, tell me true,

296 Howsoever In either case **300 tune** i.e., mood, disposition **303–4 the fiddler Apollo** i.e., Apollo, as god of music **304 catlings** catgut, of which strings for instruments were made **307 capable** able to understand **312 ignorance** ignoramus, fool.
4.1. Location: Troy. A street, in an unspecified place.
0.1, 3 ***torch, torches*** (These directions may indicate torchbearers.)
7 mind opinion **9 process** drift **10 a whole . . . days** every day for a week **13 question** discussion, parley (allowed by the truce)

14 as black defiance defiance as black **16 The one and other** i.e., Aeneas's promises of *health* and *defiance* **17 so long** for as long as this truce lasts **18 when . . . meet** i.e., when the battle gives us opportunity **20 policy** cunning. **22 face backward** i.e., bravely facing the enemy. **23, 24 Anchises, Venus** (Aeneas's parents) **25 in . . . sort** to such a degree **27 sympathize** share your feeling. **30 emulous** ambitious **34 despiteful** contemptuous **38 His . . . you** i.e., I can tell you, since the matter is at hand. **39 render** give **42 constantly** confirmedly **45 note** news, notice **46 the . . . whereof** all the causes thereof, reasons why. **50 disposition** (1) temperament (2) arrangement, ordering

Even in the soul of sound good-fellowship,
Who, in your thoughts, merits fair Helen most,
Myself or Menelaus?

DIOMEDES Both alike.
He merits well to have her that doth seek her,
Not making any scruple of her soilure,
With such a hell of pain and world of charge;
And you as well to keep her that defend her,
Not palating the taste of her dishonor,
With such a costly loss of wealth and friends.
He, like a puling cuckold, would drink up
The lees and dregs of a flat 'tamèd piece;
You, like a lecher, out of whorish loins
Are pleased to breed out your inheritors.
Both merits poised, each weighs nor less nor more;
But he as he, the heavier for a whore.

PARIS
You are too bitter to your countrywoman.

DIOMEDES
She's bitter to her country. Hear me, Paris:
For every false drop in her bawdy veins
A Grecian's life hath sunk; for every scruple
Of her contaminated carrion weight
A Trojan hath been slain. Since she could speak,
She hath not given so many good words breath
As for her Greeks and Trojans suffered death.

PARIS
Fair Diomed, you do as chapmen do,
Dispraise the thing that you desire to buy.
But we in silence hold this virtue well:
We'll not commend what we intend to sell.
Here lies our way. *Exeunt.*

✤

[4.2]

Enter Troilus and Cressida.

TROILUS
Dear, trouble not yourself. The morn is cold.

CRESSIDA
Then, sweet my lord, I'll call mine uncle down.
He shall unbolt the gates.

TROILUS Trouble him not.
To bed, to bed! Sleep kill those pretty eyes,
And give as soft attachment to thy senses
As infants' empty of all thought!

CRESSIDA
Good morrow, then.

TROILUS I prithee now, to bed.

CRESSIDA Are you aweary of me?

TROILUS
Oh, Cressida! But that the busy day,
Waked by the lark, hath roused the ribald crows,
And dreaming night will hide our joys no longer,
I would not from thee.

CRESSIDA Night hath been too brief.

TROILUS
Beshrew the witch! With venomous wights she stays
As tediously as hell, but flies the grasps of love
With wings more momentary-swift than thought.
You will catch cold, and curse me.

CRESSIDA
Prithee, tarry. You men will never tarry.
O foolish Cressid! I might have still held off,
And then you would have tarried. Hark, there's one up.

PANDARUS [*within*] What's all the doors open here?

TROILUS It is your uncle.

[*Enter Pandarus.*]

CRESSIDA
A pestilence on him! Now will he be mocking.
I shall have such a life!

PANDARUS How now, how now, how go maidenheads? Here, you maid! Where's my cousin Cressid?

CRESSIDA
Go hang yourself, you naughty mocking uncle!
You bring me to do—and then you flout me too.

PANDARUS To do what, to do what?—Let her say what.—What have I brought you to do?

CRESSIDA
Come, come, beshrew your heart! You'll ne'er be good,
Nor suffer others.

PANDARUS Ha, ha! Alas, poor wretch! Ah, poor *capocchia!* Has 't not slept tonight? Would he not—a naughty man—let it sleep? A bugbear take him!

CRESSIDA
Did not I tell you? Would he were knocked i'th' head!
One knocks.
Who's that at door? Good uncle, go and see.—
My lord, come you again into my chamber.
You smile and mock me, as if I meant naughtily.

TROILUS Ha, ha!

CRESSIDA
Come, you are deceived. I think of no such thing.
Knock.

54 soul spirit **57 He** Menelaus, or any cuckolded husband **58 Not . . . scruple** not worrying about. **soilure** dishonor, stain **59 charge** cost **61 Not palating** not tasting, being insensible of **63 puling** complaining **64 flat 'tamèd piece** wine so long opened that it is flat; hence, a used woman **65–6 out of . . . inheritors** are content to breed your heirs out of a whore's belly. **67 poised** weighed, balanced. **nor less** neither less **68 he as he** the one like the other **72 scruple** little bit. (Literally, one twenty-fourth of an ounce.) **73 carrion** putrified and rotten, like a carcass **77 chapmen** traders, merchants **80 We'll . . . sell** i.e., We won't praise Helen, even though we intend to trade her to you at a high price.

4.2. Location: Troy. The courtyard of Calchas' house.

4 Sleep kill Let sleep overpower, put to rest **5 attachment** arrest, confinement **6 infants'** i.e., infants' eyes

10 ribald offensively noisy, irreverent **13–14 Beshrew . . . hell** i.e., Curse the night! She lingers endlessly with malignant beings (since night and villainy accord) **20 What's** Why are **24 how go** what price **25 Where's . . . Cressid?** (Pandarus pretends not to recognize Cressida now that she is no longer a virgin.) **30–1 You'll . . . others** i.e., You think such dirty thoughts that you can't imagine others to be otherwise. **32–3 *capocchia*** dolt, simpleton. (Italian.) **33 Has 't** Has it. (Pandarus condescendingly uses the neuter pronoun, as one might in referring to a baby. [Also in line 34.]) **34 bugbear** hobgoblin

How earnestly they knock! Pray you, come in.
I would not for half Troy have you seen here.
Exeunt [*Troilus and Cressida*].

PANDARUS Who's there? What's the matter? Will you beat down the door? [*He opens the door.*] How now, what's the matter?

[*Enter Aeneas.*]

AENEAS Good morrow, lord, good morrow.

PANDARUS Who's there? My lord Aeneas? By my troth, I knew you not. What news with you so early?

AENEAS Is not Prince Troilus here?

PANDARUS Here? What should he do here?

AENEAS
Come, he is here, my lord. Do not deny him.
It doth import him much to speak with me.

PANDARUS Is he here, say you? It's more than I know, I'll be sworn. For my own part, I came in late. What should he do here?

AENEAS Hoo!—Nay, then. Come, come, you'll do him wrong ere you are ware. You'll be so true to him, to be false to him. Do not you know of him, but yet go fetch him hither. Go.

[*Enter Troilus.*]

TROILUS How now, what's the matter?

AENEAS
My lord, I scarce have leisure to salute you,
My matter is so rash. There is at hand
Paris your brother and Deiphobus,
The Grecian Diomed, and our Antenor
Delivered to us; and for him forthwith,
Ere the first sacrifice, within this hour,
We must give up to Diomedes' hand
The Lady Cressida.

TROILUS Is it so concluded?

AENEAS
By Priam and the general state of Troy.
They are at hand and ready to effect it.

TROILUS
How my achievements mock me!
I will go meet them. And, my lord Aeneas,
We met by chance; you did not find me here.

AENEAS
Good, good, my lord, the secrets of nature
Have not more gift in taciturnity.
Exeunt [*Troilus and Aeneas*].

PANDARUS Is't possible? No sooner got but lost? The devil take Antenor! The young prince will go mad. A plague upon Antenor! I would they had broke's neck!

Enter Cressida.

CRESSIDA
How now? What's the matter? Who was here?

PANDARUS Ah, ah!

CRESSIDA
Why sigh you so profoundly? Where's my lord?
Gone? Tell me, sweet uncle, what's the matter?

PANDARUS Would I were as deep under the earth as I am above!

CRESSIDA O the gods! What's the matter?

PANDARUS Pray thee, get thee in. Would thou hadst ne'er been born! I knew thou wouldst be his death. Oh, poor gentleman! A plague upon Antenor!

CRESSIDA Good uncle, I beseech you, on my knees I beseech you, what's the matter?

PANDARUS Thou must be gone, wench, thou must be gone. Thou art changed for Antenor. Thou must to thy father and be gone from Troilus. 'Twill be his death, 'twill be his bane; he cannot bear it.

CRESSIDA
O you immortal gods! I will not go.

PANDARUS Thou must.

CRESSIDA
I will not, uncle. I have forgot my father.
I know no touch of consanguinity;
No kin, no love, no blood, no soul so near me
As the sweet Troilus. O you gods divine!
Make Cressid's name the very crown of falsehood
If ever she leave Troilus! Time, force, and death,
Do to this body what extremes you can;
But the strong base and building of my love
Is as the very center of the earth,
Drawing all things to it. I'll go in and weep—

PANDARUS Do, do.

CRESSIDA
Tear my bright hair and scratch my praisèd cheeks,
Crack my clear voice with sobs and break my heart
With sounding "Troilus." I will not go from Troy.
[*Exeunt.*]

[4.3]

Enter Paris, Troilus, Aeneas, Deiphobus, Antenor, [*and*] *Diomedes.*

PARIS
It is great morning, and the hour prefixed
For her delivery to this valiant Greek
Comes fast upon. Good my brother Troilus,
Tell you the lady what she is to do,
And haste her to the purpose.

TROILUS Walk into her house.
I'll bring her to the Grecian presently;
And to his hand when I deliver her,
Think it an altar, and thy brother Troilus
A priest there off'ring to it his own heart. [*Exit.*]

50 should he do would he be doing **52 import** concern **57–8 You'll . . . know of him** i.e., In seeking to guard Troilus' secret, you'll protect him from knowing of a matter that concerns him. Go ahead and pretend you don't know he is here **61 salute** greet **62 rash** urgent, pressing. **66 Ere . . . sacrifice** before the first religious ceremony of the day **69 state** council **73 We met** i.e., Remember to say that we met. (This is the fiction to which Aeneas agrees.)

92 changed exchanged **94 bane** death **98 touch of consanguinity** sense or tiniest bit of kinship **110 sounding** uttering
4.3. Location: Troy. Before Cressida's house.
1 great morning broad day. **prefixed** earlier agreed upon **6 to . . . presently** to Diomedes immediately

PARIS I know what 'tis to love;
And would, as I shall pity, I could help!
Please you walk in, my lords? *Exeunt.*

✤

[4.4]

Enter Pandarus and Cressida.

PANDARUS Be moderate, be moderate.

CRESSIDA
Why tell you me of moderation?
The grief is fine, full, perfect, that I taste,
And violenteth in a sense as strong
As that which causeth it. How can I moderate it?
If I could temporize with my affection,
Or brew it to a weak and colder palate,
The like allayment could I give my grief.
My love admits no qualifying dross;
No more my grief, in such a precious loss.

Enter Troilus.

PANDARUS Here, here, here he comes. Ah, sweet ducks!

CRESSIDA Oh, Troilus! Troilus! [*Embracing him.*]

PANDARUS What a pair of spectacles is here! Let me embrace, too. "O heart," as the goodly saying is,
"O heart, heavy heart,
Why sigh'st thou without breaking?"
where he answers again,
"Because thou canst not ease thy smart
By friendship nor by speaking."
There was never a truer rhyme. Let us cast away nothing, for we may live to have need of such a verse. We see it, we see it. How now, lambs?

TROILUS
Cressid, I love thee in so strained a purity
That the blest gods, as angry with my fancy,
More bright in zeal than the devotion which
Cold lips blow to their deities, take thee from me.

CRESSIDA Have the gods envy?

PANDARUS Ay, ay, ay, ay; 'tis too plain a case.

CRESSIDA
And is it true that I must go from Troy?

TROILUS
A hateful truth.

CRESSIDA What, and from Troilus too?

TROILUS
From Troy and Troilus.

CRESSIDA Is't possible?

TROILUS
And suddenly, where injury of chance
Puts back leave-taking, jostles roughly by
All time of pause, rudely beguiles our lips
Of all rejoindure, forcibly prevents
Our locked embrasures, strangles our dear vows
Even in the birth of our own laboring breath.
We two, that with so many thousand sighs
Did buy each other, must poorly sell ourselves
With the rude brevity and discharge of one.
Injurious Time now with a robber's haste
Crams his rich thiev'ry up, he knows not how.
As many farewells as be stars in heaven,
With distinct breath and consigned kisses to them,
He fumbles up into a loose adieu,
And scants us with a single famished kiss,
Distasted with the salt of broken tears.

AENEAS (*within*) My lord, is the lady ready?

TROILUS
Hark! You are called. Some say the genius so
Cries "Come!" to him that instantly must die.—
Bid them have patience. She shall come anon.

PANDARUS Where are my tears? Rain, to lay this wind, or my heart will be blown up by the root. [*Exit.*]

CRESSIDA
I must then to the Grecians?

TROILUS No remedy.

CRESSIDA
A woeful Cressid 'mongst the merry Greeks!
When shall we see again?

TROILUS
Hear me, my love. Be thou but true of heart—

CRESSIDA
I true? How now? What wicked deem is this?

TROILUS
Nay, we must use expostulation kindly,
For it is parting from us.
I speak not "Be thou true" as fearing thee,
For I will throw my glove to Death himself
That there's no maculation in thy heart;
But "Be thou true," say I, to fashion in
My sequent protestation: Be thou true,
And I will see thee.

11 as as much as
4.4. Location: Troy. Cressida's house.
3 fine refined, pure **4 violenteth** is violent **6 temporize** compromise, come to terms **7 brew** dilute. **palate** taste **8 allayment** dilution, mitigation **9 qualifying dross** foreign matter making it less pure **14 spectacles** sights. (With suggestion of "eyeglasses.") **18 he** the heart **20 By . . . speaking** by mere friendship or words alone. **22–3 We see it** i.e., We see how verses can console **24 strained** purified as by filtering **25 as** as if. **fancy** love **26–7 More . . . deities** a love that is more zealous than the devotion which the chaste lips of vestal virgins breathe to the gods

33–4 injury . . . leave-taking injurious Fortune prevents leisurely farewells **36 rejoindure** reunion (in a farewell kiss) **37 embrasures** embraces **41 discharge of one** (1) exhalation of a single sigh (2) making of a single payment. **43 thiev'ry** stolen property. **he . . . how** every which way, distractedly. **45 With . . . them** with the words of farewell and the kisses with which those words are confirmed, sealed **46 He fumbles up** Time clumsily huddles together **47 scants** inadequately supplies **48 Distasted** rendered distasteful. **broken** interrupted with sobs **50 genius** attendant spirit supposed to be assigned to a person at birth **53 Rain . . . wind** i.e., Tears, to allay my sighs **54 by the root** i.e., as though the heart were a tree in a storm of sighs. (Sighs were thought to deprive the heart of its blood.) **57 see** see each other **59 deem** thought, surmise **60–1 we must . . . from us** i.e., we must expostulate gently, for soon even this opportunity for speech will be lost to us. **62 as fearing thee** i.e., as if not trusting your constancy **63 throw . . . to** i.e., challenge **64 maculation** stain of impurity **65 fashion in** serve as introduction for **66 sequent** ensuing

CRESSIDA
Oh, you shall be exposed, my lord, to dangers
As infinite as imminent! But I'll be true.

TROILUS
And I'll grow friend with danger. Wear this sleeve.
[*They exchange favors.*]

CRESSIDA
And you this glove. When shall I see you?

TROILUS
I will corrupt the Grecian sentinels,
To give thee nightly visitation.
But yet, be true.

CRESSIDA Oh, heavens, "Be true" again?

TROILUS Hear why I speak it, love.
The Grecian youths are full of quality;
Their loving well composed with gifts of nature,
And flowing o'er with arts and exercise.
How novelty may move, and parts with person,
Alas, a kind of godly jealousy—
Which, I beseech you, call a virtuous sin—
Makes me afeard.

CRESSIDA Oh, heavens! You love me not.

TROILUS Die I a villain, then!
In this I do not call your faith in question
So mainly as my merit. I cannot sing,
Nor heel the high lavolt, nor sweeten talk,
Nor play at subtle games—fair virtues all,
To which the Grecians are most prompt and pregnant.
But I can tell that in each grace of these
There lurks a still and dumb-discoursive devil
That tempts most cunningly. But be not tempted.

CRESSIDA Do you think I will?

TROILUS
No. But something may be done that we will not;
And sometimes we are devils to ourselves,
When we will tempt the frailty of our powers,
Presuming on their changeful potency.

AENEAS (*within*)
Nay, good my lord—

TROILUS Come, kiss, and let us part.

PARIS (*within*)
Brother Troilus!

TROILUS Good brother, come you hither,
And bring Aeneas and the Grecian with you.

CRESSIDA My lord, will you be true?

TROILUS
Who, I? Alas, it is my vice, my fault.
Whiles others fish with craft for great opinion,
I with great truth catch mere simplicity;
Whilst some with cunning gild their copper crowns,
With truth and plainness I do wear mine bare.

[*Enter Aeneas, Paris, Antenor, Deiphobus, and Diomedes.*]

Fear not my truth. The moral of my wit
Is "plain and true"; there's all the reach of it.—
Welcome, Sir Diomed. Here is the lady
Which for Antenor we deliver you.
At the port, lord, I'll give her to thy hand,
And by the way possess thee what she is.
Entreat her fair, and by my soul, fair Greek,
If e'er thou stand at mercy of my sword,
Name Cressid, and thy life shall be as safe
As Priam is in Ilium.

DIOMEDES Fair Lady Cressid,
So please you, save the thanks this prince expects.
The luster in your eye, heaven in your cheek,
Pleads your fair usage; and to Diomed
You shall be mistress, and command him wholly.

TROILUS
Grecian, thou dost not use me courteously,
To shame the zeal of my petition to thee
In praising her. I tell thee, lord of Greece,
She is as far high-soaring o'er thy praises
As thou unworthy to be called her servant.
I charge thee use her well, even for my charge;
For, by the dreadful Pluto, if thou dost not,
Though the great bulk Achilles be thy guard,
I'll cut thy throat.

DIOMEDES Oh, be not moved, Prince Troilus.
Let me be privileged by my place and message
To be a speaker free. When I am hence,
I'll answer to my lust. And know you, lord,
I'll nothing do on charge. To her own worth
She shall be prized; but that you say "Be 't so,"
I'll speak it in my spirit and honor, "No."

TROILUS
Come, to the port.—I'll tell thee, Diomed,
This brave shall oft make thee to hide thy head.—
Lady, give me your hand, and, as we walk,
To our own selves bend we our needful talk.
[*Exeunt Troilus, Cressida, and Diomedes.*] *Sound trumpet* [*within*].

70 sleeve (Sleeves were detachable and could be given as favors or tokens; *gloves* could be similarly given.) **72 corrupt** bribe **76 quality** flair, graceful manners **77 Their . . . composed** i.e., their skill in wooing is well endowed **78 arts and exercise** skills sharpened by practice. **79 parts with person** gifts and accomplishments, combined with personal charm **80 godly** divinely sanctioned, as in a marriage **85 mainly** strongly. **merit** (Troilus plays on the Protestant insistence on salvation through *faith*, line 84, not *merit*.) **86 Nor heel . . . talk** nor dance the lively dance called the lavolta, nor talk ingratiatingly **87 subtle** (1) requiring skill (2) cunning, deceptive **88 pregnant** ready, alacritous. **90 dumb-discoursive** eloquently silent **94 will not** do not desire **96 will tempt** deliberately tempt **97 Presuming . . . potency** presuming fatuously on our ability to control their unpredictable strength.

103 craft cunning. **opinion** reputation (for wisdom) **104 I . . . simplicity** I, in my use of simple truth, earn a reputation for being simple and plain **105 crowns** (1) coins (2) royal headdresses **107 truth** fidelity. **moral** maxim **108 all the reach** the full extent **111 port** gate of the city **112 possess** inform **113 Entreat her fair** Treat her with courtesy **117 So . . . expects** i.e., please save yourself the trouble of thanking Troilus for your good treatment at my hands; I'll do it for your sake, not his. **125 servant** male admirer. **126 even . . . charge** simply because I demand that you do so **128 bulk** hulk **129 moved** angry **132 answer to my lust** do what I please—with Cressida, and in responding to your challenge. **133 on charge** because you command it. **134–5 but that . . . "No"** but (I swear it by my honor) not because you tell me to. **137 brave** boast, defiance

PARIS
Hark! Hector's trumpet.
AENEAS How have we spent this morning!
The Prince must think me tardy and remiss,
That swore to ride before him to the field.
PARIS
'Tis Troilus' fault. Come, come, to field with him.
DEIPHOBUS Let us make ready straight.
AENEAS
Yea, with a bridegroom's fresh alacrity,
Let us address to tend on Hector's heels.
The glory of our Troy doth this day lie
On his fair worth and single chivalry. *Exeunt.*

✤

[4.5]

Enter Ajax, armed, Achilles, Patroclus, Agamemnon, Menelaus, Ulysses, Nestor, etc.

AGAMEMNON
Here art thou in appointment fresh and fair,
Anticipating time with starting courage.
Give with thy trumpet a loud note to Troy,
Thou dreadful Ajax, that the appallèd air
May pierce the head of the great combatant
And hale him hither.
AJAX Thou, trumpet, there's my purse.
[*He throws money to his trumpeter.*]
Now crack thy lungs and split thy brazen pipe.
Blow, villain, till thy spherèd bias cheek
Outswell the colic of puffed Aquilon.
Come, stretch thy chest, and let thy eyes spout blood;
Thou blowest for Hector. [*Trumpet sounds.*]
ULYSSES No trumpet answers.
ACHILLES 'Tis but early days.

[*Enter Diomedes, with Cressida.*]

AGAMEMNON
Is not yond Diomed, with Calchas' daughter?
ULYSSES
'Tis he. I ken the manner of his gait;
He rises on the toe. That spirit of his
In aspiration lifts him from the earth.
AGAMEMNON
Is this the Lady Cressid?
DIOMEDES Even she.
AGAMEMNON
Most dearly welcome to the Greeks, sweet lady.
[*He kisses her.*]
NESTOR
Our general doth salute you with a kiss.
ULYSSES
Yet is the kindness but particular;
'Twere better she were kissed in general.
NESTOR
And very courtly counsel. I'll begin. [*He kisses her.*]
So much for Nestor.
ACHILLES
I'll take that winter from your lips, fair lady.
Achilles bids you welcome. [*He kisses her.*]
MENELAUS
I had good argument for kissing once.
PATROCLUS
But that's no argument for kissing now;
For thus popped Paris in his hardiment,
And parted thus you and your argument.
[*He kisses her.*]
ULYSSES
Oh, deadly gall and theme of all our scorns,
For which we lose our heads to gild his horns!
PATROCLUS
The first was Menelaus' kiss; this, mine.
Patroclus kisses you. [*He kisses her again.*]
MENELAUS Oh, this is trim!
PATROCLUS
Paris and I kiss evermore for him.
MENELAUS
I'll have my kiss, sir.—Lady, by your leave.
CRESSIDA
In kissing, do you render or receive?
MENELAUS
Both take and give.
CRESSIDA I'll make my match to live,
The kiss you take is better than you give;
Therefore no kiss.
MENELAUS
I'll give you boot; I'll give you three for one.
CRESSIDA
You are an odd man; give even, or give none.
MENELAUS
An odd man, lady? Every man is odd.
CRESSIDA
No, Paris is not, for you know 'tis true
That you are odd, and he is even with you.
MENELAUS
You fillip me o'th' head.
CRESSIDA No, I'll be sworn.

140 spent consumed wastefully **146 address** get ready. **tend** attend **148 single chivalry** individual prowess.

4.5. Location: Near the Greek camp. Lists set out as an arena for combat.

1 appointment equipment, accoutrement **2 starting** bold, eager to begin **4 dreadful** inspiring dread **6 trumpet** trumpeter **8 bias** puffed out (and shaped like a weighted bowling ball used in bowls) **9 colic** i.e., swelling (like that caused by colic). **Aquilon** the north wind (here personified as distended by colic) **11 for Hector** to summon Hector. **13 days** in the day. **15 ken** recognize

21 particular single, limited to one **22 in general** by everyone. (With a play on "by the general.") **25 that winter** (Alludes to Nestor's old age.) **27 argument** theme, i.e., Helen. (But Patroclus answers in the sense of "supporting reason.") **29 popped** came in suddenly. (With sexual suggestion.) **hardiment** bold exploits, boldness. (With bawdy double meaning of "hardness.") **31–2 Oh . . . horns!** Oh, fatal bitterness and the theme that brings scorn on us all, in which we lose our lives to gild over the fact of Menelaus's having been made a cuckold! **34 trim** fine. (Said ironically.) **35 Paris . . . him** i.e., I take the kiss Menelaus hoped for, just as Paris does in kissing Helen. **38 I'll . . . to live** I'll wager my life **41 boot** odds, advantage **42 odd** (The wordplay here and in lines 43–5 includes [1] strange [2] single, no longer having a wife [3] unique, standing alone [4] odd man out [5] the opposite of *even*.) **46 fillip . . . head** i.e., touch a sensitive spot, by alluding to my cuckold's horns.

ULYSSES
It were no match, your nail against his horn.
May I, sweet lady, beg a kiss of you?

CRESSIDA
You may.

ULYSSES I do desire it.

CRESSIDA Why, beg too.

ULYSSES
Why then for Venus' sake, give me a kiss
When Helen is a maid again, and his.

CRESSIDA
I am your debtor; claim it when 'tis due.

ULYSSES
Never's my day, and then a kiss of you.

DIOMEDES
Lady, a word. I'll bring you to your father.
[They talk apart.]

NESTOR
A woman of quick sense.

ULYSSES Fie, fie upon her!
There's language in her eye, her cheek, her lip,
Nay, her foot speaks; her wanton spirits look out
At every joint and motive of her body.
Oh, these encounterers, so glib of tongue,
That give accosting welcome ere it comes,
And wide unclasp the tables of their thoughts
To every ticklish reader! Set them down
For sluttish spoils of opportunity
And daughters of the game.
Exeunt [Diomedes and Cressida].

Flourish. Enter all of Troy: [Hector, Paris, Aeneas, Helenus, Troilus, and attendants].

ALL
The Trojan's trumpet.

AGAMEMNON Yonder comes the troop.

AENEAS
Hail, all you state of Greece! What shall be done
To him that victory commands? Or do you purpose
A victor shall be known? Will you the knights
Shall to the edge of all extremity
Pursue each other, or shall they be divided
By any voice or order of the field?
Hector bade ask.

AGAMEMNON Which way would Hector have it?

AENEAS
He cares not; he'll obey conditions.

AGAMEMNON
'Tis done like Hector.

ACHILLES But securely done,
A little proudly, and great deal disprising
The knight opposed.

AENEAS If not Achilles, sir,
What is your name?

ACHILLES If not Achilles, nothing.

AENEAS
Therefore Achilles. But, whate'er, know this:
In the extremity of great and little,
Valor and pride excel themselves in Hector,
The one almost as infinite as all,
The other blank as nothing. Weigh him well,
And that which looks like pride is courtesy.
This Ajax is half made of Hector's blood,
In love whereof half Hector stays at home;
Half heart, half hand, half Hector comes to seek
This blended knight, half Trojan and half Greek.

ACHILLES
A maiden battle, then? Oh, I perceive you.

[Enter Diomedes.]

AGAMEMNON
Here is Sir Diomed. Go, gentle knight,
Stand by our Ajax. As you and Lord Aeneas
Consent upon the order of their fight,
So be it, either to the uttermost,
Or else a breath. The combatants being kin
Half stints their strife before their strokes begin.
[Ajax and Hector enter the lists.]

ULYSSES They are opposed already.

AGAMEMNON *[to Ulysses]*
What Trojan is that same that looks so heavy?

ULYSSES
The youngest son of Priam, a true knight,
Not yet mature, yet matchless firm of word,
Speaking in deeds and deedless in his tongue;
Not soon provoked, nor being provoked soon calmed;
His heart and hand both open and both free.
For what he has he gives; what thinks, he shows;
Yet gives he not till judgment guide his bounty,
Nor dignifies an impair thought with breath;
Manly as Hector, but more dangerous,
For Hector in his blaze of wrath subscribes
To tender objects, but he in heat of action

47 It . . . horn i.e., Your fingernail is not nearly tough enough to make any impression on his cuckold's horn. **49 Why, beg too** i.e., You must do more than merely *desire* a kiss; you must humble yourself as a petitionary male. **51 When . . . his** when Helen is once again the chaste wife of Menelaus. (A virtually impossible condition.) **53 Never's . . . you** i.e., I'll never claim that kiss. **55 of quick sense** of lively wit and vibrant sensuality. **58 motive** moving limb or organ **59 encounterers** seductive women **60–2 That . . . reader!** who sidle up to men without waiting to be invited, and allow their thoughts to be read avidly by every susceptible male! (With sexual suggestiveness in the image of unclasping, though *tables* are literally writing tablets, as in *Hamlet*, 1.5.108.) **63 sluttish . . . opportunity** "corrupt wenches, of whose chastity every opportunity may make a prey" (Johnson) **64 daughters of the game** i.e., prostitutes. **65 The Trojan's** Hector's **66 state** noble lords. **What . . . done** i.e., What honors shall be afforded **67 that . . . commands** that wins the victory. **68 known** adjudged and declared. **68–71 Will . . . field?** Do you desire that the combatants fight to the death, or that they be required to separate on order of the marshals, according to set regulations of the field of honor?

73 conditions whatever conditions are agreed upon. **74 securely** overconfidently **75 disprising** disdaining, underrating **79–80 In . . . Hector** i.e., Hector's valor is extremely great; his pride, extremely little **84 Ajax . . . blood** (Compare 2.2.77, note, and 4.5.121.) **88 maiden battle** combat without bloodshed. **perceive** understand **91 Consent** agree. **order** procedure, rules **93 a breath** a friendly bout for exercise. **96 heavy** sad. **99 Speaking . . . tongue** letting his deeds speak for him and never boasting **101 free** open, generous. **104 impair** unconsidered, unsuitable **106–7 subscribes . . . objects** yields mercy to the defenseless

Is more vindicative than jealous love. 108
They call him Troilus, and on him erect
A second hope, as fairly built as Hector.
Thus says Aeneas, one that knows the youth
Even to his inches, and with private soul 112
Did in great Ilium thus translate him to me. 113
Alarum. [*Hector and Ajax fight.*]

AGAMEMNON They are in action.
NESTOR Now, Ajax, hold thine own!
TROILUS Hector, thou sleep'st. Awake thee!
AGAMEMNON
His blows are well disposed. There, Ajax! 117
Trumpets cease.

DIOMEDES
You must no more.
AENEAS Princes, enough, so please you.
AJAX
I am not warm yet. Let us fight again.
DIOMEDES
As Hector pleases.
HECTOR Why, then will I no more.
Thou art, great lord, my father's sister's son,
A cousin-german to great Priam's seed. 122
The obligation of our blood forbids
A gory emulation twixt us twain. 124
Were thy commixtion Greek and Trojan so 125
That thou couldst say, "This hand is Grecian all,
And this is Trojan; the sinews of this leg
All Greek, and this all Troy; my mother's blood
Runs on the dexter cheek, and this sinister 129
Bounds in my father's," by Jove multipotent,
Thou shouldst not bear from me a Greekish member
Wherein my sword had not impressure made 132
Of our rank feud. But the just gods gainsay 133
That any drop thou borrow'dst from thy mother,
My sacred aunt, should by my mortal sword
Be drainèd! Let me embrace thee, Ajax.
By him that thunders, thou hast lusty arms! 137
Hector would have them fall upon him thus.
Cousin, all honor to thee! [*They embrace.*]
AJAX I thank thee, Hector.
Thou art too gentle and too free a man.
I came to kill thee, cousin, and bear hence
A great addition earnèd in thy death. 142
HECTOR
Not Neoptolemus so mirable, 143
On whose bright crest Fame with her loud'st "Oyez" 144
Cries, "This is he," could promise to himself 145
A thought of added honor torn from Hector. 146
AENEAS
There is expectance here from both the sides 147
What further you will do.
HECTOR We'll answer it;
The issue is embracement. Ajax, farewell. 149
[*They embrace.*]
AJAX
If I might in entreaties find success—
As seld I have the chance—I would desire 151
My famous cousin to our Grecian tents.
DIOMEDES
'Tis Agamemnon's wish, and great Achilles
Doth long to see unarmed the valiant Hector.
HECTOR
Aeneas, call my brother Troilus to me,
And signify this loving interview 156
To the expecters of our Trojan part; 157
Desire them home. Give me thy hand, my cousin. 158
I will go eat with thee and see your knights.
[*Agamemnon and the rest approach them.*]
AJAX
Great Agamemnon comes to meet us here.
HECTOR [*to Aeneas*]
The worthiest of them tell me name by name;
But for Achilles, mine own searching eyes
Shall find him by his large and portly size. 163
AGAMEMNON
Worthy of arms! As welcome as to one 164
That would be rid of such an enemy—
But that's no welcome. Understand more clear:
What's past and what's to come is strewed with husks
And formless ruin of oblivion;
But in this extant moment, faith and troth, 169
Strained purely from all hollow bias-drawing, 170
Bids thee, with most divine integrity,
From heart of very heart, great Hector, welcome.
HECTOR
I thank thee, most imperious Agamemnon. 173
AGAMEMNON [*to Troilus*]
My well-famed lord of Troy, no less to you.
MENELAUS
Let me confirm my princely brother's greeting.
You brace of warlike brothers, welcome hither.
HECTOR
Who must we answer?
AENEAS The noble Menelaus.
HECTOR
Oh, you, my lord? By Mars his gauntlet, thanks! 178

108 vindicative vindictive **112 Even . . . inches** i.e., every inch of him. **with private soul** in private confidence **113 translate** interpret **117 disposed** placed. **122 cousin-german** first cousin **124 gory emulation** bloody rivalry **125 commixtion** mixture **129 dexter** right. **sinister** left **132 impressure** impression **133 rank** hot, intemperate. **gainsay** forbid **137 By . . . thunders** i.e., By Jove **142 addition** honorable title **143–6 Not . . . Hector** i.e., Not even the much-wondered-at Achilles, on whose heraldic badge Fame herself in the role of the public crier announces "This is the man," could assure himself of added honor by defeating Hector. (*Neoptolemus* is actually the name of Achilles's son.)

147 expectance eager desire to know **149 issue** outcome **151 seld** seldom. **desire** invite **156 signify** announce **157 the expecters . . . part** those awaiting the outcome on our Trojan side **158 home** to go home. **163 portly** stately, dignified **164 of arms** (1) to bear weapons (2) to receive embracements. **as to one** as it is possible to one **169 extant** present **169–70 faith . . . bias-drawing** faithfulness and honesty, purified of all insincerities or obliquities (such as the bias weight inserted in bowling balls in the game of bowls) **173 imperious** imperial **178 By . . . gauntlet** By Mars's armored leather glove

Mock not that I affect th'untraded oath;
Your quondam wife swears still by Venus' glove.
She's well, but bade me not commend her to you.

MENELAUS
Name her not now, sir. She's a deadly theme.

HECTOR Oh, pardon! I offend.

NESTOR
I have, thou gallant Trojan, seen thee oft,
Laboring for destiny, make cruel way
Through ranks of Greekish youth, and I have seen
thee,
As hot as Perseus, spur thy Phrygian steed,
And seen thee scorning forfeits and subduements,
When thou hast hung thy advancèd sword i'th'air,
Not letting it decline on the declined,
That I have said to some my standers-by,
"Lo, Jupiter is yonder, dealing life!"
And I have seen thee pause and take thy breath,
When that a ring of Greeks have hemmed thee in,
Like an Olympian, wrestling. This have I seen;
But this thy countenance, still locked in steel,
I never saw till now. I knew thy grandsire
And once fought with him. He was a soldier good,
But, by great Mars, the captain of us all,
Never like thee. Let an old man embrace thee;
And, worthy warrior, welcome to our tents.
[*They embrace.*]

AENEAS 'Tis the old Nestor.

HECTOR
Let me embrace thee, good old chronicle,
That hast so long walked hand in hand with Time.
Most reverend Nestor, I am glad to clasp thee.

NESTOR
I would my arms could match thee in contention
As they contend with thee in courtesy.

HECTOR I would they could.

NESTOR Ha!
By this white beard, I'd fight with thee tomorrow.
Well, welcome, welcome! I have seen the time!

ULYSSES
I wonder now how yonder city stands
When we have here her base and pillar by us.

HECTOR
I know your favor, Lord Ulysses, well.
Ah, sir, there's many a Greek and Trojan dead
Since first I saw yourself and Diomed
In Ilium, on your Greekish embassy.

ULYSSES
Sir, I foretold you then what would ensue.
My prophecy is but half his journey yet,
For yonder walls, that pertly front your town,
Yon towers, whose wanton tops do buss the clouds,
Must kiss their own feet.

HECTOR I must not believe you.
There they stand yet, and modestly I think
The fall of every Phrygian stone will cost
A drop of Grecian blood. The end crowns all,
And that old common arbitrator, Time,
Will one day end it.

ULYSSES So to him we leave it.
Most gentle and most valiant Hector, welcome!
After the general, I beseech you next
To feast with me and see me at my tent.

ACHILLES
I shall forestall thee, Lord Ulysses, thou!—
Now, Hector, I have fed mine eyes on thee;
I have with exact view perused thee, Hector,
And quoted joint by joint.

HECTOR Is this Achilles?

ACHILLES I am Achilles.

HECTOR
Stand fair, I pray thee. Let me look on thee.

ACHILLES
Behold thy fill.

HECTOR Nay, I have done already.

ACHILLES
Thou art too brief. I will the second time,
As I would buy thee, view thee limb by limb.

HECTOR
Oh, like a book of sport thou'lt read me o'er;
But there's more in me than thou understand'st.
Why dost thou so oppress me with thine eye?

ACHILLES
Tell me, you heavens, in which part of his body
Shall I destroy him? Whether there, or there, or there?
That I may give the local wound a name
And make distinct the very breach whereout
Hector's great spirit flew. Answer me, heavens!

HECTOR
It would discredit the blest gods, proud man,
To answer such a question. Stand again.
Think'st thou to catch my life so pleasantly
As to prenominate in nice conjecture
Where thou wilt hit me dead?

ACHILLES I tell thee, yea.

HECTOR
Wert thou the oracle to tell me so,

179 th'untraded the unhackneyed. (Hector insists that his newly minted oath, "By Mars his gauntlet," is suited to a war fought over a woman. In line 180 he contrasts this warlike oath with Helen's favorite, "by Venus' glove.") **180 quondam** former **182 deadly theme** (1) subject for mortal strife (2) gloomy topic of discourse. **185 Laboring for destiny** employed in the service of fate, putting people to death **187 Perseus** (See the note for 1.3.42.) **188 scorning . . . subduements** i.e., ignoring those already vanquished, whose lives were forfeit; refusing easy prey **189 advancèd** raised aloft **190 the declined** those already vanquished **191 to . . . my standers-by** to some of my followers **192 dealing life** i.e., mercifully sparing the weak. **194 When that** when **195 Olympian** Olympian god, or a wrestler in the Olympic games **196 still** always **197 grandsire** i.e., Laomedon, builder of the walls of Troy and defender of the city against an earlier Greek army under Hercules **203 chronicle** i.e., storehouse of memories **211 I have . . . time!** i.e., There was a time when I could have taken you on! **214 favor** face

216–17 Since . . . embassy (Hector refers to a non-Homeric episode, early in the war, when Ulysses and Diomedes visited Troy to offer peace in return for Helen.) **220 pertly front** boldly stand before **221 wanton** insolent, reckless. (With suggestion of amorousness in the metaphor of kissing.) **buss** kiss **223 modestly** without exaggeration **231 forestall** prevent **234 quoted joint by joint** scrutinized limb by limb. **236 fair** in full view **250 pleasantly** jocosely, easily **251 prenominate** name beforehand. **nice** precise

I'd not believe thee. Henceforth guard thee well;
For I'll not kill thee there, nor there, nor there,
But, by the forge that stithied Mars his helm,
I'll kill thee everywhere, yea, o'er and o'er.—
You wisest Grecians, pardon me this brag;
His insolence draws folly from my lips.
But I'll endeavor deeds to match these words,
Or may I never—

AJAX Do not chafe thee, cousin.
And you, Achilles, let these threats alone,
Till accident or purpose bring you to't.
You may have every day enough of Hector,
If you have stomach. The general state, I fear,
Can scarce entreat you to be odd with him.

HECTOR [*to Achilles*]
I pray you, let us see you in the field.
We have had pelting wars since you refused
The Grecians' cause.

ACHILLES Dost thou entreat me, Hector?
Tomorrow do I meet thee, fell as death;
Tonight all friends.

HECTOR Thy hand upon that match.
[*They grasp hands.*]

AGAMEMNON
First, all you peers of Greece, go to my tent;
There in the full convive we. Afterwards,
As Hector's leisure and your bounties shall
Concur together, severally entreat him.
Beat loud the taborins, let the trumpets blow,
That this great soldier may his welcome know.
[*Flourish.*] *Exeunt* [*all except Troilus and Ulysses*].

TROILUS
My lord Ulysses, tell me, I beseech you,
In what place of the field doth Calchas keep?

ULYSSES
At Menelaus' tent, most princely Troilus.
There Diomed doth feast with him tonight,
Who neither looks on heaven nor on earth
But gives all gaze and bent of amorous view
On the fair Cressid.

TROILUS
Shall I, sweet lord, be bound to you so much,
After we part from Agamemnon's tent,
To bring me thither?

ULYSSES You shall command me, sir.
As gentle tell me, of what honor was
This Cressida in Troy? Had she no lover there
That wails her absence?

TROILUS
Oh, sir, to such as boasting show their scars
A mock is due. Will you walk on, my lord?
She was beloved, she loved; she is, and doth.
But still sweet love is food for fortune's tooth.
Exeunt.

[5.1]

Enter Achilles and Patroclus.

ACHILLES
I'll heat his blood with Greekish wine tonight,
Which with my scimitar I'll cool tomorrow.
Patroclus, let us feast him to the height.

PATROCLUS
Here comes Thersites.

Enter Thersites.

ACHILLES How now, thou core of envy!
Thou crusty batch of nature, what's the news?

THERSITES Why, thou picture of what thou seemest and idol of idiot-worshipers, here's a letter for thee.

ACHILLES From whence, fragment?

THERSITES Why, thou full dish of fool, from Troy.
[*He gives a letter. Achilles reads it.*]

PATROCLUS Who keeps the tent now?

THERSITES The surgeon's box, or the patient's wound.

PATROCLUS Well said, adversity! And what need these tricks?

THERSITES Prithee, be silent, boy. I profit not by thy talk. Thou art thought to be Achilles' male varlet.

PATROCLUS Male varlet, you rogue? What's that?

THERSITES Why, his masculine whore. Now, the rotten diseases of the south, the guts-griping, ruptures, catarrhs, loads o'gravel i'th' back, lethargies, cold palsies, raw eyes, dirt-rotten livers, wheezing lungs, bladders full of imposthume, sciaticas, limekilns i'th' palm, incurable bone-ache, and the riveled fee simple of the tetter, take and take again such preposterous discoveries!

PATROCLUS Why, thou damnable box of envy, thou, what mean'st thou to curse thus?

THERSITES Do I curse thee?

PATROCLUS Why, no, you ruinous butt, you whoreson indistinguishable cur, no.

256 stithied Mars his helm forged Mars's helmet **261 chafe thee** anger yourself **262–3 let . . . to't** stop making such boastful threats until, by accident or on purpose, you come face to face with Hector. **265 stomach** appetite (for fighting). **general state** i.e., Greek commanders in council **266 be odd** be at odds, undertake to fight **268 pelting** paltry **270 fell** fierce **273 convive we** let us feast together. **275 severally entreat** individually invite **276 taborins** drums **279 keep** dwell. **288 As gentle** Be so courteous as to. **honor** reputation **291 such as** those who

294 But . . . tooth i.e., Love will always prove to be the plaything (literally, the sweet tooth) of fickle Fortune.
5.1. Location: The Greek camp. Before Achilles's tent.
2 scimitar sword. (Literally, a short, curved, single-bladed sword.)
4 core central hard mass of a boil or tumor **5 batch of nature** sample of humankind in its unimproved natural state **6 picture** mere image **8 fragment** leftover, crust. **10 Who . . . now?** i.e., Who is looking after or occupying Achilles's tent these days? (Patroclus implies that Achilles can no longer be taunted with languishing here.)
11 surgeon's box (Thersites puns on *tent* in the previous line, i.e., a probe for cleaning a wound.) **12 adversity** perversity, contrariety.
18–24 guts-griping . . . discoveries! may abdominal spasms, hernias, respiratory infections, severe cases of kidney stones, lethargy, paralysis, eye inflammations, liver diseases, asthma, abscesses of the bladder, lower back pain, gout or psoriasis, syphilitic bone-ache, and incurable wrinkling caused by skin eruptions strike repeatedly with disease such unnatural perversions as are discovered here!
28 ruinous butt dilapidated cask **29 indistinguishable** misshapen

THERSITES No? Why art thou then exasperate, thou idle immaterial skein of sleave silk, thou green sarcenet flap for a sore eye, thou tassel of a prodigal's purse, thou? Ah, how the poor world is pestered with such waterflies, diminutives of nature!

PATROCLUS Out, gall!

THERSITES Finch egg!

ACHILLES
My sweet Patroclus, I am thwarted quite
From my great purpose in tomorrow's battle.
Here is a letter from Queen Hecuba,
A token from her daughter, my fair love,
Both taxing me and gaging me to keep
An oath that I have sworn. I will not break it.
Fall, Greeks; fail, fame; honor, or go or stay.
My major vow lies here; this I'll obey.
Come, come, Thersites, help to trim my tent.
This night in banqueting must all be spent.
Away, Patroclus! *Exit* [*with Patroclus*].

THERSITES With too much blood and too little brain, these two may run mad; but if with too much brain and too little blood they do, I'll be a curer of madmen. Here's Agamemnon, an honest fellow enough and one that loves quails, but he has not so much brain as earwax. And the goodly transformation of Jupiter there, his brother, the bull—the primitive statue and oblique memorial of cuckolds, a thrifty shoeing-horn in a chain, hanging at his brother's leg—to what form but that he is should wit larded with malice and malice farced with wit turn him to? To an ass were nothing, he is both ass and ox; to an ox were nothing, he's both ox and ass. To be a dog, a mule, a cat, a fitchew, a toad, a lizard, an owl, a puttock, or a herring without a roe, I would not care; but to be Menelaus! I would conspire against destiny. Ask me not what I would be if I were not Thersites, for I care not to be the louse of a lazar, so I were not Menelaus. Heyday! Sprites and fires!

Enter [*Hector, Troilus, Ajax,*] *Agamemnon, Ulysses, Nestor,* [*Menelaus,*] *and Diomed*[*es*], *with lights.*

AGAMEMNON
We go wrong, we go wrong.

AJAX No, yonder 'tis,
There, where we see the light.

HECTOR I trouble you.

AJAX
No, not a whit.

[*Enter Achilles.*]

ULYSSES Here comes himself to guide you.

ACHILLES
Welcome, brave Hector; welcome, princes all.

AGAMEMNON
So now, fair Prince of Troy, I bid good night.
Ajax commands the guard to tend on you.

HECTOR
Thanks and good night to the Greeks' general.

MENELAUS Good night, my lord.

HECTOR Good night, sweet Lord Menelaus.

THERSITES [*aside*] Sweet draft. "Sweet," quoth 'a? Sweet sink, sweet sewer.

ACHILLES
Good night and welcome, both at once, to those
That go or tarry.

AGAMEMNON Good night.

Exeunt Agamemnon [*and*] *Menelaus.*

ACHILLES
Old Nestor tarries; and you too, Diomed,
Keep Hector company an hour or two.

DIOMEDES
I cannot, lord. I have important business,
The tide whereof is now. Good night, great Hector.

HECTOR Give me your hand.

ULYSSES [*aside to Troilus*]
Follow his torch; he goes to Calchas' tent.
I'll keep you company.

TROILUS [*aside to Ulysses*] Sweet sir, you honor me.

HECTOR
And so, good night.

[*Exit Diomedes; Ulysses and Troilus following.*]

ACHILLES Come, come, enter my tent.

Exeunt [*Achilles, Hector, Ajax, and Nestor*].

THERSITES That same Diomed's a false-hearted rogue, a most unjust knave. I will no more trust him when he leers than I will a serpent when he hisses. He will spend his mouth and promise, like Brabbler the

30 exasperate exasperated, angry **30–2 thou idle . . . purse** you useless, flimsy coil of floss silk, you eye-patch of soft green silk, you fringed ornamental pendant on a spendthrift's purse **31 skein** coil. **sleave silk** floss silk, i.e., unwoven and hence worthless *(immaterial)*. **sarcenet** fine, soft silk **35 gall** (1) bitter railer (2) blister. **36 Finch egg** (The finch is a small bird.) **41 taxing** urging. **gaging** binding, pledging **43 or go** either go **45 trim** prepare **48 blood** passion, willfulness **49–50 but . . . madmen** (Thersites considers it extremely unlikely that Patroclus and Achilles should ever suffer from too much intelligence or a lack of willful behavior; it's about as likely as if he, Thersites, could cure mad folk.) **51 honest . . . enough** good enough chap **52 quails** i.e., prostitutes. (Cant term.) **53–4 transformation . . . bull** (Alludes ironically to the myth of Jupiter's rape of Europa, whom he encountered in a meadow after changing himself into a bull. Thersites has in mind the bull's horns, which are like Menelaus's cuckold's horns.) **54–5 the primitive . . . cuckolds** i.e., the prototype and indirect reminder of cuckolds in having horns **55–6 a thrifty . . . leg** i.e., a convenient tool, always available to do Agamemnon's will (the *shoeing-horn* having been suggested in Thersites's mind by the cuckold's horns) **56–8 to what . . . him to?** to what new shape other than his own should my malicious wit and witty malice transform him? (*Farced* means covered, adorned, stuffed, seasoned; or *faced,* trimmed.) **58–9 To . . . nothing** To transform him into an ass would be to accomplish nothing at all **60 fitchew** polecat **61 puttock** bird of prey of the kite kind **61–2 a herring . . . roe** i.e., a sexually emaciated or "spent" herring **64 I care not to be** I wouldn't mind being

65 lazar leper. **so** provided **66 Sprites and fires** (Thersites sees those who are entering with lights, reminding him of will-o'-the-wisps and other spirits.) **76 Sweet draft** Sweet cesspool. (An ironic echo of Hector's "sweet Lord Menelaus," line 75.) **'a** he **77 sink** privy **84 tide** time **86 his** Diomedes's **90 unjust** dishonest, perfidious **91–2 He . . . promise** He will bay loudly as though promising that he has caught the scent **92 Brabbler** (An apt name for such a noisy hound.)

hound, but when he performs, astronomers foretell it; it is prodigious, there will come some change. The sun borrows of the moon when Diomed keeps his word. I will rather leave to see Hector than not to dog him. They say he keeps a Trojan drab and uses the traitor Calchas his tent. I'll after. Nothing but lechery! All incontinent varlets! [*Exit.*]

✣

[5.2]

Enter Diomedes.

DIOMEDES What, are you up here, ho? Speak.
CALCHAS [*within*] Who calls?
DIOMEDES
Diomed. Calchas, I think. Where's your daughter?
CALCHAS [*within*] She comes to you.

[*Enter Troilus and Ulysses at a distance; after them, Thersites.*]

ULYSSES [*to Troilus*]
Stand where the torch may not discover us.
[*He and Troilus conceal themselves in one place, Thersites in another. In the ensuing dialogue, Ulysses and Troilus continue to speak in asides to each other; Thersites utters his asides in commentary on the entire scene.*]

Enter Cressida.

TROILUS
Cressid comes forth to him.
DIOMEDES [*to Cressida*] How now, my charge?
CRESSIDA
Now, my sweet guardian! Hark, a word with you.
[*She whispers.*]
TROILUS Yea, so familiar?
ULYSSES She will sing any man at first sight.
THERSITES [*aside*] And any man may sing her, if he can take her clef. She's noted.
DIOMEDES Will you remember?
CRESSIDA Remember? Yes.
DIOMEDES Nay, but do, then,
And let your mind be coupled with your words.
TROILUS What should she remember?
ULYSSES List.
CRESSIDA
Sweet honey Greek, tempt me no more to folly.
THERSITES [*aside*] Roguery!
DIOMEDES Nay, then—
CRESSIDA I'll tell you what—
DIOMEDES
Foh, foh! Come, tell a pin. You are forsworn.
CRESSIDA
In faith, I cannot. What would you have me do?
THERSITES [*aside*] A juggling trick—to be secretly open.
DIOMEDES
What did you swear you would bestow on me?
CRESSIDA
I prithee, do not hold me to mine oath.
Bid me do anything but that, sweet Greek.
DIOMEDES Good night. [*He starts to go.*]
TROILUS Hold, patience!
ULYSSES How now, Trojan?
CRESSIDA Diomed—
DIOMEDES
No, no, good night. I'll be your fool no more.
TROILUS Thy better must.
CRESSIDA Hark, one word in your ear.
TROILUS Oh, plague and madness!
ULYSSES
You are moved, Prince. Let us depart, I pray you,
Lest your displeasure should enlarge itself
To wrathful terms. This place is dangerous,
The time right deadly. I beseech you, go.
[*He tries to lead Troilus away.*]
TROILUS
Behold, I pray you!
ULYSSES Nay, good my lord, go off.
You flow to great distraction. Come, my lord.
TROILUS
I prithee, stay.
ULYSSES You have not patience. Come.
TROILUS
I pray you, stay. By hell and all hell's torments,
I will not speak a word!
DIOMEDES
And so, good night. [*He starts to go.*]
CRESSIDA Nay, but you part in anger.
TROILUS
Doth that grieve thee? Oh, witherèd truth!
ULYSSES
Why, how now, lord?
TROILUS By Jove, I will be patient.
CRESSIDA
Guardian!—Why, Greek!
DIOMEDES Foh, foh! Adieu. You palter.

93–4 astronomers . . . change i.e., it is a rare and portentous event. **95 borrows of** borrows reflected light from (reversing the natural superiority of the sun—something that will never happen) **96 leave to see** cease looking upon. **him** Diomedes. **97 drab** whore. **uses** frequents **98–9 incontinent** (1) unchaste (2) incorrigible
5.2. Location: The Greek camp. Before the tent where Calchas stays with Menelaus. See 4.5.279–87.
5 discover reveal **6 charge** person entrusted to my care. **9 sing** i.e., sing the Sirens' song to; play upon **11 clef** key. (With obscene pun on "cleft," i.e., vulva.) **noted** set to music. (With pun on the meaning "known," i.e., notorious, or "used sexually.") **17 List** Listen.

22 tell a pin i.e., don't trifle with me. **23 I cannot** i.e., I cannot do what I promised. **24 juggling trick** magic trick (since to be *secretly open* is an apparent contradiction in terms) **25 open** (1) frank (2) sexually available. **33 fool** dupe **34 Thy better must** i.e., Better men than you (including myself) must play the fool to women like Cressida. **39 wrathful terms** i.e., a fight. **42 You . . . distraction** Your overfull heart will vent itself in emotional turmoil. **49 palter** use trickery.

CRESSIDA
In faith, I do not. Come hither once again.

ULYSSES
You shake, my lord, at something. Will you go?
You will break out.

TROILUS She strokes his cheek!

ULYSSES Come, Come.

TROILUS
Nay, stay. By Jove, I will not speak a word.
There is between my will and all offenses
A guard of patience. Stay a little while.

THERSITES [*aside*] How the devil Luxury, with his fat rump and potato finger, tickles these together! Fry, lechery, fry!

DIOMEDES [*to Cressida*] But will you, then?

CRESSIDA
In faith, I will, la. Never trust me else.

DIOMEDES
Give me some token for the surety of it.

CRESSIDA I'll fetch you one. *Exit.*

ULYSSES
You have sworn patience.

TROILUS Fear me not, sweet lord.
I will not be myself, nor have cognition
Of what I feel. I am all patience.

Enter Cressida, [with Troilus' sleeve].

THERSITES [*aside*] Now the pledge; now, now, now!

CRESSIDA Here, Diomed, keep this sleeve.
[*She gives it to him.*]

TROILUS
O beauty, where is thy faith?

ULYSSES My lord—

TROILUS
I will be patient; outwardly I will.

CRESSIDA
You look upon that sleeve. Behold it well.
He loved me—O false wench!—Give't me again.
[*She takes it back again.*]

DIOMEDES Whose was 't?

CRESSIDA
It is no matter, now I ha 't again.
I will not meet with you tomorrow night.
I prithee, Diomed, visit me no more.

THERSITES [*aside*] Now she sharpens. Well said, whetstone!

DIOMEDES
I shall have it.

CRESSIDA What, this?

DIOMEDES Ay, that.

CRESSIDA
O all you gods! O pretty, pretty pledge!
Thy master now lies thinking on his bed
Of thee and me, and sighs, and takes my glove,
And gives memorial dainty kisses to it,
As I kiss thee. Nay, do not snatch it from me;
He that takes that doth take my heart withal.

DIOMEDES
I had your heart before; this follows it.

TROILUS I did swear patience.

CRESSIDA
You shall not have it, Diomed, faith, you shall not.
I'll give you something else.

DIOMEDES I will have this. Whose was it?
[*He gets the sleeve from her.*]

CRESSIDA It is no matter.

DIOMEDES Come, tell me whose it was.

CRESSIDA
'Twas one's that loved me better than you will.
But, now you have it, take it.

DIOMEDES Whose was it?

CRESSIDA
By all Diana's waiting-women yond,
And by herself, I will not tell you whose.

DIOMEDES
Tomorrow will I wear it on my helm
And grieve his spirit that dares not challenge it.

TROILUS
Wert thou the devil, and wor'st it on thy horn,
It should be challenged.

CRESSIDA
Well, well, 'tis done, 'tis past. And yet it is not;
I will not keep my word.

DIOMEDES Why, then, farewell.
Thou never shalt mock Diomed again.
[*He starts to go.*]

CRESSIDA
You shall not go. One cannot speak a word
But it straight starts you.

DIOMEDES I do not like this fooling.

THERSITES [*aside*] Nor I, by Pluto; but that that likes not you pleases me best.

DIOMEDES What, shall I come? The hour?

CRESSIDA
Ay, come—O Jove!—do come—I shall be plagued.

DIOMEDES
Farewell till then. [*Exit Diomedes.*]

CRESSIDA Good night. I prithee, come.—
Troilus, farewell! One eye yet looks on thee,
But with my heart the other eye doth see.
Ah, poor our sex! This fault in us I find:
The error of our eye directs our mind.
What error leads must err. Oh, then conclude:
Minds swayed by eyes are full of turpitude. *Exit.*

THERSITES [*aside*]
A proof of strength she could not publish more,
Unless she said, "My mind is now turned whore."

54–5 There . . . patience I have patience to interpose between my anger and the violence it would commit. **56 Luxury** Lechery **57 potato finger** (Potatoes were accounted stimulants to lechery.) **Fry** Burn (with passion) **76 sharpens** whets his appetite. **82 memorial** in loving remembrance

84 withal with it. **87 faith** in faith **94 Diana's . . . yond** i.e., yonder stars. (Diana is the moon goddess and, ironically, the goddess of chastity.) **97 grieve his spirit** afflict the spirit of him **98 wor'st** wore **104 straight starts you** immediately starts you off on some abrupt action. **105 likes** pleases **111 heart** i.e., sexual desire and longing for security **115 turpitude** wickedness. **116 A proof . . . more** She could not put the case in more forceful terms. (*Publish* here means "announce," as in publishing printed material.)

ULYSSES
All's done, my lord.
TROILUS
It is.
ULYSSES
Why stay we, then?
TROILUS
To make a recordation to my soul
Of every syllable that here was spoke.
But if I tell how these two did coact,
Shall I not lie in publishing a truth?
Sith yet there is a credence in my heart,
An esperance so obstinately strong,
That doth invert th'attest of eyes and ears,
As if those organs had deceptious functions
Created only to calumniate.
Was Cressid here?
ULYSSES
I cannot conjure, Trojan.
TROILUS
She was not, sure.
ULYSSES
Most sure she was.
TROILUS
Why, my negation hath no taste of madness.
ULYSSES
Nor mine, my lord. Cressid was here but now.
TROILUS
Let it not be believed, for womanhood!
Think, we had mothers. Do not give advantage
To stubborn critics, apt, without a theme
For depravation, to square the general sex
By Cressid's rule. Rather think this not Cressid.
ULYSSES
What hath she done, Prince, that can soil our mothers?
TROILUS
Nothing at all, unless that this were she.
THERSITES [*aside*] Will 'a swagger himself out on 's own eyes?
TROILUS
This she? No, this is Diomed's Cressida.
If beauty have a soul, this is not she;
If souls guide vows, if vows be sanctimonies,
If sanctimony be the gods' delight,
If there be rule in unity itself,
This is not she. Oh, madness of discourse,
That cause sets up with and against itself!
Bifold authority, where reason can revolt
Without perdition, and loss assume all reason
Without revolt! This is and is not Cressid.
Within my soul there doth conduce a fight
Of this strange nature, that a thing inseparate
Divides more wider than the sky and earth,
And yet the spacious breadth of this division
Admits no orifex for a point as subtle
As Ariachne's broken woof to enter.
Instance, oh, instance, strong as Pluto's gates,
Cressid is mine, tied with the bonds of heaven;
Instance, oh, instance, strong as heaven itself,
The bonds of heaven are slipped, dissolved, and loosed,
And with another knot, five-finger-tied,
The fractions of her faith, orts of her love,
The fragments, scraps, the bits and greasy relics
Of her o'ereaten faith, are bound to Diomed.
ULYSSES
May worthy Troilus be half attached
With that which here his passion doth express?
TROILUS
Ay, Greek; and that shall be divulgèd well
In characters as red as Mars his heart
Inflamed with Venus. Never did young man fancy
With so eternal and so fixed a soul.
Hark, Greek: as much as I do Cressid love,
So much by weight hate I her Diomed.
That sleeve is mine that he'll bear on his helm.
Were it a casque composed by Vulcan's skill,
My sword should bite it. Not the dreadful spout
Which shipmen do the hurricano call,
Constringed in mass by the almighty sun,
Shall dizzy with more clamor Neptune's ear
In his descent than shall my prompted sword
Falling on Diomed.
THERSITES [*aside*] He'll tickle it for his concupy.
TROILUS
O Cressid! O false Cressid! False, false, false!
Let all untruths stand by thy stainèd name,
And they'll seem glorious.
ULYSSES
Oh, contain yourself.
Your passion draws ears hither.

Enter Aeneas.

AENEAS
I have been seeking you this hour, my lord.
Hector, by this, is arming him in Troy;

119 recordation record **123 Sith** Since. **credence** belief **124 esperance** hope **125 th'attest** the witness **126 deceptious** deceiving **127 calumniate** slander, defame. **130 negation** denial **132 for** for the sake of **134 stubborn** hostile **134–6 apt . . . rule** apt enough, even when they lack grounds for negative comment, to make Cressida the standard by which all womankind is measured. (To *square* is to use a carpenter's square or measuring tool.) **139–40 Will . . . eyes?** Will he succeed, with his blustering talk, in denying the evidence of his own eyes? **143 sanctimonies** sacred things **145 If . . . itself** i.e., if an entity (like Cressida) can only be itself and not two entities **146–7 Oh . . . itself!** Oh, mad and paradoxical reasoning, that sets up an argument for and against the very proposition being debated!
148–50 Bifold . . . revolt! Inherent contradiction, when reason can revolt against itself (by denying the testimony of the senses that this is indeed Cressida) without actually seeming to contradict itself!

151 conduce take place **152 a thing inseparate** i.e., Cressida, an indivisible entity **155–6 Admits . . . enter** provides not even an orifice only as large as the tiny thickness of a spider's web. (Arachne [the normal spelling] challenged Minerva to a weaving contest; the goddess became angered, tore up Arachne's work, and turned her into a spider.) **157 Instance** Proof, evidence. **Pluto's gates** the gates of hell **161 five-finger-tied** i.e., tied indissolubly by giving her hand to Diomedes **162 fractions** fragments. **orts** leftovers, fragments **164 o'ereaten** i.e., surfeiting through overfeeding, or begnawed, eaten away **165 half attached** half as much affected (as it appears) **168 red** bloody. (Troilus will manifest his passion now in warlike deeds.) **Mars his** Mars's **169 fancy** love **172 So . . . weight** to the same extent **174 casque** headpiece, helmet **175 spout** waterspout **177 Constringed** compressed **178 dizzy** make dizzy **181 He'll . . . concupy** He'll rain ineffectual blows on Diomed's helmet, fighting it out with Diomed for the sake of his concubine (Cressida) and his concupiscence (his lust). **187 him** himself

Ajax, your guard, stays to conduct you home.

TROILUS
Have with you, Prince.—My courteous lord, adieu.
Farewell, revolted fair! And, Diomed,
Stand fast, and wear a castle on thy head!

ULYSSES I'll bring you to the gates.

TROILUS Accept distracted thanks.

Exeunt Troilus, Aeneas, and Ulysses.

THERSITES Would I could meet that rogue Diomed! I would croak like a raven; I would bode, I would bode. Patroclus will give me anything for the intelligence of this whore. The parrot will not do more for an almond than he for a commodious drab. Lechery, lechery, still wars and lechery; nothing else holds fashion. A burning devil take them! *Exit.*

✤

[5.3]

Enter Hector, [armed,] and Andromache.

ANDROMACHE
When was my lord so much ungently tempered
To stop his ears against admonishment?
Unarm, unarm, and do not fight today.

HECTOR
You train me to offend you. Get you in.
By all the everlasting gods, I'll go!

ANDROMACHE
My dreams will, sure, prove ominous to the day.

HECTOR
No more, I say.

Enter Cassandra.

CASSANDRA Where is my brother Hector?

ANDROMACHE
Here, sister, armed, and bloody in intent.
Consort with me in loud and dear petition;
Pursue we him on knees. For I have dreamt
Of bloody turbulence, and this whole night
Hath nothing been but shapes and forms of slaughter.

CASSANDRA
Oh, 'tis true.

HECTOR [*calling*] Ho! Bid my trumpet sound.

CASSANDRA
No notes of sally, for the heavens, sweet brother.

HECTOR
Begone, I say. The gods have heard me swear.

CASSANDRA
The gods are deaf to hot and peevish vows.
They are polluted off'rings, more abhorred
Than spotted livers in the sacrifice.

ANDROMACHE
Oh, be persuaded! Do not count it holy
To hurt by being just. It is as lawful,
For we would give much, to use violent thefts,
And rob in the behalf of charity.

CASSANDRA
It is the purpose that makes strong the vow,
But vows to every purpose must not hold.
Unarm, sweet Hector.

HECTOR Hold you still, I say.
Mine honor keeps the weather of my fate.
Life every man holds dear, but the dear man
Holds honor far more precious-dear than life.

Enter Troilus.

How now, young man, mean'st thou to fight today?

ANDROMACHE
Cassandra, call my father to persuade.

Exit Cassandra.

HECTOR
No, faith, young Troilus, doff thy harness, youth;
I am today i'th' vein of chivalry.
Let grow thy sinews till their knots be strong,
And tempt not yet the brushes of the war.
Unarm thee, go, and doubt thou not, brave boy,
I'll stand today for thee and me and Troy.

TROILUS
Brother, you have a vice of mercy in you,
Which better fits a lion than a man.

HECTOR
What vice is that? Good Troilus, chide me for it.

TROILUS
When many times the captive Grecian falls,
Even in the fan and wind of your fair sword,
You bid them rise and live.

HECTOR
Oh, 'tis fair play.

TROILUS Fool's play, by heaven, Hector.

HECTOR
How now, how now?

TROILUS For th' love of all the gods,
Let's leave the hermit Pity with our mothers,
And when we have our armors buckled on,
The venomed vengeance ride upon our swords,
Spur them to ruthful work, rein them from ruth.

HECTOR
Fie, savage, fie!

TROILUS Hector, then 'tis wars.

HECTOR
Troilus, I would not have you fight today.

189 Have . . . Prince I am ready to go with you, Aeneas. **lord** Ulysses **191 castle** fortress, i.e., strong helmet **195 bode** warn, prognosticate **196 intelligence of** information about **198 commodious drab** accommodating harlot. **199–200 A burning . . . them!** (1) May a devil take them all to hell! (2) May venereal disease infect them!
5.3. Location: Troy. The palace.
4 train tempt, induce **6 ominous to** prophetic regarding **9 Consort** Join. **dear** ardent **14 sally** sallying, going forth to battle. **for the heavens** for heaven's sake **16 peevish** headstrong **18 spotted** tainted and hence ill-omened

21 For . . . give because we want to give **24 vows . . . hold** not every vow must be held sacred (since not all purposes are valid). **26 keeps the weather of** keeps to the windward side of (for tactical advantage), takes precedence over **27 dear man** worthy man, man of nobility **30 father** father-in-law, i.e., Priam **31 doff thy harness** take off your armor **34 tempt** attempt, assay. **brushes** hostile encounters **38 better fits a lion** (Lions were thought to be merciful to submissive prey.) **40 captive** overpowered in battle, wretched **47 The venomed vengeance** may the envenomed spirit of vengeance **48 ruthful** lamentable, i.e., causing lamentation. **ruth** pity, mercy. **49 then 'tis wars** i.e., war is like that.

TROILUS Who should withhold me?
Not fate, obedience, nor the hand of Mars
Beck'ning with fiery truncheon my retire,
Not Priamus and Hecuba on knees,
Their eyes o'ergallèd with recourse of tears,
Nor you, my brother, with your true sword drawn
Opposed to hinder me, should stop my way,
But by my ruin.

Enter Priam and Cassandra.

CASSANDRA
Lay hold upon him, Priam, hold him fast;
He is thy crutch. Now if thou loose thy stay,
Thou on him leaning, and all Troy on thee,
Fall all together.

PRIAM Come, Hector, come. Go back.
Thy wife hath dreamt, thy mother hath had visions,
Cassandra doth foresee, and I myself
Am like a prophet suddenly enrapt
To tell thee that this day is ominous.
Therefore, come back.

HECTOR Aeneas is afield,
And I do stand engaged to many Greeks,
Even in the faith of valor, to appear
This morning to them.

PRIAM Ay, but thou shalt not go.

HECTOR I must not break my faith.
You know me dutiful; therefore, dear sir,
Let me not shame respect, but give me leave
To take that course by your consent and voice
Which you do here forbid me, royal Priam.

CASSANDRA
O Priam, yield not to him!

ANDROMACHE Do not, dear father.

HECTOR
Andromache, I am offended with you.
Upon the love you bear me, get you in.
Exit Andromache.

TROILUS
This foolish, dreaming, superstitious girl
Makes all these bodements.

CASSANDRA Oh, farewell, dear Hector!
Look how thou diest! Look how thy eye turns pale!
Look how thy wounds do bleed at many vents!
Hark, how Troy roars, how Hecuba cries out,
How poor Andromache shrills her dolors forth!
Behold, distraction, frenzy, and amazement,
Like witless antics, one another meet,
And all cry, "Hector! Hector's dead! Oh, Hector!"

TROILUS Away! away!

CASSANDRA
Farewell. Yet soft! Hector, I take my leave.
Thou dost thyself and all our Troy deceive. [*Exit.*]

HECTOR
You are amazed, my liege, at her exclaim.
Go in and cheer the town. We'll forth and fight,
Do deeds of praise, and tell you them at night.

PRIAM
Farewell. The gods with safety stand about thee!
[*Exeunt Priam and Hector separately.*] *Alarum.*

TROILUS
They are at it, hark!—Proud Diomed, believe,
I come to lose my arm, or win my sleeve.

Enter Pandarus.

PANDARUS Do you hear, my lord? Do you hear?

TROILUS What now?

PANDARUS Here's a letter come from yond poor girl.
[*He gives a letter.*]

TROILUS Let me read.

PANDARUS A whoreson phthisic, a whoreson rascally phthisic so troubles me, and the foolish fortune of this girl, and what one thing, what another, that I shall leave you one o' these days. And I have a rheum in mine eyes, too, and such an ache in my bones that, unless a man were cursed, I cannot tell what to think on't.—What says she there?

TROILUS
Words, words, mere words, no matter from the heart;
Th'effect doth operate another way.
[*He tears the letter and tosses it away.*]
Go, wind, to wind! There turn and change together.
My love with words and errors still she feeds,
But edifies another with her deeds. *Exeunt.*

✤

[5.4]

[*Alarum.*] *Enter Thersites. Excursions.*

THERSITES Now they are clapper-clawing one another. I'll go look on. That dissembling abominable varlet, Diomed, has got that same scurvy doting foolish young knave's sleeve of Troy there in his helm. I would fain see them meet, that that same young Trojan ass that loves the whore there might send that Greekish whoremasterly villain with the sleeve back to the dissembling luxurious drab, of a sleeveless errand. O'th'other side, the policy of those crafty swearing rascals—that stale old mouse-eaten dry cheese, Nestor, and that same dog-fox, Ulysses—is proved not worth a blackberry. They set me up, in policy,

53 Beck'ning . . . retire beckoning me with a flaming baton to withdraw **55 o'ergallèd . . . tears** inflamed with the flow of tears **60 loose thy stay** let go your prop **65 enrapt** carried away, inspired **69 the faith of valor** a warrior's honor **73 shame respect** i.e., violate my filial duty **80 Makes** causes. **bodements** omens of ill fortune. **84 shrills her dolors** wails her grief **86 antics** fools **89 soft** i.e., gently; wait.

91 amazed dumbstruck. **exclaim** outcry. **101 phthisic** consumptive cough **104 rheum** watery discharge **109 Th'effect . . . way** i.e., her actions belie her words. **110 Go, wind, to wind!** Go, empty words, to the air! **111 errors** deceits **112 edifies** i.e., elevates to the role of being her lover **112 s.d. *Exeunt*** (In the Folio version, Pandarus is angrily dismissed at this point using the lines printed by the Quarto at 5.10.32–4.)

5.4. Location: Between Troy and the Greek camp. The battlefield is the setting for the rest of the play.

0.1 *Excursions* sorties or issuings forth of soldiers **1 clapper-clawing** mauling, thrashing **8 luxurious drab** lecherous slut. **sleeveless** futile **9 policy** craftiness **11 dog-fox** male fox **12 set me** set. (*Me* is used colloquially.)

that mongrel cur, Ajax, against that dog of as bad a kind, Achilles. And now is the cur Ajax prouder than the cur Achilles, and will not arm today, whereupon the Grecians began to proclaim barbarism, and policy grows into an ill opinion.

[*Enter Diomedes, and Troilus following.*]

Soft! Here comes Sleeve, and t'other.

TROILUS
Fly not, for shouldst thou take the River Styx,
I would swim after.

DIOMEDES Thou dost miscall retire.
I do not fly, but advantageous care
Withdrew me from the odds of multitude.
Have at thee! [*They fight.*]

THERSITES Hold thy whore, Grecian!—Now for thy whore, Trojan!—Now the sleeve, now the sleeve!

[*Exeunt Troilus and Diomedes, fighting.*]

Enter Hector.

HECTOR
What art thou, Greek? Art thou for Hector's match?
Art thou of blood and honor?

THERSITES No, no, I am a rascal, a scurvy railing knave, a very filthy rogue.

HECTOR I do believe thee. Live. [*Exit.*]

THERSITES God-a-mercy, that thou wilt believe me; but a plague break thy neck for frighting me! What's become of the wenching rogues? I think they have swallowed one another. I would laugh at that miracle—yet, in a sort, lechery eats itself. I'll seek them. *Exit.*

[5.5]

Enter Diomedes and Servant.

DIOMEDES
Go, go, my servant, take thou Troilus' horse;
Present the fair steed to my lady Cressid.
Fellow, commend my service to her beauty;
Tell her I have chastised the amorous Trojan
And am her knight by proof.

SERVANT I go, my lord. [*Exit.*]

Enter Agamemnon.

AGAMEMNON
Renew, renew! The fierce Polydamas
Hath beat down Menon; bastard Margareton
Hath Doreus prisoner,
And stands colossus-wise, waving his beam
Upon the pashèd corpses of the kings
Epistrophus and Cedius; Polyxenes is slain,
Amphimachus and Thoas deadly hurt,
Patroclus ta'en or slain, and Palamedes
Sore hurt and bruised. The dreadful Sagittary
Appals our numbers. Haste we, Diomed,
To reinforcement, or we perish all.

Enter Nestor [*and soldiers*].

NESTOR
Go, bear Patroclus' body to Achilles,
And bid the snail-paced Ajax arm for shame.
[*Exeunt some.*]
There is a thousand Hectors in the field.
Now here he fights on Galathe his horse,
And there lacks work; anon he's there afoot,
And there they fly or die, like scalèd schools
Before the belching whale; then is he yonder,
And there the strawy Greeks, ripe for his edge,
Fall down before him, like the mower's swath.
Here, there, and everywhere he leaves and takes,
Dexterity so obeying appetite
That what he will he does, and does so much
That proof is called impossibility.

Enter Ulysses.

ULYSSES
Oh, courage, courage, princes! Great Achilles
Is arming, weeping, cursing, vowing vengeance.
Patroclus' wounds have roused his drowsy blood,
Together with his mangled Myrmidons,
That noseless, handless, hacked and chipped, come to him,
Crying on Hector. Ajax hath lost a friend
And foams at mouth, and he is armed and at it,
Roaring for Troilus, who hath done today
Mad and fantastic execution,
Engaging and redeeming of himself
With such a careless force and forceless care
As if that luck, in very spite of cunning,
Bade him win all.

Enter Ajax.

16 proclaim barbarism declare a state of anarchy; they will be governed by *policy* or statecraft no longer **19 take** enter (by way of escape). **Styx** river of the underworld **20 miscall retire** call my tactical withdrawal by the wrong name of flight. **21–2 advantageous . . . multitude** desire for better military advantage prompted me to withdraw from the general melee, where I faced heavy odds. **24 Hold** Defend your right to. **for** fight for **27 blood** noble blood **31 God-a-mercy** Thank God, thanks **35 in a sort** in a way
5.5. Location: As before; the battle continues.
5 by proof by proof of arms. **6 Renew** To it again

9 colossus-wise like the Colossus (the great bronze statue of Apollo at Rhodes, one of the seven wonders of the ancient world). **beam** lance **10 pashèd** battered **14 Sagittary** (Literally, the archer; a centaur, i.e., a monster half man, half horse, who according to medieval legends fought in the Trojan War against the Greeks.) **15 Appals our numbers** dismays our troops. **22 scalèd schools** scattering schools of scaly fish **24 strawy** like straw ready for mowing. **his edge** the edge of his sword **25 swath** felled row of grain. **26 he leaves and takes** like a mower, he drops or *leaves* one cut of the grain and rhythmically engages the next cut with his scythelike sword **29 proof** fact, accomplished deed **33 Myrmidons** soldiers of Thessaly (whom Achilles led to Troy) **35 Crying on** exclaiming against **38 execution** deeds **39–42 Engaging . . . all** committing himself to battle and emerging unhurt with such nonchalant use of strength and effortless self-defense as if Fortune herself cheered him on to victory, in defiance of his enemies' skill in arms.

AJAX
Troilus! Thou coward Troilus! *Exit.*
DIOMEDES Ay, there, there. *Exit.*
NESTOR
So, so, we draw together.

Enter Achilles.

ACHILLES Where is this Hector?
Come, come, thou boy-queller, show thy face!
Know what it is to meet Achilles angry.
Hector! Where's Hector? I will none but Hector.
Exit [*with others*].

✤

[5.6]

Enter Ajax.

AJAX
Troilus, thou coward Troilus, show thy head!

Enter Diomedes.

DIOMEDES
Troilus, I say! Where's Troilus?
AJAX What wouldst thou?
DIOMEDES I would correct him.
AJAX
Were I the general, thou shouldst have my office
Ere that correction.—Troilus, I say! What, Troilus!

Enter Troilus.

TROILUS
O traitor Diomed! Turn thy false face, thou traitor,
And pay the life thou owest me for my horse!
DIOMEDES Ha, art thou there?
AJAX
I'll fight with him alone. Stand, Diomed.
DIOMEDES
He is my prize. I will not look upon.
TROILUS
Come, both you cogging Greeks, have at you both!
[*Exit Troilus with Ajax and Diomedes, fighting.*]

[*Enter Hector.*]

HECTOR
Yea, Troilus? Oh, well fought, my youngest brother!

Enter Achilles.

ACHILLES
Now do I see thee. Ha! Have at thee, Hector!
[*They fight; Achilles tires.*]
HECTOR Pause, if thou wilt.
ACHILLES
I do disdain thy courtesy, proud Trojan.
Be happy that my arms are out of use.
My rest and negligence befriends thee now,
But thou anon shalt hear of me again;
Till when, go seek thy fortune. *Exit.*
HECTOR Fare thee well.
I would have been much more a fresher man,
Had I expected thee.

Enter Troilus.

How now, my brother!
TROILUS
Ajax hath ta'en Aeneas. Shall it be?
No, by the flame of yonder glorious heaven,
He shall not carry him. I'll be ta'en too,
Or bring him off. Fate, hear me what I say!
I reck not though thou end my life today. *Exit.*

Enter one in armor.

HECTOR
Stand, stand, thou Greek! Thou art a goodly mark.
No? Wilt thou not? I like thy armor well;
I'll frush it and unlock the rivets all,
But I'll be master of it. [*Exit one in armor.*]
Wilt thou not, beast, abide?
Why then, fly on. I'll hunt thee for thy hide.
Exit [*in pursuit*].

✤

[5.7]

Enter Achilles, with Myrmidons.

ACHILLES
Come here about me, you my Myrmidons;
Mark what I say. Attend me where I wheel.
Strike not a stroke, but keep yourselves in breath,
And when I have the bloody Hector found,
Empale him with your weapons round about;
In fellest manner execute your arms.
Follow me, sirs, and my proceedings eye.
It is decreed Hector the great must die. *Exeunt.*

Enter Thersites; Menelaus [*and*] *Paris* [*fighting*].

THERSITES The cuckold and the cuckold maker are at it. Now, bull! Now, dog! 'Loo, Paris, 'loo! Now my double-horned Spartan! 'Loo, Paris, 'loo! The bull has the game. Ware horns, ho! *Exeunt Paris and Menelaus.*

Enter Bastard [*Margareton*].

44 we draw together i.e., at last we Greeks are pulling together, with Ajax and Achilles engaged to fight. **45 boy-queller** boy killer, i.e., slayer of Patroclus
5.6. Location: As before; the battle continues.
5 Ere that correction i.e., sooner than take from me the privilege of chastising Troilus. **9 Stand** i.e., Stand aside **10 look upon** remain an onlooker. **11 cogging** deceitful

16 use practice. **24 carry** prevail over **25 bring him off** rescue him. **26 reck** care **27 mark** target. **29–30 I'll . . . of it** I'll win it, if I have to smash it and pry open the rivets to do so. **31 hide** i.e., armor.
5.7. Location: As before; the battle continues.
2 wheel execute a circling turning maneuver. **5 Empale** fence **6 fellest** fiercest. **execute your arms** bring your weapons into operation. **7 my proceedings eye** watch what I do. **10 bull** i.e., Menelaus, a cuckold, a horned creature. **'Loo** (A cry to incite a dog against the bull in the sport of bullbaiting in Shakespeare's England.) **11 Spartan** i.e., Menelaus, King of Sparta. **11–12 has the game** wins. **12 Ware** Beware

MARGARETON Turn, slave, and fight.
THERSITES What art thou?
MARGARETON A bastard son of Priam's.
THERSITES I am a bastard too; I love bastards. I am bastard begot, bastard instructed, bastard in mind, bastard in valor, in everything illegitimate. One bear will not bite another, and wherefore should one bastard? Take heed, the quarrel's most ominous to us. If the son of a whore fight for a whore, he tempts judgment. Farewell, bastard. [*Exit.*]
MARGARETON The devil take thee, coward! *Exit.*

[5.8]

Enter Hector, [dragging the one in armor he has slain].

HECTOR
Most putrefièd core, so fair without, 1
Thy goodly armor thus hath cost thy life.
Now is my day's work done. I'll take good breath.
Rest, sword; thou hast thy fill of blood and death.
[*He disarms.*]

Enter Achilles and [his] Myrmidons.

ACHILLES
Look, Hector, how the sun begins to set,
How ugly night comes breathing at his heels.
Even with the vail and dark'ning of the sun, 7
To close the day up, Hector's life is done.
HECTOR
I am unarmed. Forgo this vantage, Greek.
ACHILLES
Strike, fellows, strike! This is the man I seek.
[*They fall upon Hector and kill him.*]
So, Ilium, fall thou! Now, Troy, sink down!
Here lies thy heart, thy sinews, and thy bone.
On, Myrmidons, and cry you all amain, 13
"Achilles hath the mighty Hector slain."
Retreat [sounded].
Hark! A retire upon our Grecian part. 15
A MYRMIDON
The Trojans trumpets sound the like, my lord.
ACHILLES
The dragon wing of night o'erspreads the earth,
And, stickler-like, the armies separates. 18
My half-supped sword, that frankly would have fed, 19
Pleased with this dainty bait, thus goes to bed. 20
[*He sheathes his sword.*]
Come, tie his body to my horse's tail. 21
Along the field I will the Trojan trail.
Exeunt [with Hector's body].

5.8. Location: As before; the battle continues.
1 core i.e., the body of the Greek whom Hector has killed for his armor **7 vail** going down **13 amain** with all your might **15 retire** call to retreat **18 And . . . separates** and, like a referee, separates the armies. **19 frankly** abundantly; greedily **20 dainty bait** tasty snack **21 his** Hector's

[5.9]

[Sound retreat.] Enter Agamemnon, Ajax, Menelaus, Nestor, Diomedes, and the rest, marching. [Shout within.]

AGAMEMNON Hark! Hark! What shout is that?
NESTOR Peace, drums!
SOLDIERS (*within*)
Achilles! Achilles! Hector's slain! Achilles!
DIOMEDES
The bruit is, Hector's slain, and by Achilles. 4
AJAX
If it be so, yet bragless let it be; 5
Great Hector was a man as good as he.
AGAMEMNON
March patiently along. Let one be sent
To pray Achilles see us at our tent.
If in his death the gods have us befriended,
Great Troy is ours, and our sharp wars are ended.
Exeunt.

[5.10]

Enter Aeneas, Paris, Antenor, [and] Deiphobus.

AENEAS
Stand, ho! Yet are we masters of the field. 1
Never go home; here starve we out the night. 2

Enter Troilus.

TROILUS
Hector is slain.
ALL Hector! The gods forbid!
TROILUS
He's dead, and at the murderer's horse's tail,
In beastly sort, dragged through the shameful field.
Frown on, you heavens, effect your rage with speed!
Sit, gods, upon your thrones and smite at Troy!
I say, at once: let your brief plagues be mercy, 8
And linger not our sure destructions on! 9
AENEAS
My lord, you do discomfort all the host. 10
TROILUS
You understand me not that tell me so.
I do not speak of flight, of fear, of death, 12
But dare all imminence that gods and men 13
Address their dangers in. Hector is gone. 14
Who shall tell Priam so, or Hecuba?
Let him that will a screech owl aye be called
Go into Troy, and say their Hector's dead.

5.9. Location: The battlefield; the battle has concluded.
4 bruit rumor, noise **5 bragless** without boasting
5.10. Location: The battlefield after the battle.
1 Yet Still **2 starve we out** let us endure, outlast **8 let . . . mercy** let your afflictions end us quickly, be mercifully brief **9 linger** draw out, protract **10 discomfort** discourage. **host** army. **12 of flight** merely of disordered retreat **13 imminence** impending evils, threats of imminent disaster **14 Address . . . in** prepare to endanger us with.

There is a word will Priam turn to stone, 18
Make wells and Niobes of the maids and wives, 19
Cold statues of the youth, and, in a word,
Scare Troy out of itself. But march away.
Hector is dead. There is no more to say.
Stay yet.—You vile abominable tents,
Thus proudly pitched upon our Phrygian plains,
Let Titan rise as early as he dare, 25
I'll through and through you! And, thou great-sized
coward, 26
No space of earth shall sunder our two hates. 27
I'll haunt thee like a wicked conscience still,
That moldeth goblins swift as frenzy's thoughts. 29
Strike a free march! To Troy with comfort go. 30
Hope of revenge shall hide our inward woe.
[*They proceed to march away.*]

Enter Pandarus.

PANDARUS [*to Troilus*] But hear you, hear you!

TROILUS
Hence, broker-lackey! Ignomy and shame 33
Pursue thy life, and live aye with thy name!
Exeunt all but Pandarus.

PANDARUS A goodly medicine for my aching bones! Oh, world, world, world! Thus is the poor agent despised. O traitors and bawds, how earnestly are you set a-work, and how ill requited! Why should our endeavor be so desired and the performance so loathed?
What verse for it? What instance for it? Let me see: 40

Full merrily the humble-bee doth sing, 41
Till he hath lost his honey and his sting;
And being once subdued in armèd tail, 43
Sweet honey and sweet notes together fail.

Good traders in the flesh, set this in your painted 45
cloths: 46
As many as be here of Panders' hall, 47
Your eyes, half out, weep out at Pandar's fall; 48
Or if you cannot weep, yet give some groans,
Though not for me, yet for your aching bones. 50
Brethren and sisters of the hold-door trade, 51
Some two months hence my will shall here be made.
It should be now, but that my fear is this:
Some gallèd goose of Winchester would hiss. 54
Till then I'll sweat and seek about for eases, 55
And at that time bequeath you my diseases. [*Exit.*]

18 will Priam turn that will turn Priam **19 Niobes** (Niobe boasted that her six sons and six daughters made her superior to Latona, mother of Apollo and Diana, for which she was punished by seeing them put to death by the arrows of these two deities. While weeping, she was changed into a stone, but her tears continued to flow from the rock. *Wells* are springs.) **25 Titan** i.e., Helios, the sun-god, one of the Titans **26 coward** i.e., Achilles, cowardly slayer of Hector **27 sunder** keep apart **29 moldeth** conjures up, creates in the imagination **30 free** unregimented, quick **33 broker-lackey** pander. **Ignomy** Ignominy

40 instance illustrative example **41 humble-bee** bumblebee **43 being . . . tail** having lost its sting. (Much as a lover is emptied and perhaps infected in the sexual act.) **45–6 painted cloths** cheap wall hangings worked or painted with scenes and mottoes **47 of Panders' hall** of the liveried company of panders **48 half out** i.e., already half destroyed by weeping and venereal disease **50 aching bones** (A symptom of venereal disease, as in line 35.) **51 hold-door trade** i.e., brothel keeping **54 gallèd . . . Winchester** i.e., a prostitute having venereal disease; so called because the brothels of Southwark were under the jurisdiction of the Bishop of Winchester **55 sweat** (A common treatment for venereal disease.)

Appendix 1

Canon, Dates, and Early Texts

By "canon" we mean a listing of plays that can be ascribed to Shakespeare on the basis of reliable evidence. Such evidence is either "internal," derived from matters of style or poetics in the plays themselves (see General Introduction), or "external," derived from outside the play. The latter includes any reference by Shakespeare's contemporaries to his plays, any allusions in the plays themselves to contemporary events, the entering of Shakespeare's plays for publication in the Stationers' Register (S. R.), actual publication of the plays, and records of early performances. These matters of external evidence are also essential in attempting to date the plays.

The greatest single source of information is the First Folio text of Shakespeare's plays, sponsored by Shakespeare's fellow actors John Heminges and Henry Condell and published in 1623. It contains all the plays included in this present edition of Shakespeare except *Pericles* and *The Two Noble Kinsmen* and offers strong presumptive evidence of being a complete and accurate compilation of Shakespeare's work by men who knew him and cherished his memory. It provides the only texts we have for these eighteen plays: *The Comedy of Errors, The Two Gentlemen of Verona, The Taming of the Shrew, I Henry VI, King John, As You Like It, Twelfth Night, Julius Caesar, All's Well That Ends Well, Measure for Measure, Timon of Athens, Macbeth, Antony and Cleopatra, Coriolanus, Cymbeline, The Winter's Tale, The Tempest*, and *Henry VIII*. This includes nearly half the known canon of Shakespeare's plays. Our debt to the First Folio is incalculable and confirms our impression of its reliability.

The information of the First Folio is further confirmed by contemporary references. In 1598, a cleric and minor writer of the period named Francis Meres wrote in his *Palladis Tamia, Wit's Treasury*:

> As the soul of Euphorbus was thought to live in Pythagoras, so the sweet, witty soul of Ovid lives in mellifluous and honey-tongued Shakespeare: witness his *Venus and Adonis*, his *Lucrece*, his sugared sonnets among his private friends, etc.
>
> As Plautus and Seneca are accounted the best for comedy and tragedy among the Latins, so Shakespeare among the English is the most excellent in both kinds for the stage; for comedy, witness his *Gentlemen of Verona*, his *Errors*, his *Love's Labor's Lost*, his *Love's Labor's Won*, his *Midsummer's Night Dream*, and his *Merchant of Venice*; for tragedy his *Richard the II, Richard the III, Henry the IV, King John, Titus Andronicus* and his *Romeo and Juliet.*

Though this list was meant to offer praise, not to be an exhaustive catalogue, it is remarkably full. If the tantalizing *Love's Labor's Won* refers to *The Taming of the Shrew*, Meres's list of comedies is substantially complete down almost to 1598. It does not include the comedies that Shakespeare appears to have written around that date or soon afterward: *Much Ado About Nothing, The Merry Wives of Windsor, As You Like It*, and *Twelfth Night*. Meres correctly names all of Shakespeare's history plays except the *Henry VI* trilogy and of course the later histories, *Henry V* (1599) and *Henry VIII* (1613). He names both of Shakespeare's early tragedies that are not based on English history: *Titus Andronicus* and *Romeo and Juliet*. He tells us about the important nondramatic poems, which did not appear in the First Folio, since that volume is devoted exclusively to plays. Not much can be made of the order in which Meres names the plays, however, for we learn from other sources that *Richard III* clearly precedes *Richard II* in date of composition and that *King John* precedes the *Henry IV* plays.

Other writers of the 1590s add further confirming evidence. John Weever, in an epigram "*Ad Gulielmum Shakespeare*," published in 1599, refers to "Rose-cheeked Adonis" and "Fair fire-hot Venus," to "Chaste Lucretia" and "Proud lust-stung Tarquin," and to "*Romeo, Richard*—more whose names I know not." Richard Barnfield, in

Poems in Divers Humors (1598), praises Shakespeare for "*Venus*" and "*Lucrece*." Both Thomas Nashe and Robert Greene seemingly refer to the *Henry VI* plays, missing from Meres's list. Nashe, in his *Pierce Penniless* (1592), speculates how it would "have joyed brave Talbot (the terror of the French) to think that after he had lain two hundred years in his tomb, he should triumph again on the stage." Talbot is the hero of *1 Henry VI*, and we know of no other play on the subject. Greene, in his *Greene's Groats-worth of Wit* (1592), lashes out at an "upstart crow, beautified with our feathers, that with his '*Tiger's heart wrapped in a player's hide*' supposes he is as well able to bombast out a blank verse as the best of you, and, being an absolute *Johannes Factotum*, is in his own conceit the only Shake-scene in a country." The line about "Tiger's heart" is deliberately misquoted from *3 Henry VI*, 1.4.137. (It is possible that this famous attack on Shakespeare was actually written not by Greene himself but by Henry Chettle, his literary executor.)

The Comedy of Errors (c. 1589–1594)

The earliest known edition of *The Comedy of Errors* is in the First Folio of 1623. Its first-mentioned production, however, was on Innocents Day, December 28, 1594, when a "Comedy of Errors (like to *Plautus* his *Menechmus*)" was performed by professional actors as part of the Christmas Revels at Gray's Inn (one of the Inns of Court, where young men studied law) in London. The evening's festivities are set down in *Gesta Grayorum*, a contemporary account of the revels, though not published until 1688. According to this record, the evening was marred by such tumult and disorder that the invited guests from the Inner Temple (another of the Inns of Court) refused to stay; thereafter, the night became known as "The Night of Errors." References to sorcery and enchantment in the play leave little doubt that it was Shakespeare's.

Some scholars argue that the play was not newly written for this occasion. To them, the play seems early: slight in characterization, and full of punning wit reminiscent of *Love's Labor's Lost* and *The Two Gentlemen of Verona*. Topical clues are suggestive but not conclusive. Chief of these is the joke about France being "armed and reverted, making war against her heir" (3.2.123–4). Unquestionably, this refers to France's civil wars between Henry of Navarre and his Catholic opposition. Since Henry became a Catholic and the King of France in 1593, most scholars prefer a date before 1593. Peter Alexander (*Shakespeare's Life and Art*, 1961) has even argued for a date prior to 1589, since Henry III died in that year, leaving Henry of Navarre as nominal king rather than heir. The sad truth is that we probably cannot attach too much weight to either conclusion. Allusions to the French civil wars during the early 1590s were common but also imprecise; the joke would have seemed relevant at almost any time up to 1595. The same is probably true of the allusion to Spain's sending "whole armadas of carracks" (3.2.135–6). This is often taken to refer to the Spanish Armada, 1588, but may refer instead to the Portuguese *Madre de Dios*, captured and brought to England in 1592, or to a similar venture. In short, it is virtually impossible to prove that *The Comedy of Errors* precedes *Love's Labor's Lost, The Two Gentlemen of Verona*, or *The Taming of the Shrew*. Those scholars who think it unlikely that the young gentlemen of Gray's Inn would have bestowed their attention on a play already five years old prefer a date of 1594.

A lost play called *The History of Error* was acted before the Queen by the Children of Paul's (a company of boy actors from St. Paul's School) at Hampton Court on New Year's night, 1577. About this play we know nothing other than its suggestive title, and speculation that Shakespeare may have adapted it has been generally abandoned.

The Folio text, based probably on Shakespeare's own manuscript, is generally a good text, although, as is common in authorial manuscripts, the form of the characters' names frequently varies in the stage directions and speech prefixes. Perhaps a few performance-oriented annotations have been added to the authorial manuscript.

Love's Labor's Lost (c. 1588–1597)

Love's Labor's Lost first appeared in a Quarto dated 1598, without entry in the Stationers' Register, the official record book of the London Company of Stationers (booksellers and printers). Its title page reads:

> A PLEASANT Conceited Comedie CALLED Loues labors lost. As it vvas presented before her Highnes this last Christmas. Newly corrected and augmented *By W. Shakespere*. Imprinted at London by *W. W.* [William White] for *Cutbert Burby*. 1598.

Because the phrase "newly corrected and augmented" also appears on the title page of the second Quarto of *Romeo and Juliet*, issued in 1599 to correct an unauthorized Quarto of 1597, many scholars suspect that *Love's Labor's Lost* may similarly have appeared in an unauthorized Quarto that is now lost. Such a circumstance would explain why the existing Quarto of *Love's Labor's Lost* was not registered: if the play had already been published, even in an unauthorized version, relicensing would have been unnecessary. (The *Romeo and Juliet* second Quarto was not registered for this reason.) But it is also entirely possible that the 1598 Quarto is simply reprinting an earlier lost good Quarto and that Burby is exaggerating his claims of correcting and augmenting.

The text shows clear signs of revision. Two long passages (see textual notes at 4.3.291 and 5.2.812) give duplicate readings of the same speeches, suggesting the printer mistakenly copied both the canceled version in his copy and the revision. Speech headings are unusually confused, sometimes referring to characters by their personal names (Navarre, Armado, Holofernes) and at other times by their generic titles (King, Braggart, Pedant). Some of these errors, notably the long uncanceled passages, suggest that the printer of the 1598 Quarto or of an earlier lost Quarto, perhaps new and relatively inexperienced, was copying from Shakespeare's working draft. Whether Shakespeare wrote this draft on one occasion or whether he revised an earlier version is, however, a matter on which scholars disagree. The First Folio text was set from the Quarto and thus gives us little additional information as to when or in what stages the play was written, though it may also have had occasional reference to a playhouse manuscript.

Francis Meres refers to the play in October 1598 in his *Palladis Tamia*. The performance before Queen Elizabeth "last Christmas" was probably in late 1597. Robert Tofte tells us in his *Alba* (1598) that "*Love's Labour Lost*, I once did see a play / ycleped so." His phrasing suggests a performance seen sometime in the past, although he could mean that he saw it only once. Apart from these allusions, dating of the play must rely on its presumed internal allusions to contemporary events. The play has attracted a lot of highly speculative topical hypotheses. One such describes a "School of Night" to which Sir Walter Ralegh, Matthew Roydon, George Chapman, and others are supposed to have belonged. No objective evidence exists to prove the existence of such a school. Ralegh was tried for atheism but was acquitted. Other topical hypotheses are discussed briefly in the Introduction to the play. Some allusions to the historical King of Navarre and to his supporters, the Duc de Biron and the Duc de Longueville, are undeniable. These allusions tend to argue either for an early date (c. 1588–1589), when these persons had not yet become the chief figures in a bloody religious civil war in France and hence inappropriate subjects for light comedy, or for a date after 1594, when a satire of Navarre's perjury might seem relevant to the historical Navarre's renunciation of Protestantism in 1593. The influence of John Lyly and the children's drama also argues for an early date. If, on the other hand, the Muscovite masque in 5.2 contains a reference to the Gray's Inn (one of the Inns of Court, where young men studied law) revels of 1594, as several scholars have urged, some portions of the play may be from after that date. The hypothesis that Shakespeare revived an old play of his shortly before publication in 1598, although not universally accepted, offers at least a plausible explanation of the phrase "newly corrected and augmented" on the title page.

The Two Gentlemen of Verona (c. 1590–1594)

The Two Gentlemen of Verona was not published until the First Folio of 1623. Other than Francis Meres's listing of it in 1598 in his *Palladis Tamia* (a slender volume on contemporary literature and art, valuable because it lists most of the plays of Shakespeare that existed at that time), evidence as to dating is scarce. No convincing allusions to contemporary events have been found. From the internal evidence of style, such as the relative density and sophistication of the dialogue, most scholars prefer an early date. The influence of John Lyly's romantic comedies, such as *Campaspe* (1584) and *Endymion* (1588), is still perceptible in the play's overly ingenious wit-combat.

A notable feature of the text, its grouping of characters' names at the beginning of each scene and the absence of any other stage directions except exits, seems to indicate that the manuscript was copied at some point by the scrivener Ralph Crane, probably from an authorial manuscript still containing a number of inconsistencies. The speech prefixes are sufficiently regular, on the other hand, that the text may have been prepared for the theater or else tidied up by Crane.

The Taming of the Shrew (c. 1590–1593)

The Taming of the Shrew was not printed until the First Folio of 1623. Francis Meres does not mention the play in 1598 in his *Palladis Tamia*, unless it is the mysterious "*Loue labours wonne*" on his list. (Meres is not totally accurate, for he omits *Henry VI* from the history plays.) The play must have existed prior to 1598, however, for its style is comparable with that of *The Two Gentlemen of Verona* and other early comedies. Moreover, a play called *The Taming of a Shrew* appeared in print in 1594 (Stationers' Register, 1594). Four theories can be adduced to explain the problematic relationship of *A Shrew* to Shakespeare's play. The two least plausible theories are that Shakespeare, for some reason, reworked someone else's play shortly after its first performance or else wrote *A Shrew* himself as an early version. The third theory is that *A Shrew* represents an imitation of Shakespeare's play by some rival dramatist, who relied chiefly on his memory and who changed characters' names and the location to make the play seem his. Fourth and most plausibly, *A Shrew* may be a somewhat uncharacteristic kind of reported or memorially reconstructed Quarto, "improved" upon by a writer who also borrowed admiringly from Christopher Marlowe and other Elizabethan dramatists. In either of the latter two scenarios, Shakespeare's play would have to be dated earlier than May 1594.

The title page of *A Shrew* proclaims that "it was sundry times acted by the *Right honorable the Earle of* Pembrook his seruants." Quite possibly this derivative version was merely trying to capitalize on the original's stage success and was, in fact, describing performances of Shakespeare's play. Theater owner and manager Philip Henslowe's record of a performance of "*the Tamynge of A Shrowe*" in 1594 at Newington Butts, a mile south of London Bridge, may also refer to Shakespeare's play; certainly, the minute distinction between "A Shrew" and "The Shrew" is one that the official records of the time would overlook. The Admiral's men and the Lord Chamberlain's men, acting companies, were playing at Newington Butts at the time, either jointly or alternatingly. Since Shakespeare's company, the Lord Chamberlain's, later owned *The Shrew*, they may well have owned and acted it on this occasion in 1594, having obtained it from the Earl of Pembroke's men when that company disbanded in 1593. Many of Pembroke's leading players joined the Lord Chamberlain's, Shakespeare being quite possibly among them. (The possibility that he came to the Lord Chamberlain's from Lord Strange's men seems less certain today than it once did.) Several echoes of Shakespeare's play in other plays of the early 1590s tend to confirm a date in or before 1593. It is entirely possible, then, that *The Shrew* was acted by Pembroke's men in 1592–1593 and subsequently passed along to the Lord Chamberlain's.

The Folio text of this play is now generally thought to have been printed from Shakespeare's working manuscript or possibly from a transcript of his papers, with perhaps some theatrical annotations as well. Some signs of revision are discernible.

A Midsummer Night's Dream (c. 1595)

A Midsummer Night's Dream was entered on the Stationers' Register, the official record book of the London Company of Stationers (booksellers and printers), by Thomas Fisher on October 8, 1600, and printed by him that same year in Quarto:

A Midsommer nights dreame. As it hath beene sundry times pub*lickely acted, by the Right honoura*ble, the Lord Chamberlaine his *seruants. Written by William Shakespeare.* Imprinted at London, for *Thomas Fisher*, and are to be soulde at his shoppe, at the Signe of the White Hart, in *Fleetestreete*. 1600.

This text appears to have been set from Shakespeare's working manuscript. Its inconsistencies in time scheme and other irregularities may reflect some revision, although the inconsistencies are not noticeable in performance. A Second Quarto appeared in 1619, though falsely dated 1600; it was a reprint of the First Quarto, with some minor corrections and many new errors. A copy of this Second Quarto, evidently with some added stage directions and other minor changes from a theatrical manuscript in the company's possession, served as the basis for the First Folio text of 1623. Changes of speech assignment in the Folio text, especially in Act 5, may reflect a late revival over which Shakespeare had no control. Essentially, the First Quarto remains the authoritative text.

Other than Francis Meres's listing of the play in 1598 in his *Palladis Tamia*, external clues as to date are elusive. Possibly the worry that a lion in a play might frighten the ladies (3.1.24–31) echoes published accounts of a baptismal feast at court in August 1594, when a blackamoor was chosen to draw in a chariot in place of a lion for fear of alarming nearby spectators. The description of unruly weather (2.1.88–114) has been related to the bad summer of 1594, but complaints about the weather are perennial. On the assumption that the play celebrates some noble wedding of the period, scholars have come up with a number of suitable marriages. Chief are those of Sir Thomas Heneage to Mary, Countess of Southampton, in 1594; of William Stanley, Earl of Derby, to Elizabeth Vere, daughter of the Earl of Oxford, in 1595; and of Thomas, son of Lord Berkeley, to Elizabeth, daughter of Lord Carey, in 1596. The Countess of Southampton was the widowed mother of the young Earl of Southampton, to whom Shakespeare had dedicated his *Venus and Adonis* and *The Rape of Lucrece*. No one has ever proved convincingly, however, that the play was written for any occasion other than commercial public performance. The play makes sense for a general audience and does not need to depend on references to a private marriage. Shakespeare was, after all, in the business of writing plays for his fellow actors, who earned their livelihood chiefly by public acting before large paying audiences. In any event, the search for a court marriage is a circular argument in terms of dating; suitable court marriages can be found for any year of the decade. In the last analysis, the play has to be dated on the basis of its stylistic affinity to plays like *Romeo and Juliet* and *Richard II*, works of the "lyric" mid-1590s. The "Pyramus and Thisbe" performance in *A Midsummer Night's Dream* would seem to bear an obvious relation to *Romeo and Juliet*, although no one can say for sure which came first.

The Merchant of Venice (c. 1596–1597)

The Stationers' Register, the official record book of the London Company of Stationers (booksellers and printers), for July 22, 1598, contains an entry on behalf of the printer James Roberts for "a booke of the Marchaunt of Venyce, or otherwise called the Iewe of Venyce, Prouided, that yt bee not prynted by the said James Robertes or anye other whatsoeuer without lycence first had from the Right honorable the lord Chamberlen." Roberts evidently enjoyed a close connection with the Chamberlain's men (Shakespeare's acting company) and seemingly was granted the special favor of registering the play at this time, even though the company did not wish to see the play published until later (or until they were paid). In 1600, at any rate, Roberts transferred his rights as publisher to Thomas Heyes and printed the volume for him with the following title:

The most excellent Historie of the *Merchant of Venice*. VVith the extreame crueltie of *Shylocke* the Iewe towards the sayd Merchant, in cutting a iust pound of his flesh: and the obtayning of *Portia* by the choyse of three chests. *As it hath beene diuers times acted by the Lord Chamberlaine his Seruants*. Written by William Shakespeare. AT LONDON, Printed by *I. R.* [James Roberts] for Thomas Heyes, and are to be sold in Paules Church-yard, at the signe of the Greene Dragon. 1600.

The text of this 1600 Quarto is generally a good one, based seemingly on an accurate copy of Shakespeare's papers by the dramatist himself or some reliable transcriber. It served as copy for the Second Quarto of 1619 (printed by William Jaggard for Thomas Pavier and fraudulently dated 1600) and for the First Folio of 1623. Although some theatrical manuscript seems also to have been consulted in preparation for the Folio text, the Folio variations appear to have little authority.

Francis Meres mentions the play in 1598 in his *Palladis Tamia*. Establishing an earlier limit for dating has proven not so easy. Many scholars have urged a connection with the Roderigo Lopez affair of 1594 (see the Introduction to the play). The supposed allusion to Lopez in the lines about "a wolf, who, hanged for human slaughter" (4.1.134) may simply indicate, however, that wolves were actually hanged for attacking men in Shakespeare's day (as dogs were for killing sheep). Besides, the Lopez case remained so notorious throughout the 1590s that even a proven allusion to it in *The Merchant* would not limit the play to 1594 or 1595. Christopher Marlowe's play, *The Jew of Malta*, was revived in 1594 to exploit anti-Lopez sentiment but was also revived in 1596. There may be, moreover, an allusion in 1.1.27 to the *St. Andrew*, a Spanish ship captured at Cadiz in 1596, and Shylock's allusion to Jacob and Laban (1.3.69–88) may well echo Miles Mosse's *The Arraignment and Conviction of Usury*, 1595. If so, the likeliest date is 1596–1597.

Much Ado About Nothing (1598–1599)

"The Commedie of muche A doo about nothing a booke" was entered in the Stationers' Register, the official record book of the London Company of Stationers (booksellers and printers), on August 4, 1600, along with *As You Like It*, *Henry V*, and Ben Jonson's *Every Man in His Humor*, all marked as plays of "My lord chamberlens men" (Shakespeare's acting company) and all "to be staied"—that is, not published without further permission. Earlier in the same memorandum, written on a spare page in the Register, occurs the name of the printer James Roberts, whose registration of *The Merchant of Venice* in 1598 was similarly stayed, pending further permission to publish. Evidently, the Chamberlain's men were attempting to ensure that they were paid for any plays printed or else to prevent unauthorized publication of these very popular plays. If the latter was their motive, they were too late to forestall the appearance of an unauthorized Quarto of *Henry V* in August 1600, but they did manage to control release of the others. *Much Ado About Nothing* appeared later that same year in a seemingly authorized version:

Much adoe about Nothing. *As it hath been sundrie times publikely* acted by the right honourable, the Lord Chamberlaine his seruants. *Written by William Shakespeare*. LONDON Printed by V. S. [Valentine Sims] for Andrew Wise, and William Aspley. 1600.

Once thought to have been set up from a theatrical playbook and then used itself in the theater as a playbook before serving as copy for the First Folio of 1623, this 1600 Quarto text is now generally regarded as having been set from Shakespeare's own manuscript. The names of the actors Will Kempe and Richard Cowley appear among the speech prefixes in 4.2, indicating that Shakespeare had them in mind as he wrote; other irregularities in speech prefixes and scene headings (including "ghost" characters, such as Leonato's wife Innogen) read more like a manuscript in the last stages of revision than a playbook for a finished production. The Folio text was based on this 1600 Quarto, lightly annotated with reference to the playbook but providing little in the way of new readings other than the correction of obvious error.

Francis Meres does not mention the play in September 1598 in his *Palladis Tamia*, unless (and this seems unlikely) it is his "*Loue labours wonne*." Will Kempe, who played Dogberry, left the Chamberlain's men early in 1599. The likeliest date, then, is the winter of 1598–1599, though publication was not until 1600.

The Merry Wives of Windsor (1597–1601)

The Stationers' Register, the official record book of the London Company of Stationers (booksellers and printers), for January 18, 1602, carries an entry for "A booke called an excellent and pleasant conceited commedie of Sir John Faulstof and the merry wyves of Windesor," by assignment from John Busby to Arthur Johnson. Later that year, Thomas Creed printed the following Quarto:

A Most pleasaunt and excellent conceited Comedie, of Syr *Iohn Falstaffe*, and the merrie Wiues of *Windsor*. Entermixed with sundrie variable and pleasing humors, of Syr *Hugh* the Welch Knight, Iustice *Shallow*, and his wise Cousin M. *Slender*. With the swaggering vaine of Auncient *Pistoll*, and Corporall *Nym*. By *William Shakespeare*. As it hath bene diuers times Acted by the right Honorable my Lord Chamberlaines seruants. Both before her Maiestie, and else-where. LONDON Printed by T. C. [Thomas Creed] for Arthur Iohnson, and are to be sold at his shop in Powles Church-yard, at the signe of the Flower de Leuse and the Crowne. 1602.

This text is now generally regarded as a memorially reconstructed Quarto, perhaps assembled by the actors who played the Host and Falstaff. A Second Quarto in 1619, printed by William Jaggard for Thomas Pavier, was based on it. The First Folio text of 1623, however, was taken from a manuscript evidently transcribed by Ralph Crane (hence, the "massed entries" of characters' names at the beginnings of scenes) and based perhaps on a theatrical playbook. It is the most authoritative text. Several interesting variant readings occur in the memorially reconstructed Quarto, despite its unreliability, and seem to indicate original readings that were altered in the Folio version for reasons of prudence. We find "garmombles" in place of the Folio "germans" at 4.5.74, and "Brook" in place of the Folio "Broome" throughout as the disguise name for the jealous Ford. "Garmombles" is often interpreted as an unflattering allusion to Frederick, Count Mömpelgard (see the Introduction to the play). "Brook" is a seeming dig at the family name of the powerful Henry Brooke (a descendant of Sir John Oldcastle), eighth Lord Cobham, whose intervention probably led to the similar changing of "Oldcastle" to "Falstaff" in *Henry IV*. The First Quarto can also be used sparingly to correct errors and omissions in the Folio text when, as seems likely in a small number of instances, the omission looks like eyeskip in the Folio text, rather than actors' or reporters' interpolations in the Quarto.

On dating, two irreconcilable choices are still possible: 1597, when the Lord Chamberlain was elected to the Order of the Garter, and 1600–1601, after *Henry V* (1599), in which Nym had been introduced. (There is more on the Order of the Garter in the Introduction.) The Stationers' Register entry in January 1602 provides a forward limit in time. Recent scholarly work tends to argue for the earlier date of 1597, though Francis Meres does not mention it in 1598 in his *Palladis Tamia*.

As You Like It (1598–1600)

"As you like yt, a booke" was entered in the Stationers' Register, the official record book of the London Company of Stationers (booksellers and printers), on August 4, 1600, along with *Much Ado About Nothing*, *Henry V*, and Ben Jonson's *Every Man in His Humor*, all labeled as "My lord chamberlens mens plaies" and all ordered "to be staied" from publication until further notice. Evidently, the Chamberlain's men (Shakespeare's acting company) were anxious to ensure payment or otherwise protect their rights to these very popular plays. Despite their efforts, *Henry V* appeared in an unauthorized Quarto that same month. *As You Like It* did not appear in print, however, until the First Folio of 1623. The Folio text is a good one, based seemingly on the theatrical playbook that still retained certain authorial features (conceivably, because an autograph fair copy served as the basis for it) or on a literary transcript either of the playbook or of an authorial manuscript.

Francis Meres does not mention the play in September 1598 in his *Palladis Tamia*. However, the play contains an unusually clear allusion to Christopher Marlowe's *Hero and Leander* ("Who ever loved that loved not at first sight?" 3.5.82), of which the first extant edition appeared in 1598, although Shakespeare may well have known it earlier in manuscript or in some lost edition. Even so, other possible allusions, to the burning of satirical books in June 1599 (see 1.2.85–6) and to the new Globe Theater ("All the world's a stage," 2.7.138), point to a date between late 1598 and the summer of 1600, probably after *Much Ado About Nothing*.

Twelfth Night (1600–1602)

Twelfth Night was registered with the London Company of Stationers (booksellers and printers) in 1623 and was first published in the First Folio of that year in a good text set up from what may have been a scribal transcript of Shakespeare's draft manuscript or possibly the playbook (assuming that the scribe might omit theatrical notations). There was a brief delay in printing *Twelfth Night* in the First Folio, possibly because a transcript was being prepared. The play was first mentioned, however, in the *Diary* of a Middle Temple law student or barrister named John Manningham, who describes the festivities for Candlemas Day, February 2, 1602, as follows:

At our feast wee had a play called "Twelue Night, or What you Will," much like the Commedy of Errores, or Menechmi in Plautus, but most like and neere to that in Italian called *Inganni*. A good practise in it to make the Steward beleeve his Lady widdowe was in love with him, by couterfeyting a letter as from his Lady in generall termes, telling him what shee liked best in him, and prescribing his gesture in smiling, his apparaile, & c., and then when he came to practise making him beleeue they tooke him to be mad.

This entry was once suspected to be a forgery perpetrated by John Payne Collier, who published the *Diary* in 1831, but its authenticity is now generally accepted. The date accords with several possible allusions in the play itself. When Fabian jokes about "a pension of thousands to be paid from the Sophy" (2.5.176–7), he seems to be recalling Sir Anthony Shirley's reception by the Shah of Persia (the Sophy) between the summer of 1598 and late 1601. An account of this visit was entered in the Stationers' Register in November 1601. Viola's description of Feste as "wise enough to play the fool" (3.1.60) may recall a poem beginning "True it is, he plays the fool indeed," published in 1600–1601 by Robert Armin (who had played the role of Feste). Maria's comparison of Malvolio's smiling face to "the new map with the augmentation of the Indies" (3.2.77–8) refers to new maps published in 1599 in which America (the Indies) was increased in size. Fabian's reference to sailing north and to the icicle on a Dutchman's beard (3.2.25–6) sounds like an allusion to William Barentz's Arctic expedition, first described in English in an account entered in the Stationers' Register on June 13, 1598, though no edition survives before 1609. Leslie Hotson (*The First Night of Twelfth Night*, 1954) has argued for a first performance at court on Twelfth Night in January 1601, when Queen Elizabeth entertained Don Virginio Orsino, Duke of Bracciano, but this hypothesis has not gained general acceptance, partly because the role of Orsino in the play would scarcely flatter such a noble visitor and partly because there is no proof that any of Shakespeare's plays were originally commissioned for private performance. Nevertheless, the episode may have suggested to Shakespeare the name Orsino. All in all, a date between 1600 and early 1602 seems most likely. Francis Meres does not mention the play in 1598 in his *Palladis Tamia*.

All's Well That Ends Well (c. 1601–1605)

All's Well That Ends Well was first registered in the Stationers' Register, the official record book of the London Company of Stationers (booksellers and printers), in November 1623 and was published in the First Folio of that same year. The text contains numerous inconsistencies in speech headings, "ghost" characters, anomalies of punctuation, and vague or literary stage directions, indicating it was set from the author's working papers, but these errors are not as extensive as once thought and the text is basically sound. Shakespeare's manuscript may have been sporadically annotated by the bookkeeper. Its printing in the First Folio is unusually laden with errors.

Information on the date of the play is sparse. Francis Meres does not mention it in 1598 in his *Palladis Tamia*, unless it is the intriguing "*Loue labours wonne*" on his list. Its themes and style are more suggestive of the period of *Hamlet* and *Troilus and Cressida*. The common assumption today is that the play was written sometime around 1601–1605. It may be later than *Measure for Measure*; the two plays are closely related, but the order of composition is hard to determine. The role of Lavatch is clearly designed for the actor Robert Armin, who did not join Shakespeare's acting company until 1599 or 1600. Scholars once argued that *All's Well* is an early play later revised, but this means of explaining the inconsistencies in the text no longer seems necessary.

Measure for Measure (1603–1604)

Measure for Measure first appeared in the First Folio of 1623. The text was evidently set from scrivener Ralph Crane's copy, possibly of Shakespeare's own draft; the usual inconsistencies of composition have not yet been smoothed away by use in the theater. On the other hand, spellings tend to suggest that Crane was copying a transcript. A recent and controversial hypothesis is that Crane based his copy on a playbook in use after Shakespeare's death, which incorporated some theatrical adaptation by Thomas Middleton and some other reviser, including a song (4.1.1–6) that could have originated in *Rollo, Duke of Normandy* (c. 1617) by John Fletcher and others.

The first recorded performance (according to a Revels account document) was on December 26, 1604, St. Stephen's Night, when "a play Caled Mesur for Mesur" by "Shaxberd" was acted in the banqueting hall at Whitehall "by his Maiesties plaiers." Shakespeare's acting company, previously the Lord Chamberlain's men, had become the King's men after the accession to the throne of James I in 1603. Several allusions in the play seem to point to the summer of 1604, when the theaters, having been closed for a year because of the plague, were reopened. A reference to the King of Hungary (1.2.1–5) may reflect anxieties in England over James's negotiations for a settlement with Spain; censorship would forbid a direct mentioning of Spain. Mistress Overdone's complaint about the war, the "sweat" (plague), the "gallows" (public executions), and poverty (1.2.81–3) are all suggestive of events in 1603–1604, when war with Spain and the plague were still very much in evidence. Duke Vincentio's reticent habits have been seen as a flattering reference to James's well-known dislike of crowds. Stylistically, the play is clearly later than *Twelfth Night* (1600–1602), so that a date close to the first recorded performance in 1604 is a necessity, even if we cannot be positive about all the supposed allusions to King James.

Troilus and Cressida (c. 1601)

The textual history of *Troilus and Cressida* is complicated. On February 7, 1603, James Roberts entered in the Stationers' Register, the official record book of the London Company of Stationers (booksellers and printers), "when he hath gotten sufficient aucthority for yt, The booke of Troilus and Cresseda as yt is acted by my lord Chamberlens Men." On January 28, 1609, however, a new entry appeared in the Register, as though the first had never been made: "Richard Bonion Henry Walleys. Entred for their Copy vnder thandes of Master Segar deputy to Sir George Bucke and master warden Lownes a booke called the history of Troylus and Cressida." Later that year appeared the First Quarto with the following title:

THE Historie of Troylus and Cresseida. *As it was acted by the Kings Maiesties* seruants at the Globe. *Written by* William Shakespeare. LONDON Imprinted by *G. Eld* for *R Bonian* and *H. Walley*, and are to be sold at the spred Eagle in Paules Church-yeard, ouer against the great North doore. 1609.

Before the first printing had sold out, still in 1609, the original title leaf was replaced by two new leaves containing a new title and an epistle. The title reads:

THE Famous Historie of Troylus *and* Cresseid. *Excellently expressing the beginning* of their loues, with the conceited wooing of *Pandarus* Prince of *Licia. Written by* William Shakespeare.

The epistle is addressed "A neuer writer, to an euer reader. Newes," and begins, "Eternall reader, you haue heere a new play, neuer stal'd with the Stage, neuer clapper-clawd with the palmes of the vulger, and yet passing full of the palme comicall."

The First Folio editors originally intended *Troilus and Cressida* to follow *Romeo and Juliet*. After three pages and a title page had been set up in this position, however, the play was removed (perhaps owing to copyright difficulties) and *Timon of Athens* was inserted instead. Later, *Troilus* was placed between the Histories and the Tragedies, almost entirely without pagination. See the Introduction for some possible explanations of the unusual publishing history.

The Quarto text was evidently set from a transcript of Shakespeare's working draft, made either by Shakespeare or by a scribe, or more probably from the working draft itself. The first three pages of the Folio text, those originally intended to follow *Romeo and Juliet*, were set from this First Quarto. The remaining pages of the First Folio, however, seem to have been based on a copy of the Quarto that had been collated with a manuscript, either Shakespeare's draft or more probably the playbook, which could itself have been a transcript of Shakespeare's fair copy of his original papers. As a result, both the Quarto and Folio texts have independent textual authority. Recent editorial study has paid increasing attention to the Folio text on the theory that its readings, when not manifestly corrupt, may represent either Shakespeare's second throughts as he fair copied or at least what the Folio collator found in Shakespeare's draft or the playbook. Hence, this edition, though using the First Quarto as its control text, introduces more Folio readings than are usually found in some previous editions; the Folio readings have been rejected only when there is some textual evidence against them.

The possibility that the play may not have been publicly performed and the failure of Shakespeare's company to provide the sequel promised at the end of *Troilus* suggest that the play was written not long before the first Stationers' Register entry of February 1603. Certainly the play was not an old favorite in the company's repertoire. Failure as a stage play might have led to an attempt at quick publication, aimed at sophisticated readers. The current fad for satire would also have provided a motive for prompt publication. Stylistically, *Troilus* belongs to the period of *Hamlet* (c. 1599–1601). A seeming allusion in the Prologue of *Troilus* to the "armed" Prologue of Ben Jonson's *Poetaster* (1601) helps set a probable early limit for date of composition; although the Prologue first appears in the First Folio of 1623 and may be an addition to the original play, it probably is not much later in date of composition. George Chapman's *The Seaven Bookes of Homers Iliads*, a source of information about the Trojan war, had appeared in 1598. The play is not mentioned by Francis Meres in 1598.

Appendix 2

Sources

The Comedy of Errors

The Comedy of Errors is based chiefly on the *Menaechmi* of Plautus (c. 254–184 B.C.). Shakespeare appears to have used the Latin, which was available to him in numerous Renaissance texts. He may also have known in manuscript the translation into English by "W.W." (? William Warner), published in 1595.

A comparison of the *Menaechmi* with Shakespeare's play suggests how much he has retained and what he has changed. As in Plautus, the story concerns two separated twins, one of whom (Menaechmus the Traveler of Syracuse) has come by chance, accompanied by his servant, Messenio, to the city of Epidamnum, where his long-lost brother, Menaechmus the Citizen, lives. Menaechmus the Citizen, in the company of the parasite Peniculus, quarrels with his wife and arranges lunch with the courtesan Erotium. The confusion begins when Menaechmus the Traveler is mistaken for his twin by Erotium's cook, Cylindrus, and then by Erotium herself, who invites him to lunch and to her bed. She bids him take a cloak (which Menaechmus the Citizen had given her that morning) to the dyer's for alteration. A short time later, Peniculus, too, mistakes Menaechmus the Traveler for the Epidamnian twin, upbraids him for having dined while the parasite was absent, and threatens to tell Menaechmus's wife of his carryings-on. Erotium's maid brings Menaechmus the Traveler a chain or bracelet to be mended at the goldsmith's. Menaechmus the Citizen now returns home from a busy day to a furious wife and a vindictive Peniculus. Among other matters, the wife demands the return of her cloak, which, as she suspects, her husband stole from her and gave to Erotium. The husband, locked out of his own house by his angry wife, must now confront Erotium, who insists that she gave her chain and the cloak to him. The Citizen goes to seek the help of his friends. Menaechmus the Traveler shows up at this point and is angrily abused by the wife and by her father, both of whom consider the supposed husband to be mad. They send for a doctor, who arrives after Menaechmus the Traveler has fled; they detain Menaechmus the Citizen instead as a madman. Messenio the servant now returns to his supposed master and fights manfully with his master's captors. Finally, the two twins confront one another and unravel the mystery.

Shakespeare creates the two Dromios in place of Messenio, plays down the role of the courtesan, dignifies the part of the wife, invents the sympathetic role of Luciana her sister, eliminates the parasite and the wife's father, and replaces the courtesan's maid and cook with comic servants such as Luce, or Nell, the kitchen-wench in the household of Antipholus of Ephesus. The conventional doctor, Medicus, becomes the zany Dr. Pinch. The setting is Ephesus rather than Epidamnum. Plautus's detached ironic tone and his matter-of-fact depiction of courtesans and parasites are replaced by a thematic emphasis on patience and loyalty in marriage. The name "Dromio" may have come from John Lyly's *Mother Bombie*.

The dual identity of the servants and the superb confusion in Act 3 when Antipholus of Ephesus is locked out of his own house are derived in good part from Plautus's *Amphitruo*. In the relevant portion of that play, Amphitryon's wife Alcmena is courted by Jupiter, disguised as her husband, while Mercury guards the door in the guise of Amphitryon's slave Sosia. The real Sosia approaches but is so bewildered by Mercury's inventive wit that he begins to doubt his own identity. Later, at Jupiter's behest, Mercury again poses as Sosia to dupe

Amphitryon and to deny him entrance to his own house. Ultimately, after Alcmena has given birth to twins, one by Jupiter (Hercules) and one by Amphitryon (Iphiclus), Jupiter tells Amphitryon the truth.

The "framing" action of *The Comedy of Errors*, concerning old Egeon's painful separation from his wife and their eventual reunion, is derived not from Plautus but from the story of Apollonius of Tyre. Shakespeare later used this story for *Pericles*, and for that play his sources were chiefly two: the *Confessio Amantis* by John Gower, Book 8, and Laurence Twine's *The Pattern of Painful Adventures*, translated from a French version based in turn on a popular story in the *Gesta Romanorum*. Perhaps Shakespeare was acquainted with these same versions when he wrote *The Comedy of Errors*; in 1576, Twine's account was entered in the Stationers' Register, the official record book of the London Company of Stationers (booksellers and printers), although the earliest extant edition dates from around 1594–1595. Gower's account had been printed by William Caxton (England's first printer) in 1493 and reprinted in 1532 and 1554.

In Gower's *Confessio*, Apollonius's wife Lucina gives birth to a daughter on board ship and, having apparently died in childbirth, is put into a chest and committed to the sea. Washing ashore at Ephesus, she is restored by the physician Cerimon. She becomes a priestess in the Temple of Diana. Years later, Apollonius comes to Ephesus, is first reunited with his daughter Thaisa, and then is told in a vision to go to the Temple. There he discovers the "Abbess" to be his long-lost wife. Shakespeare has added the threatened hanging from which Egeon is finally rescued.

Love's Labor's Lost

No main source exists for *Love's Labor's Lost*. For his conception of an "academy" of aristocratic scholars, Shakespeare may have drawn on Pierre de la Primaudaye's *L'Académie française* (1577), translated into English in 1586, in which the ideals of scholarly withdrawal are discussed. The notion was, however, commonplace. Certain historical facts about Henry of Navarre may well have provided Shakespeare with a model for the play's action, especially the visit of Catherine de Medici with her daughter and the famous *l'escadron volant* (flying squadron) to Henry's court in 1578, and a similar visit in 1586 (see the Introduction to the play). Published accounts of these visits were not available when Shakespeare wrote his play, but he may well have heard the gossip. John Lyly's plays provided Shakespeare with a literary model for the saucy boyish wit of Mote, Boyet, and others, and Armado and Mote are often thought to resemble Sir Tophas and the page Epiton in Lyly's *Endymion*. Traditions of the *commedia dell' arte* provided Shakespeare with stock comic models, especially those of the *dottore* or pedant (Holofernes), his parasite (Nathaniel, the curate), the *capitano* or braggart soldier (Armado), and the rustic servant (Costard). All of these types are individualized and rendered in English terms, however. Many literary quarrels in England in the 1590s have been adduced as possible sources for Shakespeare's play, especially the controversy between Thomas Nashe and Gabriel Harvey, but the evidence remains inconclusive.

The Two Gentlemen of Verona

Shakespeare appears to have combined two kinds of stories in *The Two Gentlemen of Verona:* one of romantic love triumphing over inconstancy and one of perfect friendship triumphing over perfidy. For the story of the deserted heroine and her inconstant lover, Shakespeare's main source was evidently *Diana Enamorada*, a Spanish pastoral by Jorge de Montemayor (published c. 1559). This work was translated into French in 1578 and 1587, and was published in English in 1598 by Bartholomew Yonge. Yonge states that he began his translation some nineteen years earlier. Possibly, then, Shakespeare saw it in manuscript, or he may have relied on the Spanish original or the French translation. A play, now lost, was performed at court in 1585 called *The History of Felix & Philiomena* (i.e., Felismena). It must surely have been based on Montemayor's prose pastoral and may have provided Shakespeare with a dramatic model.

The story of Felix and Felismena is only one of the many narratives in *Diana Enamorada* that are set in contrast to the central story of Diana the shepherdess. It is told by Felismena as her own narrative, beginning in Book. 2. The story contains no character corresponding to Valentine, but Proteus and Julia find their equivalents in Felix and Felismena. The latter is attended by a maid, Rosina, like Julia's Lucetta, who is hypocritically scolded by her mistress for delivering a letter from Felix that Felismena, in fact, longs to have. Like Proteus in Shakespeare's play, Don Felix is sent off to court (in this case, the court of Princess Augusta Caesarina) to prevent his marriage to the orphaned Felismena. She follows after, appareled as a young man named Valerius (as Julia travels under the name of Sebastian). Stopping at an inn, she is invited by the host of the inn to hear some music, whereupon she happens to overhear the faithless Felix courting a lady named Celia (Shakespeare's Silvia). Disguised as Valerius, Felismena ingratiates herself with Felix's servant Fabius and takes service with Don Felix. She is sent on embassages to Celia, with whom she converses about Felix's first love. Celia falls in love with "Valerius," like Olivia in *Twelfth Night*, and subsequently dies of unrequited passion. Hereupon the distraught Felix disappears. Later, in Book 7, we hear how Felismena, disguised as an Amazonian shepherdess, rescues Felix from his attackers and is reconciled with him. Felix acknowledges her beauty to be superior to that of Celia. Shakespeare has changed some important matters, notably Celia's falling in love with "Valerius" and her dying of unrequited love; Silvia's remaining faithful to Valentine and following him into banishment are essential parts of her character in Shakespeare's account. Shakespeare also adds several new characters: the Duke of Milan (Silvia's father), Thurio, Eglamour, Lance, Speed, and the outlaws. Still, the debt to *Diana Enamorada* is considerable.

In Sir Philip Sidney's *Arcadia* (1590), Zelmane follows Felismena's example by disguising herself as a page (Daiphantus) in the service of her beloved Pyrocles. When she falls ill and is on the verge of death, Zelmane's identity is revealed to Pyrocles. *Arcadia* also offers a noble example of perfect friendship in the relation between Pyrocles and Musidorus. Shakespeare used the *Arcadia* as a source elsewhere, especially in the Gloucester plot of *King Lear*.

The story of perfect friendship has many antecedents, including the fourteenth-century *Amis and Amiloun* and Richard Edwards's play about *Damon and Pythias* (1565). The falling-out of sworn friends over a woman is the central theme of Geoffrey Chaucer's "The Knight's Tale" and of John Lyly's *Euphues* (1578). Perhaps the most suggestive example of perfect friendship is the story of Titus and Gisippus as it appears in Book 2, Chapter 12, of Sir Thomas Elyot's *The Governor* (1531). Elyot derived his account from Day 10, Novel 8, of Giovanni Boccaccio's *Decameron*. Titus and Gisippus were proverbially famous friends, like Damon and Pythias, and other Renaissance versions of the story were available (including a Latin school play of 1546[?] and a children's play at court in 1577, both now lost). Perhaps Shakespeare knew the story as a commonplace rather than having to depend on one particular literary source.

Elyot's version tells of two look-alike friends dwelling in Athens, of whom one, Gisippus, is persuaded by his kindred and acquaintances to marry. Despite a preference for the study of philosophy, he finds his fiancée most attractive. When, however, his Roman-born friend Titus falls desperately in love with the same lady and confesses as much to Gisippus, the husband-to-be generously proposes that Titus take his place on the wedding night. Because the binding element of the marriage contract is the bestowing of the ring in bed and the undoing of the girdle of virginity, the lady is now Titus's legal wife and returns with him to Rome. Gisippus, accused by the Athenians of having mismanaged the affair, follows his friend to Rome and is there wrongly accused of a murder. Titus's turn has now arrived to be magnanimous, and he insists that he be punished for the murder. Eventually, the real culprit, touched by this selflessness, confesses the crime, allowing Titus to return with Gisippus to Athens and forcibly to restore him to his rightful possessions.

Valentine's sojourn in the forest and his leadership of a band of outlaws would seem to be indebted to the tradition of Robin Hood, although no single source has been found. An analogue to the outlaw episode does appear in Henry Wotton's *A Courtly Controversy of Cupid's Cautels* (1578), where it is linked to a story of perfidy in friendship. Valentine's unwelcome rival Thurio may owe something to the braggart soldier, Captain Spavento, of the *commedia dell' arte* tradition. Silvia's father, the Duke, is a similarly conventional comic stage type.

One final analogue worthy of note is a German play, *Julio und Hyppolita*, from a collection called *Englische Comedien und Tragedien* (1620). It may have been derived from performances by English players around 1600. Although some of its lines are suggestively close to those of Shakespeare's play, we cannot determine which version is prior to the other.

The Taming of the Shrew

Scholars do not agree on the relationship of *The Taming of the Shrew* to the play called *The Taming of a Shrew*, published in 1594. *A Shrew* has been argued to be an earlier version of Shakespeare's play, or a memorial reconstruction of it, or derived from a common original. Some recent critics argue that the two versions should be treated as distinct texts. An often-held view is that *A Shrew* is derived from a now-lost earlier version of Shakespeare's play, to which the compiler added original material and borrowed or even plagiarized from other literary sources as well. If so, *A Shrew* would not appear to be a source for Shakespeare's play, as Geoffrey Bullough has argued in his *Narrative and Dramatic Sources of Shakespeare*. Apart from this question, all critics agree that Shakespeare's play consists of three elements, each with its own source: the romantic love plot of Lucentio and Bianca, the wife-taming plot of Petruchio and Kate, and the framing plot, or induction, of Christopher Sly.

The romantic love plot is derived from George Gascoigne's *Supposes*, a neoclassical comedy performed at Gray's Inn (one of the Inns of Court, where young men studied law in London) in 1566. Gascoigne's play was a rather close translation of Ludovico Ariosto's *I Suppositi* (1509), which in turn was based on two classical plays, Terence's *Eunuchus* and Plautus's *Captivi*. The heroine of Gascoigne's version (as of Ariosto's) is Polynesta, the resourceful daughter of Damon, a widower of Ferrara. Two suitors vie for Polynesta's hand: Dr. Cleander, an aged and miserly lawyer, and Erostrato, a Sicilian gentleman who has purportedly come to Ferrara to study. In fact, however, this "Erostrato" is the servant Dulippo in disguise, having changed places with his master. (These disguisings are the "supposes" of the title.) As a servant in Damon's household, "Dulippo" has secretly become the lover of Polynesta and has made her pregnant. Balia, the nurse or duenna, is their go-between. Meanwhile, "Erostrato" takes great delight in outwitting Dr. Cleander and his unattractive parasite, Pasiphilo. The counterfeit Erostrato's ruse is to produce a rich father who will guarantee a handsome dowry and thereby outbid Cleander in the contest for Polynesta's hand. The "father" he produces, however, is actually an old Sienese stranger, who is persuaded that he is in danger in Ferrara unless he cloaks his identity. Complications arise when Damon learns of his daughter's affair and throws the lover, "Dulippo," into a dungeon. The crafty Pasiphilo overhears this compromising information and resolves to cause mischief for all the principals. Moreover, when Erostrato's real father, Philogano, arrives in Ferrara, he is barred from his son's house by the counterfeit Philogano and resolves to get help. His clever servant, Litio, suggests employing the famous lawyer, Cleander. All is happily resolved when the real Dulippo proves to be the son of Dr. Cleander and the real Erostrato is revealed to be rich and socially eligible for Polynesta's hand in marriage. Cleander is even reconciled to his parasite, Pasiphilo.

Shakespeare, in his play, has almost entirely eliminated the satire of the law that is in his source. Gremio is aged and wealthy, but no shyster. The lover is not imprisoned in a dungeon. The parasite is gone, as also in *The Comedy of Errors*. Bianca does not consummate her affair with Lucentio, as does Polynesta, and hence has no need for a go-between like Balia. Shakespeare adapts a sophisticated neoclassical comedy, racy and cosmopolitan, to the moral standards of his public theater. The witless Hortensio, the tutoring in Latin, and the music lesson are Shakespeare's inventions.

The wife-taming plot of Petruchio and Kate reflects an ancient comic misogynistic tradition, still extant today in the Scottish folksong "The Cooper of Fife" or "The Wife Wrapped in Wether's Skin" (Francis James Child, *The English and Scottish Popular Ballads* [1888–1898], 5:104). Richard Hosley has argued (in *Huntington Library Quarterly, 27*, 1964) that Shakespeare's likeliest source was *A Merry Jest of a Shrewd and Curst Wife Lapped in Morel's Skin, for her Good Behavior* (printed c. 1550). In this version, the husband beats his shrewish wife with birch rods until she bleeds and faints, whereupon he wraps her in the raw salted skin of an old plow-horse named Morel. Like Kate, this shrewish wife has a gentle younger sister who is their father's favorite. This father warns the man who proposes to marry his older daughter that she is shrewish, but the suitor goes ahead and subsequently tames his wife with Morel's skin. Thereafter, at a celebratory dinner, everyone is impressed by the thoroughness of the taming.

Shakespeare avoids the misogynistic extremes of this story, despite the similarity of the narrative. Instead, he seems to have had in mind the more humanistic spirit of Erasmus's *A Merry Dialogue Declaring the Properties of Shrewd Shrews and Honest Wives* (translated 1557) and Juan Luis Vives's *The Office and Duty of an Husband* (translated 1555). Specific elements of the wife-taming plot have been traced to other possible sources. The scolding of a tailor occurs in Gerard Legh's *Accidence of Armory* (1562); a wife agrees with her husband's assertion of a patent falsehood in Don Juan Manuel's *El Conde Lucanor* (1335); and three husbands wager on the obedience of their wives in *The Book of the Knight of La Tour-Landry* (printed 1484).

The induction story, of the beggar duped into believing himself a rich lord, is an old tale occurring in the *Arabian Nights*. An interesting analogue occurs in P. Heuterus's *De Rebus Burgundicis* (1584), translated into the French of S. Goulart (1606?) and thence into the English of Edward Crimeston (1607). According to Heuterus, in 1440, Philip the Good of Burgundy actually entertained a drunken beggar in his palace "to make trial of the vanity of our life," plying him with fine clothes, bed, a feast, and the performance of "a pleasant comedy."

A Midsummer Night's Dream

No single source has been discovered that unites the various elements that we find in *A Midsummer Night's Dream*, but the four main strands of action can be individually discussed in terms of sources. The four strands are: (1) the marriage of Theseus (Duke of Athens) and Queen Hippolyta, (2) the romantic tribulations and triumphs of the four young lovers, (3) the quarrel of King Oberon and Queen Titania, together with the fairies' manipulations of human affairs, and (4) the "rude mechanicals" and their play of "Pyramus and Thisbe."

For his conception of Theseus, Shakespeare went chiefly to Geoffrey Chaucer's "The Knight's Tale" and to Thomas North's 1579 translation of "The Life of Theseus" in Plutarch's *Lives of the Noble Grecians and Romans*. Chaucer's Theseus is a duke of "wisdom" and "chivalrye," renowned for his conquest of the Amazons and his marriage to Hippolyta. Plutarch provides information concerning Theseus's other conquests (to which Oberon alludes in 2.1.77 ff.), including that of Antiopa. Shakespeare could have learned more about Theseus from Chaucer's *The Legend of Good Women* and from Ovid's *Metamorphoses*. He seems to have blended all or some of these impressions together with his own notion of a noble yet popular Renaissance ruler.

The romantic narrative of the four lovers appears to be original with Shakespeare, although one can find many analogous situations of misunderstanding and rivalry in love. Chaucer's "The Knight's Tale" tells of two friends battling over one woman. Shakespeare's own *The Two Gentlemen of Verona* gives us four lovers, properly matched at first until one of the men shifts his attentions to his friend's ladylove; eventually, all is righted when the false lover recovers his senses. Parallel situations arise in Sir Philip Sidney's *Arcadia* (1590) and in Jorge de Montemayor's *Diana Enamorada* (c. 1559), a source for *The Two Gentlemen*. What Shakespeare adds in *A Midsummer* is the intervention of the fairies in human love affairs.

Shakespeare's knowledge of fairy lore must have been extensive and is hard to trace exactly. Doubtless, much of it was from oral traditions about leprechauns, gremlins, and elves, who were thought to cause such mischief as spoiling fermentation or preventing milk from churning into butter; Puck's tricks mentioned in 2.1.34 ff. are derived from such lore. Some of the oral tales circulating about Robin Goodfellow later reached print, probably somewhat modified, in the prose pamphlet *Robin Good Fellow, His Mad Pranks and Merry Jests* (London, 1628) and a ballad, "The Mad Merry Pranks of Robbin Good-fellow" (c. 1600) in Roxburghe Ballads, vol. 2, ed. William Chappell (Hertford: Stephen Austin for the Ballad Society, 1872), p. 83. Shakespeare seems to have consulted literary sources as well. In Chaucer's "The Merchant's Tale," Pluto and Proserpina as King and Queen of the fairies intervene in the affairs of old January, his young wife May, and her lover Damyan. Fairies appear on stage in John Lyly's *Endymion* (1588), protecting true lovers and tormenting those who are morally tainted. Shakespeare later reflects this tradition in *The Merry Wives of Windsor* (1597–1601). The name Oberon probably comes from the French romance *Huon of Bordeaux* (translated by Lord Berners by about 1540), where Oberon is a dwarfish fairy King from the mysterious East who practices enchantment in a haunted wood. In Edmund Spenser's *The Faerie Queene*, Oberon is the Elfin father of Queen Gloriana (2.10. 75–76). Robert Greene's *James IV* (c. 1591) also features Oberon as the fairy King, and a lost play called *Huon of Bordeaux* was performed by Sussex's men, an acting company, at about this same time. The name "Titania" comes from Ovid's *Metamorphoses*, where it is used as a synonym for both the enchantress Circe and the chaste goddess Diana. The name "Titania" does not appear in Arthur Golding's translation (1567), suggesting that Shakespeare found it in the original. Puck, or Robin Goodfellow, is essentially the product of oral tradition, although Reginald Scot's *The Discovery of Witchcraft* (1584) discusses Robin in pejorative terms as an incubus or hobgoblin in whom intelligent people no longer believe.

Scot also reports the story of a man who finds an ass's head placed on his shoulders by enchantment. Similar legends of transformation occur in Apuleius's *The Golden Ass* (translated by William Adlington, 1566) and in the well-known story of the ass's ears bestowed by Phoebus Apollo on King Midas for his presumption. Perhaps the most suggestive possible source for Shakespeare's clownish actors, however, is Anthony Munday's play *John a Kent and John a Cumber* (c. 1587–1590). In it a group of rude artisans, led by the intrepid Turnop, stage a ludicrous interlude written by their churchwarden in praise of his millhorse. Turnop's prologue is a medley of lofty comparisons. The entertainment is presented before noble spectators, who are graciously amused. *John a Kent* also features a lot of magic trickery, a boy named Shrimp whose role is comparable to that of Puck, and a multiple love plot.

"Pyramus and Thisbe" itself is based on the *Metamorphoses* (4.55 ff.). Other versions that Shakespeare may have known include Chaucer's *The Legend of Good Women*, a poem by William Griffith in 1562, George Pettie's *A Petite Palace of Pettie His Pleasure* (1576), *A Gorgeous Gallery of Gallant Inventions* (1578), and "A New Sonnet of Pyramus and Thisbe" from Clement Robinson's *A Handful of Pleasant Delights* (1584). Several of these, especially the last three, are bad enough to have given Shakespeare materials to lampoon, though the sweep of his parody goes beyond the particular story of Pyramus and Thisbe. The occasionally stilted phraseology of Golding's translation of the *Metamorphoses* contributed to the fun. According to Kenneth Muir (*Shakespeare's Sources*, 1957), Shakespeare must also have known Thomas Mouffet's *Of the Silkworms and Their Flies* (published 1599, but possibly circulated earlier in manuscript), which contains perhaps the most ridiculous of all versions of the Pyramus and Thisbe story. Shakespeare also appears to have been spoofing the inept dramatic style and lame verse of English dramas of the 1560s, 1570s, and 1580s, especially in their treatment of tragic sentiment and high emotion; *Cambises*, *Damon and Pythias*, and *Appius and Virginia* are examples.

The Merchant of Venice

Shakespeare's probable chief source for *The Merchant of Venice* was the first story of the fourth day of *Il Pecorone (The Dunce)*, by Ser Giovanni Fiorentino. This collection of tales dates from the late fourteenth century but was first published in 1558 at Milan and was not published in English translation in Shakespeare's time. If Shakespeare was unable to read it in Italian, he may conceivably have consulted a translation in some now-lost manuscript; such translations did sometimes circulate. Behind Ser Giovanni's story lies an old tradition of a bond given for human flesh, as found in Persia, India, and the Twelve Tables of Roman Law. This legend first appears in English in the thirteenth-century *Cursor Mundi*, with a Jew as the creditor. A thirteenth-century version of the *Gesta Romanorum* (a popular collection of stories in Latin) adds a romantic love plot; the evil moneylender in this story is not Jewish. The hero pawns his own flesh to a merchant in order to win a lady. He succeeds on his third attempt, having learned to avoid a magic spell that had previously put him to sleep and cost him a large number of florins. When he goes to pay his forfeit, the lady follows him disguised as a knight, and foils the evil merchant by pointing out a quibbling distinction between flesh and blood.

Il Pecorone provided Shakespeare with a number of essential elements, although not all that he has included. Ser Giovanni's story tells of Giannetto, the adventurous youngest son of a Florentine merchant, who goes to live with his father's dearest friend, Ansaldo, in Venice. This worthy merchant gives him money to seek his fortune at sea. Unbeknownst to Ansaldo, Giannetto twice risks everything to woo the lady of Belmont: if he can succeed in sleeping with her, he will win her and her country, but, if he fails, he loses all his wealth. Twice Giannetto is given a sleeping medicine and has to forfeit everything. Returning destitute to Venice twice, he is reunited each time with Ansaldo and given the means to seek his fortune again. For the third such voyage, however, Ansaldo is driven to borrow ten thousand florins from a Jew, using the forfeiture of a pound of flesh as a guarantee. This time, one of the lady's maids warns Giannetto not to drink his wine, and he finally possesses the lady as his wife. Sometime later, remembering that the day of Ansaldo's forfeiture has arrived, Giannetto explains the predicament to his wife and is sent by her to Venice with a hundred thousand florins, but he arrives after the forfeiture has fallen due. The lady, however, following after him in the disguise of a doctor of laws, decrees that the Jew may have no blood and must take no more or no less than one pound of flesh. The Jew is jeered at and receives no money. The "doctor of laws" refuses any payment other than the ring Giannetto was given by his lady. Giving it up unwillingly, he returns to Belmont, where his lady vexes him about the ring but finally relents and tells him all. Shakespeare could thus have found in one source the wooing, the borrowing from a Jewish moneylender, the pound of flesh, the trial, and the business of the rings. The story provides no casket episode, courtship of Nerissa by Gratiano, elopement of Jessica, or clowning of Lancelot Gobbo. The Jew's motive is not prompted by the way he has been treated.

Shakespeare may also have known "The Ballad of Gernutus," a popular English work that seems to be older than the play. It has no love plot but dwells on the unnatural cruelty of a Jewish Venetian usurer who takes a bond of flesh for "a merry jest." Anthony Munday's prose *Zelauto* (1580), though its villain is a Christian rather than a Jewish moneylender, also features a bond of this sort, taken purportedly as a mere sport but with hidden malice. Truculento, the villain, takes the bond of two young men, Rodolfo and his friend Strabino, as surety for a loan. If they forfeit the loan, the young men are to lose their lands and their right eyes as well. The villain has a daughter, Brisana, whom he permits to marry Rodolfo, since Truculento expects to marry Rodolfo's sister Cornelia himself. When Cornelia instead marries Strabino, Truculento angrily takes the young men to court to demand his bond. The two brides disguise themselves as scholars and go to court, where they appeal for mercy and then foil Truculento by means of the legal quibble about blood.

Another possible source for the courtroom scene is *The Orator*, translated into English in 1596 from the French of Alexandre Sylvain. An oration, entitled "Of a Jew, who would for his debt have a pound of the flesh of a Christian," uses many specious arguments also employed by Shylock, and is forthrightly confuted in "The Christian's Answer."

Shylock's relationship to his daughter finds obvious earlier parallels in *Zelauto* and in Christopher Marlowe's play, *The Jew of Malta* (c. 1589), in which Barabas's daughter Abigail loves a Christian and ultimately renounces her faith. The actual elopement, however, is closer to the fourteenth story in Masuccio of Salerno's fifteenth-century *Il Novellino* (not published in English translation in Shakespeare's day).

The casket-choosing episode, not found in *Il Pecorone*, was a widespread legend, occurring, for example, in the story of *Barlaam and Josophat* (ninth-century Greek, translated into Latin by the thirteenth century), in Vincent of Beauvais's *Speculum Historiale*, in the *Legenda Aurea*, in Giovanni Boccaccio's *Decameron* (Day 10, Story 1), in John Gower's *Confessio Amantis*, and—closest to Shakespeare—in the *Gesta Romanorum* (translated into English in 1577 by Richard Robinson and "bettered" by him in 1595). In this last account, the choice is between a gold, silver, and lead casket, each with its own inscription. The first two inscriptions are like Shakespeare's; the third reads, "Thei that chese me, shulle fynde [in] me that God hathe disposid." The chooser, however, is a maiden, and she is not preceded by other contestants.

An old play called *The Jew* is referred to by Stephen Gosson in 1579 as containing "the greediness of worldly choosers, and bloody minds of usurers." Scholars have speculated that this was a source play for Shakespeare, but actually we have too little to go on to make a reliable judgment. Gosson was surely not referring to Robert Wilson's *The Three Ladies of London* (c. 1581) in any case, even though it is sometimes suggested as an analogue to *The Merchant of Venice*, for its Jewish figure, named Gerontus (compare Gernutus in the ballad), is an exemplary person. Besides, the probable date of this play is later than Gosson's remark.

Much Ado About Nothing

Shakespeare's probable chief source for the Hero-Claudio plot of *Much Ado* was the twenty-second story from the *Novelle* of Matteo Bandello (Lucca, 1554). A French translation by François de Belleforest, in his *Histoires Tragiques* (1569 edition), was available to Shakespeare, as was the Italian original. The story of the maiden falsely accused was, however, much older than the story by Bandello. Perhaps the earliest version that has been found is the Greek romance *Chaereas and Callirrhoe*, fourth or fifth century A.D., in which the hero Chaereas, warned by envious rivals of his wife's purported infidelity, watches at dusk while an elegantly attired stranger is admitted by the maid to the house where Callirrhoe lives. Chaereas rushes in and strikes mistakenly at his wife in the dark but is acquitted of murder when the maid confesses her part in a conspiracy to delude Chaereas. Callirrhoe is buried in a deathlike trance but awakens in time to be carried off by pirates. The story reappears in a fifteenth-century Spanish romance, *Tirante el Blanco*, in which the princess Blanche is courted seemingly by a repulsive black man. This Spanish version probably inspired the account in Canto 5 of Ludovico Ariosto's *Orlando Furioso* (1516), to which all subsequent Renaissance versions are ultimately indebted.

In Ariosto's account, as translated into English by Sir John Harington (1591), the narrator is Dalinda, maid to the virtuous Scottish princess Genevra. Dalinda tells how she has fallen guiltily in love with Polynesso, Duke of Albany, an evil man who often makes love to Dalinda in her mistress's rooms but who longs in fact to marry Genevra. Consequently, Polynesso arranges for Genevra's noble Italian suitor, Ariodante, and Ariodante's brother Lurcanio, to witness the Duke's ascent to Genevra's window by a rope ladder. The woman who admits the Duke is, of course, not Genevra but Dalinda disguised as her mistress, having been duped into believing that the Duke merely wishes to satisfy his craving for Genevra by making love to her image. Lurcanio publicly accuses the innocent Genevra and offers to fight anyone who defends her cause (compare Claudio's quarrel with Leonato). The evil Duke tries to get rid of Dalinda, but all is finally put to rights by Rinaldo (the hero of *Orlando Furioso*) and Ariodante. This account gives an unusually vivid motivation for the maid and the villain—a clearer motivation than in Shakespeare's play. A lost dramatic version, *Ariodante and Genevora*, was performed at the English court in 1583.

Shakespeare probably consulted not only Ariosto but also Edmund Spenser's *The Faerie Queene* (2.4), based on Ariosto. Spenser's emphasis is on the blind rage of Phedon, a young squire in love with Claribell. Phedon is tricked by his erstwhile friend Philemon and by Claribell's maid Pryene into believing Claribell false. Pryene's motive in dressing up as Claribell is to prove she is as beautiful as her mistress. When, after having slain Claribell for her supposed perfidy, Phedon learns the truth, he poisons Philemon and furiously pursues Pryene until he is utterly possessed by a mad frenzy.

Shakespeare's greatest debt is, however, to Bandello's story. In a number of details, the story is closer to Shakespeare's play than are those already discussed. Several names are substantially the same as in Shakespeare: the location is Messina, the father of the slandered bride is Lionato di' Lionati (compare Shakespeare's Leonato), and her lover is in the service of King Piero of Aragon (compare Don Pedro of Aragon). As in Shakespeare, a young knight (named Sir Timbreo) seeks the hand in marriage of his beloved (Fenicia) through the matchmaking offices of a noble emissary. The complication of this wooing is somewhat different in that Timbreo's friend Girondo also falls in love with Fenicia, but Girondo then plots with a mischief-loving courtier (resembling Shakespeare's Don John) to poison Timbreo's mind against Fenicia, and Girondo thereupon escorts Timbreo to a garden, where they see Girondo's servant, elegantly dressed, enter Fenicia's window. No maid takes part in the ruse, however, nor indeed is any woman seen at the window. When Fenicia is wrongly accused, she falls into a deathlike trance and is pronounced dead by a doctor, but she is revived. Her father, believing in her innocence, sends her off to a country retreat and circulates the report that she is, in fact, dead. Soon both Timbreo and Girondo are stricken with remorse, Timbreo magnanimously spares his friend's life, and both confess the truth to Fenicia's family. A year later, Timbreo marries a wife chosen for him by Lionato who turns out, of course, to be Fenicia. Girondo marries her sister Belfiore. This account does not provide any equivalent for Beatrice and Benedick. Shakespeare enhances the Friar's role and provides a brother for Leonato. Claudio and Leonato are of comparable social station in Shakespeare, whereas Bandello makes a point of Timbreo's superior social rank.

A lost play, *Panecia* (1574–1575), may have been based on Bandello's work. One other version Shakespeare may have known is George Whetstone's *The Rock of Regard* (1576), based on Ariosto and Bandello. It contains a suggestive parallel to Claudio's rejection of Hero in church. Various Italian plays in the tradition of Luigi Pasqualigo's *Il Fedele* (1579), and also a version perhaps by Anthony Munday, *Fedele and Fortunio* (published 1585), are analogous in situation, though Shakespeare need not have known any of them.

For the Beatrice-Benedick plot, no source has been discovered, apart from Shakespeare's own earlier fascination with wit-combat and candid wooing in *Love's Labor's Lost* and *The Taming of the Shrew*. Nor has a plausible source been found for Dogberry and the watch.

The Merry Wives of Windsor

The Merry Wives of Windsor is indebted to no single source that combines the various elements found in the play: the courtship of Anne Page, the hoodwinking of Falstaff by the merry wives, the horse-stealing business, and the various "humors" portraits. Nor does any one element derive from a single source. The entire play is brilliantly improvised.

Many analogues exist to the courtship of Anne Page, for it is essentially a plot in which parents and unwelcome wooers are outwitted by resourceful young people. The Bianca-Lucentio plot of Shakespeare's own *The Taming of the Shrew* is a good enough instance. Similarly, analogues have been found to the discomfiture of Falstaff. In Ser Giovanni Fiorentino's *Il Pecorone* (Day 1, Novella 2), for example, a student twice cuckolds the very professor who is instructing him in the art of love. Comically, the student reports back to the professor at every turn and is coached in his next move. He doesn't know that the lady is the professor's wife, but the professor begins to suspect and so follows after. On the first occasion, the student escapes detection by hiding under a pile of newly washed linen. The second time, he slips out the door, whereupon the neighbors arrive and, finding no intruder, berate the professor for his mad suspicions. The wife's brothers even search the linen pile at the professor's suggestion but find nothing. They thrash the professor and chain him up as a madman. Next day, intending once again to report to the professor what has happened, the student discovers the truth. This version differs markedly from Shakespeare's in that the husband is the chief comic butt. Nevertheless, Shakespeare may have known it. Although *Il Pecorone* (1558) is not known to have been translated into English in the sixteenth century, Shakespeare had already used it (or some now-lost manuscript translation) as his chief source for *The Merchant of Venice*.

Certainly available to Shakespeare was a similar story, "Two Lovers of Pisa," from *Tarlton's News Out of Purgatory* (1590). In this story, the husband is again the one who is duped. An old doctor, wedded to a beautiful young wife, becomes by chance the confidential adviser of a young man who has fallen in love with the wife. The young man reports to the husband his plans and successes in detail. The lover thrice escapes detection (when warned by the lady's maid of the husband's approach) by hiding in a vat of feathers, in a false ceiling, and in an old chest full of legal documents. When on the third occasion the jealous husband sets fire to his own house, the lover is saved by the husband's order to carry out the chest of documents. At last, the lover reveals his knowledge of the husband's identity, and everyone laughs at the old fool. Elsewhere, Tarlton's book has suggestive references to Robin Goodfellow and other prankish spirits that may have influenced the concluding scene of *The Merry Wives of Windsor*.

The story "Of Two Brethren and Their Wives" in *Riche His Farewell to Military Profession* (1581) features two wives: one of "light disposition" and much given to adultery, and the other a tedious scold. The first wife desires to rid herself of her two erstwhile lovers, a doctor and a lawyer, in order to enjoy a new liaison with a soldier, Accordingly, she pretends to encourage the lawyer's advances, but when the lawyer comes to her she feigns the approach of her husband and enjoins the lawyer to hide in a large mailbag. Meanwhile, the merry wife has arranged for the doctor to come and pick up the mailbag, on the assumption that she will be hiding in it. The doctor thus carries off the lawyer, nearly suffocating from his close confinement, into the country, where the doctor expects to enjoy his rendezvous. Instead, the soldier accosts them, cudgeling first the body in the bag and then the one who has done the laborious carrying. The lawyer is no less astonished to discover where he has arrived than is the doctor to discover what he has been carrying.

For the background of Shakespeare's horse-stealing episodes and "humors" portraits, see the Introduction to the play. The explicit comparison between Falstaff's ludicrous fate in Windsor Forest and the legend of Actaeon is ultimately indebted to Ovid's *Metamorphoses* (3, 150–304 in Arthur Golding's translation, 1567). In this account, Actaeon, grandson of Cadmus and a mighty hunter, happens to disturb Diana and her nymphs while they are bathing naked. Transformed by the vengeful Diana into a horned stag, he is hunted to death by his own hounds.

As You Like It

Shakespeare's chief source for *As You Like It* was Thomas Lodge's graceful pastoral romance, *Rosalynde: Euphues' Golden Legacy* (1590). Lodge was indebted in turn to *The Tale of Gamelyn*, a fourteenth-century poem wrongly included by some medieval scribes as "The Cook's Tale" in Chaucer's *Canterbury Tales. Gamelyn* was not printed until 1721, but Lodge clearly had access to a manuscript of it. Although Shakespeare may not have known *Gamelyn* directly, his play still retains the hearty spirit of this Robin Hood legend. (In later Robin Hood ballads, Gamelyn or Gandelyn is identified with Will Scarlet, a member of Robin Hood's band.)

Even a brief account of *Gamelyn* suggests how greatly the original tale is inspired by Robin Hood legends of outlaws valiantly defying the corrupt social order presided over by the Sheriff and his henchmen. Gamelyn, the youngest of three brothers, is denied his inheritance by his churlish eldest brother John. When Gamelyn demands his rights, John orders his men to beat Gamelyn, but the young man arms himself with a pestle and proves to be a formidable fighter. After defeating the champion wrestler in a local wrestling match (a lower-class sport befitting the social milieu of this story), Gamelyn returns home to find himself locked out by his brother. He kills the porter, flings the man's body down a well, and feasts his companions day and night for a week. John feigns a reconciliation and slyly asks if he can bind Gamelyn hand and foot merely to satisfy an oath he has sworn over the death of the porter. Gamelyn trustingly agrees and is made prisoner. After his bonds have been secretly loosed by Adam the Spencer (the steward), Gamelyn pretends to remain bound until the propitious moment for revenge and escape. The moment arrives during a feast of monks who churlishly refuse to help Gamelyn. With Adam's help, he fells many of them, ties up his brother, and escapes to the woods, where he and Adam are rescued from hunger by a band of merry outlaws. As their chief, Gamelyn becomes a champion of the poor and an enemy of rich churchmen. His brother, now sheriff, brands Gamelyn an outlaw and manages to imprison him, but Gamelyn's second brother, Sir Ote, stands bail for him. On the day of the trial, Gamelyn frees Sir Ote and hangs the sheriff and the jury. Gamelyn finally obtains his inheritance and becomes chief officer of the King's royal forests. This story is uninfluenced by the pastoral tradition and contains no love plot. Its Robin Hood traditions are very much present, nonetheless, in Shakespeare's contrasting portrayal of a tyrannical court and of a just society in banishment.

Lodge retains the primitive vigor of *Gamelyn* but adds generous infusions of pastoral sentiment in the manner of Sir Philip Sidney's *Arcadia* (1590) and sententious moralizing in the manner of John Lyly's *Euphues* (1578). The pastoralism is presented in conventional terms, with none of the genial self-reflexive satire we find in Shakespeare. Psychological motive is intricate, often more so than in Shakespeare's play. The style is also heavily influenced by Lyly's exquisitely balanced, antithetical, and ornamented prose. For his pastoralism, Lodge was indebted not only to Sidney but also to the ancient pastoral tradition that included the Greek Theocritus and the Roman Virgil, the Italian Sannazaro (*Arcadia*), and the Portuguese Jorge de Montemayor (*Diana*). Pastoralism by Lodge's time had become thoroughly imbued with artificial conventions: abject lovers writing sonnets to their disdainful mistresses, princes and princesses in shepherds' disguise, idealized landscapes, stylized debate as to the relative merits of love and friendship, youth and age, city life and country life, and so on. Some of these conventions were derived also from the vogue of sonneteering pioneered by Francesco Petrarch and can thus be described as the stereotypes of "Petrarchism." Lodge accepts these conventions and gives us typical pastoral lovers even in his hero and heroine, although the elements he derived from *Gamelyn* certainly add a contrasting note of violence and danger.

Lodge's account begins much like that of *Gamelyn*. Saladyne, the envious eldest brother, bribes the champion wrestler to do away with Rosader (Orlando) in the wrestling match. Rosader succeeds instead in killing the wrestler and in winning the heart of Rosalynde, daughter of the banished King Gerismond. When she sends him a jewel, Rosader is not at all at a loss for words; indeed, he composes a Petrarchan sonnet on the spot. The usurping King Torismond (no relation to Gerismond), despite his evil nature, is impressed by Rosader's grace and martial prowess. Rosader returns home with friends, breaks open the door, and feasts his company. The wily Saladyne overwhelms Rosader in his sleep and binds him to a post, but Rosader is untied by Adam and makes havoc among the eldest brother's guests, as in *Gamelyn*. In this case, however, the guests are Saladyne's kindred and allies, all of whom have refused to help Rosader. The sheriff tries to arrest Rosader and Adam, but they make good their escape to the Forest of Arden in France. They are saved from starvation by the kindly King Gerismond and his exiled followers. Rosalynde and King Torismond's daughter Alinda meanwhile have been banished from court and have taken abode in the forest under the names of Ganymede and Aliena. They befriend old Corydon (Corin) and young Montanus (Silvius), who is hopelessly in love with the haughty Phoebe. "Ganymede" poses as a woman to test Rosader in his wooing, and they are joined in a mock marriage. Saladyne, now repenting of his evil deeds, comes to the forest, is saved by his brother from a lion, and falls in love with Alinda (whom he helps to rescue from ruffians). The denouement is as in Shakespeare, although the triumphant return to society is more complete: King Torismond is slain, Gerismond is restored to his throne, Rosader is named heir-apparent, and all the friends are appropriately rewarded.

Despite Shakespeare's extensive indebtedness to this charming romance, there is a crucial difference: Lodge's pastoral world is never subjected to a wry or satirical exploration. Lodge offers no equivalent for Touchstone, the fool who sees the absurdity of both country and city; Jaques, the malcontent traveler; William and Audrey, the clownishly simple peasants; or Sir Oliver Martext, the ridiculous hedge-priest. Nor does Lodge tell of Le Beau, the court butterfly. Hymen is a Shakespearean addition, and the conversion of Duke Frederick by a hermit instead of his being overthrown and killed is a characteristically Shakespearean softening touch. Shakespeare's added characters are virtually all foils to the conventional pastoral vision he found in his source.

Twelfth Night

John Manningham's description of a performance of *Twelfth Night* on February 2, 1602, at the Middle Temple (one of the Inns of Court, where young men studied law in London), compares the play to Plautus's *Menaechmi* and to an Italian play called *Inganni*. The comment offers a helpful hint on sources. The *Menaechmi* had been the chief source for Shakespeare's earlier play, *The Comedy of Errors*, and that farce of mistaken identity clearly resembles *Twelfth Night* in the hilarious mix-ups resulting from the confusion of two look-alike twins. Shakespeare certainly profited from his earlier experimenting with this sort of comedy. *Twelfth Night* is not necessarily directly indebted to the *Menaechmi*, however, for Renaissance Italian comedy offered many imitations of Plautus from which Shakespeare could have taken his *Twelfth Night* plot. These include *Gl'Inganni* (1562) by Nicolò Secchi, another *Gl'Inganni* (1592) by Curzio Gonzaga, and, most important, an anonymous *Gl'Ingannati* (published 1537).

This last play was translated into French by Charles Estienne as *Les Abusés* (1543) and adapted into Spanish by Lope de Rueda in *Los Engaños* (1567). A Latin version, *Laelia*, based on the French, was performed at Cambridge in the 1590s but never printed. Obviously, *Gl'Ingannati* was widely known, and Manningham was probably referring to it in his diary. To trace Shakespeare's own reading in this matter is difficult, owing to the large number of versions available to him, but we can note the suggestive points of comparison in each.

Both *Inganni* plays feature a brother and a sister mistaken for one another. In the later play (by Gonzaga), the sister uses the disguise name of "Cesare." In Secchi's *Inganni*, the disguised sister is in love with her master, who is told that a woman the exact age of his supposed page is secretly in love with him. Another play by Secchi, *L'Interesse* (1581), has a comic duel involving a disguised heroine. Of the Italian plays considered here, however, *Gl'Ingannati* is closest to Shakespeare's play. A short prefatory entertainment included with it in most editions features the name Malevolti. In the play itself, the heroine, Lelia, disguises herself as a page in the service of Flaminio, whom she secretly loves, and is sent on embassies to Flaminio's disdainful mistress Isabella. This lady falls in love with "Fabio," as Lelia calls herself. Lelia's father, Virginio, learning of her disguise and resolving to marry her to old Gherardo (Isabella's father), seeks out Lelia but instead mistakenly arrests her long-lost twin brother, Fabrizio, who has just arrived in Modena. Fabrizio is locked up as a madman in Isabella's room, whereupon Isabella takes the opportunity to betroth herself to the person she mistakes for "Fabio." A recognition scene clears up everything and leads to the marriages of Fabrizio to Isabella and Flaminio to Lelia. This story lacks the subplot of Malvolio, Sir Toby, *et al.* Nor is there a shipwreck.

Matteo Bandello based one of the stories in his *Novelle* (1554) on *Gl'Ingannati*, and this prose version was then translated into French by François de Belleforest in his *Histoires Tragiques* (1579 edition). Shakespeare may well have read both, for he consulted these collections of stories in writing *Much Ado About Nothing*. His most direct source, however, seems to have been the story of "Apollonius and Silla" by Barnabe Riche (an English soldier and fiction writer), in *Riche His Farewell to Military Profession* (1581), which was derived from Belleforest. Riche involves his characters in more serious moral predicaments than Shakespeare allows in his festive comedy. The plot situation is much the same: Silla (the equivalent of Shakespeare's Viola) is washed ashore near Constantinople, where, disguised as "Silvio," she takes service with a duke, Apollonius (Shakespeare's Orsino), and goes on embassies to the wealthy widow Julina (Shakespeare's Olivia), who proceeds at once to fall in love with "Silvio." When Silla's twin brother, the real Silvio, arrives, he is mistaken by Julina for his twin and is invited to a rendezvous, like Shakespeare's Sebastian. The differences at this point are marked, however, for Silvio becomes Julina's lover and leaves her pregnant when he departs the next day on his quest for Silla. Apollonius is understandably furious to learn of "Silvio's" apparent success with Julina and throws his page into prison. Julina is no less distressed when she learns that the supposed father of her child is in actuality a woman. Only Silvio's eventual return to marry Julina resolves these complications. Shakespeare eschews the pregnancy, the desertion, the imprisonment, and all of Riche's stern moralizing about the bestiality of lust that accompanies this lurid tale. Moreover, he adds the plot of Malvolio, for which Riche provides little suggestion. Shakespeare changes the location to Illyria, with its hint of delirium and illusion, and provides an English flavor in the comic scenes that intensifies the festive character of the play.

Shakespeare's reading may also have included the anonymous play *Sir Clyomon and Sir Clamydes* (c. 1570–1583), Sir Philip Sidney's *Arcadia* (1590), and Emmanuel Forde's prose romance *Parismus* (1598), in which one "Violetta" borrows the disguise of a page. Scholars have suggested that the Malvolio plot may reflect an incident at Queen Elizabeth's court in which the Comptroller of the Household, Sir William Knollys, interrupted a noisy late-night party dressed in only his nightshirt and a pair of spectacles, with a copy of the Italian pornographic writer Aretino's work in his hand. A similar confrontation between revelry and sobriety occurred in 1598: Ambrose Willoughby quieted a disturbance after the Queen had gone to bed and was afterward thanked by her for doing his duty. Such incidents were no doubt common, however, and there is no compelling reason to suppose Shakespeare was sketching from current court gossip.

All's Well That Ends Well

Shakespeare's only known source for *All's Well That Ends Well* is the tale of Giglietta of Nerbone from Boccaccio's *Decameron* (c. 1348–1358), as translated into English by William Painter in *The Palace of Pleasure* (1566, 1575). Painter may have based his translation on a French intermediary by Antoine le Maçon, and Shakespeare possibly knew the Italian and French versions, although the English was the most available to him. All three are essentially the same, except for the forms of the proper names. The Helena story is also widely dispersed in folktales.

In Painter's account, Giletta is the daughter of Gerardo of Narbona, physician to the ailing Count of Rossiglione. Giletta falls in love with the Count's son, Beltramo. When the Count dies, Beltramo is "left under the royal custody of the King" and is sent to Paris. Giletta's father dies soon after, and she, refusing many favorable offers of marriage, journeys to Paris and cures the King of a fistula. The King has promised her any husband as her reward but is loath to give her Beltramo. The young man, no less reluctant, goes through with the marriage ceremony but then escapes into Italy before the marriage is consummated. In Italy he joins the Florentines in a military campaign against the Senois (Sienese). His deserted wife, now countess, returns home and governs the domain of Rossiglione with great skill. When she writes to Beltramo, offering to depart if her presence displeases him, Beltramo sets for her the "impossible" demand of obtaining his ring and begetting a son by him. Hereupon she calls together the leaders of her domain and announces her intention of going on a pilgrimage of renunciation. Despite her people's great lamentation, she departs for Florence where she inquires after Beltramo and discovers that he is paying court to a poor gentlewoman (unnamed) who dwells with her mother. Giletta offers to obtain a dowry for this daughter if she will demand the ring from Beltramo and arrange an assignation so that Giletta may secretly take her place in Beltramo's bed. Beltramo reluctantly agrees to give up the cherished ring, and Giletta becomes his lover on not one but numerous occasions. When she is pregnant, she rewards the daughter with a dowry and then remains living in Florence until she is delivered of two sons. Beltramo has meanwhile been called home by his people. Giletta arrives home in time for a great feast, at which she prostrates herself before Beltramo and proves that she has performed the terms of his "impossible" task. Beltramo is persuaded by her constancy and wit to be true to his promise and reclaim her as his wife.

Except for Helena, many of the characters' names in Shakespeare's play are derived from Painter's version. Helena is Giletta in Painter, but her father is Gerardo of Narbona (compare Shakespeare's Gerard de Narbon or Narbonne), and the young man she vainly loves is Beltramo, Count of Rossiglione (i.e., Bertram, Count of Rossillion), who is left after his father's death as a ward in the custody of the King of France. Giletta is no ward and helpless dependent, however, as in Shakespeare; she is well-to-do, is cared for by her kinsfolk after her father's death, and refuses many favorable offers of marriage before journeying to Paris to cure the King of a fistula and claim her reward. Shakespeare's Helena, on the other hand, is not rich and so can serve as an example of innate virtue or "gentleness," in contrast with Bertram's hereditary nobility. Shakespeare enhances the roles of the Countess and Lafew, and makes the King more sympathetic than in Painter to Helena's (or Giletta's) cause: in Painter, the King is reluctant to give Giletta to Beltramo, whereas in Shakespeare the King becomes a spokesman for faith in the miraculous. Other courtiers in Shakespeare's play join the King in approving of Helena, so that, however much Bertram's resistance to an enforced marriage might seem understandable in most circumstances, his refusal of Helena is made to appear willful. Lavatch, the Countess's fool, quizzically expounds questions of moral consequence that are absent in Painter. Conversely, the added character Parolles highlights the callowness and insensitivity of Bertram, and serves as a scapegoat when Bertram belatedly gains a better understanding of himself. At the same time, Shakespeare eschews Painter's easy romantic ending for one that is highly problematic: he does not offer Bertram much opportunity to show a real change of heart toward Helena, as Painter does, and thus places a greater strain on credibility in this comedy of forgiveness. Helena, because she is so far below Bertram in wealth and position, is obliged to be more aggressive than her counterpart in Painter, which raises troublesome issues of female assertiveness. She does not enjoy Giletta's prerogative of governing Rossiglione in her husband's absence and winning such love from her advisers and subjects that they all lament her public resolution to go on a pilgrimage; Helena is thrown more on her own resources and so is at once more self-reliant and self-asserting.

Another possible though minor source is the epic romance *Girart de Roussillon* set in the ninth-century Burgundian court, featuring a scene of forced marriage and an atmosphere of chivalric glory. Shakespeare may also have been thinking of the *Chanson de Roland.* Parolles's interchange with Helena in 1.1 on virginity closely resembles Donne's Paradox, "That Virginity Is a Virture," written in the 1590s.

Shakespeare gives his play a unity of construction and an economy of time not found in the sources. Characters such as the King and Diana are not discarded once their primary role has been discharged but are brought importantly into the denouement. As in his use of other Italianate fictional sources, Shakespeare compresses time: for example, Helena vows to cure the King in two days rather than eight (as in Painter), and Helena sleeps with Bertram once rather than often. No convincing source has been found for the comic exposure of Parolles.

Measure for Measure

Stories about corrupt magistrates are ancient and universal, but Shakespeare's particular story in *Measure for Measure* seems to go back to an actual incident in the sixteenth-century Italian court of Don Ferdinando de Gonzaga. A Hungarian student named Joseph Macarius, writing from Vienna, tells about an Italian citizen accused of murder whose wife submitted to the embraces of the magistrate in hopes of saving her husband. When the magistrate executed her husband despite her having fulfilled her bargain, she appealed to the Duke, who ordered the magistrate to give her a dowry and marry her. Thereafter, the Duke ordered the magistrate to be executed. This incident seems to have inspired a Senecan drama by Claude Rouillet called *Philanira* (1556), a French translation of this play (1563), a novella in the *Hecatommithi* of G. B. Giraldi Cinthio (1565), and a play by Cinthio called *Epitia* (posthumously published in 1583). Shakespeare may have known both the prose and the dramatic versions by Cinthio.

In Cinthio's story, the wise Emperor Maximian appoints his friend Juriste to govern Innsbruck, warning him to rule justly or expect no mercy from the Emperor. Juriste rules long and well, to the satisfaction of his master and the people of Innsbruck. When a young man named Vico is brought before him for ravishing a virgin, Juriste assigns the mandatory sentence of death. Vico's sister, Epitia, an extraordinarily beautiful virgin of eighteen, pleads for Vico's life, urging that his deed was one of passion and that he stands ready to marry the girl he forced. The judge, secretly inflamed with lust for Epitia, promises to consider the matter carefully. She reports this seemingly encouraging news to Vico, who urges her to persevere. When, however, the judge proposes to take her chastity in return for her brother's life, Epitia is mortified and refuses unless Juriste will marry her. During another interim in these negotiations, Vico begs his sister to save his life at any cost. She then submits to Juriste on the condition that he will both marry her and spare Vico. Next morning, however, the jailer brings her the body of her decapitated brother. She lays her complaint before the Emperor, who confronts Juriste with his guilt. Conscience-stricken, Juriste confesses and begs for mercy. At first, Epitia demands strict justice, but when the Emperor compels Juriste to marry her and then be beheaded, she reveals "her natural kindness" and begs successfully for the life of her wronger. There are several important differences between this account and Shakespeare's play: Vico is actually killed, unlike Claudio, and Epitia sleeps with Juriste and then is married to him. No equivalent to Mariana appears, or to Lucio, Pompey, Mistress Overdone, Elbow, and other characters in the comic scenes of Shakespeare's play. No duke oversees the career of Juriste and ensures that no fatal wrong will occur.

Shakespeare may also have consulted Cinthio's play *Epitia*, but his chief source was George Whetstone's two-part play *Promos and Cassandra* (1578) and a novella on the same subject. In the English play, the corrupt judge is Promos, administrator of the city of Julio under the King of Hungary. The law forbidding adultery has lain in abeyance for some years when a young gentleman named Andrugio is arrested and condemned for "incontinency." His sister Cassandra, like Epitia in Cinthio's play, lays down her precious chastity to Promos in response to her brother's piteous entreaties. Promos gives his assurance that he will marry her and save Andrugio's life. When Promos instead treacherously orders the execution of Andrugio, the jailer secretly substitutes the head of a felon, newly executed and so mutilated as to be unrecognizable even by Cassandra. (This rescue is seen as an intervention "by the providence of God.") The King sentences Promos, just as the Emperor sentences Juriste in Cinthio's play, but in Whetstone's play the King refuses Cassandra's pleas for the life of her new husband until Andrugio reveals himself to be still alive and offers to die for Promos. The King forgives Andrugio on condition that he marry Polina, whom he has wronged. The play also features a courtesan named Lamia and her man, Rosko, who ingratiate themselves with the corrupt officer (Phallax) in charge of investigating their case. Phallax is ultimately caught and dismissed from office while Lamia is publicly humiliated.

Whetstone wrote a prose novella of this same story in the *Heptameron of Civil Discourses* (1582). Shakespeare appears to have consulted it as well as the play, for the prose version mentions the names of Isabella (as the narrator of the story) and Crassus (compare *Measure for Measure*, 4.5.8), and the King's awarding of measure for measure in his sentencing of Promos—"You shall be measured with the grace you bestowed on Andrugio"—may have given Shakespeare an idea for the title of his play. Shakespeare was also indebted for a few details to a version in Thomas Lupton's *Too Good to Be True* (1581).

Even though Shakespeare's play is closely related to Whetstone's play and novella, Shakespeare has changed much. He adds the motif of the Duke's mysterious disguise. (A not very compelling analogue to this motif occurs in Sir Thomas Elyot's *The Image of Governance*, 1541.) Shakespeare introduces the use of the bed trick, found also in his presumably earlier play *All's Well That Ends Well*. Most important, Shakespeare stresses the moral and legal complexity of his story. Isabella is about to renounce the world by entering a convent. By contrast, Lucio, a Shakespearean addition, is an engaging cynic, hedonist, and slanderer. Claudio, although guilty of fornication, is only technically in violation of the laws against sexual license. Isabella does not surrender her chastity. Her breakdown in the scene with Claudio intensifies her emotional crisis and renders all the more triumphant her final ability to forgive Angelo. Angelo himself is made puritanical in temperament and is spared the actual consequences of his worst intentions so that he can be worthy of being forgiven. Isabella need not marry Angelo, since he has not actually seduced her; she is thus free to marry the Duke. No felon need be executed in Claudio's stead, for Providence provides a natural death in the prison. In the subplot, going well beyond the merest hints in Whetstone, Pompey is a brilliantly original innovation, Elbow a characteristically Shakespearean clown modeled on the earlier Dogberry of *Much Ado About Nothing*, and Escalus a significant spokesman for a moderate and practical course of equity in the law.

Troilus and Cressida

Shakespeare had access to Homer for information about the Trojan War, since George Chapman's translation of *Seven Books of the Iliads of Homer* had appeared in 1598, and earlier English translations of parts of the *Iliad* were also available. Shakespeare ends his play with the death of Hector, as do Homer and some post-Homeric historians of the war, and portrays Achilles as a figure in tragic conflict with his sense of pride, as did Homer. Thersites and Nestor are based ultimately on the *Iliad*. Ajax's ludicrous boastfulness may owe something to Homer's Ajax Telamon, as well as to Ovid's account of the quarrel between Ulysses and Ajax over Achilles's armor (*Metamorphoses*, 12–13). Yet, for Shakespeare, and for most Englishmen of his time, the chief sources of information about the Trojan War were medieval romances. These were all pro-Trojan in their bias, since Englishmen traced their own mythic history to the lineage of Aeneas and tended to look on Homer as suspiciously pro-Greek. Medieval European culture generally was far more oriented to Roman than to Greek civilization; Greek texts went almost unread. In these circumstances, a pro-Trojan account of the war emerged and grew to considerable proportions, in which non-Homeric material became increasingly important.

The central work dealing with this expanded account of the war was Benoît de Sainte-Maure's *Roman de Troie* (c. 1160), a romance freely based on earlier accounts of two supposed eyewitnesses named Dictys the Cretan and Dares the Phrygian. Benoît not only narrates the war from Troy's point of view but introduces the love story of Troilus, "Breseida," and Diomedes. Benoît found a hint for this story in the *Iliad*, in which two Trojan maidens named Chryseis and Briseis are captured and given to Agamemnon and Achilles, respectively. When Chryseis's father calls down a plague on the Greeks for refusing to return Chryseis, Agamemnon reluctantly gives her up but then seizes Briseis from Achilles, thereby precipitating Achilles's angry retirement to his tent and all that disastrously follows. Benoît freely transforms this situation into the rivalry of Troilus and Diomed, who appear in Homer but in entirely different roles.

Benoît's *Roman de Troie* became the inspiration for subsequent medieval accounts of the Trojan War. Guido delle Colonne translated Benoît in his *Historia Troiana* (completed 1287). Giovanni Boccaccio based his *Il Filostrato* (c. 1338) on Guido and Benoît but made significant alterations: the love story became the focus of attention, and Pandarus assumed the important role of go-between. (In Homer, Pandarus is a fierce warrior.) Geoffrey Chaucer based his *Troilus and Criseyde* (c. 1385–1386) on Boccaccio, giving still greater attention to the states of mind of the two lovers and endowing Pandarus with a humorous disposition. Shakespeare certainly knew Chaucer's masterpiece. He also consulted, however, at least two other medieval accounts of the war: John Lydgate's *The History, Siege, and Destruction of Troy* (first printed 1513), based on Guido and Chaucer and known also as the *Troy Book*, and William Caxton's *The Recuyell of the Histories of Troy* (printed 1474, the first book printed in English), a translation from the French of Raoul Lefevre, who had followed Guido rather closely. In Caxton, for example, Shakespeare found materials for the Trojan debate in 2.2 and for Hector's visit to the Greek camp (4.5). In addition, Shakespeare was certainly familiar with the degeneration of Cressida's character since the time of Chaucer, as reflected for example in Robert Henryson's *The Testament of Cresseid* (published 1532), in which Cressida is punished for her faithlessness by leprosy and poverty.

Shakespeare pays a good deal more attention to the war than does Chaucer and portrays the lovers as caught in a conflict beyond their control. Shakespeare's Cressida is more sardonic and experienced in the ways of the world than is Chaucer's heroine, even though Chaucer's Criseyde is a widow and Shakespeare's Cressida is unmarried. The subtle and elaborate code of courtly love evoked by Chaucer has almost completely disappeared in Shakespeare's work, leaving in its wake a more dispiriting and cynical impression. Shakespeare's Troilus is still a faithful and earnest lover, as in Chaucer, but betrayed by his own chauvinistic ideals about honor and patriotism in a way that Chaucer's Troilus is not. Pandarus is more leering, giddy, vapid, and coarse than his Chaucerian counterpart. Diomedes is also changed for the worse, being more hard and cynical.

Among the non-Chaucerian characters, Achilles is made to appear more guilty and brutal than in Shakespeare's sources: Achilles orders his Myrmidons (i.e., his soldiers) to murder the unarmed Hector, even though Hector had previously spared Achilles in battle. Lydgate and Caxton report that Achilles's Myrmidons kill Troilus, not Hector (in Caxton, Achilles cuts off Troilus's head and then drags Troilus's body behind his horse), whereas in Homer Achilles kills Hector in battle and only then do his Myrmidons desecrate the body. Shakespeare refuses to glamorize the war, just as he refuses to glamorize the love story. He also compresses time, as he did with so many of his sources. The play begins only a short time before Cressida surrenders to Troilus; she is transferred to the Greeks immediately after she and Troilus become lovers; her surrender to Diomedes follows quickly after her transfer. This telescoping provides not only dramatic unity but also a sense of sudden and violent change.

Other plays on Troilus and Cressida are known to have existed in Shakespeare's time, such as a "new" play acted by the Admiral's men, an acting company, in 1596 and another by Thomas Dekker and Henry Chettle in 1599. Shakespeare may have known and even written in response to such productions by rival theatrical companies, but today nothing is known about these lost plays.

Appendix 3

Shakespeare in Performance

Lois Potter, University of Delaware

Although we know a good deal about the conditions of performance at the time Shakespeare's plays were first produced, much of this information (summarized in the Introduction, pp. xliv–xlvii) raises as many questions as it answers. We know, for example, that Shakespeare wrote most of his plays for the Lord Chamberlain's men, first formed in 1594 after a period of plague and theater closures, and that the company (officially servants of the courtier whose duties included supervising court entertainments) was honored with the title of the King's men at the accession of James I. Elizabethan acting companies were all male, with boys or young men playing women's roles, but we know almost nothing about how they acted, or who played which parts. We know that the stages of the public, partially roofed playhouses jutted into the yard where the audience stood on three sides, looking up at the actors; the rest of the spectators sat in covered galleries looking down on them. But we are not sure whether the gallery above the stage, pictured in the contemporary illustration of the Swan Theatre interior shown on page xlvi, was meant for musicians, spectators, or both. (And of course we do not know how much the Globe's interior resembled the Swan's.) If, as appears from the illustrations of theater interiors on pages xlvi and lxiv, some spectators normally watched the action from behind the stage, the actors would have had to move a great deal during a scene, as in modern theater-in-the-round productions, to make sure that they were visible and audible to all parts of their audience.

However much information we have, we still cannot know if aspects of the theater that were common then but unusual in our eyes were taken for granted by the spectators who watched the plays in the reigns of Elizabeth and James I. Did they think of the boy actresses as boys or believe in them as women? Those who had traveled to France and Italy would have known that women played women's parts in those countries and were often as famous as the male actors. What was the acting style for love scenes between a man and a cross-dressed boy, and what was the range of responses to it? The players in the open theaters performed by day (normally beginning at 2 P.M.), but used torches and candles to indicate when the action was supposed to be taking place at night. Did audiences find it difficult to accept a convention by which actors, fully visible to the audience, declare that they are unable to see anything? There is probably no single answer. It is likely that then, as always, audience members differed in the extent to which they preferred to believe in the performance or feel superior to it.

To the audiences of Shakespeare's time, the theaters were sumptuous and impressive buildings. Their wooden interiors were painted to look like marble, and the ceiling of the Globe was apparently decorated with the signs of the zodiac (perhaps, when Hamlet and Othello addressed the heavens, they looked at both a real and an artificial sky). Visitors from abroad were taken to see plays; actors traveled with them as far as Prague; versions of them were being translated into German as early as 1618. All this indicates how much English plays and players were respected. By about 1597, the company for which Shakespeare wrote was the one most frequently invited to perform at court, evidence that it was considered the best in London.

The theater in fact offered a great deal of visual and musical pleasure even for those who could not understand the language. Vast sums of money were spent on costumes. The most valuable surviving evidence, an account book of Philip Henslowe, manager of the Rose playhouse, shows that their bright or striking colors (often red and black, with silver and gold) allowed them to stand out on a stage that depended on daylight for most of its illumination. These were not "costumes" but clothes, sometimes bought in secondhand shops and sometimes donated or sold by gentlemen patrons. Characters normally wore contemporary dress, but with some indications of historical costume, like togas for classical characters (see the contemporary drawing, usually taken to be an illustration of *Titus Andronicus*, on p. lxi). Costumes and wigs, as well as false beards, were obviously important for a theater in which twelve to fourteen actors frequently doubled in as many as thirty roles. Music was frequently used in productions and a number of writers, including Shakespeare, incorporated popular contemporary songs into their plays. Robert Johnson, who is credited with the songs to a number of Jacobean plays, may have been the company's in-house composer. Some plays may have had as much music as a modern musical comedy, though very little of it has been identified.

Shakespeare's plays were designed to show off the actors' talents: singing, playing an instrument, dancing, and fencing. Most of his most popular plays end with either a dance or a fight, and nearly all of his tragic heroes (with the interesting exceptions of Othello and Antony) have at least one heroic fight scene. Since memorization and oratory were part of every grammar school education, audiences could recognize the superior memories of the actors who learned the long and complicated speeches that Shakespeare wrote for them. The combination of great actors and a dramatist who wrote great roles for them was attractive to other playwrights, and helped to ensure the company's continuing preeminence.

Shakespeare's practice of writing plays dominated by one very large starring role probably followed Richard Burbage's rise to stardom. Many contemporary references identify him with Richard III (see the anecdote on pp. lviii–lix), and he is also known to have played Romeo, Hamlet, Othello, and Lear. John Lowin, who joined the company in 1602–1603, seems to have partnered Burbage in plays with two substantial roles. Shakespeare was unusual in that he wrote equally well for tragic and comic actors, and for the company clown, a type of performer traditionally famous for his ad-libs. Will Kemp, the most famous comedian of his day, certainly created the role of Dogberry—his name accidentally replaces the character's in one quarto of the play. It is not absolutely certain that he played Falstaff, but his departure from the Lord Chamberlain's men in 1599 is often linked with Shakespeare's writing the character out of *Henry V* after having apparently promised (at the end of *2 Henry IV*) to include him in the sequel. Those who think that Shakespeare was in agreement with Hamlet's advice to the players ("Let those that play your clowns speak no more than is set down for them") wonder whether Kemp's inability to refrain from "speaking" led to friction with his leading playwright. Kemp's successor was Robert Armin, and it is often said that the more literary quality of Shakespeare's later fools resulted from their being tailored for the new actor.

Little is known about the other chief sharers in the company, though attempts have been made to identify them with, for example, references to exceptionally thin or exceptionally fat actors. It is not known whether any particular young actor inspired Shakespeare to write his best female roles, but many boys seem to have been good enough to have a personal following. A spectator who saw *Othello* in Oxford in 1610 mentions how moved the spectators were at the sight of Desdemona after her death.

It has often been suggested that Hamlet's insistence on naturalness, and the First Player's modest claim to have "reformed" the practice of overacting at least to some extent, reflect a perceived difference between the actors for whom Shakespeare wrote and the more melodramatic ones in the company led by Philip Henslowe and its leading actor Edward Alleyn. Yet Alleyn, who created the major Marlowe roles, was no less intelligent and talented than Burbage. It was Alleyn who retired early to live the life of a gentleman (in 1597, when he was only 31), with one brief comeback in 1601–1604. Burbage, on the other hand, went on acting up to his death at the age of 46, a fact that suggests a more theatrical personality than Alleyn's. If there was a movement toward greater naturalism in the 1590s, it probably resulted from greater professionalization and better training of actors, along with greater sophistication of the audiences themselves.

As the Lord Chamberlain's men grew more successful, they looked for a more select location. In 1597 James Burbage, Richard's father, purchased part of the disused monastic site of Blackfriars in the City of London. Protests from the local residents forced him to rent out the building to boys' companies (which performed less frequently) until, early in the reign of James I, times became more favorable. Finally moving into the new premises some time after 1607, the company was able to restrict its public to those who could afford the higher admission prices. In the indoor theaters, all the spectators were seated. Comfortable spectators cause less trouble than uncomfortable ones. The smaller size may have allowed for a more "realistic" style of playing. At the same time, the company continued to use the Globe throughout the period, as well as acting at court and elsewhere, so the actors must have been able to adapt their style to circumstances. In many ways, Shakespeare's last plays are his least "realistic," since they often involve magic, but the technology available in the Blackfriars playhouse may have made the magic convincing.

Besides, if realistic acting means acting that makes one forget that one is watching a play, it is unlikely that the drama was ever truly realistic. Other dramatists' allusions to Shakespeare are obviously meant to break the dramatic illusion: "What, Hamlet, are you mad?" asks a character in *Eastward Ho!* (1605), speaking to a servant who is named Hamlet only so that someone can ask him that question. Shakespeare himself also refers to his own plays. It is likely that the lovers' suicides in "Pyramus and Thisbe," performed at the end of *A Midsummer Night's Dream*, are meant as an absurd version of the end of *Romeo and Juliet*; Malvolio's madness, in *Twelfth Night*, probably parodies Hamlet's. Perhaps a comedy can make jokes about a tragedy without destroying the atmosphere, but *Hamlet* does the same thing. When Polonius tells Hamlet about playing Julius Caesar "at the university," and being killed by Brutus, many of their audience would remember that, not long before, the two actors speaking these lines had played Caesar and Brutus, respectively, in *Julius Caesar*.

The deaths of Shakespeare in 1616 and of Burbage in 1619 may have temporarily affected Shakespeare's theatrical popularity. Burbage was so much identified with the major roles that, according to one elegy, these characters seemed to have died with him. The Earl of Pembroke may have been typical when, in a letter, he expresses reluctance to go to the theater again. John Taylor, who replaced Burbage in 1619, inherited a number of his roles. He and Lowin led the company for the next twenty years, with first John Fletcher and then Philip Massinger as their leading dramatist. The company had been called the King's men since 1603, but the name was even more appropriate under Charles I than under his father, since the actors were much closer to the court. Taylor even served as acting coach to Queen Henrietta Maria and her ladies when they put on a pastoral tragicomedy in 1633.

Though not all Puritans or parliamentarians were hostile to the theater, and not all of Charles I's courtiers approved of it, the English civil war created a further association between theater and crown. Parliament closed the theaters at the start of the war in 1642, refusing to reopen them even when hostilities had ended. Performances continued nevertheless: professionals acted illegally in the theater buildings that were still usable, or, like amateurs, legally in private houses and inns. Some also went abroad and acted for English royalists in exile. Since the prohibition applied only to plays, scenes involving popular characters (Hamlet and the gravediggers, Falstaff, Bottom) were adapted and disguised as "drolls"—comic sketches—that could be performed in a mixed program of music, dance, and drama. The 1662 frontispiece to a collection of these drolls (p. lxiv) shows how Falstaff and Mrs. Quickly were probably costumed in this period.

The Restoration and the Eighteenth Century (1660–1776)

At the Restoration of 1660, one of Charles II's first acts was to establish two licensed acting companies, one patronized by him, the other by his brother the Duke of York. Each company was assigned a selection of plays from the prewar period. Shakespeare's were among the first to be revived; indeed, actors were already playing them in London before the new theaters had opened. Although one of the speakers in Dryden's dialogue on drama (*An Essay of Dramatic Poesy*, 1665) says that Beaumont and Fletcher's plays were more popular than Shakespeare's or Jonson's, the evidence indicates that Shakespeare went on being a frequently acted dramatist throughout this period. Since the King's company seems to have received preferential treatment, it is likely that the plays awarded to them—*1 Henry IV*, *The Merry Wives of Windsor*, and Othello—were the most popular of Shakespeare's works in 1660.

It was natural that Shakespeare's works would need updating; nearly fifty years after their author's death, their language, grammar, and jokes were already becoming obsolete. Audiences saw themselves as too refined for plays with clowns and devils. Both theater managers (Thomas Killigrew and William Davenant) had been playwrights before the war, and both produced the prewar drama with extensive alterations. *The Taming of the Shrew*, as produced in 1667 by the King's company under Killigrew, was called, improbably, *Sauny the Scot*, after the new comic servant who replaced Grumio; the actor John Lacy wrote the title role for himself, exploiting the anti-Scots feeling that had been exacerbated by the Civil War. "Scenes," or scenery, the norm in the theaters of France and Italy, had already been used in prewar masques, and in the 1630s Davenant had already been planning to open a theater equipped to use it for plays. As manager of the Duke's company, he set about revising old plays to create more possibilities for spectacle. His *The Law Against Lovers* (1662) conflated *Measure for Measure* and *Much Ado About Nothing*, neither of which was well known at the period. The result was an emphasis on the romantic part of both plays, as opposed to their low comedy. He added more music and scenery in his adaptations of *Macbeth* (1664) and *The Tempest* (1667); in later revivals, these two works became almost operatic. The new theaters were rather small, and actors still played at the front of the stage, with the wings and backdrop of the new scenery stretching away behind them. Scene changes could be made quickly by rolling away one sliding backdrop to reveal another one behind it, sometimes with a new set of characters already in place. The same painted wings and backdrop were expected to serve for a number of plays, acting as a kind of shorthand to distinguish indoor from outdoor settings. The idea that each play belonged to its own particular visual world did not gain currency until well into the nineteenth century.

Charles II had insisted, in his patent for the new theaters, that the custom of boy actors—unique to England—must end. Most of the women who became actresses during the early years of the Restoration were, inevitably, untrained. The famous Nell Gwyn, mistress of Charles II, was a star of the King's company. She was considered delightful in contemporary comedies, some of which were written especially for her; however, Pepys always insisted that she was disastrous in serious roles, and there is no record of her playing Shakespeare. The new actresses could exploit their natural gifts, their beauty, and their novelty, but no one wanted to see them in character parts, especially those of elderly women. As a result, roles like the witches in *Macbeth* were taken by men, often the company's low comedians, a practice that continued for centuries. The small number of parts for attractive young women in Shakespeare now became a problem. Davenant was skillful at multiplying them. He expanded the part of Lady Macduff; Miranda, no longer the only woman in *The Tempest*, acquired a naïve younger sister, while Caliban and Ariel were likewise paired off with a female monster and spirit respectively.

Some of these changes also had a moral purpose. Davenant balanced the wickedness of Macbeth and his Lady by developing the virtuous Macduffs as foils to them. He also gave Macbeth a death speech (only one line long) to show that the dying man recognized the vanity of his ambition. Later adaptations were still more concerned with "poetic justice." This term meant simply that art ought to reward virtue and punish vice, not because this is what happens in the real world, but because art's duty is to offer virtuous models whenever possible. John Dryden, who had worked with Davenant on *The Tempest*, later wrote free adaptations of both *Antony and Cleopatra* and *Troilus and Cressida*, in which the lovers, far from being unfaithful, are only sympathetic victims of misunderstanding. His version of *Antony and Cleopatra*, called *All for Love, or, the World Well Lost* (1675–1677), largely replaced its model for much of the next century, and was often played under Shakespeare's title. Though Dryden claimed that he had made Antony's wife Octavia a virtuous foil to Cleopatra, the play's success was due less to its superior morality (indeed, its most popular scene was one in which the two women insult each other) than to its simplification of the structure, which subordinated political history to the love story. Shadwell's *Timon of Athens* (1678) provided a faithful woman as well as a faithful steward, to contrast with the mercenary friends and mistress who desert the hero. Thomas Otway's *Caius Marius* (1679) made the suicides of Romeo and Juliet more acceptable by locating them in a classical world. One of Otway's other innovations—letting the heroine revive in time to converse with the hero before they die—was to outlast the adaptation itself. Nahum Tate's *King Lear* (1681) made the virtuous Cordelia a large and dramatic role, worthy of a star actress. He also added a love interest between her and Edgar, and provided a happy ending in which Lear is restored to his throne. The adaptation remained in the repertory for 150 years, and Samuel Johnson defended it in 1765 on the grounds that, although the unjust tragic ending might be more true to life, "all reasonable beings naturally love justice." Tate's omission of the Fool, a character associated with old-fashioned theater, was not even noticed.

After 1679, the Popish Plot and uncertainty over the royal succession led to Shakespearean adaptations designed to score political points. In 1680, John Crowne wrote *The Misery of Civil War* (1680), the first of two adaptations based on the *Henry VI* plays, while Tate's *The Sicilian Usurper*, adapted from *Richard II*, fell foul of the censor, even though its deposed ruler was more sympathetic than Shakespeare's. In the following year, Tate reversed the order of scenes in *King Lear*, beginning with Edmund's first soliloquy: a bastard son claiming his right to inherit was bound to be topical in the reign of a king who had no legitimate children and whose next heir was a Roman Catholic brother. The turbulent political climate kept audiences away, and the two companies amalgamated in 1682. Very few plays of any kind survive from the last years of Charles II's reign and the three years of James II's leading to the revolution of 1688. In the reign of William and Mary (James's daughter), *King Lear* was once again so topical that it could not be staged. Mary and her sister Anne looked all too much like Lear's daughters, especially since Tate's version ends with the king's abdication in favor of his daughter and son-in-law.

Colley Cibber's *Richard III* (1699), the most successful of all adaptations, benefited from the fact that a number of Shakespeare's history plays had dropped out of the repertory by the end of the century, thus providing a quarry from which the adapter could borrow. Feeling that he had a free hand, Cibber removed Queen Margaret and, since he intended to play Richard himself, gave him some good lines from other histories, including (from *2 Henry IV*) the death speech that Shakespeare had neglected to write for his hero. This Richard, literally an actor's dream, was more theatrically popular than Shakespeare's had been, a fact that kept the version alive well into the twentieth century (the Olivier film, which also cut Margaret's role, used two recognizable Cibber lines). Cibber had some difficulties with the licenser just before the first performance because it was feared that his opening scene, showing the deposed Henry VI in the Tower, would remind its audiences of the deposed James II. He made sure to show his loyalty in his next adaptation—*King John*, under the title *Papal Tyranny*, coincided with the threatened invasion, in 1715, of James II's exiled Catholic son. As one of the managers of Drury Lane, and as poet laureate (from 1730), Cibber became a popular target for satire, and he is best remembered for Pope's attacks on him in *The Dunciad* (1743). But his entertaining autobiography, *An Apology for the Life of Colley Cibber, Comedian* (1740), is still the best source of information on the early eighteenth-century theater.

Indeed, without Cibber's book, it would be difficult to say much about Shakespearean acting at the turn of the eighteenth century. Though Thomas Betterton was recognized as the greatest actor of his age from the first years of the Restoration, those, like Samuel Pepys, who saw him at this time, praised him highly but in vague terms. Because of the division of the theatrical repertory, Betterton acquired some major Shakespearean roles, like Othello, only after the unification of the two companies in 1682, when senior actors of the King's company took the opportunity to retire. After this, he had virtually a monopoly, and went on playing a much-acclaimed Hamlet until he was seventy, as well as taking the role of Falstaff in what seems to have been his own adaptation of the *Henry IV* plays. Cibber's description of Betterton's Hamlet reacting to the first sight of his father's ghost became a point of comparison for later Hamlets well into the nineteenth century. It is clear that his effects had to do with "presence" rather than with movement—though, of course, Cibber was describing him in his last years, when he was presumably less active.

The early female performers are still more shadowy figures. Women had appeared on stage as singers, or singing actresses, in "operas" performed in the 1650s, and one of these, perhaps Margaret Hughes, may have been the first to play a Shakespearean role (probably Desdemona). Mary Sanderson, who became Mrs. Betterton, was the first Lady Macbeth. Her successor, Elizabeth Barry, was primarily a tragic actress. She is said to have owed her initial success to careful instruction by her lover, the Earl of Rochester, who recognized the importance of constant repetition and, like a modern director, insisted that she should rehearse in the dress that she was going to wear in performance. The best-loved comic actress of Cibber's youth, Anne Bracegirdle, played several Shakespearean comedy heroines alongside the Congreve roles for which she was famous. The popularity of *The Merry Wives of Windsor* may have been due not only to Betterton's playing of Falstaff but also to its two excellent roles for actresses past their first youth, probably the only women in the company experienced enough to do justice to Shakespearean comedy.

Though the history of Shakespeare editing begins in the early eighteenth century, the plays still belonged essentially to the theater; hence, the publication of acting editions, which allowed audiences to read what they were actually going to see in the theater, usually heavily cut and partially modernized. Even so, the first half of the century saw a steady return to original versions, as one role after another was suddenly revealed to be a superb vehicle for a particular actor. Shylock, for instance, had been a not-very-interesting comic miser in a not-very-interesting romantic comedy, often replaced by George Granville's adaptation, *The Jew of Venice* (1701). When Shakespeare's original was revived in 1741, Charles Macklin astonished his fellow-actors as much as the audience by emphasizing Shylock's terrifying malevolence. Although later actors would play the character more sympathetically, Macklin made him what he has been ever since: a disturbing character who cannot be assimilated into a comic structure. Something of a theorist on acting, Macklin, in teaching other actors, insisted on clear and intelligent diction. Perhaps for that reason, his Iago was the most convincing of the period.

Richard III, in Cibber's version, was the role in which David Garrick made his London debut in 1741. The actor became famous almost instantly and went on to manage the Drury Lane Theatre from 1747 to 1776. Garrick was a self-proclaimed idolater of Shakespeare whose "Jubilee" at Stratford-upon-Avon in 1769 not only inaugurated the practice of celebrations and festivals but also led contemporaries to regard him as almost equal in importance with his author. Despite his reputation for restoring Shakespeare, Garrick was as much of an adapter as his famous predecessors, turning *The Taming of the Shrew* and the last part of *The Winter's Tale* into short three-act plays and making operas out of *A Midsummer Night's Dream* and *The Tempest*. His *Macbeth* had a death speech, much more dramatic and pathetic than the one-line moral that Davenant had given him. His *Romeo and Juliet* had a pathetic farewell scene based on the one in Otway's *Caius Marius*. In response to French criticisms, he even directed a *Hamlet* in 1771 with the low comedy of the gravediggers omitted. Yet he also revived many plays not seen in their Shakespearean form since the Restoration, showing by his acting what superb roles they contained. He was equally gifted at comedy and tragedy. Two of his most popular roles were Benedick and (Tate's) King Lear. *Julius Caesar* and *Othello*, plays in which Betterton had been particularly successful, were better acted by Garrick's chief rival, Spranger Barry, a tall and handsome actor with a beautiful voice. Garrick, shorter and less romantic in appearance, was famous for his mobile and expressive features that allowed him to delineate the transitions between the "passions." It was this grasp of human psychology that he praised in Shakespeare and that others praised in him. His most significant leading lady, Hannah Pritchard, must have been equally versatile, since she was famous both as Rosalind and as Lady Macbeth. It was, however, characteristic of Garrick that he was able to form an excellent company around himself, including a number of fine actresses and low comedians. Without these conditions, it would have been impossible to revive so many of the comedies.

The Romantic Period (1776–1850)

Between Garrick's retirement in 1776 and the end of the century, the theaters changed to the point where a rapid, subtle style like Garrick's was becoming almost impossible. The Licensing Act of 1737 had limited spoken drama to Drury Lane and Covent Garden, the descendents of the two London theaters licensed in 1660 by Charles II. The late eighteenth century saw the rapid growth of a London population in search of entertainment. The two theaters responded by increasing their audience capacity until, at the end of the century, Covent Garden held over 3,000 spectators, and Drury Lane 3,600. When much of the audience was too far from the stage to see facial expressions or hear the softer tones of an actor's voice, the most successful performers were those who could establish themselves through their volume or through visual effects. Two tall and statuesque actors, John Philip Kemble and his more gifted sister, Sarah Siddons, dominated the theater of this period. Siddons's Lady Macbeth was probably the finest performance of the age: when she said that she could smell blood, at least one contemporary spectator declared that he could smell it too. Her other finest Shakespearean roles were Isabella in *Measure for Measure* and Hermione in *The Winter's Tale*, both of them strong women whose sublime moral grandeur dwarfed everyone else. Kemble's attempt to impose greater discipline and unity on theatrical productions, with more historically "correct" sets and costumes, resulted in what must have been the most genuinely classical theater yet seen in Britain. *Coriolanus*, with Kemble in the title role and Siddons as a heroically obsessed Volumnia, was the triumph of their approach. It was ironic that it should have come in an age dominated by the spirit of revolution and of the complex attitudes that are summed up as Romanticism.

It was to this spirit that Edmund Kean appealed. Those who saw him make his famous London debut as Shylock in 1814, wearing a black wig instead of the traditional red one, would have realized at once that he was going to play, not a tragic villain, but a tragic victim. He had been a singer, dancer, and Harlequin before taking London by storm, and his acting benefited from these other skills. Unlike Kemble, who expressed authority and aristocratic dignity, he excelled as Shakespeare's outsiders and outlaws: the hunchbacked Richard III (still in Cibber's softened version), the Moor Othello, and the melancholy Hamlet. Knowing his gift for pathos, he starred in an adaptation of *3 Henry VI* (where York sobs over his murdered son) and attempted to bring back the original ending of *King Lear* (where Lear grieves over the dead Cordelia), but audiences were not yet ready for either. Those who saw him at his best never forgot his haunting delivery of Richard III's forebodings before Bosworth and Othello's farewell to arms, which provided the kind of appreciative, poetic commentary on Shakespeare that characterized the best contemporary criticism.

Kean's career was short, wrecked by drink and scandal. In 1833, just as he had reached his miserable end, another actor, using the stage name of Keane, made his Covent Garden debut in the role of Othello. Ira Aldridge, a black American, may have hoped to announce himself as Kean's successor, but racial prejudice in England prevented him from being accepted as a leading tragedian. He would, however, play Othello all over Europe, and especially in Russia, in bilingual productions with local casts. Like Kean, he sought out the roles of victims and social outcasts: Aaron in his own adaptation of *Titus Andronicus*, as well as (in white make-up) Macbeth, Shylock, and King Lear; like Kean, he was also capable of singing songs in dialect or even a Russian folksong. The excitement that German and Russian spectators felt at the sight of a black actor playing a black character would become an important part of theatrical experience a century later; at this point, it was a novelty. In the 1860s Aldridge finally acted in major London theaters and might have returned to the United States after the Civil War if he had not died unexpectedly while on tour in Poland.

Meanwhile, both of the unruly London theaters were managed, in turn, by William Macready, who, as his diary makes clear, took seriously his responsibility to a dramatist he worshipped. Still more than Kemble, he behaved like a modern director, with a vision of the production as a whole. His revivals of the history plays showed the possibilities of historical reconstruction. He is best known for restoring the Fool to *King Lear* in 1838, though he gave the role to a young woman to ensure that it would be played for pathos rather than low comic effects that might distract from his own scenes. A number of fine actresses played opposite him: Helen Faucit, young, fragile, refined, who would later write a perceptive if sentimental account of her approach to acting some of Shakespeare's female characters; Fanny Kemble, a member of the famous Kemble family, whose memoirs indicate the struggle involved for women in a star-dominated theater; Charlotte Cushman, a powerful visitor from America who sometimes played male roles. The plays were still heavily cut and showed the influence of earlier adaptations, but by the end of his career, Macready could fairly claim to have restored a good deal of Shakespeare's text and to have made the theater more respectable. The repeal of the Licensing Act in 1843, which allowed smaller theaters to cater to different publics, also encouraged gentrification. Samuel Phelps, who managed the working-class Sadler's Wells Theatre from 1844 to 1869, did even more than Macready had, performing thirty-four of Shakespeare's plays; he even restored the original *Richard III*, though other actors continued to prefer the Cibber version. Charles Kean (son of Edmund), at the Princess's Theatre from 1850 to 1859, carried the historicizing process still further; his "archaeological" productions were likely to be accompanied by notes explaining the reason for the choice of period, costumes, and props.

Still, it was only rarely that anyone had the opportunity to impose a concept of Shakespearean production on an acting company in his own theater. Star actors tended to spend much of their time on tour, both in England and America, performing their favorite roles after perhaps one rehearsal with the resident company. Far from seeking new ways to interpret a play, these actors had to rely on standardized stage business (when Mr. Wopsle plays Hamlet in Dickens's *Great Expectations*, an unsympathetic audience comments loudly on each theatrical cliché as it occurs). They naturally tended to conceive of their characters in isolation and to favor tragedy over comedy, which requires ensemble playing. (Similarly, nineteenth-century critics usually focus on the analysis of individual characters.) A common practice was the pitting of one actor against another in a famous role, arguing over which one was the "true" Hamlet or Lear. In one case, the rivalry developed a nationalistic dimension. Macready's visit to America, in 1849, is notorious for the riot at Astor Place in New York, when soldiers fired on and killed some of the crowd outside the theater. The rioters had been trying to drown out Macready's performance of *Macbeth* out of a mistaken loyalty to the American tragedian, Edwin Forrest. On a visit to Britain, Forrest had hissed Macready for some foppish business with a handkerchief that the actor, as Hamlet, had used to illustrate the phrase "I must be idle." Now his personal hostility became a quarrel about effete English acting versus the manly American tradition. In fact, the distinction was largely meaningless: many well-known American actors had begun their careers in England or Ireland. While some American Shakespeareans might have seen themselves as part of the Forrest tradition, and some (like the touring performers depicted by Mark Twain in *Huckleberry Finn*) were of no tradition at all, most American actors continued to look to Europe for models.

The Victorian Era and the Early Twentieth Century (1850–1912)

The greatest American actor of the next generation, Edwin Booth, was a refined and melancholy figure whose readings of the great Shakespearean roles were psychological and poetic. Booth was the son of Junius Brutus Booth, who had acted in London opposite Edmund Kean, and the brother of John Wilkes Booth, the assassin of Abraham Lincoln. (Ironically, all three members of this acting family had once performed together in the great assassination play, *Julius Caesar*.) Though Booth briefly attempted theater management, he spent much of his time in the exhausting business of touring. He clearly thought deeply about his own roles, and about the moments when other characters interacted with him. His correspondence with the New Variorum Shakespeare editor, H.H. Furness, is quoted in many notes of that edition—an early example of successful communication between the theater and the scholarly world. Yet when Booth was alternating the two leading roles of *Othello* with Henry Irving in 1881, he sent his servant to take notes at rehearsal for him. Nothing in his experience had prepared him for a theater in which the actor-manager expected everyone to fit into a total artistic conception.

It was Irving, the first actor to be knighted, who dominated English Shakespearean acting in the late Victorian era. His pictorial sense was even stronger than that of the actor-managers who preceded him, and the technical means at his disposal in the Lyceum Theatre, which he began to manage in 1878, were much better. The old system of sliding screens in grooves, flanked by a series of wings, had been replaced by the "box set," which was built like a piece of architecture, creating a complete environment. Electric lighting, introduced in the 1880s, provided new, subtle visual effects. The elaborate and beautiful sets often required interminable scene changes and, sometimes, rearrangement of the plays to accommodate them. Irving's own performances were usually controversial. His Malvolio, like his Shylock, was a tragic figure, while his Iago was so witty and likeable that, playing opposite Booth's Othello, he stole all the sympathy from the hero. His theater offered a beautiful dream for the spectator to share: if it also disturbed the spectator, it was through its revelation of the psychological depths of character, never through its comments on social and political issues. Irving's leading lady, Ellen Terry, was both beautiful and brilliant; in most productions she was allowed to be only the former. Bernard Shaw, longing for her to appear in plays about "grownup" topics, by himself or Henrik Ibsen, resented her imprisonment in Irving's world. For Shaw and other modern thinkers, Shakespeare was becoming synonymous with nostalgia and with the moralistic and idealistic thinking that the new drama regarded as a vice. The early twentieth-century theater was finally affected by these critical attempts to reform it, but two kinds of production coexisted for some time. At His Majesty's Theatre, Herbert Beerbohm Tree, like Irving, offered psychologically based character acting in a beautiful scenic environment, recreating Cleopatra's Egypt and Henry VIII's England; having seen his lavish production of *Macbeth*, one critic commented that "Nature put up a pretty feeble imitation of what several barrels of stones and a few sheets of tin could do in His Majesty's." At the Savoy, on the other hand, Harley Granville Barker, a disciple of Bernard Shaw, developed a decorative visual style that was not tied to a specific historical period.

Meanwhile, a more experimental approach to acting was being developed in Germany. The country's unusual political structure, with small dukedoms and cities sponsoring their own theaters, made it possible for the

Duke of Saxe-Meiningen to sponsor his own company of players, sixty-six in all. His leading actors were unremarkable but, when he took them on tour in the 1880s, audiences were impressed by his handling of large groups. The Duke insisted that those who played major roles in one production should be walk-ons in another, so that crowds could be properly rehearsed instead of being assembled from those gathered around the stage door and drilled by the stage manager immediately before each performance.

Frank Benson, a young Oxford graduate, saw the Saxe-Meiningen company at Drury Lane in 1881, and was inspired to develop his own touring company—though, unlike the Duke, he acted in his own productions and consequently shaped them from a star's point of view. From 1886 on, the Bensonians became regular visitors at Stratford-upon-Avon. Shakespeare's birthplace had been briefly famous in 1769, the year of Garrick's Jubilee, but it was only in 1879, when the first Memorial Theatre was built, that tourists had any reason to visit for more than a few hours. Benson essentially created the first Stratford company, though it used the theater only during a short "Festival" season. Having a regular venue and a devoted audience enabled him to revive unusual works, if often drastically cut. In 1901 he inaugurated the new century with a "Grand Cycle" of Shakespeare's histories—the first English production of the plays as a group.

The desire to return to fuller texts and something like the original conditions of Shakespearean performance was initially associated with Germany and then with outsiders like William Poel, who founded the English Stage Society in 1894. Previously, Poel had given an experimental matinee of the First Quarto *Hamlet* at St. George's Hall in 1881. More surprisingly (though his friendship with Bernard Shaw in part explains it), the popular London actor Johnston Forbes-Robertson played an unusually full text of *Hamlet* in 1897, with characters like Reynaldo and Fortinbras appearing for the first time in centuries. Then Benson's company played an uncut *Hamlet* in 1899 and 1900. Poel, who often worked with amateurs, using all-purpose curtains rather than scenery on what was meant to be an Elizabethan stage, revived works previously considered unperformable, by Shakespeare's contemporaries as well as by Shakespeare. For example, he gave the first important *Troilus and Cressida* to be seen in London since 1734, dressing it in Elizabethan rather than classical costume. It was 1912. He had discovered the play's antiwar potential.

The Twentieth Century

World War I drastically curtailed many Shakespearean projects, including those for a gigantic celebration of the anniversary of his death in 1916, which at one point was intended to include the opening of a National Theatre. Although this theater did not come into existence until nearly 100 years after Irving had first suggested it, other developments were creating the conditions that would make Shakespeare plays, with their large casts, commercially viable.

One was the rise of repertory theaters, which could support a large company and a varied range of plays. The most famous of these was London's Royal Victoria, or "Old Vic," founded in 1914. Under a number of gifted directors (notably Robert Atkins, who had directed all the plays in the 1623 Folio by 1923, Harcourt Williams, and Tyrone Guthrie), it was the home to many legendary productions, including John Gielgud's first *Hamlet* (1929) and Olivier's first *Hamlet* (1937). At the Birmingham Repertory Theatre, Barry Jackson had already directed a modern-dress *Hamlet* in 1925. Modern dress had been common practice until the nineteenth century; it now seemed eccentric, but would by the end of the century become almost the norm. The Memorial Theatre at Stratford, after struggling to find its identity, saw some brilliant productions by Peter Brook in the 1940s and 1950s, including three plays traditionally considered minor: *Love's Labor's Lost* (1946), *Measure for Measure* (1948), and a *Titus Andronicus* (1955), starring Olivier, at which audience members regularly fainted at what was then unusual stage violence: the amputation of the hero's hand and the cutting of the villains' throats. Stratford and the Old Vic were becoming rival Shakespeare companies and in the 1960s each achieved a new status. The Memorial Theatre was renamed the Royal Shakespeare Theatre in 1960, with Peter Hall as director, whereas the Old Vic was designated the National Theatre in 1963. Olivier directed its opening production of *Hamlet*, with Peter O'Toole in the title role, and played a famous Othello in 1964. The National Theatre eventually moved into new premises in an arts complex, with three stages, on the South Bank of the Thames.

In the United States, the most exciting Shakespeare productions also occurred during a period of government subsidy: it was depression-era financing that enabled Orson Welles to direct Shakespeare on radio, and, for the Mercury Theatre, his "voodoo" *Macbeth* (1938) with an all-black cast, his anti-Fascist *Julius Caesar* (1937), and his condensation of the major history plays, *Five Kings*, which, although unsuccessful, later influenced his Falstaff film, *Chimes at Midnight* (1966). The other significant development in North America was the growth of summer Shakespeare festivals at outdoor Elizabethan-style theaters, beginning with the Elizabethan Stage at Ashland, Oregon (founded 1935), and the Guthrie-designed Festival Theatre at Stratford, Ontario (1953). Festival seasons allowed juxtapositions of related plays and the yearly performance of successive plays in a history cycle.

It was the English Stratford-upon-Avon, however, that fully seized on the history plays, performing the *Richard II–Henry V* group in 1951, during the Festival of Britain that celebrated the country's emergence from wartime and postwar rationing. For the rest of the century, the "cycle" of history plays would be recognized as a national epic, to be performed for special occasions. For the new Royal Shakespeare Company, Peter Hall and John Barton produced the *Henry VI–Richard III* group of plays—rewritten, reduced to three plays, and called *The Wars of the Roses*. They revived these, along with the other *Henry* plays, for the Shakespeare quatercentenary in 1964. The histories were produced again in 1975 by Terry Hands, with Alan Howard playing all the kings except Henry IV; in 1982 the *Henry IV* plays opened the company's new London theater at the Barbican under Trevor Nunn; and the company, now under Adrian Noble, marked the arrival of the millennium with a freshly conceived production of the *Richard II–Richard III* sequence. Just as the 1951 production showed the influence of Tillyard's essays on the histories as a unified cycle, the plays of the year 2000, deliberately disparate in style and even venue, were the product of a critical movement that emphasized discontinuity and diversity.

Contemporary Critical Approaches

By now, productions might require as much interpretation as plays. In the last half of the twentieth century, the spread of school and university education had created a substantial population that had studied at least one Shakespeare play and a smaller population, including some theater practitioners, that had read not only the plays but also the criticism. Stratford's John Barton, a former Cambridge don, directed *Twelfth Night* (1969) as if it were by Chekhov, encouraging the audience to imagine the unspoken feelings of the characters—not only Viola (Judi Dench), smiling through heartbreak, but Maria, in her apparently hopeless love for Sir Toby, and Sir Andrew in his even more hopeless love for Olivia. This attention to character, often created out of masses of tiny realistic details, informed some of the theater's most highly praised productions. Barton's *Richard II* (1973) worked very differently, externalizing the play's images in ways that were clearly independent of the characters' awareness: for instance, a glimpse of a melting snowman echoed Richard's wish that he were "a mockery king of snow" and linked the fall and rise of kings to a natural cycle of dissolution and renewal.

Other major critical approaches, easier to categorize, quickly found their way onto the stage. Political readings, often influenced by a Brechtian production style, dominated the 1960s and 1970s. These were usually Marxist and anti-authority: lines in which characters expressed high moral sentiments might be juxtaposed (legitimately) with those in which they showed themselves less noble, or (illegitimately) by setting them in a context that undermined them, as when, in Peter Zadek's *Held Henry* (Hero Henry), Henry V delivers the St. Crispin's Day speech to his bored mistress. Even before its first English publication in 1964, *Shakespeare Our Contemporary*, by the Polish critic Jan Kott, had powerfully influenced theater with his comparison of *Hamlet* and the histories to life under a totalitarian regime, *King Lear* to Theater of the Absurd, and the comedies to a Freudian nightmare. Both Brecht and Kott could be recognized behind Peter Brook's *King Lear* (1962), which, in place of the traditional sympathy with the king (a frighteningly harsh Paul Scofield), emphasized his and his followers' brutality toward Goneril's servants, and ruthlessly cut anything that might be cathartic; the Dover cliff meeting between Lear and Gloucester frankly drew on the stage imagery of Samuel Beckett's *Waiting for Godot*. Brook's *A Midsummer Night's Dream* (1970), which based its erotic treatment of Titania and Bottom on Kott's work, found a purely theatrical language for the critical commonplaces about the play's metatheatricality. Without makeup, under bright light, in a white-walled gymnasium that replaced the traditional moonlit forest, Oberon and Puck sat on trapezes and passed the aphrodisiac "flower," a metal plate, from one spinning metallic wand to another. The fact that this operation could, and occasionally did, go wrong was the point: it reminded the audience that the real magic lay in its own willingness to trust the actors. Even the "Pyramus and Thisbe" actors in the final scene were treated as serious artists, representatives of working-class culture who deserved respect. For many of his later productions, Peter Brook went abroad in search of a multilingual, multiethnic cast, searching for ways of escaping the "easy" assumptions about Shakespeare.

It was in fact race and gender rather than class that dominated Shakespeare production in the last quarter of the century. The concern with race began with the great American theatrical event of the 1940s, Margaret Webster's production of *Othello* with the charismatic Paul Robeson in the title role. After the longest run of any Shakespeare play on Broadway, it was taken on tour all over America in 1945, playing only in desegregated theaters. Although Robeson had already played Othello in London (1930), and would do so again at Stratford-upon-Avon, England, in 1959, his long period of disgrace in the politically polarized United States of the 1950s delayed the movement toward race-based casting as a norm. After initial embarrassment about racist language in Shakespeare, the theater began deliberately to explore its implications, as race became a subject for academic study. The range of *Othello* videos available by the 1990s indicates the play's performance history: besides Orson

Welles's film from 1952, these include the National Theatre production of 1964 starring Laurence Olivier and the BBC one with Antony Hopkins (1981), both with white actors in the title role; Trevor Nunn's Chekhovian version originally staged in 1989; the historic South African production by Janet Suzman, a political act at a time when apartheid still existed; and Oliver Parker's 1994 version, with Laurence Fishburne (opposite Kenneth Branagh's convincingly ordinary Iago), consciously conveying the concentrated power and sensuality associated with blackness. Confusion between "color-blind casting" (when the audience is supposed to ignore the race of both actor and character) and "race-based casting" (when the audience is being told something about race through the casting) was deliberately cultivated in Jude Kelly's *Othello* (Washington, D.C., 1997). This production enabled Patrick Stewart to achieve his otherwise unrealizable ambition of playing the title role by surrounding a white Othello with African American and Hispanic actors, yet with the play's racial references unaltered.

Just as some critics of racism felt that *Othello* and *The Merchant of Venice* had become theatrically unacceptable, some feminist responses to Shakespeare argued the same about *The Taming of the Shrew*, in which a female character is made to acquiesce in her humiliation by a husband who uses patriarchal arguments to justify his behavior. The play had usually been directed to soften its final moral, either by making it clear that the protagonists have fallen in love at first sight or by emphasizing its nature as a play within a play, safely distant from real life. A famous production by Michael Bogdanov (Royal Shakespeare Theatre, 1978) doubled the drunken tinker Sly with Petruchio and showed Kate being brutalized into a dazed submission that horrified even her husband. Obviously, the play in this version was no longer a comedy. A less obvious effect of feminism has been the increasing attention paid to Shakespeare's female characters. They tend now to be on stage more than the text directs, as when Ophelia stands appalled while her father reads Hamlet's love letters to the court or Gertrude enters in time to hear Claudius and Laertes plan to poison Hamlet, so that her decision to drink from the cup is recognized as a heroic device to save her son's life. The young Elizabeth of York, who does not appear in the text of *Richard III* although she is important to its plot, has frequently been seen and even heard in stage versions, as in the 1995 film by Richard Loncraine. The fact that women are often denied speech at crucial moments can be turned to an advantage, as when John Barton and a number of subsequent directors of *Measure for Measure* in the 1980s made Isabella silently refuse the Duke's proposal, which earlier actors and directors had assumed she would eagerly accept.

Still more important, in a theater in which women are far more likely than men to be underemployed, were devices that increased the number of Shakespearean roles for women. Cross-dressed performances, parallel to the productions focused on race, hovered between gender based and gender blind. Deborah Warner's *Richard II* in 1995, with Fiona Shaw as the title character (National Theatre, London), suggested a troubled and potentially erotic relationship between Richard and Bolingbroke without defining it further. In the all-male Cheek-by-Jowl production of *As You Like It* (1995), the audience was never certain whether it was meant to be thinking of Rosalind (Adrian Lester) as male or female. A similar confusion was exploited when Michael Kahn's *King Lear* (Washington, D.C., 1999) cast Cordelia as a deaf-mute, signing her lines, which were then interpreted by the Fool. This decision, which would have been meaningless if the audience had not known that the actress (Monique Holt) really was a deaf-mute, might be seen either as a return to the self-conscious theatricality of the Renaissance stage or as an example of identity politics.

Shakespeare on Film

Of course, the sense of identity between actor and role is strongest in the cinema, where physical appearance matters more and where audiences are particularly likely to bring with them recollections of an actor's previous roles. Films of Shakespeare plays are as old as film itself. Their transfer to videotape and then laserdisc and DVD, a process that began in the 1970s, has given them a much wider circulation and canonized some performances: Olivier's Richard III, for instance, now has much the same iconic status that Cibber gave to Betterton's Hamlet. Orson Welles's film versions of *Macbeth* (1947) and *Othello* (1952), visually remarkable as they were, have benefited from remastering to make their soundtracks more intelligible. The BBC made-for-TV versions of Shakespeare, 1979–1985, often disappointed both film and Shakespeare enthusiasts, though for different reasons, but have been widely used in schools. Kenneth Branagh's films, including a remarkable four-hour uncut *Hamlet* (1996), have been surprisingly successful in making the plays accessible to a popular audience. His *Henry V* (1989) was unfairly praised for being more "real" than Olivier's; both films were star-centered, with Olivier playing a more controlled king, Branagh a more vulnerable one. Whereas Olivier began his film with a view of an idealized Elizabethan London, then of a playhouse viewed from a superior perspective as old-fashioned and in some ways comic, Branagh introduced his Chorus (Derek Jacobi) in a room full of movie cameras, though he later allowed him to move among the actors in the film. As often in films, the moments most remembered were visual: Henry's (Branagh's) grief when, in order to enforce proper discipline, he is obliged to order the hanging of Bardolph, or the long shot, after the Battle of Agincourt, that shows Henry carrying the dead boy in a procession of English soldiers singing *Non nobis Domine*.

Branagh's youth was an asset in bringing Shakespeare to a young audience. Later filmmakers have aimed at a still younger group. *William Shakespeare's Romeo and Juliet* (directed by Baz Luhrmann, 1996), filled as it was with icons of contemporary youth culture, is perhaps the first of these, though it retains Shakespeare's language, juxtaposing it with contradictory images, so that it can be understood either as a complex visual-verbal experience or as a rather simple visual one. The *Hamlet* directed by Michael Almereyda (2000) represents its young characters as college students obsessed with modern technology: Hamlet (Ethan Hawke) is an amateur filmmaker and Ophelia is a photographer; "To be or not to be" is spoken in a video store against a background of videos labeled "Action." For students of the new field of Shakespeare in Popular Culture, Teenage Shakespeare, with the stories rewritten in contemporary language and settings, is becoming a genre in its own right. *Ten Things I Hate About You* (directed by Gil Junger, 1999) and *O* (directed by Tim Blake Nelson, 2001) retell *The Taming of the Shrew* and *Othello* in American high school settings. *The Children's Midsummer Night's Dream* (directed by Christine Edzard, 2001) has a cast of primary school children.

International Contexts and Contemporary Adaptations

Not only have the plays been adapted for every age group, they have turned out to speak an international language. This had not always been true, though English and French actors had visited each other's countries since the seventeenth century: in 1629 French actresses were booed by English audiences, still accustomed to an all-male stage; one group of English actors was booed in the Paris of 1818, but another visiting company in 1827 inspired French writers and actors to try to understand Shakespeare. English and American audiences saw *Othello* with new eyes when the Italian actor Tommaso Salvini, followed by several other famous Italians, performed on tour in the late nineteenth century. Along with the visit of the Berliner Ensemble to London in 1956, the most important influences in the late twentieth century came from Asian, especially Japanese, theater and from central and eastern Europe. Kurosawa's films, *Throne of Blood* (*Macbeth*, 1957) and *Ran* (*King Lear*, 1986), transpose Shakespearean plots into Japanese culture and images. Successful Russian films have ranged from the visually stunning colors of Yan Fried's *Twelfth Night* and Sergei Yutkevitch's *Othello* (both 1955) to Grigori Kozintsev's black-and-white *Hamlet* (1964) and *King Lear* (1971).

The opening up of contacts with central and eastern Europe after 1989 has resulted in visits from theater companies of the former eastern bloc countries. When London audiences in 1990 saw *Hamlet* by the Bulandra Theatre of Romania (directed by Alexander Tocilescu), they discovered that plays often regarded in Britain and America as "conservative" tools of the "establishment" had elsewhere been a powerful vehicle for the expression of political dissent. When first produced in 1985, Tocilescu's *Hamlet* was clearly understood to be equating the rottenness of Elsinore with the world created by Nicolae Ceaucescu, the dictator executed in 1989; Ion Caramitru, the actor who played Hamlet, had been one of the leaders of the revolution. In Czech productions of Shakespeare, similarly, actors and audience had gathered in a deliberate act of misreading directed at the occupying Russians: in *Love's Labor's Lost*, of all plays, the princess's suggestion that the courtiers disguised as Muscovites should "be gone" was the high point of the evening.

Western directors have sometimes attempted to deal with a difficult text by interpreting it as "Other," particularly as Japanese: the samurai warrior culture was the background to Barry Kyle's *The Two Noble Kinsmen* (Swan Theatre, Stratford, 1986) and to David Farr's *Coriolanus* (Royal Shakespeare Theatre, 2002), whereas Ron Daniels's *Timon of Athens* (The Other Place, Stratford, 1980) drew on the concept of a society based on gift-giving. Conversely, Yukio Ninagawa's Japanese Shakespeare productions have combined Japanese costumes with a soundtrack of European music (*Macbeth*) and interpreted *The Tempest* through the story of the famous Japanese exile, Shunkan. Such cross-cultural borrowings have sometimes been denigrated as "cultural tourism," by which critics seem to mean that it is illegitimate to appropriate the merely visual aspects of a culture to which one does not belong.

Similarly, the reconstructed "Shakespeare's Globe" in London, which opened in 1997, was accused of attempting to appropriate the emotions of another historical period. Perhaps because the opening production was *Henry V*, the "groundlings" who stood in the yard for only £5 apiece seemed to be modeling themselves on their counterparts in the Globe sequence of Olivier's film, who boo when they hear that Falstaff has been banished. Their willingness to boo the French (and, in the next season, Shylock) at first shocked the critics, and it was suggested that this theater might be suited only to comedies and histories demanding a presentational style, but productions of *Hamlet* (2000) and *King Lear* (2001) showed that it was possible to control audience response to the tragedies. Mark Rylance's *Hamlet* skillfully played his line about groundlings "capable of nothing but inexplicable dumbshow," so that he could respond to their laughter by adding "*and* noise." Whether or not the theater can really tell anyone anything about Elizabethan stage conventions and audience response, it has given considerable pleasure. Other Globes, more and less historically based, now can be found in several countries (the United States, Japan, Poland, and the Czech Republic, among others), while the open stage of Stratford, Canada, remains one of the most successful modifications of the Elizabethan model. In a reversal of the search for authenticity, the Shakespeare Theatre in Washington, D.C., has abandoned its home in the reconstructed Fortune Theatre at the Folger Shakespeare Library for a purpose-built modern auditorium. In fact, the two kinds of theater can coexist. The well-established Shakespeare festivals of Stratford, Ontario; Ashland, Oregon; and Santa Cruz, California, have added well-equipped indoor theaters to their outdoor acting spaces, and an indoor auditorium is projected as an addition to Shakespeare's Globe in London. A reconstruction of the Blackfriars Playhouse opened in Staunton, Virginia, in 2001.

Although it has been impossible to discuss the theatrical fortunes of every Shakespeare play, it may be interesting to end by reflecting how greatly these have fluctuated. If some plays, like *Hamlet* and *Macbeth*, have always been popular, the history of others is more checkered. Some of the comedies most popular today, such as *As You Like It* and *Twelfth Night*, were regarded as insipid in the eighteenth century, redeemed only by their scenes of low comedy and occasional sententious speeches. *The Merry Wives of Windsor* was the most popular comedy during the Restoration; *King John* and *Henry VIII* were more popular in the nineteenth century than *Richard II* or *2 Henry IV*. *Othello* was acted without the "willow scene" (4.3) for most of the eighteenth and nineteenth centuries, and *Troilus and Cressida* and *Titus Andronicus* were performed, if at all, only in heavily adapted versions. It is arguable that the attitude to Shakespeare that Bernard Shaw ridiculed as "Bardolatry" reached its height, not in the Victorian age, but at the end of the twentieth century, a time when any Shakespeare play, however minor, was likely to find a director and an audience. One reason might be that the subsidized theaters had been giving fewer controversial productions since 1980, emphasizing instead what the plays have in common with musical comedies and films. An important American contribution to Shakespeare in performance has taken the form of musicals like *The Boys from Syracuse* (1938), *Kiss Me Kate* (1948), and *West Side Story* (1957), based respectively on *The Comedy of Errors*, *The Taming of the Shrew*, and *Romeo and Juliet*; now, many productions of the comedies followed the Restoration practice of filling them with popular music. What was new was not the practice of adaptation but the attitude toward it. In the mid century, the plays were taken to be fixed quantities: the job of the theater director, as of the critic, was to uncover the "real" work, whether through more authentic staging, a more accurate text, or a better understanding of its meaning. By the end of the millennium, when some theorists were insisting that the text itself was unknowable, it is not surprising to find a much greater tolerance for re-creations and explorations of the plays in other forms.

Bibliography

Abbreviations Used

English Literary History	*ELH*
Publications of the Modern Language Association of America	*PMLA*
Shakespeare Quarterly	*SQ*
Shakespeare Studies	*ShakS*
Shakespeare Survey	*ShS*

Works of Reference

Abbott, E. A. *A Shakespearian Grammar*. New ed., London, 1870.

Allen, Michael J. B., and Kenneth Muir, eds. *Shakespeare's Plays in Quarto*. Berkeley, 1981.

Bentley, G. E. *The Jacobean and Caroline Stage*. 7 vols. Oxford, 1941–1968.

Bergeron, David M. *Shakespeare: A Study and Research Guide*. New York, 1975; 2nd ed., rev. David Bergeron and Geraldo de Sousa. Lawrence, Kans., 1987.

Bullough, Geoffrey, ed. *Narrative and Dramatic Sources of Shakespeare*. 8 vols. London, 1957–1975.

Chambers, E.K. *The Elizabethan Stage*. 4 vols. Oxford, 1923; rev., 1945.

———. *The Mediaeval Stage*. 2 vols. Oxford, 1903.

———. *William Shakespeare: A Study of Facts and Problems*. 2 vols. Oxford, 1930.

Dent, R. W. *Shakespeare's Proverbial Language: An Index*. Berkeley, 1981.

Garland Shakespeare Bibliographies, gen. ed. William Godshalk. Published in separate volumes for various plays, at varying dates. Garland: New York.

Greg, W. W. *A Bibliography of the English Printed Drama to the Restoration*. 4 vols. London, 1939–1959.

———, ed. *Shakespeare Quarto Facsimiles*. London, 1939–. (An incomplete set; Greg's work has been supplemented by Charlton Hinman.)

Harbage, Alfred. *Annals of English Drama, 975–1700*. Rev. S. Schoenbaum. Philadelphia, 1964; 3rd ed., Sylvia Stoler Wagonheim, 1989.

Hinman, Charlton, ed. *The Norton Facsimile: The First Folio of Shakespeare*. New York, 1968.

Hosley, Richard, ed. *Shakespeare's Holinshed*. New York, 1968.

Kökeritz, Helge. *Shakespeare's Names*. New Haven, 1959.

———. *Shakespeare's Pronunciation*. New Haven, 1953.

Long, John. *Shakespeare's Use of Music: Comedies*. Gainesville, Fla., 1955. *Final Comedies*, 1961; *Histories and Tragedies*, 1971.

McDonald, Russ. *The Bedford Companion to Shakespeare: An Introduction with Documents*. Boston, 1996; 2nd ed., 2001.

McManaway, James G., and Jeanne Addison Roberts, compilers. *A Selective Bibliography of Shakespeare*. Charlottesville, Va., 1975.

Muir, Kenneth. *Shakespeare's Sources*. 2 vols. London, 1957.

———, and S. Schoenbaum, eds. *A New Companion to Shakespeare Studies*. London and New York, 1971.

Munro, John, ed. *The Shakespeare Allusion Book*. 2 vols. London and New York, 1909; reissued 1932.

Naylor, Edward W. *Shakespeare and Music*. New ed., London, 1931.

Noble, Richmond. *Shakespeare's Biblical Knowledge*. London, 1935.

———. *Shakespeare's Use of Song*. London, 1923.

Onions, C. T. *A Shakespeare Glossary*. Rev. and enlgd. R. D. Eagleson. Oxford, 1986.

Pegasus Shakespeare Bibliographies. Annotated bibliographies of Shakespeare studies in a 12-volume series, gen. ed. Richard L. Nochimson, including *Love's Labor's Lost, A Midsummer Night's Dream,* and *The Merchant of Venice* (Clifford Chalmers Huffman), *Richard II, Henry IV, I and II,* and *Henry V* (Joseph Candido), *Hamlet* (Michael E. Mooney), *The Rape of Lucrece, Titus Andronicus, Julius Caesar, Antony and Cleopatra,* and *Coriolanus* (Clifford Chalmers Huffman and John W. Velz), *King Lear* and *Macbeth* (Rebecca W. Bushnell), and *Shakespeare and the Renaissance Stage to 1616* and *Shakespearean Stage History 1616 to 1998* (Hugh Macrae Richmond). Binghamton, N.Y. (1995) and Asheville, N.C., 1996—.

Publications of the Modern Language Association of America (PMLA). Annual Bibliography.

Rothwell, Kenneth S., and Annabelle Henkin Melzer. *Shakespeare on Screen: An International Filmography and Videography*. New York and London, 1990.

Schmidt, Alexander. *Shakespeare-Lexicon*. 5th ed. Berlin, 1962.

Seager, H. W. *Natural History in Shakespeare's Time*. London, 1896.

Seng, Peter J. *The Vocal Songs in the Plays of Shakespeare*. Cambridge, Mass., 1967.

Shakespeare Bulletin.

Shakespeare-Jahrbuch.

Shakespeare Newsletter.

Shakespeare Quarterly. Annual Bibliography.

Shakespeare Studies.

Shakespeare Survey.

Spencer, T. J. B., ed. *Shakespeare's Plutarch*. Harmondsworth, Eng., 1964.

Spevack, Marvin. *The Harvard Concordance to Shakespeare*. Cambridge, Mass., 1973.

Sternfeld, Frederick W. *Music in Shakespearean Tragedy*. London, 1963, 1967.

Thomson, J. A. K. *Shakespeare and the Classics*. London, 1952.

Wells, Stanley, ed. *Shakespeare: Select Bibliographical Guides*. London, 1973.

———, ed. *The Cambridge Companion to Shakespeare Studies*. Cambridge, Eng., 1986.

Life in Shakespeare's England

Allen, Don Cameron. *The Star-Crossed Renaissance.* Durham, N.C., 1941.

Baker, Herschel. *The Image of Man: A Study of the Idea of Human Dignity in Classical Antiquity, the Middle Ages, and the Renaissance.* Cambridge, Mass., 1961. (First published in 1947 as *The Dignity of Man.*)

———. *The Wars of Truth: Studies in the Decay of Christian Humanism in the Earlier Seventeenth Century.* Cambridge, Mass., 1952.

Bakhtin, Mikhail M. *Rabelais and His World,* trans. H. Iswolsky. Cambridge, Mass., 1968.

Barkan, Leonard. *Nature's Work of Art: The Human Body as Image of the World.* New Haven, 1975.

———. *The Gods Made Flesh: Metamorphosis and the Pursuit of Paganism.* New Haven, 1986.

Barroll, J. Leeds. *Politics, Plague, and Shakespeare's Theater: The Stuart Years.* Ithaca, N.Y., 1991.

Bindoff, S. T., et al., eds. *Elizabethan Government and Society.* Essays presented to Sir John Neale. London, 1961.

Bush, Douglas. *The Renaissance and English Humanism.* Toronto, 1939.

Buxton, John. *Elizabethan Taste.* London, 1963.

Byrne, Muriel St. Clare. *Elizabethan Life in Town and Country.* 8th ed. London, 1970.

Camden, Carroll. *The Elizabethan Woman.* Houston, 1952.

Caspari, Fritz. *Humanism and the Social Order in Tudor England.* Chicago, 1954.

Cassirer, Ernst. *The Platonic Renaissance in England,* trans. J. E. Pettegrove. Austin, Tex., 1953.

De Grazia, Margreta, Maureen Quilligan, and Peter Stallybrass, eds. *Subject and Object in Renaissance Culture.* Cambridge, Eng., 1996.

Einstein, Lewis. *Tudor Ideals.* New York, 1921.

Elizabeth I. *Collected Works,* eds. Leah S. Marcus, Janel Mueller, and Mary Beth Rose. Chicago, 2000.

Elton, G. R. *The Tudor Revolution in Government.* Cambridge, Eng., 1959.

Fumerton, Patricia, and Simon Hunt, eds. *Renaissance Culture and the Everyday.* Philadelphia, 1999.

Gallagher, Lowell. *Medusa's Gaze: Casuistry and Conscience in the Renaissance.* Stanford, 1991.

Harrison, G. B. *An Elizabethan Journal.* London, 1928; supplements.

———. *A Jacobean Journal . . . 1603–1606.* London, 1941.

———. *A Second Jacobean Journal . . . 1607 to 1610.* Ann Arbor, Mich., 1958.

Haydn, Hiram. *The Counter-Renaissance.* New York, 1950.

Helgerson, Richard. *Forms of Nationhood: The Elizbethan Writing of England.* Chicago, 1992.

Heninger, S. K., Jr. *A Handbook of Renaissance Meteorology.* Durham, N.C., 1960.

Hirst, Derek. *Authority and Conflict: England, 1603–1658.* Cambridge, Mass., 1986.

Huizinga, Johan. *The Waning of the Middle Ages.* London, 1924; Baltimore, 1955.

Hurstfield, Joel, *Elizabeth I and the Unity of England.* London, 1960.

Jones, Ann Rosalind, and Peter Stallybrass. *Renaissance Clothing and the Materials of Memory.* Cambridge, Eng., 2000.

Jordan, Constance. *Renaissance Feminism: Literary Texts and Political Models.* Ithaca, N.Y., 1990.

Judges, A. V., ed. *The Elizabethan Underworld.* London and New York, 1930. Rpt., London, 1965.

Kewes, Paulina, ed. *Plagiarism in Early Modern England.* Basingstoke, Hampshire, Eng., 2003.

Knights, L. C. *Drama and Society in the Age of Jonson.* London, 1937.

Kocher, Paul. *Science and Religion in Elizabethan England.* San Marino, Calif., 1953.

Lee, Morris. *Great Britain's Solomon: James VI and I in His Three Kingdoms.* Urbana, Ill., 1990.

Lovejoy, A. O. *The Great Chain of Being.* Cambridge, Mass., 1936.

MacCaffrey, Wallace T. *The Shaping of the Elizabethan Regime.* Princeton, 1968.

Marotti, Arthur F., ed. *Catholicism and Anti-Catholicism in Early Modern English Texts.* Basingstoke, Hampshire, Eng., 1999.

Matar, Nabil. *Turks, Moors, and Englishmen in the Age of Discovery.* New York, 1999.

Mattingly, Garrett. *The Armada.* Boston, 1959.

McEachern, Claire, and Debora Shuger, eds. *Religion and Culture in Renaissance England.* Cambridge, Eng., 1997.

McElwee, W. *The Wisest Fool in Christendom.* [About James VI and I.] New York, 1958.

McPeek, James A. S. *The Black Book of Knaves and Unthrifts in Shakespeare and Other Renaissance Authors.* Storrs, Conn., 1969.

Neale, John E. *Elizabeth I and Her Parliaments.* 2 vols. London and New York, 1953–1958.

———. *The Elizabethan House of Commons.* London, 1949.

———. *Queen Elizabeth I.* London, 1934; New York, 1957.

Nichols, John, ed. *The Progresses and Public Processions of Queen Elizabeth.* 3 vols. London, 1823.

Patterson, Annabel M. *Reading Holinshed's Chronicles.* Chicago, 1994.

Peck, Linda Levy. *Court Patronage and Corruption in Early Stuart England.* Boston, 1990.

Penrose, Boies. *Travel and Discovery in the Renaissance, 1420–1620.* Cambridge, Mass., 1955.

Quinones, Ricardo J. *The Renaissance Discovery of Time.* Cambridge, Mass., 1972.

Rowse, A. L. *The England of Elizabeth: The Structure of Society.* London, 1951.

Stallybrass, Peter, and Allon White. *The Politics and Poetics of Transgression.* Ithaca, N.Y., and London, 1986.

Stone, Lawrence. *The Crisis of the Aristocracy,* 1558–1641. Oxford, 1965.

———. *The Family, Sex and Marriage in England, 1500–1800.* London, 1977.

Stow, John. *Survey of London,* ed. C. L. Kingsford. Oxford, 1971.

Targoff, Ramie. *Common Prayer: The Language of Public Devotion in Early Modern England.* Chicago, 2001.

Tawney, R. H. *Religion and the Rise of Capitalism.* New York, 1926, 1962.

Tillyard, E. M. W. *The Elizabethan World Picture.* London, 1943, 1967.

Underdown, David. *Revel, Riot, and Rebellion: Popular Politics and Culture in England, 1603–1660.* Oxford, 1985.

Whigham, Frank. *Ambition and Privilege: The Social Tropes of Elizabethan Courtesy Theory.* Berkeley, 1984.

Willson, David Harris. *King James VI & I.* New York, 1956.

Wilson, F. P. *Elizabethan and Jacobean.* Oxford, 1945.

Wilson, J. Dover, ed. *Life in Shakespeare's England.* Cambridge, Eng., 1911; 2nd ed., 1926.

Woodbridge, Linda. *Women and the English Renaissance.* Urbana, Ill., 1984.

Wright, Louis B. *Middle-Class Culture in Elizabethan England.* Chapel Hill, N.C., 1935.

Wrightson, Keith. *English Society, 1580–1680.* New Brunswick, N.J., 1982.

Zeeveld, W. Gordon. *Foundations of Tudor Policy.* Cambridge, Mass., 1948.

Shakespeare's Predecessors and Contemporaries

See also, under *Works of Reference,* Bentley, Chambers, Greg, and Harbage; under *London Theaters and Dramatic Companies,* McMillin and MacLean; and under *Shakespeare Criticism Since 1980,* Dollimore, Garber (*Cannibals*), Goldberg, Greenblatt, Jardine, Loomba, Mullaney, Newman, and Skura.

Altman, Joel B. *The Tudor Play of Mind: Rhetorical Inquiry and the Development of Elizabethan Drama.* Berkeley, 1978.

Bamford, Karen. *Sexual Violence on the Jacobean Stage.* New York, 2000.

Barber, C. L. *Creating Elizabethan Tragedy: The Theater of Kyd and Marlowe.* Chicago, 1988.

Bartels, Emily C. *Spectacles of Strangeness: Imperialism, Alienation, and Marlowe.* Philadelphia, 1993.

Bednarz, James P. *Shakespeare and the Poets' War.* New York, 2001.

Belsey, Catherine. *The Subject of Tragedy: Identity and Difference in Renaissance Drama.* London, 1985.

Berry, Philippa. *Of Chastity and Power: Elizabethan Literature and the Unmarried Queen.* London and New York, 1989.

Bevington, David. *From "Mankind" to Marlowe: Growth of Structure in the Popular Drama of Tudor England.* Cambridge, Mass., 1962.

———. *Tudor Drama and Politics.* Cambridge, Mass., 1968.

———, and Peter Holbrook, eds. *The Politics of the Stuart Court Masque*. Cambridge, Eng., 1991.

Bowers, Fredson T. *Elizabethan Revenge Tragedy, 1587–1642*. Princeton, 1940.

Braden, Gordon. *Renaissance Tragedy and the Senecan Tradition.* New Haven, 1985.

Braunmuller, A. R., and Michael Hattaway, eds. *The Cambridge Companion to English Renaissance Drama*. Cambridge, Eng., 1990.

Bristol, Michael D. *Carnival and Theater: Plebeian Culture and the Structure of Authority in Renaissance England.* London, 1985.

Brooke, C. F. Tucker, ed. *The Shakespeare Apocrypha*. Oxford, 1908.

Brooks, Douglas A. *From Playhouse to Printing House: Drama and Authorship in Early Modern England*. Cambridge, Eng., 2000.

Bruster, Douglas. *Drama and the Market in the Age of Shakespeare*. Cambridge, Eng., 1992.

Burt, Richard. *Licensed by Authority: Ben Jonson and the Discourses of Censorship.* Ithaca, N.Y., 1993.

Bushnell, Rebecca W. *Tragedies of Tyrants: Political Thought and Theater in the English Renaissance*. Ithaca, N.Y., 1990.

Butterworth, Philip. *Theatre of Fire: Special Effects in Early English and Scottish Theatre.* London, 1998.

Caputi, Anthony. *John Marston, Satirist.* Ithaca, N.Y., 1961.

Cohen, Walter. *Drama of a Nation: Public Theater in Renaissance England and Spain.* Ithaca, N.Y., 1985.

Comensoli, Viviana, and Anna Russell, eds. *Enacting Gender on the English Renaissance Stage*. Urbana, Ill., 1999.

Cox, John D., and David Scott Kastan, eds. *A New History of Early English Drama*. New York, 1997.

Craik, T. W. *The Tudor Interlude.* Leicester, 1958, 1962.

Dawson, Anthony B., and Paul Yachnin. *The Culture of Playgoing in Shakespeare's England: A Collaborative Debate*. Cambridge, Eng., 2001.

Deats, Sara Munson. *Sex, Gender, and Desire in the Plays of Christopher Marlowe.* Newark, Del., 1997.

Dessen, Alan C. *Elizabethan Drama and the Viewer's Eye.* Chapel Hill, N.C., 1977.

Diehl, Huston. *Staging Reform, Reforming the Stage: Protestantism and Popular Theater in Early Modern England*. Ithaca, N.Y., 1997.

Dillon, Janette. *Theatre, Court and City, 1595–1610: Drama and Social Space in London*. Cambridge, Eng., 2000.

DiGangi, Mario. *The Homoerotics of Early Modern Drama*. Cambridge, Eng., 1997.

Dolan, Frances E. *Dangerous Familiars: Representations of Domestic Crime in England, 1550–1700.* Ithaca, N.Y., 1994.

Doran, Madeleine. *Endeavors of Art: A Study of Form in Elizabethan Drama.* Madison, Wis., 1954, 1972.

Farley-Hills, David. *Shakespeare and the Rival Playwrights, 1600–1606.* London, 1990.

Findlay, Alison. *A Feminist Perspective on Renaissance Drama*. Oxford, 1999.

———. *Illegitimate Power: Bastards in Renaissance Drama*. Manchester, Eng., 1994.

Finkelpearl, Philip. *John Marston of the Middle Temple*. Cambridge, Mass., 1969.

Freer, Coburn. *The Poetics of Jacobean Drama*. Baltimore, 1981.

Gardiner, H. C. *Mysteries' End.* New Haven, 1946.

Gibbons, Brian. *Jacobean City Comedy*. London, 1968.

Hall, Kim F. *Things of Darkness: Economies of Race and Gender in Early Modern England*. Ithaca, N.Y., 1995.

Hardison, O. B., Jr. *Christian Rite and Christian Drama in the Middle Ages*. Baltimore, 1965.

Hassel, R. Chris. *Renaissance Drama and the English Church Year*. Lincoln, Neb., 1979.

Hattaway, Michael. *Elizabethan Popular Theatre: Plays in Performance*. London, 1982.

Hawkins, Harriett. *Likenesses of Truth in Elizabethan and Restoration Drama*. Oxford, 1972.

Helgerson, Richard. *Adulterous Alliances: Home, State, and History in Early Modern European Drama and Painting*. Chicago, 2000.

Hendricks, Margo, and Patricia Parker, eds. *Women, "Race," and Writing in the Early Modern Period*. London and New York, 1994.

Holbrook, Peter. *Literature and Degree in Renaissance England: Nashe, Bourgeois Tragedy, Shakespeare*. Newark, Del., 1994.

Howard, Jean. *The Stage and Social Struggle in Early Modern England*. London and New York, 1994.

Hunter, G. K. *John Lyly: The Humanist as Courtier*. Cambridge, Mass., 1962.

Kastan, David Scott, and Peter Stallybrass, eds. *Staging the Renaissance: Reinterpretations of Elizabethan and Jacobean Drama.* New York and London, 1991.

Kernan, Alvin. *The Cankered Muse: Satire of the English Renaissance*. New Haven, 1959.

Kiefer, Frederick. *Writing on the Renaissance Stage: Written Words, Printed Pages, Metaphoric Books*. Newark, Del., 1996.

Kirsch, Arthur C. *Jacobean Dramatic Perspectives*. Charlottesville, Va., 1972.

Kolve, V. A. *The Play Called Corpus Christi.* Palo Alto and London, 1966.

Leggatt, Alexander. *Citizen Comedy in the Age of Shakespeare*. Toronto, 1973.

———. *Jacobean Public Theatre*. London, 1992.

Leishman, J. B., ed. *The Three Parnassus Plays (1598–1601).* London, 1949.

Levin, Harry. *The Overreacher: A Study of Christopher Marlowe*. Cambridge, Mass., 1952, 1964.

Levin, Richard. *The Multiple Plot in English Renaissance Drama*. Chicago, 1971.

Margeson, J. M. R. *The Origins of English Tragedy*. Oxford, 1967.

Marrapodi, Michele, ed., with A. J. Hoenselaars. *The Italian World of English Renaissance Drama: Cultural Exchange and Intertextuality*. Newark, Del., 1998.

Maus, Katharine Eisaman. *Inwardness and Theater in the English Renaissance Drama*. Chicago, 1995.

McAlindon, T. *English Renaissance Tragedy*. London, 1986.

McLuskie, Kathleen. *Renaissance Dramatists*. (Feminist Readings.) Atlantic Highlands, N.J., 1989.

Orgel, Stephen. *The Illusion of Power: Political Theater in the English Renaissance*. Berkeley, 1975.

———. *Impersonations: The Performance of Gender in Shakespeare's England*. Cambridge, Eng., 1996.

Orgel, Stephen, and Roy Strong. *Inigo Jones: The Theatre of the Stuart Court.* 2 vols. London and Berkeley, 1973.

Ornstein, Robert. *The Moral Vision of Jacobean Tragedy*. Madison, Wis., 1960.

Rabkin, Norman, ed: *Reinterpretations of Elizabethan Drama*. New York, 1969.

Rasmussen, Mark David, ed. *Renaissance Literature and Its Formal Engagements*. Basingstoke, Hampshire, 2002.

Rose, Mary Beth. *The Expense of Spirit: Love and Sexuality in English Renaissance Drama*. Ithaca, N.Y., 1988.

———. *Gender and Heroism in Early Modern English Literature*. Chicago, 2002.

———. ed. *Renaissance Drama as Cultural History*. Evanston, Ill., 1990.

Sanders, Wilbur. *The Dramatist and the Received Idea: Studies in the Plays of Marlowe and Shakespeare*. Cambridge, Eng., 1968.

Shannon, Laurie. *Sovereign Amity: Figures of Friendship in Shakespearean Contexts*. Chicago, 2002.

Shapiro, James. *Rival Playwrights: Marlowe, Jonson, Shakespeare.* New York, 1991.

Smith, Bruce R. *The Acoustic World of Early Modern England*. Chicago, 1999.

Smith, David L., Richard Strier, and David Bevington, eds. *The Theatrical City: Culture, Theatre and Politics in London, 1567–1649*. Cambridge, Eng., 1995.

Southern, Richard. *The Medieval Theatre in the Round*. London, 1957.

Spivack, Bernard. *Shakespeare and the Allegory of Evil*. New York, 1958.

Traub, Valerie, M. Lindsay Kaplan, and Dympna C. Callaghan, eds. *Feminist Readings of Early Modern Culture: Emerging Subjects*. Cambridge, Eng., 1996.

Vickers, Brian. *"Counterfeiting" Shakespeare: Evidence, Authorship, and John Ford's "Funerall Elegye."* Cambridge, Eng., 2002.

Waith, Eugene M. *The Herculean Hero in Marlowe, Chapman, Shakespeare, and Dryden*. New York, 1962.

Whigham, Frank. *Seizures of the Will in Early Modern English Drama*. Cambridge, Eng., 1996.

White, Paul Whitfield. *Marlowe, History, and Sexuality: New Critical Essays on Christopher Marlowe*. New York, 1998.

———. *Theatre and Reformation: Protestantism, Patronage and Playing in Tudor England.* Cambridge, Eng., 1993.
Wickham, Glynne. *Early English Stages, 1300 to 1660.* 3 vols. London, 1959–1972.
Wilson, F. P. *Marlowe and the Early Shakespeare.* Oxford, 1953.
Woodbridge, Linda. *Women and the English Renaissance: Literature and the Nature of Womankind, 1540–1620.* Urbana, Ill., 1984.
Woolf, Rosemary. *The English Mystery Plays.* Berkeley and Los Angeles, 1972.
Yachnin, Paul. *Stage-Wrights: Shakespeare, Jonson, Middleton, and the Making of Theatrical Value.* Philadelphia, 1997.
Zimmerman, Susan, ed. *Erotic Politics: Desire on the Renaissance Stage.* London and New York, 1992.

London Theaters and Dramatic Companies

See also, under *Works of Reference*, Bentley, and Chambers (*Elizabethan Stage*).
Astington, John H., ed. *The Development of Shakespeare's Theater.* New York, 1992.
Beckerman, Bernard. *Shakespeare at the Globe, 1599–1609.* New York, 1962, 1967.
Bentley, Gerald Eades. *The Profession of Dramatist in Shakespeare's Time, 1590–1642.* Princeton, 1971.
———. *The Profession of Player in Shakespeare's Time, 1590–1642.* Princeton, 1984.
Berry, Herbert. *Shakespeare's Playhouses.* New York, 1987.
Bradley, David. *From Text to Performance in the Elizabethan Theatre: Preparing the Play for the Stage.* Cambridge, Eng., 1992.
Clare, Janet. *"Art Made Tongue-Tied by Authority": Elizabethan and Jacobean Dramatic Censorship.* Manchester, Eng., 1990.
Cook, Ann Jennalie. *The Privileged Playgoers of Shakespeare's London, 1576–1642.* Princeton, 1981.
Dutton, Richard. *Mastering the Revels: The Regulation and Censorship of English Renaissance Drama.* Iowa City, 1991.
Feuillerat, Albert, ed. *Documents Relating to the Office of the Revels in the Time of Queen Elizabeth.* Louvain (Louven), Belgium, 1908.
Foakes, R. A., ed. *The Henslowe Papers: The Diary, Theatre Papers, and Bear Garden Papers.* In full and in facsimile. 3 vols. in 2. London, 1976.
Foakes, R. A., and R. T. Rickert, eds. *Henslowe's Diary.* London, 1961.
Gair, W. Reavley. *The Children of Paul's.* Cambridge, Eng., 1982.
Greg, W. W., ed. *Dramatic Documents from the Elizabethan Playhouses: Stage Plots; Actors' Parts; Prompt Books.* 2 vols. Oxford, 1931.
Gurr, Andrew. *Playgoing in Shakespeare's London.* Cambridge, Eng., 1987; 2nd ed., 1996.
———. *The Shakespearian Playing Companies.* Oxford, 1996.
——— *The Shakespearean Stage, 1574–1642.* Cambridge, Eng., 1970; 2nd ed., 1980.
Gurr, Andrew, and John Orrell. *Rebuilding Shakespeare's Globe.* London and New York, 1989.
Harbage, Alfred. *Shakespeare's Audience.* New York, 1941.
Hodges, C. Walter. *The Globe Restored.* London, 1953; 2nd ed., New York, 1968.
Hosley, Richard. "Was There a Music-room in Shakespeare's Globe?" *ShS 13* (1960), 113–23.
Ingram, William. *The Business of Playing: The Beginnings of the Adult Professional Theater in Elizabethan London.* Ithaca, N.Y., 1992.
King, T. J. *Casting Shakespeare's Plays: London Actors and Their Roles, 1590–1642.* Cambridge, Eng., 1992.
———. *Shakespearean Staging, 1599–1642.* Cambridge, Mass., 1971.
Knutson, Roslyn Lander. *The Repertory of Shakespeare's Company, 1594–1613.* Fayetteville, Ark., 1991.
———. *Playing Companies and Commerce in Shakespeare's Time.* Cambridge, Eng., 2001.
Linthicum, Marie C. *Costume in the Drama of Shakespeare and His Contemporaries.* Oxford, 1936.
Mann, David. *The Elizabethan Player: Contemporary Stage Representation.* London, 1991.
McMillin, Scott. *The Elizabethan Theatre and "The Book of Sir Thomas More."* Ithaca, N.Y., 1987.
McMillin, Scott, and Sally-Beth MacLean. *The Queen's Men and Their Plays.* Cambridge, Eng., 1998.
Nelson, Alan H. *Early Cambridge Theatres: College, University, and Town Stages, 1464–1720.* Cambridge, Eng., 1994.
Nungezer, Edwin. *A Dictionary of Actors.* London and New Haven, 1929.
Shapiro, Michael. *Children of the Revels: The Boys' Companies of Shakespeare's Time and Their Plays.* New York, 1977.
Wickham, Glynne. *Early English Stages, 1300 to 1660.* 3 vols. London, 1959–1972.

Shakespeare's Life and Work

Alexander, Peter. *Shakespeare's Life and Art.* New ed., New York, 1961.
Baldwin, T. W. *William Shakspere's Small Latine and Lesse Greeke.* 2 vols. Urbana, Ill., 1944.
Chambers, E. K. *William Shakespeare: A Study of Facts and Problems.* 2 vols. Oxford, 1930.
Eccles, Mark. *Shakespeare in Warwickshire.* Madison, Wis., 1961.
Honan, Park. *Shakespeare: A Life.* Oxford, 1998.
Matus, Irvin Leigh, *Shakespeare, In Fact.* New York, 1994.
Schoenbaum, S. *Shakespeare's Lives.* Oxford and New York, 1970.
———. *William Shakespeare: A Documentary Life.* Oxford, 1975. Also published with fewer illustrations and a slightly revised text as *A Compact Documentary Life.* 1977.
———. *William Shakespeare: Records and Images.* Oxford, 1981.
Wells, Stanley. *Shakespeare: A Life in Drama.* New York and London, 1995.
Wheeler, Richard P. "Deaths in the Family: The Loss of a Son and the Rise of Shakespearean Comedy," *SQ* 51 (2000), 127–53.

Shakespeare's Language: His Development as Poet and Dramatist

See also, under *Works of Reference*, Abbott, Onions, and Schmidt; and under *The Comedies*, Elam.
Byrne, Muriel St. Clare. "The Foundations of Elizabethan Language," *ShS 17* (1964), 223–39.
Cercignani, Fausto. *Shakespeare's Works and Elizabethan Pronunciation.* Oxford, 1981.
Charney, Maurice. *Shakespeare's Roman Plays: The Function of Imagery in the Drama.* Cambridge, Mass., 1961.
———. *Style in Hamlet.* Princeton, 1969.
Clemen, Wolfgang H. *The Development of Shakespeare's Imagery.* Cambridge, Mass., 1951.
Cruttwell, Patrick. *The Shakespearean Moment and Its Place in the Poetry of the Seventeenth Century.* London, 1954.
Desmet, Christy. *Reading Shakespeare's Characters: Rhetoric, Ethics, and Identity.* Amherst, Mass., 1992.
Dobson, E. J. *English Pronunciation, 1500–1700.* 2 vols. 2nd ed. Oxford, 1968.
Donawerth, Jane. *Shakespeare and the Sixteenth-Century Study of Language.* Urbana, Ill., 1984.
Doran, Madeleine. *Shakespeare's Dramatic Language.* Madison, Wis., 1976.
Empson, William. *The Structure of Complex Words.* London, 1951; 3rd ed., 1977.
Hulme, Hilda M. *Explorations in Shakespeare's Language.* London, 1962.
Kermode, Frank. *Shakespeare's Language.* New York, 2000.
Kökeritz, Helge. *Shakespeare's Names.* New Haven, 1959.
———. *Shakespeare's Pronunciation.* New Haven, 1953.
Lanham, Richard A. *The Motives of Eloquence: Literary Rhetoric in the Renaissance.* New Haven, 1976.
Magnussen, Lynne. *Shakespeare and Social Dialogue: Dramatic Language and Elizabethan Letters.* Cambridge, Eng., 1999.
Mahood, M. M. *Shakespeare's Wordplay.* London, 1957.
Miriam Joseph, Sister. *Shakespeare's Use of the Arts of Language.* New York, 1947. Rpt. in part as *Rhetoric in Shakespeare's Time.* 1962.
Nares, Robert. *A Glossary . . . of Shakespeare and His Contemporaries.* New ed. J. O.

Halliwell and Thomas Wright. 2 vols. London, 1859, 1905, Rpt. Detroit, 1966.
Partridge, Eric. *Shakespeare's Bawdy*. London, 1947, 1955.
Spurgeon, Caroline. *Shakespeare's Imagery and What it Tells Us*. Cambridge, Eng., 1935.
Thompson, Ann and John O. *Shakespeare: Meaning and Metaphor*. Iowa City, 1987.
Thorne, Alison. *Vision and Rhetoric in Shakespeare: Looking Through Language*. Basingstoke and New York, 2000.
Vickers, Brian. *The Artistry of Shakespeare's Prose*. London, 1968.
Willbern, David. *Poetic Will: Shakespeare and the Play of Language*. Philadelphia, 1997.
Willcock, Gladys D. "Shakespeare and Elizabethan English," *ShS* 7 (1954), 12–24.
Wright, George T. *Shakespeare's Metrical Art*. Berkeley, 1988.

Shakespeare Criticism to the 1930s

Badawi, M. M. *Coleridge: Critic of Shakespeare*. Cambridge, Eng., 1973.
Bradby, Anne, ed. *Shakespeare Criticism, 1919–35*. London, 1936.
Coleridge, S. T. *Coleridge on Shakespeare: The Text of the Lectures of 1811–12*, ed. R. A. Foakes. Charlottesville, Va., 1971.
———. *Coleridge's Writings on Shakespeare*, ed. Terence Hawkes. New York, 1959.
Evans, G. Blakemore, ed. *Shakespeare: Aspects of Influence*. Cambridge, Mass., 1976.
Hazlitt, William. *Characters of Shakespear's Plays*. London, 1817.
Johnson, Samuel. *Johnson on Shakespeare*, ed. Arthur Sherbo. Vol. 7 of *The Yale Edition of the Works of Samuel Johnson*. New Haven, 1968.
Kermode, Frank, ed. *Four Centuries of Shakespearean Criticism*. New York, 1965.
Knight, G. Wilson. *The Shakespearian Tempest*. London, 1932, 1953.
Muir, Kenneth. "Fifty Years of Shakespearian Criticism: 1900–1950," *ShS* 4 (1951), 1–25.
Rabkin, Norman, ed. *Approaches to Shakespeare*. New York, 1964.
Ralli, Augustus. *A History of Shakespearian Criticism*. 2 vols. London, 1932.
Raysor, T. M., ed. *Samuel Taylor Coleridge: Shakespearean Criticism*. 2 vols. 2nd ed. London, 1960.
Schlegel, August Wilhelm. *Lectures on Dramatic Art and Literature*, trans. John Black, 1846. Rpt., New York, 1965.
Schücking, Levin L. *Character Problems in Shakespeare's Plays*. London, 1917; trans., 1922.
Shaw, G. B. *Shaw on Shakespeare*, ed. Edwin Wilson. New York, 1961.
Sherbo, Arthur. *Samuel Johnson, Editor of Shakespeare*. Urbana, Ill., 1956.
Smith, David Nichol, ed. *Shakespeare Criticism: A Selection*. World's Classics, Oxford, 1916.
———, ed. *Eighteenth Century Essays on Shakespeare*. 2nd ed. Oxford, 1963.
Stoll, E. E. *Art and Artifice in Shakespeare*. Cambridge, Eng., 1933, 1962.
Vickers, Brian, ed. *Shakespeare: The Critical Heritage*. Several volumes. London and Boston, 1974—.
Welsford, Enid. *The Fool: His Social and Literary History*. London, 1935; rpt. 1966.
Westfall, A. V. *American Shakespearean Criticism, 1607–1865*. New York, 1939.

Shakespeare Criticism from the 1940s to the 1970s

Armstrong, Edward A. *Shakespeare's Imagination: A Study of the Psychology of Association and Inspiration*. London, 1946.
Bethell, S. L. *Shakespeare and the Popular Dramatic Tradition*. London and Durham, N.C., 1944.
Bevington, David, and Jay L. Halio, eds. *Shakespeare: Pattern of Excelling Nature*. Newark, Del., 1978.
Bloom, Allan, with Harry V. Jaffa. *Shakespeare's Politics*. New York and London, 1964.
Brown, John Russell. *Shakespeare's Plays in Performance*. London, 1966.
Bryant, J. A., Jr. *Hippolyta's View: Some Christian Aspects of Shakespeare's Plays*. Lexington, Ky., 1961.
Burckhardt, Sigurd. *Shakespearean Meanings*. Princeton, 1968.
Burke, Kenneth. *Language as Symbolic Action*. Berkeley, 1966.
Calderwood, James L. *Shakespearean Metadrama*. Minneapolis, 1971.
Coghill, Neville. *Shakespeare's Professional Skills*. Cambridge, Eng., 1964.
Colie, Rosalie L. *Shakespeare's Living Art*. Princeton, 1974.
Council, Norman. *When Honour's at the Stake: Ideas of Honour in Shakespeare's Plays*. London, 1973.
Danby, John F. *Poets on Fortune's Hill: Studies in Sidney, Shakespeare, and Beaumont and Fletcher*. London, 1952.
Dean, Leonard F., ed. *Shakespeare: Modern Essays in Criticism*. New York, 1967.
Driver, Tom F. *The Sense of History in Greek and Shakespearean Drama*. New York, 1960.
Dusinberre, Juliet. *Shakespeare and the Nature of Women*. New York, 1975. 2nd ed., 1996.
Eagleton, Terence. *Shakespeare and Society*. New York and London, 1967.
Edwards, Philip. *Shakespeare and the Confines of Art*. London and New York, 1968.
Empson, William. *The Structure of Complex Words*. London, 1951.
Fiedler, Leslie A. *The Stranger in Shakespeare*. New York, 1972.
Fly, Richard. *Shakespeare's Mediated World*. Amherst, Mass., 1976.
Frye, Roland M. *Shakespeare and Christian Doctrine*. Princeton, 1963.
Garber, Marjorie B. *Dream in Shakespeare: From Metaphor to Metamorphosis*. New Haven and London, 1974.
Goddard, Harold C. *The Meaning of Shakespeare*. Chicago, 1951.
Goldman, Michael. *Shakespeare and the Energies of Drama*. Princeton, 1972.
Granville-Barker, Harley. *Prefaces to Shakespeare*. 2 vols. Princeton, 1946–1947.
Harbage, Alfred. *As They Liked it*. New York, 1947.
———. *Shakespeare and the Rival Traditions*. New York, 1952.
Hawkes, Terence. *Shakespeare's Talking Animals: Language and Drama in Society*. London, 1973.
Hawkins, Harriett. *Poetic Freedom and Poetic Truth: Chaucer, Shakespeare, Marlowe, Milton*. Oxford, 1976.
Holland, Norman. *Psychoanalysis and Shakespeare*. New York, 1966.
———. *The Shakespearean Imagination*. New York, 1964.
Jones, Emrys. *The Origins of Shakespeare*. Oxford, 1977.
Jorgensen, Paul A. *Shakespeare's Military World*. Berkeley and Los Angeles, 1956.
Kernan, Alvin B. *The Playwright as Magician: Shakespeare's Image of the Poet in the English Public Theater*. New Haven, 1979.
———, ed. *Modern Shakespearean Criticism*. New York, 1970.
Kettle, Arnold, ed. *Shakespeare in a Changing World*. London and New York, 1964.
Knights, L. C. *Some Shakespearean Themes*. London, 1959.
Kott, Jan. *Shakespeare Our Contemporary*. New York, 1964.
Leavis, F. R. *The Common Pursuit*. London, 1952.
Levin, Richard. *New Readings vs. Old Plays: Recent Trends in the Reinterpretation of English Renaissance Drama*. Chicago, 1979.
McAlindon, T. *Shakespeare and Decorum*. London and New York, 1973.
Rabkin, Norman. *Shakespeare and the Common Understanding*. New York, 1967.
Righter, Anne. *Shakespeare and the Idea of the Play*. London, 1962.
Rossiter, A. P. *Angel with Horns*. London, 1961.
Sanders, Wilbur. *The Dramatist and the Received Idea: Studies in the Plays of Marlowe and Shakespeare*. Cambridge, Eng., 1968.
Sewell, Arthur. *Character and Society in Shakespeare*. London, 1951.
Soellner, Rolf. *Shakespeare's Patterns of Self-Knowledge*. Columbus, Ohio, 1972.
Spencer, Theodore. *Shakespeare and the Nature of Man*. New York, 1942.
Spivack, Bernard. *Shakespeare and the Allegory of Evil*. New York, 1958.
Stewart, J. I. M. *Character and Motive in Shakespeare*. London, 1949.
Stirling, Brents. *The Populace in Shakespeare*. New York, 1949.
Traversi, Derek. *An Approach to Shakespeare*. 2 vols. Rev. ed. London, 1968.
Van Laan, Thomas F. *Role-Playing in Shakespeare*. Toronto, 1978.
Watson, Curtis Brown. *Shakespeare and the Renaissance Concept of Honor*. Princeton, 1960.
Weimann, Robert. *Shakespeare and the Popular Tradition in the Theater*, ed. Robert Schwartz. Baltimore, 1978.

Whitaker, Virgil K. *Shakespeare's Use of Learning*. San Marino, Calif., 1953.

Zeeveld, W. Gordon. *The Temper of Shakespeare's Thought*. New Haven and London, 1974.

Shakespeare Criticism Since 1980, including New Historicism, Gender Studies, and Poststructuralism

See also, under *Shakespeare's Predecessors and Contemporaries*, Bednarz, Belsey, Braden, Bristol, Bruster, Cohen, Dolan, Farley-Hills, Findlay (two items), Freer, McLuskie, Orgel, Rasmussen, Rose, Shannon, and Vickers; and under *Shakespeare Criticism from the 1940s to the 1970s*, Weimann.

Adelman, Janet. *Suffocating Mothers: Fantasies of Maternal Origin in Shakespeare's Plays, "Hamlet" to "The Tempest."* Chicago, 1992.

Alexander, Catherine M. S., and Stanley Wells, eds. *Shakespeare and Race*. Cambridge, Eng., 2000.

Auden, W. H. *Lectures on Shakespeare*, ed. Arthur Kirsch. Princeton, 2000.

Bamber, Linda. *Comic Women, Tragic Men: A Study of Gender and Genre in Shakespeare*. Stanford, 1982.

Barber, C. L. *The Whole Journey: Shakespeare's Power of Development*. Berkeley, 1986.

Bate, Jonathan. *The Genius of Shakespeare*. Oxford, 1997.

Belsey, Catherine. *Shakespeare and the Loss of Eden: The Construction of Family Values in Early Modern Culture*. New Brunswick, N.J., 1999.

Berger, Harry, Jr. *Making Trifles of Terrors: Redistributing Complicities in Shakespeare*. ed. Peter Erickson. Stanford, 1997.

Bergeron, David, ed. *Pageantry in the Shakespearean Theater*. Athens, Ga., 1985.

Bevington, David. *Shakespeare*. Oxford, 2002.

Boose, Lynda E. "The Father and the Bride in Shakespeare," *PMLA* 97 (1982), 325–47.

Bristol, Michael. *Shakespeare's America, America's Shakespeare*. London and New York, 1990.

Bulman, James C., ed. *Shakespeare, Theory, and Performance*. London and New York, 1996.

Calderwood, James. *Shakespeare and the Denial of Death*. Amherst, Mass., 1987.

Callaghan, Dympna C. *Shakespeare Without Women: Representing Gender and Race on the Renaissance Stage*. London and New York, 2000.

———, ed. *A Feminist Companion to Shakespeare*. Oxford, 2000.

Callaghan, Dympna, Lorraine Helms, and Jyotsna Singh. *The Weyward Sisters: Shakespeare and Feminist Politics*. Cambridge, Eng., 1994.

Carey, John, ed. *English Renaissance Studies*. Oxford, 1980.

Cartelli, Thomas. *Repositioning Shakespeare: National Formations, Postcolonial Appropriations*. London and New York, 1999.

Cavell, Stanley. *Disowning Knowledge in Six Plays of Shakespeare*. Cambridge, Eng., 1987.

Charnes, Linda. *Notorious Identity: Materializing the Subject in Shakespeare*. Cambridge, Mass., 1993.

Cook, Ann Jennalie. *Making a Match: Courtship in Shakespeare and His Society*. Princeton, 1991.

Cox, John D. *Shakespeare and the Dramaturgy of Power*. Princeton, 1989.

Daileder, Celia R. *Eroticism on the Renaissance Stage: Transcendence, Desire, and the Limits of the Visible*. Cambridge, Eng., 1998.

Danson, Lawrence. *Shakespeare's Dramatic Genres*. Oxford, 2000.

Dawson, Anthony B. *Indirections: Shakespeare and the Art of Illusion*. Toronto, 1984.

De Grazia, Margreta, Maureen Quilligan, and Peter Stallybrass, eds. *Subject and Object in Renaissance Culture*. Cambridge, Eng., 1996.

Desmet, Christy. *Reading Shakespeare's Characters: Rhetoric, Ethics, and Identity*. Amherst, Mass., 1992.

Desmet, Christy, and Robert Sawyer, eds. *Shakespeare and Appropriation*. London and New York, 1999.

Dobson, Michael. *The Making of the National Poet: Shakespeare, Adaptation, and Authorship, 1660–1769*. Oxford, 1992.

Dolan, Frances E. *Dangerous Familiars: Representations of Domestic Crime in England, 1550–1700*. Ithaca, N.Y., 1994.

Dollimore, Jonathan. *Radical Tragedy: Religion, Ideology and Power in the Drama of Shakespeare and His Contemporaries*. Chicago, 1984; New York, 1989.

Dollimore, Jonathan, and Alan Sinfield. *Political Shakespeare: New Essays in Cultural Materialism*. Manchester, Eng., 1985.

Drakakis, John, ed. *Alternative Shakespeares*. London, 1985.

Dubrow, Heather, and Richard Strier, eds. *The Historical Renaissance: New Essays on Tudor and Stuart Literature and Culture*. Chicago, 1988.

Eagleton, Terence. *William Shakespeare*. Oxford, 1986.

Edwards, Philip, et al., eds. *Shakespeare's Styles*. Cambridge, Eng., 1980.

Engle, Lars. *Shakespearean Pragmatism: Market of His Time*. Chicago, 1993.

Erickson, Peter. *Patriarchal Structures in Shakespeare's Drama*. Berkeley, 1985.

Erickson, Peter, and Coppélia Kahn, eds. *Shakespeare's Rough Magic: Essays in Honor of C. L. Barber*. Newark, Del., 1985.

French, Marilyn. *Shakespeare's Division of Experience*. New York, 1981.

Frye, Northrop. *Northrop Frye on Shakespeare*, ed. Robert Sandler. New Haven, 1986.

Fumerton, Patricia, and Simon Hunt, eds. *Renaissance Culture and the Everyday*. Philadelphia, 1999.

Garber, Marjorie. *Coming of Age in Shakespeare*. London, 1981.

———. *Shakespeare's Ghost Writers: Literature as Uncanny Causality*. London and New York, 1987.

———, ed. *Cannibals, Witches, and Divorce: Estranging the Renaissance*. Baltimore, 1987.

Gibbons, Brian. *Shakespeare and Multiplicity*. Cambridge, Eng., 1993.

Gillies, John. *Shakespeare and the Geography of Difference*. Cambridge, Eng., 1994.

Goldberg, Jonathan. *James I and the Politics of Literature: Jonson, Shakespeare, Donne, and Their Contemporaries*. Baltimore, 1983.

———. *Sodometries: Renaissance Texts, Modern Sexualities*. Stanford, 1992.

Grady, Hugh, ed. *Shakespeare and Modernity: Early Modern to Millennium*. London and New York, 2000.

Greenblatt, Stephen. *Learning to Curse: Essays in Early Modern Culture*. London and New York, 1990.

———. *Marvelous Possessions: The Wonder of the New World*. Chicago, 1991.

———. *Renaissance Self-Fashioning: From More to Shakespeare*. Chicago, 1980.

———. *Shakespearean Negotiations: The Circulation of Social Energy in Renaissance England*. Berkeley, 1988.

Habib, Imtiaz. *Shakespeare and Race: Postcolonial Praxis in the Early Modern Period*. Lanham and Oxford, 2000.

Hall, Kim F. *Things of Darkness: Economies of Race and Gender in Early Modern England*. Ithaca, N.Y., 1994.

Hamilton, Donna B. *Shakespeare and the Politics of Protestant England*. Lexington, Ky., 1992.

Hamlin, William M. *The Image of America in Montaigne, Spenser, and Shakespeare: Renaissance Ethnography and Literary Tradition*. New York, 1995.

Hawkes, Terence. *Meaning by Shakespeare*. London and New York, 1992.

———, ed. *Alternative Shakespeares*. Vol. 2. London and New York, 1996.

Holland, Norman, et al., eds. *Shakespeare's Personality*. Berkeley, 1989.

Howard, Jean E. *Shakespeare's Art of Orchestration: Stage Technique and Audience Response*. Urbana, Ill., 1984.

———. *The Stage and Social Struggle in Early Modern England*. London, 1994.

———, and Marion F. O'Connor, eds. *Shakespeare Reproduced: The Text in History and Ideology*. London and New York, 1987.

———, and Scott Cutler Shershow, eds. *Marxist Shakespeares*. London and New York, 2000.

James, Heather. *Shakespeare's Troy: Drama, Politics, and the Translation of Empire*. Cambridge, Eng., 1997.

Jardine, Lisa. *Reading Shakespeare Historically*. London and New York, 1996.

———. *Still Harping on Daughters: Women and Drama in the Age of Shakespeare*. Sussex and Totowa, N.J., 1983; New York, 1989.

Kahn, Coppélia. *Man's Estate: Masculine Identity in Shakespeare*. Berkeley, 1981.

———. *Roman Shakespeare: Warriors, Wounds, and Women*. London and New York, 1997.

Kamps, Ivo, ed. *Materialist Shakespeare: A History*. London, 1995.

———, ed. *Shakespeare Left and Right*. New York and London, 1991.

Kastan, David Scott. *Shakespeare After Theory.* London, 1999.

———. *Shakespeare and the Book*. Cambridge, Eng., 2001.

———. *Shakespeare and the Shapes of Time.* Hanover, N.H., 1982.

———, ed. *A Companion to Shakespeare*. Oxford, 1999.

Kernan, Alvin. *Shakespeare, the King's Playwright: Theater in the Stuart Court, 1603–1613.* New Haven, 1995.

Kerrigan, William. *Shakespeare's Promises.* Baltimore, 1999.

Kirsch, Arthur. *Shakespeare and the Experience of Love*. Cambridge, Eng., 1981.

Knapp, Robert S. *Shakespeare—The Theater and the Book*. Princeton, 1989.

Knowles, Richard, ed. *Shakespeare and Carnival: After Bakhtin*. London and New York, 1998.

Lenz, Carolyn, et al., eds. *The Woman's Part: Feminist Criticism of Shakespeare*. Urbana, Ill., 1980.

Little, Arthur L., Jr. *Shakespeare Jungle Fever: National-Imperial Re-Visions of Race, Rape, and Sacrifice*. Stanford, 2000.

Loomba, Ania. *Gender, Race, Renaissance Drama*. Manchester, Eng., 1989.

Loomba, Ania, and Martin Orkin, eds. *Post-colonial Shakespeares*. London and New York, 1998.

Mahon, John W., and Thomas A. Pendleton, eds. *"Fanned and Winnowed Opinion": Shakespearean Essays Presented to Harold Jenkins.* London, 1987.

Mallin, Eric. *Inscribing the Time: Shakespeare and the End of Elizabethan England.* Berkeley, 1995.

Marcus, Leah. *Puzzling Shakespeare: Local Reading and its Discontents*. Berkeley, 1988.

Mazzio, Carla, and Douglas Trevor, eds. *Historicism, Psychoanalysis, and Early Modern Culture.* London and New York, 2000.

McDonald, Russ, ed. *Shakespeare Reread: The Texts in New Contexts*. Ithaca, N.Y., 1994.

McMullan, Gordon, and Jonathan Hope, eds. *The Politics of Tragicomedy: Shakespeare and After*. London and New York, 1992.

Melchiori,Giorgio. *Shakespeare's Garter Plays: "Edward III" to "Merry Wives of Windsor."* Newark, Del., 1994.

Miola, Robert S. *Shakespeare's Reading.* Oxford and New York, 2000.

———. *Shakespeare's Rome.* Cambridge, Eng., 1983.

Montrose, Louis. *The Purpose of Playing: Shakespeare and Cultural Politics of the Elizabethan Theatre*. Chicago, 1996.

Mullaney, Steven. *The Place of the Stage: License, Play, and Power in Renaissance England.* Chicago, 1988.

Neely, Carol Thomas. *Broken Nuptials in Shakespeare's Plays*. New Haven, 1985.

Newman, Karen. *Fashioning Femininity and the English Renaissance Drama*. Chicago, 1991.

Novy, Marianne. *Love's Argument: Gender Relations in Shakespeare*. Chapel Hill, N.C., 1984.

———, ed. *Women's Re-Visions of Shakespeare.* Urbana, Ill., 1990.

Nuttall, A. D. *A New Mimesis: Shakespeare and the Representation of Reality*. London, 1983.

Orgel, Stephen. *The Authentic Shakespeare and Other Problems of the Early Modern Stage.* London and New York, 2002.

Orgel, Stephen, and Sean Keilen, eds. *Shakespeare and History; Post-modern Shakespeare; Shakespeare and the Interpretive Tradition; Shakespeare and the Literary Tradition; Shakespeare and Gender; Political Shakespeare.* In separate volumes, New York, 1999.

Parker, Patricia. *Shakespeare from the Margins: Language, Culture, Context*. Chicago, 1996.

———, and Geoffrey Hartman, eds. *Shakespeare and the Question of Theory.* London, 1985.

Paster, Gail Kern. *The Body Embarrassed: Drama and the Disciplines of Shame in Early Modern England*. Ithaca, N.Y., 1993.

Patterson, Annabel. *Shakespeare and the Popular Voice*. Oxford, 1989.

Rabkin, Norman. *Shakespeare and the Problem of Meaning*. Chicago, 1981.

Salingar, Leo. *Dramatic Form in Shakespeare and the Jacobeans.* Cambridge, Eng., 1986.

Schwartz, Murray, and Coppélia Kahn, eds. *Representing Shakespeare: New Psychoanalytic Essays*. Baltimore, 1980.

Siemon, James R. *Shakespearean Iconoclasm.* Berkeley, 1985.

Sinfield, Alan. *Faultlines: Cultural Materialism and the Politics of Dissident Reading*. Berkeley, 1992.

Skura, Meredith Anne. *The Literary Use of the Psychoanalytic Process*. New Haven, 1981.

———. *Shakespeare the Actor and the Purposes of Playing*. Chicago, 1993.

Smith, Bruce R. *Homosexual Desire in Shakespeare's England*. Chicago, 1991.

———. *Shakespeare and Masculinity*. Oxford, 2000.

Stockholder, Kay. *Dream Works: Lovers and Families in Shakespeare's Plays*. Toronto, 1987.

Taylor, Gary. *Reinventing Shakespeare: A Cultural History from the Restoration to the Present*. New York, 1989.

Traub, Valerie. *Desire and Anxiety: Circulations of Sexuality in Shakespearean Drama*. London, 1992.

Vickers, Brian. *Appropriating Shakespeare: Contemporary Critical Quarrels*. New Haven, 1993.

Watson, Robert N. *The Rest is Silence: Death as Annihilation in the English Renaissance.* Berkeley, 1994.

———. *Shakespeare and the Hazards of Ambition.* Cambridge, Mass., 1984.

Wayne, Valerie, ed. *The Matter of Difference: Materialist Feminist Criticism of Shakespeare.* Ithaca, N.Y., 1991.

Weimann, Robert. *Author's Pen and Actor's Voice: Playing and Writing in Shakespeare's Theatre*. Cambridge, Eng., 2000.

Wells, Robin Headlam. *Shakespeare on Masculinity*. Cambridge, Eng., 2000.

———. *Shakespeare, Politics, and the State.* London, 1986.

Wheeler, Richard P. *Shakespeare's Development and the Problem Comedies: Turn and Counter-Turn*. Berkeley, 1981.

White, Paul Whitfield, and Suzanne R. Westfall, eds. *Shakespeare and Theatrical Patronage in Early Modern England.* Cambridge, Eng., 2002.

Williams, Gordon. *Shakespeare, Sex, and the Print Revolution*. London and Atlantic Highlands, N.J., 1996.

Woodbridge, Linda. *The Scythe of Saturn: Shakespeare's Magical Thinking*. Urbana, Ill., 1994.

Woodbridge, Linda, and Edward Berry, eds. *True Rites and Maimed Rites: Ritual and Anti-Ritual in Shakespeare and His Age*. Urbana, Ill., 1992.

Ziegler, Georgianna, ed. *Shakespeare's Unruly Women*. Washington, D.C., 1997.

Shakespeare in Performance; Dramaturgy

See also, under *Shakespeare Criticism from the 1940s to the 1970s*, Goldman and Granville-Barker.

Bartholomeusz, Dennis. *Macbeth and the Players*. Cambridge, Eng., 1969.

Barton, John. *Playing Shakespeare*. London, 1984.

Bevington, David. *Action is Eloquence: Shakespeare's Language of Gesture.* Cambridge, Mass., 1984.

Brockbank, Philip, ed. *Players of Shakespeare*. Cambridge, Eng., 1985.

Brown, Ivor. *Shakespeare and the Actors.* London, 1970.

Brown, John Russell. *Shakespeare's Plays in Performance*. London, 1966.

———. *Shakespeare's Dramatic Style*. London, 1970.

Bulman, J. C., and H. R. Coursen, eds. *Shakespeare on Television*. Hanover, N.H., 1988.

Carlisle, Carol Jones. *Shakespeare from the Greenroom: Actors' Criticisms of Four Major Tragedies*. Chapel Hill, N.C., 1969.

Cohn, Ruby. *Modern Shakespeare Offshoots.* Princeton, 1976.

Cook, Judith. *Shakespeare's Players*. London, 1983.

Davies, Anthony, and Stanley Wells, eds. *Shakespeare and the Moving Image: The Plays on Film and Television*. Cambridge, Eng., 1994.

Dessen, Alan C. *Recovering Shakespeare's Theatrical Vocabulary*. Cambridge, Eng., 1995.

———. *Rescripting Shakespeare: The Text, the Director, and Modern Productions*. Cambridge, Eng., 2002.

———, and Leslie Thomson. *A Dictionary of Stage Directions in English Drama, 1580–1642*. Cambridge, Eng., 1999.

Donohue, Joseph W., Jr. *Dramatic Character in the English Romantic Age*. Princeton, 1970.

Downer, Alan S. *The Eminent Tragedian, William Charles Macready*. Cambridge, Mass., 1966.

Edelman, Charles. *Brawl Ridiculous: Swordfighting in Shakespeare's Plays*. Manchester, Eng., 1992.

Hodgdon, Barbara. *The Shakespeare Trade: Performances and Appropriations*. Philadelphia, 1998.

Hogan, Charles B. *Shakespeare in the Theatre, 1701–1800*. 2 vols. Oxford, 1952–1957.

Jackson, Russell, and Robert Smallwood, eds. *Players of Shakespeare 2*. Cambridge, Eng., 1988. Followed by Vols. 3 (1993); and 4, ed. Smallwood (1998).

Jones, Emrys. *Scenic Form in Shakespeare*. Oxford, 1971.

Jorgens, Jack L. *Shakespeare on Film*. Bloomington, Ind., 1977.

Manvell, Roger. *Shakespeare and the Film*. London and New York, 1971.

McGuire, Philip C. *Speechless Dialect: Shakespeare's Open Silences*. Berkeley, 1985.

McGuire, Philip C., and David A. Samuelson. *Shakespeare: The Theatrical Dimension*. New York, 1979.

Odell, George C. D. *Shakespeare from Betterton to Irving*. 2 vols. New York, 1920, 1966.

Poel, William. *Shakespeare in the Theatre*. London, 1913, 1968.

Price, Joseph G., ed. *The Triple Bond: Plays, Mainly Shakespearean, in Performance*. University Park, Pa., 1975.

Rutter, Carol Chillington, ed. *Documents of the Rose Playhouse*. Manchester, Eng., 1999.

Rutter, Carol, et al. *Clamorous Voices: Shakespeare's Women Today*. New York, 1989.

Shapiro, Michael. *Gender in Play on the Shakespearean Stage: Boy Heroines and Female Pages*. Ann Arbor, Mich., 1994.

Shattuck, Charles H. *The Shakespeare Promptbooks: A Descriptive Catalogue*. Urbana, Ill., 1965.

———. *Shakespeare on the American Stage from the Hallams to Edwin Booth*. Washington, D.C., 1976; *from Booth and Barrett to Sothern and Marlowe*, Washington, D.C., 1987.

Slater, Ann Pasternak. *Shakespeare the Director*. Brighton, Sussex, and Totowa, N.J., 1982.

Speaight, Robert. *William Poel and the Elizabethan Revival*. London, 1954.

Sprague, Arthur Colby. *Shakespeare and the Actors*. Cambridge, Mass., 1944.

———. *Shakespearian Players and Performances*. Cambridge, Mass., 1953.

Styan, J. L. *Shakespeare's Stagecraft*. Cambridge, Eng., 1967.

Wells, Stanley. *Royal Shakespeare: Four Major Productions at Stratford-upon-Avon*. Manchester, Eng., 1977.

The Comedies

See also, under *Shakespeare Criticism Since 1980*, Drakakis (essay by Belsey), Erickson and Kahn (essay by Adelman), and Paster (Chapter 7).

Anderson, Linda. *A Kind of Wild Justice: Revenge in Shakespeare's Comedies*. Newark, Del., 1987.

Barber, C. L. *Shakespeare's Festive Comedy*. Princeton, 1959.

Barton, Anne. *The Names of Comedy*. Toronto, 1990.

Berry, Edward. *Shakespeare's Comic Rites*. Cambridge, Eng., 1984.

Berry, Ralph. *Shakespeare's Comedies: Explorations in Form*. Princeton, 1972.

———. *The Shakespearean Metaphor: Studies in Language and Form*. Totowa, N.J., 1978.

Bloom, Harold, ed., *William Shakespeare: Comedies and Romances*. New York, 1986.

Bradbury, Malcolm, and David Palmer, eds. *Shakespearian Comedy*. London, 1972.

Brown, John Russell. *Shakespeare and His Comedies*. London, 1957, 1968.

Brown, John Russell, and Bernard Harris, eds. *Early Shakespeare*. Stratford-upon-Avon Studies 3. London, 1961. (Including an essay by Frank Kermode on "The Mature Comedies.")

Bryant, J. A., Jr. *Shakespeare and the Uses of Comedy*. Lexington, Ky., 1986.

Burke, William Kenneth. *A New Approach to Shakespeare's Early Comedies: Theoretical Foundations*. New York, 1998.

Carroll, William C. *The Metamorphoses of Shakespearean Comedy*. Princeton, 1985.

Champion, Larry S. *The Evolution of Shakespeare's Comedy*. Cambridge, Mass., 1970.

Charlton, H. B. *Shakespearian Comedy*. London, 1938.

Charney, Maurice, ed. *Shakespearean Comedy*. New York, 1980.

Cody, Richard. *The Landscape of the Mind: Pastoralism and Platonic Theory in Tasso's "Aminta" and Shakespeare's Early Comedies*. Oxford, 1969.

Collins, Michael J., ed. *Shakespeare's Sweet Thunder: Essays on the Early Comedies*. Newark, Del., 1997.

Cook, Ann Jennalie. *Making a Match: Courtship in Shakespeare and His Society*. Princeton, 1991.

Cordner, Michael, Peter Holland, and John Kerrigan, eds. *English Comedy*. Cambridge, Eng., 1994.

Elam, Keir. *Shakespeare's Universe of Discourse: Language-Games in the Comedies*. Cambridge, Eng., 1984.

Evans, Bertrand. *Shakespeare's Comedies*. Oxford, 1960.

Freedman, Barbara. *Staging the Gaze: Postmodernism, Psychoanalysis, and Shakespearean Comedy*. Ithaca, N. Y., 1991.

Friedman, Michael D. *"The World Must Be Peopled": Shakespeare's Comedies of Forgiveness*. Madison, N. J., and London, 2002.

Frye, Northrop. "The Argument of Comedy," *English Institute Essays 1948*. New York, 1949.

———. *A Natural Perspective: The Development of Shakespearean Comedy and Romance*. New York, 1965.

Hall, Jonathan. *Anxious Pleasures: Shakespearean Comedy and the Nation-State*. Madison, N. J., 1995.

Hamilton, A. C. *The Early Shakespeare*. San Marino, Calif., 1967.

Hassel, R. Chris. *Faith and Folly in Shakespeare's Romantic Comedies*. Athens, Ga., 1980.

Hawkins, Sherman H. "The Two Worlds of Shakespearean Comedy," *ShakS* 3 (1967), 62–80.

Hunter, Robert G. *Shakespeare and the Comedy of Forgiveness*. New York, 1965.

Huston, J. Dennis. *Shakespeare's Comedies of Play*. New York, 1981.

Leggatt, Alexander. *English Stage Comedy, 1490–1990: Five Centuries of a Genre*. London and New York, 1998.

———. *Shakespeare's Comedy of Love*. London and New York, 1974.

Lerner, Laurence, ed. *Shakespeare's Comedies: An Anthology of Modern Criticism*. Baltimore, 1967.

Levin, Richard A. *Love and Society in Shakespearean Comedy: A Study of Dramatic Form and Content*. Newark, Del., 1985.

Miola, Robert S. *Shakespeare and Classical Comedy: The Influence of Plautus and Terence*. Oxford, 1994.

Nevo, Ruth. *Comic Transformations in Shakespeare*. London, 1980.

Newman, Karen. *Shakespeare's Rhetoric of Comic Character*. New York and London, 1985.

Palmer, David J., and Malcolm Bradbury, eds. *Shakespearian Comedy*. Statford-upon-Avon Studies 1. London, 1972.

Palmer, John. *Comic Characters of Shakespeare*. London, 1946.

Pettet, E. C. *Shakespeare and the Romance Tradition*. London, 1949.

Phialas, Peter G. *Shakespeare's Romantic Comedies*. Chapel Hill, N.C., 1966.

Richmond, Hugh M. *Shakespeare's Sexual Comedy*. Indianapolis, 1971.

Salingar, Leo. *Shakespeare and the Traditions of Comedy*. Cambridge, Eng., 1974.

Shaheen, Naseeb. *Biblical References in Shakespeare's Comedies*. Newark, Del., 1993.

Smidt, Kristian. *Unconformities in Shakespeare's Early Comedies*. London, 1986.

Stevenson, David L. *The Love-Game Comedy*. New York, 1946.

Traversi, Derek. *Shakespeare: The Early Comedies*. London, 1960.

Turner, Robert Y. *Shakespeare's Apprenticeship*. Chicago, 1974.

Westlund, Joseph. *Shakespeare's Reparative Comedies: A Psychoanalytic View of the Middle Plays*. Chicago, 1984.

Wheeler, Richard P. "Deaths in the Family: The Loss of a Son and the Rise of Shakespearean Comedy," *SQ* 51 (2000), 127–53.

Williamson, Marilyn. *The Patriarchy of Shakespeare's Comedies*. Detroit, 1986.

The Problem Plays

Campbell, Oscar James. *Shakespeare's Satire*. London and New York, 1943, 1963.

Foakes, R. A. *Shakespeare, The Dark Comedies to the Last Plays: From Satire to Celebration.* Charlottesville, Va., 1971.

Frye, Northrop. *The Myth of Deliverance: Reflections on Shakespeare's Problem Comedies.* Toronto, 1983.

Jamieson, Michael. "The Problem Plays, 1920–1970: A Retrospect," *ShS 25* (1972), 1–10.

Lawrence, W. W. *Shakespeare's Problem Comedies.* New York, 1931, 1960.

Maquerlot, Jean-Pierre. *Shakespeare and the Mannerist Tradition: A Reading of Five Problem Plays.* Cambridge, Eng., 1995. (Includes consideration of *Julius Caesar* and *Hamlet.*)

McCandless, David. *Gender and Performance in Shakespeare's Problem Comedies.* Bloomington, Ind., 1997.

Muir, Kenneth, and Stanley Wells, eds. *Aspects of Shakespeare's "Problem Plays": Articles Reprinted from "Shakespeare Survey."* Cambridge, Eng., 1982.

Schanzer, Ernest. *The Problem Plays of Shakespeare.* New York, 1963.

Thomas, Vivian. *The Moral Universe of Shakespeare's Problem Plays.* New York, 1987.

Tillyard, E. M. W. *Shakespeare's Problem Plays.* Toronto, 1949.

Wheeler, Richard P. *Shakespeare's Development and the Problem Comedies: Turn and Counter-Turn.* Berkeley, 1981.

Ure, Peter. *William Shakespeare: The Problem Plays.* London, 1961.

The Comedy of Errors

See also, under *Shakespeare Criticism Since 1980,* Hamilton (Chapter 3), and Parker; and under *The Comedies,* R. Berry, Charlton, Charney (essays by Shaw and Freedman), Cody, Collins (essays by Miola, Smith, and Thompson), Evans, Hamilton, Huston, Leggatt, Nevo, Pettet, Richmond, Salingar, Traversi, and Turner.

Barber, C. L. "Shakespearian Comedy in *The Comedy of Errors,*" *College English* 25 (1964), 493–7.

Bishop, T. G. *Shakespeare and the Theatre of Wonder.* Cambridge, Eng., 1996.

Brooks, Charles. "Shakespeare's Romantic Shrews," *SQ* 11 (1960), 351–6.

Brooks, Harold. "Themes and Structure in *The Comedy of Errors,*" *Early Shakespeare,* ed. John Russell Brown and Bernard Harris, pp. 55–71. Stratford-upon-Avon Studies 3. London, 1961.

Clubb, Louise G. "Italian Comedy and *The Comedy of Errors,*" *Comparative Literature* 19 (1967), 240–51.

Elliott, C. R. "Weirdness in *The Comedy of Errors,*" *University of Toronto Quarterly* 9 (1939), 95–106.

Enterline, Lynn. *The Tears of Narcissus: Melancholia and Masculinity in Early Modern Writing.* Stanford, 1995.

Fergusson, Francis. "Two Comedies: *The Comedy of Errors* and *Much Ado About Nothing,*" *The Human Image in Dramatic Literature,* pp. 144–57. New York, 1957.

Freedman, Barbara. "Egeon's Debt: Self-Division and Self-Redemption in *The Comedy of Errors,*" *English Literary Renaissance* 10 (1980), 360–83.

Hutson, Lorna. *The Usurer's Daughter: Male Friendship and Fictions of Women in Sixteenth-Century England.* London and New York, 1994.

Knight, G. Wilson. *The Shakespearian Tempest.* London, 1932, 1953.

Lea, Kathleen M. *Italian Popular Comedy: A Study in the Commedia dell' Arte, 1560–1620, with Special Reference to the English Stage.* Oxford, 1934.

Miola, Robert S., ed. *The Comedy of Errors: Critical Essays.* New York and London, 1997.

Salgādo, Gāmini. " 'Time's Deformed Hand': Sequence, Consequence, and Inconsequence in *The Comedy of Errors,*" *ShS 25* (1972), 81–91.

Love's Labor's Lost

See also, under *Shakespeare's Language,* Donawerth and Mahood; under *Shakespeare Criticism from the 1940s to the 1970s,* Calderwood and Hawkes; under *Shakespeare Criticism Since 1980,* Edwards et al. (essay by Hunter), Erickson and Kahn (essay by Levin), Kamps (essay by Maus), and Mazzio and Trevor (essay by Mazzio); and under *The Comedies,* Barber, R. Berry, Charlton, Cody, Collins (essay by Gilbert), Elam (Chapter 5), Hunter, Huston, Leggatt, Nevo, Palmer and Bradbury (essays by Hunt and Wells, Roberts, Swander, and Thompson), Smidt, and Stevenson.

Bevington, David. "'Jack Hath Not Jill': Failed Courtship in Lyly and Shakespeare," *ShS 42* (1990), 1–13.

Breitenberg, Mark. "The Anatomy of Masculine Desire in *Love's Labour's Lost,*" *SQ* 43 (1992), 430–49.

Burnett, Mark Thornton. "Giving and Receiving: *Love's Labour's Lost* and the Politics of Exchange," *English Literary Renaissance* 23 (1993), 287–313.

Carroll, William C. *The Great Feast of Language in "Love's Labour's Lost."* Princeton, 1976.

Ellis, Herbert A. *Shakespeares's Lusty Punning in "Love's Labour's Lost" with Contemporary Analogues.* The Hague, 1973.

Erickson, Peter B. "The Failure of Relationship Between Men and Women in *Love's Labor's Lost,*" *Women's Studies* 9 (1981): 65–81.

Evans, Malcolm. "Mercury Versus Apollo: A Reading of *Love's Labour's Lost,*" *SQ* 26 (1975), 113–27.

Frye, Northrop. "Shakespeare's Experimental Comedy," *Stratford Papers on Shakespeare 1961,* ed. B. A. W. Jackson. Toronto, 1962.

Gilbert, Mariam. *Love's Labour's Lost.* Shakespeare in Performance Series. Manchester, Eng., 1993.

Goldstien, Neal L. "*Love's Labour's Lost* and the Renaissance Vision of Love," *SQ* 25 (1974), 335–50.

Greene, Thomas M. "*Love's Labour's Lost:* The Grace of Society," *SQ* 22 (1971), 315–28. Rpt. in *The Vulnerable Text: Essays on Renaissance Literature.* New York, 1986.

Harbage, Alfred. "*Love's Labor's Lost* and the Early Shakespeare," *Philological Quarterly* 41 (1962), 18–36.

Henderson, Diana E. "Shakespeare's Laboring Lovers: Lyric and Its Discontents," *Passion Made Public: Elizabethan Lyric, Gender, and Performance,* pp. 167–213. Urbana, Ill., 1995.

Hoy, Cyrus. "*Love's Labour's Lost* and the Nature of Comedy," *SQ* 13 (1962), 31–40.

Hunter, Robert G. "The Function of the Songs at the End of *Love's Labour's Lost,*" *ShakS 7* (1974), 55–64.

Lamb, Mary Ellen. "The Nature of Topicality in *Love's Labour's Lost,*" *ShS 38* (1985), 49–59.

Montrose, Louis Adrian. *"Curious-knotted Garden": The Form, Themes and Contexts of Shakespeare's "Love's Labour's Lost."* Salzburg, 1977.

———. " 'Sport by sport o'erthrown': *Love's Labour's Lost* and the Politics of Play," *Texas Studies in Literature and Language* 18 (1977), 528–52.

Proudfoot, Richard. "*Love's Labour's Lost*: Sweet Understanding and the Five Worthies," *Essays and Studies* n.s. 37 (1984), 16–30.

Parker, Patricia. "Preposterous Reversals: *Love's Labor's Lost,*" *Modern Language Quarterly* 54 (1993), 435–82.

Westlund, Joseph. "Fancy and Achievement in *Love's Labour's Lost,*" *SQ* 18 (1967), 37–46.

Wilders, John. "The Unresolved Conflicts of *Love's Labour's Lost,*" *Essays in Criticism* 27 (1977), 20–33.

Yates, Frances A. *A Study of "Love's Labour's Lost."* Cambridge, Eng., 1936.

The Two Gentlemen of Verona

See also, under *The Comedies,* R. Berry, Bradbury and Palmer (essay by Ewbank), Champion, Charlton, Collins (essay by Carlisle and Derrick), Evans, Friedman, Hunter, Leggatt, Nevo, Pettet, and Salingar.

Brooks, Harold F. "Two Clowns in a Comedy (to Say Nothing of the Dog): Speed, Launce (and Crab) in *The Two Gentlemen of Verona,*" *English Association Essays and Studies* n.s. 16 (1963), 91–100.

Danby, John F. "Shakespeare Criticism and *Two Gentlemen of Verona,*" *Critical Quarterly* 2 (1960), 309–21.

Lindenbaum, Peter. "Education in *The Two Gentlemen of Verona,*" *Studies in English Literature* 15 (1975), 229–44.

Morse, Ruth. "*Two Gentlemen* and the Cult of Friendship," *Neuphilologische Mitteilungen* 84:2 (1983), 214–24.

Rossky, William. "*The Two Gentlemen of Verona* as Burlesque," *English Literary Renaissance* 12 (1982), 210–19.

Schleiner, Louise. "Voice, Ideology, and Gendered Subjects: The Case of *As You Like It* and *Two Gentlemen*," *SQ* 50 (1999), 285–309.

Schlueter, June, ed. *"The Two Gentlemen of Verona": Critical Essays*. London and New York, 1996.

Slights, Camille Wells. "*The Two Gentlemen of Verona* and the Courtesy Book Tradition," *ShakS 16* (1983), 13–31.

Stephenson, William E. "The Adolescent Dream-World of *The Two Gentlemen of Verona*," *SQ* 17:2 (1966), 165–8.

Weimann, Robert. "Laughing with the Audience: *The Two Gentlemen of Verona* and the Popular Tradition of Comedy," *ShS 22* (1969), 35–42.

The Taming of the Shrew

See also, under *Shakespeare's Predecessors and Contemporaries*, Marrapodi (essay by Bevington); under *Shakespeare Criticism from the 1940s to the 1970s*, Garber; under *Shakespeare Criticism Since 1980*, Auden, Fumerton and Hunt (essay by Dolan), Kahn, Lenz et al. (essay by Bean), McDonald (essay by Boose), Novy (*Love's Argument*), and Parker and Hartman (essay by Fineman); under *Shakespeare in Performance*, Rutter; and under *The Comedies*, R. Berry, Charlton, Collins (essays by Dessen and Rutter), Evans, Hawkins, Huston, Leggatt, Nevo, and Stevenson.

Boose, Lynda E. " 'Scolding Brides and Bridling Scolds': Taming the Woman's Unruly Member," *SQ* 42 (1991), 179–213.

Brunvand, Jan Harold. "The Folktale Origin of *The Taming of the Shrew*," *SQ* 17 (1966), 345–59.

Dolan, Frances E., ed. *"The Taming of the Shrew": Text and Contexts*. New York, 1996.

Haring-Smith, Tori. *From Farce to Metadrama; A Stage History of "The Taming of the Shrew," 1594–1983*. Westport, Conn., 1985.

Hosley, Richard. "Was There a 'Dramatic Epilogue' to *The Taming of the Shrew?" Studies in English Literature* 1:2 (1961), 17–34.

Hutson, Lorna. *The Usurer's Daughter: Male Friendship and Fictions of Women in Sixteenth-Century England*. London and New York, 1994.

Jayne, Sears. "The Dreaming of *The Shrew*," *SQ* 17 (1966), 41–56.

Korda, Natasha. "Household Kates: Domesticating Commodities in *The Taming of the Shrew*," *SQ* 47 (1996), 109–31.

Maguire, Laurie E. "Cultural Control in *The Taming of the Shrew*," *Renaissance Drama* n.s. 26 (1995), 83–104.

Marcus, Leah. "The Shakespearean Editor as Shrew-Tamer," *English Literary Rennaisance* 22 (1922), 177–200.

Newman, Karen. "Renaissance Family Politics and Shakespeare's *The Taming of the Shrew*," *English Literary Renaissance* 16 (1986), 86–100.

Saccio, Peter. "Shrewd and Kindly Farce," *ShS 37* (1984), 33–40.

Thompson, Ann, ed., *The Taming of the Shrew*. Cambridge, Eng., 1984.

Thorne, W. B. "Folk Elements in *The Taming of the Shrew*," *Queen's Quarterly* 75 (1968), 482–96.

A Midsummer Night's Dream

See also, under *Life in Shakespeare's England*, De Grazia, Quilligan, and Stallybrass (essay by Parker); under *Shakespeare Criticism from the 1940s to the 1970s*, Calderwood, Coghill, Garber, Granville-Barker, and Kott; under *Shakespeare Criticism Since 1980*, Callaghan (*A Feminist Companion*, essay by Loomba), Mazzio and Trevor (essay by Maus), Montrose, Parker, Paster, and Patterson (Chapter 3); and under *The Comedies*, Barber, Bloom (essay by Girard), Brown and Harris (essays by Kermode and Merchant), Carroll, Collins (essay by Halio), Evans, Huston, Leggatt, Lerner, Palmer and Bradbury (essay by Wells), and Smidt.

Bevington, David. " 'But We Are Spirits of Another Sort': The Dark Side of Love and Magic in *A Midsummer Night's Dream*," *Medieval and Renaissance Studies*, ed. Siegfried Wenzel. Chapel Hill, N.C., 1978.

Donaldson, E. Talbot. *The Swan at the Well: Shakespeare Reads Chaucer*. New Haven, 1985.

Garner, Shirley Nelson. "*A Midsummer Night's Dream*: 'Jack Shall Have Jill; Nought Shall Go Ill,' " *Women's Studies* 9 (1981), 47–63.

Girard, René. "Myth and Ritual in Shakespeare's *A Midsummer Night's Dream*," *Textual Strategies: Perspectives in Post-Structuralist Criticism*, ed. Josué V. Harari. Ithaca, N.Y., 1979.

Howard, Skiles. "Hands, Feet, and Bottoms: Decentering the Cosmic Dance in *A Midsummer Night's Dream*," *SQ* 44 (1993), 325–42.

Lamb, Mary Ellen. "*A Midsummer Night's Dream*: The Myth of Theseus and the Minotaur," *Texas Studies in Literature and Language* 21 (1979), 478–91.

———. " 'Taken by the Fairies': Fairy Practices and the Production of Popular Culture in *A Midsummer Night's Dream*," *SQ* 51 (2000), 277–312.

Montrose, Louis Adrian. " 'Shaping Fantasies': Figurations of Gender and Power in Elizabethan Culture," *Representations 2* (1.2, Spring 1983), 61–94.

Nuttall, A. D. "*A Midsummer Night's Dream*: Comedy as *Apotrope* of Myth," *ShS 53* (2000), 49–59.

Olson, Paul A. "*A Midsummer Night's Dream* and the Meaning of Court Marriage," *ELH* 24 (1957), 95–119.

Ormerod, David. "*A Midsummer Night's Dream*: The Monster in the Labyrinth," *ShakS 11* (1978), 39–52.

Pearson, D'Orsay W. " 'Unkinde' Theseus: A Study in Renaissance Mythography," *English Literary Renaissance* 4 (1974), 276–98.

Wall, Wendy. "Why Does Puck Sweep?: Fairylore, Merry Wives, and Social Struggle," *SQ* 52 (2001), 67–106.

Warren, Roger. *"A Midsummer Night's Dream": Text and Performance*. Text and Performance. London, 1983.

Williams, Gary Jay. *Our Moonlight Revels: "A Midsummer Night's Dream" in the Theatre*. Ames, Iowa, 1997.

Young, David P. *Something of Great Constancy: The Art of "A Midsummer Night's Dream."* New Haven, 1966.

The Merchant of Venice

See also, under *Shakespeare's Predecessors and Contemporaries*, Rose (ed. *Renaissance Drama*, essay by Whigham); under *Shakespeare's Language*, Donawerth; under *Shakespeare Criticism from the 1940s to the 1970s*, Burkhardt, Fiedler, and Granville-Barker; under *Shakespeare Criticism Since 1980*, Auden, Callaghan (*A Feminist Companion*, essay by Singh), Dawson, Erickson and Kahn (essays by Kahn and Wheeler), Garber (*Cannibals*, essay by Mullaney), Grady (essays by Drakakis, Freinkel, and Mallin), Howard and O'Connor (essay by Moisan), Mazzio and Trevor (essay by Siemon), Novy (*Love's Argument*, Chapter 4), Rabkin, and Wayne (essay by Leventen); and under *The Comedies*, Barber, Bradbury and Palmer (essay by Palmer), Brown and Harris (essays by J. R. Brown and Kermode), Evans, Leggatt, Levin, Nevo, and Smidt.

Auden, W. H. "Brothers and Others," *"The Dyer's Hand" and Other Essays*. New York, 1948.

Berger, Harry, Jr. "Marriage and Mercifixion in *The Merchant of Venice:* The Casket Scene Revisited," *SQ* 32 (1981), 155–62.

Boose, Lynda E. "The Comic Contract and Portia's Golden Ring," *ShakS 20* (1988), 241–54.

Bulman, James C. *The Merchant of Venice*. Shakespeare in Performance. Manchester, Eng., 1991.

Cohen, Walter. "*The Merchant of Venice* and the Possibilities of Historical Criticism," *ELH* 49 (1982), 765–89.

Danson, Lawrence. *The Harmonies of "The Merchant of Venice."* New Haven and London, 1978.

Dessen, Alan C. "The Elizabethan Stage Jew and Christian Example: Gerontus, Barabas, and Shylock," *Modern Language Quarterly* 35 (1974), 231–45.

Edelman, Charles. "Which is the Jew that Shakespeare Knew? Shylock on the Elizabethan Stage," *ShS 52* (1999), 99–106.

Engle, Lars. " 'Thrift is Blessing': Exchange and Explanation in *The Merchant of Venice*," *SQ* 37 (1986), 20–37.

Freud, Sigmund. "The Theme of the Three Caskets," *Complete Psychological Works of Sigmund Freud*, trans. James Strachey et al. London, 1973–4.

Girard, René. " 'To Entrap the Wisest': A Reading of *The Merchant of Venice*," *Literature and Society*. Selected Papers from the English Institute, 1978, ed. Edward W. Said. Baltimore, 1980.

Hutson, Lorna. *The Usurer's Daughter: Male Friendship and Fictions of Women in Sixteenth-Century England*. London and New York, 1994.

Jardine, Lisa. "Cultural Confusion and Shakespeare's Learned Heroines: 'These Are Old Paradoxes,' " *SQ* 38 (1987), 1–18.

Lever, J. W. "Shylock, Portia, and the Values of Shakespearian Comedy," *SQ* 3 (1952), 383–6.

Lewalski, Barbara K. "Biblical Allusion and Allegory in *The Merchant of Venice*," *SQ* 13 (1962), 327–43.

MacKay, Maxine. "*The Merchant of Venice:* A Reflection of the Early Conflict Between Courts of Law and Courts of Equity," *SQ* 15:4 (1964), 371–5.

Moody, A. D. *Shakespeare: "The Merchant of Venice."* London, 1964.

Newman, Karen. "Portia's Ring: Unruly Women and Structures of Exchange in *The Merchant of Venice*," *SQ* 38 (1987), 19–33.

Normand, Lawrence. "Reading the Body in *The Merchant of Venice*," *Textual Practice* 5 (1991), 55–73.

Overton, Bill. *"The Merchant of Venice": Text and Performance*. Atlantic Highlands, N.J., 1987.

Parten, Anne. "Re-establishing Sexual Order: The Ring Episode in *The Merchant of Venice*," *Women's Studies* 9 (1982), 145–55.

Pettet, E. C. "*The Merchant of Venice* and the Problem of Usury," *English Association Essays and Studies* 31 (1945), 19–33.

Shapiro, James. *Shakespeare and the Jews*. New York, 1996.

Whigham, Frank. "Ideology and Class Conduct in *The Merchant of Venice*," *Renaissance Drama* 10 (1979), 93–115.

Yaffe, Martin D. *Shylock and the Jewish Question*. Baltimore, 1997.

Much Ado About Nothing

See also, under *Shakespeare's Predecessors and Contemporaries*, Marrapodi (essay by Salingar); under *The Comedies*, R. Berry, Brown, Cordner et al. (essay by Everett), Evans, Hunter, Huston, Leggatt, Levin, Nevo, Newman, Salingar, and Stevenson; under *Shakespeare Criticism from the 1940s to the 1970s*, Rossiter; and under *Shakespeare Criticism Since 1980*, Howard and O'Connor (essay by Howard), Kirsch, Lenz et al. (essay by Hays), and Neely.

Barish, Jonas A. "Pattern and Purpose in the Prose of *Much Ado About Nothing*," *Rice U. Studies* 60:2 (1974), 19–30.

Berger, Harry, Jr. "Against the Sink-a-Pace: Sexual and Family Politics in *Much Ado About Nothing*," *SQ* 33 (1982), 302–13.

Cook, Carol. "'The Sign and Semblance of Her Honor': Reading Gender Difference in *Much Ado about Nothing*," *PMLA* 101 (1986), 186–202.

Dawson, Anthony B. "Much Ado about Signifying," *Studies in English Literature* 22 (1982), 211–21.

Dusinberre, Juliet. "Much Ado about Lying," *Shakespeare Readers, Audiences, Players*, eds. R. S. White, Charles Edelman, and Christopher Wortham. Nedlands, Australia, 1998.

Everett, Barbara. "*Much Ado About Nothing*," *Critical Quarterly* 3 (1961), 319–35.

Friedman, Michael D. "Male Bonds and Marriage in *All's Well* and *Much Ado*," *Studies in English Literature* 35 (1995), 231–49.

Jorgensen, Paul A. "*Much Ado About Nothing*," *SQ* 5 (1954), 287–95. Rpt. in *Redeeming Shakespeare's Words*. Berkeley, 1962.

Lane, Robert. " 'Foremost in report': Social Identity and Masculinity in *Much Ado About Nothing*," *Upstart Crow* 16 (1996), 31–47.

Lewalski, Barbara K. "Love, Appearance, and Reality: Much Ado About Something," *Studies in English Literature* 8 (1968), 235–51.

Mason, Pamela. *"Much Ado About Nothing": Text and Performance*. Basingstoke, 1992.

Ormerod, David. "Faith and Fashion in *Much Ado About Nothing*," *ShS 25* (1972), 93–105.

Taylor, Michael. "*Much Ado About Nothing:* The Individual in Society," *Essays in Criticism* 23 (1973), 146–53.

The Merry Wives of Windsor

See also, under *Life in Shakespeare's England*, Helgerson; under *Shakespeare's Predecessors and Contemporaries*, Helgerson; under *Shakespeare Criticism Since 1980*, Erickson and Kahn (essay by Barton), Fumerton and Hunt (essay by Helgerson), Howard and O'Connor (essay by Erickson), Kahn (Chapter 5), Knowles (essay by Hall), Melchiori, and Parker; and under *The Comedies*, Anderson, R. Berry, Carroll, Charlton, Evans, and Nevo.

Bradley, A. C. "The Rejection of Falstaff," *Oxford Lectures on Poetry*. London, 1909, 1961.

Bryant, J. A., Jr. "Falstaff and the Renewal of Windsor," *PMLA* 89 (1974), 296–301.

Carroll, William. " 'A Received Belief': Imagination in *The Merry Wives of Windsor*," *Studies in Philology* 74 (1977), 186–215.

Collington, Philip D. " 'I Would Thy Husband Were Dead': *The Merry Wives of Windsor* as Mock Domestic Tragedy," *English Literary Renaissance* 30 (2000), 184–212.

Green, William. *Shakespeare's "Merry Wives of Windsor."* Princeton, 1962.

Hinely, Jan Lawson. "Comic Scapegoats and the Falstaff of *The Merry Wives of Windsor*," *ShakS 15* (1982), 37–54.

Kegl, Rosemary. *The Rhetoric of Concealment: Figuring Gender and Class in Renaissance Literature*. Ithaca, N.Y., 1994.

Leggatt, Alexander. *Citizen Comedy in the Age of Shakespeare*. Toronto, 1973.

Parten, Anne. "Falstaff's Horns: Masculine Inadequacy and Feminine Mirth in *The Merry Wives of Windsor*," *Studies in Philology* 82 (1985), 184–99.

Roberts, Jeanne Addison. *Shakespeare's English Comedy: "The Merry Wives of Windsor" in Context*. Lincoln, Neb. 1979.

Steadman, John M. "Falstaff as Actaeon: A Dramatic Emblem," *SQ* 14 (1963), 231–44.

Wall, Wendy. "Why Does Puck Sweep?: Fairylore, Merry Wives, and Social Struggle," *SQ* 52 (2001), 67–106.

———. " 'Household stuff': The Sexual Politics of Domesticity and the Advent of English Comedy," *ELH* 65 (1998), 1–45.

As You Like It

See also, under *The Comedies*, Barber, R. Berry, Bradbury and Palmer (essay by Anne Barton), Brown, Hunter, Leggatt, Nevo, and Salingar; and under *Shakespeare Criticism Since 1980*, Belsey, Callaghan (*A Feminist Companion*, essay by Neely), Erickson, Lenz et al. (essay by Park), Mahon and Pendleton (essay by Gibbons), and McDonald (essay by Wofford).

Alpers, Paul. *What Is Pastoral?* Chicago, 1996.

Barnet, Sylvan. "Strange Events: Improbability in *As You Like It*," *ShakS 4* (1968), 119–31.

Bono, Barbara J. "Mixed Gender, Mixed Genre in Shakespeare's *As You Like It*," *Renaissance Genres: Essays on Theory, History, and Interpretation*, ed. Barbara Kiefer Lewalski. Cambridge, Mass., 1986.

Debax, Jean-Paul, and Yves Peyré, eds. *"As You Like It": Essais critiques*. Toulouse, 1998.

Doran, Madeleine. " 'Yet Am I Inland Bred,'" *SQ* 15:2 (1964), 99–114.

Fortin, René E. " 'Tongues in Trees': Symbolic Patterns in *As You Like it*," *Texas Studies in Literature and Language* 14 (1973), 569–82.

Gardner, Helen. *"As You Like It," More Talking of Shakespeare*, ed. John Garrett. London and New York, 1959.

Halio, Jay L. " 'No Clock in the Forest': Time in *As You Like It*," *Studies in English Literature* 2 (1962), 197–207.

Hayles, Nancy K. "Sexual Disguise in *As You Like It* and *Twelfth Night*," *ShS 32* (1979), 63–72.

Howard, Jean E. "Crossdressing, The Theatre, and Gender Struggle in Early Modern England," *SQ* 39 (1988), 418–40.

Kernan, Alvin B. *The Cankered Muse*. New Haven, 1959.

Knowles, Richard. "Myth and Type in *As You Like It*," *ELH* 33 (1966), 1–22.

Marshall, Cynthia. "The Doubled Jaques and Constructions of Negation in *As You Like It*," *SQ* 49 (1998), 375–92.

Montrose, Louis Adrian. " 'The Place of a Brother' in *As You Like It:* Social Process and Comic Form," *SQ* 32 (1981), 28–54.

Ronk, Martha. "Locating the Visual in *As You Like It*," *SQ* 52 (2001), 255–76.

Schleiner, Louise. "Voice, Ideology, and Gendered Subjects: The Case of *As You Like*

It and *Two Gentlemen*," *SQ* 50 (1999), 285–309.
Young, David. *The Heart's Forest*. New Haven, 1972.

Twelfth Night

See also, under *The Comedies*, Barber, E. Berry, Bradbury and Palmer (essay by Anne Barton), Brown, Brown and Harris (essay by Kermode), Hunter, Leggatt, Levin, Nevo, and Salingar; and under *Shakespeare Criticism Since 1980*, Callaghan (*A Feminist Companion*, essay by Neely), Erickson and Kahn (essay by Booth), Greenblatt (*Shakespearean Negotiations*, Chapter 3), Hamilton (Chapter 4), Hawkes (essay by Elam), Howard, and Parker and Hartman (essay by Hartman).
Arlidge, Anthony. *Shakespeare and the Prince of Love: The Feast of Misrule in the Middle Temple*. London, 2000.
Auden, W. H. "Music in Shakespeare," *"The Dyer's Hand" and Other Essays*. New York, 1948.
Bloom, Harold, ed. *Modern Critical Interpretations of "Twelfth Night."* New York, 1987.
Booth, Stephen. *Precious Nonsense: The Gettysburg Address, Ben Jonson's Epitaphs on His Children, and "Twelfth Night."* Berkeley, 1998.
Brown, John Russell. "Directions for *Twelfth Night*, or What You Will," *Tulane Drama Review* 5:4 (1961), 77–88.
Downer, Alan S. "Feste's Night," *College English* 13 (1952), 258–65.
Eagleton, Terence. "Language and Reality in *Twelfth Night*," *Critical Quarterly* 9 (1967), 217–28.
Elam, Keir. "The Fertile Eunuch: *Twelfth Night*, Early Modern Intercourse, and the Fruits of Castration," *SQ* 47 (1996), 1–36.
Hollander, John. "*Twelfth Night* and the Morality of Indulgence," *Sewanee Review* 67 (1959), 220–38.
Hutson, Lorna. "On Not Being Deceived: Rhetoric and the Body in *Twelfth Night*," *Texas Studies in Literature and Language* 38 (1996), 140–74.
Kerrigan, John. "Secrecy and Gossip in *Twelfth Night*," *ShS 50* (1997), 65–80.
Leech, Clifford. *"Twelfth Night" and Shakespearian Comedy*. Toronto, 1965.
Lewalski, Barbara K. "Thematic Patterns in *Twelfth Night*," *ShakS 1* (1965), 168–81.
Potter, Lois. *"Twelfth Night": Text and Performance*. London, 1985.
Salingar, L. D. "The Design of *Twelfth Night*," *SQ* 9 (1958), 117–39.
Shannon, Laurie J. "Nature's Bias: Renaissance Homonormativity and Elizabethan Likeness," *Modern Philology* 98 (2000), 183–210.
Wells, Stanley. *Royal Shakespeare*. Manchester, Eng., 1977. (Includes an account of John Barton's production of *Twelfth Night*.)
Welsford, Enid. *The Fool: His Social and Literary History*. London, 1935.
Williams, Porter, Jr. "Mistakes in *Twelfth Night* and Their Resolution," *PMLA* 76 (1961), 193–9.

All's Well That Ends Well

See also, under *The Comedies*, Hunter and Salingar: under *The Problem Plays*, Foakes, Frye, Muir and Wells, and Wheeler; under *Shakespeare Criticism from the 1940s to the 1970s*, Rossiter; under *Shakespeare Criticism Since 1980*, Holland et al. (essay by Adelman), Kirsch, Mahon and Pendleton (essay by Nevo), and Neely; and under *Shakespeare's Language*, Donawerth.
Calderwood, James L. "Styles of Knowing in *All's Well*," *Modern Language Quarterly* 25 (1964), 272–94.
Cole, Howard C. *The "All's Well" Story from Boccaccio to Shakespeare*. Urbana, Ill., 1981.
Desens, Marliss C. *The Bed-Trick in English Renaissance Drama: Explorations in Gender, Sexuality, and Power*. Newark, Del., 1994.
Donaldson, Ian. "*All's Well That Ends Well:* Shakespeare's Play of Endings," *Essays in Criticism* 27 (1977), 34–55.
Friedman, Michael D. "Male Bonds and Marriage in *All's Well* and *Much Ado*," *Studies in English Literature* 35 (1995), 231–49.
Haley, David. *Shakespeare's Courtly Mirror: Reflexivity and Prudence in "All's Well That Ends Well."* Newark, Del., 1993.
Halio, Jay L. *"All's Well That Ends Well," SQ* 15:1 (1964), 33–43.
Hodgdon, Barbara. "The Making of Virgins and Mothers: Sexual Signs, Substitute Scenes and Doubled Presences in *All's Well That Ends Well*," *Philological Quarterly* 66 (1987), 47–71.
Kastan, David Scott. "*All's Well That Ends Well* and the Limits of Comedy," *ELH* 52 (1985), 575–89.
King, Walter N. "Shakespeare's 'Mingled Yarn,'" *Modern Language Quarterly* 21 (1960), 33–44.
Knight, G. Wilson. *The Sovereign Flower: On Shakespeare as the Poet of Royalism*. London, 1958.
Leech, Clifford. "The Theme of Ambition in *All's Well That Ends Well*," *ELH* 21 (1954), 17–29.
Leggatt, Alexander. "*All's Well That Ends Well:* The Testing of Romance," *Modern Language Quarterly* 32 (1971), 21–41.
Lewis, Cynthia. "'Derived Honesty and Achieved Goodness': Doctrines of Grace in *All's Well That Ends Well*," *Renaissance and Reformation* (Spring, 1990), 147–70.
McCandless, David. "Helena's Bed-trick: Gender and Performance in *All's Well That Ends Well*," *SQ* 45 (1994), 449–68.
Price, Joseph G. *The Unfortunate Comedy: A Study of "All's Well That Ends Well" and Its Critics*. Toronto, 1968.
Snyder, Susan. "*All's Well That Ends Well* and Shakespeare's Helens: Text and Subtext, Subject and Object," *English Literary Renaissance* 18 (1988), 66–77.
Styan, J. L. *Shakespeare in Performance: "All's Well That Ends Well."* Manchester, Eng., 1984.
Turner, Robert Y. "Dramatic Conventions in *All's Well That Ends Well*," *PMLA* 75 (1960), 497–502.
Warren, Roger. "Why Does It End Well? Helena, Bertram, and the Sonnets," *ShS 22* (1969), 79–92.

Measure for Measure

See also, under *The Comedies*, Hunter and Newman; under *The Problem Plays*, Frye, Schanzer, and Wheeler; under *Shakespeare Criticism from the 1940s to the 1970s*, Empson, Fly, Holland, Levin (pp. 171–93), and Sewell; and under *Shakespeare Criticism Since 1980*, Cox, Dollimore, Dollimore and Sinfield (essays by Dollimore and McLuskie), Drakakis (essay by Rose), Goldberg (Chapter 5), Grady (*Shakespeare and Modernity*, essay by Engle), Hamilton (Chapter 5), Holland et al. (essay by Adelman), Kirsch, Marcus, Mullaney (Chapter 4), and Skura (pp. 243–70).
Bennett, Josephine Waters. *"Measure for Measure" as Royal Entertainment*. New York, 1966.
Bennett, Robert B. *Romance and Reformation: The Erasmian Spirit of Shakespeare's "Measure for Measure."* Newark, Del., 2000.
Brown, Carolyn E. "The Wooing of Duke Vincentio and Isabella of *Measure for Measure:* 'The Image of It Gives [Them] Content,' " *ShakS 22* (1994), 189–219.
Cacicedo, Alberto. " 'She is fast my wife': Sex, Marriage, and Ducal Authority in *Measure for Measure*," *ShakS 23* (1995), 187–209.
Chamberlain, Stephanie. "Defrocking Ecclesiastical Authority: *Measure for Measure* and the Struggle for Matrimonial Reform in Early Modern England," *Ben Jonson Journal* 7 (2000), 115–28.
Chambers, R. W. "The Jacobean Shakespeare and *Measure for Measure*," *Proceedings of the British Academy* 23 (1937), 135–92.
Coghill, Nevill. "Comic Form in *Measure for Measure*," *ShS 8* (1955), 14–27.
Desens, Marliss C. *The Bed-Trick in English Renaissance Drama: Explorations in Gender, Sexuality, and Power*. Newark, Del., 1994.
Fergusson, Francis. *The Human Image in Dramatic Literature*. Garden City, N.Y., 1957.
Gless, Darryl. *"Measure for Measure," the Law, and the Convent*. Princeton, 1979.
Lascelles, Mary. *Shakespeare's "Measure for Measure."* London, 1953.
Leavis, F. R. "The Greatness of *Measure for Measure*," *Scrutiny* 10 (1942), 234–47.
Leggatt, Alexander. "Substitution in *Measure for Measure*," *SQ* 39 (1988), 342–59.
Nagarajan, S. "*Measure for Measure* and Elizabethan Betrothals," *SQ* 14 (1963), 115–19.
Shell, Marc. *The End of Kinship: "Measure for Measure," Incest, and the Ideal of Universal Siblinghood*. Stanford, 1988.

Stevenson, David L. *The Achievement of "Measure for Measure."* Ithaca, N.Y., 1966.

Wilson, Harold S. "Action and Symbol in *Measure for Measure* and *The Tempest*." *SQ* 4 (1953), 375–84.

Wood, Nigel. "*Measure for Measure*." Theory in Practice Series. Buckingham and Philadelphia, 1996.

Troilus and Cressida

See also, under *The Problem Plays*, especially Foakes and Frye; under *Shakespeare's Predecessors and Contemporaries*, Kernan and Ornstein; under *Shakespeare Criticism from the 1940s to the 1970s*, Colie, Council, Fly, Knights, Rossiter, Spencer, and Weimann; and under *Shakespeare Criticism Since 1980*, Charnes, Dollimore, Eagleton (Chapter 3), Mallin, Novy (*Love's Argument*), Parker and Hartman (essays by Freund and Girard), Schwartz and Kahn (essay by Fineman), and Wheeler.

Adamson, Jane. "*Troilus and Cressida*." Brighton, Sussex, 1987.

Adelman, Janet. "'This is and is Not Cressid': The Characterization of Cressida," *The (M)other Tongue: Essays in Feminist Psychoanalytic Interpretation*, ed. Shirley Nelson Garner, Claire Kehane, and Madelon Sprengnether. Ithaca, N.Y., 1985.

Bayley, John. "Time and the Trojans," *Essays in Criticism* 25 (1975), 55–73.

Bowen, Barbara E. *Gender in the Theater of War: Shakespeare's "Troilus and Cressida."* New York, 1993.

Campbell, Oscar James. *Comicall Satyre and Shakespeare's "Troilus and Cressida."* San Marino, Calif., 1938.

Cox, John D. "The Error of Our Eye in *Troilus and Cressida*," *Comparative Drama* 10 (1976), 147–71.

Elton, W. R. *Shakespeare's "Troilus and Cressida" and the Inns of Court Revels*. Aldershot, 2000.

Gil, Daniel Juan. "At the Limits of the Social World: Fear and Pride in *Troilus and Cressida*," *SQ* 52 (2001), 336–59.

Greenfield, Matthew A. "Fragments of Nationalism in *Troilus and Cressida*," *SQ* 51 (2000), 181–200.

Hillman, David. "The Gastric Epic: *Troilus and Cressida*," *SQ* 48 (1997), 295–313.

Kaula, David. "Will and Reason in *Troilus and Cressida*," *SQ* 12 (1961), 271–83.

Kermode, Frank. "'Opinion' in *Troilus and Cressida*," *Teaching the Text*, eds. Susanne Kappeler and Norman Bryson. London, 1983.

Kimbrough, Robert. *Shakespeare's "Troilus and Cressida" and its Setting*. Cambridge, Mass., 1964.

Knight, G. Wilson. *The Wheel of Fire*. London, 1930, 1965.

Levine, Laura. *Men in Women's Clothing: Anti-Theatricality and Effeminization, 1579–1642*. Cambridge, Eng., 1994.

Mallin, Eric. "Emulous Factions and the Collapse of Chivalry: *Troilus and Cressida*," *Representations* 29 (1990), 145–79.

Norbrook, David. "Rhetoric, Ideology, and the Elizabethan Picture," *Renaissance Rhetoric*, ed. Peter Mack. Basingstoke and New York, 1994.

Nowottny, Winifred M. T. "'Opinion' and 'Value' in *Troilus: and Cressida*," *Essays in Criticism* 4 (1954), 282–96.

Presson, Robert K. *Shakespeare's "Troilus and Cressida" and the Legends of Troy*. Madison, Wis., 1953.

Rabkin, Norman. "*Troilus and Cressida:* The Uses of the Double Plot," *ShakS 1* (1965), 265–82.

Rutter, Carol Chillington. "Shakespeare, His Designers, and the Politics of Costume: Handing Over Cressida's Glove," *Essays in Theatre/Études théâtrales* 12 (1993–1994), 107–28.

Smith, Bruce R. "Rape, rap, rupture, rapture: R-rated futures on the global market," *Textual Practice* 9 (1995), 421–43.

Taylor, Gary. "*Troilus and Cressida:* Bibliography, Performance, and Interpretation," *ShakS 15* (1982), 99–136.

Yoder, R. A. "'Sons and Daughters of the Game': An Essay on Shakespeare's *Troilus and Cressida*," *ShS 25* (1972), 11–25.

Textual Notes

These textual notes do not offer an historical collation, either of the early quartos and folios or of more recent editions; they are simply a record of departures in this edition from the copy text. For most plays the notes give the adopted reading of this edition in bold face, followed by the rejected reading in the relevant copy text. Where two substantive early texts are involved, or where a reading from some other earlier edition has been adopted, the notes provide information on the source of the reading in square brackets. In a few texts, adopted readings of editions more recent than the First Folio are indicated by [eds.]. Alterations in lineation are not indicated, nor are some minor and obvious typographical errors; changes in punctuation are indicated when the resulting change in meaning is substantive.

Abbreviations used:

F The First Folio
Q Quarto
O Octavo
s.d. stage direction
s.p. speech prefix

The Comedy of Errors

Copy text: the First Folio. Scene divisions not marked in the Folio are provided at 1.2, 2.2, 3.2, 4.2, 4.3, and 4.4.

1.1. 0.2 [and elsewhere] ***Syracuse*** *Siracusa* **1 [and elsewhere] EGEON** *Marchant* **41 [and throughout] Epidamnum** *Epidamium* **42 the** he **102 upon** vp **116 bark** backe **123 thee** they **151 health** helpe

1.2. 0.1 ***Antipholus [of Syracuse]*** *Antipholis Erotes* ***[First] Merchant*** *a Marchant* **1 [and elsewhere] FIRST MERCHANT** *Mer.* [also called *E. Mar.*] **4 arrival** a riuall **15 travel** trauaile **30 [and elsewhere] lose** loose **32 s.d.** ***Exit*** *Exeunt* **40 unhappy** vnhappie a **66 clock** cooke **94.1** ***Exit*** *Exeunt*

2.1. 0.1 ***Antipholus [of Ephesus]*** *Antipholis Sereptus* **11 o'door** adore **12 ill** thus **45 two** too **60 thousand** hundred **63 come home** come **71 errand** arrant **106 o' love** a loue **111 Wear** Where **115.1** ***Exeunt*** *Exit*

2.2. 0.1 ***Antipholus of Syracuse*** *Antipholus Errotis* **6.1.** ***of Syracuse*** *Siracusia* **12 didst** did didst **14 S. ANTIPHOLUS** *E. Ant.* **79 men** them **97 tiring** trying **101 e'en** in **135 off** of **174 stronger** stranger **185 offered** free'd **189 elves** Owles **193 drone** *Dromio* **194 not I** I not

3.1. 71 cake cake here **75 you** your **89 her** your **91 her** your **116 [and throughout] Porcupine** *Porpentine*

3.2. 0.1 ***Luciana*** *Iuliana* **1 LUCIANA** *Iulia* **4 building** buildings **ruinous** ruinate **16 attaint** attaine **21 but** not **26 wife** wise **46 sister's** sister **49 bed** bud **them** thee **57 where** when **109 and** is **126 chalky** chalkle **136 carracks** Carrects **162 [and elsewhere] lest** least

4.1. 1 [and elsewhere] SECOND MERCHANT *Mar.* **7 [and elsewhere] ANGELO** *Gold.* **13.1** ***Enter . . . Ephesus*** *Enter Antipholus Ephes. Dromio* **17 her** their **28 carat** charect **87 then** then sir

4.2. 6 Of Oh **34 One** On **48 That** Thus **61 'a** I **66 s.d.** ***Exeunt*** *Exit*

4.3. 1 S. ANTIPHOLUS [not in F] **58 if you** if **78 s.d.** ***Exeunt*** *Exit*

4.4. 42 to prophesy the prophesie **104 those** these **106.1–2.** ***Enter . . . strives*** [after line 105 in F] **113 his** this **130.1–3.** [after line 131 in F] ***Manent*** *Manet* **143.1–2.** ***Enter . . . drawn*** *Enter Antipholus Siracusia with his Rapier drawne, and Dromio Sirac.* **146.1** ***Run all out*** [after "bound again" in line 146 in F]

5.1. 121 death depth **155 whither** whether **168 SERVANT** [not in F] **175 scissors** Cizers **180 SERVANT** *Mess.* **195 EGEON** *Mar. Fat.* **283 EGEON** *Fa.* [and elsewhere *Fath. and Father*] **330.1–2.** ***Antipholus . . . Syracuse*** *Antipholus Siracusa, and Dromio Sir.* **357–62** [these lines follow line 346 in F] **358 Antipholus'** *Antipholus* **403 ne'er** are **406 joy** go **408.1** ***Manent*** *Manet* **414.1** ***Exeunt*** *Exit*

Love's Labor's Lost

Copy text: the Quarto of 1598. The act and scene divisions here provided are not in Q. Act divisions are from F; scene divisions are editorial.

1.1. [and elsewhere] KING *Ferdinand* **18 schedule** sedule **23 too** to **24 three** thee **31 pomp** pome **62 feast** fast **70 quite** quit **79 losing** loosing **104 an** any **123 losing** loosing **127 BEROWNE** [at line 132 (*Ber.*) in Q] **130 public** publibue **possibly** possible **165 One** On **168 umpire** vmpier **180 [and elsewhere] DULL** *Constab.* **188 [and elsewhere, except for lines 219 and 221] COSTARD** *Clowne* **188 contempts** Contempls **216 welkin's** *welkis* **227 besieged** *besedged* **245 KING** [not in Q; also at lines 247, 249, 252] **254 with, with** *Which with* **264 DULL** *Antho.* **273 worst** wost

1.2. 0.1 [and elsewhere] Mote *Moth* **3 [and elsewhere] MOTE** *Boy* **4 Why,** Why? **13–14 epitheton** apethaton **97 blushing** blush-in **126 deywoman** Day womand **128 JAQUENETTA** *Maide* [and elsewhere Maid, *Ma.*] **139 DULL** *Clo.* **172 duello** [F] *Duella*

2.1. 13 [and elsewhere] PRINCESS *Queene* **32 Importunes** Importuous **34 visaged** visage **36.1** ***Exit Boyet*** [at line 35 in Q] **39 A LORD** *Lor.* [also at line 80] **Lord Longaville** *Longauill* **40 MARIA** 1. *Lady* **42–3 solemnizèd . . . Longaville**. solemnized. In *Normandie* saw I this *Longauill,* **44 parts** peerelsse **53 MARIA** *Lad.* **56 KATHARINE** 2. *Lad.* **61 Alencon's** *Alansoes* **64 ROSALINE** 3. *Lad.* **88 unpeopled** vnpeeled **90 [and elsewhere] KING** *Nauar.* **100 it—will** it will,

115–26 ROSALINE *Kather.* or *Kath.* **130 of** of, of **142 demand** pemaund **144 On** One **180 mine own** my none **190** ***Non*** *No* **195 Katharine** *Rosalin* **210 Rosaline** *Katherin* **221 KATHARINE** *La.* [also at lines 222 and 224] **246 quote** coate **254 ROSALINE** *Lad.* **255 MARIA** *Lad.* 2 **256 KATHARINE** *Lad.* 3 **257 MARIA** *Lad.* **258 KATHARINE** *Lad.*

3.1. 1 [and elsewhere] ARMADO *Bra.* **14 as if** if **15 through the nose** through: nose **18 thin-belly** thinbellies **26 penny** penne **65 voluble** volable **69 [and elsewhere] MOTE** *Pag.* **72 the mail** thee male **plain** pline **133 ounce** ouce **136 remuneration** remuration **138 carries it**. carries it **141 My** [preceded by "O" in Q; also lines 145, 147, 149, 153, 155, 172] **178 Junior** *Iunios* **188 clock** Cloake **202 sue** shue

4.1. 3 BOYET *Forr.* **6 On** Ore **42 God-i-good-e'en** God dig-you-den **49 mistress** [F] Mistrs **70–1 saw . . . saw** See . . . see **71 overcame** couercame **75 King's** King **87 Adriano** Adriana **Armado** Armatho **128.1** ***Exit*** [at line 126 in Q] **130 hit it** hit **132 mete** meate **134 ne'er** neare **136 pin** is in **144 o'th'one** ath toothen **148 is a** is **s.d.** ***Shout*** Shoot. [The s.d. follows line 149 in Q.] **149 s.d.** ***Exit*** *Exeunt*

4.2. 3 [and elsewhere] HOLOFERNES *Ped.* **8 [and elsewhere] NATHANIEL** *Curat. Nath.* **14–15 explication; facere,** explication *facere:* **29 of taste** taste **30 indiscreet** indistreell **36 Dictynna . . . Dictynna** *Dictisima . . . dictisima* **51 ignorant** ignorault **call I** cald **53 scurrility** squirilitie **65 HOLOFERNES** *Nath.* [the subsequent speech prefixes in this scene of Holofernes and Nathaniel are reversed in Q through line 147, except that the speech at line 104 is correctly assigned to Nathaniel, at lines 118–20 to *Pedan.*, and at lines 135–42 to *Ped.*] **69** ***pia mater*** primater **71 in whom** whom **72 NATHANIEL** *Holo.* **76 ingenious** ingenous **78** ***sapit*** *sapis* **81 HOLOFERNES** *Nath.* [also at lines 85, 91] **pierce-one** Person **88 Person** Parson **91** ***Fauste*** *Facile* ***pecus*** *pecas* ***omne*** *omnia* **94–5** ***Venezia . . . prezia*** *vemchie, vencha, que non te vnde, que non te perreche* **101 NATHANIEL** *Holo.* **102 HOLOFERNES** *Nath.* **stanza** stauze **104 NATHANIEL** [missing in Q] **118 apostrophus** apostraphas **119 canzonet** cangenet **120 Here** [the rest of this speech is assigned to *Nath.* in Q] **130 HOLOFERNES** *Nath.* **133 writing** written **135 Sir Nathaniel** *Ped.* Sir *Holofernes* **143 JAQUENETTA** *Mayd* **146 NATHANIEL** *Holo.* **148 HOLOFERNES** *Ped.* **156** ***ben*** *bien*

4.3. 12 melancholy mallicholie [also in line 13] **13 here my** heare my **35 wilt** will **45 KING** *Long.* **69 lose** loose **71 idolatry** ydotarie **83 quoted** coted **89 And I** And **95 ode** Odo **104 Wished** Wish **108 thorn** throne **151 coaches; in your tears** couches in your teares. **157 mote . . . mote** Moth . . . Moth **172 to . . . by** by . . . to **176 like you** like **178 Joan** Ione [Qb]; Loue [Qa] **179 me? When** mee when **184 s.d.** [after "God bless the king" in line 185 in Q] **192 Where** [Q repeats the s.p. KING] **255 and usurping** vsurping **256 doters** dooters **279 Nothing** O nothing **291 And . . . maladies** [Q follows with the following twenty-three lines that appear to be a first draft of lines 292 ff.:

And where that you haue vowd to studie (Lordes)
In that each of you haue forsworne his Booke.
Can you still dreame and poare and thereon looke.
For when would you my Lord, or you, or you,
Haue found the ground of Studies excellence,
Without the beautie of a womans face?
From womens eyes this doctrine I deriue,
They are the Ground, the Bookes, the Achadems,
From whence doth spring the true *Promethean* fire.
Why vniuersall plodding poysons vp
The nimble sprites in the arteries,
As motion and long during action tyres
The sinnowy vigour of the trauayler.
Now for not looking on a womans face,
You haue in that forsworne the vse of eyes:
And studie too, the causer of your vow.
For where is any Authour in the worlde,
Teaches such beautie as a womas eye:
Learning is but an adiunct to our selfe,
And where we are, our Learning likewise is.
Then when our selues we see in Ladies eyes,
With our selues.
Do we not likewise see our learning there?]

313 dainty Bacchus . . . taste. daintie, *Bachus* . . . taste, **316 Subtle** Subtit **333 authors** authour **335 Let** Lets **lose** loose [also in line 336] **341 standards** standars **356 betime** be time **357** ***Allons! Allons!*** Alone alone **359 forsworn** forsorne

5.1. 1 ***quod*** quid **9** ***hominem*** hominum **25 insanie** infamie **27 bone** *bene* **28** ***Bone*** **. . . Priscian** *Bome boon for boon prescian* **31** ***gaudeo*** gaudio **33** ***Quare*** *Quari* **38 lived** lyud **56 wave** wane **57 venue** vene we **66** ***manu*** *vnum* **73 wert** wart **74** ***dunghill*** *dungil* **76 Dunghill** *dunghel* **90 choice** chose **96 importunate** importunt **101 mustachio** mustachie **106 secrecy** secretie **108 antic** antique [also at line 143] **115 Nathaniel** *Holofernes* **117 rendered** rended **assistance** assistants **148** ***Allons*** Alone

5.2. 13 ne'er neare **17 ha' been a** a bin **22 You'll** Yole **28 cure . . . care** care . . . cure **43 pencils, ho!** pensalls, How? **53 [and at line 57] MARIA** *Marg.* **53 pearls** Pearle **65 hests** deuice **67 pair-taunt-like** perttaunt like **74 wantonness** wantons be **80 stabbed** stable **83 peace. Love** Peace Loue **89 sycamore** Siccamone **93 companions. Warily** companions warely, **96 they** thy **122 parle** parlee **123 love suit** Loue-feat **134 too** two **148 her** his **152 ne'er** ere **160.1** ***The . . . him*** [after line 161 in Q] **164 ever** ***euen*** **176 strangers** stranges **179 Princess** Princes **198 travel** trauaile **213 yet? No dance!** yet no dance: **217 The . . . it** [assigned in Q to *Rosa.*] **223 measure! Be** measure be **225 Price** Prise **232 [and elsewhere] PRINCESS** *Quee.* **243 KATHARINE** *Maria* [also at lines 245, 248, 249, 250, 254, 256] **260 sense, so sensible** sense so sensible, **265.1** ***Exeunt*** *Exe* **269 have; gross** haue grosse **278 Non** No **280 perhaps** perhapt **298 vailing** varling **300 woo** woe **310 run** runs **342 Construe** Consture **353 unsullied** vnsallied **375–7 foolish. When . . . eye, . . . light.** foolish when . . . eie: . . . light, **397 lady. Dart** Ladie dart **406 song** songue **408 affectation** affection **464 zany** saine **479 allowed** aloude **483 manage** nuage **485** [Q supplies a s.p. here, *"Ber."*] **501 they** thy **514 least** best **529** ***de la guerra*** *delaguar* **544 leopard's** Libbards **554 PRINCESS** *Lady* **563 this** his **582** [Q has *"Exit Curat."*] **591 Judas** *Pede.* Iudas **596 proved** proud **643 gilt** gift **669 The . . . gone** [Q prints as a s.d. or as a part of Armado's speech] **686 on, stir** or stir **691 northern** Northren **699 lose** loose **746 wholesome** holdsome **759 strange** straying **764 gravities,** grauities. **770 both—fair** both faire **774 the ambassadors** embassadours **778 this in** this **782 quote** cote **808 entitled** intiled **812 hermit** herrite **812 Hence . . . breast** [Q follows with the following six lines that appear to be a first draft of lines 813 ff.:

Berow. And what to me my Loue? and what to me?
Rosal. You must be purged to, your sinnes are rackt.
You are attaint with faultes and periurie:
Therefore if you my fauour meane to get,
A tweluemonth shall you spende and neuer rest,
But seeke the weery beddes of people sicke.]

814 A wife [assigned to *Kath.* in Q] **881** [Q supplies a s.p. here, *Brag.*] **883** [Q supplies a s.p. here, *B.*] **884 SPRING** [not in Q] **885–6** [the second and third lines of the song are transposed in Q] **906 foul** full **918 ARMADO** [not in Q] **918–19 The . . . Apollo** [printed in larger type in Q without s.p.; F adds s.p. *"Brag."* and "You that way: we this way," thus incorporating the ending into the text]

The Two Gentlemen of Verona

Copy text: the First Folio. Characters' name are grouped at the head of each scene. Act and scene divisions follow the Folio text throughout.

1.1. 26 swam swom **66 leave** loue **68 [and elsewhere] lose** loose **78 I a** I **141 testerned** cestern'd
1.2. 80–1 tune, . . . note. tune: . . . note, **97 your** you
1.3. 16 travel trauaile **24 [and elsewhere] whither** whether **50** [here F repeats speech prefix "*Pro.*"] **88 father calls** Fathers call's **91.1 *Exeunt*** *Exeunt. Finis*
2.1. 109 stead steed **136 What, are** What are
2.2. 18.1 [and elsewhere] *Panthino* *Panthion* [in F, grouped with characters' names at head of scene, as with entrance directions generally]
2.3. 27 wood would **36 tied** tide [also at lines 37, 39, and 51]
2.4. 60 know knew **106 mistress** a Mistresse **114 SERVANT** *Thur.* **118 to** too **161 braggartism** Bragadisme **163 makes** make **188.1** [at line 187 in F] **193 Is it mine eye** It is mine **207 dazzlèd** dazel'd **211 s.d. *Exit*** *Exeunt*
2.5. 1 Milan *Padua* **37 that my** that that my
3.1. 56 tenor tenure **280 master's ship** Mastership **318 kissed fasting** fasting **375.1 *Exit*** *Exeunt*
4.1. 35 had often had **49 An heir, and near** And heire and Neece,
4.2. 17.1. *Musicians* *Musitian* [grouped with characters' names at head of scene] **38 MUSICIAN** [not in F] **95 hast** has't **110 his** her
4.3. 19 abhors abhor'd **42 Recking** Wreaking
4.4. 54 hangman Hangmans **68 thou** thee **72 to** not **105 woo** woe **148 is.** is, **149 well,** well; **204 s.d. *Exit*** *Exeunt*
5.2. 7 JULIA *Pro.* **13 JULIA** *Thu.* **18 your** you **47 you, stand not** you stand, not **59 s.d. *Exit*** *Exeunt*
5.4. 26 this . . . hear! this? I see, and heare: **33 seizèd** ceazed **49 me.** me, **120 OUTLAWS** *Out-l.*

The Taming of the Shrew

Copy Text: The First Folio. The act and scene divisions are missing in the Folio except for Act 1 (before the first Induction), Act 3, Act 4 (at 4.3), and Act 5 (at 5.2).
Ind.1. 0.1 *Christopher Sly* [printed at the end of the s.d. in F as "*Christophero Sly*"] **1 [and elsewhere] SLY** *Begger* **10–11 thirdborough** Headborough **16 Breathe** Brach **21 [and elsewhere] FIRST HUNTSMAN** *Hunts.* **81 FIRST PLAYER** *2. Player* **87 SECOND PLAYER** *Sincklo* **99 FIRST PLAYER** *Plai.* **134 peasant.** peasant,
Ind. 2. 2 Lordship Lord **18 Sly's** Sies **26 [and elsewhere] THIRD SERVINGMAN** *3. Man* **27 [and elsewhere] SECOND SERVINGMAN** *2 Man* **47 [and elsewhere] FIRST SERVINGMAN** *1 Man* **53 wi'th'** with **93 Greet** Greece **98 lose** loose **99 [and elsewhere] PAGE** *Lady* **125 SERVINGMAN** *Mes.* **133 it. Is** it is
1.1. 3 fore for **13 Vincentio** *Vincentio's* **14 brought** brough **24 satiety** sacietie **25 *Mi perdonate*** *Me Pardonato* **33 Ovid be** *Ouid*; be **146 s.d. *Manent*** *Manet* **163 *captum*** *captam* **208 colored** Conlord **227 time.** time **244 your** you **248.2 *speak*** *speakes*
1.2. 17.1 *wrings* *rings* **18 masters** mistris **24 *Con . . . trovato*** *Contutti le core bene trobatto* **25 *ben*** *bene* **26 *Molto*** *multo* **onorato** *honorata* **33 pip** peepe **45 this's** this **51 grows. But** growes but **few,** few. **72 me, were she** me. Were she is **119 me and other more,** me. Other more **170 help me** helpe one **188 Antonio's** *Butonios* **189 his** my **211 ours** yours **264 feat** seeke **279 *ben*** *Been*
2.1. 8 thee tell tel **75–6 wooing.—Neighbors,** wooing neighbors: **79 unto you** vnto **104 Pisa. By report** *Pisa* by report, **153 struck** stroke **157 rascal fiddler** Rascall, Fidler **168 s.d. *Exeunt*** *Exit* **186 bonny** bony **244 askance** a sconce **322 s.d. *Exeunt*** *Exit* **328 in** me **352 Valance** Vallens **355 pail** pale **373 Marseilles** Marcellus
3.1. 28 *Sigeia* *sigeria* [also at lines 33 and 42] **43 *steterat*** *staterat* **47 [*Aside*]** *Luc.* **50 BIANCA** [not in F] **51 LUCENTIO** *Bian.* **53 BIANCA** *Hort.* **74 *B mi*** *Beeme* **76 clef** Cliffe **80 change** charge **odd** old **81 SERVANT** *Nicke*
3.2. 13 behavior. behaviour, **14 man,** man; **29 of thy** of **30 old news** newes **33 hear** heard **54 swayed** Waid **56 cheeked** chekt **60 velour** velure **128 to love** Loue **130 As I** As **150 e'er** ere **182 s.d. *Music plays*** [after line 183 in F] **199 GREMIO** *Gra.*
4.1. 23 CURTIS *Gru.* **59 Imprimis** Inprimis **81 sleekly** slickely **106 GRUMIO** *Gre.* **168.1 *Curtis*** *Curtis a Seruant* [after line 169 in F]
4.2. 4 HORTENSIO *Luc.* **6 LUCENTIO** *Hor.* [and at line 8] **7 you? First resolve** you first, resolue **8 read that I profess, *The*** reade, that I professe the **13 none** me **31 her** them **72 Take . . . alone** [assigned to "*Par.*" in F] **in** me
4.[3] [F has "*Actus Quartus. Scena Prima*" here] **48 to** too **62.1 *Enter Haberdasher*** [after 61 in F] **63 HABERDASHER** *Fel.* **81 is a** is **88 like a** like **146 where,** where **148 mete-yard** meat-yard **177 account'st** accountedst
4.4. 0.2 [*booted*] [appears at line 18.2 in F] **1 Sir** Sirs **18.2 *bareheaded*** *booted and bare headed* **68.1 *Exit*** [after line 67 in F; F also adds a s.d., "*Enter Peter,*" after line 68] **78 he's** has **91 except** expect **93 *solum*** *solem*
4.5. 14 An And **18 is** in **35 make a** make the **37 Whither** Whether **where** whether **77 she be** she
5.1. 4 [F has "*Exit*" here] **6 master's** mistris **42 brought** brough **50 master's** Mistris **62 copintank** copataine **104.1 *Exeunt*** *Exit* **139 No** Mo **143 than never** then ueuer
5.[2] [F has "*Actus Quintus*" here] **2 done** come **37 thee, lad** the lad **39 butt** But **40 butt! An** but an **45 bitter** better **two** too **52 TRANIO** *Tri.* **57 Oho** Oh, oh **62 two** too **65 for** sir **93.1 *Enter Biondello*** [after "Do what you can" in 93 in F] **132 a** fiue **136 you're** your **152 maintenance commits** maintenance. Commits

A Midsummer Night's Dream

Copy text: the First Quarto of 1600. The act and scene divisions are absent from the Quarto; the Folio provides act divisions only.
1.1. 4 wanes waues **10 New** Now **19.1 *Lysander*** Lysander *and* Helena **24 Stand forth, Demetrius** [printed as s.d. in Q] **26 Stand forth, Lysander** [printed as s.d. in Q] **74 their** there **114 [and elsewhere] lose** loose **132 Ay** Eigh **133 hear** here **136 low** loue **187 Yours would** Your words **191 I'd** ile **216 sweet** sweld **219 stranger companies** strange companions **224 s.d. *Exit Hermia*** [after line 223 in Q]
2.1. 1 [and elsewhere] PUCK *Robin* **61 [and elsewhere] TITANIA** *Qu.* **61 Fairies** Fairy **79 Aegles** Eagles **109 thin** chinne **158 the west** west **183 off** of **190 slay** stay **slayeth** stayeth **194 thee** the **201 not nor** not, not **206 lose** loose **246.1** [after line 247 in Q]
2.2. 4 leathern lethren **9 FIRST FAIRY** [not in Q] **13 CHORUS** [not in Q; also at line 24] **44 comfort** comfor **45 Be** Bet **49 good** god **53 is** it **63 human** humane **155 ate** eate
3.1. 52 BOTTOM *Cet.* **72 PUCK** *Ro.* **77 BOTTOM** *Pyra.* [also at lines 79 and 98] **78 Odors, odors** Odours, odorous **83 PUCK** *Quin.* **84 FLUTE** *Thys.* [also at lines 88 and 97] **120 ousel** Woosell **144 own** owe **156 [and elsewhere] Mote** *Moth* **157–8 Ready . . . go** [assigned to FAIRIES in Q] **170 PEASEBLOSSOM** *1. Fai.* **171 COBWEB** [not in Q] **172 MOTE** *2. Fair.* **173 MUSTARDSEED** *3. Fai.* **190 you of** you **196.1 *Exeunt*** *Exit*
3.2. 0.1 [Q: *Enter King of* Fairies, *and* Robin goodfellow] **3.1** [See previous note.] **6–7 love. / Near . . . bower,** loue, / Neere . . . bower. **15–16 brake. / When . . . take,** brake, / When . . . take: **19 mimic** Minnick **38 [and elsewhere] PUCK** *Rob.* **80 I so** I **85 sleep** slippe **213 like** life **215 rend** rent **220 passionate words** words **250 prayers** praise **260 off** of **299 gentlemen** gentleman **313 too** to **326 but** hut **344 s.d. *Exit*** *Exeunt* **406 Speak! In some bush?** Speake in some bush. **426 shalt** shat **451 To your** your
4.1. 5 [and elsewhere] BOTTOM *Clown* **20 courtesy** curtsie **24 marvelous** maruailes **54 flowerets'** flouriets **64 off** of **72 o'er** or **81 five** fine **82 ho** howe **116 Seemed** Seeme **127 this is** this **132 rite** right **137.2 *Wind . . . up*** *they all start vp. Winde hornes* **171 saw** see **177 hear** here **190 found** fonnd **198 let us** lets **205 to expound** expound **208 a patched** patcht a **213 ballad** Ballet
4.2. 0.1 [*Snout, and Starveling*] Thisby *and the rabble* **3 STARVELLING** *Flut.* **5 FLUTE** *Thys.* [and at lines 9, 13, 19] **29 no** not **34 ribbons** ribands

5.1. 34 our Or **107 [and elsewhere] THESEUS** *Duk* **122 his** this **150.1** ***Exeunt*** *Exit* [after line 153 in Q] **155 Snout** *Flute* **190 up in thee** now againe **193 love! Thou art my** loue thou art, my **205 mural down** Moon vsed **209 [and elsewhere] HIPPOLYTA** *Dutch.* **216 beasts in, a** beasts, in a **265.1** ***Enter Pyramus*** [after 267 in Q] **270 gleams** beames **309 before** before? **315 mote** moth **317 warrant** warnd **325 tomb** tumbe **347 BOTTOM** *Lyon* **363 gait** gate (also at 411) **366 lion** Lyons **367 behowls** beholds **414–15 And . . . rest** [these lines are transposed in Q]

The Merchant of Venice

Copy text: the First Quarto of 1600 [Q]. The act and scene divisions are absent from the Quarto; the Folio provides act divisions only.

1.1. 0.1 ***Salerio*** *Salaryno* [and also elsewhere *Salarino,* and abbreviated *Salar., Sala.,* and *Sal.*] ***Solanio*** *Salanio* [and abbreviated elsewhere *Sola.* and *Sol.*] **19 Peering** Piring **27 docked** docks **84 alabaster** Alablaster **85 jaundice** *Iaundies* **112 tongue** togue **113 Is** It is **128 off** of **151 back** bake

1.2. 44 Palatine Palentine [and at line 57] **53 Bone** *Boune* **58 throstle** Trassell **119.1** ***Enter a Servingman*** [after line 120 in Q]

1.3. 28 [and elsewhere] SHYLOCK *Iew* **76 compromised** compremyzd **82 peeled** pyld **110 spit** spet [also at lines 124 and 129] **125 day, another time** day another time,

2.1. 0.2 ***Morocco*** *Morochus* **25 Sophy . . . prince**, Sophy, and a Persian Prince **31 thee** the **35 page** rage

2.2. 1 [and elsewhere] LAUNCELOT *Clowne* **3 [and elsewhere in this scene] Gobbo** *Iobbe* **42 By** Be **76 murder** muder **91 fill horse** philhorse **94 last** lost **165.1** ***Exit Leonardo*** [after line 164 in Q] **168 a suit** sute **180 [and elsewhere] lose** loose

2.3. 11 did doe

2.4. 8 o'clock of clocke **9 s.d.** [after line 9 in Q] **14 Love news,** Loue, newes **20.1** ***Exit clown*** [after line 23 in Q] **39 s.d.** ***Exeunt*** *Exit*

2.5. 44 Jewess' Iewes

2.6. 26 Ho! Who's Howe whose **35 night, you** night you **59 gentlemen** gentleman **61 Who's** Whose

2.7. 18 threatens. Men threatens men **45 Spits** Spets **69 tombs** *timber*

2.8. 8 gondola Gondylo **39 Slubber** slumber

2.9. 6 rites rights **48 chaff** chaft **49 varnished** varnist **64 judgment** *iudement* **73** [Q provides a s.p.: *Arrag.*]

3.1. 19 [and elsewhere] lest least **21.1** ***Enter Shylock*** [after line 22 in Q] **46 courtesy** cursie **70 MAN** [not in Q] **74.1** [Q repeats the s.d. "*Enter* Tuball"] **100 Heard** heere **114 turquoise** Turkies

3.2. 23 eke ech **61 live. With** liue with **67 eyes** *eye* **81 vice** voyce **84 stairs** stayers **99 Veiling** vailing **101 Therefore** Therefore then **110 shuddering** shyddring **117 whether** whither **199 loved; for intermission** lou'd for intermission, **204 roof** rough **217.1–2** [after line 219 in Q] **315 BASSANIO** [not in Q] **336 e'er** ere

3.3 0.1 ***Solanio*** *Salerio* **24 SOLANIO** *Sal.*

3.4. 13 equal egall **23 Hear other things:** heere other things **49 Padua** Mantua **50 cousin's** cosin **53 traject** Tranect **80 near** nere **81 my** my my

3.5. 20 enough enow **e'en** in **26 comes** come **74 merit it,** meane it, it **81 a wife** wife **85 howsome'er** how so mere **87 s.d.** ***Exeunt*** *Exit*

4.1. 30 his state this states **31 flint** flints **35 [and elsewhere in this scene] SHYLOCK** *Iewe* **50 urine; for affection,** vrine for affection. **51 Mistress** Maisters **73 You may as well** well **74 Why he hath made the** the **bleat** bleake **75 pines** of Pines **81 more** moe **100 is** as **123 sole . . . soul** soule . . . soule **136 whilst** whilest **228 No, not** Not not **233 tenor** tenure **270 off** of **322 off** of **396 GRATIANO** *Shy.* **405.1** ***Exeunt*** *Exit*

5.1. 26 STEPHANO *Messen.* [also *Mess.* at lines 28 and 33] **41 Lorenzo** *Lorenzo, &* **49 Sweet soul** [assigned in Q to Lancelot] **51 Stephano** *Stephen* **62 choiring** quiring **87 Erebus** *Terebus* **106 wren** Renne **109 ho!** how **152 give it** giue **233 my** mine

Much Ado About Nothing

Copy text: the Quarto of 1600. The act and scene divisions are missing from the Quarto; the Folio provides act divisions only.

1.1. 0.1. ***Messina*** *Messina, Innogen, his wife* **2 Pedro** Peter [also in line 9] **40 bird-bolt** Burbolt **84 Benedick** Benedict **141 all, Leonato. Signor** all: Leonato, signior **194.1** ***Pedro*** *Pedro, Iohn the bastard* **239 [and elsewhere] lose** loose

1.2. 3 [and elsewhere] ANTONIO *Old* **6 event** euents **25 skill** shill

1.3. 46 brother's bothers **70 s.d.** ***Exeunt*** *exit*

2.1. 0.1 ***Hero*** *his wife, Hero* **0.3** ***Ursula*** [Q adds "*and a kinsman*"] **2 [and elsewhere] ANTONIO** *brother* **37 bearward** Berrord **44 Peter, for the heavens;** Peter: for the heauens, **50, 53 curtsy** cursie **67 hear** here **79.3.** ***and Don*** *or dumb* **80 a bout** about **94 BALTHASAR** *Bene.* [also at lines 97 and 99] **187 drover** Drouier **201.2** ***Leonato*** *Leonato, Iohn and Borachio, and Conrade* **311 [and elsewhere] DON PEDRO** *Prince* **369 s.d.** ***Exeunt*** *exit*

2.3. 7 s.d. [at line 5 in Q] **25 an** and **35.1** ***Claudio*** *Claudio, Musicke* **61 BALTHASAR** [not in Q] **73–6 but . . . nonny** &c. **84 lief** liue **91 s.d.** [after line 90 in Q] **139 us of** of vs **171 doffed** daft

3.1. 0.2. ***Ursula*** *Ursley* **23 s.d.** [after line 25 in Q] **63 antic** antique **111 on; I** on I

3.2. 27 can cannot **51 DON PEDRO** *Bene.* **74 [and elsewhere] DON JOHN** *Bastard* **75 e'en** den **91–2 manifest. For my brother, I . . . heart hath** manifest, for my brother (I . . . heart) hath **108 her then, tomorrow** her, then to morrow **118 her, tomorrow** her to morrow

3.3. 17 SEACOAL *Watch* 2 [also at line 27] **87 SEACOAL** *Watch* [also at lines 95, 105, 125] **134 reechy** rechie **161 SEACOAL** *Watch* 1 [also at line 165] **162 FIRST WATCH** *Watch* 2 [also at line 168] **171 SEACOAL** [missing in Q]

3.4. 17 in it

3.5. 2 [and elsewhere] DOGBERRY *Const. Dog.* **7 [and elsewhere] VERGES** *Headb.* **9 off** of **32 talking. As** talking as **50** [Q provides an "*exit*" at this point]

4.1. 4 FRIAR *Fran.* **28 DON PEDRO** *Princn* **167 tenor** tenure **202 princes** princesse

4.2. 0.1–3 [Q reads "*Enter the Constables, Borachio, and the Towne clearke in gownes.*"] **1 DOGBERRY** *Keeper* **2 [and elsewhere in this scene] VERGES** *Cowley* **4 DOGBERRY** *Andrew* **9 [and elsewhere in this scene] DOGBERRY** *Kemp* **18 CONRADE, BORACHIO** *Both* **39 SEACOAL** *Watch* 1 [also at line 53] **47 FIRST WATCH** *Watch 2* **51 VERGES** *Const.* **67 [and elsewhere] DOGBERRY** *Constable* **69 CONRADE** [missing in Q] **Off** of **73 CONRADE** *Couley* **86.1** ***Exeunt*** *exit*

5.1. 16 Bid And **97 anticly** antiquely, and **98 off** of **116 like** likt **167 there's** theirs **179 on** one **189 Lackbeard there, he** Lacke-beard, there hee **201.1.2** [after line 197 in Q] **252 VERGES** *Con.* 2

5.2. 41.1 [after line 42 in Q] **81 myself. So** my self so **97 s.d.** ***Exeunt*** *exit*

5.3. 2 A LORD *Lord* **3 CLAUDIO** [missing in Q] **10 dumb** dead **11** [Q provides a s.p. "*Claudio*" here] **12 BALTHASAR** [missing in Q] **22 CLAUDIO** *Lo.* **23 rite** right **32 speed's** speeds

5.4. 54 ANTONIO *Leo.* **97 BENEDICK** *Leon.*

The Merry Wives of Windsor

Copy text: the First Folio. Act and scene divisions follow the Folio text throughout. [Q] = readings taken from the First Quarto of 1602.

1.1. 0.1–2 [Entering characters are grouped at the heads of scenes throughout the play.] **30 compromises** compremises **41 George** *Thomas* **56 SHALLOW** *Slen.* **84 Cotswold** *Cotsall* **131 Garter** Gater **149 latten** Latin **164 careers** Car-eires **165 Latin then, too** Latten then to **235 faul** fall **236 the 'ort** the'ord [and in a few other instances dialect has been similarly regularized]

1.3. 14 lime [Q] liue **47 well** [Q] will **51 legion** [Q: legians] legend **59 oeillades** illiads **81 o'th' hoof** i'th' hoofe **82 humor** [Q] honor **93 Page** [Q] *Ford* **94 Ford** [Q] *Page* **98 Page** *Ford*

1.4. 21 whey face wee-face **23 softly-spirited** softly-sprighted **41 *un boîtier vert*** vnboyteene verd **46 *Ma*** *mai* ***fort chaud*** *for ehando* ***m'en vais*** *man voi* **47 *la cour*** *le Court* ***affaire*** *affaires* **49 *mets-le à ma*** *mette le au mon* **53 and** [Q] aad **57 *qu'ai-j'oublié*** *que ay ie oublie* **63 *Larron*** La-roone **82 *baille*** ballow **99 that, . . . mind:** that I know *Ans* mind, **115 goodyear** good-ier **134 [and elsewhere] lose** loose **149 that I will** that wee will
2.1. have I haue **23 i'th'** with The **48 What? Thou liest!** What thou liest? **55 praised** praise **59–60 Hundredth Psalm** hundred Psalms **130 and . . . of it** [Q; not in F] **137 Cathayan** *Cataian* **141 Whither** Whether [and at 3.3.139, 141] **182 gentleman.** Gentleman **199 FORD** [Q] *Shal.* **201 Brook** [Q] *Broome* [and at line 203 and elsewhere] **204 mynheers** An-heires **216 s.d. *Exeunt*** [at line 223 in F]
2.2. 4 I will . . . equipage [Q; not in F] **21 honor** honoror **23, 50 [and elsewhere] God** [Q] heauen **25 you, you** you **196 jewel. That** Iewell, that **224–5 exchange** enchange
2.3. 26 Galen *Galien* **30 Castilian** Castalion **34 Master Doctor. He** (M. Docto)rhe **51 A word** [Q] a **56 mush** much **73 PAGE, SHALLOW, AND SLENDER** *All* **77 But first** [Q; not in F]
3.1. 5 Petty-ward pittie-ward **29 God** Heauen **39 God save** [Q] 'Saue **40 God pless** [Q] 'Plesse **76–7 patience. In** patience in **84–5 for . . . appointments** [Q; not in F] **99–100 Give me . . . terrestrial; so** [Q; not in F] **105 lads** Lad
3.2. 7 [and elsewhere] MRS. PAGE *M. Pa.* [used previously for *Page*]
3.3. 3 Robert *Robin* **12 Datchet** *Dotchet* **32 cue** *Qu* **35 pumpkin** Pumpion **54 By the Lord** [Q; not in F] **58 not, Nature** not Nature **62 thee there's** thee. Ther's **68–9 Mistress** M. **72 limekiln** Limekill [also at 4.2.51] **141 whither** whether **176 foolish** foolishion **194 By** Be **208 heartily** hartly
3.4. 12 FENTON [not in F] **67 Fenton** *Fenter* **109 s.d. *Exit*** *Exeunt*
3.5. 30 sperm Spersme **57 he** be **83 By the Lord** [Q] Yes **142 s.d. *Exit*** *Exeunt*
4.1. 43 *hung* *hing* **56 *Genitivo*** *Genitiue* **57 Jenny's** Ginyes **62 "whorum"** *horum* **64 lunatics** Lunaties **73 *quae's*** *Ques*
4.2. 10 who's whose **51 MRS. PAGE** [not in F] **59 MRS. PAGE** [Q] *Mist. Ford* **68–9 [and elsewhere] Brentford** *Brainford* **91 direct** direct direct **95 misuse him** misuse **106 as lief** liefe as **111 ging** gin **118 this** thi **169 not strike** strike **180 Jeshu** [Q] yea and no
4.3. 1 Germans desire Germane desires **7 them** [Q] him **9 house** [Q] houses
4.4. 7 cold gold **25 MRS.** *M.* **30 ragg'd horns** rag'd-hornes **32 makes** make **42** [Q, reading "Horne" for "Herne"; not in F] **60 MRS. FORD** *Ford* **65 ne'er** neu'r **72 tire** time
4.5. 41 SIMPLE *Fal.* **54 Thou art** [Q] Thou are **75 Reading . . . Colnbrook** *Readins,* of *Maidenhead;* of *Cole-brooke* **86 Hue** Huy [also in line 87] **97 to say my prayers** [Q; not in F] **118 is here** here is
4.6. 39 denote deuote
5.2. 3 my daughter my
5.3. 12 Hugh Herne
5.5. 2 hot-blooded hot-bloodied **3 Jove** loue **20 hail kissing-comfits** haile-kissing Comfits **48 Bead** *Bede* **65 ring.** ring, **66 bears,** beares: **67 More** Mote **70 sapphire, pearl** Saphire-pearle **93 FAIRIES** [not in F] **105 MRS.** *M.* **179 what, son** what sonne **193 white** greene **197 green** white **201 *un garçon*** oon Garsoon ***un paysan*** oon pesant **203 green** white **204 by** bee **By** be

As You Like It

Copy text: the First Folio. Act and scene divisions follow the Folio text throughout.
1.1. 105 she hee **154 OLIVER** [not in F] **154 s.d. *Exit*** [at line 153 in F]
1.2. 3 I were were **51 goddesses and** goddesses **53 [and elsewhere] whither** whether **55 [and elsewhere] TOUCHSTONE** *Clow.* **56 father** farher **80 CELIA** *Ros.* **88 Le** the **233 love** loue; **251.1** [at line 249 in F] **280 [and occasionally elsewhere] Rosalind** *Rosaline*
1.3. 55 likelihood likelihoods **76 her** per **87.1 with Lords** *&c* **124 be** by **129 travel** trauaile **135 we in** in we **131 [and elsewhere] woo** woe
2.1. 31 antique anticke **49 much** must **50 friends** friend **59 of the** of
2.3. 10 some seeme **16 ORLANDO** [not in F] **29 ORLANDO** *Ad.* **71 seventeen** seauentie
2.4. 1 weary merry **42 thy wound** they would **65 you,** your
2.5. 1 AMIENS [not in F; also at line 35] **38.1 *All together here*** [before line 35 in F] **41–2 No . . . weather** *&c* **46 JAQUES** *Amy.*
2.7. 0.1 Lords *Lord* **38 brain** braiue **55 Not to seem** Seeme **87 comes** come **161 treble, pipes** trebble pipes, **174 AMIENS** [not in F] **182 Then** *The* **190–3 heigh-ho . . . jolly** *&c.* **201 master** masters
3.2. 26 good pood **115 graft** graffe [twice] **123 a desert** *Desert* **143 her** *his* **190 whooping** hooping **234 such fruit** fruite **241 thy** the **254 [and elsewhere] b'wi'you** buy you **340 lectures** Lectors **354 deifying** defying **362 are** art
3.3. 52–3 so. Poor men alone? No so poore men alone: No **88 TOUCHSTONE** *Ol.* **99 s.d. *Exit*** *Exeunt*
3.4. 29 a lover Louer **41 puny** puisny
3.5. 11 pretty, sure pretty sure **65 hear** here **105 erewhile** yere-while **128 I have** Haue
4.1. 1 me be me **18 my** by **27 travel** trauaile **36 gondola** Gundello **44 thousandth** thousand **72 warrant** warne **148 hyena** Hyen **202 it** in
4.2. 2 FIRST LORD *Lord* **7 SECOND LORD** *Lord* **10 SECOND LORD** [not in F]
4.3. 5.1 [after line 3 in F] **8 bid** did bid **12 tenor** tenure **79–80 bottom;** bottom **104–5 itself:** it selfe **143 In** I **156 his** this
5.1. 14 gi' ye **36 sir** sit **55 policy** police
5.2. 7 nor her nor **31 overcame** ouercome
5.3. 15 BOTH PAGES [not in F] **18 In** *In the* **ring** *rang* **24–6 In . . . spring** *In spring time, &c* [also at lines 30–2 and 36–8] **33–8** [this stanza comes after line 20 in F]
5.4. 25.1 *Exeunt* *Exit* **34.1** [after line 33 in F] **80 so to the** so ro **113 her** *his* **150 JAQUES DE BOYS** *2 Bro.* [also at line 182] **163 them** him **170 were** vvete **196 rites** rights **197 trust they'll end, in** trust, they'l end in **197.1 *Exeunt*** *Exit*

Twelfth Night

Copy text: the First Folio. Act and scene divisions follow the Folio text throughout.
1.1. 1 [and throughout] ORSINO *Duke* **10 capacity** capacitie, **11 sea, naught** sea. Nought **22 s.d.** [after 22 in F]
1.2. 15 Arion *Orion*
1.3. 51 SIR ANDREW *Ma.* **54 Mary Accost** *Mary,* accost **96 curl by** coole my **98 me** we **132 dun** dam'd **set** sit **136 That's** That
1.5. 5 [and throughout] FESTE *Clo.* **85 gagged** gag'd [also at 5.1. 376] **144 He's** Ha's **163.1 *Viola*** *Uiolenta* **296 County's** Countes **306 s.d.** [F adds *"Finis, Actus primus"*]
2.2. 20 That sure That **31 our** O **32 made of, such** made, if such
2.3. 2 *diluculo* *Deliculo* **25 leman** Lemon **39 FESTE (sings)** *Clowne sings.* **119 stoop** stope **133 a nayword** an ayword
2.4. 51 FESTE [not in F] **53 Fly . . . fly** *Fye . . . fie* **55 yew** *Ew* **88 I** It
2.5. 14 metal *Mettle* **112 staniel** stallion **118 portend?** portend, **142 born** become **achieve** atcheeues **156–7 Unhappy." Daylight** vnhappy daylight **173 dear** *deero* **203 s.d.** [F adds *"Finis Actus secundus"*]
3.1. 8 king Kings **68 wise men** wisemens **91 all ready** already **124 grece** grize
3.2. 7 thee the the **64 nine** mine
3.4. 15.1–2 s.d. [at line 14 in F, after "hither"] **25 OLIVIA** *Mal.* **65.1 *Exeunt*** *exit* **72 tang** langer **106 lose** loose **175 You** Yon **222 thee** the **228 sir. I am sure no** sir I am sure, no **249 competent** computent **397.1 *Exeunt*** *Exit*

4.1. 34 struck stroke
4.2. 6 in in in **38 clerestories** cleere stores **71 sport to** sport **101 b'wi'** buy
4.3. 1 SEBASTIAN [not in F] **35 s.d.** [F adds *"Finis Actus Quartus"*]
5.1. 5 freight fraught **141 Whither** Whether **173 He's** H'as **190.1** [after line 187 in F] **195 He's** has **200 pavane** panyn **205 help? An** helpe an **207 to** too **285 He's** has **389 tiny** *tine* **406 With hey** *hey*

All's Well That Ends Well

Copy text: the First Folio. Act divisions are from the Folio; scene divisions are editorially provided.

1.1. 1 [and elsewhere] COUNTESS *Mother* **3 [and elsewhere] BERTRAM** *Ros.* **17 [and elsewhere] losing** loosing **52 [and elsewhere] to** too **lest** least **70 Farewell. My** Farwell my **130 got** goe **148 th'one** ten **159 wear** were
1.2. 3 [and elsewhere] FIRST LORD 1. *Lo. G.* **15 [and elsewhere] SECOND LORD** 2. *Lo. E* **18 Rossillion** *Rosignoll* **52 him! He** him he **76.1** ***Exeunt*** *Exit*
1.3. 3 [and elsewhere] RINALDO *Ste.* **13 [and elsewhere] LAVATCH** *Clo.* **19 I** w **74–5** [F indicates the repetition of the line by printing a single line, followed by "*bis*"] **112 Dian no queen** Queene **115 e'er** ere **124.2 [and elsewhere]** ***Helena*** *Hellen* **125** [F has s.p. here, *Old. Cou.*, used subsequently in other s.p.] **127 rightly belong;** righlie belong **168 loneliness** louelinesse **174 th'one to th'other** 'ton tooth to th'other **180 forswear't. Howe'er,** forswear't how ere **199 intenible sieve** intemible Siue **233 Haply** Happily **247 day and** day, an
2.1. 3–4 gain all, / The gaine, all / The **5 FIRST LORD** *Lord.* G **15–16 it. When . . . shrinks, find** it, when . . . shrinkes: finde **18 SECOND LORD** *L.*G **25 SECOND LORD** *2 Lo.* E **44 with his cicatrice** his sicatrice, with **63 fee** see **94.1 [and elsewhere]** ***Helena*** *Hellen* **111 two, more dear. I** two: more deare I **146 fits** shifts **157 impostor** Impostrue **175 nay** ne **194 heaven** helpe **212 meed** deed **212.1** ***Exeunt*** *Exit*
2.2. 1 [and elsewhere in scene] COUNTESS *Lady* **60 An end, sir! To** An end sir to
2.3. 1 [and elsewhere] LAFEW *Ol. Laf.* **21 indeed. If** indeede if **34 minister, great** minister great **44** ***Mort du vinaigre*** *Mor du vinager* **51.1** ***four*** *3 or 4* **65 ALL THE LORDS** *All* **70–1 choose; but, be refused, / Let** choose, but be refused; / Let **76 s.d.** [below line 62 in F] **94 her** heere **96 HELENA** *La.* **99 LAFEW** *Ol. Lord* **125 when** whence **129 name; vileness** name? Vilenesse **130 it is** is is **137–8 word's a slave / Debauched** words, a slaue / Debosh'd **138–9 grave / A** graue: / A **140–1 tomb / Of** Tombe. / Of **168 eyes. When** eies, when **170 it, I** it: I **213 lattice** Lettice **266.1** [at line 264 in F] **293 detested** detected **301.1** ***Exeunt*** *Exit*
2.4. 11 [and elsewhere] whither whether **16 fortunes** fortune **35 me?** [F adds a s.d., *Clo.*] **56 you.** you **s.d.** *Exit Parolles* [at line 55 in F] **s.d.** ***Exeunt*** *Exit*
2.5. 16 who's whose **27 End** And **29 one** on **31 heard** hard **89 BERTRAM** [at line 90 in F] **89 men, mousieur?** men? Monsieur,
3.1. 9 SECOND LORD *French E* **17 FIRST LORD** *Fren. G* **23 to the** to'th the
3.2. 9 sold hold **18 E'en** In **19 COUNTESS** [not in F] **45 [and throughout scene] SECOND LORD** *French E* **47 [and throughout scene] FIRST LORD** *French G* **64 COUNTESS** *Old La.* **65 engrossest all** engrossest, all **111 still-piecing** still-peering
3.4. 4 RINALDO [not in F] **9–10 hie. / Bless** *hie, / Blesse* **10 peace, whilst** *peace. Whilst* **18 COUNTESS** [not in F]
3.5. 0.2 ***daughter*** *daughter, Violenta* **10 [and elsewhere] MARIANA** *Maria* **33 le** *la* **66 warrant** write **93.1.** ***Exeunt*** *Exit*
3.6. 1 [and throughout scene until line 109] FIRST LORD *Cap. E* **3 [and throughout scene until line 109] SECOND LORD** *Cap. G* **36 his** this **37 metal** mettle **ore** ours **109** FIRST LORD *Cap. G* **111, 117 SECOND LORD** *Cap. E*
3.7. 19 Resolved Resolue **41 steads** steeds **46 wicked** lawfull
4.1. 1 [and throughout scene] FIRST LORD 1. *Lord E* **69 [and throughout scene] FIRST SOLDIER** *Inter.* **90 art** are **93 SECOND SOLDIER** *Sol.* [and at line 96] **97 s.d.** ***Exeunt*** *Exit*
4.2. 6 monument. monument **31 least** lest **38 may** make **snare** scarre **56 bond** band
4.3 1 [and throughout scene] FIRST LORD *Cap.* G **2 [and throughout scene] SECOND LORD** *Cap.* E **24 nobility, . . . stream** Nobility . . . streame, **81 FIRST LORD** *Ber.* **89 effected** affected **98 he's** ha s [also at line 268] **118 Hush, hush** [assigned in F to Bertram] **125 FIRST LORD** *Cap.* **138 All's one to him** [assigned in F to Parolles] **168 poll** pole **189 sheriff's** Shrieues **199 Lordship** Lord **242 our** your **316 BERTRAM** *Count*
4.4. 16 you, your
4.5. 21 grass grace **39 name** maine **46 of** off **70 home, I** home. I **80 Marseilles** *Marcellus*
5.1. 6 s.d. ***a Gentleman*** *a gentle Astringer* [after line 6 in F]
5.2. 1 Monsieur Mr **25 similes** smiles **33 under her** vnder
5.3. 50 warped warpe **59–60 carried, / To** carried / To **60 sender turns** sender, turnes **72 COUNTESS** [not in F] **102 Plutus** *Platus* **115 conjectural** connecturall **123 tax** taze **140 KING** [not in F] **148 toll** toule **154.1** [after line 152 in F] **155 since** sir **157 s.d.** ***Diana*** *Diana, and Parrolles* [after line 157 in F] **183 them. Fairer prove** them fairer: proue **208 sickens but** sickens: but **217 infinite cunning** insuite comming **314 are** is
Epilogue 1 KING [not in F] **4 strife** *strift*

Measure for Measure

Copy text: the First Folio. Act and scene divisions are from the Folio except as indicated below.

The Names of All the Actors [at the end of the play in F]
1.1. 76 s.d. [at line 75 in F]
1.2. 58 [and elsewhere] MISTRESS OVERDONE *Bawd* **83.1** [after line 84 in F] **85 [and elsewhere] POMPEY** *Clo.* **115** [F begins "*Scena Tertia*" here] **134 morality** mortality
1.3. [F labels as "*Scena Quarta*"] **20 steeds** weedes **27 Becomes more** More **48 [and elsewhere] More** Moe **54.1** ***Exeunt*** *Exit*
1.4. [F labels as "*Scena Quinta*"] **0.1 [and elsewhere]** ***Isabella*** *Isabell* **2 [and throughout] FRANCISCA** *Nun* **5 sisterhood** Sisterstood **17 stead** steed [also at 3.2. 252] **54 givings-out** giuing-out **61–2 mind, study, and fast. / He** minde: Studie, and fast / He **72 He's** Has **78 [and elsewhere] lose** loose
2.1. 12 your our **39 breaks** brakes **90 [and elsewhere] prunes** prewyns **139.1** [at line 138 in F]
2.2. 63 back again againe **104 ere** here
2.3. 31 [and elsewhere] lest least
2.4. 9 sere feard **17 s.d.** ***Enter Servant*** [after line 17 in F] **30 s.d.** ***Enter Isabella*** [after line 30 in F] **48 metal** mettle **53 or** and **75 craftily** crafty **76 me be** be **94 all-binding** all-building
3.1. 29 thee sire, thee, fire **31 serpigo** Sapego **52 me to hear them** them to heare me **68 Though** Through **91 enew** emmew **96 damned'st** damnest **131 penury** periury **200 advisings. To . . . good a** aduisings, to . . . good; a **216 by oath** oath
3.2. 0 [not marked as a new scene in F] **8 law a** Law; a **9 on** and **26 eat, array** eate away **48 it clutched** clutch'd **74–5 bondage. If . . . patiently, why** bondage if . . . patiently: Why **109 ungenerative** generatiue **147 dearer** deare **214 See** Sea
4.1. 1 BOY [not in F] **49.1** [after line 48 in F] **61 quests** Quest **64 s.d.** ***Enter . . . Isabella*** [after line 64 in F]
4.2. 43–7 If . . . thief [assigned in F to *Clo.*] **58 yare** y'are **60.1** [at line 59 in F] **72 s.d.** ***Enter Duke*** [after line 72 in F] **100 This . . . man** [assigned in F to *Duke*] **Lordship's** Lords **101 DUKE** *Pro.* **120 PROVOST** [not in F]
4.3. 92.1 [at line 91 in F] **93 Varrius** *Angelo* **100 well** weale
4.4. 6 redeliver reliuer **15–16 proclaimed. Betimes** proclaim'd betimes **19 s.d.** [at line 18 in F]
4.5. 6 Flavius' *Flauia's*
5.1. 14 me we **34 hear!** heere. **173 s.d.** ***Enter Mariana*** [after line 173 in F] **174 her face** your face **226 promisèd** promis'd **268 s.d.** [at line 267 in F] **288.1** [after line 286 in F] **407 s.d.** ***Mariana*** *Maria* **431 confiscation** confutation **488.2** ***Juliet*** *Iulietta* **550 that's** that

Troilus and Cressida

Copy text: the Quarto of 1609. As a text seemingly based on Shakespeare's own manuscript, with many unsupplied or imprecise stage directions, mislineation, authorial punctuation, and the like, Q is a suitable copy text, even though the work of the Q compositors (three in number) reduces the reliability of that text's authority even in incidental matters. Substantively, the First Folio text (F) often gives what may perhaps be Shakespeare's later decisions in a manuscript that may also have been put to use in the theater. Some such manuscript was used to annotate a copy of Q for the Folio printers. At the same time one needs to be careful not to include in an edited text those changes in F that appear likely to have been sophistications or compositorial errors. For these limited reasons only, Q serves as copy text for these collation notes, even though many readings that substantively vary between Q and F are decided in favor of F. All adopted readings are from [F] unless otherwise indicated; [eds.] means that the reading is that of some editor since the First Folio. [Fa] refers to the first setting of the Folio text, [Fb] to the second setting. Act and scene divisions are not provided in the Quarto or the Folio. Some bracketed stage directions are from F.

Prologue [F; not in Q] **8 immures** emures [F] **12 barks** [eds.] Barke [F] **17 Antenorides** *Antenonidus* **19 Spar** [eds.] Stirre [F]

1.1. 4 [and elsewhere] Trojan [eds.] Troyan **26 the** [Q, Fa] of the [Fb] **27 [and elsewhere] ye** [eds.] yea **33 When she** [eds.] then she **is she** she is **38 [and elsewhere] Lest** [eds.] Least **55 Pour'st** [eds.] Powrest **55–7 heart / Her . . . voice; / Handlest . . . discourse—oh!—** [eds.] heart: / Her . . . voice, / Handlest . . . discourse: O **63 instead** [eds.] in steed **72 travail** [eds.] trauell **73 on of you** of you **78 not kin** [Fb] kin [Q, Fa] **79–80 what care** what **85 her. For** her for **99 woo** [eds.] woe **100 stubborn-chaste** stubborne, chast **104 resides** reides

1.2. 1 [and throughout] ALEXANDER *Man* **17 they** the **34 struck** [eds.] strooke **36.1** [F; not in Q] **48 ye** [eds.] yea **71 just . . . them; he** [eds.] iust, . . . them he **85 come** eome **87 wit** [eds.] will **117 lift** liste **125 valiantly** valianty **130 the** [eds.] thee **148 pot** por **177 s.d.** [at line 175 in Q] **180 Ilium** Ilion **189.1** [after line 190 in Q] **192 a man** man **205 man's** man **219 [and elsewhere] Who's** [eds.] Whose **224–5 indifferent well** [eds.] indifferent, well [Q, F] **225 [and elsewhere] hear** [eds.] here **236 ne'er** neuer **241.1** ***Enter common soldiers*** [F; not in Q] **245 i'th'eyes** in the eyes **249 among** amongst **256–7 so forth** such like **260 another** a **One** a man **269 too** two **280 I'll** I wil **281 bring, uncle?** [eds.] bring vncle: [Q] bring Vnkle. [F] **283.1** [F; not in Q] **291 prize** price **296 contents** content

1.3. 0.1 ***Sennet*** [F; not in Q] **2 the jaundice on** these Iaundies ore **13 every** euer **19 think** call **31 thy godly** the godlike **36 patient** ancient **48 herd** [eds.] heard **breese** Bryze **61 thy** the **67 On . . . ears** (On which heauen rides) knit all the Greekish eares **70–4** [F; not in Q] **75 basis** bases **92 ill . . . evil** influence of euill Planets **110 meets** melts **118 [and elsewhere] lose** [eds.] loose **119 includes** include **128 in** with **137 lives** stands **143 sinew** sinnow **149 awkward** sillie **159 unsquared** vnsquare **164 just** right **188 willed** wild **195 and** our **209 fineness** finesse **212 s.d.** ***Tucket*** [F; not in Q] **214.1** ***Enter Aeneas*** [F; not in Q] **219 ears** eyes **221 host** [eds.] heads **236 fame** same **238 Jove's** great *Ioues* **247 affair** affaires **250 him** with him **252 sense** seat **the** that **256 loud** alowd **262 this** his **267 That seeks** And feeds **276 compass** couple **289 or means** a meanes **294 One . . . one** A . . . no **297 this withered brawn** my withered braunes **298 will tell** tell **302 forbid** for-fend **youth** men **304 AGAMEMNON** [F; not in Q] **305 first** sir **309.1** [F; not in Q] **315 This 'tis** [F; not in Q] **324 The** True the **even as** as **327 were** weare **333 Yes** Why **334 his honor** those honours **336 this** the **340 wild** vilde **343 indices** [eds.] *indexes* [Q, F] **352 from hence receives the** receiues from hence a **354–6** [F; not in Q] **354 his** [eds.] in his [F] **359 show our foulest wares** First shew foule wares **361–2 yet . . . better** shall exceed, / By shewing the worst first **368 wear** share **370 we** it **373 did** do **377 as the worthier** for the better **388 of it** thereof **391 tar** arre **their** a

2.1. 8 there would would **11 s.d.** [F; not in Q] **14 vinewed'st** [eds.] vnsalted [Q] whinid'st [F] **17 oration** oration without booke **18 learn a** learne **19 o' thy** [eds.] ath thy [Q] **24 a fool** foole **26–7 foot. An** foot, and **27 thee** the **38, 40, 41 THERSITES, AJAX, THERSITES** [F; not in Q] **45 Thou scurvy** you scuruy **55.1** [F; not in Q] **63 I do so** so do I **71 I will** It will **75 I'll** I **88 for a** the **101 an' a** and [Q] if the [F] **out** at **105 your** [eds.] their **nails on their toes** nailes **107 war** wars **111 wit as** as **114 brach** [eds.] brooch **122 fifth** first **130.1** [F; not in Q]

2.2. 3 damage domage **4 travail** trauell **7 struck** [eds.] stroke **14, 15 surety** surely **26 Weigh** Way **27 father** fathers **30 waist** [eds.] waste **33 at** of **34 them. Should . . . father** them should . . . father; **47 Let's** Sets **52 holding** keeping **58 inclinable** attributiue **64 shores** shore **67 chose** choose **70 spoiled** soild **71 sieve** siue **74 of** with **79 stale** pale **82 launched** lansh't **86 noble** worthy **96.1** ***Enter . . . ears*** *Enter Cassandra rauing* **97 shriek** shrike **104 old** elders **106 clamor** clamours **120 th'event** [eds.] euent **149 off** of **210 strike** shrike

2.3. 1 THERSITES [not in Q] **19 dependent** depending **21.1** ***Enter Patroclus*** [F; not in Q] **24 ha'** a **25 wouldst** couldst **31 art** art not **46 thyself** *Thersites* **49 mayst** must **54–9** [F; not in Q] **62–3 commanded of Agamemnon** commanded **66 to the creator** of the Prouer **68 Patroclus** Come *Patroclus* **69 s.d.** [F; not in Q] **73–4 Now . . . all** [F; not in Q] **73 serpigo** [eds.] Suppeago [F] **78 shent** [eds.] sent [F] sate [Q] **79 appertainments** appertainings **82 so say** say so **87 the** a **88 A word, my lord** [F; not in Q] **98 council that** composure **101.1** ***Enter Patroclus*** [F; not in Q] **111 Hear** Heere **129 pettish lunes** course, and time [Q] pettish lines [F] **his flows** and flowes **as** and **130 carriage of this action** streame of his commencement **135 Bring** [Q, Fb] ring [Fa] **140 enter you** entertaine **140.1** ***Exit Ulysses*** [F; not in Q] **151 it** pride **152 clearer, Ajax** cleerer **157 I hate** I do hate **166 Why, will** Why will **179 led** lead **186 do** doth **190 Must** Shall **stale** staule **192 titled** liked **200 this** his **202 pash** push **204 'a** he **211 let** tell **humors** humorous **214 o'** of **218 'twould** two'od **219 'A . . . shares** [assigned in Q to Ajax] **221 He's . . . warm** [assigned in Q to Ajax] **Farce** Force **222 praises** praiers **in; his** his **225 You** Yon **231 thus with us** with vs thus **241 beyond all** all thy **247 bourn** boord **248 Thy** This **255 ULYSSES** *Nest.* **262 cull** call

3.1. 0.1–2 ***Music . . . Servant*** [F] *Enter Pandarus* [Q] **1 not you** you not **3 [and elsewhere] SERVANT** *Man* **25 mean, friend** mean **31 who's** who is **33 visible** [eds.] inuisible [Q, F] **37 that thou** thou **38 Cressida** *Cressid* **41 There's** theirs **52 Nell, he** *Nel.* he **76 supper you** super. You **90 poor disposer's** disposer's **106 lord** lad **107 hast** haste **113** [F; not in Q] **117 shaft confounds** *shafts confound* **120 Oh! Oh!** *oh ho* [and similarly in 122–5] **148 They're** Their **field** the field **149 woo** woe **151 these** this **159 thee** her

3.2. 3 he stays stayes **3.1** [F; not in Q] **8 a** to a **10 those** these **16 s.d.** [F; not in Q] **22 Swooning** [eds.] Sounding [Q, F] **23 Too subtle-potent** [eds.] To subtill, potent [Q, F] **28.1** [F; not in Q] **33.1** [F; not in Q] **37 unawares** vnwares **38.1** ***Pandarus and Cressida*** *pandar and Cressid* **45 thills** filles **61 Cressida** *Cressid* **67 fears** [eds.] teares **80 This is** This **91 crown it. No perfection** louer part no affection **98.1** [F; not in Q] **109 are** be **117 glance that ever—pardon** [eds.] glance; that euer pardon [Q, F] **121 grown** [eds.] grone [Q] grow [F] **131 Cunning** Comming **in** [eds.] from [Q, F] **132 My . . . from me** My very soule of councell **149–50 Where . . . what I** would be gone: / Where is my wit? I know not what I speake **156 might; that** might that **159 aye** age **175 similes, truth** simele's truth **179 Yet, after** After **184 and** or **197 witness. Here** [eds.] witnes here [Q, F] **199 pains** paine **207 with a bed** [eds.; not in Q, F]

3.3. 0.2 ***Calchas*** *Chalcas* **1 done you** done **3 to your** to **4 come** [eds.] loue **5 possessions** [eds.] possession **29 off** of **43 unplausive** vnpaulsiue **55 What, comes** [eds.] What comes [Q, F] **69.1** ***Exit*** [eds.] *Exeunt* [Q, F] **73 use** [eds.] us'd **101 shining** ayming **111 mir-**

rored [eds.] married **128 are** are. **129 abject** obiect **141 on** one **142 shrinking** shriking **153 mail** [eds.] male [Q, F] **156 one** on **159 hedge** turne **161 hindmost** him, most **162–4 Or . . . on** [F; not in Q] **163 rear** [eds.] neere [F] **165 past** passe **179 give** [eds.] goe **185 Than** That **not stirs** stirs not **198 grain . . . gold** thing **199 th'uncomprehensive deeps** the vncomprehensiue depth **225 like a** like **234 we** they **242 s.d.** ***Enter Thersites*** [after line 242 in Q] **267 ambassador to him** Ambassador **275 the most** the **279 Grecian** [not in Q] **et cetera. Do** Do **295–6 o'clock** of the clock **301 but he's** but **o'** of **306 carry** beare

4.1. 0.1 ***with a torch*** [F; not in Q] **0.2 [and elsewhere]** ***Diomedes*** [eds.] *Diomed* [Q, F] **5 you** your **18 But** Lul'd **22–3 backward. In humane gentleness,** back-ward, in humane gentlenesse: **39 Calchas'** *Calcho's* **42 do think** beleeue **46 whereof** wherefore **52 s.d.** [F; not in Q] **54 the soul** soule **55 merits** deserues **most** best **58 soilure** soyle **75 Hear** Here **78 you** they

4.2. 15 gait [eds.] gate **18 off** of **21.1** [F; not in Q] **32–3 Ah, poor** ***capoccia!*** [eds.] a poore *chipochia,* **35 s.d.** ***One knocks*** [after line 36 in Q, after 33 in F] **56 Hoo!** [eds.] Who **59.1** [F; not in Q] **65 us; and for him** him, and **74 nature** neighbor *Pandar* **79 CRESSIDA** [not in Q] **87 wouldst** wouldest **89–90 knees I beseech you** knees **110.1** [F; not in Q]

4.3. 0.2 and [F; not in Q]

4.4. 6 affection affections **50 genius so** *Genius* **51 "Come"** so **54 the root** my throate **58 my love** loue **64 there's** there is **70 Wear** were **77** [F; not in Q] **gifts** guift [F] **78 flowing** swelling **79 person** portion **106 wear** were **122 zeal** [eds.] seale **135 I'll** I **139.1–2** ***Sound trumpet*** [F; not in Q] **144–8** [F; not in Q] **144 DEIPHOBUS** [eds.] *Dio.* [F] **148 s.d.** [after line 143 in Q, F]

4.5. 0.2 ***Nestor*** [eds.] *Nester, Calcas* [Q, F] **2 time . . . courage.** [eds.] time. With starting courage, [Q, F] **16 toe** too **38 MENELAUS** [eds.] *Patr.* **44 not** nor **49 too.** [eds.] then. [Q] then? [F] **60 accosting** [eds.] a coasting [Q, F] **64.1** ***Exeunt*** [F; not in Q] **66 you** the **74 ACHILLES** [eds.; not in Q, F] **75 disprising** misprising **95** [F; not in Q] **96 AGAMEMNON** *Vlises* **99 in deeds** deeds **133 Of our rank feud** [F; not in Q] **134 drop** day **162 mine** my **164 of** all **166–71** [F; not in Q] **179 Mock . . . oath** (Mock not thy affect, the vntraded earth) **188 And seen thee scorning** Despising many **189 thy** th' **194 hemmed** shrupd **200 Let** O let **207** [F; not in Q] **253 the** an **256 stithied** stichied **276 Beat . . . taborins** To taste your bounties **282 on heaven nor on** vpon the heauen nor **288 As** But **293 she loved** my Lord

5.1. 4 core curre **12 need these** needs this **14 boy** box **15 thought** said **19 catarrhs** [F; not in Q] **i'** in **20 wheezing** whissing **26 mean'st** meanes **31 sarcenet** sacenet **32 tassel** toslell **51 Here's** her's **54 brother** be **56 hanging . . . leg** at his bare legge **58 farced** [eds.] faced [Q] forced [F] **59 he is** her's **60 dog** day **mule** Moyle **60 fitchew** Fichooke **63 not** [F; not in Q] **66.1–3** ***Enter . . . lights*** *Enter Agam: Vlysses, Nest: and Diomed with lights* **68 light** lights **68 s.d.** [F; not in Q] **71 good** God **77 sewer** [eds.] sure **78 both at once** both **98 Calchas his** *Calcas*

5.2. 4.1 ***Enter . . . Ulysses*** [F; not in Q] **5 s.d.** ***Enter Cressida*** ["*Enter Cressid*" after "to him" in line 6 in Q] **11 clef** Cliff **13 CRESSIDA** [eds.] *Cal.* **16 should** shall **35 one** a **37 pray you** pray **41 Nay** Now **42 distraction** distruction **48 Why, how now, lord?** How now my lord? **49 Adieu, you** you **57 tickles these** tickles **59 But will** Will **60 la** [eds.] lo **63 sweet** my **69** [F; not in Q] **70 CRESSIDA** *Troy.* **83 As I kiss thee** [eds.; continued as Cressida's speech in Q, F] **Nay . . . me** [eds.; assigned to Diomedes in Q, F] **87 CRESSIDA** [F; not in Q] **92 one's** [eds.] on's [Q] one [F] **94 By** And by **109 s.d.** ***Exit*** [F; not in Q] **121 coact** Court **126 had deceptious** were deceptions **137 soil** spoile **146 is** was **156 Ariachne's** *Ariachna's* [Qb] *Ariathna's* [Qa] **161 five** finde **164 bound** giuen **171 much as** [eds.] much

5.3. 14 CASSANDRA *Cres.* **20–2** [F; not in Q] **21 give** [eds.] count giue [F] **use** [eds.] as [F] **23 CASSANDRA** [F; not in Q] **29 mean'st** meanest **45 mothers** Mother **58** [F; not in Q] **85 distraction** distruction **90 s.d.** [F; not in Q] **93 of** worth **96.1** ***Pandarus*** [eds.] *Pandar* [Q, F] **104 o' these** [eds.] ath's [Q] o'th's [F] **112** [F follows with an alternate version, slightly varied, of 5.10.32–4]

5.4. 0.1 ***Alarum*** [F, at 5.2.112; not in Q] **4 young knave's** knaues **17.1** ***Enter . . . Troilus*** [F; not in Q] **26 art thou** art

5.5. 5 SERVANT *Man* **5.1** ***Enter Agamemnon*** [after "proof" in line 5 in Q] **7 Margareton** [eds.] *Margaleron* [Q, F] **11 Epistrophus** [eds.] *Epostropus* **Cedius** [eds.] *Cedus* **12 Thoas** [eds.] *Thous* **22 scalèd** scaling **schools** [eds.] sculls [Q] sculs [F] **25 the** a **41 luck** lust **43 AJAX** [F; not in Q]

5.6. 1 AJAX [F; not in Q] **2 DIOMEDES** [F; not in Q] **7 the** [eds.] thy [Q, F] **11.1** ***Exit Troilus*** [F; not in Q] **11.2** ***Enter Hector*** [F; not in Q] **13 ACHILLES** [F; not in Q] **21 s.d.** ***Enter Troilus*** [eds.; after line 21 in Q, F] **26 reck** [eds.] wreake **thou end** I end

5.7. 1 ACHILLES [F; not in Q] **8 s.d.** ***Exeunt*** [eds.] *Exit* **and** [F; not in Q] **10 'Loo** [eds.] lowe **10–11 double-horned Spartan** [eds.] double hen'd spartan [Q] double hen'd sparrow [F] **12 s.d.** ***Exeunt*** [eds.] *Exit* **13 [and throughout scene] MARGARETON** [eds.] *Bast.* [Q, F]

5.8. 3 good my **4.2** ***his*** [F; not in Q] **11 Now** next, come **15 part** prat **16 MYRMIDON** [eds.] *One.* [Q] *Gree.* [F] **Trojan trumpets** Troyans trumpet

5.9. 0.1 ***Sound retreat*** [F; not in Q] **0.3** ***Shout*** [F, at the end of scene 8; not in Q] **1 shout is that** is this **3 slain! Achilles!** [F subst.] slaine *Achilles,* **6 a man as good** as good a man

5.10. 0.1 ***and*** [F; not in Q] **2 Never** *Troy.* Neuer **2.1** [placement as in F; before line 2 in Q] **3 TROILUS** [F; not in Q] **7 smite** [eds.] smile [Q, F] **20 Cold** Could [Q] Coole [F] **21 Scare** [eds.] Scarre [Q, F] **21–2 But . . . dead** [F; not in Q] **23 yet. You vile abominable tents,** [F, subst.] yet you proud abhominable tents: [Q] **33 broker-lackey!** broker, lacky, **Ignomy and** ignomyny **36 world, world, world** world, world **39 desired** lou'd **50 your** my **51 hold-door** hold-ore **56 s.d. [*Exit*]** *Exeunt* [F; not in Q]

Glossary

Shakespearean Words and Meanings of Frequent Occurrence

A

'A: he (unaccented form).
Abate: lessen, diminish; blunt, reduce; deprive; bar, leave out of account, except; depreciate; humble.
Abuse (N): insult, error, misdeed, offense, crime; imposture, deception; also the modern sense.
Abuse (V): deceive, misapply, put to a bad use; maltreat; frequently the modern sense.
Addition: something added to one's name to denote rank; mark of distinction; title.
Admiration: wonder; object of wonder.
Admire: wonder at.
Advantage (N): profit, convenience, benefit; opportunity, favorable opportunity; pecuniary profit; often shades toward the modern sense.
Advantage (V): profit, be of benefit to, benefit; augment.
Advice: reflection, consideration, deliberation, consultation.
Affect: aim at, aspire to, incline toward; be fond of, be inclined; love; act upon contagiously (as a disease). (PAST PART.) **Affected**: disposed, inclined, in love, loved.
Affection: passion, love; emotion, feeling, mental tendency, disposition; wish, inclination; affectation.
Alarum: signal calling soldiers to arms (in stage directions).
An: if; but; **an if:** if, though, even if.
Anon: at once, soon; presently, by and by.
Answer: return, requite; atone for; render an account of, account for; obey, agree with; also the modern sense.
Apparent: evident, plain; seeming.
Argument: subject, theme, reason, cause; story; excuse.
As: according as; as far as; namely; as if; in the capacity of; that; so that; that is, that they.
Assay: try, attempt; accost, address; challenge.
Atone: reconcile; set at one.
Attach: arrest, seize.
Aweful, awful: commanding reverential fear or respect; profoundly respectful or reverential.

B

Band: bond, fetters, manacle (leash for a dog). **Band** and **bond** are etymologically the same word; **band** was formerly used in both senses.
Basilisk: fabulous reptile said to kill by its look. The basilisk of popular superstition was a creature with legs, wings, a serpentine and winding tail, and a crest or comb somewhat like a cock. It was the offspring of a cock's egg hatched under a toad or serpent.
Bate: blunt, abate, reduce; deduct, except.
Battle: army; division of an army.
Beshrew: curse, blame; used as a mild curse, "Bad or ill luck to."
Bias: tendency, bent, inclination, swaying influence; term in bowling applied to the form of the bowl, the oblique line in which it runs, and the kind of impetus given to cause it to run obliquely.
Blood: nature, vigor; supposed source of emotion; passion; spirit, animation; one of the four humors (see **humor**).
Boot (N): advantage, profit; something given in addition to the bargain; booty, plunder.
Boot (V): profit, avail.
Brave (ADJ.): fine, gallant; splendid, finely arrayed, showy; ostentatiously defiant.
Brave (V): challenge, defy; make splendid.
Brook: tolerate, endure.

C

Can: can do; know; be skilled; sometimes used for *did.*
Capable: comprehensive; sensible, impressible, susceptible; capable of; gifted, intelligent.
Careful: anxious, full of care; provident; attentive.
Carry: manage, execute; be successful, win; conquer; sustain; endure.
Censure (N): judgment, opinion; critical opinion, unfavorable opinion.
Censure (V): judge, estimate; pass sentence or judgment.
Character (N): writing, printing, record; handwriting; cipher; face, features (bespeaking inward qualities).
Character (V): write, engrave, inscribe.
Check (N): reproof; restraint.
Check (V): reprove, restrain, keep from; control.

Circumstance: condition, state of affairs, particulars; adjunct details; detailed narration, argument, or discourse; formality, ceremony.

Clip: embrace; surround.

Close: secret, private; concealed; uncommunicative; enclosed.

Cog: cheat.

Coil: noise, disturbance, turmoil; fuss, to-do, bustle.

Color: appearance; pretext, pretense; excuse.

Companion: fellow (used contemptuously).

Complete: accomplished, fully endowed; perfect, perfect in quality; also frequently the modern sense.

Complexion: external appearance; temperament, disposition; the four complexions—sanguine, choleric, phlegmatic, and melancholy—corresponding to the four humors (see **humor**); also the modern sense.

Composition: compact, agreement, constitution.

Compound: settle, agree.

Conceit: conception, idea, thought; mental faculty, wit; fancy, imagination; opinion, estimate; device, invention, design.

Condition: temperament, disposition; characteristic, property, quality; social or official position, rank or status; covenant, treaty, contract.

Confound: waste, spend, invalidate, destroy; undo, ruin; mingle indistinguishably, mix, blend.

Confusion: destruction, overthrow, ruin; mental agitation.

Continent: that which contains or encloses; earth, globe; sum, summary.

Contrive: plot; plan; spend or pass (time).

Conversation: conduct, deportment; social intercourse, association.

Converse: hold intercourse; associate with, have to do with.

Cope: encounter, meet; have to do with.

Copy: model, pattern; example; minutes or memoranda.

Cousin: any relative not belonging to one's immediate family.

Cry you mercy: beg your pardon.

Cuckold: husband whose wife is unfaithful.

Curious: careful, fastidious; anxious, concerned; made with care, skillfully, intricately, or daintily wrought; particular.

Cursed, curst: shrewish, perverse, spiteful.

D

Dainty: minute; scrupulous, particular; particular about (with **of**); refined, elegant; also the modern sense.

Date: duration, termination, term of existence; limit or end of a term or period, term.

Dear: precious; best; costly; important; affectionate; hearty; grievous, dire; also the modern sense.

Debate: discuss; fight.

Decay (N): downfall, ruin; cause of ruin.

Decay (V): perish, be destroyed; destroy.

Defeat (N): destruction, ruin.

Defeat (V): destroy, disfigure, ruin.

Defy: challenge, challenge to a fight; reject; despise.

Demand (N): inquiry; request.

Demand (V): inquire, question; request.

Deny: refuse (to do something); refuse permission; refuse to accept; refuse admittance; disown.

Depart (N): departure.

Depart (V): part; go away from, leave, quit; take leave (of one another); **depart with, withal:** part with, give up.

Derive: gain, obtain; draw upon, direct (to); descend; pass by descent, be descended or inherited; trace the origin of.

Difference: diversity of opinion, disagreement, dissension, dispute; characteristic or distinguishing feature; alteration or addition to a coat of arms to distinguish a younger or lateral branch of a family.

Digest: arrange, perfect; assimilate, amalgamate; disperse, dissipate; comprehend, understand; put up with (FIG. from the physical sense of digesting food).

Discourse (N): reasoning, reflection; talk, act of conversing, conversation; faculty of conversing; familiar intercourse; relating (as by speech).

Discourse (V): speak, talk, converse; pass (the time) in talk; say, utter, tell, give forth; narrate, relate.

Discover: uncover, expose to view; divulge, reveal, make known; spy out, reconnoiter; betray; distinguish, discern; also the modern sense.

Dispose (N): disposal; temperament, bent of mind, disposition; external manner.

Dispose (V): distribute, manage, make use of; deposit, put or stow away; regulate, order, direct; come to terms. (PAST PART.) **Disposed:** in a good frame of mind; inclined to be merry.

Dispute: discuss, reason; strive against, resist.

Distemper (V): disturb; (N): disorder, ill humor; illness.

Doit: old Dutch coin, one-half an English farthing.

Doubt (N): suspicion, apprehension; fear, danger, risk; also the modern sense.

Doubt (V): suspect, apprehend; fear; also the modern sense.

Doubtful: inclined to suspect, suspicious, apprehensive; not to be relied on; almost certain.

Duty: reverence, respect, expression of respect; submission to authority, obedience; due.

E

Earnest: money paid as an installment to secure a bargain; partial payment; often used with *quibble* in the modern sense.

Ease: comfort, assistance, leisure; idleness, sloth, inactivity; also the modern sense.

Ecstasy: frenzy, madness, state of being beside oneself, excitement, bewilderment; swoon; rapture.

Element: used to refer to the simple substances of which all material bodies were thought to be composed; specifically earth, air, fire, and water, corresponding to the four humors (see **humor**); atmosphere, sky; atmospheric agencies or powers; that one of the four elements which is the natural abode of a creature; hence, natural surroundings, sphere.

Engage: pledge, pawn, mortgage; bind by a promise, swear to; entangle, involve; enlist; embark on an enterprise.

Engine: mechanical contrivance; artifice, device, plot.

Enlarge: give free scope to; set at liberty, release.

Entertain: keep up, maintain, accept; take into one's service; treat; engage (someone's) attention or thought; occupy, while or pass away pleasurably; engage (as an enemy); receive.

Envious: malicious, spiteful, malignant.

Envy: ill-will, malice; hate; also the modern sense.

Even: uniform; direct, straightforward; exact, precise; equable, smooth, comfortable; equal, equally balanced.

Event: outcome; affair, business; also frequently the modern sense.

Exclaim: protest, rail; accuse, blame (with **on**), reproach.

Excursion: stage battle or skirmish (in stage directions).

Excuse: seek to extenuate (a fault); maintain the innocence of; clear oneself, justify or vindicate oneself; decline.

F

Fact: deed, act; crime.

Faction: party, class, group, set (of persons); party strife, dissension; factious quarrel, intrigue.

Fail: die, die out; err, be at fault; omit, leave undone.

Fair (N): fair thing; one of the fair sex; someone beloved; beauty (the abstract concept).

Fair (ADJ.): just; clear, distinct; beautiful; of light complexion or color of hair.

Fair (ADV): fairly.

Fairly: beautifully, handsomely; courteously, civilly; properly, honorably, honestly; becomingly, appropriately; favorably, fortunately; softly, gently, kindly.

Fall: let fall, drop; happen, come to pass; befall; shades frequently toward the modern senses.

Falsely: wrongly; treacherously; improperly.

Fame: report; rumor; reputation.

Familiar (N): intimate friend; familiar or attendant spirit, demon associated with, and obedient to, a person.

Familiar (ADJ.): intimate, friendly; belonging to household or family, domestic; well-known; habitual, ordinary, trivial; plain, easily understood.

Fancy: fantasticalness; imaginative conception, flight of imagination; amorous inclination or passion, love; liking, taste.

Fantasy: fancy, imagination; caprice, whim.

Favor: countenance, face; complexion; aspect, appearance; leave, permission, pardon; attraction, charm, good will; **in favor:** benevolently.

Fear (N): dread, apprehension; dreadfulness; object of dread or fear.

Fear (V): be apprehensive or concerned about, mistrust, doubt; frighten, make afraid.

Fearful: exciting or inspiring fear, terrible, dreadful; timorous, apprehensive, full of fear.

Feature: shape or form of body, figure; shapeliness, comeliness.

Fellow: companion; partaker, sharer (of); equal, match; customary form of address to a servant or an inferior (sometimes used contemptuously or condescendingly).

Fine (N): end, conclusion; **in fine:** finally.

Fine (ADJ.): highly accomplished or skillful; exquisitely fashioned, delicate; refined, subtle; frequently the modern sense.

Flaw: fragment; crack, fissure; tempest, squall, gust of wind; outburst of passion.

Flesh (V): reward a hawk or hound with a piece of flesh of the game killed to excite its eagerness of the chase; hence, to inflame by a foretaste of success; initiate or inure to bloodshed (used for a first time in battle); harden, train.

Flourish: fanfare of trumpets (in stage directions).

Fond: foolish, doting; **fond of:** eager for; also the modern sense.

Fool: term of endearment and pity; frequently the modern sense.

For that, for why: because.

Forfend: forbid, avert.

Free: generous, magnanimous; candid, open; guiltless, innocent.

Front: forehead, face; foremost line of battle; beginning.

Furnish: equip, fit out (furnish forth); endow; dress, decorate, embellish.

G

Gear: apparel, dress; stuff, substance, thing, article; discourse, talk; matter, business, affair.

Get: beget.

Gloss: specious fair appearance; lustrous surface.

Go to: expression of remonstrance, impatience, disapprobation, or derision.

Grace (N): kindness, favor, charm, divine favor; fortune, luck; beneficent virtue; sense of duty or propriety; mercy, pardon; embellish; **do grace:** reflect credit on, do honor to, do a favor for.

Grace (V): gratify, delight; honor, favor.

Groat: coin equal to four pence.

H

Habit: dress, garb, costume; bearing, demeanor, manner; occasionally in the modern sense.

Happily: haply, perchance, perhaps; fortunately.

Hardly: with difficulty.

Have at: I shall come at (you) (i.e., listen to me), I shall attack (a person or thing); let me at.

Have with: I shall go along with; let me go along with; come along.

Having: possession, property, wealth, estate; endowments, accomplishments.

Head: armed force.

Hind: servant, slave; rustic, boor, clown.

His: its. **His** was historically the possessive form of both the masculine and neuter pronouns. **Its,** although not common in Shakespeare's time, occurs in the plays occasionally.

Holp: helped (archaic past tense).

Home: fully, satisfactorily, thoroughly, plainly, effectually; to the quick.

Honest: holding an honorable position, honorable, respectable; decent, kind, seemly, befitting, proper; chaste; genuine; loosely used as an epithet of approbation.

Humor: mood, temper, cast of mind, temperament, disposition; vagary, fancy, whim; moisture (the literal sense); a physiological and, by transference, a psychological term applied to the four chief fluids of the human body—phlegm, blood, bile or choler, and black bile or melancholy. A person's disposition and temporary state of mind were determined according to the relative proportions of these fluids in the body; consequently, a person was said to be phlegmatic, sanguine, choleric, or melancholy.

I

Image: likeness; visible form; representation; embodiment, type; mental picture, creation of the imagination.

Influence: supposed flowing from the stars or heavens of an ethereal fluid, acting upon the characters and destinies of men (used metaphorically).

Inform: take shape, give form to, imbue, inspire; instruct, teach; charge (against).

Instance: evidence, proof, sign, confirmation; motive, cause.

Invention: power of mental creation, the creative faculty; work of the imagination, artistic creation, premeditated design; device, plan, scheme.

J

Jar (N): discord in music; quarrel, discord.
Jar (V): be out of tune; be discordant, quarrel.
Jump: agree, tally, coincide, fit exactly; risk, hazard.

K

Keep: continue, carry on; dwell, lodge, guard, defend, care for, employ, be with; restrain, control; confine in prison.
Kind (N): nature, established order of things; manner, fashion, respect; race, class, kindred, family; **by kind:** naturally.
Kind (ADJ.): natural; favorable; affectionate.
Kindly (ADJ.): natural, appropriate; agreeable; innate; benign.
Kindly (ADV): naturally; gently, courteously.

L

Large: liberal, bounteous, lavish; free, unrestrained; **at large:** at length, in full; in full detail, as a whole, in general.
Late: lately.
Learn: teach; inform (someone of something); also the modern sense.
Let: hinder.
Level: aim; also shades toward the modern sense.
Liberal: possessed of the characteristics and qualities of wellborn persons; genteel, becoming, refined; free in speech; unrestrained by prudence or decorum; licentious.
Lie: be in bed; be still; be confined, be kept in prison; dwell, sojourn, reside, lodge.
Like: please, feel affection; liken, compare.
List (N): strip of cloth, selvedge; limit, boundary; desire.
List (V): choose, desire, please; listen to.
Liver: the seat of love and of violent passions generally (see also **spleen**).
'Long of: owing to, on account of.
Look: power to see; take care, see to it; expect; seek, search for.

M

Make: do; have to do (with); consider; go; be effective, make up, complete; also the modern sense.
Manage: management, conduct, administration; action and paces to which a horse is trained; short gallop at full speed.
Marry: mild interjection equivalent to "Indeed!" Originally, an oath by the Virgin Mary.
May: can; also frequently the modern sense to denote probability; **might** has corresponding meanings and uses.
Mean, means (N): instrument, agency, method; effort; opportunity (for doing something); something interposed or intervening; money, wealth (frequently in the plural form); middle position, medium; tenor or alto part in singing (usually in the singular form).
Mean (ADJ.): average, moderate, middle; of low degree, station, or position; undignified, base.
Measure (N): grave or stately dance, graceful motion; tune, melody, musical accompaniment; treatment meted out; moderation, proportion; limit; distance, reach.
Measure (V): judge, estimate; traverse.
Mere: absolute, sheer; pure, unmixed; downright, sincere.
Mew (up): coop up (as used of a hawk), shut up, imprison, confine.
Mind (N): thoughts, judgment, opinion, message; purpose, intention, desire; disposition; also the modern sense of the mental faculty.
Mind (V): remind; perceive, notice, attend; intend.
Minion: saucy woman, hussy; follower; favorite, favored person, darling (often used contemptuously).
Misdoubt (N): suspicion.
Misdoubt (V): mistrust, suspect.
Model: pattern, replica, likeness.
Modern: ordinary, commonplace, everyday.
Modest: moderate, marked by moderation, becoming; characterized by decency and propriety; chaste.
Moiety: half; share; small part, lesser share; portion, part of.
Mortal: fatal; deadly, of or for death; belonging to mankind; human, pertaining to human affairs.
Motion: power of movement; suggestion, proposal; movement of the soul; impulse, prompting; also the modern sense.
Move: make angry; urge, incite, instigate, arouse, prompt; propose, make a proposal to, apply to, appeal to, suggest; also the modern sense.
Muse: wonder, marvel; grumble, complain.

N

Napkin: handkerchief.
Natural: related by blood; having natural or kindly feeling; also the modern sense.
Naught: useless, worthless; wicked, naughty.
Naughty: wicked; good for nothing, worthless.
Nerves: sinews.
Nice: delicate; fastidious, dainty, particular, scrupulous; minute, subtle; shy, coy; reluctant, unwilling; unimportant, insignificant, trivial; accurate, precise; wanton, lascivious.
Nothing (ADJ.): not at all.

O

Of: from, away from; during; on; by; as regards; instead of; **out of:** compelled by; made from.
Offer: make an attack; menace; venture, dare, presume.
Opinion: censure; reputation or credit; favorable estimate of oneself; self-conceit, arrogance; self-confidence; public opinion, reputation; also the modern sense.
Or: before; also used conjunctively where no alternative is implied; **or . . . or:** either . . . or; whether . . . or.
Out (ADV): without, outside; abroad; fully, quite; at an end, finished; at variance, aligned the wrong way.
Out (INTERJ.): an expression of reproach, impatience, indignation, or anger.
Owe: own; also the modern sense.

P

Pack (V): load; depart, begone; conspire.
Pageant: show, spectacle, spectacular entertainment; device on a moving carriage.
Pain: punishment, penalty; labor, trouble, effort; also frequently the modern sense.
Painted: specious, unreal, counterfeit.
Parle (N): parley, conference, talk; bugle call for parley.

Part (V): depart, part from; divide.
Particular (N): detail; personal interest or concern; details of a private nature; single person.
Party: faction, side, part, cause; partner, ally.
Pass (V): pass through, traverse; exceed; surpass; pledge.
Passing (ADJ. and ADV.): surpassing, surpassingly, exceedingly.
Passion (N): powerful or violent feeling, violent sorrow or grief; painful affection or disorder of the body; sorrow; feelings or desires of love; passionate speech or outburst.
Passion (V): sorrow, grieve.
Peevish: silly, senseless, childish; perverse, obstinate, stubborn; sullen.
Perforce: by violence or compulsion; forcibly; necessarily.
Phoenix: mythical Arabian bird believed to be the only one of its kind; it lived five or six hundred years, after which it burned itself to ashes and reemerged to live through another cycle.
Physic: medical faculty; healing art, medical treatment; remedy, medicine, healing property.
Pitch: height; specifically, the height to which a falcon soars before swooping on its prey (often used figuratively); tarlike substance.
Policy: conduct of affairs (especially public affairs); prudent management; stratagem, trick; contrivance; craft, cunning.
Port: bearing, demeanor; state, style of living, social station; gate.
Possess: have or give possession or command (of something); inform, acquaint; also the modern sense.
Post (N): courier, messenger; post-horse; haste.
Post (V): convey swiftly; hasten, ignore through haste (with **over** or **off**).
Practice (N): execution; exercise (especially for instruction); stratagem, intrigue; conspiracy, plot, treachery.
Practice (V): perform, take part in; use stratagem, craft, or artifice; scheme, plot; play a joke on.
Pregnant: resourceful; disposed, inclined; clear, obvious.
Present (ADJ.): ready, immediate, prompt, instant.
Present (V): represent.
Presently: immediately, at once.
Prevent: forestall, anticipate, foresee; also the modern sense.
Process: drift, tenor, gist; narrative, story; formal command, mandate.
Proof: test, trial, experiment; experience; issue, result; proved or tested strength of armor or arms; also the modern sense.
Proper: (one's or its) own; peculiar, exclusive; excellent; honest, respectable; handsome, elegant, fine, good-looking.
Proportion: symmetry; size; form, carriage, appearance, shape; portion, allotment; rhythm.
Prove: make trial of; put to test; show or find out by experience.
Purchase (N): acquisition; spoil, booty.
Purchase (V): acquire, gain, obtain; strive, exert oneself; redeem, exempt.

Q

Quaint: skilled, clever; pretty, fine, dainty; handsome, elegant; carefully or ingeniously wrought or elaborated.
Quality: that which constitutes (something); essential being; good natural gifts; accomplishment, attainment, property; art, skill; rank, position; profession, occupation, business; party, side; manner, style; cause, occasion.
Quick: living (used substantively to mean "living flesh"); alive; lively, sharp, piercing; hasty, impatient; with child.
Quillets: verbal niceties, subtle distinctions.
Quit: requite, reward; set at liberty; acquit, remit; pay for, clear off.

R

Rack (V): stretch or strain beyond normal extent or capacity to endure; strain oneself; distort.
Rage (N): madness, insanity; vehement pain; angry disposition; violent passion or appetite; poetic enthusiasm; warlike ardor or fury.
Rage (V): behave wantonly or riotously; act with fury or violence; enrage; pursue furiously.
Range: extend or lie in the same plane (with); occupy a position; rove, roam; be inconstant; traverse.
Rank (ADJ.): coarsely luxuriant; puffed up, swollen, fat, abundant; full, copious; rancid; lustful; corrupt, foul.
Rate (N): estimate; value or worth; estimation, consideration; standard, style.
Rate (V): allot; calculate, estimate, compute; reckon, consider; be of equal value (with); chide, scold, berate; drive away by chiding or scolding.
Recreant (N): traitor, coward, cowardly wretch (also as ADJ.).
Remorse: pity, compassion; also the modern sense.
Remove: removal, absence; period of absence; change.
Require: ask, inquire of, request.
Resolve: dissolve, melt, dissipate; answer; free from doubt or uncertainty, convince; inform; decide; also the modern sense.
Respect (N): consideration, reflection, act of seeing, view; attention, notice; decency, modest deportment; also the modern sense.
Respect (V): esteem, value, prize; regard, consider; heed, pay attention to; also the modern sense.
Round: spherical; plain, direct, brusque; fair; honest.
Roundly: plainly, unceremoniously.
Rub: obstacle (a term in the game of bowls); unevenness; inequality.

S

Sack: generic term for Spanish and Canary wines; sweet white wine.
Sad: grave, serious; also the modern sense.
Sadness: seriousness; also the modern sense.
Sans: without (French preposition).
Scope: object, aim, limit; freedom, license; free play.
Seal: bring to completion or conclusion; conclude, confirm, ratify, stamp; also the modern sense.
Sennet: a series of notes sounded on a trumpet to herald the approach or departure of a procession (used in stage directions).
Sense: mental faculty, mind; mental perception, import, rational meaning; physical perception; sensual nature; **common sense:** ordinary or untutored perception, observation or knowledge.
Sensible: capable of physical feeling or perception, sensitive; capable of or exhibiting emotion; rational; capable of being perceived.
Serve: be sufficient; be favorable; succeed; satisfy the need for; serve a turn; answer the purpose.

Several: separate, distinct, different; particular, private; various.
Shadow: shade, shelter; reflection; likeness, image; ghost; representation, picture of the imagination, phantom; also the modern sense.
Shift: change; stratagem, strategy, trick, contrivance, device to serve a purpose; **make shift:** manage.
Shrewd: malicious, mischievous, ill-natured; shrewish; bad, of evil import, grievous; severe.
Sirrah: ordinary or customary form of address to inferiors or servants; disrespectful form of address.
Sith: since.
Smock: woman's undergarment; used typically for "a woman."
Something: somewhat.
Sometime: sometimes, from time to time; once, formerly; at times, at one time.
Speed (N): fortune, success; protecting and assisting power; also the modern sense.
Speed (V): fare (well or ill); succeed; be successful; assist, guard, favor.
Spleen: the seat of emotions and passions; violent passion; fiery temper; malice; anger, rage; impulse, fit of passion; caprice; impetuosity (see also **liver**).
Spoil: destruction, ruin; plunder; slaughter, massacre.
Starve: die of cold or hunger; be benumbed with cold; paralyze, disable; allow or cause to die.
State: degree, rank; social position, station; pomp, splendor, outward display, clothes; court, household of a great person; shades into the modern sense.
Stay: wait, wait for; sustain; stand; withhold, withstand; stop.
Stead: assist; be of use to, benefit, help.
Still: always, ever, continuously or continually, constant or constantly; silent, mute; also modern senses.
Stomach: appetite, inclination, disposition; resentment; angry temper, resentful feeling; proud spirit, courage.
Straight: immediately.
Strange: belonging to another country or person, foreign, unfriendly; new, fresh; ignorant; estranged.
Success: issue, outcome (good or bad); sequel, succession, descent (as from father to son).
Suggest: tempt; prompt; seduce.
Suggestion: temptation.

T

Table: memorandum, tablet; surface on which something is written or drawn.
Take: strike; bewitch; charm; infect; destroy; repair to for refuge; modern senses.
Tall: goodly, fine; strong in fight, valiant.
Target: shield.
Tax: censure, blame, accuse.
Tell: count; relate.
Thorough: through.
Throughly: thoroughly.
Toward: in preparation; forthcoming, about to take place; modern senses.
Toy: trifle, idle fancy; folly.
Train: lure, entice, allure, attract.
Trencher: wooden dish or plate.
Trow: think, suppose, believe; know.

U

Undergo: undertake, perform; modern sense.
Undo: ruin.
Unfold: disclose, tell, make known, reveal; communicate.
Unhappy: evil, mischievous; fatal, ill-fated; miserable.
Unjust: untrue, dishonest; unjustified, groundless; faithless, false.
Unkind: unnatural, cruel, faulty; compare **kind.**
Use (N): custom, habit; interest paid.
Use (V): make practice of; be accustomed; put out at interest.

V

Vail: lower, let fall.
Vantage: advantage; opportunity; benefit, profit; superiority.
Virtue: general excellence; valor, bravery; merit, goodness, honor; good accomplishment, excellence in culture; power; essence, essential part.

W

Want: lack; be in need of; be without.
Watch: be awake, lie awake, sit up at night, lose sleep; keep from sleep (TRANS.).
Weed: garment, clothes.
Welkin: sky, heavens.
Wink: close the eyes; close the eyes in sleep; have the eyes closed; seem not to see.
Withal: with; with it, this, or these; together with this; at the same time.
Wot: know.

Index

Page ranges in **bold** indicate the page range for the entire play. Page references followed by *n* indicate a footnote. *See* and *See also* cross-references indicate entries throughout the four-volume set.